OpenGL
Programming Guide
Second Edition

*The Official Guide to
Learning OpenGL, Version 1.1*

OpenGL Architecture Review Board
Mason Woo   Jackie Neider   Tom Davis

ADDISON-WESLEY

An imprint of Addison Wesley Longman, Inc.

Reading, Massachusetts • Harlow, England • Menlo Park, California
Berkeley, California • Don Mills, Ontario • Sydney
Bonn • Amsterdam • Tokyo • Mexico City

Library of Congress Cataloging-in-Publication Data

Woo, Mason
    OpenGL programming guide: the official guide to learning OpenGL, version 1.1/Mason Woo, Jackie Neider, Tom Davis 2nd ed.
       p.   cm.
    Neider's name appears first on the earlier edition.
    Includes index.
    ISBN 0-201-46138-2
    1. Computer graphics. 2. OpenGL. I. Neider, Jackie. II. Davis, Tom. III. Title.
T385.N435   1996
006.6'93–dc21   96–39420
                                                      CIP

Sponsoring Editor: Mary Treseler
Project Manager: John Fuller
Production Assistant: Melissa Lima
Cover Design: Jean Seal

Set in 10-point Stone Serif

6 7 8 9 1011 MA   01 00 99 98
6th Printing December 1998

Addison-Wesley books are available for bulk purchases by corporations, institutions, and other organizations. For more information please contact the Corporate, Government, and Special Sales Department at (800) 238-9682.

For my family—Felicity, Max, Sarah, and Scout.

—JLN

For my family—Ellyn, Ricky, and Lucy.

—TRD

To Tom Doeppner and Andy van Dam, who started me along this path.

—MW

Contents

About This Guide

The OpenGL graphics system is a software interface to graphics hardware. (The GL stands for Graphics Library.) It allows you to create interactive programs that produce color images of moving three-dimensional objects. With OpenGL, you can control computer-graphics technology to produce realistic pictures or ones that depart from reality in imaginative ways. This guide explains how to program with the OpenGL graphics system to deliver the visual effect you want.

What This Guide Contains

This guide has 14 chapters, one more than the ideal number. The first five chapters present basic information that you need to understand to be able to draw a properly colored and lit three-dimensional object on the screen.

- Chapter 1, **"Introduction to OpenGL,"** provides a glimpse into the kinds of things OpenGL can do. It also presents a simple OpenGL program and explains essential programming details you need to know for subsequent chapters.

- Chapter 2, **"State Management and Drawing Geometric Objects,"** explains how to create a three-dimensional geometric description of an object that is eventually drawn on the screen.

- Chapter 3, **"Viewing,"** describes how such three-dimensional models are transformed before being drawn onto a two-dimensional screen. You can control these transformations to show a particular view of a model.

- Chapter 4, **"Color,"** describes how to specify the color and shading method used to draw an object.

- Chapter 5, **"Lighting,"** explains how to control the lighting conditions surrounding an object and how that object responds to light (that is, how it reflects or absorbs light). Lighting is an important topic, since objects usually don't look three-dimensional until they're lit.

The remaining chapters explain how to optimize or add sophisticated features to your three-dimensional scene. You might choose not to take advantage of many of these features until you're more comfortable with OpenGL. Particularly advanced topics are noted in the text where they occur.

- Chapter 6, **"Blending, Antialiasing, Fog, and Polygon Offset,"** describes techniques essential to creating a realistic scene—alpha blending (to create transparent objects), antialiasing (to eliminate jagged edges), atmospheric effects (to simulate fog or smog), and polygon offset (to remove visual artifacts when highlighting the edges of filled polygons).

- Chapter 7, **"Display Lists,"** discusses how to store a series of OpenGL commands for execution at a later time. You'll want to use this feature to increase the performance of your OpenGL program.

- Chapter 8, **"Drawing Pixels, Bitmaps, Fonts, and Images,"** discusses how to work with sets of two-dimensional data as bitmaps or images. One typical use for bitmaps is describing characters in fonts.

- Chapter 9, **"Texture Mapping,"** explains how to map one- and two-dimensional images called textures onto three-dimensional objects. Many marvelous effects can be achieved through texture mapping.

- Chapter 10, **"The Framebuffer,"** describes all the possible buffers that can exist in an OpenGL implementation and how you can control them. You can use the buffers for such effects as hidden-surface elimination, stenciling, masking, motion blur, and depth-of-field focusing.

- Chapter 11, **"Tessellators and Quadrics,"** shows how to use the tessellation and quadrics routines in the GLU (OpenGL Utility Library).

- Chapter 12, **"Evaluators and NURBS,"** gives an introduction to advanced techniques for efficiently generating curves or surfaces.

- Chapter 13, **"Selection and Feedback,"** explains how you can use OpenGL's selection mechanism to select an object on the screen. It also explains the feedback mechanism, which allows you to collect the drawing information OpenGL produces rather than having it be used to draw on the screen.

- Chapter 14, **"Now That You Know,"** describes how to use OpenGL in several clever and unexpected ways to produce interesting results. These techniques are drawn from years of experience with both OpenGL and the technological precursor to OpenGL, the Silicon Graphics IRIS Graphics Library.

In addition, there are several appendices that you will likely find useful.

- Appendix A, **"Order of Operations,"** gives a technical overview of the operations OpenGL performs, briefly describing them in the order in which they occur as an application executes.

- Appendix B, **"State Variables,"** lists the state variables that OpenGL maintains and describes how to obtain their values.

- Appendix C, **"OpenGL and Window Systems,"** briefly describes the routines available in window-system specific libraries, which are extended to support OpenGL rendering. WIndow system interfaces to the X Window System, Apple MacIntosh, IBM OS/2, and Microsoft Windows NT and Windows 95 are discussed here.

- Appendix D, **"Basics of GLUT: The OpenGL Utility Toolkit,"** discusses the library that handles window system operations. GLUT is portable and it makes code examples shorter and more comprehensible.

- Appendix E, **"Calculating Normal Vectors,"** tells you how to calculate normal vectors for different types of geometric objects.

- Appendix F, **"Homogeneous Coordinates and Transformation Matrices,"** explains some of the mathematics behind matrix transformations.

- Appendix G, **"Programming Tips,"** lists some programming tips based on the intentions of the designers of OpenGL that you might find useful.

- Appendix H, **"OpenGL Invariance,"** describes when and where an OpenGL implementation must generate the exact pixel values described in the OpenGL specification.

Finally, an extensive Glossary defines the key terms used in this guide.

What's New in This Edition

To the question, "What's new in this edition?" the wiseacre answer is "About 100 pages." The more informative answer follows.

- Detailed information about the following new features of OpenGL Version 1.1 has been added.

  - Vertex arrays

  - Texturing enhancements, including texture objects (including residency and prioritization), internal texture image format, texture subimages, texture proxies, and copying textures from frame buffer data

  - Polygon offset

  - Logical operation in RGBA mode

- Program examples have been converted to Mark Kilgard's GLUT, which stands for Graphics Library Utility Toolkit. GLUT is an increasingly popular windowing toolkit, which is well-documented and has been ported to different window systems.

- More detail about some topics that were in the first edition, especially coverage of the OpenGL Utility (GLU) Library.

  - An entire chapter on GLU tessellators and quadrics

  - A section (in Chapter 3) on the use of **gluProject()** and **gluUnProject()**, which mimics or reverses the operations of the geometric processing pipeline (This has been the subject of frequent discussions on the Internet newsgroup on OpenGL, *comp.graphics.api.opengl*.)

  - Expanded coverage (and more diagrams) about images

  - Changes to GLU NURBS properties

  - Error handling and vendor-specific extensions to OpenGL

  - Appendix C expanded to include OpenGL interfaces to several window/operating systems

  The first edition's appendix on the OpenGL Utility Library was removed, and its information has been integrated into other chapters.

- A much larger and more informative index

- Bug fixes and minor topic reordering. Moving the display list chapter is the most noticeable change.

What You Should Know Before Reading This Guide

This guide assumes only that you know how to program in the C language and that you have some background in mathematics (geometry, trigonometry, linear algebra, calculus, and differential geometry). Even if you have little or no experience with computer-graphics technology, you should be able to follow most of the discussions in this book. Of course, computer graphics is a huge subject, so you may want to enrich your learning experience with supplemental reading.

- *Computer Graphics: Principles and Practice* by James D. Foley, Andries van Dam, Steven K. Feiner, and John F. Hughes (Reading, MA: Addison-Wesley, 1990)—This book is an encyclopedic treatment of the subject of computer graphics. It includes a wealth of information but is probably best read after you have some experience with the subject.

- *3D Computer Graphics: A User's Guide for Artists and Designers* by Andrew S. Glassner (New York: Design Press, 1989)—This book is a nontechnical, gentle introduction to computer graphics. It focuses on the visual effects that can be achieved rather than on the techniques needed to achieve them.

Once you begin programming with OpenGL, you might want to obtain the *OpenGL Reference Manual* by the OpenGL Architecture Review Board (Reading, MA: Addison-Wesley Developers Press, 1996), which is designed as a companion volume to this guide. The *Reference Manual* provides a technical view of how OpenGL operates on data that describes a geometric object or an image to produce an image on the screen. It also contains full descriptions of each set of related OpenGL commands—the parameters used by the commands, the default values for those parameters, and what the commands accomplish. Many OpenGL implementations have this same material on-line, in the form of *man* pages or other help documents, and it's probably more up-to-date. There is also a http version on the World Wide Web; consult Silicon Graphics OpenGL Web Site (see page xxii) for the latest pointer.

OpenGL is really a hardware-independent specification of a programming interface, and you use a particular implementation of it on a particular kind of hardware. This guide explains how to program with any OpenGL implementation. However, since implementations may vary slightly—in performance and in providing additional, optional features, for example—you might want to investigate whether supplementary documentation is available for the particular implementation you're using. In addition, you might have OpenGL-related utilities, toolkits, programming and debugging support, widgets, sample programs, and demos available to you with your system.

How to Obtain the Sample Code

This guide contains many sample programs to illustrate the use of particular OpenGL programming techniques. These programs make use of Mark Kilgard's OpenGL Utility Toolkit (GLUT). GLUT is documented in *OpenGL Programming for the X Window System* by Mark Kilgard (Reading, MA: Addison-Wesley Developers Press, 1996). The section "OpenGL-Related Libraries" on page 14 and Appendix D gives more information about using GLUT. If you have access to the Internet, you can obtain the source code for both the sample programs and GLUT for free via anonymous ftp (file-transfer protocol).

For the source code examples found in this book, grab this file:

```
ftp://sgigate.sgi.com/pub/opengl/opengl1_1.tar.Z
```

The files you receive are compressed *tar* archives. To uncompress and extract the files, type

```
uncompress opengl1_1.tar
tar xf opengl1_1.tar
```

For Mark Kilgard's source code for an X Window System version of GLUT, you need to know what the most current version is. The filename will be *glut-i.j.tar.Z*, where *i* is the major revision number and *j* is the minor revision number of the most recent version. Check the directory for the right numbers, then grab this file:

```
ftp://sgigate.sgi.com/pub/opengl/xjournal/GLUT/glut-i.j.tar.Z
```

This file must also be uncompressed and extracted by using the *tar* command. The sample programs and GLUT library are created as subdirectories from wherever you are in the file directory structure.

Other ports of GLUT (for example, for Microsoft Windows NT) are springing up. A good place to start searching for the latest developments in GLUT and for OpenGL, in general, is Silicon Graphics' OpenGL Web Site:

```
http://www.sgi.com/Technology/openGL
```

Many implementations of OpenGL might also include the code samples as part of the system. This source code is probably the best source for your implementation, because it might have been optimized for your system.

Read your machine-specific OpenGL documentation to see where the code samples can be found.

Errata

Although this book is ideal and perfec in every conceivable way, there is a a pointer to an errata list from the Silicon Graphics OpenGL Web Site:

`http://www.sgi.com/Technology/openGL`

The authors are quite certain there will be a little note there to reassure the reader of the pristeen quality of this book.

Style Conventions

These style conventions are used in this guide:

- **Bold**—Command and routine names and matrices
- *Italics*—Variables, arguments, parameter names, spatial dimensions, matrix components, and the first occurrence of key terms
- Regular—Enumerated types and defined constants

Code examples are set off from the text in a monospace font, and command summaries are shaded with gray boxes.

In a command summary, braces are used to identify choices among data types. In the following example, **glCommand** has four possible suffixes: s, i, f, and d, which stand for the data types GLshort, GLint, GLfloat, and GLdouble. In the function prototype for **glCommand**, *TYPE* is a wildcard that represents the data type indicated by the suffix.

void **glCommand**{sifd}(*TYPE x1*, *TYPE y1*, *TYPE x2*, *TYPE y2*);

Acknowledgments

The second edition of this book required the support of many individuals. The impetus for the second edition began with Paula Womack and Tom McReynolds of Silicon Graphics, who recognized the need for a revision and also contributed some of the new material. John Schimpf, OpenGL Product Manager at Silicon Graphics, was instrumental in getting the revision off and running.

Thanks to many people at Silicon Graphics: Allen Akin, Brian Cabral, Norman Chin, Kathleen Danielson, Craig Dunwoody, Michael Gold, Paul Ho, Deanna Hohn, Brian Hook, Kevin Hunter, David Koller, Zicheng Liu, Rob Mace, Mark Segal, Pierre Tardif, and David Yu for putting up with intrusions and inane questions. Thanks to Dave Orton and Kurt Akeley for executive-level support. Thanks to Kay Maitz and Renate Kempf for document production support. And thanks to Cindy Ahuna, for always keeping an eye out for free food.

Special thanks are due to the reviewers who volunteered and trudged through the six hundred pages of technical material that constitute the second edition: Bill Armstrong of Evans & Sutherland, Patrick Brown of IBM, Jim Cobb of Parametric Technology, Mark Kilgard of Silicon Graphics, Dale Kirkland of Intergraph, and Andy Vesper of Digital Equipment. Their careful diligence has greatly improved the quality of this book.

Thanks to Mike Heck of Template Graphics Software, Gilman Wong of Microsoft, and Suzy Deffeyes of IBM for their contributions to the technical information in Appendix C.

The continued success of the OpenGL owes much to the commitment of the OpenGL Architecture Review Board (ARB) participants. They guide the evolution of the OpenGL standard and update the specification to reflect the needs and desires of the graphics industry. Active contributors of the OpenGL ARB include Fred Fisher of AccelGraphics; Bill Clifford, Dick

Coulter, and Andy Vesper of Digital Equipment Corporation; Bill Armstrong of Evans & Sutherland; Kevin LeFebvre and Randi Rost of Hewlett-Packard; Pat Brown and Bimal Poddar of IBM; Igor Sinyak of Intel; Dale Kirkland of Intergraph; Henri Warren of Megatek; Otto Berkes, Drew Bliss, Hock San Lee, and Steve Wright of Microsoft; Ken Garnett of NCD; Jim Cobb of Parametric Technology; Craig Dunwoody, Chris Frazier, and Paula Womack of Silicon Graphics; Tim Misner and Bill Sweeney of Sun Microsystems; Mike Heck of Template Graphics Software; and Andy Bigos, Phil Huxley, and Jeremy Morris of 3Dlabs.

The second edition of this book would not have been possible without the first edition, and neither edition would have been possible without the creation of OpenGL.

Thanks to the chief architects of OpenGL: Mark Segal and Kurt Akeley. Special recognition goes to the pioneers who heavily contributed to the initial design and functionality of OpenGL: Allen Akin, David Blythe, Jim Bushnell, Dick Coulter, John Dennis, Raymond Drewry, Fred Fisher, Chris Frazier, Momi Furuya, Bill Glazier, Kipp Hickman, Paul Ho, Rick Hodgson, Simon Hui, Lesley Kalmin, Phil Karlton, On Lee, Randi Rost, Kevin P. Smith, Murali Sundaresan, Pierre Tardif, Linas Vepstas, Chuck Whitmer, Jim Winget, and Wei Yen.

Assembling the set of colorplates was no mean feat. The sequence of plates based on the cover image (Plate 1 through Plate 9) was created by Thad Beier, Seth Katz, and Mason Woo. Plate 10 through Plate 12b are snapshots of programs created by Mason. Gavin Bell, Kevin Goldsmith, Linda Roy, and Mark Daly created the fly-through program used for Plate 24. The model for Plate 25 was created by Barry Brouillette of Silicon Graphics; Doug Voorhies, also of Silicon Graphics, performed some image processing for the final image. Plate 26 was created by John Rohlf and Michael Jones, both of Silicon Graphics. Plate 27 was created by Carl Korobkin of Silicon Graphics. Plate 28 is a snapshot from a program written by Gavin Bell with contributions from the Open Inventor team at Silicon Graphics—Alain Dumesny, Dave Immel, David Mott, Howard Look, Paul Isaacs, Paul Strauss, and Rikk Carey. Plate 29 and Plate 30 are snapshots from a visual simulation program created by the Silicon Graphics IRIS Performer team—Craig Phillips, John Rohlf, Sharon Clay, Jim Helman, and Michael Jones—from a database produced for Silicon Graphics by Paradigm Simulation, Inc. Plate 31 is a snapshot from skyfly, the precursor to Performer, which was created by John Rohlf, Sharon Clay, and Ben Garlick, all of Silicon Graphics.

Several other people played special roles in creating this book. If we were to list other names as authors on the front of this book, Kurt Akeley and Mark

Segal would be there, as honorary yeoman. They helped define the structure and goals of the book, provided key sections of material for it, reviewed it when everybody else was too tired of it to do so, and supplied that all-important humor and support throughout the process. Kay Maitz provided invaluable production and design assistance. Kathy Gochenour very generously created many of the illustrations for this book. Susan Riley copyedited the manuscript, which is a brave task, indeed.

And now, each of the authors would like to take the 15 minutes that have been allotted to them by Andy Warhol to say thank you.

I'd like to thank my managers at Silicon Graphics—Dave Larson and Way Ting—and the members of my group—Patricia Creek, Arthur Evans, Beth Fryer, Jed Hartman, Ken Jones, Robert Reimann, Eve Stratton (aka Margaret-Anne Halse), John Stearns, and Josie Wernecke—for their support during this lengthy process. Last but surely not least, I want to thank those whose contributions toward this project are too deep and mysterious to elucidate: Yvonne Leach, Kathleen Lancaster, Caroline Rose, Cindy Kleinfeld, and my parents, Florence and Ferdinand Neider.

—JLN

In addition to my parents, Edward and Irene Davis, I'd like to thank the people who taught me most of what I know about computers and computer graphics—Doug Engelbart and Jim Clark.

—TRD

I'd like to thank the many past and current members of Silicon Graphics whose accommodation and enlightenment were essential to my contribution to this book: Gerald Anderson, Wendy Chin, Bert Fornaciari, Bill Glazier, Jill Huchital, Howard Look, Bill Mannel, David Marsland, Dave Orton, Linda Roy, Keith Seto, and Dave Shreiner. Very special thanks to Karrin Nicol, Leilani Gayles, Kevin Dankwardt, Kiyoshi Hasegawa, and Raj Singh for their guidance throughout my career. I also bestow much gratitude to my teammates on the Stanford B ice hockey team for periods of glorious distraction throughout the initial writing of this book. Finally, I'd like to thank my family, especially my mother, Bo, and my late father, Henry.

—MW

Figures

Tables

Examples

Chapter 1

Introduction to OpenGL

Chapter Objectives

After reading this chapter, you'll be able to do the following:

- Appreciate in general terms what OpenGL does

- Identify different levels of rendering complexity

- Understand the basic structure of an OpenGL program

- Recognize OpenGL command syntax

- Identify the sequence of operations of the OpenGL rendering pipeline

- Understand in general terms how to animate graphics in an OpenGL program

This chapter introduces OpenGL. It has the following major sections:

- "What Is OpenGL?" on page 2 explains what OpenGL is, what it does and doesn't do, and how it works.

- "A Smidgen of OpenGL Code" on page 5 presents a small OpenGL program and briefly discusses it. This section also defines a few basic computer-graphics terms.

- "OpenGL Command Syntax" on page 7 explains some of the conventions and notations used by OpenGL commands.

- "OpenGL as a State Machine" on page 9 describes the use of state variables in OpenGL and the commands for querying, enabling, and disabling states.

- "OpenGL Rendering Pipeline" on page 10 shows a typical sequence of operations for processing geometric and image data.

- "OpenGL-Related Libraries" on page 14 describes sets of OpenGL-related routines, including an auxiliary library specifically written for this book to simplify programming examples.

- "Animation" on page 20 explains in general terms how to create pictures on the screen that move.

What Is OpenGL?

OpenGL is a software interface to graphics hardware. This interface consists of about 150 distinct commands that you use to specify the objects and operations needed to produce interactive three-dimensional applications.

OpenGL is designed as a streamlined, hardware-independent interface to be implemented on many different hardware platforms. To achieve these qualities, no commands for performing windowing tasks or obtaining user input are included in OpenGL; instead, you must work through whatever windowing system controls the particular hardware you're using. Similarly, OpenGL doesn't provide high-level commands for describing models of three-dimensional objects. Such commands might allow you to specify relatively complicated shapes such as automobiles, parts of the body, airplanes, or molecules. With OpenGL, you must build up your desired model from a small set of *geometric primitives*—points, lines, and polygons.

A sophisticated library that provides these features could certainly be built on top of OpenGL. The OpenGL Utility Library (GLU) provides many of the modeling features, such as quadric surfaces and NURBS curves and surfaces. GLU is a standard part of every OpenGL implementation. Also, there is a higher-level, object-oriented toolkit, Open Inventor, which is built atop OpenGL, and is available separately for many implementations of OpenGL. (See "OpenGL-Related Libraries" on page 14 for more information about Open Inventor.)

Now that you know what OpenGL *doesn't* do, here's what it *does* do. Take a look at the color plates—they illustrate typical uses of OpenGL. They show the scene on the cover of this book, *rendered* (which is to say, drawn) by a computer using OpenGL in successively more complicated ways. The following list describes in general terms how these pictures were made.

- Plate 1 shows the entire scene displayed as a *wireframe* model—that is, as if all the objects in the scene were made of wire. Each *line* of wire corresponds to an edge of a primitive (typically a polygon). For example, the surface of the table is constructed from triangular polygons that are positioned like slices of pie.

  Note that you can see portions of objects that would be obscured if the objects were solid rather than wireframe. For example, you can see the entire model of the hills outside the window even though most of this model is normally hidden by the wall of the room. The globe appears to be nearly solid because it's composed of hundreds of colored blocks, and you see the wireframe lines for all the edges of all the blocks, even those forming the back side of the globe. The way the globe is constructed gives you an idea of how complex objects can be created by assembling lower-level objects.

- Plate 2 shows a *depth-cued* version of the same wireframe scene. Note that the lines farther from the eye are dimmer, just as they would be in real life, thereby giving a visual cue of *depth*. OpenGL uses atmospheric effects (collectively referred to as *fog*) to achieve depth cueing.

- Plate 3 shows an *antialiased* version of the wireframe scene. Antialiasing is a technique for reducing the jagged edges (also known as *jaggies*) created when approximating smooth edges using *pixels*—short for picture *elements*—which are confined to a rectangular grid. Such jaggies are usually the most visible with near-horizontal or near-vertical lines.

- Plate 4 shows a *flat-shaded*, *unlit* version of the scene. The objects in the scene are now shown as solid. They appear "flat" in the sense that only one color is used to render each polygon, so they don't appear smoothly rounded. There are no effects from any light sources.

- Plate 5 shows a *lit, smooth-shaded* version of the scene. Note how the scene looks much more realistic and three-dimensional when the objects are shaded to respond to the light sources in the room as if the objects were smoothly rounded.

- Plate 6 adds *shadows* and *textures* to the previous version of the scene. Shadows aren't an explicitly defined feature of OpenGL (there is no "shadow command"), but you can create them yourself using the techniques described in Chapter 14. *Texture mapping* allows you to apply a two-dimensional image onto a three-dimensional object. In this scene, the top on the table surface is the most vibrant example of texture mapping. The wood grain on the floor and table surface are all texture mapped, as well as the wallpaper and the toy top (on the table).

- Plate 7 shows a *motion-blurred* object in the scene. The sphinx (or dog, depending on your Rorschach tendencies) appears to be captured moving forward, leaving a blurred trace of its path of motion.

- Plate 8 shows the scene as it's drawn for the cover of the book from a different viewpoint. This plate illustrates that the image really is a snapshot of models of three-dimensional objects.

- Plate 9 brings back the use of fog, which was seen in Plate 2, to show the presence of smoke particles in the air. Note how the same effect in Plate 2 now has a more dramatic impact in Plate 9.

- Plate 10 shows the *depth-of-field effect*, which simulates the inability of a camera lens to maintain all objects in a photographed scene in focus. The camera focuses on a particular spot in the scene. Objects that are significantly closer or farther than that spot are somewhat blurred.

The color plates give you an idea of the kinds of things you can do with the OpenGL graphics system. The following list briefly describes the major graphics operations which OpenGL performs to render an image on the screen. (See "OpenGL Rendering Pipeline" on page 10 for detailed information about this order of operations.)

1. Construct shapes from geometric primitives, thereby creating mathematical descriptions of objects. (OpenGL considers points, lines, polygons, images, and bitmaps to be primitives.)

2. Arrange the objects in three-dimensional space and select the desired vantage point for viewing the composed scene.

3. Calculate the color of all the objects. The color might be explicitly assigned by the application, determined from specified lighting conditions, obtained by pasting a texture onto the objects, or some combination of these three actions.

4. Convert the mathematical description of objects and their associated color information to pixels on the screen. This process is called *rasterization*.

During these stages, OpenGL might perform other operations, such as eliminating parts of objects that are hidden by other objects. In addition, after the scene is rasterized but before it's drawn on the screen, you can perform some operations on the pixel data if you want.

In some implementations (such as with the X Window System), OpenGL is designed to work even if the computer that displays the graphics you create isn't the computer that runs your graphics program. This might be the case if you work in a networked computer environment where many computers are connected to one another by a digital network. In this situation, the computer on which your program runs and issues OpenGL drawing commands is called the *client*, and the computer that receives those commands and performs the drawing is called the *server*. The format for transmitting OpenGL commands (called the *protocol*) from the client to the server is always the same, so OpenGL programs can work across a *network* even if the client and server are different kinds of computers. If an OpenGL program isn't running across a network, then there's only one computer, and it is both the client and the server.

A Smidgen of OpenGL Code

Because you can do so many things with the OpenGL graphics system, an OpenGL program can be complicated. However, the basic structure of a useful program can be simple: Its tasks are to initialize certain states that control how OpenGL renders and to specify objects to be rendered.

Before you look at some OpenGL code, let's go over a few terms. *Rendering*, which you've already seen used, is the process by which a computer creates images from models. These *models*, or objects, are constructed from geometric primitives—points, lines, and polygons—that are specified by their *vertices*.

The final rendered image consists of pixels drawn on the screen; a pixel is the smallest visible element the display hardware can put on the screen.

Information about the pixels (for instance, what color they're supposed to be) is organized in memory into bitplanes. A *bitplane* is an area of memory that holds one *bit* of information for every pixel on the screen; the bit might indicate how red a particular pixel is supposed to be, for example. The bitplanes are themselves organized into a *framebuffer*, which holds all the information that the graphics display needs to control the color and intensity of all the pixels on the screen.

Now look at what an OpenGL program might look like. Example 1-1 renders a white rectangle on a black background, as shown in Figure 1-1.

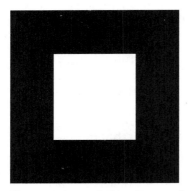

Figure 1-1   White Rectangle on a Black Background

Example 1-1   Chunk of OpenGL Code

```
#include <whateverYouNeed.h>

main() {

    InitializeAWindowPlease();

    glClearColor (0.0, 0.0, 0.0, 0.0);
    glClear (GL_COLOR_BUFFER_BIT);
    glColor3f (1.0, 1.0, 1.0);
    glOrtho(0.0, 1.0, 0.0, 1.0, -1.0, 1.0);
    glBegin(GL_POLYGON);
        glVertex3f (0.25, 0.25, 0.0);
        glVertex3f (0.75, 0.25, 0.0);
        glVertex3f (0.75, 0.75, 0.0);
        glVertex3f (0.25, 0.75, 0.0);
    glEnd();
    glFlush();
```

```
        UpdateTheWindowAndCheckForEvents();
}
```

The first line of the **main()** routine initializes a *window* on the screen:
The **InitializeAWindowPlease()** routine is meant as a placeholder for
window system-specific routines, which are generally not OpenGL calls.
The next two lines are OpenGL commands that clear the window to black:
glClearColor() establishes what color the window will be cleared to, and
glClear() actually clears the window. Once the clearing color is set, the
window is cleared to that color whenever **glClear()** is called. This clearing
color can be changed with another call to **glClearColor()**. Similarly, the
glColor3f() command establishes what color to use for drawing objects—in
this case, the color is white. All objects drawn after this point use this color,
until it's changed with another call to set the color.

The next OpenGL command used in the program, **glOrtho()**, specifies
the *coordinate system* OpenGL assumes as it draws the final image and how
the image gets mapped to the screen. The next calls, which are bracketed
by **glBegin()** and **glEnd()**, define the object to be drawn—in this example,
a polygon with four vertices. The polygon's "corners" are defined by the
glVertex3f() commands. As you might be able to guess from the arguments,
which are (x, y, z) coordinates, the polygon is a rectangle on the z=0 plane.

Finally, **glFlush()** ensures that the drawing commands are actually executed
rather than stored in a *buffer* awaiting additional OpenGL commands. The
UpdateTheWindowAndCheckForEvents() placeholder routine manages
the contents of the window and begins event processing.

Actually, this piece of OpenGL code isn't well structured. You may be
asking, "What happens if I try to move or resize the window?" Or, "Do I
need to reset the coordinate system each time I draw the rectangle?" Later
in this chapter, you will see replacements for both
InitializeAWindowPlease() and
UpdateTheWindowAndCheckForEvents() that actually work but will
require restructuring the code to make it efficient.

OpenGL Command Syntax

As you might have observed from the simple program in the previous
section, OpenGL commands use the prefix **gl** and initial capital letters for
each word making up the command name (recall **glClearColor()**, for
example). Similarly, OpenGL defined constants begin with GL_, use all

capital letters, and use underscores to separate words (like GL_COLOR_BUFFER_BIT).

You might also have noticed some seemingly extraneous letters appended to some command names (for example, the **3f** in **glColor3f()** and **glVertex3f()**). It's true that the **Color** part of the command name **glColor3f()** is enough to define the command as one that sets the current color. However, more than one such command has been defined so that you can use different types of arguments. In particular, the **3** part of the suffix indicates that three arguments are given; another version of the **Color** command takes four arguments. The **f** part of the suffix indicates that the arguments are floating-point numbers. Having different formats allows OpenGL to accept the user's data in his or her own data format.

Some OpenGL commands accept as many as 8 different data types for their arguments. The letters used as suffixes to specify these data types for ISO C implementations of OpenGL are shown in Table 1-1, along with the corresponding OpenGL type definitions. The particular implementation of OpenGL that you're using might not follow this scheme exactly; an implementation in C++ or Ada, for example, wouldn't need to.

Suffix	Data Type	Typical Corresponding C-Language Type	OpenGL Type Definition
b	8-bit integer	signed char	GLbyte
s	16-bit integer	short	GLshort
i	32-bit integer	int or long	GLint, GLsizei
f	32-bit floating-point	float	GLfloat, GLclampf
d	64-bit floating-point	double	GLdouble, GLclampd
ub	8-bit unsigned integer	unsigned char	GLubyte, GLboolean
us	16-bit unsigned integer	unsigned short	GLushort
ui	32-bit unsigned integer	unsigned int or unsigned long	GLuint, GLenum, GLbitfield

Table 1-1   Command Suffixes and Argument Data Types

Thus, the two commands

```
glVertex2i(1, 3);
glVertex2f(1.0, 3.0);
```

are equivalent, except that the first specifies the vertex's coordinates as 32-bit integers, and the second specifies them as single-precision floating-point numbers.

Note: Implementations of OpenGL have leeway in selecting which C data type to use to represent OpenGL data types. If you resolutely use the OpenGL defined data types throughout your application, you will avoid mismatched types when porting your code between different implementations.

Some OpenGL commands can take a final letter **v**, which indicates that the command takes a pointer to a vector (or array) of values rather than a series of individual arguments. Many commands have both vector and nonvector versions, but some commands accept only individual arguments and others require that at least some of the arguments be specified as a vector. The following lines show how you might use a vector and a nonvector version of the command that sets the current color:

```
glColor3f(1.0, 0.0, 0.0);

GLfloat color_array[] = {1.0, 0.0, 0.0};
glColor3fv(color_array);
```

Finally, OpenGL defines the typedef GLvoid. This is most often used for OpenGL commands that accept pointers to arrays of values.

In the rest of this guide (except in actual code examples), OpenGL commands are referred to by their base names only, and an asterisk is included to indicate that there may be more to the command name. For example, **glColor*()** stands for all variations of the command you use to set the current color. If we want to make a specific point about one version of a particular command, we include the suffix necessary to define that version. For example, **glVertex*v()** refers to all the vector versions of the command you use to specify vertices.

OpenGL as a State Machine

OpenGL is a state machine. You put it into various states (or modes) that then remain in effect until you change them. As you've already seen, the current color is a state variable. You can set the current color to white, red, or any other color, and thereafter every object is drawn with that color until you set the current color to something else. The current color is only one of many state variables that OpenGL maintains. Others control such things as the current viewing and projection transformations, line and polygon stipple patterns, polygon drawing modes, pixel-packing conventions, positions and characteristics of lights, and material properties of the objects being drawn. Many state variables refer to modes that are enabled or disabled with the command **glEnable()** or **glDisable()**.

Each state variable or mode has a default value, and at any point you can query the system for each variable's current value. Typically, you use one of the six following commands to do this: **glGetBooleanv()**, **glGetDoublev()**, **glGetFloatv()**, **glGetIntegerv()**, **glGetPointerv()**, or **glIsEnabled()**. Which of these commands you select depends on what data type you want the answer to be given in. Some state variables have a more specific query command (such as **glGetLight*()**, **glGetError()**, or **glGetPolygonStipple()**). In addition, you can save a collection of state variables on an attribute stack with **glPushAttrib()** or **glPushClientAttrib()**, temporarily modify them, and later restore the values with **glPopAttrib()** or **glPopClientAttrib()**. For temporary state changes, you should use these commands rather than any of the query commands, since they're likely to be more efficient.

See Appendix B for the complete list of state variables you can query. For each variable, the appendix also lists a suggested **glGet*()** command that returns the variable's value, the attribute class to which it belongs, and the variable's default value.

OpenGL Rendering Pipeline

Most implementations of OpenGL have a similar order of operations, a series of processing stages called the OpenGL rendering pipeline. This ordering, as shown in Figure 1-2, is not a strict rule of how OpenGL is implemented but provides a reliable guide for predicting what OpenGL will do.

If you are new to three-dimensional graphics, the upcoming description may seem like drinking water out of a fire hose. You can skim this now, but come back to Figure 1-2 as you go through each chapter in this book.

The following diagram shows the Henry Ford assembly line approach, which OpenGL takes to processing data. Geometric data (vertices, lines, and polygons) follow the path through the row of boxes that includes evaluators and per-vertex operations, while pixel data (pixels, images, and bitmaps) are treated differently for part of the process. Both types of data undergo the same final steps (rasterization and per-fragment operations) before the final pixel data is written into the framebuffer.

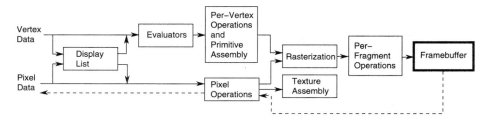

Figure 1-2   Order of Operations

Now you'll see more detail about the key stages in the OpenGL rendering pipeline.

Display Lists

All data, whether it describes geometry or pixels, can be saved in a *display list* for current or later use. (The alternative to retaining data in a display list is processing the data immediately—also known as *immediate mode*.) When a display list is executed, the retained data is sent from the display list just as if it were sent by the application in immediate mode. (See Chapter 7, "Display Lists," for more information about display lists.)

Evaluators

All geometric primitives are eventually described by vertices. Parametric curves and surfaces may be initially described by control points and polynomial functions called basis functions. Evaluators provide a method to derive the vertices used to represent the surface from the control points. The method is a polynomial mapping, which can produce surface normal, texture coordinates, colors, and spatial coordinate values from the control points. (See Chapter 12, "Evaluators and NURBS," to learn more about evaluators.)

Per-Vertex Operations

For vertex data, next is the "per-vertex operations" stage, which converts the vertices into primitives. Some vertex data (for example, spatial coordinates) are transformed by 4 x 4 floating-point matrices. Spatial coordinates are projected from a position in the 3D world to a position on your screen. (See Chapter 3, "Viewing," for details about the transformation matrices.)

If advanced features are enabled, this stage is even busier. If texturing is used, texture coordinates may be generated and transformed here. If lighting is enabled, the lighting calculations are performed using the transformed vertex, surface normal, light source position, material properties, and other lighting information to produce a color value.

Primitive Assembly

Clipping, a major part of primitive assembly, is the elimination of portions of geometry which fall outside a half-space, defined by a plane. Point clipping simply passes or rejects vertices; line or polygon clipping can add additional vertices depending upon how the line or polygon is clipped.

In some cases, this is followed by perspective division, which makes distant geometric objects appear smaller than closer objects. Then viewport and depth (z coordinate) operations are applied. If culling is enabled and the primitive is a polygon, it then may be rejected by a culling test. Depending upon the polygon mode, a polygon may be drawn as points or lines. (See "Polygon Details" on page 55.)

The results of this stage are complete geometric primitives, which are the transformed and clipped vertices with related color, depth, and sometimes texture-coordinate values and guidelines for the rasterization step.

Pixel Operations

While geometric data takes one path through the OpenGL rendering pipeline, pixel data takes a different route. Pixels from an array in system memory are first unpacked from one of a variety of formats into the proper number of components. Next the data is scaled, biased, and processed by a pixel map. The results are clamped and then either written into texture memory or sent to the rasterization step. (See "Imaging Pipeline" on page 296.)

If pixel data is read from the frame buffer, pixel-transfer operations (scale, bias, mapping, and clamping) are performed. Then these results are packed into an appropriate format and returned to an array in system memory.

There are special pixel copy operations to copy data in the framebuffer to other parts of the framebuffer or to the texture memory. A single pass is made through the pixel transfer operations before the data is written to the texture memory or back to the framebuffer.

Texture Assembly

An OpenGL application may wish to apply texture images onto geometric objects to make them look more realistic. If several texture images are used, it's wise to put them into texture objects so that you can easily switch among them.

Some OpenGL implementations may have special resources to accelerate texture performance. There may be specialized, high-performance texture memory. If this memory is available, the texture objects may be prioritized to control the use of this limited and valuable resource. (See Chapter 9, "Texture Mapping.")

Rasterization

Rasterization is the conversion of both geometric and pixel data into *fragments*. Each fragment square corresponds to a pixel in the framebuffer. Line and polygon stipples, line width, point size, shading model, and coverage calculations to support antialiasing are taken into consideration as vertices are connected into lines or the interior pixels are calculated for a filled polygon. Color and depth values are assigned for each fragment square.

Fragment Operations

Before values are actually stored into the framebuffer, a series of operations are performed that may alter or even throw out fragments. All these operations can be enabled or disabled.

The first operation which may be encountered is texturing, where a *texel* (texture element) is generated from texture memory for each fragment and applied to the fragment. Then fog calculations may be applied, followed by the scissor test, the alpha test, the stencil test, and the depth-buffer test (the depth buffer is for hidden-surface removal). Failing an enabled test may end the continued processing of a fragment's square. Then, blending, dithering, logical operation, and masking by a bitmask may be performed. (See Chapter 6, "Blending, Antialiasing, Fog, and Polygon Offset" and Chapter 10, "The Framebuffer.") Finally, the thoroughly processed fragment is drawn into the appropriate buffer, where it has finally advanced to be a pixel and achieved its final resting place.

OpenGL-Related Libraries

OpenGL provides a powerful but primitive set of rendering commands, and all higher-level drawing must be done in terms of these commands. Also, OpenGL programs have to use the underlying mechanisms of the windowing system. A number of libraries exist to allow you to simplify your programming tasks, including the following:

- The OpenGL Utility Library (GLU) contains several routines that use lower-level OpenGL commands to perform such tasks as setting up matrices for specific viewing orientations and projections, performing polygon tessellation, and rendering surfaces. This library is provided as part of every OpenGL implementation. Portions of the GLU are described in the *OpenGL Reference Manual*. The more useful GLU routines are described in this guide, where they're relevant to the topic being discussed, such as in all of Chapter 11 and in the section "The GLU NURBS Interface" on page 455. GLU routines use the prefix **glu**.

- For every window system, there is a library that extends the functionality of that window system to support OpenGL rendering. For machines that use the X Window System, the OpenGL Extension to the X Window System (GLX) is provided as an adjunct to OpenGL. GLX routines use the prefix **glX**. For Microsoft Windows, the WGL routines provide the Windows to OpenGL interface. All WGL routines use the prefix **wgl**. For IBM OS/2, the PGL is the Presentation Manager to OpenGL interface, and its routines use the prefix **pgl**.

  All these window system extension libraries are described in more detail in both Appendix C. In addition, the GLX routines are also described in the *OpenGL Reference Manual*.

- The OpenGL Utility Toolkit (GLUT) is a window system-independent toolkit, written by Mark Kilgard, to hide the complexities of differing window system APIs. GLUT is the subject of the next section, and it's described in more detail in Mark Kilgard's book *OpenGL Programming for the X Window System* (ISBN 0-201-48359-9). GLUT routines use the prefix **glut.** "How to Obtain the Sample Code" on page v describes how to obtain the source code for GLUT, using ftp.

- Open Inventor is an object-oriented toolkit based on OpenGL which provides objects and methods for creating interactive three-dimensional graphics applications. Open Inventor, which is written in C++, provides prebuilt objects and a built-in event model for user interaction, high-level application components for creating and editing three-dimensional scenes, and the ability to print objects and exchange data in other graphics formats. Open Inventor is separate from OpenGL.

Include Files

For all OpenGL applications, you want to include the gl.h header file in every file. Almost all OpenGL applications use GLU, the aforementioned OpenGL Utility Library, which requires inclusion of the glu.h header file. So almost every OpenGL source file begins with

```
#include <GL/gl.h>
#include <GL/glu.h>
```

If you are directly accessing a window interface library to support OpenGL, such as GLX, AGL, PGL, or WGL, you must include additional header files. For example, if you are calling GLX, you may need to add these lines to your code

```
#include <X11/Xlib.h>
#include <GL/glx.h>
```

If you are using GLUT for managing your window manager tasks, you should include

```
#include <GL/glut.h>
```

Note that glut.h includes gl.h, glu.h, and glx.h automatically, so including all three files is redundant. GLUT for Microsoft Windows includes the appropriate header file to access WGL.

GLUT, the OpenGL Utility Toolkit

As you know, OpenGL contains rendering commands but is designed to be independent of any window system or operating system. Consequently, it contains no commands for opening windows or reading events from the keyboard or mouse. Unfortunately, it's impossible to write a complete graphics program without at least opening a window, and most interesting programs require a bit of user input or other services from the operating system or window system. In many cases, complete programs make the most interesting examples, so this book uses GLUT to simplify opening windows, detecting input, and so on. If you have an implementation of OpenGL and GLUT on your system, the examples in this book should run without change when linked with them.

In addition, since OpenGL drawing commands are limited to those that generate simple geometric primitives (points, lines, and polygons), GLUT includes several routines that create more complicated three-dimensional objects such as a sphere, a torus, and a teapot. This way, snapshots of program output can be interesting to look at. (Note that the OpenGL Utility Library, GLU, also has quadrics routines that create some of the same three-dimensional objects as GLUT, such as a sphere, cylinder, or cone.)

GLUT may not be satisfactory for full-featured OpenGL applications, but you may find it a useful starting point for learning OpenGL. The rest of this section briefly describes a small subset of GLUT routines so that you can follow the programming examples in the rest of this book. (See Appendix D for more details about this subset of GLUT, or see Chapters 4 and 5 of *OpenGL Programming for the X Window System* for information about the rest of GLUT.)

Window Management

Five routines perform tasks necessary to initialize a window.

- **glutInit**(int *argc*, char **argv*) initializes GLUT and processes any command line arguments (for X, this would be options like -display and -geometry). **glutInit**() should be called before any other GLUT routine.

- **glutInitDisplayMode**(unsigned int *mode*) specifies whether to use an *RGBA* or color-index color model. You can also specify whether you want a single- or double-buffered window. (If you're working in color-index mode, you'll want to load certain colors into the color map; use **glutSetColor**() to do this.) Finally, you can use this routine to indicate that you want the window to have an associated depth, stencil, and/or accumulation buffer. For example, if you want a window with double buffering, the RGBA color model, and a depth buffer, you might call **glutInitDisplayMode**(*GLUT_DOUBLE* | *GLUT_RGB* | *GLUT_DEPTH*).

- **glutInitWindowPosition**(int *x*, int *y*) specifies the screen location for the upper-left corner of your window.

- **glutInitWindowSize**(int *width*, int *size*) specifies the size, in pixels, of your window.

- int **glutCreateWindow**(char **string*) creates a window with an OpenGL context. It returns a unique identifier for the new window. Be warned: Until **glutMainLoop()** is called (see next section), the window is not yet displayed.

The Display Callback

glutDisplayFunc(void (**func*)(void)) is the first and most important event callback function you will see. Whenever GLUT determines the contents of the window need to be redisplayed, the callback function registered by **glutDisplayFunc()** is executed. Therefore, you should put all the routines you need to redraw the scene in the display callback function.

If your program changes the contents of the window, sometimes you will have to call **glutPostRedisplay**(void), which gives **glutMainLoop()** a nudge to call the registered display callback at its next opportunity.

Running the Program

The very last thing you must do is call **glutMainLoop**(void). All windows that have been created are now shown, and rendering to those windows is now effective. Event processing begins, and the registered display callback is triggered. Once this loop is entered, it is never exited!

Example 1-2 shows how you might use GLUT to create the simple program shown in Example 1-1. Note the restructuring of the code. To maximize efficiency, operations that need only be called once (setting the background color and coordinate system) are now in a procedure called **init()**. Operations to render (and possibly re-render) the scene are in the **display()** procedure, which is the registered GLUT display callback.

Example 1-2   Simple OpenGL Program Using GLUT: hello.c

```c
#include <GL/gl.h>
#include <GL/glut.h>

void display(void)
{
/*  clear all pixels  */
    glClear (GL_COLOR_BUFFER_BIT);

/*  draw white polygon (rectangle) with corners at
 *  (0.25, 0.25, 0.0) and (0.75, 0.75, 0.0)
 */
    glColor3f (1.0, 1.0, 1.0);
    glBegin(GL_POLYGON);
        glVertex3f (0.25, 0.25, 0.0);
        glVertex3f (0.75, 0.25, 0.0);
        glVertex3f (0.75, 0.75, 0.0);
        glVertex3f (0.25, 0.75, 0.0);
    glEnd();

/*  don't wait!
 *  start processing buffered OpenGL routines
 */
    glFlush ();
}

void init (void)
{
/*  select clearing (background) color       */
    glClearColor (0.0, 0.0, 0.0, 0.0);

/*  initialize viewing values  */
    glMatrixMode(GL_PROJECTION);
    glLoadIdentity();
    glOrtho(0.0, 1.0, 0.0, 1.0, -1.0, 1.0);
}
```

```
/*
 * Declare initial window size, position, and display mode
 * (single buffer and RGBA).  Open window with "hello"
 * in its title bar.  Call initialization routines.
 * Register callback function to display graphics.
 * Enter main loop and process events.
 */
int main(int argc, char** argv)
{
    glutInit(&argc, argv);
    glutInitDisplayMode (GLUT_SINGLE | GLUT_RGB);
    glutInitWindowSize (250, 250);
    glutInitWindowPosition (100, 100);
    glutCreateWindow ("hello");
    init ();
    glutDisplayFunc(display);
    glutMainLoop();
    return 0;    /* ISO C requires main to return int. */
}
```

Handling Input Events

You can use these routines to register callback commands that are invoked when specified events occur.

- **glutReshapeFunc**(void (*$func$)(int w, int h)) indicates what action should be taken when the window is resized.

- **glutKeyboardFunc**(void (*$func$)(unsigned char key, int x, int y)) and **glutMouseFunc**(void (*$func$)(int $button$, int $state$, int x, int y)) allow you to link a keyboard key or a mouse button with a routine that's invoked when the key or mouse button is pressed or released.

- **glutMotionFunc**(void (*$func$)(int x, int y)) registers a routine to call back when the mouse is moved while a mouse button is also pressed.

Managing a Background Process

You can specify a function that's to be executed if no other events are pending—for example, when the event loop would otherwise be idle—with **glutIdleFunc**(void (*func)(void)). This routine takes a pointer to the function as its only argument. Pass in NULL (zero) to disable the execution of the function.

Drawing Three-Dimensional Objects

GLUT includes several routines for drawing these three-dimensional objects:

cone	icosahedron	teapot
cube	octahedron	tetrahedron
dodecahedron	sphere	torus

You can draw these objects as wireframes or as solid shaded objects with surface normals defined. For example, the routines for a cube and a sphere are as follows:

void **glutWireCube**(GLdouble *size*);

void **glutSolidCube**(GLdouble *size*);

void **glutWireSphere**(GLdouble *radius*, GLint *slices*, GLint *stacks*);

void **glutSolidSphere**(GLdouble *radius*, GLint *slices*, GLint *stacks*);

All these models are drawn centered at the origin of the world coordinate system. (See Appendix D for information on the prototypes of all these drawing routines.)

Animation

One of the most exciting things you can do on a graphics computer is draw pictures that move. Whether you're an engineer trying to see all sides of a mechanical part you're designing, a pilot learning to fly an airplane using simulation, or merely a computer-game aficionado, it's clear that *animation* is an important part of computer graphics.

In a movie theater, motion is achieved by taking a sequence of pictures and projecting them at 24 per second on the screen. Each frame is moved into position behind the lens, the shutter is opened, and the frame is displayed. The shutter is momentarily closed while the film is advanced to the next frame, then that frame is displayed, and so on. Although you're watching 24 different frames each second, your brain blends them all into a smooth animation. (The old Charlie Chaplin movies were shot at 16 frames per second and are noticeably jerky.) In fact, most modern projectors display each picture twice at a rate of 48 per second to reduce flickering. Computer-graphics screens typically refresh (redraw the picture) approximately 60 to 76 times per second, and some even run at about 120 refreshes per second. Clearly, 60 per second is smoother than 30, and 120 is marginally better than 60. Refresh rates faster than 120, however, are beyond the point of diminishing returns, since the human eye is only so good.

The key reason that motion picture projection works is that each frame is complete when it is displayed. Suppose you try to do computer animation of your million-frame movie with a program like this:

```
open_window();
for (i = 0; i < 1000000; i++) {
    clear_the_window();
    draw_frame(i);
    wait_until_a_24th_of_a_second_is_over();
}
```

If you add the time it takes for your system to clear the screen and to draw a typical frame, this program gives more and more disturbing results depending on how close to 1/24 second it takes to clear and draw. Suppose the drawing takes nearly a full 1/24 second. Items drawn first are visible for the full 1/24 second and present a solid image on the screen; items drawn toward the end are instantly cleared as the program starts on the next frame. They present at best a ghostlike image, since for most of the 1/24 second your eye is viewing the cleared background instead of the items that were unlucky enough to be drawn last. The problem is that this program doesn't display completely drawn frames; instead, you watch the drawing as it happens.

Most OpenGL implementations provide *double-buffering*—hardware or software that supplies two complete color buffers. One is displayed while the other is being drawn. When the drawing of a frame is complete, the two buffers are swapped, so the one that was being viewed is now used for drawing, and vice versa. This is like a movie projector with only two frames in a loop; while one is being projected on the screen, an artist is desperately erasing and redrawing the frame that's not visible. As long as the artist is quick enough, the viewer notices no difference between this setup and one where all the frames are already drawn and the projector is simply displaying them one after the other. With double-buffering, every frame is shown only when the drawing is complete; the viewer never sees a partially drawn frame.

A modified version of the preceding program that does display smoothly animated graphics might look like this:

```
open_window_in_double_buffer_mode();
for (i = 0; i < 1000000; i++) {
    clear_the_window();
    draw_frame(i);
    swap_the_buffers();
}
```

The Refresh That Pauses

For some OpenGL implementations, in addition to simply swapping the viewable and drawable buffers, the **swap_the_buffers()** routine waits until the current screen refresh period is over so that the previous buffer is completely displayed. This routine also allows the new buffer to be completely displayed, starting from the beginning. Assuming that your system refreshes the display 60 times per second, this means that the fastest frame rate you can achieve is 60 frames per second (*fps*), and if all your frames can be cleared and drawn in under 1/60 second, your animation will run smoothly at that rate.

What often happens on such a system is that the frame is too complicated to draw in 1/60 second, so each frame is displayed more than once. If, for example, it takes 1/45 second to draw a frame, you get 30 fps, and the graphics are idle for 1/30–1/45=1/90 second per frame, or one-third of the time.

In addition, the video refresh rate is constant, which can have some unexpected performance consequences. For example, with the 1/60 second per refresh monitor and a constant frame rate, you can run at 60 fps, 30 fps, 20 fps, 15 fps, 12 fps, and so on (60/1, 60/2, 60/3, 60/4, 60/5, ...). That means that if you're writing an application and gradually adding features (say it's a flight simulator, and you're adding ground scenery), at first each feature you add has no effect on the overall performance—you still get 60 fps. Then, all of a sudden, you add one new feature, and the system can't quite draw the whole thing in 1/60 of a second, so the animation slows from 60 fps to 30 fps because it misses the first possible buffer-swapping time. A similar thing happens when the drawing time per frame is more than 1/30 second—the animation drops from 30 to 20 fps.

If the scene's complexity is close to any of the magic times (1/60 second, 2/60 second, 3/60 second, and so on in this example), then because of random variation, some frames go slightly over the time and some slightly under. Then the frame rate is irregular, which can be visually disturbing. In this case, if you can't simplify the scene so that all the frames are fast enough, it might be better to add an intentional, tiny delay to make sure they all miss, giving a constant, slower, frame rate. If your frames have drastically different complexities, a more sophisticated approach might be necessary.

Motion = Redraw + Swap

The structure of real animation programs does not differ too much from this description. Usually, it is easier to redraw the entire buffer from scratch for each frame than to figure out which parts require redrawing. This is especially true with applications such as three-dimensional flight simulators where a tiny change in the plane's orientation changes the position of everything outside the window.

In most animations, the objects in a scene are simply redrawn with different transformations—the *viewpoint* of the viewer moves, or a car moves down the road a bit, or an object is rotated slightly. If significant recomputation is required for non-drawing operations, the attainable frame rate often slows down. Keep in mind, however, that the idle time after the **swap_the_buffers()** routine can often be used for such calculations.

OpenGL doesn't have a **swap_the_buffers()** command because the feature might not be available on all hardware and, in any case, it's highly dependent on the window system. For example, if you are using the X Window System and accessing it directly, you might use the following GLX routine:

```
void glXSwapBuffers(Display *dpy, Window window);
```

(See Appendix C for equivalent routines for other window systems.)

If you are using the GLUT library, you'll want to call this routine:

```
void glutSwapBuffers(void);
```

Example 1-3 illustrates the use of **glutSwapBuffers**() in an example that draws a spinning square as shown in Figure 1-3. The following example also shows how to use GLUT to control an input device and turn on and off an idle function. In this example, the mouse buttons toggle the spinning on and off.

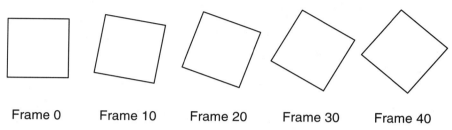

Frame 0   Frame 10   Frame 20   Frame 30   Frame 40

Figure 1-3   Double-Buffered Rotating Square

Example 1-3   Double-Buffered Program: double.c

```
#include <GL/gl.h>
#include <GL/glu.h>
#include <GL/glut.h>
#include <stdlib.h>

static GLfloat spin = 0.0;

void init(void)
{
   glClearColor (0.0, 0.0, 0.0, 0.0);
   glShadeModel (GL_FLAT);
}

void display(void)
{
   glClear(GL_COLOR_BUFFER_BIT);
   glPushMatrix();
   glRotatef(spin, 0.0, 0.0, 1.0);
   glColor3f(1.0, 1.0, 1.0);
   glRectf(-25.0, -25.0, 25.0, 25.0);
   glPopMatrix();
   glutSwapBuffers();
}
```

```
void spinDisplay(void)
{
    spin = spin + 2.0;
    if (spin > 360.0)
        spin = spin - 360.0;
    glutPostRedisplay();
}

void reshape(int w, int h)
{
    glViewport (0, 0, (GLsizei) w, (GLsizei) h);
    glMatrixMode(GL_PROJECTION);
    glLoadIdentity();
    glOrtho(-50.0, 50.0, -50.0, 50.0, -1.0, 1.0);
    glMatrixMode(GL_MODELVIEW);
    glLoadIdentity();
}

void mouse(int button, int state, int x, int y)
{
    switch (button) {
        case GLUT_LEFT_BUTTON:
            if (state == GLUT_DOWN)
                glutIdleFunc(spinDisplay);
            break;
        case GLUT_MIDDLE_BUTTON:
            if (state == GLUT_DOWN)
                glutIdleFunc(NULL);
            break;
        default:
            break;
    }
}
```

```
/*
 *  Request double buffer display mode.
 *  Register mouse input callback functions
 */
int main(int argc, char** argv)
{
   glutInit(&argc, argv);
   glutInitDisplayMode (GLUT_DOUBLE | GLUT_RGB);
   glutInitWindowSize (250, 250);
   glutInitWindowPosition (100, 100);
   glutCreateWindow (argv[0]);
   init ();
   glutDisplayFunc(display);
   glutReshapeFunc(reshape);
   glutMouseFunc(mouse);
   glutMainLoop();
   return 0;
}
```

Chapter 2

State Management and Drawing Geometric Objects

Chapter Objectives

After reading this chapter, you'll be able to do the following:

- Clear the window to an arbitrary color

- Force any pending drawing to complete

- Draw with any geometric primitive—points, lines, and polygons—in two or three dimensions

- Turn states on and off and query state variables

- Control the display of those primitives—for example, draw dashed lines or outlined polygons

- Specify *normal vectors* at appropriate points on the surface of solid objects

- Use *vertex arrays* to store and access a lot of geometric data with only a few function calls

- Save and restore several state variables at once

Although you can draw complex and interesting pictures using OpenGL, they're all constructed from a small number of primitive graphical items. This shouldn't be too surprising—look at what Leonardo da Vinci accomplished with just pencils and paintbrushes.

At the highest level of abstraction, there are three basic drawing operations: clearing the window, drawing a geometric object, and drawing a raster object. Raster objects, which include such things as two-dimensional images, bitmaps, and character fonts, are covered in Chapter 8. In this chapter, you learn how to clear the screen and to draw geometric objects, including points, straight lines, and flat polygons.

You might think to yourself, "Wait a minute. I've seen lots of computer graphics in movies and on television, and there are plenty of beautifully shaded curved lines and surfaces. How are those drawn, if all OpenGL can draw are straight lines and flat polygons?" Even the image on the cover of this book includes a round table and objects on the table that have curved surfaces. It turns out that all the curved lines and surfaces you've seen are approximated by large numbers of little flat polygons or straight lines, in much the same way that the globe on the cover is constructed from a large set of rectangular blocks. The globe doesn't appear to have a smooth surface because the blocks are relatively large compared to the globe. Later in this chapter, we show you how to construct curved lines and surfaces from lots of small geometric primitives.

This chapter has the following major sections:

- "A Drawing Survival Kit" on page 29 explains how to clear the window and force drawing to be completed. It also gives you basic information about controlling the color of geometric objects and describing a coordinate system.

- "Describing Points, Lines, and Polygons" on page 37 shows you what the set of primitive geometric objects is and how to draw them.

- "Basic State Management" on page 48 describes how to turn on and off some states (modes) and query state variables.

- "Displaying Points, Lines, and Polygons" on page 49 explains what control you have over the details of how primitives are drawn—for example, what diameter points have, whether lines are solid or dashed, and whether polygons are outlined or filled.

- "Normal Vectors" on page 63 discusses how to specify normal vectors for geometric objects and (briefly) what these vectors are for.

- "Vertex Arrays" on page 65 shows you how to put lots of geometric data into just a few arrays and how, with only a few function calls, to render the geometry it describes. Reducing function calls may increase the efficiency and performance of rendering.

- "Attribute Groups" on page 78 reveals how to query the current value of state variables and how to save and restore several related state values all at once.

- "Some Hints for Building Polygonal Models of Surfaces" on page 81 explores the issues and techniques involved in constructing polygonal approximations to surfaces.

One thing to keep in mind as you read the rest of this chapter is that with OpenGL, unless you specify otherwise, every time you issue a drawing command, the specified object is drawn. This might seem obvious, but in some systems, you first make a list of things to draw. When your list is complete, you tell the graphics hardware to draw the items in the list. The first style is called *immediate-mode* graphics and is the default OpenGL style. In addition to using immediate mode, you can choose to save some commands in a list (called a *display list*) for later drawing. Immediate-mode graphics are typically easier to program, but display lists are often more efficient. Chapter 7 tells you how to use display lists and why you might want to use them.

A Drawing Survival Kit

This section explains how to clear the window in preparation for drawing, set the color of objects that are to be drawn, and force drawing to be completed. None of these subjects has anything to do with geometric objects in a direct way, but any program that draws geometric objects has to deal with these issues.

Clearing the Window

Drawing on a computer screen is different from drawing on paper in that the paper starts out white, and all you have to do is draw the picture. On a computer, the memory holding the picture is usually filled with the last picture you drew, so you typically need to clear it to some background color before you start to draw the new scene. The color you use for the background depends on the application. For a word processor, you might clear to white (the color of the paper) before you begin to draw the text. If you're drawing a view from a spaceship, you clear to the black of space before beginning to draw the stars, planets, and alien spaceships. Sometimes you might not need to clear the screen at all; for example, if the image is the inside of a room, the entire graphics window gets covered as you draw all the walls.

At this point, you might be wondering why we keep talking about *clearing* the window—why not just draw a rectangle of the appropriate color that's large enough to cover the entire window? First, a special command to clear a window can be much more efficient than a general-purpose drawing command. In addition, as you'll see in Chapter 3, OpenGL allows you to set the coordinate system, viewing position, and viewing direction arbitrarily, so it might be difficult to figure out an appropriate size and location for a window-clearing rectangle. Finally, on many machines, the graphics hardware consists of multiple buffers in addition to the buffer containing colors of the pixels that are displayed. These other buffers must be cleared from time to time, and it's convenient to have a single command that can clear any combination of them. (See Chapter 10 for a discussion of all the possible buffers.)

You must also know how the colors of pixels are stored in the graphics hardware known as *bitplanes*. There are two methods of storage. Either the red, green, blue, and alpha (RGBA) values of a pixel can be directly stored in the bitplanes, or a single index value that references a color lookup table is stored. RGBA color-display mode is more commonly used, so most of the examples in this book use it. (See Chapter 4, "Color," for more information about both display modes.) You can safely ignore all references to alpha values until Chapter 6, "Blending, Antialiasing, Fog, and Polygon Offset."

As an example, these lines of code clear an RGBA mode window to black:

```
glClearColor(0.0, 0.0, 0.0, 0.0);
glClear(GL_COLOR_BUFFER_BIT);
```

The first line sets the clearing color to black, and the next command clears the entire window to the current clearing color. The single parameter to **glClear()** indicates which buffers are to be cleared. In this case, the program clears only the color buffer, where the image displayed on the screen is kept. Typically, you set the clearing color once, early in your application, and then you clear the buffers as often as necessary. OpenGL keeps track of the current clearing color as a state variable rather than requiring you to specify it each time a buffer is cleared.

Chapter 4 and Chapter 10 talk about how other buffers are used. For now, all you need to know is that clearing them is simple. For example, to clear both the color buffer and the depth buffer, you would use the following sequence of commands:

```
glClearColor(0.0, 0.0, 0.0, 0.0);
glClearDepth(1.0);
glClear(GL_COLOR_BUFFER_BIT | GL_DEPTH_BUFFER_BIT);
```

In this case, the call to **glClearColor()** is the same as before, the **glClearDepth()** command specifies the value to which every pixel of the depth buffer is to be set, and the parameter to the **glClear()** command now consists of the bitwise OR of all the buffers to be cleared. The following summary of **glClear()** includes a table that lists the buffers that can be cleared, their names, and the chapter where each type of buffer is discussed.

---

void **glClearColor**(GLclampf *red*, GLclampf *green*, GLclampf *blue*, GLclampf *alpha*);

Sets the current clearing color for use in clearing color buffers in RGBA mode. (See Chapter 4 for more information on RGBA mode.) The *red*, *green*, *blue*, and *alpha* values are clamped if necessary to the range [0,1]. The default clearing color is (0, 0, 0, 0), which is black.

---

void **glClear**(GLbitfield *mask*);

Clears the specified buffers to their current clearing values. The *mask* argument is a bitwise-ORed combination of the values listed in Table 2-1.

Buffer	Name	Reference
Color buffer	GL_COLOR_BUFFER_BIT	Chapter 4
Depth buffer	GL_DEPTH_BUFFER_BIT	Chapter 10
Accumulation buffer	GL_ACCUM_BUFFER_BIT	Chapter 10
Stencil buffer	GL_STENCIL_BUFFER_BIT	Chapter 10

Table 2-1   Clearing Buffers

Before issuing a command to clear multiple buffers, you have to set the values to which each buffer is to be cleared if you want something other than the default RGBA color, depth value, accumulation color, and stencil index. In addition to the **glClearColor()** and **glClearDepth()** commands that set the current values for clearing the color and depth buffers, **glClearIndex()**, **glClearAccum()**, and **glClearStencil()** specify the *color index*, accumulation color, and stencil index used to clear the corresponding buffers. (See Chapter 4 and Chapter 10 for descriptions of these buffers and their uses.)

OpenGL allows you to specify multiple buffers because clearing is generally a slow operation, since every pixel in the window (possibly millions) is touched, and some graphics hardware allows sets of buffers to be cleared simultaneously. Hardware that doesn't support simultaneous clears performs them sequentially. The difference between

```
glClear(GL_COLOR_BUFFER_BIT | GL_DEPTH_BUFFER_BIT);
```

and

```
glClear(GL_COLOR_BUFFER_BIT);
glClear(GL_DEPTH_BUFFER_BIT);
```

is that although both have the same final effect, the first example might run faster on many machines. It certainly won't run more slowly.

Specifying a Color

With OpenGL, the description of the shape of an object being drawn is independent of the description of its color. Whenever a particular geometric object is drawn, it's drawn using the currently specified coloring scheme. The coloring scheme might be as simple as "draw everything in fire-engine red," or might be as complicated as "assume the object is made out of blue plastic, that there's a yellow spotlight pointed in such and such a direction, and that there's a general low-level reddish-brown light everywhere else." In general, an OpenGL programmer first sets the color or coloring scheme and then draws the objects. Until the color or coloring scheme is changed, all objects are drawn in that color or using that coloring scheme. This method helps OpenGL achieve higher drawing performance than would result if it didn't keep track of the current color.

For example, the pseudocode

```
set_current_color(red);
draw_object(A);
draw_object(B);
set_current_color(green);
set_current_color(blue);
draw_object(C);
```

draws objects A and B in red, and object C in blue. The command on the fourth line that sets the current color to green is wasted.

Coloring, lighting, and shading are all large topics with entire chapters or large sections devoted to them. To draw geometric primitives that can be seen, however, you need some basic knowledge of how to set the current color; this information is provided in the next paragraphs. (See Chapter 4 and Chapter 5 for details on these topics.)

To set a color, use the command **glColor3f()**. It takes three parameters, all of which are floating-point numbers between 0.0 and 1.0. The parameters are, in order, the red, green, and blue *components* of the color. You can think of these three values as specifying a "mix" of colors: 0.0 means don't use any of that component, and 1.0 means use all you can of that component. Thus, the code

```
glColor3f(1.0, 0.0, 0.0);
```

makes the brightest red the system can draw, with no green or blue components. All zeros makes black; in contrast, all ones makes white. Setting all three components to 0.5 yields gray (halfway between black and white). Here are eight commands and the colors they would set.

```
glColor3f(0.0, 0.0, 0.0);      black
glColor3f(1.0, 0.0, 0.0);      red
glColor3f(0.0, 1.0, 0.0);      green
glColor3f(1.0, 1.0, 0.0);      yellow
glColor3f(0.0, 0.0, 1.0);      blue
glColor3f(1.0, 0.0, 1.0);      magenta
glColor3f(0.0, 1.0, 1.0);      cyan
glColor3f(1.0, 1.0, 1.0);      white
```

You might have noticed earlier that the routine to set the clearing color, **glClearColor()**, takes four parameters, the first three of which match the parameters for **glColor3f()**. The fourth parameter is the alpha value; it's covered in detail in "Blending" on page 214. For now, set the fourth parameter of **glClearColor()** to 0.0, which is its default value.

Forcing Completion of Drawing

As you saw in "OpenGL Rendering Pipeline" on page 10, most modern graphics systems can be thought of as an assembly line. The main central processing unit (CPU) issues a drawing command. Perhaps other hardware does geometric transformations. Clipping is performed, followed by shading and/or texturing. Finally, the values are written into the bitplanes for display. In high-end architectures, each of these operations is performed by a different piece of hardware that's been designed to perform its particular task quickly. In such an architecture, there's no need for the CPU to wait for each drawing command to complete before issuing the next one. While the CPU is sending a vertex down the pipeline, the transformation hardware is working on transforming the last one sent, the one before that is being clipped, and so on. In such a system, if the CPU waited for each command to complete before issuing the next, there could be a huge performance penalty.

In addition, the application might be running on more than one machine. For example, suppose that the main program is running elsewhere (on a machine called the client) and that you're viewing the results of the drawing on your workstation or terminal (the server), which is connected by a network to the client. In that case, it might be horribly inefficient to send each command over the network one at a time, since considerable overhead is often associated with each network transmission. Usually, the client gathers a collection of commands into a single network packet before sending it. Unfortunately, the network code on the client typically has no way of knowing that the graphics program is finished drawing a frame or scene. In the worst case, it waits forever for enough additional drawing commands to fill a packet, and you never see the completed drawing.

For this reason, OpenGL provides the command **glFlush()**, which forces the client to send the network packet even though it might not be full. Where there is no network and all commands are truly executed immediately on the server, **glFlush()** might have no effect. However, if you're writing a program that you want to work properly both with and without a network, include a call to **glFlush()** at the end of each frame or scene. Note that **glFlush()** doesn't wait for the drawing to complete—it just forces the drawing to begin execution, thereby guaranteeing that all previous commands *execute* in finite time even if no further rendering commands are executed.

There are other situations where **glFlush()** is useful.

- Software renderers that build image in system memory and don't want to constantly update the screen.

- Implementations that gather sets of rendering commands to amortize start-up costs. The aforementioned network transmission example is one instance of this.

> void **glFlush**(void);
>
> Forces previously issued OpenGL commands to begin execution, thus guaranteeing that they complete in finite time.

A few commands—for example, commands that swap buffers in double-buffer mode—automatically flush pending commands onto the network before they can occur.

If **glFlush()** isn't sufficient for you, try **glFinish()**. This command flushes the network as **glFlush()** does and then waits for notification from the graphics hardware or network indicating that the drawing is complete in the framebuffer. You might need to use **glFinish()** if you want to synchronize tasks—for example, to make sure that your three-dimensional rendering is on the screen before you use Display PostScript to draw labels on top of the rendering. Another example would be to ensure that the drawing is complete before it begins to accept user input. After you issue a **glFinish()** command, your graphics process is blocked until it receives notification from the graphics hardware that the drawing is complete. Keep in mind that excessive use of **glFinish()** can reduce the performance of your application, especially if you're running over a network, because it requires round-trip communication. If **glFlush()** is sufficient for your needs, use it instead of **glFinish()**.

> void **glFinish**(void);
>
> Forces all previously issued OpenGL commands to complete. This command doesn't return until all effects from previous commands are fully realized.

Coordinate System Survival Kit

Whenever you initially open a window or later move or resize that window, the window system will send an event to notify you. If you are using GLUT, the notification is automated; whatever routine has been registered to **glutReshapeFunc()** will be called. You must register a callback function that will

*   Reestablish the rectangular region that will be the new rendering canvas

*   Define the coordinate system to which objects will be drawn

In Chapter 3, "Viewing," you'll see how to define three-dimensional coordinate systems, but right now, just create a simple, basic two-dimensional coordinate system into which you can draw a few objects. Call **glutReshapeFunc(reshape)**, where **reshape()** is the following function shown in Example 2-1.

Example 2-1   Reshape Callback Function

```
void reshape (int w, int h)
{
   glViewport (0, 0, (GLsizei) w, (GLsizei) h);
   glMatrixMode (GL_PROJECTION);
   glLoadIdentity ();
   gluOrtho2D (0.0, (GLdouble) w, 0.0, (GLdouble) h);
}
```

The internals of GLUT will pass this function two arguments: the width and height, in pixels, of the new, moved, or resized window. **glViewport()** adjusts the pixel rectangle for drawing to be the entire new window. The next three routines adjust the coordinate system for drawing so that the lower-left corner is (0, 0), and the upper-right corner is (*w*, *h*) (See Figure 2-1).

To explain it another way, think about a piece of graphing paper. The *w* and *h* values in **reshape()** represent how many columns and rows of squares are on your graph paper. Then you have to put axes on the graph paper. The **gluOrtho2D()** routine puts the origin, (0, 0), all the way in the lowest, leftmost square, and makes each square represent one unit. Now when you render the points, lines, and polygons in the rest of this chapter, they will appear on this paper in easily predictable squares. (For now, keep all your objects two-dimensional.)

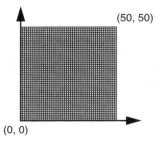

Figure 2-1   Coordinate System Defined by w = 50, h = 50

Describing Points, Lines, and Polygons

This section explains how to describe OpenGL geometric primitives. All geometric primitives are eventually described in terms of their *vertices*—coordinates that define the points themselves, the endpoints of line segments, or the corners of polygons. The next section discusses how these primitives are displayed and what control you have over their display.

What Are Points, Lines, and Polygons?

You probably have a fairly good idea of what a mathematician means by the terms *point*, *line*, and *polygon*. The OpenGL meanings are similar, but not quite the same.

One difference comes from the limitations of computer-based calculations. In any OpenGL implementation, floating-point calculations are of finite precision, and they have round-off errors. Consequently, the coordinates of OpenGL points, lines, and polygons suffer from the same problems.

Another more important difference arises from the limitations of a raster graphics display. On such a display, the smallest displayable unit is a pixel, and although pixels might be less than 1/100 of an inch wide, they are still much larger than the mathematician's concepts of infinitely small (for points) or infinitely thin (for lines). When OpenGL performs calculations, it assumes points are represented as vectors of floating-point numbers. However, a point is typically (but not always) drawn as a single pixel, and many different points with slightly different coordinates could be drawn by OpenGL on the same pixel.

Points

A point is represented by a set of floating-point numbers called a *vertex*. All internal calculations are done as if vertices are three-dimensional. Vertices specified by the user as two-dimensional (that is, with only x and y coordinates) are assigned a z coordinate equal to zero by OpenGL.

Advanced

OpenGL works in the *homogeneous coordinates* of three-dimensional projective geometry, so for internal calculations, all vertices are represented with four floating-point coordinates (x, y, z, w). If w is different from zero, these coordinates correspond to the Euclidean three-dimensional point $(x/w, y/w, z/w)$. You can specify the w coordinate in OpenGL commands, but that's rarely done. If the *w* coordinate isn't specified, it's understood to be 1.0. (See Appendix F for more information about homogeneous coordinate systems.)

Lines

In OpenGL, the term *line* refers to a *line segment*, not the mathematician's version that extends to infinity in both directions. There are easy ways to specify a connected series of line segments, or even a closed, connected series of segments (see Figure 2-2). In all cases, though, the lines constituting the connected series are specified in terms of the vertices at their endpoints.

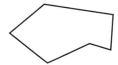

Figure 2-2   Two Connected Series of Line Segments

Polygons

Polygons are the areas enclosed by single closed loops of line segments, where the line segments are specified by the vertices at their endpoints. Polygons are typically drawn with the pixels in the interior filled in, but you can also draw them as outlines or a set of points. (See "Polygon Details" on page 55.)

In general, polygons can be complicated, so OpenGL makes some strong restrictions on what constitutes a primitive polygon. First, the edges of OpenGL polygons can't intersect (a mathematician would call a polygon satisfying this condition a *simple polygon*). Second, OpenGL polygons must be *convex*, meaning that they cannot have indentations. Stated precisely, a region is convex if, given any two points in the interior, the line segment joining them is also in the interior. See Figure 2-3 for some examples of valid and invalid polygons. OpenGL, however, doesn't restrict the number of line segments making up the boundary of a convex polygon. Note that polygons with holes can't be described. They are *nonconvex*, and they can't be drawn with a boundary made up of a single closed loop. Be aware that if you present OpenGL with a nonconvex filled polygon, it might not draw it as you expect. For instance, on most systems no more than the *convex hull* of the polygon would be filled. On some systems, less than the convex hull might be filled.

Valid   Invalid

Figure 2-3   Valid and Invalid Polygons

The reason for the OpenGL restrictions on valid polygon types is that it's simpler to provide fast polygon-rendering hardware for that restricted class of polygons. Simple polygons can be rendered quickly. The difficult cases are hard to detect quickly. So for maximum performance, OpenGL crosses its fingers and assumes the polygons are simple.

Many real-world surfaces consist of nonsimple polygons, nonconvex polygons, or polygons with holes. Since all such polygons can be formed from unions of simple convex polygons, some routines to build more complex objects are provided in the GLU library. These routines take complex descriptions and tessellate them, or break them down into groups of the simpler OpenGL polygons that can then be rendered. (See "Polygon Tessellation" on page 410 for more information about the *tessellation* routines.)

Since OpenGL vertices are always three-dimensional, the points forming the boundary of a particular polygon don't necessarily lie on the same plane in space. (Of course, they do in many cases—if all the z coordinates are zero, for example, or if the polygon is a *triangle*.) If a polygon's vertices don't lie in the same plane, then after various rotations in space, changes in the viewpoint, and projection onto the display screen, the points might no longer form a simple convex polygon. For example, imagine a four-point *quadrilateral* where the points are slightly out of plane, and look at it almost edge-on. You can get a nonsimple polygon that resembles a bow tie, as shown in Figure 2-4, which isn't guaranteed to be rendered correctly. This situation isn't all that unusual if you approximate curved surfaces by quadrilaterals made of points lying on the true surface. You can always avoid the problem by using triangles, since any three points always lie on a plane.

Figure 2-4   Nonplanar Polygon Transformed to Nonsimple Polygon

Rectangles

Since rectangles are so common in graphics applications, OpenGL provides a filled-rectangle drawing primitive, **glRect*()**. You can draw a rectangle as a polygon, as described in "OpenGL Geometric Drawing Primitives" on page 42, but your particular implementation of OpenGL might have optimized **glRect*()** for rectangles.

---
void **glRect**{sifd}(*TYPE x1, TYPE y1, TYPE x2, TYPE y2*);
void **glRect**{sifd}**v**(*TYPE *v1, TYPE *v2*);

Draws the rectangle defined by the corner points (*x1, y1*) and (*x2, y2*). The rectangle lies in the plane *z*=0 and has sides parallel to the *x*- and *y*-axes. If the vector form of the function is used, the corners are given by two pointers to arrays, each of which contains an (*x, y*) pair.

Note that although the rectangle begins with a particular orientation in three-dimensional space (in the *x-y* plane and parallel to the axes), you can change this by applying rotations or other transformations. (See Chapter 3 for information about how to do this.)

Curves and Curved Surfaces

Any smoothly curved line or surface can be approximated—to any arbitrary degree of accuracy—by short line segments or small polygonal regions. Thus, subdividing curved lines and surfaces sufficiently and then approximating them with straight line segments or flat polygons makes them appear curved (see Figure 2-5). If you're skeptical that this really works, imagine subdividing until each line segment or polygon is so tiny that it's smaller than a pixel on the screen.

Figure 2-5   Approximating Curves

Even though curves aren't geometric primitives, OpenGL does provide some direct support for subdividing and drawing them. (See Chapter 12 for information about how to draw curves and curved surfaces.)

Specifying Vertices

With OpenGL, all geometric objects are ultimately described as an ordered set of vertices. You use the **glVertex*()** command to specify a vertex.

---

void **glVertex**{234}{sifd}[v](*TYPE coords*);

Specifies a vertex for use in describing a geometric object. You can supply up to four coordinates (*x, y, z, w*) for a particular vertex or as few as two (*x, y*) by selecting the appropriate version of the command. If you use a version that doesn't explicitly specify *z* or *w*, *z* is understood to be 0 and *w* is understood to be 1. Calls to **glVertex*()** are only effective between a **glBegin()** and **glEnd()** pair.

Example 2-2 provides some examples of using **glVertex*()**.

Example 2-2   Legal Uses of glVertex*()

```
glVertex2s(2, 3);
glVertex3d(0.0, 0.0, 3.1415926535898);
glVertex4f(2.3, 1.0, -2.2, 2.0);

GLdouble dvect[3] = {5.0, 9.0, 1992.0};
glVertex3dv(dvect);
```

The first example represents a vertex with three-dimensional coordinates (2, 3, 0). (Remember that if it isn't specified, the *z* coordinate is understood to be 0.) The coordinates in the second example are (0.0, 0.0, 3.1415926535898) (double-precision floating-point numbers). The third example represents the vertex with three-dimensional coordinates (1.15, 0.5, −1.1). (Remember that the *x, y,* and *z* coordinates are eventually divided by the *w* coordinate.) In the final example, *dvect* is a pointer to an array of three double-precision floating-point numbers.

On some machines, the vector form of **glVertex*()** is more efficient, since only a single parameter needs to be passed to the graphics subsystem. Special hardware might be able to send a whole series of coordinates in a single batch. If your machine is like this, it's to your advantage to arrange your data so that the vertex coordinates are packed sequentially in memory. In this case, there may be some gain in performance by using the vertex array operations of OpenGL. (See "Vertex Arrays" on page 65.)

OpenGL Geometric Drawing Primitives

Now that you've seen how to specify vertices, you still need to know how to tell OpenGL to create a set of points, a line, or a polygon from those vertices. To do this, you bracket each set of vertices between a call to **glBegin()** and a call to **glEnd()**. The argument passed to **glBegin()** determines what sort of geometric primitive is constructed from the vertices. For example, Example 2-3 specifies the vertices for the polygon shown in Figure 2-6.

Example 2-3   Filled Polygon

```
glBegin(GL_POLYGON);
    glVertex2f(0.0, 0.0);
    glVertex2f(0.0, 3.0);
    glVertex2f(4.0, 3.0);
    glVertex2f(6.0, 1.5);
    glVertex2f(4.0, 0.0);
glEnd();
```

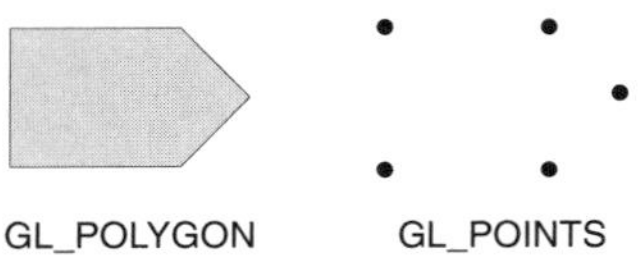

GL_POLYGON   GL_POINTS

Figure 2-6   Drawing a Polygon or a Set of Points

If you had used GL_POINTS instead of GL_POLYGON, the primitive would have been simply the five points shown in Figure 2-6. Table 2-2 in the following function summary for **glBegin()** lists the ten possible arguments and the corresponding type of primitive.

void **glBegin**(GLenum *mode*);

Marks the beginning of a vertex-data list that describes a geometric primitive. The type of primitive is indicated by *mode*, which can be any of the values shown in Table 2-2.

Value	Meaning
GL_POINTS	individual points
GL_LINES	pairs of vertices interpreted as individual line segments
GL_LINE_STRIP	series of connected line segments
GL_LINE_LOOP	same as above, with a segment added between last and first vertices
GL_TRIANGLES	triples of vertices interpreted as triangles
GL_TRIANGLE_STRIP	linked strip of triangles
GL_TRIANGLE_FAN	linked fan of triangles
GL_QUADS	quadruples of vertices interpreted as four-sided polygons
GL_QUAD_STRIP	linked strip of quadrilaterals
GL_POLYGON	boundary of a simple, convex polygon

Table 2-2   Geometric Primitive Names and Meanings

void **glEnd**(void);

Marks the end of a vertex-data list.

Figure 2-7 shows examples of all the geometric primitives listed in Table 2-2. The paragraphs that follow the figure describe the pixels that are drawn for each of the objects. Note that in addition to points, several types of lines and polygons are defined. Obviously, you can find many ways to draw the same primitive. The method you choose depends on your vertex data.

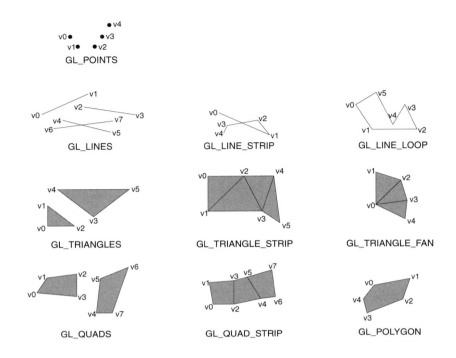

Figure 2-7   Geometric Primitive Types

As you read the following descriptions, assume that n vertices (v_0, v_1, v_2, ... , v_{n-1}) are described between a **glBegin()** and **glEnd()** pair.

GL_POINTS   Draws a point at each of the n vertices.

GL_LINES   Draws a series of unconnected line segments. Segments are drawn between v_0 and v_1, between v_2 and v_3, and so on. If n is odd, the last segment is drawn between v_{n-3} and v_{n-2}, and v_{n-1} is ignored.

GL_LINE_STRIP   Draws a line segment from v_0 to v_1, then from v_1 to v_2, and so on, finally drawing the segment from v_{n-2} to v_{n-1}. Thus, a total of $n-1$ line segments are drawn. Nothing is drawn unless n is larger than 1. There are no restrictions on the vertices describing a line strip (or a line loop); the lines can intersect arbitrarily.

GL_LINE_LOOP   Same as GL_LINE_STRIP, except that a final line segment is drawn from v_{n-1} to v_0, completing a loop.

GL_TRIANGLES   Draws a series of triangles (three-sided polygons) using
                      vertices v_0, v_1, v_2, then v_3, v_4, v_5, and so on. If n isn't an
                      exact multiple of 3, the final one or two vertices are
                      ignored.

GL_TRIANGLE_STRIP

                      Draws a series of triangles (three-sided polygons) using
                      vertices v_0, v_1, v_2, then v_2, v_1, v_3 (note the order), then
                      v_2, v_3, v_4, and so on. The ordering is to ensure that the
                      triangles are all drawn with the same orientation so that
                      the strip can correctly form part of a surface. Preserving
                      the orientation is important for some operations, such
                      as culling. (See "Reversing and Culling Polygon Faces"
                      on page 56) n must be at least 3 for anything to be
                      drawn.

GL_TRIANGLE_FAN

                      Same as GL_TRIANGLE_STRIP, except that the vertices
                      are v_0, v_1, v_2, then v_0, v_2, v_3, then v_0, v_3, v_4, and so on
                      (see Figure 2-7).

GL_QUADS   Draws a series of quadrilaterals (four-sided polygons)
                      using vertices v_0, v_1, v_2, v_3, then v_4, v_5, v_6, v_7, and so on.
                      If n isn't a multiple of 4, the final one, two, or three
                      vertices are ignored.

GL_QUAD_STRIP   Draws a series of quadrilaterals (four-sided polygons)
                      beginning with v_0, v_1, v_3, v_2, then v_2, v_3, v_5, v_4, then v_4,
                      v_5, v_7, v_6, and so on (see Figure 2-7). n must be at least 4
                      before anything is drawn. If n is odd, the final vertex is
                      ignored.

GL_POLYGON   Draws a polygon using the points v_0, ... , v_{n-1} as vertices.
                      n must be at least 3, or nothing is drawn. In addition,
                      the polygon specified must not intersect itself and must
                      be convex. If the vertices don't satisfy these conditions,
                      the results are unpredictable.

Restrictions on Using glBegin() and glEnd()

The most important information about vertices is their coordinates, which
are specified by the **glVertex*()** command. You can also supply additional
vertex-specific data for each vertex—a color, a normal vector, texture
coordinates, or any combination of these—using special commands. In

addition, a few other commands are valid between a **glBegin()** and **glEnd()** pair. Table 2-3 contains a complete list of such valid commands.

Command	Purpose of Command	Reference
glVertex*()	set vertex coordinates	Chapter 2
glColor*()	set current color	Chapter 4
glIndex*()	set current color index	Chapter 4
glNormal*()	set normal vector coordinates	Chapter 2
glTexCoord*()	set texture coordinates	Chapter 9
glEdgeFlag*()	control drawing of edges	Chapter 2
glMaterial*()	set material properties	Chapter 5
glArrayElement()	extract vertex array data	Chapter 2
glEvalCoord*(), glEvalPoint*()	generate coordinates	Chapter 12
glCallList(), glCallLists()	execute display list(s)	Chapter 7

Table 2-3   Valid Commands between glBegin() and glEnd()

No other OpenGL commands are valid between a **glBegin()** and **glEnd()** pair, and making most other OpenGL calls generates an error. Some vertex array commands, such as **glEnableClientState()** and **glVertexPointer()**, when called between **glBegin()** and **glEnd()**, have undefined behavior but do not necessarily generate an error. (Also, routines related to OpenGL, such as **glX*()** routines have undefined behavior between **glBegin()** and **glEnd()**.) These cases should be avoided, and debugging them may be more difficult.

Note, however, that only OpenGL commands are restricted; you can certainly include other programming-language constructs (except for calls, such as the aforementioned **glX*()** routines). For example, Example 2-4 draws an outlined circle.

Example 2-4   Other Constructs between glBegin() and glEnd()

```
#define PI 3.1415926535898
GLint circle_points = 100;
glBegin(GL_LINE_LOOP);
```

```
for (i = 0; i < circle_points; i++) {
   angle = 2*PI*i/circle_points;
   glVertex2f(cos(angle), sin(angle));
}
glEnd();
```

Note: This example isn't the most efficient way to draw a circle, especially if you intend to do it repeatedly. The graphics commands used are typically very fast, but this code calculates an angle and calls the **sin()** and **cos()** routines for each vertex; in addition, there's the loop overhead. (Another way to calculate the vertices of a circle is to use a GLU routine; see "Quadrics: Rendering Spheres, Cylinders, and Disks" on page 428.) If you need to draw lots of circles, calculate the coordinates of the vertices once and save them in an array and create a display list (see Chapter 7), or use vertex arrays to render them.

Unless they are being compiled into a display list, all **glVertex*()** commands should appear between some **glBegin()** and **glEnd()** combination. (If they appear elsewhere, they don't accomplish anything.) If they appear in a display list, they are executed only if they appear between a **glBegin()** and a **glEnd()**. (See Chapter 7 for more information about display lists.)

Although many commands are allowed between **glBegin()** and **glEnd()**, vertices are generated only when a **glVertex*()** command is issued. At the moment **glVertex*()** is called, OpenGL assigns the resulting vertex the current color, texture coordinates, normal vector information, and so on. To see this, look at the following code sequence. The first point is drawn in red, and the second and third ones in blue, despite the extra color commands.

```
glBegin(GL_POINTS);
   glColor3f(0.0, 1.0, 0.0);                    /* green */
   glColor3f(1.0, 0.0, 0.0);                    /* red */
   glVertex(...);
   glColor3f(1.0, 1.0, 0.0);                    /* yellow */
   glColor3f(0.0, 0.0, 1.0);                    /* blue */
   glVertex(...);
   glVertex(...);
glEnd();
```

You can use any combination of the 24 versions of the **glVertex*()** command between **glBegin()** and **glEnd()**, although in real applications all the calls in any particular instance tend to be of the same form. If your vertex-data specification is consistent and repetitive (for example, **glColor*,**

glVertex*, **glColor***, **glVertex***,...), you may enhance your program's performance by using vertex arrays. (See "Vertex Arrays" on page 65.)

Basic State Management

In the previous section, you saw an example of a state variable, the current RGBA color, and how it can be associated with a primitive. OpenGL maintains many states and state variables. An object may be rendered with lighting, texturing, hidden surface removal, fog, or some other states affecting its appearance.

By default, most of these states are initially inactive. These states may be costly to activate; for example, turning on texture mapping will almost certainly slow down the speed of rendering a primitive. However, the quality of the image will improve and look more realistic, due to the enhanced graphics capabilities.

To turn on and off many of these states, use these two simple commands:

---
void **glEnable**(GLenum *cap*);
void **glDisable**(GLenum *cap*);

---

glEnable() turns on a capability, and **glDisable()** turns it off. There are over 40 enumerated values that can be passed as a parameter to **glEnable()** or **glDisable()**. Some examples of these are GL_BLEND (which controls blending RGBA values), GL_DEPTH_TEST (which controls depth comparisons and updates to the depth buffer), GL_FOG (which controls fog), GL_LINE_STIPPLE (patterned lines), GL_LIGHTING (you get the idea), and so forth.

You can also check if a state is currently enabled or disabled.

GLboolean **glIsEnabled**(GLenum *capability*)

Returns GL_TRUE or GL_FALSE, depending upon whether the queried capability is currently activated.

The states you have just seen have two settings: on and off. However, most OpenGL routines set values for more complicated state variables. For example, the routine **glColor3f()** sets three values, which are part of the GL_CURRENT_COLOR state. There are five querying routines used to find out what values are set for many states:

---

void **glGetBooleanv**(GLenum *pname*, GLboolean **params*);
void **glGetIntegerv**(GLenum *pname*, GLint **params*);
void **glGetFloatv**(GLenum *pname*, GLfloat **params*);
void **glGetDoublev**(GLenum *pname*, GLdouble **params*);
void **glGetPointerv**(GLenum *pname*, GLvoid ***params*);

Obtains Boolean, integer, floating-point, double-precision, or pointer state variables. The *pname* argument is a symbolic constant indicating the state variable to return, and *params* is a pointer to an array of the indicated type in which to place the returned data. See the tables in Appendix B for the possible values for *pname*. For example, to get the current RGBA color, a table in Appendix B suggests you use **glGetIntegerv**(GL_CURRENT_COLOR, *params*) or **glGetFloatv**(GL_CURRENT_COLOR, *params*). A type conversion is performed if necessary to return the desired variable as the requested data type.

These querying routines handle most, but not all, requests for obtaining state information. (See "The Query Commands" on page 536 for an additional 16 querying routines.)

Displaying Points, Lines, and Polygons

By default, a point is drawn as a single pixel on the screen, a line is drawn solid and one pixel wide, and polygons are drawn solidly filled in. The following paragraphs discuss the details of how to change these default display modes.

Point Details

To control the size of a rendered point, use **glPointSize()** and supply the desired size in pixels as the argument.

---
void **glPointSize**(GLfloat *size*);

Sets the width in pixels for rendered points; *size* must be greater than 0.0 and by default is 1.0.

The actual collection of pixels on the screen which are drawn for various point widths depends on whether antialiasing is enabled. (Antialiasing is a technique for smoothing points and lines as they're rendered; see "Antialiasing" on page 226 for more detail.) If antialiasing is disabled (the default), fractional widths are rounded to integer widths, and a screen-aligned square region of pixels is drawn. Thus, if the width is 1.0, the square is 1 pixel by 1 pixel; if the width is 2.0, the square is 2 pixels by 2 pixels, and so on.

With antialiasing enabled, a circular *group* of pixels is drawn, and the pixels on the boundaries are typically drawn at less than full intensity to give the edge a smoother appearance. In this mode, non-integer widths aren't rounded.

Most OpenGL implementations support very large point sizes. The maximum size for antialiased points is queryable, but the same information is not available for standard, aliased points. A particular implementation, however, might limit the size of standard, aliased points to not less than its maximum antialiased point size, rounded to the nearest integer value. You can obtain this floating-point value by using GL_POINT_SIZE_RANGE with **glGetFloatv**().

Line Details

With OpenGL, you can specify lines with different widths and lines that are *stippled* in various ways—dotted, dashed, drawn with alternating dots and dashes, and so on.

Wide Lines

---
void **glLineWidth**(GLfloat *width*);

Sets the width in pixels for rendered lines; *width* must be greater than 0.0 and by default is 1.0.

The actual rendering of lines is affected by the antialiasing mode, in the same way as for points. (See "Antialiasing" on page 226.) Without antialiasing, widths of 1, 2, and 3 draw lines 1, 2, and 3 pixels wide. With antialiasing enabled, non-integer line widths are possible, and pixels on the boundaries are typically drawn at less than full intensity. As with point sizes, a particular OpenGL implementation might limit the width of nonantialiased lines to its maximum antialiased line width, rounded to the nearest integer value. You can obtain this floating-point value by using GL_LINE_WIDTH_RANGE with **glGetFloatv()**.

Note: Keep in mind that by default lines are 1 pixel wide, so they appear wider on lower-resolution screens. For computer displays, this isn't typically an issue, but if you're using OpenGL to render to a high-resolution plotter, 1-pixel lines might be nearly invisible. To obtain resolution-independent line widths, you need to take into account the physical dimensions of pixels.

Advanced

With nonantialiased wide lines, the line width isn't measured perpendicular to the line. Instead, it's measured in the y direction if the absolute value of the slope is less than 1.0; otherwise, it's measured in the x direction. The rendering of an antialiased line is exactly equivalent to the rendering of a filled rectangle of the given width, centered on the exact line.

Stippled Lines

To make stippled (dotted or dashed) lines, you use the command **glLineStipple()** to define the *stipple* pattern, and then you enable line stippling with **glEnable()**.

```
glLineStipple(1, 0x3F07);
glEnable(GL_LINE_STIPPLE);
```

---

void **glLineStipple**(GLint *factor*, GLushort *pattern*);

Sets the current stippling pattern for lines. The *pattern* argument is a 16-bit series of 0s and 1s, and it's repeated as necessary to stipple a given line. A 1 indicates that drawing occurs, and 0 that it does not, on a pixel-by-pixel basis, beginning with the low-order bit of the pattern. The pattern can be stretched out by using *factor*, which multiplies each subseries of consecutive 1s and 0s. Thus, if three consecutive 1s appear in the pattern, they're stretched to six if *factor* is 2. *factor* is clamped to lie between 1 and 255. Line stippling must be enabled by passing GL_LINE_STIPPLE to **glEnable()**; it's disabled by passing the same argument to **glDisable()**.

With the preceding example and the pattern 0x3F07 (which translates to 0011111100000111 in binary), a line would be drawn with 3 pixels on, then 5 off, 6 on, and 2 off. (If this seems backward, remember that the low-order bit is used first.) If *factor* had been 2, the pattern would have been elongated: 6 pixels on, 10 off, 12 on, and 4 off. Figure 2-8 shows lines drawn with different patterns and repeat factors. If you don't enable line stippling, drawing proceeds as if *pattern* were 0xFFFF and *factor* 1. (Use **glDisable()** with GL_LINE_STIPPLE to disable stippling.) Note that stippling can be used in combination with wide lines to produce wide stippled lines.

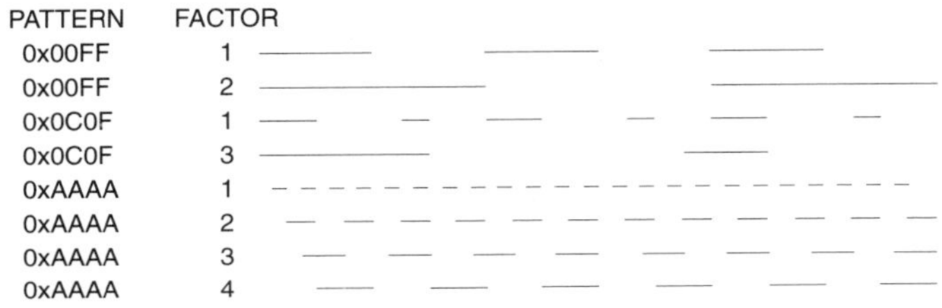

PATTERN	FACTOR			
0x00FF	1			
0x00FF	2			
0x0C0F	1			
0x0C0F	3			
0xAAAA	1			
0xAAAA	2			
0xAAAA	3			
0xAAAA	4			

Figure 2-8   Stippled Lines

One way to think of the stippling is that as the line is being drawn, the pattern is shifted by 1 bit each time a pixel is drawn (or *factor* pixels are drawn, if *factor* isn't 1). When a series of connected line segments is drawn between a single **glBegin()** and **glEnd()**, the pattern continues to shift as one segment turns into the next. This way, a stippling pattern continues across a series of connected line segments. When **glEnd()** is executed, the pattern is reset, and—if more lines are drawn before stippling is disabled—the stippling restarts at the beginning of the pattern. If you're drawing lines with GL_LINES, the pattern resets for each independent line.

Example 2-5 illustrates the results of drawing with a couple of different stipple patterns and line widths. It also illustrates what happens if the lines are drawn as a series of individual segments instead of a single connected line strip. The results of running the program appear in Figure 2-9.

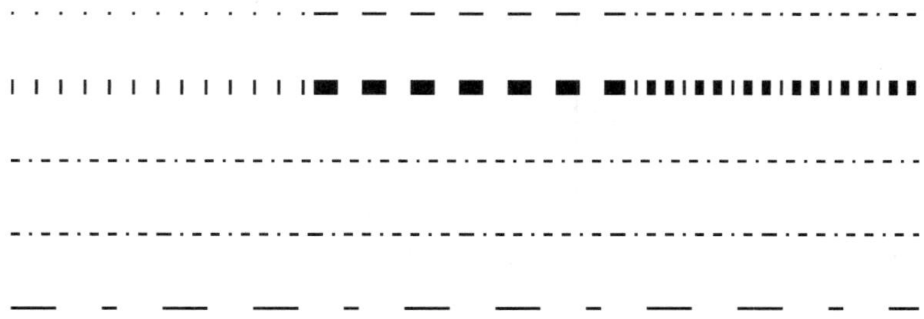

Figure 2-9   Wide Stippled Lines

Example 2-5   Line Stipple Patterns: lines.c

```
#include <GL/gl.h>
#include <GL/glut.h>

#define drawOneLine(x1,y1,x2,y2)  glBegin(GL_LINES);  \
   glVertex2f ((x1),(y1)); glVertex2f ((x2),(y2)); glEnd();

void init(void)
{
   glClearColor (0.0, 0.0, 0.0, 0.0);
   glShadeModel (GL_FLAT);
}

void display(void)
{
   int i;

   glClear (GL_COLOR_BUFFER_BIT);
/* select white for all lines  */
   glColor3f (1.0, 1.0, 1.0);

/* in 1st row, 3 lines, each with a different stipple  */
   glEnable (GL_LINE_STIPPLE);

   glLineStipple (1, 0x0101);  /*  dotted  */
   drawOneLine (50.0, 125.0, 150.0, 125.0);
   glLineStipple (1, 0x00FF);  /*  dashed  */
   drawOneLine (150.0, 125.0, 250.0, 125.0);
   glLineStipple (1, 0x1C47);  /*  dash/dot/dash  */
   drawOneLine (250.0, 125.0, 350.0, 125.0);
```

```
    /* in 2nd row, 3 wide lines, each with different stipple */
    glLineWidth (5.0);
    glLineStipple (1, 0x0101);  /*  dotted  */
    drawOneLine (50.0, 100.0, 150.0, 100.0);
    glLineStipple (1, 0x00FF);  /*  dashed  */
    drawOneLine (150.0, 100.0, 250.0, 100.0);
    glLineStipple (1, 0x1C47);  /*  dash/dot/dash  */
    drawOneLine (250.0, 100.0, 350.0, 100.0);
    glLineWidth (1.0);

 /* in 3rd row, 6 lines, with dash/dot/dash stipple  */
 /* as part of a single connected line strip         */
    glLineStipple (1, 0x1C47);  /*  dash/dot/dash  */
    glBegin (GL_LINE_STRIP);
    for (i = 0; i < 7; i++)
       glVertex2f (50.0 + ((GLfloat) i * 50.0), 75.0);
    glEnd ();

 /* in 4th row, 6 independent lines with same stipple  */
    for (i = 0; i < 6; i++) {
       drawOneLine (50.0 + ((GLfloat) i * 50.0), 50.0,
          50.0 + ((GLfloat)(i+1) * 50.0), 50.0);
    }

 /* in 5th row, 1 line, with dash/dot/dash stipple    */
 /* and a stipple repeat factor of 5                  */
    glLineStipple (5, 0x1C47);  /*  dash/dot/dash  */
    drawOneLine (50.0, 25.0, 350.0, 25.0);

    glDisable (GL_LINE_STIPPLE);
    glFlush ();
}

void reshape (int w, int h)
{
    glViewport (0, 0, (GLsizei) w, (GLsizei) h);
    glMatrixMode (GL_PROJECTION);
    glLoadIdentity ();
    gluOrtho2D (0.0, (GLdouble) w, 0.0, (GLdouble) h);
}
```

```
int main(int argc, char** argv)
{
    glutInit(&argc, argv);
    glutInitDisplayMode (GLUT_SINGLE | GLUT_RGB);
    glutInitWindowSize (400, 150);
    glutInitWindowPosition (100, 100);
    glutCreateWindow (argv[0]);
    init ();
    glutDisplayFunc(display);
    glutReshapeFunc(reshape);
    glutMainLoop();
    return 0;
}
```

Polygon Details

Polygons are typically drawn by filling in all the pixels enclosed within the boundary, but you can also draw them as outlined polygons or simply as points at the vertices. A filled polygon might be solidly filled or stippled with a certain pattern. Although the exact details are omitted here, filled polygons are drawn in such a way that if adjacent polygons share an edge or vertex, the pixels making up the edge or vertex are drawn exactly once—they're included in only one of the polygons. This is done so that partially transparent polygons don't have their edges drawn twice, which would make those edges appear darker (or brighter, depending on what color you're drawing with). Note that it might result in narrow polygons having no filled pixels in one or more rows or columns of pixels. Antialiasing polygons is more complicated than for points and lines. (See "Antialiasing" on page 226 for details.)

Polygons as Points, Outlines, or Solids

A polygon has two sides—front and back—and might be rendered differently depending on which side is facing the viewer. This allows you to have cutaway views of solid objects in which there is an obvious distinction between the parts that are inside and those that are outside. By default, both front and back faces are drawn in the same way. To change this, or to draw only outlines or vertices, use **glPolygonMode()**.

---

void **glPolygonMode**(GLenum *face*, GLenum *mode*);

Controls the drawing mode for a polygon's front and back faces. The parameter *face* can be GL_FRONT_AND_BACK, GL_FRONT, or GL_BACK; *mode* can be GL_POINT, GL_LINE, or GL_FILL to indicate whether the polygon should be drawn as points, outlined, or filled. By default, both the front and back faces are drawn filled.

For example, you can have the *front faces* filled and the *back faces* outlined with two calls to this routine:

```
glPolygonMode(GL_FRONT, GL_FILL);
glPolygonMode(GL_BACK, GL_LINE);
```

Reversing and Culling Polygon Faces

By convention, polygons whose vertices appear in counterclockwise order on the screen are called front-facing. You can construct the surface of any "reasonable" solid—a mathematician would call such a surface an orientable manifold (spheres, donuts, and teapots are orientable; Klein bottles and Möbius strips aren't)—from polygons of consistent orientation. In other words, you can use all clockwise polygons, or all counterclockwise polygons. (This is essentially the mathematical definition of *orientable*.)

Suppose you've consistently described a model of an orientable surface but that you happen to have the clockwise orientation on the outside. You can swap what OpenGL considers the back face by using the function **glFrontFace**(), supplying the desired orientation for front-facing polygons.

---

void **glFrontFace**(GLenum *mode*);

Controls how front-facing polygons are determined. By default, *mode* is GL_CCW, which corresponds to a counterclockwise orientation of the ordered vertices of a projected polygon in window coordinates. If *mode* is GL_CW, faces with a clockwise orientation are considered front-facing.

In a completely enclosed surface constructed from opaque polygons with a consistent orientation, none of the back-facing polygons are ever visible—they're always obscured by the front-facing polygons. If you are outside this surface, you might enable *culling* to discard polygons that OpenGL determines are back-facing. Similarly, if you are inside the object, only back-facing polygons are visible. To instruct OpenGL to discard front- or back-facing polygons, use the command **glCullFace()** and enable culling with **glEnable()**.

---

void **glCullFace**(GLenum *mode*);

Indicates which polygons should be discarded (culled) before they're converted to screen coordinates. The mode is either GL_FRONT, GL_BACK, or GL_FRONT_AND_BACK to indicate front-facing, back-facing, or all polygons. To take effect, culling must be enabled using **glEnable()** with GL_CULL_FACE; it can be disabled with **glDisable()** and the same argument.

Advanced

In more technical terms, the decision of whether a face of a polygon is front- or back-facing depends on the sign of the polygon's area computed in window coordinates. One way to compute this area is

$$a = \frac{1}{2} \sum_{i=0}^{n-1} x_i y_{i \oplus 1} - x_{i \oplus 1} y_i$$

where x_i and y_i are the x and y window coordinates of the ith vertex of the n-vertex polygon and $i \oplus 1$ is $(i+1) \bmod n$. Assuming that GL_CCW has been specified, if $a > 0$, the polygon corresponding to that vertex is considered to be front-facing; otherwise, it's back-facing. If GL_CW is specified and if $a < 0$, then the corresponding polygon is front-facing; otherwise, it's back-facing.

Try This

- Modify Example 2-5 by adding some filled polygons. Experiment with different colors. Try different polygon modes. Also enable culling to see its effect.

Stippling Polygons

By default, filled polygons are drawn with a solid pattern. They can also be filled with a 32-bit by 32-bit *window-aligned* stipple pattern, which you specify with **glPolygonStipple()**.

---

void **glPolygonStipple**(const GLubyte *_mask_);

Defines the current stipple pattern for filled polygons. The argument _mask_ is a pointer to a 32×32 bitmap that's interpreted as a mask of 0s and 1s. Where a 1 appears, the corresponding pixel in the polygon is drawn, and where a 0 appears, nothing is drawn. Figure 2-10 shows how a stipple pattern is constructed from the characters in _mask_. Polygon stippling is enabled and disabled by using **glEnable()** and **glDisable()** with GL_POLYGON_STIPPLE as the argument. The interpretation of the _mask_ data is affected by the **glPixelStore*()** GL_UNPACK* modes. (See "Controlling Pixel-Storage Modes" on page 298.)

In addition to defining the current polygon stippling pattern, you must enable stippling:

```
glEnable(GL_POLYGON_STIPPLE);
```

Use **glDisable()** with the same argument to disable polygon stippling.

Figure 2-11 shows the results of polygons drawn unstippled and then with two different stippling patterns. The program is shown in Example 2-6. The reversal of white to black (from Figure 2-10 to Figure 2-11) occurs because the program draws in white over a black background, using the pattern in Figure 2-10 as a stencil.

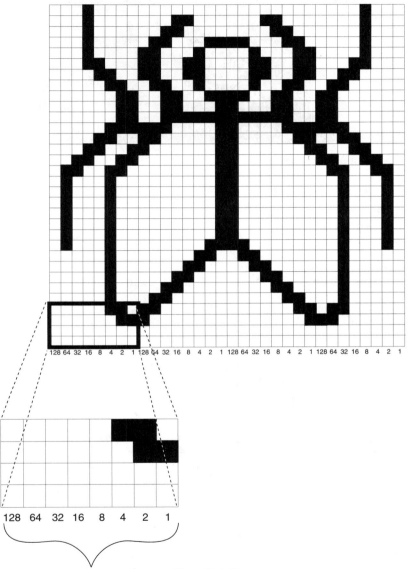

By default, for each byte the most significant bit is first.
Bit ordering can be changed by calling **glPixelStore*()**.

Figure 2-10   Constructing a Polygon Stipple Pattern

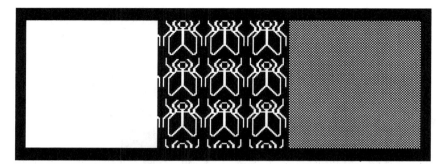

Figure 2-11   Stippled Polygons

Example 2-6   Polygon Stipple Patterns: polys.c

```c
#include <GL/gl.h>
#include <GL/glut.h>
void display(void)
{
    GLubyte fly[] = {
        0x00, 0x00, 0x00, 0x00, 0x00, 0x00, 0x00, 0x00,
        0x03, 0x80, 0x01, 0xC0, 0x06, 0xC0, 0x03, 0x60,
        0x04, 0x60, 0x06, 0x20, 0x04, 0x30, 0x0C, 0x20,
        0x04, 0x18, 0x18, 0x20, 0x04, 0x0C, 0x30, 0x20,
        0x04, 0x06, 0x60, 0x20, 0x44, 0x03, 0xC0, 0x22,
        0x44, 0x01, 0x80, 0x22, 0x44, 0x01, 0x80, 0x22,
        0x44, 0x01, 0x80, 0x22, 0x44, 0x01, 0x80, 0x22,
        0x44, 0x01, 0x80, 0x22, 0x44, 0x01, 0x80, 0x22,
        0x66, 0x01, 0x80, 0x66, 0x33, 0x01, 0x80, 0xCC,
        0x19, 0x81, 0x81, 0x98, 0x0C, 0xC1, 0x83, 0x30,
        0x07, 0xe1, 0x87, 0xe0, 0x03, 0x3f, 0xfc, 0xc0,
        0x03, 0x31, 0x8c, 0xc0, 0x03, 0x33, 0xcc, 0xc0,
        0x06, 0x64, 0x26, 0x60, 0x0c, 0xcc, 0x33, 0x30,
        0x18, 0xcc, 0x33, 0x18, 0x10, 0xc4, 0x23, 0x08,
        0x10, 0x63, 0xC6, 0x08, 0x10, 0x30, 0x0c, 0x08,
        0x10, 0x18, 0x18, 0x08, 0x10, 0x00, 0x00, 0x08};
    GLubyte halftone[] = {
        0xAA, 0xAA, 0xAA, 0xAA, 0x55, 0x55, 0x55, 0x55,
        0xAA, 0xAA, 0xAA, 0xAA, 0x55, 0x55, 0x55, 0x55,
        0xAA, 0xAA, 0xAA, 0xAA, 0x55, 0x55, 0x55, 0x55,
        0xAA, 0xAA, 0xAA, 0xAA, 0x55, 0x55, 0x55, 0x55,
        0xAA, 0xAA, 0xAA, 0xAA, 0x55, 0x55, 0x55, 0x55,
        0xAA, 0xAA, 0xAA, 0xAA, 0x55, 0x55, 0x55, 0x55,
        0xAA, 0xAA, 0xAA, 0xAA, 0x55, 0x55, 0x55, 0x55,
        0xAA, 0xAA, 0xAA, 0xAA, 0x55, 0x55, 0x55, 0x55,
        0xAA, 0xAA, 0xAA, 0xAA, 0x55, 0x55, 0x55, 0x55,
```

```
         0xAA, 0xAA, 0xAA, 0xAA, 0x55, 0x55, 0x55, 0x55,
         0xAA, 0xAA, 0xAA, 0xAA, 0x55, 0x55, 0x55, 0x55,
         0xAA, 0xAA, 0xAA, 0xAA, 0x55, 0x55, 0x55, 0x55,
         0xAA, 0xAA, 0xAA, 0xAA, 0x55, 0x55, 0x55, 0x55,
         0xAA, 0xAA, 0xAA, 0xAA, 0x55, 0x55, 0x55, 0x55,
         0xAA, 0xAA, 0xAA, 0xAA, 0x55, 0x55, 0x55, 0x55,
         0xAA, 0xAA, 0xAA, 0xAA, 0x55, 0x55, 0x55, 0x55};

   glClear (GL_COLOR_BUFFER_BIT);
   glColor3f (1.0, 1.0, 1.0);

/*  draw one solid, unstippled rectangle,       */
/*  then two stippled rectangles                */
   glRectf (25.0, 25.0, 125.0, 125.0);
   glEnable (GL_POLYGON_STIPPLE);
   glPolygonStipple (fly);
   glRectf (125.0, 25.0, 225.0, 125.0);
   glPolygonStipple (halftone);
   glRectf (225.0, 25.0, 325.0, 125.0);
   glDisable (GL_POLYGON_STIPPLE);

   glFlush ();
}

void init (void)
{
   glClearColor (0.0, 0.0, 0.0, 0.0);
   glShadeModel (GL_FLAT);
}

void reshape (int w, int h)
{
   glViewport (0, 0, (GLsizei) w, (GLsizei) h);
   glMatrixMode (GL_PROJECTION);
   glLoadIdentity ();
   gluOrtho2D (0.0, (GLdouble) w, 0.0, (GLdouble) h);
}

int main(int argc, char** argv)
{
   glutInit(&argc, argv);
   glutInitDisplayMode (GLUT_SINGLE | GLUT_RGB);
   glutInitWindowSize (350, 150);
   glutCreateWindow (argv[0]);
   init ();
   glutDisplayFunc(display);
   glutReshapeFunc(reshape);
```

```
glutMainLoop();
return 0;
}
```

You might want to use display lists to store polygon stipple patterns to maximize efficiency. (See "Display-List Design Philosophy" on page 257.)

Marking Polygon Boundary Edges

Advanced

OpenGL can render only convex polygons, but many nonconvex polygons arise in practice. To draw these nonconvex polygons, you typically subdivide them into convex polygons—usually triangles, as shown in Figure 2-12—and then draw the triangles. Unfortunately, if you decompose a general polygon into triangles and draw the triangles, you can't really use **glPolygonMode()** to draw the polygon's outline, since you get all the triangle outlines inside it. To solve this problem, you can tell OpenGL whether a particular vertex precedes a boundary edge; OpenGL keeps track of this information by passing along with each vertex a bit indicating whether that vertex is followed by a boundary edge. Then, when a polygon is drawn in GL_LINE mode, the nonboundary edges aren't drawn. In Figure 2-12, the dashed lines represent added edges.

Figure 2-12   Subdividing a Nonconvex Polygon

By default, all vertices are marked as preceding a boundary edge, but you can manually control the setting of the *edge flag* with the command **glEdgeFlag*()**. This command is used between **glBegin()** and **glEnd()** pairs, and it affects all the vertices specified after it until the next **glEdgeFlag()** call is made. It applies only to vertices specified for polygons, triangles, and quads, not to those specified for strips of triangles or quads.

> void **glEdgeFlag**(GLboolean *flag*);
> void **glEdgeFlagv**(const GLboolean **flag*);
>
> Indicates whether a vertex should be considered as initializing a boundary edge of a polygon. If *flag* is GL_TRUE, the edge flag is set to TRUE (the default), and any vertices created are considered to precede boundary edges until this function is called again with *flag* being GL_FALSE.

As an example, Example 2-7 draws the outline shown in Figure 2-13.

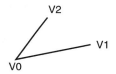

Figure 2-13   Outlined Polygon Drawn Using Edge Flags

Example 2-7   Marking Polygon Boundary Edges

```
glPolygonMode(GL_FRONT_AND_BACK, GL_LINE);
glBegin(GL_POLYGON);
    glEdgeFlag(GL_TRUE);
    glVertex3fv(V0);
    glEdgeFlag(GL_FALSE);
    glVertex3fv(V1);
    glEdgeFlag(GL_TRUE);
    glVertex3fv(V2);
glEnd();
```

Normal Vectors

A *normal vector* (or *normal*, for short) is a vector that points in a direction that's perpendicular to a surface. For a flat surface, one perpendicular direction is the same for every point on the surface, but for a general curved surface, the normal direction might be different at each point on the surface. With OpenGL, you can specify a normal for each polygon or for each vertex. Vertices of the same polygon might share the same normal (for a flat surface) or have different normals (for a curved surface). But you can't assign normals anywhere other than at the vertices.

An object's normal vectors define the orientation of its surface in space—in particular, its orientation relative to light sources. These vectors are used by OpenGL to determine how much light the object receives at its vertices. Lighting—a large topic by itself—is the subject of Chapter 5, and you might want to review the following information after you've read that chapter. Normal vectors are discussed briefly here because you define normal vectors for an object at the same time you define the object's geometry.

You use **glNormal*()** to set the current normal to the value of the argument passed in. Subsequent calls to **glVertex*()** cause the specified vertices to be assigned the current normal. Often, each vertex has a different normal, which necessitates a series of alternating calls, as in Example 2-8.

Example 2-8   Surface Normals at Vertices

```
glBegin (GL_POLYGON);
    glNormal3fv(n0);
    glVertex3fv(v0);
    glNormal3fv(n1);
    glVertex3fv(v1);
    glNormal3fv(n2);
    glVertex3fv(v2);
    glNormal3fv(n3);
    glVertex3fv(v3);
glEnd();
```

---

void **glNormal3**{bsidf}(*TYPE nx, TYPE ny, TYPE nz*);
void **glNormal3**{bsidf}**v**(const *TYPE* *v);

Sets the current normal vector as specified by the arguments. The nonvector version (without the **v**) takes three arguments, which specify an (*nx, ny, nz*) vector that's taken to be the normal. Alternatively, you can use the vector version of this function (with the **v**) and supply a single array of three elements to specify the desired normal. The **b**, **s**, and **i** versions scale their parameter values linearly to the range [–1.0,1.0].

There's no magic to finding the normals for an object—most likely, you have to perform some calculations that might include taking derivatives—but there are several techniques and tricks you can use to achieve certain effects. Appendix E explains how to find normal vectors for surfaces. If you already know how to do this, if you can count on always being supplied with normal vectors, or if you don't want to use the lighting facility provided by OpenGL lighting facility, you don't need to read this appendix.

Note that at a given point on a surface, two vectors are perpendicular to the surface, and they point in opposite directions. By convention, the normal is the one that points to the outside of the surface being modeled. (If you get inside and outside reversed in your model, just change every normal vector from (x, y, z) to $(-x, -y, -z)$).

Also, keep in mind that since normal vectors indicate direction only, their length is mostly irrelevant. You can specify normals of any length, but eventually they have to be converted to having a length of 1 before lighting calculations are performed. (A vector that has a length of 1 is said to be of unit length, or *normalized*.) In general, you should supply normalized normal vectors. To make a normal vector of unit length, divide each of its x, y, z components by the length of the normal: $\sqrt{x^2 + y^2 + z^2}$.

Normal vectors remain normalized as long as your model transformations include only rotations and translations. (See Chapter 3 for a discussion of transformations.) If you perform irregular transformations (such as scaling or multiplying by a shear matrix), or if you specify nonunit-length normals, then you should have OpenGL automatically normalize your normal vectors after the transformations. To do this, call **glEnable()** with GL_NORMALIZE as its argument. By default, automatic normalization is disabled. Note that automatic normalization typically requires additional calculations that might reduce the performance of your application.

Vertex Arrays

You may have noticed that OpenGL requires many function calls to render geometric primitives. Drawing a 20-sided polygon requires 22 function calls: one call to **glBegin()**, one call for each of the vertices, and a final call to **glEnd()**. In the two previous code examples, additional information (polygon boundary edge flags or surface normals) added function calls for each vertex. This can quickly double or triple the number of function calls required for one geometric object. For some systems, function calls have a great deal of overhead and can hinder performance.

An additional problem is the redundant processing of vertices that are shared between adjacent polygons. For example, the cube in Figure 2-14 has six faces and eight shared vertices. Unfortunately, using the standard method of describing this object, each vertex would have to be specified three times: once for every face that uses it. So 24 vertices would be processed, even though eight would be enough.

Figure 2-14   Six Sides; Eight Shared Vertices

OpenGL has vertex array routines that allow you to specify a lot of vertex-related data with just a few arrays and to access that data with equally few function calls. Using vertex array routines, all 20 vertices in a 20-sided polygon could be put into one array and called with one function. If each vertex also had a surface normal, all 20 surface normals could be put into another array and also called with one function.

Arranging data in vertex arrays may increase the performance of your application. Using vertex arrays reduces the number of function calls, which improves performance. Also, using vertex arrays may allow non-redundant processing of shared vertices. (Vertex sharing is not supported on all implementations of OpenGL.)

Note: Vertex arrays are standard in version 1.1 of OpenGL but were not part of the OpenGL 1.0 specification. With OpenGL 1.0, some vendors have implemented vertex arrays as an extension.

There are three steps to using vertex arrays to render geometry.

1. Activate (enable) up to six arrays, each to store a different type of data: vertex coordinates, RGBA colors, color indices, surface normals, texture coordinates, or polygon edge flags.

2. Put data into the array or arrays. The arrays are accessed by the addresses of (that is, pointers to) their memory locations. In the client-server model, this data is stored in the client's address space.

3. Draw geometry with the data. OpenGL obtains the data from all activated arrays by dereferencing the pointers. In the client-server model, the data is transferred to the server's address space. There are three ways to do this:

   a. Accessing individual array elements (randomly hopping around)

   b. Creating a list of individual array elements (methodically hopping around)

   c. Processing sequential array elements

The dereferencing method you choose may depend upon the type of problem you encounter.

Interleaved vertex array data is another common method of organization. Instead of having up to six different arrays, each maintaining a different type of data (color, surface normal, coordinate, and so on), you might have the different types of data mixed into a single array. (See "Interleaved Arrays" on page 75 for two methods of solving this.)

Step 1: Enabling Arrays

The first step is to call **glEnableClientState()** with an enumerated parameter, which activates the chosen array. In theory, you may need to call this up to six times to activate the six available arrays. In practice, you'll probably activate only between one to four arrays. For example, it is unlikely that you would activate both GL_COLOR_ARRAY and GL_INDEX_ARRAY, since your program's display mode supports either RGBA mode or color-index mode, but probably not both simultaneously.

---

void **glEnableClientState**(GLenum *array*)

Specifies the array to enable. Symbolic constants GL_VERTEX_ARRAY, GL_COLOR_ARRAY, GL_INDEX_ARRAY, GL_NORMAL_ARRAY, GL_TEXTURE_COORD_ARRAY, and GL_EDGE_FLAG_ARRAY are acceptable parameters.

If you use lighting, you may want to define a surface normal for every vertex. (See "Normal Vectors" on page 63.) To use vertex arrays for that case, you activate both the surface normal and vertex coordinate arrays:

```
glEnableClientState(GL_NORMAL_ARRAY);
glEnableClientState(GL_VERTEX_ARRAY);
```

Suppose that you want to turn off lighting at some point and just draw the geometry using a single color. You want to call **glDisable()** to turn off lighting states (see Chapter 5). Now that lighting has been deactivated, you also want to stop changing the values of the surface normal state, which is wasted effort. To do that, you call

```
glDisableClientState(GL_NORMAL_ARRAY);
```

---

void **glDisableClientState**(GLenum *array*);

Specifies the array to disable. Accepts the same symbolic constants as **glEnableClientState**().

You might be asking yourself why the architects of OpenGL created these new (and long!) command names, **gl*ClientState**(). Why can't you just call **glEnable**() and **glDisable**()? One reason is that **glEnable**() and **glDisable**() can be stored in a display list, but the specification of vertex arrays cannot, because the data remains on the client's side.

Step 2: Specifying Data for the Arrays

There is a straightforward way by which a single command specifies a single array in the client space. There are six different routines to specify arrays—one routine for each kind of array. There is also a command that can specify several client-space arrays at once, all originating from a single interleaved array.

---

void **glVertexPointer**(GLint *size*, GLenum *type*, GLsizei *stride*,
                 const GLvoid **pointer*);

Specifies where spatial coordinate data can be accessed. *pointer* is the memory address of the first coordinate of the first vertex in the array. *type* specifies the data type (GL_SHORT, GL_INT, GL_FLOAT, or GL_DOUBLE) of each coordinate in the array. *size* is the number of coordinates per vertex, which must be 2, 3, or 4. *stride* is the byte offset between consecutive vertexes. If *stride* is 0, the vertices are understood to be tightly packed in the array.

To access the other five arrays, there are five similar routines:

---

void **glColorPointer**(GLint *size*, GLenum *type*, GLsizei *stride*,
              const GLvoid **pointer*);
void **glIndexPointer**(GLenum *type*, GLsizei *stride*, const GLvoid **pointer*);
void **glNormalPointer**(GLenum *type*, GLsizei *stride*,
              const GLvoid **pointer*);
void **glTexCoordPointer**(GLint *size*, GLenum *type*, GLsizei *stride*,
              const GLvoid **pointer*);
void **glEdgeFlagPointer**(GLsizei *stride*, const GLvoid **pointer*);

The main differences among the routines are whether size and type are unique or must be specified. For example, a surface normal always has three components, so it is redundant to specify its size. An edge flag is always a single Boolean, so neither size nor type needs to be mentioned. Table 2-4 displays legal values for size and data types.

Command	Sizes	Values for *type* Argument
glVertexPointer	2, 3, 4	GL_SHORT, GL_INT, GL_FLOAT, GL_DOUBLE
glNormalPointer	3	GL_BYTE, GL_SHORT, GL_INT, GL_FLOAT, GL_DOUBLE
glColorPointer	3, 4	GL_BYTE, GL_UNSIGNED_BYTE, GL_SHORT, GL_UNSIGNED_SHORT, GL_INT, GL_UNSIGNED_INT, GL_FLOAT, GL_DOUBLE
glIndexPointer	1	GL_UNSIGNED_BYTE, GL_SHORT, GL_INT, GL_FLOAT, GL_DOUBLE
glTexCoordPointer	1, 2, 3, 4	GL_SHORT, GL_INT, GL_FLOAT, GL_DOUBLE
glEdgeFlagPointer	1	no type argument (type of data must be GLboolean)

Table 2-4   Vertex Array Sizes (Values per Vertex) and Data Types

Example 2-9 uses vertex arrays for both RGBA colors and vertex coordinates. RGB floating-point values and their corresponding (x, y) integer coordinates are loaded into the GL_COLOR_ARRAY and GL_VERTEX_ARRAY.

Example 2-9   Enabling and Loading Vertex Arrays: varray.c

```
static GLint vertices[] = {25, 25,
                           100, 325,
                           175, 25,
                           175, 325,
                           250, 25,
                           325, 325};
static GLfloat colors[] = {1.0, 0.2, 0.2,
                           0.2, 0.2, 1.0,
                           0.8, 1.0, 0.2,
                           0.75, 0.75, 0.75,
                           0.35, 0.35, 0.35,
                           0.5, 0.5, 0.5};
```

```
glEnableClientState (GL_COLOR_ARRAY);
glEnableClientState (GL_VERTEX_ARRAY);

glColorPointer (3, GL_FLOAT, 0, colors);
glVertexPointer (2, GL_INT, 0, vertices);
```

Stride

With a stride of zero, each type of vertex array (RGB color, color index, vertex coordinate, and so on) must be tightly packed. The data in the array must be homogeneous; that is, the data must be all RGB color values, all vertex coordinates, or all some other data similar in some fashion.

Using a stride of other than zero can be useful, especially when dealing with interleaved arrays. In the following array of GLfloats, there are six vertices. For each vertex, there are three RGB color values, which alternate with the (x, y, z) vertex coordinates.

```
static GLfloat intertwined[] =
     {1.0, 0.2, 1.0, 100.0, 100.0, 0.0,
      1.0, 0.2, 0.2, 0.0, 200.0, 0.0,
      1.0, 1.0, 0.2, 100.0, 300.0, 0.0,
      0.2, 1.0, 0.2, 200.0, 300.0, 0.0,
      0.2, 1.0, 1.0, 300.0, 200.0, 0.0,
      0.2, 0.2, 1.0, 200.0, 100.0, 0.0};
```

Stride allows a vertex array to access its desired data at regular intervals in the array. For example, to reference only the color values in the *intertwined* array, the following call starts from the beginning of the array (which could also be passed as &*intertwined[0]*) and jumps ahead 6 * **sizeof**(GLfloat) bytes, which is the size of both the color and vertex coordinate values. This jump is enough to get to the beginning of the data for the next vertex.

```
glColorPointer (3, GL_FLOAT, 6 * sizeof(GLfloat), intertwined);
```

For the vertex coordinate pointer, you need to start from further in the array, at the fourth element of *intertwined* (remember that C programmers start counting at zero).

```
glVertexPointer(3, GL_FLOAT,6*sizeof(GLfloat), &intertwined[3]);
```

Step 3: Dereferencing and Rendering

Until the contents of the vertex arrays are dereferenced, the arrays remain on the client side, and their contents are easily changed. In Step 3, contents of the arrays are obtained, sent down to the server, and then sent down the graphics processing pipeline for rendering.

There are three ways to obtain data: from a single array element (indexed location), from a sequence of array elements, and from an ordered list of array elements.

Dereference a Single Array Element

---

void **glArrayElement**(GLint *ith*)

Obtains the data of one (the *ith*) vertex for all currently enabled arrays. For the vertex coordinate array, the corresponding command would be **glVertex**[*size*][*type*]**v**(), where *size* is one of [2,3,4], and *type* is one of [s,i,f,d] for GLshort, GLint, GLfloat, and GLdouble respectively. Both size and type were defined by **glVertexPointer**(). For other enabled arrays, **glArrayElement**() calls **glEdgeFlagv**(), **glTexCoord**[*size*][*type*]**v**(), **glColor**[*size*][*type*]**v**(), **glIndex**[*type*]**v**(), and **glNormal**[*type*]**v**(). If the vertex coordinate array is enabled, the **glVertex*v**() routine is executed last, after the execution (if enabled) of up to five corresponding array values.

---

glArrayElement() is usually called between **glBegin**() and **glEnd**(). (If called outside, **glArrayElement**() sets the current state for all enabled arrays, except for vertex, which has no current state.) In Example 2-10, a triangle is drawn using the third, fourth, and sixth vertices from enabled vertex arrays (again, remember that C programmers begin counting array locations with zero).

Example 2-10   Using glArrayElement() to Define Colors and Vertices

```
glEnableClientState (GL_COLOR_ARRAY);
glEnableClientState (GL_VERTEX_ARRAY);
glColorPointer (3, GL_FLOAT, 0, colors);
glVertexPointer (2, GL_INT, 0, vertices);

glBegin(GL_TRIANGLES);
glArrayElement (2);
glArrayElement (3);
glArrayElement (5);
glEnd();
```

When executed, the latter five lines of code has the same effect as

```
glBegin(GL_TRIANGLES);
```

```
glColor3fv(colors+(2*3*sizeof(GLfloat));
glVertex3fv(vertices+(2*2*sizeof(GLint));
glColor3fv(colors+(3*3*sizeof(GLfloat));
glVertex3fv(vertices+(3*2*sizeof(GLint));
glColor3fv(colors+(5*3*sizeof(GLfloat));
glVertex3fv(vertices+(5*2*sizeof(GLint));
glEnd();
```

Since **glArrayElement()** is only a single function call per vertex, it may reduce the number of function calls, which increases overall performance.

Be warned that if the contents of the array are changed between **glBegin()** and **glEnd()**, there is no guarantee that you will receive original data or changed data for your requested element. To be safe, don't change the contents of any array element which might be accessed until the primitive is completed.

Dereference a List of Array Elements

glArrayElement() is good for randomly "hopping around" your data arrays. A similar routine, **glDrawElements()**, is good for hopping around your data arrays in a more orderly manner.

---

void **glDrawElements**(GLenum *mode*, GLsizei *count*, GLenum *type*,
void **indices*);

Defines a sequence of geometric primitives using *count* number of elements, whose indices are stored in the array *indices*. *type* must be one of GL_UNSIGNED_BYTE, GL_UNSIGNED_SHORT, or GL_UNSIGNED_INT, indicating the data type of the *indices* array. *mode* specifies what kind of primitives are constructed and is one of the same values that is accepted by **glBegin()**; for example, GL_POLYGON, GL_LINE_LOOP, GL_LINES, GL_POINTS, and so on.

The effect of **glDrawElements()** is almost the same as this command sequence:

```
int i;
glBegin (mode);
for (i = 0; i < count; i++)
    glArrayElement(indices[i]);
glEnd();
```

glDrawElements() additionally checks to make sure *mode*, *count*, and *type* are valid. Also, unlike the preceding sequence, executing

glDrawElements() leaves several states indeterminate. After execution of **glDrawElements()**, current RGB color, color index, normal coordinates, texture coordinates, and edge flag are indeterminate if the corresponding array has been enabled.

With **glDrawElements()**, the vertices for each face of the cube can be placed in an array of indices. Example 2-11 shows two ways to use **glDrawElements()** to render the cube. Figure 2-15 shows the numbering of the vertices used in Example 2-11.

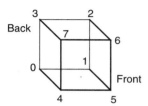

Figure 2-15   Cube with Numbered Vertices

Example 2-11   Two Ways to Use glDrawElements()

```
static GLubyte frontIndices = {4, 5, 6, 7};
static GLubyte rightIndices = {1, 2, 6, 5};
static GLubyte bottomIndices = {0, 1, 5, 4};
static GLubyte backIndices = {0, 3, 2, 1};
static GLubyte leftIndices = {0, 4, 7, 3};
static GLubyte topIndices = {2, 3, 7, 6};

glDrawElements(GL_QUADS, 4, GL_UNSIGNED_BYTE, frontIndices);
glDrawElements(GL_QUADS, 4, GL_UNSIGNED_BYTE, rightIndices);
glDrawElements(GL_QUADS, 4, GL_UNSIGNED_BYTE, bottomIndices);
glDrawElements(GL_QUADS, 4, GL_UNSIGNED_BYTE, backIndices);
glDrawElements(GL_QUADS, 4, GL_UNSIGNED_BYTE, leftIndices);
glDrawElements(GL_QUADS, 4, GL_UNSIGNED_BYTE, topIndices);
```

Or better still, crunch all the indices together:

```
static GLubyte allIndices = {4, 5, 6, 7, 1, 2, 6, 5,
                             0, 1, 5, 4, 0, 3, 2, 1,
                             0, 4, 7, 3, 2, 3, 7, 6};

glDrawElements(GL_QUADS, 24, GL_UNSIGNED_BYTE, allIndices);
```

Note: It is an error to encapsulate **glDrawElements()** between a **glBegin()/glEnd()** pair.

With both **glArrayElement()** and **glDrawElements()**, it is also possible that your OpenGL implementation caches recently processed vertices, allowing your application to "share" or "reuse" vertices. Take the aforementioned cube, for example, which has six faces (polygons) but only eight vertices. Each vertex is used by exactly three faces. Without **glArrayElement()** or **glDrawElements()**, rendering all six faces would require processing twenty-four vertices, even though sixteen vertices would be redundant. Your implementation of OpenGL may be able to minimize redundancy and process as few as eight vertices. (Reuse of vertices may be limited to all vertices within a single **glDrawElements()** call or, for **glArrayElement()**, within one **glBegin()**/**glEnd()** pair.)

Dereference a Sequence of Array Elements

While **glArrayElement()** and **glDrawElements()** "hop around" your data arrays, **glDrawArrays()** plows straight through them.

---

void **glDrawArrays**(GLenum *mode*, GLint *first*, GLsizei *count*);

Constructs a sequence of geometric primitives using array elements starting at *first* and ending at *first+count*-1 of each enabled array. *mode* specifies what kinds of primitives are constructed and is one of the same values accepted by **glBegin()**; for example, GL_POLYGON, GL_LINE_LOOP, GL_LINES, GL_POINTS, and so on.

The effect of **glDrawArrays()** is almost the same as this command sequence:

```
int i;
glBegin (mode);
for (i = 0; i < count; i++)
   glArrayElement(first + i);
glEnd();
```

As is the case with **glDrawElements()**, **glDrawArrays()** also performs error checking on its parameter values and leaves the current RGB color, color index, normal coordinates, texture coordinates, and edge flag with indeterminate values if the corresponding array has been enabled.

Try This

- Change the icosahedron drawing routine in Example 2-13 (on page 84) to use vertex arrays.

Interleaved Arrays

Advanced

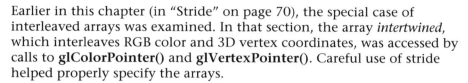

Earlier in this chapter (in "Stride" on page 70), the special case of interleaved arrays was examined. In that section, the array *intertwined*, which interleaves RGB color and 3D vertex coordinates, was accessed by calls to **glColorPointer()** and **glVertexPointer()**. Careful use of stride helped properly specify the arrays.

```
static GLfloat intertwined[] =
     {1.0, 0.2, 1.0, 100.0, 100.0, 0.0,
      1.0, 0.2, 0.2, 0.0, 200.0, 0.0,
      1.0, 1.0, 0.2, 100.0, 300.0, 0.0,
      0.2, 1.0, 0.2, 200.0, 300.0, 0.0,
      0.2, 1.0, 1.0, 300.0, 200.0, 0.0,
      0.2, 0.2, 1.0, 200.0, 100.0, 0.0};
```

There is also a behemoth routine, **glInterleavedArrays()**, that can specify several vertex arrays at once. **glInterleavedArrays()** also enables and disables the appropriate arrays (so it combines both Steps 1 and 2). The array *intertwined* exactly fits one of the fourteen data interleaving configurations supported by **glInterleavedArrays()**. So to specify the contents of the array *intertwined* into the RGB color and vertex arrays and enable both arrays, call

```
glInterleavedArrays (GL_C3F_V3F, 0, intertwined);
```

This call to **glInterleavedArrays()** enables the GL_COLOR_ARRAY and GL_VERTEX_ARRAY arrays. It disables the GL_INDEX_ARRAY, GL_TEXTURE_COORD_ARRAY, GL_NORMAL_ARRAY, and GL_EDGE_FLAG_ARRAY.

This call also has the same effect as calling **glColorPointer()** and **glVertexPointer()** to specify the values for six vertices into each array. Now you are ready for Step 3: Calling **glArrayElement()**, **glDrawElements()**, or **glDrawArrays()** to dereference array elements.

---

void **glInterleavedArrays**(GLenum *format*, GLsizei *stride*, void **pointer*)

Initializes all six arrays, disabling arrays that are not specified in *format*, and enabling the arrays that are specified. *format* is one of 14 symbolic constants, which represent 14 data configurations; Table 2-5 displays *format* values. *stride* specifies the byte offset between consecutive vertexes. If *stride* is 0, the vertexes are understood to be tightly packed in the array. *pointer* is the memory address of the first coordinate of the first vertex in the array.

Note that **glInterleavedArrays()** does not support edge flags.

The mechanics of **glInterleavedArrays()** are intricate and require reference to Example 2-12 and Table 2-5. In that example and table, you'll see e_t, e_c, and e_n, which are the boolean values for the enabled or disabled texture coordinate, color, and normal arrays, and you'll see s_t, s_c, and s_v, which are the sizes (number of components) for the texture coordinate, color, and vertex arrays. t_c is the data type for RGBA color, which is the only array that can have non-float interleaved values. p_c, p_n, and p_v are the calculated strides for jumping over individual color, normal, and vertex values, and s is the stride (if one is not specified by the user) to jump from one array element to the next.

The effect of **glInterleavedArrays()** is the same as calling the command sequence in Example 2-12 with many values defined in Table 2-5. All pointer arithmetic is performed in units of **sizeof**(GL_UNSIGNED_BYTE).

Example 2-12   Effect of glInterleavedArrays(format, stride, pointer)

```
int str;
/*  set et, ec, en, st, sc, sv, tc, pc, pn, pv, and s
 *  as a function of Table 2-5 and the value of format
 */
str = stride;
if (str == 0)
   str = s;
glDisableClientState(GL_EDGE_FLAG_ARRAY);
glDisableClientState(GL_INDEX_ARRAY);
if (et) {
   glEnableClientState(GL_TEXTURE_COORD_ARRAY);
   glTexCoordPointer(st, GL_FLOAT, str, pointer);
}
```

```
else
   glDisableClientState(GL_TEXTURE_COORD_ARRAY);
if (e_c) {
   glEnableClientState(GL_COLOR_ARRAY);
   glColorPointer(s_c, t_c, str, pointer+p_c);
}
else
   glDisableClientState(GL_COLOR_ARRAY);
if (e_n) {
   glEnableClientState(GL_NORMAL_ARRAY);
   glNormalPointer(GL_FLOAT, str, pointer+p_n);
}
else
   glDisableClientState(GL_NORMAL_ARRAY);
glEnableClientState(GL_VERTEX_ARRAY);
glVertexPointer(s_v, GL_FLOAT, str, pointer+p_v);
```

In Table 2-5, T and F are True and False. f is **sizeof**(GL_FLOAT). c is 4 times **sizeof**(GL_UNSIGNED_BYTE), rounded up to the nearest multiple of f.

format	e_t	e_c	e_n	s_t	s_c	s_v	t_c	p_c	p_n	p_v	s
GL_V2F	F	F	F			2				0	2f
GL_V3F	F	F	F			3				0	3f
GL_C4UB_V2F	F	T	F		4	2	GL_UNSIGNED_BYTE	0		c	c+2f
GL_C4UB_V3F	F	T	F		4	3	GL_UNSIGNED_BYTE	0		c	c+3f
GL_C3F_V3F	F	T	F		3	3	GL_FLOAT	0		3f	6f
GL_N3F_V3F	F	F	T			3			0	3f	6f
GL_C4F_N3F_V3F	F	T	T		4	3	GL_FLOAT	0	4f	7f	10f
GL_T2F_V3F	T	F	F	2		3				2f	5f
GL_T4F_V4F	T	F	F	4		4				4f	8f
GL_T2F_C4UB_V3F	T	T	F	2	4	3	GL_UNSIGNED_BYTE	2f		c+2f	c+5f
GL_T2F_C3F_V3F	T	T	F	2	3	3	GL_FLOAT	2f		5f	8f
GL_T2F_N3F_V3F	T	F	T	2		3			2f	5f	8f
GL_T2F_C4F_N3F_V3F	T	T	T	2	4	3	GL_FLOAT	2f	6f	9f	12f
GL_T4F_C4F_N3F_V4F	T	T	T	4	4	4	GL_FLOAT	4f	8f	11f	15f

Table 2-5   Variables that Direct glInterleavedArrays()

Start by learning the simpler formats, GL_V2F, GL_V3F, and GL_C3F_V3F. If you use any of the formats with C4UB, you may have to use a struct data type or do some delicate type casting and pointer math to pack four unsigned bytes into a single 32-bit word.

For some OpenGL implementations, use of interleaved arrays may increase application performance. With an interleaved array, the exact layout of your data is known. You know your data is tightly packed and may be accessed in one chunk. If interleaved arrays are not used, the stride and size information has to be examined to detect whether data is tightly packed.

Note: **glInterleavedArrays()** only enables and disables vertex arrays and specifies values for the vertex-array data. It does not render anything. You must still complete Step 3 and call **glArrayElement()**, **glDrawElements()**, or **glDrawArrays()** to dereference the pointers and render graphics.

Attribute Groups

In "Basic State Management" on page 48, you saw how to set or query an individual state or state variable. Well, you can also save and restore the values of a collection of related state variables with a single command.

OpenGL groups related state variables into an *attribute group*. For example, the GL_LINE_BIT attribute consists of five state variables: the line width, the GL_LINE_STIPPLE enable status, the line stipple pattern, the line stipple repeat counter, and the GL_LINE_SMOOTH enable status. (See "Antialiasing" on page 226.) With the commands **glPushAttrib()** and **glPopAttrib()**, you can save and restore all five state variables, all at once.

Some state variables are in more than one attribute group. For example, the state variable, GL_CULL_FACE, is part of both the polygon and the enable attribute groups.

In OpenGL Version 1.1, there are now two different attribute stacks. In addition to the original attribute stack (which saves the values of server state variables), there is also a client attribute stack, accessible by the commands **glPushClientAttrib()** and **glPopClientAttrib()**.

In general, it's faster to use these commands than to get, save, and restore the values yourself. Some values might be maintained in the hardware, and getting them might be expensive. Also, if you're operating on a remote client, all the attribute data has to be transferred across the network connection and back as it is obtained, saved, and restored. However, your OpenGL implementation keeps the attribute stack on the server, avoiding unnecessary network delays.

There are about twenty different attribute groups, which can be saved and restored by **glPushAttrib**() and **glPopAttrib**(). There are two client attribute groups, which can be saved and restored by **glPushClientAttrib**() and **glPopClientAttrib**(). For both server and client, the attributes are stored on a stack, which has a depth of at least 16 saved attribute groups. (The actual stack depths for your implementation can be obtained using GL_MAX_ATTRIB_STACK_DEPTH and GL_MAX_CLIENT_ATTRIB_STACK_DEPTH with **glGetIntegerv**().) Pushing a full stack or popping an empty one generates an error.

(See the tables in Appendix B to find out exactly which attributes are saved for particular mask values; that is, which attributes are in a particular attribute group.)

---

void **glPushAttrib**(GLbitfield *mask*);
void **glPopAttrib**(void);

---

glPushAttrib() saves all the attributes indicated by bits in *mask* by pushing them onto the attribute stack. **glPopAttrib**() restores the values of those state variables that were saved with the last **glPushAttrib**(). Table 2-7 lists the possible mask bits that can be logically ORed together to save any combination of attributes. Each bit corresponds to a collection of individual state variables. For example, GL_LIGHTING_BIT refers to all the state variables related to lighting, which include the current material color, the ambient, diffuse, specular, and emitted light, a list of the lights that are enabled, and the directions of the spotlights. When **glPopAttrib**() is called, all those variables are restored.

The special mask, GL_ALL_ATTRIB_BITS, is used to save and restore all the state variables in all the attribute groups.

Mask Bit	Attribute Group
GL_ACCUM_BUFFER_BIT	accum-buffer
GL_ALL_ATTRIB_BITS	--
GL_COLOR_BUFFER_BIT	color-buffer
GL_CURRENT_BIT	current
GL_DEPTH_BUFFER_BIT	depth-buffer
GL_ENABLE_BIT	enable

Table 2-6   Attribute Groups

Mask Bit	Attribute Group
GL_EVAL_BIT	eval
GL_FOG_BIT	fog
GL_HINT_BIT	hint
GL_LIGHTING_BIT	lighting
GL_LINE_BIT	line
GL_LIST_BIT	list
GL_PIXEL_MODE_BIT	pixel
GL_POINT_BIT	point
GL_POLYGON_BIT	polygon
GL_POLYGON_STIPPLE_BIT	polygon-stipple
GL_SCISSOR_BIT	scissor
GL_STENCIL_BUFFER_BIT	stencil-buffer
GL_TEXTURE_BIT	texture
GL_TRANSFORM_BIT	transform
GL_VIEWPORT_BIT	viewport

Table 2-6   Attribute Groups (continued)

void **glPushClientAttrib**(GLbitfield *mask*);
void **glPopClientAttrib**(void);

glPushClientAttrib() saves all the attributes indicated by bits in *mask* by pushing them onto the client attribute stack. **glPopClientAttrib()** restores the values of those state variables that were saved with the last **glPushClientAttrib()**. Table 2-7 lists the possible mask bits that can be logically ORed together to save any combination of client attributes.

There are two client attribute groups, feedback and select, that cannot be saved or restored with the stack mechanism.

Mask Bit	Attribute Group
GL_CLIENT_PIXEL_STORE_BIT	pixel-store
GL_CLIENT_VERTEX_ARRAY_BIT	vertex-array
GL_ALL_CLIENT_ATTRIB_BITS	--
can't be pushed or popped	feedback
can't be pushed or popped	select

Table 2-7   Client Attribute Groups

Some Hints for Building Polygonal Models of Surfaces

Following are some techniques that you might want to use as you build polygonal approximations of surfaces. You might want to review this section after you've read Chapter 5 on lighting and Chapter 7 on display lists. The lighting conditions affect how models look once they're drawn, and some of the following techniques are much more efficient when used in conjunction with display lists. As you read these techniques, keep in mind that when lighting calculations are enabled, normal vectors must be specified to get proper results.

Constructing polygonal approximations to surfaces is an art, and there is no substitute for experience. This section, however, lists a few pointers that might make it a bit easier to get started.

- Keep polygon orientations consistent. Make sure that when viewed from the outside, all the polygons on the surface are oriented in the same direction (all clockwise or all counterclockwise). Consistent orientation is important for polygon culling and two-sided lighting. Try to get this right the first time, since it's excruciatingly painful to fix the problem later. (If you use **glScale*()** to reflect geometry around some axis of symmetry, you might change the orientation with **glFrontFace()** to keep the orientations consistent.)

- When you subdivide a surface, watch out for any nontriangular polygons. The three vertices of a triangle are guaranteed to lie on a plane; any polygon with four or more vertices might not. Nonplanar polygons can be viewed from some orientation such that the edges cross each other, and OpenGL might not render such polygons correctly.

- There's always a trade-off between the display speed and the quality of the image. If you subdivide a surface into a small number of polygons, it renders quickly but might have a jagged appearance; if you subdivide it into millions of tiny polygons, it probably looks good but might take a long time to render. Ideally, you can provide a parameter to the subdivision routines that indicates how fine a subdivision you want, and if the object is farther from the eye, you can use a coarser subdivision. Also, when you subdivide, use large polygons where the surface is relatively flat, and small polygons in regions of high curvature.

- For high-quality images, it's a good idea to subdivide more on the silhouette edges than in the interior. If the surface is to be rotated relative to the eye, this is tougher to do, since the silhouette edges keep moving. Silhouette edges occur where the normal vectors are perpendicular to the vector from the surface to the viewpoint—that is, when their vector dot product is zero. Your subdivision algorithm might choose to subdivide more if this dot product is near zero.

- Try to avoid T-intersections in your models (see Figure 2-16). As shown, there's no guarantee that the line segments AB and BC lie on exactly the same pixels as the segment AC. Sometimes they do, and sometimes they don't, depending on the transformations and orientation. This can cause cracks to appear intermittently in the surface.

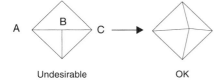

Figure 2-16   Modifying an Undesirable T-intersection

- If you're constructing a closed surface, make sure to use exactly the same numbers for coordinates at the beginning and end of a closed loop, or you can get gaps and cracks due to numerical round-off. Here's a two-dimensional example of bad code:

```
/* don't use this code */
#define PI 3.14159265
#define EDGES 30

/* draw a circle */
glBegin(GL_LINE_STRIP);
for (i = 0; i <= EDGES; i++)
    glVertex2f(cos((2*PI*i)/EDGES), sin((2*PI*i)/EDGES));
glEnd();
```

The edges meet exactly only if your machine manages to calculate the sine and cosine of 0 and of (2*PI*EDGES/EDGES) and gets exactly the same values. If you trust the floating-point unit on your machine to do this right, the authors have a bridge they'd like to sell you.... To correct the code, make sure that when i == EDGES, you use 0 for the sine and cosine, not 2*PI*EDGES/EDGES. (Or simpler still, use GL_LINE_LOOP instead of GL_LINE_STRIP, and change the loop termination condition to i < EDGES.)

An Example: Building an Icosahedron

To illustrate some of the considerations that arise in approximating a surface, let's look at some example code sequences. This code concerns the vertices of a regular icosahedron (which is a Platonic solid composed of twenty faces that span twelve vertices, each face of which is an equilateral triangle). An icosahedron can be considered a rough approximation for a sphere. Example 2-13 defines the vertices and triangles making up an icosahedron and then draws the icosahedron.

Example 2-13 Drawing an Icosahedron

```
#define X .525731112119133606
#define Z .850650808352039932

static GLfloat vdata[12][3] = {
   {-X, 0.0, Z}, {X, 0.0, Z}, {-X, 0.0, -Z}, {X, 0.0, -Z},
   {0.0, Z, X}, {0.0, Z, -X}, {0.0, -Z, X}, {0.0, -Z, -X},
   {Z, X, 0.0}, {-Z, X, 0.0}, {Z, -X, 0.0}, {-Z, -X, 0.0}
};
static GLuint tindices[20][3] = {
   {0,4,1}, {0,9,4}, {9,5,4}, {4,5,8}, {4,8,1},
   {8,10,1}, {8,3,10}, {5,3,8}, {5,2,3}, {2,7,3},
   {7,10,3}, {7,6,10}, {7,11,6}, {11,0,6}, {0,1,6},
   {6,1,10}, {9,0,11}, {9,11,2}, {9,2,5}, {7,2,11} };
int i;

glBegin(GL_TRIANGLES);
for (i = 0; i < 20; i++) {
   /* color information here */
   glVertex3fv(&vdata[tindices[i][0]][0]);
   glVertex3fv(&vdata[tindices[i][1]][0]);
   glVertex3fv(&vdata[tindices[i][2]][0]);
}
glEnd();
```

The strange numbers *X* and *Z* are chosen so that the distance from the origin to any of the vertices of the icosahedron is 1.0. The coordinates of the twelve vertices are given in the array *vdata[][]*, where the zeroth vertex is *{–X, 0.0, Z}*, the first is *{X, 0.0, Z}*, and so on. The array *tindices[][]* tells how to link the vertices to make triangles. For example, the first triangle is made from the zeroth, fourth, and first vertex. If you take the vertices for triangles in the order given, all the triangles have the same orientation.

The line that mentions color information should be replaced by a command that sets the color of the *i*th face. If no code appears here, all faces are drawn in the same color, and it'll be impossible to discern the three-dimensional quality of the object. An alternative to explicitly specifying colors is to define surface normals and use lighting, as described in the next subsection.

Note: In all the examples described in this section, unless the surface is to be drawn only once, you should probably save the calculated vertex and normal coordinates so that the calculations don't need to be repeated each time that the surface is drawn. This can be done using your own data structures or by constructing display lists. (See Chapter 7.)

Calculating Normal Vectors for a Surface

If a surface is to be lit, you need to supply the vector normal to the surface. Calculating the normalized cross product of two vectors on that surface provides normal vector. With the flat surfaces of an icosahedron, all three vertices defining a surface have the same normal vector. In this case, the normal needs to be specified only once for each set of three vertices. The code in Example 2-14 can replace the "color information here" line in Example 2-13 for drawing the icosahedron.

Example 2-14   Generating Normal Vectors for a Surface

```
GLfloat d1[3], d2[3], norm[3];
for (j = 0; j < 3; j++) {
   d1[j] = vdata[tindices[i][0]][j] - vdata[tindices[i][1]][j];
   d2[j] = vdata[tindices[i][1]][j] - vdata[tindices[i][2]][j];
}
normcrossprod(d1, d2, norm);
glNormal3fv(norm);
```

The function **normcrossprod()** produces the normalized cross product of two vectors, as shown in Example 2-15.

Example 2-15   Calculating the Normalized Cross Product of Two Vectors

```
void normalize(float v[3]) {
   GLfloat d = sqrt(v[0]*v[0]+v[1]*v[1]+v[2]*v[2]);
   if (d == 0.0) {
      error("zero length vector");
      return;
   }
   v[0] /= d; v[1] /= d; v[2] /= d;
}
```

```
void normcrossprod(float v1[3], float v2[3], float out[3])
{
    GLint i, j;
    GLfloat length;

    out[0] = v1[1]*v2[2] - v1[2]*v2[1];
    out[1] = v1[2]*v2[0] - v1[0]*v2[2];
    out[2] = v1[0]*v2[1] - v1[1]*v2[0];
    normalize(out);
}
```

If you're using an icosahedron as an approximation for a shaded sphere, you'll want to use normal vectors that are perpendicular to the true surface of the sphere, rather than being perpendicular to the faces. For a sphere, the normal vectors are simple; each points in the same direction as the vector from the origin to the corresponding vertex. Since the icosahedron vertex data is for an icosahedron of radius 1, the normal and vertex data is identical. Here is the code that would draw an icosahedral approximation of a smoothly shaded sphere (assuming that lighting is enabled, as described in Chapter 5):

```
glBegin(GL_TRIANGLES);
for (i = 0; i < 20; i++) {
    glNormal3fv(&vdata[tindices[i][0]][0]);
    glVertex3fv(&vdata[tindices[i][0]][0]);
    glNormal3fv(&vdata[tindices[i][1]][0]);
    glVertex3fv(&vdata[tindices[i][1]][0]);
    glNormal3fv(&vdata[tindices[i][2]][0]);
    glVertex3fv(&vdata[tindices[i][2]][0]);
}
glEnd();
```

Improving the Model

A twenty-sided approximation to a sphere doesn't look good unless the image of the sphere on the screen is quite small, but there's an easy way to increase the accuracy of the approximation. Imagine the icosahedron inscribed in a sphere, and subdivide the triangles as shown in Figure 2-17. The newly introduced vertices lie slightly inside the sphere, so push them to the surface by normalizing them (dividing them by a factor to make them have length 1). This subdivision process can be repeated for arbitrary accuracy. The three objects shown in Figure 2-17 use 20, 80, and 320 approximating triangles, respectively.

Figure 2-17   Subdividing to Improve a Polygonal Approximation to a Surface

Example 2-16 performs a single subdivision, creating an 80-sided spherical approximation.

Example 2-16 Single Subdivision

```
void drawtriangle(float *v1, float *v2, float *v3)
{
   glBegin(GL_TRIANGLES);
      glNormal3fv(v1); vlVertex3fv(v1);
      glNormal3fv(v2); vlVertex3fv(v2);
      glNormal3fv(v3); vlVertex3fv(v3);
   glEnd();
}

void subdivide(float *v1, float *v2, float *v3)
{
   GLfloat v12[3], v23[3], v31[3];
   GLint i;

   for (i = 0; i < 3; i++) {
      v12[i] = v1[i]+v2[i];
      v23[i] = v2[i]+v3[i];
      v31[i] = v3[i]+v1[i];
   }
   normalize(v12);
   normalize(v23);
   normalize(v31);
   drawtriangle(v1, v12, v31);
   drawtriangle(v2, v23, v12);
   drawtriangle(v3, v31, v23);
   drawtriangle(v12, v23, v31);
}
```

```
for (i = 0; i < 20; i++) {
    subdivide(&vdata[tindices[i][0]][0],
            &vdata[tindices[i][1]][0],
            &vdata[tindices[i][2]][0]);
}
```

Example 2-17 is a slight modification of Example 2-16 which recursively subdivides the triangles to the proper depth. If the depth value is 0, no subdivisions are performed, and the triangle is drawn as is. If the depth is 1, a single subdivision is performed, and so on.

Example 2-17   Recursive Subdivision

```
void subdivide(float *v1, float *v2, float *v3, long depth)
{
    GLfloat v12[3], v23[3], v31[3];
    GLint i;

    if (depth == 0) {
        drawtriangle(v1, v2, v3);
        return;
    }
    for (i = 0; i < 3; i++) {
        v12[i] = v1[i]+v2[i];
        v23[i] = v2[i]+v3[i];
        v31[i] = v3[i]+v1[i];
    }
    normalize(v12);
    normalize(v23);
    normalize(v31);
    subdivide(v1, v12, v31, depth-1);
    subdivide(v2, v23, v12, depth-1);
    subdivide(v3, v31, v23, depth-1);
    subdivide(v12, v23, v31, depth-1);
}
```

Generalized Subdivision

A recursive subdivision technique such as the one described in Example 2-17 can be used for other types of surfaces. Typically, the recursion ends either if a certain depth is reached or if some condition on the curvature is satisfied (highly curved parts of surfaces look better with more subdivision).

To look at a more general solution to the problem of subdivision, consider an arbitrary surface parameterized by two variables *u[0]* and *u[1]*. Suppose that two routines are provided:

```
void surf(GLfloat u[2], GLfloat vertex[3], GLfloat normal[3]);
float curv(GLfloat u[2]);
```

If **surf()** is passed *u[]*, the corresponding three-dimensional vertex and normal vectors (of length 1) are returned. If *u[]* is passed to **curv()**, the curvature of the surface at that point is calculated and returned. (See an introductory textbook on differential geometry for more information about measuring surface curvature.)

Example 2-18 shows the recursive routine that subdivides a triangle either until the maximum depth is reached or until the maximum curvature at the three vertices is less than some cutoff.

Example 2-18   Generalized Subdivision

```
void subdivide(float u1[2], float u2[2], float u3[2],
               float cutoff, long depth)
{
   GLfloat v1[3], v2[3], v3[3], n1[3], n2[3], n3[3];
   GLfloat u12[2], u23[2], u32[2];
   GLint i;

   if (depth == maxdepth || (curv(u1) < cutoff &&
       curv(u2) < cutoff && curv(u3) < cutoff)) {
      surf(u1, v1, n1); surf(u2, v2, n2); surf(u3, v3, n3);
      glBegin(GL_POLYGON);
         glNormal3fv(n1); glVertex3fv(v1);
         glNormal3fv(n2); glVertex3fv(v2);
         glNormal3fv(n3); glVertex3fv(v3);
      glEnd();
      return;
   }
   for (i = 0; i < 2; i++) {
      u12[i] = (u1[i] + u2[i])/2.0;
      u23[i] = (u2[i] + u3[i])/2.0;
      u31[i] = (u3[i] + u1[i])/2.0;
   }
   subdivide(u1, u12, u31, cutoff, depth+1);
   subdivide(u2, u23, u12, cutoff, depth+1);
   subdivide(u3, u31, u23, cutoff, depth+1);
   subdivide(u12, u23, u31, cutoff, depth+1);
}
```

Chapter 3

Viewing

Chapter Objectives

After reading this chapter, you'll be able to do the following:

- View a *geometric model* in any orientation by transforming it in three-dimensional space

- Control the location in three-dimensional space from which the model is viewed

- Clip undesired portions of the model out of the scene that's to be viewed

- Manipulate the appropriate matrix stacks that control model transformation for viewing and project the model onto the screen

- Combine multiple transformations to mimic sophisticated systems in motion, such as a solar system or an articulated robot arm

- Reverse or mimic the operations of the geometric processing pipeline

Chapter 2 explained how to instruct OpenGL to draw the geometric models you want displayed in your scene. Now you must decide how you want to position the models in the scene, and you must choose a vantage point from which to view the scene. You can use the default positioning and vantage point, but most likely you want to specify them.

Look at the image on the cover of this book. The program that produced that image contained a single geometric description of a building block. Each block was carefully positioned in the scene: Some blocks were scattered on the floor, some were stacked on top of each other on the table, and some were assembled to make the globe. Also, a particular viewpoint had to be chosen. Obviously, we wanted to look at the corner of the room containing the globe. But how far away from the scene—and where exactly—should the viewer be? We wanted to make sure that the final image of the scene contained a good view out the window, that a portion of the floor was visible, and that all the objects in the scene were not only visible but presented in an interesting arrangement. This chapter explains how to use OpenGL to accomplish these tasks: how to position and orient models in three-dimensional space and how to establish the location—also in three-dimensional space—of the viewpoint. All of these factors help determine exactly what image appears on the screen.

You want to remember that the point of computer graphics is to create a two-dimensional image of three-dimensional objects (it has to be two-dimensional because it's drawn on a flat screen), but you need to think in three-dimensional coordinates while making many of the decisions that determine what gets drawn on the screen. A common mistake people make when creating three-dimensional graphics is to start thinking too soon that the final image appears on a flat, two-dimensional screen. Avoid thinking about which pixels need to be drawn, and instead try to visualize three-dimensional space. Create your models in some three-dimensional universe that lies deep inside your computer, and let the computer do its job of calculating which pixels to color.

A series of three computer operations convert an object's three-dimensional coordinates to pixel positions on the screen.

- Transformations, which are represented by matrix multiplication, include modeling, viewing, and projection operations. Such operations include rotation, translation, scaling, reflecting, orthographic projection, and perspective projection. Generally, you use a combination of several transformations to draw a scene.

- Since the scene is rendered on a rectangular window, objects (or parts of objects) that lie outside the window must be clipped. In three-dimensional computer graphics, clipping occurs by throwing out objects on one side of a clipping plane.

- Finally, a correspondence must be established between the transformed coordinates and screen pixels. This is known as a *viewport* transformation.

This chapter describes all of these operations, and how to control them, in the following major sections:

- "Overview: The Camera Analogy" on page 94 gives an overview of the transformation process by describing the analogy of taking a photograph with a camera, presents a simple example program that transforms an object, and briefly describes the basic OpenGL transformation commands.

- "Viewing and Modeling Transformations" on page 104 explains in detail how to specify and to imagine the effect of viewing and modeling transformations. These transformations orient the model and the camera relative to each other to obtain the desired final image.

- "Projection Transformations" on page 120 describes how to specify the shape and orientation of the *viewing volume*. The viewing volume determines how a scene is projected onto the screen (with a perspective or orthographic projection) and which objects or parts of objects are clipped out of the scene.

- "Viewport Transformation" on page 125 explains how to control the conversion of three-dimensional model coordinates to screen coordinates.

- "Troubleshooting Transformations" on page 129 presents some tips for discovering why you might not be getting the desired effect from your modeling, viewing, projection, and viewport transformations.

- "Manipulating the Matrix Stacks" on page 132 discusses how to save and restore certain transformations. This is particularly useful when you're drawing complicated objects that are built up from simpler ones.

- "Additional Clipping Planes" on page 136 describes how to specify additional clipping planes beyond those defined by the viewing volume.

- "Examples of Composing Several Transformations" on page 139 walks you through a couple of more complicated uses for transformations.

- "Reversing or Mimicking Transformations" on page 147 shows you how to take a transformed point in window coordinates and reverse the transformation to obtain its original object coordinates. The transformation itself (without reversal) can also be emulated.

Overview: The Camera Analogy

The transformation process to produce the desired scene for viewing is analogous to taking a photograph with a camera. As shown in Figure 3-1, the steps with a camera (or a computer) might be the following.

1. Set up your tripod and pointing the camera at the scene (viewing transformation).

2. Arrange the scene to be photographed into the desired composition (modeling transformation).

3. Choose a camera lens or adjust the zoom (projection transformation).

4. Determine how large you want the final photograph to be—for example, you might want it enlarged (viewport transformation).

After these steps are performed, the picture can be snapped or the scene can be drawn.

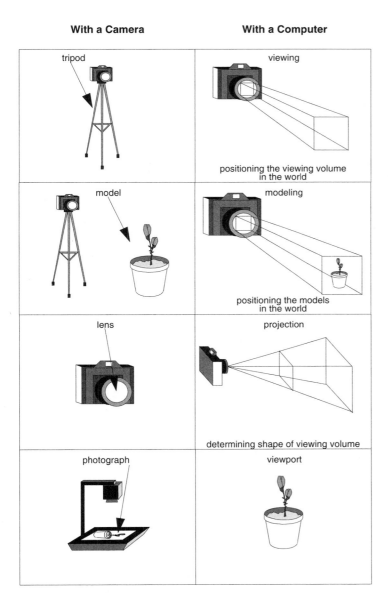

With a Camera

With a Computer

tripod

viewing

positioning the viewing volume
in the world

model

modeling

positioning the models
in the world

lens

projection

determining shape of viewing volume

photograph

viewport

Figure 3-1   The Camera Analogy

Note that these steps correspond to the order in which you specify the
desired transformations in your program, not necessarily the order in which
the relevant mathematical operations are performed on an object's vertices.

The viewing transformations must precede the modeling transformations in your code, but you can specify the projection and viewport transformations at any point before drawing occurs. Figure 3-2 shows the order in which these operations occur on your computer.

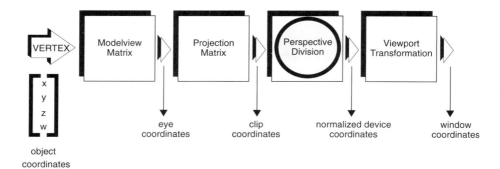

Figure 3-2   Stages of Vertex Transformation

To specify viewing, modeling, and projection transformations, you construct a 4×4 matrix **M**, which is then multiplied by the coordinates of each vertex *v* in the scene to accomplish the transformation

v′=Mv

(Remember that vertices always have four coordinates (*x, y, z, w*), though in most cases *w* is 1 and for two-dimensional data *z* is 0.) Note that viewing and modeling transformations are automatically applied to surface normal vectors, in addition to vertices. (Normal vectors are used only in *eye coordinates*.) This ensures that the normal vector's relationship to the vertex data is properly preserved.

The viewing and modeling transformations you specify are combined to form the modelview matrix, which is applied to the incoming *object coordinates* to yield eye coordinates. Next, if you've specified additional clipping planes to remove certain objects from the scene or to provide cutaway views of objects, these clipping planes are applied.

After that, OpenGL applies the projection matrix to yield *clip coordinates*. This transformation defines a viewing volume; objects outside this volume are clipped so that they're not drawn in the final scene. After this point, the *perspective division* is performed by dividing coordinate values by *w*, to produce *normalized device coordinates*. (See Appendix F for more information about the meaning of the *w* coordinate and how it affects matrix transformations.) Finally, the transformed coordinates are converted to *window coordinates* by applying the viewport transformation. You can manipulate the dimensions of the viewport to cause the final image to be enlarged, shrunk, or stretched.

You might correctly suppose that the x and y coordinates are sufficient to determine which pixels need to be drawn on the screen. However, all the transformations are performed on the z coordinates as well. This way, at the end of this transformation process, the z values correctly reflect the depth of a given vertex (measured in distance away from the screen). One use for this depth value is to eliminate unnecessary drawing. For example, suppose two vertices have the same x and y values but different z values. OpenGL can use this information to determine which surfaces are obscured by other surfaces and can then avoid drawing the hidden surfaces. (See Chapter 10 for more information about this technique, which is called *hidden-surface removal*.)

As you've probably guessed by now, you need to know a few things about matrix mathematics to get the most out of this chapter. If you want to brush up on your knowledge in this area, you might consult a textbook on linear algebra.

A Simple Example: Drawing a Cube

Example 3-1 draws a cube that's scaled by a modeling transformation (see Figure 3-3). The viewing transformation, **gluLookAt()**, positions and aims the camera towards where the cube is drawn. A projection transformation and a viewport transformation are also specified. The rest of this section walks you through Example 3-1 and briefly explains the transformation commands it uses. The succeeding sections contain the complete, detailed discussion of all OpenGL's transformation commands.

Figure 3-3   Transformed Cube

Example 3-1   Transformed Cube: cube.c

```c
#include <GL/gl.h>
#include <GL/glu.h>
#include <GL/glut.h>

void init(void)
{
   glClearColor (0.0, 0.0, 0.0, 0.0);
   glShadeModel (GL_FLAT);
}

void display(void)
{
   glClear (GL_COLOR_BUFFER_BIT);
   glColor3f (1.0, 1.0, 1.0);
   glLoadIdentity ();               /* clear the matrix */
         /* viewing transformation  */
   gluLookAt (0.0, 0.0, 5.0, 0.0, 0.0, 0.0, 0.0, 1.0, 0.0);
   glScalef (1.0, 2.0, 1.0);        /* modeling transformation */
   glutWireCube (1.0);
   glFlush ();
}

void reshape (int w, int h)
{
   glViewport (0, 0, (GLsizei) w, (GLsizei) h);
   glMatrixMode (GL_PROJECTION);
   glLoadIdentity ();
   glFrustum (-1.0, 1.0, -1.0, 1.0, 1.5, 20.0);
   glMatrixMode (GL_MODELVIEW);
}

int main(int argc, char** argv)
{
   glutInit(&argc, argv);
   glutInitDisplayMode (GLUT_SINGLE | GLUT_RGB);
   glutInitWindowSize (500, 500);
   glutInitWindowPosition (100, 100);
   glutCreateWindow (argv[0]);
   init ();
   glutDisplayFunc(display);
   glutReshapeFunc(reshape);
   glutMainLoop();
   return 0;
}
```

The Viewing Transformation

Recall that the viewing transformation is analogous to positioning and aiming a camera. In this code example, before the viewing transformation can be specified, the *current matrix* is set to the identity matrix with **glLoadIdentity()**. This step is necessary since most of the transformation commands multiply the current matrix by the specified matrix and then set the result to be the current matrix. If you don't clear the current matrix by loading it with the identity matrix, you continue to combine previous transformation matrices with the new one you supply. In some cases, you do want to perform such combinations, but you also need to clear the matrix sometimes.

In Example 3-1, after the matrix is initialized, the viewing transformation is specified with **gluLookAt()**. The arguments for this command indicate where the camera (or eye position) is placed, where it is aimed, and which way is up. The arguments used here place the camera at (0, 0, 5), aim the camera lens towards (0, 0, 0), and specify the *up-vector* as (0, 1, 0). The up-vector defines a unique orientation for the camera.

If **gluLookAt()** was not called, the camera has a default position and orientation. By default, the camera is situated at the origin, points down the negative z-axis, and has an up-vector of (0, 1, 0). So in Example 3-1, the overall effect is that **gluLookAt()** moves the camera 5 units along the z-axis. (See "Viewing and Modeling Transformations" on page 104 for more information about viewing transformations.)

The Modeling Transformation

You use the modeling transformation to position and orient the model. For example, you can rotate, translate, or scale the model—or perform some combination of these operations. In Example 3-1, **glScalef()** is the modeling transformation that is used. The arguments for this command specify how scaling should occur along the three axes. If all the arguments are 1.0, this command has no effect. In Example 3-1, the cube is drawn twice as large in the *y* direction. Thus, if one corner of the cube had originally been at (3.0, 3.0, 3.0), that corner would wind up being drawn at (3.0, 6.0, 3.0). The effect of this modeling transformation is to transform the cube so that it isn't a cube but a rectangular box.

Try This

- Change the **gluLookAt()** call in Example 3-1 to the modeling transformation **glTranslatef()** with parameters (0.0, 0.0, -5.0). The result should look exactly the same as when you used **gluLookAt()**. Why are the effects of these two commands similar?

Note that instead of moving the camera (with a viewing transformation) so that the cube could be viewed, you could have moved the cube away from the camera (with a modeling transformation). This duality in the nature of viewing and modeling transformations is why you need to think about the effect of both types of transformations simultaneously. It doesn't make sense to try to separate the effects, but sometimes it's easier to think about them one way rather than the other. This is also why modeling and viewing transformations are combined into the *modelview matrix* before the transformations are applied. (See "Viewing and Modeling Transformations" on page 104 for more detail on how to think about modeling and viewing transformations and how to specify them to get the result you want.)

Also note that the modeling and viewing transformations are included in the **display()** routine, along with the call that's used to draw the cube, **glutWireCube()**. This way, **display()** can be used repeatedly to draw the contents of the window if, for example, the window is moved or uncovered, and you've ensured that each time, the cube is drawn in the desired way, with the appropriate transformations. The potential repeated use of **display()** underscores the need to load the identity matrix before performing the viewing and modeling transformations, especially when other transformations might be performed between calls to **display()**.

The Projection Transformation

Specifying the projection transformation is like choosing a lens for a camera. You can think of this transformation as determining what the field of view or viewing volume is and therefore what objects are inside it and to some extent how they look. This is equivalent to choosing among wide-angle, normal, and telephoto lenses, for example. With a wide-angle lens, you can include a wider scene in the final photograph than with a telephoto lens, but a telephoto lens allows you to photograph objects as though they're closer to you than they actually are. In computer graphics, you don't have to pay $10,000 for a 2000-millimeter telephoto lens; once you've bought your graphics workstation, all you need to do is use a smaller number for your field of view.

In addition to the field-of-view considerations, the projection transformation determines how objects are *projected* onto the screen, as its name suggests. Two basic types of projections are provided for you by OpenGL, along with several corresponding commands for describing the relevant parameters in different ways. One type is the *perspective* projection, which matches how you see things in daily life. Perspective makes objects that are farther away appear smaller; for example, it makes railroad tracks appear to converge in the distance. If you're trying to make realistic pictures, you'll want to choose perspective projection, which is specified with the **glFrustum()** command in this code example.

The other type of projection is *orthographic*, which maps objects directly onto the screen without affecting their relative size. Orthographic projection is used in architectural and computer-aided design applications where the final image needs to reflect the measurements of objects rather than how they might look. Architects create perspective drawings to show how particular buildings or interior spaces look when viewed from various vantage points; the need for orthographic projection arises when blueprint plans or elevations are generated, which are used in the construction of buildings. (See "Projection Transformations" on page 120 for a discussion of ways to specify both kinds of projection transformations.)

Before **glFrustum()** can be called to set the projection transformation, some preparation needs to happen. As shown in the **reshape()** routine in Example 3-1, the command called **glMatrixMode()** is used first, with the argument GL_PROJECTION. This indicates that the current matrix specifies the projection transformation; the following transformation calls then affect the *projection matrix*. As you can see, a few lines later **glMatrixMode()** is called again, this time with GL_MODELVIEW as the argument. This indicates that succeeding transformations now affect the modelview matrix instead of the projection matrix. (See "Manipulating the Matrix Stacks" on page 132 for more information about how to control the projection and modelview matrices.)

Note that **glLoadIdentity()** is used to initialize the current projection matrix so that only the specified projection transformation has an effect. Now **glFrustum()** can be called, with arguments that define the parameters of the projection transformation. In this example, both the projection transformation and the viewport transformation are contained in the **reshape()** routine, which is called when the window is first created and whenever the window is moved or reshaped. This makes sense, since both projecting (the width to height aspect ratio of the projection viewing volume) and applying the viewport relate directly to the screen, and specifically to the size or aspect ratio of the window on the screen.

Try This

- Change the **glFrustum()** call in Example 3-1 to the more commonly used Utility Library routine **gluPerspective()** with parameters (60.0,

1.0, 1.5, 20.0). Then experiment with different values, especially for *fovy* and *aspect*.

The Viewport Transformation

Together, the projection transformation and the viewport transformation determine how a scene gets mapped onto the computer screen. The projection transformation specifies the mechanics of how the mapping should occur, and the viewport indicates the shape of the available screen area into which the scene is mapped. Since the viewport specifies the region the image occupies on the computer screen, you can think of the viewport transformation as defining the size and location of the final processed photograph—for example, whether the photograph should be enlarged or shrunk.

The arguments to **glViewport()** describe the origin of the available screen space within the window—(0, 0) in this example—and the width and height of the available screen area, all measured in pixels on the screen. This is why this command needs to be called within **reshape()**—if the window changes size, the viewport needs to change accordingly. Note that the width and height are specified using the actual width and height of the window; often, you want to specify the viewport this way rather than giving an absolute size. (See "Viewport Transformation" on page 125 for more information about how to define the viewport.)

Drawing the Scene

Once all the necessary transformations have been specified, you can draw the scene (that is, take the photograph). As the scene is drawn, OpenGL transforms each vertex of every object in the scene by the modeling and viewing transformations. Each vertex is then transformed as specified by the projection transformation and clipped if it lies outside the viewing volume described by the projection transformation. Finally, the remaining transformed vertices are divided by *w* and mapped onto the viewport.

General-Purpose Transformation Commands

This section discusses some OpenGL commands that you might find useful as you specify desired transformations. You've already seen a couple of these commands, **glMatrixMode()** and **glLoadIdentity()**. The other two commands described here—**glLoadMatrix*()** and **glMultMatrix*()**—allow you to specify any transformation matrix directly and then to multiply the current matrix by that specified matrix. More specific transformation commands—such as **gluLookAt()** and **glScale*()**—are described in later sections.

As described in the preceding section, you need to state whether you want to modify the modelview or projection matrix before supplying a transformation command. You choose the matrix with **glMatrixMode()**. When you use nested sets of OpenGL commands that might be called repeatedly, remember to reset the matrix mode correctly. (The **glMatrixMode()** command can also be used to indicate the *texture matrix*; texturing is discussed in detail in "The Texture Matrix Stack" on page 371.)

---

void **glMatrixMode**(GLenum *mode*);

Specifies whether the modelview, projection, or texture matrix will be modified, using the argument GL_MODELVIEW, GL_PROJECTION, or GL_TEXTURE for *mode*. Subsequent transformation commands affect the specified matrix. Note that only one matrix can be modified at a time. By default, the modelview matrix is the one that's modifiable, and all three matrices contain the identity matrix.

You use the **glLoadIdentity()** command to clear the currently modifiable matrix for future transformation commands, since these commands modify the current matrix. Typically, you always call this command before specifying projection or viewing transformations, but you might also call it before specifying a modeling transformation.

---

void **glLoadIdentity**(void);

Sets the currently modifiable matrix to the 4×4 identity matrix.

If you want to specify explicitly a particular matrix to be loaded as the current matrix, use **glLoadMatrix*()**. Similarly, use **glMultMatrix*()** to multiply the current matrix by the matrix passed in as an argument. The argument for both these commands is a vector of sixteen values (m_1, m_2, ... , m_{16}) that specifies a matrix **M** as follows:

$$\mathbf{M} = \begin{bmatrix} m_1 & m_5 & m_9 & m_{13} \\ m_2 & m_6 & m_{10} & m_{14} \\ m_3 & m_7 & m_{11} & m_{15} \\ m_4 & m_8 & m_{12} & m_{16} \end{bmatrix}$$

Remember that you might be able to maximize efficiency by using display lists to store frequently used matrices (and their inverses) rather than recomputing them. (See "Display-List Design Philosophy" on page 257.) (OpenGL implementations often must compute the inverse of the modelview matrix so that normals and clipping planes can be correctly transformed to eye coordinates.)

Caution: If you're programming in C and you declare a matrix as $m[4][4]$, then the element $m[i][j]$ is in the ith column and jth row of the OpenGL transformation matrix. This is the reverse of the standard C convention in which $m[i][j]$ is in row i and column j. To avoid confusion, you should declare your matrices as $m[16]$.

---

void **glLoadMatrix**{fd}(const *TYPE* *m*);

Sets the sixteen values of the current matrix to those specified by *m*.

---

void **glMultMatrix**{fd}(const *TYPE* *m*);

Multiplies the matrix specified by the sixteen values pointed to by *m* by the current matrix and stores the result as the current matrix.

Note: All matrix multiplication with OpenGL occurs as follows: Suppose the current matrix is **C** and the matrix specified with **glMultMatrix*()** or any of the transformation commands is **M**. After multiplication, the final matrix is always **CM**. Since matrix multiplication isn't generally commutative, the order makes a difference.

Viewing and Modeling Transformations

Viewing and modeling transformations are inextricably related in OpenGL and are in fact combined into a single modelview matrix. (See "A Simple Example: Drawing a Cube" on page 97.) One of the toughest problems newcomers to computer graphics face is understanding the effects of combined three-dimensional transformations. As you've already seen, there are alternative ways to think about transformations—do you want to move the camera in one direction, or move the object in the opposite direction? Each way of thinking about transformations has advantages and disadvantages, but in some cases one way more naturally matches the effect of the intended transformation. If you can find a natural approach for your particular application, it's easier to visualize the necessary transformations and then write the corresponding code to specify the matrix manipulations. The first part of this section discusses how to think about transformations; later, specific commands are presented. For now, we use only the matrix-manipulation commands you've already seen. Finally, keep in mind that you must call **glMatrixMode()** with GL_MODELVIEW as its argument prior to performing modeling or viewing transformations.

Thinking about Transformations

Let's start with a simple case of two transformations: a 45-degree counterclockwise rotation about the origin around the z-axis, and a translation down the x-axis. Suppose that the object you're drawing is small compared to the translation (so that you can see the effect of the translation), and that it's originally located at the origin. If you rotate the object first and then translate it, the rotated object appears on the x-axis. If you translate it down the x-axis first, however, and then rotate about the origin, the object is on the line y=x, as shown in Figure 3-4. In general, the order of transformations is critical. If you do transformation A and then transformation B, you almost always get something different than if you do them in the opposite order.

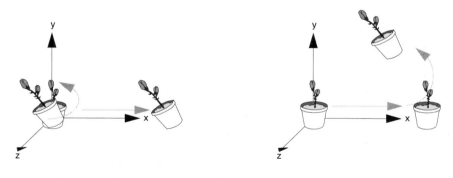

Rotate then Translate   Translate then Rotate

Figure 3-4   Rotating First or Translating First

Now let's talk about the order in which you specify a series of transformations. All viewing and modeling transformations are represented as 4×4 matrices. Each successive **glMultMatrix*()** or transformation command multiplies a new 4×4 matrix **M** by the current modelview matrix **C** to yield **CM**. Finally, vertices v are multiplied by the current modelview matrix. This process means that the last transformation command called in your program is actually the first one applied to the vertices: **CMv**. Thus, one way of looking at it is to say that you have to specify the matrices in the reverse order. Like many other things, however, once you've gotten used to thinking about this correctly, backward will seem like forward.

Consider the following code sequence, which draws a single point using three transformations:

```
glMatrixMode(GL_MODELVIEW);
glLoadIdentity();
glMultMatrixf(N);                      /* apply transformation N */
glMultMatrixf(M);                      /* apply transformation M */
glMultMatrixf(L);                      /* apply transformation L */
glBegin(GL_POINTS);
glVertex3f(v);                         /* draw transformed vertex v */
glEnd();
```

With this code, the modelview matrix successively contains **I**, **N**, **NM**, and finally **NML**, where **I** represents the identity matrix. The transformed vertex is **NMLv**. Thus, the vertex transformation is **N(M(Lv))**—that is, **v** is multiplied first by **L**, the resulting **Lv** is multiplied by **M**, and the resulting **MLv** is multiplied by **N**. Notice that the transformations to vertex **v** effectively occur in the opposite order than they were specified. (Actually, only a single multiplication of a vertex by the modelview matrix occurs; in this example, the **N**, **M**, and **L** matrices are already multiplied into a single matrix before it's applied to **v**.)

Grand, Fixed Coordinate System

Thus, if you like to think in terms of a grand, fixed coordinate system—in which matrix multiplications affect the position, orientation, and scaling of your model—you have to think of the multiplications as occurring in the opposite order from how they appear in the code. Using the simple example shown on the left side of Figure 3-4 (a rotation about the origin and a translation along the *x*-axis), if you want the object to appear on the axis after the operations, the rotation must occur first, followed by the translation. To do this, you'll need to reverse the order of operations, so the code looks something like this (where **R** is the rotation matrix and **T** is the translation matrix):

```
glMatrixMode(GL_MODELVIEW);
glLoadIdentity();
glMultMatrixf(T);                      /* translation */
glMultMatrixf(R);                      /* rotation */
draw_the_object();
```

Moving a Local Coordinate System

Another way to view matrix multiplications is to forget about a grand, fixed coordinate system in which your model is transformed and instead imagine that a local coordinate system is tied to the object you're drawing. All operations occur relative to this changing coordinate system. With this approach, the matrix multiplications now appear in the natural order in the code. (Regardless of which analogy you're using, the code is the same, but how you think about it differs.) To see this in the translation-rotation example, begin by visualizing the object with a coordinate system tied to it. The translation operation moves the object and its coordinate system down the x-axis. Then, the rotation occurs about the (now-translated) origin, so the object rotates in place in its position on the axis.

This approach is what you should use for applications such as articulated robot arms, where there are joints at the shoulder, elbow, and wrist, and on each of the fingers. To figure out where the tips of the fingers go relative to the body, you'd like to start at the shoulder, go down to the wrist, and so on, applying the appropriate rotations and translations at each joint. Thinking about it in reverse would be far more confusing.

This second approach can be problematic, however, in cases where scaling occurs, and especially so when the scaling is nonuniform (scaling different amounts along the different axes). After uniform scaling, translations move a vertex by a multiple of what they did before, since the coordinate system is stretched. Nonuniform scaling mixed with rotations may make the axes of the local coordinate system nonperpendicular.

As mentioned earlier, you normally issue viewing transformation commands in your program before any modeling transformations. This way, a vertex in a model is first transformed into the desired orientation and then transformed by the viewing operation. Since the matrix multiplications must be specified in reverse order, the viewing commands need to come first. Note, however, that you don't need to specify either viewing or modeling transformations if you're satisfied with the default conditions. If there's no viewing transformation, the "camera" is left in the default position at the origin, pointed toward the negative z-axis; if there's no modeling transformation, the model isn't moved, and it retains its specified position, orientation, and size.

Since the commands for performing modeling transformations can be used to perform viewing transformations, modeling transformations are *discussed* first, even if viewing transformations are actually *issued* first. This order for discussion also matches the way many programmers think when planning their code: Often, they write all the code necessary to compose the scene, which involves transformations to position and orient objects correctly relative to each other. Next, they decide where they want the viewpoint to be relative to the scene they've composed, and then they write the viewing transformations accordingly.

Modeling Transformations

The three OpenGL routines for modeling transformations are **glTranslate*()**, **glRotate*()**, and **glScale*()**. As you might suspect, these routines transform an object (or coordinate system, if you're thinking of it that way) by moving, rotating, stretching, shrinking, or reflecting it. All three commands are equivalent to producing an appropriate translation, rotation, or scaling matrix, and then calling **glMultMatrix*()** with that matrix as the argument. However, these three routines might be faster than using **glMultMatrix*()**. OpenGL automatically computes the matrices for you. (See Appendix F if you're interested in the details.)

In the command summaries that follow, each matrix multiplication is described in terms of what it does to the vertices of a geometric object using the fixed coordinate system approach, and in terms of what it does to the local coordinate system that's attached to an object.

Translate

void **glTranslate**{fd}(*TYPE x, TYPE y, TYPE z*);

Multiplies the current matrix by a matrix that moves (translates) an object by the given *x*, *y*, and *z* values (or moves the local coordinate system by the same amounts).

Figure 3-5 shows the effect of **glTranslate*()**.

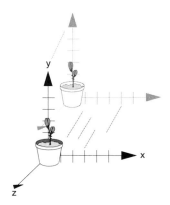

Figure 3-5   Translating an Object

Note that using (0.0, 0.0, 0.0) as the argument for **glTranslate*()** is the identity operation—that is, it has no effect on an object or its local coordinate system.

Rotate

void **glRotate**{fd}(TYPE *angle*, TYPE *x*, TYPE *y*, TYPE *z*);

Multiplies the current matrix by a matrix that rotates an object (or the local coordinate system) in a counterclockwise direction about the ray from the origin through the point (*x, y, z*). The *angle* parameter specifies the angle of rotation in degrees.

The effect of **glRotatef**(45.0, 0.0, 0.0, 1.0), which is a rotation of 45 degrees about the *z*-axis, is shown in Figure 3-6.

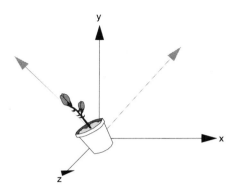

Figure 3-6   Rotating an Object

Note that an object that lies farther from the axis of rotation is more dramatically rotated (has a larger orbit) than an object drawn near the axis. Also, if the *angle* argument is zero, the **glRotate*()** command has no effect.

Scale

void **glScale**{fd}(*TYPE x, TYPE y, TYPE z*);

Multiplies the current matrix by a matrix that stretches, shrinks, or reflects an object along the axes. Each *x*, *y*, and *z* coordinate of every point in the object is multiplied by the corresponding argument *x*, *y*, or *z*. With the local coordinate system approach, the local coordinate axes are stretched, shrunk, or reflected by the *x*, *y*, and *z* factors, and the associated object is transformed with them.

Figure 3-7 shows the effect of **glScalef**(2.0, -0.5, 1.0).

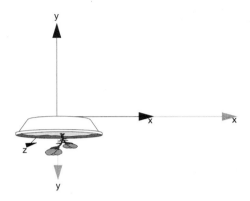

Figure 3-7   Scaling and Reflecting an Object

glScale*() is the only one of the three modeling transformations that changes the apparent size of an object: Scaling with values greater than 1.0 stretches an object, and using values less than 1.0 shrinks it. Scaling with a –1.0 value reflects an object across an axis. The identity values for scaling are (1.0, 1.0, 1.0). In general, you should limit your use of **glScale*()** to those cases where it is necessary. Using **glScale*()** decreases the performance of lighting calculations, because the normal vectors have to be renormalized after transformation.

Note: A scale value of zero collapses all object coordinates along that axis to zero. It's usually not a good idea to do this, because such an operation cannot be undone. Mathematically speaking, the matrix cannot be inverted, and inverse matrices are required for certain lighting operations. (See Chapter 5.) Sometimes collapsing coordinates does make sense, however; the calculation of shadows on a planar surface is a typical application. (See "Shadows" on page 519.) In general, if a coordinate system is to be collapsed, the projection matrix should be used rather than the modelview matrix.

A Modeling Transformation Code Example

Example 3-2 is a portion of a program that renders a triangle four times, as shown in Figure 3-8. These are the four transformed triangles.

- A solid wireframe triangle is drawn with no modeling transformation.

- The same triangle is drawn again, but with a dashed line stipple and translated (to the left—along the negative x-axis).

- A triangle is drawn with a long dashed line stipple, with its height (*y*-axis) halved and its width (*x*-axis) increased by 50%.

- A rotated triangle, made of dotted lines, is drawn.

Figure 3-8   Modeling Transformation Example

Example 3-2   Using Modeling Transformations: model.c

```
glLoadIdentity();
glColor3f(1.0, 1.0, 1.0);
draw_triangle();                        /* solid lines */

glEnable(GL_LINE_STIPPLE);              /* dashed lines */
glLineStipple(1, 0xF0F0);
glLoadIdentity();
glTranslatef(-20.0, 0.0, 0.0);
draw_triangle();

glLineStipple(1, 0xF00F);               /*long dashed lines */
glLoadIdentity();
glScalef(1.5, 0.5, 1.0);
draw_triangle();

glLineStipple(1, 0x8888);               /* dotted lines */
glLoadIdentity();
glRotatef (90.0, 0.0, 0.0, 1.0);
draw_triangle ();
glDisable (GL_LINE_STIPPLE);
```

Note the use of **glLoadIdentity()** to isolate the effects of modeling transformations; initializing the matrix values prevents successive transformations from having a cumulative effect. Even though using **glLoadIdentity()** repeatedly has the desired effect, it may be inefficient, because you may have to respecify viewing or modeling transformations. (See "Manipulating the Matrix Stacks" on page 132 for a better way to isolate transformations.)

Note: Sometimes, programmers who want a continuously rotating object attempt to achieve this by repeatedly applying a rotation matrix that has small values. The problem with this technique is that because of round-off errors, the product of thousands of tiny rotations gradually drifts away from the value you really want (it might even become something that isn't a rotation). Instead of using this technique, increment the angle and issue a new rotation command with the new angle at each update step.

Viewing Transformations

A viewing transformation changes the position and orientation of the viewpoint. If you recall the camera analogy, the viewing transformation positions the camera tripod, pointing the camera toward the model. Just as you move the camera to some position and rotate it until it points in the desired direction, viewing transformations are generally composed of translations and rotations. Also remember that to achieve a certain scene composition in the final image or photograph, you can either move the camera or move all the objects in the opposite direction. Thus, a modeling transformation that rotates an object counterclockwise is equivalent to a viewing transformation that rotates the camera clockwise, for example. Finally, keep in mind that the viewing transformation commands must be called before any modeling transformations are performed, so that the modeling transformations take effect on the objects first.

You can manufacture a viewing transformation in any of several ways, as described next. You can also choose to use the default location and orientation of the viewpoint, which is at the origin, looking down the negative z-axis.

- Use one or more modeling transformation commands (that is, **glTranslate*()** and **glRotate*()**). You can think of the effect of these transformations as moving the camera position or as moving all the objects in the world, relative to a stationary camera.

- Use the Utility Library routine **gluLookAt()** to define a line of sight. This routine encapsulates a series of rotation and translation commands.

- Create your own utility routine that encapsulates rotations and translations. Some applications might require custom routines that allow you to specify the viewing transformation in a convenient way. For example, you might want to specify the roll, pitch, and heading rotation angles of a plane in flight, or you might want to specify a transformation in terms of polar coordinates for a camera that's orbiting around an object.

Using glTranslate*() and glRotate*()

When you use modeling transformation commands to emulate viewing transformations, you're trying to move the viewpoint in a desired way while keeping the objects in the world stationary. Since the viewpoint is initially located at the origin and since objects are often most easily constructed there as well (see Figure 3-9), in general you have to perform some transformation so that the objects can be viewed. Note that, as shown in the figure, the camera initially points down the negative z-axis. (You're seeing the back of the camera.)

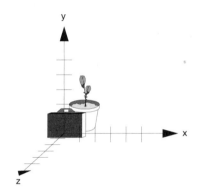

Figure 3-9   Object and Viewpoint at the Origin

In the simplest case, you can move the viewpoint backward, away from the objects; this has the same effect as moving the objects forward, or away from the viewpoint. Remember that by default forward is down the negative z-axis; if you rotate the viewpoint, forward has a different meaning. So, to put 5 units of distance between the viewpoint and the objects by moving the viewpoint, as shown in Figure 3-10, use

```
glTranslatef(0.0, 0.0, -5.0);
```

This routine moves the objects in the scene -5 units along the z axis. This is also equivalent to moving the camera +5 units along the z axis.

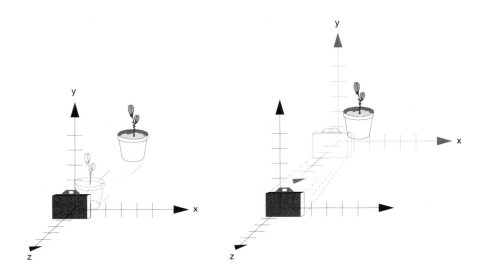

Figure 3-10   Separating the Viewpoint and the Object

Now suppose you want to view the objects from the side. Should you issue a rotate command before or after the translate command? If you're thinking in terms of a grand, fixed coordinate system, first imagine both the object and the camera at the origin. You could rotate the object first and then move it away from the camera so that the desired side is visible. Since you know that with the fixed coordinate system approach, commands have to be issued in the opposite order in which they should take effect, you know that you need to write the translate command first in your code and follow it with the rotate command.

Now let's use the local coordinate system approach. In this case, think about moving the object and its local coordinate system away from the origin; then, the rotate command is carried out using the now-translated coordinate system. With this approach, commands are issued in the order in which they're applied, so once again the translate command comes first. Thus, the sequence of transformation commands to produce the desired result is

```
glTranslatef(0.0, 0.0, -5.0);
glRotatef(90.0, 0.0, 1.0, 0.0);
```

If you're having trouble keeping track of the effect of successive matrix multiplications, try using both the fixed and local coordinate system approaches and see whether one makes more sense to you. Note that with the fixed coordinate system, rotations always occur about the grand origin, whereas with the local coordinate system, rotations occur about the origin of the local system. You might also try using the **gluLookAt()** utility routine described in the next section.

Using the gluLookAt() Utility Routine

Often, programmers construct a scene around the origin or some other convenient location, then they want to look at it from an arbitrary point to get a good view of it. As its name suggests, the **gluLookAt()** utility routine is designed for just this purpose. It takes three sets of arguments, which specify the location of the viewpoint, define a reference point toward which the camera is aimed, and indicate which direction is up. Choose the viewpoint to yield the desired view of the scene. The reference point is typically somewhere in the middle of the scene. (If you've built your scene at the origin, the reference point is probably the origin.) It might be a little trickier to specify the correct up-vector. Again, if you've built some real-world scene at or around the origin and if you've been taking the positive *y*-axis to point upward, then that's your up-vector for **gluLookAt()**. However, if you're designing a flight simulator, up is the direction perpendicular to the plane's wings, from the plane toward the sky when the plane is right-side up on the ground.

The **gluLookAt()** routine is particularly useful when you want to pan across a landscape, for instance. With a viewing volume that's symmetric in both *x* and *y*, the (*eyex, eyey, eyez*) point specified is always in the center of the image on the screen, so you can use a series of commands to move this point slightly, thereby panning across the scene.

---

void **gluLookAt**(GLdouble *eyex*, GLdouble *eyey*, GLdouble *eyez*, GLdouble *centerx*, GLdouble *centery*, GLdouble *centerz*, GLdouble *upx*, GLdouble *upy*, GLdouble *upz*);

Defines a viewing matrix and multiplies it to the right of the current matrix. The desired viewpoint is specified by *eyex, eyey*, and *eyez*. The *centerx, centery*, and *centerz* arguments specify any point along the desired line of sight, but typically they're some point in the center of the scene being looked at. The *upx, upy*, and *upz* arguments indicate which direction is up (that is, the direction from the bottom to the top of the viewing volume).

In the default position, the camera is at the origin, is looking down the negative *z*-axis, and has the positive *y*-axis as straight up. This is the same as calling

```
gluLookat (0.0, 0.0, 0.0, 0.0, 0.0, -100.0, 0.0, 1.0, 0.0);
```

The *z* value of the reference point is -100.0, but could be any negative *z*, because the line of sight will remain the same. In this case, you don't actually want to call **gluLookAt()**, because this is the default (see Figure 3-11) and you are already there! (The lines extending from the camera represent the viewing volume, which indicates its field of view.)

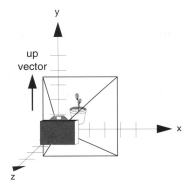

Figure 3-11   Default Camera Position

Figure 3-12 shows the effect of a typical **gluLookAt()** routine. The camera position (*eyex, eyey, eyez*) is at (4, 2, 1). In this case, the camera is looking right at the model, so the reference point is at (2, 4, -3). An orientation vector of (2, 2, -1) is chosen to rotate the viewpoint to this 45-degree angle.

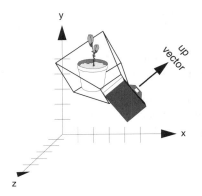

Figure 3-12   Using gluLookAt()

So, to achieve this effect, call

```
gluLookAt(4.0, 2.0, 1.0, 2.0, 4.0, -3.0, 2.0, 2.0, -1.0);
```

Note that **gluLookAt()** is part of the Utility Library rather than the basic OpenGL library. This isn't because it's not useful, but because it encapsulates several basic OpenGL commands—specifically, **glTranslate*()** and **glRotate*()**. To see this, imagine a camera located at an arbitrary viewpoint and oriented according to a line of sight, both as specified with **gluLookAt()** and a scene located at the origin. To "undo" what **gluLookAt()** does, you need to transform the camera so that it sits at the origin and points down the negative z-axis, the default position. A simple translate moves the camera to the origin. You can easily imagine a series of rotations about each of the three axes of a fixed coordinate system that would orient the camera so that it pointed toward negative z values. Since OpenGL allows rotation about an arbitrary axis, you can accomplish any desired rotation of the camera with a single **glRotate*()** command.

Note: You can have only one active viewing transformation. You cannot try to combine the effects of two viewing transformations, any more than a camera can have two tripods. If you want to change the position of the camera, make sure you call **glLoadIdentity()** to wipe away the effects of any current viewing transformation.

Advanced

To transform any arbitrary vector so that it's coincident with another arbitrary vector (for instance, the negative z-axis), you need to do a little mathematics. The axis about which you want to rotate is given by the cross product of the two normalized vectors. To find the angle of rotation, normalize the initial two vectors. The cosine of the desired angle between the vectors is equal to the dot product of the normalized vectors. The angle of rotation around the axis given by the cross product is always between 0 and 180 degrees. (See Appendix E for definitions of cross and dot products.)

Note that computing the angle between two normalized vectors by taking the inverse cosine of their dot product is not very accurate, especially for small angles. But it should work well enough to get you started.

Creating a Custom Utility Routine

Advanced

For some specialized applications, you might want to define your own transformation routine. Since this is rarely done and in any case is a fairly advanced topic, it's left mostly as an exercise for the reader. The following exercises suggest two custom viewing transformations that might be useful.

Try This

- Suppose you're writing a flight simulator and you'd like to display the world from the point of view of the pilot of a plane. The world is described in a coordinate system with the origin on the runway and the plane at coordinates (x, y, z). Suppose further that the plane has some *roll*, *pitch*, and *heading* (these are rotation angles of the plane relative to its center of gravity).

  Show that the following routine could serve as the viewing transformation:

```
void pilotView{GLdouble planex, GLdouble planey,
            GLdouble planez, GLdouble roll,
            GLdouble pitch, GLdouble heading)
{
    glRotated(roll, 0.0, 0.0, 1.0);
    glRotated(pitch, 0.0, 1.0, 0.0);
    glRotated(heading, 1.0, 0.0, 0.0);
    glTranslated(-planex, -planey, -planez);
}
```

- Suppose your application involves orbiting the camera around an object that's centered at the origin. In this case, you'd like to specify the viewing transformation by using polar coordinates. Let the *distance* variable define the radius of the orbit, or how far the camera is from the origin. (Initially, the camera is moved *distance* units along the positive z-axis.) The *azimuth* describes the angle of rotation of the camera about the object in the *x-y* plane, measured from the positive *y*-axis. Similarly, *elevation* is the angle of rotation of the camera in the *y-z* plane, measured from the positive *z*-axis. Finally, *twist* represents the rotation of the viewing volume around its line of sight.

  Show that the following routine could serve as the viewing transformation:

```
void polarView{GLdouble distance, GLdouble twist,
            GLdouble elevation, GLdouble azimuth)
{
    glTranslated(0.0, 0.0, -distance);
    glRotated(-twist, 0.0, 0.0, 1.0);
    glRotated(-elevation, 1.0, 0.0, 0.0);
    glRotated(azimuth, 0.0, 0.0, 1.0);
}
```

Projection Transformations

The previous section described how to compose the desired modelview matrix so that the correct modeling and viewing transformations are applied. This section explains how to define the desired projection matrix, which is also used to transform the vertices in your scene. Before you issue any of the transformation commands described in this section, remember to call

```
glMatrixMode(GL_PROJECTION);
glLoadIdentity();
```

so that the commands affect the projection matrix rather than the modelview matrix and so that you avoid compound projection transformations. Since each projection transformation command completely describes a particular transformation, typically you don't want to combine a projection transformation with another transformation.

The purpose of the projection transformation is to define a *viewing volume*, which is used in two ways. The viewing volume determines how an object is projected onto the screen (that is, by using a perspective or an orthographic projection), and it defines which objects or portions of objects are clipped out of the final image. You can think of the viewpoint we've been talking about as existing at one end of the viewing volume. At this point, you might want to reread "A Simple Example: Drawing a Cube" on page 97 for its overview of all the transformations, including projection transformations.

Perspective Projection

The most unmistakable characteristic of perspective projection is foreshortening: the farther an object is from the camera, the smaller it appears in the final image. This occurs because the viewing volume for a perspective projection is a *frustum* of a pyramid (a truncated pyramid whose top has been cut off by a plane parallel to its base). Objects that fall within the viewing volume are projected toward the apex of the pyramid, where the camera or viewpoint is. Objects that are closer to the viewpoint appear larger because they occupy a proportionally larger amount of the viewing volume than those that are farther away, in the larger part of the frustum. This method of projection is commonly used for animation, visual simulation, and any other applications that strive for some degree of realism because it's similar to how our eye (or a camera) works.

The command to define a frustum, **glFrustum()**, calculates a matrix that accomplishes perspective projection and multiplies the current projection matrix (typically the identity matrix) by it. Recall that the viewing volume is used to clip objects that lie outside of it; the four sides of the frustum, its top, and its base correspond to the six clipping planes of the viewing volume, as shown in Figure 3-13. Objects or parts of objects outside these planes are clipped from the final image. Note that **glFrustum()** doesn't require you to define a symmetric viewing volume.

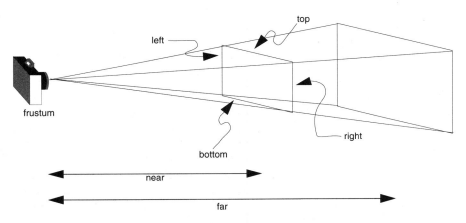

Figure 3-13   Perspective Viewing Volume Specified by glFrustum()

---

void **glFrustum**(GLdouble *left*, GLdouble *right*, GLdouble *bottom*,
         GLdouble *top*, GLdouble *near*, GLdouble *far*);

Creates a matrix for a perspective-view frustum and multiplies the current matrix by it. The frustum's viewing volume is defined by the parameters: (*left, bottom, -near*) and (*right, top, -near*) specify the (*x, y, z*) coordinates of the lower-left and upper-right corners of the near clipping plane; *near* and *far* give the distances from the viewpoint to the near and far clipping planes. They should always be positive.

The frustum has a default orientation in three-dimensional space. You can perform rotations or translations on the projection matrix to alter this orientation, but this is tricky and nearly always avoidable.

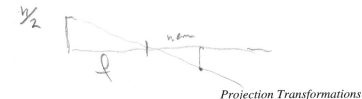

Advanced

Also, the frustum doesn't have to be symmetrical, and its axis isn't necessarily aligned with the *z*-axis. For example, you can use **glFrustum()** to draw a picture as if you were looking through a rectangular window of a house, where the window was above and to the right of you. Photographers use such a viewing volume to create false perspectives. You might use it to have the hardware calculate images at much higher than normal resolutions, perhaps for use on a printer. For example, if you want an image that has twice the resolution of your screen, draw the same picture four times, each time using the frustum to cover the entire screen with one-quarter of the image. After each quarter of the image is rendered, you can read the pixels back to collect the data for the higher-resolution image. (See Chapter 8 for more information about reading pixel data.)

Although it's easy to understand conceptually, **glFrustum()** isn't intuitive to use. Instead, you might try the Utility Library routine **gluPerspective()**. This routine creates a viewing volume of the same shape as **glFrustum()** does, but you specify it in a different way. Rather than specifying corners of the near clipping plane, you specify the angle of the field of view (Θ, or theta, in Figure 3-14) in the *y* direction and the aspect ratio of the width to height (*x/y*). (For a square portion of the screen, the aspect ratio is 1.0.) These two parameters are enough to determine an untruncated pyramid along the line of sight, as shown in Figure 3-14. You also specify the distance between the viewpoint and the near and far clipping planes, thereby truncating the pyramid. Note that **gluPerspective()** is limited to creating frustums that are symmetric in both the *x*- and *y*-axes along the line of sight, but this is usually what you want.

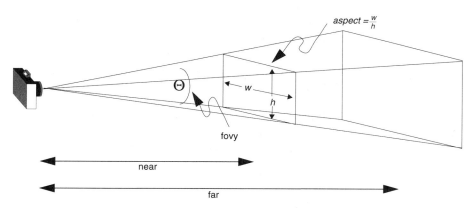

Figure 3-14   Perspective Viewing Volume Specified by gluPerspective()

void **gluPerspective**(GLdouble *fovy*, GLdouble *aspect*,
  GLdouble *near*, GLdouble *far*);

Creates a matrix for a symmetric perspective-view frustum and multiplies the current matrix by it. *fovy* is the angle of the field of view in the *x-z* plane; its value must be in the range [0.0,180.0]. *aspect* is the aspect ratio of the frustum, its width divided by its height. *near* and *far* values the distances between the viewpoint and the clipping planes, along the negative *z*-axis. They should always be positive.

Just as with **glFrustum**(), you can apply rotations or translations to change the default orientation of the viewing volume created by **gluPerspective**(). With no such transformations, the viewpoint remains at the origin, and the line of sight points down the negative *z*-axis.

With **gluPerspective**(), you need to pick appropriate values for the field of view, or the image may look distorted. For example, suppose you're drawing to the entire screen, which happens to be 11 inches high. If you choose a field of view of 90 degrees, your eye has to be about 7.8 inches from the screen for the image to appear undistorted. (This is the distance that makes the screen subtend 90 degrees.) If your eye is farther from the screen, as it usually is, the perspective doesn't look right. If your drawing area occupies less than the full screen, your eye has to be even closer. To get a perfect field of view, figure out how far your eye normally is from the screen and how big the window is, and calculate the angle the window subtends at that size and distance. It's probably smaller than you would guess. Another way to think about it is that a 94-degree field of view with a 35-millimeter camera requires a 20-millimeter lens, which is a very wide-angle lens. (See "Troubleshooting Transformations" on page 129 for more details on how to calculate the desired field of view.)

The preceding paragraph mentions inches and millimeters—do these really have anything to do with OpenGL? The answer is, in a word, no. The projection and other transformations are inherently unitless. If you want to think of the near and far clipping planes as located at 1.0 and 20.0 meters, inches, kilometers, or leagues, it's up to you. The only rule is that you have to use a consistent unit of measurement. Then the resulting image is drawn to scale.

Orthographic Projection

With an orthographic projection, the viewing volume is a rectangular parallelepiped, or more informally, a box (see Figure 3-15). Unlike perspective projection, the size of the viewing volume doesn't change from one end to the other, so distance from the camera doesn't affect how large an object appears. This type of projection is used for applications such as creating architectural blueprints and computer-aided design, where it's crucial to maintain the actual sizes of objects and angles between them as they're projected.

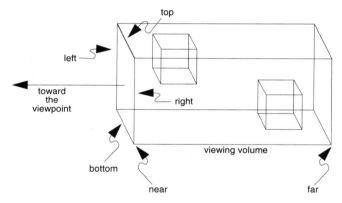

Figure 3-15   Orthographic Viewing Volume

The command **glOrtho()** creates an orthographic parallel viewing volume. As with **glFrustum()**, you specify the corners of the near clipping plane and the distance to the far clipping plane.

---

void **glOrtho**(GLdouble *left*, GLdouble *right*, GLdouble *bottom*,
                 GLdouble *top*, GLdouble *near*, GLdouble *far*);

Creates a matrix for an orthographic parallel viewing volume and multiplies the current matrix by it. (*left, bottom, -near*) and (*right, top, -near*) are points on the near clipping plane that are mapped to the lower-left and upper-right corners of the viewport window, respectively. (*left, bottom, -far*) and (*right, top, -far*) are points on the far clipping plane that are mapped to the same respective corners of the viewport. Both *near* and *far* can be positive or negative.

With no other transformations, the direction of projection is parallel to the z-axis, and the viewpoint faces toward the negative z-axis. Note that this means that the values passed in for *far* and *near* are used as negative z values if these planes are in front of the viewpoint, and positive if they're behind the viewpoint.

For the special case of projecting a two-dimensional image onto a two-dimensional screen, use the Utility Library routine **gluOrtho2D()**. This routine is identical to the three-dimensional version, **glOrtho()**, except that all the z coordinates for objects in the scene are assumed to lie between −1.0 and 1.0. If you're drawing two-dimensional objects using the two-dimensional vertex commands, all the z coordinates are zero; thus, none of the objects are clipped because of their z values.

---

void **gluOrtho2D**(GLdouble *left*, GLdouble *right*,
            GLdouble *bottom*, GLdouble *top*);

Creates a matrix for projecting two-dimensional coordinates onto the screen and multiplies the current projection matrix by it. The clipping region is a rectangle with the lower-left corner at (*left, bottom*) and the upper-right corner at (*right, top*).

Viewing Volume Clipping

After the vertices of the objects in the scene have been transformed by the modelview and projection matrices, any primitives that lie outside the viewing volume are clipped. The six clipping planes used are those that define the sides and ends of the viewing volume. You can specify additional clipping planes and locate them wherever you choose. (See "Additional Clipping Planes" on page 136 for information about this relatively advanced topic.) Keep in mind that OpenGL reconstructs the edges of polygons that get clipped.

Viewport Transformation

Recalling the camera analogy, you know that the viewport transformation corresponds to the stage where the size of the developed photograph is chosen. Do you want a wallet-size or a poster-size photograph? Since this is computer graphics, the viewport is the rectangular region of the window where the image is drawn. Figure 3-16 shows a viewport that occupies most of the screen. The viewport is measured in window coordinates, which reflect the position of pixels on the screen relative to the lower-left corner of the window. Keep in mind that all vertices have been transformed by the modelview and projection matrices by this point, and vertices outside the viewing volume have been clipped.

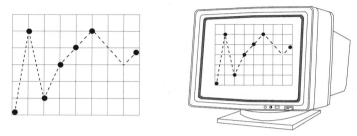

Figure 3-16   Viewport Rectangle

Defining the Viewport

The window system, not OpenGL, is responsible for opening a window on the screen. However, by default the viewport is set to the entire pixel rectangle of the window that's opened. You use the **glViewport()** command to choose a smaller drawing region; for example, you can subdivide the window to create a split-screen effect for multiple views in the same window.

---

void **glViewport**(GLint *x*, GLint *y*, GLsizei *width*, GLsizei *height*);

Defines a pixel rectangle in the window into which the final image is mapped. The (*x, y*) parameter specifies the lower-left corner of the viewport, and *width* and *height* are the size of the viewport rectangle. By default, the initial viewport values are (*0, 0, winWidth, winHeight*), where *winWidth* and *winHeight* are the size of the window.

The aspect ratio of a viewport should generally equal the aspect ratio of the viewing volume. If the two ratios are different, the projected image will be distorted when mapped to the viewport, as shown in Figure 3-17. Note that subsequent changes to the size of the window don't explicitly affect the viewport. Your application should detect window resize events and modify the viewport appropriately.

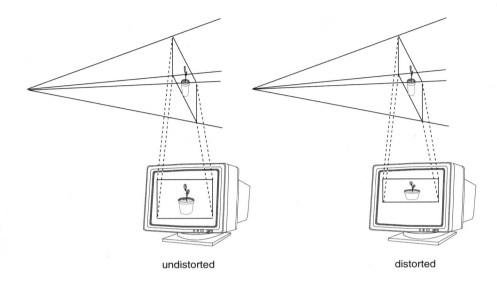

undistorted   distorted

Figure 3-17   Mapping the Viewing Volume to the Viewport

In Figure 3-17, the left figure shows a projection that maps a square image onto a square viewport using these routines:

```
gluPerspective(fovy, 1.0, near, far);
glViewport(0, 0, 400, 400);
```

However, in the right figure, the window has been resized to a nonequilateral rectangular viewport, but the projection is unchanged. The image appears compressed along the *x*-axis.

```
gluPerspective(fovy, 1.0, near, far);
glViewport (0, 0, 400, 200);
```

To avoid the distortion, modify the aspect ratio of the projection to match the viewport:

```
gluPerspective(fovy, 2.0, near, far);
glViewport(0, 0, 400, 200);
```

Try This

- Modify an existing program so that an object is drawn twice, in different viewports. You might draw the object with different projection and/or viewing transformations for each viewport. To create two side-by-side viewports, you might issue these commands, along

with the appropriate modeling, viewing, and projection transformations:

```
glViewport (0, 0, sizex/2, sizey);
      .
      .
      .
glViewport (sizex/2, 0, sizex/2, sizey);
```

The Transformed Depth Coordinate

The depth (z) coordinate is encoded during the viewport transformation (and later stored in the depth buffer). You can scale z values to lie within a desired range with the **glDepthRange**() command. (Chapter 10 discusses the depth buffer and the corresponding uses for the depth coordinate.) Unlike x and y window coordinates, z window coordinates are treated by OpenGL as though they always range from 0.0 to 1.0.

---

void **glDepthRange**(GLclampd *near*, GLclampd *far*);

Defines an encoding for z coordinates that's performed during the viewport transformation. The *near* and *far* values represent adjustments to the minimum and maximum values that can be stored in the depth buffer. By default, they're 0.0 and 1.0, respectively, which work for most applications. These parameters are clamped to lie within [0,1].

In perspective projection, the transformed depth coordinate (like the x and y coordinates) is subject to perspective division by the w coordinate. As the transformed depth coordinate moves farther away from the near clipping plane, its location becomes increasingly less precise. (See Figure 3-18.)

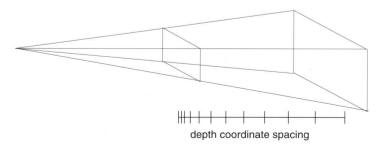

depth coordinate spacing

Figure 3-18   Perspective Projection and Transformed Depth Coordinates

Therefore, perspective division affects the accuracy of operations which rely upon the transformed depth coordinate, especially depth-buffering, which is used for hidden surface removal.

Troubleshooting Transformations

It's pretty easy to get a camera pointed in the right direction, but in computer graphics, you have to specify position and direction with coordinates and angles. As we can attest, it's all too easy to achieve the well-known black-screen effect. Although any number of things can go wrong, often you get this effect—which results in absolutely nothing being drawn in the window you open on the screen—from incorrectly aiming the "camera" and taking a picture with the model behind you. A similar problem arises if you don't choose a field of view that's wide enough to view your objects but narrow enough so they appear reasonably large.

If you find yourself exerting great programming effort only to create a black window, try these diagnostic steps.

1. Check the obvious possibilities. Make sure your system is plugged in. Make sure you're drawing your objects with a color that's different from the color with which you're clearing the screen. Make sure that whatever states you're using (such as lighting, texturing, alpha blending, logical operations, or antialiasing) are correctly turned on or off, as desired.

2. Remember that with the projection commands, the near and far coordinates measure distance from the viewpoint and that (by default) you're looking down the negative z axis. Thus, if the near value is 1.0 and the far 3.0, objects must have z coordinates between −1.0 and −3.0 in order to be visible. To ensure that you haven't clipped everything out of your scene, temporarily set the near and far clipping planes to some absurdly inclusive values, such as 0.001 and 1000000.0. This alters appearance for operations such as depth-buffering and fog, but it might uncover inadvertently clipped objects.

3. Determine where the viewpoint is, in which direction you're looking, and where your objects are. It might help to create a real three-dimensional space—using your hands, for instance—to figure these things out.

4. Make sure you know where you're rotating about. You might be rotating about some arbitrary location unless you translated back to the origin first. It's OK to rotate about any point unless you're expecting to rotate about the origin.

5. Check your aim. Use **gluLookAt()** to aim the viewing volume at your objects. Or draw your objects at or near the origin, and use **glTranslate*()** as a viewing transformation to move the camera far enough in the z direction only so that the objects fall within the viewing volume. Once you've managed to make your objects visible, try to change the viewing volume incrementally to achieve the exact result you want, as described next.

Even after you've aimed the camera in the correct direction and you can see your objects, they might appear too small or too large. If you're using **gluPerspective()**, you might need to alter the angle defining the field of view by changing the value of the first parameter for this command. You can use trigonometry to calculate the desired field of view given the size of the object and its distance from the viewpoint: The tangent of half the desired angle is half the size of the object divided by the distance to the object (see Figure 3-19). Thus, you can use an arctangent routine to compute half the desired angle. Example 3-3 assumes such a routine, **atan2()**, which calculates the arctangent given the length of the opposite and adjacent sides of a right triangle. This result then needs to be converted from radians to degrees.

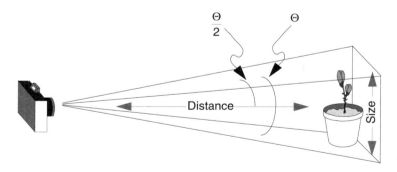

Figure 3-19   Using Trigonometry to Calculate the Field of View

Example 3-3 Calculating Field of View

```
#define PI 3.1415926535

double calculateAngle(double size, double distance)
{
    double radtheta, degtheta;

    radtheta = 2.0 * atan2 (size/2.0, distance);
    degtheta = (180.0 * radtheta) / PI;
    return (degtheta);
}
```

Of course, typically you don't know the exact size of an object, and the distance can only be determined between the viewpoint and a single point in your scene. To obtain a fairly good approximate value, find the bounding box for your scene by determining the maximum and minimum x, y, and z coordinates of all the objects in your scene. Then calculate the radius of a bounding sphere for that box, and use the center of the sphere to determine the distance and the radius to determine the size.

For example, suppose all the coordinates in your object satisfy the equations $-1 \leq x \leq 3$, $5 \leq y \leq 7$, and $-5 \leq z \leq 5$. Then the center of the bounding box is $(1, 6, 0)$, and the radius of a bounding sphere is the distance from the center of the box to any corner—say $(3, 7, 5)$—or

$$\sqrt{(3-1)^2 + (7-6)^2 + (5-0)^2} = \sqrt{30} = 5.477$$

If the viewpoint is at $(8, 9, 10)$, the distance between it and the center is

$$\sqrt{(8-1)^2 + (9-6)^2 + (10-0)^2} = \sqrt{158} = 12.570$$

The tangent of the half angle is 5.477 divided by 12.570, which equals 0.4357, so the half angle is 23.54 degrees.

Remember that the field-of-view angle affects the optimal position for the viewpoint, if you're trying to achieve a realistic image. For example, if your calculations indicate that you need a 179-degree field of view, the viewpoint must be a fraction of an inch from the screen to achieve realism. If your calculated field of view is too large, you might need to move the viewpoint farther away from the object.

Manipulating the Matrix Stacks

The modelview and projection matrices you've been creating, loading, and multiplying have only been the visible tips of their respective icebergs. Each of these matrices is actually the topmost member of a stack of matrices (see Figure 3-20).

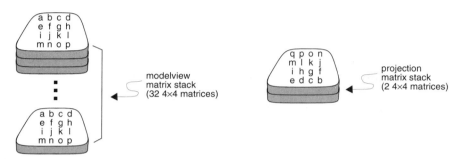

Figure 3-20   Modelview and Projection Matrix Stacks

A stack of matrices is useful for constructing hierarchical models, in which complicated objects are constructed from simpler ones. For example, suppose you're drawing an automobile that has four wheels, each of which is attached to the car with five bolts. You have a single routine to draw a wheel and another to draw a bolt, since all the wheels and all the bolts look the same. These routines draw a wheel or a bolt in some convenient position and orientation, say centered at the origin with its axis coincident with the z axis. When you draw the car, including the wheels and bolts, you want to call the wheel-drawing routine four times with different transformations in effect each time to position the wheels correctly. As you draw each wheel, you want to draw the bolts five times, each time translated appropriately relative to the wheel.

Suppose for a minute that all you have to do is draw the car body and the wheels. The English description of what you want to do might be something like this:

> Draw the car body. Remember where you are, and translate to the right front wheel. Draw the wheel and throw away the last translation so your current position is back at the origin of the car body. Remember where you are, and translate to the left front wheel....

Similarly, for each wheel, you want to draw the wheel, remember where you are, and successively translate to each of the positions that bolts are drawn, throwing away the transformations after each bolt is drawn.

Since the transformations are stored as matrices, a matrix stack provides an ideal mechanism for doing this sort of successive remembering, translating, and throwing away. All the matrix operations that have been described so far (**glLoadMatrix**(), **glMultMatrix**(), **glLoadIdentity**() and the commands that create specific transformation matrices) deal with the current matrix, or the top matrix on the stack. You can control which matrix is on top with the commands that perform stack operations: **glPushMatrix**(), which copies the current matrix and adds the copy to the top of the stack, and **glPopMatrix**(), which discards the top matrix on the stack, as shown in Figure 3-21. (Remember that the current matrix is always the matrix on the top.) In effect, **glPushMatrix**() means "remember where you are" and **glPopMatrix**() means "go back to where you were."

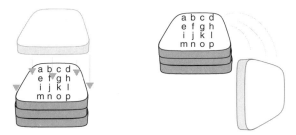

Figure 3-21   Pushing and Popping the Matrix Stack

---

void **glPushMatrix**(void);

Pushes all matrices in the current stack down one level. The current stack is determined by **glMatrixMode**(). The topmost matrix is copied, so its contents are duplicated in both the top and second-from-the-top matrix. If too many matrices are pushed, an error is generated.

---

void **glPopMatrix**(void);

Pops the top matrix off the stack, destroying the contents of the popped matrix. What was the second-from-the-top matrix becomes the top matrix. The current stack is determined by **glMatrixMode**(). If the stack contains a single matrix, calling **glPopMatrix**() generates an error.

Example 3-4 draws an automobile, assuming the existence of routines that draw the car body, a wheel, and a bolt.

Example 3-4   Pushing and Popping the Matrix

```
draw_wheel_and_bolts()
{
    long i;

    draw_wheel();
    for(i=0;i<5;i++){
        glPushMatrix();
            glRotatef(72.0*i,0.0,0.0,1.0);
            glTranslatef(3.0,0.0,0.0);
            draw_bolt();
        glPopMatrix();
    }
}

draw_body_and_wheel_and_bolts()
{
    draw_car_body();
    glPushMatrix();
        glTranslatef(40,0,30);      /*move to first wheel position*/
        draw_wheel_and_bolts();
    glPopMatrix();
    glPushMatrix();
        glTranslatef(40,0,-30);     /*move to 2nd wheel position*/
        draw_wheel_and_bolts();
    glPopMatrix();
    ...                             /*draw last two wheels similarly*/
}
```

This code assumes the wheel and bolt axes are coincident with the *z*-axis, that the bolts are evenly spaced every 72 degrees, 3 units (maybe inches) from the center of the wheel, and that the front wheels are 40 units in front of and 30 units to the right and left of the car's origin.

A stack is more efficient than an individual matrix, especially if the stack is implemented in hardware. When you push a matrix, you don't need to copy the current data back to the main process, and the hardware may be able to copy more than one element of the matrix at a time. Sometimes you might want to keep an identity matrix at the bottom of the stack so that you don't need to call **glLoadIdentity()** repeatedly.

The Modelview Matrix Stack

As you've seen earlier in "Viewing and Modeling Transformations" on page 104, the modelview matrix contains the cumulative product of multiplying viewing and modeling transformation matrices. Each viewing or modeling transformation creates a new matrix that multiplies the current modelview matrix; the result, which becomes the new current matrix, represents the composite transformation. The modelview matrix stack contains at least thirty-two 4×4 matrices; initially, the topmost matrix is the identity matrix. Some implementations of OpenGL may support more than thirty-two matrices on the stack. To find the maximum allowable number of matrices, you can use the query command **glGetIntegerv**(GL_MAX_MODELVIEW_STACK_DEPTH, GLint *params*).

The Projection Matrix Stack

The projection matrix contains a matrix for the projection transformation, which describes the viewing volume. Generally, you don't want to compose projection matrices, so you issue **glLoadIdentity()** before performing a projection transformation. Also for this reason, the projection matrix stack need be only two levels deep; some OpenGL implementations may allow more than two 4×4 matrices. To find the stack depth, call **glGetIntegerv**(GL_MAX_PROJECTION_STACK_DEPTH, GLint *params*).

One use for a second matrix in the stack would be an application that needs to display a help window with text in it, in addition to its normal window showing a three-dimensional scene. Since text is most easily positioned with an orthographic projection, you could change temporarily to an orthographic projection, display the help, and then return to your previous projection:

```
glMatrixMode(GL_PROJECTION);
glPushMatrix();                    /*save the current projection*/
    glLoadIdentity();
    glOrtho(...);                  /*set up for displaying help*/
    display_the_help();
glPopMatrix();
```

Note that you'd probably have to also change the modelview matrix appropriately.

Advanced

If you know enough mathematics, you can create custom projection matrices that perform arbitrary projective transformations. For example, the OpenGL and its Utility Library have no built-in mechanism for two-point perspective. If you were trying to emulate the drawings in drafting texts, you might need such a projection matrix.

Additional Clipping Planes

In addition to the six clipping planes of the viewing volume (left, right, bottom, top, near, and far), you can define up to six additional clipping planes to further restrict the viewing volume, as shown in Figure 3-22. This is useful for removing extraneous objects in a scene—for example, if you want to display a cutaway view of an object.

Each plane is specified by the coefficients of its equation: $Ax+By+Cz+D = 0$. The clipping planes are automatically transformed appropriately by modeling and viewing transformations. The clipping volume becomes the intersection of the viewing volume and all *half-spaces* defined by the additional clipping planes. Remember that polygons that get clipped automatically have their edges reconstructed appropriately by OpenGL.

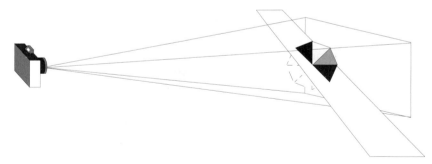

Figure 3-22   Additional Clipping Planes and the Viewing Volume

---

void **glClipPlane**(GLenum *plane*, const GLdouble *equation*);

Defines a clipping plane. The *equation* argument points to the four coefficients of the plane equation, $Ax+By+Cz+D = 0$. All points with eye coordinates (x_e, y_e, z_e, w_e) that satisfy $(A\ B\ C\ D)M^{-1}\ (x_e\ y_e\ z_e\ w_e)^T >= 0$ lie in the half-space defined by the plane, where **M** is the current modelview matrix at the time **glClipPlane**() is called. All points not in this half-space are clipped away. The *plane* argument is GL_CLIP_PLANE*i*, where *i* is an integer specifying which of the available clipping planes to define. *i* is a number between 0 and one less than the maximum number of additional clipping planes.

You need to enable each additional clipping plane you define:

```
glEnable(GL_CLIP_PLANEi);
```

You can disable a plane with

```
glDisable(GL_CLIP_PLANEi);
```

All implementations of OpenGL must support at least six additional clipping planes, although some implementations may allow more. You can use **glGetIntegerv**() with GL_MAX_CLIP_PLANES to find how many clipping planes are supported.

Note: Clipping performed as a result of **glClipPlane**() is done in eye coordinates, not in clip coordinates. This difference is noticeable if the projection matrix is singular (that is, a real projection matrix that flattens three-dimensional coordinates to two-dimensional ones). Clipping performed in eye coordinates continues to take place in three dimensions even when the projection matrix is singular.

A Clipping Plane Code Example

Example 3-5 renders a wireframe sphere with two clipping planes that slice away three-quarters of the original sphere, as shown in Figure 3-23.

Figure 3-23   Clipped Wireframe Sphere

Example 3-5   Wireframe Sphere with Two Clipping Planes: clip.c

```
#include <GL/gl.h>
#include <GL/glu.h>
#include <GL/glut.h>

void init(void)
{
   glClearColor (0.0, 0.0, 0.0, 0.0);
   glShadeModel (GL_FLAT);
}

void display(void)
{
   GLdouble eqn[4] = {0.0, 1.0, 0.0, 0.0};
   GLdouble eqn2[4] = {1.0, 0.0, 0.0, 0.0};

   glClear(GL_COLOR_BUFFER_BIT);
   glColor3f (1.0, 1.0, 1.0);
   glPushMatrix();
   glTranslatef (0.0, 0.0, -5.0);

/*    clip lower half -- y < 0          */
   glClipPlane (GL_CLIP_PLANE0, eqn);
   glEnable (GL_CLIP_PLANE0);
/*    clip left half -- x < 0           */
   glClipPlane (GL_CLIP_PLANE1, eqn2);
   glEnable (GL_CLIP_PLANE1);

   glRotatef (90.0, 1.0, 0.0, 0.0);
   glutWireSphere(1.0, 20, 16);
   glPopMatrix();
   glFlush ();
}
```

```
void reshape (int w, int h)
{
   glViewport (0, 0, (GLsizei) w, (GLsizei) h);
   glMatrixMode (GL_PROJECTION);
   glLoadIdentity ();
   gluPerspective(60.0, (GLfloat) w/(GLfloat) h, 1.0, 20.0);
   glMatrixMode (GL_MODELVIEW);
}

int main(int argc, char** argv)
{
   glutInit(&argc, argv);
   glutInitDisplayMode (GLUT_SINGLE | GLUT_RGB);
   glutInitWindowSize (500, 500);
   glutInitWindowPosition (100, 100);
   glutCreateWindow (argv[0]);
   init ();
   glutDisplayFunc(display);
   glutReshapeFunc(reshape);
   glutMainLoop();
   return 0;
}
```

Try This

- Try changing the coefficients that describe the clipping planes in Example 3-5.

- Try calling a modeling transformation, such as **glRotate*()**, to affect **glClipPlane()**. Make the clipping plane move independently of the objects in the scene.

Examples of Composing Several Transformations

This section demonstrates how to combine several transformations to achieve a particular result. The two examples discussed are a solar system, in which objects need to rotate on their axes as well as in orbit around each other, and a robot arm, which has several joints that effectively transform coordinate systems as they move relative to each other.

Building a Solar System

The program described in this section draws a simple solar system with a planet and a sun, both using the same sphere-drawing routine. To write this program, you need to use **glRotate*()** for the revolution of the planet around the sun and for the rotation of the planet around its own axis. You also need **glTranslate*()** to move the planet out to its orbit, away from the origin of the solar system. Remember that you can specify the desired size of the two spheres by supplying the appropriate arguments for the **glutWireSphere()** routine.

To draw the solar system, you first want to set up a projection and a viewing transformation. For this example, **gluPerspective()** and **gluLookAt()** are used.

Drawing the sun is straightforward, since it should be located at the origin of the grand, fixed coordinate system, which is where the sphere routine places it. Thus, drawing the sun doesn't require translation; you can use **glRotate*()** to make the sun rotate about an arbitrary axis. To draw a planet rotating around the sun, as shown in Figure 3-24, requires several modeling transformations. The planet needs to rotate about its own axis once a day. And once a year, the planet completes one revolution around the sun.

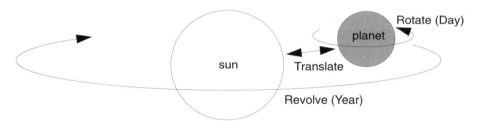

Figure 3-24   Planet and Sun

To determine the order of modeling transformations, visualize what happens to the local coordinate system. An initial **glRotate*()** rotates the local coordinate system that initially coincides with the grand coordinate system. Next, **glTranslate*()** moves the local coordinate system to a position on the planet's orbit; the distance moved should equal the radius of the orbit. Thus, the initial **glRotate*()** actually determines where along the orbit the planet is (or what time of year it is).

A second **glRotate*()** rotates the local coordinate system around the local axes, thus determining the time of day for the planet. Once you've issued all these transformation commands, the planet can be drawn.

In summary, these are the OpenGL commands to draw the sun and planet; the full program is shown in Example 3-6.

```
glPushMatrix();
glutWireSphere(1.0, 20, 16);        /* draw sun */
glRotatef ((GLfloat) year, 0.0, 1.0, 0.0);
glTranslatef (2.0, 0.0, 0.0);
glRotatef ((GLfloat) day, 0.0, 1.0, 0.0);
glutWireSphere(0.2, 10, 8);          /* draw smaller planet */
glPopMatrix();
```

Example 3-6   Planetary System: planet.c

```
#include <GL/gl.h>
#include <GL/glu.h>
#include <GL/glut.h>

static int year = 0, day = 0;

void init(void)
{
   glClearColor (0.0, 0.0, 0.0, 0.0);
   glShadeModel (GL_FLAT);
}

void display(void)
{
   glClear (GL_COLOR_BUFFER_BIT);
   glColor3f (1.0, 1.0, 1.0);

   glPushMatrix();
   glutWireSphere(1.0, 20, 16);    /* draw sun */
   glRotatef ((GLfloat) year, 0.0, 1.0, 0.0);
   glTranslatef (2.0, 0.0, 0.0);
   glRotatef ((GLfloat) day, 0.0, 1.0, 0.0);
   glutWireSphere(0.2, 10, 8);      /* draw smaller planet */
   glPopMatrix();
   glutSwapBuffers();
}
```

```
void reshape (int w, int h)
{
    glViewport (0, 0, (GLsizei) w, (GLsizei) h);
    glMatrixMode (GL_PROJECTION);
    glLoadIdentity ();
    gluPerspective(60.0, (GLfloat) w/(GLfloat) h, 1.0, 20.0);
    glMatrixMode(GL_MODELVIEW);
    glLoadIdentity();
    gluLookAt (0.0, 0.0, 5.0, 0.0, 0.0, 0.0, 0.0, 1.0, 0.0);
}

void keyboard (unsigned char key, int x, int y)
{
    switch (key) {
        case 'd':
            day = (day + 10) % 360;
            glutPostRedisplay();
            break;
        case 'D':
            day = (day - 10) % 360;
            glutPostRedisplay();
            break;
        case 'y':
            year = (year + 5) % 360;
            glutPostRedisplay();
            break;
        case 'Y':
            year = (year - 5) % 360;
            glutPostRedisplay();
            break;
        default:
            break;
    }
}

int main(int argc, char** argv)
{
    glutInit(&argc, argv);
    glutInitDisplayMode (GLUT_DOUBLE | GLUT_RGB);
    glutInitWindowSize (500, 500);
    glutInitWindowPosition (100, 100);
    glutCreateWindow (argv[0]);
    init ();
    glutDisplayFunc(display);
    glutReshapeFunc(reshape);
    glutKeyboardFunc(keyboard);
    glutMainLoop();
```

```
    return 0;
}
```

Try This

- Try adding a moon to the planet. Or try several moons and additional planets. Hint: Use **glPushMatrix()** and **glPopMatrix()** to save and restore the position and orientation of the coordinate system at appropriate moments. If you're going to draw several moons around a planet, you need to save the coordinate system prior to positioning each moon and restore the coordinate system after each moon is drawn.

- Try tilting the planet's axis.

Building an Articulated Robot Arm

This section discusses a program that creates an articulated robot arm with two or more segments. The arm should be connected with pivot points at the shoulder, elbow, or other joints. Figure 3-25 shows a single joint of such an arm.

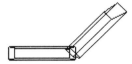

Figure 3-25   Robot Arm

You can use a scaled cube as a segment of the robot arm, but first you must call the appropriate modeling transformations to orient each segment. Since the origin of the local coordinate system is initially at the center of the cube, you need to move the local coordinate system to one edge of the cube. Otherwise, the cube rotates about its center rather than the pivot point.

After you call **glTranslate*()** to establish the pivot point and **glRotate*()** to pivot the cube, translate back to the center of the cube. Then the cube is scaled (flattened and widened) before it is drawn. The **glPushMatrix()** and **glPopMatrix()** restrict the effect of **glScale*()**. Here's what your code might look like for this first segment of the arm (the entire program is shown in Example 3-7):

```
glTranslatef (-1.0, 0.0, 0.0);
glRotatef ((GLfloat) shoulder, 0.0, 0.0, 1.0);
glTranslatef (1.0, 0.0, 0.0);
glPushMatrix();
glScalef (2.0, 0.4, 1.0);
glutWireCube (1.0);
glPopMatrix();
```

To build a second segment, you need to move the local coordinate system to the next pivot point. Since the coordinate system has previously been rotated, the *x*-axis is already oriented along the length of the rotated arm. Therefore, translating along the *x*-axis moves the local coordinate system to the next pivot point. Once it's at that pivot point, you can use the same code to draw the second segment as you used for the first one. This can be continued for an indefinite number of segments (shoulder, elbow, wrist, fingers).

```
glTranslatef (1.0, 0.0, 0.0);
glRotatef ((GLfloat) elbow, 0.0, 0.0, 1.0);
glTranslatef (1.0, 0.0, 0.0);
glPushMatrix();
glScalef (2.0, 0.4, 1.0);
glutWireCube (1.0);
glPopMatrix();
```

Example 3-7   Robot Arm: robot.c

```
#include <GL/gl.h>
#include <GL/glu.h>
#include <GL/glut.h>

static int shoulder = 0, elbow = 0;

void init(void)
{
   glClearColor (0.0, 0.0, 0.0, 0.0);
   glShadeModel (GL_FLAT);
}
```

```
void display(void)
{
    glClear (GL_COLOR_BUFFER_BIT);
    glPushMatrix();
    glTranslatef (-1.0, 0.0, 0.0);
    glRotatef ((GLfloat) shoulder, 0.0, 0.0, 1.0);
    glTranslatef (1.0, 0.0, 0.0);
    glPushMatrix();
    glScalef (2.0, 0.4, 1.0);
    glutWireCube (1.0);
    glPopMatrix();

    glTranslatef (1.0, 0.0, 0.0);
    glRotatef ((GLfloat) elbow, 0.0, 0.0, 1.0);
    glTranslatef (1.0, 0.0, 0.0);
    glPushMatrix();
    glScalef (2.0, 0.4, 1.0);
    glutWireCube (1.0);
    glPopMatrix();

    glPopMatrix();
    glutSwapBuffers();
}

void reshape (int w, int h)
{
    glViewport (0, 0, (GLsizei) w, (GLsizei) h);
    glMatrixMode (GL_PROJECTION);
    glLoadIdentity ();
    gluPerspective(65.0, (GLfloat) w/(GLfloat) h, 1.0, 20.0);
    glMatrixMode(GL_MODELVIEW);
    glLoadIdentity();
    glTranslatef (0.0, 0.0, -5.0);
}

void keyboard (unsigned char key, int x, int y)
{
    switch (key) {
        case 's':   /*  s key rotates at shoulder  */
            shoulder = (shoulder + 5) % 360;
            glutPostRedisplay();
            break;
        case 'S':
            shoulder = (shoulder - 5) % 360;
            glutPostRedisplay();
            break;
        case 'e':   /*  e key rotates at elbow  */
```

```
          elbow = (elbow + 5) % 360;
          glutPostRedisplay();
          break;
      case 'E':
          elbow = (elbow - 5) % 360;
          glutPostRedisplay();
          break;
      default:
          break;
   }
}

int main(int argc, char** argv)
{
   glutInit(&argc, argv);
   glutInitDisplayMode (GLUT_DOUBLE | GLUT_RGB);
   glutInitWindowSize (500, 500);
   glutInitWindowPosition (100, 100);
   glutCreateWindow (argv[0]);
   init ();
   glutDisplayFunc(display);
   glutReshapeFunc(reshape);
   glutKeyboardFunc(keyboard);
   glutMainLoop();
   return 0;
}
```

Try This

- Modify Example 3-7 to add additional segments onto the robot arm.

- Modify Example 3-7 to add additional segments at the same position. For example, give the robot arm several "fingers" at the wrist, as shown in Figure 3-26. Hint: Use **glPushMatrix()** and **glPopMatrix()** to save and restore the position and orientation of the coordinate system at the wrist. If you're going to draw fingers at the wrist, you need to save the current matrix prior to positioning each finger and restore the current matrix after each finger is drawn.

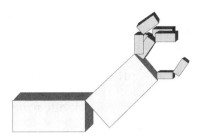

Figure 3-26   Robot Arm with Fingers

Reversing or Mimicking Transformations

The geometric processing pipeline is very good at using viewing and projection matrices and a viewport for clipping to transform the world (or object) coordinates of a vertex into window (or screen) coordinates. However, there are situations in which you want to reverse that process. A common situation is when an application user utilizes the mouse to choose a location in three dimensions. The mouse returns only a two-dimensional value, which is the screen location of the cursor. Therefore, the application will have to reverse the transformation process to determine from where in three-dimensional space this screen location originated.

The Utility Library routine **gluUnProject()** performs this reversal of the transformations. Given the three-dimensional window coordinates for a location and all the transformations that affected them, **gluUnProject()** returns the world coordinates from where it originated.

---

int **gluUnProject**(GLdouble *winx*, GLdouble *winy*, GLdouble *winz*, const GLdouble *modelMatrix[16]*, const GLdouble *projMatrix[16]*, const GLint *viewport[4]*, GLdouble **objx*, GLdouble **objy*, GLdouble **objz*);

Map the specified window coordinates (*winx, winy, winz*) into object coordinates, using transformations defined by a modelview matrix (*modelMatrix*), projection matrix (*projMatrix*), and viewport (*viewport*). The resulting object coordinates are returned in *objx, objy,* and *objz*. The function returns GL_TRUE, indicating success, or GL_FALSE, indicating failure (such as an noninvertible matrix). This operation does not attempt to clip the coordinates to the viewport or eliminate depth values that fall outside of **glDepthRange()**.

There are inherent difficulties in trying to reverse the transformation process. A two-dimensional screen location could have originated from anywhere on an entire line in three-dimensional space. To disambiguate the result, **gluUnProject()** requires that a window depth coordinate (*winz*) be provided and that *winz* be specified in terms of **glDepthRange()**. For the default values of **glDepthRange()**, *winz* at 0.0 will request the world coordinates of the transformed point at the near clipping plane, while *winz* at 1.0 will request the point at the far clipping plane.

Example 3-8 demonstrates **gluUnProject()** by reading the mouse position and determining the three-dimensional points at the near and far clipping planes from which it was transformed. The computed world coordinates are printed to standard output, but the rendered window itself is just black.

Example 3-8   Reversing the Geometric Processing Pipeline: unproject.c

```
#include <GL/gl.h>
#include <GL/glu.h>
#include <GL/glut.h>
#include <stdlib.h>
#include <stdio.h>

void display(void)
{
   glClear(GL_COLOR_BUFFER_BIT);
   glFlush();
}

void reshape(int w, int h)
{
   glViewport (0, 0, (GLsizei) w, (GLsizei) h);
   glMatrixMode(GL_PROJECTION);
   glLoadIdentity();
   gluPerspective (45.0, (GLfloat) w/(GLfloat) h, 1.0, 100.0);
   glMatrixMode(GL_MODELVIEW);
   glLoadIdentity();
}

void mouse(int button, int state, int x, int y)
{
   GLint viewport[4];
   GLdouble mvmatrix[16], projmatrix[16];
   GLint realy;  /*  OpenGL y coordinate position  */
   GLdouble wx, wy, wz;  /*  returned world x, y, z coords  */
```

```
    switch (button) {
       case GLUT_LEFT_BUTTON:
          if (state == GLUT_DOWN) {
             glGetIntegerv (GL_VIEWPORT, viewport);
             glGetDoublev (GL_MODELVIEW_MATRIX, mvmatrix);
             glGetDoublev (GL_PROJECTION_MATRIX, projmatrix);
/*  note viewport[3] is height of window in pixels  */
             realy = viewport[3] - (GLint) y - 1;
             printf ("Coordinates at cursor are (%4d, %4d)\n",
                x, realy);
             gluUnProject ((GLdouble) x, (GLdouble) realy, 0.0,
                mvmatrix, projmatrix, viewport, &wx, &wy, &wz);
             printf ("World coords at z=0.0 are (%f, %f, %f)\n",
                wx, wy, wz);
             gluUnProject ((GLdouble) x, (GLdouble) realy, 1.0,
                mvmatrix, projmatrix, viewport, &wx, &wy, &wz);
            printf ("World coords at z=1.0 are (%f, %f, %f)\n",
                wx, wy, wz);
          }
          break;
       case GLUT_RIGHT_BUTTON:
          if (state == GLUT_DOWN)
             exit(0);
          break;
       default:
          break;
    }
}

int main(int argc, char** argv)
{
   glutInit(&argc, argv);
   glutInitDisplayMode (GLUT_SINGLE | GLUT_RGB);
   glutInitWindowSize (500, 500);
   glutInitWindowPosition (100, 100);
   glutCreateWindow (argv[0]);
   glutDisplayFunc(display);
   glutReshapeFunc(reshape);
   glutMouseFunc(mouse);
   glutMainLoop();
   return 0;
}
```

gluProject() is another Utility Library routine, which is related to
gluUnProject(). gluProject() mimics the actions of the transformation
pipeline. Given three-dimensional world coordinates and all the

transformations that affect them, **gluProject()** returns the transformed window coordinates.

---

int **gluProject**(GLdouble *objx*, GLdouble *objy*, GLdouble *objz*, const GLdouble *modelMatrix[16]*, const GLdouble *projMatrix[16]*, const GLint *viewport[4]*, GLdouble **winx*, GLdouble **winy*, GLdouble **winz*);

Map the specified object coordinates (*objx, objy, objz*) into window coordinates, using transformations defined by a modelview matrix (*modelMatrix*), projection matrix (*projMatrix*), and viewport (*viewport*). The resulting window coordinates are returned in *winx, winy,* and *winz*. The function returns GL_TRUE, indicating success, or GL_FALSE, indicating failure.

Chapter 4

Color

Chapter Objectives

After reading this chapter, you'll be able to do the following:

- Decide between using RGBA or color-index mode for your application

- Specify desired colors for drawing objects

- Use smooth shading to draw a single polygon with more than one color

The goal of almost all OpenGL applications is to draw color pictures in a window on the screen. The window is a rectangular array of pixels, each of which contains and displays its own color. Thus, in a sense, the point of all the calculations performed by an OpenGL implementation—calculations that take into account OpenGL commands, state information, and values of parameters—is to determine the final color of every pixel that's to be drawn in the window. This chapter explains the commands for specifying colors and how OpenGL interprets them in the following major sections:

- "Color Perception" on page 152 discusses how the eye perceives color.

- "Computer Color" on page 154 describes the relationship between pixels on a computer *monitor* and their colors; it also defines the two display modes, RGBA and color index.

- "RGBA versus Color-Index Mode" on page 156 explains how the two display modes use graphics hardware and how to decide which mode to use.

- "Specifying a Color and a Shading Model" on page 162 describes the OpenGL commands you use to specify the desired color or shading model.

Color Perception

Physically, light is composed of photons—tiny particles of light, each traveling along its own path, and each vibrating at its own frequency (or wavelength, or energy—any one of frequency, wavelength, or energy determines the others). A photon is completely characterized by its position, direction, and frequency/wavelength/energy. Photons with wavelengths ranging from about 390 nanometers (nm) (violet) and 720 nm (red) cover the colors of the visible spectrum, forming the colors of a rainbow (violet, indigo, blue, green, yellow, orange, red). However, your eyes perceive lots of colors that aren't in the rainbow—white, black, brown, and pink, for example. How does this happen?

What your eye actually sees is a mixture of photons of different frequencies. Real light sources are characterized by the distribution of photon frequencies they emit. Ideal white light consists of an equal amount of light of all frequencies. Laser light is usually very pure, and all photons have almost identical frequencies (and direction and phase, as well). Light from a sodium-vapor lamp has more light in the yellow frequency. Light from most stars in space has a distribution that depends heavily on their temperatures (black-body radiation). The frequency distribution of light from most sources in your immediate environment is more complicated.

The human eye perceives color when certain cells in the retina (called *cone cells*, or just *cones*) become excited after being struck by photons. The three different kinds of cone cells respond best to three different wavelengths of light: one type of cone cell responds best to red light, one type to green, and the other to blue. (A person who is color-blind is usually missing one or more types of cone cells.) When a given mixture of photons enters the eye, the cone cells in the retina register different degrees of excitation depending on their types, and if a different mixture of photons comes in that happens to excite the three types of cone cells to the same degrees, its color is indistinguishable from that of the first mixture.

Since each color is recorded by the eye as the levels of excitation of the cone cells by the incoming photons, the eye can perceive colors that aren't in the spectrum produced by a prism or rainbow. For example, if you send a mixture of red and blue photons so that both the red and blue cones in the retina are excited, your eye sees it as magenta, which isn't in the spectrum. Other combinations give browns, turquoises, and mauves, none of which appear in the color spectrum.

A computer-graphics monitor emulates visible colors by lighting pixels with a combination of red, green, and blue light in proportions that excite the red-, green-, and blue-sensitive cones in the retina in such a way that it matches the excitation levels generated by the photon mix it's trying to emulate. If humans had more types of cone cells, some that were yellow-sensitive for example, color monitors would probably have a yellow gun as well, and we'd use RGBY (red, green, blue, yellow) quadruples to specify colors. And if everyone were color-blind in the same way, this chapter would be simpler.

To display a particular color, the monitor sends the right amounts of red, green, and blue light to appropriately stimulate the different types of cone cells in your eye. A color monitor can send different proportions of red, green, and blue to each of the pixels, and the eye sees a million or so pinpoints of light, each with its own color.

This section considers only how the eye perceives combinations of photons that enter it. The situation for light bouncing off materials and entering the eye is even more complex—white light bouncing off a red ball will appear red, or yellow light shining through blue glass appears almost black, for example. (See "Real-World and OpenGL Lighting" on page 173 for a discussion of these effects.)

Computer Color

On a color computer screen, the hardware causes each pixel on the screen to emit different amounts of red, green, and blue light. These are called the R, G, and B values. They're often packed together (sometimes with a fourth value, called alpha, or A), and the packed value is called the RGB (or RGBA) value. (See "Blending" on page 214 for an explanation of the alpha values.) The color information at each pixel can be stored either in *RGBA mode*, in which the R, G, B, and possibly A values are kept for each pixel, or in *color-index mode*, in which a single number (called the color index) is stored for each pixel. Each color index indicates an entry in a table that defines a particular set of R, G, and B values. Such a table is called a *color map*.

In color-index mode, you might want to alter the values in the color map. Since color maps are controlled by the window system, there are no OpenGL commands to do this. All the examples in this book initialize the color-display mode at the time the window is opened by using routines from the GLUT library. (See Appendix D for details.)

There is a great deal of variation among the different graphics hardware platforms in both the size of the pixel array and the number of colors that can be displayed at each pixel. On any graphics system, each pixel has the same amount of memory for storing its color, and all the memory for all the pixels is called the *color buffer*. The size of a buffer is usually measured in bits, so an 8-bit buffer could store 8 bits of data (256 possible different colors) for each pixel. The size of the possible buffers varies from machine to machine. (See Chapter 10 for more information.)

The R, G, and B values can range from 0.0 (none) to 1.0 (full intensity). For example, R = 0.0, G = 0.0, and B = 1.0 represents the brightest possible blue. If R, G, and B are all 0.0, the pixel is black; if all are 1.0, the pixel is drawn in the brightest white that can be displayed on the screen. *Blending* green and blue creates shades of cyan. Blue and red combine for magenta. Red and green create yellow. To help you create the colors you want from the R, G, and B components, look at the color cube shown in Plate 12. The axes of this cube represent intensities of red, blue, and green. A black-and-white version of the cube is shown in Figure 4-1.

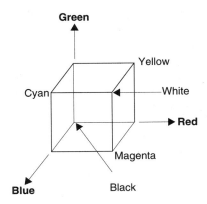

Figure 4-1   The Color Cube in Black and White

The commands to specify a color for an object (in this case, a point) can be as simple as this:

```
glColor3f (1.0, 0.0, 0.0);   /* the current RGB color is red: */
                             /* full red, no green, no blue. */
glBegin (GL_POINTS);
    glVertex3fv (point_array);
glEnd ();
```

In certain modes (for example, if lighting or texturing calculations are performed), the assigned color might go through other operations before arriving in the framebuffer as a value representing a color for a pixel. In fact, the color of a pixel is determined by a lengthy sequence of operations.

Early in a program's execution, the color-display mode is set to either RGBA mode or color-index mode. Once the color-display mode is initialized, it can't be changed. As the program executes, a color (either a color index or an RGBA value) is determined on a per-vertex basis for each geometric primitive. This color is either a color you've explicitly specified for a vertex or, if lighting is enabled, is determined from the interaction of the transformation matrices with the surface normals and other material properties. In other words, a red ball with a blue light shining on it looks different from the same ball with no light on it. (See Chapter 5 for details.) After the relevant lighting calculations are performed, the chosen shading model is applied. As explained in "Specifying a Color and a Shading Model" on page 162, you can choose flat or smooth shading, each of which has different effects on the eventual color of a pixel.

Next, the primitives are *rasterized*, or converted to a two-dimensional image. Rasterizing involves determining which squares of an integer grid in window coordinates are occupied by the primitive and then assigning color and other values to each such square. A grid square along with its associated values of color, z (depth), and texture coordinates is called a *fragment*. Pixels are elements of the framebuffer; a fragment comes from a primitive and is combined with its corresponding pixel to yield a new pixel. Once a fragment is constructed, texturing, fog, and antialiasing are applied—if they're enabled—to the fragments. After that, any specified alpha blending, *dithering*, and bitwise logical operations are carried out using the fragment and the pixel already stored in the framebuffer. Finally, the fragment's color value (either color index or RGBA) is written into the pixel and displayed in the window using the window's color-display mode.

RGBA versus Color-Index Mode

In either color-index or RGBA mode, a certain amount of color data is stored at each pixel. This amount is determined by the number of bitplanes in the framebuffer. A *bitplane* contains 1 bit of data for each pixel. If there are 8color bitplanes, there are 8 color bits per pixel, and hence $2^8 = 256$ different values or colors that can be stored at the pixel.

Bitplanes are often divided evenly into storage for R, G, and B components (that is, a 24-bitplane system devotes 8 bits each to red, green, and blue), but this isn't always true. To find out the number of bitplanes available on your system for red, green, blue, alpha, or color-index values, use **glGetIntegerv()** with GL_RED_BITS, GL_GREEN_BITS, GL_BLUE_BITS, GL_ALPHA_BITS, and GL_INDEX_BITS.

Note: Color intensities on most computer screens aren't perceived as linear by the human eye. Consider colors consisting of just a red component, with green and blue set to zero. As the intensity varies from 0.0 (off) to 1.0 (full on), the number of electrons striking the pixels increases, but the question is, does 0.5 look like halfway between 0.0 and 1.0? To test this, write a program that draws alternate pixels in a checkerboard pattern to intensities 0.0 and 1.0, and compare it with a region drawn solidly in color 0.5. From a reasonable distance from the screen, the two regions should appear to have the same intensity. If they look noticeably different, you need to use whatever correction mechanism is provided on your particular system. For example, many systems have a table to adjust intensities so that 0.5 appears to be halfway between 0.0 and 1.0. The mapping generally used is an exponential one, with the exponent referred to as gamma (hence the term *gamma correction*). Using the same gamma for the red, green, and blue components gives pretty good results, but three different gamma values might give slightly better results. (For more details on this topic, see Foley, van Dam, et al. *Computer Graphics: Principles and Practice*. Reading, MA: Addison-Wesley Developers Press, 1990.)

RGBA Display Mode

In RGBA mode, the hardware sets aside a certain number of bitplanes for each of the R, G, B, and A components (not necessarily the same number for each component) as shown in Figure 4-2. The R, G, and B values are typically stored as integers rather than floating-point numbers, and they're scaled to the number of available bits for storage and retrieval. For example, if a system has 8 bits available for the R component, integers between 0 and 255 can be stored; thus, 0, 1, 2, ..., 255 in the bitplanes would correspond to R values of 0/255 = 0.0, 1/255, 2/255, ..., 255/255 = 1.0. Regardless of the number of bitplanes, 0.0 specifies the minimum intensity, and 1.0 specifies the maximum intensity.

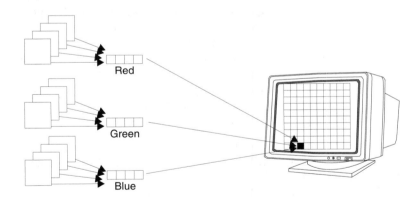

Figure 4-2   RGB Values from the Bitplanes

Note: The alpha value (the A in RGBA) has no direct effect on the color displayed on the screen. It can be used for many things, including blending and transparency, and it can have an effect on the values of R, G, and B that are written. (See "Blending" on page 214 for more information about alpha values.)

The number of distinct colors that can be displayed at a single pixel depends on the number of bitplanes and the capacity of the hardware to interpret those bitplanes. The number of distinct colors can't exceed 2^n, where n is the number of bitplanes. Thus, a machine with 24 bitplanes for RGB can display up to 16.77 million distinct colors.

Dithering

Advanced

Some graphics hardware uses dithering to increase the number of apparent colors. Dithering is the technique of using combinations of some colors to create the effect of other colors. To illustrate how dithering works, suppose your system has only 1 bit each for R, G, and B and thus can display only eight colors: black, white, red, blue, green, yellow, cyan, and magenta. To display a pink region, the hardware can fill the region in a checkerboard manner, alternating red and white pixels. If your eye is far enough away from the screen that it can't distinguish individual pixels, the region appears pink—the average of red and white. Redder pinks can be achieved by filling a higher proportion of the pixels with red, whiter pinks would use more white pixels, and so on.

With this technique, there are no pink pixels. The only way to achieve the effect of "pinkness" is to cover a region consisting of multiple pixels—you can't dither a single pixel. If you specify an RGB value for an unavailable color and fill a polygon, the hardware fills the pixels in the interior of the polygon with a mixture of nearby colors whose average appears to your eye to be the color you want. (Remember, though, that if you're reading pixel information out of the framebuffer, you get the actual red and white pixel values, since there aren't any pink ones. See Chapter 8 for more information about reading pixel values.)

Figure 4-3 illustrates some simple dithering of black and white pixels to make shades of gray. From left to right, the 4×4 patterns at the top represent dithering patterns for 50 percent, 19 percent, and 69 percent gray. Under each pattern, you can see repeated reduced copies of each pattern, but these black and white squares are still bigger than most pixels. If you look at them from across the room, you can see that they blur together and appear as three levels of gray.

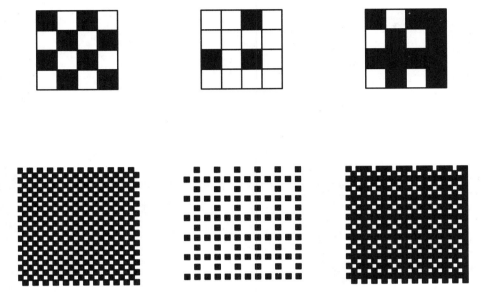

Figure 4-3   Dithering Black and White to Create Gray

With about 8 bits each of R, G, and B, you can get a fairly high-quality image without dithering. Just because your machine has 24 color bitplanes, however, doesn't mean that dithering won't be desirable. For example, if you are running in double-buffer mode, the bitplanes might be divided into two sets of twelve, so there are really only 4 bits each per R, G, and B component. Without dithering, 4-bit-per-component color can give less than satisfactory results in many situations.

You enable or disable dithering by passing GL_DITHER to **glEnable()** or **glDisable()**. Note that dithering, unlike many other features, is enabled by default.

Color-Index Display Mode

With color-index mode, OpenGL uses a color map (or *lookup table*), which is similar to using a palette to mix paints to prepare for a paint-by-number scene. A painter's palette provides spaces to mix paints together; similarly, a computer's color map provides indices where the primary red, green, and blue values can be mixed, as shown in Figure 4-4.

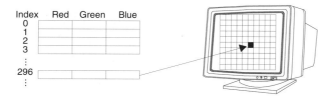

Figure 4-4   A Color Map

A painter filling in a paint-by-number scene chooses a color from the color palette and fills the corresponding numbered regions with that color. A computer stores the color index in the bitplanes for each pixel. Then those bitplane values reference the color map, and the screen is painted with the corresponding red, green, and blue values from the color map, as shown in Figure 4-5.

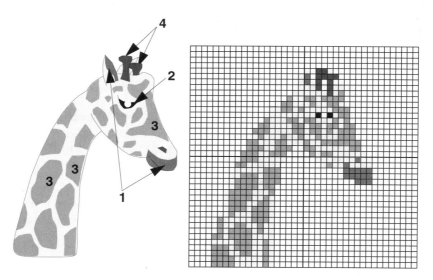

Figure 4-5   Using a Color Map to Paint a Picture

In color-index mode, the number of simultaneously available colors is limited by the size of the color map and the number of bitplanes available. The size of the color map is determined by the amount of hardware dedicated to it. The size of the color map is always a power of 2, and typical sizes range from 256 (2^8) to 4096 (2^{12}), where the exponent is the number of bitplanes being used. If there are 2^n indices in the color map and m available bitplanes, the number of usable entries is the smaller of 2^n and 2^m.

With RGBA mode, each pixel's color is independent of other pixels. However, in color-index mode, each pixel with the same index stored in its bitplanes shares the same color-map location. If the contents of an entry in the color map change, then all pixels of that color index change their color.

Choosing between RGBA and Color-Index Mode

You should base your decision to use RGBA or color-index mode on what hardware is available and on what your application needs. For most systems, more colors can be simultaneously represented with RGBA mode than with color-index mode. Also, for several effects, such as shading, lighting, texture mapping, and fog, RGBA provides more flexibility than color-index mode.

You might prefer to use color-index mode in the following cases:

- If you're porting an existing application that makes significant use of color-index mode, it might be easier to not change to RGBA mode.

- If you have a small number of bitplanes available, RGBA mode may produce noticeably coarse shades of colors. For example, if you have only 8 bitplanes, in RGBA mode, you may have only 3 bits for red, 3 bits for green, and 2 bits for blue. You'd only have 8 (2^3) shades of red and green, and only 4 shades of blue. The gradients between color shades are likely to be very obvious.

  In this situation, if you have limited shading requirements, you can use the color lookup table to load more shades of colors. For example, if you need only shades of blue, you can use color-index mode and store up to 256 (2^8) shades of blue in the color-lookup table, which is much better than the 4 shades you would have in RGBA mode. Of course, this example would use up your entire color-lookup table, so you would have no shades of red, green, or other combined colors.

- Color-index mode can be useful for various tricks, such as color-map animation and drawing in layers. (See Chapter 14 for more information.)

In general, use RGBA mode wherever possible. It works with texture mapping and works better with lighting, shading, fog, antialiasing, and blending.

Changing between Display Modes

In the best of all possible worlds, you might want to avoid making a choice between RGBA and color-index display mode. For example, you may want to use color-index mode for a color-map animation effect and then, when needed, immediately change the scene to RGBA mode for texture mapping.

Or similarly, you may desire to switch between single and double buffering. For example, you may have very few bitplanes; let's say 8 bitplanes. In single-buffer mode, you'll have 256 (2^8) colors, but if you are using double-buffer mode to eliminate flickering from your animated program, you may only have 16 (2^4) colors. Perhaps you want to draw a moving object without flicker and are willing to sacrifice colors for using double-buffer mode (maybe the object is moving so fast that the viewer won't notice the details). But when the object comes to rest, you will want to draw it in single-buffer mode so that you can use more colors.

Unfortunately, most window systems won't allow an easy switch. For example, with the X Window System, the color-display mode is an attribute of the X Visual. An X Visual must be specified before the window is created. Once it is specified, it cannot be changed for the life of the window. After you create a window with a double-buffered, RGBA display mode, you're stuck with it.

A tricky solution to this problem is to create more than one window, each with a different display mode. Then you must control the visibility of the windows (for example, mapping or unmapping an X Window, or managing or unmanaging a Motif or Athena widget) and draw the object into the appropriate, visible window.

Specifying a Color and a Shading Model

OpenGL maintains a current color (in RGBA mode) and a current color index (in color-index mode). Unless you're using a more complicated coloring model such as lighting or texture mapping, each object is drawn using the current color (or color index). Look at the following pseudocode sequence:

```
set_color(RED);
draw_item(A);
draw_item(B);
set_color(GREEN);
set_color(BLUE);
draw_item(C);
```

Items A and B are drawn in red, and item C is drawn in blue. The fourth line, which sets the current color to green, has no effect (except to waste a bit of time). With no lighting or texturing, when the current color is set, all items drawn afterward are drawn in that color until the current color is changed to something else.

Specifying a Color in RGBA Mode

In RGBA mode, use the **glColor*()** command to select a current color.

void **glColor3**{b s i f d ub us ui} (*TYPE r, TYPE g, TYPE b*);
void **glColor4**{b s i f d ub us ui} (*TYPE r, TYPE g, TYPE b, TYPE a*);
void **glColor3**{b s i f d ub us ui}**v** (const *TYPE *v*);
void **glColor4**{b s i f d ub us ui}**v** (const *TYPE *v*);

Sets the current red, green, blue, and alpha values. This command can have up to three suffixes, which differentiate variations of the parameters accepted. The first suffix is either 3 or 4, to indicate whether you supply an alpha value in addition to the red, green, and blue values. If you don't supply an alpha value, it's automatically set to 1.0. The second suffix indicates the data type for parameters: byte, short, integer, float, double, unsigned byte, unsigned short, or unsigned integer. The third suffix is an optional **v**, which indicates that the argument is a pointer to an array of values of the given data type.

For the versions of **glColor*()** that accept floating-point data types, the values should typically range between 0.0 and 1.0, the minimum and maximum values that can be stored in the framebuffer. Unsigned-integer color components, when specified, are linearly mapped to floating-point values such that the largest representable value maps to 1.0 (full intensity), and zero maps to 0.0 (zero intensity). Signed-integer color components, when specified, are linearly mapped to floating-point values such that the most positive representable value maps to 1.0, and the most negative representable value maps to −1.0 (see Table 4-1).

Neither floating-point nor signed-integer values are clamped to the range [0,1] before updating the current color or current lighting material parameters. After lighting calculations, resulting color values outside the range [0,1] are clamped to the range [0,1] before they are interpolated or written into a color buffer. Even if lighting is disabled, the color components are clamped before rasterization.

Suffix	Data Type	Minimum Value	Min Value Maps to	Maximum Value	Max Value Maps to
b	1-byte integer	−128	−1.0	127	1.0
s	2-byte integer	−32,768	−1.0	32,767	1.0
i	4-byte integer	−2,147,483,648	−1.0	2,147,483,647	1.0
ub	unsigned 1-byte integer	0	0.0	255	1.0
us	unsigned 2-byte integer	0	0.0	65,535	1.0
ui	unsigned 4-byte integer	0	0.0	4,294,967,295	1.0

Table 4-1   Converting Color Values to Floating-Point Numbers

Specifying a Color in Color-Index Mode

In color-index mode, use the **glIndex*()** command to select a single-valued color index as the current color index.

---
void **glIndex**{sifd ub}(TYPE *c*);
void **glIndex**{sifd ub}**v**(const TYPE **c*);

Sets the current color index to *c*. The first suffix for this command indicates the data type for parameters: short, integer, float, double, or unsigned byte. The second, optional suffix is **v**, which indicates that the argument is an array of values of the given data type (the array contains only one value).

In "Clearing the Window" on page 29, you saw the specification of **glClearColor()**. For color-index mode, there is a corresponding **glClearIndex()**.

void **glClearIndex**(GLfloat *cindex*);

Sets the current clearing color in color-index mode. In a color-index mode window, a call to **glClear**(GL_COLOR_BUFFER_BIT) will use *cindex* to clear the buffer. The default clearing index is 0.0.

Note: OpenGL does not have any routines to load values into the color-lookup table. Window systems typically already have such operations. GLUT has the routine **glutSetColor()** to call the window-system specific commands.

Advanced

The current index is stored as a floating-point value. Integer values are converted directly to floating-point values, with no special mapping. Index values outside the representable range of the color-index buffer aren't clamped. However, before an index is dithered (if enabled) and written to the framebuffer, it's converted to fixed-point format. Any bits in the integer portion of the resulting fixed-point value that don't correspond to bits in the framebuffer are masked out.

Specifying a Shading Model

A line or a filled polygon primitive can be drawn with a single color (flat shading) or with many different colors (smooth shading, also called *Gouraud shading*). You specify the desired shading technique with **glShadeModel()**.

void **glShadeModel** (GLenum *mode*);

Sets the shading model. The mode parameter can be either GL_SMOOTH (the default) or GL_FLAT.

With flat shading, the color of one particular vertex of an independent primitive is duplicated across all the primitive's vertices to render that primitive. With smooth shading, the color at each vertex is treated individually. For a line primitive, the colors along the line segment are interpolated between the vertex colors. For a polygon primitive, the colors for the interior of the polygon are interpolated between the vertex colors. Example 4-1 draws a smooth-shaded triangle, as shown in Plate 11.

Example 4-1   Drawing a Smooth-Shaded Triangle: smooth.c

```
#include <GL/gl.h>
#include <GL/glut.h>

void init(void)
{
   glClearColor (0.0, 0.0, 0.0, 0.0);
   glShadeModel (GL_SMOOTH);
}

void triangle(void)
{
   glBegin (GL_TRIANGLES);
   glColor3f (1.0, 0.0, 0.0);
   glVertex2f (5.0, 5.0);
   glColor3f (0.0, 1.0, 0.0);
   glVertex2f (25.0, 5.0);
   glColor3f (0.0, 0.0, 1.0);
   glVertex2f (5.0, 25.0);
   glEnd();
}

void display(void)
{
   glClear (GL_COLOR_BUFFER_BIT);
   triangle ();
   glFlush ();
}

void reshape (int w, int h)
{
   glViewport (0, 0, (GLsizei) w, (GLsizei) h);
   glMatrixMode (GL_PROJECTION);
   glLoadIdentity ();
   if (w <= h)
      gluOrtho2D (0.0, 30.0, 0.0, 30.0*(GLfloat) h/(GLfloat) w);
   else
      gluOrtho2D (0.0, 30.0*(GLfloat) w/(GLfloat) h, 0.0, 30.0);
   glMatrixMode(GL_MODELVIEW);
}
```

```
int main(int argc, char** argv)
{
   glutInit(&argc, argv);
   glutInitDisplayMode (GLUT_SINGLE | GLUT_RGB);
   glutInitWindowSize (500, 500);
   glutInitWindowPosition (100, 100);
   glutCreateWindow (argv[0]);
   init ();
   glutDisplayFunc(display);
   glutReshapeFunc(reshape);
   glutMainLoop();
   return 0;
}
```

With smooth shading, neighboring pixels have slightly different color values. In RGBA mode, adjacent pixels with slightly different values look similar, so the color changes across a polygon appear gradual. In color-index mode, adjacent pixels may reference different locations in the color-index table, which may not have similar colors at all. Adjacent color-index entries may contain wildly different colors, so a smooth-shaded polygon in color-index mode can look psychedelic.

To avoid this problem, you have to create a color ramp of smoothly changing colors among a contiguous set of indices in the color map. Remember that loading colors into a color map is performed through your window system rather than OpenGL. If you use GLUT, you can use **glutSetColor()** to load a single index in the color map with specified red, green, and blue values. The first argument for **glutSetColor()** is the index, and the others are the red, green, and blue values. To load thirty-two contiguous color indices (from color index 16 to 47) with slightly differing shades of yellow, you might call

```
for (i = 0; i < 32; i++) {
   glutSetColor (16+i, 1.0*(i/32.0), 1.0*(i/32.0), 0.0);
}
```

Now, if you render smooth-shaded polygons that use only the colors from index 16 to 47, those polygons have gradually differing shades of yellow.

With flat shading, the color of a single vertex defines the color of an entire primitive. For a line segment, the color of the line is the current color when the second (ending) vertex is specified. For a polygon, the color used is the one that's in effect when a particular vertex is specified, as shown in Table 4-2. The table counts vertices and polygons starting from 1. OpenGL follows these rules consistently, but the best way to avoid uncertainty about how a flat-shaded primitive will be drawn is to specify only one color for the primitive.

Type of Polygon	Vertex Used to Select the Color for the ith Polygon
single polygon	1
triangle strip	i+2
triangle fan	i+2
independent triangle	3i
quad strip	2i+2
independent quad	4i

Table 4-2   How OpenGL Selects a Color for the ith Flat-Shaded Polygon

Chapter 5

Lighting

Chapter Objectives

After reading this chapter, you'll be able to do the following:

- Understand how real-world lighting conditions are approximated by OpenGL

- Render illuminated objects by defining the desired light sources and lighting model

- Define the material properties of the objects being illuminated

- Manipulate the matrix stack to control the position of light sources

As you saw in Chapter 4, OpenGL computes the color of each pixel in a final, displayed scene that's held in the framebuffer. Part of this computation depends on what lighting is used in the scene and on how objects in the scene reflect or absorb that light. As an example of this, recall that the ocean has a different color on a bright, sunny day than it does on a gray, cloudy day. The presence of sunlight or clouds determines whether you see the ocean as bright turquoise or murky gray-green. In fact, most objects don't even look three-dimensional until they're lit. Figure 5-1 shows two versions of the exact same scene (a single sphere), one with lighting and one without.

Figure 5-1   A Lit and an Unlit Sphere

As you can see, an unlit sphere looks no different from a two-dimensional disk. This demonstrates how critical the interaction between objects and light is in creating a three-dimensional scene.

With OpenGL, you can manipulate the lighting and objects in a scene to create many different kinds of effects. This chapter begins with a primer on hidden-surface removal. Then it explains how to control the lighting in a scene, discusses the OpenGL conceptual model of lighting, and describes in detail how to set the numerous illumination parameters to achieve certain effects. Toward the end of the chapter, the mathematical computations that determine how lighting affects color are presented.

This chapter contains the following major sections:

- "A Hidden-Surface Removal Survival Kit" on page 171 describes the basics of removing hidden surfaces from view.

- "Real-World and OpenGL Lighting" on page 173 explains in general terms how light behaves in the world and how OpenGL models this behavior.

- "A Simple Example: Rendering a Lit Sphere" on page 176 introduces the OpenGL lighting facility by presenting a short program that renders a lit sphere.

- "Creating Light Sources" on page 180 explains how to define and position light sources.

- "Selecting a Lighting Model" on page 192 discusses the elements of a lighting model and how to specify them.

- "Defining Material Properties" on page 195 explains how to describe the properties of objects so that they interact with light in a desired way.

- "The Mathematics of Lighting" on page 205 presents the mathematical calculations used by OpenGL to determine the effect of lights in a scene.

- "Lighting in Color-Index Mode" on page 209 discusses the differences between using RGBA mode and color-index mode for lighting.

A Hidden-Surface Removal Survival Kit

With this section, you begin to draw shaded, three-dimensional objects, in earnest. With shaded polygons, it becomes very important to draw the objects that are closer to our viewing position and to eliminate objects obscured by others nearer to the eye.

When you draw a scene composed of three-dimensional objects, some of them might obscure all or parts of others. Changing your viewpoint can change the obscuring relationship. For example, if you view the scene from the opposite direction, any object that was previously in front of another is now behind it. To draw a realistic scene, these obscuring relationships must be maintained. Suppose your code works like this:

```
while (1) {
    get_viewing_point_from_mouse_position();
    glClear(GL_COLOR_BUFFER_BIT);
    draw_3d_object_A();
    draw_3d_object_B();
}
```

For some mouse positions, object A might obscure object B. For others, the reverse may hold. If nothing special is done, the preceding code always draws object B second (and thus on top of object A) no matter what viewing position is selected. In a worst case scenario, if objects A and B intersect one another so that part of object A obscures object B and part of B obscures A, changing the drawing order does not provide a solution.

The elimination of parts of solid objects that are obscured by others is called *hidden-surface removal*. (Hidden-line removal, which does the same job for objects represented as wireframe skeletons, is a bit trickier and isn't discussed here. See "Hidden-Line Removal" on page 521 for details.) The easiest way to achieve hidden-surface removal is to use the depth buffer (sometimes called a z-buffer). (Also see Chapter 10.)

A depth buffer works by associating a depth, or distance, from the view plane (usually the near clipping plane), with each pixel on the window. Initially, the depth values for all pixels are set to the largest possible distance (usually the far clipping plane) using the **glClear()** command with GL_DEPTH_BUFFER_BIT. Then the objects in the scene are drawn in any order.

Graphical calculations in hardware or software convert each surface that's drawn to a set of pixels on the window where the surface will appear if it isn't obscured by something else. In addition, the distance from the view plane is computed. With depth buffering enabled, before each pixel is drawn a comparison is done with the depth value already stored at the pixel. If the new pixel is closer than (in front of) what's there, the new pixel's color and depth values replace those that are currently written into the pixel. If the new pixel's depth is greater than what's currently there, the new pixel is obscured, and the color and depth information for the incoming pixel is discarded.

To use depth buffering, you need to enable depth buffering. This has to be done only once. Before drawing, each time you draw the scene, you need to clear the depth buffer and then draw the objects in the scene in any order.

To convert the preceding code example so that it performs hidden-surface removal, modify it to the following:

```
glutInitDisplayMode (GLUT_DEPTH | .... );
glEnable(GL_DEPTH_TEST);
...
while (1) {
    glClear(GL_COLOR_BUFFER_BIT | GL_DEPTH_BUFFER_BIT);
    get_viewing_point_from_mouse_position();
    draw_3d_object_A();
    draw_3d_object_B();
}
```

The argument to **glClear()** clears both the depth and color buffers.

Depth-buffer testing can affect the performance of your application. Since information is discarded rather than used for drawing, hidden-surface removal can increase your performance slightly. However, the implementation of your depth buffer probably has the greatest effect on performance. A "software" depth buffer (implemented with processor memory) may be much slower than one implemented with a specialized hardware depth buffer.

Real-World and OpenGL Lighting

When you look at a physical surface, your eye's perception of the color depends on the distribution of photon energies that arrive and trigger your cone cells. (See "Color Perception" on page 152.) Those photons come from a light source or combination of sources, some of which are absorbed and some of which are reflected by the surface. In addition, different surfaces may have very different properties—some are shiny and preferentially reflect light in certain directions, while others scatter incoming light equally in all directions. Most surfaces are somewhere in between.

OpenGL approximates light and lighting as if light can be broken into red, green, and blue components. Thus, the color of light sources is characterized by the amount of red, green, and blue light they emit, and the material of surfaces is characterized by the percentage of the incoming red, green, and blue components that is reflected in various directions. The OpenGL lighting equations are just an approximation but one that works fairly well and can be computed relatively quickly. If you desire a more accurate (or just different) lighting model, you have to do your own calculations in software. Such software can be enormously complex, as a few hours of reading any optics textbook should convince you.

In the OpenGL lighting model, the light in a scene comes from several light sources that can be individually turned on and off. Some light comes from a particular direction or position, and some light is generally scattered about the scene. For example, when you turn on a light bulb in a room, most of the light comes from the bulb, but some light comes after bouncing off one, two, three, or more walls. This bounced light (called *ambient*) is assumed to be so scattered that there is no way to tell its original direction, but it disappears if a particular light source is turned off.

Finally, there might be a general ambient light in the scene that comes from no particular source, as if it had been scattered so many times that its original source is impossible to determine.

In the OpenGL model, the light sources have an effect only when there are surfaces that absorb and reflect light. Each surface is assumed to be composed of a material with various properties. A material might emit its own light (like headlights on an automobile), it might scatter some incoming light in all directions, and it might reflect some portion of the incoming light in a preferential direction like a mirror or other shiny surface.

The OpenGL lighting model considers the lighting to be divided into four independent components: emissive, ambient, diffuse, and specular. All four components are computed independently and then added together.

Ambient, Diffuse, and Specular Light

Ambient illumination is light that's been scattered so much by the environment that its direction is impossible to determine—it seems to come from all directions. Backlighting in a room has a large ambient component, since most of the light that reaches your eye has first bounced off many surfaces. A spotlight outdoors has a tiny ambient component; most of the light travels in the same direction, and since you're outdoors, very little of the light reaches your eye after bouncing off other objects. When ambient light strikes a surface, it's scattered equally in all directions.

The *diffuse* component is the light that comes from one direction, so it's brighter if it comes squarely down on a surface than if it barely glances off the surface. Once it hits a surface, however, it's scattered equally in all directions, so it appears equally bright, no matter where the eye is located. Any light coming from a particular position or direction probably has a diffuse component.

Finally, *specular* light comes from a particular direction, and it tends to bounce off the surface in a preferred direction. A well-collimated laser beam bouncing off a high-quality mirror produces almost 100 percent specular reflection. Shiny metal or plastic has a high specular component, and chalk or carpet has almost none. You can think of specularity as shininess.

Although a light source delivers a single distribution of frequencies, the ambient, diffuse, and specular components might be different. For example, if you have a white light in a room with red walls, the scattered light tends to be red, although the light directly striking objects is white. OpenGL allows you to set the red, green, and blue values for each component of light independently.

Material Colors

The OpenGL lighting model makes the approximation that a material's color depends on the percentages of the incoming red, green, and blue light it reflects. For example, a perfectly red ball reflects all the incoming red light and absorbs all the green and blue light that strikes it. If you view such a ball in white light (composed of equal amounts of red, green, and blue light), all the red is reflected, and you see a red ball. If the ball is viewed in pure red light, it also appears to be red. If, however, the red ball is viewed in pure green light, it appears black (all the green is absorbed, and there's no incoming red, so no light is reflected).

Like lights, materials have different ambient, diffuse, and specular colors, which determine the ambient, diffuse, and specular reflectances of the material. A material's ambient reflectance is combined with the ambient component of each incoming light source, the diffuse reflectance with the light's diffuse component, and similarly for the specular reflectance and component. Ambient and diffuse reflectances define the color of the material and are typically similar if not identical. Specular reflectance is usually white or gray, so that specular highlights end up being the color of the light source's specular intensity. If you think of a white light shining on a shiny red plastic sphere, most of the sphere appears red, but the shiny highlight is white.

In addition to ambient, diffuse, and specular colors, materials have an *emissive* color, which simulates light originating from an object. In the OpenGL lighting model, the emissive color of a surface adds intensity to the object, but is unaffected by any light sources. Also, the emissive color does not introduce any additional light into the overall scene.

RGB Values for Lights and Materials

The color components specified for lights mean something different than for materials. For a light, the numbers correspond to a percentage of full intensity for each color. If the R, G, and B values for a light's color are all 1.0, the light is the brightest possible white. If the values are 0.5, the color is still white, but only at half intensity, so it appears gray. If R=G=1 and B=0 (full red and green with no blue), the light appears yellow.

For materials, the numbers correspond to the reflected proportions of those colors. So if R=1, G=0.5, and B=0 for a material, that material reflects all the incoming red light, half the incoming green, and none of the incoming blue light. In other words, if an OpenGL light has components (LR, LG, LB), and a material has corresponding components (MR, MG, MB), then, ignoring all other reflectivity effects, the light that arrives at the eye is given by (LR*MR, LG*MG, LB*MB).

Similarly, if you have two lights that send (R1, G1, B1) and (R2, G2, B2) to the eye, OpenGL adds the components, giving (R1+R2, G1+G2, B1+B2). If any of the sums are greater than 1 (corresponding to a color brighter than the equipment can display), the component is clamped to 1.

A Simple Example: Rendering a Lit Sphere

These are the steps required to add lighting to your scene.

1. Define normal vectors for each vertex of all the objects. These normals determine the orientation of the object relative to the light sources.

2. Create, select, and position one or more light sources.

3. Create and select a *lighting model*, which defines the level of global ambient light and the effective location of the viewpoint (for the purposes of lighting calculations).

4. Define material properties for the objects in the scene.

Example 5-1 accomplishes these tasks. It displays a sphere illuminated by a single light source, as shown earlier in Figure 5-1.

Example 5-1   Drawing a Lit Sphere: light.c

```
#include <GL/gl.h>
#include <GL/glu.h>
#include <GL/glut.h>

void init(void)
{
    GLfloat mat_specular[] = { 1.0, 1.0, 1.0, 1.0 };
    GLfloat mat_shininess[] = { 50.0 };
    GLfloat light_position[] = { 1.0, 1.0, 1.0, 0.0 };
```

```
   glClearColor (0.0, 0.0, 0.0, 0.0);
   glShadeModel (GL_SMOOTH);

   glMaterialfv(GL_FRONT, GL_SPECULAR, mat_specular);
   glMaterialfv(GL_FRONT, GL_SHININESS, mat_shininess);
   glLightfv(GL_LIGHT0, GL_POSITION, light_position);

   glEnable(GL_LIGHTING);
   glEnable(GL_LIGHT0);
   glEnable(GL_DEPTH_TEST);
}

void display(void)
{
   glClear (GL_COLOR_BUFFER_BIT | GL_DEPTH_BUFFER_BIT);
   glutSolidSphere (1.0, 20, 16);
   glFlush ();
}

void reshape (int w, int h)
{
   glViewport (0, 0, (GLsizei) w, (GLsizei) h);
   glMatrixMode (GL_PROJECTION);
   glLoadIdentity();
   if (w <= h)
      glOrtho (-1.5, 1.5, -1.5*(GLfloat)h/(GLfloat)w,
         1.5*(GLfloat)h/(GLfloat)w, -10.0, 10.0);
   else
      glOrtho (-1.5*(GLfloat)w/(GLfloat)h,
         1.5*(GLfloat)w/(GLfloat)h, -1.5, 1.5, -10.0, 10.0);
   glMatrixMode(GL_MODELVIEW);
   glLoadIdentity();
}

int main(int argc, char** argv)
{
   glutInit(&argc, argv);
   glutInitDisplayMode (GLUT_SINGLE | GLUT_RGB | GLUT_DEPTH);
   glutInitWindowSize (500, 500);
   glutInitWindowPosition (100, 100);
   glutCreateWindow (argv[0]);
   init ();
   glutDisplayFunc(display);
   glutReshapeFunc(reshape);
   glutMainLoop();
   return 0;
}
```

The lighting-related calls are in the **init**() command; they're discussed briefly in the following paragraphs and in more detail later in the chapter. One thing to note about Example 5-1 is that it uses RGBA color mode, not color-index mode. The OpenGL lighting calculation is different for the two modes, and in fact the lighting capabilities are more limited in color-index mode. Thus, RGBA is the preferred mode when doing lighting, and all the examples in this chapter use it. (See "Lighting in Color-Index Mode" on page 209 for more information about lighting in color-index mode.)

Define Normal Vectors for Each Vertex of Every Object

An object's normals determine its orientation relative to the light sources. For each vertex, OpenGL uses the assigned normal to determine how much light that particular vertex receives from each light source. In this example, the normals for the sphere are defined as part of the **glutSolidSphere**() routine. (See "Normal Vectors" on page 63 for more details on how to define normals.)

Create, Position, and Enable One or More Light Sources

Example 5-1 uses only one, white light source; its location is specified by the **glLightfv**() call. This example uses the default color for light zero (GL_LIGHT0), which is white; if you want a differently colored light, use **glLight*()** to indicate this. You can include at least eight different light sources in your scene of various colors; the default color of these other lights is black. (The particular implementation of OpenGL you're using might allow more than eight.) You can also locate the lights wherever you desire—you can position them near the scene, as a desk lamp would be, or an infinite distance away, like the sun. In addition, you can control whether a light produces a narrow, focused beam or a wider beam. Remember that each light source adds significantly to the calculations needed to render the scene, so performance is affected by the number of lights in the scene. (See "Creating Light Sources" on page 180 for more information about how to create lights with the desired characteristics.)

After you've defined the characteristics of the lights you want, you have to turn them on with the **glEnable**() command. You also need to call **glEnable**() with GL_LIGHTING as a parameter to prepare OpenGL to perform lighting calculations. (See "Enabling Lighting" on page 195 for more information.)

Select a Lighting Model

As you might expect, the **glLightModel*()** command describes the parameters of a lighting model. In Example 5-1, the only element of the lighting model that's defined explicitly is the global ambient light. The lighting model also defines whether the viewer of the scene should be considered to be an infinite distance away or local to the scene, and whether lighting calculations should be performed differently for the front and back surfaces of objects in the scene. Example 5-1 uses the default settings for these two aspects of the model—an infinite viewer and one-sided lighting. Using a local viewer adds significantly to the complexity of the calculations that must be performed, because OpenGL must calculate the angle between the viewpoint and each object. With an infinite viewer, however, the angle is ignored, and the results are slightly less realistic. Further, since in this example, the back surface of the sphere is never seen (it's the inside of the sphere), one-sided lighting is sufficient. (See "Selecting a Lighting Model" on page 192 for a more detailed description of the elements of an OpenGL lighting model.)

Define Material Properties for the Objects in the Scene

An object's material properties determine how it reflects light and therefore what material it seems to be made of. Because the interaction between an object's material surface and incident light is complex, specifying material properties so that an object has a certain desired appearance is an art. You can specify a material's ambient, diffuse, and specular colors and how shiny it is. In this example, only these last two material properties—the specular material color and shininess—are explicitly specified (with the **glMaterialfv()** calls). (See "Defining Material Properties" on page 195 for a description and examples of all the material-property parameters.)

Some Important Notes

As you write your own lighting program, remember that you can use the default values for some lighting parameters; others need to be changed. Also, don't forget to enable whatever lights you define and to enable lighting calculations. Finally, remember that you might be able to use display lists to maximize efficiency as you change lighting conditions. (See "Display-List Design Philosophy" on page 257.)

Creating Light Sources

Light sources have a number of properties, such as color, position, and direction. The following sections explain how to control these properties and what the resulting light looks like. The command used to specify all properties of lights is **glLight*()**; it takes three arguments: to identify the light whose property is being specified, the property, and the desired value for that property.

---

void **glLight**{if}(GLenum *light*, GLenum *pname*, TYPE *param*);
void **glLight**{if}**v**(GLenum *light*, GLenum *pname*, TYPE **param*);

Creates the light specified by *light*, which can be GL_LIGHT0, GL_LIGHT1, ... , or GL_LIGHT7. The characteristic of the light being set is defined by *pname*, which specifies a named parameter (see Table 5-1). *param* indicates the values to which the *pname* characteristic is set; it's a pointer to a group of values if the vector version is used, or the value itself if the nonvector version is used. The nonvector version can be used to set only single-valued light characteristics.

Parameter Name	Default Value	Meaning
GL_AMBIENT	(0.0, 0.0, 0.0, 1.0)	ambient RGBA intensity of light
GL_DIFFUSE	(1.0, 1.0, 1.0, 1.0)	diffuse RGBA intensity of light
GL_SPECULAR	(1.0, 1.0, 1.0, 1.0)	specular RGBA intensity of light
GL_POSITION	(0.0, 0.0, 1.0, 0.0)	(x, y, z, w) position of light
GL_SPOT_DIRECTION	(0.0, 0.0, −1.0)	(x, y, z) direction of spotlight
GL_SPOT_EXPONENT	0.0	spotlight exponent
GL_SPOT_CUTOFF	180.0	spotlight cutoff angle
GL_CONSTANT_ATTENUATION	1.0	constant attenuation factor
GL_LINEAR_ATTENUATION	0.0	linear attenuation factor

Table 5-1   Default Values for pname Parameter of glLight*()

Parameter Name	Default Value	Meaning
GL_QUADRATIC_ATTENUATION	0.0	quadratic attenuation factor

Table 5-1   Default Values for pname Parameter of glLight*() (continued)

Note: The default values listed for GL_DIFFUSE and GL_SPECULAR in Table 5-1 apply only to GL_LIGHT0. For other lights, the default value is (0.0, 0.0, 0.0, 1.0) for both GL_DIFFUSE and GL_SPECULAR.

Example 5-2 shows how to use **glLight*()**:

Example 5-2   Defining Colors and Position for a Light Source

```
GLfloat light_ambient[]  = { 0.0, 0.0, 0.0, 1.0 };
GLfloat light_diffuse[]  = { 1.0, 1.0, 1.0, 1.0 };
GLfloat light_specular[] = { 1.0, 1.0, 1.0, 1.0 };
GLfloat light_position[] = { 1.0, 1.0, 1.0, 0.0 };

glLightfv(GL_LIGHT0, GL_AMBIENT, light_ambient);
glLightfv(GL_LIGHT0, GL_DIFFUSE, light_diffuse);
glLightfv(GL_LIGHT0, GL_SPECULAR, light_specular);
glLightfv(GL_LIGHT0, GL_POSITION, light_position);
```

As you can see, arrays are defined for the parameter values, and **glLightfv()** is called repeatedly to set the various parameters. In this example, the first three calls to **glLightfv()** are superfluous, since they're being used to specify the default values for the GL_AMBIENT, GL_DIFFUSE, and GL_SPECULAR parameters.

Note: Remember to turn on each light with **glEnable()**. (See "Enabling Lighting" on page 195 for more information about how to do this.)

All the parameters for **glLight*()** and their possible values are explained in the following sections. These parameters interact with those that define the overall lighting model for a particular scene and an object's material properties. (See "Selecting a Lighting Model" on page 192 and "Defining Material Properties" on page 195 for more information about these two topics. "The Mathematics of Lighting" on page 205 explains how all these parameters interact mathematically.)

Color

OpenGL allows you to associate three different color-related parameters—GL_AMBIENT, GL_DIFFUSE, and GL_SPECULAR—with any particular light. The GL_AMBIENT parameter refers to the RGBA intensity of the ambient light that a particular light source adds to the scene. As you can see in Table 5-1, by default there is no ambient light since GL_AMBIENT is (0.0, 0.0, 0.0, 1.0). This value was used in Example 5-1. If this program had specified blue ambient light as

```
GLfloat light_ambient[] = { 0.0, 0.0, 1.0, 1.0};
glLightfv(GL_LIGHT0, GL_AMBIENT, light_ambient);
```

the result would have been as shown in the left side of Plate 13a.

The GL_DIFFUSE parameter probably most closely correlates with what you naturally think of as "the color of a light." It defines the RGBA color of the diffuse light that a particular light source adds to a scene. By default, GL_DIFFUSE is (1.0, 1.0, 1.0, 1.0) for GL_LIGHT0, which produces a bright, white light as shown in the left side of Plate 13a. The default value for any other light (GL_LIGHT1, ... , GL_LIGHT7) is (0.0, 0.0, 0.0, 0.0).

The GL_SPECULAR parameter affects the color of the specular highlight on an object. Typically, a real-world object such as a glass bottle has a specular highlight that's the color of the light shining on it (which is often white). Therefore, if you want to create a realistic effect, set the GL_SPECULAR parameter to the same value as the GL_DIFFUSE parameter. By default, GL_SPECULAR is (1.0, 1.0, 1.0, 1.0) for GL_LIGHT0 and (0.0, 0.0, 0.0, 0.0) for any other light.

Note: The alpha component of these colors is not used until blending is enabled. (See Chapter 6.) Until then, the alpha value can be safely ignored.

Position and Attenuation

As previously mentioned, you can choose whether to have a light source that's treated as though it's located infinitely far away from the scene or one that's nearer to the scene. The first type is referred to as a *directional* light source; the effect of an infinite location is that the rays of light can be considered parallel by the time they reach an object. An example of a real-world directional light source is the sun. The second type is called a *positional* light source, since its exact position within the scene determines the effect it has on a scene and, specifically, the direction from which the light rays come. A desk lamp is an example of a positional light source. You can see the difference between directional and positional lights in Plate 12b. The light used in Example 5-1 is a directional one:

```
GLfloat light_position[] = { 1.0, 1.0, 1.0, 0.0 };
glLightfv(GL_LIGHT0, GL_POSITION, light_position);
```

As shown, you supply a vector of four values (x, y, z, w) for the GL_POSITION parameter. If the last value, w, is zero, the corresponding light source is a directional one, and the (x, y, z) values describe its direction. This direction is transformed by the modelview matrix. By default, GL_POSITION is (0, 0, 1, 0), which defines a directional light that points along the negative z-axis. (Note that nothing prevents you from creating a directional light with the direction of (0, 0, 0), but such a light won't help you much.)

If the w value is nonzero, the light is positional, and the (x, y, z) values specify the location of the light in homogeneous object coordinates. (See Appendix F.) This location is transformed by the modelview matrix and stored in eye coordinates. (See "Controlling a Light's Position and Direction" on page 187 for more information about how to control the transformation of the light's location.) Also, by default, a positional light radiates in all directions, but you can restrict it to producing a cone of illumination by defining the light as a spotlight. (See "Spotlights" on page 184 for an explanation of how to define a light as a spotlight.)

Note: Remember that the colors across the face of a smooth-shaded polygon are determined by the colors calculated for the vertices. Because of this, you probably want to avoid using large polygons with local lights. If you locate the light near the middle of the polygon, the vertices might be too far away to receive much light, and the whole polygon will look darker than you intended. To avoid this problem, break up the large polygon into smaller ones.

For real-world lights, the intensity of light decreases as distance from the light increases. Since a directional light is infinitely far away, it doesn't make sense to attenuate its intensity over distance, so attenuation is disabled for a directional light. However, you might want to attenuate the light from a positional light. OpenGL attenuates a light source by multiplying the contribution of that source by an attenuation factor:

$$\text{attenuation factor} = \frac{1}{k_c + k_l d + k_q d^2}$$

where

d = distance between the light's position and the vertex

k_c = GL_CONSTANT_ATTENUATION

k_l = GL_LINEAR_ATTENUATION

k_q = GL_QUADRATIC_ATTENUATION

By default, k_c is 1.0 and both k_l and k_q are zero, but you can give these parameters different values:

```
glLightf(GL_LIGHT0, GL_CONSTANT_ATTENUATION, 2.0);
glLightf(GL_LIGHT0, GL_LINEAR_ATTENUATION, 1.0);
glLightf(GL_LIGHT0, GL_QUADRATIC_ATTENUATION, 0.5);
```

Note that the ambient, diffuse, and specular contributions are all attenuated. Only the emission and global ambient values aren't attenuated. Also note that since attenuation requires an additional division (and possibly more math) for each calculated color, using attenuated lights may slow down application performance.

Spotlights

As previously mentioned, you can have a positional light source act as a spotlight—that is, by restricting the shape of the light it emits to a cone. To create a spotlight, you need to determine the spread of the cone of light you desire. (Remember that since spotlights are positional lights, you also have to locate them where you want them. Again, note that nothing prevents you from creating a directional spotlight, but it won't give you the result you want.) To specify the angle between the axis of the cone and a ray along the edge of the cone, use the GL_SPOT_CUTOFF parameter. The angle of the cone at the apex is then twice this value, as shown in Figure 5-2.

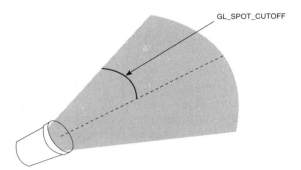

GL_SPOT_CUTOFF

Figure 5-2 GL_SPOT_CUTOFF Parameter

Note that no light is emitted beyond the edges of the cone. By default, the spotlight feature is disabled because the GL_SPOT_CUTOFF parameter is 180.0. This value means that light is emitted in all directions (the angle at the cone's apex is 360 degrees, so it isn't a cone at all). The value for GL_SPOT_CUTOFF is restricted to being within the range [0.0,90.0] (unless it has the special value 180.0). The following line sets the cutoff parameter to 45 degrees:

```
glLightf(GL_LIGHT0, GL_SPOT_CUTOFF, 45.0);
```

You also need to specify a spotlight's direction, which determines the axis of the cone of light:

```
GLfloat spot_direction[] = { -1.0, -1.0, 0.0 };
glLightfv(GL_LIGHT0, GL_SPOT_DIRECTION, spot_direction);
```

The direction is specified in object coordinates. By default, the direction is (0.0, 0.0, −1.0), so if you don't explicitly set the value of GL_SPOT_DIRECTION, the light points down the negative z-axis. Also, keep in mind that a spotlight's direction is transformed by the modelview matrix just as though it were a normal vector, and the result is stored in eye coordinates. (See "Controlling a Light's Position and Direction" on page 187 for more information about such transformations.)

In addition to the spotlight's cutoff angle and direction, there are two ways you can control the intensity distribution of the light within the cone. First, you can set the attenuation factor described earlier, which is multiplied by the light's intensity. You can also set the GL_SPOT_EXPONENT parameter, which by default is zero, to control how concentrated the light is. The light's intensity is highest in the center of the cone. It's attenuated toward the edges of the cone by the cosine of the angle between the direction of the light and the direction from the light to the vertex being lit, raised to the power of the spot exponent. Thus, higher spot exponents result in a more focused light source. (See "The Mathematics of Lighting" on page 205 for more details on the equations used to calculate light intensity.)

Multiple Lights

As mentioned, you can have at least eight lights in your scene (possibly more, depending on your OpenGL implementation). Since OpenGL needs to perform calculations to determine how much light each vertex receives from each light source, increasing the number of lights adversely affects performance. The constants used to refer to the eight lights are GL_LIGHT0, GL_LIGHT1, GL_LIGHT2, GL_LIGHT3, and so on. In the preceding discussions, parameters related to GL_LIGHT0 were set. If you want an additional light, you need to specify its parameters; also, remember that the default values are different for these other lights than they are for GL_LIGHT0, as explained in Table 5-1. Example 5-3 defines a white attenuated spotlight.

Example 5-3   Second Light Source

```
GLfloat light1_ambient[] = { 0.2, 0.2, 0.2, 1.0 };
GLfloat light1_diffuse[] = { 1.0, 1.0, 1.0, 1.0 };
GLfloat light1_specular[] = { 1.0, 1.0, 1.0, 1.0 };
GLfloat light1_position[] = { -2.0, 2.0, 1.0, 1.0 };
GLfloat spot_direction[] = { -1.0, -1.0, 0.0 };

glLightfv(GL_LIGHT1, GL_AMBIENT, light1_ambient);
glLightfv(GL_LIGHT1, GL_DIFFUSE, light1_diffuse);
glLightfv(GL_LIGHT1, GL_SPECULAR, light1_specular);
glLightfv(GL_LIGHT1, GL_POSITION, light1_position);
glLightf(GL_LIGHT1, GL_CONSTANT_ATTENUATION, 1.5);
glLightf(GL_LIGHT1, GL_LINEAR_ATTENUATION, 0.5);
glLightf(GL_LIGHT1, GL_QUADRATIC_ATTENUATION, 0.2);

glLightf(GL_LIGHT1, GL_SPOT_CUTOFF, 45.0);
glLightfv(GL_LIGHT1, GL_SPOT_DIRECTION, spot_direction);
glLightf(GL_LIGHT1, GL_SPOT_EXPONENT, 2.0);

glEnable(GL_LIGHT1);
```

If these lines were added to Example 5-1, the sphere would be lit with two lights, one directional and one spotlight.

Try This

Modify Example 5-1 in the following manner:

- Change the first light to be a positional colored light rather than a directional white one.

- Add an additional colored spotlight. Hint: Use some of the code shown in the preceding section.

- Measure how these two changes affect performance.

Controlling a Light's Position and Direction

OpenGL treats the position and direction of a light source just as it treats the position of a geometric primitive. In other words, a light source is subject to the same matrix transformations as a primitive. More specifically, when **glLight*()** is called to specify the position or the direction of a light source, the position or direction is transformed by the current modelview matrix and stored in eye coordinates. This means you can manipulate a light source's position or direction by changing the contents of the modelview matrix. (The projection matrix has no effect on a light's position or direction.) This section explains how to achieve the following three different effects by changing the point in the program at which the light position is set, relative to modeling or viewing transformations:

- A light position that remains fixed

- A light that moves around a stationary object

- A light that moves along with the viewpoint

Keeping the Light Stationary

In the simplest example, as in Example 5-1, the light position remains fixed. To achieve this effect, you need to set the light position after whatever viewing and/or modeling transformation you use. In Example 5-4, the relevant code from the **init()** and **reshape()** routines might look like this.

Example 5-4   Stationary Light Source

```
glViewport (0, 0, (GLsizei) w, (GLsizei) h);
glMatrixMode (GL_PROJECTION);
glLoadIdentity();
```

```
if (w <= h)
    glOrtho (-1.5, 1.5, -1.5*h/w, 1.5*h/w, -10.0, 10.0);
else
    glOrtho (-1.5*w/h, 1.5*w/h, -1.5, 1.5, -10.0, 10.0);
glMatrixMode (GL_MODELVIEW);
glLoadIdentity();

/* later in init() */
GLfloat light_position[] = { 1.0, 1.0, 1.0, 1.0 };
glLightfv(GL_LIGHT0, GL_POSITION, position);
```

As you can see, the viewport and projection matrices are established first. Then, the identity matrix is loaded as the modelview matrix, after which the light position is set. Since the identity matrix is used, the originally specified light position (1.0, 1.0, 1.0) isn't changed by being multiplied by the modelview matrix. Then, since neither the light position nor the modelview matrix is modified after this point, the direction of the light remains (1.0, 1.0, 1.0).

Independently Moving the Light

Now suppose you want to rotate or translate the light position so that the light moves relative to a stationary object. One way to do this is to set the light position after the modeling transformation, which is itself changed specifically to modify the light position. You can begin with the same series of calls in **init()** early in the program. Then you need to perform the desired modeling transformation (on the modelview stack) and reset the light position, probably in **display()**. Example 5-5 shows what **display()** might be.

Example 5-5   Independently Moving Light Source

```
static GLdouble spin;

void display(void)
{
    GLfloat light_position[] = { 0.0, 0.0, 1.5, 1.0 };
    glClear(GL_COLOR_BUFFER_BIT | GL_DEPTH_BUFFER_BIT);

    glPushMatrix();
        gluLookAt (0.0, 0.0, 5.0, 0.0, 0.0, 0.0, 0.0, 1.0, 0.0);
        glPushMatrix();
            glRotated(spin, 1.0, 0.0, 0.0);
            glLightfv(GL_LIGHT0, GL_POSITION, light_position);
        glPopMatrix();
        glutSolidTorus (0.275, 0.85, 8, 15);
```

```
      glPopMatrix();
      glFlush();
}
```

spin is a global variable and is probably controlled by an input device.
display() causes the scene to be redrawn with the light rotated *spin* degrees
around a stationary torus. Note the two pairs of **glPushMatrix()** and
glPopMatrix() calls, which are used to isolate the viewing and modeling
transformations, all of which occur on the modelview stack. Since in
Example 5-5 the viewpoint remains constant, the current matrix is pushed
down the stack and then the desired viewing transformation is loaded with
gluLookAt(). The matrix stack is pushed again before the modeling
transformation **glRotated()** is specified. Then the light position is set in the
new, rotated coordinate system so that the light itself appears to be rotated
from its previous position. (Remember that the light position is stored in
eye coordinates, which are obtained after transformation by the modelview
matrix.) After the rotated matrix is popped off the stack, the torus is drawn.

Example 5-6 is a program that rotates a light source around an object. When
the left mouse button is pressed, the light position rotates an additional 30
degrees. A small, unlit, wireframe cube is drawn to represent the position of
the light in the scene.

Example 5-6   Moving a Light with Modeling Transformations: movelight.c

```
#include <GL/gl.h>
#include <GL/glu.h>
#include "glut.h"

static int spin = 0;

void init(void)
{
   glClearColor (0.0, 0.0, 0.0, 0.0);
   glShadeModel (GL_SMOOTH);
   glEnable(GL_LIGHTING);
   glEnable(GL_LIGHT0);
   glEnable(GL_DEPTH_TEST);
}

/*  Here is where the light position is reset after the modeling
 *  transformation (glRotated) is called.  This places the
 *  light at a new position in world coordinates.  The cube
 *  represents the position of the light.
 */
```

```c
void display(void)
{
   GLfloat position[] = { 0.0, 0.0, 1.5, 1.0 };

   glClear (GL_COLOR_BUFFER_BIT | GL_DEPTH_BUFFER_BIT);
   glPushMatrix ();
   glTranslatef (0.0, 0.0, -5.0);

   glPushMatrix ();
   glRotated ((GLdouble) spin, 1.0, 0.0, 0.0);
   glLightfv (GL_LIGHT0, GL_POSITION, position);

   glTranslated (0.0, 0.0, 1.5);
   glDisable (GL_LIGHTING);
   glColor3f (0.0, 1.0, 1.0);
   glutWireCube (0.1);
   glEnable (GL_LIGHTING);
   glPopMatrix ();

   glutSolidTorus (0.275, 0.85, 8, 15);
   glPopMatrix ();
   glFlush ();
}

void reshape (int w, int h)
{
   glViewport (0, 0, (GLsizei) w, (GLsizei) h);
   glMatrixMode (GL_PROJECTION);
   glLoadIdentity();
   gluPerspective(40.0, (GLfloat) w/(GLfloat) h, 1.0, 20.0);
   glMatrixMode(GL_MODELVIEW);
   glLoadIdentity();
}

void mouse(int button, int state, int x, int y)
{
   switch (button) {
      case GLUT_LEFT_BUTTON:
         if (state == GLUT_DOWN) {
            spin = (spin + 30) % 360;
            glutPostRedisplay();
         }
         break;
      default:
         break;
   }
}
```

```
int main(int argc, char** argv)
{
   glutInit(&argc, argv);
   glutInitDisplayMode (GLUT_SINGLE | GLUT_RGB | GLUT_DEPTH);
   glutInitWindowSize (500, 500);
   glutInitWindowPosition (100, 100);
   glutCreateWindow (argv[0]);
   init ();
   glutDisplayFunc(display);
   glutReshapeFunc(reshape);
   glutMouseFunc(mouse);
   glutMainLoop();
   return 0;
}
```

Moving the Light Source Together with Your Viewpoint

To create a light that moves along with the viewpoint, you need to set the light position before the viewing transformation. Then the viewing transformation affects both the light and the viewpoint in the same way. Remember that the light position is stored in eye coordinates, and this is one of the few times when eye coordinates are critical. In Example 5-7, the light position is defined in **init**(), which stores the light position at (0, 0, 0) in eye coordinates. In other words, the light is shining from the lens of the camera.

Example 5-7   Light Source That Moves with the Viewpoint

```
GLfloat light_position() = { 0.0, 0.0, 0.0, 1.0 };

glViewport(0, 0, (GLint) w, (GLint) h);
glMatrixMode(GL_PROJECTION);
glLoadIdentity();
gluPerspective(40.0, (GLfloat) w/(GLfloat) h, 1.0, 100.0);
glMatrixMode(GL_MODELVIEW);
glLoadIdentity();
glLightfv(GL_LIGHT0, GL_POSITION, light_position);
```

If the viewpoint is now moved, the light will move along with it, maintaining (0, 0, 0) distance, relative to the eye. In the continuation of Example 5-7, which follows next, the global variables (*ex*, *ey*, *ez*) and (*upx*, *upy*, *upz*) control the position of the viewpoint and up vector. The **display**() routine that's called from the event loop to redraw the scene might be this:

```
static GLdouble ex, ey, ez, upx, upy, upz;

void display(void)
{
    glClear(GL_COLOR_BUFFER_MASK | GL_DEPTH_BUFFER_MASK);
    glPushMatrix();
        gluLookAt (ex, ey, ez, 0.0, 0.0, 0.0, upx, upy, upz);
        glutSolidTorus (0.275, 0.85, 8, 15);
    glPopMatrix();
    glFlush();
}
```

When the lit torus is redrawn, both the light position and the viewpoint are moved to the same location. As the values passed to **gluLookAt()** change and the eye moves, the object will never appear dark, because it is always being illuminated from the eye position. Even though you haven't respecified the light position, the light moves because the eye coordinate system has changed.

This method of moving the light can be very useful for simulating the illumination from a miner's hat. Another example would be carrying a candle or lantern. The light position specified by the call to **glLightfv**(GL_LIGHTi, GL_POSITION, position) would be the x, y, and z distance from the eye position to the illumination source. Then as the eye position moves, the light will remain the same relative distance away.

Try This

Modify Example 5-6 in the following manner:

- Make the light translate past the object instead of rotating around it. Hint: Use **glTranslated()** rather than the first **glRotated()** in **display()**, and choose an appropriate value to use instead of *spin*.

- Change the attenuation so that the light decreases in intensity as it's moved away from the object. Hint: Add calls to **glLight*()** to set the desired attenuation parameters.

Selecting a Lighting Model

The OpenGL notion of a lighting model has three components:

- The global ambient light intensity

- Whether the viewpoint position is local to the scene or whether it should be considered to be an infinite distance away

- Whether lighting calculations should be performed differently for both the front and back faces of objects

This section explains how to specify a lighting model. It also discusses how to enable lighting—that is, how to tell OpenGL that you want lighting calculations performed.

The command used to specify all properties of the lighting model is **glLightModel*()**. **glLightModel*()** has two arguments: the lighting model property and the desired value for that property.

---

void **glLightModel**{if}(GLenum *pname*, *TYPE param*);
void **glLightModel**{if}**v**(GLenum *pname*, *TYPE *param*);

Sets properties of the lighting model. The characteristic of the lighting model being set is defined by *pname*, which specifies a named parameter (see Table 5-1). *param* indicates the values to which the *pname* characteristic is set; it's a pointer to a group of values if the vector version is used, or the value itself if the nonvector version is used. The nonvector version can be used to set only single-valued lighting model characteristics, not for GL_LIGHT_MODEL_AMBIENT.

Parameter Name	Default Value	Meaning
GL_LIGHT_MODEL_AMBIENT	(0.2, 0.2, 0.2, 1.0)	ambient RGBA intensity of the entire scene
GL_LIGHT_MODEL_LOCAL_VIEWER	0.0 or GL_FALSE	how specular reflection angles are computed
GL_LIGHT_MODEL_TWO_SIDE	0.0 or GL_FALSE	choose between one-sided or two-sided lighting

Table 5-2   Default Values for pname Parameter of glLightModel*()

Global Ambient Light

As discussed earlier, each light source can contribute ambient light to a scene. In addition, there can be other ambient light that's not from any particular source. To specify the RGBA intensity of such global ambient light, use the GL_LIGHT_MODEL_AMBIENT parameter as follows:

```
GLfloat lmodel_ambient[] = { 0.2, 0.2, 0.2, 1.0 };
glLightModelfv(GL_LIGHT_MODEL_AMBIENT, lmodel_ambient);
```

In this example, the values used for *lmodel_ambient* are the default values for GL_LIGHT_MODEL_AMBIENT. Since these numbers yield a small amount of white ambient light, even if you don't add a specific light source to your scene, you can still see the objects in the scene. Plate 14a shows the effect of different amounts of global ambient light.

Local or Infinite Viewpoint

The location of the viewpoint affects the calculations for highlights produced by specular reflectance. More specifically, the intensity of the highlight at a particular vertex depends on the normal at that vertex, the direction from the vertex to the light source, and the direction from the vertex to the viewpoint. Keep in mind that the viewpoint isn't actually being moved by calls to lighting commands (you need to change the projection transformation, as described in "Projection Transformations" on page 120); instead, different assumptions are made for the lighting calculations as if the viewpoint were moved.

With an infinite viewpoint, the direction between it and any vertex in the scene remains constant. A local viewpoint tends to yield more realistic results, but since the direction has to be calculated for each vertex, overall performance is decreased with a local viewpoint. By default, an infinite viewpoint is assumed. Here's how to change to a local viewpoint:

```
glLightModeli(GL_LIGHT_MODEL_LOCAL_VIEWER, GL_TRUE);
```

This call places the viewpoint at (0, 0, 0) in eye coordinates. To switch back to an infinite viewpoint, pass in GL_FALSE as the argument.

Two-sided Lighting

Lighting calculations are performed for all polygons, whether they're front-facing or back-facing. Since you usually set up lighting conditions with the front-facing polygons in mind, however, the back-facing ones typically aren't correctly illuminated. In Example 5-1 where the object is a sphere, only the front faces are ever seen, since they're the ones on the outside of the sphere. So, in this case, it doesn't matter what the back-facing polygons look like. If the sphere is going to be cut away so that its inside surface will be visible, however, you might want to have the inside surface be fully lit according to the lighting conditions you've defined; you might also want to supply a different material description for the back faces. When you turn on two-sided lighting with

```
glLightModeli(GL_LIGHT_MODEL_TWO_SIDE, GL_TRUE);
```

OpenGL reverses the surface normals for back-facing polygons; typically, this means that the surface normals of visible back- and front-facing polygons face the viewer, rather than pointing away. As a result, all polygons are illuminated correctly. However, these additional operations usually make two-sided lighting perform more slowly than the default one-sided lighting.

To turn two-sided lighting off, pass in GL_FALSE as the argument in the preceding call. (See "Defining Material Properties" on page 195 for information about how to supply material properties for both faces.) You can also control which faces OpenGL considers to be front-facing with the command **glFrontFace()**. (See "Reversing and Culling Polygon Faces" on page 56 for more information.)

Enabling Lighting

With OpenGL, you need to explicitly enable (or disable) lighting. If lighting isn't enabled, the current color is simply mapped onto the current vertex, and no calculations concerning normals, light sources, the lighting model, and material properties are performed. Here's how to enable lighting:

```
glEnable(GL_LIGHTING);
```

To disable lighting, call **glDisable()** with GL_LIGHTING as the argument.

You also need to explicitly enable each light source that you define, after you've specified the parameters for that source. Example 5-1 uses only one light, GL_LIGHT0:

```
glEnable(GL_LIGHT0);
```

Defining Material Properties

You've seen how to create light sources with certain characteristics and how to define the desired lighting model. This section describes how to define the material properties of the objects in the scene: the ambient, diffuse, and specular colors, the shininess, and the color of any emitted light. (See "The

Mathematics of Lighting" on page 205 for the equations used in the lighting and material-property calculations.) Most of the material properties are conceptually similar to ones you've already used to create light sources. The mechanism for setting them is similar, except that the command used is called **glMaterial*()**.

---

void **glMaterial**{if}(GLenum *face*, GLenum *pname*, TYPE *param*);
void **glMaterial**{if}v(GLenum *face*, GLenum *pname*, TYPE **param*);

Specifies a current material property for use in lighting calculations. *face* can be GL_FRONT, GL_BACK, or GL_FRONT_AND_BACK to indicate which face of the object the material should be applied to. The particular material property being set is identified by *pname* and the desired values for that property are given by *param*, which is either a pointer to a group of values (if the vector version is used) or the actual value (if the nonvector version is used). The nonvector version works only for setting GL_SHININESS. The possible values for pname are shown in Table 5-3. Note that GL_AMBIENT_AND_DIFFUSE allows you to set both the ambient and diffuse material colors simultaneously to the same RGBA value.

Parameter Name	Default Value	Meaning
GL_AMBIENT	(0.2, 0.2, 0.2, 1.0)	ambient color of material
GL_DIFFUSE	(0.8, 0.8, 0.8, 1.0)	diffuse color of material
GL_AMBIENT_AND_DIFFUSE		ambient and diffuse color of material
GL_SPECULAR	(0.0, 0.0, 0.0, 1.0)	specular color of material
GL_SHININESS	0.0	specular exponent
GL_EMISSION	(0.0, 0.0, 0.0, 1.0)	emissive color of material
GL_COLOR_INDEXES	(0,1,1)	ambient, diffuse, and specular color indices

Table 5-3   Default Values for pname Parameter of glMaterial*()

As discussed in "Selecting a Lighting Model" on page 192, you can choose to have lighting calculations performed differently for the front- and back-facing polygons of objects. If the back faces might indeed be seen, you can supply different material properties for the front and the back surfaces by using the *face* parameter of **glMaterial*()**. See Plate 14b for an example of an object drawn with different inside and outside material properties.

To give you an idea of the possible effects you can achieve by manipulating material properties, see Plate 16. This figure shows the same object drawn with several different sets of material properties. The same light source and lighting model are used for the entire figure. The sections that follow discuss the specific properties used to draw each of these spheres.

Note that most of the material properties set with **glMaterial*()** are (R, G, B, A) colors. Regardless of what alpha values are supplied for other parameters, the alpha value at any particular vertex is the diffuse-material alpha value (that is, the alpha value given to GL_DIFFUSE with the **glMaterial*()** command, as described in the next section). (See "Blending" on page 214 for a complete discussion of alpha values.) Also, none of the RGBA material properties apply in color-index mode. (See "Lighting in Color-Index Mode" on page 209 for more information about what parameters are relevant in color-index mode.)

Diffuse and Ambient Reflection

The GL_DIFFUSE and GL_AMBIENT parameters set with **glMaterial*()** affect the color of the diffuse and ambient light reflected by an object. Diffuse reflectance plays the most important role in determining what you perceive the color of an object to be. It's affected by the color of the incident diffuse light and the angle of the incident light relative to the normal direction. (It's most intense where the incident light falls perpendicular to the surface.) The position of the viewpoint doesn't affect diffuse reflectance at all.

Ambient reflectance affects the overall color of the object. Because diffuse reflectance is brightest where an object is directly illuminated, ambient reflectance is most noticeable where an object receives no direct illumination. An object's total ambient reflectance is affected by the global ambient light and ambient light from individual light sources. Like diffuse reflectance, ambient reflectance isn't affected by the position of the viewpoint.

For real-world objects, diffuse and ambient reflectance are normally the same color. For this reason, OpenGL provides you with a convenient way of assigning the same value to both simultaneously with **glMaterial*()**:

```
GLfloat mat_amb_diff[] = { 0.1, 0.5, 0.8, 1.0 };
glMaterialfv(GL_FRONT_AND_BACK, GL_AMBIENT_AND_DIFFUSE,
          mat_amb_diff);
```

In this example, the RGBA color (0.1, 0.5, 0.8, 1.0)—a deep blue color—represents the current ambient and diffuse reflectance for both the front- and back-facing polygons.

In Plate 16, the first row of spheres has no ambient reflectance (0.0, 0.0, 0.0, 0.0), and the second row has a significant amount of it (0.7, 0.7, 0.7, 1.0).

Specular Reflection

Specular reflection from an object produces highlights. Unlike ambient and diffuse reflection, the amount of specular reflection seen by a viewer does depend on the location of the viewpoint—it's brightest along the direct angle of reflection. To see this, imagine looking at a metallic ball outdoors in the sunlight. As you move your head, the highlight created by the sunlight moves with you to some extent. However, if you move your head too much, you lose the highlight entirely.

OpenGL allows you to set the effect that the material has on reflected light (with GL_SPECULAR) and control the size and brightness of the highlight (with GL_SHININESS). You can assign a number in the range of [0.0, 128.0] to GL_SHININESS—the higher the value, the smaller and brighter (more focused) the highlight. (See "The Mathematics of Lighting" on page 205 for the details of how specular highlights are calculated.)

In Plate 16, the spheres in the first column have no specular reflection. In the second column, GL_SPECULAR and GL_SHININESS are assigned values as follows:

```
GLfloat mat_specular[] = { 1.0, 1.0, 1.0, 1.0 };
GLfloat low_shininess[] = { 5.0 };
glMaterialfv(GL_FRONT, GL_SPECULAR, mat_specular);
glMaterialfv(GL_FRONT, GL_SHININESS, low_shininess);
```

In the third column, the GL_SHININESS parameter is increased to 100.0.

Emission

By specifying an RGBA color for GL_EMISSION, you can make an object appear to be giving off light of that color. Since most real-world objects (except lights) don't emit light, you'll probably use this feature mostly to simulate lamps and other light sources in a scene. In Plate 16, the spheres in the fourth column have a reddish, grey value for GL_EMISSION:

```
GLfloat mat_emission[] = {0.3, 0.2, 0.2, 0.0};
glMaterialfv(GL_FRONT, GL_EMISSION, mat_emission);
```

Notice that the spheres appear to be slightly glowing; however, they're not actually acting as light sources. You would need to create a light source and position it at the same location as the sphere to create that effect.

Changing Material Properties

Example 5-1 uses the same material properties for all vertices of the only object in the scene (the sphere). In other situations, you might want to assign different material properties for different vertices on the same object. More likely, you have more than one object in the scene, and each object has different material properties. For example, the code that produced Plate 16 has to draw twelve different objects (all spheres), each with different material properties. Example 5-8 shows a portion of the code in **display()**.

Example 5-8   Different Material Properties: material.c

```
   GLfloat no_mat[] = { 0.0, 0.0, 0.0, 1.0 };
   GLfloat mat_ambient[] = { 0.7, 0.7, 0.7, 1.0 };
   GLfloat mat_ambient_color[] = { 0.8, 0.8, 0.2, 1.0 };
   GLfloat mat_diffuse[] = { 0.1, 0.5, 0.8, 1.0 };
   GLfloat mat_specular[] = { 1.0, 1.0, 1.0, 1.0 };
   GLfloat no_shininess[] = { 0.0 };
   GLfloat low_shininess[] = { 5.0 };
   GLfloat high_shininess[] = { 100.0 };
   GLfloat mat_emission[] = {0.3, 0.2, 0.2, 0.0};

   glClear(GL_COLOR_BUFFER_BIT | GL_DEPTH_BUFFER_BIT);

/*  draw sphere in first row, first column
 *  diffuse reflection only; no ambient or specular
 */
   glPushMatrix();
   glTranslatef (-3.75, 3.0, 0.0);
   glMaterialfv(GL_FRONT, GL_AMBIENT, no_mat);
   glMaterialfv(GL_FRONT, GL_DIFFUSE, mat_diffuse);
   glMaterialfv(GL_FRONT, GL_SPECULAR, no_mat);
   glMaterialfv(GL_FRONT, GL_SHININESS, no_shininess);
   glMaterialfv(GL_FRONT, GL_EMISSION, no_mat);
   glutSolidSphere(1.0, 16, 16);
   glPopMatrix();
```

```
/*  draw sphere in first row, second column
 *  diffuse and specular reflection; low shininess; no ambient
 */
   glPushMatrix();
   glTranslatef (-1.25, 3.0, 0.0);
   glMaterialfv(GL_FRONT, GL_AMBIENT, no_mat);
   glMaterialfv(GL_FRONT, GL_DIFFUSE, mat_diffuse);
   glMaterialfv(GL_FRONT, GL_SPECULAR, mat_specular);
   glMaterialfv(GL_FRONT, GL_SHININESS, low_shininess);
   glMaterialfv(GL_FRONT, GL_EMISSION, no_mat);
   glutSolidSphere(1.0, 16, 16);
   glPopMatrix();

/*  draw sphere in first row, third column
 *  diffuse and specular reflection; high shininess; no ambient
 */
   glPushMatrix();
   glTranslatef (1.25, 3.0, 0.0);
   glMaterialfv(GL_FRONT, GL_AMBIENT, no_mat);
   glMaterialfv(GL_FRONT, GL_DIFFUSE, mat_diffuse);
   glMaterialfv(GL_FRONT, GL_SPECULAR, mat_specular);
   glMaterialfv(GL_FRONT, GL_SHININESS, high_shininess);
   glMaterialfv(GL_FRONT, GL_EMISSION, no_mat);
   glutSolidSphere(1.0, 16, 16);
   glPopMatrix();

/*  draw sphere in first row, fourth column
 *  diffuse reflection; emission; no ambient or specular refl.
 */
   glPushMatrix();
   glTranslatef (3.75, 3.0, 0.0);
   glMaterialfv(GL_FRONT, GL_AMBIENT, no_mat);
   glMaterialfv(GL_FRONT, GL_DIFFUSE, mat_diffuse);
   glMaterialfv(GL_FRONT, GL_SPECULAR, no_mat);
   glMaterialfv(GL_FRONT, GL_SHININESS, no_shininess);
   glMaterialfv(GL_FRONT, GL_EMISSION, mat_emission);
   glutSolidSphere(1.0, 16, 16);
   glPopMatrix();
```

As you can see, **glMaterialfv()** is called repeatedly to set the desired material property for each sphere. Note that it only needs to be called to change a property that needs to be respecified. The second, third, and fourth spheres use the same ambient and diffuse properties as the first sphere, so these properties do not need to be respecified. Since **glMaterial*()** has a performance cost associated with its use, Example 5-8 could be rewritten to minimize material-property changes.

Another technique for minimizing performance costs associated with changing material properties is to use **glColorMaterial()**.

---

void **glColorMaterial**(GLenum *face*, GLenum *mode*);

Causes the material property (or properties) specified by *mode* of the specified material face (or faces) specified by *face* to track the value of the current color at all times. A change to the current color (using **glColor*()**) immediately updates the specified material properties. The *face* parameter can be GL_FRONT, GL_BACK, or GL_FRONT_AND_BACK (the default). The *mode* parameter can be GL_AMBIENT, GL_DIFFUSE, GL_AMBIENT_AND_DIFFUSE (the default), GL_SPECULAR, or GL_EMISSION. At any given time, only one mode is active. **glColorMaterial()** has no effect on color-index lighting.

Note that **glColorMaterial()** specifies two independent values: the first specifies which face or faces are updated, and the second specifies which material property or properties of those faces are updated. OpenGL does *not* maintain separate *mode* variables for each face.

After calling **glColorMaterial()**, you need to call **glEnable()** with GL_COLOR_MATERIAL as the parameter. Then, you can change the current color using **glColor*()** (or other material properties, using **glMaterial*()**) as needed as you draw:

```
glEnable(GL_COLOR_MATERIAL);
glColorMaterial(GL_FRONT, GL_DIFFUSE);
/* now glColor* changes diffuse reflection  */
glColor3f(0.2, 0.5, 0.8);
/* draw some objects here */
glColorMaterial(GL_FRONT, GL_SPECULAR);
/* glColor* no longer changes diffuse reflection  */
/* now glColor* changes specular reflection  */
glColor3f(0.9, 0.0, 0.2);
/* draw other objects here */
glDisable(GL_COLOR_MATERIAL);
```

You should use **glColorMaterial()** whenever you need to change a single material parameter for most vertices in your scene. If you need to change more than one material parameter, as was the case for Plate 16, use **glMaterial*()**. When you don't need the capabilities of **glColorMaterial()** anymore, be sure to disable it so that you don't get undesired material properties and don't incur the performance cost associated with it. The performance value in using **glColorMaterial()** varies, depending on your OpenGL implementation. Some implementations may be able to optimize the vertex routines so that they can quickly update material properties based on the current color.

Example 5-9 shows an interactive program that uses **glColorMaterial()** to change material parameters. Pressing each of the three mouse buttons changes the color of the diffuse reflection.

Example 5-9   Using glColorMaterial(): colormat.c

```
#include <GL/gl.h>
#include <GL/glu.h>
#include "glut.h"

GLfloat diffuseMaterial[4] = { 0.5, 0.5, 0.5, 1.0 };

void init(void)
{
   GLfloat mat_specular[] = { 1.0, 1.0, 1.0, 1.0 };
   GLfloat light_position[] = { 1.0, 1.0, 1.0, 0.0 };

   glClearColor (0.0, 0.0, 0.0, 0.0);
   glShadeModel (GL_SMOOTH);
   glEnable(GL_DEPTH_TEST);
   glMaterialfv(GL_FRONT, GL_DIFFUSE, diffuseMaterial);
   glMaterialfv(GL_FRONT, GL_SPECULAR, mat_specular);
   glMaterialf(GL_FRONT, GL_SHININESS, 25.0);
   glLightfv(GL_LIGHT0, GL_POSITION, light_position);
   glEnable(GL_LIGHTING);
   glEnable(GL_LIGHT0);

   glColorMaterial(GL_FRONT, GL_DIFFUSE);
   glEnable(GL_COLOR_MATERIAL);
}

void display(void)
{
   glClear(GL_COLOR_BUFFER_BIT | GL_DEPTH_BUFFER_BIT);
   glutSolidSphere(1.0, 20, 16);
   glFlush ();
}
```

```
void reshape (int w, int h)
{
   glViewport (0, 0, (GLsizei) w, (GLsizei) h);
   glMatrixMode (GL_PROJECTION);
   glLoadIdentity();
   if (w <= h)
      glOrtho (-1.5, 1.5, -1.5*(GLfloat)h/(GLfloat)w,
         1.5*(GLfloat)h/(GLfloat)w, -10.0, 10.0);
   else
      glOrtho (-1.5*(GLfloat)w/(GLfloat)h,
         1.5*(GLfloat)w/(GLfloat)h, -1.5, 1.5, -10.0, 10.0);
   glMatrixMode(GL_MODELVIEW);
   glLoadIdentity();
}

void mouse(int button, int state, int x, int y)
{
   switch (button) {
      case GLUT_LEFT_BUTTON:
         if (state == GLUT_DOWN) {        /*  change red  */
            diffuseMaterial[0] += 0.1;
            if (diffuseMaterial[0] > 1.0)
               diffuseMaterial[0] = 0.0;
            glColor4fv(diffuseMaterial);
            glutPostRedisplay();
         }
         break;
      case GLUT_MIDDLE_BUTTON:
         if (state == GLUT_DOWN) {        /*  change green  */
            diffuseMaterial[1] += 0.1;
            if (diffuseMaterial[1] > 1.0)
               diffuseMaterial[1] = 0.0;
            glColor4fv(diffuseMaterial);
            glutPostRedisplay();
         }
         break;
      case GLUT_RIGHT_BUTTON:
         if (state == GLUT_DOWN) {        /*  change blue  */
            diffuseMaterial[2] += 0.1;
            if (diffuseMaterial[2] > 1.0)
               diffuseMaterial[2] = 0.0;
            glColor4fv(diffuseMaterial);
            glutPostRedisplay();
         }
         break;
```

```
              default:
                 break;
          }
   }

   int main(int argc, char** argv)
   {
      glutInit(&argc, argv);
      glutInitDisplayMode (GLUT_SINGLE | GLUT_RGB | GLUT_DEPTH);
      glutInitWindowSize (500, 500);
      glutInitWindowPosition (100, 100);
      glutCreateWindow (argv[0]);
      init ();
      glutDisplayFunc(display);
      glutReshapeFunc(reshape);
      glutMouseFunc(mouse);
      glutMainLoop();
      return 0;
   }
```

Try This

Modify Example 5-8 in the following manner:

- Change the global ambient light in the scene. Hint: Alter the value of the GL_LIGHT_MODEL_AMBIENT parameter.

- Change the diffuse, ambient, and specular reflection parameters, the shininess exponent, and the emission color. Hint: Use the **glMaterial*()** command, but avoid making excessive calls.

- Use two-sided materials and add a user-defined clipping plane so that you can see the inside and outside of a row or column of spheres. (See "Additional Clipping Planes" on page 136, if you need to recall user-defined clipping planes.) Hint: Turn on two-sided lighting with GL_LIGHT_MODEL_TWO_SIDE, set the desired material properties, and add a clipping plane.

- Remove all the **glMaterialfv()** calls, and use the more efficient **glColorMaterial()** calls to achieve the same lighting.

The Mathematics of Lighting

Advanced

This section presents the equations used by OpenGL to perform lighting calculations to determine colors when in RGBA mode. (See "The Mathematics of Color-Index Mode Lighting" on page 210 for corresponding calculations for color-index mode.) You don't need to read this section if you're willing to experiment to obtain the lighting conditions you want. Even after reading this section, you'll probably have to experiment, but you'll have a better idea of how the values of parameters affect a vertex's color. Remember that if lighting is not enabled, the color of a vertex is simply the current color; if it is enabled, the lighting computations described here are carried out in eye coordinates.

In the following equations, mathematical operations are performed separately on the R, G, and B components. Thus, for example, when three terms are shown as added together, the R values, the G values, and the B values for each term are separately added to form the final RGB color $(R_1+R_2+R_3, G_1+G_2+G_3, B_1+B_2+B_3)$. When three terms are multiplied, the calculation is $(R_1R_2R_3, G_1G_2G_3, B_1B_2B_3)$. (Remember that the final A or alpha component at a vertex is equal to the material's diffuse alpha value at that vertex.)

The color produced by lighting a vertex is computed as follows:

vertex color = the material emission at that vertex +

the global ambient light scaled by the material's ambient property at that vertex +

the ambient, diffuse, and specular contributions from all the light sources, properly attenuated

After lighting calculations are performed, the color values are clamped (in RGBA mode) to the range [0,1].

Note that OpenGL lighting calculations don't take into account the possibility of one object blocking light from another; as a result shadows aren't automatically created. (See "Shadows" on page 519 for a technique to create shadows.) Also keep in mind that with OpenGL, illuminated objects don't radiate light onto other objects.

Material Emission

The material emission term is the simplest. It's the RGB value assigned to the GL_EMISSION parameter.

Scaled Global Ambient Light

The second term is computed by multiplying the global ambient light (as defined by the GL_LIGHT_MODEL_AMBIENT parameter) by the material's ambient property (GL_AMBIENT value as assigned with **glMaterial*()**):

$$ambient_{light\ model} * ambient_{material}$$

Each of the R, G, and B values for these two parameters are multiplied separately to compute the final RGB value for this term: (R_1R_2, G_1G_2, B_1B_2).

Contributions from Light Sources

Each light source may contribute to a vertex's color, and these contributions are added together. The equation for computing each light source's contribution is as follows:

contribution = attenuation factor * spotlight effect *

(ambient term + diffuse term + specular term)

Attenuation Factor

The *attenuation factor* was described in "Position and Attenuation" on page 182:

$$attenuation\ factor = \frac{1}{k_c + k_l d + k_q d^2}$$

where

d = distance between the light's position and the vertex

k_c = GL_CONSTANT_ATTENUATION

k_l = GL_LINEAR_ATTENUATION

k_q = GL_QUADRATIC_ATTENUATION

If the light is a directional one, the attenuation factor is 1.

Spotlight Effect

The *spotlight effect* evaluates to one of three possible values, depending on whether the light is actually a spotlight and whether the vertex lies inside or outside the cone of illumination produced by the spotlight:

- 1 if the light isn't a spotlight (GL_SPOT_CUTOFF is 180.0).

- 0 if the light is a spotlight, but the vertex lies outside the cone of illumination produced by the spotlight.

- $(\max \{\mathbf{v} \cdot \mathbf{d}, 0\})^{\text{GL\_SPOT\_EXPONENT}}$ where:

  $\mathbf{v} = (v_x, v_y, v_z)$ is the unit vector that points from the spotlight (GL_POSITION) to the vertex.

  $\mathbf{d} = (d_x, d_y, d_z)$ is the spotlight's direction (GL_SPOT_DIRECTION), assuming the light is a spotlight and the vertex lies inside the cone of illumination produced by the spotlight.

  The dot product of the two vectors $\mathbf{v}$ and $\mathbf{d}$ varies as the cosine of the angle between them; hence, objects directly in line get maximum illumination, and objects off the axis have their illumination drop as the cosine of the angle.

To determine whether a particular vertex lies within the cone of illumination, OpenGL evaluates $(\max \{\mathbf{v} \cdot \mathbf{d}, 0\})$ where $\mathbf{v}$ and $\mathbf{d}$ are as defined in the preceding discussion. If this value is less than the cosine of the spotlight's cutoff angle (GL_SPOT_CUTOFF), then the vertex lies outside the cone; otherwise, it's inside the cone.

Ambient Term

The ambient term is simply the ambient color of the light scaled by the ambient material property:

$$\text{ambient}_{\text{light}} * \text{ambient}_{\text{material}}$$

Diffuse Term

The diffuse term needs to take into account whether light falls directly on the vertex, the diffuse color of the light, and the diffuse material property:

$$(\max \{\mathbf{L} \cdot \mathbf{n}, 0\}) * \text{diffuse}_{\text{light}} * \text{diffuse}_{\text{material}}$$

where:

$\mathbf{L} = (\mathbf{L}_x, \mathbf{L}_y, \mathbf{L}_z)$ is the unit vector that points from the vertex to the light position (GL_POSITION).

$\mathbf{n} = (\mathbf{n}_x, \mathbf{n}_y, \mathbf{n}_z)$ is the unit normal vector at the vertex.

Specular Term

The specular term also depends on whether light falls directly on the vertex. If $\mathbf{L} \cdot \mathbf{n}$ is less than or equal to zero, there is no specular component at the vertex. (If it's less than zero, the light is on the wrong side of the surface.) If there's a specular component, it depends on the following:

- The unit normal vector at the vertex (n_x, n_y, n_z).

- The sum of the two unit vectors that point between (1) the vertex and the light position (or light direction) and (2) the vertex and the viewpoint (assuming that GL_LIGHT_MODEL_LOCAL_VIEWER is true; if it's not true, the vector (0, 0, 1) is used as the second vector in the sum). This vector sum is normalized (by dividing each component by the magnitude of the vector) to yield $\mathbf{s} = (s_x, s_y, s_z)$.

- The specular exponent (GL_SHININESS).

- The specular color of the light (GL_SPECULAR$_{light}$).

- The specular property of the material (GL_SPECULAR$_{material}$).

Using these definitions, here's how OpenGL calculates the specular term:

$$(\max \{\mathbf{s} \cdot \mathbf{n}, 0\})^{shininess} * specular_{light} * specular_{material}$$

However, if $\mathbf{L} \cdot \mathbf{n} = 0$, the specular term is 0.

Putting It All Together

Using the definitions of terms described in the preceding paragraphs, the following represents the entire lighting calculation in RGBA mode:

vertex color = emission$_{material}$ +

    ambient$_{light\ model}$ * ambient$_{material}$ +

$$\sum_{i=0}^{n-1}\left(\frac{1}{k_c + k_1 d + k_q d^2}\right)_i * (spotlight\ effect)_i *$$

    [ambient$_{light}$ *ambient$_{material}$ +

    $(\max \{ \mathbf{L} \cdot \mathbf{n}, 0\})$ * diffuse$_{light}$ * diffuse$_{material}$ +

    $(\max \{ \mathbf{s} \cdot \mathbf{n}, 0\})^{shininess}$ * specular$_{light}$ * specular$_{material}$]$_i$

Lighting in Color-Index Mode

In color-index mode, the parameters comprising RGBA values either have no effect or have a special interpretation. Since it's much harder to achieve certain effects in color-index mode, you should use RGBA whenever possible. In fact, the only light-source, lighting-model, or material parameters in an RGBA form that are used in color-index mode are the light-source parameters GL_DIFFUSE and GL_SPECULAR and the material parameter GL_SHININESS. GL_DIFFUSE and GL_SPECULAR (d_l and s_l, respectively) are used to compute color-index diffuse and specular light intensities (d_{ci} and s_{ci}) as follows:

$$d_{ci} = 0.30 \ R(d_l) + 0.59 \ G(d_l) + 0.11 \ B(d_l)$$

$$s_{ci} = 0.30 \ R(s_l) + 0.59 \ G(s_l) + 0.11 \ B(s_l)$$

where $R(x)$, $G(x)$, and $B(x)$ refer to the red, green, and blue components, respectively, of color x. The weighting values 0.30, 0.59, and 0.11 reflect the "perceptual" weights that red, green, and blue have for your eye—your eye is most sensitive to green and least sensitive to blue.

To specify material colors in color-index mode, use **glMaterial*()** with the special parameter GL_COLOR_INDEXES, as follows:

```
GLfloat mat_colormap[] = { 16.0, 47.0, 79.0 };
glMaterialfv(GL_FRONT, GL_COLOR_INDEXES, mat_colormap);
```

The three numbers supplied for GL_COLOR_INDEXES specify the color indices for the ambient, diffuse, and specular material colors, respectively. In other words, OpenGL regards the color associated with the first index (16.0 in this example) as the pure ambient color, with the second index (47.0) as the pure diffuse color, and with the third index (79.0) as the pure specular color. (By default, the ambient color index is 0.0, and the diffuse and specular color indices are both 1.0. Note that **glColorMaterial()** has no effect on color-index lighting.)

As it draws a scene, OpenGL uses colors associated with indices in between these numbers to shade objects in the scene. Therefore, you must build a color ramp between the indicated indices (in this example, between indices 16 and 47, and then between 47 and 79). Often, the color ramp is built smoothly, but you might want to use other formulations to achieve different effects. Here's an example of a smooth color ramp that starts with a black ambient color and goes through a magenta diffuse color to a white specular color:

```
for (i = 0; i < 32; i++) {
    glutSetColor (16 + i, 1.0 * (i/32.0), 0.0, 1.0 * (i/32.0));
    glutSetColor (48 + i, 1.0, 1.0 * (i/32.0), 1.0);
}
```

The GLUT library command **glutSetColor()** takes four arguments. It associates the color index indicated by the first argument to the RGB triplet specified by the last three arguments. When $i = 0$, the color index 16 is assigned the RGB value (0.0, 0.0, 0.0), or black. The color ramp builds smoothly up to the diffuse material color at index 47 (when $i = 31$), which is assigned the pure magenta RGB value (1.0, 0.0, 1.0). The second loop builds the ramp between the magenta diffuse color and the white (1.0, 1.0, 1.0) specular color (index 79). Plate 15 shows the result of using this color ramp with a single lit sphere.

The Mathematics of Color-Index Mode Lighting

Advanced

As you might expect, since the allowable parameters are different for color-index mode than for RGBA mode, the calculations are different as well. Since there's no material emission and no ambient light, the only terms of interest from the RGBA equations are the diffuse and specular contributions from the light sources and the shininess. Even these need to be modified, however, as explained next.

Begin with the diffuse and specular terms from the RGBA equations. In the diffuse term, instead of diffuse$_{light}$ * diffuse$_{material}$, substitute d_{ci} as defined in the previous section for color-index mode. Similarly, in the specular term, instead of specular$_{light}$ * specular$_{material}$, use s_{ci} as defined in the previous section. (Calculate the attenuation, spotlight effect, and all other components of these terms as before.) Call these modified diffuse and specular terms d and s, respectively. Now let $s' = \min\{ s, 1 \}$, and then compute

$$c = a_m + d(1-s')(d_m-a_m) + s'(s_m-a_m)$$

where a_m, d_m, and s_m are the ambient, diffuse, and specular material indexes specified using GL_COLOR_INDEXES. The final color index is

$$c' = \min \{ c, s_m \}$$

After lighting calculations are performed, the color-index values are converted to fixed-point (with an unspecified number of bits to the right of the binary point). Then the integer portion is masked (bitwise ANDed) with 2^n-1, where n is the number of bits in a color in the color-index buffer.

Chapter 6

Blending, Antialiasing, Fog, and Polygon Offset

Chapter Objectives

After reading this chapter, you'll be able to do the following:

- Blend colors to achieve such effects as making objects appear translucent

- Smooth jagged edges of lines and polygons with antialiasing

- Create scenes with realistic atmospheric effects

- Draw geometry at or near the same depth, but avoid unaesthetic artifacts from intersecting geometry

The preceding chapters have given you the basic information you need to create a computer-graphics scene; you've learned how to do the following:

- Draw geometric shapes

- Transform those geometric shapes so that they can be viewed from whatever perspective you wish

- Specify how the geometric shapes in your scene should be colored and shaded

- Add lights and indicate how they should affect the shapes in your scene

Now you're ready to get a little fancier. This chapter discusses four techniques that can add extra detail and polish to your scene. None of these techniques is hard to use—in fact, it's probably harder to explain them than to use them. Each of these techniques is described in its own major section:

- "Blending" on page 214 tells you how to specify a blending function that combines color values from a source and a destination. The final effect is that parts of your scene appear translucent.

- "Antialiasing" on page 226 explains this relatively subtle technique that alters colors so that the edges of points, lines, and polygons appear smooth rather than angular and jagged.

- "Fog" on page 239 describes how to create the illusion of depth by computing the color values of an object based on its distance from the viewpoint. Thus, objects that are far away appear to fade into the background, just as they do in real life.

- If you've tried to draw a wireframe outline atop a shaded object and used the same vertices, you've probably noticed some ugly visual artifacts. "Polygon Offset" on page 247 shows you how to tweak (offset) depth values to make an outlined, shaded object look beautiful.

Blending

You've already seen alpha values (alpha is the A in RGBA), but they've been ignored until now. Alpha values are specified with **glColor*()**, when using **glClearColor()** to specify a clearing color and when specifying certain lighting parameters such as a material property or light-source intensity. As you learned in Chapter 4, the pixels on a monitor screen emit red, green, and blue light, which is controlled by the red, green, and blue color values.

So how does an alpha value affect what gets drawn in a window on the screen?

When blending is enabled, the alpha value is often used to combine the color value of the fragment being processed with that of the pixel already stored in the framebuffer. Blending occurs after your scene has been rasterized and converted to fragments, but just before the final pixels are drawn in the framebuffer. Alpha values can also be used in the alpha test to accept or reject a fragment based on its alpha value. (See Chapter 10 for more information about this process.)

Without blending, each new fragment overwrites any existing color values in the framebuffer, as though the fragment were opaque. With blending, you can control how (and how much of) the existing color value should be combined with the new fragment's value. Thus you can use alpha blending to create a translucent fragment that lets some of the previously stored color value "show through." Color blending lies at the heart of techniques such as transparency, digital compositing, and painting.

Note: Alpha values aren't specified in color-index mode, so blending operations aren't performed in color-index mode.

The most natural way to think of blending operations is to think of the RGB components of a fragment as representing its color and the alpha component as representing opacity. Transparent or translucent surfaces have lower opacity than opaque ones and, therefore, lower alpha values. For example, if you're viewing an object through green glass, the color you see is partly green from the glass and partly the color of the object. The percentage varies depending on the transmission properties of the glass: If the glass transmits 80 percent of the light that strikes it (that is, has an opacity of 20 percent), the color you see is a combination of 20 percent glass color and 80 percent of the color of the object behind it. You can easily imagine situations with multiple translucent surfaces. If you look at an automobile, for instance, its interior has one piece of glass between it and your viewpoint; some objects behind the automobile are visible through two pieces of glass.

The Source and Destination Factors

During blending, color values of the incoming fragment (the *source*) are combined with the color values of the corresponding currently stored pixel (the *destination*) in a two-stage process. First you specify how to compute source and destination factors. These factors are RGBA quadruplets that are multiplied by each component of the R, G, B, and A values in the source and destination, respectively. Then the corresponding components in the two sets of RGBA quadruplets are added. To show this mathematically, let the source and destination blending factors be (S_r, S_g, S_b, S_a) and (D_r, D_g, D_b, D_a), respectively, and the RGBA values of the source and destination be indicated with a subscript of s or d. Then the final, blended RGBA values are given by

$$(R_sS_r+R_dD_r, \; G_sS_g+G_dD_g, \; B_sS_b+B_dD_b, \; A_sS_a+A_dD_a)$$

Each component of this quadruplet is eventually clamped to [0,1].

Now consider how the source and destination blending factors are generated. You use **glBlendFunc()** to supply two constants: one that specifies how the source factor should be computed and one that indicates how the destination factor should be computed. To have blending take effect, you also need to enable it:

```
glEnable(GL_BLEND);
```

Use **glDisable()** with GL_BLEND to disable blending. Also note that using the constants GL_ONE (source) and GL_ZERO (destination) gives the same results as when blending is disabled; these values are the default.

---

void **glBlendFunc**(GLenum *sfactor*, GLenum *dfactor*);

Controls how color values in the fragment being processed (the source) are combined with those already stored in the framebuffer (the destination). The argument *sfactor* indicates how to compute a source blending factor; *dfactor* indicates how to compute a destination blending factor. The possible values for these arguments are explained in Table 6-1. The blend factors are assumed to lie in the range [0,1]; after the color values in the source and destination are combined, they're clamped to the range [0,1].

Note: In Table 6-1, the RGBA values of the source and destination are indicated with the subscripts s and d, respectively. Subtraction of quadruplets means subtracting them componentwise. The Relevant Factor column indicates whether the corresponding constant can be used to specify the source or destination blend factor.

Constant	Relevant Factor	Computed Blend Factor
GL_ZERO	source or destination	$(0, 0, 0, 0)$
GL_ONE	source or destination	$(1, 1, 1, 1)$
GL_DST_COLOR	source	(R_d, G_d, B_d, A_d)
GL_SRC_COLOR	destination	(R_s, G_s, B_s, A_s)
GL_ONE_MINUS_DST_COLOR	source	$(1, 1, 1, 1)-(R_d, G_d, B_d, A_d)$
GL_ONE_MINUS_SRC_COLOR	destination	$(1, 1, 1, 1)-(R_s, G_s, B_s, A_s)$
GL_SRC_ALPHA	source or destination	(A_s, A_s, A_s, A_s)
GL_ONE_MINUS_SRC_ALPHA	source or destination	$(1, 1, 1, 1)-(A_s, A_s, A_s, A_s)$
GL_DST_ALPHA	source or destination	(A_d, A_d, A_d, A_d)
GL_ONE_MINUS_DST_ALPHA	source or destination	$(1, 1, 1, 1)-(A_d, A_d, A_d, A_d)$
GL_SRC_ALPHA_SATURATE	source	$(f, f, f, 1); f=\min(A_s, 1-A_d)$

Table 6-1   Source and Destination Blending Factors

Sample Uses of Blending

Not all combinations of source and destination factors make sense. Most applications use a small number of combinations. The following paragraphs describe typical uses for particular combinations of source and destination factors. Some of these examples use only the incoming alpha value, so they work even when alpha values aren't stored in the framebuffer. Also note that often there's more than one way to achieve some of these effects.

- One way to draw a picture composed half of one image and half of another, equally blended, is to set the source factor to GL_ONE and the destination factor to GL_ZERO, and draw the first image. Then set the source factor to GL_SRC_ALPHA and destination factor to GL_ONE_MINUS_SRC_ALPHA, and draw the second image with alpha equal to 0.5. This pair of factors probably represents the most commonly used blending operation. If the picture is supposed to be blended with 0.75 of the first image and 0.25 of the second, draw the first image as before, and draw the second with an alpha of 0.25.

- To blend three different images equally, set the destination factor to GL_ONE and the source factor to GL_SRC_ALPHA. Draw each of the images with an alpha equal to 0.3333333. With this technique, each image is only one-third of its original brightness, which is noticeable where the images don't overlap.

- Suppose you're writing a paint program, and you want to have a brush that gradually adds color so that each brush stroke blends in a little more color with whatever is currently in the image (say 10 percent color with 90 percent image on each pass). To do this, draw the image of the brush with alpha of 10 percent and use GL_SRC_ALPHA (source) and GL_ONE_MINUS_SRC_ALPHA (destination). Note that you can vary the alphas across the brush to make the brush add more of its color in the middle and less on the edges, for an antialiased brush shape. (See "Antialiasing" on page 226.) Similarly, erasers can be implemented by setting the eraser color to the background color.

- The blending functions that use the source or destination colors—GL_DST_COLOR or GL_ONE_MINUS_DST_COLOR for the source factor and GL_SRC_COLOR or GL_ONE_MINUS_SRC_COLOR for the destination factor—effectively allow you to modulate each color component individually. This operation is equivalent to applying a simple filter—for example, multiplying the red component by 80 percent, the green component by 40 percent, and the blue component by 72 percent would simulate viewing the scene through a photographic filter that blocks 20 percent of red light, 60 percent of green, and 28 percent of blue.

- Suppose you want to draw a picture composed of three translucent surfaces, some obscuring others, and all over a solid background. Assume the farthest surface transmits 80 percent of the color behind it, the next transmits 40 percent, and the closest transmits 90 percent. To compose this picture, draw the background first with the default source and destination factors, and then change the blending factors to GL_SRC_ALPHA (source) and GL_ONE_MINUS_SRC_ALPHA (destination). Next, draw the farthest surface with an alpha of 0.2, then the middle surface with an alpha of 0.6, and finally the closest surface with an alpha of 0.1.

- If your system has alpha planes, you can render objects one at a time (including their alpha values), read them back, and then perform interesting matting or compositing operations with the fully rendered objects. (See "Compositing 3D Rendered Images" by Tom Duff, SIGGRAPH 1985 Proceedings, p. 41–44, for examples of this technique.) Note that objects used for picture composition can come from any source—they can be rendered using OpenGL commands, rendered using techniques such as ray-tracing or radiosity that are implemented in another graphics library, or obtained by scanning in existing images.

- You can create the effect of a nonrectangular raster image by assigning different alpha values to individual fragments in the image. In most cases, you would assign an alpha of 0 to each "invisible" fragment and an alpha of 1.0 to each opaque fragment. For example, you can draw a polygon in the shape of a tree and apply a texture map of foliage; the viewer can see through parts of the rectangular texture that aren't part of the tree if you've assigned them alpha values of 0. This method, sometimes called *billboarding*, is much faster than creating the tree out of three-dimensional polygons. An example of this technique is shown in Figure 6-1: The tree is a single rectangular polygon that can be rotated about the center of the trunk, as shown by the outlines, so that it's always facing the viewer. (See "Texture Functions" on page 354 for more information about blending textures.)

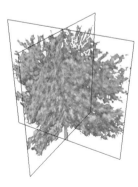

Figure 6-1   Creating a Nonrectangular Raster Image

- Blending is also used for *antialiasing*, which is a rendering technique to reduce the jagged appearance of primitives drawn on a raster screen. (See "Antialiasing" on page 226 for more information.)

A Blending Example

Example 6-1 draws two overlapping colored triangles, each with an alpha of 0.75. Blending is enabled and the source and destination blending factors are set to GL_SRC_ALPHA and GL_ONE_MINUS_SRC_ALPHA, respectively.

When the program starts up, a yellow triangle is drawn on the left and then a cyan triangle is drawn on the right so that in the center of the window, where the triangles overlap, cyan is blended with the original yellow. You can change which triangle is drawn first by typing 't' in the window.

Example 6-1 Blending Example: alpha.c

```
#include <GL/gl.h>
#include <GL/glu.h>
#include <GL/glut.h>
#include <stdlib.h>

static int leftFirst = GL_TRUE;

/*  Initialize alpha blending function.  */
static void init(void)
{
   glEnable (GL_BLEND);
   glBlendFunc (GL_SRC_ALPHA, GL_ONE_MINUS_SRC_ALPHA);
   glShadeModel (GL_FLAT);
   glClearColor (0.0, 0.0, 0.0, 0.0);
}

static void drawLeftTriangle(void)
{
/* draw yellow triangle on LHS of screen */
   glBegin (GL_TRIANGLES);
      glColor4f(1.0, 1.0, 0.0, 0.75);
      glVertex3f(0.1, 0.9, 0.0);
      glVertex3f(0.1, 0.1, 0.0);
      glVertex3f(0.7, 0.5, 0.0);
   glEnd();
}
```

```
static void drawRightTriangle(void)
{
/* draw cyan triangle on RHS of screen */
   glBegin (GL_TRIANGLES);
       glColor4f(0.0, 1.0, 1.0, 0.75);
       glVertex3f(0.9, 0.9, 0.0);
       glVertex3f(0.3, 0.5, 0.0);
       glVertex3f(0.9, 0.1, 0.0);
   glEnd();
}

void display(void)
{
   glClear(GL_COLOR_BUFFER_BIT);

   if (leftFirst) {
      drawLeftTriangle();
      drawRightTriangle();
   }
   else {
      drawRightTriangle();
      drawLeftTriangle();
   }
   glFlush();
}

void reshape(int w, int h)
{
   glViewport(0, 0, (GLsizei) w, (GLsizei) h);
   glMatrixMode(GL_PROJECTION);
   glLoadIdentity();
   if (w <= h)
      gluOrtho2D (0.0, 1.0, 0.0, 1.0*(GLfloat)h/(GLfloat)w);
   else
      gluOrtho2D (0.0, 1.0*(GLfloat)w/(GLfloat)h, 0.0, 1.0);
}

void keyboard(unsigned char key, int x, int y)
{
   switch (key) {
      case 't':
      case 'T':
         leftFirst = !leftFirst;
         glutPostRedisplay();
         break;
      case 27:  /*  Escape key  */
         exit(0);
```

```
                  break;
              default:
                  break;
          }
      }

      int main(int argc, char** argv)
      {
          glutInit(&argc, argv);
          glutInitDisplayMode (GLUT_SINGLE | GLUT_RGB);
          glutInitWindowSize (200, 200);
          glutCreateWindow (argv[0]);
          init();
          glutReshapeFunc (reshape);
          glutKeyboardFunc (keyboard);
          glutDisplayFunc (display);
          glutMainLoop();
          return 0;
      }
```

The order in which the triangles are drawn affects the color of the overlapping region. When the left triangle is drawn first, cyan fragments (the source) are blended with yellow fragments, which are already in the framebuffer (the destination). When the right triangle is drawn first, yellow is blended with cyan. Because the alpha values are all 0.75, the actual blending factors become 0.75 for the source and 1.0 − 0.75 = 0.25 for the destination. In other words, the source fragments are somewhat translucent, but they have more effect on the final color than the destination fragments.

Three-Dimensional Blending with the Depth Buffer

As you saw in the previous example, the order in which polygons are drawn greatly affects the blended result. When drawing three-dimensional translucent objects, you can get different appearances depending on whether you draw the polygons from back to front or from front to back. You also need to consider the effect of the depth buffer when determining the correct order. (See "A Hidden-Surface Removal Survival Kit" on page 171 for an introduction to the depth buffer. Also see "Depth Test" on page 391 for more information.) The depth buffer keeps track of the distance between the viewpoint and the portion of the object occupying a given pixel in a window on the screen; when another candidate color arrives for that pixel, it's drawn only if its object is closer to the viewpoint, in which case its depth value is stored in the depth buffer. With this method, obscured (or hidden) portions of surfaces aren't necessarily drawn and therefore aren't used for blending.

If you want to render both opaque and translucent objects in the same scene, then you want to use the depth buffer to perform hidden-surface removal for any objects that lie behind the opaque objects. If an opaque object hides either a translucent object or another opaque object, you want the depth buffer to eliminate the more distant object. If the translucent object is closer, however, you want to blend it with the opaque object. You can generally figure out the correct order to draw the polygons if everything in the scene is stationary, but the problem can quickly become too hard if either the viewpoint or the object is moving.

The solution is to enable depth buffering but make the depth buffer read-only while drawing the translucent objects. First you draw all the opaque objects, with the depth buffer in normal operation. Then you preserve these depth values by making the depth buffer read-only. When the translucent objects are drawn, their depth values are still compared to the values established by the opaque objects, so they aren't drawn if they're behind the opaque ones. If they're closer to the viewpoint, however, they don't eliminate the opaque objects, since the depth-buffer values can't change. Instead, they're blended with the opaque objects. To control whether the depth buffer is writable, use **glDepthMask()**; if you pass GL_FALSE as the argument, the buffer becomes read-only, whereas GL_TRUE restores the normal, writable operation.

Example 6-2 demonstrates how to use this method to draw opaque and translucent three-dimensional objects. In the program, typing 'a' triggers an animation sequence in which a translucent cube moves through an opaque sphere. Pressing the 'r' key resets the objects in the scene to their initial positions. To get the best results when transparent objects overlap, draw the objects from back to front.

Example 6-2   Three-Dimensional Blending: alpha3D.c

```
#include <stdlib.h>
#include <stdio.h>
#include <GL/gl.h>
#include <GL/glu.h>
#include <GL/glut.h>

#define MAXZ 8.0
#define MINZ -8.0
#define ZINC 0.4
```

```
static float solidZ = MAXZ;
static float transparentZ = MINZ;
static GLuint sphereList, cubeList;

static void init(void)
{
   GLfloat mat_specular[] = { 1.0, 1.0, 1.0, 0.15 };
   GLfloat mat_shininess[] = { 100.0 };
   GLfloat position[] = { 0.5, 0.5, 1.0, 0.0 };

   glMaterialfv(GL_FRONT, GL_SPECULAR, mat_specular);
   glMaterialfv(GL_FRONT, GL_SHININESS, mat_shininess);
   glLightfv(GL_LIGHT0, GL_POSITION, position);

   glEnable(GL_LIGHTING);
   glEnable(GL_LIGHT0);
   glEnable(GL_DEPTH_TEST);

   sphereList = glGenLists(1);
   glNewList(sphereList, GL_COMPILE);
      glutSolidSphere (0.4, 16, 16);
   glEndList();

   cubeList = glGenLists(1);
   glNewList(cubeList, GL_COMPILE);
      glutSolidCube (0.6);
   glEndList();
}

void display(void)
{
   GLfloat mat_solid[] = { 0.75, 0.75, 0.0, 1.0 };
   GLfloat mat_zero[] = { 0.0, 0.0, 0.0, 1.0 };
   GLfloat mat_transparent[] = { 0.0, 0.8, 0.8, 0.6 };
   GLfloat mat_emission[] = { 0.0, 0.3, 0.3, 0.6 };

   glClear (GL_COLOR_BUFFER_BIT | GL_DEPTH_BUFFER_BIT);

   glPushMatrix ();
      glTranslatef (-0.15, -0.15, solidZ);
      glMaterialfv(GL_FRONT, GL_EMISSION, mat_zero);
      glMaterialfv(GL_FRONT, GL_DIFFUSE, mat_solid);
      glCallList (sphereList);
   glPopMatrix ();

   glPushMatrix ();
      glTranslatef (0.15, 0.15, transparentZ);
```

```
      glRotatef (15.0, 1.0, 1.0, 0.0);
      glRotatef (30.0, 0.0, 1.0, 0.0);
      glMaterialfv(GL_FRONT, GL_EMISSION, mat_emission);
      glMaterialfv(GL_FRONT, GL_DIFFUSE, mat_transparent);
      glEnable (GL_BLEND);
      glDepthMask (GL_FALSE);
      glBlendFunc (GL_SRC_ALPHA, GL_ONE);
      glCallList (cubeList);
      glDepthMask (GL_TRUE);
      glDisable (GL_BLEND);
   glPopMatrix ();

   glutSwapBuffers();
}

void reshape(int w, int h)
{
   glViewport(0, 0, (GLint) w, (GLint) h);
   glMatrixMode(GL_PROJECTION);
   glLoadIdentity();
   if (w <= h)
      glOrtho (-1.5, 1.5, -1.5*(GLfloat)h/(GLfloat)w,
            1.5*(GLfloat)h/(GLfloat)w, -10.0, 10.0);
   else
      glOrtho (-1.5*(GLfloat)w/(GLfloat)h,
            1.5*(GLfloat)w/(GLfloat)h, -1.5, 1.5, -10.0, 10.0);
   glMatrixMode(GL_MODELVIEW);
   glLoadIdentity();
}

void animate(void)
{
   if (solidZ <= MINZ || transparentZ >= MAXZ)
      glutIdleFunc(NULL);
   else {
      solidZ -= ZINC;
      transparentZ += ZINC;
      glutPostRedisplay();
   }
}

void keyboard(unsigned char key, int x, int y)
{
   switch (key) {
      case 'a':
      case 'A':
         solidZ = MAXZ;
```

```
                transparentZ = MINZ;
                glutIdleFunc(animate);
                break;
           case 'r':
           case 'R':
                solidZ = MAXZ;
                transparentZ = MINZ;
                glutPostRedisplay();
                break;
           case 27:
              exit(0);
        }
    }

int main(int argc, char** argv)
{
     glutInit(&argc, argv);
     glutInitDisplayMode (GLUT_SINGLE | GLUT_RGB | GLUT_DEPTH);
     glutInitWindowSize(500, 500);
     glutCreateWindow(argv[0]);
     init();
     glutReshapeFunc(reshape);
     glutKeyboardFunc(keyboard);
     glutDisplayFunc(display);
     glutMainLoop();
     return 0;
}
```

Antialiasing

You might have noticed in some of your OpenGL pictures that lines,
especially nearly horizontal or nearly vertical ones, appear jagged. These
jaggies appear because the ideal line is approximated by a series of pixels
that must lie on the pixel grid. The jaggedness is called *aliasing*, and this
section describes antialiasing techniques to reduce it. Figure 6-2 shows two
intersecting lines, both aliased and antialiased. The pictures have been
magnified to show the effect.

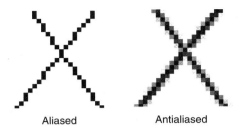

Aliased Antialiased

Figure 6-2   Aliased and Antialiased Lines

Figure 6-3 shows how a diagonal line 1 pixel wide covers more of some pixel squares than others. In fact, when performing antialiasing, OpenGL calculates a *coverage* value for each fragment based on the fraction of the pixel square on the screen that it would cover. The figure shows these coverage values for the line. In RGBA mode, OpenGL multiplies the fragment's alpha value by its coverage. You can then use the resulting alpha value to blend the fragment with the corresponding pixel already in the framebuffer. In color-index mode, OpenGL sets the least significant 4 bits of the color index based on the fragment's coverage (0000 for no coverage and 1111 for complete coverage). It's up to you to load your color map and apply it appropriately to take advantage of this coverage information.

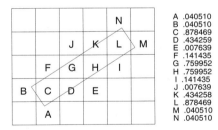

A .040510
B .040510
C .878469
D .434259
E .007639
F .141435
G .759952
H .759952
I .141435
J .007639
K .434258
L .878469
M .040510
N .040510

Figure 6-3   Determining Coverage Values

The details of calculating coverage values are complex, difficult to specify in general, and in fact may vary slightly depending on your particular implementation of OpenGL. You can use the **glHint()** command to exercise some control over the trade-off between image quality and speed, but not all implementations will take the hint.

---

void **glHint**(GLenum *target*, GLenum *hint*);

Controls certain aspects of OpenGL behavior. The *target* parameter indicates which behavior is to be controlled; its possible values are shown in Table 6-2. The *hint* parameter can be GL_FASTEST to indicate that the most efficient option should be chosen, GL_NICEST to indicate the highest-quality option, or GL_DONT_CARE to indicate no preference. The interpretation of hints is implementation-dependent; an implementation can ignore them entirely. (For more information about the relevant topics, see "Antialiasing" on page 226 for the details on sampling and "Fog" on page 239 for details on fog.)

The GL_PERSPECTIVE_CORRECTION_HINT target parameter refers to how color values and texture coordinates are interpolated across a primitive: either linearly in screen space (a relatively simple calculation) or in a perspective-correct manner (which requires more computation). Often, systems perform linear color interpolation because the results, while not technically correct, are visually acceptable; however, in most cases textures require perspective-correct interpolation to be visually acceptable. Thus, an implementation can choose to use this parameter to control the method used for interpolation. (See Chapter 3 for a discussion of perspective projection, Chapter 4 for a discussion of color, and Chapter 9 for a discussion of texture mapping.)

Parameter	Meaning
GL_POINT_SMOOTH_HINT, GL_LINE_SMOOTH_HINT, GL_POLYGON_SMOOTH_HINT	Specify the desired sampling quality of points, lines, or polygons during antialiasing operations
GL_FOG_HINT	Specifies whether fog calculations are done per pixel (GL_NICEST) or per vertex (GL_FASTEST)
GL_PERSPECTIVE_CORRECTION_HINT	Specifies the desired quality of color and texture-coordinate interpolation

Table 6-2   Values for Use with glHint()

Antialiasing Points or Lines

To antialias points or lines, you need to turn on antialiasing with **glEnable()**, passing in GL_POINT_SMOOTH or GL_LINE_SMOOTH, as appropriate. You might also want to provide a quality hint with **glHint()**. (Remember that you can set the size of a point or the width of a line. You can also stipple a line. See "Line Details" on page 50.) Next follow the procedures described in one of the following sections, depending on whether you're in RGBA or color-index mode.

Antialiasing in RGBA Mode

In RGBA mode, you need to enable blending. The blending factors you most likely want to use are GL_SRC_ALPHA (source) and GL_ONE_MINUS_SRC_ALPHA (destination). Alternatively, you can use GL_ONE for the destination factor to make lines a little brighter where they intersect. Now you're ready to draw whatever points or lines you want antialiased. The antialiased effect is most noticeable if you use a fairly high alpha value. Remember that since you're performing blending, you might need to consider the rendering order as described in "Three-Dimensional Blending with the Depth Buffer" on page 222. However, in most cases, the ordering can be ignored without significant adverse effects. Example 6-3 initializes the necessary modes for antialiasing and then draws two intersecting diagonal lines. When you run this program, press the 'r' key to rotate the lines so that you can see the effect of antialiasing on lines of different slopes. Note that the depth buffer isn't enabled in this example.

Example 6-3   Antialiased lines: aargb.c

```
#include <GL/gl.h>
#include <GL/glu.h>
#include <GL/glut.h>
#include <stdlib.h>
#include <stdio.h>

static float rotAngle = 0.;

/*  Initialize antialiasing for RGBA mode, including alpha
 *  blending, hint, and line width.  Print out implementation
 *  specific info on line width granularity and width.
 */
void init(void)
{
   GLfloat values[2];
   glGetFloatv (GL_LINE_WIDTH_GRANULARITY, values);
   printf ("GL_LINE_WIDTH_GRANULARITY value is %3.1f\n",
      values[0]);
```

```
        glGetFloatv (GL_LINE_WIDTH_RANGE, values);
        printf ("GL_LINE_WIDTH_RANGE values are %3.1f %3.1f\n",
            values[0], values[1]);

        glEnable (GL_LINE_SMOOTH);
        glEnable (GL_BLEND);
        glBlendFunc (GL_SRC_ALPHA, GL_ONE_MINUS_SRC_ALPHA);
        glHint (GL_LINE_SMOOTH_HINT, GL_DONT_CARE);
        glLineWidth (1.5);

        glClearColor(0.0, 0.0, 0.0, 0.0);
    }

    /* Draw 2 diagonal lines to form an X */
    void display(void)
    {
        glClear(GL_COLOR_BUFFER_BIT);

        glColor3f (0.0, 1.0, 0.0);
        glPushMatrix();
        glRotatef(-rotAngle, 0.0, 0.0, 0.1);
        glBegin (GL_LINES);
            glVertex2f (-0.5, 0.5);
            glVertex2f (0.5, -0.5);
        glEnd ();
        glPopMatrix();

        glColor3f (0.0, 0.0, 1.0);
        glPushMatrix();
        glRotatef(rotAngle, 0.0, 0.0, 0.1);
        glBegin (GL_LINES);
            glVertex2f (0.5, 0.5);
            glVertex2f (-0.5, -0.5);
        glEnd ();
        glPopMatrix();

        glFlush();
    }
```

```
void reshape(int w, int h)
{
    glViewport(0, 0, (GLint) w, (GLint) h);
    glMatrixMode(GL_PROJECTION);
    glLoadIdentity();
    if (w <= h)
        gluOrtho2D (-1.0, 1.0,
            -1.0*(GLfloat)h/(GLfloat)w, 1.0*(GLfloat)h/(GLfloat)w);
    else
        gluOrtho2D (-1.0*(GLfloat)w/(GLfloat)h,
            1.0*(GLfloat)w/(GLfloat)h, -1.0, 1.0);
    glMatrixMode(GL_MODELVIEW);
    glLoadIdentity();
}

void keyboard(unsigned char key, int x, int y)
{
    switch (key) {
        case 'r':
        case 'R':
            rotAngle += 20.;
            if (rotAngle >= 360.) rotAngle = 0.;
            glutPostRedisplay();
            break;
        case 27:  /*  Escape Key  */
            exit(0);
            break;
        default:
            break;
    }
}

int main(int argc, char** argv)
{
    glutInit(&argc, argv);
    glutInitDisplayMode (GLUT_SINGLE | GLUT_RGB);
    glutInitWindowSize (200, 200);
    glutCreateWindow (argv[0]);
    init();
    glutReshapeFunc (reshape);
    glutKeyboardFunc (keyboard);
    glutDisplayFunc (display);
    glutMainLoop();
    return 0;
}
```

Antialiasing in Color-Index Mode

The tricky part about antialiasing in color-index mode is loading and using the color map. Since the last 4 bits of the color index indicate the coverage value, you need to load sixteen contiguous indices with a color ramp from the background color to the object's color. (The ramp has to start with an index value that's a multiple of 16.) Then you clear the color buffer to the first of the sixteen colors in the ramp and draw your points or lines using colors in the ramp. Example 6-4 demonstrates how to construct the color ramp to draw antialiased lines in color-index mode. In this example, two color ramps are created: one contains shades of green and the other shades of blue.

Example 6-4   Antialiasing in Color-Index Mode: aaindex.c

```
#include <GL/gl.h>
#include <GL/glu.h>
#include <GL/glut.h>
#include <stdlib.h>

#define RAMPSIZE 16
#define RAMP1START 32
#define RAMP2START 48

static float rotAngle = 0.;

/*  Initialize antialiasing for color-index mode,
 *  including loading a green color ramp starting
 *  at RAMP1START, and a blue color ramp starting
 *  at RAMP2START. The ramps must be a multiple of 16.
 */
void init(void)
{
   int i;

   for (i = 0; i < RAMPSIZE; i++) {
      GLfloat shade;
      shade = (GLfloat) i/(GLfloat) RAMPSIZE;
      glutSetColor(RAMP1START+(GLint)i, 0., shade, 0.);
      glutSetColor(RAMP2START+(GLint)i, 0., 0., shade);
   }
   glEnable (GL_LINE_SMOOTH);
   glHint (GL_LINE_SMOOTH_HINT, GL_DONT_CARE);
   glLineWidth (1.5);

   glClearIndex ((GLfloat) RAMP1START);
}
```

```
/*  Draw 2 diagonal lines to form an X */
void display(void)
{
   glClear(GL_COLOR_BUFFER_BIT);

   glIndexi(RAMP1START);
   glPushMatrix();
   glRotatef(-rotAngle, 0.0, 0.0, 0.1);
   glBegin (GL_LINES);
      glVertex2f (-0.5, 0.5);
      glVertex2f (0.5, -0.5);
   glEnd ();
   glPopMatrix();

   glIndexi(RAMP2START);
   glPushMatrix();
   glRotatef(rotAngle, 0.0, 0.0, 0.1);
   glBegin (GL_LINES);
      glVertex2f (0.5, 0.5);
      glVertex2f (-0.5, -0.5);
   glEnd ();
   glPopMatrix();

   glFlush();
}


void reshape(int w, int h)
{
   glViewport(0, 0, (GLsizei) w, (GLsizei) h);
   glMatrixMode(GL_PROJECTION);
   glLoadIdentity();
   if (w <= h)
      gluOrtho2D (-1.0, 1.0,
         -1.0*(GLfloat)h/(GLfloat)w, 1.0*(GLfloat)h/(GLfloat)w);
   else
      gluOrtho2D (-1.0*(GLfloat)w/(GLfloat)h,
         1.0*(GLfloat)w/(GLfloat)h, -1.0, 1.0);
   glMatrixMode(GL_MODELVIEW);
   glLoadIdentity();
}
```

```
void keyboard(unsigned char key, int x, int y)
{
   switch (key) {
      case 'r':
      case 'R':
         rotAngle += 20.;
         if (rotAngle >= 360.) rotAngle = 0.;
         glutPostRedisplay();
         break;
      case 27:  /*  Escape Key */
         exit(0);
         break;
      default:
         break;
   }
}

int main(int argc, char** argv)
{
   glutInit(&argc, argv);
   glutInitDisplayMode (GLUT_SINGLE | GLUT_INDEX);
   glutInitWindowSize (200, 200);
   glutCreateWindow (argv[0]);
   init();
   glutReshapeFunc (reshape);
   glutKeyboardFunc (keyboard);
   glutDisplayFunc (display);
   glutMainLoop();
   return 0;
}
```

Since the color ramp goes from the background color to the object's color, the antialiased lines look correct only in the areas where they are drawn on top of the background. When the blue line is drawn, it erases part of the green line at the point where the lines intersect. To fix this, you would need to redraw the area where the lines intersect using a ramp that goes from green (the color of the line in the framebuffer) to blue (the color of the line being drawn). However, this requires additional calculations and it is usually not worth the effort since the intersection area is small. Note that this is not a problem in RGBA mode, since the colors of object being drawn are blended with the color already in the framebuffer.

You may also want to enable the depth test when drawing antialiased points and lines in color-index mode. In this example, the depth test is disabled since both of the lines lie in the same z-plane. However, if you want to draw a three-dimensional scene, you should enable the depth buffer so that the resulting pixel colors correspond to the "nearest" objects.

The trick described in "Three-Dimensional Blending with the Depth Buffer" on page 222 can also be used to mix antialiased points and lines with aliased, depth-buffered polygons. To do this, draw the polygons first, then make the depth buffer read-only and draw the points and lines. The points and lines intersect nicely with each other but will be obscured by nearer polygons.

Try This

- Take a previous program, such as the robot arm or solar system examples described in "Examples of Composing Several Transformations" on page 139, and draw wireframe objects with antialiasing. Try it in either RGBA or color-index mode. Also try different line widths or point sizes to see their effects.

Antialiasing Polygons

Antialiasing the edges of filled polygons is similar to antialiasing points and lines. When different polygons have overlapping edges, you need to blend the color values appropriately. You can either use the method described in this section, or you can use the accumulation buffer to perform antialiasing for your entire scene. Using the accumulation buffer, which is described in Chapter 10, is easier from your point of view, but it's much more computation-intensive and therefore slower. However, as you'll see, the method described here is rather cumbersome.

Note: If you draw your polygons as points at the vertices or as outlines—that is, by passing GL_POINT or GL_LINE to **glPolygonMode()**—point or line antialiasing is applied, if enabled as described earlier. The rest of this section addresses polygon antialiasing when you're using GL_FILL as the polygon mode.

In theory, you can antialias polygons in either RGBA or color-index mode. However, object intersections affect polygon antialiasing more than they affect point or line antialiasing, so rendering order and blending accuracy become more critical. In fact, they're so critical that if you're antialiasing more than one polygon, you need to order the polygons from front to back and then use **glBlendFunc()** with GL_SRC_ALPHA_SATURATE for the source factor and GL_ONE for the destination factor. Thus, antialiasing polygons in color-index mode normally isn't practical.

To antialias polygons in RGBA mode, you use the alpha value to represent coverage values of polygon edges. You need to enable polygon antialiasing by passing GL_POLYGON_SMOOTH to **glEnable()**. This causes pixels on the edges of the polygon to be assigned fractional alpha values based on their coverage, as though they were lines being antialiased. Also, if you desire, you can supply a value for GL_POLYGON_SMOOTH_HINT.

Now you need to blend overlapping edges appropriately. First, turn off the depth buffer so that you have control over how overlapping pixels are drawn. Then set the blending factors to GL_SRC_ALPHA_SATURATE (source) and GL_ONE (destination). With this specialized blending function, the final color is the sum of the destination color and the scaled source color; the scale factor is the smaller of either the incoming source alpha value or one minus the destination alpha value. This means that for a pixel with a large alpha value, successive incoming pixels have little effect on the final color because one minus the destination alpha is almost zero. With this method, a pixel on the edge of a polygon might be blended eventually with the colors from another polygon that's drawn later. Finally, you need to sort all the polygons in your scene so that they're ordered from front to back before drawing them.

Example 6-5 shows how to antialias filled polygons; clicking the left mouse button toggles the antialiasing on and off. Note that backward-facing polygons are culled and that the alpha values in the color buffer are cleared to zero before any drawing. Pressing the 't' key toggles the antialiasing on and off.

Note: Your color buffer must store alpha values for this technique to work correctly. Make sure you request GLUT_ALPHA and receive a legitimate window.

Example 6-5 Antialiasing Filled Polygons: aapoly.c

```
#include <GL/gl.h>
#include <GL/glu.h>
#include <GL/glut.h>
#include <stdlib.h>
#include <stdio.h>
#include <string.h>

GLboolean polySmooth = GL_TRUE;
```

```c
static void init(void)
{
    glCullFace (GL_BACK);
    glEnable (GL_CULL_FACE);
    glBlendFunc (GL_SRC_ALPHA_SATURATE, GL_ONE);
    glClearColor (0.0, 0.0, 0.0, 0.0);
}

#define NFACE 6
#define NVERT 8
void drawCube(GLdouble x0, GLdouble x1, GLdouble y0,
              GLdouble y1, GLdouble z0, GLdouble z1)
{
    static GLfloat v[8][3];
    static GLfloat c[8][4] = {
        {0.0, 0.0, 0.0, 1.0}, {1.0, 0.0, 0.0, 1.0},
        {0.0, 1.0, 0.0, 1.0}, {1.0, 1.0, 0.0, 1.0},
        {0.0, 0.0, 1.0, 1.0}, {1.0, 0.0, 1.0, 1.0},
        {0.0, 1.0, 1.0, 1.0}, {1.0, 1.0, 1.0, 1.0}
    };

/*  indices of front, top, left, bottom, right, back faces  */
    static GLubyte indices[NFACE][4] = {
        {4, 5, 6, 7}, {2, 3, 7, 6}, {0, 4, 7, 3},
        {0, 1, 5, 4}, {1, 5, 6, 2}, {0, 3, 2, 1}
    };

    v[0][0] = v[3][0] = v[4][0] = v[7][0] = x0;
    v[1][0] = v[2][0] = v[5][0] = v[6][0] = x1;
    v[0][1] = v[1][1] = v[4][1] = v[5][1] = y0;
    v[2][1] = v[3][1] = v[6][1] = v[7][1] = y1;
    v[0][2] = v[1][2] = v[2][2] = v[3][2] = z0;
    v[4][2] = v[5][2] = v[6][2] = v[7][2] = z1;

#ifdef GL_VERSION_1_1
    glEnableClientState (GL_VERTEX_ARRAY);
    glEnableClientState (GL_COLOR_ARRAY);
    glVertexPointer (3, GL_FLOAT, 0, v);
    glColorPointer (4, GL_FLOAT, 0, c);
    glDrawElements(GL_QUADS, NFACE*4, GL_UNSIGNED_BYTE, indices);
    glDisableClientState (GL_VERTEX_ARRAY);
    glDisableClientState (GL_COLOR_ARRAY);
#else
    printf ("If this is GL Version 1.0, ");
    printf ("vertex arrays are not supported.\n");
    exit(1);
#endif
}
```

```
/*  Note:  polygons must be drawn from front to back
 *  for proper blending.
 */
void display(void)
{
   if (polySmooth) {
      glClear (GL_COLOR_BUFFER_BIT);
      glEnable (GL_BLEND);
      glEnable (GL_POLYGON_SMOOTH);
      glDisable (GL_DEPTH_TEST);
   }
   else {
      glClear (GL_COLOR_BUFFER_BIT | GL_DEPTH_BUFFER_BIT);
      glDisable (GL_BLEND);
      glDisable (GL_POLYGON_SMOOTH);
      glEnable (GL_DEPTH_TEST);
   }

   glPushMatrix ();
      glTranslatef (0.0, 0.0, -8.0);
      glRotatef (30.0, 1.0, 0.0, 0.0);
      glRotatef (60.0, 0.0, 1.0, 0.0);
      drawCube(-0.5, 0.5, -0.5, 0.5, -0.5, 0.5);
   glPopMatrix ();

   glFlush ();
}

void reshape(int w, int h)
{
   glViewport(0, 0, (GLsizei) w, (GLsizei) h);
   glMatrixMode(GL_PROJECTION);
   glLoadIdentity();
   gluPerspective(30.0, (GLfloat) w/(GLfloat) h, 1.0, 20.0);
   glMatrixMode(GL_MODELVIEW);
   glLoadIdentity();
}
```

```
void keyboard(unsigned char key, int x, int y)
{
    switch (key) {
        case 't':
        case 'T':
            polySmooth = !polySmooth;
            glutPostRedisplay();
            break;
        case 27:
            exit(0);   /*  Escape key  */
            break;
        default:
            break;
    }
}

int main(int argc, char** argv)
{
    glutInit(&argc, argv);
    glutInitDisplayMode (GLUT_SINGLE | GLUT_RGB
                         | GLUT_ALPHA | GLUT_DEPTH);
    glutInitWindowSize(200, 200);
    glutCreateWindow(argv[0]);
    init ();
    glutReshapeFunc (reshape);
    glutKeyboardFunc (keyboard);
    glutDisplayFunc (display);
    glutMainLoop();
    return 0;
}
```

Fog

Computer images sometimes seem unrealistically sharp and well defined. Antialiasing makes an object appear more realistic by smoothing its edges. Additionally, you can make an entire image appear more natural by adding fog, which makes objects fade into the distance. *Fog* is a general term that describes similar forms of atmospheric effects; it can be used to simulate haze, mist, smoke, or pollution. (See Plate 9.) Fog is essential in visual-simulation applications, where limited visibility needs to be approximated. It's often incorporated into flight-simulator displays.

When fog is enabled, objects that are farther from the viewpoint begin to fade into the fog color. You can control the density of the fog, which determines the rate at which objects fade as the distance increases, as well as the fog's color. Fog is available in both RGBA and color-index modes, although the calculations are slightly different in the two modes. Since fog is applied after matrix transformations, lighting, and texturing are performed, it affects transformed, lit, and textured objects. Note that with large simulation programs, fog can improve performance, since you can choose not to draw objects that would be too fogged to be visible.

All types of geometric primitives can be fogged, including points and lines. Using the fog effect on points and lines is also called *depth-cuing* (as shown in Plate 2) and is popular in molecular modeling and other applications.

Using Fog

Using fog is easy. You enable it by passing GL_FOG to **glEnable()**, and you choose the color and the equation that controls the density with **glFog*()**. If you want, you can supply a value for GL_FOG_HINT with **glHint()**, as described on Table 6-2. Example 6-6 draws five red spheres, each at a different distance from the viewpoint. Pressing the 'f' key selects among the three different fog equations, which are described in the next section.

Example 6-6   Five Fogged Spheres in RGBA Mode: fog.c

```
#include <GL/gl.h>
#include <GL/glu.h>
#include <math.h>
#include <GL/glut.h>
#include <stdlib.h>
#include <stdio.h>

static GLint fogMode;

static void init(void)
{
    GLfloat position[] = { 0.5, 0.5, 3.0, 0.0 };

    glEnable(GL_DEPTH_TEST);

    glLightfv(GL_LIGHT0, GL_POSITION, position);
    glEnable(GL_LIGHTING);
    glEnable(GL_LIGHT0);
    {
        GLfloat mat[3] = {0.1745, 0.01175, 0.01175};
        glMaterialfv (GL_FRONT, GL_AMBIENT, mat);
```

```
        mat[0] = 0.61424; mat[1] = 0.04136; mat[2] = 0.04136;
        glMaterialfv (GL_FRONT, GL_DIFFUSE, mat);
        mat[0] = 0.727811; mat[1] = 0.626959; mat[2] = 0.626959;
        glMaterialfv (GL_FRONT, GL_SPECULAR, mat);
        glMaterialf (GL_FRONT, GL_SHININESS, 0.6*128.0);
    }

    glEnable(GL_FOG);
    {
        GLfloat fogColor[4] = {0.5, 0.5, 0.5, 1.0};

        fogMode = GL_EXP;
        glFogi (GL_FOG_MODE, fogMode);
        glFogfv (GL_FOG_COLOR, fogColor);
        glFogf (GL_FOG_DENSITY, 0.35);
        glHint (GL_FOG_HINT, GL_DONT_CARE);
        glFogf (GL_FOG_START, 1.0);
        glFogf (GL_FOG_END, 5.0);
    }
    glClearColor(0.5, 0.5, 0.5, 1.0);  /* fog color */
}

static void renderSphere (GLfloat x, GLfloat y, GLfloat z)
{
    glPushMatrix();
    glTranslatef (x, y, z);
    glutSolidSphere(0.4, 16, 16);
    glPopMatrix();
}

/* display() draws 5 spheres at different z positions.
 */
void display(void)
{
    glClear(GL_COLOR_BUFFER_BIT | GL_DEPTH_BUFFER_BIT);
    renderSphere (-2., -0.5, -1.0);
    renderSphere (-1., -0.5, -2.0);
    renderSphere (0., -0.5, -3.0);
    renderSphere (1., -0.5, -4.0);
    renderSphere (2., -0.5, -5.0);
    glFlush();
}

void reshape(int w, int h)
{
    glViewport(0, 0, (GLsizei) w, (GLsizei) h);
    glMatrixMode(GL_PROJECTION);
```

```
            glLoadIdentity();
            if (w <= h)
               glOrtho (-2.5, 2.5, -2.5*(GLfloat)h/(GLfloat)w,
                   2.5*(GLfloat)h/(GLfloat)w, -10.0, 10.0);
            else
               glOrtho (-2.5*(GLfloat)w/(GLfloat)h,
                   2.5*(GLfloat)w/(GLfloat)h, -2.5, 2.5, -10.0, 10.0);
            glMatrixMode(GL_MODELVIEW);
            glLoadIdentity ();
         }

         void keyboard(unsigned char key, int x, int y)
         {
            switch (key) {
               case 'f':
               case 'F':
                  if (fogMode == GL_EXP) {
                     fogMode = GL_EXP2;
                     printf ("Fog mode is GL_EXP2\n");
                  }
                  else if (fogMode == GL_EXP2) {
                     fogMode = GL_LINEAR;
                     printf ("Fog mode is GL_LINEAR\n");
                  }
                  else if (fogMode == GL_LINEAR) {
                     fogMode = GL_EXP;
                     printf ("Fog mode is GL_EXP\n");
                  }
                  glFogi (GL_FOG_MODE, fogMode);
                  glutPostRedisplay();
                  break;
               case 27:
                  exit(0);
                  break;
               default:
                  break;
            }
         }

         int main(int argc, char** argv)
         {
            glutInit(&argc, argv);
            glutInitDisplayMode (GLUT_SINGLE | GLUT_RGB | GLUT_DEPTH);
            glutInitWindowSize(500, 500);
            glutCreateWindow(argv[0]);
            init();
            glutReshapeFunc (reshape);
```

```
    glutKeyboardFunc (keyboard);
    glutDisplayFunc (display);
    glutMainLoop();
    return 0;
}
```

Fog Equations

Fog blends a fog color with an incoming fragment's color using a fog
blending factor. This factor, *f*, is computed with one of these three
equations and then clamped to the range [0,1].

$$f = e^{-(density \cdot z)} \quad \text{(GL\_EXP)}$$

$$f = e^{-(density \cdot z)^2} \quad \text{(GL\_EXP2)}$$

$$f = \frac{end - z}{end - start} \quad \text{(GL\_LINEAR)}$$

In these three equations, *z* is the eye-coordinate distance between the
viewpoint and the fragment center. The values for *density*, *start*, and *end* are
all specified with **glFog*()**. The *f* factor is used differently, depending on
whether you're in RGBA mode or color-index mode, as explained in the
next subsections.

---

void **glFog**{if}(GLenum *pname, TYPE param*);
void **glFog**{if}**v**(GLenum *pname, TYPE *params*);

Sets the parameters and function for calculating fog. If *pname* is
GL_FOG_MODE, then *param* is either GL_EXP (the default), GL_EXP2,
or GL_LINEAR to select one of the three fog factors. If *pname* is
GL_FOG_DENSITY, GL_FOG_START, or GL_FOG_END, then *param*
is (or points to, with the vector version of the command) a value for
density, *start*, or *end* in the equations. (The default values are 1, 0, and 1,
respectively.) In RGBA mode, *pname* can be GL_FOG_COLOR, in which
case *params* points to four values that specify the fog's RGBA color
values. The corresponding value for *pname* in color-index mode is
GL_FOG_INDEX, for which *param* is a single value specifying the fog's
color index.

Figure 6-4 plots the fog-density equations for various values of the parameters.

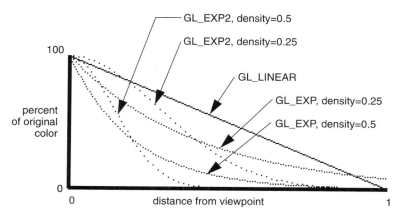

Figure 6-4   Fog-Density Equations

Fog in RGBA Mode

In RGBA mode, the fog factor f is used as follows to calculate the final fogged color:

$$C = f\,C_i + (1 - f)\,C_f$$

where C_i represents the incoming fragment's RGBA values and C_f the fog-color values assigned with GL_FOG_COLOR.

Fog in Color-Index Mode

In color-index mode, the final fogged color index is computed as follows:

$$I = I_i + (1 - f)\,I_f$$

where I_i is the incoming fragment's color index and I_f is the fog's color index as specified with GL_FOG_INDEX.

To use fog in color-index mode, you have to load appropriate values in a color ramp. The first color in the ramp is the color of the object without fog, and the last color in the ramp is the color of the completely fogged object. You probably want to use **glClearIndex()** to initialize the background color index so that it corresponds to the last color in the ramp; this way, totally fogged objects blend into the background. Similarly, before objects are drawn, you should call **glIndex*()** and pass in the index of the first color in the ramp (the unfogged color). Finally, to apply fog to different colored objects in the scene, you need to create several color ramps and call **glIndex*()** before each object is drawn to set the current color index to the start of each color ramp. Example 6-7 illustrates how to initialize appropriate conditions and then apply fog in color-index mode.

Example 6-7   Fog in Color-Index Mode: fogindex.c

```
#include <GL/gl.h>
#include <GL/glu.h>
#include <math.h>
#include <GL/glut.h>
#include <stdlib.h>
#include <stdio.h>

/*  Initialize color map and fog.  Set screen clear color
 *  to end of color ramp.
 */
#define NUMCOLORS 32
#define RAMPSTART 16

static void init(void)
{
   int i;

   glEnable(GL_DEPTH_TEST);

   for (i = 0; i < NUMCOLORS; i++) {
      GLfloat shade;
      shade = (GLfloat) (NUMCOLORS-i)/(GLfloat) NUMCOLORS;
      glutSetColor (RAMPSTART + i, shade, shade, shade);
   }
   glEnable(GL_FOG);

   glFogi (GL_FOG_MODE, GL_LINEAR);
   glFogi (GL_FOG_INDEX, NUMCOLORS);
   glFogf (GL_FOG_START, 1.0);
   glFogf (GL_FOG_END, 6.0);
   glHint (GL_FOG_HINT, GL_NICEST);
   glClearIndex((GLfloat) (NUMCOLORS+RAMPSTART-1));
}

static void renderSphere (GLfloat x, GLfloat y, GLfloat z)
{
   glPushMatrix();
   glTranslatef (x, y, z);
   glutWireSphere(0.4, 16, 16);
```

```
            glPopMatrix();
     }

    /*  display() draws 5 spheres at different z positions.
     */
     void display(void)
     {
        glClear(GL_COLOR_BUFFER_BIT | GL_DEPTH_BUFFER_BIT);
        glIndexi (RAMPSTART);

        renderSphere (-2., -0.5, -1.0);
        renderSphere (-1., -0.5, -2.0);
        renderSphere (0., -0.5, -3.0);
        renderSphere (1., -0.5, -4.0);
        renderSphere (2., -0.5, -5.0);

        glFlush();
     }

    void reshape(int w, int h)
    {
        glViewport(0, 0, w, h);
        glMatrixMode(GL_PROJECTION);
        glLoadIdentity();
        if (w <= h)
            glOrtho (-2.5, 2.5, -2.5*(GLfloat)h/(GLfloat)w,
                2.5*(GLfloat)h/(GLfloat)w, -10.0, 10.0);
        else
            glOrtho (-2.5*(GLfloat)w/(GLfloat)h,
                2.5*(GLfloat)w/(GLfloat)h, -2.5, 2.5, -10.0, 10.0);
        glMatrixMode(GL_MODELVIEW);
        glLoadIdentity ();
    }

    void keyboard(unsigned char key, int x, int y)
    {

        switch (key) {
           case 27:
              exit(0);
        }
    }

    int main(int argc, char** argv)
    {
        glutInit(&argc, argv);
        glutInitDisplayMode (GLUT_SINGLE | GLUT_INDEX | GLUT_DEPTH);
```

```
    glutInitWindowSize(500, 500);
    glutCreateWindow(argv[0]);
    init();
    glutReshapeFunc (reshape);
    glutKeyboardFunc (keyboard);
    glutDisplayFunc (display);
    glutMainLoop();
    return 0;
}
```

Polygon Offset

If you want to highlight the edges of a solid object, you might try to draw
the object with polygon mode GL_FILL and then draw it again, but in a
different color with polygon mode GL_LINE. However, because lines and
filled polygons are not rasterized in exactly the same way, the depth values
generated for pixels on a line are usually not the same as the depth values
for a polygon edge, even between the same two vertices. The highlighting
lines may fade in and out of the coincident polygons, which is sometimes
called "stitching" and is visually unpleasant.

The visual unpleasantness can be eliminated by using polygon offset, which
adds an appropriate offset to force coincident z values apart to cleanly
separate a polygon edge from its highlighting line. (The stencil buffer,
described in "Stencil Test" on page 385, can also be used to eliminate
stitching. However, polygon offset is almost always faster than stenciling.)
Polygon offset is also useful for applying decals to surfaces, rendering
images with hidden-line removal. In addition to lines and filled polygons,
this technique can also be used with points.

There are three different ways to turn on polygon offset, one for each type
of polygon rasterization mode: GL_FILL, GL_LINE, or GL_POINT. You
enable the polygon offset by passing the appropriate parameter to
glEnable(), either GL_POLYGON_OFFSET_FILL,
GL_POLYGON_OFFSET_LINE, or GL_POLYGON_OFFSET_POINT. You
must also call **glPolygonMode()** to set the current polygon rasterization
method.

void **glPolygonOffset**(GLfloat *factor*, GLfloat *units*);

When enabled, the depth value of each fragment is added to a calculated offset value. The offset is added before the depth test is performed and before the depth value is written into the depth buffer. The offset value o is calculated by:

$$o = m * factor + r * units$$

where m is the maximum depth slope of the polygon and r is the smallest value guaranteed to produce a resolvable difference in window coordinate depth values. The value r is an implementation-specific constant.

To achieve a nice rendering of the highlighted solid object without visual artifacts, you can either add a positive offset to the solid object (push it away from you) or a negative offset to the wireframe (pull it towards you). The big question is: "How much offset is enough?" Unfortunately, the offset required depends upon various factors, including the depth slope of each polygon and the width of the lines in the wireframe.

OpenGL calculates the depth slope (see Figure 6-5) of a polygon for you, but it's important that you understand what the depth slope is, so that you choose a reasonable value for *factor*. The depth slope is the change in z (depth) values divided by the change in either x or y coordinates, as you traverse a polygon. The depth values are in window coordinates, clamped to the range [0, 1]. To estimate the maximum depth slope of a polygon (m in the offset equation), use this formula:

$$m = max \left\{ \left| \frac{\partial z}{\partial x} \right|, \left| \frac{\partial z}{\partial y} \right| \right\}$$

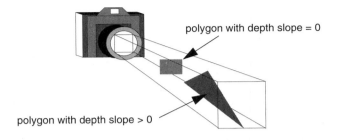

polygon with depth slope = 0

polygon with depth slope > 0

Figure 6-5   Polygons and Their Depth Slopes

For polygons that are parallel to the near and far clipping planes, the depth slope is zero. For the polygons in your scene with a depth slope near zero, only a small, constant offset is needed. To create a small, constant offset, you can pass *factor*=0.0 and *units*=1.0 to **glPolygonOffset()**.

For polygons that are at a great angle to the clipping planes, the depth slope can be significantly greater than zero, and a larger offset may be needed. Small, non-zero values for *factor,* such as 0.75 or 1.0, are probably enough to generate distinct depth values and eliminate the unpleasant visual artifacts.

Example 6-8 shows a portion of code, where a display list (which presumably draws a solid object) is first rendered with lighting, the default GL_FILL polygon mode, and polygon offset with *factor* of 1.0 and *units* of 1.0. These values ensure that the offset is enough for all polygons in your scene, regardless of depth slope. (These values may actually be a little more offset than the minimum needed, but too much offset is less noticeable than too little.) Then, to highlight the edges of the first object, the object is rendered as an unlit wireframe with the offset disabled.

Example 6-8   Polygon Offset to Eliminate Visual Artifacts: polyoff.c

```
glEnable(GL_LIGHTING);
glEnable(GL_LIGHT0);
glEnable(GL_POLYGON_OFFSET_FILL);
glPolygonOffset(1.0, 1.0);
glCallList (list);
glDisable(GL_POLYGON_OFFSET_FILL);

glDisable(GL_LIGHTING);
glDisable(GL_LIGHT0);
glColor3f (1.0, 1.0, 1.0);
```

```
glPolygonMode(GL_FRONT_AND_BACK, GL_LINE);
glCallList (list);
glPolygonMode(GL_FRONT_AND_BACK, GL_FILL);
```

In a few situations, the simplest values for *factor* and *units* (1.0 and 1.0) aren't the answers. For instance, if the width of the lines that are highlighting the edges are greater than one, then increasing the value of *factor* may be necessary. Also, since depth values are unevenly transformed into window coordinates when using perspective projection (see "The Transformed Depth Coordinate" on page 128), less offset is needed for polygons that are closer to the near clipping plane, and more offset is needed for polygons that are further away. Once again, experimenting with the value of *factor* may be warranted.

Chapter 7

Display Lists

Chapter Objectives

After reading this chapter, you'll be able to do the following:

- Understand how display lists can be used along with commands in immediate mode to organize your data and improve performance

- Maximize performance by knowing how and when to use display lists

A *display list* is a group of OpenGL commands that have been stored for later execution. When a display list is invoked, the commands in it are executed in the order in which they were issued. Most OpenGL commands can be either stored in a display list or issued in *immediate mode*, which causes them to be executed immediately. You can freely mix immediate-mode programming and display lists within a single program. The programming examples you've seen so far have used immediate mode. This chapter discusses what display lists are and how best to use them. It has the following major sections:

- "Why Use Display Lists?" on page 252 explains when to use display lists.

- "An Example of Using a Display List" on page 253 gives a brief example, showing the basic commands for using display lists.

- "Display-List Design Philosophy" on page 257 explains why certain design choices were made (such as making display lists uneditable) and what performance optimizations you might expect to see when using display lists.

- "Creating and Executing a Display List" on page 259 discusses in detail the commands for creating, executing, and deleting display lists.

- "Executing Multiple Display Lists" on page 267 shows how to execute several display lists in succession, using a small character set as an example.

- "Managing State Variables with Display Lists" on page 273 illustrates how to use display lists to save and restore OpenGL commands that set state variables.

Why Use Display Lists?

Display lists may improve performance since you can use them to store OpenGL commands for later execution. It is often a good idea to cache commands in a display list if you plan to redraw the same geometry multiple times, or if you have a set of state changes that need to be applied multiple times. Using display lists, you can define the geometry and/or state changes once and execute them multiple times.

To see how you can use display lists to store geometry just once, consider drawing a tricycle. The two wheels on the back are the same size but are offset from each other. The front wheel is larger than the back wheels and also in a different location. An efficient way to render the wheels on the tricycle would be to store the geometry for one wheel in a display list then execute the list three times. You would need to set the modelview matrix appropriately each time before executing the list to calculate the correct size and location for the wheels.

When running OpenGL programs remotely to another machine on the network, it is especially important to cache commands in a display list. In this case, the server is a different machine than the host. (See "What Is OpenGL?" on page 2 for a discussion of the OpenGL client-server model.) Since display lists are part of the server state and therefore reside on the server machine, you can reduce the cost of repeatedly transmitting that data over a network if you store repeatedly used commands in a display list.

When running locally, you can often improve performance by storing frequently used commands in a display list. Some graphics hardware may store display lists in dedicated memory or may store the data in an optimized form that is more compatible with the graphics hardware or software. (See "Display-List Design Philosophy" on page 257 for a detailed discussion of these optimizations.)

An Example of Using a Display List

A display list is a convenient and efficient way to name and organize a set of OpenGL commands. For example, suppose you want to draw a torus and view it from different angles. The most efficient way to do this would be to store the torus in a display list. Then whenever you want to change the view, you would change the modelview matrix and execute the display list to draw the torus. Example 7-1 illustrates this.

Example 7-1   Creating a Display List: torus.c

```
#include <GL/gl.h>
#include <GL/glu.h>
#include <stdio.h>
#include <math.h>
#include <GL/glut.h>
#include <stdlib.h>
```

```
GLuint theTorus;

/* Draw a torus */
static void torus(int numc, int numt)
{
    int i, j, k;
    double s, t, x, y, z, twopi;

    twopi = 2 * (double)M_PI;
    for (i = 0; i < numc; i++) {
        glBegin(GL_QUAD_STRIP);
        for (j = 0; j <= numt; j++) {
            for (k = 1; k >= 0; k--) {
                s = (i + k) % numc + 0.5;
                t = j % numt;

                x = (1+.1*cos(s*twopi/numc))*cos(t*twopi/numt);
                y = (1+.1*cos(s*twopi/numc))*sin(t*twopi/numt);
                z = .1 * sin(s * twopi / numc);
                glVertex3f(x, y, z);
            }
        }
        glEnd();
    }
}

/* Create display list with Torus and initialize state*/
static void init(void)
{
    theTorus = glGenLists (1);
    glNewList(theTorus, GL_COMPILE);
    torus(8, 25);
    glEndList();

    glShadeModel(GL_FLAT);
    glClearColor(0.0, 0.0, 0.0, 0.0);
}

void display(void)
{
    glClear(GL_COLOR_BUFFER_BIT);
    glColor3f (1.0, 1.0, 1.0);
    glCallList(theTorus);
    glFlush();
}
```

```
void reshape(int w, int h)
{
    glViewport(0, 0, (GLsizei) w, (GLsizei) h);
    glMatrixMode(GL_PROJECTION);
    glLoadIdentity();
    gluPerspective(30, (GLfloat) w/(GLfloat) h, 1.0, 100.0);
    glMatrixMode(GL_MODELVIEW);
    glLoadIdentity();
    gluLookAt(0, 0, 10, 0, 0, 0, 0, 1, 0);
}

/* Rotate about x-axis when "x" typed; rotate about y-axis
   when "y" typed; "i" returns torus to original view */
void keyboard(unsigned char key, int x, int y)
{
    switch (key) {
    case 'x':
    case 'X':
        glRotatef(30.,1.0,0.0,0.0);
        glutPostRedisplay();
        break;
    case 'y':
    case 'Y':
        glRotatef(30.,0.0,1.0,0.0);
        glutPostRedisplay();
        break;
    case 'i':
    case 'I':
        glLoadIdentity();
        gluLookAt(0, 0, 10, 0, 0, 0, 0, 1, 0);
        glutPostRedisplay();
        break;
    case 27:
        exit(0);
        break;
    }
}

int main(int argc, char **argv)
{
    glutInitWindowSize(200, 200);
    glutInit(&argc, argv);
    glutInitDisplayMode(GLUT_SINGLE | GLUT_RGB);
    glutCreateWindow(argv[0]);
    init();
    glutReshapeFunc(reshape);
    glutKeyboardFunc(keyboard);
```

```
glutDisplayFunc(display);
glutMainLoop();
return 0;
}
```

Let's start by looking at **init()**. It creates a display list for the torus and initializes the viewing matrices and other rendering state. Note that the routine for drawing a torus (**torus()**) is bracketed by **glNewList()** and **glEndList()**, which defines a display list. The argument *listName* for **glNewList()** is an integer index, generated by **glGenLists()**, that uniquely identifies this display list.

The user can rotate the torus about the x- or y-axis by pressing the 'x' or 'y' key when the window has focus. Whenever this happens, the callback function **keyboard()** is called, which concatenates a 30-degree rotation matrix (about the x- or y-axis) with the current modelview matrix. Then **glutPostRedisplay()** is called, which will cause **glutMainLoop()** to call **display()** and render the torus after other events have been processed. When the 'i' key is pressed, **keyboard()** restores the initial modelview matrix and returns the torus to its original location.

The **display()** function is very simple: It clears the window and then calls **glCallList()** to execute the commands in the display list. If we hadn't used display lists, **display()** would have to reissue the commands to draw the torus each time it was called.

A display list contains only OpenGL commands. In Example 7-1, only the **glBegin()**, **glVertex()**, and **glEnd()** calls are stored in the display list. The parameters for the calls are evaluated, and their values are copied into the display list when it is created. All the trigonometry to create the torus is done only once, which should increase rendering performance. However, the values in the display list can't be changed later. And once a command has been stored in a list it is not possible to remove it. Neither can you add any new commands to the list after it has been defined. You can delete the entire display list and create a new one, but you can't edit it.

Note: Display lists also work well with GLU commands, since those operations are ultimately broken down into low-level OpenGL commands, which can easily be stored in display lists. Use of display lists with GLU is particularly important for optimizing performance of GLU tessellators and NURBS.

Display-List Design Philosophy

To optimize performance, an OpenGL display list is a cache of commands rather than a dynamic database. In other words, once a display list is created, it can't be modified. If a display list were modifiable, performance could be reduced by the overhead required to search through the display list and perform memory management. As portions of a modifiable display list were changed, memory allocation and deallocation might lead to memory fragmentation. Any modifications that the OpenGL implementation made to the display-list commands in order to make them more efficient to render would need to be redone. Also, the display list may be difficult to access, cached somewhere over a network or a system bus.

The way in which the commands in a display list are optimized may vary from implementation to implementation. For example, a command as simple as **glRotate*()** might show a significant improvement if it's in a display list, since the calculations to produce the rotation matrix aren't trivial (they can involve square roots and trigonometric functions). In the display list, however, only the final rotation matrix needs to be stored, so a display-list rotation command can be executed as fast as the hardware can execute **glMultMatrix*()**. A sophisticated OpenGL implementation might even concatenate adjacent transformation commands into a single matrix multiplication.

Although you're not guaranteed that your OpenGL implementation optimizes display lists for any particular uses, the execution of display lists isn't slower than executing the commands contained within them individually. There is some overhead, however, involved in jumping to a display list. If a particular list is small, this overhead could exceed any execution advantage. The most likely possibilities for optimization are listed next, with references to the chapters where the topics are discussed.

- Matrix operations (Chapter 3). Most matrix operations require OpenGL to compute inverses. Both the computed matrix and its inverse might be stored by a particular OpenGL implementation in a display list.

- Raster bitmaps and images (Chapter 8). The format in which you specify raster data isn't likely to be one that's ideal for the hardware. When a display list is compiled, OpenGL might transform the data into the representation preferred by the hardware. This can have a significant effect on the speed of raster character drawing, since character strings usually consist of a series of small bitmaps.

- Lights, material properties, and lighting models (Chapter 5). When you draw a scene with complex lighting conditions, you might change the materials for each item in the scene. Setting the materials can be slow, since it might involve significant calculations. If you put the material definitions in display lists, these calculations don't have to be done each time you switch materials, since only the results of the calculations need to be stored; as a result, rendering lit scenes might be faster. (See "Encapsulating Mode Changes" on page 275 for more details on using display lists to change such values as lighting conditions.)

- Textures (Chapter 9). You might be able to maximize efficiency when defining textures by compiling them into a display list, since the display list may allow the texture image to be cached in dedicated texture memory. Then the texture image would not have to be recopied each time it was needed. Also, the hardware texture format might differ from the OpenGL format, and the conversion can be done at display-list compile time rather than during display.

  In OpenGL version 1.0, the display list is the primary method to manage textures. However, if the OpenGL implementation that you are using is version 1.1 or greater, then you should store the texture in a *texture object* instead. (Some version 1.0 implementations have a vendor-specific extension to support texture objects. If your implementation supports texture objects, you are encouraged to use them.)

- Polygon stipple patterns (Chapter 2).

Some of the commands to specify the properties listed here are context-sensitive, so you need to take this into account to ensure optimum performance. For example, when GL_COLOR_MATERIAL is enabled, some of the material properties will track the current color. (See Chapter 5.) Any **glMaterial*()** calls that set the same material properties are ignored.

It may improve performance to store state settings with geometry. For example, suppose you want to apply a transformation to some geometric objects and then draw the result. Your code may look like this:

```
glNewList(1, GL_COMPILE);
draw_some_geometric_objects();
glEndList();

glLoadMatrix(M);
glCallList(1);
```

However, if the geometric objects are to be transformed in the same way each time, it is better to store the matrix in the display list. For example, if you were to write your code as follows, some implementations may be able to improve performance by transforming the objects when they are defined instead of each time they are drawn:

```
glNewList(1, GL_COMPILE);
glLoadMatrix(M);
draw_some_geometric_objects();
glEndList();

glCallList(1);
```

A more likely situation occurs when rendering images. As you will see in Chapter 8, you can modify pixel transfer state variables and control the way images and bitmaps are rasterized. If the commands that set these state variables precede the definition of the image or bitmap in the display list, the implementation may be able to perform some of the operations ahead of time and cache the result.

Remember that display lists have some disadvantages. Very small lists may not perform well since there is some overhead when executing a list. Another disadvantage is the immutability of the contents of a display list. To optimize performance, an OpenGL display list can't be changed and its contents can't be read. If the application needs to maintain data separately from the display list (for example, for continued data processing), then a lot of additional memory may be required.

Creating and Executing a Display List

As you've already seen, **glNewList()** and **glEndList()** are used to begin and end the definition of a display list, which is then invoked by supplying its identifying index with **glCallList()**. In Example 7-2, a display list is created in the **init()** routine. This display list contains OpenGL commands to draw a red triangle. Then in the **display()** routine, the display list is executed ten times. In addition, a line is drawn in immediate mode. Note that the display list allocates memory to store the commands and the values of any necessary variables.

Example 7-2   Using a Display List: list.c

```
#include <GL/gl.h>
#include <GL/glu.h>
```

```
#include <GL/glut.h>
#include <stdlib.h>

GLuint listName;

static void init (void)
{
   listName = glGenLists (1);
   glNewList (listName, GL_COMPILE);
      glColor3f (1.0, 0.0, 0.0);  /*  current color red  */
      glBegin (GL_TRIANGLES);
      glVertex2f (0.0, 0.0);
      glVertex2f (1.0, 0.0);
      glVertex2f (0.0, 1.0);
      glEnd ();
      glTranslatef (1.5, 0.0, 0.0); /*  move position  */
   glEndList ();
   glShadeModel (GL_FLAT);
}

static void drawLine (void)
{
   glBegin (GL_LINES);
   glVertex2f (0.0, 0.5);
   glVertex2f (15.0, 0.5);
   glEnd ();
}

void display(void)
{
   GLuint i;

   glClear (GL_COLOR_BUFFER_BIT);
   glColor3f (0.0, 1.0, 0.0);  /*  current color green  */
   for (i = 0; i < 10; i++)    /*  draw 10 triangles   */
      glCallList (listName);
   drawLine ();  /*  is this line green?  NO!  */
                 /*  where is the line drawn?  */
   glFlush ();
}

void reshape(int w, int h)
{
   glViewport(0, 0, w, h);
   glMatrixMode(GL_PROJECTION);
   glLoadIdentity();
```

```
   if (w <= h)
      gluOrtho2D (0.0, 2.0, -0.5 * (GLfloat) h/(GLfloat) w,
         1.5 * (GLfloat) h/(GLfloat) w);
   else
      gluOrtho2D (0.0, 2.0*(GLfloat) w/(GLfloat) h, -0.5, 1.5);
   glMatrixMode(GL_MODELVIEW);
   glLoadIdentity();
}

void keyboard(unsigned char key, int x, int y)
{
   switch (key) {
      case 27:
         exit(0);
   }
}

int main(int argc, char** argv)
{
   glutInit(&argc, argv);
   glutInitDisplayMode (GLUT_SINGLE | GLUT_RGB);
   glutInitWindowSize(650, 50);
   glutCreateWindow(argv[0]);
   init ();
   glutReshapeFunc (reshape);
   glutKeyboardFunc (keyboard);
   glutDisplayFunc (display);
   glutMainLoop();
   return 0;
}
```

The **glTranslatef()** routine in the display list alters the position of the next object to be drawn. Without it, calling the display list twice would just draw the triangle on top of itself. The **drawLine()** routine, which is called in immediate mode, is also affected by the ten **glTranslatef()** calls that precede it. So if you call transformation commands within a display list, don't forget to take into account the effect those commands will have later in your program.

Only one display list can be created at a time. In other words, you must eventually follow **glNewList()** with **glEndList()** to end the creation of a display list before starting another one. As you might expect, calling **glEndList()** without having started a display list generates the error GL_INVALID_OPERATION. (See "Error Handling" on page 501 for more information about processing errors.)

Naming and Creating a Display List

Each display list is identified by an integer index. When creating a display list, you want to be careful that you don't accidentally choose an index that's already in use, thereby overwriting an existing display list. To avoid accidental deletions, use **glGenLists()** to generate one or more unused indices.

GLuint **glGenLists**(GLsizei *range*);

Allocates *range* number of contiguous, previously unallocated display-list indices. The integer returned is the index that marks the beginning of a contiguous block of empty display-list indices. The returned indices are all marked as empty and used, so subsequent calls to **glGenLists()** don't return these indices until they're deleted. Zero is returned if the requested number of indices isn't available, or if range is zero.

In the following example, a single index is requested, and if it proves to be available, it's used to create a new display list:

```
listIndex = glGenLists(1);
if (listIndex != 0) {
   glNewList(listIndex,GL_COMPILE);
      . . .
   glEndList();
}
```

Note: Zero is not a valid display-list index.

---

void **glNewList** (GLuint *list*, GLenum *mode*);

Specifies the start of a display list. OpenGL routines that are called subsequently (until **glEndList()** is called to end the display list) are stored in a display list, except for a few restricted OpenGL routines that can't be stored. (Those restricted routines are executed immediately, during the creation of the display list.) *list* is a nonzero positive integer that uniquely identifies the display list. The possible values for *mode* are GL_COMPILE and GL_COMPILE_AND_EXECUTE. Use GL_COMPILE if you don't want the OpenGL commands executed as they're placed in the display list; to cause the commands to be executed immediately as well as placed in the display list for later use, specify GL_COMPILE_AND_EXECUTE.

void **glEndList** (void);

Marks the end of a display list.

When a display list is created it is stored with the current OpenGL context. Thus, when the context is destroyed, the display list is also destroyed. Some windowing systems allow multiple contexts to share display lists. In this case, the display list is destroyed when the last context in the *share group* is destroyed.

What's Stored in a Display List

When you're building a display list, only the values for expressions are stored in the list. If values in an array are subsequently changed, the display-list values don't change. In the following code fragment, the display list contains a command to set the current RGBA color to black (0.0, 0.0, 0.0). The subsequent change of the value of the *color_vector* array to red (1.0, 0.0, 0.0) has no effect on the display list because the display list contains the values that were in effect when it was created.

```
GLfloat color_vector[3] = {0.0, 0.0, 0.0};
glNewList(1, GL_COMPILE);
    glColor3fv(color_vector);
glEndList();
color_vector[0] = 1.0;
```

Not all OpenGL commands can be stored and executed from within a display list. For example, commands that set client state and commands that retrieve state values aren't stored in a display list. (Many of these commands are easily identifiable because they return values in parameters passed by reference or return a value directly.) If these commands are called when making a display list, they're executed immediately.

Here are the OpenGL commands that aren't stored in a display list (also, note that **glNewList()** generates an error if it's called while you're creating a display list). Some of these commands haven't been described yet; you can look in the index to see where they're discussed.

glColorPointer()	glFlush()	glNormalPointer()
glDeleteLists()	glGenLists()	glPixelStore()
glDisableClientState()	glGet*()	glReadPixels()

glEdgeFlagPointer()	glIndexPointer()	glRenderMode()
glEnableClientState()	glInterleavedArrays()	glSelectBuffer()
glFeedbackBuffer()	glIsEnabled()	glTexCoordPointer()
glFinish()	glIsList()	glVertexPointer()

To understand more clearly why these commands can't be stored in a display list, remember that when you're using OpenGL across a network, the client may be on one machine and the server on another. After a display list is created, it resides with the server, so the server can't rely on the client for any information related to the display list. If querying commands, such as **glGet*()** or **glIs*()**, were allowed in a display list, the calling program would be surprised at random times by data returned over the network. Without parsing the display list as it was sent, the calling program wouldn't know where to put the data. Thus, any command that returns a value can't be stored in a display list. In addition, commands that change client state, such as **glPixelStore()**, **glSelectBuffer()**, and the commands to define vertex arrays, can't be stored in a display list.

The operation of some OpenGL commands depends upon client state. For example, the vertex array specification routines (such as **glVertexPointer()** **glColorPointer()**, and **glInterleavedArrays()**) set client state pointers and cannot be stored in a display list. **glArrayElement()**, **glDrawArrays()**, and **glDrawElements()** send data to the server state to construct primitives from elements in the enabled arrays, so these operations can be stored in a display list. (See "Vertex Arrays" on page 65.) The vertex array data stored in this display list is obtained by dereferencing data from the pointers, not by storing the pointers themselves. Therefore, subsequent changes to the data in the vertex arrays will not affect the definition of the primitive in the display list.

In addition, any commands that use the pixel storage modes use the modes that are in effect when they are placed in the display list. (See "Controlling Pixel-Storage Modes" on page 298.) Other routines that rely upon client state—such as **glFlush()** and **glFinish()**—can't be stored in a display list because they depend upon the client state that is in effect when they are executed.

Executing a Display List

After you've created a display list, you can execute it by calling **glCallList()**. Naturally, you can execute the same display list many times, and you can mix calls to execute display lists with calls to perform immediate-mode graphics, as you've already seen.

---

void **glCallList** (GLuint *list*);

This routine executes the display list specified by *list*. The commands in the display list are executed in the order they were saved, just as if they were issued without using a display list. If *list* hasn't been defined, nothing happens.

You can call **glCallList()** from anywhere within a program, as long as an OpenGL context that can access the display list is active (that is, the context that was active when the display list was created or a context in the same share group). A display list can be created in one routine and executed in a different one, since its index uniquely identifies it. Also, there is no facility to save the contents of a display list into a data file, nor a facility to create a display list from a file. In this sense, a display list is designed for temporary use.

Hierarchical Display Lists

You can create a *hierarchical display list*, which is a display list that executes another display list by calling **glCallList()** between a **glNewList()** and **glEndList()** pair. A hierarchical display list is useful for an object made of components, especially if some of those components are used more than once. For example, this is a display list that renders a bicycle by calling other display lists to render parts of the bicycle:

```
glNewList(listIndex,GL_COMPILE);
    glCallList(handlebars);
    glCallList(frame);
    glTranslatef(1.0,0.0,0.0);
    glCallList(wheel);
    glTranslatef(3.0,0.0,0.0);
    glCallList(wheel);
glEndList();
```

To avoid infinite recursion, there's a limit on the nesting level of display lists; the limit is at least 64, but it might be higher, depending on the implementation. To determine the nesting limit for your implementation of OpenGL, call

```
glGetIntegerv(GL_MAX_LIST_NESTING, GLint *data);
```

OpenGL allows you to create a display list that calls another list that hasn't been created yet. Nothing happens when the first list calls the second, undefined one.

You can use a hierarchical display list to approximate an editable display list by wrapping a list around several lower-level lists. For example, to put a polygon in a display list while allowing yourself to be able to easily edit its vertices, you could use the code in Example 7-3.

Example 7-3   Hierarchical Display List

```
glNewList(1,GL_COMPILE);
   glVertex3f(v1);
glEndList();
glNewList(2,GL_COMPILE);
   glVertex3f(v2);
glEndList();
glNewList(3,GL_COMPILE);
   glVertex3f(v3);
glEndList();

glNewList(4,GL_COMPILE);
   glBegin(GL_POLYGON);
      glCallList(1);
      glCallList(2);
      glCallList(3);
   glEnd();
glEndList();
```

To render the polygon, call display list number 4. To edit a vertex, you need only recreate the single display list corresponding to that vertex. Since an index number uniquely identifies a display list, creating one with the same index as an existing one automatically deletes the old one. Keep in mind that this technique doesn't necessarily provide optimal memory usage or peak performance, but it's acceptable and useful in some cases.

Managing Display List Indices

So far, we've recommended the use of **glGenLists()** to obtain unused display-list indices. If you insist upon avoiding **glGenLists()**, then be sure to use **glIsList()** to determine whether a specific index is in use.

GLboolean **glIsList**(GLuint *list*);

Returns GL_TRUE if list is already used for a display list and GL_FALSE otherwise.

You can explicitly delete a specific display list or a contiguous range of lists with **glDeleteLists()**. Using **glDeleteLists()** makes those indices available again.

---

void **glDeleteLists**(GLuint *list*, GLsizei *range*);

Deletes *range* display lists, starting at the index specified by *list*. An attempt to delete a list that has never been created is ignored.

Executing Multiple Display Lists

OpenGL provides an efficient mechanism to execute several display lists in succession. This mechanism requires that you put the display-list indices in an array and call **glCallLists()**. An obvious use for such a mechanism occurs when display-list indices correspond to meaningful values. For example, if you're creating a font, each display-list index might correspond to the ASCII value of a character in that font. To have several such fonts, you would need to establish a different initial display-list index for each font. You can specify this initial index by using **glListBase()** before calling **glCallLists()**.

---

void **glListBase**(GLuint *base*);

Specifies the offset that's added to the display-list indices in **glCallLists()** to obtain the final display-list indices. The default display-list base is 0. The list base has no effect on **glCallList()**, which executes only one display list or on **glNewList()**.

---

void **glCallLists**(GLsizei *n*, GLenum *type*, const GLvoid **lists*);

Executes *n* display lists. The indices of the lists to be executed are computed by adding the offset indicated by the current display-list base (specified with **glListBase()**) to the signed integer values in the array pointed to by *lists*.

The *type* parameter indicates the data type of the values in *lists*. It can be set to GL_BYTE, GL_UNSIGNED_BYTE, GL_SHORT, GL_UNSIGNED_SHORT, GL_INT, GL_UNSIGNED_INT, or GL_FLOAT, indicating that *lists* should be treated as an array of bytes, unsigned bytes, shorts, unsigned shorts, integers, unsigned integers, or floats, respectively. *Type* can also be GL_2_BYTES, GL_3_BYTES, or GL_4_BYTES, in which case sequences of 2, 3, or 4 bytes are read from *lists* and then shifted and added together, byte by byte, to calculate the display-list offset. The following algorithm is used (where *byte[0]* is the start of a byte sequence).

```
/* b = 2, 3, or 4; bytes are numbered 0, 1, 2, 3 in array */
offset = 0;
for (i = 0; i < b; i++) {
   offset = offset << 8;
   offset += byte[i];
}
index = offset + listbase;
```

For multiple-byte data, the highest-order data comes first as bytes are taken from the array in order.

As an example of the use of multiple display lists, look at the program fragments in Example 7-4 taken from the full program in Example 7-5. This program draws characters with a stroked font (a set of letters made from line segments). The routine **initStrokedFont()** sets up the display-list indices for each letter so that they correspond with their ASCII values.

Example 7-4   Defining Multiple Display Lists

```
void initStrokedFont(void)
{
   GLuint base;

   base = glGenLists(128);
   glListBase(base);
   glNewList(base+'A', GL_COMPILE);
      drawLetter(Adata); glEndList();
```

```
glNewList(base+'E', GL_COMPILE);
    drawLetter(Edata); glEndList();
glNewList(base+'P', GL_COMPILE);
    drawLetter(Pdata); glEndList();
glNewList(base+'R', GL_COMPILE);
    drawLetter(Rdata); glEndList();
glNewList(base+'S', GL_COMPILE);
    drawLetter(Sdata); glEndList();
glNewList(base+' ', GL_COMPILE);        /* space character */
    glTranslatef(8.0, 0.0, 0.0);
glEndList();
}
```

The **glGenLists()** command allocates 128 contiguous display-list indices. The first of the contiguous indices becomes the display-list base. A display list is made for each letter; each display-list index is the sum of the base and the ASCII value of that letter. In this example, only a few letters and the space character are created.

After the display lists have been created, **glCallLists()** can be called to execute the display lists. For example, you can pass a character string to the subroutine **printStrokedString()**:

```
void printStrokedString(GLbyte *s)
{
   GLint len = strlen(s);
   glCallLists(len, GL_BYTE, s);
}
```

The ASCII value for each letter in the string is used as the offset into the display-list indices. The current list base is added to the ASCII value of each letter to determine the final display-list index to be executed. The output produced by Example 7-5 is shown in Figure 7-1.

Figure 7-1   Stroked Font That Defines the Characters A, E, P, R, S

Example 7-5   Multiple Display Lists to Define a Stroked Font: stroke.c

```
#include <GL/gl.h>
#include <GL/glu.h>
#include <GL/glut.h>
```

```c
#include <stdlib.h>
#include <string.h>

#define PT     1
#define STROKE 2
#define END    3

typedef struct charpoint {
   GLfloat   x, y;
   int       type;
} CP;

CP Adata[] = {
   { 0, 0, PT}, {0, 9, PT}, {1, 10, PT}, {4, 10, PT},
   {5, 9, PT}, {5, 0, STROKE}, {0, 5, PT}, {5, 5, END}
};

CP Edata[] = {
   {5, 0, PT}, {0, 0, PT}, {0, 10, PT}, {5, 10, STROKE},
   {0, 5, PT}, {4, 5, END}
};

CP Pdata[] = {
   {0, 0, PT}, {0, 10, PT}, {4, 10, PT}, {5, 9, PT}, {5, 6, PT},
   {4, 5, PT}, {0, 5, END}
};

CP Rdata[] = {
   {0, 0, PT}, {0, 10, PT}, {4, 10, PT}, {5, 9, PT}, {5, 6, PT},
   {4, 5, PT}, {0, 5, STROKE}, {3, 5, PT}, {5, 0, END}
};

CP Sdata[] = {
   {0, 1, PT}, {1, 0, PT}, {4, 0, PT}, {5, 1, PT}, {5, 4, PT},
   {4, 5, PT}, {1, 5, PT}, {0, 6, PT}, {0, 9, PT}, {1, 10, PT},
   {4, 10, PT}, {5, 9, END}
};

/*  drawLetter() interprets the instructions from the array
 *  for that letter and renders the letter with line segments.
 */
static void drawLetter(CP *l)
{
   glBegin(GL_LINE_STRIP);
   while (1) {
      switch (l->type) {
```

```
        case PT:
            glVertex2fv(&l->x);
            break;
        case STROKE:
            glVertex2fv(&l->x);
            glEnd();
            glBegin(GL_LINE_STRIP);
            break;
        case END:
            glVertex2fv(&l->x);
            glEnd();
            glTranslatef(8.0, 0.0, 0.0);
            return;
    }
    l++;
    }
}

/*  Create a display list for each of 6 characters     */
static void init (void)
{
    GLuint base;

    glShadeModel (GL_FLAT);

    base = glGenLists (128);
    glListBase(base);
    glNewList(base+'A', GL_COMPILE); drawLetter(Adata);
    glEndList();
    glNewList(base+'E', GL_COMPILE); drawLetter(Edata);
    glEndList();
    glNewList(base+'P', GL_COMPILE); drawLetter(Pdata);
    glEndList();
    glNewList(base+'R', GL_COMPILE); drawLetter(Rdata);
    glEndList();
    glNewList(base+'S', GL_COMPILE); drawLetter(Sdata);
    glEndList();
    glNewList(base+' ', GL_COMPILE);
    glTranslatef(8.0, 0.0, 0.0); glEndList();
}

char *test1 = "A SPARE SERAPE APPEARS AS";
char *test2 = "APES PREPARE RARE PEPPERS";
```

```
static void printStrokedString(char *s)
{
   GLsizei len = strlen(s);
   glCallLists(len, GL_BYTE, (GLbyte *)s);
}

void display(void)
{
   glClear(GL_COLOR_BUFFER_BIT);
   glColor3f(1.0, 1.0, 1.0);
   glPushMatrix();
   glScalef(2.0, 2.0, 2.0);
   glTranslatef(10.0, 30.0, 0.0);
   printStrokedString(test1);
   glPopMatrix();
   glPushMatrix();
   glScalef(2.0, 2.0, 2.0);
   glTranslatef(10.0, 13.0, 0.0);
   printStrokedString(test2);
   glPopMatrix();
   glFlush();
}

void reshape(int w, int h)
{
   glViewport(0, 0, (GLsizei) w, (GLsizei) h);
   glMatrixMode (GL_PROJECTION);
   glLoadIdentity ();
   gluOrtho2D (0.0, (GLdouble) w, 0.0, (GLdouble) h);
}

void keyboard(unsigned char key, int x, int y)
{
   switch (key) {
      case ' ':
         glutPostRedisplay();
         break;
      case 27:
         exit(0);
   }
}

int main(int argc, char** argv)
{
   glutInit(&argc, argv);
   glutInitDisplayMode (GLUT_SINGLE | GLUT_RGB);
   glutInitWindowSize (440, 120);
```

```
    glutCreateWindow (argv[0]);
    init ();
    glutReshapeFunc(reshape);
    glutKeyboardFunc(keyboard);
    glutDisplayFunc(display);
    glutMainLoop();
    return 0;
}
```

Managing State Variables with Display Lists

A display list can contain calls that change the value of OpenGL state
variables. These values change as the display list is executed, just as if the
commands were called in immediate mode and the changes persist after
execution of the display list is completed. As previously seen in Example 7-2
and in Example 7-6, which follows, the changes to the current color and
current matrix made during the execution of the display list remain in
effect after it has been called.

Example 7-6 Persistence of State Changes after Execution of a Display List

```
glNewList(listIndex,GL_COMPILE);
    glColor3f(1.0, 0.0, 0.0);
    glBegin(GL_POLYGON);
        glVertex2f(0.0,0.0);
        glVertex2f(1.0,0.0);
        glVertex2f(0.0,1.0);
    glEnd();
    glTranslatef(1.5,0.0,0.0);
glEndList();
```

So if you now call the following sequence, the line drawn after the display
list is drawn with red as the current color and translated by an additional
(1.5, 0.0, 0.0):

```
glCallList(listIndex);
glBegin(GL_LINES);
    glVertex2f(2.0,-1.0);
    glVertex2f(1.0,0.0);
glEnd();
```

Sometimes you want state changes to persist, but other times you want to
save the values of state variables before executing a display list and then
restore these values after the list has executed. Remember that you cannot

use **glGet*()** in a display list, so you must use another way to query and store the values of state variables.

You can use **glPushAttrib()** to save a group of state variables and **glPopAttrib()** to restore the values when you're ready for them. To save and restore the current matrix, use **glPushMatrix()** and **glPopMatrix()** as described in "Manipulating the Matrix Stacks" on page 132. These push and pop routines can be legally cached in a display list. To restore the state variables in Example 7-6, you might use the code shown in Example 7-7.

Example 7-7   Restoring State Variables within a Display List

```
glNewList(listIndex,GL_COMPILE);
   glPushMatrix();
   glPushAttrib(GL_CURRENT_BIT);
   glColor3f(1.0, 0.0, 0.0);
   glBegin(GL_POLYGON);
      glVertex2f(0.0,0.0);
      glVertex2f(1.0,0.0);
      glVertex2f(0.0,1.0);
   glEnd();
   glTranslatef(1.5,0.0,0.0);
   glPopAttrib();
   glPopMatrix();
glEndList();
```

If you use the display list from Example 7-7, which restores values, the code in Example 7-8 draws a green, untranslated line. With the display list in Example 7-6, which doesn't save and restore values, the line is drawn red, and its position is translated ten times (1.5, 0.0, 0.0).

Example 7-8   The Display List May or May Not Affect drawLine()

```
void display(void)
{
   GLint i;

   glClear(GL_COLOR_BUFFER_BIT);
   glColor3f(0.0, 1.0, 0.0);   /* set current color to green   */
   for (i = 0; i < 10; i++)
      glCallList(listIndex);   /* display list called 10 times */
   drawLine();                 /* how and where does this line appear? */
   glFlush();
}
```

Encapsulating Mode Changes

You can use display lists to organize and store groups of commands to change various modes or set various parameters. When you want to switch from one group of settings to another, using display lists might be more efficient than making the calls directly, since the settings might be cached in a format that matches the requirements of your graphics system.

Display lists may be more efficient than immediate mode for switching among various lighting, lighting-model, and material-parameter settings. You might also use display lists for stipple patterns, fog parameters, and clipping-plane equations. In general, you'll find that executing display lists is at least as fast as making the relevant calls directly, but remember that some overhead is involved in jumping to a display list.

Example 7-9 shows how to use display lists to switch among three different line stipples. First, you call **glGenLists()** to allocate a display list for each stipple pattern and create a display list for each pattern. Then, you use **glCallList()** to switch from one stipple pattern to another.

Example 7-9   Display Lists for Mode Changes

```
GLuint offset;
offset = glGenLists(3);

glNewList (offset, GL_COMPILE);
    glDisable (GL_LINE_STIPPLE);
glEndList ();

glNewList (offset+1, GL_COMPILE);
    glEnable (GL_LINE_STIPPLE);
    glLineStipple (1, 0x0F0F);
glEndList ();

glNewList (offset+2, GL_COMPILE);
    glEnable (GL_LINE_STIPPLE);
    glLineStipple (1, 0x1111);
glEndList ();


#define drawOneLine(x1,y1,x2,y2) glBegin(GL_LINES); \
    glVertex2f ((x1),(y1)); glVertex2f ((x2),(y2)); glEnd();

glCallList (offset);
drawOneLine (50.0, 125.0, 350.0, 125.0);
```

```
glCallList (offset+1);
drawOneLine (50.0, 100.0, 350.0, 100.0);

glCallList (offset+2);
drawOneLine (50.0, 75.0, 350.0, 75.0);
```

Chapter 8

Drawing Pixels, Bitmaps, Fonts, and Images

Chapter Objectives

After reading this chapter, you'll be able to do the following:

- Position and draw bitmapped data

- Read pixel data (bitmaps and images) from the framebuffer into processor memory and from memory into the framebuffer

- Copy pixel data from one color buffer to another, or to another location in the same buffer

- Magnify or reduce an image as it's written to the framebuffer

- Control pixel-data formatting and perform other transformations as the data is moved to and from the framebuffer

So far, most of the discussion in this guide has concerned the rendering of geometric data—points, lines, and polygons. Two other important classes of data that can be rendered by OpenGL are

- Bitmaps, typically used for characters in fonts

- Image data, which might have been scanned in or calculated

Both bitmaps and image data take the form of rectangular arrays of pixels. One difference between them is that a *bitmap* consists of a single bit of information about each pixel, and image data typically includes several pieces of data per pixel (the complete red, green, blue, and alpha color components, for example). Also, bitmaps are like masks in that they're used to overlay another image, but image data simply overwrites or is blended with whatever data is in the framebuffer.

This chapter describes how to draw pixel data (bitmaps and images) from processor memory to the framebuffer and how to read pixel data from the framebuffer into processor memory. It also describes how to copy pixel data from one position to another, either from one buffer to another or within a single buffer. This chapter contains the following major sections:

- "Bitmaps and Fonts" on page 279 describes the commands for positioning and drawing bitmapped data. Such data may describe a font.

- "Images" on page 289 presents the basic information about drawing, reading and copying pixel data.

- "Imaging Pipeline" on page 296 describes the operations that are performed on images and bitmaps when they are read from the framebuffer and when they are written to the framebuffer.

- "Reading and Drawing Pixel Rectangles" on page 309 covers all the details of how pixel data is stored in memory and how to transform it as it's moved into or out of memory.

- "Tips for Improving Pixel Drawing Rates" on page 314 lists tips for getting better performance when drawing pixel rectangles.

In most cases, the necessary pixel operations are simple, so the first three sections might be all you need to read for your application. However, pixel manipulation can be complex—there are many ways to store pixel data in memory, and you can apply any of several transformations to pixels as they're moved to and from the framebuffer. These details are the subject of the fourth section of this chapter. Most likely, you'll want to read this section only when you actually need to make use of the information. The

Chapter 8: Drawing Pixels, Bitmaps, Fonts, and Images

last section provides useful tips to get the best performance when rendering bitmaps and images.

Bitmaps and Fonts

A bitmap is a rectangular array of 0s and 1s that serves as a drawing mask for a corresponding rectangular portion of the window. Suppose you're drawing a bitmap and that the current raster color is red. Wherever there's a 1 in the bitmap, the corresponding pixel is replaced by a red pixel (or combined with a red pixel, depending on which per-fragment operations are in effect. (See "Testing and Operating on Fragments" on page 382.) If there's a 0 in the bitmap, the contents of the pixel are unaffected. The most common use of bitmaps is for drawing characters on the screen.

OpenGL provides only the lowest level of support for drawing strings of characters and manipulating fonts. The commands **glRasterPos*()** and **glBitmap()** position and draw a single bitmap on the screen. In addition, through the display-list mechanism, you can use a sequence of character codes to index into a corresponding series of bitmaps representing those characters. (See Chapter 7 for more information about display lists.) You'll have to write your own routines to provide any other support you need for manipulating bitmaps, fonts, and strings of characters.

Consider Example 8-1, which draws the character F three times on the screen. Figure 8-1 shows the F as a bitmap and its corresponding bitmap data.

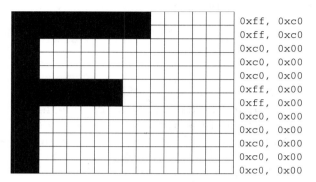

	0xff, 0xc0
	0xff, 0xc0
	0xc0, 0x00
	0xc0, 0x00
	0xc0, 0x00
	0xff, 0x00
	0xff, 0x00
	0xc0, 0x00
	0xc0, 0x00
	0xc0, 0x00
	0xc0, 0x00
	0xc0, 0x00

Figure 8-1   Bitmapped F and Its Data

Example 8-1   Drawing a Bitmapped Character: drawf.c

```
#include <GL/gl.h>
#include <GL/glu.h>
#include <GL/glut.h>
#include <stdlib.h>

GLubyte rasters[24] = {
    0xc0, 0x00, 0xc0, 0x00, 0xc0, 0x00, 0xc0, 0x00, 0xc0, 0x00,
    0xff, 0x00, 0xff, 0x00, 0xc0, 0x00, 0xc0, 0x00, 0xc0, 0x00,
    0xff, 0xc0, 0xff, 0xc0};

void init(void)
{
    glPixelStorei (GL_UNPACK_ALIGNMENT, 1);
    glClearColor (0.0, 0.0, 0.0, 0.0);
}

void display(void)
{
    glClear(GL_COLOR_BUFFER_BIT);
    glColor3f (1.0, 1.0, 1.0);
    glRasterPos2i (20, 20);
    glBitmap (10, 12, 0.0, 0.0, 11.0, 0.0, rasters);
    glBitmap (10, 12, 0.0, 0.0, 11.0, 0.0, rasters);
    glBitmap (10, 12, 0.0, 0.0, 11.0, 0.0, rasters);
    glFlush();
}

void reshape(int w, int h)
{
    glViewport(0, 0, (GLsizei) w, (GLsizei) h);
```

```
    glMatrixMode(GL_PROJECTION);
    glLoadIdentity();
    glOrtho (0, w, 0, h, -1.0, 1.0);
    glMatrixMode(GL_MODELVIEW);
}

void keyboard(unsigned char key, int x, int y)
{
    switch (key) {
        case 27:
            exit(0);
    }
}

int main(int argc, char** argv)
{
    glutInit(&argc, argv);
    glutInitDisplayMode(GLUT_SINGLE | GLUT_RGB);
    glutInitWindowSize(100, 100);
    glutInitWindowPosition(100, 100);
    glutCreateWindow(argv[0]);
    init();
    glutReshapeFunc(reshape);
    glutKeyboardFunc(keyboard);
    glutDisplayFunc(display);
    glutMainLoop();
    return 0;
}
```

In Figure 8-1, note that the visible part of the F character is at most 10 bits wide. Bitmap data is always stored in chunks that are multiples of 8 bits, but the width of the actual bitmap doesn't have to be a multiple of 8. The bits making up a bitmap are drawn starting from the lower-left corner: First, the bottom row is drawn, then the next row above it, and so on. As you can tell from the code, the bitmap is stored in memory in this order—the array of rasters begins with 0xc0, 0x00, 0xc0, 0x00 for the bottom two rows of the F and continues to 0xff, 0xc0, 0xff, 0xc0 for the top two rows.

The commands of interest in this example are **glRasterPos2i()** and **glBitmap()**; they're discussed in detail in the next section. For now, ignore the call to **glPixelStorei()**; it describes how the bitmap data is stored in computer memory. (See "Controlling Pixel-Storage Modes" on page 298 for more information.)

The Current Raster Position

The *current raster position* is the origin where the next bitmap (or image) is to be drawn. In the F example, the raster position was set by calling **glRasterPos*()** with coordinates (20, 20), which is where the lower-left corner of the F was drawn:

```
glRasterPos2i(20, 20);
```

---

void **glRasterPos{234}{sifd}**(*TYPE x, TYPE y, TYPE z, TYPE w*);
void **glRasterPos{234}{sifd}v**(*TYPE *coords*);

Sets the current raster position. The *x, y, z,* and *w* arguments specify the coordinates of the raster position. If the vector form of the function is used, the *coords* array contains the coordinates of the raster position. If **glRasterPos2*()** is used, *z* is implicitly set to zero and *w* is implicitly set to one; similarly, with **glRasterPos3*()**, *w* is set to one.

The coordinates of the raster position are transformed to screen coordinates in exactly the same way as coordinates supplied with a **glVertex*()** command (that is, with the modelview and perspective matrices). After transformation, they either define a valid spot in the viewport, or they're clipped out because the coordinates were outside the viewing volume. If the transformed point is clipped out, the current raster position is invalid.

Note: If you want to specify the raster position in screen coordinates, you'll want to make sure you've specified the modelview and projection matrices for simple 2D rendering, with something like this sequence of commands, where *width* and *height* are also the size (in pixels) of the viewport:

```
glMatrixMode(GL_PROJECTION);
glLoadIdentity();
gluOrtho2D(0.0, (GLfloat) width, 0.0, (GLfloat) height);
glMatrixMode(GL_MODELVIEW);
glLoadIdentity();
```

To obtain the current raster position, you can use the query command **glGetFloatv()** with GL_CURRENT_RASTER_POSITION as the first argument. The second argument should be a pointer to an array that can hold the (*x, y, z, w*) values as floating-point numbers. Call **glGetBooleanv()** with GL_CURRENT_RASTER_POSITION_VALID as the first argument to determine whether the current raster position is valid.

Drawing the Bitmap

Once you've set the desired raster position, you can use the **glBitmap()** command to draw the data.

---

void **glBitmap**(GLsizei *width*, GLsizei *height*, GLfloat x_{bo},
            GLfloat y_{bo}, GLfloat x_{bi},
            GLfloat y_{bi}, const GLubyte **bitmap*);

Draws the bitmap specified by *bitmap*, which is a pointer to the bitmap image. The origin of the bitmap is placed at the current raster position. If the current raster position is invalid, nothing is drawn, and the raster position remains invalid. The *width* and *height* arguments indicate the width and height, in pixels, of the bitmap. The width need not be a multiple of 8, although the data is stored in unsigned characters of 8 bits each. (In the F example, it wouldn't matter if there were garbage bits in the data beyond the tenth bit; since **glBitmap()** was called with a width of 10, only 10 bits of the row are rendered.) Use x_{bo} and y_{bo} to define the origin of the bitmap (positive values move the origin up and to the right of the raster position; negative values move it down and to the left); x_{bi} and y_{bi} indicate the *x* and *y* increments that are added to the raster position after the bitmap is rasterized (see Figure 8-2).

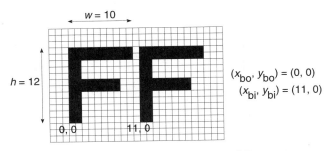

$(x_{bo}, y_{bo}) = (0, 0)$
$(x_{bi}, y_{bi}) = (11, 0)$

Figure 8-2   Bitmap and Its Associated Parameters

Allowing the origin of the bitmap to be placed arbitrarily makes it easy for characters to extend below the origin (typically used for characters with descenders, such as g, j, and y), or to extend beyond the left of the origin (used for various swash characters, which have extended flourishes, or for characters in fonts that lean to the left).

After the bitmap is drawn, the current raster position is advanced by x_{bi} and y_{bi} in the *x*- and *y*-directions, respectively. (If you just want to advance the current raster position without drawing anything, call **glBitmap()** with the *bitmap* parameter set to NULL and with the *width* and *height* set to zero.) For standard Latin fonts, y_{bi} is typically 0.0 and x_{bi} is positive (since successive characters are drawn from left to right). For Hebrew, where characters go from right to left, the x_{bi} values would typically be negative. Fonts that draw successive characters vertically in columns would use zero for x_{bi} and nonzero values for y_{bi}. In Figure 8-2, each time the F is drawn, the current raster position advances by 11 pixels, allowing a 1-pixel space between successive characters.

Since x_{bo}, y_{bo}, x_{bi}, and y_{bi} are floating-point values, characters need not be an integral number of pixels apart. Actual characters are drawn on exact pixel boundaries, but the current raster position is kept in floating point so that each character is drawn as close as possible to where it belongs. For example, if the code in the F example was modified so that x_{bi} is 11.5 instead of 12, and if more characters were drawn, the space between letters would alternate between 1 and 2 pixels, giving the best approximation to the requested 1.5-pixel space.

Note: You can't rotate bitmap fonts because the bitmap is always drawn aligned to the *x* and *y* framebuffer axes.

Choosing a Color for the Bitmap

You are familiar with using **glColor*()** and **glIndex*()** to set the current color or index to draw geometric primitives. The same commands are used to set different state variables, GL_CURRENT_RASTER_COLOR and GL_CURRENT_RASTER_INDEX, for rendering bitmaps. The raster color state variables are set when **glRasterPos*()** is called, which can lead to a trap. In the following sequence of code, what is the color of the bitmap?

```
glColor3f(1.0, 1.0, 1.0);   /* white */
glRasterPos3fv(position);
glColor3f(1.0, 0.0, 0.0);   /* red  */
glBitmap(....);
```

The bitmap is white! The GL_CURRENT_RASTER_COLOR is set to white when **glRasterPos3fv()** is called. The second call to **glColor3f()** changes the value of GL_CURRENT_COLOR for future geometric rendering, but the color used to render the bitmap is unchanged.

To obtain the current raster color or index, you can use the query commands **glGetFloatv()** or **glGetIntegerv()** with

GL_CURRENT_RASTER_COLOR or GL_CURRENT_RASTER_INDEX as the first argument.

Fonts and Display Lists

Display lists are discussed in general terms in Chapter 7. However, a few of the display-list management commands have special relevance for drawing strings of characters. As you read this section, keep in mind that the ideas presented here apply equally well to characters that are drawn using bitmap data and those drawn using geometric primitives (points, lines, and polygons). (See "Executing Multiple Display Lists" on page 267 for an example of a geometric font.)

A font typically consists of a set of characters, where each character has an identifying number (usually the ASCII code) and a drawing method. For a standard ASCII character set, the capital letter A is number 65, B is 66, and so on. The string "DAB" would be represented by the three indices 68, 65, 66. In the simplest approach, display-list number 65 draws an A, number 66 draws a B, and so on. Then to draw the string 68, 65, 66, just execute the corresponding display lists.

You can use the command **glCallLists()** in just this way:

```
void glCallLists(GLsizei n, GLenum type, const GLvoid *lists);
```

The first argument, *n*, indicates the number of characters to be drawn, *type* is usually GL_BYTE, and *lists* is an array of character codes.

Since many applications need to draw character strings in multiple fonts and sizes, this simplest approach isn't convenient. Instead, you'd like to use 65 as A no matter what font is currently active. You could force font 1 to encode A, B, and C as 1065, 1066, 1067, and font 2 as 2065, 2066, 2067, but then any numbers larger than 256 would no longer fit in an 8-bit byte. A better solution is to add an offset to every entry in the string and to choose the display list. In this case, font 1 has A, B, and C represented by 1065, 1066, and 1067, and in font 2, they might be 2065, 2066, and 2067. Then to draw characters in font 1, set the offset to 1000 and draw display lists 65, 66, and 67. To draw that same string in font 2, set the offset to 2000 and draw the same lists.

To set the offset, use the command **glListBase()**. For the preceding examples, it should be called with 1000 or 2000 as the (only) argument.

Now what you need is a contiguous list of unused display-list numbers, which you can obtain from **glGenLists()**:

```
GLuint glGenLists(GLsizei range);
```

This function returns a block of *range* display-list identifiers. The returned lists are all marked as "used" even though they're empty, so that subsequent calls to **glGenLists()** never return the same lists (unless you've explicitly deleted them previously). Therefore, if you use 4 as the argument and if **glGenLists()** returns 81, you can use display-list identifiers 81, 82, 83, and 84 for your characters. If **glGenLists()** can't find a block of unused identifiers of the requested length, it returns 0. (Note that the command **glDeleteLists()** makes it easy to delete all the lists associated with a font in a single operation.)

Most American and European fonts have a small number of characters (fewer than 256), so it's easy to represent each character with a different code that can be stored in a single byte. Asian fonts, among others, may require much larger character sets, so a byte-per-character encoding is impossible. OpenGL allows strings to be composed of 1-, 2-, 3-, or 4-byte characters through the *type* parameter in **glCallLists()**. This parameter can have any of the following values:

GL_BYTE	GL_UNSIGNED_BYTE
GL_SHORT	GL_UNSIGNED_SHORT
GL_INT	GL_UNSIGNED_INT
GL_FLOAT	GL_2_BYTES
GL_3_BYTES	GL_4_BYTES

(See "Executing Multiple Display Lists" on page 267 for more information about these values.)

Defining and Using a Complete Font

The **glBitmap()** command and the display-list mechanism described in the previous section make it easy to define a raster font. In Example 8-2, the upper-case characters of an ASCII font are defined. In this example, each character has the same width, but this is not always the case. Once the characters are defined, the program prints the message "THE QUICK BROWN FOX JUMPS OVER A LAZY DOG".

The code in Example 8-2 is similar to the F example, except that each character's bitmap is stored in its own display list. The display list identifier, when combined with the offset returned by **glGenLists()**, is equal to the ASCII code for the character.

Example 8-2   Drawing a Complete Font: font.c

```
#include <GL/gl.h>
#include <GL/glu.h>
#include <GL/glut.h>
#include <stdlib.h>
#include <string.h>

GLubyte space[] =
    {0x00, 0x00, 0x00, 0x00, 0x00, 0x00, 0x00, 0x00, 0x00, 0x00, 0x00, 0x00, 0x00};

GLubyte letters[][13] = {
    {0x00, 0x00, 0xc3, 0xc3, 0xc3, 0xc3, 0xff, 0xc3, 0xc3, 0xc3, 0x66, 0x3c, 0x18},
    {0x00, 0x00, 0xfe, 0xc7, 0xc3, 0xc3, 0xc7, 0xfe, 0xc7, 0xc3, 0xc3, 0xc7, 0xfe},
    {0x00, 0x00, 0x7e, 0xe7, 0xc0, 0xc0, 0xc0, 0xc0, 0xc0, 0xc0, 0xc0, 0xe7, 0x7e},
    {0x00, 0x00, 0xfc, 0xce, 0xc7, 0xc3, 0xc3, 0xc3, 0xc3, 0xc3, 0xc7, 0xce, 0xfc},
    {0x00, 0x00, 0xff, 0xc0, 0xc0, 0xc0, 0xc0, 0xfc, 0xc0, 0xc0, 0xc0, 0xc0, 0xff},
    {0x00, 0x00, 0xc0, 0xc0, 0xc0, 0xc0, 0xc0, 0xc0, 0xfc, 0xc0, 0xc0, 0xc0, 0xff},
    {0x00, 0x00, 0x7e, 0xe7, 0xc3, 0xc3, 0xcf, 0xc0, 0xc0, 0xc0, 0xc0, 0xe7, 0x7e},
    {0x00, 0x00, 0xc3, 0xc3, 0xc3, 0xc3, 0xc3, 0xff, 0xc3, 0xc3, 0xc3, 0xc3, 0xc3},
    {0x00, 0x00, 0x7e, 0x18, 0x18, 0x18, 0x18, 0x18, 0x18, 0x18, 0x18, 0x18, 0x7e},
    {0x00, 0x00, 0x7c, 0xee, 0xc6, 0x06, 0x06, 0x06, 0x06, 0x06, 0x06, 0x06, 0x06},
    {0x00, 0x00, 0xc3, 0xc6, 0xcc, 0xd8, 0xf0, 0xe0, 0xf0, 0xd8, 0xcc, 0xc6, 0xc3},
    {0x00, 0x00, 0xff, 0xc0, 0xc0, 0xc0, 0xc0, 0xc0, 0xc0, 0xc0, 0xc0, 0xc0, 0xc0},
    {0x00, 0x00, 0xc3, 0xc3, 0xc3, 0xc3, 0xc3, 0xc3, 0xdb, 0xff, 0xff, 0xe7, 0xc3},
    {0x00, 0x00, 0xc7, 0xc7, 0xcf, 0xcf, 0xdf, 0xdb, 0xfb, 0xf3, 0xf3, 0xe3, 0xe3},
    {0x00, 0x00, 0x7e, 0xe7, 0xc3, 0xc3, 0xc3, 0xc3, 0xc3, 0xc3, 0xc3, 0xe7, 0x7e},
    {0x00, 0x00, 0xc0, 0xc0, 0xc0, 0xc0, 0xc0, 0xfe, 0xc7, 0xc3, 0xc3, 0xc7, 0xfe},
    {0x00, 0x00, 0x3f, 0x6e, 0xdf, 0xdb, 0xc3, 0xc3, 0xc3, 0xc3, 0xc3, 0x66, 0x3c},
    {0x00, 0x00, 0xc3, 0xc6, 0xcc, 0xd8, 0xf0, 0xfe, 0xc7, 0xc3, 0xc3, 0xc7, 0xfe},
    {0x00, 0x00, 0x7e, 0xe7, 0x03, 0x03, 0x07, 0x7e, 0xe0, 0xc0, 0xc0, 0xe7, 0x7e},
    {0x00, 0x00, 0x18, 0x18, 0x18, 0x18, 0x18, 0x18, 0x18, 0x18, 0x18, 0x18, 0xff},
    {0x00, 0x00, 0x7e, 0xe7, 0xc3, 0xc3, 0xc3, 0xc3, 0xc3, 0xc3, 0xc3, 0xc3, 0xc3},
    {0x00, 0x00, 0x18, 0x3c, 0x3c, 0x66, 0x66, 0xc3, 0xc3, 0xc3, 0xc3, 0xc3, 0xc3},
    {0x00, 0x00, 0xc3, 0xe7, 0xff, 0xff, 0xdb, 0xdb, 0xc3, 0xc3, 0xc3, 0xc3, 0xc3},
    {0x00, 0x00, 0xc3, 0x66, 0x66, 0x3c, 0x3c, 0x18, 0x3c, 0x3c, 0x66, 0x66, 0xc3},
    {0x00, 0x00, 0x18, 0x18, 0x18, 0x18, 0x18, 0x18, 0x3c, 0x3c, 0x66, 0x66, 0xc3},
    {0x00, 0x00, 0xff, 0xc0, 0xc0, 0x60, 0x30, 0x7e, 0x0c, 0x06, 0x03, 0x03, 0xff}
};

GLuint fontOffset;
```

```
void makeRasterFont(void)
{
   GLuint i, j;
   glPixelStorei(GL_UNPACK_ALIGNMENT, 1);

   fontOffset = glGenLists (128);
   for (i = 0,j = 'A'; i < 26; i++,j++) {
      glNewList(fontOffset + j, GL_COMPILE);
      glBitmap(8, 13, 0.0, 2.0, 10.0, 0.0, letters[i]);
      glEndList();
   }
   glNewList(fontOffset + ' ', GL_COMPILE);
   glBitmap(8, 13, 0.0, 2.0, 10.0, 0.0, space);
   glEndList();
}

void init(void)
{
   glShadeModel (GL_FLAT);
   makeRasterFont();
}

void printString(char *s)
{
   glPushAttrib (GL_LIST_BIT);
   glListBase(fontOffset);
   glCallLists(strlen(s), GL_UNSIGNED_BYTE, (GLubyte *) s);
   glPopAttrib ();
}

/* Everything above this line could be in a library
 * that defines a font.  To make it work, you've got
 * to call makeRasterFont() before you start making
 * calls to printString().
 */
void display(void)
{
   GLfloat white[3] = { 1.0, 1.0, 1.0 };

   glClear(GL_COLOR_BUFFER_BIT);
   glColor3fv(white);
```

```
    glRasterPos2i(20, 60);
    printString("THE QUICK BROWN FOX JUMPS");
    glRasterPos2i(20, 40);
    printString("OVER A LAZY DOG");
    glFlush ();
}

void reshape(int w, int h)
{
    glViewport(0, 0, (GLsizei) w, (GLsizei) h);
    glMatrixMode(GL_PROJECTION);
    glLoadIdentity();
    glOrtho (0.0, w, 0.0, h, -1.0, 1.0);
    glMatrixMode(GL_MODELVIEW);
}

void keyboard(unsigned char key, int x, int y)
{
    switch (key) {
        case 27:
            exit(0);
    }
}

int main(int argc, char** argv)
{
    glutInit(&argc, argv);
    glutInitDisplayMode(GLUT_SINGLE | GLUT_RGB);
    glutInitWindowSize(300, 100);
    glutInitWindowPosition (100, 100);
    glutCreateWindow(argv[0]);
    init();
    glutReshapeFunc(reshape);
    glutKeyboardFunc(keyboard);
    glutDisplayFunc(display);
    glutMainLoop();
    return 0;
}
```

Images

An image is similar to a bitmap, but instead of containing only a single bit
for each pixel in a rectangular region of the screen, an image can contain
much more information. For example, an image can contain a complete (R,

G, B, A) color stored at each pixel. Images can come from several sources, such as

- A photograph that's digitized with a scanner

- An image that was first generated on the screen by a graphics program using the graphics hardware and then read back, pixel by pixel

- A software program that generated the image in memory pixel by pixel

The images you normally think of as pictures come from the color buffers. However, you can read or write rectangular regions of pixel data from or to the depth buffer or the stencil buffer. (See Chapter 10 for an explanation of these other buffers.)

In addition to simply being displayed on the screen, images can be used for texture maps, in which case they're essentially pasted onto polygons that are rendered on the screen in the normal way. (See Chapter 9 for more information about this technique.)

Reading, Writing, and Copying Pixel Data

OpenGL provides three basic commands that manipulate image data:

- **glReadPixels()**—Reads a rectangular array of pixels from the framebuffer and stores the data in processor memory.

- **glDrawPixels()**—Writes a rectangular array of pixels from data kept in processor memory into the framebuffer at the current raster position specified by **glRasterPos*()**.

- **glCopyPixels()**—Copies a rectangular array of pixels from one part of the framebuffer to another. This command behaves similarly to a call to **glReadPixels()** followed by a call to **glDrawPixels()**, but the data is never written into processor memory.

For the aforementioned commands, the order of pixel data processing operations is shown in Figure 8-3:

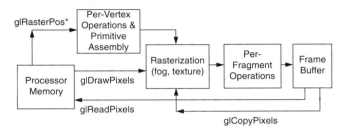

Figure 8-3   Simplistic Diagram of Pixel Data Flow

The basic ideas in Figure 8-3 are correct. The coordinates of **glRasterPos*()**, which specify the current raster position used by **glDrawPixels()** and **glCopyPixels()**, are transformed by the geometric processing pipeline. Both **glDrawPixels()** and **glCopyPixels()** are affected by rasterization and per-fragment operations. (But when drawing or copying a pixel rectangle, there's almost never a reason to have fog or texture enabled.)

However, additional steps arise because there are many kinds of framebuffer data, many ways to store pixel information in computer memory, and various data conversions that can be performed during the reading, writing, and copying operations. These possibilities translate to many different modes of operation. If all your program does is copy images on the screen or read them into memory temporarily so that they can be copied out later, you can ignore most of these modes. However, if you want your program to modify the data while it's in memory—for example, if you have an image stored in one format but the window requires a different format—or if you want to save image data to a file for future restoration in another session or on another kind of machine with significantly different graphical capabilities, you have to understand the various modes.

The rest of this section describes the basic commands in detail. The following sections discuss the details of the series of imaging operations that comprise the Imaging Pipeline: pixel-storage modes, pixel-transfer operations, and pixel-mapping operations.

Reading Pixel Data from Frame Buffer to Processor Memory

void **glReadPixels**(GLint *x*, GLint *y*, GLsizei *width*, GLsizei *height*,
GLenum *format*, GLenum *type*, GLvoid **pixels*);

Reads pixel data from the framebuffer rectangle whose lower-left corner is at (*x, y*) and whose dimensions are *width* and *height* and stores it in the array pointed to by *pixels*. *format* indicates the kind of pixel data elements that are read (an index value or an R, G, B, or A component value, as listed in Table 8-1), and *type* indicates the data type of each element (see Table 8-2).

If you are using **glReadPixels**() to obtain RGBA or color-index information, you may need to clarify which buffer you are trying to access. For example, if you have a double-buffered window, you need to specify whether you are reading data from the front buffer or back buffer. To control the current read source buffer, call **glReadBuffer**(). (See "Selecting Color Buffers for Writing and Reading" on page 379.)

format Constant	Pixel Format
GL_COLOR_INDEX	A single color index
GL_RGB	A red color component, followed by a green color component, followed by a blue color component
GL_RGBA	A red color component, followed by a green color component, followed by a blue color component, followed by an alpha color component
GL_RED	A single red color component
GL_GREEN	A single green color component
GL_BLUE	A single blue color component
GL_ALPHA	A single alpha color component
GL_LUMINANCE	A single luminance component
GL_LUMINANCE_ALPHA	A luminance component followed by an alpha color component
GL_STENCIL_INDEX	A single stencil index
GL_DEPTH_COMPONENT	A single depth component

Table 8-1   Pixel Formats for glReadPixels() or glDrawPixels()

type Constant	Data Type
GL_UNSIGNED_BYTE	unsigned 8-bit integer
GL_BYTE	signed 8-bit integer
GL_BITMAP	single bits in unsigned 8-bit integers using the same format as **glBitmap()**
GL_UNSIGNED_SHORT	unsigned 16-bit integer
GL_SHORT	signed 16-bit integer
GL_UNSIGNED_INT	unsigned 32-bit integer
GL_INT	signed 32-bit integer
GL_FLOAT	single-precision floating point

Table 8-2   Data Types for glReadPixels() or glDrawPixels()

Remember that, depending on the format, anywhere from one to four elements are read (or written). For example, if the format is GL_RGBA and you're reading into 32-bit integers (that is, if *type* is equal to GL_UNSIGNED_INT or GL_INT), then every pixel read requires 16 bytes of storage (four components × four bytes/component).

Each element of the image is stored in memory as indicated by Table 8-2. If the element represents a continuous value, such as a red, green, blue, or *luminance* component, each value is scaled to fit into the available number of bits. For example, assume the red component is initially specified as a floating-point value between 0.0 and 1.0. If it needs to be packed into an unsigned byte, only 8 bits of precision are kept, even if more bits are allocated to the red component in the framebuffer. GL_UNSIGNED_SHORT and GL_UNSIGNED_INT give 16 and 32 bits of precision, respectively. The normal (signed) versions of GL_BYTE, GL_SHORT, and GL_INT have 7, 15, and 31 bits of precision, since the negative values are typically not used.

If the element is an index (a color index or a stencil index, for example), and the type is not GL_FLOAT, the value is simply masked against the available bits in the type. The signed versions—GL_BYTE, GL_SHORT, and GL_INT—have masks with one fewer bit. For example, if a color index is to be stored in a signed 8-bit integer, it's first masked against 0x7f. If the type is GL_FLOAT, the index is simply converted into a single-precision floating-point number (for example, the index 17 is converted to the float 17.0).

Writing Pixel Data from Processor Memory to Frame Buffer

---

void **glDrawPixels**(GLsizei *width*, GLsizei *height*, GLenum *format*,
GLenum *type*, const GLvoid **pixels*);

Draws a rectangle of pixel data with dimensions *width* and *height*. The pixel rectangle is drawn with its lower-left corner at the current raster position. *format* and *type* have the same meaning as with **glReadPixels()**. (For legal values for *format* and *type*, see Table 8-1 and Table 8-2.) The array pointed to by *pixels* contains the pixel data to be drawn. If the current raster position is invalid, nothing is drawn, and the raster position remains invalid.

Example 8-3 is a portion of a program, which uses **glDrawPixels()** to draw an pixel rectangle in the lower-left corner of a window. **makeCheckImage()** creates a 64-by-64 RGB array of a black-and-white checkerboard image. **glRasterPos2i(0,0)** positions the lower-left corner of the image. For now, ignore **glPixelStorei()**.

Example 8-3   Use of glDrawPixels(): image.c

```
#define checkImageWidth 64
#define checkImageHeight 64
GLubyte checkImage[checkImageHeight][checkImageWidth][3];

void makeCheckImage(void)
{
    int i, j, c;

    for (i = 0; i < checkImageHeight; i++) {
        for (j = 0; j < checkImageWidth; j++) {
            c = ((((i&0x8)==0)^((j&0x8))==0))*255;
            checkImage[i][j][0] = (GLubyte) c;
            checkImage[i][j][1] = (GLubyte) c;
            checkImage[i][j][2] = (GLubyte) c;
        }
    }
}

void init(void)
{
    glClearColor (0.0, 0.0, 0.0, 0.0);
    glShadeModel(GL_FLAT);
    makeCheckImage();
    glPixelStorei(GL_UNPACK_ALIGNMENT, 1);
}
```

```
void display(void)
{
   glClear(GL_COLOR_BUFFER_BIT);
   glRasterPos2i(0, 0);
   glDrawPixels(checkImageWidth, checkImageHeight, GL_RGB,
                GL_UNSIGNED_BYTE, checkImage);
   glFlush();
}
```

When using **glDrawPixels()** to write RGBA or color-index information, you may need to control the current drawing buffers with **glDrawBuffer()**, which, along with **glReadBuffer()**, is also described in "Selecting Color Buffers for Writing and Reading" on page 379.

Copying Pixel Data within the Frame Buffer

---

void **glCopyPixels**(GLint *x*, GLint *y*, GLsizei *width*, GLsizei *height*,
                    GLenum *buffer*);

Copies pixel data from the framebuffer rectangle whose lower-left corner is at (*x, y*) and whose dimensions are *width* and *height*. The data is copied to a new position whose lower-left corner is given by the current raster position. *buffer* is either GL_COLOR, GL_STENCIL, or GL_DEPTH, specifying the framebuffer that is used. **glCopyPixels()** behaves similarly to a **glReadPixels()** followed by a **glDrawPixels()**, with the following translation for the *buffer* to *format* parameter:

- If *buffer* is GL_DEPTH or GL_STENCIL, then GL_DEPTH_COMPONENT or GL_STENCIL_INDEX is used, respectively.

- If GL_COLOR is specified, GL_RGBA or GL_COLOR_INDEX is used, depending on whether the system is in RGBA or color-index mode.

Note that there's no need for a *format* or *data* parameter for **glCopyPixels()**, since the data is never copied into processor memory. The read source buffer and the destination buffer of **glCopyPixels()** are specified by **glReadBuffer()** and **glDrawBuffer()** respectively. Both **glDrawPixels()** and **glCopyPixels()** are used in Example 8-4 on page 306.

For all three functions, the exact conversions of the data going to or from the framebuffer depend on the modes in effect at the time. See the next section for details.

Imaging Pipeline

This section discusses the complete Imaging Pipeline: the pixel-storage modes and pixel-transfer operations, which include how to set up an arbitrary mapping to convert pixel data. You can also magnify or reduce a pixel rectangle before it's drawn by calling **glPixelZoom()**. The order of these operations is shown in Figure 8-4.

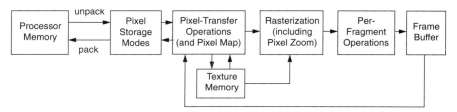

Figure 8-4   Imaging Pipeline

When **glDrawPixels()** is called, the data is first unpacked from processor memory according to the pixel-storage modes that are in effect and then the pixel-transfer operations are applied. The resulting pixels are then rasterized. During rasterization, the pixel rectangle may be zoomed up or down, depending on the current state. Finally, the fragment operations are applied and the pixels are written into the framebuffer. (See "Testing and Operating on Fragments" on page 382 for a discussion of the fragment operations.)

When **glReadPixels()** is called, data is read from the framebuffer, the pixel-transfer operations are performed, and then the resulting data is packed into processor memory.

glCopyPixels() applies all the pixel-transfer operations during what would be the **glReadPixels()** activity. The resulting data is written as it would be by **glDrawPixels()**, but the transformations aren't applied a second time. Figure 8-5 shows how **glCopyPixels()** moves pixel data, starting from the frame buffer.

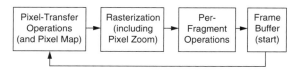

Figure 8-5   glCopyPixels() Pixel Path

From "Drawing the Bitmap" on page 283 and Figure 8-6, you see that rendering bitmaps is simpler than rendering images. Neither the pixel-transfer operations nor the pixel-zoom operation are applied.

Figure 8-6   glBitmap() Pixel Path

Note that the pixel-storage modes and pixel-transfer operations are applied to textures as they are read from or written to texture memory. Figure 8-7 shows the effect on **glTexImage*()**, **glTexSubImage*()**, and **glGetTexImage()**.

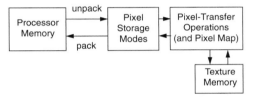

Figure 8-7   glTexImage*(), glTexSubImage*(), and glGetTexImage() Pixel Paths

As seen in Figure 8-8, when pixel data is copied from the framebuffer into texture memory (**glCopyTexImage*()** or **glCopyTexSubImage*()**), only pixel-transfer operations are applied. (See Chapter 9 for more information on textures.)

Figure 8-8   glCopyTexImage*() and glCopyTexSubImage*() Pixel Paths

Pixel Packing and Unpacking

Packing and unpacking refer to the way that pixel data is written to and read from processor memory.

An image stored in memory has between one and four chunks of data, called *elements*. The data might consist of just the color index or the luminance (luminance is the weighted sum of the red, green, and blue values), or it might consist of the red, green, blue, and alpha components for each pixel. The possible arrangements of pixel data, or *formats*, determine the number of elements stored for each pixel and their order.

Some elements (such as a color index or a stencil index) are integers, and others (such as the red, green, blue, and alpha components, or the depth component) are floating-point values, typically ranging between 0.0 and 1.0. Floating-point components are usually stored in the framebuffer with lower resolution than a full floating-point number would require (for example, color components may be stored in 8 bits). The exact number of bits used to represent the components depends on the particular hardware being used. Thus, it's often wasteful to store each component as a full 32-bit floating-point number, especially since images can easily contain a million pixels.

Elements can be stored in memory as various data types, ranging from 8-bit bytes to 32-bit integers or floating-point numbers. OpenGL explicitly defines the conversion of each component in each format to each of the possible data types. Keep in mind that you may lose data if you try to store a high-resolution component in a type represented by a small number of bits.

Controlling Pixel-Storage Modes

Image data is typically stored in processor memory in rectangular two- or three-dimensional arrays. Often, you want to display or store a subimage that corresponds to a subrectangle of the array. In addition, you might need to take into account that different machines have different byte-ordering conventions. Finally, some machines have hardware that is far more efficient at moving data to and from the framebuffer if the data is aligned on 2-byte, 4-byte, or 8-byte boundaries in processor memory. For such machines, you probably want to control the byte alignment. All the issues raised in this paragraph are controlled as pixel-storage modes, which are discussed in the next subsection. You specify these modes by using

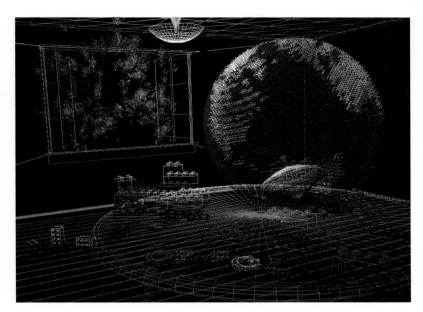

Plate 1. The scene from the cover of this book, with the objects rendered as wireframe models. See Chapter 2.

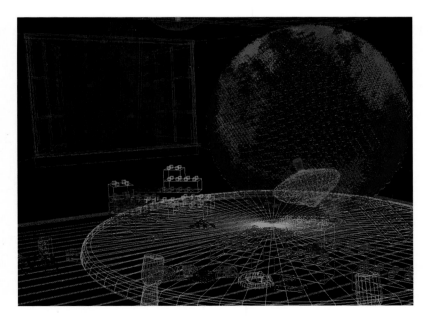

Plate 2. The same scene using fog for depth-cueing (lines further from the eye are dimmer). See Chapter 6.

Plate 3. The same scene with antialiased lines that smooth the jagged edges. See Chapter 6.

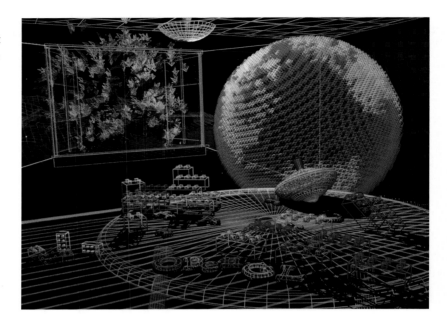

Plate 4. The scene drawn with flat-shaded polygons (a single color for each filled polygon). See Chapter 4.

Plate 5. The scene rendered with lighting and smooth-shaded polygons. See Chapters 4 and 5.

Plate 6. The scene with texture maps and shadows added. See Chapters 9 and 14.

Plate 7. The scene drawn with one of the objects motion-blurred. The accumulation buffer is used to compose the sequence of images needed to blur the moving object. See Chapter 10.

Plate 8. A close-up shot—the scene is rendered from a new viewpoint. See Chapter 3.

Plate 9. The scene drawn using atmospheric effects (fog) to simulate a smoke-filled room. See Chapter 6.

Plate 10. Teapots drawn with jittered viewing volumes into the accumulation buffer for a depth-of-field effect. The gold teapot is in sharpest focus. See Chapter 10.

Plate 11. A smooth-shaded triangle. The three vertices at the corners are drawn in red, green, and blue; the rest of the triangle is smoothly shaded between these three colors. See Chapter 4.

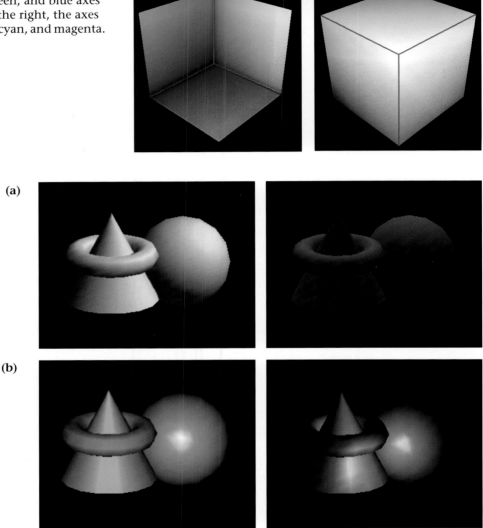

Plate 12. The color cube. On the left, the red, green, and blue axes are shown; on the right, the axes denote yellow, cyan, and magenta. See Chapter 4.

(a)

(b)

Plate 13. Objects drawn with gray material parameters and colored light sources. **(a)** The scene on the left has pale blue ambient light and a white diffuse light source. The scene on the right has a pale blue diffuse light source and almost no ambient light. **(b)** On the left, an infinite light source is used; on the right, a local light source is used. With the infinite light source, the highlight (specular reflection) is centered on both the cone and the sphere because the angle between the object and the line of sight is ignored. With a local light source, the angle is taken into account, so the highlights are located appropriately on both objects. See Chapter 5.

(a)

(b)

Plate 15. A lighted sphere drawn using color index mode. See Chapter 5.

Plate 14. Gray teapots drawn with different lighting conditions. **(a)** Each of the three teapots is drawn with increasing ambient light. **(b)** The teapots are clipped to expose their interiors. The top teapot uses one-sided lighting, the middle one uses two-sided lighting with the same material for both front and back faces, and the bottom teapot uses two-sided lighting and different materials for the front and back faces. See Chapter 5.

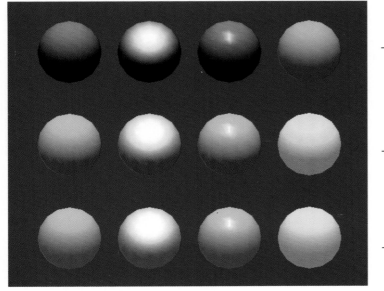

— No ambient reflection.

— Grey ambient reflection.

— Blue ambient reflection.

Plate 16. Twelve spheres, each with different material parameters. The row properties are as labeled above. The first column uses a blue diffuse material color with no specular properties. The second column adds white specular reflection with a low shininess exponent. The third column uses a high shininess exponent and thus has a more concentrated highlight. The fourth column uses the blue diffuse color and, instead of specular reflection, adds an emissive component. See Chapter 5.

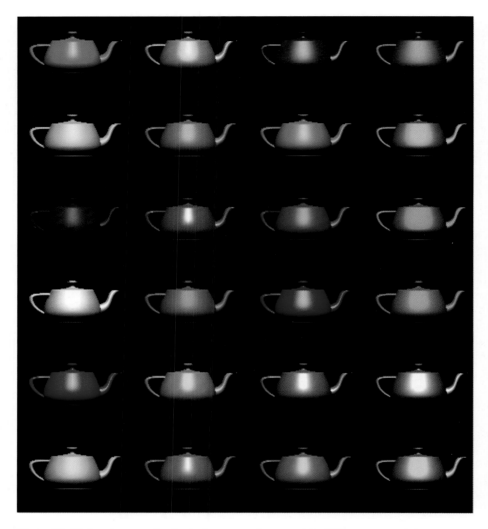

Plate 17. Lighted, smooth-shaded teapots drawn with different material properties that approximate real materials. The first column has materials that resemble (from top to bottom) emerald, jade, obsidian, pearl, ruby, and turquoise. The second column resembles brass, bronze, chrome, copper, gold, and silver. The third column represents various colors of plastic: black, cyan, green, red, white, and yellow. The fourth column is drawn with similar colors of rubber. See Chapter 5.

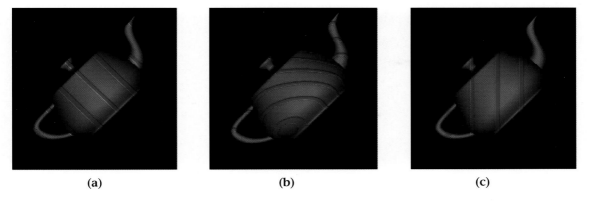

(a)   (b)   (c)

Plate 18. Lighted, green teapots drawn using automatic texture-coordinate generation and a red contour texture map. **(a)** The texture contour stripes are parallel to the plane x = 0, relative to the transformed object (that is, using GL_OBJECT_LINEAR). As the object moves, the texture appears to be attached to it. **(b)** A different planar equation (x + y + z = 0) is used, so the stripes have a different orientation. **(c)** The texture coordinates are calculated relative to eye coordinates and hence aren't fixed to the object (GL_EYE_LINEAR). As the object moves, it appears to "swim" through the texture. See Chapter 9.

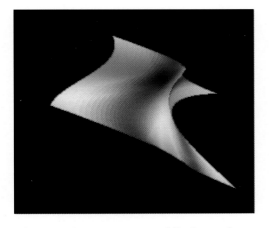

Plate 19. A texture-mapped Bezier surface mesh created using evaluators. See Chapters 9 and 12.

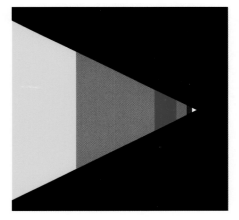

Plate 20. A single polygon drawn using a set of mipmapped textures. In this case, each texture is simply a different color. The polygon is actually a rectangle oriented so that it recedes into the distance, appearing to become progressively smaller. As the visible area of the polygon becomes smaller, correspondingly smaller mipmaps are used. See Chapter 9.

Plate 21. An environment-mapped object. On the left is the original texture, a processed photograph of a coffee shop in Palo Alto, taken with a very wide-angle lens. Below is a goblet with the environment map applied; because of the mapping, the goblet appears to reflect the coffee shop off its surface. See Chapter 9.

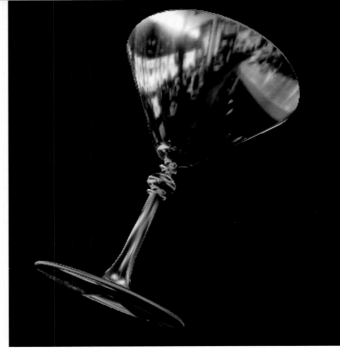

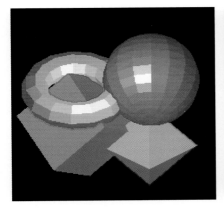
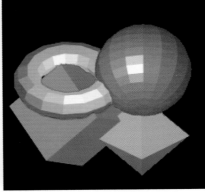

Plate 22. A scene with several flat-shaded objects. On the left, the scene is aliased. On the right, the accumulation buffer is used for scene antialiasing: the scene is rendered several times, each time jittered less than one pixel, and the images are accumulated and then averaged. See Chapter 10.

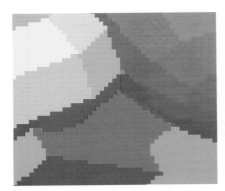

Plate 23. A magnification of the previous scenes. The left image shows the aliased, jagged edges. In the right image, the edges are blurred, or antialiased, and hence less jagged. See Chapter 10.

Plate 24. A scene drawn with texture mapping, lighting, and shadows. The paintings, floor, ceiling, and benches are texture-mapped. Note the use of spotlights and shadows. See Chapters 5, 9, and 14.

Plate 25. A lighted, smooth-shaded model on a texture-mapped surface. See Chapters 4, 5, and 9.

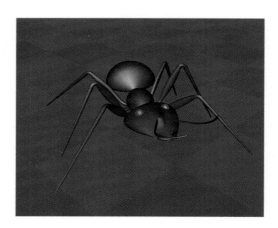

Plate 26. A dramatically lit and shadowed scene, with most of the surfaces textured. The iris is a polygonal model. See Chapters 2, 5, 9, and 14.

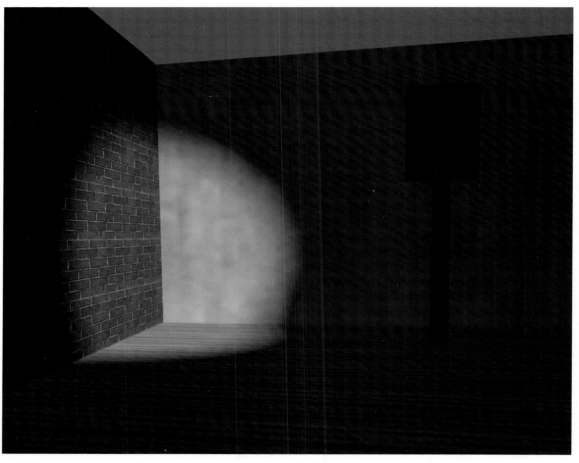

Plate 27. Sophisticated use of texturing. All surfaces are texture-mapped. In addition, the attenuated spotlight effect is created using a projected texture. See Chapters 9 and 14.

Plate 28. Lit, smooth-shaded three-dimensional font. The font is created by extruding a two-dimensional shape along a specified axis. See Chapters 2, 4, and 5.

Plates 29 and 30. Two scenes snapped from a visual simulation program. The hills are composed of just a few polygons, but all the polygons are texture-mapped. Similarly, the buildings are composed of only a few textured rectangular walls. See Chapters 2, 3, and 9.

Plate 31. Another scene from a different visual simulation program. The hills are textured, and the scene is rendered with fog. The airplanes, obviously, are polygonal. See Chapters 2, 3, 6, and 9.

glPixelStore*(), which you've already seen used in a couple of example programs.

All the possible pixel-storage modes are controlled with the **glPixelStore*()** command. Typically, several successive calls are made with this command to set several parameter values.

---

void **glPixelStore**{if}(GLenum *pname*, *TYPE param*);

Sets the pixel-storage modes, which affect the operation of **glDrawPixels()**, **glReadPixels()**, **glBitmap()**, **glPolygonStipple()**, **glTexImage1D()**, **glTexImage2D()**, **glTexSubImage1D()**, **glTexSubImage2D()**, and **glGetTexImage()**. The possible parameter names for *pname* are shown in Table 8-3, along with their data type, initial value, and valid range of values. The GL_UNPACK* parameters control how data is unpacked from memory by **glDrawPixels()**, **glBitmap()**, **glPolygonStipple()**, **glTexImage1D()**, **glTexImage2D()**, **glTexSubImage1D()**, and **glTexSubImage2D()**. The GL_PACK* parameters control how data is packed into memory by **glReadPixels()** and **glGetTexImage()**.

Parameter Name	Type	Initial Value	Valid Range
GL_UNPACK_SWAP_BYTES, GL_PACK_SWAP_BYTES	GLboolean	FALSE	TRUE/FALSE
GL_UNPACK_LSB_FIRST, GL_PACK_LSB_FIRST	GLboolean	FALSE	TRUE/FALSE
GL_UNPACK_ROW_LENGTH, GL_PACK_ROW_LENGTH	GLint	0	any nonnegative integer
GL_UNPACK_SKIP_ROWS, GL_PACK_SKIP_ROWS	GLint	0	any nonnegative integer
GL_UNPACK_SKIP_PIXELS, GL_PACK_SKIP_PIXELS	GLint	0	any nonnegative integer
GL_UNPACK_ALIGNMENT, GL_PACK_ALIGNMENT	GLint	4	1, 2, 4, 8

Table 8-3   glPixelStore() Parameters

Since the corresponding parameters for packing and unpacking have the same meanings, they're discussed together in the rest of this section and referred to without the GL_PACK or GL_UNPACK prefix. For example,

*SWAP_BYTES refers to GL_PACK_SWAP_BYTES and GL_UNPACK_SWAP_BYTES.

If the *SWAP_BYTES parameter is FALSE (the default), the ordering of the bytes in memory is whatever is native for the OpenGL client; otherwise, the bytes are reversed. The byte reversal applies to any size element, but really only has a meaningful effect for multibyte elements.

Note: As long as your OpenGL application doesn't share images with other machines, you can ignore the issue of byte ordering. If your application must render an OpenGL image that was created on a different machine and the "endianness" of the two machines differs, byte ordering can be swapped using *SWAP_BYTES. However, *SWAP_BYTES does not allow you to reorder elements (for example, to swap red and green).

The *LSB_FIRST parameter applies when drawing or reading 1-bit images or bitmaps, for which a single bit of data is saved or restored for each pixel. If *LSB_FIRST is FALSE (the default), the bits are taken from the bytes starting with the most significant bit; otherwise, they're taken in the opposite order. For example, if *LSB_FIRST is FALSE, and the byte in question is 0x31, the bits, in order, are {0, 0, 1, 1, 0, 0, 0, 1}. If *LSB_FIRST is TRUE, the order is {1, 0, 0, 0, 1, 1, 0, 0}.

Sometimes you want to draw or read only a subrectangle of the entire rectangle of image data stored in memory. If the rectangle in memory is larger than the subrectangle that's being drawn or read, you need to specify the actual length (measured in pixels) of the larger rectangle with *ROW_LENGTH. If *ROW_LENGTH is zero (which it is by default), the row length is understood to be the same as the width that's specified with **glReadPixels()**, **glDrawPixels()**, or **glCopyPixels()**. You also need to specify the number of rows and pixels to skip before starting to copy the data for the subrectangle. These numbers are set using the parameters *SKIP_ROWS and *SKIP_PIXELS, as shown in Figure 8-9. By default, both parameters are 0, so you start at the lower-left corner.

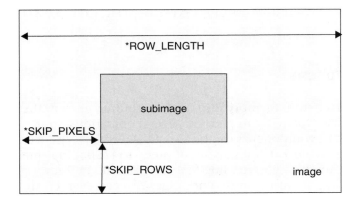

Figure 8-9   *SKIP_ROWS, *SKIP_PIXELS, and *ROW_LENGTH Parameters

Often a particular machine's hardware is optimized for moving pixel data to and from memory, if the data is saved in memory with a particular byte alignment. For example, in a machine with 32-bit words, hardware can often retrieve data much faster if it's initially aligned on a 32-bit boundary, which typically has an address that is a multiple of 4. Likewise, 64-bit architectures might work better when the data is aligned to 8-byte boundaries. On some machines, however, byte alignment makes no difference.

As an example, suppose your machine works better with pixel data aligned to a 4-byte boundary. Images are most efficiently saved by forcing the data for each row of the image to begin on a 4-byte boundary. If the image is 5 pixels wide and each pixel consists of 1 byte each of red, green, and blue information, a row requires $5 \times 3 = 15$ bytes of data. Maximum display efficiency can be achieved if the first row, and each successive row, begins on a 4-byte boundary, so there is 1 byte of waste in the memory storage for each row. If your data is stored like this, set the *ALIGNMENT parameter appropriately (to 4, in this case).

If *ALIGNMENT is set to 1, the next available byte is used. If it's 2, a byte is skipped if necessary at the end of each row so that the first byte of the next row has an address that's a multiple of 2. In the case of bitmaps (or 1-bit images) where a single bit is saved for each pixel, the same byte alignment works, although you have to count individual bits. For example, if you're saving a single bit per pixel, the row length is 75, and the alignment is 4, then each row requires 75/8, or 9 3/8 bytes. Since 12 is the smallest multiple of 4 that is bigger than 9 3/8, 12 bytes of memory are used for each row. If the alignment is 1, then 10 bytes are used for each row, as 9 3/8 is rounded up to the next byte. (There is a simple use of **glPixelStorei**() in Example 8-4 on page 306.)

Pixel-Transfer Operations

As image data is transferred from memory into the framebuffer, or from the framebuffer into memory, OpenGL can perform several operations on it. For example, the ranges of components can be altered—normally, the red component is between 0.0 and 1.0, but you might prefer to keep it in some other range; or perhaps the data you're using from a different graphics system stores the red component in a different range. You can even create maps to perform arbitrary conversion of color indices or color components during pixel transfer. Conversions such as these performed during the transfer of pixels to and from the framebuffer are called pixel-transfer operations. They're controlled with the **glPixelTransfer***() and **glPixelMap***() commands.

Be aware that although the color, depth, and stencil buffers have many similarities, they don't behave identically, and a few of the modes have special cases for special buffers. All the mode details are covered in this section and the sections that follow, including all the special cases.

Some of the pixel-transfer function characteristics are set with **glPixelTransfer***(). The other characteristics are specified with **glPixelMap***(), which is described in the next section.

---

void **glPixelTransfer**{if}(GLenum *pname*, *TYPE param*);

Sets pixel-transfer modes that affect the operation of **glDrawPixels**(), **glReadPixels**(), **glCopyPixels**(), **glTexImage1D**(), **glTexImage2D**(), **glCopyTexImage1D**(), **glCopyTexImage2D**(), **glTexSubImage1D**(), **glTexSubImage2D**(), **glCopyTexSubImage1D**(), **glCopyTexSubImage2D**(), and **glGetTexImage**(). The parameter *pname* must be one of those listed in the first column of Table 8-4, and its value, *param*, must be in the valid range shown.

Parameter Name	Type	Initial Value	Valid Range
GL_MAP_COLOR	GLboolean	FALSE	TRUE/FALSE
GL_MAP_STENCIL	GLboolean	FALSE	TRUE/FALSE

Table 8-4   glPixelTransfer*() Parameters

Parameter Name	Type	Initial Value	Valid Range
GL_INDEX_SHIFT	GLint	0	$(-\infty, \infty)$
GL_INDEX_OFFSET	GLint	0	$(-\infty, \infty)$
GL_RED_SCALE	GLfloat	1.0	$(-\infty, \infty)$
GL_GREEN_SCALE	GLfloat	1.0	$(-\infty, \infty)$
GL_BLUE_SCALE	GLfloat	1.0	$(-\infty, \infty)$
GL_ALPHA_SCALE	GLfloat	1.0	$(-\infty, \infty)$
GL_DEPTH_SCALE	GLfloat	1.0	$(-\infty, \infty)$
GL_RED_BIAS	GLfloat	0	$(-\infty, \infty)$
GL_GREEN_BIAS	GLfloat	0	$(-\infty, \infty)$
GL_BLUE_BIAS	GLfloat	0	$(-\infty, \infty)$
GL_ALPHA_BIAS	GLfloat	0	$(-\infty, \infty)$
GL_DEPTH_BIAS	GLfloat	0	$(-\infty, \infty)$

Table 8-4   glPixelTransfer*() Parameters (continued)

If the GL_MAP_COLOR or GL_MAP_STENCIL parameter is TRUE, then mapping is enabled. See the next subsection to learn how the mapping is done and how to change the contents of the maps. All the other parameters directly affect the pixel component values.

A scale and bias can be applied to the red, green, blue, alpha, and depth components. For example, you may wish to scale red, green, and blue components that were read from the framebuffer before converting them to a luminance format in processor memory. Luminance is computed as the sum of the red, green, and blue components, so if you use the default value for GL_RED_SCALE, GL_GREEN_SCALE and GL_BLUE_SCALE, the components all contribute equally to the final intensity or luminance value. If you want to convert RGB to luminance, according to the NTSC standard, you set GL_RED_SCALE to .30, GL_GREEN_SCALE to .59, and GL_BLUE_SCALE to .11.

Indices (color and stencil) can also be transformed. In the case of indices a shift and offset are applied. This is useful if you need to control which portion of the color table is used during rendering.

Pixel Mapping

All the color components, color indices, and stencil indices can be modified by means of a table lookup before they are placed in screen memory. The command for controlling this mapping is **glPixelMap*()**.

---

void **glPixelMap**{ui us f}**v**(GLenum *map*, GLint *mapsize*,
             const *TYPE* *values*);

Loads the pixel map indicated by *map* with *mapsize* entries, whose values are pointed to by *values*. Table 8-5 lists the map names and values; the default sizes are all 1 and the default values are all 0. Each map's size must be a power of 2.

Map Name	Address	Value
GL_PIXEL_MAP_I_TO_I	color index	color index
GL_PIXEL_MAP_S_TO_S	stencil index	stencil index
GL_PIXEL_MAP_I_TO_R	color index	R
GL_PIXEL_MAP_I_TO_G	color index	G
GL_PIXEL_MAP_I_TO_B	color index	B
GL_PIXEL_MAP_I_TO_A	color index	A
GL_PIXEL_MAP_R_TO_R	R	R
GL_PIXEL_MAP_G_TO_G	G	G
GL_PIXEL_MAP_B_TO_B	B	B
GL_PIXEL_MAP_A_TO_A	A	A

Table 8-5   glPixelMap*() Parameter Names and Values

The maximum size of the maps is machine-dependent. You can find the sizes of the pixel maps supported on your machine with **glGetIntegerv()**. Use the query argument GL_MAX_PIXEL_MAP_TABLE to obtain the maximum size for all the pixel map tables, and use GL_PIXEL_MAP_*_TO_*_SIZE to obtain the current size of the specified map. The six maps whose address is a color index or stencil index must always be sized to an integral power of 2. The four RGBA maps can be any size from 1 through GL_MAX_PIXEL_MAP_TABLE.

To understand how a table works, consider a simple example. Suppose that you want to create a 256-entry table that maps color indices to color indices using GL_PIXEL_MAP_I_TO_I. You create a table with an entry for each of the values between 0 and 255 and initialize the table with **glPixelMap*()**. Assume you're using the table for thresholding and want to map indices below 101 (indices 0 to 100) to 0, and all indices 101 and above to 255. In this case, your table consists of 101 0s and 155 255s. The pixel map is enabled using the routine **glPixelTransfer*()** to set the parameter GL_MAP_COLOR to TRUE. Once the pixel map is loaded and enabled, incoming color indices below 101 come out as 0, and incoming pixels between 101 and 255 are mapped to 255. If the incoming pixel is larger than 255, it's first masked by 255, throwing out all the bits above the eighth, and the resulting masked value is looked up in the table. If the incoming index is a floating-point value (say 88.14585), it's rounded to the nearest integer value (giving 88), and that number is looked up in the table (giving 0).

Using pixel maps, you can also map stencil indices or convert color indices to RGB. (See "Reading and Drawing Pixel Rectangles" on page 309 for information about the conversion of indices.)

Magnifying, Reducing, or Flipping an Image

After the pixel-storage modes and pixel-transfer operations are applied, images and bitmaps are rasterized. Normally, each pixel in an image is written to a single pixel on the screen. However, you can arbitrarily magnify, reduce, or even flip (reflect) an image by using **glPixelZoom()**.

---

void **glPixelZoom**(GLfloat $zoom_x$, GLfloat $zoom_y$);

Sets the magnification or reduction factors for pixel-write operations (**glDrawPixels()** or **glCopyPixels()**), in the x- and y-dimensions. By default, $zoom_x$ and $zoom_y$ are 1.0. If they're both 2.0, each image pixel is drawn to 4 screen pixels. Note that fractional magnification or reduction factors are allowed, as are negative factors. Negative zoom factors reflect the resulting image about the current raster position.

During rasterization, each image pixel is treated as a $zoom_x \times zoom_y$ rectangle, and fragments are generated for all the pixels whose centers lie within the rectangle. More specifically, let (x_{rp}, y_{rp}) be the current raster position. If a particular group of elements (index or components) is the nth in a row and belongs to the mth column, consider the region in window coordinates bounded by the rectangle with corners at

$(x_{rp} + zoom_x * n, y_{rp} + zoom_y * m)$ and $(x_{rp} + zoom_x(n+1), y_{rp} + zoom_y(m+1))$

Any fragments whose centers lie inside this rectangle (or on its bottom or left boundaries) are produced in correspondence with this particular group of elements.

A negative zoom can be useful for flipping an image. OpenGL describes images from the bottom row of pixels to the top (and from left to right). If you have a "top to bottom" image, such as a frame of video, you may want to use **glPixelZoom**(1.0, -1.0) to make the image right side up for OpenGL. Be sure that you reposition the current raster position appropriately, if needed.

Example 8-4 shows the use of **glPixelZoom**(). A checkerboard image is initially drawn in the lower-left corner of the window. Pressing a mouse button and moving the mouse uses **glCopyPixels**() to copy the lower-left corner of the window to the current cursor location. (If you copy the image onto itself, it looks wacky!) The copied image is zoomed, but initially it is zoomed by the default value of 1.0, so you won't notice. The 'z' and 'Z' keys increase and decrease the zoom factors by 0.5. Any window damage causes the contents of the window to be redrawn. Pressing the 'r' key resets the image and the zoom factors.

Example 8-4   Drawing, Copying, and Zooming Pixel Data: image.c

```
#include <GL/gl.h>
#include <GL/glu.h>
#include <GL/glut.h>
#include <stdlib.h>
#include <stdio.h>

#define checkImageWidth 64
#define checkImageHeight 64
GLubyte checkImage[checkImageHeight][checkImageWidth][3];

static GLdouble zoomFactor = 1.0;
static GLint height;

void makeCheckImage(void)
{
    int i, j, c;

    for (i = 0; i < checkImageHeight; i++) {
        for (j = 0; j < checkImageWidth; j++) {
            c = ((((i&0x8)==0)^((j&0x8))==0))*255;
            checkImage[i][j][0] = (GLubyte) c;
```

```
            checkImage[i][j][1] = (GLubyte) c;
            checkImage[i][j][2] = (GLubyte) c;
         }
      }
}

void init(void)
{
   glClearColor (0.0, 0.0, 0.0, 0.0);
   glShadeModel(GL_FLAT);
   makeCheckImage();
   glPixelStorei(GL_UNPACK_ALIGNMENT, 1);
}

void display(void)
{
   glClear(GL_COLOR_BUFFER_BIT);
   glRasterPos2i(0, 0);
   glDrawPixels(checkImageWidth, checkImageHeight, GL_RGB,
               GL_UNSIGNED_BYTE, checkImage);
   glFlush();
}

void reshape(int w, int h)
{
   glViewport(0, 0, (GLsizei) w, (GLsizei) h);
   height = (GLint) h;
   glMatrixMode(GL_PROJECTION);
   glLoadIdentity();
   gluOrtho2D(0.0, (GLdouble) w, 0.0, (GLdouble) h);
   glMatrixMode(GL_MODELVIEW);
   glLoadIdentity();
}

void motion(int x, int y)
{
   static GLint screeny;

   screeny = height - (GLint) y;
   glRasterPos2i (x, screeny);
   glPixelZoom (zoomFactor, zoomFactor);
   glCopyPixels (0, 0, checkImageWidth, checkImageHeight,
               GL_COLOR);
   glPixelZoom (1.0, 1.0);
   glFlush ();
}
```

```
void keyboard(unsigned char key, int x, int y)
{
    switch (key) {
        case 'r':
        case 'R':
            zoomFactor = 1.0;
            glutPostRedisplay();
            printf ("zoomFactor reset to 1.0\n");
            break;
        case 'z':
            zoomFactor += 0.5;
            if (zoomFactor >= 3.0)
                zoomFactor = 3.0;
            printf ("zoomFactor is now %4.1f\n", zoomFactor);
            break;
        case 'Z':
            zoomFactor -= 0.5;
            if (zoomFactor <= 0.5)
                zoomFactor = 0.5;
            printf ("zoomFactor is now %4.1f\n", zoomFactor);
            break;
        case 27:
            exit(0);
            break;
        default:
            break;
    }
}

int main(int argc, char** argv)
{
    glutInit(&argc, argv);
    glutInitDisplayMode(GLUT_SINGLE | GLUT_RGB);
    glutInitWindowSize(250, 250);
    glutInitWindowPosition(100, 100);
    glutCreateWindow(argv[0]);
    init();
    glutDisplayFunc(display);
    glutReshapeFunc(reshape);
    glutKeyboardFunc(keyboard);
    glutMotionFunc(motion);
    glutMainLoop();
    return 0;
}
```

Reading and Drawing Pixel Rectangles

This section describes the reading and drawing processes in detail. The pixel conversions performed when going from framebuffer to memory (reading) are similar but not identical to the conversions performed when going in the opposite direction (drawing), as explained in the following sections. You may wish to skip this section the first time through, especially if you do not plan to use the pixel-transfer operations right away.

The Pixel Rectangle Drawing Process

Figure 8-10 and the following list describe the operation of drawing pixels into the framebuffer.

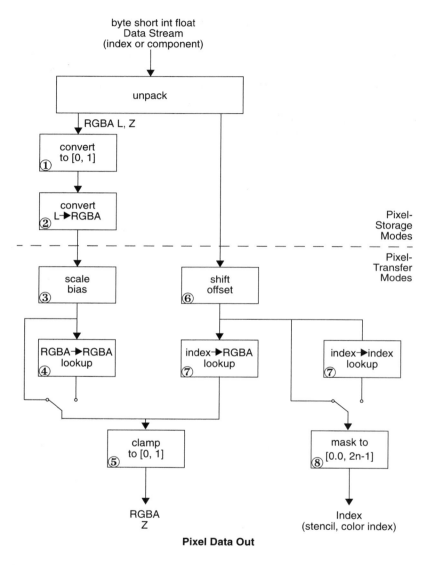

Figure 8-10   Drawing Pixels with glDrawPixels()

1. If the pixels aren't indices (that is, the format isn't GL_COLOR_INDEX or GL_STENCIL_INDEX), the first step is to convert the components to floating-point format if necessary. (See Table 4-1 on page 164 for the details of the conversion.)

2. If the format is GL_LUMINANCE or GL_LUMINANCE_ALPHA, the luminance element is converted into R, G, and B, by using the luminance value for each of the R, G, and B components. In GL_LUMINANCE_ALPHA format, the alpha value becomes the A value. If GL_LUMINANCE is specified, the A value is set to 1.0.

3. Each component (R, G, B, A, or depth) is multiplied by the appropriate scale, and the appropriate bias is added. For example, the R component is multiplied by the value corresponding to GL_RED_SCALE and added to the value corresponding to GL_RED_BIAS.

4. If GL_MAP_COLOR is true, each of the R, G, B, and A components is clamped to the range [0.0,1.0], multiplied by an integer one less than the table size, truncated, and looked up in the table. (See "Tips for Improving Pixel Drawing Rates" on page 314 for more details.)

5. Next, the R, G, B, and A components are clamped to [0.0,1.0], if they weren't already, and converted to fixed-point with as many bits to the left of the binary point as there are in the corresponding framebuffer component.

6. If you're working with index values (stencil or color indices), then the values are first converted to fixed-point (if they were initially floating-point numbers) with some unspecified bits to the right of the binary point. Indices that were initially fixed-point remain so, and any bits to the right of the binary point are set to zero.

   The resulting index value is then shifted right or left by the absolute value of GL_INDEX_SHIFT bits; the value is shifted left if GL_INDEX_SHIFT > 0 and right otherwise. Finally, GL_INDEX_OFFSET is added to the index.

7. The next step with indices depends on whether you're using RGBA mode or color-index mode. In RGBA mode, a color index is converted to RGBA using the color components specified by GL_PIXEL_MAP_I_TO_R, GL_PIXEL_MAP_I_TO_G, GL_PIXEL_MAP_I_TO_B, and GL_PIXEL_MAP_I_TO_A. (See "Pixel Mapping" on page 304 for details.) Otherwise, if GL_MAP_COLOR is GL_TRUE, a color index is looked up through the table GL_PIXEL_MAP_I_TO_I. (If GL_MAP_COLOR is GL_FALSE, the index is unchanged.) If the image is made up of stencil indices rather than

color indices, and if GL_MAP_STENCIL is GL_TRUE, the index is looked up in the table corresponding to GL_PIXEL_MAP_S_TO_S. If GL_MAP_STENCIL is FALSE, the stencil index is unchanged.

8. Finally, if the indices haven't been converted to RGBA, the indices are then masked to the number of bits of either the color-index or stencil buffer, whichever is appropriate.

The Pixel Rectangle Reading Process

Many of the conversions done during the pixel rectangle drawing process are also done during the pixel rectangle reading process. The pixel reading process is shown in Figure 8-11 and described in the following list.

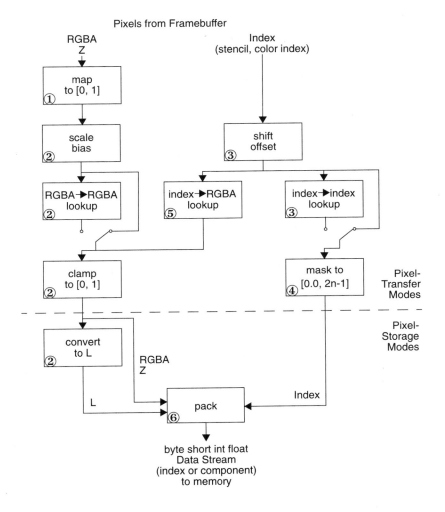

Figure 8-11   Reading Pixels with glReadPixels()

1. If the pixels to be read aren't indices (that is, the format isn't GL_COLOR_INDEX or GL_STENCIL_INDEX), the components are mapped to [0.0,1.0]—that is, in exactly the opposite way that they are when written.

2. Next, the scales and biases are applied to each component. If GL_MAP_COLOR is GL_TRUE, they're mapped and again clamped to [0.0,1.0]. If luminance is desired instead of RGB, the R, G, and B components are added (L = R + G + B).

3. If the pixels are indices (color or stencil), they're shifted, offset, and, if GL_MAP_COLOR is GL_TRUE, also mapped.

4. If the storage format is either GL_COLOR_INDEX or GL_STENCIL_INDEX, the pixel indices are masked to the number of bits of the storage type (1, 8, 16, or 32) and packed into memory as previously described.

5. If the storage format is one of the component kind (such as luminance or RGB), the pixels are always mapped by the index-to-RGBA maps. Then, they're treated as though they had been RGBA pixels in the first place (including potential conversion to luminance).

6. Finally, for both index and component data, the results are packed into memory according to the GL_PACK* modes set with **glPixelStore*()**.

The scaling, bias, shift, and offset values are the same as those used when drawing pixels, so if you're both reading and drawing pixels, be sure to reset these components to the appropriate values before doing a read or a draw. Similarly, the various maps must be properly reset if you intend to use maps for both reading and drawing.

Note: It might seem that luminance is handled incorrectly in both the reading and drawing operations. For example, luminance is not usually equally dependent on the R, G, and B components as it may be assumed from both Figure 8-10 and Figure 8-11. If you wanted your luminance to be calculated such that the R component contributed 30 percent, the G 59 percent, and the B 11 percent, you can set GL_RED_SCALE to .30, GL_RED_BIAS to 0.0, and so on. The computed L is then .30R + .59G + .11B.

Tips for Improving Pixel Drawing Rates

As you can see, OpenGL has a rich set of features for reading, drawing and manipulating pixel data. Although these features are often very useful, they can also decrease performance. Here are some tips for improving pixel draw rates.

• For best performance, set all pixel-transfer parameters to their default values, and set pixel zoom to (1.0,1.0).

- A series of fragment operations is applied to pixels as they are drawn into the framebuffer. (See "Testing and Operating on Fragments" on page 382.) For optimum performance disable all fragment operations.

- While performing pixel operations, disable other costly states, such as texturing and lighting.

- If you use an image format and type that matches the framebuffer, you can reduce the amount of work that the OpenGL implementation has to do. For example, if you are writing images to an RGB framebuffer with 8 bits per component, call **glDrawPixels()** with *format* set to RGB and *type* set to UNSIGNED_BYTE.

- For some implementations, unsigned image formats are faster to use than signed image formats.

- It is usually faster to draw a large pixel rectangle than to draw several small ones, since the cost of transferring the pixel data can be amortized over many pixels.

- If possible, reduce the amount of data that needs to be copied by using small data types (for example, use GL_UNSIGNED_BYTE) and fewer components (for example, use format GL_LUMINANCE_ALPHA).

- Pixel-transfer operations, including pixel mapping and values for scale, bias, offset, and shift other than the defaults, may decrease performance.

Chapter 9

Texture Mapping

Chapter Objectives

After reading this chapter, you'll be able to do the following:

- Understand what texture mapping can add to your scene

- Specify a texture image

- Control how a texture image is filtered as it's applied to a fragment

- Create and manage texture images in texture objects and, if available, control a high-performance working set of those texture objects

- Specify how the color values in the image combine with those of the fragment to which it's being applied

- Supply texture coordinates to indicate how the texture image should be aligned to the objects in your scene

- Use automatic texture coordinate generation to produce effects like contour maps and environment maps

So far, every geometric primitive has been drawn as either a solid color or smoothly shaded between the colors at its vertices—that is, they've been drawn without texture mapping. If you want to draw a large brick wall without texture mapping, for example, each brick must be drawn as a separate polygon. Without texturing, a large flat wall—which is really a single rectangle—might require thousands of individual bricks, and even then the bricks may appear too smooth and regular to be realistic.

Texture mapping allows you to glue an image of a brick wall (obtained, perhaps, by scanning in a photograph of a real wall) to a polygon and to draw the entire wall as a single polygon. Texture mapping ensures that all the right things happen as the polygon is transformed and rendered. For example, when the wall is viewed in perspective, the bricks may appear smaller as the wall gets farther from the viewpoint. Other uses for texture mapping include depicting vegetation on large polygons representing the ground in flight simulation; wallpaper patterns; and textures that make polygons look like natural substances such as marble, wood, or cloth. The possibilities are endless. Although it's most natural to think of applying textures to polygons, textures can be applied to all primitives—points, lines, polygons, bitmaps, and images. Plates 6, 8, 18–21, 24–27, and 29–31 all demonstrate the use of textures.

Because there are so many possibilities, texture mapping is a fairly large, complex subject, and you must make several programming choices when using it. For instance, you can map textures to surfaces made of a set of polygons or to curved surfaces, and you can repeat a texture in one or both directions to cover the surface. A texture can even be one-dimensional. In addition, you can automatically map a texture onto an object in such a way that the texture indicates contours or other properties of the item being viewed. Shiny objects can be textured so that they appear to be in the center of a room or other environment, reflecting the surroundings off their surfaces. Finally, a texture can be applied to a surface in different ways. It can be painted on directly (like a decal placed on a surface), used to modulate the color the surface would have been painted otherwise, or used to blend a texture color with the surface color. If this is your first exposure to texture mapping, you might find that the discussion in this chapter moves fairly quickly. As an additional reference, you might look at the chapter on texture mapping in *Fundamentals of Three-Dimensional Computer Graphics* by Alan Watt (Reading, MA: Addison-Wesley Publishing Company, 1990).

Textures are simply rectangular arrays of data—for example, color data, luminance data, or color and alpha data. The individual values in a texture array are often called *texels*. What makes texture mapping tricky is that a rectangular texture can be mapped to nonrectangular regions, and this must be done in a reasonable way.

Figure 9-1 illustrates the texture-mapping process. The left side of the figure represents the entire texture, and the black outline represents a quadrilateral shape whose corners are mapped to those spots on the texture. When the quadrilateral is displayed on the screen, it might be distorted by applying various transformations—rotations, translations, scaling, and projections. The right side of the figure shows how the texture-mapped quadrilateral might appear on your screen after these transformations. (Note that this quadrilateral is concave and might not be rendered correctly by OpenGL without prior tessellation. See Chapter 11 for more information about tessellating polygons.)

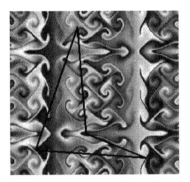 

Figure 9-1   Texture-Mapping Process

Notice how the texture is distorted to match the distortion of the quadrilateral. In this case, it's stretched in the x direction and compressed in the y direction; there's a bit of rotation and shearing going on as well. Depending on the texture size, the quadrilateral's distortion, and the size of the screen image, some of the texels might be mapped to more than one fragment, and some fragments might be covered by multiple texels. Since the texture is made up of discrete texels (in this case, 256×256 of them), filtering operations must be performed to map texels to fragments. For example, if many texels correspond to a fragment, they're averaged down to fit; if texel boundaries fall across fragment boundaries, a weighted average of the applicable texels is performed. Because of these calculations, texturing is computationally expensive, which is why many specialized graphics systems include hardware support for texture mapping.

An application may establish texture objects, with each texture object representing a single texture (and possible associated mipmaps). Some implementations of OpenGL can support a special *working set* of texture objects that have better performance than texture objects outside the working set. These high-performance texture objects are said to be *resident* and may have special hardware and/or software acceleration available. You may use OpenGL to create and delete texture objects and to determine which textures constitute your working set.

This chapter covers the OpenGL's texture-mapping facility in the following major sections.

- "An Overview and an Example" on page 321 gives a brief, broad look at the steps required to perform texture mapping. It also presents a relatively simple example of texture mapping.

- "Specifying the Texture" on page 326 explains how to specify one- or two-dimensional textures. It also discusses how to use a texture's borders, how to supply a series of related textures of different sizes, and how to control the filtering methods used to determine how an applied texture is mapped to screen coordinates.

- "Filtering" on page 344 details how textures are either magnified or minified as they are applied to the pixels of polygons. Minification using special mipmap textures is also explained.

- "Texture Objects" on page 346 describes how to put texture images into objects so that you can control several textures at one time. With texture objects, you may be able to create a working set of high-performance textures, which are said to be resident. You may also prioritize texture objects to increase or decrease the likelihood that a texture object is resident.

- "Texture Functions" on page 354 discusses the methods used for painting a texture onto a surface. You can choose to have the texture color values replace those that would be used if texturing wasn't in effect, or you can have the final color be a combination of the two.

- "Assigning Texture Coordinates" on page 357 describes how to compute and assign appropriate texture coordinates to the vertices of an object. It also explains how to control the behavior of coordinates that lie outside the default range—that is, how to repeat or clamp textures across a surface.

- "Automatic Texture-Coordinate Generation" on page 364 shows how to have OpenGL automatically generate texture coordinates so that you can achieve such effects as contour and environment maps.

- "Advanced Features" on page 371 explains how to manipulate the texture matrix stack and how to use the q texture coordinate.

Version 1.1 of OpenGL introduces several new texture-mapping operations:

- Thirty-eight additional internal texture image formats

- Texture proxy, to query whether there are enough resources to accommodate a given texture image

- Texture subimage, to replace all or part of an existing texture image rather than completely deleting and creating a texture to achieve the same effect

- Specifying texture data from framebuffer memory (as well as from processor memory)

- Texture objects, including resident textures and prioritizing

If you try to use one of these texture-mapping operations and can't find it, check the version number of your implementation of OpenGL to see if it actually supports it. (See "Which Version Am I Using?" on page 503.)

An Overview and an Example

This section gives an overview of the steps necessary to perform texture mapping. It also presents a relatively simple texture-mapping program. Of course, you know that texture mapping can be a very involved process.

Steps in Texture Mapping

To use texture mapping, you perform these steps.

1. Create a texture object and specify a texture for that object.

2. Indicate how the texture is to be applied to each pixel.

3. Enable texture mapping.

4. Draw the scene, supplying both texture and geometric coordinates.

Keep in mind that texture mapping works only in RGBA mode. Texture mapping results in color-index mode are undefined.

Create a Texture Object and Specify a Texture for That Object

A texture is usually thought of as being two-dimensional, like most images, but it can also be one-dimensional. The data describing a texture may consist of one, two, three, or four elements per texel, representing anything from a modulation constant to an (R, G, B, A) quadruple.

In Example 9-1, which is very simple, a single texture object is created to maintain a single two-dimensional texture. This example does not find out how much memory is available. Since only one texture is created, there is no attempt to prioritize or otherwise manage a working set of texture objects. Other advanced techniques, such as texture borders or mipmaps, are not used in this simple example.

Indicate How the Texture Is to Be Applied to Each Pixel

You can choose any of four possible functions for computing the final RGBA value from the fragment color and the texture-image data. One possibility is simply to use the texture color as the final color; this is the *decal* mode, in which the texture is painted on top of the fragment, just as a decal would be applied. (Example 9-1 uses decal mode.) The *replace* mode, a variant of the decal mode, is a second method. Another method is to use the texture to *modulate*, or scale, the fragment's color; this technique is useful for combining the effects of lighting with texturing. Finally, a constant color can be blended with that of the fragment, based on the texture value.

Enable Texture Mapping

You need to enable texturing before drawing your scene. Texturing is enabled or disabled using **glEnable()** or **glDisable()** with the symbolic constant GL_TEXTURE_1D or GL_TEXTURE_2D for one- or two-dimensional texturing, respectively. (If both are enabled, GL_TEXTURE_2D is the one that is used.)

Draw the Scene, Supplying Both Texture and Geometric Coordinates

You need to indicate how the texture should be aligned relative to the fragments to which it's to be applied before it's "glued on." That is, you need to specify both texture coordinates and geometric coordinates as you specify the objects in your scene. For a two-dimensional texture map, for example, the texture coordinates range from 0.0 to 1.0 in both directions, but the coordinates of the items being textured can be anything. For the brick-wall example, if the wall is square and meant to represent one copy of the texture, the code would probably assign texture coordinates $(0, 0)$, $(1, 0)$, $(1, 1)$, and $(0, 1)$ to the four corners of the wall. If the wall is large, you might want to paint several copies of the texture map on it. If you do so, the texture map must be designed so that the bricks on the left edge match up nicely with the bricks on the right edge, and similarly for the bricks on the top and those on the bottom.

You must also indicate how texture coordinates outside the range [0.0,1.0] should be treated. Do the textures repeat to cover the object, or are they clamped to a boundary value?

A Sample Program

One of the problems with showing sample programs to illustrate texture mapping is that interesting textures are large. Typically, textures are read from an image file, since specifying a texture programmatically could take hundreds of lines of code. In Example 9-1, the texture—which consists of alternating white and black squares, like a checkerboard—is generated by the program. The program applies this texture to two squares, which are then rendered in perspective, one of them facing the viewer squarely and the other tilting back at 45 degrees, as shown in Figure 9-2. In object coordinates, both squares are the same size.

Figure 9-2   Texture-Mapped Squares

Example 9-1   Texture-Mapped Checkerboard: checker.c

```
#include <GL/gl.h>
#include <GL/glu.h>
#include <GL/glut.h>
#include <stdlib.h>
#include <stdio.h>

/*  Create checkerboard texture  */
#define checkImageWidth 64
#define checkImageHeight 64
```

```
static GLubyte checkImage[checkImageHeight][checkImageWidth][4];

static GLuint texName;

void makeCheckImage(void)
{
    int i, j, c;

    for (i = 0; i < checkImageHeight; i++) {
        for (j = 0; j < checkImageWidth; j++) {
            c = ((((i&0x8)==0)^((j&0x8))==0))*255;
            checkImage[i][j][0] = (GLubyte) c;
            checkImage[i][j][1] = (GLubyte) c;
            checkImage[i][j][2] = (GLubyte) c;
            checkImage[i][j][3] = (GLubyte) 255;
        }
    }
}

void init(void)
{
    glClearColor (0.0, 0.0, 0.0, 0.0);
    glShadeModel(GL_FLAT);
    glEnable(GL_DEPTH_TEST);

    makeCheckImage();
    glPixelStorei(GL_UNPACK_ALIGNMENT, 1);

    glGenTextures(1, &texName);
    glBindTexture(GL_TEXTURE_2D, texName);

    glTexParameteri(GL_TEXTURE_2D, GL_TEXTURE_WRAP_S, GL_REPEAT);
    glTexParameteri(GL_TEXTURE_2D, GL_TEXTURE_WRAP_T, GL_REPEAT);
    glTexParameteri(GL_TEXTURE_2D, GL_TEXTURE_MAG_FILTER,
                    GL_NEAREST);
    glTexParameteri(GL_TEXTURE_2D, GL_TEXTURE_MIN_FILTER,
                    GL_NEAREST);
    glTexImage2D(GL_TEXTURE_2D, 0, GL_RGBA, checkImageWidth,
                 checkImageHeight, 0, GL_RGBA, GL_UNSIGNED_BYTE,
                 checkImage);
}

void display(void)
{
    glClear(GL_COLOR_BUFFER_BIT | GL_DEPTH_BUFFER_BIT);
    glEnable(GL_TEXTURE_2D);
    glTexEnvf(GL_TEXTURE_ENV, GL_TEXTURE_ENV_MODE, GL_DECAL);
```

```
   glBindTexture(GL_TEXTURE_2D, texName);
   glBegin(GL_QUADS);
   glTexCoord2f(0.0, 0.0); glVertex3f(-2.0, -1.0, 0.0);
   glTexCoord2f(0.0, 1.0); glVertex3f(-2.0, 1.0, 0.0);
   glTexCoord2f(1.0, 1.0); glVertex3f(0.0, 1.0, 0.0);
   glTexCoord2f(1.0, 0.0); glVertex3f(0.0, -1.0, 0.0);

   glTexCoord2f(0.0, 0.0); glVertex3f(1.0, -1.0, 0.0);
   glTexCoord2f(0.0, 1.0); glVertex3f(1.0, 1.0, 0.0);
   glTexCoord2f(1.0, 1.0); glVertex3f(2.41421, 1.0, -1.41421);
   glTexCoord2f(1.0, 0.0); glVertex3f(2.41421, -1.0, -1.41421);
   glEnd();
   glFlush();
   glDisable(GL_TEXTURE_2D);
}

void reshape(int w, int h)
{
   glViewport(0, 0, (GLsizei) w, (GLsizei) h);
   glMatrixMode(GL_PROJECTION);
   glLoadIdentity();
   gluPerspective(60.0, (GLfloat) w/(GLfloat) h, 1.0, 30.0);
   glMatrixMode(GL_MODELVIEW);
   glLoadIdentity();
   glTranslatef(0.0, 0.0, -3.6);
}

void keyboard (unsigned char key, int x, int y)
{
   switch (key) {
      case 27:
         exit(0);
         break;
      default:
         break;
   }
}

int main(int argc, char** argv)
{
   glutInit(&argc, argv);
   glutInitDisplayMode(GLUT_SINGLE | GLUT_RGB | GLUT_DEPTH);
   glutInitWindowSize(250, 250);
   glutInitWindowPosition(100, 100);
   glutCreateWindow(argv[0]);
   init();
   glutDisplayFunc(display);
```

```
    glutReshapeFunc(reshape);
    glutKeyboardFunc(keyboard);
    glutMainLoop();
    return 0;
}
```

The checkerboard texture is generated in the routine **makeCheckImage()**, and all the texture-mapping initialization occurs in the routine **init()**. **glGenTextures()** and **glBindTexture()** name and create a texture object for a texture image. (See "Texture Objects" on page 346.) The single, full-resolution texture map is specified by **glTexImage2D()**, whose parameters indicate the size of the image, type of the image, location of the image, and other properties of it. (See "Specifying the Texture" on page 326 for more information about **glTexImage2D()**.)

The four calls to **glTexParameter*()** specify how the texture is to be wrapped and how the colors are to be filtered if there isn't an exact match between pixels in the texture and pixels on the screen. (See "Repeating and Clamping Textures" on page 360 and "Filtering" on page 344.)

In **display()**, **glEnable()** turns on texturing. **glTexEnv*()** sets the drawing mode to GL_DECAL so that the textured polygons are drawn using the colors from the texture map (rather than taking into account what color the polygons would have been drawn without the texture).

Then, two polygons are drawn. Note that texture coordinates are specified along with vertex coordinates. The **glTexCoord*()** command behaves similarly to the **glNormal()** command. **glTexCoord*()** sets the current texture coordinates; any subsequent vertex command has those texture coordinates associated with it until **glTexCoord*()** is called again.

Note: The checkerboard image on the tilted polygon might look wrong when you compile and run it on your machine—for example, it might look like two triangles with different projections of the checkerboard image on them. If so, try setting the parameter GL_PERSPECTIVE_CORRECTION_HINT to GL_NICEST and running the example again. To do this, use **glHint()**.

Specifying the Texture

The command **glTexImage2D()** defines a two-dimensional texture. It takes several arguments, which are described briefly here and in more detail in the subsections that follow. The related command for one-dimensional textures, **glTexImage1D()**, is described in "One-Dimensional Textures" on page 335.

---

void **glTexImage2D**(GLenum *target*, GLint *level*, GLint *internalFormat*,
           GLsizei *width*, GLsizei *height*, GLint *border*,
           GLenum *format*, GLenum *type*,
           const GLvoid **pixels*);

Defines a two-dimensional texture. The *target* parameter is set to either the constant GL_TEXTURE_2D or GL_PROXY_TEXTURE_2D. You use the *level* parameter if you're supplying multiple resolutions of the texture map; with only one resolution, *level* should be 0. (See "Multiple Levels of Detail" on page 338 for more information about using multiple resolutions.)

The next parameter, *internalFormat*, indicates which of the R, G, B, and A components or luminance or intensity values are selected for use in describing the texels of an image. The value of *internalFormat* is an integer from 1 to 4, or one of thirty-eight symbolic constants. The thirty-eight symbolic constants that are also legal values for *internalFormat* are GL_ALPHA, GL_ALPHA4, GL_ALPHA8, GL_ALPHA12, GL_ALPHA16, GL_LUMINANCE, GL_LUMINANCE4, GL_LUMINANCE8, GL_LUMINANCE12, GL_LUMINANCE16, GL_LUMINANCE_ALPHA, GL_LUMINANCE4_ALPHA4, GL_LUMINANCE6_ALPHA2, GL_LUMINANCE8_ALPHA8, GL_LUMINANCE12_ALPHA4, GL_LUMINANCE12_ALPHA12, GL_LUMINANCE16_ALPHA16, GL_INTENSITY, GL_INTENSITY4, GL_INTENSITY8, GL_INTENSITY12, GL_INTENSITY16, GL_RGB, GL_R3_G3_B2, GL_RGB4, GL_RGB5, GL_RGB8, GL_RGB10, GL_RGB12, GL_RGB16, GL_RGBA, GL_RGBA2, GL_RGBA4, GL_RGB5_A1, GL_RGBA8, GL_RGB10_A2, GL_RGBA12, and GL_RGBA16. (See "Texture Functions" on page 354 for a discussion of how these selected components are applied.)

If *internalFormat* is one of the thirty-eight symbolic constants, then you are asking for specific components and perhaps the resolution of those components. For example, if *internalFormat* is GL_R3_G3_B2, you are asking that texels be 3 bits of red, 3 bits of green, and 2 bits of blue, but OpenGL is not guaranteed to deliver this. OpenGL is only obligated to choose an internal representation that closely approximates what is requested, but an exact match is usually not required. By definition, GL_LUMINANCE, GL_LUMINANCE_ALPHA, GL_RGB, and GL_RGBA are lenient, because they do not ask for a specific resolution. (For compatibility with the OpenGL release 1.0, the numeric values 1, 2, 3, and 4, for *internalFormat*, are equivalent to the symbolic constants GL_LUMINANCE, GL_LUMINANCE_ALPHA, GL_RGB, and GL_RGBA, respectively.)

The *width* and *height* parameters give the dimensions of the texture image; *border* indicates the width of the border, which is either zero (no border) or one. (See "Using a Texture's Borders" on page 337.) Both *width* and *height* must have the form 2^m+2b, where m is a nonnegative integer (which can have a different value for *width* than for *height*) and b is the value of *border*. The maximum size of a texture map depends on the implementation of OpenGL, but it must be at least 64×64 (or 66×66 with borders).

The *format* and *type* parameters describe the format and data type of the texture image data. They have the same meaning as they do for **glDrawPixels()**. (See "Imaging Pipeline" on page 296.) In fact, texture data is in the same format as the data used by **glDrawPixels()**, so the settings of **glPixelStore*()** and **glPixelTransfer*()** are applied. (In Example 9-1, the call

```
glPixelStorei(GL_UNPACK_ALIGNMENT, 1);
```

is made because the data in the example isn't padded at the end of each texel row.) The *format* parameter can be GL_COLOR_INDEX, GL_RGB, GL_RGBA, GL_RED, GL_GREEN, GL_BLUE, GL_ALPHA, GL_LUMINANCE, or GL_LUMINANCE_ALPHA—that is, the same formats available for **glDrawPixels()** with the exceptions of GL_STENCIL_INDEX and GL_DEPTH_COMPONENT.

Similarly, the *type* parameter can be GL_BYTE, GL_UNSIGNED_BYTE, GL_SHORT, GL_UNSIGNED_SHORT, GL_INT, GL_UNSIGNED_INT, GL_FLOAT, or GL_BITMAP.

Finally, *pixels* contains the texture-image data. This data describes the texture image itself as well as its border.

The internal format of a texture image may affect the performance of texture operations. For example, some implementations perform texturing with GL_RGBA faster than GL_RGB, because the color components align the processor memory better. Since this varies, you should check specific information about your implementation of OpenGL.

The internal format of a texture image also may control how much memory a texture image consumes. For example, a texture of internal format

GL_RGBA8 uses 32 bits per texel, while a texture of internal format GL_R3_G3_B2 only uses 8 bits per texel. Of course, there is a corresponding trade-off between memory consumption and color resolution.

Note: Although texture-mapping results in color-index mode are undefined, you can still specify a texture with a GL_COLOR_INDEX image. In that case, pixel-transfer operations are applied to convert the indices to RGBA values by table lookup before they're used to form the texture image.

The number of texels for both the width and height of a texture image, not including the optional border, must be a power of 2. If your original image does not have dimensions that fit that limitation, you can use the OpenGL Utility Library routine **gluScaleImage()** to alter the size of your textures.

---

int **gluScaleImage**(GLenum *format*, GLint *widthin*, GLint *heightin*,
        GLenum *typein*, const void **datain*, GLint *widthout*,
        GLint *heightout*, GLenum *typeout*, void **dataout*);

Scales an image using the appropriate pixel-storage modes to unpack the data from *datain*. The *format*, *typein*, and *typeout* parameters can refer to any of the formats or data types supported by **glDrawPixels()**. The image is scaled using linear interpolation and box filtering (from the size indicated by *widthin* and *heightin* to *widthout* and *heightout*), and the resulting image is written to *dataout*, using the pixel GL_PACK* storage modes. The caller of **gluScaleImage()** must allocate sufficient space for the output buffer. A value of 0 is returned on success, and a GLU error code is returned on failure.

The framebuffer itself can also be used as a source for texture data. **glCopyTexImage2D()** reads a rectangle of pixels from the framebuffer and uses it for a new texture.

---

void **glCopyTexImage2D**(GLenum *target*, GLint *level*,
        GLint *internalFormat*,
        GLint *x*, GLint *y*, GLsizei *width*, GLsizei *height*,
        GLint *border*);

Creates a two-dimensional texture, using framebuffer data to define the texels. The pixels are read from the current GL_READ_BUFFER and are processed exactly as if **glCopyPixels()** had been called but stopped before final conversion. The settings of **glPixelTransfer*()** are applied.

The *target* parameter must be set to the constant GL_TEXTURE_2D. The *level*, *internalFormat*, and *border* parameters have the same effects that they have for **glTexImage2D()**. The texture array is taken from a screen-aligned pixel rectangle with the lower-left corner at coordinates specified by the (*x*, *y*) parameters. The *width* and *height* parameters specify the size of this pixel rectangle. Both *width* and *height* must have the form 2^m+2b, where m is a nonnegative integer (which can have a different value for *width* than for *height*) and b is the value of *border*.

The next sections give more detail about texturing, including the use of the *target*, *border*, and *level* parameters. The *target* parameter can be used to accurately query the size of a texture (by creating a texture proxy with **glTexImage*D()**) and whether a texture possibly can be used within the texture resources of an OpenGL implementation. Redefining a portion of a texture is described in "Replacing All or Part of a Texture Image" on page 332. One-dimensional textures are discussed in "One-Dimensional Textures" on page 335. The texture border, which has its size controlled by the *border* parameter, is detailed in "Using a Texture's Borders" on page 337. The *level* parameter is used to specify textures of different resolutions and is incorporated into the special technique of *mipmapping*, which is explained in "Multiple Levels of Detail" on page 338. Mipmapping requires understanding how to filter textures as they're applied; filtering is the subject of "Filtering" on page 344.

Texture Proxy

To an OpenGL programmer who uses textures, size is important. Texture resources are typically limited and vary among OpenGL implementations. There is a special texture proxy target to evaluate whether sufficient resources are available.

glGetIntegerv(GL_MAX_TEXTURE_SIZE,...) tells you the largest dimension (width or height, without borders) of a texture image, typically the size of the largest square texture supported. However, GL_MAX_TEXTURE_SIZE does not consider the effect of the internal format of a texture. A texture image that stores texels using the GL_RGBA16 internal format may be using 64 bits per texel, so its image may have to be 16 times smaller than an image with the GL_LUMINANCE4 internal format. (Also, images requiring borders or mipmaps may further reduce the amount of available memory.)

A special place holder, or *proxy*, for a texture image allows the program to query more accurately whether OpenGL can accommodate a texture of a desired internal format. To use the proxy to query OpenGL, call **glTexImage2D()** with a *target* parameter of GL_PROXY_TEXTURE_2D and the given *level, internalFormat, width, height, border, format,* and *type.* (For one-dimensional textures, use corresponding 1D routines and symbolic constants.) For a proxy, you should pass NULL as the pointer for the *pixels* array.

To find out whether there are enough resources available for your texture, after the texture proxy has been created, query the texture state variables with **glGetTexLevelParameter*()**. If there aren't enough resources to accommodate the texture proxy, the texture state variables for width, height, border width, and component resolutions are set to 0.

---

void **glGetTexLevelParameter**{if}**v**(GLenum *target*, GLint *level*,
            GLenum *pname*, *TYPE *params*);

Returns in *params* texture parameter values for a specific level of detail, specified as *level*. *target* defines the target texture and is one of GL_TEXTURE_1D, GL_TEXTURE_2D, GL_PROXY_TEXTURE_1D, or GL_PROXY_TEXTURE_2D. Accepted values for *pname* are GL_TEXTURE_WIDTH, GL_TEXTURE_HEIGHT, GL_TEXTURE_BORDER, GL_TEXTURE_INTERNAL_FORMAT, GL_TEXTURE_RED_SIZE, GL_TEXTURE_GREEN_SIZE, GL_TEXTURE_BLUE_SIZE, GL_TEXTURE_ALPHA_SIZE, GL_TEXTURE_LUMINANCE_SIZE, or GL_TEXTURE_INTENSITY_SIZE.

GL_TEXTURE_COMPONENTS is also accepted for *pname*, but only for backward compatibility with OpenGL Release 1.0—GL_TEXTURE_INTERNAL_FORMAT is the recommended symbolic constant for Release 1.1.

Example 9-2 demonstrates how to use the texture proxy to find out if there are enough resources to create a 64×64 texel texture with RGBA components with 8 bits of resolution. If this succeeds, then **glGetTexLevelParameteriv()** stores the internal format (in this case, GL_RGBA8) into the variable *format*.

Example 9-2   Querying Texture Resources with a Texture Proxy

```
GLint format;

glTexImage2D(GL_PROXY_TEXTURE_2D, 0, GL_RGBA8,
             64, 64, 0, GL_RGBA, GL_UNSIGNED_BYTE, NULL);
glGetTexLevelParameteriv(GL_PROXY_TEXTURE_2D, 0,
                         GL_TEXTURE_INTERNAL_FORMAT, &format);
```

Note: There is one major limitation about texture proxies: The texture proxy tells you if there is space for your texture, but only if all texture resources are available (in other words, if it's the only texture in town). If other textures are using resources, then the texture proxy query may respond affirmatively, but there may not be enough space to make your texture resident (that is, part of a possibly high-performance working set of textures). (See "Texture Objects" on page 346 for more information about managing resident textures.)

Replacing All or Part of a Texture Image

Creating a texture may be more computationally expensive than modifying an existing one. In OpenGL Release 1.1, there are new routines to replace all or part of a texture image with new information. This can be helpful for certain applications, such as using real-time, captured video images as texture images. For that application, it makes sense to create a single texture and use **glTexSubImage2D()** to repeatedly replace the texture data with new video images. Also, there are no size restrictions for **glTexSubImage2D()** that force the height or width to be a power of two. This is helpful for processing video images, which generally do not have sizes that are powers of two.

---

void **glTexSubImage2D**(GLenum *target*, GLint *level*, GLint *xoffset*,
  GLint *yoffset*, GLsizei *width*, GLsizei *height*,
  GLenum *format*, GLenum *type*, const GLvoid **pixels*);

Defines a two-dimensional texture image that replaces all or part of a contiguous subregion (in 2D, it's simply a rectangle) of the current, existing two-dimensional texture image. The *target* parameter must be set to GL_TEXTURE_2D.

The *level*, *format*, and *type* parameters are similar to the ones used for **glTexImage2D()**. *level* is the mipmap level-of-detail number. It is not an error to specify a width or height of zero, but the subimage will have no effect. *format* and *type* describe the format and data type of the texture image data. The subimage is also affected by modes set by **glPixelStore*()** and **glPixelTransfer*()**.

pixels contains the texture data for the subimage. *width* and *height* are the dimensions of the subregion that is replacing all or part of the current texture image. *xoffset* and *yoffset* specify the texel offset in the *x* and *y* directions (with (0, 0) at the lower-left corner of the texture) and specify where to put the subimage within the existing texture array. This region may not include any texels outside the range of the originally defined texture array.

In Example 9-3, some of the code from Example 9-1 has been modified so that pressing the 's' key drops a smaller checkered subimage into the existing image. (The resulting texture is shown in Figure 9-3.) Pressing the 'r' key restores the original image. Example 9-3 shows the two routines, **makeCheckImages()** and **keyboard()**, that have been substantially changed. (See "Texture Objects" on page 346 for more information about **glBindTexture()**.)

Figure 9-3   Texture with Subimage Added

Example 9-3   Replacing a Texture Subimage: texsub.c

```
/*  Create checkerboard textures   */
#define checkImageWidth 64
#define checkImageHeight 64
#define subImageWidth 16
#define subImageHeight 16
static GLubyte checkImage[checkImageHeight][checkImageWidth][4];
static GLubyte subImage[subImageHeight][subImageWidth][4];

void makeCheckImages(void)
{
   int i, j, c;

   for (i = 0; i < checkImageHeight; i++) {
      for (j = 0; j < checkImageWidth; j++) {
         c = ((((i&0x8)==0)^((j&0x8))==0))*255;
         checkImage[i][j][0] = (GLubyte) c;
         checkImage[i][j][1] = (GLubyte) c;
         checkImage[i][j][2] = (GLubyte) c;
         checkImage[i][j][3] = (GLubyte) 255;
      }
```

```
        }
    for (i = 0; i < subImageHeight; i++) {
        for (j = 0; j < subImageWidth; j++) {
            c = (((((i&0x4)==0)^((j&0x4))==0))*255;
            subImage[i][j][0] = (GLubyte) c;
            subImage[i][j][1] = (GLubyte) 0;
            subImage[i][j][2] = (GLubyte) 0;
            subImage[i][j][3] = (GLubyte) 255;
        }
    }
}

void keyboard (unsigned char key, int x, int y)
{
    switch (key) {
        case 's':
        case 'S':
            glBindTexture(GL_TEXTURE_2D, texName);
            glTexSubImage2D(GL_TEXTURE_2D, 0, 12, 44,
                         subImageWidth, subImageHeight, GL_RGBA,
                         GL_UNSIGNED_BYTE, subImage);
            glutPostRedisplay();
            break;
        case 'r':
        case 'R':
            glBindTexture(GL_TEXTURE_2D, texName);
            glTexImage2D(GL_TEXTURE_2D, 0, GL_RGBA,
                      checkImageWidth, checkImageHeight, 0,
                      GL_RGBA, GL_UNSIGNED_BYTE, checkImage);
            glutPostRedisplay();
            break;
        case 27:
            exit(0);
            break;
        default:
            break;
    }
}
```

Once again, the framebuffer itself can be used as a source for texture data; this time, a texture subimage. **glCopyTexSubImage2D()** reads a rectangle of pixels from the framebuffer and replaces a portion of an existing texture array. (**glCopyTexSubImage2D()** is kind of a cross between **glCopyTexImage2D()** and **glTexSubImage2D()**.)

void **glCopyTexSubImage2D**(GLenum *target*, GLint *level*,
 GLint *xoffset*, GLint *yoffset*, GLint *x*, GLint *y*,
 GLsizei *width*, GLsizei *height*);

Uses image data from the framebuffer to replace all or part of a contiguous subregion of the current, existing two-dimensional texture image. The pixels are read from the current GL_READ_BUFFER and are processed exactly as if **glCopyPixels()** had been called, stopping before final conversion. The settings of **glPixelStore*()** and **glPixelTransfer*()** are applied.

The *target* parameter must be set to GL_TEXTURE_2D. *level* is the mipmap level-of-detail number. *xoffset* and *yoffset* specify the texel offset in the x and y directions (with (0, 0) at the lower-left corner of the texture) and specify where to put the subimage within the existing texture array. The subimage texture array is taken from a screen-aligned pixel rectangle with the lower-left corner at coordinates specified by the (*x*, *y*) parameters. The *width* and *height* parameters specify the size of this subimage rectangle.

One-Dimensional Textures

Sometimes a one-dimensional texture is sufficient—for example, if you're drawing textured bands where all the variation is in one direction. A one-dimensional texture behaves like a two-dimensional one with *height* = 1, and without borders along the top and bottom. All the two-dimensional texture and subtexture definition routines have corresponding one-dimensional routines. To create a simple one-dimensional texture, use **glTexImage1D()**.

void **glTexImage1D**(GLenum *target*, GLint *level*, GLint *internalFormat*,
 GLsizei *width*, GLint *border*, GLenum *format*,
 GLenum *type*, const GLvoid **pixels*);

Defines a one-dimensional texture. All the parameters have the same meanings as for **glTexImage2D()**, except that the image is now a one-dimensional array of texels. As before, the value of *width* is 2^m (or 2^m+2, if there's a border), where m is a nonnegative integer. You can supply mipmaps, proxies (set *target* to GL_PROXY_TEXTURE_1D), and the same filtering options are available as well.

For a sample program that uses a one-dimensional texture map, see Example 9-6 on page 365.

To replace all or some of the texels of a one-dimensional texture, use **glTexSubImage1D()**.

---

void **glTexSubImage1D**(GLenum *target*, GLint *level*, GLint *xoffset*,
                GLsizei *width*, GLenum *format*,
                GLenum *type*, const GLvoid **pixels*);

Defines a one-dimensional texture array that replaces all or part of a contiguous subregion (in 1D, a row) of the current, existing one-dimensional texture image. The *target* parameter must be set to GL_TEXTURE_1D.

The *level*, *format*, and *type* parameters are similar to the ones used for **glTexImage1D()**. *level* is the mipmap level-of-detail number. *format* and *type* describe the format and data type of the texture image data. The subimage is also affected by modes set by **glPixelStore*()** or **glPixelTransfer*()**.

pixels contains the texture data for the subimage. *width* is the number of texels that replace part or all of the current texture image. *xoffset* specifies the texel offset for where to put the subimage within the existing texture array.

To use the framebuffer as the source of a new or replacement for an old one-dimensional texture, use either **glCopyTexImage1D()** or **glCopyTexSubImage1D()**.

---

void **glCopyTexImage1D**(GLenum *target*, GLint *level*,
                GLint *internalFormat*, GLint *x*, GLint *y*,
                GLsizei *width*, GLint *border*);

Creates a one-dimensional texture, using framebuffer data to define the texels. The pixels are read from the current GL_READ_BUFFER and are processed exactly as if **glCopyPixels()** had been called but stopped before final conversion. The settings of **glPixelStore*()** and **glPixelTransfer*()** are applied.

The *target* parameter must be set to the constant GL_TEXTURE_1D. The *level*, *internalFormat*, and *border* parameters have the same effects that they have for **glCopyTexImage2D()**. The texture array is taken from a row of pixels with the lower-left corner at coordinates specified by the (*x*, *y*) parameters. The *width* parameter specifies the number of pixels in this row. The value of *width* is 2^m (or 2^m+2 if there's a border), where m is a nonnegative integer.

void **glCopyTexSubImage1D**(GLenum *target*, GLint *level*, GLint *xoffset*, GLint *x*, GLint *y*, GLsizei *width*);

Uses image data from the framebuffer to replace all or part of a contiguous subregion of the current, existing one-dimensional texture image. The pixels are read from the current GL_READ_BUFFER and are processed exactly as if **glCopyPixels()** had been called but stopped before final conversion. The settings of **glPixelStore*()** and **glPixelTransfer*()** are applied.

The *target* parameter must be set to GL_TEXTURE_1D. *level* is the mipmap level-of-detail number. *xoffset* specifies the texel offset and specifies where to put the subimage within the existing texture array. The subimage texture array is taken from a row of pixels with the lower-left corner at coordinates specified by the (*x*, *y*) parameters. The *width* parameter specifies the number of pixels in this row.

Using a Texture's Borders

Advanced

If you need to apply a larger texture map than your implementation of OpenGL allows, you can, with a little care, effectively make larger textures by tiling with several different textures. For example, if you need a texture twice as large as the maximum allowed size mapped to a square, draw the square as four subsquares, and load a different texture before drawing each piece.

Since only a single texture map is available at one time, this approach might lead to problems at the edges of the textures, especially if some form of linear filtering is enabled. The texture value to be used for pixels at the edges must be averaged with something beyond the edge, which, ideally, should come from the adjacent texture map. If you define a border for each texture whose texel values are equal to the values of the texels on the edge of the adjacent texture map, then the correct behavior results when linear filtering takes place.

To do this correctly, notice that each map can have eight neighbors—one adjacent to each edge, and one touching each corner. The values of the texels in the corner of the border need to correspond with the texels in the texture maps that touch the corners. If your texture is an edge or corner of the whole tiling, you need to decide what values would be reasonable to put in the borders. The easiest reasonable thing to do is to copy the value of the adjacent texel in the texture map. Remember that the border values need to be supplied at the same time as the texture-image data, so you need to figure this out ahead of time.

A texture's border color is also used if the texture is applied in such a way that it only partially covers a primitive. (See "Repeating and Clamping Textures" on page 360 for more information about this situation.)

Multiple Levels of Detail

Advanced

Textured objects can be viewed, like any other objects in a scene, at different distances from the viewpoint. In a dynamic scene, as a textured object moves farther from the viewpoint, the texture map must decrease in size along with the size of the projected image. To accomplish this, OpenGL has to filter the texture map down to an appropriate size for mapping onto the object, without introducing visually disturbing artifacts. For example, to render a brick wall, you may use a large (say 128×128 texel) texture image when it is close to the viewer. But if the wall is moved farther away from the viewer until it appears on the screen as a single pixel, then the filtered textures may appear to change abruptly at certain transition points.

To avoid such artifacts, you can specify a series of prefiltered texture maps of decreasing resolutions, called *mipmaps*, as shown in Figure 9-4. The term *mipmap* was coined by Lance Williams, when he introduced the idea in his paper, *"Pyramidal Parametrics"* (SIGGRAPH 1983 Proceedings). *Mip* stands for the Latin *multim im parvo*, meaning "many things in a small place." Mipmapping uses some clever methods to pack image data into memory.

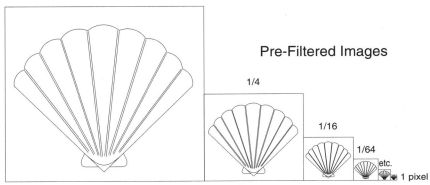

Original Texture

Pre-Filtered Images

1/4

1/16

1/64

etc.

1 pixel

Figure 9-4   Mipmaps

When using mipmapping, OpenGL automatically determines which texture map to use based on the size (in pixels) of the object being mapped. With this approach, the level of detail in the texture map is appropriate for the image that's drawn on the screen—as the image of the object gets smaller, the size of the texture map decreases. Mipmapping requires some extra computation and texture storage area; however, when it's not used, textures that are mapped onto smaller objects might shimmer and flash as the objects move.

To use mipmapping, you must provide all sizes of your texture in powers of 2 between the largest size and a 1×1 map. For example, if your highest-resolution map is 64×16, you must also provide maps of size 32×8, 16×4, 8×2, 4×1, 2×1, and 1×1. The smaller maps are typically filtered and averaged-down versions of the largest map in which each texel in a smaller texture is an average of the corresponding four texels in the larger texture. (Since OpenGL doesn't require any particular method for calculating the smaller maps, the differently sized textures could be totally unrelated. In practice, unrelated textures would make the transitions between mipmaps extremely noticeable.)

To specify these textures, call **glTexImage2D()** once for each resolution of the texture map, with different values for the *level*, *width*, *height*, and *image* parameters. Starting with zero, *level* identifies which texture in the series is specified; with the previous example, the largest texture of size 64×16 would be declared with *level* = 0, the 32×8 texture with *level* = 1, and so on. In addition, for the mipmapped textures to take effect, you need to choose one of the appropriate filtering methods described in the next section.

Example 9-4 illustrates the use of a series of six texture maps decreasing in size from 32×32 to 1×1. This program draws a rectangle that extends from the foreground far back in the distance, eventually disappearing at a point, as shown in Plate 20. Note that the texture coordinates range from 0.0 to 8.0 so 64 copies of the texture map are required to tile the rectangle, eight in each direction. To illustrate how one texture map succeeds another, each map has a different color.

Example 9-4   Mipmap Textures: mipmap.c

```
#include <GL/gl.h>
#include <GL/glu.h>
#include <GL/glut.h>
#include <stdlib.h>

GLubyte mipmapImage32[32][32][4];
GLubyte mipmapImage16[16][16][4];
GLubyte mipmapImage8[8][8][4];
GLubyte mipmapImage4[4][4][4];
GLubyte mipmapImage2[2][2][4];
GLubyte mipmapImage1[1][1][4];

static GLuint texName;

void makeImages(void)
{
    int i, j;

    for (i = 0; i < 32; i++) {
        for (j = 0; j < 32; j++) {
            mipmapImage32[i][j][0] = 255;
            mipmapImage32[i][j][1] = 255;
            mipmapImage32[i][j][2] = 0;
            mipmapImage32[i][j][3] = 255;
        }
    }
    for (i = 0; i < 16; i++) {
        for (j = 0; j < 16; j++) {
            mipmapImage16[i][j][0] = 255;
            mipmapImage16[i][j][1] = 0;
            mipmapImage16[i][j][2] = 255;
            mipmapImage16[i][j][3] = 255;
        }
    }
    for (i = 0; i < 8; i++) {
        for (j = 0; j < 8; j++) {
```

```
                mipmapImage8[i][j][0] = 255;
                mipmapImage8[i][j][1] = 0;
                mipmapImage8[i][j][2] = 0;
                mipmapImage8[i][j][3] = 255;
            }
        }
    for (i = 0; i < 4; i++) {
        for (j = 0; j < 4; j++) {
                mipmapImage4[i][j][0] = 0;
                mipmapImage4[i][j][1] = 255;
                mipmapImage4[i][j][2] = 0;
                mipmapImage4[i][j][3] = 255;
            }
        }
    for (i = 0; i < 2; i++) {
        for (j = 0; j < 2; j++) {
                mipmapImage2[i][j][0] = 0;
                mipmapImage2[i][j][1] = 0;
                mipmapImage2[i][j][2] = 255;
                mipmapImage2[i][j][3] = 255;
            }
        }
    mipmapImage1[0][0][0] = 255;
    mipmapImage1[0][0][1] = 255;
    mipmapImage1[0][0][2] = 255;
    mipmapImage1[0][0][3] = 255;
}

void init(void)
{
    glEnable(GL_DEPTH_TEST);
    glShadeModel(GL_FLAT);

    glTranslatef(0.0, 0.0, -3.6);
    makeImages();
    glPixelStorei(GL_UNPACK_ALIGNMENT, 1);

    glGenTextures(1, &texName);
    glBindTexture(GL_TEXTURE_2D, texName);
    glTexParameteri(GL_TEXTURE_2D, GL_TEXTURE_WRAP_S, GL_REPEAT);
    glTexParameteri(GL_TEXTURE_2D, GL_TEXTURE_WRAP_T, GL_REPEAT);
    glTexParameteri(GL_TEXTURE_2D, GL_TEXTURE_MAG_FILTER,
                    GL_NEAREST);
    glTexParameteri(GL_TEXTURE_2D, GL_TEXTURE_MIN_FILTER,
                    GL_NEAREST_MIPMAP_NEAREST);
    glTexImage2D(GL_TEXTURE_2D, 0, GL_RGBA, 32, 32, 0,
                 GL_RGBA, GL_UNSIGNED_BYTE, mipmapImage32);
```

```
        glTexImage2D(GL_TEXTURE_2D, 1, GL_RGBA, 16, 16, 0,
                    GL_RGBA, GL_UNSIGNED_BYTE, mipmapImage16);
        glTexImage2D(GL_TEXTURE_2D, 2, GL_RGBA, 8, 8, 0,
                    GL_RGBA, GL_UNSIGNED_BYTE, mipmapImage8);
        glTexImage2D(GL_TEXTURE_2D, 3, GL_RGBA, 4, 4, 0,
                    GL_RGBA, GL_UNSIGNED_BYTE, mipmapImage4);
        glTexImage2D(GL_TEXTURE_2D, 4, GL_RGBA, 2, 2, 0,
                    GL_RGBA, GL_UNSIGNED_BYTE, mipmapImage2);
        glTexImage2D(GL_TEXTURE_2D, 5, GL_RGBA, 1, 1, 0,
                    GL_RGBA, GL_UNSIGNED_BYTE, mipmapImage1);

        glTexEnvf(GL_TEXTURE_ENV, GL_TEXTURE_ENV_MODE, GL_DECAL);
        glEnable(GL_TEXTURE_2D);
    }

    void display(void)
    {
        glClear(GL_COLOR_BUFFER_BIT | GL_DEPTH_BUFFER_BIT);
        glBindTexture(GL_TEXTURE_2D, texName);
        glBegin(GL_QUADS);
        glTexCoord2f(0.0, 0.0); glVertex3f(-2.0, -1.0, 0.0);
        glTexCoord2f(0.0, 8.0); glVertex3f(-2.0, 1.0, 0.0);
        glTexCoord2f(8.0, 8.0); glVertex3f(2000.0, 1.0, -6000.0);
        glTexCoord2f(8.0, 0.0); glVertex3f(2000.0, -1.0, -6000.0);
        glEnd();
        glFlush();
    }

    void reshape(int w, int h)
    {
        glViewport(0, 0, (GLsizei) w, (GLsizei) h);
        glMatrixMode(GL_PROJECTION);
        glLoadIdentity();
        gluPerspective(60.0, (GLfloat)w/(GLfloat)h, 1.0, 30000.0);
        glMatrixMode(GL_MODELVIEW);
        glLoadIdentity();
    }

    void keyboard (unsigned char key, int x, int y)
    {
        switch (key) {
          case 27:
             exit(0);
             break;
          default:
             break;
        }
```

```
}

int main(int argc, char** argv)
{
    glutInit(&argc, argv);
    glutInitDisplayMode(GLUT_SINGLE | GLUT_RGB | GLUT_DEPTH);
    glutInitWindowSize(500, 500);
    glutInitWindowPosition(50, 50);
    glutCreateWindow(argv[0]);
    init();
    glutDisplayFunc(display);
    glutReshapeFunc(reshape);
    glutKeyboardFunc(keyboard);
    glutMainLoop();
    return 0;
}
```

Example 9-4 illustrates mipmapping by making each mipmap a different color so that it's obvious when one map is replaced by another. In a real situation, you define mipmaps so that the transition is as smooth as possible. Thus, the maps of lower resolution are usually filtered versions of an original, high-resolution map. The construction of a series of such mipmaps is a software process, and thus isn't part of OpenGL, which is simply a rendering library. However, since mipmap construction is such an important operation, however, the OpenGL Utility Library contains two routines that aid in the manipulation of images to be used as mipmapped textures.

Assuming you have constructed the level 0, or highest-resolution map, the routines **gluBuild1DMipmaps()** and **gluBuild2DMipmaps()** construct and define the pyramid of mipmaps down to a resolution of 1×1 (or 1, for one-dimensional texture maps). If your original image has dimensions that are not exact powers of 2, **gluBuild*DMipmaps()** helpfully scales the image to the nearest power of 2.

| int **gluBuild1DMipmaps**(GLenum *target*, GLint *components*, GLint *width*, |
| GLenum *format*, GLenum *type*, void **data*); |
| int **gluBuild2DMipmaps**(GLenum *target*, GLint *components*, GLint *width*, |
| GLint *height*, GLenum *format*, GLenum *type*, |
| void **data*); |

Constructs a series of mipmaps and calls **glTexImage*D**() to load the images. The parameters for *target*, *components*, *width*, *height*, *format*, *type*, and *data* are exactly the same as those for **glTexImage1D**() and **glTexImage2D**(). A value of 0 is returned if all the mipmaps are constructed successfully; otherwise, a GLU error code is returned.

Filtering

Texture maps are square or rectangular, but after being mapped to a polygon or surface and transformed into screen coordinates, the individual texels of a texture rarely correspond to individual pixels of the final screen image. Depending on the transformations used and the texture mapping applied, a single pixel on the screen can correspond to anything from a tiny portion of a texel (magnification) to a large collection of texels (minification), as shown in Figure 9-5. In either case, it's unclear exactly which texel values should be used and how they should be averaged or interpolated. Consequently, OpenGL allows you to specify any of several filtering options to determine these calculations. The options provide different trade-offs between speed and image quality. Also, you can specify independently the filtering methods for magnification and minification.

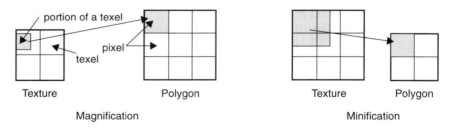

Figure 9-5   Texture Magnification and Minification

In some cases, it isn't obvious whether magnification or minification is called for. If the mipmap needs to be stretched (or shrunk) in both the *x* and *y* directions, then magnification (or minification) is needed. If the mipmap needs to be stretched in one direction and shrunk in the other, OpenGL makes a choice between magnification and minification that in most cases gives the best result possible. It's best to try to avoid these situations by using texture coordinates that map without such distortion. (See "Computing Appropriate Texture Coordinates" on page 358.)

The following lines are examples of how to use **glTexParameter*()** to specify the magnification and minification filtering methods:

```
glTexParameteri(GL_TEXTURE_2D, GL_TEXTURE_MAG_FILTER,
                GL_NEAREST);
glTexParameteri(GL_TEXTURE_2D, GL_TEXTURE_MIN_FILTER,
                GL_NEAREST);
```

The first argument to **glTexParameter*()** is either GL_TEXTURE_2D or GL_TEXTURE_1D, depending on whether you're working with two- or one-dimensional textures. For the purposes of this discussion, the second argument is either GL_TEXTURE_MAG_FILTER or GL_TEXTURE_MIN_FILTER to indicate whether you're specifying the filtering method for magnification or minification. The third argument specifies the filtering method; Table 9-1 lists the possible values.

Parameter	Values
GL_TEXTURE_MAG_FILTER	GL_NEAREST or GL_LINEAR
GL_TEXTURE_MIN_FILTER	GL_NEAREST, GL_LINEAR, GL_NEAREST_MIPMAP_NEAREST, GL_NEAREST_MIPMAP_LINEAR, GL_LINEAR_MIPMAP_NEAREST, or GL_LINEAR_MIPMAP_LINEAR

Table 9-1   Filtering Methods for Magnification and Minification

If you choose GL_NEAREST, the texel with coordinates nearest the center of the pixel is used for both magnification and minification. This can result in aliasing artifacts (sometimes severe). If you choose GL_LINEAR, a weighted linear average of the 2×2 array of texels that lie nearest to the center of the pixel is used, again for both magnification and minification. When the texture coordinates are near the edge of the texture map, the nearest 2×2 array of texels might include some that are outside the texture map. In these cases, the texel values used depend on whether GL_REPEAT or GL_CLAMP is in effect and whether you've assigned a border for the texture. (See "Using a Texture's Borders" on page 337.) GL_NEAREST requires less computation than GL_LINEAR and therefore might execute more quickly, but GL_LINEAR provides smoother results.

With magnification, even if you've supplied mipmaps, the largest texture map (*level* = 0) is always used. With minification, you can choose a filtering method that uses the most appropriate one or two mipmaps, as described in the next paragraph. (If GL_NEAREST or GL_LINEAR is specified with minification, the largest texture map is used.)

As shown in Table 9-1, four additional filtering choices are available when minifying with mipmaps. Within an individual mipmap, you can choose the nearest texel value with GL_NEAREST_MIPMAP_NEAREST, or you can interpolate linearly by specifying GL_LINEAR_MIPMAP_NEAREST. Using the nearest texels is faster but yields less desirable results. The particular mipmap chosen is a function of the amount of minification required, and there's a cutoff point from the use of one particular mipmap to the next. To avoid a sudden transition, use GL_NEAREST_MIPMAP_LINEAR or GL_LINEAR_MIPMAP_LINEAR to linearly interpolate texel values from the two nearest best choices of mipmaps. GL_NEAREST_MIPMAP_LINEAR selects the nearest texel in each of the two maps and then interpolates linearly between these two values. GL_LINEAR_MIPMAP_LINEAR uses linear interpolation to compute the value in each of two maps and then interpolates linearly between these two values. As you might expect, GL_LINEAR_MIPMAP_LINEAR generally produces the smoothest results, but it requires the most computation and therefore might be the slowest.

Texture Objects

Texture objects are an important new feature in release 1.1 of OpenGL. A texture object stores texture data and makes it readily available. You can now control many textures and go back to textures that have been previously loaded into your texture resources. Using texture objects is usually the fastest way to apply textures, resulting in big performance gains, because it is almost always much faster to bind (reuse) an existing texture object than it is to reload a texture image using **glTexImage*D()**.

Also, some implementations support a limited *working set* of high-performance textures. You can use texture objects to load your most often used textures into this limited area.

To use texture objects for your texture data, take these steps.

1. Generate texture names.

2. Initially bind (create) texture objects to texture data, including the image arrays and texture properties.

3. If your implementation supports a working set of high-performance textures, see if you have enough space for all your texture objects. If there isn't enough space, you may wish to establish priorities for each texture object so that more often used textures stay in the working set.

4. Bind and rebind texture objects, making their data currently available for rendering textured models.

Naming A Texture Object

Any nonzero unsigned integer may be used as a texture name. To avoid accidentally reusing names, consistently use **glGenTextures()** to provide unused texture names.

---

void **glGenTextures**(GLsizei *n*, GLuint **textureNames*);

Returns *n* currently unused names for texture objects in the array *textureNames*. The names returned in *textureNames* do not have to be a contiguous set of integers.

The names in *textureNames* are marked as used, but they acquire texture state and dimensionality (1D or 2D) only when they are first bound.

Zero is a reserved texture name and is never returned as a texture name by **glGenTextures()**.

glIsTexture() determines if a texture name is actually in use. If a texture name was returned by **glGenTextures()** but has not yet been bound (calling **glBindTexture()** with the name at least once), then **glIsTexture()** returns GL_FALSE.

GLboolean **glIsTexture**(GLuint *textureName*);

Returns GL_TRUE if *textureName* is the name of a texture that has been bound and has not been subsequently deleted. Returns GL_FALSE if *textureName* is zero or *textureName* is a nonzero value that is not the name of an existing texture.

Creating and Using Texture Objects

The same routine, **glBindTexture()**, both creates and uses texture objects. When a texture name is initially bound (used with **glBindTexture()**), a new texture object is created with default values for the texture image and texture properties. Subsequent calls to **glTexImage*()**, **glTexSubImage*()**, **glCopyTexImage*()**, **glCopyTexSubImage*()**, **glTexParameter*()**, and **glPrioritizeTextures()** store data in the texture object. The texture object may contain a texture image and associated mipmap images (if any), including associated data such as width, height, border width, internal format, resolution of components, and texture properties. Saved texture properties include minification and magnification filters, wrapping modes, border color, and texture priority.

When a texture object is subsequently bound once again, its data becomes the current texture state. (The state of the previously bound texture is replaced.)

---

void **glBindTexture**(GLenum *target*, GLuint *textureName*);

---

glBindTexture() does three things. When using *textureName* of an unsigned integer other than zero for the first time, a new texture object is created and assigned that name. When binding to a previously created texture object, that texture object becomes active. When binding to a *textureName* value of zero, OpenGL stops using texture objects and returns to the unnamed default texture.

When a texture object is initially bound (that is, created), it assumes the dimensionality of *target*, which is either GL_TEXTURE_1D or GL_TEXTURE_2D. Immediately upon its initial binding, the state of texture object is equivalent to the state of the default GL_TEXTURE_1D or GL_TEXTURE_2D (depending upon its dimensionality) at the initialization of OpenGL. In this initial state, texture properties such as minification and magnification filters, wrapping modes, border color, and texture priority are set to their default values.

In Example 9-5, two texture objects are created in **init()**. In **display()**, each texture object is used to render a different four-sided polygon.

Example 9-5   Binding Texture Objects: texbind.c

```
#define checkImageWidth 64
#define checkImageHeight 64
static GLubyte checkImage[checkImageHeight][checkImageWidth][4];
```

```
static GLubyte otherImage[checkImageHeight][checkImageWidth][4];

static GLuint texName[2];

void makeCheckImages(void)
{
    int i, j, c;

    for (i = 0; i < checkImageHeight; i++) {
        for (j = 0; j < checkImageWidth; j++) {
            c = ((((i&0x8)==0)^((j&0x8))==0))*255;
            checkImage[i][j][0] = (GLubyte) c;
            checkImage[i][j][1] = (GLubyte) c;
            checkImage[i][j][2] = (GLubyte) c;
            checkImage[i][j][3] = (GLubyte) 255;
            c = (((((i&0x10)==0)^((j&0x10))==0))*255;
            otherImage[i][j][0] = (GLubyte) c;
            otherImage[i][j][1] = (GLubyte) 0;
            otherImage[i][j][2] = (GLubyte) 0;
            otherImage[i][j][3] = (GLubyte) 255;
        }
    }
}

void init(void)
{
    glClearColor (0.0, 0.0, 0.0, 0.0);
    glShadeModel(GL_FLAT);
    glEnable(GL_DEPTH_TEST);

    makeCheckImages();
    glPixelStorei(GL_UNPACK_ALIGNMENT, 1);

    glGenTextures(2, texName);
    glBindTexture(GL_TEXTURE_2D, texName[0]);
    glTexParameteri(GL_TEXTURE_2D, GL_TEXTURE_WRAP_S, GL_CLAMP);
    glTexParameteri(GL_TEXTURE_2D, GL_TEXTURE_WRAP_T, GL_CLAMP);
    glTexParameteri(GL_TEXTURE_2D, GL_TEXTURE_MAG_FILTER,
                    GL_NEAREST);
    glTexParameteri(GL_TEXTURE_2D, GL_TEXTURE_MIN_FILTER,
                    GL_NEAREST);
    glTexImage2D(GL_TEXTURE_2D, 0, GL_RGBA, checkImageWidth,
                 checkImageHeight, 0, GL_RGBA, GL_UNSIGNED_BYTE,
                 checkImage);

    glBindTexture(GL_TEXTURE_2D, texName[1]);
    glTexParameteri(GL_TEXTURE_2D, GL_TEXTURE_WRAP_S, GL_CLAMP);
```

```
        glTexParameteri(GL_TEXTURE_2D, GL_TEXTURE_WRAP_T, GL_CLAMP);
        glTexParameteri(GL_TEXTURE_2D, GL_TEXTURE_MAG_FILTER,
                        GL_NEAREST);
        glTexParameteri(GL_TEXTURE_2D, GL_TEXTURE_MIN_FILTER,
                        GL_NEAREST);
        glTexEnvf(GL_TEXTURE_ENV, GL_TEXTURE_ENV_MODE, GL_DECAL);
        glTexImage2D(GL_TEXTURE_2D, 0, GL_RGBA, checkImageWidth,
                     checkImageHeight, 0, GL_RGBA, GL_UNSIGNED_BYTE,
                     otherImage);
        glEnable(GL_TEXTURE_2D);
}

void display(void)
{
        glClear(GL_COLOR_BUFFER_BIT | GL_DEPTH_BUFFER_BIT);
        glBindTexture(GL_TEXTURE_2D, texName[0]);
        glBegin(GL_QUADS);
        glTexCoord2f(0.0, 0.0); glVertex3f(-2.0, -1.0, 0.0);
        glTexCoord2f(0.0, 1.0); glVertex3f(-2.0, 1.0, 0.0);
        glTexCoord2f(1.0, 1.0); glVertex3f(0.0, 1.0, 0.0);
        glTexCoord2f(1.0, 0.0); glVertex3f(0.0, -1.0, 0.0);
        glEnd();
        glBindTexture(GL_TEXTURE_2D, texName[1]);
        glBegin(GL_QUADS);
        glTexCoord2f(0.0, 0.0); glVertex3f(1.0, -1.0, 0.0);
        glTexCoord2f(0.0, 1.0); glVertex3f(1.0, 1.0, 0.0);
        glTexCoord2f(1.0, 1.0); glVertex3f(2.41421, 1.0, -1.41421);
        glTexCoord2f(1.0, 0.0); glVertex3f(2.41421, -1.0, -1.41421);
        glEnd();
        glFlush();
}
```

Whenever a texture object is bound once again, you may edit the contents of the bound texture object. Any commands you call that change the texture image or other properties change the contents of the currently bound texture object as well as the current texture state.

In Example 9-5, after completion of **display()**, you are still bound to the texture named by the contents of *texName[1]*. Be careful that you don't call a spurious texture routine that changes the data in that texture object.

When using mipmaps, all related mipmaps of a single texture image must be put into a single texture object. In Example 9-4, levels 0–5 of a mipmapped texture image are put into a single texture object named *texName*.

Cleaning Up Texture Objects

As you bind and unbind texture objects, their data still sits around somewhere among your texture resources. If texture resources are limited, deleting textures may be one way to free up resources.

---

void **glDeleteTextures**(GLsizei *n*, const GLuint **textureNames*);

Deletes *n* texture objects, named by elements in the array *textureNames*. The freed texture names may now be reused (for example, by **glGenTextures**()).

If a texture that is currently bound is deleted, the binding reverts to the default texture, as if **glBindTexture**() were called with zero for the value of *textureName*. Attempts to delete nonexistent texture names or the texture name of zero are ignored without generating an error.

A Working Set of Resident Textures

Some OpenGL implementations support a working set of high-performance textures, which are said to be resident. Typically, these implementations have specialized hardware to perform texture operations and a limited hardware cache to store texture images. In this case, using texture objects is recommended, because you are able to load many textures into the working set and then control them.

If all the textures required by the application exceed the size of the cache, some textures cannot be resident. If you want to find out if a single texture is currently resident, bind its object, and then use **glGetTexParameter*v**() to find out the value associated with the GL_TEXTURE_RESIDENT state. If you want to know about the texture residence status of many textures, use **glAreTexturesResident**().

GLboolean **glAreTexturesResident**(GLsizei *n*, const
GLuint*textureNames, GLboolean *residences);

Queries the texture residence status of the *n* texture objects, named in the array *textureNames*. *residences* is an array in which texture residence status is returned for the corresponding texture objects in the array *textureNames*. If all the named textures in *textureNames* are resident, the **glAreTexturesResident**() function returns GL_TRUE, and the contents of the array *residences* are undisturbed. If any texture in *textureNames* is not resident, then **glAreTexturesResident**() returns GL_FALSE and the elements in *residences*, which correspond to nonresident texture objects in *textureNames*, are also set to GL_FALSE.

Note that **glAreTexturesResident**() returns the current residence status. Texture resources are very dynamic, and texture residence status may change at any time. Some implementations cache textures when they are first used. It may be necessary to draw with the texture before checking residency.

If your OpenGL implementation does not establish a working set of high-performance textures, then the texture objects are always considered resident. In that case, **glAreTexturesResident**() always returns GL_TRUE and basically provides no information.

Texture Residence Strategies

If you can create a working set of textures and want to get the best texture performance possible, you really have to know the specifics of your implementation and application. For example, with a visual simulation or video game, you have to maintain performance in all situations. In that case, you should never access a nonresident texture. For these applications, you want to load up all your textures upon initialization and make them all resident. If you don't have enough texture memory available, you may need to reduce the size, resolution, and levels of mipmaps for your texture images, or you may use **glTexSubImage***() to repeatedly reuse the same texture memory.

For applications that create textures "on the fly," nonresident textures may be unavoidable. If some textures are used more frequently than others, you may assign a higher priority to those texture objects to increase their likelihood of being resident. Deleting texture objects also frees up space. Short of that, assigning a lower priority to a texture object may make it first in line for being moved out of the working set, as resources dwindle. **glPrioritizeTextures()** is used to assign priorities to texture objects.

---

void **glPrioritizeTextures**(GLsizei *n*, const GLuint **textureNames*,
const GLclampf **priorities*);

Assigns the *n* texture objects, named in the array *textureNames*, the texture residence priorities in the corresponding elements of the array *priorities*. The priority values in the array *priorities* are clamped to the range [0.0, 1.0] before being assigned. Zero indicates the lowest priority; these textures are least likely to be resident. One indicates the highest priority.

glPrioritizeTextures() does not require that any of the textures in *textureNames* be bound. However, the priority might not have any effect on a texture object until it is initially bound.

glTexParameter*() also may be used to set a single texture's priority, but only if the texture is currently bound. In fact, use of **glTexParameter*()** is the only way to set the priority of a default texture.

If texture objects have equal priority, typical implementations of OpenGL apply a least recently used (LRU) strategy to decide which texture objects to move out of the working set. If you know that your OpenGL implementation has this behavior, then having equal priorities for all texture objects creates a reasonable LRU system for reallocating texture resources.

If your implementation of OpenGL doesn't use an LRU strategy for texture objects of equal priority (or if you don't know how it decides), you can implement your own LRU strategy by carefully maintaining the texture object priorities. When a texture is used (bound), you can maximize its priority, which reflects its recent use. Then, at regular (time) intervals, you can degrade the priorities of all texture objects.

Note: Fragmentation of texture memory can be a problem, especially if you're deleting and creating lots of new textures. Although it is even possible that you can load all the texture objects into a working set by binding them in one sequence, binding them in a different sequence may leave some textures nonresident.

Texture Functions

In all the examples so far in this chapter, the values in the texture map have been used directly as colors to be painted on the surface being rendered. You can also use the values in the texture map to modulate the color that the surface would be rendered without texturing, or to blend the color in the texture map with the original color of the surface. You choose one of four texturing functions by supplying the appropriate arguments to glTexEnv*().

---

void **glTexEnv**{if}(GLenum *target*, GLenum *pname*, TYPE *param*);
void **glTexEnv**{if}**v**(GLenum *target*, GLenum *pname*, TYPE **param*);

Sets the current texturing function. *target* must be GL_TEXTURE_ENV. If *pname* is GL_TEXTURE_ENV_MODE, *param* can be GL_DECAL, GL_REPLACE, GL_MODULATE, or GL_BLEND, to specify how texture values are to be combined with the color values of the fragment being processed. If *pname* is GL_TEXTURE_ENV_COLOR, *param* is an array of four floating-point values representing R, G, B, and A components. These values are used only if the GL_BLEND texture function has been specified as well.

The combination of the texturing function and the base internal format determine how the textures are applied for each component of the texture. The texturing function operates on selected components of the texture and the color values that would be used with no texturing. (Note that the selection is performed after the pixel-transfer function has been applied.) Recall that when you specify your texture map with glTexImage*D(), the third argument is the internal format to be selected for each texel.

Table 9-2 and Table 9-3 show how the texturing function and base internal format determine the texturing application formula used for each component of the texture. There are six base internal formats (the letters in parentheses represent their values in the tables): GL_ALPHA (A), GL_LUMINANCE (L), GL_LUMINANCE_ALPHA (L and A), GL_INTENSITY (I), GL_RGB (C), and GL_RGBA (C and A). Other internal formats specify desired resolutions of the texture components and can be matched to one of these six base internal formats.

Base Internal Format	Replace Texture Function	Modulate Texture Function
GL_ALPHA	$C = C_f,$ $A = A_t$	$C = C_f,$ $A = A_f A_t$
GL_LUMINANCE	$C = L_t,$ $A = A_f$	$C = C_f L_t,$ $A = A_f$
GL_LUMINANCE_ALPHA	$C = L_t,$ $A = A_t$	$C = C_f L_t,$ $A = A_f A_t$
GL_INTENSITY	$C = I_t,$ $A = I_t$	$C = C_f I_t,$ $A = A_f I_t$
GL_RGB	$C = C_t,$ $A = A_f$	$C = C_f C_t,$ $A = A_f$
GL_RGBA	$C = C_t,$ $A = A_t$	$C = C_f C_t,$ $A = A_f A_t$

Table 9-2   Replace and Modulate Texture Functions

Base Internal Format	Decal Texture Function	Blend Texture Function
GL_ALPHA	undefined	$C = C_f,$ $A = A_f A_t$
GL_LUMINANCE	undefined	$C = C_f(1-L_t) + C_c L_t,$ $A = A_f$
GL_LUMINANCE_ALPHA	undefined	$C = C_f(1-L_t) + C_c L_t,$ $A = A_f A_t$
GL_INTENSITY	undefined	$C = C_f(1-I_t) + C_c I_t,$ $A = A_f(1-I_t) + A_c I_t,$
GL_RGB	$C = C_t,$ $A = A_f$	$C = C_f(1-C_t) + C_c C_t,$ $A = A_f$
GL_RGBA	$C = C_f(1-A_t) + C_t A_t,$ $A = A_f$	$C = C_f(1-C_t) + C_c C_t,$ $A = A_f A_t$

Table 9-3   Decal and Blend Texture Functions

Note: In Table 9-2 and Table 9-3, a subscript of t indicates a texture value, f indicates the incoming fragment value, c indicates the values assigned with GL_TEXTURE_ENV_COLOR, and no subscript indicates the final, computed value. Also in the tables, multiplication of a color triple by a scalar means multiplying each of the R, G, and B components by the scalar; multiplying (or adding) two color triples means multiplying (or adding) each component of the second by the corresponding component of the first.

The decal texture function makes sense only for the RGB and RGBA internal formats (remember that texture mapping doesn't work in color-index mode). With the RGB internal format, the color that would have been painted in the absence of any texture mapping (the fragment's color) is replaced by the texture color, and its alpha is unchanged. With the RGBA internal format, the fragment's color is blended with the texture color in a ratio determined by the texture alpha, and the fragment's alpha is unchanged. You use the decal texture function in situations where you want to apply an opaque texture to an object—if you were drawing a soup can with an opaque label, for example. The decal texture function also can be used to apply an alpha blended texture, such as an insignia onto an airplane wing.

The replacement texture function is similar to decal; in fact, for the RGB internal format, they are exactly the same. With all the internal formats, the component values are either replaced or left alone.

For modulation, the fragment's color is modulated by the contents of the texture map. If the base internal format is GL_LUMINANCE, GL_LUMINANCE_ALPHA, or GL_INTENSITY, the color values are multiplied by the same value, so the texture map modulates between the fragment's color (if the luminance or intensity is 1) to black (if it's 0). For the GL_RGB and GL_RGBA internal formats, each of the incoming color components is multiplied by a corresponding (possibly different) value in the texture. If there's an alpha value, it's multiplied by the fragment's alpha. Modulation is a good texture function for use with lighting, since the lit polygon color can be used to attenuate the texture color. Most of the texture-mapping examples in the color plates use modulation for this reason. White, specular polygons are often used to render lit, textured objects, and the texture image provides the diffuse color.

The blending texture function is the only function that uses the color specified by GL_TEXTURE_ENV_COLOR. The luminance, intensity, or color value is used somewhat like an alpha value to blend the fragment's color with the GL_TEXTURE_ENV_COLOR. (See "Sample Uses of Blending" on page 217 for the billboarding example, which uses a blended texture.)

Assigning Texture Coordinates

As you draw your texture-mapped scene, you must provide both object coordinates and texture coordinates for each vertex. After transformation, the object coordinates determine where on the screen that particular vertex is rendered. The texture coordinates determine which texel in the texture map is assigned to that vertex. In exactly the same way that colors are interpolated between two vertices of shaded polygons and lines, texture coordinates are also interpolated between vertices. (Remember that textures are rectangular arrays of data.)

Texture coordinates can comprise one, two, three, or four coordinates. They're usually referred to as the $s, t, r,$ and q coordinates to distinguish them from object coordinates ($x, y, z,$ and w) and from evaluator coordinates (u and v; see Chapter 12). For one-dimensional textures, you use the s coordinate; for two-dimensional textures, you use s and t. In Release 1.1, the r coordinate is ignored. (Some implementations have 3D texture mapping as an extension, and that extension uses the r coordinate.) The q coordinate, like w, is typically given the value 1 and can be used to create homogeneous coordinates; it's described as an advanced feature in "The q Coordinate" on page 372. The command to specify texture coordinates, **glTexCoord*()**, is similar to **glVertex*()**, **glColor*()**, and **glNormal*()**—it comes in similar variations and is used the same way between **glBegin()** and **glEnd()** pairs. Usually, texture-coordinate values range from 0 to 1; values can be assigned outside this range, however, with the results described in "Repeating and Clamping Textures" on page 360.

void **glTexCoord**{1234}{sifd}(*TYPE coords*);
void **glTexCoord**{1234}{sifd}**v**(*TYPE *coords*);

Sets the current texture coordinates (*s, t, r, q*). Subsequent calls to **glVertex*()** result in those vertices being assigned the current texture coordinates. With **glTexCoord1*()**, the *s* coordinate is set to the specified value, *t* and *r* are set to 0, and *q* is set to 1. Using **glTexCoord2*()** allows you to specify *s* and *t*; *r* and *q* are set to 0 and 1, respectively. With **glTexCoord3*()**, *q* is set to 1 and the other coordinates are set as specified. You can specify all coordinates with **glTexCoord4*()**. Use the appropriate suffix (s, i, f, or d) and the corresponding value for *TYPE* (GLshort, GLint, GLfloat, or GLdouble) to specify the coordinates' data type. You can supply the coordinates individually, or you can use the vector version of the command to supply them in a single array. Texture coordinates are multiplied by the 4×4 texture matrix before any texture mapping occurs. (See "The Texture Matrix Stack" on page 371.) Note that integer texture coordinates are interpreted directly rather than being mapped to the range [–1,1] as normal coordinates are.

The next section discusses how to calculate appropriate texture coordinates. Instead of explicitly assigning them yourself, you can choose to have texture coordinates calculated automatically by OpenGL as a function of the vertex coordinates. (See "Automatic Texture-Coordinate Generation" on page 364.)

Computing Appropriate Texture Coordinates

Two-dimensional textures are square or rectangular images that are typically mapped to the polygons that make up a polygonal model. In the simplest case, you're mapping a rectangular texture onto a model that's also rectangular—for example, your texture is a scanned image of a brick wall, and your rectangle is to represent a brick wall of a building. Suppose the brick wall is square and the texture is square, and you want to map the whole texture to the whole wall. The texture coordinates of the texture square are (0, 0), (1, 0), (1, 1), and (0, 1) in counterclockwise order. When you're drawing the wall, just give those four coordinate sets as the texture coordinates as you specify the wall's vertices in counterclockwise order.

Now suppose that the wall is two-thirds as high as it is wide, and that the texture is again square. To avoid distorting the texture, you need to map the wall to a portion of the texture map so that the aspect ratio of the texture is preserved. Suppose that you decide to use the lower two-thirds of the texture map to texture the wall. In this case, use texture coordinates of (0,0), (1,0), (1,2/3), and (0,2/3) for the texture coordinates as the wall vertices are traversed in a counterclockwise order.

As a slightly more complicated example, suppose you'd like to display a tin can with a label wrapped around it on the screen. To obtain the texture, you purchase a can, remove the label, and scan it in. Suppose the label is 4 units tall and 12 units around, which yields an aspect ratio of 3 to 1. Since textures must have aspect ratios of 2^n to 1, you can either simply not use the top third of the texture, or you can cut and paste the texture until it has the necessary aspect ratio. Suppose you decide not to use the top third. Now suppose the tin can is a cylinder approximated by thirty polygons of length 4 units (the height of the can) and width 12/30 (1/30 of the circumference of the can). You can use the following texture coordinates for each of the thirty approximating rectangles:

1: (0, 0), (1/30, 0), (1/30, 2/3), (0, 2/3)

2: (1/30, 0), (2/30, 0), (2/30, 2/3), (1/30, 2/3)

3: (2/30, 0), (3/30, 0), (3/30, 2/3), (2/30, 2/3)

. . .

30: (29/30, 0), (1, 0), (1, 2/3), (29/30, 2/3)

Only a few curved surfaces such as cones and cylinders can be mapped to a flat surface without geodesic distortion. Any other shape requires some distortion. In general, the higher the curvature of the surface, the more distortion of the texture is required.

If you don't care about texture distortion, it's often quite easy to find a reasonable mapping. For example, consider a sphere whose surface coordinates are given by $(\cos\theta\cos\phi, \cos\theta\sin\phi, \sin\theta)$, where $0\leq\theta\leq2\pi$, and $0\leq\phi\leq\pi$. The θ-ϕ rectangle can be mapped directly to a rectangular texture map, but the closer you get to the poles, the more distorted the texture is. The entire top edge of the texture map is mapped to the north pole, and the entire bottom edge to the south pole. For other surfaces, such as that of a torus (doughnut) with a large hole, the natural surface coordinates map to the texture coordinates in a way that produces only a little distortion, so it might be suitable for many applications. Figure 9-6 shows two tori, one with a small hole (and therefore a lot of distortion near the center) and one with a large hole (and only a little distortion).

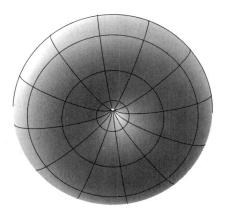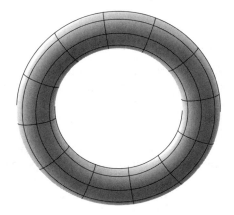

Figure 9-6   Texture-Map Distortion

If you're texturing spline surfaces generated with evaluators (see Chapter 12), the u and v parameters for the surface can sometimes be used as texture coordinates. In general, however, there's a large artistic component to successfully mapping textures to polygonal approximations of curved surfaces.

Repeating and Clamping Textures

You can assign texture coordinates outside the range [0,1] and have them either clamp or repeat in the texture map. With repeating textures, if you have a large plane with texture coordinates running from 0.0 to 10.0 in both directions, for example, you'll get 100 copies of the texture tiled together on the screen. During repeating, the integer part of texture coordinates is ignored, and copies of the texture map tile the surface. For most applications where the texture is to be repeated, the texels at the top of the texture should match those at the bottom, and similarly for the left and right edges.

The other possibility is to clamp the texture coordinates: Any values greater than 1.0 are set to 1.0, and any values less than 0.0 are set to 0.0. Clamping is useful for applications where you want a single copy of the texture to appear on a large surface. If the surface-texture coordinates range from 0.0 to 10.0 in both directions, one copy of the texture appears in the lower corner of the surface. If you've chosen GL_LINEAR as the filtering method (see "Filtering" on page 344), an equally weighted combination of the border color and the texture color is used, as follows.

- When repeating, the 2×2 array wraps to the opposite edge of the texture. Thus, texels on the right edge are averaged with those on the left, and top and bottom texels are also averaged.

- If there is a border, then the texel from the border is used in the weighting. Otherwise, GL_TEXTURE_BORDER_COLOR is used. (If you've chosen GL_NEAREST as the filtering method, the border color is completely ignored.)

Note that if you are using clamping, you can avoid having the rest of the surface affected by the texture. To do this, use alpha values of 0 for the edges (or borders, if they are specified) of the texture. The decal texture function directly uses the texture's alpha value in its calculations. If you are using one of the other texture functions, you may also need to enable blending with good source and destination factors. (See "Blending" on page 214.)

To see the effects of wrapping, you must have texture coordinates that venture beyond [0.0, 1.0]. Start with Example 9-1, and modify the texture coordinates for the squares by mapping the texture coordinates from 0.0 to 3.0 as follows:

```
glBegin(GL_QUADS);
   glTexCoord2f(0.0, 0.0); glVertex3f(-2.0, -1.0, 0.0);
   glTexCoord2f(0.0, 3.0); glVertex3f(-2.0, 1.0, 0.0);
   glTexCoord2f(3.0, 3.0); glVertex3f(0.0, 1.0, 0.0);
   glTexCoord2f(3.0, 0.0); glVertex3f(0.0, -1.0, 0.0);

   glTexCoord2f(0.0, 0.0); glVertex3f(1.0, -1.0, 0.0);
   glTexCoord2f(0.0, 3.0); glVertex3f(1.0, 1.0, 0.0);
   glTexCoord2f(3.0, 3.0); glVertex3f(2.41421, 1.0, -1.41421);
   glTexCoord2f(3.0, 0.0); glVertex3f(2.41421, -1.0, -1.41421);
glEnd();
```

With GL_REPEAT wrapping, the result is as shown in Figure 9-7.

Figure 9-7   Repeating a Texture

In this case, the texture is repeated in both the *s* and *t* directions, since the following calls are made to **glTexParameter*()**:

```
glTexParameteri(GL_TEXTURE_2D, GL_TEXTURE_WRAP_S, GL_REPEAT);
glTexParameteri(GL_TEXTURE_2D, GL_TEXTURE_WRAP_T, GL_REPEAT);
```

If GL_CLAMP is used instead of GL_REPEAT for each direction, you see something similar to Figure 9-8.

Figure 9-8   Clamping a Texture

You can also clamp in one direction and repeat in the other, as shown in Figure 9-9.

Figure 9-9   Repeating and Clamping a Texture

You've now seen all the possible arguments for **glTexParameter*()**, which is summarized here.

void **glTexParameter**{if}(GLenum *target*, GLenum *pname*, *TYPE param*);
void **glTexParameter**{if}**v**(GLenum *target*, GLenum *pname*,
                TYPE *param);

Sets various parameters that control how a texture is treated as it's
applied to a fragment or stored in a texture object. The *target* parameter is
either GL_TEXTURE_2D or GL_TEXTURE_1D to indicate a two- or
one-dimensional texture. The possible values for *pname* and *param* are
shown in Table 9-4. You can use the vector version of the command to
supply an array of values for GL_TEXTURE_BORDER_COLOR, or you can
supply individual values for other parameters using the nonvector
version. If these values are supplied as integers, they're converted to
floating-point according to Table 4-1 on page 164; they're also clamped
to the range [0,1].

Parameter	Values
GL_TEXTURE_WRAP_S	GL_CLAMP, GL_REPEAT
GL_TEXTURE_WRAP_T	GL_CLAMP, GL_REPEAT
GL_TEXTURE_MAG_FILTER	GL_NEAREST, GL_LINEAR
GL_TEXTURE_MIN_FILTER	GL_NEAREST, GL_LINEAR, GL_NEAREST_MIPMAP_NEAREST, GL_NEAREST_MIPMAP_LINEAR, GL_LINEAR_MIPMAP_NEAREST, GL_LINEAR_MIPMAP_LINEAR
GL_TEXTURE_BORDER_COLOR	any four values in [0.0, 1.0]
GL_TEXTURE_PRIORITY	[0.0, 1.0] for the current texture object

Table 9-4   glTexParameter*() Parameters

Try This

Figure 9-8 and Figure 9-9 are drawn using GL_NEAREST for the minification
and magnification filter. What happens if you change the filter values to
GL_LINEAR? Why?

Automatic Texture-Coordinate Generation

You can use texture mapping to make contours on your models or to simulate the reflections from an arbitrary environment on a shiny model. To achieve these effects, let OpenGL automatically generate the texture coordinates for you, rather than explicitly assigning them with **glTexCoord*()**. To generate texture coordinates automatically, use the command **glTexGen()**.

---

void **glTexGen**{ifd}(GLenum *coord*, GLenum *pname*, TYPE *param*);
void **glTexGen**{ifd}**v**(GLenum *coord*, GLenum *pname*, TYPE **param*);

Specifies the functions for automatically generating texture coordinates. The first parameter, *coord*, must be GL_S, GL_T, GL_R, or GL_Q to indicate whether texture coordinate *s*, *t*, *r*, or *q* is to be generated. The *pname* parameter is GL_TEXTURE_GEN_MODE, GL_OBJECT_PLANE, or GL_EYE_PLANE. If it's GL_TEXTURE_GEN_MODE, *param* is an integer (or, in the vector version of the command, points to an integer) that's either GL_OBJECT_LINEAR, GL_EYE_LINEAR, or GL_SPHERE_MAP. These symbolic constants determine which function is used to generate the texture coordinate. With either of the other possible values for *pname*, *param* is a pointer to an array of values (for the vector version) specifying parameters for the texture-generation function.

The different methods of texture-coordinate generation have different uses. Specifying the reference plane in object coordinates is best for when a texture image remains fixed to a moving object. Thus, GL_OBJECT_LINEAR would be used for putting a wood grain on a table top. Specifying the reference plane in eye coordinates (GL_EYE_LINEAR) is best for producing dynamic contour lines on moving objects. GL_EYE_LINEAR may be used by specialists in geosciences, who are drilling for oil or gas. As the drill goes deeper into the ground, the drill may be rendered with different colors to represent the layers of rock at increasing depths. GL_SPHERE_MAP is predominantly used for environment mapping. (See "Environment Mapping" on page 369.)

Creating Contours

When GL_TEXTURE_GEN_MODE and GL_OBJECT_LINEAR are specified, the generation function is a linear combination of the object coordinates of the vertex (x_0, y_0, z_0, w_0):

generated coordinate $= p_1x_0 + p_2y_0 + p_3z_0 + p_4w_0$

The $p_1, ..., p_4$ values are supplied as the *param* argument to **glTexGen*v()**, with *pname* set to GL_OBJECT_PLANE. With $p_1, ..., p_4$ correctly normalized, this function gives the distance from the vertex to a plane. For example, if $p_2 = p_3 = p_4 = 0$ and $p_1 = 1$, the function gives the distance between the vertex and the plane $x = 0$. The distance is positive on one side of the plane, negative on the other, and zero if the vertex lies on the plane.

Initially in Example 9-6, equally spaced contour lines are drawn on a teapot; the lines indicate the distance from the plane $x = 0$. The coefficients for the plane $x = 0$ are in this array:

```
static GLfloat xequalzero[] = {1.0, 0.0, 0.0, 0.0};
```

Since only one property is being shown (the distance from the plane), a one-dimensional texture map suffices. The texture map is a constant green color, except that at equally spaced intervals it includes a red mark. Since the teapot is sitting on the *x-y* plane, the contours are all perpendicular to its base. Plate 18a shows the picture drawn by the program.

In the same example, pressing the 's' key changes the parameters of the reference plane to

```
static GLfloat slanted[] = {1.0, 1.0, 1.0, 0.0};
```

the contour stripes are parallel to the plane $x + y + z = 0$, slicing across the teapot at an angle, as shown in Plate 18b. To restore the reference plane to its initial value, $x = 0$, press the 'x' key.

Example 9-6   Automatic Texture-Coordinate Generation: texgen.c

```
#include <GL/gl.h>
#include <GL/glu.h>
#include <GL/glut.h>
#include <stdlib.h>
#include <stdio.h>

#define stripeImageWidth 32
GLubyte stripeImage[4*stripeImageWidth];
```

```
static GLuint texName;

void makeStripeImage(void)
{
   int j;

   for (j = 0; j < stripeImageWidth; j++) {
      stripeImage[4*j] = (GLubyte) ((j<=4) ? 255 : 0);
      stripeImage[4*j+1] = (GLubyte) ((j>4) ? 255 : 0);
      stripeImage[4*j+2] = (GLubyte) 0;
      stripeImage[4*j+3] = (GLubyte) 255;
   }
}

/*  planes for texture coordinate generation  */
static GLfloat xequalzero[] = {1.0, 0.0, 0.0, 0.0};
static GLfloat slanted[] = {1.0, 1.0, 1.0, 0.0};
static GLfloat *currentCoeff;
static GLenum currentPlane;
static GLint currentGenMode;

void init(void)
{
   glClearColor (0.0, 0.0, 0.0, 0.0);
   glEnable(GL_DEPTH_TEST);
   glShadeModel(GL_SMOOTH);

   makeStripeImage();
   glPixelStorei(GL_UNPACK_ALIGNMENT, 1);

   glGenTextures(1, &texName);
   glBindTexture(GL_TEXTURE_1D, texName);
   glTexParameteri(GL_TEXTURE_1D, GL_TEXTURE_WRAP_S, GL_REPEAT);
   glTexParameteri(GL_TEXTURE_1D, GL_TEXTURE_MAG_FILTER,
                   GL_LINEAR);
   glTexParameteri(GL_TEXTURE_1D, GL_TEXTURE_MIN_FILTER,
                   GL_LINEAR);
   glTexImage1D(GL_TEXTURE_1D, 0, GL_RGBA, stripeImageWidth, 0,
                GL_RGBA, GL_UNSIGNED_BYTE, stripeImage);

   glTexEnvf(GL_TEXTURE_ENV, GL_TEXTURE_ENV_MODE, GL_MODULATE);
   currentCoeff = xequalzero;
   currentGenMode = GL_OBJECT_LINEAR;
   currentPlane = GL_OBJECT_PLANE;
   glTexGeni(GL_S, GL_TEXTURE_GEN_MODE, currentGenMode);
   glTexGenfv(GL_S, currentPlane, currentCoeff);
```

```
   glEnable(GL_TEXTURE_GEN_S);
   glEnable(GL_TEXTURE_1D);
   glEnable(GL_CULL_FACE);
   glEnable(GL_LIGHTING);
   glEnable(GL_LIGHT0);
   glEnable(GL_AUTO_NORMAL);
   glEnable(GL_NORMALIZE);
   glFrontFace(GL_CW);
   glCullFace(GL_BACK);
   glMaterialf (GL_FRONT, GL_SHININESS, 64.0);
}

void display(void)
{
   glClear(GL_COLOR_BUFFER_BIT | GL_DEPTH_BUFFER_BIT);

   glPushMatrix ();
   glRotatef(45.0, 0.0, 0.0, 1.0);
   glBindTexture(GL_TEXTURE_1D, texName);
   glutSolidTeapot(2.0);
   glPopMatrix ();
   glFlush();
}

void reshape(int w, int h)
{
   glViewport(0, 0, (GLsizei) w, (GLsizei) h);
   glMatrixMode(GL_PROJECTION);
   glLoadIdentity();
   if (w <= h)
      glOrtho (-3.5, 3.5, -3.5*(GLfloat)h/(GLfloat)w,
               3.5*(GLfloat)h/(GLfloat)w, -3.5, 3.5);
   else
      glOrtho (-3.5*(GLfloat)w/(GLfloat)h,
               3.5*(GLfloat)w/(GLfloat)h, -3.5, 3.5, -3.5, 3.5);
   glMatrixMode(GL_MODELVIEW);
   glLoadIdentity();
}

void keyboard (unsigned char key, int x, int y)
{
   switch (key) {
      case 'e':
      case 'E':
         currentGenMode = GL_EYE_LINEAR;
         currentPlane = GL_EYE_PLANE;
         glTexGeni(GL_S, GL_TEXTURE_GEN_MODE, currentGenMode);
```

```
                    glTexGenfv(GL_S, currentPlane, currentCoeff);
                    glutPostRedisplay();
                    break;
                case 'o':
                case 'O':
                    currentGenMode = GL_OBJECT_LINEAR;
                    currentPlane = GL_OBJECT_PLANE;
                    glTexGeni(GL_S, GL_TEXTURE_GEN_MODE, currentGenMode);
                    glTexGenfv(GL_S, currentPlane, currentCoeff);
                    glutPostRedisplay();
                    break;
                case 's':
                case 'S':
                    currentCoeff = slanted;
                    glTexGenfv(GL_S, currentPlane, currentCoeff);
                    glutPostRedisplay();
                    break;
                case 'x':
                case 'X':
                    currentCoeff = xequalzero;
                    glTexGenfv(GL_S, currentPlane, currentCoeff);
                    glutPostRedisplay();
                    break;
                case 27:
                    exit(0);
                    break;
                default:
                    break;
        }
    }

    int main(int argc, char** argv)
    {
        glutInit(&argc, argv);
        glutInitDisplayMode (GLUT_SINGLE | GLUT_RGB | GLUT_DEPTH);
        glutInitWindowSize(256, 256);
        glutInitWindowPosition(100, 100);
        glutCreateWindow (argv[0]);
        init ();
        glutDisplayFunc(display);
        glutReshapeFunc(reshape);
        glutKeyboardFunc(keyboard);
        glutMainLoop();
        return 0;
    }
```

You enable texture-coordinate generation for the *s* coordinate by passing GL_TEXTURE_GEN_S to **glEnable()**. To generate other coordinates, enable them with GL_TEXTURE_GEN_T, GL_TEXTURE_GEN_R, or GL_TEXTURE_GEN_Q. Use **glDisable()** with the appropriate constant to disable coordinate generation. Also note the use of GL_REPEAT to cause the contour lines to be repeated across the teapot.

The GL_OBJECT_LINEAR function calculates the texture coordinates in the model's coordinate system. Initially in Example 9-6, the GL_OBJECT_LINEAR function is used, so the contour lines remain perpendicular to the base of the teapot, no matter how the teapot is rotated or viewed. However, if you press the 'e' key, the texture generation mode is changed from GL_OBJECT_LINEAR to GL_EYE_LINEAR, and the contour lines are calculated relative to the eye coordinate system. (Pressing the 'o' key restores GL_OBJECT_LINEAR as the texture generation mode.) If the reference plane is $x = 0$, the result is a teapot with red stripes parallel to the *y-z* plane from the eye's point of view, as shown in Plate 18c. Mathematically, you are multiplying the vector (p_1 p_2 p_3 p_4) by the inverse of the modelview matrix to obtain the values used to calculate the distance to the plane. The texture coordinate is generated with the following function:

generated coordinate = $p_1' x_e + p_2' y_e + p_3' z_e + p_4' w_e$

where $(p_1' p_2' p_3' p_4') = (p_1 p_2 p_3 p_4)\mathbf{M}^{-1}$

In this case, (x_e, y_e, z_e, w_e) are the eye coordinates of the vertex, and p_1, ..., p_4 are supplied as the *param* argument to **glTexGen*()** with *pname* set to GL_EYE_PLANE. The primed values are calculated only at the time they're specified so this operation isn't as computationally expensive as it looks.

In all these examples, a single texture coordinate is used to generate contours. The *s* and *t* texture coordinates can be generated independently, however, to indicate the distances to two different planes. With a properly constructed two-dimensional texture map, the resulting two sets of contours can be viewed simultaneously. For an added level of complexity, you can calculate the *s* coordinate using GL_OBJECT_LINEAR and the *t* coordinate using GL_EYE_LINEAR.

Environment Mapping

The goal of environment mapping is to render an object as if it were perfectly reflective, so that the colors on its surface are those reflected to the eye from its surroundings. In other words, if you look at a perfectly polished, perfectly reflective silver object in a room, you see the walls, floor, and other objects in the room reflected off the object. (A classic example of using environment mapping is the evil, morphing cyborg in the film *Terminator 2*.) The objects whose reflections you see depend on the position of your eye and on the position and surface angles of the silver object. To perform environment mapping, all you have to do is create an appropriate texture map and then have OpenGL generate the texture coordinates for you.

Environment mapping is an approximation based on the assumption that the items in the environment are far away compared to the surfaces of the shiny object—that is, it's a small object in a large room. With this assumption, to find the color of a point on the surface, take the ray from the eye to the surface, and reflect the ray off the surface. The direction of the reflected ray completely determines the color to be painted there. Encoding a color for each direction on a flat texture map is equivalent to putting a polished perfect sphere in the middle of the environment and taking a picture of it with a camera that has a lens with a very long focal length placed far away. Mathematically, the lens has an infinite focal length and the camera is infinitely far away. The encoding therefore covers a circular region of the texture map, tangent to the top, bottom, left, and right edges of the map. The texture values outside the circle make no difference, as they are never accessed in environment mapping.

To make a perfectly correct environment texture map, you need to obtain a large silvered sphere, take a photograph of it in some environment with a camera located an infinite distance away and with a lens that has an infinite focal length, and scan in the photograph. To approximate this result, you can use a scanned-in photograph of an environment taken with an extremely wide-angle (or fish-eye) lens. Plate 21 shows a photograph taken with such a lens and the results when that image is used as an environment map.

Once you've created a texture designed for environment mapping, you need to invoke OpenGL's environment-mapping algorithm. This algorithm finds the point on the surface of the sphere with the same tangent surface as the point on the object being rendered, and it paints the object's point with the color visible on the sphere at the corresponding point.

To automatically generate the texture coordinates to support environment mapping, use this code in your program:

```
glTexGeni(GL_S, GL_TEXTURE_GEN_MODE, GL_SPHERE_MAP);
glTexGeni(GL_T, GL_TEXTURE_GEN_MODE, GL_SPHERE_MAP);
```

```
glEnable(GL_TEXTURE_GEN_S);
glEnable(GL_TEXTURE_GEN_T);
```

The GL_SPHERE_MAP constant creates the proper texture coordinates for the environment mapping. As shown, you need to specify it for both the *s* and *t* directions. However, you don't have to specify any parameters for the texture-coordinate generation function.

The GL_SPHERE_MAP texture function generates texture coordinates using the following mathematical steps.

1. **u** is the unit vector pointing from the origin to the vertex (in eye coordinates).

2. **n'** is the current normal vector, after transformation to eye coordinates.

3. **r** is the reflection vector, $(r_x \ r_y \ r_z)^T$, which is calculated by $\mathbf{u} - 2\mathbf{n'}\mathbf{n'}^T\mathbf{u}$.

4. Then an interim value, *m*, is calculated by $m = 2\sqrt{r_x^2 + r_y^2 + (r_z + 1)^2}$.

5. Finally, the *s* and *t* texture coordinates are calculated by $s = r_x/m + \frac{1}{2}$ and $t = r_y/m + \frac{1}{2}$.

Advanced Features

Advanced

This section describes how to manipulate the texture matrix stack and how to use the *q* coordinate. Both techniques are considered advanced, since you don't need them for many applications of texture mapping.

The Texture Matrix Stack

Just as your model coordinates are transformed by a matrix before being rendered, texture coordinates are multiplied by a 4×4 matrix before any texture mapping occurs. By default, the texture matrix is the identity, so the texture coordinates you explicitly assign or those that are automatically generated remain unchanged. By modifying the texture matrix while redrawing an object, however, you can make the texture slide over the surface, rotate around it, stretch and shrink, or any combination of the three. In fact, since the texture matrix is a completely general 4×4 matrix, effects such as perspective can be achieved.

When the four texture coordinates (s, t, r, q) are multiplied by the texture matrix, the resulting vector ($s'\,t'\,r'\,q'$) is interpreted as homogeneous texture coordinates. In other words, the texture map is indexed by s'/q' and t'/q'. (Remember that r'/q' is ignored in standard OpenGL, but may be used by implementations that support a 3D texture extension.) The texture matrix is actually the top matrix on a stack, which must have a stack depth of at least two matrices. All the standard matrix-manipulation commands such as **glPushMatrix()**, **glPopMatrix()**, **glMultMatrix()**, and **glRotate*()** can be applied to the texture matrix. To modify the current texture matrix, you need to set the matrix mode to GL_TEXTURE, as follows:

```
glMatrixMode(GL_TEXTURE); /* enter texture matrix mode */
glRotated(...);
/* ... other matrix manipulations ... */
glMatrixMode(GL_MODELVIEW); /* back to modelview mode */
```

The *q* Coordinate

The mathematics of the q coordinate in a general four-dimensional texture coordinate is as described in the previous section. You can make use of q in cases where more than one projection or perspective transformation is needed. For example, suppose you want to model a spotlight that has some nonuniform pattern—brighter in the center, perhaps, or noncircular, because of flaps or lenses that modify the shape of the beam. You can emulate shining such a light on a flat surface by making a texture map that corresponds to the shape and intensity of a light, and then projecting it on the surface in question using projection transformations. Projecting the cone of light onto surfaces in the scene requires a perspective transformation ($q \neq 1$), since the lights might shine on surfaces that aren't perpendicular to them. A second perspective transformation occurs because the viewer sees the scene from a different (but perspective) point of view. (See Plate 27 for an example, and see "Fast Shadows and Lighting Effects Using Texture Mapping" by Mark Segal, Carl Korobkin, Rolf van Widenfelt, Jim Foran, and Paul Haeberli, SIGGRAPH 1992 Proceedings, (*Computer Graphics*, 26:2, July 1992, p. 249–252) for more details.)

Another example might arise if the texture map to be applied comes from a photograph that itself was taken in perspective. As with spotlights, the final view depends on the combination of two perspective transformations.

Chapter 10

The Framebuffer

Chapter Objectives

After reading this chapter, you'll be able to do the following:

- Understand what buffers make up the framebuffer and how they're used

- Clear selected buffers and enable them for writing

- Control the parameters of the scissoring, alpha, stencil, and depth-buffer tests that are applied to pixels

- Perform dithering and logical operations

- Use the accumulation buffer for such purposes as scene antialiasing

An important goal of almost every graphics program is to draw pictures on the screen. The screen is composed of a rectangular array of pixels, each capable of displaying a tiny square of color at that point in the image. After the rasterization stage (including texturing and fog), the data are not yet pixels, but are fragments. Each fragment has coordinate data which corresponds to a pixel, as well as color and depth values. Then each fragment undergoes a series of tests and operations, some of which have been previously described (See "Blending" in Chapter 6) and others that are discussed in this chapter.

If the tests and operations are survived, the fragment values are ready to become pixels. To draw these pixels, you need to know what color they are, which is the information that's stored in the color buffer. Whenever data is stored uniformly for each pixel, such storage for all the pixels is called a *buffer*. Different buffers might contain different amounts of data per pixel, but within a given buffer, each pixel is assigned the same amount of data. A buffer that stores a single bit of information about pixels is called a *bitplane*.

As shown in Figure 10-1, the lower-left pixel in an OpenGL window is pixel (0, 0), corresponding to the window coordinates of the lower-left corner of the 1×1 region occupied by this pixel. In general, pixel (x, y) fills the region bounded by x on the left, $x+1$ on the right, y on the bottom, and $y+1$ on the top.

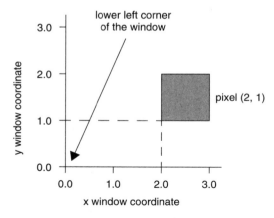

Figure 10-1   Region Occupied by a Pixel

As an example of a buffer, let's look more closely at the color buffer, which holds the color information that's to be displayed on the screen. Assume that the screen is 1280 pixels wide and 1024 pixels high and that it's a full 24-bit color screen—in other words, there are 2^{24} (or 16,777,216) different colors that can be displayed. Since 24 bits translates to 3 bytes (8 bits/byte), the color buffer in this example has to store at least 3 bytes of data for each of the 1,310,720 (1280*1024) pixels on the screen. A particular hardware system might have more or fewer pixels on the physical screen as well as more or less color data per pixel. Any particular color buffer, however, has the same amount of data saved for each pixel on the screen.

The color buffer is only one of several buffers that hold information about a pixel. For example, in "A Hidden-Surface Removal Survival Kit" on page 171, you learned that the depth buffer holds depth information for each pixel. The color buffer itself can consist of several subbuffers. The *framebuffer* on a system comprises all of these buffers. With the exception of the color buffer(s), you don't view these other buffers directly; instead, you use them to perform such tasks as hidden-surface elimination, antialiasing of an entire scene, stenciling, drawing smooth motion, and other operations.

This chapter describes all the buffers that can exist in an OpenGL implementation and how they're used. It also discusses the series of tests and pixel operations that are performed before any data is written to the viewable color buffer. Finally, it explains how to use the accumulation buffer, which is used to accumulate images that are drawn into the color buffer. This chapter has the following major sections.

- "Buffers and Their Uses" on page 376 describes the possible buffers, what they're for, and how to clear them and enable them for writing.

- "Testing and Operating on Fragments" on page 382 explains the scissoring, alpha, stencil, and depth-buffer tests that occur after a pixel's position and color have been calculated but before this information is drawn on the screen. Several operations—blending, dithering, and logical operations—can also be performed before a fragment updates the screen.

- "The Accumulation Buffer" on page 394 describes how to perform several advanced techniques using the accumulation buffer. These techniques include antialiasing an entire scene, using motion blur, and simulating photographic depth of field.

Buffers and Their Uses

An OpenGL system can manipulate the following buffers:

- Color buffers: front-left, front-right, back-left, back-right, and any number of auxiliary color buffers

- Depth buffer

- Stencil buffer

- Accumulation buffer

Your particular OpenGL implementation determines which buffers are available and how many bits per pixel each holds. Additionally, you can have multiple visuals, or window types, that have different buffers available. Table 10-1 lists the parameters to use with **glGetIntegerv()** to query your OpenGL system about per-pixel buffer storage for a particular visual.

Note: If you're using the X Window System, you're guaranteed, at a minimum, to have a visual with one color buffer for use in RGBA mode with associated stencil, depth, and accumulation buffers that have color components of nonzero size. Also, if your X Window System implementation supports a Pseudo-Color visual, you are also guaranteed to have one OpenGL visual that has a color buffer for use in color-index mode with associated depth and stencil buffers. You'll probably want to use **glXGetConfig()** to query your visuals; see Appendix C and the *OpenGL Reference Manual* for more information about this routine.

Parameter	Meaning
GL_RED_BITS, GL_GREEN_BITS, GL_BLUE_BITS, GL_ALPHA_BITS	Number of bits per R, G, B, or A component in the color buffers
GL_INDEX_BITS	Number of bits per index in the color buffers
GL_DEPTH_BITS	Number of bits per pixel in the depth buffer
GL_STENCIL_BITS	Number of bits per pixel in the stencil buffer
GL_ACCUM_RED_BITS, GL_ACCUM_GREEN_BITS, GL_ACCUM_BLUE_BITS, GL_ACCUM_ALPHA_BITS	Number of bits per R, G, B, or A component in the accumulation buffer

Table 10-1   Query Parameters for Per-Pixel Buffer Storage

Color Buffers

The color buffers are the ones to which you usually draw. They contain either color-index or RGB color data and may also contain alpha values. An OpenGL implementation that supports stereoscopic viewing has left and right color buffers for the left and right stereo images. If stereo isn't supported, only the left buffers are used. Similarly, double-buffered systems have front and back buffers, and a single-buffered system has the front buffers only. Every OpenGL implementation must provide a front-left color buffer.

Optional, nondisplayable auxiliary color buffers may also be supported. OpenGL doesn't specify any particular uses for these buffers, so you can define and use them however you please. For example, you might use them for saving an image that you use repeatedly. Then rather than redrawing the image, you can just copy it from an auxiliary buffer into the usual color buffers. (See the description of **glCopyPixels()** in "Reading, Writing, and Copying Pixel Data" on page 290 for more information about how to do this.)

You can use GL_STEREO or GL_DOUBLEBUFFER with **glGetBooleanv()** to find out if your system supports stereo (that is, has left and right buffers) or double-buffering (has front and back buffers). To find out how many, if any, auxiliary buffers are present, use **glGetIntegerv()** with GL_AUX_BUFFERS.

Depth Buffer

The depth buffer stores a depth value for each pixel. As described in "A Hidden-Surface Removal Survival Kit" on page 171, depth is usually measured in terms of distance to the eye, so pixels with larger depth-buffer values are overwritten by pixels with smaller values. This is just a useful convention, however, and the depth buffer's behavior can be modified as described in "Depth Test" on page 391. The depth buffer is sometimes called the *z buffer* (the z comes from the fact that x and y values measure horizontal and vertical displacement on the screen, and the z value measures distance perpendicular to the screen).

Stencil Buffer

One use for the stencil buffer is to restrict drawing to certain portions of the screen, just as a cardboard stencil can be used with a can of spray paint to make fairly precise painted images. For example, if you want to draw an image as it would appear through an odd-shaped windshield, you can store an image of the windshield's shape in the stencil buffer, and then draw the entire scene. The stencil buffer prevents anything that wouldn't be visible through the windshield from being drawn. Thus, if your application is a driving simulation, you can draw all the instruments and other items inside the automobile once, and as the car moves, only the outside scene need be updated.

Accumulation Buffer

The accumulation buffer holds RGBA color data just like the color buffers do in RGBA mode. (The results of using the accumulation buffer in color-index mode are undefined.) It's typically used for accumulating a series of images into a final, composite image. With this method, you can perform operations like scene antialiasing by supersampling an image and then averaging the samples to produce the values that are finally painted into the pixels of the color buffers. You don't draw directly into the accumulation buffer; accumulation operations are always performed in rectangular blocks, which are usually transfers of data to or from a color buffer.

Clearing Buffers

In graphics programs, clearing the screen (or any of the buffers) is typically one of the most expensive operations you can perform—on a 1280×1024 monitor, it requires touching well over a million pixels. For simple graphics applications, the clear operation can take more time than the rest of the drawing. If you need to clear not only the color buffer but also the depth and stencil buffers, the clear operation can be three times as expensive.

To address this problem, some machines have hardware that can clear more than one buffer at once. The OpenGL clearing commands are structured to take advantage of architectures like this. First, you specify the values to be written into each buffer to be cleared. Then you issue a single command to perform the clear operation, passing in a list of all the buffers to be cleared. If the hardware is capable of simultaneous clears, they all occur at once; otherwise, each buffer is cleared sequentially.

The following commands set the clearing values for each buffer.

---

void **glClearColor**(GLclampf *red*, GLclampf *green*, GLclampf *blue*,
              GLclampf *alpha*);
void **glClearIndex**(GLfloat *index*);
void **glClearDepth**(GLclampd *depth*);
void **glClearStencil**(GLint *s*);
void **glClearAccum**(GLfloat *red*, GLfloat *green*, GLfloat *blue*,
              GLfloat *alpha*);

Specifies the current clearing values for the color buffer (in RGBA mode), the color buffer (in color-index mode), the depth buffer, the stencil buffer, and the accumulation buffer. The GLclampf and GLclampd types (clamped GLfloat and clamped GLdouble) are clamped to be between 0.0 and 1.0. The default depth-clearing value is 1.0; all the other default clearing values are 0. The values set with the clear commands remain in effect until they're changed by another call to the same command.

After you've selected your clearing values and you're ready to clear the buffers, use **glClear()**.

---

void **glClear**(GLbitfield *mask*);

Clears the specified buffers. The value of *mask* is the bitwise logical OR of some combination of GL_COLOR_BUFFER_BIT, GL_DEPTH_BUFFER_BIT, GL_STENCIL_BUFFER_BIT, and GL_ACCUM_BUFFER_BIT to identify which buffers are to be cleared. GL_COLOR_BUFFER_BIT clears either the RGBA color or the color-index buffer, depending on the mode of the system at the time. When you clear the color or color-index buffer, all the color buffers that are enabled for writing (see the next section) are cleared. The pixel ownership test, scissor test, and dithering, if enabled, are applied to the clearing operation. Masking operations, such as **glColorMask()** and **glIndexMask()**, are also effective. The alpha test, stencil test, and depth test do not affect the operation of **glClear()**.

Selecting Color Buffers for Writing and Reading

The results of a drawing or reading operation can go into or come from any of the color buffers: front, back, front-left, back-left, front-right, back-right, or any of the auxiliary buffers. You can choose an individual buffer to be the drawing or reading target. For drawing, you can also set the target to draw into more than one buffer at the same time. You use **glDrawBuffer()** to select the buffers to be written and **glReadBuffer()** to select the buffer as the source for **glReadPixels()**, **glCopyPixels()**, **glCopyTexImage*()**, and **glCopyTexSubImage*()**.

If you are using double-buffering, you usually want to draw only in the back buffer (and swap the buffers when you're finished drawing). In some situations, you might want to treat a double-buffered window as though it were single-buffered by calling **glDrawBuffer()** to enable you to draw to both front and back buffers at the same time.

glDrawBuffer() is also used to select buffers to render stereo images (GL*LEFT and GL*RIGHT) and to render into auxiliary buffers (GL_AUX*i*).

---

void **glDrawBuffer**(GLenum *mode*);

Selects the color buffers enabled for writing or clearing. Disables buffers enabled by previous calls to **glDrawBuffer()**. More than one buffer may be enabled at one time. The value of *mode* can be one of the following:

GL_FRONT	GL_FRONT_LEFT	GL_AUX*i*
GL_BACK	GL_FRONT_RIGHT	GL_FRONT_AND_BACK
GL_LEFT	GL_BACK_LEFT	GL_NONE
GL_RIGHT	GL_BACK_RIGHT	

Arguments that omit LEFT or RIGHT refer to both the left and right buffers; similarly, arguments that omit FRONT or BACK refer to both. The *i* in GL_AUX*i* is a digit identifying a particular auxiliary buffer.

By default, *mode* is GL_FRONT for single-buffered contexts and GL_BACK for double-buffered contexts.

Note: You can enable drawing to nonexistent buffers as long as you enable drawing to at least one buffer that does exist. If none of the specified buffers exist, an error results.

---

void **glReadBuffer**(GLenum *mode*);

Selects the color buffer enabled as the source for reading pixels for subsequent calls to **glReadPixels()**, **glCopyPixels()**, **glCopyTexImage*()**, and **glCopyTexSubImage*()**. Disables buffers enabled by previous calls to **glReadBuffer()**. The value of *mode* can be one of the following:

GL_FRONT	GL_FRONT_LEFT	GL_AUX*i*
GL_BACK	GL_FRONT_RIGHT	

GL_LEFT   GL_BACK_LEFT
GL_RIGHT   GL_BACK_RIGHT

By default, *mode* is GL_FRONT for single-buffered contexts and GL_BACK for double-buffered contexts.

Note: You must enable reading from a buffer that does exist or an error results.

Masking Buffers

Before OpenGL writes data into the enabled color, depth, or stencil buffers, a masking operation is applied to the data, as specified with one of the following commands. A bitwise logical AND is performed with each mask and the corresponding data to be written.

---

void **glIndexMask**(GLuint *mask*);
void **glColorMask**(GLboolean *red*, GLboolean *green*, GLboolean *blue*,
                 GLboolean *alpha*);
void **glDepthMask**(GLboolean *flag*);
void **glStencilMask**(GLuint *mask*);

Sets the masks used to control writing into the indicated buffers. The mask set by **glIndexMask**() applies only in color-index mode. If a 1 appears in *mask*, the corresponding bit in the color-index buffer is written; where a 0 appears, the bit isn't written. Similarly, **glColorMask**() affects drawing in RGBA mode only. The *red*, *green*, *blue*, and *alpha* values control whether the corresponding component is written. (GL_TRUE means it is written.) If *flag* is GL_TRUE for **glDepthMask**(), the depth buffer is enabled for writing; otherwise, it's disabled. The mask for **glStencilMask**() is used for stencil data in the same way as the mask is used for color-index data in **glIndexMask**(). The default values of all the GLboolean masks are GL_TRUE, and the default values for the two GLuint masks are all 1's.

You can do plenty of tricks with color masking in color-index mode. For example, you can use each bit in the index as a different layer and set up interactions between arbitrary layers with appropriate settings of the color map. You can create overlays and underlays, and do so-called color-map animations. (See Chapter 14 for examples of using color masking.) Masking in RGBA mode is useful less often, but you can use it for loading separate image files into the red, green, and blue bitplanes, for example.

You've seen one use for disabling the depth buffer in "Three-Dimensional Blending with the Depth Buffer" on page 222. Disabling the depth buffer for writing can also be useful if a common background is desired for a series of frames, and you want to add some features that may be obscured by parts of the background. For example, suppose your background is a forest, and you would like to draw repeated frames with the same trees, but with objects moving among them. After the trees are drawn with their depths recorded in the depth buffer, then the image of the trees is saved, and the new items are drawn with the depth buffer disabled for writing. As long as the new items don't overlap each other, the picture is correct. To draw the next frame, restore the image of the trees and continue. You don't need to restore the values in the depth buffer. This trick is most useful if the background is extremely complex—so complex that it's much faster just to recopy the image into the color buffer than to recompute it from the geometry.

Masking the stencil buffer can allow you to use a multiple-bit stencil buffer to hold multiple stencils (one per bit). You might use this technique to perform capping as explained in "Stencil Test" on page 385 or to implement the Game of Life as described in "Life in the Stencil Buffer" on page 526.

Note: The mask specified by **glStencilMask()** controls which stencil bitplanes are written. This mask isn't related to the mask that's specified as the third parameter of **glStencilFunc()**, which specifies which bitplanes are considered by the stencil function.

Testing and Operating on Fragments

When you draw geometry, text, or images on the screen, OpenGL performs several calculations to rotate, translate, scale, determine the lighting, project the object(s) into perspective, figure out which pixels in the window are affected, and determine what colors those pixels should be drawn. Many of the earlier chapters in this book give some information about how to control these operations. After OpenGL determines that an individual fragment should be generated and what its color should be, several processing stages remain that control how and whether the fragment is drawn as a pixel into the framebuffer. For example, if it's outside a rectangular region or if it's farther from the viewpoint than the pixel that's already in the framebuffer, it isn't drawn. In another stage, the fragment's color is blended with the color of the pixel already in the framebuffer.

This section describes both the complete set of tests that a fragment must pass before it goes into the framebuffer and the possible final operations that can be performed on the fragment as it's written. The tests and operations occur in the following order; if a fragment is eliminated in an early test, none of the later tests or operations take place.

1. Scissor test

2. Alpha test

3. Stencil test

4. Depth test

5. Blending

6. Dithering

7. Logical operation

Each of these tests and operations is described in detail in the following sections.

Scissor Test

You can define a rectangular portion of your window and restrict drawing to take place within it by using the **glScissor()** command. If a fragment lies inside the rectangle, it passes the scissor test.

---

void **glScissor**(GLint *x*, GLint *y*, GLsizei *width*, GLsizei *height*);

Sets the location and size of the scissor rectangle (also known as the scissor box). The parameters define the lower-left corner (x, y), and the width and height of the rectangle. Pixels that lie inside the rectangle pass the scissor test. Scissoring is enabled and disabled by passing GL_SCISSOR_TEST to **glEnable()** and **glDisable()**. By default, the rectangle matches the size of the window and scissoring is disabled.

The scissor test is just a version of a stencil test using a rectangular region of the screen. It's fairly easy to create a blindingly fast hardware implementation of scissoring, while a given system might be much slower at stenciling—perhaps because the stenciling is performed in software.

Advanced

An advanced use of scissoring is performing nonlinear projection. First divide the window into a regular grid of subregions, specifying viewport and scissor parameters that limit rendering to one region at a time. Then project the entire scene to each region using a different projection matrix.

To determine whether scissoring is enabled and to obtain the values that define the scissor rectangle, you can use GL_SCISSOR_TEST with **glIsEnabled()** and GL_SCISSOR_BOX with **glGetIntegerv()**.

Alpha Test

In RGBA mode, the alpha test allows you to accept or reject a fragment based on its alpha value. The alpha test is enabled and disabled by passing GL_ALPHA_TEST to **glEnable()** and **glDisable()**. To determine whether the alpha test is enabled, use GL_ALPHA_TEST with **glIsEnabled()**.

If enabled, the test compares the incoming alpha value with a reference value. The fragment is accepted or rejected depending on the result of the comparison. Both the reference value and the comparison function are set with **glAlphaFunc()**. By default, the reference value is zero, the comparison function is GL_ALWAYS, and the alpha test is disabled. To obtain the alpha comparison function or reference value, use GL_ALPHA_TEST_FUNC or GL_ALPHA_TEST_REF with **glGetIntegerv()**.

---

void **glAlphaFunc**(GLenum *func*, GLclampf *ref*);

Sets the reference value and comparison function for the alpha test. The reference value *ref* is clamped to be between zero and one. The possible values for *func* and their meaning are listed in Table 10-2.

Parameter	Meaning
GL_NEVER	Never accept the fragment
GL_ALWAYS	Always accept the fragment
GL_LESS	Accept fragment if fragment alpha < reference alpha
GL_LEQUAL	Accept fragment if fragment alpha ≤ reference alpha
GL_EQUAL	Accept fragment if fragment alpha = reference alpha

Table 10-2   glAlphaFunc() Parameter Values

Parameter	Meaning
GL_GEQUAL	Accept fragment if fragment alpha $\geq$ reference alpha
GL_GREATER	Accept fragment if fragment alpha > reference alpha
GL_NOTEQUAL	Accept fragment if fragment alpha $\neq$ reference alpha

Table 10-2   glAlphaFunc() Parameter Values (continued)

One application for the alpha test is to implement a transparency algorithm. Render your entire scene twice, the first time accepting only fragments with alpha values of one, and the second time accepting fragments with alpha values that aren't equal to one. Turn the depth buffer on during both passes, but disable depth buffer writing during the second pass.

Another use might be to make decals with texture maps where you can see through certain parts of the decals. Set the alphas in the decals to 0.0 where you want to see through, set them to 1.0 otherwise, set the reference value to 0.5 (or anything between 0.0 and 1.0), and set the comparison function to GL_GREATER. The decal has see-through parts, and the values in the depth buffer aren't affected. This technique, called billboarding, is described in "Sample Uses of Blending" on page 217.

Stencil Test

The stencil test takes place only if there is a stencil buffer. (If there is no stencil buffer, the stencil test always passes.) Stenciling applies a test that compares a reference value with the value stored at a pixel in the stencil buffer. Depending on the result of the test, the value in the stencil buffer is modified. You can choose the particular comparison function used, the reference value, and the modification performed with the **glStencilFunc()** and **glStencilOp()** commands.

---

void **glStencilFunc**(GLenum *func*, GLint *ref*, GLuint *mask*);

Sets the comparison function (*func*), reference value (*ref*), and a mask (*mask*) for use with the stencil test. The reference value is compared to the value in the stencil buffer using the comparison function, but the comparison applies only to those bits where the corresponding bits of the mask are 1. The function can be GL_NEVER, GL_ALWAYS, GL_LESS, GL_LEQUAL, GL_EQUAL, GL_GEQUAL, GL_GREATER, or

GL_NOTEQUAL. If it's GL_LESS, for example, then the fragment passes if *ref* is less than the value in the stencil buffer. If the stencil buffer contains *s* bitplanes, the low-order *s* bits of *mask* are bitwise ANDed with the value in the stencil buffer and with the reference value before the comparison is performed. The masked values are all interpreted as nonnegative values. The stencil test is enabled and disabled by passing GL_STENCIL_TEST to **glEnable()** and **glDisable()**. By default, *func* is GL_ALWAYS, *ref* is 0, *mask* is all 1's, and stenciling is disabled.

---

void **glStencilOp**(GLenum *fail*, GLenum *zfail*, GLenum *zpass*);

Specifies how the data in the stencil buffer is modified when a fragment passes or fails the stencil test. The three functions *fail*, *zfail*, and *zpass* can be GL_KEEP, GL_ZERO, GL_REPLACE, GL_INCR, GL_DECR, or GL_INVERT. They correspond to keeping the current value, replacing it with zero, replacing it with the reference value, incrementing it, decrementing it, and bitwise-inverting it. The result of the increment and decrement functions is clamped to lie between zero and the maximum unsigned integer value (2^s-1 if the stencil buffer holds *s* bits). The *fail* function is applied if the fragment fails the stencil test; if it passes, then *zfail* is applied if the depth test fails and *zpass* if the depth test passes, or if no depth test is performed. (See "Depth Test" on page 391.) By default, all three stencil operations are GL_KEEP.

Stencil Queries

You can obtain the values for all six stencil-related parameters by using the query function **glGetIntegerv()** and one of the values shown in Table 10-3. You can also determine whether the stencil test is enabled by passing GL_STENCIL_TEST to **glIsEnabled()**.

Query Value	Meaning
GL_STENCIL_FUNC	Stencil function
GL_STENCIL_REF	Stencil reference value
GL_STENCIL_VALUE_MASK	Stencil mask
GL_STENCIL_FAIL	Stencil fail action
GL_STENCIL_PASS_DEPTH_FAIL	Stencil pass and depth buffer fail action

Table 10-3   Query Values for the Stencil Test

Query Value	Meaning
GL_STENCIL_PASS_DEPTH_PASS	Stencil pass and depth buffer pass action

Table 10-3   Query Values for the Stencil Test (continued)

Stencil Examples

Probably the most typical use of the stencil test is to mask out an irregularly shaped region of the screen to prevent drawing from occurring within it (as in the windshield example in "Buffers and Their Uses" on page 376). To do this, fill the stencil mask with zeros, and then draw the desired shape in the stencil buffer with 1's. You can't draw geometry directly into the stencil buffer, but you can achieve the same result by drawing into the color buffer and choosing a suitable value for the *zpass* function (such as GL_REPLACE). (You can use **glDrawPixels()** to draw pixel data directly into the stencil buffer.) Whenever drawing occurs, a value is also written into the stencil buffer (in this case, the reference value). To prevent the stencil-buffer drawing from affecting the contents of the color buffer, set the color mask to zero (or GL_FALSE). You might also want to disable writing into the depth buffer.

After you've defined the stencil area, set the reference value to one, and the comparison function such that the fragment passes if the reference value is equal to the stencil-plane value. During drawing, don't modify the contents of the stencil planes.

Example 10-1 demonstrates how to use the stencil test in this way. Two tori are drawn, with a diamond-shaped cutout in the center of the scene. Within the diamond-shaped stencil mask, a sphere is drawn. In this example, drawing into the stencil buffer takes place only when the window is redrawn, so the color buffer is cleared after the stencil mask has been created.

Example 10-1   Using the Stencil Test: stencil.c

```
#include <GL/gl.h>
#include <GL/glu.h>
#include <GL/glut.h>
#include <stdlib.h>

#define YELLOWMAT    1
#define BLUEMAT 2

void init (void)
```

```
{
    GLfloat yellow_diffuse[] = { 0.7, 0.7, 0.0, 1.0 };
    GLfloat yellow_specular[] = { 1.0, 1.0, 1.0, 1.0 };

    GLfloat blue_diffuse[] = { 0.1, 0.1, 0.7, 1.0 };
    GLfloat blue_specular[] = { 0.1, 1.0, 1.0, 1.0 };

    GLfloat position_one[] = { 1.0, 1.0, 1.0, 0.0 };

    glNewList(YELLOWMAT, GL_COMPILE);
    glMaterialfv(GL_FRONT, GL_DIFFUSE, yellow_diffuse);
    glMaterialfv(GL_FRONT, GL_SPECULAR, yellow_specular);
    glMaterialf(GL_FRONT, GL_SHININESS, 64.0);
    glEndList();

    glNewList(BLUEMAT, GL_COMPILE);
    glMaterialfv(GL_FRONT, GL_DIFFUSE, blue_diffuse);
    glMaterialfv(GL_FRONT, GL_SPECULAR, blue_specular);
    glMaterialf(GL_FRONT, GL_SHININESS, 45.0);
    glEndList();

    glLightfv(GL_LIGHT0, GL_POSITION, position_one);

    glEnable(GL_LIGHT0);
    glEnable(GL_LIGHTING);
    glEnable(GL_DEPTH_TEST);

    glClearStencil(0x0);
    glEnable(GL_STENCIL_TEST);
}

/* Draw a sphere in a diamond-shaped section in the
 * middle of a window with 2 tori.
 */
void display(void)
{
    glClear(GL_COLOR_BUFFER_BIT | GL_DEPTH_BUFFER_BIT);

/* draw blue sphere where the stencil is 1 */
    glStencilFunc (GL_EQUAL, 0x1, 0x1);
    glStencilOp (GL_KEEP, GL_KEEP, GL_KEEP);
    glCallList (BLUEMAT);
    glutSolidSphere (0.5, 15, 15);

/* draw the tori where the stencil is not 1 */
    glStencilFunc (GL_NOTEQUAL, 0x1, 0x1);
    glPushMatrix();
```

```
        glRotatef (45.0, 0.0, 0.0, 1.0);
        glRotatef (45.0, 0.0, 1.0, 0.0);
        glCallList (YELLOWMAT);
        glutSolidTorus (0.275, 0.85, 15, 15);
        glPushMatrix();
            glRotatef (90.0, 1.0, 0.0, 0.0);
            glutSolidTorus (0.275, 0.85, 15, 15);
        glPopMatrix();
    glPopMatrix();
}


/*  Whenever the window is reshaped, redefine the
 *  coordinate system and redraw the stencil area.
 */
void reshape(int w, int h)
{
    glViewport(0, 0, (GLsizei) w, (GLsizei) h);

/* create a diamond shaped stencil area */
    glMatrixMode(GL_PROJECTION);
    glLoadIdentity();
    if (w <= h)
        gluOrtho2D(-3.0, 3.0, -3.0*(GLfloat)h/(GLfloat)w,
                    3.0*(GLfloat)h/(GLfloat)w);
    else
        gluOrtho2D(-3.0*(GLfloat)w/(GLfloat)h,
                    3.0*(GLfloat)w/(GLfloat)h, -3.0, 3.0);
    glMatrixMode(GL_MODELVIEW);
    glLoadIdentity();

    glClear(GL_STENCIL_BUFFER_BIT);
    glStencilFunc (GL_ALWAYS, 0x1, 0x1);
    glStencilOp (GL_REPLACE, GL_REPLACE, GL_REPLACE);
    glBegin(GL_QUADS);
        glVertex2f (-1.0, 0.0);
        glVertex2f (0.0, 1.0);
        glVertex2f (1.0, 0.0);
        glVertex2f (0.0, -1.0);
    glEnd();

    glMatrixMode(GL_PROJECTION);
    glLoadIdentity();
    gluPerspective(45.0, (GLfloat) w/(GLfloat) h, 3.0, 7.0);
    glMatrixMode(GL_MODELVIEW);
    glLoadIdentity();
    glTranslatef(0.0, 0.0, -5.0);
}
```

```
/* Main Loop
 * Be certain to request stencil bits.
 */
int main(int argc, char** argv)
{
    glutInit(&argc, argv);
    glutInitDisplayMode (GLUT_SINGLE | GLUT_RGB
                           | GLUT_DEPTH | GLUT_STENCIL);
    glutInitWindowSize (400, 400);
    glutInitWindowPosition (100, 100);
    glutCreateWindow (argv[0]);
    init ();
    glutReshapeFunc(reshape);
    glutDisplayFunc(display);
    glutMainLoop();
    return 0;
}
```

The following examples illustrate other uses of the stencil test. (See Chapter 14 for additional ideas.)

- Capping—Suppose you're drawing a closed convex object (or several of them, as long as they don't intersect or enclose each other) made up of several polygons, and you have a clipping plane that may or may not slice off a piece of it. Suppose that if the plane does intersect the object, you want to cap the object with some constant-colored surface, rather than seeing the inside of it. To do this, clear the stencil buffer to zeros, and begin drawing with stenciling enabled and the stencil comparison function set to always accept fragments. Invert the value in the stencil planes each time a fragment is accepted. After all the objects are drawn, regions of the screen where no capping is required have zeros in the stencil planes, and regions requiring capping are nonzero. Reset the stencil function so that it draws only where the stencil value is nonzero, and draw a large polygon of the capping color across the entire screen.

- Overlapping translucent polygons—Suppose you have a translucent surface that's made up of polygons that overlap slightly. If you simply use alpha blending, portions of the underlying objects are covered by more than one transparent surface, which doesn't look right. Use the stencil planes to make sure that each fragment is covered by at most one portion of the transparent surface. Do this by clearing the stencil planes to zeros, drawing only when the stencil plane is zero, and incrementing the value in the stencil plane when you draw.

- Stippling—Suppose you want to draw an image with a stipple pattern. (See "Displaying Points, Lines, and Polygons" on page 49 for more information about stippling.) You can do this by writing the stipple pattern into the stencil buffer, and then drawing conditionally on the contents of the stencil buffer. After the original stipple pattern is drawn, the stencil buffer isn't altered while drawing the image, so the object gets stippled by the pattern in the stencil planes.

Depth Test

For each pixel on the screen, the depth buffer keeps track of the distance between the viewpoint and the object occupying that pixel. Then if the specified depth test passes, the incoming depth value replaces the one already in the depth buffer.

The depth buffer is generally used for hidden-surface elimination. If a new candidate color for that pixel appears, it's drawn only if the corresponding object is closer than the previous object. In this way, after the entire scene has been rendered, only objects that aren't obscured by other items remain. Initially, the clearing value for the depth buffer is a value that's as far from the viewpoint as possible, so the depth of any object is nearer than that value. If this is how you want to use the depth buffer, you simply have to enable it by passing GL_DEPTH_TEST to **glEnable()** and remember to clear the depth buffer before you redraw each frame. (See "Clearing Buffers" on page 378.) You can also choose a different comparison function for the depth test with **glDepthFunc()**.

---

void **glDepthFunc**(GLenum *func*);

Sets the comparison function for the depth test. The value for *func* must be GL_NEVER, GL_ALWAYS, GL_LESS, GL_LEQUAL, GL_EQUAL, GL_GEQUAL, GL_GREATER, or GL_NOTEQUAL. An incoming fragment passes the depth test if its z value has the specified relation to the value already stored in the depth buffer. The default is GL_LESS, which means that an incoming fragment passes the test if its z value is less than that already stored in the depth buffer. In this case, the z value represents the distance from the object to the viewpoint, and smaller values mean the corresponding objects are closer to the viewpoint.

Blending, Dithering, and Logical Operations

Once an incoming fragment has passed all the tests described in the previous section, it can be combined with the current contents of the color buffer in one of several ways. The simplest way, which is also the default, is to overwrite the existing values. Alternatively, if you're using RGBA mode and you want the fragment to be translucent or antialiased, you might average its value with the value already in the buffer (blending). On systems with a small number of available colors, you might want to dither color values to increase the number of colors available at the cost of a loss in resolution. In the final stage, you can use arbitrary bitwise logical operations to combine the incoming fragment and the pixel that's already written.

Blending

Blending combines the incoming fragment's R, G, B, and alpha values with those of the pixel already stored at the location. Different blending operations can be applied, and the blending that occurs depends on the values of the incoming alpha value and the alpha value (if any) stored at the pixel. (See "Blending" on page 214 for an extensive discussion of this topic.)

Dithering

On systems with a small number of color bitplanes, you can improve the color resolution at the expense of spatial resolution by dithering the color in the image. Dithering is like halftoning in newspapers. Although *The New York Times* has only two colors—black and white—it can show photographs by representing the shades of gray with combinations of black and white dots. Comparing a newspaper image of a photo (having no shades of gray) with the original photo (with grayscale) makes the loss of spatial resolution obvious. Similarly, systems with a small number of color bitplanes may dither values of red, green, and blue on neighboring pixels for the perception of a wider range of colors.

The dithering operation that takes place is hardware-dependent; all OpenGL allows you to do is to turn it on and off. In fact, on some machines, enabling dithering might do nothing at all, which makes sense if the machine already has high color resolution. To enable and disable dithering, pass GL_DITHER to **glEnable()** and **glDisable()**. Dithering is enabled by default.

Dithering applies in both RGBA and color-index mode. The colors or color indices alternate in some hardware-dependent way between the two nearest possibilities. For example, in color-index mode, if dithering is enabled and the color index to be painted is 4.4, then 60% of the pixels may be painted with index 4 and 40% of the pixels with index 5. (Many dithering algorithms are possible, but a dithered value produced by any algorithm must depend upon only the incoming value and the fragment's x and y coordinates.) In RGBA mode, dithering is performed separately for each component (including alpha). To use dithering in color-index mode, you generally need to arrange the colors in the color map appropriately in ramps, otherwise, bizarre images might result.

Logical Operations

The final operation on a fragment is the *logical operation*, such as an OR, XOR, or INVERT, which is applied to the incoming fragment values (source) and/or those currently in the color buffer (destination). Such fragment operations are especially useful on bit-blt-type machines, on which the primary graphics operation is copying a rectangle of data from one place in the window to another, from the window to processor memory, or from memory to the window. Typically, the copy doesn't write the data directly into memory but instead allows you to perform an arbitrary logical operation on the incoming data and the data already present; then it replaces the existing data with the results of the operation.

Since this process can be implemented fairly cheaply in hardware, many such machines are available. As an example of using a logical operation, XOR can be used to draw on an image in an undoable way; simply XOR the same drawing again, and the original image is restored. As another example, when using color-index mode, the color indices can be interpreted as bit patterns. Then you can compose an image as combinations of drawings on different layers, use writemasks to limit drawing to different sets of bitplanes, and perform logical operations to modify different layers.

You enable and disable logical operations by passing GL_INDEX_LOGIC_OP or GL_COLOR_LOGIC_OP to **glEnable()** and **glDisable()** for color-index mode or RGBA mode, respectively. You also must choose among the sixteen logical operations with **glLogicOp()**, or you'll just get the effect of the default value, GL_COPY. (For backward compatibility with OpenGL Version 1.0, **glEnable**(GL_LOGIC_OP) also enables logical operation in color-index mode.)

---

void **glLogicOp**(GLenum *opcode*);

Selects the logical operation to be performed, given an incoming (source) fragment and the pixel currently stored in the color buffer (destination). Table 10-4 shows the possible values for *opcode* and their meaning (*s* represents source and *d* destination). The default value is GL_COPY.

Parameter	Operation	Parameter	Operation
GL_CLEAR	0	GL_AND	$s \wedge d$
GL_COPY	s	GL_OR	$s \vee d$
GL_NOOP	d	GL_NAND	$\neg(s \wedge d)$
GL_SET	1	GL_NOR	$\neg(s \vee d)$
GL_COPY_INVERTED	$\neg s$	GL_XOR	$s\ XOR\ d$
GL_INVERT	$\neg d$	GL_EQUIV	$\neg(s\ XOR\ d)$
GL_AND_REVERSE	$s \wedge \neg d$	GL_AND_INVERTED	$\neg s \wedge d$
GL_OR_REVERSE	$s \vee \neg d$	GL_OR_INVERTED	$\neg s \vee d$

Table 10-4   Sixteen Logical Operations

The Accumulation Buffer

Advanced

The accumulation buffer can be used for such things as scene antialiasing, motion blur, simulating photographic depth of field, and calculating the soft shadows that result from multiple light sources. Other techniques are possible, especially in combination with some of the other buffers. (See *The Accumulation Buffer: Hardware Support for High-Quality Rendering* by Paul Haeberli and Kurt Akeley (SIGGRAPH 1990 Proceedings, p. 309–318) for more information on the uses for the accumulation buffer.)

OpenGL graphics operations don't write directly into the accumulation buffer. Typically, a series of images is generated in one of the standard color buffers, and these are accumulated, one at a time, into the accumulation buffer. When the accumulation is finished, the result is copied back into a color buffer for viewing. To reduce rounding errors, the accumulation buffer may have higher precision (more bits per color) than the standard color buffers. Rendering a scene several times obviously takes longer than rendering it once, but the result is higher quality. You can decide what trade-off between quality and rendering time is appropriate for your application.

You can use the accumulation buffer the same way a photographer can use film for multiple exposures. A photographer typically creates a multiple exposure by taking several pictures of the same scene without advancing the film. If anything in the scene moves, that object appears blurred. Not surprisingly, a computer can do more with an image than a photographer can do with a camera. For example, a computer has exquisite control over the viewpoint, but a photographer can't shake a camera a predictable and controlled amount. (See "Clearing Buffers" on page 378 for information about how to clear the accumulation buffer; use **glAccum()** to control it.)

---

void **glAccum**(GLenum *op*, GLfloat *value*);

Controls the accumulation buffer. The *op* parameter selects the operation, and *value* is a number to be used in that operation. The possible operations are GL_ACCUM, GL_LOAD, GL_RETURN, GL_ADD, and GL_MULT.

- GL_ACCUM reads each pixel from the buffer currently selected for reading with **glReadBuffer()**, multiplies the R, G, B, and alpha values by *value*, and adds the result to the accumulation buffer.

- GL_LOAD does the same thing, except that the values replace those in the accumulation buffer rather than being added to them.

- GL_RETURN takes values from the accumulation buffer, multiplies them by *value*, and places the result in the color buffer(s) enabled for writing.

- GL_ADD and GL_MULT simply add or multiply the value of each pixel in the accumulation buffer by *value* and then return it to the accumulation buffer. For GL_MULT, *value* is clamped to be in the range [−1.0,1.0]. For GL_ADD, no clamping occurs.

Scene Antialiasing

To perform scene antialiasing, first clear the accumulation buffer and enable the front buffer for reading and writing. Then loop several times (say, *n*) through code that jitters and draws the image (*jittering* is moving the image to a slightly different position), accumulating the data with

```
glAccum(GL_ACCUM, 1.0/n);
```

and finally calling

```
glAccum(GL_RETURN, 1.0);
```

Note that this method is a bit faster if, on the first pass through the loop, GL_LOAD is used and clearing the accumulation buffer is omitted. See Table 10-5 for possible jittering values. With this code, the image is drawn *n* times before the final image is drawn. If you want to avoid showing the user the intermediate images, draw into a color buffer that's not displayed, accumulate from that, and use the GL_RETURN call to draw into a displayed buffer (or into a back buffer that you subsequently swap to the front).

You could instead present a user interface that shows the viewed image improving as each additional piece is accumulated and that allows the user to halt the process when the image is good enough. To accomplish this, in the loop that draws successive images, call **glAccum()** with GL_RETURN after each accumulation, using 16.0/1.0, 16.0/2.0, 16.0/3.0, ... as the second argument. With this technique, after one pass, 1/16 of the final image is shown, after two passes, 2/16 is shown, and so on. After the GL_RETURN, the code should check to see if the user wants to interrupt the process. This interface is slightly slower, since the resultant image must be copied in after each pass.

To decide what *n* should be, you need to trade off speed (the more times you draw the scene, the longer it takes to obtain the final image) and quality (the more times you draw the scene, the smoother it gets, until you make maximum use of the accumulation buffer's resolution). Plates 22 and 23 show improvements made using scene antialiasing.

Example 10-2 defines two routines for jittering that you might find useful: **accPerspective()** and **accFrustum()**. The routine **accPerspective()** is used in place of **gluPerspective()**, and the first four parameters of both routines are the same. To jitter the viewing frustum for scene antialiasing, pass the *x* and *y* jitter values (of less than one pixel) to the fifth and sixth parameters of **accPerspective()**. Also pass 0.0 for the seventh and eighth parameters to **accPerspective()** and a nonzero value for the ninth parameter (to prevent division by zero inside **accPerspective()**). These last three parameters are used for depth-of-field effects, which are described later in this chapter.

Example 10-2 Routines for Jittering the Viewing Volume: accpersp.c

```
#define PI_ 3.14159265358979323846

void accFrustum(GLdouble left, GLdouble right, GLdouble bottom,
    GLdouble top, GLdouble near, GLdouble far, GLdouble pixdx,
    GLdouble pixdy, GLdouble eyedx, GLdouble eyedy,
    GLdouble focus)
{
    GLdouble xwsize, ywsize;
    GLdouble dx, dy;
    GLint viewport[4];

    glGetIntegerv (GL_VIEWPORT, viewport);

    xwsize = right - left;
    ywsize = top - bottom;
    dx = -(pixdx*xwsize/(GLdouble) viewport[2] +
            eyedx*near/focus);
    dy = -(pixdy*ywsize/(GLdouble) viewport[3] +
            eyedy*near/focus);

    glMatrixMode(GL_PROJECTION);
    glLoadIdentity();
    glFrustum (left + dx, right + dx, bottom + dy, top + dy,
        near, far);
    glMatrixMode(GL_MODELVIEW);
    glLoadIdentity();
    glTranslatef (-eyedx, -eyedy, 0.0);
}

void accPerspective(GLdouble fovy, GLdouble aspect,
    GLdouble near, GLdouble far, GLdouble pixdx, GLdouble pixdy,
    GLdouble eyedx, GLdouble eyedy, GLdouble focus)
{
    GLdouble fov2,left,right,bottom,top;
    fov2 = ((fovy*PI_) / 180.0) / 2.0;

    top = near / (fcos(fov2) / fsin(fov2));
    bottom = -top;
    right = top * aspect;
    left = -right;
```

```
        accFrustum (left, right, bottom, top, near, far,
            pixdx, pixdy, eyedx, eyedy, focus);
}
```

Example 10-3 uses these two routines to perform scene antialiasing.

Example 10-3 Scene Antialiasing: accpersp.c

```
#include <GL/gl.h>
#include <GL/glu.h>
#include <stdlib.h>
#include <math.h>
#include <GL/glut.h>
#include "jitter.h"

void init(void)
{
    GLfloat mat_ambient[] = { 1.0, 1.0, 1.0, 1.0 };
    GLfloat mat_specular[] = { 1.0, 1.0, 1.0, 1.0 };
    GLfloat light_position[] = { 0.0, 0.0, 10.0, 1.0 };
    GLfloat lm_ambient[] = { 0.2, 0.2, 0.2, 1.0 };

    glMaterialfv(GL_FRONT, GL_AMBIENT, mat_ambient);
    glMaterialfv(GL_FRONT, GL_SPECULAR, mat_specular);
    glMaterialf(GL_FRONT, GL_SHININESS, 50.0);
    glLightfv(GL_LIGHT0, GL_POSITION, light_position);
    glLightModelfv(GL_LIGHT_MODEL_AMBIENT, lm_ambient);

    glEnable(GL_LIGHTING);
    glEnable(GL_LIGHT0);
    glEnable(GL_DEPTH_TEST);
    glShadeModel (GL_FLAT);

    glClearColor(0.0, 0.0, 0.0, 0.0);
    glClearAccum(0.0, 0.0, 0.0, 0.0);
}

void displayObjects(void)
{
    GLfloat torus_diffuse[] = { 0.7, 0.7, 0.0, 1.0 };
    GLfloat cube_diffuse[] = { 0.0, 0.7, 0.7, 1.0 };
    GLfloat sphere_diffuse[] = { 0.7, 0.0, 0.7, 1.0 };
    GLfloat octa_diffuse[] = { 0.7, 0.4, 0.4, 1.0 };

    glPushMatrix ();
    glTranslatef (0.0, 0.0, -5.0);
    glRotatef (30.0, 1.0, 0.0, 0.0);
```

```
    glPushMatrix ();
    glTranslatef (-0.80, 0.35, 0.0);
    glRotatef (100.0, 1.0, 0.0, 0.0);
    glMaterialfv(GL_FRONT, GL_DIFFUSE, torus_diffuse);
    glutSolidTorus (0.275, 0.85, 16, 16);
    glPopMatrix ();

    glPushMatrix ();
    glTranslatef (-0.75, -0.50, 0.0);
    glRotatef (45.0, 0.0, 0.0, 1.0);
    glRotatef (45.0, 1.0, 0.0, 0.0);
    glMaterialfv(GL_FRONT, GL_DIFFUSE, cube_diffuse);
    glutSolidCube (1.5);
    glPopMatrix ();

    glPushMatrix ();
    glTranslatef (0.75, 0.60, 0.0);
    glRotatef (30.0, 1.0, 0.0, 0.0);
    glMaterialfv(GL_FRONT, GL_DIFFUSE, sphere_diffuse);
    glutSolidSphere (1.0, 16, 16);
    glPopMatrix ();

    glPushMatrix ();
    glTranslatef (0.70, -0.90, 0.25);
    glMaterialfv(GL_FRONT, GL_DIFFUSE, octa_diffuse);
    glutSolidOctahedron ();
    glPopMatrix ();

    glPopMatrix ();
}

#define ACSIZE  8

void display(void)
{
    GLint viewport[4];
    int jitter;

    glGetIntegerv (GL_VIEWPORT, viewport);

    glClear(GL_ACCUM_BUFFER_BIT);
    for (jitter = 0; jitter < ACSIZE; jitter++) {
       glClear(GL_COLOR_BUFFER_BIT | GL_DEPTH_BUFFER_BIT);
       accPerspective (50.0,
          (GLdouble) viewport[2]/(GLdouble) viewport[3],
          1.0, 15.0, j8[jitter].x, j8[jitter].y, 0.0, 0.0, 1.0);
       displayObjects ();
```

```
          glAccum(GL_ACCUM, 1.0/ACSIZE);
   }
   glAccum (GL_RETURN, 1.0);
   glFlush();
}

void reshape(int w, int h)
{
   glViewport(0, 0, (GLsizei) w, (GLsizei) h);
}

/*  Main Loop
 *  Be certain you request an accumulation buffer.
 */
int main(int argc, char** argv)
{
   glutInit(&argc, argv);
   glutInitDisplayMode (GLUT_SINGLE | GLUT_RGB
                        | GLUT_ACCUM | GLUT_DEPTH);
   glutInitWindowSize (250, 250);
   glutInitWindowPosition (100, 100);
   glutCreateWindow (argv[0]);
   init();
   glutReshapeFunc(reshape);
   glutDisplayFunc(display);
   glutMainLoop();
   return 0;
}
```

You don't have to use a perspective projection to perform scene antialiasing. You can antialias a scene with orthographic projection simply by using **glTranslate*()** to jitter the scene. Keep in mind that **glTranslate*()** operates in world coordinates, but you want the apparent motion of the scene to be less than one pixel, measured in screen coordinates. Thus, you must reverse the world-coordinate mapping by calculating the jittering translation values, using its width or height in world coordinates divided by its viewport size. Then multiply that world-coordinate value by the amount of jitter to determine how much the scene should be moved in world coordinates to get a predictable jitter of less than one pixel. Example 10-4 shows how the **display()** and **reshape()** routines might look with a world-coordinate width and height of 4.5.

Example 10-4   Jittering with an Orthographic Projection: accanti.c

```
#define ACSIZE   8

void display(void)
{
    GLint viewport[4];
    int jitter;

    glGetIntegerv (GL_VIEWPORT, viewport);

    glClear(GL_ACCUM_BUFFER_BIT);
    for (jitter = 0; jitter < ACSIZE; jitter++) {
        glClear(GL_COLOR_BUFFER_BIT | GL_DEPTH_BUFFER_BIT);
        glPushMatrix ();
/*      Note that 4.5 is the distance in world space between
 *      left and right and bottom and top.
 *      This formula converts fractional pixel movement to
 *      world coordinates.
 */
        glTranslatef (j8[jitter].x*4.5/viewport[2],
                      j8[jitter].y*4.5/viewport[3], 0.0);
        displayObjects ();
        glPopMatrix ();
        glAccum(GL_ACCUM, 1.0/ACSIZE);
    }
    glAccum (GL_RETURN, 1.0);
    glFlush();
}

void reshape(int w, int h)
{
    glViewport(0, 0, (GLsizei) w, (GLsizei) h);
    glMatrixMode(GL_PROJECTION);
    glLoadIdentity();
    if (w <= h)
        glOrtho (-2.25, 2.25, -2.25*h/w, 2.25*h/w, -10.0, 10.0);
    else
        glOrtho (-2.25*w/h, 2.25*w/h, -2.25, 2.25, -10.0, 10.0);
    glMatrixMode(GL_MODELVIEW);
    glLoadIdentity();
}
```

Motion Blur

Similar methods can be used to simulate motion blur, as shown in Plate 7 and Figure 10-2. Suppose your scene has some stationary and some moving objects in it, and you want to make a motion-blurred image extending over a small interval of time. Set up the accumulation buffer in the same way, but instead of spatially jittering the images, jitter them temporally. The entire scene can be made successively dimmer by calling

```
glAccum (GL_MULT, decayFactor);
```

as the scene is drawn into the accumulation buffer, where *decayFactor* is a number from 0.0 to 1.0. Smaller numbers for *decayFactor* cause the object to appear to be moving faster. You can transfer the completed scene with the object's current position and "vapor trail" of previous positions from the accumulation buffer to the standard color buffer with

```
glAccum (GL_RETURN, 1.0);
```

The image looks correct even if the items move at different speeds, or if some of them are accelerated. As before, the more jitter points (temporal, in this case) you use, the better the final image, at least up to the point where you begin to lose resolution due to finite precision in the accumulation buffer. You can combine motion blur with antialiasing by jittering in both the spatial and temporal domains, but you pay for higher quality with longer rendering times.

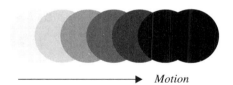

$\longrightarrow$ *Motion*

Figure 10-2   Motion-Blurred Object

Depth of Field

A photograph made with a camera is in perfect focus only for items lying on a single plane a certain distance from the film. The farther an item is from this plane, the more out of focus it is. The depth of field for a camera is a region about the plane of perfect focus where items are out of focus by a small enough amount.

Under normal conditions, everything you draw with OpenGL is in focus (unless your monitor's bad, in which case everything is out of focus). The accumulation buffer can be used to approximate what you would see in a photograph where items are more and more blurred as their distance from a plane of perfect focus increases. It isn't an exact simulation of the effects produced in a camera, but the result looks similar to what a camera would produce.

To achieve this result, draw the scene repeatedly using calls with different argument values to **glFrustum()**. Choose the arguments so that the position of the viewpoint varies slightly around its true position and so that each frustum shares a common rectangle that lies in the plane of perfect focus, as shown in Figure 10-3. The results of all the renderings should be averaged in the usual way using the accumulation buffer.

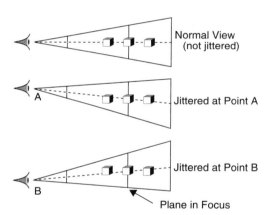

Figure 10-3   Jittered Viewing Volume for Depth-of-Field Effects

Plate 10 shows an image of five teapots drawn using the depth-of-field effect. The gold teapot (second from the left) is in focus, and the other teapots get progressively blurrier, depending upon their distance from the focal plane (gold teapot). The code to draw this image is shown in Example 10-5 (which assumes **accPerspective()** and **accFrustum()** are defined as described in Example 10-2). The scene is drawn eight times, each with a slightly jittered viewing volume, by calling **accPerspective()**. As you recall, with scene antialiasing, the fifth and sixth parameters jitter the viewing volumes in the x and y directions. For the depth-of-field effect, however, you want to jitter the volume while holding it stationary at the focal plane. The focal plane is the depth value defined by the ninth (last) parameter to **accPerspective()**, which is $z = 5.0$ in this example. The amount of blur is determined by multiplying the *x* and *y* jitter values (seventh and eighth parameters of **accPerspective()**) by a constant. Determining the constant is not a science; experiment with values until the depth of field is as pronounced as you want. (Note that in Example 10-5, the fifth and sixth parameters to **accPerspective()** are set to 0.0, so scene antialiasing is turned off.)

Example 10-5   Depth-of-Field Effect: dof.c

```
#include <GL/gl.h>
#include <GL/glu.h>
#include <GL/glut.h>
#include <stdlib.h>
#include <math.h>
#include "jitter.h"

void init(void)
{
    GLfloat ambient[] = { 0.0, 0.0, 0.0, 1.0 };
    GLfloat diffuse[] = { 1.0, 1.0, 1.0, 1.0 };
    GLfloat specular[] = { 1.0, 1.0, 1.0, 1.0 };
    GLfloat position[] = { 0.0, 3.0, 3.0, 0.0 };

    GLfloat lmodel_ambient[] = { 0.2, 0.2, 0.2, 1.0 };
    GLfloat local_view[] = { 0.0 };

    glLightfv(GL_LIGHT0, GL_AMBIENT, ambient);
    glLightfv(GL_LIGHT0, GL_DIFFUSE, diffuse);
    glLightfv(GL_LIGHT0, GL_POSITION, position);

    glLightModelfv(GL_LIGHT_MODEL_AMBIENT, lmodel_ambient);
    glLightModelfv(GL_LIGHT_MODEL_LOCAL_VIEWER, local_view);

    glFrontFace (GL_CW);
    glEnable(GL_LIGHTING);
    glEnable(GL_LIGHT0);
    glEnable(GL_AUTO_NORMAL);
    glEnable(GL_NORMALIZE);
    glEnable(GL_DEPTH_TEST);

    glClearColor(0.0, 0.0, 0.0, 0.0);
    glClearAccum(0.0, 0.0, 0.0, 0.0);
/*  make teapot display list */
    teapotList = glGenLists(1);
    glNewList (teapotList, GL_COMPILE);
    glutSolidTeapot (0.5);
```

```
    glEndList ();
}

void renderTeapot (GLfloat x, GLfloat y, GLfloat z,
    GLfloat ambr, GLfloat ambg, GLfloat ambb,
    GLfloat difr, GLfloat difg, GLfloat difb,
    GLfloat specr, GLfloat specg, GLfloat specb, GLfloat shine)
{
    GLfloat mat[4];

    glPushMatrix();
    glTranslatef (x, y, z);
    mat[0] = ambr; mat[1] = ambg; mat[2] = ambb; mat[3] = 1.0;
    glMaterialfv (GL_FRONT, GL_AMBIENT, mat);
    mat[0] = difr; mat[1] = difg; mat[2] = difb;
    glMaterialfv (GL_FRONT, GL_DIFFUSE, mat);
    mat[0] = specr; mat[1] = specg; mat[2] = specb;
    glMaterialfv (GL_FRONT, GL_SPECULAR, mat);
    glMaterialf (GL_FRONT, GL_SHININESS, shine*128.0);
    glCallList(teapotList);
    glPopMatrix();
}

void display(void)
{
    int jitter;
    GLint viewport[4];

    glGetIntegerv (GL_VIEWPORT, viewport);
    glClear(GL_ACCUM_BUFFER_BIT);

    for (jitter = 0; jitter < 8; jitter++) {
        glClear(GL_COLOR_BUFFER_BIT | GL_DEPTH_BUFFER_BIT);
        accPerspective (45.0,
            (GLdouble) viewport[2]/(GLdouble) viewport[3],
            1.0, 15.0, 0.0, 0.0,
            0.33*j8[jitter].x, 0.33*j8[jitter].y, 5.0);

/*      ruby, gold, silver, emerald, and cyan teapots    */
        renderTeapot (-1.1, -0.5, -4.5, 0.1745, 0.01175,
                        0.01175, 0.61424, 0.04136, 0.04136,
                        0.727811, 0.626959, 0.626959, 0.6);
        renderTeapot (-0.5, -0.5, -5.0, 0.24725, 0.1995,
                        0.0745, 0.75164, 0.60648, 0.22648,
                        0.628281, 0.555802, 0.366065, 0.4);
```

```
          renderTeapot (0.2, -0.5, -5.5, 0.19225, 0.19225,
                        0.19225, 0.50754, 0.50754, 0.50754,
                        0.508273, 0.508273, 0.508273, 0.4);
          renderTeapot (1.0, -0.5, -6.0, 0.0215, 0.1745, 0.0215,
                        0.07568, 0.61424, 0.07568, 0.633,
                        0.727811, 0.633, 0.6);
          renderTeapot (1.8, -0.5, -6.5, 0.0, 0.1, 0.06, 0.0,
                        0.50980392, 0.50980392, 0.50196078,
                        0.50196078, 0.50196078, .25);
          glAccum (GL_ACCUM, 0.125);
      }
      glAccum (GL_RETURN, 1.0);
      glFlush();
  }

  void reshape(int w, int h)
  {
      glViewport(0, 0, (GLsizei) w, (GLsizei) h);
  }

  /*  Main Loop
   *  Be certain you request an accumulation buffer.
   */
  int main(int argc, char** argv)
  {
      glutInit(&argc, argv);
      glutInitDisplayMode (GLUT_SINGLE | GLUT_RGB
                           | GLUT_ACCUM | GLUT_DEPTH);
      glutInitWindowSize (400, 400);
      glutInitWindowPosition (100, 100);
      glutCreateWindow (argv[0]);
      init();
      glutReshapeFunc(reshape);
      glutDisplayFunc(display);
      glutMainLoop();
      return 0;
  }
```

Soft Shadows

To accumulate soft shadows due to multiple light sources, render the
shadows with one light turned on at a time, and accumulate them together.
This can be combined with spatial jittering to antialias the scene at the same
time. (See "Shadows" on page 519 for more information about drawing
shadows.)

Jittering

If you need to take nine or sixteen samples to antialias an image, you might think that the best choice of points is an equally spaced grid across the pixel. Surprisingly, this is not necessarily true. In fact, sometimes it's a good idea to take points that lie in adjacent pixels. You might want a uniform distribution or a normalized distribution, clustering toward the center of the pixel. (The aforementioned SIGGRAPH paper discusses these issues.) In addition, Table 10-5 shows a few sets of reasonable jittering values to be used for some selected sample counts. Most of the examples in the table are uniformly distributed in the pixel, and all lie within the pixel.

Count	Values
2	{0.25, 0.75}, {0.75, 0.25}
3	{0.5033922635, 0.8317967229}, {0.7806016275, 0.2504380877}, {0.2261828938, 0.4131553612}
4	{0.375, 0.25}, {0.125, 0.75}, {0.875, 0.25}, {0.625, 0.75}
5	{0.5, 0.5}, {0.3, 0.1}, {0.7, 0.9}, {0.9, 0.3}, {0.1, 0.7}
6	{0.4646464646, 0.4646464646}, {0.1313131313, 0.7979797979}, {0.5353535353, 0.8686868686}, {0.8686868686, 0.5353535353}, {0.7979797979, 0.1313131313}, {0.2020202020, 0.2020202020}
8	{0.5625, 0.4375}, {0.0625, 0.9375}, {0.3125, 0.6875}, {0.6875, 0.8125}, {0.8125, 0.1875}, {0.9375, 0.5625}, {0.4375, 0.0625}, {0.1875, 0.3125}
9	{0.5, 0.5}, {0.1666666666, 0.9444444444}, {0.5, 0.1666666666}, {0.5, 0.8333333333}, {0.1666666666, 0.2777777777}, {0.8333333333, 0.3888888888}, {0.1666666666, 0.6111111111}, {0.8333333333, 0.7222222222}, {0.8333333333, 0.0555555555}
12	{0.4166666666, 0.625}, {0.9166666666, 0.875}, {0.25, 0.375}, {0.4166666666, 0.125}, {0.75, 0.125}, {0.0833333333, 0.125}, {0.75, 0.625}, {0.25, 0.875}, {0.5833333333, 0.375}, {0.9166666666, 0.375}, {0.0833333333, 0.625}, {0.583333333, 0.875}

Table 10-5   Sample Jittering Values

Count	Values
16	{0.375, 0.4375}, {0.625, 0.0625}, {0.875, 0.1875}, {0.125, 0.0625}, {0.375, 0.6875}, {0.875, 0.4375}, {0.625, 0.5625}, {0.375, 0.9375}, {0.625, 0.3125}, {0.125, 0.5625}, {0.125, 0.8125}, {0.375, 0.1875}, {0.875, 0.9375}, {0.875, 0.6875}, {0.125, 0.3125}, {0.625, 0.8125}

Table 10-5   Sample Jittering Values (continued)

Chapter 11

Tessellators and Quadrics

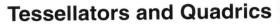

Chapter Objectives

After reading this chapter, you'll be able to do the following:

- Render concave filled polygons by first tessellating them into convex polygons, which can be rendered using standard OpenGL routines.

- Use the GLU library to create quadrics objects to render and model the surfaces of spheres and cylinders and to tessellate disks (circles) and partial disks (arcs).

The OpenGL library (GL) is designed for low-level operations, both streamlined and accessible to hardware acceleration. The OpenGL Utility Library (GLU) complements the OpenGL library, supporting higher-level operations. Some of the GLU operations are covered in other chapters. Mipmapping (**gluBuild*DMipmaps()**) and image scaling (**gluScaleImage()**) are discussed along with other facets of texture mapping in Chapter 9. Several matrix transformation GLU routines (**gluOrtho2D()**, **gluPerspective()**, **gluLookAt()**, **gluProject()**, and **gluUnProject()**) are described in Chapter 3. The use of **gluPickMatrix()** is explained in Chapter 13. The GLU NURBS facilities, which are built atop OpenGL evaluators, are covered in Chapter 12. Only two GLU topics remain: polygon tessellators and quadric surfaces, and those topics are discussed in this chapter.

To optimize performance, the basic OpenGL only renders convex polygons, but the GLU contains routines to tessellate concave polygons into convex ones, which the basic OpenGL can handle. Where the basic OpenGL operates upon simple primitives, such as points, lines, and filled polygons, the GLU can create higher-level objects, such as the surfaces of spheres, cylinders, and cones.

This chapter has the following major sections.

- "Polygon Tessellation" on page 410 explains how to tessellate convex polygons into easier-to-render convex polygons.

- "Quadrics: Rendering Spheres, Cylinders, and Disks" on page 428 describes how to generate spheres, cylinders, circles and arcs, including data such as surface normals and texture coordinates.

Polygon Tessellation

As discussed in "Describing Points, Lines, and Polygons" on page 37, OpenGL can directly display only simple convex polygons. A polygon is simple if the edges intersect only at vertices, there are no duplicate vertices, and exactly two edges meet at any vertex. If your application requires the display of concave polygons, polygons containing holes, or polygons with intersecting edges, those polygons must first be subdivided into simple convex polygons before they can be displayed. Such subdivision is called *tessellation*, and the GLU provides a collection of routines that perform tessellation. These routines take as input arbitrary contours, which describe hard-to-render polygons, and they return some combination of triangles, triangle meshes, triangle fans, or lines.

Figure 11-1 shows some contours of polygons that require tessellation: from left to right, a concave polygon, a polygon with a hole, and a self-intersecting polygon.

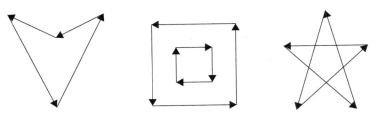

Figure 11-1   Contours That Require Tessellation

If you think a polygon may need tessellation, follow these typical steps.

1. Create a new tessellation object with **gluNewTess()**.

2. Use **gluTessCallback()** several times to register callback functions to perform operations during the tessellation. The trickiest case for a callback function is when the tessellation algorithm detects an intersection and must call the function registered for the GLU_TESS_COMBINE callback.

3. Specify tessellation properties by calling **gluTessProperty()**. The most important property is the winding rule, which determines the regions that should be filled and those that should remain unshaded.

4. Create and render tessellated polygons by specifying the contours of one or more closed polygons. If the data for the object is static, encapsulate the tessellated polygons in a display list. (If you don't have to recalculate the tessellation over and over again, using display lists is more efficient.)

5. If you need to tessellate something else, you may reuse your tessellation object. If you are forever finished with your tessellation object, you may delete it with **gluDeleteTess()**.

Note: The tessellator described here was introduced in version 1.2 of the GLU. If you are using an older version of the GLU, you must use routines described in "Describing GLU Errors" on page 426. To query which version of GLU you have, use **gluGetString(GLU_VERSION)**, which returns a string with your GLU version number. If you don't seem to have **gluGetString()** in your GLU, then you have GLU 1.0, which did not yet have the **gluGetString()** routine.

Create a Tessellation Object

As a complex polygon is being described and tessellated, it has associated data, such as the vertices, edges, and callback functions. All this data is tied to a single tessellation object. To perform tessellation, your program first has to create a tessellation object using the routine **gluNewTess()**.

GLUtesselator* **gluNewTess**(void);

Creates a new tessellation object and returns a pointer to it. A null pointer is returned if the creation fails.

A single tessellation object can be reused for all your tessellations. This object is required only because library routines might need to do their own tessellations, and they should be able to do so without interfering with any tessellation that your program is doing. It might also be useful to have multiple tessellation objects if you want to use different sets of callbacks for different tessellations. A typical program, however, allocates a single tessellation object and uses it for all its tessellations. There's no real need to free it because it uses a small amount of memory. On the other hand, it never hurts to be tidy.

Tessellation Callback Routines

After you create a tessellation object, you must provide a series of callback routines to be called at appropriate times during the tessellation. After specifying the callbacks, you describe the contours of one or more polygons using GLU routines. When the description of the contours is complete, the tessellation facility invokes your callback routines as necessary.

Any functions that are omitted are simply not called during the tessellation, and any information they might have returned to your program is lost. All are specified by the single routine **gluTessCallback()**.

---

void **gluTessCallback**(GLUtesselator **tessobj*, GLenum *type*, void (*fn*)());

Associates the callback function *fn* with the tessellation object *tessobj*. The type of the callback is determined by the parameter *type*, which can be GLU_TESS_BEGIN, GLU_TESS_BEGIN_DATA, GLU_TESS_EDGE_FLAG, GLU_TESS_EDGE_FLAG_DATA, GLU_TESS_VERTEX, GLU_TESS_VERTEX_DATA, GLU_TESS_END, GLU_TESS_END_DATA, GLU_TESS_COMBINE, GLU_TESS_COMBINE_DATA, GLU_TESS_ERROR, and GLU_TESS_ERROR_DATA. The twelve possible callback functions have the following prototypes:

GLU_TESS_BEGIN   void **begin**(GLenum *type*);

GLU_TESS_BEGIN_DATA   void **begin**(GLenum *type*,
                                        void **user_data*);

GLU_TESS_EDGE_FLAG   void **edgeFlag**(GLboolean *flag*);

GLU_TESS_EDGE_FLAG_DATA void **edgeFlag**(GLboolean *flag*,
                                        void **user_data*);

GLU_TESS_VERTEX   void **vertex**(void **vertex_data*);

GLU_TESS_VERTEX_DATA   void **vertex**(void **vertex_data*,
                                        void **user_data*);

GLU_TESS_END   void **end**(void);

GLU_TESS_END_DATA   void **end**(void **user_data*);

GLU_TESS_ERROR   void **error**(GLenum *errno*);

GLU_TESS_ERROR_DATA   void **error**(GLenum *errno*, void
user_data);

GLU_TESS_COMBINE   void **combine**(GLdouble *coords*[3],
                                        void **vertex_data*[4],
                                        GLfloat *weight*[4],
                                        void ***outData*);

GLU_TESS_COMBINE_DATA   void **combine**(GLdouble *coords*[3],
                                        void **vertex_data*[4],
                                        GLfloat *weight*[4],
                                        void ***outData*,
                                        void **user_data*);

To change a callback routine, simply call **gluTessCallback**() with the new routine. To eliminate a callback routine without replacing it with a new one, pass **gluTessCallback**() a null pointer for the appropriate function.

As tessellation proceeds, the callback routines are called in a manner similar to how you use the OpenGL commands **glBegin()**, **glEdgeFlag*()**, **glVertex*()**, and **glEnd()**. (See "Marking Polygon Boundary Edges" on page 62 for more information about **glEdgeFlag*()**.) The combine callback is used to create new vertices where edges intersect. The error callback is invoked during the tessellation only if something goes wrong.

For every tessellator object created, a GLU_TESS_BEGIN callback is invoked with one of four possible parameters: GL_TRIANGLE_FAN, GL_TRIANGLE_STRIP, GL_TRIANGLES, and GL_LINE_LOOP. When the tessellator decomposes the polygons, the tessellation algorithm will decide which type of triangle primitive is most efficient to use. (If the GLU_TESS_BOUNDARY_ONLY property is enabled, then GL_LINE_LOOP is used for rendering.)

Since edge flags make no sense in a triangle fan or triangle strip, if there is a callback associated with GLU_TESS_EDGE_FLAG that enables edge flags, the GLU_TESS_BEGIN callback is called only with GL_TRIANGLES. The GLU_TESS_EDGE_FLAG callback works exactly analogously to the OpenGL **glEdgeFlag*()** call.

After the GLU_TESS_BEGIN callback routine is called and before the callback associated with GLU_TESS_END is called, some combination of the GLU_TESS_EDGE_FLAG and GLU_TESS_VERTEX callbacks is invoked (usually by calls to **gluTessVertex()**, which is described on page 423). The associated edge flags and vertices are interpreted exactly as they are in OpenGL between **glBegin()** and the matching **glEnd()**.

If something goes wrong, the error callback is passed a GLU error number. A character string describing the error is obtained using the routine **gluErrorString()**. (See "Describing GLU Errors" on page 426 for more information about this routine.)

Example 11-1 shows a portion of tess.c, where a tessellation object is created and several callbacks are registered.

Example 11-1   Registering Tessellation Callbacks: tess.c

```
/*  a portion of init() */

tobj = gluNewTess();
gluTessCallback(tobj, GLU_TESS_VERTEX,
                    (GLvoid (*) ()) &glVertex3dv);
gluTessCallback(tobj, GLU_TESS_BEGIN,
                    (GLvoid (*) ()) &beginCallback);
gluTessCallback(tobj, GLU_TESS_END,
                    (GLvoid (*) ()) &endCallback);
```

```
gluTessCallback(tobj, GLU_TESS_ERROR,
                (GLvoid (*) ()) &errorCallback);

/*  the callback routines registered by gluTessCallback() */

void beginCallback(GLenum which)
{
   glBegin(which);
}

void endCallback(void)
{
   glEnd();
}

void errorCallback(GLenum errorCode)
{
   const GLubyte *estring;

   estring = gluErrorString(errorCode);
   fprintf (stderr, "Tessellation Error: %s\n", estring);
   exit (0);
}
```

In Example 11-1, the registered GLU_TESS_VERTEX callback is simply **glVertex3dv()**, and only the coordinates at each vertex are passed along. However, if you want to specify more information at every vertex, such as a color value, a surface normal vector, or texture coordinate, you'll have to make a more complex callback routine. Example 11-2 shows the start of another tessellated object, further along in program tess.c. The registered function **vertexCallback()** expects to receive a parameter that is a pointer to six double-length floating point values: the x, y, and z coordinates and the red, green, and blue color values, respectively, for that vertex.

Example 11-2 Vertex and Combine Callbacks: tess.c

```
/*  a different portion of init() */
   gluTessCallback(tobj, GLU_TESS_VERTEX,
                   (GLvoid (*) ()) &vertexCallback);
   gluTessCallback(tobj, GLU_TESS_BEGIN,
                   (GLvoid (*) ()) &beginCallback);
   gluTessCallback(tobj, GLU_TESS_END,
                   (GLvoid (*) ()) &endCallback);
   gluTessCallback(tobj, GLU_TESS_ERROR,
                   (GLvoid (*) ()) &errorCallback);
   gluTessCallback(tobj, GLU_TESS_COMBINE,
                   (GLvoid (*) ()) &combineCallback);
```

```
/*  new callback routines registered by these calls */
void vertexCallback(GLvoid *vertex)
{
   const GLdouble *pointer;

   pointer = (GLdouble *) vertex;
   glColor3dv(pointer+3);
   glVertex3dv(vertex);
}

void combineCallback(GLdouble coords[3],
                     GLdouble *vertex_data[4],
                     GLfloat weight[4], GLdouble **dataOut )
{
   GLdouble *vertex;
   int i;

   vertex = (GLdouble *) malloc(6 * sizeof(GLdouble));
   vertex[0] = coords[0];
   vertex[1] = coords[1];
   vertex[2] = coords[2];
   for (i = 3; i < 7; i++)
      vertex[i] = weight[0] * vertex_data[0][i]
                  + weight[1] * vertex_data[1][i]
                  + weight[2] * vertex_data[2][i]
                  + weight[3] * vertex_data[3][i];
   *dataOut = vertex;
}
```

Example 11-2 also shows the use of the GLU_TESS_COMBINE callback.
Whenever the tessellation algorithm examines the input contours, detects
an intersection, and decides it must create a new vertex, the
GLU_TESS_COMBINE callback is invoked. The callback is also called when
the tessellator decides to merge features of two vertices that are very close
to one another. The newly created vertex is a linear combination of up to
four existing vertices, referenced by *vertex_data*[0..3] in Example 11-2. The
coefficients of the linear combination are given by *weight*[0..3]; these
weights sum to 1.0. *coords* gives the location of the new vertex.

The registered callback routine must allocate memory for another vertex,
perform a weighted interpolation of data using *vertex_data* and *weight*, and
return the new vertex pointer as *dataOut*. **combineCallback()** in
Example 11-2 interpolates the RGB color value. The function allocates a
six-element array, puts the *x*, *y*, and *z* coordinates in the first three elements,
and then puts the weighted average of the RGB color values in the last three
elements.

User-Specified Data

Six kinds of callbacks can be registered. Since there are two versions of each kind of callback, there are twelve callbacks in all. For each kind of callback, there is one with user-specified data and one without. The user-specified data is given by the application to **gluTessBeginPolygon()** and is then passed, unaltered, to each *DATA callback routine. With GLU_TESS_BEGIN_DATA, the user-specified data may be used for "per-polygon" data. If you specify both versions of a particular callback, the callback with *user_data* is used, and the other is ignored. So, although there are twelve callbacks, you can have a maximum of six callback functions active at any time.

For instance, Example 11-2 uses smooth shading, so **vertexCallback()** specifies an RGB color for every vertex. If you want to do lighting and smooth shading, the callback would specify a surface normal for every vertex. However, if you want lighting and flat shading, you might specify only one surface normal for every polygon, not for every vertex. In that case, you might choose to use the GLU_TESS_BEGIN_DATA callback and pass the vertex coordinates and surface normal in the *user_data* pointer.

Tessellation Properties

Prior to tessellation and rendering, you may use **gluTessProperty()** to set several properties to affect the tessellation algorithm. The most important and complicated of these properties is the winding rule, which determines what is considered "interior" and "exterior."

---

void **gluTessProperty**(GLUtesselator *tessobj*, GLenum *property*,
             GLdouble *value*);

For the tessellation object *tessobj*, the current value of *property* is set to *value*. *property* is one of GLU_TESS_BOUNDARY_ONLY, GLU_TESS_TOLERANCE, or GLU_TESS_WINDING_RULE.

If *property* is GLU_TESS_BOUNDARY_ONLY, *value* is either GL_TRUE or GL_FALSE. When set to GL_TRUE, polygons are no longer tessellated into filled polygons; line loops are drawn to outline the contours that separate the polygon interior and exterior. The default value is GL_FALSE. (See **gluTessNormal()** to see how to control the winding direction of the contours.)

If *property* is GLU_TESS_TOLERANCE, *value* is a distance used to calculate whether two vertices are close together enough to be merged by the GLU_TESS_COMBINE callback. The tolerance value is multiplied by the largest coordinate magnitude of an input vertex to determine the maximum distance any feature can move as a result of a single merge operation. Feature merging may not be supported by your implementation, and the tolerance value is only a hint. The default tolerance value is zero.

The GLU_TESS_WINDING_RULE *property* determines which parts of the polygon are on the interior and which are the exterior and should not be filled. *value* can be one of GLU_TESS_WINDING_ODD (the default), GLU_TESS_WINDING_NONZERO, GLU_TESS_WINDING_POSITIVE, GLU_TESS_WINDING_NEGATIVE, or GLU_TESS_WINDING_ABS_GEQ_TWO.

Winding Numbers and Winding Rules

For a single contour, the winding number of a point is the signed number of revolutions we make around that point while traveling once around the contour (where a counterclockwise revolution is positive and a clockwise revolution is negative). When there are several contours, the individual winding numbers are summed. This procedure associates a signed integer value with each point in the plane. Note that the winding number is the same for all points in a single region.

Figure 11-2 shows three sets of contours and winding numbers for points inside those contours. In the left set, all three contours are counterclockwise, so each nested interior region adds one to the winding number. For the middle set, the two interior contours are drawn clockwise, so the winding number decreases and actually becomes negative.

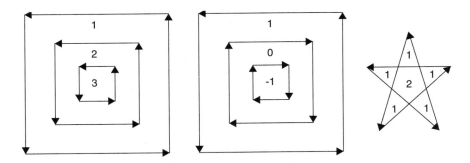

Figure 11-2   Winding Numbers for Sample Contours

The winding rule classifies a region as *inside* if its winding number belongs to the chosen category (odd, nonzero, positive, negative, or "absolute value of greater than or equal to two"). The odd and nonzero rules are common ways to define the interior. The positive, negative, and "absolute value>=2" winding rules have some limited use for polygon CSG (computational solid geometry) operations.

The program tesswind.c demonstrates the effects of winding rules. The four sets of contours shown in Figure 11-3 are rendered. The user can then cycle through the different winding rule properties to see their effects. For each winding rule, the dark areas represent interiors. Note the effect of clockwise and counterclockwise winding.

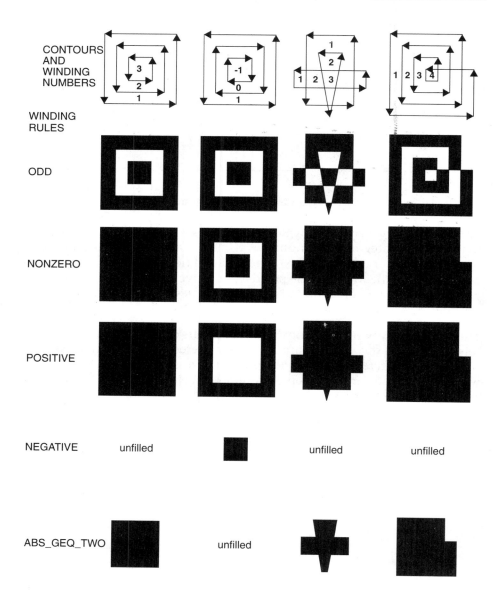

Figure 11-3   How Winding Rules Define Interiors

CSG Uses for Winding Rules

GLU_TESS_WINDING_ODD and GLU_TESS_WINDING_NONZERO are the most commonly used winding rules. They work for the most typical cases of shading.

The winding rules are also designed for computational solid geometry (CSG) operations. Thy make it easy to find the union, difference, or intersection (Boolean operations) of several contours.

First, assume that each contour is defined so that the winding number is zero for each exterior region and one for each interior region. (Each contour must not intersect itself.) Under this model, counterclockwise contours define the outer boundary of the polygon, and clockwise contours define holes. Contours may be nested, but a nested contour must be oriented oppositely from the contour that contains it.

If the original polygons do not satisfy this description, they can be converted to this form by first running the tessellator with the GLU_TESS_BOUNDARY_ONLY property turned on. This returns a list of contours satisfying the restriction just described. By creating two tessellator objects, the callbacks from one tessellator can be fed directly as input to the other.

Given two or more polygons of the preceding form, CSG operations can be implemented as follows.

- UNION—To calculate the union of several contours, draw all input contours as a single polygon. The winding number of each resulting region is the number of original polygons that cover it. The union can be extracted by using the GLU_TESS_WINDING_NONZERO or GLU_TESS_WINDING_POSITIVE winding rules. Note that with the nonzero winding rule, we would get the same result if all contour orientations were reversed.

- INTERSECTION—This only works for two contours at a time. Draw a single polygon using two contours. Extract the result using GLU_TESS_WINDING_ABS_GEQ_TWO.

- DIFFERENCE—Suppose you want to compute A diff (B union C union D). Draw a single polygon consisting of the unmodified contours from A, followed by the contours of B, C, and D, with their vertex order reversed. To extract the result, use the GLU_TESS_WINDING_POSITIVE winding rule. (If B, C, and D are the result of a GLU_TESS_BOUNDARY_ONLY operation, an alternative to reversing the vertex order is to use **gluTessNormal()** to reverse the sign of the supplied normal.

Other Tessellation Property Routines

There are complementary routines, which work alongside **gluTessProperty()**. **gluGetTessProperty()** retrieves the current values of tessellator properties. If the tessellator is being used to generate wire frame outlines instead of filled polygons, **gluTessNormal()** can be used to determine the winding direction of the tessellated polygons.

---

void **gluGetTessProperty**(GLUtesselator *tessobj*, GLenum *property*, GLdouble **value*);

For the tessellation object *tessobj*, the current value of *property* is returned to *value*. Values for *property* and *value* are the same as for **gluTessProperty()**.

---

void **gluTessNormal**(GLUtesselator *tessobj*, GLdouble *x*, GLdouble *y*, GLdouble *z*);

For the tessellation object *tessobj*, **gluTessNormal()** defines a normal vector, which controls the winding direction of generated polygons. Before tessellation, all input data is projected into a plane perpendicular to the normal. Then, all output triangles are oriented counterclockwise, with respect to the normal. (Clockwise orientation can be obtained by reversing the sign of the supplied normal.) The default normal is (0, 0, 0).

If you have some knowledge about the location and orientation of the input data, then using **gluTessNormal()** can increase the speed of the tessellation. For example, if you know that all polygons lie on the x-y plane, call **gluTessNormal**(*tessobj*, 0, 0, 1).

The default normal is (0, 0, 0), and its effect is not immediately obvious. In this case, it is expected that the input data lies approximately in a plane, and a plane is fitted to the vertices, no matter how they are truly connected. The sign of the normal is chosen so that the sum of the signed areas of all input contours is nonnegative (where a counterclockwise contour has a positive area). Note that if the input data does not lie approximately in a plane, then projection perpendicular to the computed normal may substantially change the geometry.

Polygon Definition

After all the tessellation properties have been set and the callback actions have been registered, it is finally time to describe the vertices that compromise input contours and tessellate the polygons.

---

void **gluTessBeginPolygon** (GLUtesselator *tessobj*, void **user_data*);
void **gluTessEndPolygon** (GLUtesselator *tessobj*);

Begins and ends the specification of a polygon to be tessellated and associates a tessellation object, *tessobj*, with it. *user_data* points to a user-defined data structure, which is passed along all the GLU_TESS_*_DATA callback functions that have been bound.

Calls to **gluTessBeginPolygon**() and **gluTessEndPolygon**() surround the definition of one or more contours. When **gluTessEndPolygon**() is called, the tessellation algorithm is implemented, and the tessellated polygons are generated and rendered. The callback functions and tessellation properties that were bound and set to the tessellation object using **gluTessCallback**() and **gluTessProperty**() are used.

---

void **gluTessBeginContour** (GLUtesselator *tessobj*);
void **gluTessEndContour** (GLUtesselator *tessobj*);

Begins and ends the specification of a closed contour, which is a portion of a polygon. A closed contour consists of zero or more calls to **gluTessVertex**(), which defines the vertices. The last vertex of each contour is automatically linked to the first.

In practice, a minimum of three vertices is needed for a meaningful contour.

---

void **gluTessVertex** (GLUtesselator *tessobj*, GLdouble *coords*[3],
                 void **vertex_data*);

Specifies a vertex in the current contour for the tessellation object. *coords* contains the three-dimensional vertex coordinates, and *vertex_data* is a pointer that's sent to the callback associated with GLU_TESS_VERTEX or GLU_TESS_VERTEX_DATA. Typically, *vertex_data* contains vertex coordinates, surface normals, texture coordinates, color information, or whatever else the application may find useful.

In the program tess.c, a portion of which is shown in Example 11-3, two polygons are defined. One polygon is a rectangular contour with a triangular hole inside, and the other is a smooth-shaded, self-intersecting, five-pointed star. For efficiency, both polygons are stored in display lists. The first polygon consists of two contours; the outer one is wound counterclockwise, and the "hole" is wound clockwise. For the second polygon, the *star* array contains both the coordinate and color data, and its tessellation callback, **vertexCallback()**, uses both.

It is important that each vertex is in a different memory location because the vertex data is not copied by **gluTessVertex()**; only the pointer (*vertex_data*) is saved. A program that reuses the same memory for several vertices may not get the desired result.

Note: In **gluTessVertex()**, it may seem redundant to specify the vertex coordinate data twice, for both the *coords* and *vertex_data* parameters; however, both are necessary. *coords* refers only to the vertex coordinates. *vertex_data* uses the coordinate data, but may also use other information for each vertex.

Example 11-3   Polygon Definition: tess.c

```
GLdouble rect[4][3] = {50.0, 50.0, 0.0,
                       200.0, 50.0, 0.0,
                       200.0, 200.0, 0.0,
                       50.0, 200.0, 0.0};
GLdouble tri[3][3] = {75.0, 75.0, 0.0,
                      125.0, 175.0, 0.0,
                      175.0, 75.0, 0.0};
GLdouble star[5][6] = {250.0, 50.0, 0.0, 1.0, 0.0, 1.0,
                       325.0, 200.0, 0.0, 1.0, 1.0, 0.0,
                       400.0, 50.0, 0.0, 0.0, 1.0, 1.0,
                       250.0, 150.0, 0.0, 1.0, 0.0, 0.0,
                       400.0, 150.0, 0.0, 0.0, 1.0, 0.0};

startList = glGenLists(2);
tobj = gluNewTess();
gluTessCallback(tobj, GLU_TESS_VERTEX,
                (GLvoid (*) ()) &glVertex3dv);
gluTessCallback(tobj, GLU_TESS_BEGIN,
                (GLvoid (*) ()) &beginCallback);
gluTessCallback(tobj, GLU_TESS_END,
                (GLvoid (*) ()) &endCallback);
gluTessCallback(tobj, GLU_TESS_ERROR,
                (GLvoid (*) ()) &errorCallback);
```

```
glNewList(startList, GL_COMPILE);
glShadeModel(GL_FLAT);
gluTessBeginPolygon(tobj, NULL);
   gluTessBeginContour(tobj);
      gluTessVertex(tobj, rect[0], rect[0]);
      gluTessVertex(tobj, rect[1], rect[1]);
      gluTessVertex(tobj, rect[2], rect[2]);
      gluTessVertex(tobj, rect[3], rect[3]);
   gluTessEndContour(tobj);
   gluTessBeginContour(tobj);
      gluTessVertex(tobj, tri[0], tri[0]);
      gluTessVertex(tobj, tri[1], tri[1]);
      gluTessVertex(tobj, tri[2], tri[2]);
   gluTessEndContour(tobj);
gluTessEndPolygon(tobj);
glEndList();

gluTessCallback(tobj, GLU_TESS_VERTEX,
                (GLvoid (*) ()) &vertexCallback);
gluTessCallback(tobj, GLU_TESS_BEGIN,
                (GLvoid (*) ()) &beginCallback);
gluTessCallback(tobj, GLU_TESS_END,
                (GLvoid (*) ()) &endCallback);
gluTessCallback(tobj, GLU_TESS_ERROR,
                (GLvoid (*) ()) &errorCallback);
gluTessCallback(tobj, GLU_TESS_COMBINE,
                (GLvoid (*) ()) &combineCallback);

glNewList(startList + 1, GL_COMPILE);
glShadeModel(GL_SMOOTH);
gluTessProperty(tobj, GLU_TESS_WINDING_RULE,
                GLU_TESS_WINDING_POSITIVE);
gluTessBeginPolygon(tobj, NULL);
   gluTessBeginContour(tobj);
      gluTessVertex(tobj, star[0], star[0]);
      gluTessVertex(tobj, star[1], star[1]);
      gluTessVertex(tobj, star[2], star[2]);
      gluTessVertex(tobj, star[3], star[3]);
      gluTessVertex(tobj, star[4], star[4]);
   gluTessEndContour(tobj);
gluTessEndPolygon(tobj);
glEndList();
```

Deleting a Tessellator Object

If you no longer need a tessellation object, you can delete it and free all associated memory with **gluDeleteTess()**.

---

void **gluDeleteTess**(GLUtesselator *tessobj*);

Deletes the specified tessellation object, *tessobj*, and frees all associated memory.

Tessellator Performance Tips

For best performance, remember these rules.

1. Cache the output of the tessellator in a display list or other user structure. To obtain the post-tessellation vertex coordinates, tessellate the polygons while in feedback mode. (See "Feedback" on page 491.)

2. Use **gluTessNormal()** to supply the polygon normal.

3. Use the same tessellator object to render many polygons rather than allocate a new tessellator for each one. (In a multithreaded, multiprocessor environment, you may get better performance using several tessellators.)

Describing GLU Errors

The GLU provides a routine for obtaining a descriptive string for an error code. This routine is not limited to tessellation but is also used for NURBS and quadrics errors, as well as errors in the base GL. (See "Error Handling" on page 501 for information about OpenGL's error handling facility.)

Backward Compatibility

If you are using the 1.0 or 1.1 version of GLU, you have a much less powerful tessellator available. The 1.0/1.1 tessellator handles only simple nonconvex polygons or simple polygons containing holes. It does not properly tessellate intersecting contours (no COMBINE callback), nor process per-polygon data.

The 1.0/1.1 tessellator has some similarities to the current tessellator. **gluNewTess()** and **gluDeleteTess()** are used for both tessellators. The main vertex specification routine remains **gluTessVertex()**. The callback mechanism is controlled by **gluTessCallback()**, although there are only five callback functions that can be registered, a subset of the current twelve.

Here are the prototypes for the 1.0/1.1 tessellator. The 1.0/1.1 tessellator still works in GLU 1.2, but its use is no longer recommended.

---

void **gluBeginPolygon**(GLUtriangulatorObj *tessobj*);
void **gluNextContour**(GLUtriangulatorObj *tessobj*, GLenum *type*);
void **gluEndPolygon**(GLUtriangulatorObj *tessobj*);

The outermost contour must be specified first, and it does not require an initial call to **gluNextContour()**. For polygons without holes, only one contour is defined, and **gluNextContour()** is not used. If a polygon has multiple contours (that is, holes or holes within holes), the contours are specified one after the other, each preceded by **gluNextContour()**. **gluTessVertex()** is called for each vertex of a contour.

For **gluNextContour()**, type can be GLU_EXTERIOR, GLU_INTERIOR, GLU_CCW, GLU_CW, or GLU_UNKNOWN. These serve only as hints to the tessellation. If you get them right, the tessellation might go faster. If you get them wrong, they're ignored, and the tessellation still works. For polygons with holes, one contour is the exterior contour and the other's interior. The first contour is assumed to be of type GLU_EXTERIOR. Choosing clockwise and counterclockwise orientation is arbitrary in three dimensions; however, there are two different orientations in any plane, and the GLU_CCW and GLU_CW types should be used consistently. Use GLU_UNKNOWN if you don't have a clue.

It is highly recommended that you convert GLU 1.0/1.1 code to the new tessellation interface for GLU 1.2 by following these steps.

1. Change references to the major data structure type from GLUtriangulatorObj to GLUtesselator. In GLU 1.2, GLUtriangulatorObj and GLUtesselator are defined to be the same type.

2. Convert **gluBeginPolygon()** to two commands: **gluTessBeginPolygon()** and **gluTessBeginContour()**. All contours must be explicitly started, including the first one.

3. Convert **gluNextContour()** to both **gluTessEndContour()** and **gluTessBeginContour()**. You have to end the previous contour before starting the next one.

4. Convert **gluEndPolygon()** to both **gluTessEndContour()** and **gluTessEndPolygon()**. The final contour must be closed.

5. Change references to constants to **gluTessCallback()**. In GLU 1.2, GLU_BEGIN, GLU_VERTEX, GLU_END, GLU_ERROR, and GLU_EDGE_FLAG are defined as synonyms for GLU_TESS_BEGIN, GLU_TESS_VERTEX, GLU_TESS_END, GLU_TESS_ERROR, and GLU_TESS_EDGE_FLAG.

Quadrics: Rendering Spheres, Cylinders, and Disks

The base OpenGL library only provides support for modeling and rendering simple points, lines, and convex filled polygons. Neither 3D objects, nor commonly used 2D objects such as circles, are directly available.

Throughout this book, you've been using GLUT to create some 3D objects. The GLU also provides routines to model and render tessellated, polygonal approximations for a variety of 2D and 3D shapes (spheres, cylinders, disks, and parts of disks), which can be calculated with quadric equations. This includes routines to draw the quadric surfaces in a variety of styles and orientations. Quadric surfaces are defined by the following general quadratic equation:

$$a_1 x^2 + a_2 y^2 + a_3 z^2 + a_4 xy + a_5 yz + a_6 xz + a_7 x + a_8 y + a_9 z + a_{10} = 0$$

(See David Rogers' *Procedural Elements for Computer Graphics.* New York, NY: McGraw-Hill Book Company, 1985.) Creating and rendering a quadric surface is similar to using the tessellator. To use a quadrics object, follow these steps.

1. To create a quadrics object, use **gluNewQuadric()**.

2. Specify the rendering attributes for the quadrics object (unless you're satisfied with the default values).

    a. Use **gluQuadricOrientation()** to control the winding direction and differentiate the interior from the exterior.

    b. Use **gluQuadricDrawStyle()** to choose between rendering the object as points, lines, or filled polygons.

    c. For lit quadrics objects, use **gluQuadricNormals()** to specify one normal per vertex or one normal per face. The default is that no normals are generated at all.

d. For textured quadrics objects, use **gluQuadricTexture()** if you want to generate texture coordinates.

3. Prepare for problems by registering an error-handling routine with **gluQuadricCallback()**. Then, if an error occurs during rendering, the routine you've specified is invoked.

4. Now invoke the rendering routine for the desired type of quadrics object: **gluSphere()**, **gluCylinder()**, **gluDisk()**, or **gluPartialDisk()**. For best performance for static data, encapsulate the quadrics object in a display list.

5. When you're completely finished with it, destroy this object with **gluDeleteQuadric()**. If you need to create another quadric, it's best to reuse your quadrics object.

Manage Quadrics Objects

A quadrics object consists of parameters, attributes, and callbacks that are stored in a data structure of type GLUquadricObj. A quadrics object may generate vertices, normals, texture coordinates, and other data, all of which may be used immediately or stored in a display list for later use. The following routines create, destroy, and report upon errors of a quadrics object.

GLUquadricObj* **gluNewQuadric** (void);

Creates a new quadrics object and returns a pointer to it. A null pointer is returned if the routine fails.

void **gluDeleteQuadric** (GLUquadricObj *qobj);

Destroys the quadrics object *qobj* and frees up any memory used by it.

void **gluQuadricCallback** (GLUquadricObj *qobj, GLenum *which*, void (*fn*)());

Defines a function *fn* to be called in special circumstances. GLU_ERROR is the only legal value for *which*, so *fn* is called when an error occurs. If *fn* is NULL, any existing callback is erased.

For GLU_ERROR, *fn* is called with one parameter, which is the error code. **gluErrorString()** can be used to convert the error code into an ASCII string.

Control Quadrics Attributes

The following routines affect the kinds of data generated by the quadrics routines. Use these routines before you actually specify the primitives.

Example 11-4, quadric.c, on page 433, demonstrates changing the drawing style and the kind of normals generated as well as creating quadrics objects, error handling, and drawing the primitives.

---

void **gluQuadricDrawStyle** (GLUquadricObj *qobj*, GLenum *drawStyle*);

For the quadrics object *qobj*, *drawStyle* controls the rendering style. Legal values for *drawStyle* are GLU_POINT, GLU_LINE, GLU_SILHOUETTE, and GLU_FILL.

GLU_POINT and GLU_LINE specify that primitives should be rendered as a point at every vertex or a line between each pair of connected vertices.

GLU_SILHOUETTE specifies that primitives are rendered as lines, except that edges separating coplanar faces are not drawn. This is most often used for **gluDisk()** and **gluPartialDisk()**.

GLU_FILL specifies rendering by filled polygons, where the polygons are drawn in a counterclockwise fashion with respect to their normals. This may be affected by **gluQuadricOrientation()**.

---

void **gluQuadricOrientation** (GLUquadricObj *qobj*, GLenum *orientation*);

For the quadrics object *qobj*, *orientation* is either GLU_OUTSIDE (the default) or GLU_INSIDE, which controls the direction in which normals are pointing.

For **gluSphere()** and **gluCylinder()**, the definitions of outside and inside are obvious. For **gluDisk()** and **gluPartialDisk()**, the positive *z* side of the disk is considered to be outside.

---

void **gluQuadricNormals** (GLUquadricObj *qobj*, GLenum *normals*);

For the quadrics object *qobj*, *normals* is one of GLU_NONE (the default), GLU_FLAT, or GLU_SMOOTH.

gluQuadricNormals() is used to specify when to generate normal vectors. GLU_NONE means that no normals are generated and is intended for use without lighting. GLU_FLAT generates one normal for each facet, which is often best for lighting with flat shading. GLU_SMOOTH generates one normal for every vertex of the quadric, which is usually best for lighting with smooth shading.

---

void **gluQuadricTexture** (GLUquadricObj *_qobj_,
GLboolean _textureCoords_);

For the quadrics object _qobj_, _textureCoords_ is either GL_FALSE (the default) or GL_TRUE. If the value of _textureCoords_ is GL_TRUE, then texture coordinates are generated for the quadrics object. The manner in which the texture coordinates are generated varies, depending upon the type of quadrics object rendered.

Quadrics Primitives

The following routines actually generate the vertices and other data that constitute a quadrics object. In each case, _qobj_ refers to a quadrics object created by **gluNewQuadric()**.

---

void **gluSphere** (GLUquadricObj *_qobj_, GLdouble _radius_,
GLint _slices_, GLint _stacks_);

Draws a sphere of the given _radius_, centered around the origin, (0, 0, 0). The sphere is subdivided around the z axis into a number of _slices_ (similar to longitude) and along the z axis into a number of _stacks_ (latitude).

If texture coordinates are also generated by the quadrics facility, the t coordinate ranges from 0.0 at z = -radius to 1.0 at z = radius, with t increasing linearly along longitudinal lines. Meanwhile, s ranges from 0.0 at the $+y$ axis, to 0.25 at the $+x$ axis, to 0.5 at the $-y$ axis, to 0.75 at the $-x$ axis, and back to 1.0 at the $+y$ axis.

---

void **gluCylinder** (GLUquadricObj *_qobj_, GLdouble _baseRadius_,
GLdouble _topRadius_, GLdouble _height_,
GLint _slices_, GLint _stacks_);

Draws a cylinder oriented along the z axis, with the base of the cylinder at z = 0 and the top at z = height. Like a sphere, the cylinder is subdivided around the z axis into a number of _slices_ and along the z axis into a number of _stacks_. _baseRadius_ is the radius of the cylinder at z = 0.

topRadius is the radius of the cylinder at *z* = height. If *topRadius* is set to zero, then a cone is generated.

If texture coordinates are generated by the quadrics facility, then the *t* coordinate ranges linearly from 0.0 at *z* = 0 to 1.0 at *z* = *height*. The *s* texture coordinates are generated the same way as they are for a sphere.

Note: The cylinder is not closed at the top or bottom. The disks at the base and at the top are not drawn.

---

void **gluDisk** (GLUquadricObj *qobj*, GLdouble *innerRadius*,
 GLdouble *outerRadius*, GLint *slices*, GLint *rings*);

Draws a disk on the *z* = 0 plane, with a radius of *outerRadius* and a concentric circular hole with a radius of *innerRadius*. If *innerRadius* is 0, then no hole is created. The disk is subdivided around the *z* axis into a number of *slices* (like slices of pizza) and also about the *z* axis into a number of concentric *rings*.

With respect to orientation, the +*z* side of the disk is considered to be "outside"; that is, any normals generated point along the +*z* axis. Otherwise, the normals point along the -*z* axis.

If texture coordinates are generated by the quadrics facility, then the texture coordinates are generated linearly such that where R=*outerRadius*, the values for *s* and *t* at (R, 0, 0) is (1, 0.5), at (0, R, 0) they are (0.5, 1), at (-R, 0, 0) they are (0, 0.5), and at (0, -R, 0) they are (0.5, 0).

---

void **gluPartialDisk** (GLUquadricObj *qobj*, GLdouble *innerRadius*,
 GLdouble *outerRadius*, GLint *slices*, GLint *rings*,
 GLdouble *startAngle*, GLdouble *sweepAngle*);

Draws a partial disk on the *z* = 0 plane. A partial disk is similar to a complete disk, in terms of *outerRadius*, *innerRadius*, *slices*, and *rings*. The difference is that only a portion of a partial disk is drawn, starting from *startAngle* through *startAngle*+*sweepAngle* (where *startAngle* and *sweepAngle* are measured in degrees, where 0 degrees is along the +*y* axis, 90 degrees along the +*x* axis, 180 along the -*y* axis, and 270 along the -*x* axis).

A partial disk handles orientation and texture coordinates in the same way as a complete disk.

Note: For all quadrics objects, it's better to use the *Radius*, *height*, and similar arguments to scale them rather than the **glScale*()** command so that the unit-length normals that are generated don't have to be renormalized. Set the *rings* and *stacks* arguments to values other than one to force lighting calculations at a finer granularity, especially if the material specularity is high.

Example 11-4 shows each of the quadrics primitives being drawn, as well as the effects of different drawing styles.

Example 11-4   Quadrics Objects: quadric.c

```c
#include <GL/gl.h>
#include <GL/glu.h>
#include <GL/glut.h>
#include <stdio.h>
#include <stdlib.h>

GLuint startList;

void errorCallback(GLenum errorCode)
{
    const GLubyte *estring;

    estring = gluErrorString(errorCode);
    fprintf(stderr, "Quadric Error: %s\n", estring);
    exit(0);
}

void init(void)
{
    GLUquadricObj *qobj;
    GLfloat mat_ambient[] = { 0.5, 0.5, 0.5, 1.0 };
    GLfloat mat_specular[] = { 1.0, 1.0, 1.0, 1.0 };
    GLfloat mat_shininess[] = { 50.0 };
    GLfloat light_position[] = { 1.0, 1.0, 1.0, 0.0 };
    GLfloat model_ambient[] = { 0.5, 0.5, 0.5, 1.0 };

    glClearColor(0.0, 0.0, 0.0, 0.0);

    glMaterialfv(GL_FRONT, GL_AMBIENT, mat_ambient);
    glMaterialfv(GL_FRONT, GL_SPECULAR, mat_specular);
    glMaterialfv(GL_FRONT, GL_SHININESS, mat_shininess);
    glLightfv(GL_LIGHT0, GL_POSITION, light_position);
    glLightModelfv(GL_LIGHT_MODEL_AMBIENT, model_ambient);

    glEnable(GL_LIGHTING);
```

```
    glEnable(GL_LIGHT0);
    glEnable(GL_DEPTH_TEST);

/* Create 4 display lists, each with a different quadric object.
 * Different drawing styles and surface normal specifications
 * are demonstrated.
 */
    startList = glGenLists(4);
    qobj = gluNewQuadric();
    gluQuadricCallback(qobj, GLU_ERROR, errorCallback);

    gluQuadricDrawStyle(qobj, GLU_FILL); /* smooth shaded */
    gluQuadricNormals(qobj, GLU_SMOOTH);
    glNewList(startList, GL_COMPILE);
        gluSphere(qobj, 0.75, 15, 10);
    glEndList();

    gluQuadricDrawStyle(qobj, GLU_FILL); /* flat shaded */
    gluQuadricNormals(qobj, GLU_FLAT);
    glNewList(startList+1, GL_COMPILE);
        gluCylinder(qobj, 0.5, 0.3, 1.0, 15, 5);
    glEndList();

    gluQuadricDrawStyle(qobj, GLU_LINE); /* wireframe */
    gluQuadricNormals(qobj, GLU_NONE);
    glNewList(startList+2, GL_COMPILE);
        gluDisk(qobj, 0.25, 1.0, 20, 4);
    glEndList();

    gluQuadricDrawStyle(qobj, GLU_SILHOUETTE);
    gluQuadricNormals(qobj, GLU_NONE);
    glNewList(startList+3, GL_COMPILE);
        gluPartialDisk(qobj, 0.0, 1.0, 20, 4, 0.0, 225.0);
    glEndList();
}

void display(void)
{
    glClear (GL_COLOR_BUFFER_BIT | GL_DEPTH_BUFFER_BIT);
    glPushMatrix();

    glEnable(GL_LIGHTING);
    glShadeModel (GL_SMOOTH);
    glTranslatef(-1.0, -1.0, 0.0);
    glCallList(startList);

    glShadeModel (GL_FLAT);
```

```
   glTranslatef(0.0, 2.0, 0.0);
   glPushMatrix();
   glRotatef(300.0, 1.0, 0.0, 0.0);
   glCallList(startList+1);
   glPopMatrix();

   glDisable(GL_LIGHTING);
   glColor3f(0.0, 1.0, 1.0);
   glTranslatef(2.0, -2.0, 0.0);
   glCallList(startList+2);

   glColor3f(1.0, 1.0, 0.0);
   glTranslatef(0.0, 2.0, 0.0);
   glCallList(startList+3);

   glPopMatrix();
   glFlush();
}

void reshape (int w, int h)
{
   glViewport(0, 0, (GLsizei) w, (GLsizei) h);
   glMatrixMode(GL_PROJECTION);
   glLoadIdentity();
   if (w <= h)
      glOrtho(-2.5, 2.5, -2.5*(GLfloat)h/(GLfloat)w,
         2.5*(GLfloat)h/(GLfloat)w, -10.0, 10.0);
   else
      glOrtho(-2.5*(GLfloat)w/(GLfloat)h,
         2.5*(GLfloat)w/(GLfloat)h, -2.5, 2.5, -10.0, 10.0);
   glMatrixMode(GL_MODELVIEW);
   glLoadIdentity();
}

void keyboard(unsigned char key, int x, int y)
{
   switch (key) {
      case 27:
         exit(0);
         break;
   }
}

int main(int argc, char** argv)
{
   glutInit(&argc, argv);
   glutInitDisplayMode(GLUT_SINGLE | GLUT_RGB | GLUT_DEPTH);
```

```
        glutInitWindowSize(500, 500);
        glutInitWindowPosition(100, 100);
        glutCreateWindow(argv[0]);
        init();
        glutDisplayFunc(display);
        glutReshapeFunc(reshape);
        glutKeyboardFunc(keyboard);
        glutMainLoop();
        return 0;
    }
```

Chapter 12

Evaluators and NURBS

Chapter Objectives

Advanced

After reading this chapter, you'll be able to do the following:

- Use OpenGL evaluator commands to draw basic curves and surfaces

- Use the GLU's higher-level NURBS facility to draw more complex curves and surfaces

Note that this chapter presumes a number of prerequisites; they're listed in "Prerequisites" on page 439.

At the lowest level, graphics hardware draws points, line segments, and polygons, which are usually triangles and quadrilaterals. Smooth curves and surfaces are drawn by approximating them with large numbers of small line segments or polygons. However, many useful curves and surfaces can be described mathematically by a small number of parameters such as a few *control points*. Saving the 16 control points for a surface requires much less storage than saving 1000 triangles together with the normal vector information at each vertex. In addition, the 1000 triangles only approximate the true surface, but the control points accurately describe the real surface.

Evaluators provide a way to specify points on a curve or surface (or part of one) using only the control points. The curve or surface can then be rendered at any precision. In addition, normal vectors can be calculated for surfaces automatically. You can use the points generated by an evaluator in many ways—to draw dots where the surface would be, to draw a wireframe version of the surface, or to draw a fully lighted, shaded, and even textured version.

You can use evaluators to describe any polynomial or rational polynomial splines or surfaces of any degree. These include almost all splines and spline surfaces in use today, including B-splines, NURBS (Non-Uniform Rational B-Spline) surfaces, Bézier curves and surfaces, and Hermite splines. Since evaluators provide only a low-level description of the points on a curve or surface, they're typically used underneath utility libraries that provide a higher-level interface to the programmer. The GLU's NURBS facility is such a higher-level interface—the NURBS routines encapsulate lots of complicated code. Much of the final rendering is done with evaluators, but for some conditions (trimming curves, for example) the NURBS routines use planar polygons for rendering.

This chapter contains the following major sections.

- "Prerequisites" on page 439 discusses what knowledge is assumed for this chapter. It also gives several references where you can obtain this information.

- "Evaluators" on page 440 explains how evaluators work and how to control them using the appropriate OpenGL commands.

- "The GLU NURBS Interface" on page 455 describes the GLU routines for creating NURBS surfaces.

Prerequisites

Evaluators make splines and surfaces that are based on a Bézier (or Bernstein) basis. The defining formulas for the functions in this basis are given in this chapter, but the discussion doesn't include derivations or even lists of all their interesting mathematical properties. If you want to use evaluators to draw curves and surfaces using other bases, you must know how to convert your basis to a Bézier basis. In addition, when you render a Bézier surface or part of it using evaluators, you need to determine the granularity of your subdivision. Your decision needs to take into account the trade-off between high-quality (highly subdivided) images and high speed. Determining an appropriate subdivision strategy can be quite complicated—too complicated to be discussed here.

Similarly, a complete discussion of NURBS is beyond the scope of this book. The GLU NURBS interface is documented here, and programming examples are provided for readers who already understand the subject. In what follows, you already should know about NURBS control points, knot sequences, and trimming curves.

If you lack some of these prerequisites, the following references will help.

- Farin, Gerald E., *Curves and Surfaces for Computer-Aided Geometric Design, Fourth Edition*. San Diego, CA: Academic Press, 1996.

- Farin, Gerald E., *NURB Curves and Surfaces: from Projective Geometry to Practical Use*. Wellesley, MA: A. K. Peters Ltd., 1995.

- Farin, Gerald E., editor, *NURBS for Curve and Surface Design*, Society for Industrial and Applied Mathematics, Philadelphia, PA, 1991.

- Hoschek, Josef and Dieter Lasser, *Fundamentals of Computer Aided Geometric Design*. Wellesley, MA: A. K. Peters Ltd., 1993.

- Piegl, Les and Wayne Tiller, *The NURBS Book*. New York, NY: Springer-Verlag, 1995.

Note: Some terms used in this chapter might have slightly different meanings in other books on spline curves and surfaces, since there isn't total agreement among the practitioners of this art. Generally, the OpenGL meanings are a bit more restrictive. For example, OpenGL evaluators always use Bézier bases; in other contexts, evaluators might refer to the same concept, but with an arbitrary basis.

Evaluators

A Bézier curve is a vector-valued function of one variable

$$C(u) = [X(u) \quad Y(u) \quad Z(u)]$$

where u varies in some domain (say [0,1]). A Bézier surface patch is a vector-valued function of two variables

$$S(u,v) = [X(u,v) \quad Y(u,v) \quad Z(u,v)]$$

where u and v can both vary in some domain. The range isn't necessarily three-dimensional as shown here. You might want two-dimensional output for curves on a plane or texture coordinates, or you might want four-dimensional output to specify RGBA information. Even one-dimensional output may make sense for gray levels.

For each u (or u and v, in the case of a surface), the formula for C() (or S()) calculates a point on the curve (or surface). To use an evaluator, first define the function C() or S(), enable it, and then use the **glEvalCoord1()** or **glEvalCoord2()** command instead of **glVertex*()**. This way, the curve or surface vertices can be used like any other vertices—to form points or lines, for example. In addition, other commands automatically generate series of vertices that produce a regular mesh uniformly spaced in u (or in u and v). One- and two-dimensional evaluators are similar, but the description is somewhat simpler in one dimension, so that case is discussed first.

One-Dimensional Evaluators

This section presents an example of using one-dimensional evaluators to draw a curve. It then describes the commands and equations that control evaluators.

One-Dimensional Example: A Simple Bézier Curve

The program shown in Example 12-1 draws a cubic Bézier curve using four control points, as shown in Figure 12-1.

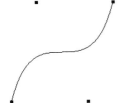

Figure 12-1   Bézier Curve

Example 12-1   Bézier Curve with Four Control Points: bezcurve.c

```
#include <GL/gl.h>
#include <GL/glu.h>
#include <stdlib.h>
#include <GL/glut.h>

GLfloat ctrlpoints[4][3] = {
        { -4.0, -4.0, 0.0}, { -2.0, 4.0, 0.0},
        {2.0, -4.0, 0.0}, {4.0, 4.0, 0.0}};

void init(void)
{
   glClearColor(0.0, 0.0, 0.0, 0.0);
   glShadeModel(GL_FLAT);
   glMap1f(GL_MAP1_VERTEX_3, 0.0, 1.0, 3, 4, &ctrlpoints[0][0]);
   glEnable(GL_MAP1_VERTEX_3);
}

void display(void)
{
   int i;

   glClear(GL_COLOR_BUFFER_BIT);
   glColor3f(1.0, 1.0, 1.0);
   glBegin(GL_LINE_STRIP);
      for (i = 0; i <= 30; i++)
         glEvalCoord1f((GLfloat) i/30.0);
   glEnd();
   /* The following code displays the control points as dots. */
   glPointSize(5.0);
   glColor3f(1.0, 1.0, 0.0);
   glBegin(GL_POINTS);
      for (i = 0; i < 4; i++)
         glVertex3fv(&ctrlpoints[i][0]);
```

```
        glEnd();
        glFlush();
}

void reshape(int w, int h)
{
    glViewport(0, 0, (GLsizei) w, (GLsizei) h);
    glMatrixMode(GL_PROJECTION);
    glLoadIdentity();
    if (w <= h)
        glOrtho(-5.0, 5.0, -5.0*(GLfloat)h/(GLfloat)w,
                5.0*(GLfloat)h/(GLfloat)w, -5.0, 5.0);
    else
        glOrtho(-5.0*(GLfloat)w/(GLfloat)h,
                5.0*(GLfloat)w/(GLfloat)h, -5.0, 5.0, -5.0, 5.0);
    glMatrixMode(GL_MODELVIEW);
    glLoadIdentity();
}

int main(int argc, char** argv)
{
    glutInit(&argc, argv);
    glutInitDisplayMode (GLUT_SINGLE | GLUT_RGB);
    glutInitWindowSize (500, 500);
    glutInitWindowPosition (100, 100);
    glutCreateWindow (argv[0]);
    init ();
    glutDisplayFunc(display);
    glutReshapeFunc(reshape);
    glutMainLoop();
    return 0;
}
```

A cubic Bézier curve is described by four control points, which appear in this example in the *ctrlpoints[][]* array. This array is one of the arguments to **glMap1f()**. All the arguments for this command are as follows:

GL_MAP1_VERTEX_3

> Three-dimensional control points are provided and three-dimensional vertices are produced

0.0
> Low value of parameter u

1.0
> High value of parameter u

3
> The number of floating-point values to advance in the data between one control point and the next

4	The order of the spline, which is the degree+1; in this case, the degree is 3 (since this is a cubic curve)
&ctrlpoints[0][0]	Pointer to the first control point's data

Note that the second and third arguments control the parameterization of the curve—as the variable u ranges from 0.0 to 1.0, the curve goes from one end to the other. The call to **glEnable()** enables the one-dimensional evaluator for three-dimensional vertices.

The curve is drawn in the routine **display()** between the **glBegin()** and **glEnd()** calls. Since the evaluator is enabled, the command **glEvalCoord1f()** is just like issuing a **glVertex()** command with the coordinates of a vertex on the curve corresponding to the input parameter u.

Defining and Evaluating a One-Dimensional Evaluator

The Bernstein polynomial of degree n (or order $n+1$) is given by

$$B_i^n(u) = \binom{n}{i} u^i (1-u)^{n-i}$$

If P_i represents a set of control points (one-, two-, three-, or even four-dimensional), then the equation

$$C(u) = \sum_{i=0}^{n} B_i^n(u) P_i$$

represents a Bézier curve as u varies from 0.0 to 1.0. To represent the same curve but allowing u to vary between u_1 and u_2 instead of 0.0 and 1.0, evaluate

$$C\left(\frac{u - u_1}{u_2 - u_1}\right)$$

The command **glMap1()** defines a one-dimensional evaluator that uses these equations.

---

void **glMap1**{fd}(GLenum *target*, TYPE *u1*, TYPE *u2*, GLint *stride*, GLint *order*, const TYPE **points*);

Defines a one-dimensional evaluator. The *target* parameter specifies what the control points represent, as shown in Table 12-1, and therefore how many values need to be supplied in *points*. The points can represent vertices, RGBA color data, normal vectors, or texture coordinates. For example, with GL_MAP1_COLOR_4, the evaluator generates color data along a curve in four-dimensional (RGBA) color space. You also use the parameter values listed in Table 12-1 to enable each defined evaluator before you invoke it. Pass the appropriate value to **glEnable()** or **glDisable()** to enable or disable the evaluator.

The second two parameters for **glMap1*()**, *u1* and *u2*, indicate the range for the variable *u*. The variable *stride* is the number of single- or double-precision values (as appropriate) in each block of storage. Thus, it's an offset value between the beginning of one control point and the beginning of the next.

The *order* is the degree plus one, and it should agree with the number of control points. The *points* parameter points to the first coordinate of the first control point. Using the example data structure for **glMap1*()**, use the following for *points*:

```
(GLfloat *) (&ctlpoints[0].x)
```

Parameter	Meaning
GL_MAP1_VERTEX_3	x, y, z vertex coordinates
GL_MAP1_VERTEX_4	x, y, z, w vertex coordinates
GL_MAP1_INDEX	color index
GL_MAP1_COLOR_4	R, G, B, A
GL_MAP1_NORMAL	normal coordinates
GL_MAP1_TEXTURE_COORD_1	s texture coordinates
GL_MAP1_TEXTURE_COORD_2	s, t texture coordinates
GL_MAP1_TEXTURE_COORD_3	s, t, r texture coordinates
GL_MAP1_TEXTURE_COORD_4	s, t, r, q texture coordinates

Table 12-1   Types of Control Points for glMap1*()

More than one evaluator can be evaluated at a time. If you have both a GL_MAP1_VERTEX_3 and a GL_MAP1_COLOR_4 evaluator defined and enabled, for example, then calls to **glEvalCoord1()** generate both a position and a color. Only one of the vertex evaluators can be enabled at a time, although you might have defined both of them. Similarly, only one of the texture evaluators can be active. Other than that, however, evaluators can be used to generate any combination of vertex, normal, color, and texture-coordinate data. If more than one evaluator of the same type is defined and enabled, the one of highest dimension is used.

Use **glEvalCoord1*()** to evaluate a defined and enabled one-dimensional map.

---

void **glEvalCoord1**{fd}(*TYPE u*);
void **glEvalCoord1**{fd}**v**(*TYPE *u*);

Causes evaluation of the enabled one-dimensional maps. The argument *u* is the value (or a pointer to the value, in the vector version of the command) of the domain coordinate.

For evaluated vertices, values for color, color index, normal vectors, and texture coordinates are generated by evaluation. Calls to **glEvalCoord*()** do not use the current values for color, color index, normal vectors, and texture coordinates. **glEvalCoord*()** also leaves those values unchanged.

Defining Evenly Spaced Coordinate Values in One Dimension

You can use **glEvalCoord1()** with any values for *u*, but by far the most common use is with evenly spaced values, as shown previously in Example 12-1. To obtain evenly spaced values, define a one-dimensional grid using **glMapGrid1*()** and then apply it using **glEvalMesh1()**.

---

void **glMapGrid1**{fd}(GLint *n*, *TYPE u1*, *TYPE u2*);

Defines a grid that goes from *u1* to *u2* in *n* steps, which are evenly spaced.

---

void **glEvalMesh1**(GLenum *mode*, GLint *p1*, GLint *p2*);

Applies the currently defined map grid to all enabled evaluators. The *mode* can be either GL_POINT or GL_LINE, depending on whether you want to draw points or a connected line along the curve. The call has exactly the same effect as issuing a **glEvalCoord1()** for each of the steps between and including *p1* and *p2*, where $0 <= p1, p2 <= n$. Programmatically, it's equivalent to the following:

```
glBegin(GL_POINTS);      /* OR glBegin(GL_LINE_STRIP); */
for (i = p1; i <= p2; i++)
    glEvalCoord1(u1 + i*(u2-u1)/n);
glEnd();
```

except that if $i = 0$ or $i = n$, then **glEvalCoord1()** is called with exactly $u1$ or $u2$ as its parameter.

Two-Dimensional Evaluators

In two dimensions, everything is similar to the one-dimensional case, except that all the commands must take two parameters, u and v, into account. Points, colors, normals, or texture coordinates must be supplied over a surface instead of a curve. Mathematically, the definition of a Bézier surface patch is given by

$$S(u, v) = \sum_{i=0}^{n} \sum_{j=0}^{m} B_i^n(u) B_j^m(v) P_{ij}$$

where P_{ij} are a set of $m*n$ control points, and the B_i are the same Bernstein polynomials for one dimension. As before, the P_{ij} can represent vertices, normals, colors, or texture coordinates.

The procedure to use two-dimensional evaluators is similar to the procedure for one dimension.

1. Define the evaluator(s) with **glMap2*()**.

2. Enable them by passing the appropriate value to **glEnable()**.

3. Invoke them either by calling **glEvalCoord2()** between a **glBegin()** and **glEnd()** pair or by specifying and then applying a mesh with **glMapGrid2()** and **glEvalMesh2()**.

Defining and Evaluating a Two-Dimensional Evaluator

Use **glMap2*()** and **glEvalCoord2*()** to define and then invoke a two-dimensional evaluator.

---

void **glMap2{fd}**(GLenum *target*, TYPE *u1*, TYPE *u2*, GLint *ustride*,
          GLint *uorder*, TYPE *v1*, TYPE *v2*, GLint *vstride*,
          GLint *vorder*, TYPE *points*);

The *target* parameter can have any of the values in Table 12-1, except that the string MAP1 is replaced with MAP2. As before, these values are also used with **glEnable()** to enable the corresponding evaluator. Minimum and maximum values for both u and v are provided as $u1$, $u2$, $v1$, and $v2$. The parameters *ustride* and *vstride* indicate the number of single- or double-precision values (as appropriate) between independent settings for these values, allowing users to select a subrectangle of control points out of a much larger array. For example, if the data appears in the form

```
GLfloat ctlpoints[100][100][3];
```

and you want to use the 4x4 subset beginning at ctlpoints[20][30], choose *ustride* to be 100*3 and *vstride* to be 3. The starting point, *points*, should be set to &ctlpoints[20][30][0]. Finally, the order parameters, *uorder* and *vorder*, can be different, allowing patches that are cubic in one direction and quadratic in the other, for example.

---

void **glEvalCoord2**{fd}(*TYPE u, TYPE v*);
void **glEvalCoord2**{fd}**v**(*TYPE *values*);

Causes evaluation of the enabled two-dimensional maps. The arguments *u* and *v* are the values (or a pointer to the *values* u and v, in the vector version of the command) for the domain coordinates. If either of the vertex evaluators is enabled (GL_MAP2_VERTEX_3 or GL_MAP2_VERTEX_4), then the normal to the surface is computed analytically. This normal is associated with the generated vertex if automatic normal generation has been enabled by passing GL_AUTO_NORMAL to **glEnable**(). If it's disabled, the corresponding enabled normal map is used to produce a normal. If no such map exists, the current normal is used.

Two-Dimensional Example: A Bézier Surface

Example 12-2 draws a wireframe Bézier surface using evaluators, as shown in Figure 12-2. In this example, the surface is drawn with nine curved lines in each direction. Each curve is drawn as 30 segments. To get the whole program, add the **reshape**() and **main**() routines from Example 12-1.

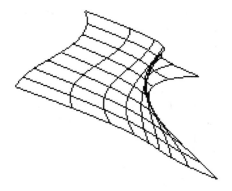

Figure 12-2   Bézier Surface

Example 12-2   Bézier Surface: bezsurf.c

```
#include <GL/gl.h>
#include <GL/glu.h>
#include <stdlib.h>
#include <GL/glut.h>

GLfloat ctrlpoints[4][4][3] = {
    {{-1.5, -1.5, 4.0}, {-0.5, -1.5, 2.0},
     {0.5, -1.5, -1.0}, {1.5, -1.5, 2.0}},
    {{-1.5, -0.5, 1.0}, {-0.5, -0.5, 3.0},
     {0.5, -0.5, 0.0}, {1.5, -0.5, -1.0}},
    {{-1.5, 0.5, 4.0}, {-0.5, 0.5, 0.0},
     {0.5, 0.5, 3.0}, {1.5, 0.5, 4.0}},
    {{-1.5, 1.5, -2.0}, {-0.5, 1.5, -2.0},
     {0.5, 1.5, 0.0}, {1.5, 1.5, -1.0}}
};

void display(void)
{
    int i, j;

    glClear(GL_COLOR_BUFFER_BIT | GL_DEPTH_BUFFER_BIT);
    glColor3f(1.0, 1.0, 1.0);
    glPushMatrix ();
    glRotatef(85.0, 1.0, 1.0, 1.0);
    for (j = 0; j <= 8; j++) {
        glBegin(GL_LINE_STRIP);
        for (i = 0; i <= 30; i++)
            glEvalCoord2f((GLfloat)i/30.0, (GLfloat)j/8.0);
        glEnd();
```

```
        glBegin(GL_LINE_STRIP);
        for (i = 0; i <= 30; i++)
            glEvalCoord2f((GLfloat)j/8.0, (GLfloat)i/30.0);
        glEnd();
    }
    glPopMatrix ();
    glFlush();
}

void init(void)
{
    glClearColor (0.0, 0.0, 0.0, 0.0);
    glMap2f(GL_MAP2_VERTEX_3, 0, 1, 3, 4,
            0, 1, 12, 4, &ctrlpoints[0][0][0]);
    glEnable(GL_MAP2_VERTEX_3);
    glMapGrid2f(20, 0.0, 1.0, 20, 0.0, 1.0);
    glEnable(GL_DEPTH_TEST);
    glShadeModel(GL_FLAT);
}
```

Defining Evenly Spaced Coordinate Values in Two Dimensions

In two dimensions, the **glMapGrid2*()** and **glEvalMesh2()** commands are similar to the one-dimensional versions, except that both *u* and *v* information must be included.

---

void **glMapGrid2**{fd}(GLint *nu*, *TYPE u1*, *TYPE u2*,
          GLint *nv*, *TYPE v1*, *TYPE v2*);
void **glEvalMesh2**(GLenum *mode*, GLint *i1*, GLint *i2*, GLint *j1*, GLint *j2*);

Defines a two-dimensional map grid that goes from *u1* to *u2* in *nu* evenly spaced steps, from *v1* to *v2* in *nv* steps (**glMapGrid2*()**), and then applies this grid to all enabled evaluators (**glEvalMesh2()**). The only significant difference from the one-dimensional versions of these two commands is that in **glEvalMesh2()** the *mode* parameter can be GL_FILL as well as GL_POINT or GL_LINE. GL_FILL generates filled polygons using the quad-mesh primitive. Stated precisely, **glEvalMesh2()** is nearly equivalent to one of the following three code fragments. (It's nearly equivalent because when *i* is equal to *nu* or *j* to *nv*, the parameter is exactly equal to *u2* or *v2*, not to *u1+nu*(u2–u1)/nu*, which might be slightly different due to round-off error.)

```
glBegin(GL_POINTS);                          /* mode == GL_POINT */
for (i = nu1; i <= nu2; i++)
    for (j = nv1; j <= nv2; j++)
        glEvalCoord2(u1 + i*(u2-u1)/nu, v1+j*(v2-v1)/nv);
glEnd();
```

or

```
for (i = nu1; i <= nu2; i++) {      /* mode == GL_LINE */
    glBegin(GL_LINES);
        for (j = nv1; j <= nv2; j++)
            glEvalCoord2(u1 + i*(u2-u1)/nu, v1+j*(v2-v1)/nv);
    glEnd();
}
for (j = nv1; j <= nv2; j++) {
    glBegin(GL_LINES);
    for (i = nu1; i <= nu2; i++)
        glEvalCoord2(u1 + i*(u2-u1)/nu, v1+j*(v2-v1)/nv);
    glEnd();
}
```

or

```
for (i = nu1; i < nu2; i++) {       /* mode == GL_FILL */
    glBegin(GL_QUAD_STRIP);
    for (j = nv1; j <= nv2; j++) {
        glEvalCoord2(u1 + i*(u2-u1)/nu, v1+j*(v2-v1)/nv);
        glEvalCoord2(u1 + (i+1)*(u2-u1)/nu, v1+j*(v2-v1)/nv);
    glEnd();
}
```

Example 12-3 shows the differences necessary to draw the same Bézier
surface as Example 12-2, but using **glMapGrid2()** and **glEvalMesh2()** to
subdivide the square domain into a uniform 8x8 grid. This program also
adds lighting and shading, as shown in Figure 12-3.

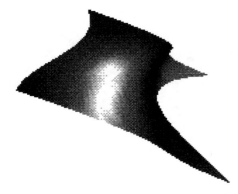

Figure 12-3   Lit, Shaded Bézier Surface Drawn with a Mesh

Example 12-3   Lit, Shaded Bézier Surface Using a Mesh: bezmesh.c

```
void initlights(void)
{
   GLfloat ambient[] = {0.2, 0.2, 0.2, 1.0};
   GLfloat position[] = {0.0, 0.0, 2.0, 1.0};
   GLfloat mat_diffuse[] = {0.6, 0.6, 0.6, 1.0};
   GLfloat mat_specular[] = {1.0, 1.0, 1.0, 1.0};
   GLfloat mat_shininess[] = {50.0};

   glEnable(GL_LIGHTING);
   glEnable(GL_LIGHT0);

   glLightfv(GL_LIGHT0, GL_AMBIENT, ambient);
   glLightfv(GL_LIGHT0, GL_POSITION, position);

   glMaterialfv(GL_FRONT, GL_DIFFUSE, mat_diffuse);
   glMaterialfv(GL_FRONT, GL_SPECULAR, mat_specular);
   glMaterialfv(GL_FRONT, GL_SHININESS, mat_shininess);
}

void display(void)
{
   glClear(GL_COLOR_BUFFER_BIT | GL_DEPTH_BUFFER_BIT);
   glPushMatrix();
   glRotatef(85.0, 1.0, 1.0, 1.0);
   glEvalMesh2(GL_FILL, 0, 20, 0, 20);
   glPopMatrix();
   glFlush();
}
```

```
void init(void)
{
    glClearColor(0.0, 0.0, 0.0, 0.0);
    glEnable(GL_DEPTH_TEST);
    glMap2f(GL_MAP2_VERTEX_3, 0, 1, 3, 4,
            0, 1, 12, 4, &ctrlpoints[0][0][0]);
    glEnable(GL_MAP2_VERTEX_3);
    glEnable(GL_AUTO_NORMAL);
    glMapGrid2f(20, 0.0, 1.0, 20, 0.0, 1.0);
    initlights();
}
```

Using Evaluators for Textures

Example 12-4 enables two evaluators at the same time: The first generates three-dimensional points on the same Bézier surface as Example 12-3, and the second generates texture coordinates. In this case, the texture coordinates are the same as the *u* and *v* coordinates of the surface, but a special flat Bézier patch must be created to do this.

The flat patch is defined over a square with corners at (0, 0), (0, 1), (1, 0), and (1, 1); it generates (0, 0) at corner (0, 0), (0, 1) at corner (0, 1), and so on. Since it's of order two (linear degree plus one), evaluating this texture at the point (*u*, *v*) generates texture coordinates (*s*, *t*). It's enabled at the same time as the vertex evaluator, so both take effect when the surface is drawn. (See Plate 19.) If you want the texture to repeat three times in each direction, change every 1.0 in the array *texpts[][][]* to 3.0. Since the texture wraps in this example, the surface is rendered with nine copies of the texture map.

Example 12-4   Using Evaluators for Textures: texturesurf.c

```
#include <GL/gl.h>
#include <GL/glu.h>
#include <stdlib.h>
#include <GL/glut.h>
#include <math.h>

GLfloat ctrlpoints[4][4][3] = {
    {{ -1.5, -1.5, 4.0}, { -0.5, -1.5, 2.0},
     {0.5, -1.5, -1.0}, {1.5, -1.5, 2.0}},
    {{ -1.5, -0.5, 1.0}, { -0.5, -0.5, 3.0},
     {0.5, -0.5, 0.0}, {1.5, -0.5, -1.0}},
    {{ -1.5, 0.5, 4.0}, { -0.5, 0.5, 0.0},
```

```
         {0.5, 0.5, 3.0}, {1.5, 0.5, 4.0}},
      {{ -1.5, 1.5, -2.0}, { -0.5, 1.5, -2.0},
       {0.5, 1.5, 0.0}, {1.5, 1.5, -1.0}}
};
GLfloat texpts[2][2][2] = {{{0.0, 0.0}, {0.0, 1.0}},
                           {{1.0, 0.0}, {1.0, 1.0}}};

void display(void)
{
   glClear(GL_COLOR_BUFFER_BIT | GL_DEPTH_BUFFER_BIT);
   glColor3f(1.0, 1.0, 1.0);
   glEvalMesh2(GL_FILL, 0, 20, 0, 20);
   glFlush();
}
#define imageWidth 64
#define imageHeight 64
GLubyte image[3*imageWidth*imageHeight];

void makeImage(void)
{
   int i, j;
   float ti, tj;

   for (i = 0; i < imageWidth; i++) {
      ti = 2.0*3.14159265*i/imageWidth;
      for (j = 0; j < imageHeight; j++) {
         tj = 2.0*3.14159265*j/imageHeight;
         image[3*(imageHeight*i+j)] =
               (GLubyte) 127*(1.0+sin(ti));
         image[3*(imageHeight*i+j)+1] =
               (GLubyte) 127*(1.0+cos(2*tj));
         image[3*(imageHeight*i+j)+2] =
               (GLubyte) 127*(1.0+cos(ti+tj));
      }
   }
}

void init(void)
{
   glMap2f(GL_MAP2_VERTEX_3, 0, 1, 3, 4,
           0, 1, 12, 4, &ctrlpoints[0][0][0]);
   glMap2f(GL_MAP2_TEXTURE_COORD_2, 0, 1, 2, 2,
           0, 1, 4, 2, &texpts[0][0][0]);
   glEnable(GL_MAP2_TEXTURE_COORD_2);
   glEnable(GL_MAP2_VERTEX_3);
   glMapGrid2f(20, 0.0, 1.0, 20, 0.0, 1.0);
   makeImage();
```

```
        glTexEnvf(GL_TEXTURE_ENV, GL_TEXTURE_ENV_MODE, GL_DECAL);
        glTexParameteri(GL_TEXTURE_2D, GL_TEXTURE_WRAP_S, GL_REPEAT);
        glTexParameteri(GL_TEXTURE_2D, GL_TEXTURE_WRAP_T, GL_REPEAT);
        glTexParameteri(GL_TEXTURE_2D, GL_TEXTURE_MAG_FILTER,
                    GL_NEAREST);
        glTexParameteri(GL_TEXTURE_2D, GL_TEXTURE_MIN_FILTER,
                    GL_NEAREST);
        glTexImage2D(GL_TEXTURE_2D, 0, 3, imageWidth, imageHeight, 0,
                    GL_RGB, GL_UNSIGNED_BYTE, image);
        glEnable(GL_TEXTURE_2D);
        glEnable(GL_DEPTH_TEST);
        glShadeModel (GL_FLAT);
    }

    void reshape(int w, int h)
    {
        glViewport(0, 0, (GLsizei) w, (GLsizei) h);
        glMatrixMode(GL_PROJECTION);
        glLoadIdentity();
        if (w <= h)
            glOrtho(-4.0, 4.0, -4.0*(GLfloat)h/(GLfloat)w,
                    4.0*(GLfloat)h/(GLfloat)w, -4.0, 4.0);
        else
            glOrtho(-4.0*(GLfloat)w/(GLfloat)h,
                    4.0*(GLfloat)w/(GLfloat)h, -4.0, 4.0, -4.0, 4.0);
        glMatrixMode(GL_MODELVIEW);
        glLoadIdentity();
        glRotatef(85.0, 1.0, 1.0, 1.0);
    }

    int main(int argc, char** argv)
    {
        glutInit(&argc, argv);
        glutInitDisplayMode (GLUT_SINGLE | GLUT_RGB | GLUT_DEPTH);
        glutInitWindowSize (500, 500);
        glutInitWindowPosition (100, 100);
        glutCreateWindow (argv[0]);
        init ();
        glutDisplayFunc(display);
        glutReshapeFunc(reshape);
        glutMainLoop();
        return 0;
    }
```

The GLU NURBS Interface

Although evaluators are the only OpenGL primitive available to draw curves and surfaces directly, and even though they can be implemented very efficiently in hardware, they're often accessed by applications through higher-level libraries. The GLU provides a NURBS (Non-Uniform Rational B-Spline) interface built on top of the OpenGL evaluator commands.

A Simple NURBS Example

If you understand NURBS, writing OpenGL code to manipulate NURBS curves and surfaces is relatively easy, even with lighting and texture mapping. Follow these steps to draw NURBS curves or untrimmed NURBS surfaces. (See "Trim a NURBS Surface" on page 464 for information about trimmed surfaces.)

1. If you intend to use lighting with a NURBS surface, call **glEnable()** with GL_AUTO_NORMAL to automatically generate surface normals. (Or you can calculate your own.)

2. Use **gluNewNurbsRenderer()** to create a pointer to a NURBS object, which is referred to when creating your NURBS curve or surface.

3. If desired, call **gluNurbsProperty()** to choose rendering values, such as the maximum size of lines or polygons that are used to render your NURBS object.

4. Call **gluNurbsCallback()** if you want to be notified when an error is encountered. (Error checking may slightly degrade performance but is still highly recommended.)

5. Start your curve or surface by calling **gluBeginCurve()** or **gluBeginSurface()**.

6. Generate and render your curve or surface. Call **gluNurbsCurve()** or **gluNurbsSurface()** at least once with the control points (rational or nonrational), knot sequence, and order of the polynomial basis function for your NURBS object. You might call these functions additional times to specify surface normals and/or texture coordinates.

7. Call **gluEndCurve()** or **gluEndSurface()** to complete the curve or surface.

Example 12-5 renders a NURBS surface in the shape of a symmetrical hill with control points ranging from –3.0 to 3.0. The basis function is a cubic

B-spline, but the knot sequence is nonuniform, with a multiplicity of 4 at each endpoint, causing the basis function to behave like a Bézier curve in each direction. The surface is lighted, with a dark gray diffuse reflection and white specular highlights. Figure 12-4 shows the surface as a lit wireframe.

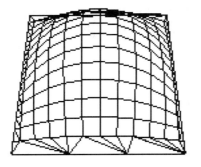 

Figure 12-4   NURBS Surface

Example 12-5   NURBS Surface: surface.c

```
#include <GL/gl.h>
#include <GL/glu.h>
#include <GL/glut.h>
#include <stdlib.h>
#include <stdio.h>

GLfloat ctlpoints[4][4][3];
int showPoints = 0;

GLUnurbsObj *theNurb;

void init_surface(void)
{
    int u, v;
    for (u = 0; u < 4; u++) {
        for (v = 0; v < 4; v++) {
            ctlpoints[u][v][0] = 2.0*((GLfloat)u - 1.5);
            ctlpoints[u][v][1] = 2.0*((GLfloat)v - 1.5);

            if ( (u == 1 || u == 2) && (v == 1 || v == 2))
                ctlpoints[u][v][2] = 3.0;
            else
                ctlpoints[u][v][2] = -3.0;
        }
    }
}
```

```
void nurbsError(GLenum errorCode)
{
    const GLubyte *estring;

    estring = gluErrorString(errorCode);
    fprintf (stderr, "Nurbs Error: %s\n", estring);
    exit (0);
}

void init(void)
{
    GLfloat mat_diffuse[] = { 0.7, 0.7, 0.7, 1.0 };
    GLfloat mat_specular[] = { 1.0, 1.0, 1.0, 1.0 };
    GLfloat mat_shininess[] = { 100.0 };

    glClearColor (0.0, 0.0, 0.0, 0.0);
    glMaterialfv(GL_FRONT, GL_DIFFUSE, mat_diffuse);
    glMaterialfv(GL_FRONT, GL_SPECULAR, mat_specular);
    glMaterialfv(GL_FRONT, GL_SHININESS, mat_shininess);

    glEnable(GL_LIGHTING);
    glEnable(GL_LIGHT0);
    glEnable(GL_DEPTH_TEST);
    glEnable(GL_AUTO_NORMAL);
    glEnable(GL_NORMALIZE);

    init_surface();

    theNurb = gluNewNurbsRenderer();
    gluNurbsProperty(theNurb, GLU_SAMPLING_TOLERANCE, 25.0);
    gluNurbsProperty(theNurb, GLU_DISPLAY_MODE, GLU_FILL);
    gluNurbsCallback(theNurb, GLU_ERROR,
                    (GLvoid (*)()) nurbsError);
}

void display(void)
{
    GLfloat knots[8] = {0.0, 0.0, 0.0, 0.0, 1.0, 1.0, 1.0, 1.0};
    int i, j;

    glClear(GL_COLOR_BUFFER_BIT | GL_DEPTH_BUFFER_BIT);

    glPushMatrix();
    glRotatef(330.0, 1.,0.,0.);
    glScalef (0.5, 0.5, 0.5);

    gluBeginSurface(theNurb);
```

```
        gluNurbsSurface(theNurb,
                   8, knots, 8, knots,
                   4 * 3, 3, &ctlpoints[0][0][0],
                   4, 4, GL_MAP2_VERTEX_3);
        gluEndSurface(theNurb);

        if (showPoints) {
           glPointSize(5.0);
           glDisable(GL_LIGHTING);
           glColor3f(1.0, 1.0, 0.0);
           glBegin(GL_POINTS);
           for (i = 0; i < 4; i++) {
              for (j = 0; j < 4; j++) {
                 glVertex3f(ctlpoints[i][j][0],
                         ctlpoints[i][j][1], ctlpoints[i][j][2]);
              }
           }
           glEnd();
           glEnable(GL_LIGHTING);
        }
        glPopMatrix();
        glFlush();
}

void reshape(int w, int h)
{
    glViewport(0, 0, (GLsizei) w, (GLsizei) h);
    glMatrixMode(GL_PROJECTION);
    glLoadIdentity();
    gluPerspective (45.0, (GLdouble)w/(GLdouble)h, 3.0, 8.0);
    glMatrixMode(GL_MODELVIEW);
    glLoadIdentity();
    glTranslatef (0.0, 0.0, -5.0);
}
```

```
void keyboard(unsigned char key, int x, int y)
{
   switch (key) {
      case 'c':
      case 'C':
         showPoints = !showPoints;
         glutPostRedisplay();
         break;
      case 27:
         exit(0);
         break;
      default:
         break;
   }
}

int main(int argc, char** argv)
{
   glutInit(&argc, argv);
   glutInitDisplayMode(GLUT_SINGLE | GLUT_RGB | GLUT_DEPTH);
   glutInitWindowSize (500, 500);
   glutInitWindowPosition (100, 100);
   glutCreateWindow(argv[0]);
   init();
   glutReshapeFunc(reshape);
   glutDisplayFunc(display);
   glutKeyboardFunc (keyboard);
   glutMainLoop();
   return 0;
}
```

Manage a NURBS Object

As shown in Example 12-5, **gluNewNurbsRenderer()** returns a new NURBS
object, whose type is a pointer to a GLUnurbsObj structure. You must make
this object before using any other NURBS routine. When you're done with
a NURBS object, you may use **gluDeleteNurbsRenderer()** to free up the
memory that was used.

GLUnurbsObj* **gluNewNurbsRenderer** (void);

Creates a new NURBS object, *nobj*. Returns a pointer to the new object, or
zero, if OpenGL cannot allocate memory for a new NURBS object.

void **gluDeleteNurbsRenderer** (GLUnurbsObj *nobj*);

Destroys the NURBS object *nobj*.

Control NURBS Rendering Properties

A set of properties associated with a NURBS object affects the way the object is rendered. These properties include how the surface is rasterized (for example, filled or wireframe) and the precision of tessellation.

void **gluNurbsProperty**(GLUnurbsObj *nobj*, GLenum *property*,
GLfloat *value*);

Controls attributes of a NURBS object, *nobj*. The *property* argument specifies the property and can be GLU_DISPLAY_MODE, GLU_CULLING, GLU_SAMPLING_METHOD, GLU_SAMPLING_TOLERANCE, GLU_PARAMETRIC_TOLERANCE, GLU_U_STEP, GLU_V_STEP, or GLU_AUTO_LOAD_MATRIX. The *value* argument indicates what the property should be.

The default value for GLU_DISPLAY_MODE is GLU_FILL, which causes the surface to be rendered as polygons. If GLU_OUTLINE_POLYGON is used for the display-mode property, only the outlines of polygons created by tessellation are rendered. GLU_OUTLINE_PATCH renders the outlines of patches and trimming curves. (See "Create a NURBS Curve or Surface" on page 462.)

GLU_CULLING can speed up performance by not performing tessellation if the NURBS object falls completely outside the viewing volume; set this property to GL_TRUE to enable culling (the default is GL_FALSE).

Since a NURBS object is rendered as primitives, it's sampled at different values of its parameter(s) (*u* and *v*) and broken down into small line segments or polygons for rendering. If *property* is GLU_SAMPLING_METHOD, then *value* is set to one of GLU_PATH_LENGTH (which is the default), GLU_PARAMETRIC_ERROR, or GLU_DOMAIN_DISTANCE, which specifies how a NURBS curve or surface should be tessellated. When *value* is set to GLU_PATH_LENGTH, the surface is rendered so that the maximum length, in pixels, of the edges of tessellated polygons is no greater than what is specified by GLU_SAMPLING_TOLERANCE. When set to GLU_PARAMETRIC_ERROR, then the value specified by GLU_PARAMETRIC_TOLERANCE is the maximum distance, in pixels, between tessellated polygons and the surfaces they approximate. When set to GLU_DOMAIN_DISTANCE, the application specifies, in parametric coordinates, how many sample points per unit length are taken in the *u* and *v* dimensions, using the values for GLU_U_STEP and GLU_V_STEP.

If *property* is GLU_SAMPLING_TOLERANCE and the sampling method is GLU_PATH_LENGTH, *value* controls the maximum length, in pixels, to use for tessellated polygons. The default value of 50.0 makes the largest sampled line segment or polygon edge 50.0 pixels long. If *property* is GLU_PARAMETRIC_TOLERANCE and the sampling method is GLU_PARAMETRIC_ERROR, *value* controls the maximum distance, in pixels, between the tessellated polygons and the surfaces they approximate. The default value for GLU_PARAMETRIC_TOLERANCE is 0.5, which makes the tessellated polygons within one-half pixel of the approximated surface. If the sampling method is GLU_DOMAIN_DISTANCE and *property* is either GLU_U_STEP or GLU_V_STEP, then *value* is the number of sample points per unit length taken along the u or v dimension, respectively, in parametric coordinates. The default for both GLU_U_STEP and GLU_V_STEP is 100.

The GLU_AUTO_LOAD_MATRIX property determines whether the projection matrix, modelview matrix, and viewport are downloaded from the OpenGL server (GL_TRUE, the default), or whether the application must supply these matrices with **gluLoadSamplingMatrices()** (GL_FALSE).

---

void **gluLoadSamplingMatrices** (GLUnurbsObj **nobj*, const GLfloat *modelMatrix*[16], const GLfloat *projMatrix*[16], const GLint *viewport*[4]);

If the GLU_AUTO_LOAD_MATRIX is turned off, the modelview and projection matrices and the viewport specified in **gluLoadSamplingMatrices()** are used to compute sampling and culling matrices for each NURBS curve or surface.

If you need to query the current value for a NURBS property, you may use **gluGetNurbsProperty()**.

---

void **gluGetNurbsProperty** (GLUnurbsObj **nobj*, GLenum *property*,
              GLfloat **value*);

Given the *property* to be queried for the NURBS object *nobj*, return its current *value*.

Handle NURBS Errors

Since there are 37 different errors specific to NURBS functions, it's a good idea to register an error callback to let you know if you've stumbled into one of them. In Example 12-5, the callback function was registered with

```
gluNurbsCallback(theNurb, GLU_ERROR, (GLvoid (*)()) nurbsError);
```

---

void **gluNurbsCallback** (GLUnurbsObj *nobj*, GLenum *which*,
void (**fn*)(GLenum *errorCode*));

---

which is the type of callback; it must be GLU_ERROR. When a NURBS function detects an error condition, *fn* is invoked with the error code as its only argument. *errorCode* is one of 37 error conditions, named GLU_NURBS_ERROR1 through GLU_NURBS_ERROR37. Use **gluErrorString()** to describe the meaning of those error codes.

In Example 12-5, the **nurbsError()** routine was registered as the error callback function:

```
void nurbsError(GLenum errorCode)
{
    const GLubyte *estring;

    estring = gluErrorString(errorCode);
    fprintf (stderr, "Nurbs Error: %s\n", estring);
    exit (0);
}
```

Create a NURBS Curve or Surface

To render a NURBS surface, **gluNurbsSurface()** is bracketed by **gluBeginSurface()** and **gluEndSurface()**. The bracketing routines save and restore the evaluator state.

```
void gluBeginSurface (GLUnurbsObj *nobj);
void gluEndSurface (GLUnurbsObj *nobj);
```

After **gluBeginSurface()**, one or more calls to **gluNurbsSurface()** defines the attributes of the surface. Exactly one of these calls must have a surface type of GL_MAP2_VERTEX_3 or GL_MAP2_VERTEX_4 to generate vertices. Use **gluEndSurface()** to end the definition of a surface. Trimming of NURBS surfaces is also supported between **gluBeginSurface()** and **gluEndSurface()**. (See "Trim a NURBS Surface" on page 464.)

```
void gluNurbsSurface (GLUnurbsObj *nobj, GLint uknot_count,
                GLfloat *uknot, GLint vknot_count, GLfloat *vknot,
                GLint u_stride, GLint v_stride, GLfloat *ctlarray,
                GLint uorder, GLint vorder, GLenum type);
```

Describes the vertices (or surface normals or texture coordinates) of a NURBS surface, *nobj*. Several of the values must be specified for both *u* and *v* parametric directions, such as the knot sequences (*uknot* and *vknot*), knot counts (*uknot_count* and *vknot_count*), and order of the polynomial (*uorder* and *vorder*) for the NURBS surface. Note that the number of control points isn't specified. Instead, it's derived by determining the number of control points along each parameter as the number of knots minus the order. Then, the number of control points for the surface is equal to the number of control points in each parametric direction, multiplied by one another. The *ctlarray* argument points to an array of control points.

The last parameter, *type*, is one of the two-dimensional evaluator types. Commonly, you might use GL_MAP2_VERTEX_3 for nonrational or GL_MAP2_VERTEX_4 for rational control points, respectively. You might also use other types, such as GL_MAP2_TEXTURE_COORD_* or GL_MAP2_NORMAL to calculate and assign texture coordinates or surface normals. For example, to create a lighted (with surface normals) and textured NURBS surface, you may need to call this sequence:

```
gluBeginSurface(nobj);
    gluNurbsSurface(nobj, ..., GL_MAP2_TEXTURE_COORD_2);
    gluNurbsSurface(nobj, ..., GL_MAP2_NORMAL);
    gluNurbsSurface(nobj, ..., GL_MAP2_VERTEX_3);
gluEndSurface(nobj);
```

The *u_stride* and *v_stride* arguments represent the number of floating-point values between control points in each parametric direction. The evaluator type, as well as its order, affects the *u_stride* and *v_stride* values. In Example 12-5, *u_stride* is 12 (4 * 3) because there are three coordinates for each vertex (set by GL_MAP2_VERTEX_3) and four control points in the parametric *v* direction; *v_stride* is 3 because each vertex had three coordinates, and *v* control points are adjacent to one another.

Drawing a NURBS curve is similar to drawing a surface, except that all calculations are done with one parameter, *u*, rather than two. Also, for curves, **gluBeginCurve()** and **gluEndCurve()** are the bracketing routines.

---

void **gluBeginCurve** (GLUnurbsObj **nobj*);
void **gluEndCurve** (GLUnurbsObj **nobj*);

After **gluBeginCurve()**, one or more calls to **gluNurbsCurve()** define the attributes of the surface. Exactly one of these calls must have a surface type of GL_MAP1_VERTEX_3 or GL_MAP1_VERTEX_4 to generate vertices. Use **gluEndCurve()** to end the definition of a surface.

---

void **gluNurbsCurve** (GLUnurbsObj **nobj*, GLint *uknot_count*,
                        GLfloat **uknot*, GLint *u_stride*, GLfloat **ctlarray*,
                        GLint *uorder*, GLenum *type*);

Defines a NURBS curve for the object *nobj*. The arguments have the same meaning as those for **gluNurbsSurface()**. Note that this routine requires only one knot sequence and one declaration of the order of the NURBS object. If this curve is defined within a **gluBeginCurve()**/**gluEndCurve()** pair, then the type can be any of the valid one-dimensional evaluator types (such as GL_MAP1_VERTEX_3 or GL_MAP1_VERTEX_4).

Trim a NURBS Surface

To create a trimmed NURBS surface with OpenGL, start as if you were creating an untrimmed surface. After calling **gluBeginSurface()** and **gluNurbsSurface()** but before calling **gluEndSurface()**, start a trim by calling **gluBeginTrim()**.

void **gluBeginTrim** (GLUnurbsObj *nobj*);
void **gluEndTrim** (GLUnurbsObj *nobj*);

Marks the beginning and end of the definition of a trimming loop. A trimming loop is a set of oriented, trimming curve segments (forming a closed curve) that defines the boundaries of a NURBS surface.

You can create two kinds of trimming curves, a piecewise linear curve with **gluPwlCurve()** or a NURBS curve with **gluNurbsCurve()**. A piecewise linear curve doesn't look like what's conventionally called a curve, because it's a series of straight lines. A NURBS curve for trimming must lie within the unit square of parametric (u, v) space. The type for a NURBS trimming curve is usually GLU_MAP1_TRIM2. Less often, the type is GLU_MAP1_TRIM3, where the curve is described in a two-dimensional homogeneous space (u', v', w') by $(u, v) = (u'/w', v'/w')$.

void **gluPwlCurve** (GLUnurbsObj *nobj*, GLint *count*, GLfloat *array*, GLint *stride*, GLenum *type*);

Describes a piecewise linear trimming curve for the NURBS object *nobj*. There are *count* points on the curve, and they're given by *array*. The *type* can be either GLU_MAP1_TRIM_2 (the most common) or GLU_MAP1_TRIM_3 ((u, v, w) homogeneous parameter space). The type affects whether *stride*, the number of floating-point values to the next vertex, is 2 or 3.

You need to consider the orientation of trimming curves—that is, whether they're counterclockwise or clockwise—to make sure you include the desired part of the surface. If you imagine walking along a curve, everything to the left is included and everything to the right is trimmed away. For example, if your trim consists of a single counterclockwise loop, everything inside the loop is included. If the trim consists of two nonintersecting counterclockwise loops with nonintersecting interiors, everything inside either of them is included. If it consists of a counterclockwise loop with two clockwise loops inside it, the trimming region has two holes in it. The outermost trimming curve must be counterclockwise. Often, you run a trimming curve around the entire unit square to include everything within it, which is what you get by default by not specifying any trimming curves.

Trimming curves must be closed and nonintersecting. You can combine trimming curves, so long as the endpoints of the trimming curves meet to form a closed curve. You can nest curves, creating islands that float in space. Be sure to get the curve orientations right. For example, an error results if you specify a trimming region with two counterclockwise curves, one enclosed within another: The region between the curves is to the left of one and to the right of the other, so it must be both included and excluded, which is impossible. Figure 12-5 illustrates a few valid possibilities.

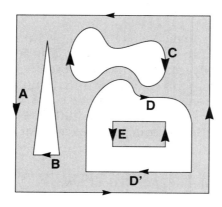

```
gluBeginSurface();
    gluNurbsSurface(...);
    gluBeginTrim();
        gluPwlCurve(...);  /* A */
    gluEndTrim();
    gluBeginTrim();
        gluPwlCurve(...);  /* B */
    gluEndTrim();
    gluBeginTrim();
        gluNurbsCurve(...);/* C */
    gluEndTrim();
    gluBeginTrim();
        gluNurbsCurve(...);/* D */
        gluPwlCurve(...);  /* D' */
    gluEndTrim();
    gluBeginTrim();
        gluPwlCurve(...);  /* E */
    gluEndTrim();
gluEndSurface();
```

Figure 12-5   Parametric Trimming Curves

Figure 12-6 shows the same small hill as in Figure 12-4, this time with a trimming curve that's a combination of a piecewise linear curve and a NURBS curve. The program that creates this figure is similar to that shown in Example 12-5; the differences are in the routines shown in Example 12-6.

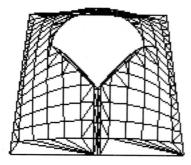

Figure 12-6   Trimmed NURBS Surface

Example 12-6 Trimming a NURBS Surface: trim.c

```c
void display(void)
{
   GLfloat knots[8] = {0.0, 0.0, 0.0, 0.0, 1.0, 1.0, 1.0, 1.0};
   GLfloat edgePt[5][2] = /* counter clockwise */
      {{0.0, 0.0}, {1.0, 0.0}, {1.0, 1.0}, {0.0, 1.0},
       {0.0, 0.0}};
   GLfloat curvePt[4][2] = /* clockwise */
      {{0.25, 0.5}, {0.25, 0.75}, {0.75, 0.75}, {0.75, 0.5}};
   GLfloat curveKnots[8] =
      {0.0, 0.0, 0.0, 0.0, 1.0, 1.0, 1.0, 1.0};
   GLfloat pwlPt[4][2] = /* clockwise */
      {{0.75, 0.5}, {0.5, 0.25}, {0.25, 0.5}};

   glClear(GL_COLOR_BUFFER_BIT | GL_DEPTH_BUFFER_BIT);
   glPushMatrix();
   glRotatef(330.0, 1.,0.,0.);
   glScalef (0.5, 0.5, 0.5);

   gluBeginSurface(theNurb);
   gluNurbsSurface(theNurb, 8, knots, 8, knots,
                   4 * 3, 3, &ctlpoints[0][0][0],
                   4, 4, GL_MAP2_VERTEX_3);
   gluBeginTrim (theNurb);
      gluPwlCurve (theNurb, 5, &edgePt[0][0], 2,
                   GLU_MAP1_TRIM_2);
   gluEndTrim (theNurb);
   gluBeginTrim (theNurb);
      gluNurbsCurve (theNurb, 8, curveKnots, 2,
                     &curvePt[0][0], 4, GLU_MAP1_TRIM_2);
      gluPwlCurve (theNurb, 3, &pwlPt[0][0], 2,
                   GLU_MAP1_TRIM_2);
   gluEndTrim (theNurb);
   gluEndSurface(theNurb);

   glPopMatrix();
   glFlush();
}
```

In Example 12-6, **gluBeginTrim()** and **gluEndTrim()** bracket each trimming curve. The first trim, with vertices defined by the array *edgePt[][]*, goes counterclockwise around the entire unit square of parametric space. This ensures that everything is drawn, provided it isn't removed by a clockwise trimming curve inside of it. The second trim is a combination of a NURBS trimming curve and a piecewise linear trimming curve. The NURBS curve ends at the points (0.9, 0.5) and (0.1, 0.5), where it is met by the piecewise linear curve, forming a closed clockwise curve.

Chapter 13

Selection and Feedback

Chapter Objectives

After reading this chapter, you'll be able to do the following:

- Create applications that allow the user to select a region of the screen or pick an object drawn on the screen

- Use the OpenGL feedback mode to obtain the results of rendering calculations

Some graphics applications simply draw static images of two- and three-dimensional objects. Other applications allow the user to identify objects on the screen and then to move, modify, delete, or otherwise manipulate those objects. OpenGL is designed to support exactly such interactive applications. Since objects drawn on the screen typically undergo multiple rotations, translations, and perspective transformations, it can be difficult for you to determine which object a user is selecting in a three-dimensional scene. To help you, OpenGL provides a selection mechanism that automatically tells you which objects are drawn inside a specified region of the window. You can use this mechanism together with a special utility routine to determine which object within the region the user is specifying, or *picking*, with the cursor.

Selection is actually a mode of operation for OpenGL; feedback is another such mode. In feedback mode, you use your graphics hardware and OpenGL to perform the usual rendering calculations. Instead of using the calculated results to draw an image on the screen, however, OpenGL returns (or feeds back) the drawing information to you. For example, if you want to draw three-dimensional objects on a plotter rather than the screen, you would draw the items in feedback mode, collect the drawing instructions, and then convert them to commands the plotter can understand.

In both selection and feedback modes, drawing information is returned to the application rather than being sent to the framebuffer, as it is in rendering mode. Thus, the screen remains frozen—no drawing occurs—while OpenGL is in selection or feedback mode. In these modes, the contents of the color, depth, stencil, and accumulation buffers are not affected. This chapter explains each of these modes in its own section:

- "Selection" on page 470 discusses how to use selection mode and related routines to allow a user of your application to pick an object drawn on the screen.

- "Feedback" on page 491 describes how to obtain information about what would be drawn on the screen and how that information is formatted.

Selection

Typically, when you're planning to use OpenGL's selection mechanism, you first draw your scene into the framebuffer, and then you enter selection mode and redraw the scene. However, once you're in selection mode, the contents of the framebuffer don't change until you exit selection mode.

When you exit selection mode, OpenGL returns a list of the primitives that intersect the viewing volume (remember that the viewing volume is defined by the current modelview and projection matrices and any additional clipping planes, as explained in Chapter 3.) Each primitive that intersects the viewing volume causes a selection *hit*. The list of primitives is actually returned as an array of integer-valued *names* and related data—the *hit records*—that correspond to the current contents of the *name stack*. You construct the name stack by loading names onto it as you issue primitive drawing commands while in selection mode. Thus, when the list of names is returned, you can use it to determine which primitives might have been selected on the screen by the user.

In addition to this selection mechanism, OpenGL provides a utility routine designed to simplify selection in some cases by restricting drawing to a small region of the viewport. Typically, you use this routine to determine which objects are drawn near the cursor, so that you can identify which object the user is picking. (You can also delimit a selection region by specifying additional clipping planes. Remember that these planes act in world space, not in screen space.) Since picking is a special case of selection, selection is described first in this chapter, and then picking.

The Basic Steps

To use the selection mechanism, you need to perform the following steps.

1. Specify the array to be used for the returned hit records with **glSelectBuffer()**.

2. Enter selection mode by specifying GL_SELECT with **glRenderMode()**.

3. Initialize the name stack using **glInitNames()** and **glPushName()**.

4. Define the viewing volume you want to use for selection. Usually this is different from the viewing volume you originally used to draw the scene, so you probably want to save and then restore the current transformation state with **glPushMatrix()** and **glPopMatrix()**.

5. Alternately issue primitive drawing commands and commands to manipulate the name stack so that each primitive of interest has an appropriate name assigned.

6. Exit selection mode and process the returned selection data (the hit records).

The following paragraphs describe **glSelectBuffer()** and **glRenderMode()**. In the next section, the commands to manipulate the name stack are described.

---

void **glSelectBuffer**(GLsizei *size*, GLuint **buffer*);

Specifies the array to be used for the returned selection data. The *buffer* argument is a pointer to an array of unsigned integers into which the data is put, and *size* indicates the maximum number of values that can be stored in the array. You need to call **glSelectBuffer()** before entering selection mode.

GLint **glRenderMode**(GLenum *mode*);

Controls whether the application is in rendering, selection, or feedback mode. The *mode* argument can be one of GL_RENDER (the default), GL_SELECT, or GL_FEEDBACK. The application remains in a given mode until **glRenderMode()** is called again with a different argument. Before entering selection mode, **glSelectBuffer()** must be called to specify the selection array. Similarly, before entering feedback mode, **glFeedbackBuffer()** must be called to specify the feedback array. The return value for **glRenderMode()** has meaning if the current render mode (that is, not the *mode* parameter) is either GL_SELECT or GL_FEEDBACK. The return value is the number of selection hits or the number of values placed in the feedback array when either mode is exited; a negative value means that the selection or feedback array has overflowed. You can use GL_RENDER_MODE with **glGetIntegerv()** to obtain the current mode.

Creating the Name Stack

As mentioned in the previous section, the name stack forms the basis for the selection information that's returned to you. To create the name stack, first initialize it with **glInitNames()**, which simply clears the stack, and then add integer names to it while issuing corresponding drawing commands. As you might expect, the commands to manipulate the stack allow you to push a name onto it (**glPushName()**), pop a name off of it (**glPopName()**), and replace the name on the top of the stack with a different one (**glLoadName()**). Example 13-1 shows what your name-stack manipulation code might look like with these commands.

Example 13-1 Creating a Name Stack

```
glInitNames();
glPushName(0);

glPushMatrix();    /* save the current transformation state */

    /* create your desired viewing volume here */

    glLoadName(1);
    drawSomeObject();
    glLoadName(2);
    drawAnotherObject();
    glLoadName(3);
    drawYetAnotherObject();
    drawJustOneMoreObject();

glPopMatrix ();    /* restore the previous transformation state*/
```

In this example, the first two objects to be drawn have their own names, and the third and fourth objects share a single name. With this setup, if either or both of the third and fourth objects causes a selection hit, only one hit record is returned to you. You can have multiple objects share the same name if you don't need to differentiate between them when processing the hit records.

---

void **glInitNames**(void);

Clears the name stack so that it's empty.

---

void **glPushName**(GLuint *name*);

Pushes *name* onto the name stack. Pushing a name beyond the capacity of the stack generates the error GL_STACK_OVERFLOW. The name stack's depth can vary among different OpenGL implementations, but it must be able to contain at least sixty-four names. You can use the parameter GL_NAME_STACK_DEPTH with **glGetIntegerv()** to obtain the depth of the name stack.

---

void **glPopName**(void);

Pops one name off the top of the name stack. Popping an empty stack generates the error GL_STACK_UNDERFLOW.

---
void **glLoadName**(GLuint *name*);

Replaces the value on the top of the name stack with *name*. If the stack is empty, which it is right after **glInitNames()** is called, **glLoadName()** generates the error GL_INVALID_OPERATION. To avoid this, if the stack is initially empty, call **glPushName()** at least once to put something on the name stack before calling **glLoadName()**.

Calls to **glPushName()**, **glPopName()**, and **glLoadName()** are ignored if you're not in selection mode. You might find that it simplifies your code to use these calls throughout your drawing code, and then use the same drawing code for both selection and normal rendering modes.

The Hit Record

In selection mode, a primitive that intersects the viewing volume causes a selection hit. Whenever a name-stack manipulation command is executed or **glRenderMode()** is called, OpenGL writes a hit record into the selection array if there's been a hit since the last time the stack was manipulated or **glRenderMode()** was called. With this process, objects that share the same name—for example, an object that's composed of more than one primitive—don't generate multiple hit records. Also, hit records aren't guaranteed to be written into the array until **glRenderMode()** is called.

Note: In addition to primitives, valid coordinates produced by **glRasterPos()** can cause a selection hit. Also, in the case of polygons, no hit occurs if the polygon would have been culled.

Each hit record consists of four items, in order.

*   The number of names on the name stack when the hit occurred.

*   Both the minimum and maximum window-coordinate z values of all vertices of the primitives that intersected the viewing volume since the last recorded hit. These two values, which lie in the range [0,1], are each multiplied by $2^{32}-1$ and rounded to the nearest unsigned integer.

*   The contents of the name stack at the time of the hit, with the bottommost element first.

When you enter selection mode, OpenGL initializes a pointer to the beginning of the selection array. Each time a hit record is written into the array, the pointer is updated accordingly. If writing a hit record would cause the number of values in the array to exceed the *size* argument specified with

glSelectBuffer(), OpenGL writes as much of the record as fits in the array and sets an overflow flag. When you exit selection mode with **glRenderMode()**, this command returns the number of hit records that were written (including a partial record if there was one), clears the name stack, resets the overflow flag, and resets the stack pointer. If the overflow flag had been set, the return value is –1.

A Selection Example

In Example 13-2, four triangles (green, red, and two yellow triangles, created by calling **drawTriangle()**) and a wireframe box representing the viewing volume (**drawViewVolume()**) are drawn to the screen. Then the triangles are rendered again (**selectObjects()**), but this time in selection mode. The corresponding hit records are processed in **processHits()**, and the selection array is printed out. The first triangle generates a hit, the second one doesn't, and the third and fourth ones together generate a single hit.

Example 13-2   Selection Example: select.c

```
#include <GL/gl.h>
#include <GL/glu.h>
#include <GL/glut.h>
#include <stdlib.h>
#include <stdio.h>

void drawTriangle (GLfloat x1, GLfloat y1, GLfloat x2,
    GLfloat y2, GLfloat x3, GLfloat y3, GLfloat z)
{
   glBegin (GL_TRIANGLES);
   glVertex3f (x1, y1, z);
   glVertex3f (x2, y2, z);
   glVertex3f (x3, y3, z);
   glEnd ();
}

void drawViewVolume (GLfloat x1, GLfloat x2, GLfloat y1,
                  GLfloat y2, GLfloat z1, GLfloat z2)
{
   glColor3f (1.0, 1.0, 1.0);
   glBegin (GL_LINE_LOOP);
   glVertex3f (x1, y1, -z1);
   glVertex3f (x2, y1, -z1);
   glVertex3f (x2, y2, -z1);
```

```
        glVertex3f (x1, y2, -z1);
        glEnd ();

        glBegin (GL_LINE_LOOP);
        glVertex3f (x1, y1, -z2);
        glVertex3f (x2, y1, -z2);
        glVertex3f (x2, y2, -z2);
        glVertex3f (x1, y2, -z2);
        glEnd ();

        glBegin (GL_LINES);  /*  4 lines    */
        glVertex3f (x1, y1, -z1);
        glVertex3f (x1, y1, -z2);
        glVertex3f (x1, y2, -z1);
        glVertex3f (x1, y2, -z2);
        glVertex3f (x2, y1, -z1);
        glVertex3f (x2, y1, -z2);
        glVertex3f (x2, y2, -z1);
        glVertex3f (x2, y2, -z2);
        glEnd ();
}

void drawScene (void)
{
    glMatrixMode (GL_PROJECTION);
    glLoadIdentity ();
    gluPerspective (40.0, 4.0/3.0, 1.0, 100.0);

    glMatrixMode (GL_MODELVIEW);
    glLoadIdentity ();
    gluLookAt (7.5, 7.5, 12.5, 2.5, 2.5, -5.0, 0.0, 1.0, 0.0);
    glColor3f (0.0, 1.0, 0.0);   /*  green triangle     */
    drawTriangle (2.0, 2.0, 3.0, 2.0, 2.5, 3.0, -5.0);
    glColor3f (1.0, 0.0, 0.0);   /*  red triangle       */
    drawTriangle (2.0, 7.0, 3.0, 7.0, 2.5, 8.0, -5.0);
    glColor3f (1.0, 1.0, 0.0);   /*  yellow triangles   */
    drawTriangle (2.0, 2.0, 3.0, 2.0, 2.5, 3.0, 0.0);
    drawTriangle (2.0, 2.0, 3.0, 2.0, 2.5, 3.0, -10.0);
    drawViewVolume (0.0, 5.0, 0.0, 5.0, 0.0, 10.0);
}

void processHits (GLint hits, GLuint buffer[])
{
    unsigned int i, j;
    GLuint names, *ptr;

    printf ("hits = %d\n", hits);
```

```
   ptr = (GLuint *) buffer;
   for (i = 0; i < hits; i++) { /*  for each hit   */
      names = *ptr;
      printf (" number of names for hit = %d\n", names); ptr++;
      printf("   z1 is %g;", (float) *ptr/0x7fffffff); ptr++;
      printf(" z2 is %g\n", (float) *ptr/0x7fffffff); ptr++;
      printf ("   the name is ");
      for (j = 0; j < names; j++) {        /*  for each name */
         printf ("%d ", *ptr); ptr++;
      }
      printf ("\n");
   }
}

#define BUFSIZE 512

void selectObjects(void)
{
   GLuint selectBuf[BUFSIZE];
   GLint hits;

   glSelectBuffer (BUFSIZE, selectBuf);
   (void) glRenderMode (GL_SELECT);

   glInitNames();
   glPushName(0);

   glPushMatrix ();
   glMatrixMode (GL_PROJECTION);
   glLoadIdentity ();
   glOrtho (0.0, 5.0, 0.0, 5.0, 0.0, 10.0);
   glMatrixMode (GL_MODELVIEW);
   glLoadIdentity ();
   glLoadName(1);
   drawTriangle (2.0, 2.0, 3.0, 2.0, 2.5, 3.0, -5.0);
   glLoadName(2);
   drawTriangle (2.0, 7.0, 3.0, 7.0, 2.5, 8.0, -5.0);
   glLoadName(3);
   drawTriangle (2.0, 2.0, 3.0, 2.0, 2.5, 3.0, 0.0);
   drawTriangle (2.0, 2.0, 3.0, 2.0, 2.5, 3.0, -10.0);
   glPopMatrix ();
   glFlush ();

   hits = glRenderMode (GL_RENDER);
   processHits (hits, selectBuf);
}
```

```
void init (void)
{
    glEnable(GL_DEPTH_TEST);
    glShadeModel(GL_FLAT);
}

void display(void)
{
    glClearColor (0.0, 0.0, 0.0, 0.0);
    glClear(GL_COLOR_BUFFER_BIT | GL_DEPTH_BUFFER_BIT);
    drawScene ();
    selectObjects ();
    glFlush();
}

int main(int argc, char** argv)
{
    glutInit(&argc, argv);
    glutInitDisplayMode (GLUT_SINGLE | GLUT_RGB | GLUT_DEPTH);
    glutInitWindowSize (200, 200);
    glutInitWindowPosition (100, 100);
    glutCreateWindow (argv[0]);
    init();
    glutDisplayFunc(display);
    glutMainLoop();
    return 0;
}
```

Picking

As an extension of the process described in the previous section, you can use selection mode to determine if objects are picked. To do this, you use a special picking matrix in conjunction with the projection matrix to restrict drawing to a small region of the viewport, typically near the cursor. Then you allow some form of input, such as clicking a mouse button, to initiate selection mode. With selection mode established and with the special picking matrix used, objects that are drawn near the cursor cause selection hits. Thus, during picking you're typically determining which objects are drawn near the cursor.

Picking is set up almost exactly like regular selection mode is, with the following major differences.

- Picking is usually triggered by an input device. In the following code examples, pressing the left mouse button invokes a function that performs picking.

- You use the utility routine **gluPickMatrix()** to multiply a special picking matrix onto the current projection matrix. This routine should be called prior to multiplying a standard projection matrix (such as **gluPerspective()** or **glOrtho()**). You'll probably want to save the contents of the projection matrix first, so the sequence of operations may look like this:

```
glMatrixMode (GL_PROJECTION);
glPushMatrix ();
glLoadIdentity ();
gluPickMatrix (...);
gluPerspective, glOrtho, gluOrtho2D, or glFrustum
    /* ... draw scene for picking ; perform picking ... */
glPopMatrix();
```

Another completely different way to perform picking is described in "Object Selection Using the Back Buffer" on page 508. This technique uses color values to identify different components of an object.

---

void **gluPickMatrix**(GLdouble *x*, GLdouble *y*, GLdouble *width*, GLdouble *height*, GLint *viewport[4]*);

Creates a projection matrix that restricts drawing to a small region of the viewport and multiplies that matrix onto the current matrix stack. The center of the picking region is (x, y) in window coordinates, typically the cursor location. *width* and *height* define the size of the picking region in screen coordinates. (You can think of the width and height as the sensitivity of the picking device.) *viewport[]* indicates the current viewport boundaries, which can be obtained by calling

```
glGetIntegerv(GL_VIEWPORT, GLint *viewport);
```

Advanced

The net result of the matrix created by **gluPickMatrix()** is to transform the clipping region into the unit cube $-1 \leq (x, y, z) \leq 1$ (or $-w \leq (wx, wy, wz) \leq w$). The picking matrix effectively performs an orthogonal transformation that maps a subregion of this unit cube to the unit cube. Since the transformation is arbitrary, you can make picking work for different sorts of regions—for example, for rotated rectangular portions of the window. In certain situations, you might find it easier to specify additional clipping planes to define the picking region.

Example 13-3 illustrates simple picking. It also demonstrates how to use multiple names to identify different components of a primitive, in this case the row and column of a selected object. A 3×3 grid of squares is drawn, with each square a different color. The board[3][3] array maintains the current amount of blue for each square. When the left mouse button is pressed, the **pickSquares()** routine is called to identify which squares were picked by the mouse. Two names identify each square in the grid—one identifies the row, and the other the column. Also, when the left mouse button is pressed, the color of all squares under the cursor position changes.

Example 13-3   Picking Example: picksquare.c

```
#include <GL/gl.h>
#include <GL/glu.h>
#include <stdlib.h>
#include <stdio.h>
#include <GL/glut.h>

int board[3][3];    /*   amount of color for each square   */

/*   Clear color value for every square on the board    */
void init(void)
{
   int i, j;
   for (i = 0; i < 3; i++)
      for (j = 0; j < 3; j ++)
         board[i][j] = 0;
   glClearColor (0.0, 0.0, 0.0, 0.0);
}
```

```
void drawSquares(GLenum mode)
{
    GLuint i, j;
    for (i = 0; i < 3; i++) {
        if (mode == GL_SELECT)
            glLoadName (i);
        for (j = 0; j < 3; j ++) {
            if (mode == GL_SELECT)
                glPushName (j);
            glColor3f ((GLfloat) i/3.0, (GLfloat) j/3.0,
                        (GLfloat) board[i][j]/3.0);
            glRecti (i, j, i+1, j+1);
            if (mode == GL_SELECT)
                glPopName ();
        }
    }
}


/*  processHits prints out the contents of the
 *  selection array.
 */
void processHits (GLint hits, GLuint buffer[])
{
    unsigned int i, j;
    GLuint ii, jj, names, *ptr;

    printf ("hits = %d\n", hits);
    ptr = (GLuint *) buffer;
    for (i = 0; i < hits; i++) { /*  for each hit  */
        names = *ptr;
        printf (" number of names for this hit = %d\n", names);
            ptr++;
        printf("   z1 is %g;", (float) *ptr/0x7fffffff); ptr++;
        printf(" z2 is %g\n", (float) *ptr/0x7fffffff); ptr++;
        printf ("   names are ");
        for (j = 0; j < names; j++) { /*  for each name */
            printf ("%d ", *ptr);
            if (j == 0)  /*  set row and column  */
                ii = *ptr;
            else if (j == 1)
                jj = *ptr;
            ptr++;
        }
        printf ("\n");
        board[ii][jj] = (board[ii][jj] + 1) % 3;
    }
}
```

```
#define BUFSIZE 512

void pickSquares(int button, int state, int x, int y)
{
   GLuint selectBuf[BUFSIZE];
   GLint hits;
   GLint viewport[4];

   if (button != GLUT_LEFT_BUTTON || state != GLUT_DOWN)
      return;

   glGetIntegerv (GL_VIEWPORT, viewport);

   glSelectBuffer (BUFSIZE, selectBuf);
   (void) glRenderMode (GL_SELECT);

   glInitNames();
   glPushName(0);

   glMatrixMode (GL_PROJECTION);
   glPushMatrix ();
   glLoadIdentity ();
/*  create 5x5 pixel picking region near cursor location      */
   gluPickMatrix ((GLdouble) x, (GLdouble) (viewport[3] - y),
                  5.0, 5.0, viewport);
   gluOrtho2D (0.0, 3.0, 0.0, 3.0);
   drawSquares (GL_SELECT);

   glMatrixMode (GL_PROJECTION);
   glPopMatrix ();
   glFlush ();

   hits = glRenderMode (GL_RENDER);
   processHits (hits, selectBuf);
   glutPostRedisplay();
}

void display(void)
{
   glClear(GL_COLOR_BUFFER_BIT);
   drawSquares (GL_RENDER);
   glFlush();
}

void reshape(int w, int h)
{
   glViewport(0, 0, w, h);
```

```
    glMatrixMode(GL_PROJECTION);
    glLoadIdentity();
    gluOrtho2D (0.0, 3.0, 0.0, 3.0);
    glMatrixMode(GL_MODELVIEW);
    glLoadIdentity();
}

int main(int argc, char** argv)
{
    glutInit(&argc, argv);
    glutInitDisplayMode (GLUT_SINGLE | GLUT_RGB);
    glutInitWindowSize (100, 100);
    glutInitWindowPosition (100, 100);
    glutCreateWindow (argv[0]);
    init ();
    glutMouseFunc (pickSquares);
    glutReshapeFunc (reshape);
    glutDisplayFunc(display);
    glutMainLoop();
    return 0;
}
```

Picking with Multiple Names and a Hierarchical Model

Multiple names can also be used to choose parts of a hierarchical object in a scene. For example, if you were rendering an assembly line of automobiles, you might want the user to move the mouse to pick the third bolt on the left front tire of the third car in line. A different name can be used to identify each level of hierarchy: which car, which tire, and finally which bolt. As another example, one name can be used to describe a single molecule among other molecules, and additional names can differentiate individual atoms within that molecule.

Example 13-4 is a modification of Example 3-4 which draws an automobile with four identical wheels, each of which has five identical bolts. Code has been added to manipulate the name stack with the object hierarchy.

Example 13-4   Creating Multiple Names

```
draw_wheel_and_bolts()
{
    long i;

    draw_wheel_body();
    for (i = 0; i < 5; i++) {
        glPushMatrix();
```

```
            glRotate(72.0*i, 0.0, 0.0, 1.0);
            glTranslatef(3.0, 0.0, 0.0);
            glPushName(i);
                draw_bolt_body();
            glPopName();
        glPopMatrix();
    }
  }

draw_body_and_wheel_and_bolts()
{
    draw_car_body();
    glPushMatrix();
        glTranslate(40, 0, 20);   /* first wheel position*/
        glPushName(1);            /* name of wheel number 1 */
            draw_wheel_and_bolts();
        glPopName();
    glPopMatrix();
    glPushMatrix();
        glTranslate(40, 0, -20); /* second wheel position */
        glPushName(2);            /* name of wheel number 2 */
            draw_wheel_and_bolts();
        glPopName();
    glPopMatrix();

    /* draw last two wheels similarly */
}
```

Example 13-5 uses the routines in Example 13-4 to draw three different cars, numbered 1, 2, and 3.

Example 13-5 Using Multiple Names

```
draw_three_cars()
{
    glInitNames();
    glPushMatrix();
        translate_to_first_car_position();
        glPushName(1);
            draw_body_and_wheel_and_bolts();
        glPopName();
    glPopMatrix();

    glPushMatrix();
        translate_to_second_car_position();
        glPushName(2);
            draw_body_and_wheel_and_bolts();
        glPopName();
```

```
        glPopMatrix();

        glPushMatrix();
            translate_to_third_car_position();
            glPushName(3);
                draw_body_and_wheel_and_bolts();
            glPopName();
        glPopMatrix();
}
```

Assuming that picking is performed, the following are some possible name-stack return values and their interpretations. In these examples, at most one hit record is returned; also, $d1$ and $d2$ are depth values.

2 $d1$ $d2$ 2 1	Car 2, wheel 1
1 $d1$ $d2$ 3	Car 3 body
3 $d1$ $d2$ 1 1 0	Bolt 0 on wheel 1 on car 1
empty	The pick was outside all cars

The last interpretation assumes that the bolt and wheel don't occupy the same picking region. A user might well pick both the wheel and the bolt, yielding two hits. If you receive multiple hits, you have to decide which hit to process, perhaps by using the depth values to determine which picked object is closest to the viewpoint. The use of depth values is explored further in the next section.

Picking and Depth Values

Example 13-6 demonstrates how to use depth values when picking to determine which object is picked. This program draws three overlapping rectangles in normal rendering mode. When the left mouse button is pressed, the **pickRects()** routine is called. This routine returns the cursor position, enters selection mode, initializes the name stack, and multiplies the picking matrix onto the stack before the orthographic projection matrix. A selection hit occurs for each rectangle the cursor is over when the left mouse button is clicked. Finally, the contents of the selection buffer are examined to identify which named objects were within the picking region near the cursor.

The rectangles in this program are drawn at different depth, or z, values. Since only one name is used to identify all three rectangles, only one hit can be recorded. However, if more than one rectangle is picked, that single hit has different minimum and maximum z values.

Example 13-6 Picking with Depth Values: pickdepth.c

```c
#include <GL/gl.h>
#include <GL/glu.h>
#include <GL/glut.h>
#include <stdlib.h>
#include <stdio.h>

void init(void)
{
   glClearColor(0.0, 0.0, 0.0, 0.0);
   glEnable(GL_DEPTH_TEST);
   glShadeModel(GL_FLAT);
   glDepthRange(0.0, 1.0);   /* The default z mapping */
}

void drawRects(GLenum mode)
{
   if (mode == GL_SELECT)
      glLoadName(1);
   glBegin(GL_QUADS);
   glColor3f(1.0, 1.0, 0.0);
   glVertex3i(2, 0, 0);
   glVertex3i(2, 6, 0);
   glVertex3i(6, 6, 0);
   glVertex3i(6, 0, 0);
   glEnd();
   if (mode == GL_SELECT)
      glLoadName(2);
   glBegin(GL_QUADS);
   glColor3f(0.0, 1.0, 1.0);
   glVertex3i(3, 2, -1);
   glVertex3i(3, 8, -1);
   glVertex3i(8, 8, -1);
   glVertex3i(8, 2, -1);
   glEnd();
   if (mode == GL_SELECT)
      glLoadName(3);
   glBegin(GL_QUADS);
   glColor3f(1.0, 0.0, 1.0);
   glVertex3i(0, 2, -2);
   glVertex3i(0, 7, -2);
   glVertex3i(5, 7, -2);
   glVertex3i(5, 2, -2);
   glEnd();
}
```

```
void processHits(GLint hits, GLuint buffer[])
{
    unsigned int i, j;
    GLuint names, *ptr;

    printf("hits = %d\n", hits);
    ptr = (GLuint *) buffer;
    for (i = 0; i < hits; i++) {   /* for each hit  */
        names = *ptr;
        printf(" number of names for hit = %d\n", names); ptr++;
        printf("  z1 is %g;", (float) *ptr/0x7fffffff); ptr++;
        printf(" z2 is %g\n", (float) *ptr/0x7fffffff); ptr++;
        printf("    the name is ");
        for (j = 0; j < names; j++) {   /* for each name */
            printf("%d ", *ptr); ptr++;
        }
        printf("\n");
    }
}

#define BUFSIZE 512

void pickRects(int button, int state, int x, int y)
{
    GLuint selectBuf[BUFSIZE];
    GLint hits;
    GLint viewport[4];

    if (button != GLUT_LEFT_BUTTON || state != GLUT_DOWN)
        return;
    glGetIntegerv(GL_VIEWPORT, viewport);

    glSelectBuffer(BUFSIZE, selectBuf);
    (void) glRenderMode(GL_SELECT);

    glInitNames();
    glPushName(0);

    glMatrixMode(GL_PROJECTION);
    glPushMatrix();
    glLoadIdentity();
/*  create 5x5 pixel picking region near cursor location */
    gluPickMatrix((GLdouble) x, (GLdouble) (viewport[3] - y),
                  5.0, 5.0, viewport);
    glOrtho(0.0, 8.0, 0.0, 8.0, -0.5, 2.5);
    drawRects(GL_SELECT);
    glPopMatrix();
```

```
        glFlush();

        hits = glRenderMode(GL_RENDER);
        processHits(hits, selectBuf);
}

void display(void)
{
    glClear(GL_COLOR_BUFFER_BIT | GL_DEPTH_BUFFER_BIT);
    drawRects(GL_RENDER);
    glFlush();
}

void reshape(int w, int h)
{
    glViewport(0, 0, (GLsizei) w, (GLsizei) h);
    glMatrixMode(GL_PROJECTION);
    glLoadIdentity();
    glOrtho(0.0, 8.0, 0.0, 8.0, -0.5, 2.5);
    glMatrixMode(GL_MODELVIEW);
    glLoadIdentity();
}

int main(int argc, char **argv)
{
    glutInit(&argc, argv);
    glutInitDisplayMode(GLUT_SINGLE | GLUT_RGB | GLUT_DEPTH);
    glutInitWindowSize (200, 200);
    glutInitWindowPosition (100, 100);
    glutCreateWindow(argv[0]);
    init();
    glutMouseFunc(pickRects);
    glutReshapeFunc(reshape);
    glutDisplayFunc(display);
    glutMainLoop();
    return 0;
}
```

Try This

- Modify Example 13-6 to add additional calls to **glPushName()** so that
  multiple names are on the stack when the selection hit occurs. What
  will the contents of the selection buffer be?

- By default, **glDepthRange()** sets the mapping of the z values to
  [0.0,1.0]. Try modifying the **glDepthRange()** values and see how it
  affects the z values that are returned in the selection array.

Hints for Writing a Program That Uses Selection

Most programs that allow a user to interactively edit some geometry provide a mechanism for the user to pick items or groups of items for editing. For two-dimensional drawing programs (for example, text editors, page-layout programs, and circuit-design programs), it might be easier to do your own picking calculations instead of using the OpenGL picking mechanism. Often, it's easy to find bounding boxes for two-dimensional objects and to organize them in some hierarchical data structure to speed up searches. For example, picking that uses the OpenGL style in a VLSI layout program containing millions of rectangles can be relatively slow. However, using simple bounding-box information when rectangles are typically aligned with the screen could make picking in such a program extremely fast. The code is probably simpler to write, too.

As another example, since only geometric objects cause hits, you might want to create your own method for picking text. Setting the current raster position is a geometric operation, but it effectively creates only a single pickable point at the current raster position, which is typically at the lower-left corner of the text. If your editor needs to manipulate individual characters within a text string, some other picking mechanism must be used. You could draw little rectangles around each character during picking mode, but it's almost certainly easier to handle text as a special case.

If you decide to use OpenGL picking, organize your program and its data structures so that it's easy to draw appropriate lists of objects in either selection or normal drawing mode. This way, when the user picks something, you can use the same data structures for the pick operation that you use to display the items on the screen. Also, consider whether you want to allow the user to select multiple objects. One way to do this is to store a bit for each item indicating whether it's selected (however, this method requires traversing your entire list of items to find the selected items). You might find it useful to maintain a list of pointers to selected items to speed up this search. It's probably a good idea to keep the selection bit for each item as well, since when you're drawing the entire picture, you might want to draw selected items differently (for example, in a different color or with a selection box around them). Finally, consider the selection user interface. You might want to allow the user to do the following:

- Select an item

- Sweep-select a group of items (see the next paragraphs for a description of this behavior)

- Add an item to the selection

- Add a sweep selection to the current selections

- Delete an item from a selection

- Choose a single item from a group of overlapping items

A typical solution for a two-dimensional drawing program might work as follows.

1. All selection is done by pointing with the mouse cursor and using the left mouse button. In what follows, *cursor* means the cursor tied to the mouse, and *button* means the left mouse button.

2. Clicking on an item selects it and deselects all other currently selected items. If the cursor is on top of multiple items, the smallest is selected. (In three dimensions, many other strategies work to disambiguate a selection.)

3. Clicking down where there is no item, holding the button down while dragging the cursor, and then releasing the button selects all the items in a screen-aligned rectangle whose corners are determined by the cursor positions when the button went down and where it came up. This is called a *sweep selection*. All items not in the swept-out region are deselected. (You must decide whether an item is selected only if it's completely within the sweep region, or if any part of it falls within the region. The completely within strategy usually works best.)

4. If the Shift key is held down and the user clicks on an item that isn't currently selected, that item is added to the selected list. If the clicked-upon item is selected, it's deleted from the selection list.

5. If a sweep selection is performed with the Shift key pressed, the items swept out are added to the current selection.

6. In an extremely cluttered region, it's often hard to do a sweep selection. When the button goes down, the cursor might lie on top of some item, and normally that item would be selected. You can make any operation a sweep selection, but a typical user interface interprets a button-down on an item plus a mouse motion as a select-plus-drag operation. To solve this problem, you can have an enforced sweep selection by holding down, say, the Alt key. With this, the following set of operations constitutes a sweep selection: Alt-button down, sweep, button up. Items under the cursor when the button goes down are ignored.

7. If the Shift key is held during this sweep selection, the items enclosed in the sweep region are added to the current selection.

8. Finally, if the user clicks on multiple items, select just one of them. If the cursor isn't moved (or maybe not moved more than a pixel), and the user clicks again in the same place, deselect the item originally selected, and select a different item under the cursor. Use repeated clicks at the same point to cycle through all the possibilities.

Different rules can apply in particular situations. In a text editor, you probably don't have to worry about characters on top of each other, and selections of multiple characters are always contiguous characters in the document. Thus, you need to mark only the first and last selected characters to identify the complete selection. With text, often the best way to handle selection is to identify the positions between characters rather than the characters themselves. This allows you to have an empty selection when the beginning and end of the selection are between the same pair of characters; it also allows you to put the cursor before the first character in the document or after the final one with no special-case code.

In three-dimensional editors, you might provide ways to rotate and zoom between selections, so sophisticated schemes for cycling through the possible selections might be unnecessary. On the other hand, selection in three dimensions is difficult because the cursor's position on the screen usually gives no indication of its depth.

Feedback

Feedback is similar to selection in that once you're in either mode, no pixels are produced and the screen is frozen. Drawing does not occur; instead, information about primitives that would have been rendered is sent back to the application. The key difference between selection and feedback modes is what information is sent back. In selection mode, assigned names are returned to an array of integer values. In feedback mode, information about transformed primitives is sent back to an array of floating-point values. The values sent back to the feedback array consist of tokens that specify what type of primitive (point, line, polygon, image, or bitmap) has been processed and transformed, followed by vertex, color, or other data for that primitive. The values returned are fully transformed by lighting and viewing operations. Feedback mode is initiated by calling **glRenderMode()** with GL_FEEDBACK as the argument.

Here's how you enter and exit feedback mode.

1. Call **glFeedbackBuffer()** to specify the array to hold the feedback information. The arguments to this command describe what type of data and how much of it gets written into the array.

2. Call **glRenderMode()** with GL_FEEDBACK as the argument to enter feedback mode. (For this step, you can ignore the value returned by **glRenderMode()**.) After this point, primitives aren't rasterized to produce pixels until you exit feedback mode, and the contents of the framebuffer don't change.

3. Draw your primitives. While issuing drawing commands, you can make several calls to **glPassThrough()** to insert markers into the returned feedback data and thus facilitate parsing.

4. Exit feedback mode by calling **glRenderMode()** with GL_RENDER as the argument if you want to return to normal drawing mode. The integer value returned by **glRenderMode()** is the number of values stored in the feedback array.

5. Parse the data in the feedback array.

---

void **glFeedbackBuffer**(GLsizei *size*, GLenum *type*, GLfloat **buffer*);

Establishes a buffer for the feedback data: *buffer* is a pointer to an array where the data is stored. The *size* argument indicates the maximum number of values that can be stored in the array. The *type* argument describes the information fed back for each vertex in the feedback array; its possible values and their meaning are shown in Table 13-1. **glFeedbackBuffer()** must be called before feedback mode is entered. In the table, *k* is 1 in color-index mode and 4 in RGBA mode.

type **Argument**	Coordinates	Color	Texture	Total Values
GL_2D	x, y	-	-	2
GL_3D	x, y, z	-	-	3
GL_3D_COLOR	x, y, z	k	-	3 + k
GL_3D_COLOR_TEXTURE	x, y, z	k	4	7 + k
GL_4D_COLOR_TEXTURE	x, y, z, w	k	4	8 + k

Table 13-1   glFeedbackBuffer() *type* Values

The Feedback Array

In feedback mode, each primitive that would be rasterized (or each call to **glBitmap()**, **glDrawPixels()**, or **glCopyPixels()**, if the raster position is valid) generates a block of values that's copied into the feedback array. The number of values is determined by the *type* argument to **glFeedbackBuffer()**, as listed in Table 13-1. Use the appropriate value for the type of primitives you're drawing: GL_2D or GL_3D for unlit two- or three-dimensional primitives, GL_3D_COLOR for lit, three-dimensional primitives, and GL_3D_COLOR_TEXTURE or GL_4D_COLOR_TEXTURE for lit, textured, three- or four-dimensional primitives.

Each block of feedback values begins with a code indicating the primitive type, followed by values that describe the primitive's vertices and associated data. Entries are also written for pixel rectangles. In addition, pass-through markers that you've explicitly created can be returned in the array; the next section explains these markers in more detail. Table 13-2 shows the syntax for the feedback array; remember that the data associated with each returned vertex is as described in Table 13-1. Note that a polygon can have *n* vertices returned. Also, the *x, y, z* coordinates returned by feedback are window coordinates; if *w* is returned, it's in clip coordinates. For bitmaps and pixel rectangles, the coordinates returned are those of the current raster position. In the table, note that GL_LINE_RESET_TOKEN is returned only when the line stipple is reset for that line segment.

Primitive Type	Code	Associated Data
Point	GL_POINT_TOKEN	vertex
Line	GL_LINE_TOKEN or GL_LINE_RESET_TOKEN	vertex vertex
Polygon	GL_POLYGON_TOKEN	*n* vertex vertex ... vertex
Bitmap	GL_BITMAP_TOKEN	vertex
Pixel Rectangle	GL_DRAW_PIXEL_TOKEN or GL_COPY_PIXEL_TOKEN	vertex
Pass-through	GL_PASS_THROUGH_TOKEN	a floating-point number

Table 13-2   Feedback Array Syntax

Using Markers in Feedback Mode

Feedback occurs after transformations, lighting, polygon culling, and interpretation of polygons by **glPolygonMode()**. It might also occur after polygons with more than three edges are broken up into triangles (if your particular OpenGL implementation renders polygons by performing this decomposition). Thus, it might be hard for you to recognize the primitives you drew in the feedback data you receive. To help parse the feedback data, call **glPassThrough()** as needed in your sequence of drawing commands to insert a marker. You might use the markers to separate the feedback values returned from different primitives, for example. This command causes GL_PASS_THROUGH_TOKEN to be written into the feedback array, followed by the floating-point value you pass in as an argument.

---

void **glPassThrough**(GLfloat *token*);

Inserts a marker into the stream of values written into the feedback array, if called in feedback mode. The marker consists of the code GL_PASS_THROUGH_TOKEN followed by a single floating-point value, *token*. This command has no effect when called outside of feedback mode. Calling **glPassThrough()** between **glBegin()** and **glEnd()** generates a GL_INVALID_OPERATION error.

A Feedback Example

Example 13-7 demonstrates the use of feedback mode. This program draws a lit, three-dimensional scene in normal rendering mode. Then, feedback mode is entered, and the scene is redrawn. Since the program draws lit, untextured, three-dimensional objects, the type of feedback data is GL_3D_COLOR. Since RGBA mode is used, each unclipped vertex generates seven values for the feedback buffer: x, y, z, r, g, b, and a.

In feedback mode, the program draws two lines as part of a line strip and then inserts a pass-through marker. Next, a point is drawn at (−100.0, −100.0, −100.0), which falls outside the orthographic viewing volume and thus doesn't put any values into the feedback array. Finally, another pass-through marker is inserted, and another point is drawn.

Example 13-7   Feedback Mode: feedback.c

```c
#include <GL/gl.h>
#include <GL/glu.h>
#include <GL/glut.h>
#include <stdlib.h>
#include <stdio.h>

void init(void)
{
   glEnable(GL_LIGHTING);
   glEnable(GL_LIGHT0);
}

void drawGeometry (GLenum mode)
{
   glBegin (GL_LINE_STRIP);
   glNormal3f (0.0, 0.0, 1.0);
   glVertex3f (30.0, 30.0, 0.0);
   glVertex3f (50.0, 60.0, 0.0);
   glVertex3f (70.0, 40.0, 0.0);
   glEnd ();
   if (mode == GL_FEEDBACK)
      glPassThrough (1.0);
   glBegin (GL_POINTS);
   glVertex3f (-100.0, -100.0, -100.0);   /*  will be clipped  */
   glEnd ();
   if (mode == GL_FEEDBACK)
      glPassThrough (2.0);
   glBegin (GL_POINTS);
   glNormal3f (0.0, 0.0, 1.0);
   glVertex3f (50.0, 50.0, 0.0);
   glEnd ();
}

void print3DcolorVertex (GLint size, GLint *count,
                         GLfloat *buffer)
{
   int i;

   printf ("   ");
   for (i = 0; i < 7; i++) {
      printf ("%4.2f ", buffer[size-(*count)]);
      *count = *count - 1;
   }
   printf ("\n");
}
```

```
void printBuffer(GLint size, GLfloat *buffer)
{
    GLint count;
    GLfloat token;

    count = size;
    while (count) {
        token = buffer[size-count]; count--;
        if (token == GL_PASS_THROUGH_TOKEN) {
            printf ("GL_PASS_THROUGH_TOKEN\n");
            printf ("  %4.2f\n", buffer[size-count]);
            count--;
        }
        else if (token == GL_POINT_TOKEN) {
            printf ("GL_POINT_TOKEN\n");
            print3DcolorVertex (size, &count, buffer);
        }
        else if (token == GL_LINE_TOKEN) {
            printf ("GL_LINE_TOKEN\n");
            print3DcolorVertex (size, &count, buffer);
            print3DcolorVertex (size, &count, buffer);
        }
        else if (token == GL_LINE_RESET_TOKEN) {
            printf ("GL_LINE_RESET_TOKEN\n");
            print3DcolorVertex (size, &count, buffer);
            print3DcolorVertex (size, &count, buffer);
        }
    }
}

void display(void)
{
    GLfloat feedBuffer[1024];
    GLint size;

    glMatrixMode (GL_PROJECTION);
    glLoadIdentity ();
    glOrtho (0.0, 100.0, 0.0, 100.0, 0.0, 1.0);

    glClearColor (0.0, 0.0, 0.0, 0.0);
    glClear(GL_COLOR_BUFFER_BIT);
    drawGeometry (GL_RENDER);

    glFeedbackBuffer (1024, GL_3D_COLOR, feedBuffer);
    (void) glRenderMode (GL_FEEDBACK);
    drawGeometry (GL_FEEDBACK);
```

```
    size = glRenderMode (GL_RENDER);
    printBuffer (size, feedBuffer);
}

int main(int argc, char** argv)
{
    glutInit(&argc, argv);
    glutInitDisplayMode(GLUT_SINGLE | GLUT_RGB);
    glutInitWindowSize (100, 100);
    glutInitWindowPosition (100, 100);
    glutCreateWindow(argv[0]);
    init();
    glutDisplayFunc(display);
    glutMainLoop();
    return 0;
}
```

Running this program generates the following output:

```
GL_LINE_RESET_TOKEN
  30.00 30.00 0.00 0.84 0.84 0.84 1.00
  50.00 60.00 0.00 0.84 0.84 0.84 1.00
GL_LINE_TOKEN
  50.00 60.00 0.00 0.84 0.84 0.84 1.00
  70.00 40.00 0.00 0.84 0.84 0.84 1.00
GL_PASS_THROUGH_TOKEN
  1.00
GL_PASS_THROUGH_TOKEN
  2.00
GL_POINT_TOKEN
  50.00 50.00 0.00 0.84 0.84 0.84 1.00
```

Thus, the line strip drawn with these commands results in two primitives:

```
glBegin(GL_LINE_STRIP);
    glNormal3f (0.0, 0.0, 1.0);
    glVertex3f (30.0, 30.0, 0.0);
    glVertex3f (50.0, 60.0, 0.0);
    glVertex3f (70.0, 40.0, 0.0);
glEnd();
```

The first primitive begins with GL_LINE_RESET_TOKEN, which indicates that the primitive is a line segment and that the line stipple is reset. The second primitive begins with GL_LINE_TOKEN, so it's also a line segment, but the line stipple isn't reset and hence continues from where the previous line segment left off. Each of the two vertices for these lines generates seven values for the feedback array. Note that the RGBA values for all four vertices in these two lines are (0.84, 0.84, 0.84, 1.0), which is a very light gray color with the maximum alpha value. These color values are a result of the interaction of the surface normal and lighting parameters.

Since no feedback data is generated between the first and second pass-through markers, you can deduce that any primitives drawn between the first two calls to **glPassThrough()** were clipped out of the viewing volume. Finally, the point at (50.0, 50.0, 0.0) is drawn, and its associated data is copied into the feedback array.

Note: In both feedback and selection modes, information on objects is returned prior to any fragment tests. Thus, objects that would not be drawn due to failure of the scissor, alpha, depth, or stencil tests may still have their data processed and returned in both feedback and selection modes.

Try This

Make changes to Example 13-7 and see how they affect the feedback values that are returned. For example, change the coordinate values of **glOrtho()**. Change the lighting variables, or eliminate lighting altogether and change the feedback type to GL_3D. Or add more primitives to see what other geometry (such as filled polygons) contributes to the feedback array.

Chapter 14

Now That You Know

Chapter Objectives

This chapter doesn't have objectives in the same way that previous chapters do. It's simply a collection of topics that describe ideas you might find useful for your application. Some topics, such as error handling, don't fit into other categories, but are too short for an entire chapter.

OpenGL is kind of a bag of low-level tools; now that you know about those tools, you can use them to implement higher-level functions. This chapter presents several examples of such higher-level capabilities.

This chapter discusses a variety of techniques based on OpenGL commands that illustrate some of the not-so-obvious uses to which you can put these commands. The examples are in no particular order and aren't related to each other. The idea is to read the section headings and skip to the examples that you find interesting. For your convenience, the headings are listed and explained briefly here.

Note: Most of the examples in the rest of this guide are complete and can be compiled and run as is. In this chapter, however, there are no complete programs, and you have to do a bit of work on your own to make them run.

- "Error Handling" on page 501 tells you how to check for OpenGL error conditions.

- "Which Version Am I Using?" on page 503 describes how to find out details about the implementation, including the version number. This can be useful for writing applications that are backward compatible with earlier versions of OpenGL.

- "Extensions to the Standard" on page 505 presents techniques to identify and use vendor-specific extensions to the OpenGL standard.

- "Cheesy Translucency" on page 506 explains how to use polygon stippling to achieve translucency; this is particularly useful when you don't have blending hardware available.

- "An Easy Fade Effect" on page 506 shows how to use polygon stippling to create the effect of a fade into the background.

- "Object Selection Using the Back Buffer" on page 508 describes how to use the back buffer in a double-buffered system to handle simple object picking.

- "Cheap Image Transformation" on page 509 discusses how to draw a distorted version of a bitmapped image by drawing each pixel as a quadrilateral.

- "Displaying Layers" on page 511 explains how to display multiple different layers of materials and indicate where the materials overlap.

- "Antialiased Characters" on page 512 describes how to draw smoother fonts.

- "Drawing Round Points" on page 514 describes how to draw near-round points.

- "Interpolating Images" on page 514 shows how to smoothly blend from one image to the another.

- "Making Decals" on page 515 explains how to draw two images, where one is a sort of decal that should always appear on top of the other.

- "Drawing Filled, Concave Polygons Using the Stencil Buffer" on page 516 tells you how to draw concave polygons, nonsimple polygons, and polygons with holes by using the stencil buffer.

- "Finding Interference Regions" on page 518 describes how to determine where three-dimensional pieces overlap.

- "Shadows" on page 519 describes how to draw shadows of lit objects.

- "Hidden-Line Removal" on page 521 discusses how to draw a wireframe object with hidden lines removed by using the stencil buffer.

- "Texture-Mapping Applications" on page 523 describes several clever uses for texture mapping, such as rotating and warping images.

- "Drawing Depth-Buffered Images" on page 523 tells you how to combine images in a depth-buffered environment.

- "Dirichlet Domains" on page 524 explains how to find the Dirichlet domain of a set of points using the depth buffer.

- "Life in the Stencil Buffer" on page 526 explains how to implement the Game of Life using the stencil buffer.

- "Alternative Uses for glDrawPixels() and glCopyPixels()" on page 527 describes how to use these two commands for such effects as fake video, airbrushing, and transposed images.

Error Handling

The truth is, your program will make mistakes. Use of error-handling routines are essential during development and are highly recommended for commercially released applications. (Unless you can give a 100% guarantee your program will never generate an OpenGL error condition. Get real!) OpenGL has simple error-handling routines for the base GL and GLU libraries.

When OpenGL detects an error (in either the base GL or GLU), it records a current error code. The command that caused the error is ignored, so it has no effect on OpenGL state or on the framebuffer contents. (If the error recorded was GL_OUT_OF_MEMORY, however, the results of the command are undefined.) Once recorded, the current error code isn't cleared—that is, additional errors aren't recorded—until you call the query command **glGetError()**, which returns the current error code. After you've queried and cleared the current error code, or if there's no error to begin with, **glGetError()** returns GL_NO_ERROR.

GLenum **glGetError**(void);

Returns the value of the error flag. When an error occurs in either the GL or GLU, the error flag is set to the appropriate error code value. If GL_NO_ERROR is returned, there has been no detectable error since the last call to **glGetError()**, or since the GL was initialized. No other errors are recorded until **glGetError()** is called, the error code is returned, and the flag is reset to GL_NO_ERROR.

It is strongly recommended that you call **glGetError()** at least once in each **display()** routine. Table 14-1 lists the basic defined OpenGL error codes.

Error Code	Description
GL_INVALID_ENUM	GLenum argument out of range
GL_INVALID_VALUE	Numeric argument out of range
GL_INVALID_OPERATION	Operation illegal in current state
GL_STACK_OVERFLOW	Command would cause a stack overflow
GL_STACK_UNDERFLOW	Command would cause a stack underflow
GL_OUT_OF_MEMORY	Not enough memory left to execute command

Table 14-1   OpenGL Error Codes

There are also thirty-seven GLU NURBS errors (with non-descriptive constant names, GLU_NURBS_ERROR1, GLU_NURBS_ERROR2, and so on), fourteen tessellator errors (GLU_TESS_MISSING_BEGIN_POLYGON, GLU_TESS_MISSING_END_POLYGON, GLU_TESS_MISSING_BEGIN_CONTOUR, GLU_TESS_MISSING_END_CONTOUR, GLU_TESS_COORD_TOO_LARGE, GLU_TESS_NEED_COMBINE_CALLBACK, and eight generically named GLU_TESS_ERROR*), and GLU_INCOMPATIBLE_GL_VERSION. Also, the GLU defines the error codes GLU_INVALID_ENUM, GLU_INVALID_VALUE, and GLU_OUT_OF_MEMORY, which have the same meaning as the related OpenGL codes.

To obtain a printable, descriptive string corresponding to either a GL or GLU error code, use the GLU routine **gluErrorString**().

---

const GLubyte* **gluErrorString**(GLenum *errorCode*);

Returns a pointer to a descriptive string that corresponds to the OpenGL or GLU error number passed in *errorCode*.

In Example 14-1, a simple error handling routine is shown.

Example 14-1   Querying and Printing an Error

```
GLenum errCode;
const GLubyte *errString;

if ((errCode = glGetError()) != GL_NO_ERROR) {
   errString = gluErrorString(errCode);
   fprintf (stderr, "OpenGL Error: %s\n", errString);
}
```

Note: The string returned by **gluErrorString**() must not be altered or freed by the application.

Which Version Am I Using?

The portability of OpenGL applications is one of OpenGL's attractive features. However, new versions of OpenGL introduce new features, which may introduce backward compatibility problems. In addition, you may want your application to perform equally well on a variety of implementations. For example, you might make texture mapping the default rendering mode on one machine, but only have flat shading on another. You can use **glGetString**() to obtain release information about your OpenGL implementation.

---

const GLubyte* **glGetString**(GLenum *name*);

Returns a pointer to a string that describes an aspect of the OpenGL implementation. *name* can be one of the following: GL_VENDOR, GL_RENDERER, GL_VERSION, or GL_EXTENSIONS.

GL_VENDOR returns the name of the company responsible for the OpenGL implementation. GL_RENDERER returns an identifier of the renderer, which is usually the hardware platform. For more about GL_EXTENSIONS, see the next section, "Extensions to the Standard" on page 505.

GL_VERSION returns a string that identifies the version number of this implementation of OpenGL. The version string is laid out as follows:

<version number><space><vendor-specific information>

The version number is either of the form

major_number.minor_number

    or

major_number.minor_number.release_number

where the numbers all have one or more digits. The vendor-specific information is optional. For example, if this OpenGL implementation is from the fictitious XYZ Corporation, the string returned might be

1.1.4 XYZ-OS 3.2

which means that this implementation is XYZ's fourth release of an OpenGL library that conforms to the specification for OpenGL Version 1.1. It probably also means this is release 3.2 of XYZ's proprietary operating system.

Another way to query the version number for OpenGL is to look for the symbolic constant (use the preprocessor statement #ifdef) named GL_VERSION_1_1. The absence of the constant GL_VERSION_1_1 means that you have OpenGL Version 1.0.

Note: If running from client to server, such as when performing indirect rendering with the OpenGL extension to the X Window System, the client and server may be different versions. If your client version is ahead of your server, your client might request an operation that is not supported on your server.

Utility Library Version

gluGetString() is a query function for the Utility Library (GLU) and is similar to **glGetString()**.

---

const GLubyte* **gluGetString**(GLenum *name*);

Returns a pointer to a string that describes an aspect of the OpenGL implementation. *name* can be one of the following: GLU_VERSION, or GLU_EXTENSIONS.

Note that **gluGetString()** was not available in GLU 1.0. Another way to query the version number for GLU is to look for the symbolic constant GLU_VERSION_1_1. The absence of the constant GLU_VERSION_1_1 means that you have GLU 1.0.

Extensions to the Standard

OpenGL has a formal written specification that describes what operations comprise the library. An individual vendor or a group of vendors may decide to include additional functionality to their released implementation.

New routine and symbolic constant names clearly indicate whether a feature is part of the OpenGL standard or a vendor-specific extension. To make a vendor-specific name, the vendor appends a company identifier (in uppercase) and, if needed, additional information, such as a machine name. For example, if XYZ Corporation wants to add a new routine and symbolic constant, they might be of the form **glCommandXYZ()** and GL_DEFINITION_XYZ. If XYZ Corporation wants to have an extension that is available only on its FooBar graphics board, then the names might be **glCommandXYZfb()** and GL_DEFINITION_XYZ_FB.

If two of more vendors agree to implement the same extension, then the procedures and constants are suffixed with the more generic EXT (**glCommandEXT()** and GL_DEFINITION_EXT).

If you want to know if a particular extension is supported on your implementation, use **glGetString**(GL_EXTENSIONS). This returns a list of all the extensions in the implementation, separated by spaces. If you want to find out if a specific extension is supported, use the code in Example 14-2 to search through the list and match the extension name. Return GL_TRUE, if it is; GL_FALSE, if it isn't.

Example 14-2   Find Out If An Extension Is Supported

```
static GLboolean QueryExtension(char *extName)
{
   char *p = (char *) glGetString(GL_EXTENSIONS);
```

```
char *end = p + strlen(p);
while (p < end) {
  int n = strcspn(p, " ");
  if ((strlen(extName)==n) && (strncmp(extName,p,n)==0)) {
    return GL_TRUE;
  }
  p += (n + 1);
}
return GL_FALSE;
}
```

Cheesy Translucency

You can use polygon stippling to simulate a translucent material. This is an especially good solution for systems that don't have blending hardware. Since polygon stipple patterns are 32x32 bits, or 1024 bits, you can go from opaque to transparent in 1023 steps. (In practice, that's many more steps than you need!) For example, if you want a surface that lets through 29 percent of the light, simply make up a stipple pattern where 29 percent (roughly 297) of the pixels in the mask are zero and the rest are one. Even if your surfaces have the same translucency, don't use the same stipple pattern for each one, as they cover exactly the same bits on the screen. Make up a different pattern for each by randomly selecting the appropriate number of pixels to be zero. (See "Displaying Points, Lines, and Polygons" on page 49 for more information about polygon stippling.)

If you don't like the effect with random pixels turned on, you can use regular patterns, but they don't work as well when transparent surfaces are stacked. This is often not a problem because most scenes have relatively few translucent regions that overlap. In a picture of an automobile with translucent windows, your line of sight can go through at most two windows, and usually it's only one.

An Easy Fade Effect

Suppose you have an image that you want to fade gradually to some background color. Define a series of polygon stipple patterns, each of which has more bits turned on so that they represent denser and denser patterns. Then use these patterns repeatedly with a polygon large enough to cover the region over which you want to fade. For example, suppose you want to fade to black in 16 steps. First define 16 different pattern arrays:

```
GLubyte stips[16][4*32];
```

Then load them in such a way that each has one-sixteenth of the pixels in a 32×32 stipple pattern turned on and that the bitwise OR of all the stipple patterns is all ones. After that, the following code does the trick:

```
draw_the_picture();
glColor3f(0.0, 0.0, 0.0);        /* set color to black */
for (i = 0; i < 16; i++) {
    glPolygonStipple(&stips[i][0]);
    draw_a_polygon_large_enough_to_cover_the_whole_region();
}
```

In some OpenGL implementations, you might get better performance by first compiling the stipple patterns into display lists. During your initialization, do something like this:

```
#define STIP_OFFSET 100
for (i = 0; i < 16; i++) {
    glNewList(i+STIP_OFFSET, GL_COMPILE);
    glPolygonStipple(&stips[i][0]);
    glEndList();
}
```

Then, replace this line in the first code fragment

```
glPolygonStipple(&stips[i][0]);
```

with

```
glCallList(i);
```

By compiling the command to set the stipple into a display list, OpenGL might be able to rearrange the data in the *stips[ ][ ]* array into the hardware-specific form required for maximum stipple-setting speed.

Another application for this technique is if you're drawing a changing picture and want to leave some blur behind that gradually fades out to give some indication of past motion. For example, suppose you're simulating a planetary system and you want to leave trails on the planets to show a recent portion of their path. Again, assuming you want to fade in sixteen steps, set up the stipple patterns as before (using the display-list version, say), and have the main simulation loop look something like this:

```
current_stipple = 0;
while (1) {                              /* loop forever */
    draw_the_next_frame();
    glCallList(current_stipple++);
    if (current_stipple == 16) current_stipple = 0;
    glColor3f(0.0, 0.0, 0.0);        /* set color to black */
    draw_a_polygon_large_enough_to_cover_the_whole_region();
}
```

Each time through the loop, you clear one-sixteenth of the pixels. Any pixel that hasn't had a planet on it for sixteen frames is certain to be cleared to black. Of course, if your system supports blending in hardware, it's easier to blend in a certain amount of background color with each frame. (See "Displaying Points, Lines, and Polygons" on page 49 for polygon stippling details, Chapter 7 for more information about display lists, and "Blending" on page 214 for information about blending.)

Object Selection Using the Back Buffer

Although the OpenGL selection mechanism (see "Selection" on page 470) is powerful and flexible, it can be cumbersome to use. Often, the situation is simple: Your application draws a scene composed of a substantial number of objects; the user points to an object with the mouse, and the application needs to find the item under the tip of the cursor.

One way to do this requires your application to be running in double-buffer mode. When the user picks an object, the application redraws the entire scene in the back buffer, but instead of using the normal colors for objects, it encodes some kind of object identifier for each object's color. The application then simply reads back the pixel under the cursor, and the value of that pixel encodes the number of the picked object. If many picks are expected for a single, static picture, you can read the entire color buffer once and look in your copy for each attempted pick, rather than read back each pixel individually.

Note that this scheme has an advantage over standard selection in that it picks the object that's in front if multiple objects appear at the same pixel, one behind the other. Since the image with false colors is drawn in the back buffer, the user never sees it; you can redraw the back buffer (or copy it from the front buffer) before swapping the buffers. In color-index mode, the encoding is simple—send the object identifier as the index. In RGBA mode, encode the bits of the identifier into the R, G, and B components.

Be aware that you can run out of identifiers if there are too many objects in the scene. For example, suppose you're running in color-index mode on a system that has 4-bit buffers for color-index information (16 possible different indices) in each of the color buffers, but the scene has thousands of pickable items. To address this issue, the picking can be done in a few passes. To think about this in concrete terms, assume there are fewer than 4096 items, so all the object identifiers can be encoded in 12 bits. In the first pass, draw the scene using indices composed of the 4 high-order bits, then use the second and third passes to draw the middle 4 bits and the 4 low-order bits. After each pass, read the pixel under the cursor, extract the bits, and pack them together at the end to get the object identifier.

With this method, the picking takes three times as long, but that's often acceptable. Note that after you have the high-order 4 bits, you eliminate 15/16 of all objects, so you really need to draw only 1/16 of them for the second pass. Similarly, after the second pass, 255 of the 256 possible items have been eliminated. The first pass thus takes about as long as drawing a single frame does, but the second and third passes can be up to 16 and 256 times as fast.

If you're trying to write portable code that works on different systems, break up your object identifiers into chunks that fit on the lowest common denominator of those systems. Also, keep in mind that your system might perform automatic dithering in RGB mode. If this is the case, turn off dithering.

Cheap Image Transformation

If you want to draw a distorted version of a bitmapped image (perhaps simply stretched or rotated, or perhaps drastically modified by some mathematical function), there are many possibilities. You can use the image as a texture map, which allows you to scale, rotate, or otherwise distort the image. If you just want to scale the image, you can use **glPixelZoom()**.

In many cases, you can achieve good results by drawing the image of each pixel as a quadrilateral. Although this scheme doesn't produce images that are as nice as those you would get by applying a sophisticated filtering algorithm (and it might not be sufficient for sophisticated users), it's a lot quicker.

To make the problem more concrete, assume that the original image is m pixels by n pixels, with coordinates chosen from $[0, m-1] \times [0, n-1]$. Let the distortion functions be $x(m,n)$ and $y(m,n)$. For example, if the distortion is simply a zooming by a factor of 3.2, then $x(m,n) = 3.2*m$ and $y(m,n) = 3.2*n$. The following code draws the distorted image:

```
glShadeModel(GL_FLAT);
glScale(3.2, 3.2, 1.0);
for (j=0; j < n; j++) {
    glBegin(GL_QUAD_STRIP);
    for (i=0; i <= m; i++) {
        glVertex2i(i,j);
        glVertex2i(i, j+1);
        set_color(i,j);
    }
    glEnd();
}
```

This code draws each transformed pixel in a solid color equal to that pixel's color and scales the image size by 3.2. The routine **set_color()** stands for whatever the appropriate OpenGL command is to set the color of the image pixel.

The following is a slightly more complex version that distorts the image using the functions $x(i,j)$ and $y(i,j)$:

```
glShadeModel(GL_FLAT);
for (j=0; j < n; j++) {
    glBegin(GL_QUAD_STRIP);
    for (i=0; i <= m; i++) {
        glVertex2i(x(i,j), y(i,j));
        glVertex2i(x(i,j+1), y(i,j+1));
        set_color(i,j);
    }
    glEnd();
}
```

An even better distorted image can be drawn with the following code:

```
glShadeModel(GL_SMOOTH);
for (j=0; j < (n-1); j++) {
    glBegin(GL_QUAD_STRIP);
    for (i=0; i < m; i++) {
        set_color(i,j);
        glVertex2i(x(i,j), y(i,j));
        set_color(i,j+1);
        glVertex2i(x(i,j+1), y(i,j+1));
    }
```

```
    glEnd();
}
```

This code smoothly interpolates color across each quadrilateral. Note that this version produces one fewer quadrilateral in each dimension than do the flat-shaded versions, because the color image is being used to specify colors at the quadrilateral vertices. In addition, you can antialias the polygons with the appropriate blending function (GL_SRC_ALPHA, GL_ONE) to get an even nicer image.

Displaying Layers

In some applications such as semiconductor layout programs, you want to display multiple different layers of materials and indicate where the materials overlap each other.

As a simple example, suppose you have three different substances that can be layered. At any point, eight possible combinations of layers can occur, as shown in Table 14-2.

	Layer 1	Layer 2	Layer 3	Color
0	absent	absent	absent	black
1	present	absent	absent	red
2	absent	present	absent	green
3	present	present	absent	blue
4	absent	absent	present	pink
5	present	absent	present	yellow
6	absent	present	present	white
7	present	present	present	gray

Table 14-2   Eight Combinations of Layers

You want your program to display eight different colors, depending on the layers present. One arbitrary possibility is shown in the last column of the table. To use this method, use color-index mode and load your color map so that entry 0 is black, entry 1 is red, entry 2 is green, and so on. Note that if the numbers from 0 through 7 are written in binary, the 4 bit is turned on whenever layer 3 appears, the 2 bit whenever layer 2 appears, and the 1 bit whenever layer 1 appears.

To clear the window, set the writemask to 7 (all three layers) and set the clearing color to 0. To draw your image, set the color to 7, and then when you want to draw something in layer *n*, set the writemask to *n*. In other types of applications, it might be necessary to selectively erase in a layer, in which case you would use the writemasks just discussed, but set the color to 0 instead of 7. (See "Masking Buffers" on page 381 for more information about writemasks.)

Antialiased Characters

Using the standard technique for drawing characters with **glBitmap()**, drawing each pixel of a character is an all-or-nothing affair—the pixel is either turned on or not. If you're drawing black characters on a white background, for example, the resulting pixels are either black or white, never a shade of gray. Much smoother, higher-quality images can be achieved if intermediate colors are used when rendering characters (grays, in this example).

Assuming that you're drawing black characters on a white background, imagine a highly magnified picture of the pixels on the screen, with a high-resolution character outline superimposed on it, as shown in the left side of Figure 14-1.

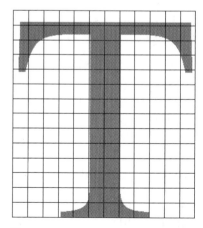

Figure 14-1   Antialiased Characters

Notice that some of the pixels are completely enclosed by the character's outline and should be painted black; some pixels are completely outside the outline and should be painted white; but many pixels should ideally be painted some shade of gray, where the darkness of the gray corresponds to the amount of black in the pixel. If this technique is used, the resulting image on the screen looks better.

If speed and memory usage are of no concern, each character can be drawn as a small image instead of as a bitmap. If you're using RGBA mode, however, this method might require up to 32 bits per pixel of the character to be stored and drawn, instead of the 1 bit per pixel in a standard character. Alternatively, you could use one 8-bit index per pixel and convert these indices to RGBA by table lookup during transfer. In many cases, a compromise is possible that allows you to draw the character with a few gray levels between black and white (say, two or three), and the resulting font description requires only 2 or 3 bits per pixel of storage.

The numbers in the right side of Figure 14-1 indicate the approximate percentage coverage of each pixel: 0 means approximately empty, 1 means approximately one-third coverage, 2 means two-thirds, and 3 means completely covered. If pixels labeled 0 are painted white, pixels labeled 3 are painted black, and pixels labeled 1 and 2 are painted one-third and two-thirds black, respectively, the resulting character looks quite good. Only 2 bits are required to store the numbers 0, 1, 2, and 3, so for 2 bits per pixel, four levels of gray can be saved.

There are basically two methods to implement antialiased characters, depending on whether you're in RGBA or color-index mode.

In RGBA mode, define three different character bitmaps, corresponding to where 1, 2, and 3 appear in Figure 14-1. Set the color to white, and clear for the background. Set the color to one-third gray (RGB = (0.666, 0.666, 0.666)), and draw all the pixels with a 1 in them. Then set RGB = (0.333, 0.333, 0.333), draw with the 2 bitmap, and use RGB = (0.0, 0.0, 0.0) for the 3 bitmap. What you're doing is defining three different fonts and redrawing the string three times, where each pass fills in the bits of the appropriate color densities.

In color-index mode, you can do exactly the same thing, but if you're willing to set up the color map correctly and use writemasks, you can get away with only two bitmaps per character and two passes per string. In the preceding example, set up one bitmap that has a 1 wherever 1 or 3 appears in the character. Set up a second bitmap that has a 1 wherever a 2 or a 3 appears. Load the color map so that 0 gives white, 1 gives light gray, 2 gives dark gray, and 3 gives black. Set the color to 3 (11 in binary) and the writemask to 1, and draw the first bitmap. Then change the writemask to 2, and draw the second. Where 0 appears in Figure 14-1, nothing is drawn in the framebuffer. Where 1, 2, and 3 appear, 1, 2, and 3 appear in the framebuffer.

For this example with only four gray levels, the savings is small—two passes instead of three. If eight gray levels were used instead, the RGBA method would require seven passes, and the color-map masking technique would require only three. With sixteen gray levels, the comparison is fifteen passes to four passes. (See "Masking Buffers" on page 381 for more information about writemasks and "Bitmaps and Fonts" on page 279 for more information about drawing bitmaps.)

Try This

- Can you see how to do RGBA rendering using no more images than the optimized color-index case? Hint: How are RGB fragments normally merged into the color buffer when antialiasing is desired?

Drawing Round Points

Draw near-round, aliased points by enabling point antialiasing, turning blending off, and using an alpha function that passes only fragments with alpha greater than 0.5. (See "Antialiasing" on page 226 and "Blending" on page 214 for more information about these topics.)

Interpolating Images

Suppose you have a pair of images (where *image* can mean a bitmap image, or a picture generated using geometry in the usual way), and you want to smoothly blend from one to the other. This can be done easily using the alpha component and appropriate blending operations. Let's say you want to accomplish the blending in ten steps, where image A is shown in frame 0 and image B is shown in frame 9. The obvious approach is to draw image A with alpha equal to $(9-i)/9$ and image B with an alpha of $i/9$ in frame i.

The problem with this method is that both images must be drawn in each frame. A faster approach is to draw image A in frame 0. To get frame 1, blend in 1/9 of image B and 8/9 of what's there. For frame 2, blend in 1/8 of image

B with 7/8 of what's there. For frame 3, blend in 1/7 of image B with 6/7 of what's there, and so on. For the last step, you're just drawing 1/1 of image B blended with 0/1 of what's left, yielding image B exactly.

To see that this works, if for frame i you have

$$\frac{(9-i)\,A}{9} + \frac{iB}{9}$$

and you blend in $B/(9-i)$ with $(8-i)/(9-i)$ of what's there, you get

$$\frac{B}{9-i} + \frac{8-i}{9-i}\left[\frac{(9-i)\,A}{9} + \frac{iB}{9}\right] = \frac{9-(i+1)\,A}{9} + \frac{(i+1)\,B}{9}$$

(See "Blending" on page 214.)

Making Decals

Suppose you're drawing a complex three-dimensional picture using depth-buffering to eliminate the hidden surfaces. Suppose further that one part of your picture is composed of coplanar figures A and B, where B is a sort of decal that should always appear on top of figure A.

Your first approach might be to draw B after you've drawn A, setting the depth-buffering function to replace on greater or equal. Due to the finite precision of the floating-point representations of the vertices, however, round-off error can cause polygon B to be sometimes a bit in front and sometimes a bit behind figure A. Here's one solution to this problem.

1. Disable the depth buffer for writing, and render A.

2. Enable the depth buffer for writing, and render B.

3. Disable the color buffer for writing, and render A again.

4. Enable the color buffer for writing.

Note that during the entire process, the depth-buffer test is enabled. In step 1, A is rendered wherever it should be, but none of the depth-buffer values are changed; thus, in step 2, wherever B appears over A, B is guaranteed to be drawn. Step 3 simply makes sure that all of the depth values under A are updated correctly, but since RGBA writes are disabled, the color pixels are unaffected. Finally, step 4 returns the system to the default state (writing is enabled both in the depth buffer and in the color buffer).

If a stencil buffer is available, the following simpler technique works.

1. Configure the stencil buffer to write one if the depth test passes, and zero otherwise. Render A.

2. Configure the stencil buffer to make no stencil value change, but to render only where stencil values are one. Disable the depth-buffer test and its update. Render B.

With this method, it's not necessary to initialize the contents of the stencil buffer at any time, because the stencil value of all pixels of interest (that is, those rendered by A) are set when A is rendered. Be sure to reenable the depth test and disable the stencil test before additional polygons are drawn. (See "Selecting Color Buffers for Writing and Reading" on page 379, "Depth Test" on page 391, and "Stencil Test" on page 385.)

Drawing Filled, Concave Polygons Using the Stencil Buffer

Consider the concave polygon 1234567 shown in Figure 14-2. Imagine that it's drawn as a series of triangles: 123, 134, 145, 156, 167, all of which are shown in the figure. The heavier line represents the original polygon boundary. Drawing all these triangles divides the buffer into nine regions A, B, C, ..., I, where region I is outside all the triangles.

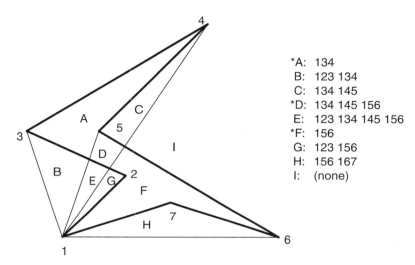

Figure 14-2   Concave Polygon

*A: 134
 B: 123 134
 C: 134 145
*D: 134 145 156
 E: 123 134 145 156
*F: 156
 G: 123 156
 H: 156 167
 I: (none)

In the text of the figure, each of the region names is followed by a list of the triangles that cover it. Regions A, D, and F make up the original polygon; note that these three regions are covered by an odd number of triangles. Every other region is covered by an even number of triangles (possibly zero). Thus, to render the inside of the concave polygon, you just need to render regions that are enclosed by an odd number of triangles. This can be done using the stencil buffer, with a two-pass algorithm.

First, clear the stencil buffer and disable writing into the color buffer. Next, draw each of the triangles in turn, using the GL_INVERT function in the stencil buffer. (For best performance, use triangle fans.) This flips the value between zero and a nonzero value every time a triangle is drawn that covers a pixel. After all the triangles are drawn, if a pixel is covered an even number of times, the value in the stencil buffers is zero; otherwise, it's nonzero. Finally, draw a large polygon over the whole region (or redraw the triangles), but allow drawing only where the stencil buffer is nonzero.

Note: There's a slight generalization of the preceding technique, where you don't need to start with a polygon vertex. In the 1234567 example, let P be any point on or off the polygon. Draw the triangles: P12, P23, P34, P45, P56, P67, and P71. Regions covered by an odd number of triangles are inside; other regions are outside. This is a generalization in that if P happens to be one of the polygon's edges, one of the triangles is empty.

This technique can be used to fill both nonsimple polygons (polygons whose edges cross each other) and polygons with holes. The following example illustrates how to handle a complicated polygon with two regions, one four-sided and one five-sided. Assume further that there's a triangular and a four-sided hole (it doesn't matter in which regions the holes lie). Let the two regions be abcd and efghi, and the holes jkl and mnop. Let z be any point on the plane. Draw the following triangles:

zab zbc zcd zda zef zfg zgh zhi zie zjk zkl zlj zmn zno zop zpm

Mark regions covered by an odd number of triangles as *in*, and those covered by an even number as *out*. (See "Stencil Test" on page 385 for more information about the stencil buffer.)

Finding Interference Regions

If you're designing a mechanical part made from smaller three-dimensional pieces, you often want to display regions where the pieces overlap. In many cases, such regions indicate design errors where parts of a machine interfere with each other. In the case of moving parts, it can be even more valuable, since a search for interfering regions can be done through a complete mechanical cycle of the design. The method for doing this is complicated, and the description here might be too brief. Complete details can be found in the paper *Interactive Inspection of Solids: Cross-sections and Interferences*, by Jarek Rossignac, Abe Megahed, and Bengt-Olaf Schneider (SIGGRAPH 1992 Proceedings).

The method is related to the capping algorithm described in "Stencil Test" on page 385. The idea is to pass an arbitrary clipping plane through the objects that you want to test for interference, and then determine when a portion of the clipping plane is inside more than one object at a time. For a static image, the clipping plane can be moved manually to highlight interfering regions; for a dynamic image, it might be easier to use a grid of clipping planes to search for all possible interferences.

Draw each of the objects you want to check and clip them against the clipping plane. Note which pixels are inside the object at that clipping plane using an odd-even count in the stencil buffer, as explained in the preceding section. (For properly formed objects, a point is inside the object if a ray drawn from that point to the eye intersects an odd number of surfaces of the object.) To find interferences, you need to find pixels in the framebuffer where the clipping plane is in the interior of two or more regions at once; in other words, in the intersection of the interiors of any pair of objects.

If multiple objects need to be tested for mutual intersection, store 1 bit every time some intersection appears, and another bit wherever the clipping buffer is inside any of the objects (the union of the objects' interiors). For each new object, determine its interior, find the intersection of that interior with the union of the interiors of the objects so far tested, and keep track of the intersection points. Then add the interior points of the new object to the union of the other objects' interiors.

You can perform the operations described in the preceding paragraph by using different bits in the stencil buffer together with various masking operations. Three bits of stencil buffer are required per pixel—one for the toggling to determine the interior of each object, one for the union of all interiors discovered so far, and one for the regions where interference has occurred so far. To make this discussion more concrete, assume the 1 bit of the stencil buffer is for toggling interior/exterior, the 2 bit is the running union, and the 4 bit is for interferences so far. For each object that you're going to render, clear the 1 bit (using a stencil mask of one and clearing to zero), then toggle the 1 bit by keeping the stencil mask as one and using the GL_INVERT stencil operation.

You can find intersections and unions of the bits in the stencil buffers using the stenciling operations. For example, to make bits in buffer 2 be the union of the bits in buffers 1 and 2, mask the stencil to those 2 bits, and draw something over the entire object with the stencil function set to pass if anything nonzero occurs. This happens if the bits in buffer 1, buffer 2, or both are turned on. If the comparison succeeds, write a 1 in buffer 2. Also, make sure that drawing in the color buffer is disabled. An intersection calculation is similar—set the function to pass only if the value in the two buffers is equal to 3 (bits turned on in both buffers 1 and 2). Write the result into the correct buffer. (See "Stencil Test" on page 385.)

Shadows

Every possible projection of three-dimensional space to three-dimensional space can be achieved with a suitable 4×4 invertible matrix and homogeneous coordinates. If the matrix isn't invertible but has rank 3, it projects three-dimensional space onto a two-dimensional plane. Every such possible projection can be achieved with a suitable rank-3 4×4 matrix. To find the shadow of an arbitrary object on an arbitrary plane from an arbitrary light source (possibly at infinity), you need to find a matrix representing that projection, multiply it on the matrix stack, and draw the object in the shadow color. Keep in mind that you need to project onto each plane that you're calling the "ground."

As a simple illustration, assume the light is at the origin, and the equation of the ground plane is $ax+by+c+d=0$. Given a vertex S=$(sx,sy,sz,1)$, the line from the light through S includes all points αS, where α is an arbitrary real number. The point where this line intersects the plane occurs when

$$\alpha(a*sz+b*sy+c*sz) + d = 0,$$

so

$$\alpha = -d/(a*sx+b*sy+c*sz).$$

Plugging this back into the line, we get

$$-d(sx,sy,sz)/(a*sx+b*sy+c*sz)$$

for the point of intersection.

The matrix that maps S to this point for every S is

$$\begin{bmatrix} -d & 0 & 0 & a \\ 0 & -d & 0 & b \\ 0 & 0 & -d & c \\ 0 & 0 & 0 & 0 \end{bmatrix}$$

This matrix can be used if you first translate the world so that the light is at the origin.

If the light is from an infinite source, all you have is a point S and a direction D = (dx,dy,dz). Points along the line are given by

$$S + \alpha D$$

Proceeding as before, the intersection of this line with the plane is given by

$$a(sx+\alpha dx)+b(sy+\alpha dy)+c(sz+\alpha dz)+d = 0$$

Solving for α, plugging that back into the equation for a line, and then determining a projection matrix gives

$$\begin{bmatrix} b*dy+c*dz & -a*dy & -a*dz & 0 \\ -b*dx & a*dx+c*dz & -b*dz & 0 \\ -c*dx & -c*dy & a*dx+b*dy & 0 \\ -d*dx & -d*dy & -d*dz & a*dx+b*dy*c*dz \end{bmatrix}$$

This matrix works given the plane and an arbitrary direction vector. There's no need to translate anything first. (See Chapter 3 and Appendix F.)

Hidden-Line Removal

If you want to draw a wireframe object with hidden lines removed, one approach is to draw the outlines using lines and then fill the interiors of the polygons making up the surface with polygons having the background color. With depth-buffering enabled, this interior fill covers any outlines that would be obscured by faces closer to the eye. This method would work, except that there's no guarantee that the interior of the object falls entirely inside the polygon's outline; in fact, it might overlap it in various places.

There's an easy, two-pass solution using either polygon offset or the stencil buffer. Polygon offset is usually the preferred technique, since polygon offset is almost always faster than stencil buffer. Both methods are described here, so you can see how both approaches to the problem work.

Hidden-Line Removal with Polygon Offset

To use polygon offset to accomplish hidden-line removal, the object is drawn twice. The highlighted edges are drawn in the foreground color, using filled polygons but with the polygon mode GL_LINE to rasterize it as a wireframe. Then the filled polygons are drawn with the default polygon mode, which fills the interior of the wireframe, and with enough polygon offset to nudge the filled polygons a little farther from the eye. With the polygon offset, the interior recedes just enough that the highlighted edges are drawn without unpleasant visual artifacts.

```
glEnable(GL_DEPTH_TEST);
glPolygonMode(GL_FRONT_AND_BACK, GL_LINE);
set_color(foreground);
draw_object_with_filled_polygons();

glPolygonMode(GL_FRONT_AND_BACK, GL_FILL);
glEnable(GL_POLYGON_OFFSET_FILL);
glPolygonOffset(1.0, 1.0);
set_color(background);
draw_object_with_filled_polygons();
glDisable(GL_POLYGON_OFFSET_FILL);
```

You may need to adjust the amount of offset needed (for wider lines, for example). (See "Polygon Offset" on page 247 for more information.)

Hidden-Line Removal with the Stencil Buffer

Using the stencil buffer for hidden-line removal is a more complicated procedure. For each polygon, you'll need to clear the stencil buffer, and then draw the outline both in the framebuffer and in the stencil buffer. Then when you fill the interior, enable drawing only where the stencil buffer is still clear. To avoid doing an entire stencil-buffer clear for each polygon, an easy way to clear it is simply to draw 0's into the buffer using the same polygon outline. In this way, you need to clear the entire stencil buffer only once.

For example, the following code represents the inner loop you might use to perform such hidden-line removal. Each polygon is outlined in the foreground color, filled with the background color, and then outlined again in the foreground color. The stencil buffer is used to keep the fill color of each polygon from overwriting its outline. To optimize performance, the stencil and color parameters are changed only twice per loop by using the same values both times the polygon outline is drawn.

```
glEnable(GL_STENCIL_TEST);
glEnable(GL_DEPTH_TEST);
glClear(GL_STENCIL_BUFFER_BIT);
glStencilFunc(GL_ALWAYS, 0, 1);
glStencilOp(GL_INVERT, GL_INVERT, GL_INVERT);
set_color(foreground);
for (i=0; i < max; i++) {
    outline_polygon(i);
    set_color(background);
    glStencilFunc(GL_EQUAL, 0, 1);
    glStencilOp(GL_KEEP, GL_KEEP, GL_KEEP);
    fill_polygon(i);
    set_color(foreground);
    glStencilFunc(GL_ALWAYS, 0, 1);
    glStencilOp(GL_INVERT, GL_INVERT, GL_INVERT);
    outline_polygon(i);
}
```

(See "Stencil Test" on page 385.)

Texture-Mapping Applications

Texture mapping is quite powerful, and it can be used in some interesting ways. Here are a few advanced applications of texture mapping.

- Antialiased text—Define a texture map for each character at a relatively high resolution, and then map them onto smaller areas using the filtering provided by texturing. This also makes text appear correctly on surfaces that aren't aligned with the screen, but are tilted and have some perspective distortion.

- Antialiased lines—These can be done like antialiased text: Make the line in the texture several pixels wide, and use the texture filtering to antialias the lines.

- Image scaling and rotation—If you put an image into a texture map and use that texture to map onto a polygon, rotating and scaling the polygon effectively rotates and scales the image.

- Image warping—As in the preceding example, store the image as a texture map, but map it to some spline-defined surface (use evaluators). As you warp the surface, the image follows the warping.

- Projecting images—Put the image in a texture map, and project it as a spotlight, creating a slide projector effect. (See "The q Coordinate" on page 372 for more information about how to model a spotlight using textures.)

(See Chapter 3 for information about rotating and scaling, Chapter 9 for more information about creating textures, and Chapter 12 for details on evaluators.)

Drawing Depth-Buffered Images

For complex static backgrounds, the rendering time for the geometric description of the background can be greater than the time it takes to draw a pixel image of the rendered background. If there's a fixed background and a relatively simple changing foreground, you may want to draw the background and its associated depth-buffered version as an image rather than render it geometrically. The foreground might also consist of items that are time-consuming to render, but whose framebuffer images and depth buffers are available. You can render these items into a depth-buffered environment using a two-pass algorithm.

For example, if you're drawing a model of a molecule made of spheres, you might have an image of a beautifully rendered sphere and its associated depth-buffer values that were calculated using Phong shading or ray-tracing or by using some other scheme that isn't directly available through OpenGL. To draw a complex model, you might be required to draw hundreds of such spheres, which should be depth-buffered together.

To add a depth-buffered image to the scene, first draw the image's depth-buffer values into the depth buffer using **glDrawPixels()**. Then enable depth-buffering, set the writemask to zero so that no drawing occurs, and enable stenciling such that the stencil buffers get drawn whenever a write to the depth buffer occurs.

Then draw the image into the color buffer, masked by the stencil buffer you've just written so that writing occurs only when there's a 1 in the stencil buffer. During this write, set the stenciling function to zero out the stencil buffer so that it's automatically cleared when it's time to add the next image to the scene. If the objects are to be moved nearer to or farther from the viewer, you need to use an orthographic projection; in these cases, you use GL_DEPTH_BIAS with **glPixelTransfer*()** to move the depth image. (See "Coordinate System Survival Kit" on page 35, "Depth Test" on page 391, "Stencil Test" on page 385, and Chapter 8 for details on **glDrawPixels()** and **glPixelTransfer*()**.)

Dirichlet Domains

Given a set S of points on a plane, the Dirichlet domain or Voronoi polygon of one of the points is the set of all points in the plane closer to that point than to any other point in the set S. These points provide the solution to many problems in computational geometry. Figure 14-3 shows outlines of the Dirichlet domains for a set of points.

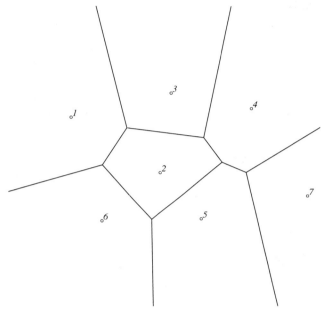

Figure 14-3 Dirichlet Domains

If you draw a depth-buffered cone with its apex at the point in a different color than each of the points in S, the Dirichlet domain for each point is drawn in that color. The easiest way to do this is to precompute a cone's depth in an image and use the image as the depth-buffer values as described in the preceding section. You don't need an image to draw in the framebuffer as in the case of shaded spheres, however. While you're drawing into the depth buffer, use the stencil buffer to record the pixels where drawing should occur by first clearing it and then writing nonzero values wherever the depth test succeeds. To draw the Dirichlet region, draw a polygon over the entire window, but enable drawing only where the stencil buffers are nonzero.

You can do this perhaps more easily by rendering cones of uniform color with a simple depth buffer, but a good cone might require thousands of polygons. The technique described in this section can render much higher-quality cones much more quickly. (See "A Hidden-Surface Removal Survival Kit" on page 171 and "Depth Test" on page 391.)

Life in the Stencil Buffer

The Game of Life, invented by John Conway, is played on a rectangular grid where each grid location is "alive" or "dead." To calculate the next generation from the current one, count the number of live neighbors for each grid location (the eight adjacent grid locations are neighbors). A grid location is alive in generation $n+1$ if it was alive in generation n and has exactly two or three live neighbors, or if it was dead in generation n and has exactly three live neighbors. In all other cases, it is dead in generation $n+1$. This game generates some incredibly interesting patterns given different initial configurations. (See Martin Gardner, "Mathematical Games," *Scientific American*, vol. 223, no. 4, October 1970, p. 120–123.) Figure 14-4 shows six generations from a game.

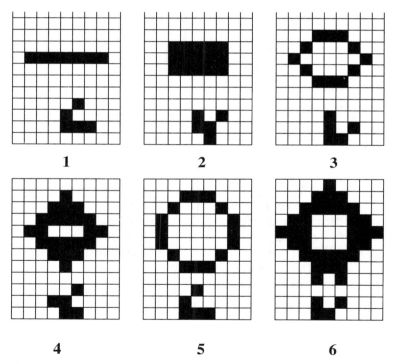

Figure 14-4   Six Generations from the Game of Life

One way to create this game using OpenGL is to use a multipass algorithm. Keep the data in the color buffer, one pixel for each grid point. Assume that black (all zeros) is the background color, and the color of a live pixel is nonzero. Initialize by clearing the depth and stencil buffers to zero, set the depth-buffer writemask to zero, and set the depth comparison function so that it passes on not-equal. To iterate, read the image off the screen, enable drawing into the depth buffer, and set the stencil function so that it increments whenever a depth comparison succeeds but leaves the stencil buffer unchanged otherwise. Disable drawing into the color buffer.

Next, draw the image eight times, offset one pixel in each vertical, horizontal, and diagonal direction. When you're done, the stencil buffer contains a count of the number of live neighbors for each pixel. Enable drawing to the color buffer, set the color to the color for live cells, and set the stencil function to draw only if the value in the stencil buffer is 3 (three live neighbors). In addition, if this drawing occurs, decrement the value in the stencil buffer. Then draw a rectangle covering the image; this paints each cell that has exactly three live neighbors with the "alive" color.

At this point, the stencil buffers contain 0, 1, 2, 4, 5, 6, 7, 8, and the values under the 2's are correct. The values under 0, 1, 4, 5, 6, 7, and 8 must be cleared to the "dead" color. Set the stencil function to draw whenever the value is not 2, and to zero the stencil values in all cases. Then draw a large polygon of the "dead" color across the entire image. You're done.

For a usable demonstration program, you might want to zoom the grid up to a size larger than a single pixel; it's hard to see detailed patterns with a single pixel per grid point. (See "Coordinate System Survival Kit" on page 35, "Depth Test" on page 391, and "Stencil Test" on page 385.)

Alternative Uses for glDrawPixels() and glCopyPixels()

You might think of **glDrawPixels()** as a way to draw a rectangular region of pixels to the screen. Although this is often what it's used for, some other interesting uses are outlined here.

- Video—Even if your machine doesn't have special video hardware, you can display short movie clips by repeatedly drawing frames with **glDrawPixels()** in the same region of the back buffer and then swapping the buffers. The size of the frames you can display with reasonable performance using this method depends on your hardware's drawing speed, so you might be limited to 100×100 pixel movies (or smaller) if you want smooth fake video.

- Airbrush—In a paint program, your airbrush (or paintbrush) shape can be simulated using alpha values. The color of the paint is represented as the color values. To paint with a circular brush in blue, repeatedly draw a blue square with **glDrawPixels()** where the alpha values are largest in the center and taper to zero at the edges of a circle centered in the square. Draw using a blending function that uses alpha of the incoming color and (1–alpha) of the color already at the pixel. If the alpha values in the brush are all much less than one, you have to paint over an area repeatedly to get a solid color. If the alpha values are near one, each brush stroke pretty much obliterates the colors underneath.

- Filtered Zooms—If you zoom a pixel image by a nonintegral amount, OpenGL effectively uses a box filter, which can lead to rather severe aliasing effects. To improve the filtering, jitter the resulting image by amounts less than a pixel and redraw it multiple times, using alpha blending to average the resulting pixels. The result is a filtered zoom.

- Transposing Images—You can swap same-size images in place with **glCopyPixels()** using the XOR operation. With this method, you can avoid having to read the images back into processor memory. If A and B represent the two images, the operation looks like this:

  a. A = A XOR B

  b. B = A XOR B

  c. A = A XOR B

Order of Operations

This book describes all the operations performed between when vertices are initially specified and fragments are finally written into the framebuffer. The chapters of this book are arranged in an order that facilitates learning rather than in the exact order in which these operations are actually performed. Sometimes the exact order of operations doesn't matter—for example, surfaces can be converted to polygons and then transformed, or transformed first and then converted to polygons, with identical results—and different implementations of OpenGL might do things differently.

This appendix describes a possible order; any implementation is required to give equivalent results. If you want more details than are presented here, see the *OpenGL Reference Manual*.

This appendix has the following major sections:

Overview

This section gives an overview of the order of operations, as shown in Figure A-1. Geometric data (vertices, lines, and polygons) follows the path through the row of boxes that include evaluators and per-vertex operations, while pixel data (pixels, images, and bitmaps) is treated differently for part of the process. Both types of data undergo the rasterization and per-fragment operations before the final pixel data is written into the framebuffer.

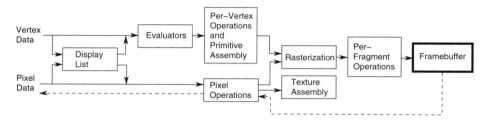

Figure A-1   Order of Operations

All data, whether it describes geometry or pixels, can be saved in a display list or processed immediately. When a display list is executed, the data is sent from the display list just as if it were sent by the application.

All geometric primitives are eventually described by vertices. If evaluators are used, that data is converted to vertices and treated as vertices from then on. Vertex data may also be stored in and used from specialized vertex arrays. Per-vertex calculations are performed on each vertex, followed by rasterization to fragments. For pixel data, pixel operations are performed, and the results are either stored in the texture memory, used for polygon stippling, or rasterized to fragments.

Finally, the fragments are subjected to a series of per-fragment operations, after which the final pixel values are drawn into the framebuffer.

Geometric Operations

Geometric data, whether it comes from a display list, an evaluator, the vertices of a rectangle, or as raw data, consists of a set of vertices and the type of primitive it describes (a vertex, line, or polygon). Vertex data includes not only the (x, y, z, w) coordinates, but also a normal vector, texture coordinates, a RGBA color, a color index, material properties, and edge-flag data. All these elements except the vertex's coordinates can be specified in any order, and default values exist as well. As soon as the vertex command **glVertex*()** is issued, the components are padded, if necessary, to four dimensions (using $z = 0$ and $w = 1$), and the current values of all the elements are associated with the vertex. The complete set of vertex data is then processed. (If vertex arrays are used, vertex data may be batch processed and processed vertices may be reused.)

Per-Vertex Operations

In the per-vertex operations stage of processing, each vertex's spatial coordinates are transformed by the modelview matrix, while the normal vector is transformed by that matrix's inverse transpose and renormalized if specified. If automatic texture generation is enabled, new texture coordinates are generated from the transformed vertex coordinates, and they replace the vertex's old texture coordinates. The texture coordinates are then transformed by the current texture matrix and passed on to the primitive assembly step.

Meanwhile, the lighting calculations, if enabled, are performed using the transformed vertex and normal vector coordinates, and the current material, lights, and lighting model. These calculations generate new colors or indices that are clamped or masked to the appropriate range and passed on to the primitive assembly step.

Primitive Assembly

Primitive assembly differs, depending on whether the primitive is a point, a line, or a polygon. If flat shading is enabled, the colors or indices of all the vertices in a line or polygon are set to the same value. If special clipping planes are defined and enabled, they're used to clip primitives of all three types. (The clipping-plane equations are transformed by the inverse transpose of the modelview matrix when they're specified.) Point clipping simply passes or rejects vertices; line or polygon clipping can add additional vertices depending on how the line or polygon is clipped. After this clipping, the spatial coordinates of each vertex are transformed by the projection matrix, and the results are clipped against the standard viewing planes $x = \pm w$, $y = \pm w$, and $z = \pm w$.

If selection is enabled, any primitive not eliminated by clipping generates a selection-hit report, and no further processing is performed. Without selection, perspective division by *w* occurs and the viewport and depth-range operations are applied. Also, if the primitive is a polygon, it's then subjected to a culling test (if culling is enabled). A polygon might convert to vertices or lines, depending on the polygon mode.

Finally, points, lines, and polygons are rasterized to fragments, taking into account polygon or line stipples, line width, and point size. Rasterization involves determining which squares of an integer grid in window coordinates are occupied by the primitive. If antialiasing is enabled, coverage (the portion of the square that is occupied by the primitive) is also computed. Color and depth values are also assigned to each such square. If polygon offset is enabled, depth values are slightly modified by a calculated offset value.

Pixel Operations

Pixels from host memory are first unpacked into the proper number of components. The OpenGL unpacking facility handles a number of different formats. Next, the data is scaled, biased, and processed using a pixel map. The results are clamped to an appropriate range depending on the data type and then either written in the texture memory for use in texture mapping or rasterized to fragments.

If pixel data is read from the framebuffer, pixel-transfer operations (scale, bias, mapping, and clamping) are performed. The results are packed into an appropriate format and then returned to processor memory.

The pixel copy operation is similar to a combination of the unpacking and transfer operations, except that packing and unpacking is unnecessary, and only a single pass is made through the transfer operations before the data is written back into the framebuffer.

Texture Memory

OpenGL Version 1.1 provides additional control over texture memory. Texture image data can be specified from framebuffer memory, as well as processor memory. All or a portion of a texture image may be replaced. Texture data may be stored in texture objects, which can be loaded into texture memory. If there are too many texture objects to fit into texture memory at the same time, the textures that have the highest priorities remain in the texture memory.

Fragment Operations

If texturing is enabled, a texel is generated from texture memory for each fragment and applied to the fragment. Then fog calculations are performed, if they're enabled, followed by the application of coverage (antialiasing) values, if antialiasing is enabled.

Next comes scissoring, followed by the alpha test (in RGBA mode only), the stencil test, and the depth-buffer test. If in RGBA mode, blending is performed. Blending is followed by dithering and logical operation. All these operations may be disabled.

The fragment is then masked by a color mask or an index mask, depending on the mode, and drawn into the appropriate buffer. If fragments are being written into the stencil or depth buffer, masking occurs after the stencil and depth tests, and the results are drawn into the framebuffer without performing the blending, dithering, or logical operation.

Odds and Ends

Matrix operations deal with the current matrix stack, which can be the modelview, the projection, or the texture matrix stack. The commands **glMultMatrix*()**, **glLoadMatrix*()**, and **glLoadIdentity()** are applied to the top matrix on the stack, while **glTranslate*()**, **glRotate*()**, **glScale*()**, **glOrtho()**, and **glFrustum()** are used to create a matrix that's multiplied by the top matrix. When the modelview matrix is modified, its inverse transpose is also generated for normal vector transformation.

The commands that set the current raster position are treated exactly like a vertex command up until when rasterization would occur. At this point, the value is saved and is used in the rasterization of pixel data.

The various **glClear()** commands bypass all operations except scissoring, dithering, and writemasking.

State Variables

This appendix lists the queryable OpenGL state variables, their default values, and the commands for obtaining the values of these variables. The *OpenGL Reference Manual* contains detailed information on all the commands and constants discussed in this appendix. This appendix has these major sections:

- "The Query Commands" on page 536
- "OpenGL State Variables" on page 537

The Query Commands

In addition to the basic commands to obtain the values of simple state variables (commands such as **glGetIntegerv()** and **glIsEnabled()**, which are described in "Basic State Management" on page 48), there are other specialized commands to return more complex state variables. The prototypes for these specialized commands are listed here. Some of these routines, such as **glGetError()** and **glGetString()**, have been discussed in more detail elsewhere in the book.

To find out when you need to use these commands and their corresponding symbolic constants, use the tables in the next section, "OpenGL State Variables" on page 537. Also see the *OpenGL Reference Manual*.

void **glGetClipPlane**(GLenum *plane*, GLdouble **equation*);

GLenum **glGetError**(void);

void **glGetLight**{if}**v**(GLenum *light*, GLenum *pname*, TYPE **params*);

void **glGetMap**{ifd}**v**(GLenum *target*, GLenum *query*, TYPE **v*);

void **glGetMaterial**{if}**v**(GLenum *face*, GLenum *pname*, TYPE **params*);

void **glGetPixelMap**{f ui us}**v**(GLenum *map*, TYPE **values*);

void **glGetPolygonStipple**(GLubyte **mask*);

const GLubyte * **glGetString**(GLenum *name*);

void **glGetTexEnv**{if}**v**(GLenum *target*, GLenum *pname*, TYPE **params*);

void **glGetTexGen**{ifd}**v**(GLenum *coord*, GLenum *pname*, TYPE **params*);

void **glGetTexImage**(GLenum *target*, GLint *level*, GLenum *format*, GLenum *type*, GLvoid **pixels*);

void **glGetTexLevelParameter**{if}**v**(GLenum *target*, GLint *level*, GLenum *pname*, TYPE **params*);

void **glGetTexParameter**{if}**v**(GLenum *target*, GLenum *pname*, TYPE **params*);

void **gluGetNurbsProperty**(GLUnurbsObj **nobj*, GLenum *property*, GLfloat **value*);

const GLubyte * **gluGetString**(GLenum *name*);

void **gluGetTessProperty**(GLUtesselator **tess*, GLenum *which*, GLdouble **data*);

OpenGL State Variables

The following pages contain tables that list the names of queryable state variables. For each variable, the tables list a description of it, its attribute group, its initial or minimum value, and the suggested **glGet*()** command to use for obtaining it. State variables that can be obtained using **glGetBooleanv()**, **glGetIntegerv()**, **glGetFloatv()**, or **glGetDoublev()** are listed with just one of these commands—the one that's most appropriate given the type of data to be returned. (Some vertex array variables can be queried only with **glGetPointerv()**.) These state variables can't be obtained using **glIsEnabled()**. However, state variables for which **glIsEnabled()** is listed as the query command can also be obtained using **glGetBooleanv()**, **glGetIntegerv()**, **glGetFloatv()**, and **glGetDoublev()**. State variables for which any other command is listed as the query command can be obtained only by using that command.

If one or more attribute groups are listed, the state variable belongs to the listed group or groups. If no attribute group is listed, the variable doesn't belong to any group. **glPushAttrib()**, **glPushClientAttrib()**, **glPopAttrib()**, and **glPopClientAttrib()** may be used to save and restore all state values that belong to an attribute group. (See "Attribute Groups" on page 78 for more information.)

All queryable state variables, except the implementation-dependent ones, have initial values. If no initial value is listed, you need to consult either the section where that variable is discussed or the *OpenGL Reference Manual* to determine its initial value.

Current Values and Associated Data

State Variable	Description	Attribute Group	Initial Value	Get Command
GL_CURRENT_COLOR	Current color	current	1, 1, 1, 1	glGetIntegerv(), glGetFloatv()
GL_CURRENT_INDEX	Current color index	current	1	glGetIntegerv(), glGetFloatv()
GL_CURRENT_TEXTURE_COORDS	Current texture coordinates	current	0, 0, 0, 1	glGetFloatv()
GL_CURRENT_NORMAL	Current normal	current	0, 0, 1	glGetFloatv()
GL_CURRENT_RASTER_POSITION	Current raster position	current	0, 0, 0, 1	glGetFloatv()
GL_CURRENT_RASTER_DISTANCE	Current raster distance	current	0	glGetFloatv()
GL_CURRENT_RASTER_COLOR	Color associated with raster position	current	1, 1, 1, 1	glGetIntegerv(), glGetFloatv()
GL_CURRENT_RASTER_INDEX	Color index associated with raster position	current	1	glGetIntegerv(), glGetFloatv()
GL_CURRENT_RASTER_TEXTURE_COORDS	Texture coordinates associated with raster position	current	0, 0, 0, 1	glGetFloatv()
GL_CURRENT_RASTER_POSITION_VALID	Raster position valid bit	current	GL_TRUE	glGetBooleanv()
GL_EDGE_FLAG	Edge flag	current	GL_TRUE	glGetBooleanv()

Table B-1   State Variables for Current Values and Associated Data

Vertex Array

State Variable	Description	Attribute Group	Initial Value	Get Command
GL_VERTEX_ARRAY	Vertex array enable	vertex-array	GL_FALSE	glIsEnabled()
GL_VERTEX_ARRAY_SIZE	Coordinates per vertex	vertex-array	4	glGetIntegerv()
GL_VERTEX_ARRAY_TYPE	Type of vertex coordinates	vertex-array	GL_FLOAT	glGetIntegerv()
GL_VERTEX_ARRAY_STRIDE	Stride between vertices	vertex-array	0	glGetIntegerv()
GL_VERTEX_ARRAY_POINTER	Pointer to the vertex array	vertex-array	NULL	glGetPointerv()
GL_NORMAL_ARRAY	Normal array enable	vertex-array	GL_FALSE	glIsEnabled()
GL_NORMAL_ARRAY_TYPE	Type of normal coordinates	vertex-array	GL_FLOAT	glGetIntegerv()
GL_NORMAL_ARRAY_STRIDE	Stride between normals	vertex-array	0	glGetIntegerv()
GL_NORMAL_ARRAY_POINTER	Pointer to the normal array	vertex-array	NULL	glGetPointerv()
GL_COLOR_ARRAY	RGBA color array enable	vertex-array	GL_FALSE	glIsEnabled()
GL_COLOR_ARRAY_SIZE	Colors per vertex	vertex-array	4	glGetIntegerv()
GL_COLOR_ARRAY_TYPE	Type of color components	vertex-array	GL_FLOAT	glGetIntegerv()
GL_COLOR_ARRAY_STRIDE	Stride between colors	vertex-array	0	glGetIntegerv()
GL_COLOR_ARRAY_POINTER	Pointer to the color array	vertex-array	NULL	glGetPointerv()
GL_INDEX_ARRAY	Color-index array enable	vertex-array	GL_FALSE	glIsEnabled()

Table B-2   Vertex Array State Variables

State Variable	Description	Attribute Group	Initial Value	Get Command
GL_INDEX_ARRAY_TYPE	Type of color indices	vertex-array	GL_FLOAT	glGetIntegerv()
GL_INDEX_ARRAY_STRIDE	Stride between color indices	vertex-array	0	glGetIntegerv()
GL_INDEX_ARRAY_POINTER	Pointer to the index array	vertex-array	NULL	glGetPointerv()
GL_TEXTURE_COORD_ARRAY	Texture coordinate array enable	vertex-array	GL_FALSE	glIsEnabled()
GL_TEXTURE_COORD_ARRAY_SIZE	Texture coordinates per element	vertex-array	4	glGetIntegerv()
GL_TEXTURE_COORD_ARRAY_TYPE	Type of texture coordinates	vertex-array	GL_FLOAT	glGetIntegerv()
GL_TEXTURE_COORD_ARRAY_STRIDE	Stride between texture coordinates	vertex-array	0	glGetIntegerv()
GL_TEXTURE_COORD_ARRAY_POINTER	Pointer to the texture coordinate array	vertex-array	NULL	glGetPointerv()
GL_EDGE_FLAG_ARRAY	Edge flag array enable	vertex-array	GL_FALSE	glIsEnabled()
GL_EDGE_FLAG_ARRAY_STRIDE	Stride between edge flags	vertex-array	0	glGetIntegerv()
GL_EDGE_FLAG_ARRAY_POINTER	Pointer to the edge flag array	vertex-array	NULL	glGetPointerv()

Table B-2   Vertex Array State Variables (continued)

Transformation

State Variable	Description	Attribute Group	Initial Value	Get Command
GL_MODELVIEW_MATRIX	Modelview matrix stack	—	Identity	glGetFloatv()
GL_PROJECTION_MATRIX	Projection matrix stack	—	Identity	glGetFloatv()
GL_TEXTURE_MATRIX	Texture matrix stack	—	Identity	glGetFloatv()
GL_VIEWPORT	Viewport origin and extent	viewport	—	glGetIntegerv()
GL_DEPTH_RANGE	Depth range near and far	viewport	0, 1	glGetFloatv()
GL_MODELVIEW_STACK_DEPTH	Modelview matrix stack pointer	—	1	glGetIntegerv()
GL_PROJECTION_STACK_DEPTH	Projection matrix stack pointer	—	1	glGetIntegerv()
GL_TEXTURE_STACK_DEPTH	Texture matrix stack pointer	—	1	glGetIntegerv()
GL_MATRIX_MODE	Current matrix mode	transform	GL_MODELVIEW	glGetIntegerv()
GL_NORMALIZE	Current normal normalization on/off	transform/ enable	GL_FALSE	glIsEnabled()
GL_CLIP_PLANE*i*	User clipping plane coefficients	transform	0, 0, 0, 0	glGetClipPlane()
GL_CLIP_PLANE*i*	*i*th user clipping plane enabled	transform/ enable	GL_FALSE	glIsEnabled()

Table B-3   Transformation State Variables

Coloring

State Variable	Description	Attribute Group	Initial Value	Get Command
GL_FOG_COLOR	Fog color	fog	0, 0, 0, 0	glGetFloatv()
GL_FOG_INDEX	Fog index	fog	0	glGetFloatv()
GL_FOG_DENSITY	Exponential fog density	fog	1.0	glGetFloatv()
GL_FOG_START	Linear fog start	fog	0.0	glGetFloatv()
GL_FOG_END	Linear fog end	fog	1.0	glGetFloatv()
GL_FOG_MODE	Fog mode	fog	GL_EXP	glGetIntegerv()
GL_FOG	True if fog enabled	fog/enable	GL_FALSE	glIsEnabled()
GL_SHADE_MODEL	glShadeModel() setting	lighting	GL_SMOOTH	glGetIntegerv()

Table B-4   Coloring State Variables

Lighting

See also Table 5-1 on page 180 and Table 5-3 on page 196 for initial values.

State Variable	Description	Attribute Group	Initial Value	Get Command
GL_LIGHTING	True if lighting is enabled	lighting /enable	GL_FALSE	glIsEnabled()
GL_COLOR_MATERIAL	True if color tracking is enabled	lighting	GL_FALSE	glIsEnabled()
GL_COLOR_MATERIAL_PARAMETER	Material properties tracking current color	lighting	GL_AMBIENT_ AND_DIFFUSE	glGetIntegerv()
GL_COLOR_MATERIAL_FACE	Face(s) affected by color tracking	lighting	GL_FRONT_ AND_BACK	glGetIntegerv()
GL_AMBIENT	Ambient material color	lighting	(0.2, 0.2, 0.2, 1.0)	glGetMaterialfv()
GL_DIFFUSE	Diffuse material color	lighting	(0.8, 0.8, 0.8, 1.0)	glGetMaterialfv()
GL_SPECULAR	Specular material color	lighting	(0.0, 0.0, 0.0, 1.0)	glGetMaterialfv()
GL_EMISSION	Emissive material color	lighting	(0.0, 0.0, 0.0, 1.0)	glGetMaterialfv()
GL_SHININESS	Specular exponent of material	lighting	0.0	glGetMaterialfv()
GL_LIGHT_MODEL_AMBIENT	Ambient scene color	lighting	(0.2, 0.2, 0.2, 1.0)	glGetFloatv()
GL_LIGHT_MODEL_LOCAL_VIEWER	Viewer is local	lighting	GL_FALSE	glGetBooleanv()
GL_LIGHT_MODEL_TWO_SIDE	Use two-sided lighting	lighting	GL_FALSE	glGetBooleanv()

Table B-5   Lighting State Variables

State Variable	Description	Attribute Group	Initial Value	Get Command
GL_AMBIENT	Ambient intensity of light i	lighting	(0.0,0.0,0.0,1.0)	glGetLightfv()
GL_DIFFUSE	Diffuse intensity of light i	lighting	—	glGetLightfv()
GL_SPECULAR	Specular intensity of light i	lighting	—	glGetLightfv()
GL_POSITION	Position of light i	lighting	(0.0, 0.0, 1.0, 0.0)	glGetLightfv()
GL_CONSTANT_ATTENUATION	Constant attenuation factor	lighting	1.0	glGetLightfv()
GL_LINEAR_ATTENUATION	Linear attenuation factor	lighting	0.0	glGetLightfv()
GL_QUADRATIC_ATTENUATION	Quadratic attenuation factor	lighting	0.0	glGetLightfv()
GL_SPOT_DIRECTION	Spotlight direction of light i	lighting	(0.0, 0.0, −1.0)	glGetLightfv()
GL_SPOT_EXPONENT	Spotlight exponent of light i	lighting	0.0	glGetLightfv()
GL_SPOT_CUTOFF	Spotlight angle of light i	lighting	180.0	glGetLightfv()
GL_LIGHTi	True if light i enabled	lighting /enable	GL_FALSE	glIsEnabled()
GL_COLOR_INDEXES	c_a, c_d and c_s for color-index lighting	lighting /enable	0, 1, 1	glGetMaterialfv()

Table B-5   Lighting State Variables (continued)

Rasterization

State Variable	Description	Attribute Group	Initial Value	Get Command
GL_POINT_SIZE	Point size	point	1.0	glGetFloatv()
GL_POINT_SMOOTH	Point antialiasing on	point/enable	GL_FALSE	glIsEnabled()
GL_LINE_WIDTH	Line width	line	1.0	glGetFloatv()
GL_LINE_SMOOTH	Line antialiasing on	line/enable	GL_FALSE	glIsEnabled()
GL_LINE_STIPPLE_PATTERN	Line stipple	line	1's	glGetIntegerv()
GL_LINE_STIPPLE_REPEAT	Line stipple repeat	line	1	glGetIntegerv()
GL_LINE_STIPPLE	Line stipple enable	line/enable	GL_FALSE	glIsEnabled()
GL_CULL_FACE	Polygon culling enabled	polygon/enable	GL_FALSE	glIsEnabled()
GL_CULL_FACE_MODE	Cull front-/back-facing polygons	polygon	GL_BACK	glGetIntegerv()
GL_FRONT_FACE	Polygon front-face CW/CCW indicator	polygon	GL_CCW	glGetIntegerv()
GL_POLYGON_SMOOTH	Polygon antialiasing on	polygon/enable	GL_FALSE	glIsEnabled()
GL_POLYGON_MODE	Polygon rasterization mode (front and back)	polygon	GL_FILL	glGetIntegerv()
GL_POLYGON_OFFSET_FACTOR	Polygon offset factor	polygon	0	glGetFloatv()
GL_POLYGON_OFFSET_BIAS	Polygon offset bias	polygon	0	glGetFloatv()

Table B-6   Rasterization State Variables

State Variable	Description	Attribute Group	Initial Value	Get Command
GL_POLYGON_OFFSET_POINT	Polygon offset enable for GL_POINT mode rasterization	polygon/enable	GL_FALSE	glIsEnabled()
GL_POLYGON_OFFSET_LINE	Polygon offset enable for GL_LINE mode rasterization	polygon/enable	GL_FALSE	glIsEnabled()
GL_POLYGON_OFFSET_FILL	Polygon offset enable for GL_FILL mode rasterization	polygon/enable	GL_FALSE	glIsEnabled()
GL_POLYGON_STIPPLE	Polygon stipple enable	polygon/enable	GL_FALSE	glIsEnabled()
—	Polygon stipple pattern	polygon-stipple	1's	glGetPolygon-Stipple()

Table B-6   Rasterization State Variables (continued)

Texturing

State Variable	Description	Attribute Group	Initial Value	Get Command
GL_TEXTURE_x	True if x-D texturing enabled (x is 1D or 2D)	texture/ enable	GL_FALSE	glIsEnabled()
GL_TEXTURE_BINDING_x	Texture object bound to GL_TEXTURE_x (x is 1D or 2D)	texture	GL_FALSE	glGetIntegerv()
GL_TEXTURE	x-D texture image at level of detail i	—	—	glGetTexImage()
GL_TEXTURE_WIDTH	x-D texture image i's width	—	0	glGetTexLevelParameter*()
GL_TEXTURE_HEIGHT	x-D texture image i's height	—	0	glGetTexLevelParameter*()
GL_TEXTURE_BORDER	x-D texture image i's border width	—	0	glGetTexLevelParameter*()
GL_TEXTURE_INTERNAL _FORMAT	x-D texture image i's internal image format	—	1	glGetTexLevelParameter*()
GL_TEXTURE_RED_SIZE	x-D texture image i's red resolution	—	0	glGetTexLevelParameter*()
GL_TEXTURE_GREEN_SIZE	x-D texture image i's green resolution	—	0	glGetTexLevelParameter*()
GL_TEXTURE_BLUE_SIZE	x-D texture image i's blue resolution	—	0	glGetTexLevelParameter*()
GL_TEXTURE_ALPHA_SIZE	x-D texture image i's alpha resolution	—	0	glGetTexLevelParameter*()

Table B-7   Texturing State Variables

State Variable	Description	Attribute Group	Initial Value	Get Command
GL_TEXTURE_LUMINANCE_SIZE	x-D texture image i's luminance resolution	—	0	glGetTexLevelParameter*()
GL_TEXTURE_INTENSITY_SIZE	x-D texture image i's intensity resolution	—	0	glGetTexLevelParameter*()
GL_TEXTURE_BORDER_COLOR	Texture border color	texture	0, 0, 0, 0	glGetTexParameter*()
GL_TEXTURE_MIN_FILTER	Texture minification function	texture	GL_NEAREST_MIPMAP_LINEAR	glGetTexParameter*()
GL_TEXTURE_MAG_FILTER	Texture magnification function	texture	GL_LINEAR	glGetTexParameter*()
GL_TEXTURE_WRAP_x	Texture wrap mode (x is S or T)	texture	GL_REPEAT	glGetTexParameter*()
GL_TEXTURE_PRIORITY	Texture object priority	texture	1	glGetTexParameter*()
GL_TEXTURE_RESIDENCY	Texture residency	texture	GL_FALSE	glGetTexParameteriv()
GL_TEXTURE_ENV_MODE	Texture application function	texture	GL_MODULATE	glGetTexEnviv()
GL_TEXTURE_ENV_COLOR	Texture environment color	texture	0, 0, 0, 0	glGetTexEnvfv()
GL_TEXTURE_GEN_x	Texgen enabled (x is S, T, R, or Q)	texture/ enable	GL_FALSE	glIsEnabled()
GL_EYE_PLANE	Texgen plane equation coefficients	texture	—	glGetTexGenfv()
GL_OBJECT_PLANE	Texgen object linear coefficients	texture	—	glGetTexGenfv()

Table B-7   Texturing State Variables (continued)

State Variable	Description	Attribute Group	Initial Value	Get Command
GL_TEXTURE_GEN_MODE	Function used for texgen	texture	GL_EYE_LINEAR	glGetTexGeniv()

Table B-7   Texturing State Variables (continued)

Pixel Operations

State Variable	Description	Attribute Group	Initial Value	Get Command
GL_SCISSOR_TEST	Scissoring enabled	scissor/enable	GL_FALSE	glIsEnabled()
GL_SCISSOR_BOX	Scissor box	scissor	—	glGetIntegerv()
GL_ALPHA_TEST	Alpha test enabled	color-buffer/enable	GL_FALSE	glIsEnabled()
GL_ALPHA_TEST_FUNC	Alpha test function	color-buffer	GL_ALWAYS	glGetIntegerv()
GL_ALPHA_TEST_REF	Alpha test reference value	color-buffer	0	glGetIntegerv()
GL_STENCIL_TEST	Stenciling enabled	stencil-buffer/enable	GL_FALSE	glIsEnabled()
GL_STENCIL_FUNC	Stencil function	stencil-buffer	GL_ALWAYS	glGetIntegerv()
GL_STENCIL_VALUE_MASK	Stencil mask	stencil-buffer	1's	glGetIntegerv()
GL_STENCIL_REF	Stencil reference value	stencil-buffer	0	glGetIntegerv()

Table B-8   Pixel Operations

State Variable	Description	Attribute Group	Initial Value	Get Command
GL_STENCIL_FAIL	Stencil fail action	stencil-buffer	GL_KEEP	glGetIntegerv()
GL_STENCIL_PASS_DEPTH_FAIL	Stencil depth buffer fail action	stencil-buffer	GL_KEEP	glGetIntegerv()
GL_STENCIL_PASS_DEPTH_PASS	Stencil depth buffer pass action	stencil-buffer	GL_KEEP	glGetIntegerv()
GL_DEPTH_TEST	Depth buffer enabled	depth-buffer/enable	GL_FALSE	glIsEnabled()
GL_DEPTH_FUNC	Depth buffer test function	depth-buffer	GL_LESS	glGetIntegerv()
GL_BLEND	Blending enabled	color-buffer/enable	GL_FALSE	glIsEnabled()
GL_BLEND_SRC	Blending source function	color-buffer	GL_ONE	glGetIntegerv()
GL_BLEND_DST	Blending destination function	color-buffer	GL_ZERO	glGetIntegerv()
GL_DITHER	Dithering enabled	color-buffer/enable	GL_TRUE	glIsEnabled()
GL_INDEX_LOGIC_OP	Color index logical operation enabled	color-buffer/enable	GL_FALSE	glIsEnabled()
GL_COLOR_LOGIC_OP	RGBA color logical operation enabled	color-buffer/enable	GL_FALSE	glIsEnabled()
GL_LOGIC_OP_MODE	Logical operation function	color-buffer	GL_COPY	glGetIntegerv()

Table B-8   Pixel Operations (continued)

Framebuffer Control

State Variable	Description	Attribute Group	Initial Value	Get Command
GL_DRAW_BUFFER	Buffers selected for drawing	color-buffer	—	glGetIntegerv()
GL_INDEX_WRITEMASK	Color-index writemask	color-buffer	1's	glGetIntegerv()
GL_COLOR_WRITEMASK	Color write enables; R, G, B, or A	color-buffer	GL_TRUE	glGetBooleanv()
GL_DEPTH_WRITEMASK	Depth buffer enabled for writing	depth-buffer	GL_TRUE	glGetBooleanv()
GL_STENCIL_WRITEMASK	Stencil-buffer writemask	stencil-buffer	1's	glGetIntegerv()
GL_COLOR_CLEAR_VALUE	Color-buffer clear value (RGBA mode)	color-buffer	0, 0, 0, 0	glGetFloatv()
GL_INDEX_CLEAR_VALUE	Color-buffer clear value (color-index mode)	color-buffer	0	glGetFloatv()
GL_DEPTH_CLEAR_VALUE	Depth-buffer clear value	depth-buffer	1	glGetIntegerv()
GL_STENCIL_CLEAR_VALUE	Stencil-buffer clear value	stencil-buffer	0	glGetIntegerv()
GL_ACCUM_CLEAR_VALUE	Accumulation-buffer clear value	accum-buffer	0	glGetFloatv()

Table B-9   Framebuffer Control State Variables

Pixels

State Variable	Description	Attribute Group	Initial Value	Get Command
GL_UNPACK_SWAP_BYTES	Value of GL_UNPACK_SWAP_BYTES	pixel-store	GL_FALSE	glGetBooleanv()
GL_UNPACK_LSB_FIRST	Value of GL_UNPACK_LSB_FIRST	pixel-store	GL_FALSE	glGetBooleanv()
GL_UNPACK_ROW_LENGTH	Value of GL_UNPACK_ROW_LENGTH	pixel-store	0	glGetIntegerv()
GL_UNPACK_SKIP_ROWS	Value of GL_UNPACK_SKIP_ROWS	pixel-store	0	glGetIntegerv()
GL_UNPACK_SKIP_PIXELS	Value of GL_UNPACK_SKIP_PIXELS	pixel-store	0	glGetIntegerv()
GL_UNPACK_ALIGNMENT	Value of GL_UNPACK_ALIGNMENT	pixel-store	4	glGetIntegerv()
GL_PACK_SWAP_BYTES	Value of GL_PACK_SWAP_BYTES	pixel-store	GL_FALSE	glGetBooleanv()
GL_PACK_LSB_FIRST	Value of GL_PACK_LSB_FIRST	pixel-store	GL_FALSE	glGetBooleanv()
GL_PACK_ROW_LENGTH	Value of GL_PACK_ROW_LENGTH	pixel-store	0	glGetIntegerv()
GL_PACK_SKIP_ROWS	Value of GL_PACK_SKIP_ROWS	pixel-store	0	glGetIntegerv()
GL_PACK_SKIP_PIXELS	Value of GL_PACK_SKIP_PIXELS	pixel-store	0	glGetIntegerv()
GL_PACK_ALIGNMENT	Value of GL_PACK_ALIGNMENT	pixel-store	4	glGetIntegerv()
GL_MAP_COLOR	True if colors are mapped	pixel	GL_FALSE	glGetBooleanv()
GL_MAP_STENCIL	True if stencil values are mapped	pixel	GL_FALSE	glGetBooleanv()
GL_INDEX_SHIFT	Value of GL_INDEX_SHIFT	pixel	0	glGetIntegerv()

Table B-10   Pixel State Variables

State Variable	Description	Attribute Group	Initial Value	Get Command
GL_INDEX_OFFSET	Value of GL_INDEX_OFFSET	pixel	0	glGetIntegerv()
GL_x_SCALE	Value of GL_x_SCALE; x is GL_RED, GL_GREEN, GL_BLUE, GL_ALPHA, or GL_DEPTH	pixel	1	glGetFloatv()
GL_x_BIAS	Value of GL_x_BIAS; x is one of GL_RED, GL_GREEN, GL_BLUE, GL_ALPHA, or GL_DEPTH	pixel	0	glGetFloatv()
GL_ZOOM_X	x zoom factor	pixel	1.0	glGetFloatv()
GL_ZOOM_Y	y zoom factor	pixel	1.0	glGetFloatv()
GL_x	glPixelMap() translation tables; x is a map name from Table 8-1	—	0's	glGetPixelMap*()
GL_x_SIZE	Size of table x	—	1	glGetIntegerv()
GL_READ_BUFFER	Read source buffer	pixel	—	glGetIntegerv()

Table B-10   Pixel State Variables   (continued)

Evaluators

State Variable	Description	Attribute Group	Initial Value	Get Command
GL_ORDER	1D map order	—	1	glGetMapiv()
GL_ORDER	2D map orders	—	1, 1	glGetMapiv()
GL_COEFF	1D control points	—	—	glGetMapfv()
GL_COEFF	2D control points	—	—	glGetMapfv()
GL_DOMAIN	1D domain endpoints	—	—	glGetMapfv()
GL_DOMAIN	2D domain endpoints	—	—	glGetMapfv()
GL_MAP1_x	1D map enables: x is map type	eval/enable	GL_FALSE	glIsEnabled()
GL_MAP2_x	2D map enables: x is map type	eval/enable	GL_FALSE	glIsEnabled()
GL_MAP1_GRID_DOMAIN	1D grid endpoints	eval	0, 1	glGetFloatv()
GL_MAP2_GRID_DOMAIN	2D grid endpoints	eval	0, 1; 0, 1	glGetFloatv()
GL_MAP1_GRID_SEGMENTS	1D grid divisions	eval	1	glGetFloatv()
GL_MAP2_GRID_SEGMENTS	2D grid divisions	eval	1,1	glGetFloatv()
GL_AUTO_NORMAL	True if automatic normal generation enabled	eval	GL_FALSE	glIsEnabled()

Table B-11   Evaluator State Variables

Hints

State Variable	Description	Attribute Group	Initial Value	Get Command
GL_PERSPECTIVE_CORRECTION_HINT	Perspective correction hint	hint	GL_DONT_CARE	glGetIntegerv()
GL_POINT_SMOOTH_HINT	Point smooth hint	hint	GL_DONT_CARE	glGetIntegerv()
GL_LINE_SMOOTH_HINT	Line smooth hint	hint	GL_DONT_CARE	glGetIntegerv()
GL_POLYGON_SMOOTH_HINT	Polygon smooth hint	hint	GL_DONT_CARE	glGetIntegerv()
GL_FOG_HINT	Fog hint	hint	GL_DONT_CARE	glGetIntegerv()

Table B-12   Hint State Variables

Implementation-Dependent Values

State Variable	Description	Attribute Group	Minimum Value	Get Command
GL_MAX_LIGHTS	Maximum number of lights	—	8	glGetIntegerv()
GL_MAX_CLIP_PLANES	Maximum number of user clipping planes	—	6	glGetIntegerv()
GL_MAX_MODELVIEW_STACK_DEPTH	Maximum modelview-matrix stack depth	—	32	glGetIntegerv()
GL_MAX_PROJECTION_STACK_DEPTH	Maximum projection-matrix stack depth	—	2	glGetIntegerv()
GL_MAX_TEXTURE_STACK_DEPTH	Maximum depth of texture matrix stack	—	2	glGetIntegerv()
GL_SUBPIXEL_BITS	Number of bits of subpixel precision in x and y	—	4	glGetIntegerv()
GL_MAX_TEXTURE_SIZE	See discussion in "Texture Proxy" on page 330	—	64	glGetIntegerv()
GL_MAX_PIXEL_MAP_TABLE	Maximum size of a glPixelMap() translation table	—	32	glGetIntegerv()
GL_MAX_NAME_STACK_DEPTH	Maximum selection-name stack depth	—	64	glGetIntegerv()
GL_MAX_LIST_NESTING	Maximum display-list call nesting	—	64	glGetIntegerv()
GL_MAX_EVAL_ORDER	Maximum evaluator polynomial order	—	8	glGetIntegerv()

Table B-13 Implementation-Dependent State Variables

State Variable	Description	Attribute Group	Minimum Value	Get Command
GL_MAX_VIEWPORT_DIMS	Maximum viewport dimensions	—	—	glGetIntegerv()
GL_MAX_ATTRIB_STACK_DEPTH	Maximum depth of the attribute stack	—	16	glGetIntegerv()
GL_MAX_CLIENT_ATTRIB_STACK_DEPTH	Maximum depth of the client attribute stack	—	16	glGetIntegerv()
GL_AUX_BUFFERS	Number of auxiliary buffers	—	0	glGetBooleanv()
GL_RGBA_MODE	True if color buffers store RGBA	—	—	glGetBooleanv()
GL_INDEX_MODE	True if color buffers store indices	—	—	glGetBooleanv()
GL_DOUBLEBUFFER	True if front and back buffers exist	—	—	glGetBooleanv()
GL_STEREO	True if left and right buffers exist	—	—	glGetBooleanv()
GL_POINT_SIZE_RANGE	Range (low to high) of antialiased point sizes	—	1, 1	glGetFloatv()
GL_POINT_SIZE_GRANULARITY	Antialiased point-size granularity	—	—	glGetFloatv()
GL_LINE_WIDTH_RANGE	Range (low to high) of antialiased line widths	—	1, 1	glGetFloatv()
GL_LINE_WIDTH_GRANULARITY	Antialiased line-width granularity	—	—	glGetFloatv()

Table B-13   Implementation-Dependent State Variables (continued)

Implementation-Dependent Pixel Depths

State Variable	Description	Attribute Group	Minimum Value	Get Command
GL_RED_BITS	Number of bits per red component in color buffers	—	—	glGetIntegerv()
GL_GREEN_BITS	Number of bits per green component in color buffers	—	—	glGetIntegerv()
GL_BLUE_BITS	Number of bits per blue component in color buffers	—	—	glGetIntegerv()
GL_ALPHA_BITS	Number of bits per alpha component in color buffers	—	—	glGetIntegerv()
GL_INDEX_BITS	Number of bits per index in color buffers	—	—	glGetIntegerv()
GL_DEPTH_BITS	Number of depth-buffer bitplanes	—	—	glGetIntegerv()
GL_STENCIL_BITS	Number of stencil bitplanes	—	—	glGetIntegerv()
GL_ACCUM_RED_BITS	Number of bits per red component in the accumulation buffer	—	—	glGetIntegerv()
GL_ACCUM_GREEN_BITS	Number of bits per green component in the accumulation buffer	—	—	glGetIntegerv()
GL_ACCUM_BLUE_BITS	Number of bits per blue component in the accumulation buffer	—	—	glGetIntegerv()
GL_ACCUM_ALPHA_BITS	Number of bits per alpha component in the accumulation buffer	—	—	glGetIntegerv()

Table B-14   Implementation-Dependent Pixel-Depth State Variables

Miscellaneous

State Variable	Description	Attribute Group	Initial Value	Get Command
GL_LIST_BASE	Setting of glListBase()	list	0	glGetIntegerv()
GL_LIST_INDEX	Number of display list under construction; 0 if none	—	0	glGetIntegerv()
GL_LIST_MODE	Mode of display list under construction; undefined if none	—	0	glGetIntegerv()
GL_ATTRIB_STACK_DEPTH	Attribute stack pointer	—	0	glGetIntegerv()
GL_CLIENT_ATTRIB_STACK_DEPTH	Client attribute stack pointer	—	0	glGetIntegerv()
GL_NAME_STACK_DEPTH	Name stack depth	—	0	glGetIntegerv()
GL_RENDER_MODE	glRenderMode() setting	—	GL_RENDER	glGetIntegerv()
GL_SELECTION_BUFFER_POINTER	Pointer to selection buffer	select	0	glGetPointerv()
GL_SELECTION_BUFFER_SIZE	Size of selection buffer	select	0	glGetIntegerv()
GL_FEEDBACK_BUFFER_POINTER	Pointer to feedback buffer	feedback	0	glGetPointerv()
GL_FEEDBACK_BUFFER_SIZE	Size of feedback buffer	feedback	0	glGetIntegerv()
GL_FEEDBACK_BUFFER_TYPE	Type of feedback buffer	feedback	GL_2D	glGetIntegerv()
—	Current error code(s)	—	0	glGetError()

Table B-15   Miscellaneous State Variables

OpenGL and Window Systems

OpenGL is available on many different platforms and works with many different window systems. OpenGL is designed to complement window systems, not duplicate their functionality. Therefore, OpenGL performs geometric and image rendering in two and three dimensions, but it does not manage windows or handle input events.

However, the basic definitions of most window systems don't support a library as sophisticated as OpenGL, with its complex and diverse pixel formats, including depth, stencil, and accumulation buffers, as well as double-buffering. For most window systems, some routines are added to extend the window system to support OpenGL.

This appendix introduces the extensions defined for several window and operating systems: the X Window System, the Apple Mac OS, OS/2 Warp from IBM, and Microsoft Windows NT and Windows 95. You need to have some knowledge of the window systems to fully understand this appendix.

This appendix has the following major sections:

- "GLX: OpenGL Extension for the X Window System" on page 562

- "AGL: OpenGL Extension to the Apple Macintosh" on page 566

- "PGL: OpenGL Extension for IBM OS/2 Warp" on page 570

- "WGL: OpenGL Extension for Microsoft Windows NT and Windows 95" on page 574

GLX: OpenGL Extension for the X Window System

In the X Window System, OpenGL rendering is made available as an extension to X in the formal X sense. GLX is an extension to the X protocol (and its associated API) for communicating OpenGL commands to an extended X server. Connection and authentication are accomplished with the normal X mechanisms.

As with other X extensions, there is a defined network protocol for OpenGL's rendering commands encapsulated within the X byte stream, so client-server OpenGL rendering is supported. Since performance is critical in three-dimensional rendering, the OpenGL extension to X allows OpenGL to bypass the X server's involvement in data encoding, copying, and interpretation and instead render directly to the graphics pipeline.

The X Visual is the key data structure to maintain pixel format information about the OpenGL window. A variable of data type XVisualInfo keeps track of pixel information, including pixel type (RGBA or color index), single or double-buffering, resolution of colors, and presence of depth, stencil, and accumulation buffers. The standard X Visuals (for example, PseudoColor, TrueColor) do not describe the pixel format details, so each implementation must extend the number of X Visuals supported.

The GLX routines are discussed in more detail in the *OpenGL Reference Manual*. Integrating OpenGL applications with the X Window System and the Motif widget set is discussed in great detail in *OpenGL Programming for the X Window System* by Mark Kilgard (Reading, MA: Addison-Wesley Developers Press, 1996), which includes full source code examples. If you absolutely want to learn about the internals of GLX, you may want to read the GLX specification, which can be found at

```
ftp://sgigate.sgi.com/pub/opengl/doc/
```

Initialization

Use **glXQueryExtension()** and **glXQueryVersion()** to determine whether the GLX extension is defined for an X server and, if so, which version is present. **glXQueryExtensionsString()** returns extension information about the client-server connection. **glXGetClientString()** returns information about the client library, including extensions and version number. **glXQueryServerString()** returns similar information about the server.

glXChooseVisual() returns a pointer to an XVisualInfo structure describing the visual that meets the client's specified attributes. You can query a visual about its support of a particular OpenGL attribute with **glXGetConfig**().

Controlling Rendering

Several GLX routines are provided for creating and managing an OpenGL rendering context. You can use such a context to render off-screen if you want. Routines are also provided for such tasks as synchronizing execution between the X and OpenGL streams, swapping front and back buffers, and using an X font.

Managing an OpenGL Rendering Context

An OpenGL rendering context is created with **glXCreateContext**(). One of the arguments to this routine allows you to request a direct rendering context that bypasses the X server as described previously. (Note that to do direct rendering, the X server connection must be local, and the OpenGL implementation needs to support direct rendering.) **glXCreateContext**() also allows display-list and texture-object indices and definitions to be shared by multiple rendering contexts. You can determine whether a GLX context is direct with **glXIsDirect**().

To make a rendering context current, use **glXMakeCurrent**(); **glXGetCurrentContext**() returns the current context. You can also obtain the current drawable with **glXGetCurrentDrawable**() and the current X Display with **glXGetCurrentDisplay**(). Remember that only one context can be current for any thread at any one time. If you have multiple contexts, you can copy selected groups of OpenGL state variables from one context to another with **glXCopyContext**(). When you're finished with a particular context, destroy it with **glXDestroyContext**().

Off-Screen Rendering

To render off-screen, first create an X Pixmap and then pass this as an argument to **glXCreateGLXPixmap**(). Once rendering is completed, you can destroy the association between the X and GLX Pixmaps with **glXDestroyGLXPixmap**(). (Off-screen rendering isn't guaranteed to be supported for direct renderers.)

Synchronizing Execution

To prevent X requests from executing until any outstanding OpenGL rendering is completed, call **glXWaitGL()**. Then, any previously issued OpenGL commands are guaranteed to be executed before any X rendering calls made after **glXWaitGL()**. Although the same result can be achieved with **glFinish()**, **glXWaitGL()** doesn't require a round trip to the server and thus is more efficient in cases where the client and server are on separate machines.

To prevent an OpenGL command sequence from executing until any outstanding X requests are completed, use **glXWaitX()**. This routine guarantees that previously issued X rendering calls are executed before any OpenGL calls made after **glXWaitX()**.

Swapping Buffers

For drawables that are double-buffered, the front and back buffers can be exchanged by calling **glXSwapBuffers()**. An implicit **glFlush()** is done as part of this routine.

Using an X Font

A shortcut for using X fonts in OpenGL is provided with the command **glXUseXFont()**. This routine builds display lists, each of which calls **glBitmap()**, for each requested character from the specified font and font size.

GLX Prototypes

Initialization

Determine whether the GLX extension is defined on the X server:

Bool **glXQueryExtension** (Display *dpy*, int *errorBase*, int *eventBase*);

Query version and extension information for client and server:

Bool **glXQueryVersion** (Display *dpy*, int *major*, int *minor*);

const char* **glXGetClientString** (Display *dpy*, int *name*);

const char* **glXQueryServerString** (Display *dpy*, int *screen*, int *name*);

const char* **glXQueryExtensionsString** (Display *dpy*, int *screen*);

Obtain the desired visual:

XVisualInfo* **glXChooseVisual** (Display *dpy*, int *screen*,
int *attribList*);

int **glXGetConfig** (Display *dpy*, XVisualInfo *visual*, int *attrib*,
int *value*);

Controlling Rendering

Manage or query an OpenGL rendering context:

GLXContext **glXCreateContext** (Display *dpy*, XVisualInfo *visual*,
GLXContext *shareList*, Bool *direct*);

void **glXDestroyContext** (Display *dpy*, GLXContext *context*);

void **glXCopyContext** (Display *dpy*, GLXContext *source*,
GLXContext *dest*, unsigned long *mask*);

Bool **glXIsDirect** (Display *dpy*, GLXContext *context*);

Bool **glXMakeCurrent** (Display *dpy*, GLXDrawable *draw*,
GLXContext *context*);

GLXContext **glXGetCurrentContext** (void);

Display* **glXGetCurrentDisplay** (void);

GLXDrawable **glXGetCurrentDrawable** (void);

Perform off-screen rendering:

GLXPixmap **glXCreateGLXPixmap** (Display *dpy*, XVisualInfo *visual*,
Pixmap *pixmap*);

void **glXDestroyGLXPixmap** (Display *dpy*, GLXPixmap *pix*);

Synchronize execution:

void **glXWaitGL** (void);

void **glXWaitX** (void);

Exchange front and back buffers:

void **glXSwapBuffers** (Display *dpy*, GLXDrawable *drawable*);

Use an X font:

void **glXUseXFont** (Font *font*, int *first*, int *count*, int *listBase*);

AGL: OpenGL Extension to the Apple Macintosh

This section covers the routines defined as the OpenGL extension to the Apple Macintosh (AGL), as defined by Template Graphics Software. An understanding of the way the Macintosh handles graphics rendering (QuickDraw) is required. The *Macintosh Toolbox Essentials* and *Imaging With QuickDraw* manuals from the *Inside Macintosh* series are also useful to have at hand.

For more information (including how to obtain the OpenGL software library for the Power Macintosh), you may want to check out the web site for OpenGL information at Template Graphics Software:

http://www.sd.tgs.com/Products/opengl.htm

For the Macintosh, OpenGL rendering is made available as a library that is either compiled in or resident as an extension for an application that wishes to make use of it. OpenGL is implemented in software for systems that do not possess hardware acceleration. Where acceleration is available (through the QuickDraw 3D Accelerator), those capabilities that match the OpenGL pipeline are used with the remaining functionality being provided through software rendering.

The data type AGLPixelFmtID (the AGL equivalent to XVisualInfo) maintains pixel information, including pixel type (RGBA or color index), single- or double-buffering, resolution of colors, and presence of depth, stencil, and accumulation buffers.

In contrast to other OpenGL implementations on other systems (such as the X Window System), the client/server model is not used. However, you may still need to call **glFlush()** since some hardware accelerators buffer the OpenGL pipeline and require a flush to empty it.

Initialization

Use **aglQueryVersion()** to determine what version of OpenGL for the Macintosh is available.

The capabilities of underlying graphics devices and your requirements for rendering buffers are resolved using **aglChoosePixelFmt()**. Use **aglListPixelFmts()** to find the particular formats supported by a graphics device. Given a pixel format, you can determine which attributes are available by using **aglGetConfig()**.

Rendering and Contexts

Several AGL routines are provided for creating and managing an OpenGL rendering context. You can use such a context to render into either a window or an off-screen graphics world. Routines are also provided that allow you to swap front and back rendering buffers, adjust buffers in response to a move, resize or graphics device change event, and use Macintosh fonts. For software rendering (and in some cases, hardware-accelerated rendering) the rendering buffers are created in your application memory space. For the application to work properly you must provide sufficient memory for these buffers in your application's SIZE resource.

Managing an OpenGL Rendering Context

An OpenGL rendering context is created (at least one context per window being rendered into) with **aglCreateContext()**. This takes the pixel format you selected as a parameter and uses it to initialize the context.

Use **aglMakeCurrent()** to make a rendering context current. Only one context can be current for a thread of control at any time. This indicates which drawable is to be rendered into and which context to use with it. It's possible for more than one context to be used (not simultaneously) with a particular drawable. Two routines allow you to determine which is the current rendering context and drawable being rendered into: **aglGetCurrentContext()** and **aglGetCurrentDrawable()**.

If you have multiple contexts, you can copy selected groups of OpenGL state variables from one context to another with **aglCopyContext()**. When a particular context is finished with, it should be destroyed by calling **aglDestroyContext()**.

On-screen Rendering

With the OpenGL extensions for the Apple Macintosh you can choose whether window clipping is performed when writing to the screen and whether the cursor is hidden during screen writing operations. This is important since these two items may affect how fast rendering can be performed. Call **aglSetOptions()** to select these options.

Off-screen Rendering

To render off-screen, first create an off-screen graphics world in the usual way, and pass the handle into **aglCreateAGLPixmap()**. This routine returns a drawable that can be used with **aglMakeCurrent**(). Once rendering is completed, you can destroy the association with **aglDestroyAGLPixmap**().

Swapping Buffers

For drawables that are double-buffered (as per the pixel format of the current rendering context), call **aglSwapBuffers**() to exchange the front and back buffers. An implicit **glFlush**() is performed as part of this routine.

Updating the Rendering Buffers

The Apple Macintosh toolbox requires you to perform your own event handling and does not provide a way for libraries to automatically hook in to the event stream. So that the drawables maintained by OpenGL can adjust to changes in drawable size, position and pixel depth, **aglUpdateCurrent**() is provided.

This routine must be called by your event processing code whenever one of these events occurs in the current drawable. Ideally the scene should be rerendered after a update call to take into account the changes made to the rendering buffers.

Using an Apple Macintosh Font

A shortcut for using Macintosh fonts is provided with **aglUseFont**(). This routine builds display lists, each of which calls **glBitmap**(), for each requested character from the specified font and font size.

Error Handling

An error-handling mechanism is provided for the Apple Macintosh OpenGL extension. When an error occurs you can call **aglGetError**() to get a more precise description of what caused the error.

AGL Prototypes

Initialization

Determine AGL version:

> GLboolean **aglQueryVersion** (int *major*, int *minor*);

Pixel format selection, availability, and capability:

> AGLPixelFmtID **aglChoosePixelFmt** (GDHandle *dev*, int *ndev*, int *attribs*);

> int **aglListPixelFmts** (GDHandle *dev*, AGLPixelFmtID ***fmts*);

> GLboolean **aglGetConfig** (AGLPixelFmtID *pix*, int *attrib*, int *value*);

Controlling Rendering

Manage an OpenGL rendering context:

> AGLContext **aglCreateContext** (AGLPixelFmtID *pix*, AGLContext *shareList*);

> GLboolean **aglDestroyContext** (AGLContext *context*);

> GLboolean **aglCopyContext** (AGLContext *source*, AGLContext *dest*, GLuint *mask*);

> GLboolean **aglMakeCurrent** (AGLDrawable *drawable*, AGLContext *context*);

> GLboolean **aglSetOptions** (int *opts*);

> AGLContext **aglGetCurrentContext** (void);

> AGLDrawable **aglGetCurrentDrawable** (void);

Perform off-screen rendering:

> AGLPixmap **aglCreateAGLPixmap** (AGLPixelFmtID *pix*, GWorldPtr *pixmap*);

> GLboolean **aglDestroyAGLPixmap** (AGLPixmap *pix*);

Exchange front and back buffers:

> GLboolean **aglSwapBuffers** (AGLDrawable *drawable*);

Update the current rendering buffers:

> GLboolean **aglUpdateCurrent** (void);

Use a Macintosh font:

> GLboolean **aglUseFont** (int *familyID*, int *size*, int *first*, int *count*, int *listBase*);

Find the cause of an error:

> GLenum **aglGetError** (void);

PGL: OpenGL Extension for IBM OS/2 Warp

OpenGL rendering for IBM OS/2 Warp is accomplished by using PGL routines added to integrate OpenGL into the standard IBM Presentation Manager. OpenGL with PGL supports both a direct OpenGL context (which is often faster) and an indirect context (which allows some integration of Gpi and OpenGL rendering).

The data type VISUALCONFIG (the PGL equivalent to XVisualInfo) maintains the visual configuration, including pixel type (RGBA or color index), single- or double-buffering, resolution of colors, and presence of depth, stencil, and accumulation buffers.

To get more information (including how to obtain the OpenGL software library for IBM OS/2 Warp, Version 3.0), you may want to start at

`http://www.austin.ibm.com/software/OpenGL/`

Packaged along with the software is the document, *OpenGL On OS/2 Warp*, which provides more detailed information. OpenGL support is included with the base operating system with OS/2 Warp Version 4.

Initialization

Use **pglQueryCapability()** and **pglQueryVersion()** to determine whether the OpenGL is supported on this machine and, if so, how it is supported and which version is present. **pglChooseConfig()** returns a pointer to an VISUALCONFIG structure describing the visual configuration that best meets the client's specified attributes. A list of the particular visual configurations supported by a graphics device can be found using **pglQueryConfigs()**.

Controlling Rendering

Several PGL routines are provided for creating and managing an OpenGL rendering context, capturing the contents of a bitmap, synchronizing execution between the Presentation Manager and OpenGL streams, swapping front and back buffers, using a color palette, and using an OS/2 logical font.

Managing an OpenGL Rendering Context

An OpenGL rendering context is created with **pglCreateContext()**. One of the arguments to this routine allows you to request a direct rendering context that bypasses the Gpi and render to a PM window, which is generally faster. You can determine whether a OpenGL context is direct with **pglIsIndirect()**.

To make a rendering context current, use **pglMakeCurrent()**; **pglGetCurrentContext()** returns the current context. You can also obtain the current window with **pglGetCurrentWindow()**. You can copy some OpenGL state variables from one context to another with **pglCopyContext()**. When you're finished with a particular context, destroy it with **pglDestroyContext()**.

Access the Bitmap of the Front Buffer

To lock access to the bitmap representation of the contents of the front buffer, use **pglGrabFrontBitmap()**. An implicit **glFlush()** is performed, and you can read the bitmap, but its contents are effectively read-only. Immediately after access is completed, you should call **pglReleaseFrontBitmap()** to restore write access to the front buffer.

Synchronizing Execution

To prevent Gpi rendering requests from executing until any outstanding OpenGL rendering is completed, call **pglWaitGL()**. Then, any previously issued OpenGL commands are guaranteed to be executed before any Gpi rendering calls made after **pglWaitGL()**.

To prevent an OpenGL command sequence from executing until any outstanding Gpi requests are completed, use **pglWaitPM()**. This routine guarantees that previously issued Gpi rendering calls are executed before any OpenGL calls made after **pglWaitPM()**.

Note: OpenGL and Gpi rendering can be integrated in the same window only if the OpenGL context is an indirect context.

Swapping Buffers

For windows that are double-buffered, the front and back buffers can be exchanged by calling **pglSwapBuffers()**. An implicit **glFlush()** is done as part of this routine.

Using a Color Index Palette

When you are running in 8-bit (256 color) mode, you have to worry about color palette management. For windows with a color index Visual Configuration, call **pglSelectColorIndexPalette()** to tell OpenGL what color-index palette you want to use with your context. A color palette must be selected before the context is initially bound to a window. In RGBA mode, OpenGL sets up a palette automatically.

Using an OS/2 Logical Font

A shortcut for using OS/2 logical fonts in OpenGL is provided with the command **pglUseFont()**. This routine builds display lists, each of which calls **glBitmap()**, for each requested character from the specified font and font size.

PGL Prototypes

Initialization

Determine whether OpenGL is supported and, if so, its version number:

> long **pglQueryCapability** (HAB *hab*);

> void **pglQueryVersion** (HAB *hab*, int *major, int *minor);

Visual configuration selection, availability and capability:

> PVISUALCONFIG **pglChooseConfig** (HAB *hab*, int *attribList);

> PVISUALCONFIG * **pglQueryConfigs** (HAB *hab*);

Controlling Rendering

Manage or query an OpenGL rendering context:

> HGC **pglCreateContext** (HAB *hab*, PVISUALCONFIG *pVisualConfig*, HGC *shareList*, Bool isDirect);

> Bool **pglDestroyContext** (HAB *hab*, HGC *hgc*);

> Bool **pglCopyContext** (HAB *hab*, HGC *source*, HGC *dest*, GLuint *mask*);

> Bool **pglMakeCurrent** (HAB *hab*, HGC *hgc*, HWND *hwnd*);

> long **pglIsIndirect** (HAB *hab*, HGC *hgc*);

HGC **pglGetCurrentContext** (HAB *hab*);

HWND **pglGetCurrentWindow** (HAB *hab*);

Access and release the bitmap of the front buffer:

Bool **pglGrabFrontBitmap** (HAB *hab*, HPS **hps*, HBITMAP **phbitmap*);

Bool **pglReleaseFrontBitmap** (HAB *hab*);

Synchronize execution:

HPS **pglWaitGL** (HAB *hab*);

void **pglWaitPM** (HAB *hab*);

Exchange front and back buffers:

void **pglSwapBuffers** (HAB *hab*, HWND *hwnd*);

Finding a color-index palette:

void **pglSelectColorIndexPalette** (HAB *hab*, HPAL, *hpal*, HGC *hgc*);

Use an OS/2 logical font:

Bool **pglUseFont** (HAB *hab*, HPS *hps*, FATTRS **fontAttribs*,
long *logicalId*, int *first*, int *count*, int *listBase*);

WGL: OpenGL Extension for Microsoft Windows NT and Windows 95

OpenGL rendering is supported on systems that run Microsoft Windows NT and Windows 95. The functions and routines of the Win32 library are necessary to initialize the pixel format and control rendering for OpenGL. Some routines, which are prefixed by **wgl**, extend Win32 so that OpenGL can be fully supported.

For Win32/WGL, the PIXELFORMATDESCRIPTOR is the key data structure to maintain pixel format information about the OpenGL window. A variable of data type PIXELFORMATDESCRIPTOR keeps track of pixel information, including pixel type (RGBA or color index), single- or double-buffering, resolution of colors, and presence of depth, stencil, and accumulation buffers.

To get more information about WGL, you may want to start with technical articles available through the Microsoft Developer Network at

```
http://www.microsoft.com/msdn/
```

Initialization

Use **GetVersion()** or the newer **GetVersionEx()** to determine version information. **ChoosePixelFormat()** tries to find a PIXELFORMATDESCRIPTOR with specified attributes. If a good match for the requested pixel format is found, then **SetPixelFormat()** should be called to actually use the pixel format. You should select a pixel format in the device context before calling **wglCreateContext()**.

If you want to find out details about a given pixel format, use **DescribePixelFormat()** or, for overlays or underlays, **wglDescribeLayerPlane()**.

Controlling Rendering

Several WGL routines are provided for creating and managing an OpenGL rendering context, rendering to a bitmap, swapping front and back buffers, finding a color palette, and using either bitmap or outline fonts.

Managing an OpenGL Rendering Context

wglCreateContext() creates an OpenGL rendering context for drawing on the device in the selected pixel format of the device context. (To create an OpenGL rendering context for overlay or underlay windows, use **wglCreateLayerContext()** instead.) To make a rendering context current, use **wglMakeCurrent()**; **wglGetCurrentContext()** returns the current context. You can also obtain the current device context with **wglGetCurrentDC()**. You can copy some OpenGL state variables from one context to another with **wglCopyContext()** or make two contexts share the same display lists and texture objects with **wglShareLists()**. When you're finished with a particular context, destroy it with **wglDestroyContext()**.

OpenGL Rendering to a Bitmap

Win32 has a few routines to allocate (and deallocate) bitmaps, to which you can render OpenGL directly. **CreateDIBitmap()** creates a device-dependent bitmap (DDB) from a device-independent bitmap (DIB). **CreateDIBSection()** creates a device-independent bitmap (DIB) that applications can write to directly. When finished with your bitmap, you can use **DeleteObject()** to free it up.

Synchronizing Execution

If you want to combine GDI and OpenGL rendering, be aware there are no equivalents to functions like **glXWaitGL()**, **glXWaitX()**, or **pglWaitGL()** in Win32. Although **glXWaitGL()** has no equivalent in Win32, you can achieve the same effect by calling **glFinish()**, which waits until all pending OpenGL commands are executed, or by calling **GdiFlush()**, which waits until all GDI drawing has completed.

Swapping Buffers

For windows that are double-buffered, the front and back buffers can be exchanged by calling **SwapBuffers()** or **wglSwapLayerBuffers()**; the latter for overlays and underlays.

Finding a Color Palette

To access the color palette for the standard (non-layer) bitplanes, use the standard GDI functions to set the palette entries. For overlay or underlay layers, use **wglRealizeLayerPalette()**, which maps palette entries from a given color-index layer plane into the physical palette or initializes the palette of an RGBA layer plane. **wglGetLayerPaletteEntries()** is used to query the entries in palettes of layer planes.

Using a Bitmap or Outline Font

WGL has two routines, **wglUseFontBitmaps()** and **wglUseFontOutlines()**, for converting system fonts to use with OpenGL. Both routines build a display list for each requested character from the specified font and font size.

WGL Prototypes

Initialization

Determine version information:

> BOOL **GetVersion** (LPOSVERSIONINFO *lpVersionInformation*);

> BOOL **GetVersionEx** (LPOSVERSIONINFO *lpVersionInformation*);

Pixel format availability, selection, and capability:

> int **ChoosePixelFormat** (HDC *hdc*,
> CONST PIXELFORMATDESCRIPTOR * *ppfd*);

> BOOL **SetPixelFormat** (HDC *hdc*, int *iPixelFormat*,
> CONST PIXELFORMATDESCRIPTOR * *ppfd*);

> int **DescribePixelFormat** (HDC *hdc*, int *iPixelFormat*, UINT *nBytes*,
> LPPIXELFORMATDESCRIPTOR *ppfd*);

> BOOL **wglDescribeLayerPlane** (HDC *hdc*, int *iPixelFormat*,
> int *iLayerPlane*, UINT *nBytes*, LPLAYERPLANEDESCRIPTOR *plpd*);

Controlling Rendering

Manage or query an OpenGL rendering context:

> HGLRC **wglCreateContext** (HDC *hdc*);

> HGLRC **wglCreateLayerContext** (HDC *hdc*, int *iLayerPlane*);

> BOOL **wglShareLists** (HGLRC *hglrc1*, HGLRC *hglrc2*);

> BOOL **wglDeleteContext** (HGLRC *hglrc*);

> BOOL **wglCopyContext** (HGLRC *hglrcSource*, HGLRC *hlglrcDest*,
> UINT *mask*);

BOOL **wglMakeCurrent** (HDC *hdc*, HGLRC *hglrc*);

HGLRC **wglGetCurrentContext** (VOID) ;

HDC **wglGetCurrentDC** (VOID);

Access and release the bitmap of the front buffer:

HBITMAP **CreateDIBitmap** (HDC *hdc*,
CONST BITMAPINFOHEADER **lpbmih*, DWORD *fdwInit*,
CONST VOID **lpbInit*, CONST BITMAPINFO **lpbmi*, UINT *fuUsage*);

HBITMAP **CreateDIBSection** (HDC *hdc*, CONST BITMAPINFO **pbmi*,
UINT *iUsage*, VOID **ppvBits*, HANDLE *hSection*, DWORD *dwOffset*);

BOOL **DeleteObject** (HGDIOBJ *hObject*);

Exchange front and back buffers:

BOOL **SwapBuffers** (HDC *hdc*);

BOOL **wglSwapLayerBuffers** (HDC *hdc*, UINT *fuPlanes*);

Finding a color palette for overlay or underlay layers:

int **wglGetLayerPaletteEntries** (HDC *hdc*, int *iLayerPlane*, int *iStart*,
int *cEntries*, CONST COLORREF **pcr*);

BOOL **wglRealizeLayerPalette** (HDC *hdc*, int *iLayerPlane*,
BOOL *bRealize*);

Use a bitmap or an outline font:

BOOL **wglUseFontBitmaps** (HDC *hdc*, DWORD *first*, DWORD *count*,
DWORD *listBase*);

BOOL **wglUseFontOutlines** (HDC *hdc*, DWORD *first*, DWORD *count*,
DWORD *listBase*, FLOAT *deviation*, FLOAT *extrusion*, int *format*,
LPGLYPHMETRICSFLOAT *lpgmf*);

Basics of GLUT: The OpenGL Utility Toolkit

This appendix describes a subset of Mark Kilgard's OpenGL Utility Toolkit (GLUT), which is fully documented in his book, *OpenGL Programming for the X Window System* (Reading, MA: Addison-Wesley Developers Press, 1996). GLUT has become a popular library for OpenGL programmers, because it standardizes and simplifies window and event management. GLUT has been ported atop a variety of OpenGL implementations, including both the X Window System and Microsoft Windows NT.

This appendix has the following major sections:

(See "How to Obtain the Sample Code" on page v for information about how to obtain the source code for GLUT.)

With GLUT, your application structures its event handling to use callback functions. (This method is similar to using the Xt Toolkit, also known as the X Intrinsics, with a widget set.) For example, first you open a window and register callback routines for specific events. Then, you create a main loop without an exit. In that loop, if an event occurs, its registered callback functions are executed. Upon completion of the callback functions, flow of control is returned to the main loop.

Initializing and Creating a Window

Before you can open a window, you must specify its characteristics: Should it be single-buffered or double-buffered? Should it store colors as RGBA values or as color indices? Where should it appear on your display? To specify the answers to these questions, call **glutInit()**, **glutInitDisplayMode()**, **glutInitWindowSize()**, and **glutInitWindowPosition()** before you call **glutCreateWindow()** to open the window.

---

void **glutInit**(int *argc*, char ****argv*);

---

glutInit() should be called before any other GLUT routine, because it initializes the GLUT library. **glutInit()** will also process command line options, but the specific options are window system dependent. For the X Window System, -iconic, -geometry, and -display are examples of command line options, processed by **glutInit()**. (The parameters to the **glutInit()** should be the same as those to **main()**.)

---

void **glutInitDisplayMode**(unsigned int *mode*);

Specifies a display mode (such as RGBA or color-index, or single- or double-buffered) for windows created when **glutCreateWindow()** is called. You can also specify that the window have an associated depth, stencil, and/or accumulation buffer. The *mask* argument is a bitwise ORed combination of GLUT_RGBA or GLUT_INDEX, GLUT_SINGLE or GLUT_DOUBLE, and any of the buffer-enabling flags: GLUT_DEPTH, GLUT_STENCIL, or GLUT_ACCUM. For example, for a double-buffered, RGBA-mode window with a depth and stencil buffer, use GLUT_DOUBLE | GLUT_RGBA | GLUT_DEPTH | GLUT_STENCIL. The default value is GLUT_RGBA | GLUT_SINGLE (an RGBA, single-buffered window).

void **glutInitWindowSize**(int *width*, int *height*);
void **glutInitWindowPosition**(int *x*, int *y*);

Requests windows created by **glutCreateWindow**() to have an initial size
and position. The arguments (*x, y*) indicate the location of a corner of the
window, relative to the entire display. The *width* and *height* indicate the
window's size (in pixels). The initial window size and position are hints
and may be overridden by other requests.

int **glutCreateWindow**(char **name*);

Opens a window with previously set characteristics (display mode, width,
height, and so on). The string *name* may appear in the title bar if your
window system does that sort of thing. The window is not initially
displayed until **glutMainLoop**() is entered, so do not render into the
window until then.

The value returned is a unique integer identifier for the window. This
identifier can be used for controlling and rendering to multiple windows
(each with an OpenGL rendering context) from the same application.

Handling Window and Input Events

After the window is created, but before you enter the main loop, you should
register callback functions using the following routines.

void **glutDisplayFunc**(void (**func*)(void));

Specifies the function that's called whenever the contents of the window
need to be redrawn. The contents of the window may need to be redrawn
when the window is initially opened, when the window is popped and
window damage is exposed, and when **glutPostRedisplay**() is explicitly
called.

void **glutReshapeFunc**(void (*func*)(int *width*, int *height*));

Specifies the function that's called whenever the window is resized or moved. The argument *func* is a pointer to a function that expects two arguments, the new width and height of the window. Typically, *func* calls **glViewport**(), so that the display is clipped to the new size, and it redefines the projection matrix so that the aspect ratio of the projected image matches the viewport, avoiding aspect ratio distortion. If **glutReshapeFunc**() isn't called or is deregistered by passing NULL, a default reshape function is called, which calls **glViewport**(*0, 0, width, height*).

void **glutKeyboardFunc**(void (*func*)(unsigned int *key*, int *x*, int *y*);

Specifies the function, *func*, that's called when a key that generates an ASCII character is pressed. The *key* callback parameter is the generated ASCII value. The *x* and *y* callback parameters indicate the location of the mouse (in window-relative coordinates) when the key was pressed.

void **glutMouseFunc**(void (*func*)(int *button*, int *state*, int *x*, int *y*));

Specifies the function, *func*, that's called when a mouse button is pressed or released. The *button* callback parameter is one of GLUT_LEFT_BUTTON, GLUT_MIDDLE_BUTTON, or GLUT_RIGHT_BUTTON. The *state* callback parameter is either GLUT_UP or GLUT_DOWN, depending upon whether the mouse has been released or pressed. The *x* and *y* callback parameters indicate the location (in window-relative coordinates) of the mouse when the event occurred.

void **glutMotionFunc**(void (*func*)(int *x*, int *y*));

Specifies the function, *func*, that's called when the mouse pointer moves within the window while one or more mouse buttons is pressed. The *x* and *y* callback parameters indicate the location (in window-relative coordinates) of the mouse when the event occurred.

void **glutPostRedisplay**(void);

Marks the current window as needing to be redrawn. At the next opportunity, the callback function registered by **glutDisplayFunc**() will be called.

Loading the Color Map

If you're using color-index mode, you might be surprised to discover there's no OpenGL routine to load a color into a color lookup table. This is because the process of loading a color map depends entirely on the window system. GLUT provides a generalized routine to load a single color index with an RGB value, **glutSetColor()**.

---

void **glutSetColor**(GLint *index*, GLfloat *red*, GLfloat *green*, GLfloat *blue*);

Loads the index in the color map, *index*, with the given *red*, *green*, and *blue* values. These values are normalized to lie in the range [0.0,1.0].

Initializing and Drawing Three-Dimensional Objects

Many sample programs in this guide use three-dimensional models to illustrate various rendering properties. The following drawing routines are included in GLUT to avoid having to reproduce the code to draw these models in each program. The routines render all their graphics in immediate mode. Each three-dimensional model comes in two flavors: wireframe without surface normals, and solid with shading and surface normals. Use the solid version when you're applying lighting. Only the teapot generates texture coordinates.

---

void **glutWireSphere**(GLdouble *radius*, GLint *slices*, GLint *stacks*);
void **glutSolidSphere**(GLdouble *radius*, GLint *slices*, GLint *stacks*);

---

void **glutWireCube**(GLdouble *size*);
void **glutSolidCube**(GLdouble *size*);

---

void **glutWireTorus**(GLdouble *innerRadius*, GLdouble *outerRadius*,
        GLint *nsides*, GLint *rings*);
void **glutSolidTorus**(GLdouble *innerRadius*, GLdouble *outerRadius*,
        GLint *nsides*, GLint *rings*);

---

void **glutWireIcosahedron**(void);
void **glutSolidIcosahedron**(void);

---

void **glutWireOctahedron**(void);
void **glutSolidOctahedron**(void);

---

void **glutWireTetrahedron**(void);
void **glutSolidTetrahedron**(void);

---

void **glutWireDodecahedron**(GLdouble *radius*);
void **glutSolidDodecahedron**(GLdouble *radius*);

---

void **glutWireCone**(GLdouble *radius*, GLdouble *height*, GLint *slices*,
      GLint *stacks*);
void **glutSolidCone**(GLdouble *radius*, GLdouble *height*, GLint *slices*,
      GLint *stacks*);

---

void **glutWireTeapot**(GLdouble *size*);
void **glutSolidTeapot**(GLdouble *size*);

Managing a Background Process

You can specify a function that's to be executed if no other events are pending—for example, when the event loop would otherwise be idle—with **glutIdleFunc**(). This is particularly useful for continuous animation or other background processing.

---

void **glutIdleFunc**(void (*func*)(void));

Specifies the function, *func*, to be executed if no other events are pending. If NULL (zero) is passed in, execution of *func* is disabled.

Running the Program

After all the setup is completed, GLUT programs enter an event processing loop, **glutMainLoop()**.

---

void **glutMainLoop**(void);

Enters the GLUT processing loop, never to return. Registered callback functions will be called when the corresponding events instigate them.

Calculating Normal Vectors

This appendix describes how to calculate normal vectors for surfaces. You need to define normals to use the OpenGL lighting facility, which is described in Chapter 5. "Normal Vectors" on page 63 introduces normals and the OpenGL command for specifying them. This appendix goes through the details of calculating them. It has the following major sections:

Since normals are perpendicular to a surface, you can find the normal at a particular point on a surface by first finding the flat plane that just touches the surface at that point. The normal is the vector that's perpendicular to that plane. On a perfect sphere, for example, the normal at a point on the surface is in the same direction as the vector from the center of the sphere to that point. For other types of surfaces, there are other, better means for determining the normals, depending on how the surface is specified.

Recall that smooth curved surfaces are approximated by a large number of small flat polygons. If the vectors perpendicular to these polygons are used as the surface normals in such an approximation, the surface appears faceted, since the normal direction is discontinuous across the polygonal boundaries. In many cases, however, an exact mathematical description exists for the surface, and true surface normals can be calculated at every point. Using the true normals improves the rendering considerably, as shown in Figure E-1. Even if you don't have a mathematical description, you can do better than the faceted look shown in the figure. The two major sections in this appendix describe how to calculate normal vectors for these two cases:

- "Finding Normals for Analytic Surfaces" on page 588 explains what to do when you have a mathematical description of a surface.

- "Finding Normals from Polygonal Data" on page 591 covers the case when you have only the polygonal data to describe a surface.

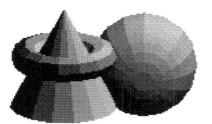 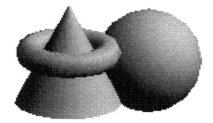

Figure E-1   Rendering with Polygonal Normals vs. True Normals

Finding Normals for Analytic Surfaces

Analytic surfaces are smooth, differentiable surfaces that are described by a mathematical equation (or set of equations). In many cases, the easiest surfaces to find normals for are analytic surfaces for which you have an explicit definition in the following form:

$$V(s,t) = [\ X(s,t)\ \ Y(s,t)\ \ Z(s,t)\ ]$$

where s and t are constrained to be in some domain, and X, Y, and Z are differentiable functions of two variables. To calculate the normal, find

$$\frac{\partial V}{\partial s} \text{ and } \frac{\partial V}{\partial t}$$

which are vectors tangent to the surface in the s and t directions. The cross product

$$\frac{\partial V}{\partial s} \times \frac{\partial V}{\partial t}$$

is perpendicular to both and, hence, to the surface. The following shows how to calculate the cross product of two vectors. (Watch out for the degenerate cases where the cross product has zero length!)

$$\begin{bmatrix} v_x & v_y & v_z \end{bmatrix} \times \begin{bmatrix} w_x & w_y & w_z \end{bmatrix} = \begin{bmatrix} (v_y w_z - w_y v_z) & (w_x v_z - v_x w_z) & (v_x w_y - w_x v_y) \end{bmatrix}$$

You should probably normalize the resulting vector. To normalize a vector $[x\ y\ z]$, calculate its length

$$\text{Length} = \sqrt{x^2 + y^2 + z^2}$$

and divide each component of the vector by the length.

As an example of these calculations, consider the analytic surface

$$V(s,t) = [\ s^2\ \ t^3\ \ 3{-}st\ ]$$

From this we have

$$\frac{\partial V}{\partial s} = \begin{bmatrix} 2s & 0 & -t \end{bmatrix}, \quad \frac{\partial V}{\partial t} = \begin{bmatrix} 0 & 3t^2 & -s \end{bmatrix}, \text{ and } \frac{\partial V}{\partial s} \times \frac{\partial V}{\partial t} = \begin{bmatrix} -3t^3 & 2s^2 & 6st^2 \end{bmatrix}$$

So, for example, when $s=1$ and $t=2$, the corresponding point on the surface is (1, 8, 1), and the vector (−24, 2, 24) is perpendicular to the surface at that point. The length of this vector is 34, so the unit normal vector is (−24/34, 2/34, 24/34) = (−0.70588, 0.058823, 0.70588).

For analytic surfaces that are described implicitly, as F(x, y, z) = 0, the problem is harder. In some cases, you can solve for one of the variables, say z = G(x, y), and put it in the explicit form given previously:

$$\mathbf{V}(s, t) = \begin{bmatrix} s & t & \mathbf{G}(s, t) \end{bmatrix}$$

Then continue as described earlier.

If you can't get the surface equation in an explicit form, you might be able to make use of the fact that the normal vector is given by the gradient

$$\nabla F = \begin{bmatrix} \dfrac{\partial F}{\partial x} & \dfrac{\partial F}{\partial y} & \dfrac{\partial F}{\partial z} \end{bmatrix}$$

evaluated at a particular point (x, y, z). Calculating the gradient might be easy, but finding a point that lies on the surface can be difficult. As an example of an implicitly defined analytic function, consider the equation of a sphere of radius 1 centered at the origin:

$$x^2 + y^2 + z^2 - 1 = 0$$

This means that

$$\mathbf{F}(x, y, z) = x^2 + y^2 + z^2 - 1$$

which can be solved for z to yield

$$z = \pm\sqrt{1 - x^2 - y^2}$$

Thus, normals can be calculated from the explicit form

$$\mathbf{V}(s, t) = \begin{bmatrix} s & t & \sqrt{1 - s^2 - t^2} \end{bmatrix}$$

as described previously.

If you could not solve for z, you could have used the gradient

$$\nabla F = \begin{bmatrix} 2x & 2y & 2z \end{bmatrix}$$

as long as you could find a point on the surface. In this case, it's not so hard to find a point—for example, (2/3, 1/3, 2/3) lies on the surface. Using the gradient, the normal at this point is (4/3, 2/3, 4/3). The unit-length normal is (2/3, 1/3, 2/3), which is the same as the point on the surface, as expected.

Finding Normals from Polygonal Data

As mentioned previously, you often want to find normals for surfaces that are described with polygonal data such that the surfaces appear smooth rather than faceted. In most cases, the easiest way for you to do this (though it might not be the most efficient way) is to calculate the normal vectors for each of the polygonal facets and then to average the normals for neighboring facets. Use the averaged normal for the vertex that the neighboring facets have in common. Figure E-2 shows a surface and its polygonal approximation. (Of course, if the polygons represent the exact surface and aren't merely an approximation—if you're drawing a cube or a cut diamond, for example—don't do the averaging. Calculate the normal for each facet as described in the following paragraphs, and use that same normal for each vertex of the facet.)

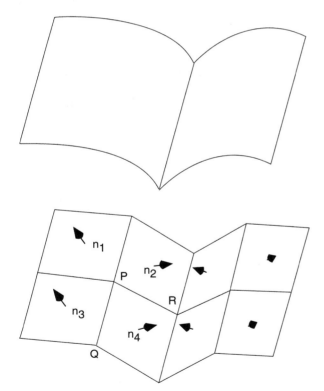

Figure E-2   Averaging Normal Vectors

To find the normal for a flat polygon, take any three vertices v_1, v_2, and v_3 of the polygon that do not lie in a straight line. The cross product

$$[v_1 - v_2] \times [v_2 - v_3]$$

is perpendicular to the polygon. (Typically, you want to normalize the resulting vector.) Then you need to average the normals for adjoining facets to avoid giving too much weight to one of them. For instance, in the example shown in Figure E-2, if n_1, n_2, n_3, and n_4 are the normals for the four polygons meeting at point P, calculate $n_1+n_2+n_3+n_4$ and then normalize it. (You can get a better average if you weight the normals by the size of the angles at the shared intersection.) The resulting vector can be used as the normal for point P.

Sometimes, you need to vary this method for particular situations. For instance, at the boundary of a surface (for example, point Q in Figure E-2), you might be able to choose a better normal based on your knowledge of what the surface should look like. Sometimes the best you can do is to average the polygon normals on the boundary as well. Similarly, some models have some smooth parts and some sharp corners (point R is on such an edge in Figure E-2). In this case, the normals on either side of the crease shouldn't be averaged. Instead, polygons on one side of the crease should be drawn with one normal, and polygons on the other side with another.

Homogeneous Coordinates and Transformation Matrices

This appendix presents a brief discussion of homogeneous coordinates. It also lists the form of the transformation matrices used for rotation, scaling, translation, perspective projection, and orthographic projection. These topics are introduced and discussed in Chapter 3. For a more detailed discussion of these subjects, see almost any book on three-dimensional computer graphics—for example, *Computer Graphics: Principles and Practice* by Foley, van Dam, Feiner, and Hughes (Reading, MA: Addison-Wesley, 1990)—or a text on projective geometry—for example, *The Real Projective Plane*, by H. S. M. Coxeter, 2nd ed. (Cambridge: Cambridge University Press, 1961). In the discussion that follows, the term *homogeneous coordinates* always means three-dimensional homogeneous coordinates, although projective geometries exist for all dimensions.

This appendix has the following major sections:

Homogeneous Coordinates

OpenGL commands usually deal with two- and three-dimensional vertices, but in fact all are treated internally as three-dimensional homogeneous vertices comprising four coordinates. Every column vector $(x, y, z, w)^T$ represents a homogeneous vertex if at least one of its elements is nonzero. If the real number a is nonzero, then $(x, y, z, w)^T$ and $(ax, ay, az, aw)^T$ represent the same homogeneous vertex. (This is just like fractions: $x/y = (ax)/(ay)$.) A three-dimensional euclidean space point $(x, y, z)^T$ becomes the homogeneous vertex with coordinates $(x, y, z, 1.0)^T$, and the two-dimensional euclidean point $(x, y)^T$ becomes $(x, y, 0.0, 1.0)^T$.

As long as w is nonzero, the homogeneous vertex $(x, y, z, w)^T$ corresponds to the three-dimensional point $(x/w, y/w, z/w)^T$. If $w = 0.0$, it corresponds to no euclidean point, but rather to some idealized "point at infinity." To understand this point at infinity, consider the point (1, 2, 0, 0), and note that the sequence of points (1, 2, 0, 1), (1, 2, 0, 0.01), and (1, 2.0, 0.0, 0.0001), corresponds to the euclidean points (1, 2), (100, 200), and (10000, 20000). This sequence represents points rapidly moving toward infinity along the line $2x = y$. Thus, you can think of (1, 2, 0, 0) as the point at infinity in the direction of that line.

Note: OpenGL might not handle homogeneous clip coordinates with $w < 0$ correctly. To be sure that your code is portable to all OpenGL systems, use only nonnegative w values.

Transforming Vertices

Vertex transformations (such as rotations, translations, scaling, and shearing) and projections (such as perspective and orthographic) can all be represented by applying an appropriate 4×4 matrix to the coordinates representing the vertex. If **v** represents a homogeneous vertex and **M** is a 4×4 transformation matrix, then **Mv** is the image of **v** under the transformation by **M**. (In computer-graphics applications, the transformations used are usually nonsingular—in other words, the matrix **M** can be inverted. This isn't required, but some problems arise with nonsingular transformations.)

After transformation, all transformed vertices are clipped so that x, y, and z are in the range $[-w, w]$ (assuming $w > 0$). Note that this range corresponds in euclidean space to $[-1.0, 1.0]$.

Transforming Normals

Normal vectors aren't transformed in the same way as vertices or position vectors. Mathematically, it's better to think of normal vectors not as vectors, but as planes perpendicular to those vectors. Then, the transformation rules for normal vectors are described by the transformation rules for perpendicular planes.

A homogeneous plane is denoted by the row vector (a, b, c, d), where at least one of a, b, c, or d is nonzero. If q is a nonzero real number, then (a, b, c, d) and (qa, qb, qc, qd) represent the same plane. A point $(x, y, z, w)^T$ is on the plane (a, b, c, d) if $ax+by+cz+dw = 0$. (If $w = 1$, this is the standard description of a euclidean plane.) In order for (a, b, c, d) to represent a euclidean plane, at least one of a, b, or c must be nonzero. If they're all zero, then $(0, 0, 0, d)$ represents the "plane at infinity," which contains all the "points at infinity."

If $\mathbf{p}$ is a homogeneous plane and $\mathbf{v}$ is a homogeneous vertex, then the statement "$\mathbf{v}$ lies on plane $\mathbf{p}$" is written mathematically as $\mathbf{pv} = 0$, where $\mathbf{pv}$ is normal matrix multiplication. If $\mathbf{M}$ is a nonsingular vertex transformation (that is, a 4×4 matrix that has an inverse $\mathbf{M}^{-1}$), then $\mathbf{pv} = 0$ is equivalent to $\mathbf{pM}^{-1}\mathbf{Mv} = 0$, so $\mathbf{Mv}$ lies on the plane $\mathbf{pM}^{-1}$. Thus, $\mathbf{pM}^{-1}$ is the image of the plane under the vertex transformation $\mathbf{M}$.

If you like to think of normal vectors as vectors instead of as the planes perpendicular to them, let $\mathbf{v}$ and $\mathbf{n}$ be vectors such that $\mathbf{v}$ is perpendicular to $\mathbf{n}$. Then, $\mathbf{n}^T\mathbf{v} = 0$. Thus, for an arbitrary nonsingular transformation $\mathbf{M}$, $\mathbf{n}^T\mathbf{M}^{-1}\mathbf{Mv} = 0$, which means that $\mathbf{n}^T\mathbf{M}^{-1}$ is the transpose of the transformed normal vector. Thus, the transformed normal vector is $(\mathbf{M}^{-1})^T\mathbf{n}$. In other words, normal vectors are transformed by the inverse transpose of the transformation that transforms points. Whew!

Transformation Matrices

Although any nonsingular matrix $\mathbf{M}$ represents a valid projective transformation, a few special matrices are particularly useful. These matrices are listed in the following subsections.

Translation

The call **glTranslate*(x, y, z)** generates T, where

$$T = \begin{bmatrix} 1 & 0 & 0 & x \\ 0 & 1 & 0 & y \\ 0 & 0 & 1 & z \\ 0 & 0 & 0 & 1 \end{bmatrix} \text{ and } T^{-1} = \begin{bmatrix} 1 & 0 & 0 & -x \\ 0 & 1 & 0 & -y \\ 0 & 0 & 1 & -z \\ 0 & 0 & 0 & 1 \end{bmatrix}$$

Scaling

The call **glScale*(x, y, z)** generates S, where

$$S = \begin{bmatrix} x & 0 & 0 & 0 \\ 0 & y & 0 & 0 \\ 0 & 0 & z & 0 \\ 0 & 0 & 0 & 1 \end{bmatrix} \text{ and } S^{-1} = \begin{bmatrix} \frac{1}{x} & 0 & 0 & 0 \\ 0 & \frac{1}{y} & 0 & 0 \\ 0 & 0 & \frac{1}{z} & 0 \\ 0 & 0 & 0 & 1 \end{bmatrix}$$

Notice that S^{-1} is defined only if x, y, and z are all nonzero.

Rotation

The call **glRotate*(a, x, y, z)** generates R as follows:

Let $v = (x, y, z)^T$, and $u = v/\|v\| = (x', y', z')^T$.

Also let

$$S = \begin{bmatrix} 0 & -z' & y' \\ z' & 0 & -x' \\ -y' & x' & 0 \end{bmatrix} \text{ and } M = uu^T + (\cos a)(I - u u^T) + (\sin a) S$$

Then

$$R = \begin{bmatrix} m & m & m & 0 \\ m & m & m & 0 \\ m & m & m & 0 \\ 0 & 0 & 0 & 1 \end{bmatrix}$$ where m represents elements from M, which is a 3×3 matrix.

The **R** matrix is always defined. If $x=y=z=0$, then **R** is the identity matrix. You can obtain the inverse of **R**, **R^{-1}**, by substituting $-a$ for a, or by transposition.

The **glRotate*()** command generates a matrix for rotation about an arbitrary axis. Often, you're rotating about one of the coordinate axes; the corresponding matrices are as follows:

glRotate*(a, 1, 0, 0): $\begin{bmatrix} 1 & 0 & 0 & 0 \\ 0 & \cos a & -\sin a & 0 \\ 0 & \sin a & \cos a & 0 \\ 0 & 0 & 0 & 1 \end{bmatrix}$

glRotate*(a, 0, 1, 0): $\begin{bmatrix} \cos a & 0 & \sin a & 0 \\ 0 & 1 & 0 & 0 \\ -\sin a & 0 & \cos a & 0 \\ 0 & 0 & 0 & 1 \end{bmatrix}$

glRotate*(a, 0, 0, 1): $\begin{bmatrix} \cos a & -\sin a & 0 & 0 \\ \sin a & \cos a & 0 & 0 \\ 0 & 0 & 1 & 0 \\ 0 & 0 & 0 & 1 \end{bmatrix}$

As before, the inverses are obtained by transposition.

Perspective Projection

The call **glFrustum(**l, r, b, t, n, f**)** generates **R**, where

$$
\mathbf{R} = \begin{bmatrix} \dfrac{2n}{r-l} & 0 & \dfrac{r+l}{r-l} & 0 \\[2mm] 0 & \dfrac{2n}{t-b} & \dfrac{t+b}{t-b} & 0 \\[2mm] 0 & 0 & \dfrac{-(f+n)}{f-n} & \dfrac{-2fn}{f-n} \\[2mm] 0 & 0 & -1 & 0 \end{bmatrix}
\quad \text{and } \mathbf{R}^{-1} = \begin{bmatrix} \dfrac{r-l}{2n} & 0 & 0 & \dfrac{r+l}{2n} \\[2mm] 0 & \dfrac{t-b}{2n} & 0 & \dfrac{t+b}{2n} \\[2mm] 0 & 0 & 0 & -1 \\[2mm] 0 & 0 & \dfrac{-(f-n)}{2fn} & \dfrac{f+n}{2fn} \end{bmatrix}
$$

R is defined as long as $l \neq r$, $t \neq b$, and $n \neq f$.

Orthographic Projection

The call **glOrtho(**l, r, b, t, n, f**)** generates **R**, where

$$
\mathbf{R} = \begin{bmatrix} \dfrac{2}{r-l} & 0 & 0 & -\dfrac{r+l}{r-l} \\[2mm] 0 & \dfrac{2}{t-b} & 0 & -\dfrac{t+b}{t-b} \\[2mm] 0 & 0 & \dfrac{-2}{f-n} & \dfrac{f+n}{f-n} \\[2mm] 0 & 0 & 0 & 1 \end{bmatrix}
\quad \text{and } \mathbf{R}^{-1} = \begin{bmatrix} \dfrac{r-l}{2} & 0 & 0 & \dfrac{r+l}{2} \\[2mm] 0 & \dfrac{t-b}{2} & 0 & \dfrac{t+b}{2} \\[2mm] 0 & 0 & \dfrac{f-n}{-2} & \dfrac{n+f}{2} \\[2mm] 0 & 0 & 0 & 1 \end{bmatrix}
$$

R is defined as long as $l \neq r$, $t \neq b$, and $n \neq f$.

Appendix F: Homogeneous Coordinates and Transformation Matrices

Programming Tips

This appendix lists some tips and guidelines that you might find useful. Keep in mind that these tips are based on the intentions of the designers of the OpenGL, not on any experience with actual applications and implementations! This appendix has the following major sections:

- "OpenGL Correctness Tips" on page 600

- "OpenGL Performance Tips" on page 602

- "GLX Tips" on page 603

OpenGL Correctness Tips

- Perform error checking often. Call **glGetError()** at least once each time the scene is rendered to make certain error conditions are noticed.

- Do not count on the error behavior of an OpenGL implementation—it might change in a future release of OpenGL. For example, OpenGL 1.1 ignores matrix operations invoked between **glBegin()** and **glEnd()** commands, but a future version might not. Put another way, OpenGL error semantics may change between upward-compatible revisions.

- If you need to collapse all geometry to a single plane, use the projection matrix. If the modelview matrix is used, OpenGL features that operate in eye coordinates (such as lighting and application-defined clipping planes) might fail.

- Do not make extensive changes to a single matrix. For example, do not animate a rotation by continually calling **glRotate*()** with an incremental angle. Rather, use **glLoadIdentity()** to initialize the given matrix for each frame, then call **glRotate*()** with the desired complete angle for that frame.

- Count on multiple passes through a rendering database to generate the same pixel fragments only if this behavior is guaranteed by the invariance rules established for a compliant OpenGL implementation. (See Appendix H for details on the invariance rules.) Otherwise, a different set of fragments might be generated.

- Do not expect errors to be reported while a display list is being defined. The commands within a display list generate errors only when the list is executed.

- Place the near frustum plane as far from the viewpoint as possible to optimize the operation of the depth buffer.

- Call **glFlush()** to force all previous OpenGL commands to be executed. Do not count on **glGet*()** or **glIs*()** to flush the rendering stream. Query commands flush as much of the stream as is required to return valid data but don't guarantee completing all pending rendering commands.

- Turn dithering off when rendering predithered images (for example, when **glCopyPixels()** is called).

- Make use of the full range of the accumulation buffer. For example, if accumulating four images, scale each by one-quarter as it's accumulated.

- If exact two-dimensional rasterization is desired, you must carefully specify both the orthographic projection and the vertices of primitives that are to be rasterized. The orthographic projection should be specified with integer coordinates, as shown in the following example:

```
gluOrtho2D(0, width, 0, height);
```

where *width* and *height* are the dimensions of the viewport. Given this projection matrix, polygon vertices and pixel image positions should be placed at integer coordinates to rasterize predictably. For example, **glRecti**(0, 0, 1, 1) reliably fills the lower left pixel of the viewport, and **glRasterPos2i**(0, 0) reliably positions an unzoomed image at the lower left of the viewport. Point vertices, line vertices, and bitmap positions should be placed at half-integer locations, however. For example, a line drawn from (*x1*, 0.5) to (*x2*, 0.5) will be reliably rendered along the bottom row of pixels into the viewport, and a point drawn at (0.5, 0.5) will reliably fill the same pixel as **glRecti**(0, 0, 1, 1).

An optimum compromise that allows all primitives to be specified at integer positions, while still ensuring predictable rasterization, is to translate *x* and *y* by 0.375, as shown in the following code fragment. Such a translation keeps polygon and pixel image edges safely away from the centers of pixels, while moving line vertices close enough to the pixel centers.

```
glViewport(0, 0, width, height);
glMatrixMode(GL_PROJECTION);
glLoadIdentity();
gluOrtho2D(0, width, 0, height);
glMatrixMode(GL_MODELVIEW);
glLoadIdentity();
glTranslatef(0.375, 0.375, 0.0);
/* render all primitives at integer positions */
```

- Avoid using negative *w* vertex coordinates and negative *q* texture coordinates. OpenGL might not clip such coordinates correctly and might make interpolation errors when shading primitives defined by such coordinates.

- Do not assume the precision of operations, based upon the data type of parameters to OpenGL commands. For example, if you are using **glRotated**(), you should not assume that geometric processing pipeline operates with double-precision floating point. It is possible that the parameters to **glRotated**() are converted to a different data type before processing.

OpenGL Performance Tips

- Use **glColorMaterial()** when only a single material property is being varied rapidly (at each vertex, for example). Use **glMaterial()** for infrequent changes, or when more than a single material property is being varied rapidly.

- Use **glLoadIdentity()** to initialize a matrix, rather than loading your own copy of the identity matrix.

- Use specific matrix calls such as **glRotate*()**, **glTranslate*()**, and **glScale*()** rather than composing your own rotation, translation, or scale matrices and calling **glMultMatrix()**.

- Use query functions when your application requires just a few state values for its own computations. If your application requires several state values from the same attribute group, use **glPushAttrib()** and **glPopAttrib()** to save and restore them.

- Use display lists to encapsulate potentially expensive state changes.

- Use display lists to encapsulate the rendering calls of rigid objects that will be drawn repeatedly.

- Use texture objects to encapsulate texture data. Place all the **glTexImage*()** calls (including mipmaps) required to completely specify a texture and the associated **glTexParameter*()** calls (which set texture properties) into a texture object. Bind this texture object to select the texture.

- If the situation allows it, use **gl*TexSubImage()** to replace all or part of an existing texture image rather than the more costly operations of deleting and creating an entire new image.

- If your OpenGL implementation supports a high-performance working set of resident textures, try to make all your textures resident; that is, make them fit into the high-performance texture memory. If necessary, reduce the size or internal format resolution of your textures until they all fit into memory. If such a reduction creates intolerably fuzzy textured objects, you may give some textures lower priority, which will, when push comes to shove, leave them out of the working set.

- Use evaluators even for simple surface tessellations to minimize network bandwidth in client-server environments.

- Provide unit-length normals if it's possible to do so, and avoid the overhead of GL_NORMALIZE. Avoid using **glScale*()** when doing lighting because it almost always requires that GL_NORMALIZE be enabled.

- Set **glShadeModel()** to GL_FLAT if smooth shading isn't required.

- Use a single **glClear()** call per frame if possible. Do not use **glClear()** to clear small subregions of the buffers; use it only for complete or near-complete clears.

- Use a single call to **glBegin**(GL_TRIANGLES) to draw multiple independent triangles rather than calling **glBegin**(GL_TRIANGLES) multiple times, or calling **glBegin**(GL_POLYGON). Even if only a single triangle is to be drawn, use GL_TRIANGLES rather than GL_POLYGON. Use a single call to **glBegin**(GL_QUADS) in the same manner rather than calling **glBegin**(GL_POLYGON) repeatedly. Likewise, use a single call to **glBegin**(GL_LINES) to draw multiple independent line segments rather than calling **glBegin**(GL_LINES) multiple times.

- Some OpenGL implementations benefit from storing vertex data in vertex arrays. Use of vertex arrays reduces function call overhead. Some implementations can improve performance by batch processing or reusing processed vertices.

- In general, use the vector forms of commands to pass precomputed data, and use the scalar forms of commands to pass values that are computed near call time.

- Avoid making redundant mode changes, such as setting the color to the same value between each vertex of a flat-shaded polygon.

- Be sure to disable expensive rasterization and per-fragment operations when drawing or copying images. OpenGL will even apply textures to pixel images if asked to!

- Unless absolutely needed, avoid having different front and back polygon modes.

GLX Tips

- Use **glXWaitGL()** rather than **glFinish()** to force X rendering commands to follow GL rendering commands.

- Likewise, use **glXWaitX()** rather than **XSync()** to force GL rendering commands to follow X rendering commands.

- Be careful when using **glXChooseVisual()**, because boolean selections are matched exactly. Since some implementations won't export visuals with all combinations of boolean capabilities, you should call **glXChooseVisual()** several times with different boolean values before you give up. For example, if no single-buffered visual with the required characteristics is available, check for a double-buffered visual with the same capabilities. It might be available, and it's easy to use.

OpenGL Invariance

OpenGL is not a pixel-exact specification. It therefore doesn't guarantee an exact match between images produced by different OpenGL implementations. However, OpenGL does specify exact matches, in some cases, for images produced by the same implementation. This appendix describes the invariance rules that define these cases.

The obvious and most fundamental case is repeatability. A conforming OpenGL implementation generates the same results each time a specific sequence of commands is issued from the same initial conditions. Although such repeatability is useful for testing and verification, it's often not useful to application programmers, because it's difficult to arrange for equivalent initial conditions. For example, rendering a scene twice, the second time after swapping the front and back buffers, doesn't meet this requirement. So repeatability can't be used to guarantee a stable, double-buffered image.

A simple and useful algorithm that counts on invariant execution is erasing a line by redrawing it in the background color. This algorithm works only if rasterizing the line results in the same fragment x,y pairs being generated in both the foreground and background color cases. OpenGL requires that the coordinates of the fragments generated by rasterization be invariant with respect to framebuffer contents, which color buffers are enabled for drawing, the values of matrices other than those on the top of the matrix stacks, the scissor parameters, all writemasks, all clear values, the current color, index, normal, texture coordinates, and edge-flag values, the current raster color, raster index, and raster texture coordinates, and the material properties. It is further required that exactly the same fragments be generated, including the fragment color values, when framebuffer contents, color buffer enables, matrices other than those on the top of the matrix stacks, the scissor parameters, writemasks, or clear values differ.

OpenGL further suggests, but doesn't require, that fragment generation be invariant with respect to the matrix mode, the depths of the matrix stacks, the alpha test parameters (other than alpha test enable), the stencil parameters (other than stencil enable), the depth test parameters (other than depth test enable), the blending parameters (other than enable), the logical operation (but not logical operation enable), and the pixel-storage and pixel-transfer parameters. Because invariance with respect to several enables isn't recommended, you should use other parameters to disable functions when invariant rendering is required. For example, to render invariantly with blending enabled and disabled, set the blending parameters to GL_ONE and GL_ZERO to disable blending rather than calling **glDisable**(GL_BLEND). Alpha testing, stencil testing, depth testing, and the logical operation all can be disabled in this manner.

Finally, OpenGL requires that per-fragment arithmetic, such as blending and the depth test, is invariant to all OpenGL state except the state that directly defines it. For example, the only OpenGL parameters that affect how the arithmetic of blending is performed are the source and destination blend parameters and the blend enable parameter. Blending is invariant to all other state changes. This invariance holds for the scissor test, the alpha test, the stencil test, the depth test, blending, dithering, logical operations, and buffer writemasking.

As a result of all these invariance requirements, OpenGL can guarantee that images rendered into different color buffers, either simultaneously or separately using the same command sequence, are pixel identical. This holds for all the color buffers in the framebuffer or all the color buffers in an off-screen buffer, but it isn't guaranteed between the framebuffer and off-screen buffers.

Glossary

accumulation buffer

Memory (bitplanes) that is used to accumulate a series of images generated in the color buffer. Using the accumulation buffer may significantly improve the quality of the image, but also take correspondingly longer to render. The accumulation buffer is used for effects such as depth of field, motion blur, and full-scene antialiasing.

aliasing

A rendering technique that assigns to pixels the color of the primitive being rendered, regardless of whether that primitive covers all or only a portion of the pixel's area. This results in jagged edges, or jaggies.

alpha

A fourth color component. The alpha component is never displayed directly and is typically used to control color blending. By convention, OpenGL alpha corresponds to the notion of opacity rather than transparency, meaning that an alpha value of 1.0 implies complete opacity, and an alpha value of 0.0 complete transparency.

ambient

Ambient light is nondirectional and distributed uniformly throughout space. Ambient light falling upon a surface approaches from all directions. The light is reflected from the object independent of surface location and orientation with equal intensity in all directions.

animation

Generating repeated renderings of a scene, with smoothly changing viewpoint and/or object positions, quickly enough so that the illusion of motion is achieved. OpenGL animation is almost always done using double-buffering.

antialiasing

A rendering technique that assigns pixel colors based on the fraction of the pixel's area that's covered by the primitive being rendered. Antialiased rendering reduces or eliminates the jaggies that result from aliased rendering.

application-specific clipping

Clipping of primitives against planes in eye coordinates; the planes are specified by the application using **glClipPlane()**.

attribute group

A set of related state variables, which OpenGL can save or restore together at one time.

back faces

See *faces*.

bit

Binary digit. A state variable having only two possible values: 0 or 1. Binary numbers are constructions of one or more bits.

bitmap

A rectangular array of bits. Also, the primitive rendered by the **glBitmap()** command, which uses its *bitmap* parameter as a mask.

bitplane

A rectangular array of bits mapped one-to-one with pixels. The framebuffer is a stack of bitplanes.

blending

Reduction of two color components to one component, usually as a linear interpolation between the two components.

buffer

A group of bitplanes that store a single component (such as depth or green) or a single index (such as the color index or the stencil index). Sometimes the red, green, blue, and alpha buffers together are referred to as the color buffer, rather than the color buffers.

C

God's programming language.

C++

The object-oriented programming language of a pagan deity.

client

The computer from which OpenGL commands are issued. The computer that issues OpenGL commands can be connected via a network to a different computer that executes the commands, or commands can be issued and executed on the same computer. See also *server*.

client memory

The main memory (where program variables are stored) of the client computer.

clip coordinates

The coordinate system that follows transformation by the projection matrix and precedes perspective division. View-volume clipping is done in clip coordinates, but application-specific clipping is not.

clipping

Elimination of the portion of a geometric primitive that's outside the half-space defined by a clipping plane. Points are simply rejected if outside. The portion of a line or of a polygon that's outside the half-space is eliminated, and additional vertices are generated as necessary to complete the primitive within the clipping half-space. Geometric primitives and the current raster position (when specified) are always clipped against the six half-spaces defined by the left, right, bottom, top, near, and far planes of the view volume. Applications can specify optional application-specific clipping planes to be applied in eye coordinates.

color index

A single value that represents a color by name, rather than by value. OpenGL color indices are treated as continuous values (for example, floating-point numbers), while operations such as interpolation and dithering are performed on them. Color indices stored in the framebuffer are always integer values, however. Floating-point indices are converted to integers by rounding to the nearest integer value.

color-index mode

An OpenGL context is in color-index mode if its color buffers store color indices rather than red, green, blue, and alpha color components.

color map

A table of index-to-RGB mappings that's accessed by the display hardware. Each color index is read from the color buffer, converted to an RGB triple by lookup in the color map, and sent to the monitor.

components

Single, continuous (for example, floating-point) values that represent intensities or quantities. Usually, a component value of zero represents the minimum value or intensity, and a component value of one represents the maximum value or intensity, though other ranges are sometimes used. Because component values are interpreted in a normalized range, they are specified independent of actual resolution. For example, the RGB triple (1, 1, 1) is white, regardless of whether the color buffers store 4, 8, or 12 bits each.

Out-of-range components are typically clamped to the normalized range, not truncated or otherwise interpreted. For example, the RGB triple (1.4, 1.5, 0.9) is clamped to (1.0, 1.0, 0.9) before it's used to update the color buffer. Red, green, blue, alpha, and depth are always treated as components, never as indices.

concave

Not *convex*.

context

A complete set of OpenGL state variables. Note that framebuffer contents are not part of OpenGL state, but that the configuration of the framebuffer is.

convex

A polygon is convex if no straight line in the plane of the polygon intersects the polygon more than twice.

convex hull

The smallest convex region enclosing a specified group of points. In two dimensions, the convex hull is found conceptually by stretching a rubber band around the points so that all of the points lie within the band.

coordinate system

In *n*-dimensional space, a set of *n* linearly independent vectors anchored to a point (called the origin). A group of coordinates specifies a point in space (or a vector from the origin) by indicating how far to travel along each vector to reach the point (or tip of the vector).

culling

The process of eliminating a front face or back face of a polygon so that it isn't drawn.

current matrix

A matrix that transforms coordinates in one coordinate system to coordinates of another system. There are three current matrices in OpenGL: the modelview matrix transforms object coordinates (coordinates specified by the programmer) to eye coordinates; the perspective matrix transforms eye coordinates to clip coordinates; the texture matrix transforms specified or generated texture coordinates as described by the matrix. Each current matrix is the top element on a stack of matrices. Each of the three stacks can be manipulated with OpenGL matrix-manipulation commands.

current raster position

A window coordinate position that specifies the placement of an image primitive when it's rasterized. The current raster position and other current raster parameters are updated when **glRasterPos()** is called.

decal

A method of calculating color values during texture application, where the texture colors replace the fragment colors or, if alpha blending is enabled, the texture colors are blended with the fragment colors, using only the alpha value.

depth

Generally refers to the *z* window coordinate.

depth buffer

Memory that stores the depth value at every pixel. To perform hidden-surface removal, the depth buffer records the depth value of the object that lies closest to the observer at every pixel. The depth value of every new fragment uses the recorded value for depth comparison and must pass the comparison test before being rendered.

depth-cuing

A rendering technique that assigns color based on distance from the viewpoint.

diffuse

Diffuse lighting and reflection accounts for the directionality of a light source. The intensity of light striking a surface varies with the angle between the orientation of the object and the direction of the light source. A diffuse material scatters that light evenly in all directions.

directional light source

See *infinite light source*.

display list

A named list of OpenGL commands. Display lists are always stored on the server, so display lists can be used to reduce network traffic in client-server environments. The contents of a display list may be preprocessed and might therefore execute more efficiently than the same set of OpenGL commands executed in immediate mode. Such preprocessing is especially important for computing intensive commands such as NURBS or polygon tessellation.

dithering

A technique for increasing the perceived range of colors in an image at the cost of spatial resolution. Adjacent pixels are assigned differing color values; when viewed from a distance, these colors seem to blend into a single intermediate color. The technique is similar to the halftoning used in black-and-white publications to achieve shades of gray.

double-buffering

OpenGL contexts with both front and back color buffers are double-buffered. Smooth animation is accomplished by rendering into only the back buffer (which isn't displayed), then causing the front and back buffers to be swapped. See **glutSwapBuffers()** in Appendix D.

edge flag

A Boolean value at a vertex which marks whether that vertex precedes a boundary edge. **glEdgeFlag*()** may be used to mark an edge as not on the boundary. When a polygon is drawn in GL_LINE mode, only boundary edges are drawn.

element

A single component or index.

emission

The color of an object which is self-illuminating or self-radiating. The intensity of an emissive material is not attributed to any external light source.

evaluated

The OpenGL process of generating object-coordinate vertices and parameters from previously specified Bézier equations.

execute

An OpenGL command is executed when it's called in immediate mode or when the display list that it's a part of is called.

eye coordinates

The coordinate system that follows transformation by the modelview matrix and precedes transformation by the projection matrix. Lighting and application-specific clipping are done in eye coordinates.

faces

The sides of a polygon. Each polygon has two faces: a front face and a back face. Only one face or the other is ever visible in the window. Whether the back or front face is visible is effectively determined after the polygon is projected onto the window. After this projection, if the polygon's edges are directed clockwise, one of the faces is visible; if directed counterclockwise, the other face is visible. Whether clockwise corresponds to front or back (and counterclockwise corresponds to back or front) is determined by the OpenGL programmer.

flat shading

Refers to a primitive colored with a single, constant color across its extent, rather than smoothly interpolated colors across the primitive. See *Gouraud shading*.

fog

A rendering technique that can be used to simulate atmospheric effects such as haze, fog, and smog by fading object colors to a background color based on distance from the viewer. Fog also aids in the perception of distance from the viewer, giving a depth cue.

fonts

Groups of graphical character representations generally used to display strings of text. The characters may be roman letters, mathematical symbols, Asian ideograms, Egyptian hieroglyphics, and so on.

fragment

Fragments are generated by the rasterization of primitives. Each fragment corresponds to a single pixel and includes color, depth, and sometimes texture-coordinate values.

framebuffer

All the buffers of a given window or context. Sometimes includes all the pixel memory of the graphics hardware accelerator.

front faces

See *faces*.

frustum

The view volume warped by perspective division.

gamma correction

A function applied to colors stored in the framebuffer to correct for the nonlinear response of the eye (and sometimes of the monitor) to linear changes in color-intensity values.

geometric model

The object-coordinate vertices and parameters that describe an object. Note that OpenGL doesn't define a syntax for geometric models, but rather a syntax and semantics for the rendering of geometric models.

geometric object

See *geometric model*.

geometric primitive

A point, a line, or a polygon.

Gouraud shading

Smooth interpolation of colors across a polygon or line segment. Colors are assigned at vertices and linearly interpolated across the primitive to produce a relatively smooth variation in color. Also called smooth shading.

group

Each pixel of an image in client memory is represented by a group of one, two, three, or four elements. Thus, in the context of a client memory image, a group and a pixel are the same thing.

half-spaces

A plane divides space into two half-spaces.

hidden-line removal

A technique to determine which portions of a wireframe object should be visible. The lines that comprise the wireframe are considered to be edges of opaque surfaces, which may obscure other edges that are farther away from the viewer.

hidden-surface removal

A technique to determine which portions of an opaque, shaded object should be visible and which portions should be obscured. A test of the depth coordinate, using the depth buffer for storage, is a common method of hidden-surface removal.

homogeneous coordinates

A set of $n+1$ coordinates used to represent points in n-dimensional projective space. Points in projective space can be thought of as points in euclidean space together with some points at infinity. The coordinates are homogeneous because a scaling of each of the coordinates by the same nonzero constant doesn't alter the point to which the coordinates refer. Homogeneous coordinates are useful in the calculations of projective geometry, and thus in computer graphics, where scenes must be projected onto a window.

image

A rectangular array of pixels, either in client memory or in the framebuffer.

image primitive

A bitmap or an image.

immediate mode

Execution of OpenGL commands when they're called, rather than from a display list. No immediate-mode bit exists; the mode in immediate mode refers to use of OpenGL, rather than to a specific bit of OpenGL state.

index

A single value that's interpreted as an absolute value, rather than as a normalized value in a specified range (as is a component). Color indices are the names of colors, which are dereferenced by the display hardware using the color map. Indices are typically masked rather than clamped when out of range. For example, the index 0xf7 is masked to 0x7 when written to a 4-bit buffer (color or stencil). Color indices and stencil indices are always treated as indices, never as components.

indices

Preferred plural of index. (The choice between the plural forms indices or indexes—as well as matrices or matrixes and vertices or vertexes—has engendered much debate between the authors and principal reviewers of this guide. The authors' compromise solution is to use the -ices form but to state clearly for the record that the use of indice [*sic*], matrice [*sic*], and vertice [*sic*] for the singular forms is an abomination.)

infinite light source

A directional source of illumination. The radiating light from an infinite light source strikes all objects as parallel rays.

interpolation

Calculation of values (such as color or depth) for interior pixels, given the values at the boundaries (such as at the vertices of a polygon or a line).

IRIS GL

Silicon Graphics proprietary graphics library, developed from 1982 through 1992. OpenGL was designed with IRIS GL as a starting point.

IRIS Inventor

See *Open Inventor*.

jaggies

Artifacts of aliased rendering. The edges of primitives that are rendered with aliasing are jagged rather than smooth. A near-horizontal aliased line, for example, is rendered as a set of horizontal lines on adjacent pixel rows rather than as a smooth, continuous line.

jittering

A pseudo-random displacement (shaking) of the objects in a scene, used in conjunction with the accumulation buffer to achieve special effects.

lighting

The process of computing the color of a vertex based on current lights, material properties, and lighting-model modes.

line

A straight region of finite width between two vertices. (Unlike mathematical lines, OpenGL lines have finite width and length.) Each segment of a strip of lines is itself a line.

local light source

A source of illumination which has an exact position. The radiating light from a local light source emanates from that position. Other names for a local light source are point light source or positional light source. A spotlight is a special kind of local light source.

logical operation

Boolean mathematical operations between the incoming fragment's RGBA color or color-index values and the RGBA color or color-index values already stored at the corresponding location in the framebuffer. Examples of logical operations include AND, OR, XOR, NAND, and INVERT.

luminance

The perceived brightness of a surface. Often refers to a weighted average of red, green, and blue color values that gives the perceived brightness of the combination.

matrices

Preferred plural of matrix. See *indices*.

matrix

A two-dimensional array of values. OpenGL matrices are all 4×4, though when stored in client memory they're treated as 1×16 single-dimension arrays.

modelview matrix

The 4×4 matrix that transforms points, lines, polygons, and raster positions from object coordinates to eye coordinates.

modulate

A method of calculating color values during texture application, where the texture and the fragment colors are combined.

monitor

The device that displays the image in the framebuffer.

motion blurring

A technique that uses the accumulation buffer to simulate what appears on film when you take a picture of a moving object or when you move the camera while taking a picture of a stationary object. In animations without motion blur, moving objects can appear jerky.

network

A connection between two or more computers that allows each to transfer data to and from the others.

nonconvex

A polygon is nonconvex if there exists a line in the plane of the polygon that intersects the polygon more than twice.

normal

A three-component plane equation that defines the angular orientation, but not position, of a plane or surface.

normalized

To normalize a normal vector, divide each of the components by the square root of the sum of their squares. Then, if the normal is thought of as a vector from the origin to the point (nx', ny', nz'), this vector has unit length.

factor = sqrt(nx^2 + ny^2 + nz^2)

nx' = nx / factor

ny' = ny / factor

nz' = nz / factor

normal vectors

See *normal*.

NURBS

Non-Uniform Rational B-Spline. A common way to specify parametric curves and surfaces. (See GLU NURBS routines in Chapter 12.)

object

An object-coordinate model that's rendered as a collection of primitives.

object coordinates

Coordinate system prior to any OpenGL transformation.

Open Inventor

An object-oriented 3D toolkit, built on top of OpenGL, based on a 3D scene database and user interaction components. It includes objects such as cubes, polygons, text, materials, cameras, lights, trackballs and handle boxes.

orthographic

Nonperspective projection, as in some engineering drawings, with no foreshortening.

parameters

Values passed as arguments to OpenGL commands. Sometimes parameters are passed by reference to an OpenGL command.

perspective division

The division of x, y, and z by w, carried out in clip coordinates.

pixel

Picture element. The bits at location (x, y) of all the bitplanes in the framebuffer constitute the single pixel (x, y). In an image in client memory, a pixel is one group of elements. In OpenGL window coordinates, each pixel corresponds to a 1.0×1.0 screen area. The coordinates of the lower-left corner of the pixel are x,y are (x, y), and of the upper-right corner are $(x+1, y+1)$.

point

An exact location in space, which is rendered as a finite-diameter dot.

point light source

See *local light source*.

polygon

A near-planar surface bounded by edges specified by vertices. Each triangle of a triangle mesh is a polygon, as is each quadrilateral of a quadrilateral mesh. The rectangle specified by **glRect*()** is also a polygon.

positional light source

See *local light source.*

primitive

A point, a line, a polygon, a bitmap, or an image. (Note: Not just a point, a line, or a polygon!)

projection matrix

The 4×4 matrix that transforms points, lines, polygons, and raster positions from eye coordinates to clip coordinates.

proxy texture

A placeholder for a texture image, which is used to determine if there are enough resources to support a texture image of a given size and internal format resolution.

quadrilateral

A polygon with four edges.

rasterized

Converted a projected point, line, or polygon, or the pixels of a bitmap or image, to fragments, each corresponding to a pixel in the framebuffer. Note that all primitives are rasterized, not just points, lines, and polygons.

rectangle

A quadrilateral whose alternate edges are parallel to each other in object coordinates. Polygons specified with **glRect*()** are always rectangles; other quadrilaterals might be rectangles.

rendering

Conversion of primitives specified in object coordinates to an image in the framebuffer. Rendering is the primary operation of OpenGL—it's what OpenGL does.

resident texture

A texture image that is cached in special, high-performance texture memory. If an OpenGL implementation does not have special, high-performance texture memory, then all texture images are deemed resident textures.

RGBA

Red, Green, Blue, Alpha.

RGBA mode

An OpenGL context is in RGBA mode if its color buffers store red, green, blue, and alpha color components, rather than color indices.

server

The computer on which OpenGL commands are executed. This might differ from the computer from which commands are issued. See *client*.

shading

The process of interpolating color within the interior of a polygon, or between the vertices of a line, during rasterization.

shininess

The exponent associated with specular reflection and lighting. Shininess controls the degree with which the specular highlight decays.

single-buffering

OpenGL contexts that don't have back color buffers are single-buffered. You can use these contexts for animation, but take care to avoid visually disturbing flashes when rendering.

singular matrix

A matrix that has no inverse. Geometrically, such a matrix represents a transformation that collapses points along at least one line to a single point.

specular

Specular lighting and reflection incorporates reflection off shiny objects and the position of the viewer. Maximum specular reflectance occurs when the angle between the viewer and the direction of the reflected light is zero. A specular material scatters light with greatest intensity in the direction of the reflection, and its brightness decays, based upon the exponential value shininess.

spotlight

A special type of local light source that has a direction (where it points to) as well as a position. A spotlight simulates a cone of light, which may have a fall-off in intensity, based upon distance from the center of the cone.

stencil buffer

Memory (bitplanes) that is used for additional per-fragment testing, along with the depth buffer. The stencil test may be used for masking regions, capping solid geometry, and overlapping translucent polygons.

stereo

Enhanced three-dimensional perception of a rendered image by computing separate images for each eye. Stereo requires special hardware, such as two synchronized monitors or special glasses to alternate viewed frames for each eye. Some implementations of OpenGL support stereo by having both left and right buffers for color data.

stipple

A one- or two-dimensional binary pattern that defeats the generation of fragments where its value is zero. Line stipples are one-dimensional and are applied relative to the start of a line. Polygon stipples are two-dimensional and are applied with a fixed orientation to the window.

tessellation

Reduction of a portion of an analytic surface to a mesh of polygons, or of a portion of an analytic curve to a sequence of lines.

texel

A texture element. A texel is obtained from texture memory and represents the color of the texture to be applied to a corresponding fragment.

textures

One- or two-dimensional images that are used to modify the color of fragments produced by rasterization.

texture mapping

The process of applying an image (the texture) to a primitive. Texture mapping is often used to add realism to a scene. For example, you can apply a picture of a building facade to a polygon representing a wall.

texture matrix

The 4×4 matrix that transforms texture coordinates from the coordinates in which they're specified to the coordinates that are used for interpolation and texture lookup.

texture object

A named cache that stores texture data, such as the image array, associated mipmaps, and associated texture parameter values: width, height, border width, internal format, resolution of components, minification and magnification filters, wrapping modes, border color, and texture priority.

transformations

The warping of spaces. In OpenGL, transformations are limited to projective transformations that include anything that can be represented by a 4×4 matrix. Such transformations include rotations, translations, (nonuniform) scalings along the coordinate axes, perspective transformations, and combinations of these.

triangle

A polygon with three edges. Triangles are always convex.

vertex

A point in three-dimensional space.

vertex array

Where a block of vertex data (vertex coordinates, texture coordinates, surface normals, RGBA colors, color indices, and edge flags) may be stored in an array and then used to specify multiple geometric primitives through the execution of a single OpenGL command.

vertices

Preferred plural of vertex. See *indices*.

viewpoint

The origin of either the eye- or the clip-coordinate system, depending on context. (For example, when discussing lighting, the viewpoint is the origin of the eye-coordinate system. When discussing projection, the viewpoint is the origin of the clip-coordinate system.) With a typical projection matrix, the eye-coordinate and clip-coordinate origins are at the same location.

view volume

The volume in clip coordinates whose coordinates satisfy the three conditions

$-w \leq x \leq w$

$-w \leq y \leq w$

$-w \leq z \leq w$

Geometric primitives that extend outside this volume are clipped.

VRML

VRML stands for Virtual Reality Modeling Language, which is (according to the VRML Mission Statement) "a universal description language for multi-participant simulations." VRML is specifically designed to allow people to navigate through three-dimensional worlds thatare placed on the World Wide Web. The first versions of VRML are subsets of the Open Inventor file format with additions to allow hyperlinking to the Web (to URLs—Universal Resource Locators).

window

A subregion of the framebuffer, usually rectangular, whose pixels all have the same buffer configuration. An OpenGL context renders to a single window at a time.

window-aligned

When referring to line segments or polygon edges, implies that these are parallel to the window boundaries. (In OpenGL, the window is rectangular, with horizontal and vertical edges). When referring to a polygon pattern, implies that the pattern is fixed relative to the window origin.

window coordinates

The coordinate system of a window. It's important to distinguish between the names of pixels, which are discrete, and the window-coordinate system, which is continuous. For example, the pixel at the lower-left corner of a window is pixel (0, 0); the window coordinates of the center of this pixel are (0.5, 0.5, z). Note that window coordinates include a depth, or z, component, and that this component is continuous as well.

wireframe

A representation of an object that contains line segments only. Typically, the line segments indicate polygon edges.

working set

On machines with special hardware that increases texture performance, this is the group of texture objects that are currently resident. The performance of textures within the working set outperforms the textures outside the working set.

X Window System

A window system used by many of the machines on which OpenGL is implemented. GLX is the name of the OpenGL extension to the X Window System. (See Appendix C.)

E

triangle
  fan, specifying, 43, 45
  specifying, 43, 45
  strip, specifying, 43, 45
  tessellated polygons decomposed into, 414
trimming
  curves and curved surfaces, 464–468
  sample program, 467
two-sided lighting, 194

U

up-vector, 99
Utility Library, OpenGL, see GLU
Utility Toolkit, OpenGL, see GLUT

V

van Dam, Andries, xxi, 157, 593
van Widenfelt, Rolf, 372
vendor-specific extensions, 505
versions, 503–505
  GLU, 504
vertex, 37
  also see vertex arrays
  evaluators, generating with, 440
  feedback mode, 493
  per-vertex operations pipeline stage, 12, 531
  specifying, 41
  tessellation, specifying for, 415, 423
  transformation pipeline, 96
vertex arrays, 65–77
  dereference a list of array elements, 72
  dereference a sequence of array elements, 74
  dereference a single element, 71
  disabling, 68
  display list use, 264
  enabling, 67
  interleaved arrays, 75
  interleaved arrays, specifying, 76
  performance tips, 603
  querying, 537
  reuse of vertices, 74

sample program, 69
specifying data, 68
steps to use, 66
stride between data, 70, 76
video
  fake, 527
  flipping an image with glPixelZoom(), 306
  textured images, 332
viewing
  camera analogy, 94–95
viewing transformations, 99, 104, 113–118
  connection to modeling transformations, 100
  default position, 99
  different methods, 118
  pilot view, 119
  polar view, 119
  tripod analogy, 94
  up-vector, 99
viewing volume, 121
  clipping, 125, 136
  jittering, 397, 400
viewpoint
  lighting, for, 194
viewport transformations, 97, 102, 125–128
  photograph analogy, 94
  rendering pipeline stage, 12, 532
visual simulation
  fog, use of, 239
Voronoi polygons, 524

W

w coordinates, 37, 96, 102
  avoiding negative values, 601
  lighting, use with, 183
  perspective division, 128, 532
warping images, 523
Watt, Alan, 318
web sites
  IBM OS/2 software and documentation, 570
  Microsoft Developer Network, 574
  Silicon Graphics' OpenGL, xxii
  Template Graphics Software, 566

WGL, 14, 574
  wglCopyContext(), 575, 576
  wglCreateContext(), 574, 575, 576
  wglCreateLayerContext(), 575, 576
  wglDeleteContext(), 576
  wglDescribeLayerPlane(), 574, 576
  wglDestroyContext(), 575
  wglGetCurrentContext(), 575, 577
  wglGetCurrentDC(), 575, 577
  wglGetLayerPaletteEntries(), 576, 577
  wglMakeCurrent(), 575, 577
  wglRealizeLayerPalette(), 575, 577
  wglShareLists(), 575, 576
  wglSwapLayerBuffers(), 575, 577
  wglUseFontBitmaps(), 576, 577
  wglUseFontOutlines(), 576, 577
Williams, Lance, 338
Win32
  ChoosePixelFormat(), 574, 576
  CreateDIBitmap(), 575, 577
  CreateDIBSection(), 575, 577
  DeleteObject(), 575, 577
  DescribePixelFormat(), 574, 576
  GetVersion(), 574, 576
  GetVersionEx(), 574, 576
  SetPixelFormat(), 574, 576
  SwapBuffers(), 575, 577
winding rules, 418–422
  computational solid geometry, used for, 421
  reversing winding direction, 422
window coordinates, 97, 126
  feedback mode, 493
  polygon offset, 248
window management
  glViewport() called, when window resized, 126
  using GLUT, 16, 35
working set of textures, 332, 346, 351
  fragmentation of texture memory, 353
writemask, See masking (buffers)
writing pixel data, See pixel data (drawing)

X

X Window System, 14, 562
  client-server rendering, 5
  minimum framebuffer configuration, 376
  X Visual, 162, 562

Z

z buffer, See depth buffer
z coordinates, See depth coordinates
zooming images, 305
  filtered, 528

W9-BXA-783

WEBSTER'S
NEW WORLD™

OFFICE PROFESSIONAL'S
DESK REFERENCE

WEBSTER'S
NEW WORLD™

OFFICE PROFESSIONAL'S
DESK REFERENCE

Edited by Anthony S. Vlamis

MACMILLAN • USA

Macmillan General Reference
A Pearson Education Macmillan Company
1633 Broadway
New York, NY 10019-6785

A Webster's New World™ Book

Macmillan is a registered trademark of Macmillan USA.

Webster's New World is a registered trademark of Macmillan USA.

ISBN 0-02-862883-7

Library of Congress Catalog Card Number 99-70262

Manufactured in the United States of America

03   02   01   00   99   4   3   2   1

This book is printed on 50# Husky Offset.

About the Author/Contributors

Anthony S. Vlamis (residing in River Vale, New Jersey) has been in the field of business, professional, technical, and reference publishing for 25 years. A former executive editor at Simon & Schuster, Prentice-Hall, Amacom Books, and Van Nostrand Reinhold, he edited and published hundreds of titles in the business, industrial engineering, finance, and technology areas. He was a founder of Alexander Publishing and Marketing, a newsletter publisher and direct-marketing services agency. He is the author of *Smart Leadership* published by the American Management Association.

Susan Heyboer O'Keefe is co-founder and editor of the monthly newsletter *Secrets and Strategies for the Office Professional* (Economics Press) and editor of Stroman and Wilson's *Administrative Assistant's and Secretary's Handbook* (AMACOM Books).

Florence Stone has over 25 years of experience in management publishing at the American Management Association, most recently as senior editor responsible for all the organization's newsletters and journals. She is author of the new AMACOM book *Coaching, Counseling & Mentoring*. During her association with AMA, she has become an authority on supervisory and middle management problems and concerns.

Geoffrey Steck heads Alexander Publishing Inc., headquartered in Englewood, New Jersey. The firm provides direct-marketing support, motivational and business skills training, and editorial and publishing services such as the monthly newsletter *Secrets & Strategies for Office Professionals* (formerly *Secretary's Letter*), the magazine *Leadership—with a Human Touch*, and the biweekly *First-Rate Customer Service Manager's Memo*.

E. Alexander Saenz is a New York–based communications specialist for one of the world's largest banks and regularly writes for the mutual fund industry. As a freelance writer in the business and finance area, his writings have also appeared in a variety of professional books and journals including *Management Review* and the *Take-Charge Assistant*.

M. Faunette Johnston is an experienced reference editor working on such titles as *Pocket Style Guide, Dictionary of Quotations, Dictionary of Science, Pocket Book of Facts, Dictionary of Computer Terms,* and *Pocket Internet Directory and Dictionary.* She has a Master's degree in Communications Development from Colorado State University.

Other contributors include: Susan C. Bauer, Jeanette L. Bely, Murray Bromberg, Linda A. Bruce, Lois M. Burns, William W. Cook, Rose A. Doherty, Julie Eichenberger, Joyce Gold, Charlotte B. Holmquest, Audrey Katz, Milton Katz, Ruth Kimball Kent, Doreen La Blanc, Sheryl Lindsell-Roberts, James C. Matthews, John I. McCollum, Ardis R. Morton, Emojean G. Novotny, Barry Persky, Naomi Dornfeld Platt, Warren T. Schimmel, Abba Spero.

CONTENTS

CHAPTER 5 Computers   165

SIDEBARS AND TABLES

1

COMMUNICATIONS

◆

- **Face-to-Face Customer/Client Relations**
  - Basic Communication Techniques
  - The Protocol of Introductions
- **Basic Principles of Organization and Effectiveness**
  - Telephone Techniques
  - Answering Services, Answering Machines, and Voice Mail
  - Long-Distance Services
  - Memos
  - Minutes of a Meeting
- **Correspondence**
  - Letters
  - Faxes
  - E-mail
- **For More Information**

An office professional always has needed strong communication skills—but never before has the ability to communicate been so critical to an office professional's job. The responsibilities of this position have grown tremendously—and likely will continue to grow. Those office professionals who will benefit most from these ever-increasing opportunities for recognition—including promotions and raises—are those with communication strengths. They are the office professionals who can communicate effectively with customers and vendors. They are the professionals who have the interpersonal communication skills to work well with all members of their organization, from peers to technicians, to other managers, to senior executives, to the CEO. And they have the ability to network outside the organization to bring ideas for operating improvement to their workplace.

This book examines the traditional tasks of office professionals and also explores new and growing responsibilities. The subject of communication is an ideal place to begin. Today's office professionals serve in their managers' place in certain meetings and act as representatives of their operating group in project team meetings. They are the contacts with clients—international as well as domestic. Assistants' roles have given them the opportunities to utilize their communication skills to make good impressions, not only with their bosses but also with others who make promotion decisions.

FACE-TO-FACE CUSTOMER/ CLIENT RELATIONS

Good customer relations is a competitive advantage—and one to which you can contribute.

You, as the office professional, create the first impression when a client or customer visits the office. You are usually the first person visitors meet; by your welcome, you can help a visitor believe that he or she has chosen well the organization with which to do business. You can ignore the presence of a visitor or glare at him as he enters the office area, or you can continue to socialize while the visitor waits to get your attention. *Or* you can greet the visitor and ask if you can assist her.

If the visitor has an appointment, all you need to do is make the person comfortable until your boss is free. But if the visit is unexpected, and if your boss is tied up elsewhere or away from the office, you might have to make the customer feel welcome. Introduce yourself and offer to help. If you don't know the answer to the person's question, contact someone within the organization who can help. Keep a list of persons within your organization by your phone so that you can refer the visitor's problem to someone who can answer his or her questions.

Adapt your response to the customer's own style. On some occasions, a friendly, informal style works best. At other times, it is better to be completely professional.

BASIC COMMUNICATION TECHNIQUES

An important function of every office professional involves receiving guests—important or otherwise. How smoothly you handle this duty can dramatically affect everything that happens after your greeting.

If an individual seems rushed, respond by being as efficient as you can be. If someone seems relaxed and is smiling and happy, smile back and soften your tone. Professionals who have studied such responses call this pacing, establishing rapport, or mirroring. Although this technique is used most often by salespeople, it can work as effectively for office professionals in the course of their work.

Use the "Magic Mirror" Approach

Psychologists conclude that, in the short run, 90 percent of what's communicated between people comes from body language and tone of voice. So show visitors what they like best to see: themselves.

How do you use mirroring? When someone first approaches your desk, pay attention to his or her mood and deportment, and then adapt your responses accordingly. Affect a non-intimidating manner if the person seems at ease. If the person seems intent and formal, respond formally. If the person appears jolly, extend a cheery greeting. If the person seems frazzled, be empathetic.

A reminder: You're not ridiculing visitors when you mirror them. You're trying to make them feel comfortable, showing them that although they're in unfamiliar surroundings, they've come across someone who is like themselves and who can identify with their feelings.

Add the Personal Touch

The next crucial decision when you greet someone is whether to shake hands.

Some individuals feel awkward shaking hands with members of the opposite sex or with people perceived as subordinates. If the situation feels awkward, or if you sense an awkwardness in the other person, don't press the issue.

Otherwise, extend your hand. Grip the person's hand firmly but not tightly. Let him or her dictate how long you shake.

People usually welcome a touch that reassures and relaxes, as long as it's respectful. But be sensitive to persons of other cultures who do not like being touched by strangers. If you expect cultural differences, either discover the proper behavior and follow it, or keep your gestures as neutral as possible.

THE PROTOCOL OF INTRODUCTIONS

Introducing people correctly is important because it makes people feel at ease, fosters interesting conversations, feeds the ego of the introduced, and enhances your professional image.

Introductions have to do with communicating naturally and gracefully, and making people feel that they are valuable and important—skills every businessperson must have.

On various occasions in business you must introduce one person to another, whether in team or group meetings, in visits to suppliers or customer organizations, in professional association meetings, or in social occasions in which family members might be invited. The key to making introductions is to remember that the person lesser in age, rank, achievement, and so on should be introduced to the higher; a member of your organization to a client or customer; someone from your country to a visitor from a foreign country; and someone without an official title (for example, judge or senator) to the person with the title. If you find yourself introducing family members to office colleagues, you would introduce family members to your business associates.

Besides greeting visitors to your office, you might be responsible for taking visitors to meet with others or leading tours of the office if your boss is busy or unavailable. During the course of your travel through the office, you might have to introduce a visitor to those within your organization. Keep these tips in mind:

- Always introduce people with whom you are standing or walking when another person joins you.

- If you can remember the first name and not the last, use the first name: "Jerry, this is an old friend from my Chicago days. George, this is Jerry Perkins, one of the partners." (No one will notice that you didn't mention George's last name.)

- If you can remember the last name but not the first, bluff around it: "Jerry, this is an old friend, the very respectable Mr. Anderson, the best squash player in Chicago."

- If you can't remember any part of the name, laugh and admit it: "I'm sorry, but I can't even remember my mother's name. I'm hopeless!" The people with you should laugh, put out their hands to shake, and give their own names.

- If you get the feeling that someone is having difficulty remembering your name, extend your hand to the person standing next to him or her and introduce yourself. In other words, alleviate the embarrassment and give your name right away.

- Write down a difficult-to-pronounce name phonetically as soon as you're able, and practice saying it aloud several times. You might be asked to introduce an international colleague at a corporate function—practice. Or, write the name on a card, and as you take the person around, glance at the card to make sure you're pronouncing his or her name correctly.

- If you're being introduced and the person doing it makes a mistake with your name, whisper in his or her ear to correct the error. Don't allow him or her to continue inaccurately. If you correct someone with a big smile on your face, he or she won't feel intimidated—just grateful.

BASIC PRINCIPLES OF ORGANIZATION AND EFFECTIVENESS

We communicate our professionalism not only in the work we do, but also in our greetings to visitors, as mentioned. But with other communications we must be alert to the impression we leave others. Over the telephone, always exhibit a professional demeanor when talking to others, whether they are internal callers or external callers. Likewise, memos and written communications should display carefulness and conscientiousness. This is what professionalism is all about.

TELEPHONE TECHNIQUES

The telephone is the most frequently used audio communication medium in the business world, and dependency on this instrument continues to grow.

Receptionists use the phone all day; assistants answer calls directed to them as well as their bosses.

The reputation and goodwill of the employer and the firm might depend upon your approach and skill in using the telephone. Although most people begin to use the telephone in early childhood, perhaps the majority still need to be trained in proper telephone techniques. An impressive way to point out defects in techniques—and one that results in a rapid and desirable change—is to make a recording or tape of a telephone conversation. Such a recording emphasizes the faults in telephone techniques and vividly points out areas needing improvement. Many organizations—even those that aren't efficiently organized—lose customers, money, and goodwill simply because of employees' poor telephone habits.

Speaking Clearly and Pleasantly
People talking on a phone have no visual image on which to base impressions. The frame of reference is based entirely upon the voice coming over the wires. If these sounds are jarring or unpleasant, a busy executive might quickly lose

patience and discontinue association with the firm in question. On the other hand, a pleasant and understanding voice coming over an inanimate instrument can accomplish wonders. The power of the spoken word can and does exert a great impact upon the listener. Knowing how to pick the right tone of professionalism, friendliness, matter-of-factness, or even irritation is the key to good telephone relationships.

To enhance your telephone personality, inject variety and flexibility into the voice, and convey mood and attitude conversations. These qualities can be obtained through pitch, inflection, and emphasis. A high-pitched voice might convey an impression of childishness and immaturity, or of impatience and irritability. On the other hand, a voice that is well-modulated carries the impression of culture and polish. Pitch in speaking (as in pitch in music), refers to the key in which one speaks. Everyone has a range of tone within which a pleasant speaking voice is possible, and this can be consciously controlled. Each person must be conscious of his or her own range and practice utilizing it. An individual is said to speak in a *modulated* voice when the pitch falls in the lower half of the possible range. This tonal range carries best and is easiest to hear over the telephone.

In cultivating an interesting telephone personality, the speaker must enunciate clearly and distinctly. A garbled and indistinct speech pattern will annoy the listener who cannot understand what is being said. Do not be afraid to move your lips: You can't form rounded vowel sounds or distinct consonants unless the lips accomplish their function—however, it is not necessary to exaggerate or to become stilted. Your telephone voice should reflect your personality and transmit alertness and pleasantness. Your voice should be natural, distinct, and expressive—and neither too loud nor too soft. Avoid repetitious, mechanical words and phrases.

Answering Promptly

Answering a business telephone call is similar to welcoming a visitor. Therefore, it is essential that each call be greeted by a prompt, effective, and pleasing answer. Some disagreement exists about the impact of voice mail on customer relations. Still, most organizations have some version of voice mail in their offices. You'll want to set your system to reflect the attitude of your organization and your manager toward answering calls: Do they prefer to pick up calls after the first ring, or is it acceptable to answer after the third or even fourth ring?

The telephone should sit on the desk so that it is readily accessible. If you are left-handed, place the telephone on your left side; if you are right-handed, the phone belongs on the right side of your desk. You want it within reach, which means that you don't have to reach across your computer to pick it up. Keep a pad and pencil or pen handy to jot down necessary information.

Assistants might be juggling many things when the phone rings, and consequently put the call on hold as soon as they pick it up. Don't do this unless

it is absolutely imperative. Many callers find this practice infuriating. Instead, allow voice mail to pick up a call, or arrange for a colleague to pick up your phone after three rings. A co-worker can take a message after explaining that you are presently busy and will return the call as soon as you are free.
Use the same procedure if you step away from your desk for some time.

Never leave a telephone unattended. An unanswered telephone becomes an instrument of failure—failure to the company because of the loss of customers and failure of the individuals responsible.

A receptionist might or might not handle incoming calls in addition to greeting visitors (and notifying staff that the visitors have arrived). If this is part of the receptionist's responsibility, he or she should complete a discussion on the phone before turning to help a visitor. A receptionist never should ask a caller to wait while they attend to a visitor or staff member.

The matter isn't so clear-cut for other office staff when handling incoming calls represents 50 percent or more of the job. You can put a caller on hold for a brief period, either to address another issue or to search for materials pertinent to the telephone conversation.

On the Phone

When you pick up the phone, identify your office and yourself immediately. Let the caller know that he or she has reached the person he intended to reach. Don't just say, "Hello." This advice applies to assistants as well as receptionists, who should simply identify the company, ask whom the caller wishes to contact, and speedily connect the call to the individual the caller wants.

If you pick up your boss's line, you might want to let the caller know that it is your boss's line by saying, "Mr. Crawford's line," or "Ms. Erick's line." If you want, you then can identify yourself—"This is Ms. O'Brien, his assistant"—or say, "Mr. O'Connor is away from his phone. May I help you? I'm Ms. O'Brien, his assistant."

Many phones in today's offices have caller ID. This is very helpful in giving you direction about whether to put another call on hold or to just let it ring through to voice mail. Let's say that you are planning for a corporate retreat, and you have several calls out to local people as well as the hotel folks in Florida. If you're on the phone with a local caterer, you can let the line ring through if you see it's another local call. If it's your boss, you might put the other call on hold and pick up, or if it's long distance, you might finish and answer the other line.

Handling Incoming Calls

The wise telephone user develops a keen ear and learns to recognize the voices of important or frequent callers. However, a word of caution: Do not become too sure of an infallible ear, for voices might sound different over the telephone. If you know the voice beyond a doubt, use the caller's name when speaking. If you identify the voice correctly, the caller will be pleased that you have recognized and addressed him or her by name. Then speak *to* the person at the other end of the wire, not *at* the telephone. If you are incorrect in identifying the voice before divulging any information, little harm will occur because the caller will make the correction. Apologize tactfully and take up the business at hand. However, when the name of the caller is not revealed and/or the nature of the business is not identified, you always can ask politely, "Who is calling, please?" or "May I ask what this refers to?"

Some executives prefer their support staff to screen incoming calls. Do so with tact and discretion. In some cases, the executive will speak with anyone who calls, but wants to know beforehand who is calling and the nature of the business. The screener must obtain this information before transferring the call to the executive. Avoid curtness and rudeness in doing so. It is correct to say, for example, "May I tell Mr. Brown who is calling?" or "Ms. Winslow is talking on another line. Would you care to wait, or may I have her call you? I believe her other call may take some time." Also consider saying, "Mr. Zobkiw is in conference. May I help you?" Be sincere and courteous in your explanation, but do not divulge information unnecessarily. Your goal is simply to find out tactfully who is calling.

Although some executives answer the telephone themselves (especially those with direct lines), many depend on a receptionist or their own assistant to answer all incoming calls. Whoever takes these calls, therefore, must be familiar with the executive's preferences. Learn which calls the assistant is expected to handle, which are to be referred to the executive, and which should be transferred to someone else. Telephone callers must be classified accurately and quickly. Every call is important, and you must ascertain enough information to classify the call. Never allow a caller to get to the end of a long inquiry before being referred to the proper person. To forestall this, make a discreet vocal sound that causes the caller to pause slightly so that you can say, "Mr. Chan in the shipping department should be able to help you with this. Please let me transfer your call to him."

Routing the Call

The following sections describe calls that the office professional usually can handle.

Requests for information. Such calls might come to the office receptionist or an assistant within the office. Either can handle the information if it's not confidential and if no doubt exists about the request. For instance, some organizations include a main number to handle requests for product information if they do not have a designated customer service operation. If they have placed an advertisement for a job vacancy, the company might want to set aside a phone to receive such calls without identifying the organization. If the latter is the case, then those who might pick up the phone will be told in advance not to identify their organization.

Sometimes, you might have to check with the employer before imparting information. If any complications arise, it is always wiser to turn the call over to the executive. In certain situations, the assistant can ask for a letter of request and respond upon its receipt and approval.

Requests for appointments. Such calls likely will go directly to the person with whom the caller wants an appointment, or to his or her assistant. If the assistant answers the call, he or she can place the appointment tentatively on the manager's calendar, and confirm once the manager returns.

After you have received and routed the call, take down the message or information. Remember always to write clearly, and always get the phone number and verify the caller's name. This information will help in returning calls.

You also might decide to transfer the call directly to the recipient or other appropriate person. Let the caller know you are transferring; if the caller would rather not be switched over, provide another phone number to call directly (or take a message). If the caller agrees to a transfer, make sure that the right office is reached, and give the person in that office sufficient information before hanging up so that the caller will not need to repeat it.

When taking calls from persons who wish to speak to the executive directly, the screener must know how to handle the following situations tactfully, discreetly, and diplomatically:

- *The employer is in and free.* Inform the executive of the caller. On occasion, if the caller is well-known to the employer and is someone to whom the executive talks frequently, the assistant may signal the executive to pick up the telephone.

- *The employer is in but does not want to be disturbed.* Tell the caller that the executive is engaged at the moment, and ask whether you can take a message to him or her as soon as the employer is free.

- *The employer is in another office in the building.* The assistant should ascertain whether the executive will be available for telephone calls when away from the office. Generally, only the most urgent calls should be transferred under such circumstances.

Taking Messages

It is good practice to keep a written record of all incoming calls, particularly when the executive is away from the office. Indicate the time the call was received; the name, business affiliation, and telephone number of the caller; and the message. Then sign the note with your initials. If the message comes from an out-of-town caller, also record the area code or the telephone operator's number. When taking a message, read it back to the caller to avoid errors or misunderstandings. Always take messages verbatim. Be patient and pleasant, but persistent. Ask the caller to spell out both first and last names, if necessary. If numbers are involved, repeat the sequence for verification.

A good way to keep track of these messages is to use a special phone message book that is available from most office supply stores and catalogs. This a spiral-bound book provides perforated rows of message slips that you can tear out and give to the recipient, as well as carbon copies of the message for later reference.

When taking a call, place the phone message slip on the executive's desk immediately. The heads-up assistant also should anticipate the executive's needs by attaching to the slips any material (possibly annotated) necessary for reference to conclude the transaction successfully—this can include back correspondence, a bill, price lists, or whatever might assist the executive in handling the call intelligently.

To handle the incoming calls more efficiently, the office staff should know where the executive will be when away from the office, whether urgent messages can be relayed, and the expected time of return to the office.

In taking calls for other persons in the office, it is helpful if you can state when that person will return or whether the call can be transferred somewhere else. Offer whatever information is possible; otherwise, the caller might get the impression of being put off with an excuse. Be courteous and use discretion in explaining an absence from the office. It is less offensive to say, "Ms. Jones is away from her desk just now. May I have her call you, or would you prefer to leave a message?" than to say bluntly, "She's out," or "This is her coffee break," or "I don't know where she is." The office professional must always use tact in dealing with callers, whether it be for one's own executive or for another co-worker.

Taking Action

If you promise the caller some definite action, you must see to it that the promise is kept. If the caller is told that the executive will call back, then this information must be conveyed to the employer so that the call can be made. A broken promise can result in a canceled order or a lost customer—and it might take many months to regain lost goodwill.

If, for some reason, you can't deliver on the action, it's always safe to call back and let the caller know the information might be delayed or is not available. He or she might be disappointed but will appreciate the effort made by the follow-up call.

On some calls that the office staff can handle, more information might be needed than is within immediate reach. In such a case, leave the telephone to look up the necessary information, and inform the caller of this fact and of the length of time that it could take to obtain the material. Offer the caller a choice of waiting or of being called back. The caller never should be left waiting for an unreasonable amount of time. If you make a promise to call back with the needed information, you must honor the promise.

If the caller is waiting to speak to the executive, the assistant should reassure the caller periodically that the call will be connected as soon as the employer is free. When you're ready to transfer the call, thank the caller for waiting.

Completing the Incoming Call

At the completion of the call, indicate its end by summing up the details. Use the caller's name when saying a pleasant "Good-bye." It is courteous to wait for the caller to end the call. Permitting the caller to say "Good-bye" first also allows time for last-minute orders or special instructions. Replace the receiver gently in its cradle—the most pleasant "Good-bye" can be spoiled by the jarring sound of a receiver dropped into position. Do not hang up until your caller has done so first.

ANSWERING SERVICES, ANSWERING MACHINES, AND VOICE MAIL

As mentioned earlier, office staff today frequently rely on answering services, answering machines, or voice mail to handle incoming calls when they are too busy to pick up or are away from the phones.

Answering Services

Before the advent of modern electronics, the outside answering service offered the only viable way to get calls answered when no business "insiders" were available. Services still exist as an option for all sorts of businesses, but these are used primarily when a human touch or human judgment concerning off-hours callers is important to the enterprise.

Many professionals (such as doctors, dentists, accountants, and financial advisors) still use answering services. These individuals prefer an answering service for two reasons: The call might be an emergency, and they might need to be notified immediately. The caller also might need the reassurance that the person being called will understand the urgency of his or her request. A pager might alert the owner that someone wants to speak with him or her, but it doesn't communicate the compelling need for the call to be returned, which an answering service hopefully will do. A person might leave an urgent message on voice mail, but he or she can't be sure that the person being called regularly checks messages.

A good answering service should act as if it were the company—in effect, as if it were a message center at another location. When choosing one to serve your company, look (and listen) for courteous, professional-sounding operators who are able to identify themselves as you would like to be identified when they're covering your company's calls.

Procedure setup is critical when using an answering service to ensure that you are notified of emergencies. Make sure that you've set up an acceptable routine for doing so.

Answering Machines

Chip-sized electronics make some fairly inexpensive machines quite sophisticated, adding features such as mailboxes for several people or departments. Despite their popularity, keep in mind some answering machine cautions:

- Don't overdo the outgoing message you record. Write it down and practice saying it before you record. You might announce your regular business hours and perhaps an alternative means to contact the company (such as a fax number). But then get quickly to the business of taking a message if that's what you want to do.

- Be prepared to retrieve messages when you push the playback button. Quickly convey each to the appropriate individual, or at least acknowledge receipt to the original caller.

Answering machines don't have all the functions of most voice-mail systems, however. Although they work well for smaller organizations, voice mail is more appropriate for larger organizations.

Voice Mail

By far the most common systems in use today, voice-mail systems work like answering machines on a grand scale. The system might be internal, using computers or equipment in your company, or it might be a service provided by the local phone company. Most offer a slew of options that make them either another valuable workplace tool or a maze that can turn off callers with their impersonality.

The guidelines for good answering machine messages apply systemwide to voice-mail setups—in fact, they're doubly important because a caller might face two tiers of messaging before he or she gets to leave one. You know what annoys you when you're caught in voice mail limbo. Remedy it in your system.

Telephone Directories

Once a mainstay of business information, the mushrooming of telephone numbers and telephone-related ways of contacting companies and individuals— fax lines, e-mail, Web sites, cell phones, pagers, and so on—has diminished the usefulness of the local directory. Still, these are good places to begin the search for contact information about a firm or individual.

Local directories are usually available free to local service subscribers, at least one per phone listing. Libraries often have out-of-town directories, or you

CREATING GREAT VOICE-MAIL MESSAGES

You want callers who get your voice mail to want to leave a message. You also want those whom you call to return your call when you leave a message on voice mail.

Here's how to marshal the many phone skills you already have to handle voice mail easily and effectively:

- *Put a smile in your voice.* What works as a good phone tip for "live" conversations works even better for voice mail. A smile on your face adds pleasantness to your voice. Imagine that the person you're talking to can see you that very moment. This will help add expression and variation to your words.

- *Address the individual by name.* This gives the call a personal touch. The individual also will pay greater attention to your message, having heard his or her name first.

- *Who, what, when, where, and why?* You know the purpose of your call; the other person doesn't. Make your message specific: Do you want the other person to return your call, or will you call back? Do you want that person to have information ready for the call back? Say so now.

- *Time is of the essence.* Just as you consider time zones when you make a call, keep them in mind when leaving messages. Whenever you mention a time, frame it with a "my time" or "your time" reference so there's no mistake.

- *Postmark your voice mail.* Although some voice mail services automatically date and time stamp messages, others do not. The best bet is always to add that information to your voice message. It might not seem necessary at the moment, but if a person is collecting more than a day's worth of mail at once, undated messages can be very confusing. Postmarking your mail is essential when you leave instructions such as "I need this information tomorrow."

- *Sign your letter.* Unless it's your mother, the other person might not recognize your voice. Leave your full name, even if you speak to the person frequently. What might seem like overkill to you can save frustration for the person who can't place you by your first name alone.

- *Sign off by leaving your phone number.* Even if you're sure that the other person already has your number, state it anyway. This saves the time of looking it up.

might acquire one for a modest fee for areas where your company might have greater than passing interest.

Most local directories now are arranged in general sections to facilitate your information search. As a rule, the introductory section contains useful information about phone company services and might present some local highlights. The White Pages embody the comprehensive phone number listing, although the number listed might represent one of many ways to reach the company or individual you seek. Remember that the printed book is dated as soon as it rolls off the press—new numbers are issued daily.

This is why phone companies put their directories, both White and Yellow Pages, online—so they can always be up-to-date. One site for all Yellow Pages in the United States is www.bigbook.com. Another site that offers online White Pages is www.whowhere.com. Still, we need paper editions because we don't always have access to the Internet.

Government-related phone information often is listed in a section of its own. Paid listings in the Yellow Pages might provide more detailed information about phoning businesses you wish to contact.

Personal Phone Directories

For numbers you use all the time, such as those for clients or vendors, you'll want to have a system for keeping personal numbers organized and handy. You could have a low-tech recipe box full of 3 × 5 cards or a Rolodex with handwritten contact information. You also can go high-tech by keeping an address book on your desktop in Outlook or another scheduler or database. Card files, such as Rolodex cards, are very popular because they offer an organized way to store and access cards, plus easy replacement or addition of addresses and numbers. If you travel or move between offices, you might even want to investigate a portable desktop address book. Most are the size of large calculators, run on battery power, and can store hundreds of names, addresses, and numbers.

Many office professionals also keep business cards. Some are organized separately (in a binder designed specifically to hold business cards in plastic sleeves) or as part of a card file system. At office supply stores, you even can buy a hole punch for business cards that will punch the slots required to fit it into a Rolodex system.

The key to any personal system is using it to keep information as up-to-date as possible. The record should identify individuals by noting title and company affiliations as well as address and phone number options, including extension listings, fax numbers, toll-free numbers, cell phones, pager numbers, e-mail addresses, and the like. Personal data (spouse: Connie; one son: Alex; likes fishing) also might go into the record.

TIP: Be aware of what information is available on what scale. You don't want to publish personal home numbers or information in the company phone list, nor do you want to restrict access of general information. You must counterbalance the capability of recording many things in a semi-public company database with the need for privacy. Certain information to which you are privy might not warrant general circulation—particularly information about other employees. The in-house telephone list, if you have one, should be bare bones for general perusal.

Assembling Data for Outgoing Calls

To place outgoing calls quickly for the employer, the office support staff should master all the telephone techniques needed to do this skillfully. Be absolutely certain of the telephone number before calling. Then assemble all the information that might be necessary to conduct the business transaction when the call is put through. You might have to obtain materials from the files to refresh the executive's memory on previous business, or you might need to get other information that will help in making a successful call. All pertinent material should be placed on the executive's desk before the call is made. Don't call someone unless you have the materials you need in front of you. It is unfair to make the person you are calling have to wait while you hunt for the pertinent information.

If you are placing a call for someone else, it is also a good practice to be sure they will be free and available to take the call as soon as it goes through. Delays not only lower the prestige of the company and the executive and cause annoyance, but they also can prove costly to the firm making the call.

Even today, the question frequently arises about which executive should answer first. Courtesy prescribes that the caller should be on the line, ready to talk, when the person called is put on the line by his or her own staff member—particularly if the person called outranks the caller. Put the executive on the line immediately, if possible. This can be done readily if the assistant identifies the employer when the call is answered. The assistant at the other end then can transfer the call to the person called without delay, or immediately can inform the caller about how to reach that individual.

LONG-DISTANCE SERVICES

In addition to business calls within the local community or surrounding areas, you might have to place calls to more distant points.

When you call long distance, keep in mind that different types of long-distance calls exist, called *classes*. These classes determine how calls are billed; rates can vary, depending on time of day, area called, use of a live operator, direct dial, and so on. Keep in mind that long-distance calls do add up—and make for a large proportion of business expense. Try to be organized and aware of the cost, and avoid use of high-priced calls (such as operator assistance) when possible. Also, make sure you try to look up a number first instead of just calling directory assistance.

AREA CODES

U.S. Domestic

Until 1990, all area codes had either a "1" or a "0" as the middle number. However, with rapid population and technology growth in many regions, area codes now contain all numbers. This list might change because area codes are added and change often.

Alabama			Colorado	
north	205		Denver	303
south	334		southeast	719
Alaska	907		west and northwest	970
Arizona	520		Connecticut	
Phoenix	602		east	860
			west	203
Arkansas	870		Delaware	302
Little Rock	501			
California			District of Columbia	202
central	209		Florida	
Los Angeles	213		east and central	407
Los Angeles west	562		Gainesville	352
north and central	530		Miami	305
	916		north	904
northwest	707		south	941
northwest and central	510		southeast	561
	925			954
Pasadena	818		west and central	813
south	310		Georgia	
San Diego	619		Atlanta	404
San Francisco	415		Atlanta northwest	770
southeast	760		north	706
southwest	714		south	912
	805			
	949		Guam	671
west and central	408		Hawaii	808
	650			
	909		Idaho	208

Illinois		Massachusetts (cont'd)	
central	217	northeast	508
Chicago	312	southeast	978
	630	west	413
	708	Michigan	
	773	central	517
	847	Detroit	313
north	815	northeast	810
northwest	309	northwest	906
south	618	Oakland county	248
Indiana		southeast	734
central	765	west	616
Indianapolis	317	Minnesota	
north	219	Minneapolis	320
south	812	St. Paul	612
Iowa		north	218
central	515	south	507
east	319	Mississippi	228
west	712	Jackson	601
Kansas		Missouri	
Kansas City	913	east	573
north	785	northwest	816
south	316	St. Louis	314
Kentucky		southwest	417
east	606	Montana	406
west	502	Nebraska	
Louisiana		east	402
northwest	318	west	308
southeast	504	Nevada	702
Maine	207	New Hampshire	603
Maryland		New Jersey	
east	410	central	732
	443	northwest	201
west	240		973
	301	northwest and central	908
Massachusetts		south	609
Boston	617	New Mexico	505
	781		

continues

New York			South Carolina	
northeast	518		coastal	843
northwest	315		north and central	803
south and central	607		northwest	864
southeast	914		South Dakota	605
west	716			
New York City	718		Tennessee	
cellular	917		east	423
Long Island	516		north and central	615
Manhattan	212		south and central	931
			west	901
North Carolina			Texas	
central	910		Arlington	817
east	919		Dallas	214
west	704			972
			east central	254
North Dakota	701		Houston	281
				713
Ohio			north and central	940
Cleveland	216		northeast	903
Dayton	937		northwest	806
north and central	440		San Antonio	210
northeast	330		south and central	512
northwest	419		southeast	409
southeast and central	614		southwest	830
southwest	513			956
			west	915
Oklahoma				
northeast	918		Utah	801
west and central	405			
			Vermont	802
Oregon	541			
northwest	503		Virginia	
			central	804
Pennsylvania			east	757
east	717		north	703
Philadelphia	215		west	540
southeast	610			
southwest	412		Washington	
	724		east	509
west	814		northwest	253
				425
Puerto Rico	787		Seattle	206
			southwest	360
Rhode Island	401			

West Virginia	304	Wisconsin (cont'd)	
Wisconsin		southeast	920
Milwaukee	414	southwest	608
north	715	Wyoming	307

Canadian Domestic

Alberta	403	Ontario (cont'd)	
British Columbia	250	northwest	807
Vancouver	604	southeast	905
		southwest	519
Manitoba	204	Toronto	416
New Brunswick	506	Quebec	450
Newfoundland	709	Montreal	514
		Quebec City	418
Nova Scotia/Prince		Sherbrooke	819
Edward Island	902	Saskatchewan	306
Ontario		Yukon/Northwest	
central	705	Territories	867
east	613		

Caribbean Domestic

Anguilla	264	Jamaica	876
Antigua and Barbuda	268	Montserrat	664
The Bahamas	242	Northern Mariana Islands	670
Barbados	246	St. Kitts/Nevis	869
Bermuda	441	St. Lucia	758
British Virgin Islands	284	St. Vincent/Grenadines	784
Caribbean Islands	809	Trinidad and Tobago	868
Cayman Islands	345	Turks and Caicos Islands	649
Dominica	767	U.S. Virgin Islands	340
Grenada	473		

Time Differences

Check the differences in time when planning to place a long-distance call. Be aware not only that this country is divided into time zones, but also understand that differences in time exist in all countries. For example, the United States (excluding Alaska and Hawaii) is divided into four standard time zones:

800 NUMBERS FOR LONG-DISTANCE SERVICE PROVIDERS

Chances are, you won't ever have to price or select long-distance service for your office or company, but sometimes billing questions, travel concerns, or other questions require a call to a long-distance provider.

Amnex	800-287-2646
AT&T	800-222-0400
Cable & Wireless	800-486-8686
Frontier	800-836-7000
INS	800-469-4000
LCI	800-860-1020
LDDS WorldCom	800-264-1000
MCI	800-950-5555
Network Phoenix	800-800-3002
One Star	800-950-4357
Sprint	800-877-4646
UniDial Communications/Solutions	800-832-7999
U.S. Long Distance	800-460-1111

Eastern, Central, Mountain, and Pacific. Each zone is one hour earlier than the zone immediately to the east of it: When it is noon Eastern Standard Time, it is 11 A.M. in the Central zone. Likewise, 10 A.M. in Mountain zone is 9 A.M. Pacific time. Greenwich Mean Time (which is the mean solar time of the meridian at Greenwich, England) is used as the basis for standard time throughout most of the world.

Teleconferencing

When you set up a teleconference, bring the telephone numbers of those who will be in conference with you. Depending on the number of individuals on the teleconference and the existing equipment, you might be able to set up the phone conference from a typical office phone, or you might need to work through either a telephone service company or your company's switchboard.

INTERNATIONAL COUNTRY AND CITY CALLING CODES

Albania	355		Santa Fe	42
Durres	52		Tandil	293
Elbassan	545		Armenia	374
Korce	824			
Shkoder	224		Aruba	297
Tirana	42		All cities	8
Algeria	213		Ascension Island	247
Adrar	7			
Ain Defla	3		Australia	61
Bejaia	5		Adelaide	8
Guerrar	9		Ballarat	53
			Brisbane	7
American Samoa	684		Canberra	6
			Darwin	89
Andorra	376		Geelong	52
			Gold Coast	75
Angola	244		Hobart	02
Luanda	2		Launceston	03
			Melbourne	3
Anguilla	264		Newcastle	49
			Perth	9
Antarctica			Sydney	2
Casey Base	67212		Toowoomba	76
Scott Base	672		Townsville	77
			Wollongong	42
Antigua and Barbuda	268			
			Austria	43
Argentina	54		Bludenz	5552
Babia Blanca	91		Graz	316
Buenos Aires	1		Innsbruck	512
Cordoba	51		Kitzbuhel	5356
Corrientes	783		Klagenfurt	463
La Plata	21		Krems An Der Donau	2732
Mar Del Plata	23		Linz Donau	70
Mendoza	61		Neunkirchen	
Merlo	220		Niederosterreich	2635
Posadas	752		St. Polten	2742
Resistencia	722		Salzburg	662
Rio Cuatro	586		Vienna	1
Rosario	41		Villach	4242
San Juan	64			
San Rafael	627			

continues

Wels	7242	Mons	65
Wiener Neustadt	2622	Namur	81
		Ostend	59
Azerbaijan	994	Verviers	87
Baku	12		
Daskasan	216	Belize	501
Sumgayit	164	Belize City	2
		Belmopan	8
The Bahamas	242	Benque Viejo Del	
		Carmen	93
Bahrain	973	Corozal Town	4
Bangladesh	880	Dangriga	5
Barisal	431	Independence	6
Bogra	51	Orange Walk	3
Chittagong	31	Punta Gorda	7
Comilla	81	San Ignacio	92
Dhaka	2	Stan Creek	5
Khulna	41		
Maulabi Bazar	861	Benin	229
Mymensingh	91		
Narayangon	671	Bermuda	441
Rajshaki	721	Bhutan	975
Sylhet	821		
		Bolivia	591
Barbados	246	Cochabamba	42
		Cotoga	388
Belarus	375	Guayaramerin	855
Loev	2347	La Belgica	923
Minsk	172	La Paz	2
Mogilev	222	Mineros	984
		Montero	92
Belgium	32	Oruro	52
Antwerp	3	Portachuelo	924
Bruges	50	Saavedra	924
Brussels	2	Santa Cruz	3
Charleroi	71	Sucre	64
Courtrai	56	Trinidad	46
Ghent	9	Warnes	923
Hasselt	11		
La Louviere	64	Bosnia Herzegovina	387
Leuven	16	Mostar	88
Libramont	61	Sarajevo	71
Liege	41	Zenica	72
Malines	15		

Botswana	267	Burkina Faso	226
Jwaneng	380	Burundi	257
Kanye	340	Bujumbura	2
Lobatse	330	Buruchi	50
Mahalapye	410	Gitega	40
Mochudi	377	Muyinga	30
Molepolole	320	Rutana	50
Orapa	270		
Palapye	420	Cambodia	855
Serowe	430	Phnom Penh	23
Brazil	55	Cameroon	327
Belem	91	Cape Verde Islands	238
Belo Horizonte	31		
Brasilia	61	Cayman Islands	345
Curitiba	41	Central African Rep.	236
Fortaleza	85		
Goiania	62	Chad	235
Niteroi	21	Moundou	69
Pelotas	532	N'djamena	51
Porto Alegre	51	Chile	56
Recife	81	Chiguayante	41
Rio de Janeiro	21	Concepcion	41
Salvador	71	La Serena	51
Santo Andre	11	Penco	41
Santos	132	Recreo	32
Sao Paulo	11	San Bernardo	2
Vitoria	27	Santiago	2
		Talcahuano	41
British Virgin Islands	284	Valparaiso	32
		Vina del Mar	32
Brunei	673	China	86
Bandar Seri Bagawan	2	Beijing	10
Kuala Belait	3	Fuzhou	591
Mumong	3	Guangzhou	20
Tutong	4	Shanghai	21
Bulgaria	359	Christmas Island	672
Kardjali	361	Christmas	4
Pazardjik	34		
Plovdiv	32	Cocos Islands	672
Sofia	2	Cocos	3
Varna	52		

continues

INTERNATIONAL COUNTRY AND CITY CALLING CODES *continued*

Colombia	57	Platres	5	
Armenia	67	Polis	6	
Barranquilla	58	Czech Republic	42	
Bogota	1	Brno	5	
Bucaramanga	76	Havirov	6994	
Cali	2	Ostrava	69	
Cartagena	5	Prague	2	
Cartago	656			
Cucuta	75	Denmark	45	
Giradot	834	Djibouti	253	
Ibague	82			
Manizales	68	Dominica	767	
Medellin	4	Dominican Republic	809	
Neiva	88			
Palmira	22	Ecuador	593	
Pereira	63	Ambato	3	
Santa Marta	54	Cayambe	2	
		Cuenca	7	
Comoros	269	Esmeraldas	6	
Congo	242	Guayaquil	4	
		Ibarra	6	
Cook Islands	682	Loja	7	
Costa Rica	506	Machachi	2	
		Machala	7	
Croatia	385	Manta	4	
Dubrovnik	20	Portoviejo	5	
Rijeka	51	Quevedo	5	
Split	21	Quito	2	
Zagreb	41	Salinas	4	
Cuba	53	Santo Domingo	2	
Havana City	7	Tulcan	6	
Santiago de				
Cuba Santia	226	Egypt	20	
		Alexandria	3	
Cyprus	53	Aswan	97	
Famagusta	392	Asyut	88	
Kyrenia	581	Benha	13	
Larnaca	4	Cairo	2	
Lefkonico	3	Damanhour	5	
Limassol	5	El Mahallah	43	
Nicosia	2	El Mansoura	50	
Paphos	6	Luxor	95	

Port Said	66	French Antilles	596
Shebin El Kom	48	French Guiana	594
Sohag	93		
Tanta	40	French Polynesia	689
El Salvador	503	Gabon	241
Equatorial Guinea	240	Gambia	220
Bata	8	Georgia	995
Malabo	9	Suhumi	881
Qaliub	2	Tblisi	883
Eritrea	291	Germany	49
Estonia	372	Bad Homburg	6172
Rakvere	32	Berlin	30
Tallinn	2	Bonn	228
Tartu	7	Bremen	421
Ethiopia	251	Cologne	221
Addis Ababa	1	Cottbus	355
Awassa	6	Dresden	351
Dire Dawa	5	Dusseldorf	211
Jimma	77	Erfurt	361
Nazareth	2	Essen	201
		Frankfurt am Main	69
Faroe Islands	298	Frankfurt an der Oder	335
Falkland Islands	500	Gera	365
		Halle	345
Fiji Islands	679	Hamburg	50
Finland	358	Heidelberg	6221
Helsinki	09	Karl-Stadt	9353
Joensuu	013	Koblenz	261
Jyvaskyla	014	Leipzig	341
Kuopio	017	Magdeburg	391
Lahti	03	Mannheim	621
Lappeenranta	05	Munich	89
Oulu	08	Neubrandenburg	395
Pori	02	Nurnberg	911
Vaasa	06	Potsdam	331
France	33	Rostock	381
Aix-en-Provence	4	Saal	38223
Bordeaux	5	Schwerin	385
Cherbourg	2	Stuttgart	711
Paris	1	Wiesbaden	611

continues

Ghana	233	Labe	51
Accra	21	Mamou	68
Koforidua	81	Guinea-Bissau	245
Kumasi	51		
Takoradi	31	Guyana	592
Gibraltar	350	Anna Regina	71
		Bartica	5
Greece	30	Beteryerwaging	20
Argos	751	Georgetown	2
Athens	1	Ituni	41
Corfu	661	Linden	4
Corinth	741	Mabaruma	77
Iraklion	81	Mahaica	28
Kavala	51	Mahaicony	21
Larissa	41	New Amsterdam	3
Patrai	61	New Hope	66
Rodos	241	Rosignol	30
Salonica	31	Timehri	61
Sparti	731	Vreed-En-Hoop	64
Tripolis	71	Whim	37
Volos	421	Haiti	509
Zagora	426		
Greenland	299	Honduras	504
Grenada	473	Hong Kong	852
Guadeloupe	590	Hungary	36
Basse-Terre	81	Abasar	37
Capesterre	86	Balatonaliga	84
Gosier	84	Budapest	1
Grand Bourg	97	Dorgicse	80
Jarry	26	Fertoboz	99
Pointe-a-Pitre	8	Gyor	96
		Kaposvar	82
Guam	671	Kazincbarcika	48
Guatamala	502	Komlo	72
Guatamala City	2	Miskolc	46
		Nagykanizsa	93
Guinea	224	Szekesfehervar	22
Conakry	4	Szolnok	56
Faranah	81	Varpalota	80
Kindia	61	Zalaegerszeg	92

Iceland	354	Surabaya	31
Akureyri	6	Tanjungkarang	721
Hafnarfjorður	1	Yogyakarta	274
Husavik	6	Iran	98
Keflavik Naval Base	2	Abadan	631
Sandgerði	2	Ahwaz	61
Selfoss	8	Arak	861
Siglufjorður	6	Esfahan	31
Stokkseyri	8	Ghazvin	281
Suðavik	4	Ghome	251
Vik	8	Hamadan	81
India	91	Karadj	261
Ahmedabad	79	Kerman	341
Amritsar	183	Mashad	51
Bangalore	80	Rasht	231
Baroda	265	Rezaiyeh	441
Bhopal	755	Shiraz	71
Bombay	22	Tabriz	41
Calcutta	33	Tehran	21
Chandigarh	172	Iraq	964
Hyderabad	40	Baghdad	1
Jaipur	141	Basra	40
Jullunder	181	Kerbela	32
Kanpur	512	Kirkuk	50
Madras	44	Mousil	60
New Delhi	11	Najaf	33
Poona	212	Ireland, Republic of	353
Surat	261	Arklow	402
Indonesia	62	Cork	21
Bandung	22	Dingle	66
Cirebon	231	Donegal	72-75
Denpasar	361	Drogheda	41
Jakarta	21	Dublin	1
Madiun	351	Dundalk	42
Malang	341	Ennis	65
Medan	61	Galway	91
Padang	751	Kildare	45
Palembang	711	Killarney	64
Sekurang	778	Limerick	61
Semarang	24	Sligo	71
Solo	271		

continues

Tipperary	62	Verona	45
Tralee	66	Vatican City	6
Tullamore	502	Ivory Coast	225
Waterford	51		
Wexford	53	Jamaica	876
Israel	972	Japan	81
Afula	6	Chiba	43
Ako	4	Fuchu	423
Ashkelon	7	Hiroshima	82
Bat Yam	3	Kawasaki	44
Beer Sheva	7	Kobe	78
Dimona	7	Kyoto	75
Hadera	6	Nagasaki	958
Haifa	4	Nagoya	52
Holon	3	Naha	98
Jerusalem	2	Osaka	6
Nazareth	6	Sapporo	11
Netania	9	Sasebo	956
Ramat Gan	3	Tachikawa	425
Rehovot	8	Tokyo	3
Tel Aviv	3	Yokohama	45
Tiberias	6	Yokosuka	468
Tsefat	6	Jordan	962
Italy	39	Amman	6
Bari	80	Aqaba	3
Bologna	51	Irbid	2
Brindisi	831	Jerash	4
Capri	81	Karak	3
Como	31	Maa'n	3
Florence	55	Mafruq	4
Genoa	10	Ramtha	2
Milan	2	Sueeleh	6
Naples	81	Sult	5
Padova	49	Zerqa	9
Palermo	91	Kazakhstan	7
Pisa	50	Alma-Ata	3272
Rome	6	Chimkent	325
Torino	11	Guryev	312
Trieste	40	Petropavlovsk	315
Venice	41		

Kenya	254	Laos	856
Anmer	2845	Vientiane	21
Bamburi	11	Latvia	371
Embakasi	2	Daugavpils	54
Gigiri	2	Jelgava	30
Kabete	2	Liepaja	34
Karen	2882	Riga	2
Kiambu	154	Ventspils	36
Kikuyu	154		
Kisumu	35	Lebanon	961
Langata	2	Beirut	1
Mombasa	11	Tripoli	6
Nairobi	2	Zahle	8
Nakuru	37	Lesotho	266
Shanzu	11		
Thika	151	Liberia	231
Uthiru	2	Libya	218
Kiribati	686	Angelat	282
		Benghazi	61
Korea, North	850	Benina	63
Pyong Yang	2	Derna	81
Korea, South	82	Misuratha	51
Chuncheon	361	Sabratha	24
Chung Ju	431	Sebha	71
Icheon	336	Taigura	26
Inchon	32	Tripoli	2133
Kwangju	62	Zawai	23
Masan	551	Zuara	25
Osan	339	Liechtenstein	41
Pohang	562	Kaunas	7
Pusan	51	Klaipeda	6
Seoul	2	Panevezys	54
Suwon	331	Siauliai	1
Taegu	53	Vilnius	2
Uijongbu	351		
Ulsan	522	Lithuania	370
Wonju	371	Luxembourg	352
Kuwait	965	Macau	853
Kyrgyzstan	7	Montserrat	664
Osh	33222		

continues

INTERNATIONAL COUNTRY AND CITY CALLING CODES *continued*

Morocco	212	Okahandja	6228
Agadir	88	Olympia	61
Beni-Mellal	348	Otjiwarongo	651
Berrechid	2	Pioneerspark	61
Casablanca	2	Swakopmund	641
El Jadida	334	Tsumeb	671
Fez	5	Windhoek	61
Kenitra	73	Nauru	674
Marrakech	4		
Meknes	55	Nepal	977
Mohammedia	332	Bhaktapur	1
Nador	660	Dhangadi	91
Oujda	668	Gorkha	64
Rabat	7	Kathmandu	1
Tangiers	99	Nepalgunj	81
Tetouan	996	Netherlands	31
Mozambique	258	Amsterdam	20
Beira	3	Arnhem	85
Chimolo	51	Eindhoven	40
Chokwe	21	Groningen	50
Maputo	1	Haarlem	23
Matola	4	The Hague	70
Nampula	6	Heemstede	23
Quelimane	4	Hillegersberg	10
Tete	52	Hoensbroek	45
Xai-Xai	22	Hoogkerk	50
		Hoogvliet	10
Myanmar	95	Loosduinen	70
Bassein	42	Nijmegen	80
Mandalay	2	Oud Zuilen	30
Monywa	71	Rotterdam	10
Prome	53	Utrecht	30
Rangoon	1		
		Netherlands Antilles	599
Namibia	264	Bonaire	7
Gobabis	681	Curacao	9
Grootfontein	6731	Saba	46
Industria	61	St. Eustatius	38
Keetmanshoop	631	St. Maarten	5
Luderitz	6331		
Mariental	661	New Caledonia	687

New Zealand	64	Norfolk Island	672
Auckland	9	Norway	47
Christchurch	3		
Dunedin	3	Oman	968
Hamilton	7	Pakistan	92
Hastings	6	Abbotabad	5921
Invercargill	3	Bahawaipur	621
Napier	6	Faisalabad	411
Nelson	3	Gujranwala	431
New Plymouth	6	Hyderabad	221
Palmerston, N	6	Islamabad	51
Rotorua	7	Karachi	21
Tauranga	7	Lahore	42
Timaru	3	Multan	61
Wanganui	6	Okara	442
Wellington	4	Peshawar	521
Whangarei	9	Quetta	81
Nicaragua	505	Sahiwal	441
Boaco	54	Sargodha	451
Chinandega	341	Sialkot	432
Diriamba	4222	Sukkur	71
Esteli	71	Palau	680
Granada	55		
Jinotepe	41	Panama	507
Leon	311	Papua New Guinea	675
Managua	2		
Masatepe	44	Paraguay	595
Masaya	52	Asuncion	21
Nandaime	4522	Ayolas	72
Rivas	46	Capiata	28
San Juan Del Sur	4682	Concepcion	31
San Marcos, Titipapa	53	Coronel Bogado	74
		Coronel Oviedo	521
Niger	227	Encarnacion	71
Nigeria	234	Hernandarias	63
Badagry	1	Ita	24
Kaduna	62	Pedro J. Caballero	36
Lagos	1	Pilar	86
Port Hartcourt	84	San Antonio	27
		San Ignacio	82
Niue Island	683		

continues

Peru	51	Portugal	351
Arequipa	54	Almada	1
Ayacucho	6491	Angra Do Heroismo	95
Callao	14	Barreiro	1
Chiclayo	74	Braga	53
Chimbote	44	Caldas Da Rainha	62
Cuzco	84	Coimbra	39
Huancavelica	6495	Estoril	1
Huancayo	64	Evora	66
Ica	34	Faro	89
Iquitos	94	Lajes Air Force Base	95
Lima	14	Lisbon	1
Piura	74	Madalena	92
Tacna	54	Madeira Islands	91
Trujillo	44	Motijo	1
		Ponta Delgada	96
Philippines	63	Porto	2
Angeles	455	Santa Cruz	92
Bacolad	34	Setubal	65
Baguio City	74	Velas	95
Cebu City	32	Vila Do Porto	96
Dagupan	75		
Davao	82	Puerto Rico	787
Iloilo City	33	Qatar	974
Lucena	42		
Manila	2	Reunion Island	262
Poland	48	Romania	40
Bialystok	85	Arad	57
Bydgoszcz	52	Bacau	34
Crakow	12	Brasov	68
Gdansk	58	Bucharest	0
Katowice	3	Cluj-Napoca	64
Lodz	42	Constanta	41
Lublin	81	Craiova	51
Olsztyn	89	Galati	36
Poznan	61	Iasi	32
Radom	48	Oradea	59
Sopot	58	Pitesti	48
Torun	56	Ploiesti	44
Warsaw	22	Satu-Mare	61
		Sibiu	69

Timisoara	56	Sierra Leone	232	
Tirgu Mures	65	Freetown	22	
Russia	7	Singapore	65	
Magadan	413	Slovak Republic	42	
Moscow	095	Bratislava	7	
St. Petersburg	812.	Presov	91	
Rwanda	250	Slovenia	386	
St. Helena	290	Ljubljana	61	
St. Kitts/Nevis	869	Maribor	62	
St. Lucia	758	Solomon Islands	677	
St. Pierre and Miquelon	508	South Africa	27	
St. Vincent and		Bloemfontein	51	
Grenadines	784	Cape Town	21	
		De Aar	571	
San Marino	378	Durban	31	
Sao Tome	239	East London	431	
Saudi Arabia	966	Gordons Bay	24	
Abha	7	Johannesburg	11	
Abqaiq	3	La Lucia	31	
Al Khobar	3	Pretoria	12	
Al Markazi	2	Sasolburg	16	
Al Ulaya	1	Somerset West	24	
Damman	3	Uitenhage	41	
Dhahran	3	Welkom	57	
Hofuf	3	Spain	34	
Jeddah	2	Barcelona	3	
Khamis Mushait	7	Bilbao	4	
Mecca	2	Cadiz	56	
Medina	4	Ceuta	56	
Najran	7	Granada	58	
Qatif	3	Igualada	3	
Riyadh	1	Las Palmas de		
Taif	2	Gran Canaria	28	
Yenbu	4	Leon	87	
Senegal	221	Madrid	1	
		Malaga	5	
Seychelles	248	Melilla	52	
		Palma de Mallorca	71	
		Pamplona	48	

continues

INTERNATIONAL COUNTRY AND CITY CALLING CODES *continued*

Santa Cruz de Tenerife	22	Switzerland	41
Sandander	42	Baden	56
Seville	5	Basel	61
Torremolinos	52	Berne	31
Valencia	6	Davos	81
		Fribourg	37
Sri Lanka	94	Geneva	22
Ambalangoda	97	Interlaken	36
Colombo Central	1	Lausanne	21
Galle	9	Lucerne	41
Havelock Town	1	Lugano	91
Kandy	8	Montreux	21
Katugastota	8	Neuchatel	38
Kotte	1	St. Gallen	71
Maradana	1	St. Mortiz	82
Matara	41	Winterthur	52
Negombo	31	Zurich	1
Panadura	34		
Trincomalee	26	Syria	963
		Aleppo	21
Suriname	597	Banias	43
		Damascus	11
Swaziland	268	Deir Ezzor	51
Villaverde de		Gableh	491
Gualalimar	67	Halab	21
		Hama	33
Sweden	46	Hasake	52
Alingsas	322	Homs	31
Boras	33	Idleb	23
Boteborg	31	Jebleh	41
Eskilstuna	16	Jisr Shogoor	441
Gamleby	493	Kamishly	53
Helsingborg	42	Kerdaha	492
Karlstad	54	Kuneitra	141
Linkoping	13	Lattakia	412
Lund	46	Nebek	12
Malmo	40	Rakka	22
Norrkoping	11	Safita	32
Stockholm	8	Sweida	16
Sundsvall	60	Tartous	43
Trelleborg	410	Yabroud	192
Uppsala	18	Zabadani	131
Vasteras	21		

Taiwan	886	Togo	228
Changhua	4	Tonga Islands	676
Chunan	37		
Chunghsing-Hsintsun	49	Trinidad and Tobago	868
Chungli	3	Tunisia	216
Fengyuan	4	Agareb	4
Hsiaying	6	Beja	8
Hualien	38	Bizerte	2
Kaohsiung	7	Carthage	1
Keelung	2	Chebba	4
Lotung	39	Gabes	5
Pingtung	8	Gafsa	6
Taichung	4	Haffouz	7
Tainan	6	Hamman-Sousse	3
Taipei	2	Kairouan	7
Taitung	89	Kef	8
Taoyuan	3	Khenis	3
Tajikistan	7	Medenine	5
Dushanbe	3772	Tabarka	8
		Tozeur	6
Tanzania	255	Tunis	1
Dar Es Salaam	51		
Dodoma	61	Turkey	90
Mwanza	68	Adana	322
Tanga	53	Ankara	312
		Antalya	242
Thailand	66	Bursa	224
Bangkok	2	Eskisehir	222
Burirum	44	Gaziantep	851
Chanthaburi	39	Istanbul Asya	216
Chiang Mai	53	Istanbul Avrupa	212
Chiang Rai	54	Izmir	232
Kamphaengphet	55	Izmit	262
Lampang	54	Kayseri	352
Nakhon Sawan	56	Konya	332
Nong Khai	42	Malatya	422
Pattani	73	Samsun	362
Pattaya	38		
Ratchaburi	32	Turkmenistan	7
Saraburi	36	Ashkhabad	3632
Tak	55	Chardzhou	378
Ubon Ratchathani	45		

continues

INTERNATIONAL COUNTRY AND CITY CALLING CODES *continued*

Turks and Caicos		London	181
Islands	649	Manchester	161
		Nottingham	115
Tuvalu	688	Prestwick	1292
		Sheffield	114
Uganda	256	Southampton	1703
Entebbe	42		
Jinja	43	Uruguay	598
Kampala	41	Canelones	32
Kyambogo	41	Florida	352
		Las Piedras	324
Ukraine	380	Maldonado	42
Kharkov	572	Mercedes	532
Kiev	44	Minas	442
L'viv	322	Montevideo	2
		Paysandu	722
United Arab Emirates	971	Punta Del Este	42
Abu Dhabi	2	San Jose	342
Ajman	6	San Jose De Carrasco	38
Al Ain	3		
Aweer	58	U.S. Virgin Islands	340
Dhayd	6		
Dibba	9	Uzbekistan	7
Dubai	4	Karshi	375
Falaj-al-Moalla	6	Samarkand	3662
Fujairah	9	Tashkent	3712
Khawanij	487		
Ras-al-Khaimah	7	Vanuatu	678
Sharjah	6		
Tarif	88	Vatican City	6 & 39
Umm-al-Qaiwain	6	Venezuela	58
		Barcelona	81
United Kingdom	44	Barquisimeto	51
Belfast	1232	Cabimas	64
Birmingham	121	Caracas	2
Bournemouth	1202	Ciudad Bolivar	85
Cardiff	1222	Coro	68
Durham	191	Cumana	93
Edinburgh	131	Los Teques	32
Glasgow	141	Maiquetia	31
Gloucester	1452	Maracaibo	61
Ipswich	1473	Maracay	43
Liverpool	151	Maturin	91
London	171	Merida	74

Puerto Cabello	42	Taiz	4
San Cristobal	76	Yarim	4
Valencia	41	Zabid	3
Vietnam	84	Zaire	243
Hanoi	4	Kinshasa	12
Ho Chi Minh City	8	Lubumbashi	2
Virgin Islands	284	Zambia	260
Wallis and Futuna		Chingola	2
Islands	681	Kitwe	2
		Luanshya	2
Western Samoa	685	Lusaka	1
Yemen	967	Ndola	2
Aden	2	Zimbabwe	263
Almahrah	5	Bulawayo	9
Amran	7	Harare	4
Sana'a	1	Mutare	20

Setting up anything but a basic conference call requires more than a little preplanning. A teleconference deserves at least the same degree of thoughtful preparation as the face-to-face meeting it is intended to replace.

Cellular Guidelines

The etiquette of cellular phone use fundamentally relies on common sense. For instance, you should not pull out your cellular phone in a quiet restaurant and begin yakking in a loud voice. You also shouldn't answer your cellular phone in the middle of a conversation. Check the caller number. If it is a call you must take, excuse yourself and step aside so you don't interrupt the conversation around you. Find a private place where you won't disturb others and then take the call. At the least, if you are with others, excuse yourself for a moment to take the call. Tell the caller that you are busy and that you will call him or her back as soon as you are free.

What if your boss calls you on his or her cellular phone? That call is important. If you get interrupted, don't leave the vicinity of your phone or pick up the phone and make a call yourself. It's likely that your boss will call back.

Because cellular rates are still higher than regular telephone rates, your boss might prefer to have you call him or her on the office phone instead of calling you. Discuss this with your boss and decide how you will handle cellular calls, either incoming or outgoing.

The cell phone system still suffers from frequent service interruptions, so it's wise to avoid putting incoming cell phone callers on hold. Likewise, when transferring a call, try to be quick and prepare the party receiving the transfer by telling them that their caller is on a cell phone.

Always keep in mind that the confidentiality of a cell phone conversation is easily compromised—by malicious intent or just by pranksters. Watch what you say. Discourage any indiscreet caller from speaking too freely. Wait until a secure line can be used to spell out important confidential details or reveal account numbers, credit card information, and the like.

MEMOS

A memo, short for memorandum, is basically written correspondence between company employees that is less formal than a traditional letter. A memo might be short or long, single- or multipage. An office assistant might be asked to compose memos as well as type them for executives.

Ideally, memos should be no more than a single page or two. Anything longer really needs more formatting than a typical memo—more like a report. Some managers believe that a memo is needed to record every decision they make, or that everyone within their organization—from janitor to CEO— needs to receive a memo on an issue, regardless of whether it is relevant to their work. Sending unnecessary memos only adds to the junk mail in your office. Limit copies of memos to those with a need to know. Send memos only when the recipient must know the information in the memo to do his or her job, when he or she needs to respond to the work you have done, or when he or she needs to appreciate the work you are doing.

Depending on distribution lists and the amount of contents, many memos today can be sent as e-mail.

Office memos are used for various purposes:

■ To supplement face-to-face discussions on complex issues

■ To avoid making unnecessary telephone calls for business that might not be urgent

■ To create a written record

Memos not only avoid situations that might be misunderstood, but they also protect people by having a written record. Usually, office memos are brief and direct. However, some exceptions exist, depending upon the nature, purpose, and scope of the subject discussed and the writer's purpose and intent. For instance, memos should not be used to inform employees of anything related to their position, whether it is a promotion or a layoff. These subjects should be discussed in person, although you might want to record the particulars in a memo after the fact.

TIP: The plural form of memorandum may be either *memorandums* (add an "s") or *memoranda* (add an "a" for the Latin form). When composing or writing, be consistent and use only one form for the plural.

Types of Memos

Memos come to our desks two ways: through the mail room and through our computer network as e-mail:

- *E-mail*. As companies become more global, distribution of paper memos is decreasing. E-mail offers a much faster way to send a message to individuals who are not located at one site, but rather at various corporate locations around the world.

- *Paper memos*. Although e-mail memos can be printed and stored in a file drawer, some managers still feel more comfortable issuing memos on paper. The speed with which these memos on paper are read depends on corporate culture. As organizations become more electronic, it is less likely that memos on paper will get as speedy attention as e-mail.

Different organizations have different formats for their memos. See examples of each type on pages 40 and 42. However, all the principles of writing and business correspondence apply to memos, just as they do to letters.

One principle includes the issue of confidentiality. As assistant, you might be privy to confidential correspondence—including memos. It is your professional responsibility to keep to yourself what you see in these memos.

Parts of a Memo

All memos, whether in print or e-mail, should be composed of a few essential parts. Formats might differ, but the parts still include the name of the sender, the name of the recipient(s), the date, the subject, the body, and sometimes end references (for example, reference initials, distribution of copies, and so on).

To/From

The To/From section can be reversed. Some feel that using "To" first is more courteous to the reader. However, follow the company preferences. Omit personal titles (Mr., Ms.), but use professional titles (Prof., Dr., and so on).

In e-mail memos, the "To" sometimes is omitted if it's clear who the memo is reaching by the other addresses. If not, it's appropriate to note the person to whom the memo is being distributed, as in, "All employees," or "All employees at the main location," or "All members of Joe Stack's product development team."

INTEROFFICE COMMUNICATION

TO: Horace Denize, Executive Director

FROM: Julia Brown, Chairperson, Board of Directors

DATE: October 15, 200_

SUBJECT: Organizational Meeting

A Board of Directors meeting has been scheduled for Wednesday, October 30, 1999, in Conference Room A, East Building.

The agenda will include:

- Approval of Minutes
- Report for the Chairperson
- Discussion of Goals
- New Business

Since this is the first meeting, your attendance is necessary. Please bring business report No. 23-A, located in the central database file.

JB/TS 8.8a

Distribution:

Jerome L. Abrams
Bennette Von Brun
Josephine D'Allo
Maye Santiago
Norman Zapper

Sample Typed Memo

In formal use, a name and a title exist in both the "To" and "From" sections, as in the following:

TO: Horace Denize, Executive Director

FROM: Julia Brown, Chairperson, Board of Directors

No salutation, complimentary close, or signature exists. However, the person sending the memorandum might initial it between the name and title, or at the end of the "From" line.

Date

The date always should be included in e-mail memos because the date the memo was prepared or sent could differ from the date you read it or the date your e-mail system tags it.

Follow a standard format; do not use shortcuts. Type the date in one of the two following ways:

September 19, 1999

9/29/99

Subject

The "Subject" line provides a short description of what the memorandum is about. It focuses attention and serves as a subject category for filing and retrieval. This line should be brief and to the point: Delete unnecessary words.

Body

This section contains the main idea and purpose of the memo. If enumerations are present, use an acceptable format, such as (1), (2); or (a), (b).

You might use some special keyboarding symbols before the enumeration to capture the reader's attention. These include dashes (—) and bullets (■).

- Call Mr. Gomez and make an appointment.

- Cancel the Simmons' contract (No. 23-A).

- Print file #23.A-9 (4.1).

This technique calls immediate attention to enumerations and enhances the appearance. Numbering and/or lettering the items or points also makes it easier for the reader to follow the sequential development of ideas and comments.

Reference Information

Several types of reference information might be located at the end of a memo. These include reference initials, copy notations, enclosures, filing code, and word processing code. Reference initials may be typed in lowercase or uppercase.

At times, the composer or originator of a document might be someone other than the executive or principal. If this is the case, use the following:

MC:CH:MI (Executive, composer or originator, transcriber)

Word/Information Processing Codes
Many documents are electronically stored and processed. For ease of retrieval in these cases, codes are necessary:

MJ/e 8.8

MJ/CH 8.8a

A colon (:) may be substituted for the slash (/). The code 8.8 represents month, day, disk number, or another meaning, such as file No. 8.8. Because such codes are not necessarily standardized, the office should create a system.

```
Author:  Samuel Walt
Date:    1/27/00  1:27 AM
Priority: Normal
TO: Rose Wilt/CPG; Len Texman/CPG
CC: Michael James/DC; John Wilson/DC
BCC: Harrison DeWitt/VP Finance
Subject: Meeting/Project X
------------------- Message Contents --------------------

The next meeting of the Project X team will be held in Room
79A at 9:00 a.m. Tuesday, January 19. Let me know if you
can make presentations on your assignments at that time.
```

Sample E-mail Memo

Copies and Distribution
This final section of the memo alphabetically lists the names of those who were sent copies. The list may be ordered by seniority or by rank: Follow the company policy and check with your superior. The omission of a name might be an oversight, or it might be deliberate.

With e-mail, copies may be sent through a network to various terminals. If this procedure is used, the usual distribution lists should be keyed into a database. The receipt of a transmission easily can be acknowledged by return transmission; a reply also can be keyed. If electronic messages are stored, keep an index. These data then can serve as boilerplates and standard paragraphs that can be inserted into other future memorandums without rekeying.

Formatting a Memo
Paper memos often are typed on plain paper or on printed forms that contain standard parts. If plain paper is used for one or more pages, use quality paper. If the memorandum is short, use a half-sheet. If a preprinted form is used, align the typing evenly with the printed headings.

TIPS FOR WRITING EFFECTIVE MEMOS

- If your company has guidelines for memos, follow that standard format.

- Set a consistent, professional, and objective tone in your memos.

- Be clear about the information you're conveying.

- Be direct in your requests.

- Make sure that your expectations of the recipients are reasonable and attainable.

- Focus on one single idea or objective; do not digress.

- Keep your memos brief and free of unnecessary details.

- Although more informal than business letters, memos still should follow the principles of good writing.

- Proofread carefully, checking all facts and figures before sending.

- Remember, memos are often the only written record of an event or conversation.

The background for e-mail memos can vary, depending on templates available through a company's communication network. Beyond this, the formatting of memos, whether on paper or e-mail, is similar.

Margins on paper are usually 1 inch from all sides—left, right, top, and bottom. If the memo is electronic, the template will have set margins.

For printed forms, the left margin should begin evenly with the "To/From" element printed on the form.

Whether using typed or preprinted forms, begin two or three spaces from the colon. Triple-space between the subject line and the beginning of the text. Single-space the content of each paragraph, but double-space between paragraphs.

MINUTES OF A MEETING

If you work as an assistant to an executive or for an organization with either a board of directors or another group that meets formally, you might be called upon to produce minutes of a meeting. *Minutes* is a term used to describe an official record of the proceedings of a meeting. Keeping minutes of meetings is always advisable. Although the minutes might not be disseminated, they should be filed in case they are needed at a later date.

Producing minutes usually involves "taking" them and then typing them. To take minutes, you should be present at the meeting. If you will type them up later, take detailed notes or use shorthand. If the meeting is conducted by phone or involves legalities, you often will take a formal transcription. However, it is helpful to take notes to maintain the structure of the meeting and isolate key points and issues. The minutes you type up are not meant to serve as a word-for-word account of the meeting; rather they act as a written record of the items discussed, issues raised, and business conducted.

Types of Meetings

Basically two types of meetings exist: formal and informal. A formal meeting is a preplanned, structured event, such as an annual conference or convention. Usually a prepared agenda is drawn up. An informal meeting may be short and may be announced only a short time before it is held; it usually takes place on company premises. To inform staff members of a quickly scheduled meeting, the assistant might use electronic calendaring, e-mail, or, if on very short notice, the telephone. In such a case, always confirm by sending a follow-up e-mail.

A formal meeting requires a slight knowledge of formal meeting flow, such as the formal reading or acceptance of the minutes from the previous meeting; a formal recorder or recording secretary, the opening of old business and new business; and votes, including motions and seconds. It's not required that you know *Robert's Rules of Order* inside and out, but it might be helpful to get an idea—and might make it easier to keep up!

Preparing the Minutes

The most important phase of preparing minutes involves the accurate recording and reporting of the actions taken and what was said. At times, it is difficult to report what is done. For informal meetings, the minutes are compact and simple; for formal meetings, the minutes are complex. If you find that grouping the minutes around a central theme is clearer, do so. On the other hand, the executive might prefer chronological order.

Corporate minutes (official minutes of a formal nature) must be prepared in the order of occurrence, showing details and the exact wording of motions, resolutions, and so forth. By law, corporations are required to keep minutes of stockholders and directors meetings. These minutes are legal records and should be protected from tampering.

When preparing corporate minutes, use watermarked paper and place the finalized minutes in binders. Any corrections resulting from a subsequent meeting should be written. Incorrect portions should be ruled out in ink and initialed in the margin. The official assistant of the corporate officer takes responsibility for the completeness and accuracy of corporate minutes, but the office professional is the one who will prepare and type them.

Format of Minutes

Follow these suggestions in preparing minutes:

1. Use plain white paper. For official corporate minutes, don't use letterhead, but do use watermarked second sheets.

2. Center and capitalize the title.

Meeting of the Executive Committee

April 2, 200_

ATTENDANCE

The weekly meeting of the executive committee was held in the office of Cortez Diaz, first Vice-President of Operations, at 10:00 a.m. on April 2, 2001. Mr. Diaz presided. Present were James Madison, Frederick McAllison, Yolanda Smith, Anne Marie Johnson, and Lewis Smith. Paricia Mendea was absent.

ITEMS COVERED

1. Contract No. 23-a.1 was approved in the amount of $125,000,000.

2. Yolanda Smith gave an update report on Contract No. 24. Further information is to be presented at the May 21 meeting.

3. Ann Marie Johnson reviewed the service budget for the first quarter. Recommendations were made. A feasibility study is to be conducted for implementation of an improved MIS.

4. Lewis Smith presented the proposed budget for the Xavius Project, a government grant. A draft copy of his recommendations will be distributed before the May 21 meeting. This item will be discussed and voted upon at the May 21 meeting.

ADJOURNMENT

The meeting was adjourned at 12:00 p.m.

James Madison
———————————————
James Madison, Recorder

Sample Minutes of a Weekly Committee Meeting

3. Double-space the text to allow for official corrections, if necessary. Allow a 1½-inch left margin, a 1-inch right margin, and a generous top margin. The left margin should allow for hole-punching or binding. Be consistent.

4. Indent five to ten spaces.

5. List the name of the presiding officer and the recorder. The recorder should sign the minutes.

6. Follow the agenda's subject headings as closely as possible.

7. List absences and indicate quorums.

8. Follow the company's policy on capitalization of words such as "committee," "department," and so on.

9. Paginate at the bottom consecutively.

10. If a formal resolution, motion, or vote is passed, record it word for word.

11. Record the time of adjournment.

12. Use businesslike language. Avoid descriptive adjectives such as "outstanding."

13. List and summarize the gist of what was said, making a new bullet or paragraph for each point.

14. Transcribe minutes while they are still fresh in your mind.

15. Prepare a rough draft for approval before finalizing. To avoid confusion, make sure you name the electronic file in an organized way.

16. File a hard copy, just in case.

CORRESPONDENCE

We tend to think of correspondence in terms of letters. Not so—today, correspondence also includes electronic communications, including e-mail and faxed documents. The latter can be a problem if a hard copy is needed. For instance, most courts still do not accept faxed copies of contracts.

LETTERS

The task of typing letters has evolved radically with the proliferation of computers in the workplace. Still, the form that letters take and even some of the keyboarding terms associated with the day of the typewritten letter still hold sway. Why? Because the fundamental purpose of a business letter remains unchanged.

BASIC PRINCIPLES OF WRITING LETTERS

The biggest stumbling block to clear writing isn't a matter of technique or writing ability; it's a matter of mental attitude. The reason more people don't write better is because they are too self-centered.

In good writing, one person—and one person alone—is important: the reader. Yet, what happens when the average businessperson sits down to write a letter or report? Somewhere inside, an insidious thought occurs: "What will the reader think of me?"

The more that thought interferes with concentrating on the reader, the poorer the writing will be. In writing of any kind, the important thing is to plant an idea in the reader's mind, or to stimulate feelings or emotions.

Write to express, not to impress. Write in the same language you would use if you were carrying on a conversation across your desk. Keep it simple. Write from a "you" perspective. ("Your letter of January 15 was very much appreciated, Ms. Jones," not "I appreciated your letter.") If possible, keep the tone pleasant and friendly. Get politely to the point, wrap it up, and wish your correspondent well.

In a very real sense, letters that leave a business office are ambassadors of goodwill. The impression that an individual letter creates could mean the difference between the gain or loss of a prospective client or an influential friend for your company. This impression depends as much on the appearance of the letter as on its tone or contents.

Letter Styles

It has often been said that an ideal letter should resemble a picture in an appropriate frame. That still holds true today, especially given the use of stylish letterhead paper that includes more than the firm's logo and address. Some letterhead includes the names of the company officers in the left margin; others list product lines in the right margin. Some have a watermark mid-center.

Some organizations have different letterhead for different divisions of the organization. Access to these variations might come through the company network, or you might be able to requisition the paper stock you need from the company supply closet. Letters must be arranged and then typed or keyboarded according to the style of the letterhead as well as the letter style that the company has chosen. Most organizations have a procedural manual for their employees, illustrating the letter style and explaining how they want the various parts of the business letter to appear.

Given office technology, letters should not contain misspellings or other errors—check every piece of correspondence. Some software programs

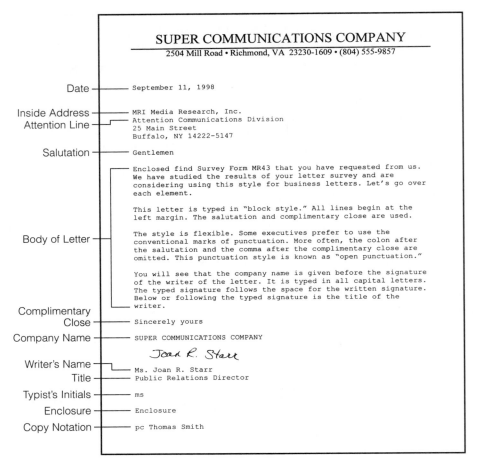

Letter 1: Block Style with Open Punctuation

require spellchecking; others use a color to raise a question about a spelling or other error.

After you have finished typing your letter, use the print preview function to view it before printing. This also will help you center your letter on the paper when it is printed. Does the finished product look professional?

Regardless of the technology you're using, you still should follow one of the accepted modern letter styles. Each is addressed in the following sections.

Block Style (Letter 1)
The block style letter, also called a full block style letter, aligns all lines at the left margin. Paragraphs are not indented.

Modified Block Style (Letters 2 and 3)
The modified block style letter places the dateline, the complimentary close, and the sender's name and title in the center of the page. Paragraphs may be

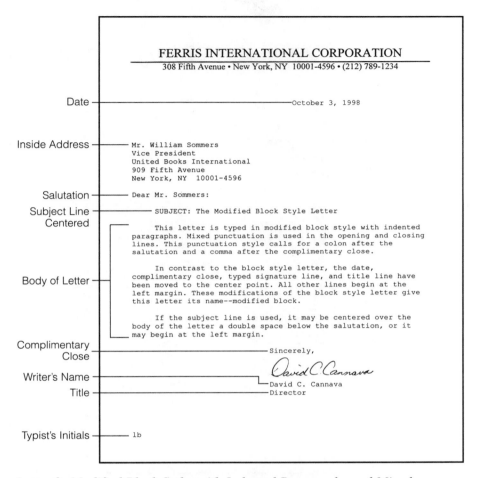

FERRIS INTERNATIONAL CORPORATION
308 Fifth Avenue • New York, NY 10001-4596 • (212) 789-1234

Date ———————————————————————————— October 3, 1998

Inside Address ——————— Mr. William Sommers
Vice President
United Books International
909 Fifth Avenue
New York, NY 10001-4596

Salutation ——————— Dear Mr. Sommers:

Subject Line
Centered ——————— SUBJECT: The Modified Block Style Letter

This letter is typed in modified block style with indented
paragraphs. Mixed punctuation is used in the opening and closing
lines. This punctuation style calls for a colon after the
salutation and a comma after the complimentary close.

In contrast to the block style letter, the date,
complimentary close, typed signature line, and title line have
been moved to the center point. All other lines begin at the
left margin. These modifications of the block style letter give
this letter its name--modified block.

Body of Letter

If the subject line is used, it may be centered over the
body of the letter a double space below the salutation, or it
may begin at the left margin.

Complimentary
Close ——————————————— Sincerely,

David C Cannava

Writer's Name ———————— David C. Cannava
Title ———————————————— Director

Typist's Initials ——————— lb

Letter 2: Modified Block Style, with Indented Paragraphs and Mixed Punctuation

indented, or they may begin at the left margin. On computers, the trend is not to indent unless a very short letter is double-spaced.

Simplified Letter Style (Letter 4)

The simplified letter style, traditionally known as the AMS (Administrative Management Society) letter, is the most modern letter style. This style eliminates the salutation and the complimentary close. A subject line typed on the third line below the inside address in all capital letters replaces the salutation. All lines begin at the left margin. The sender's name and title are typed in all capital letters three or four lines below the body of the letter. This style of letter eliminates salutation problems (whether to use Ms., Gentlemen, or Ladies and Gentlemen).

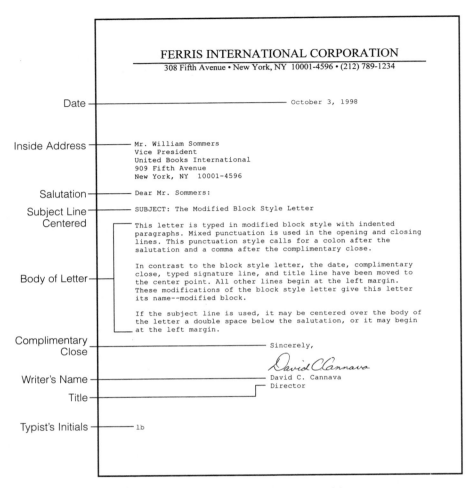

Letter 3: Modified Block Style, with Blocked Paragraphs and Mixed Punctuation

Business Letter Punctuation

Two punctuation styles exist for business letters. In *mixed punctuation style,* a colon is placed after the salutation and a comma is placed after the complimentary close. In *open punctuation style,* no punctuation is used after the salutation or the complimentary close.

Basic Parts of a Business Letter

Although companies use different looks in their letters, the letters themselves have the following elements in common:

Letter 4: Simplified Style

Letterhead

Most business letters still go on preprinted letterhead. The format of the letterhead differs with each firm, but the contents of the letterhead remain fairly standard: the company name, the street address, the name of the city and state, and the ZIP code. Other elements that might appear in the letterhead are the telephone number (with area code) of the firm, and the names and titles of the corporate officers.

Dateline

The dateline begins on about the third line below the company letterhead, or on line 14 (counting down from the top of the page), whichever is more eye-appealing for letter placement. The dateline consists of the month, the day, and the year. The month is always spelled in full, the date and the year are given as numerals, and the date is followed by a comma.

Preferred style	October 3, 2001
Military style	3 October 2001
Unacceptable styles	October 3rd, 2001
	Oct. 3, 2001

A letter from a foreign country more likely will follow the military style, with the day of the month first, followed by the month, and finally the year.

Inside Address

A complete inside address is very important to ensure not only that the letter is directed to the correct person, but also that accurate files can be established. The inside address may be typed anywhere from three to twelve lines below the date line, depending on the length of the letter; it aligns with the left margin for all letter styles.

The inside address should include the following elements: person's name, person's title, name of company or organization, street address, city name, state name, and ZIP code. If the letter addresses a company or organization, or a person at a company or organization, the inside address should be typed exactly as it appears in the addressee's letterhead.

If you are unable to determine a specific person's name, then you may use an *attention line* with a business title. In this way, the letter will be directed to the proper person. The attention line is the second line of the inside address.

If the address includes an apartment number or room number, type these elements on the same line as the street. State names should be abbreviated in the address according to the two-letter state abbreviations. The nine-digit ZIP code is typed one or two spaces after the state abbreviation.

Mr. John Alexander, President
ABZ Company
1234 East Sixth Street, Room 1410
Buffalo, NY 14222-5147

The ABZ Company
Attention Sales Manager
1234 East Sixth Street
Buffalo, NY 14222-5147

Mr. John Alexander
National Sales Manager
ABZ Company
P.O. Box 1614
Buffalo, NY 14222-5147

Mr. John Alexander
666 Fifth Avenue, Apt. 4D
Buffalo, NY 14222-5147

Follow these general guidelines when typing the inside address:

- Type names as they appear in the letterhead; always check the spelling of proper names by referring to your files.

- The number (#) symbol is not necessary when typing the house number, room number, or post office box number. House numbers (with the exception of "one") are typed in figures.

    One East Sixth Street

    2 East Sixth Street

- When street names are numbers, write out names below ten, and use figures for names above ten.

- When figures are used in street addresses, it is not necessary to use endings such as *st, d, nd,* or *rd* after the numbered street name.

    1234 East 12 Street

- Type the city name, state name, and ZIP code on the same line.

- Type the city name in full, followed by a comma and then the two-letter state abbreviation.

- Type the ZIP code one or two spaces after the two-letter state abbreviation. No punctuation follows the state abbreviation.

Salutation

The salutation is typed two lines below the last line of the inside address. The salutation is omitted in the simplified letter. In all other letter styles, the salutation is typed, starting at the left margin and followed by a colon if mixed punctuation is used.

Capitalization of salutations. Capitalize the first word, the title, and any noun in the salutation:

Dear Mr. Jones

My dear Professor Clark

Dear Ms. Morgan

Your Excellency

Abbreviations in salutations. Abbreviate Mr., Ms., Messrs., and Dr.. Write out other titles, such as Captain, Professor, Father, Reverend, and so on.

Forms of salutations. For the forms of salutations to use in addressing church or government officials, judges, doctors, and so on, see the Grammar and Punctuation Guide at the back of this book.

When an organization is comprised of men and women, the salutation used is still "Gentlemen" if the correspondence is addressed to a company.

Although some groups frown upon this style, it is still used simply because a more acceptable salutation has not yet evolved. Alternative salutations that are becoming more popular include "Ladies and Gentlemen," or the appropriate title or function: Dear Treasurer, Dear Review Committee, and so on.

Guidelines for Salutations

Addressee	*Salutation*
Firm's name	Gentlemen
Firm's name, with an attention line	Gentlemen
Married woman, a widow, or a divorced woman who uses the title Mrs.	Dear Mrs. Jones
Unmarried woman	Dear Ms. Jones
Unknown whether a woman is married or single	Dear Ms. Jones
Group comprised of men and women	Ladies and Gentlemen
Married couple	Dear Mr. and Mrs. Jones
Man and a woman	Dear Mr. Jones and Ms. Black
	Dear Sir and Madam

Body of the Letter

The part of the letter containing the message is known as the *body*. The body is typed a double space below the salutation, or a double space below the subject line. The paragraphs should be blocked or indented, depending upon the letter style used. Paragraphs are single-spaced. Occasionally, short letters are typed in double space.

Whether the lines are single-spaced or double-spaced, use only double spacing between paragraphs.

Tabulated matter in body of the letter. Tabulated matter in the body of a letter is indented at least five spaces from both the left and right margins.

Enumerated paragraphs. Enumerated paragraphs are also indented five spaces from both the right and left margins. These paragraphs begin with a number followed by a period. Two spaces after the period, begin typing the paragraph. Single-space each enumerated paragraph, but double-space between the enumerated paragraphs. (If each enumerated paragraph contains only one line, you may single-space between paragraphs.)

1.

2.

Complimentary Closing

The complimentary closing is typed two lines below the last line of the body of the letter.

Capitalize only the first word in the complimentary closing. Follow the complimentary closing with a comma, unless open punctuation is used; in that case, no punctuation is needed.

Placement of complimentary closing. The placement of the complimentary closing depends upon which letter style is used (see Letters 1–3 and 5).

Degrees of formality. As with the salutation, degrees of formality also are recognized in complimentary closings.

- *Formal tone:* Yours truly, Yours very truly, Very truly yours

- *More formal tone:* Respectfully yours, Yours respectfully, Very respectfully yours, Yours very respectfully

- *Less formal and more personal tone:* Sincerely, Cordially, Sincerely yours, Cordially yours, Yours sincerely

Signature and Title

When a company name appears as part of the signature, it is typed in all capitals a double space below the complimentary closing. The typewritten signature then is typed on the fourth line below the company name or the complimentary closing. Place the penned signature in the intervening space. If a letter is unusually short, place the typed signature on the sixth or eighth line below the company name or the complimentary closing. If the signer's handwriting is unusually large, the signature may be typed from five to eight lines below the company name or complimentary closing.

The writer's title may appear on the same line with the typed signature, or on the line below the typed signature, whichever gives a better balance to the page.

Yours very truly,

Clarence Brown

Clarence Brown, Manager

Yours very truly,

Clarence Brown

Clarence Brown
Manager

In the simplified letter style, beginning at the left margin, type the writer's name and title on the fifth line below the body of the letter in all capital letters, or type the name on the fifth line and the title on the sixth line (see Letter 4).

Joseph H. Feng

JOSEPH H. FENG
ASSISTANT MANAGER

Division or department. Frequently, a division or department is used in the closing lines of a letter; it is typed below the typed signature and title, as follows:

Very truly yours,

R. M. Brown, Supervisor
Plastics Division

More than one signature. When a letter requires two signatures, use either of the following forms:

Sincerely yours,

Ms. Jane R. Jones
District Manager

Milton Trout
General Manager

Sincerely yours,

Ms. Jane R. Jones
District Manager

Milton Trout
General Manager

Signature for the employer. If, as an assistant, you are required to sign a letter for your employer, you may use either one of the following forms:

Sincerely yours,

Secretary to Ms. Jones

Sincerely yours,

Ms. Kristi Hart
Secretary to Ms. Jones

Signing someone else's name. When signing someone else's name, it is not necessary to write "per" or "by." Simply sign the individual's name, and then write your initials. If your employer has a facsimile signature, use it.

When the individual signing a letter for another person is not the person's assistant, use either one of these forms:

Sincerely yours,

For Milton Trout
General Manager

Sincerely yours,

Milton Trout
General Manager

Academic, military, and professional titles. These titles should appear in the typewritten signatures, as follows:

Yours truly,

Grace Johnson

Ms. Grace Johnson, C.P.S.

Yours truly,

James Simpson

James Simpson, M.D.

Yours truly,

Laura Wilson

Laura Wilson, Ph.D.
Professor of Humanities

Yours truly,

Leonard Richardson

Leonard J. Richardson
Colonel, USAF

    The salutations in replies to each of these would be, respectively, Dear Ms. Johnson, Dear Dr. Simpson, Dear Professor Wilson, and Dear Colonel Richardson.

    Courtesy titles. When a first name could be a man's or a woman's name, or if initials are used, call ahead to clarify or omit the use the courtesy title.

Sincerely,

Dale Harrington

Mr. Dale Harrington

Sincerely yours,

Dale Harrington

Mr. D. K. Harrington

    If the letter requires the addressee to sign and return it, the name of the addressee will be at the end of the letter with space above for his or her signature. Below this will be space set aside for the date of signature. On the other side of the letter, the sender will have signed his or her name on another line; beneath will be the typed name. Beneath this will be a line under which the word "Date" appears.

TIP: If you have a name that is common in either gender, you might try a courtesy title in the signature line of letters, (Ms. or Mr.). This helps in the reply and any follow-up calls.

Reference Initials

Today, most firms prefer only the typist's reference initials. Occasionally, two sets of initials appear: The first set represents the author of the written document and the second set is that of the typist. If both sets of initials are used, the first set is typed in capital letters and the second set in lowercase with either a slash or a colon separating the sets.

As middle managers increasingly prepare their own letters, reference initials are disappearing. However, if you are preparing a letter for your manager or another person, it is important that you use reference initials.

Reference initials are typed at the left margin a double space below the typewritten signature and title. Illustrations are as follows:

JRJ:lm   JRJ (author of document) and lm (typist)

JRJ/lm   JRJ (author of document) and lm (typist)

lm   (typist's initials only)

File Name Notation

With most letters being prepared on computers and stored in a computer record for future reference, you might want to actually put the file name on the correspondence. (Because it's computer-generated, use a smaller type size to make it less apparent, if possible.) Put the file name on a line of its own below the reference initials.

Before you do this, make sure that your computer can handle file names of more than eight characters. Furthermore, be aware that the letters after the dot represent the application extension, not the place to show it's a letter (for instance, you would name a file letter.doc, not jones.let). If you must e-mail files back and forth, this is doubly important.

Avoid emoticons (little smilies common in e-mail communication to show humor or emotion) in your business memos, as tempting as it may be to use them. Save these for your personal correspondence on the Net.

Other Elements in a Business Letter

In addition to the standard parts in all business letters, other elements sometimes are included.

Attention Line

The writer might want to direct the letter to a particular person or department within the firm. When the inside address is directed to a firm name and the writer wants a certain person or specific department also to be aware of the contents of the letter, an attention line should be used.

The post office recommends putting the attention line first in an address. For consistency, use that form in the letter as well. The word "attention" must appear; however, no punctuation is necessary after it.

ACE Recruitment International
Attention Mr. Samuel Jones
8225 Dunwoody Place
Atlanta, GA 30339-7329

Subject Line

When a subject line is used, it should be typed a double space below the salutation.

The subject line may be typed starting at the left margin, centered, or indented five spaces, depending on the style of the letter. The word "Subject" may precede the subject line, typed in all uppercase or typed in initial caps. Today, many businesses prefer to type the subject line in all uppercase, without the word "Subject" preceding it.

If the simplified letter style is used, the subject line should replace the salutation and be typed on the third line below the last line of the inside address. The subject line should be typed at the left margin in all uppercase. The word "Subject" does not precede the subject line.

Reply Reference Notation

Place the notation as you would a subject line. The word "Reference" (or "Re"), followed by a colon and two spaces, may be shown before the notation.

Enclosure Notation

Whenever an item is to be enclosed with a letter, this should be indicated on the letter by typing an enclosure notation two lines below the reference initials at the left margin. This tells the recipient to check the envelope or package for additional items.

When more than one item is enclosed, any one of the following forms may be used:

Enclosures 2   Enc. 2

Enclosures (2)

Important enclosures should be listed:

Enclosure: check   Enclosures:
                               1. check
Enclosures: check contract   2. contract

Copy Notation

When a copy is prepared for the information of a person other than the addressee of the letter, a notation followed by the name of the person receiving the copy is typed at the left margin, a double space below the reference initials or enclosure notation. If more than one person is to receive a copy, the names should be listed either in order of importance in the company or in alphabetical order. Common examples follow:

ms	ms
Enclosure	cc Raymond Smith
cc: Raymond Smith	
Albert Wayne	

Some organizations keep a record of their correspondence by preparing a photocopy of outgoing communications. The following notations may be used:

pc: Rosemarie Sweeting	pc Rosemarie Sweeting

Other organizations make no distinction as to the type of copy made and use the following notations:

c: Sandra Delgado	c Sandra Delgado

Blind Copies

In some instances, it is necessary to send a copy of a letter to one or more persons without the knowledge of the addressee. This is known as a blind copy *(bcc,* for *blind carbon copy).* To make this special notation, type the bcc notation for only the blind copy recipients at the bottom of the letter at the left margin. Make sure the firm's file copy shows all the bcc notations.

Postscript

A postscript often is used to emphasize a special point by setting it apart from the rest of the letter, or to relay a personal message to the recipient of the letter.

A postscript should be typed as a single-spaced paragraph a double space below the last notation. Acceptable forms include PS:, P.S., or neither. Indent the paragraph if the paragraphs of the letter are indented.

Mailing Notation

Any special mailing delivery (airmail, special delivery, registered, certified, express mail, by fax) should be typed midway between the date and the inside address. This should appear in all uppercase at the left margin.

Multiple Page Letters

When a letter consists of more than one page, the second sheets or successive pages are typed on paper of the same size, color, and quality as the letterhead. If possible, leave at least two lines of a paragraph at the bottom of the page, and carry at least two lines to the next page. Do not end a page with a divided word.

Each successive page requires a *heading*. The heading consists of the name of the addressee, the page number of the letter, and the date, typed on the

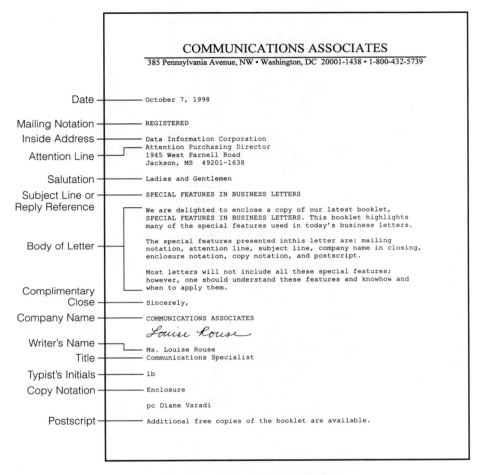

Letter 5: Block Style, with Open Punctuation Special Features

seventh line from the top edge of the paper. Triple-space after the heading and continue typing the remainder of the letter. Use the same-side margins as for the first page.

Two formats exist for headings for the second and subsequent pages of multiple-page letters: block style and horizontal style. The block style heading is typed at the left margin:

    Ms. Jane R. Smith
    Page 2
    October 7, xxxx

In the horizontal style, the name of the addressee is typed at the left margin, the page number is centered, and the dateline ends at the right margin:

    Ms. Jane R. Smith   2   October 7, xxxx

This all can be done automatically by using headers and footers. Just prepare the headers to contain the date and correct page numbers automatically.

> **TIP:** If you want to be sure that a letter will look good on letterhead, print it first on plain paper. Then hold the letter up to the light against a blank sheet of letterhead. You'll be able to see how well the margins work—in particular, the top and bottom margins, depending on letterhead style. Some letterhead pages have deep top margins; others include corporate information on the bottom.

Using Templates

When you use templates, set them up so they contain all the standard parts and margins. Then all you do is type your letters. If you use more than one template with different margins or spacing, you will want to set up style sheets and template files to hold the various templates.

Doing Mass Mailings

Among your responsibilities might be conducting mass mailings for your company. For example, your task might be to handle a list of 100 names. Here's how to set up a mail merge. You key the letter, replacing areas that would be personalized (such as the inside address, greeting, and even text in the body of the letter) with codes that tell the program what to put there. Then you compile a file of addresses, greetings, and other information that fits the required codes for the master letter. When you merge the two, the program automatically creates each individual letter with the information from the address file. You often can create these address files from databases from the start.

> **TIP:** Not every software program calls the combining of a list of addresses into their respective letters a *mail merge*. To see if your software program has the function, check the help menu for keywords such as *personalized mailings*.

Mail-merge letters are pretty standard. Most people recognize that they were on a large list, even if their letter was personalized. Still, any attempt to personalize these letters is a nice touch.

One way to add a personal touch is to have the person sending the letter sign each one—and sometimes even add a little note in his or her own handwriting.

If you are talking about 200 letters, however, you might want to scan in a signature—most word processing programs will let you set a signature as an image. Alternatively, you can use a stamp with the person's signature.

Envelopes

When preparing business envelopes, you must observe several guidelines because the post office optical character readers (OCRs) are programmed to scan a specific area of the envelope. The address must be completely within the read zone, blocked, and single-spaced. Two-letter state abbreviations must be used. Nine-digit ZIP codes should be used, if available. Apartment and room numbers should follow the street address on the same line. The U.S. Postal Service prefers, but does not require, the use of all capital letters and no punctuation in envelope addresses.

The OCR will be happy to direct your mail to its proper destination, but it first must locate the delivery address and read it. The "eye" of the OCR looks for the address within an imaginary rectangle on each piece of mail. Make some quick measurements—if the delivery address is located within the following boundaries, the OCR won't have any trouble finding it:

Sides of rectangle	$\frac{1}{2}$ inch from the right and left edge
Bottom of rectangle	$\frac{5}{8}$ inch up from the bottom edge
Top of rectangle	$2\frac{3}{4}$ inches up from bottom edge

Non-Address Information

Because the OCR looks for the address in a particular area, extraneous printing can confuse it. Thus, the space below and on either side of the delivery address line, within the OCR read area, should be clear of all printing and other markings that are not actually part of the address (such as the return address, special notations, advertising copy, company logos, and so on). Positioning such information as far away from the address as possible helps.

Bar Code Clear Area

After reading an address, the OCR prints the appropriate bar code on the bottom of the mail piece for other postal scanners to use to direct the mail. The OCR rejects the mail and delays delivery if it sees some other type of printing where the bar code goes. Leave blank an area measuring $\frac{5}{8}$ inch high and $4\frac{3}{4}$ inches wide from the right corner of the mail piece.

The two standard-size envelopes are as follows:

- No. $6\frac{3}{4}$ envelope measures $6\frac{1}{2} \times 3\frac{5}{8}$ inches
- No. 10 envelope measures $\frac{9}{12} \times 4\frac{1}{8}$ inches

Special notations to the addressee (confidential, hold for arrival, personal) should be typed in all uppercase about three lines below the return address.

Special mailing notations (airmail, special delivery, registered, certified) should be typed below the stamp (about line nine) to end five to six spaces from the right edge of the envelope; these notations also should be typed in all uppercase.

```
Mr. L.M. Smith
245 Main Street
Glendale, NY 11385-7342


                                                REGISTERED

               Data Information Center
               Attention Purchasing Director
               1945 W. Parnell Road
               Jackson, MS 49201-1638
```

Traditional Method for Addressing a No. 10 Envelope

```
Mr. L.M. Smith
245 Main Street
Glendale, NY 11385-7342

HOLD FOR ARRIVAL

             Ms. Roberta Rogers
             987 Kingston Drive, Apt. 7
             Des Moines, IA 50310-3636
```

Traditional Method for Addressing a No. 6¾ Envelope

Although most assistants use a computer for their correspondence, they often keep their old reliable typewriter to type addresses on letters. Still, it's possible to do envelopes with your printer if you use print labels. Many brands that fit into laser printers come in white, colored, and clear versions.

FAXES

Faxes have made a tremendous difference in the way in which we do business—in particular, the tempo of communications. A letter that might take several days to reach us can be in our hands in a few minutes. If a negative side exists to faxes, it is that this convenience is often used when there is no need for urgency.

If you are to be successful in your position, you must be familiar with your firm's fax machine. If your computer has the capability, you also must be able to fax directly from your computer. Suppose that your boss must call an emergency directors meeting. You know that many of your firm's trustees don't check their e-mail regularly. Rather than e-mail, you might want to fax them, either from your computer or from your company's fax machine.

Given the importance of faxes, you should get the fax number—as well as e-mail address—for everyone with whom your boss does business.

Fax Protocol

Part of faxing is knowing what is appropriate to fax. Letters, agendas, messages, and other business-related faxing are always appropriate, depending on the receiver and the topic. However, with the proliferation of fax machines, the unsolicited fax has become an unwelcome intruder. Unsolicited faxes often include business-related messages, discounts, special offers, announcements, and so on. Even if these must be sent out to a group of clients or customers, they are not always welcome or appropriate.

Junk faxes tie up lines, use supplies, run up phone bills, and sidetrack the fax's very purpose—getting important messages in a timely fashion.

Junk faxes can range from an unasked-for cartoon from a colleague on another floor of your office to a copy of a chain letter, to a corporate advertisement about special discount pricing. What distinguishes junk faxes from worthwhile documents isn't their quantity, but their worth. A fax from your CEO or a client firm about a new product would not be junk mail because it would have an impact on your work.

> **TIP:** Be guided by this rule proffered by the *New York Times:* "Fax unto others as you would have others fax unto you."

State and federal laws on junk faxes are still in development, but you still can fight junk faxes. Send back a message to the senders of the junk faxes to cease and desist; tell them that their messages are tying up your machine and not building goodwill.

Dealing with the Fax Machine

Some assistants take on the responsibility for their department's fax machine; other machines are serviced by a supplier. Even if you have an outside supplier, you should know some basics about the machine: how to insert paper, how to program autodial lists for common groups (such as a board or a group of remote employees), and the like.

TIP: If you have an older fax machine, it will use rolls of thermal paper. When the faxes come off, they often curl. Don't send these rolls of thermal fax paper originals back through the fax machine. They can cause jams, and the treated paper can damage scanners. Photocopy the fax, and then fax the copy.

Want to fax faster? A fax moves quickly over lighter portions of the document and more slowly over darker portions. To fax faster, make sure that whatever you're transmitting has no unnecessary large portions of solid black (such as letterhead or a fax cover sheet with large black or colored portions). Sometimes, copiers can leave black edges, as can fax machines. Trim these off if they'll cause problems.

Fax-photocopier teamwork. Does your photocopier have a feature that enables you to reduce/enlarge images? Reduce airy and easy-to-read documents before faxing. A tighter original can cut transmission time. Teach others to do the same when faxing to you, and you'll save paper.

On the cover sheet, note the percentage that the document has been reduced. This allows easier re-enlarging if the recipient desires.

Incoming fax jam? If you're deluged with faxes and plan to put a second machine to work fielding calls, don't publicize the new number. Instead, arrange with the phone company to have the existing fax line roll or automatically switch to the new line when the established number's busy. When you order the new lines from the phone company, make sure you let the company know how and in what order you want multiple lines to roll.

Efficient Faxing

Let's face it, faxing can be a real time drain. Numbers don't connect, machines jam, machines on the other end are busy, and, even when everything seems normal, your boss calls from the business trip furious that she didn't receive anything. Or, she received three pages and went to the meeting to discover that pages four and five were missing. Or, she asked at the hotel front desk and was sent to the business center where you faxed it—and it was closed. By the time you call and resend, and resend and call, it's lunchtime! If you plan ahead and establish a routine, you can easily fax and verify, making both your boss and yourself look like stars.

Use cover sheets. Use a cover sheet for all fax transmissions. Identify all relevant information from your end: your company and mailing address, the individual sender, fax and voice line numbers, date of transmission, and total number of pages (including the cover sheet). If you have a long fax, it's useful to number each page as 1 of 10, 2 of 10, and so forth—especially if you're faxing something important and need to easily verify that it arrived. For example, if you are faxing a report to your boss at a hotel in England, you want to verify that it arrived (if it didn't, you could be in trouble), and you want to easily and quickly verify if any pages are missing. With a numbering system, the person on the other end can easily determine what, if anything, needs to be re-sent.

When you address your cover sheet, make sure that you address it to a specific person, not just a department or a company. If you are sending to a hotel, identify whether the person is a guest or on staff. You should note "hold for arrival" if the person is checking in later that day.

Often, if you are sending a letter or written message with your fax, you can combine the fax cover and letter into one document. Office supply companies also stock the sticky fax notes that can be placed directly on the first page of the fax. These are useful but sometimes can jam the machine, so be careful.

Verify the receipt. Be proactive in making sure that your fax has arrived. Call to confirm its receipt so you can quickly right any wrongs from your end. In larger organizations in which the fax goes to a central location and then must be distributed, the intended recipient can hustle things along from that end.

Actually look at the transmission-confirmation report that you get from your machine (and review the autodial log you get if you do the paper check). Keep in mind, though, that the transmission log isn't gospel. If it's really important, check on the receiving end. The transmission log might show that the other fax machine received it, but the other fax machine could have stored but not printed it, run out of paper, or experienced some other malfunction.

As fax numbers proliferate, a misdialed eleven-number string is more likely to connect to another fax machine and send your document to a total stranger. One-touch speed dialing also might send material rocketing off to J while K waits impatiently for the material you promised to send immediately.

> **TIP:** Remember, faxes aren't confidential! If you need to fax a confidential document, the best thing to do is phone the receiver or the assistant or other office professional picking it up on the other end. Have this person pick up the document directly from the fax machine. If you are faxing to a hotel and security is important, phone ahead and make sure the person who receives it immediately seals it in envelope. In special circumstances, you can always ask the hotel to hand-deliver the fax to the recipient's office or room.

Sending Large or Multiple Faxes

On occasions, you will do a mass faxing yourself. Suppose that you are organizing a meeting of customers for your manager. You want to remind them to make their reservations in time to get rooms at the hotel where the meeting will be held. The reminder note has a registration form attached that you've taken from the conference brochure.

TIPS FOR EFFICIENT FAXES

- Keep faxes short.

- Use a cover sheet when faxing to a large organization.

- Do not use a cover sheet when faxing to a small organization.

- As a cover sheet or not, the first page should include the following, typed or written clearly at the top of the page: addressee's name, your own name, and the total number of pages being faxed.

- Always use 1-inch margins.

- Reduce oversized documents (including those that do not have 1-inch margins) on a copy machine before faxing them.

- Number the pages being faxed, even if the document is already paginated—this is especially important if you're faxing only a portion of a document.

- Do not put folded, stapled, or otherwise mutilated documents through the fax machine. Make a copy, and then run the copy through the fax machine.

- Do not exceed your machine's paper feeder capacity.

- Check for incoming faxes frequently.

- Clear incoming faxes from the machine as they are delivered to prevent paper jams.

- Make sure you have enough paper in the machine to last the entire work day.

Here are some points to remember:

- If you are using the registration form from the brochure, check to see whether it has fax-back information if you want the customers to fax it back.

- Check your machine's instruction manual for how to set up phone lists for multiple mailings on the machine.

- Find out whether your machine has automatic transmission. By timing transmissions for hours when rates are lower, senders can gain substantial savings. If your machine includes a polling feature, this also represents a more efficient way to send the same document to multiple locations when measured by staff time and cost.

- If you have lots of faxes, use an automatic dialing system, and fax before or after regular business hours to avoid busy-signal delays. You also might snag the company some savings in off-peak phone rates.

- Faxing the wrong kind of document can be ineffective and costly. For example, computer printouts, which are difficult to read in the original, become almost impossible to understand when faxed. Often, blueprints or architectural renderings and other artwork lose necessary clarity when faxed. Odd-sized originals that reduce disproportionately when faxed can lose important details.

- Lengthy documents (five or more pages) not needed in a rush often are better sent through the mail, especially over long distances. The pages of multipage documents can get mixed up or lost easily, which can hurt rather than help communication.

Choosing Fax Over Regular Mail

Faxes are more public than postal correspondence, and many people prefer the privacy of a letter received in the mail. Find out before you fax.

Timing is the key issue when choosing between mail and fax, however. If someone needs something right away, fax it. Cost isn't an issue because a fax costs no more than a long-distance phone call.

Remember the intangibles. The big-production, super-sales brochure or extra-elegant report quickly turns into just more sheets of fax paper when it's printed out at the recipients' end. And the impression they get turns out to be much less than you meant to make. The advantages of rushing the real thing by mail might outweigh its cost and the immediacy of a fax.

Also remember that sometimes you can get better impact by faxing something that otherwise would be mailed. A faxed thank-you for the sale, the appointment, or the information might be appropriate. This can be a real attention-getter, and it allows for a degree of informality that a letter doesn't. Likewise, consider faxing birthday and company anniversary greetings, congrats on a promotion, or celebratory greetings. Just remember, as in any other situation, use a little judgment. The medium depends on the recipient, the sender, and the occasion.

ARE FAXES LEGALLY BINDING?

Many courts have refused to accept faxed documents as evidence. Thermal paper faxes are least likely to be accepted in a court of law because of the poor quality of reproduction. But with plain-resolution paper, faxes might look as clean and clear as a typed document and stand up to the legal test.

Fax Formatting

What kinds of faxes are reader-friendly? Unfortunately, fewer than you might think. Clarity is not everything with faxes; it's virtually the only thing. Here are some tips for creating reader-friendly faxes.

- *Plain Jane wins the day.* Numbers are often the very reason for a fax, but whether you fax words or numbers, choose a plain, clean typeface that leaves little chance for misreading. Sans-serif typefaces such as Helvetica and Courier hold up very well when faxed, but serif typefaces such as Times Roman do not.

- *Don't be bold.* The process of faxing alone makes the print on the end product appear bolder. Additional boldface type sometimes can turn the print into unreadable black blobs. Stick to regular or lightface type.

- *No italics for emphasis.* Italic type comes out even more ragged in fax than regular type. To emphasize key lines, apply underscore.

- *Get the points.* What's legible on this end might not be legible on the receiving end. This is just as true for point size as for other elements of design. Try for a minimum of 12-point type when faxing. The 10-point type, usually quite legible in the original, gets hard to read on the other end of the transmission.

- *The acid test.* Still not sure that what you've created is readable? Then fax filled-in copies of the suspicious form or document to yourself. Or, at least run them through the fax machine on copy mode. Can you read everything clearly? If not, then the recipient won't either—it's time to redesign.

E-MAIL

E-mail has rapidly become an indispensable tool in business communications. Because technology is constantly advancing—and because the Internet is currently the red-hot communication highway—this growth will doubtless continue.

As the use of e-mail grows, it will continue to affect the way business is done—and certainly the way communications are handled. In many organizations, e-mail has replaced interoffice memos and traditional mail. Not only does it enable us to communicate swiftly, but we can send it with attachments to support our communications, from spreadsheets to graphics.

Even in offices such as consulting firms or investment banks (which don't use lots of technology or e-mail), some individuals are using e-mail as the new way of corresponding. It has replaced letters in many areas and is replacing faxes as well because you can easily attach and send spreadsheets and other documents. E-mail also is much more confidential (although many companies have policies allowing them to monitor employee e-mail). When you get into e-mail etiquette, approach it from the correspondence angle: E-mail enables you to bcc, cc, and send out multiple copies.

In a nutshell, e-mail in offices uses computers and networks hooked to the Internet (or, in some cases, to individual modems and phone lines) to transmit messages from one computer to another; this turns the computer into an electronic mailbox. The transmittals do not require paper. Systems operate 24 hours a day, so time differences do not cause any difficulty. Messages can be sent to multiple destinations simultaneously and can be stored, retrieved, and often printed out virtually at will. Messages travel over the Internet; depending on the traffic and the speed of your connection, they can arrive almost simultaneously.

Most offices have dedicated e-mail systems that run on internal networks. With this system, each user gets an individual mail account or mailbox to send and receive mail both internally and, if set up over the Internet, to anyone else with an e-mail address. Companies use e-mail for in-house communications but also for many customers, prospects, and employees who can be contacted via computer workstations and terminals in their places of business or their homes.

As with any new technology, the etiquette, rules, procedures, legal issues, and such surrounding e-mail messaging are still in transition. Beyond that, here's a roundup of simple guidelines that have evolved so far.

You will use e-mail in many ways, from short memos to remind people about the date for the next team meeting, to the distribution of a report (as an attachment) for the meeting's attendees, to an announcement to potential customers about the product that the team has developed. You or your boss might e-mail someone down the hall or across the ocean. Rather than call someone with a question and risk telephone tag, it's so much easier to send your question as e-mail.

As you use e-mail, keep some points in mind. First and foremost, e-mail messages are still very public and are best kept straightforward. Further, e-mail is a form of professional communication and, as such, should be treated professionally. Avoid jargon and the cute stuff. E-mail has fostered a shorthand of its own (such as LOL = Laughing Out Loud) and visual representations, called *emoticons* (the little sideways happy or sad faces made up of punctuation marks are the best known). These are out of place in most business communications.

Don't abuse e-mail. Don't rehash a previously sent message. Keep your e-mail messages brief, ideally to one page or screen.

To grab the reader's attention, use the subject line wisely. E-mail scammers and junk e-mailers do this to tempt you. For your business e-mail correspondence, be as specific as you can in the subject line to involve your reader(s). For example, "Per Diem Allowance Increase" is better than "Travel Changes."

Divide your message into paragraphs: Don't force everything into one big run-on paragraph. If bullets, indents, or spaces between ideas will increase clarity, use them. Finally, organize your e-mail files.

Just as with paper files, dump, "deadfile," or otherwise deal with e-mail that has been on the system too long. How long is too long? In the ethereal world of electronic communication, thirty to sixty days probably represents the outside limit. Anything on the system longer should be archived in some other way: paper, disk, or another electronic backup format.

FOR MORE INFORMATION

If you can't find what you need from the phone numbers and Web sites listed in this chapter, you may need to expand your search.

- For more information on communications, business etiquette, or face-to-face skills, check your local library in the business communications or self help sections.

- For more information on formal letters, see the CD-ROM that accompanies this book. "1001 Essential Letters" gives examples, templates, and other valuable information for letter-writing help.

- For more information on dialing international calls, check your telephone directory. It will provide specific instructions.

- For more information on conducting formal meetings, including parliamentary procedure and formal minutes, check your local library or bookstore in the reference book section.

2

OTHER OFFICE DOCUMENTS

◆

- **Business Reports**
  - Types of Business Reports
  - Format and Preparation
  - Parts of a Business Report
  - Visual Aids
  - Types of Visuals
  - The Four Cs of Chart Design
- **Presentations**
  - Presentation and Graphics Software
- **Web Pages**
- **Company Newsletters**
- **For More Information**

Although a great number of office communications happen via phone, fax, and e-mail, today's office professional must be familiar with many other kinds of documents in order to function. These communications include everything from spreadsheets to reports to slides. The office professional might be supporting a corporate executive who gives presentations or a team that needs materials for training. Whatever the duties, they should have an idea of the technology available and its capabilities for creating the most effective work in the most efficient manner.

Today's office environment is more electronic and more technology-based than ever. Yet it's also true that there are more and more reports generated in the traditional format of words on paper. That means professional documents, including reports, letters, and spreadsheets, are prepared with the aid of computers, but executed or produced by the "brain-sweat" and talent of the office professionals.

In this chapter, we will discuss the preparation of reports: annual reports, business presentations, newsletters, sales reports, and other business documents.

BUSINESS REPORTS

A business report is a lengthy, in-depth communication, containing facts and ideas, that is usually prepared internally for co-workers, a superior, a committee, or a team. Reports can appear in several forms, and there is no authoritative list of all types of reports. Reports may be analytical, compartmentalized, or in the form of a catalog. The procedures here put the elements together to produce an effective, quality report. Reports may be produced by an outside printer or publisher (such as a corporation's annual report), produced internally on desktop publishing systems (such as an employee newsletter or committee report), or produced internally in regular word processing software (such as a white paper or another special report for a superior). The office professional might be responsible for anything from typing the information to simply having the files prepared to send out.

TYPES OF BUSINESS REPORTS

There are many types of business reports—here are just a few types you'll see in use in today's offices:

- *Corporate Report.* This category includes memorandum reports, letter reports, and mega-reports (very lengthy, complex reports, containing hundreds of pages). A corporate report might introduce and analyze a specific problem (the company's exposure to Y2K liability, for example), discuss it, and provide impetus for its resolution. The content may be technical or general. One office support person may have responsibility for the production of the entire report, including careful proofreading, checking for accuracy, duplication, binding, collating, and distribution.

- *White Paper.* A white paper often refers to a government report. Examples include Health Maintenance Organizations (HMOs), privatizing Social Security funds, or a detailed authoritative report on any single subject (process re-engineering or corporate environmental responsibility, for example). White papers usually involve citations to outside sources, and may contain a bibliography and footnotes as well.

- *Project or Committee Report.* This report is usually the collective or collaborative work of a team of people. One person is typically assigned the responsibility for integrating the material, seeing that it has a single voice or sound (as if one person wrote the text), and preparing it to look like a formally prepared document. A typical report might deal with safety issues in the workplace, proposed locations for a new plant, or entry of the company's products into the Euromarket.

- *Executive Summary.* An executive summary is a brief description and summation of a report's contents. Significant data are summarized. A summary of this type is used for problem-solving and defines the problem, determines how it should be solved, and what the benefits are. Usually, detailed data are not given. The summary may be part of a longer report. An example of an executive summary is one seen in a research report recommending investment in a particular company. Another might be a one-page review of sales that precedes a consolidated financial report in which the details on the operating results or revenues of the company's divisions or domestic and international operations are given. Executive summaries digest the contents of the larger report, telling the reader the key facts in a concise way. Their purpose is to give the reader the gist of the entire document or report at a glance. So, the executive summary is quite often one of the most important elements of the report and is carefully prepared to communicate the facts of the report in a terse style.

- *Abstract.* An abstract, like an executive summary, is a brief description or overview of the contents of a report. There are two types of abstracts: informative and descriptive. An *informative abstract* is a summary, an internal discussion. A *descriptive abstract* lists the elements covered in a complete report without stating the supporting data; it is an external discussion or framework.

FORMAT AND PREPARATION

Careful formatting and preparation of a business report are musts. Fortunately, the software bundled with office computers make report preparation much easier than it used to be. However, it's also true that software allows the user to include so many bells and whistles in a report that it can look "amateurish" and be difficult to read. You must be consistent in form, type style (e.g., italics, bold), and fonts to produce a quality document.

Even with computer software capability, it's often best to think about the report before beginning its preparation at the keyboard. Should the document contain headers and footers, with the title of the report on the right-hand header and the section head on the left-hand header? Do you want automatic page numbering to appear; if so, where on the page? All of this preparation is fairly manageable with today's word processing programs. In fact, inserting charts, checklists, and graphics is easy as well. You can even import spreadsheets or illustrations with a simple click of the mouse. Moving text is the same simple maneuver of highlight, edit, cut, and paste. Remember, too, that there are templates available in most word processing programs for reports, memos, newsletters, and brochures.

Today's wide range of business services also helps the office professional think of how the report will be presented. Will it be spiral-bound or presented in a folder? Give thought to the paper, type style and font, format, and presentation, as well as the special features of the report and the care and use of the equipment to be used in preparing the report.

Paper

Reports should use a good quality of paper, usually 8½" × 11" white paper with 24 percent rag content. This is a better quality paper than copier paper or regular printer paper—it is closer to letterhead-quality paper. The higher the rag content of paper, the longer its life.

A watermark imprinted on rag-content paper tells the brand of paper and the percentage of cotton fiber in it. To read the watermark, hold a blank piece of paper up to a light source. The right side of the paper shows a readable watermark. Use either 16-, 20-, or 24-pound paper. Print on the face of the paper showing the readable watermark.

If you are looking for a higher quality paper to print a report on, check with an office supply expert. They can recommend papers that will not only look good, but also will run through a laser printer or copier without jamming. Multiple originals can be generated by computers, and many offices use photocopiers to produce quality copies.

Here are some rules of thumb for selecting paper. Is it a throwaway report for the sales force? If so, you might simply use a photocopy machine to make duplicates of the original. If it is a report that will be read by everyone in management, letterhead may be needed. If you use letterhead for the first sheet in lengthy reports, you can use blank letterhead for the additional pages. If the report is for the Board of Directors, the CEO, or other shareholders, you might want to have the whole thing handled outside by a commercial print shop. It can be printed on expensive paper and bound in a report cover, which is a good idea for reports that contain graphics and other color charts that look best on coated papers.

Of course, you must consider budgets, there are hybrid methods of combining inside and outside work to save on costs. For example, you could have the local print shop handle the printing of color graphs and charts for the report, collate them into the text portion you prepared in the office, and bind the whole thing for you. You wouldn't want to do this for the annual report unless instructed to do so because here is where the company usually puts its best efforts into presentation.

Choosing Type

A 10-point font is preferred for reports because its large size makes it easier to read. As for design, the conventional roman typeface is still the most widely acceptable. A sturdy, modern sans-serif design is clean, easy to read, and makes single-spaced or tightly packed data appear less crowded. It's often used for report titles, headings, and captions for figures and tables. Italic type or underscoring may be used to highlight certain words in the text of a report. The underscoring equals and should be interpreted as the word(s) being in italics. In all cases, the style must be good letter quality. The format must be consistent throughout the report.

Of course, these are guidelines; you should be guided by the application and use of the material. A short sales report that contains numbers that are to be scanned quickly (for example, a weekly sales report), could be done in 12- or even 14-point type. If you plan to use callouts (marginal notations or excerpts that summarize key points in the text), drop to a smaller font, usually 8-point type, or 2 points below the body type.

Remember that while you may be creative with the use of fonts and want to try something different once in awhile, the best way to go is clean, crisp, and uncluttered. No more than three fonts on a page is a good rule. If you are working in a funky organization, then the rules may not apply. Also, the corporate culture may be avant-garde. Consider the in-your-face style of *Wired* magazine and some of its more recent imitators. Just remember that those pioneers employ professional graphic artists who have a lot of experience under their belts. It may look easy to create at the cutting edge of design, but the best designs for most of us in business are clean, crisp, and simple with a lot of white space.

PARTS OF A BUSINESS REPORT

The business report may include all or some of the following formal sections, along with the main body: letter or memorandum of transmittal, title page, preface, table of contents, list of tables and/or figures, bibliography, appendices, and index.

Although the report itself may contain no words authored by you, the way it looks is directly influenced by your hand. The look reflects on you as the report designer—your efforts make the information or data look good, not only to the readers but to the people who wrote the text.

A word here about writing. Although usually not necessary, if you notice some erroneous data, bad grammar, or spelling, it's a good idea to call it to the boss's attention and explain how you will fix it. Another opportunity exists with the collaborative report, written by several writers. You can see whether everything reads as if it were one voice or author. If not, then some tweaking or copy editing will often improve the way it reads, to everyone's delight. You make the authors look better, the readers are impressed, and most folks appreciate the wordsmithing.

Parts of the business report are discussed in the following paragraphs.

Letter of transmittal. A letter of transmittal is used to introduce the reader to the report. The content of the letter should tell the reader what the topic of the report is, why it was written, how it was compiled, who worked on it, and what major findings or conclusions resulted from the research. The letter of transmittal appears directly after the title page, and it may be typed in any acceptable business letter or memorandum format.

Title page. The title page usually contains the name or title of the report, the name and title of the person or organization for whom it was written, the name and title of the person or group who wrote it, and the date it was submitted. The title page may also include more information, if necessary. As a general rule, place the main title in all uppercase letters, approximately 2 inches from the top of the page. Put the date 2 inches from the bottom of the page. Space the other information equally between the top and bottom margins, typed in lowercase letters, with the first letter of each main word capitalized. Center each line horizontally. There are various formats for title pages. For an acceptable style, see the following figure.

Preface. The preface, also called the *foreword,* is optional. It allows the writer to give a personal message to the reader. The author may, for example, provide special information that may not appear in the body of the report, such as the methods used, points of emphasis, pragmatic considerations, or reasons for treatment of content.

Table of contents. The table of contents (TOC) is one of the last things prepared, after all pages of the report are completed and numbered. The table of contents lists, in chronological order, the numbers and titles of the sections or chapters in the report, and the pages on which they begin. It should not be confused with the index, which is arranged alphabetically and includes more items. If your computer software has a table-of-contents feature, generate the TOC that way.

To format the table of contents, type the heading "TABLE OF CONTENTS" in all uppercase, centered 2 inches from the top edge of the paper.

```
INTRODUCING INFORMATION PROCESSING INTO THE BUSINESS CURRICULUM AT
                   ST. ANN'S TECHNICAL COLLEGE




                         The Effect of Change
      The State University of New York Program in Office Management
                                  by
                      Technical Consultants, Inc.




                          August 16, 200_
```

Example of a Title Page

Type "Page" a triple space below the heading. Begin typing the contents a double space below "Page" at the left margin. Use the same margins that you use in typing the body of the report. A good style is to use all uppercase letters when typing those entries of the contents page that refer to the major sections of the report. The sections of lesser importance should be indented under their main headings and listed in the same sequence as they appear in the report.

Example of a Table of Contents

Only the initial letters of main words should be uppercase. Leaders should be used to guide the reader's eye across the page from a content's entry to the page number. See the above figure for an example.

   List of illustrations. When a report contains several tables, charts, and/or other figures by way of illustration, separate lists of these should be included after the table of contents. Number each title or figure, and give the full caption or title of each. A computer spreadsheet or word processing program with a table-numbering feature may aid you here. If the number of illustrations is not significant, they can be listed in, or simply added to the end of, the table of contents. Conversely, should the report contain both tables and figures (and many of each), individual lists may make sense. The list of tables would precede the list of figures, each list on its own page.

Body of the Report

Whether you design it yourself or use a template from your word processing application, organization and presentation of the information is key. Here are some guidelines rooted in the classic style of setting up reports.

Margins. Margins for reports and manuscripts are a minimum of 1 inch; however, many authors prefer margins of 1¼ inches. When the report is to be bound on the left side, allow for the binding by making the left margin 1½ inches wide and reducing the right margin accordingly.

The top margin on the first page should be at least 2 inches; on the other pages, it should be 1 inch. If the report is to be bound at the top, allow an additional one-half inch for this. Keep the bottom margins at least 1 inch deep; in some cases, you may want to make them as much as 1½ inches deep.

Spacing. Usually, reports are double-spaced and the first line of each paragraph is indented. The following figure presents a page from a report.

In the text itself, when a long quote (of three lines or more) is set apart from the rest of the text as a separate paragraph, it should be single spaced, the quote marks should be dropped, and the paragraph should be indented an extra five spaces inside the right and left margins. Further indent the first line of the quotation to show a paragraph indention. Copy the indented quotation in single spacing, and omit the quotation marks. The indention tells the reader that the material is a quote.

If listings are included in your report, single-space them. Center the items on the page. If listings contain widely separated columns, use leaders to assist the eye in reading the material.

Allow at least two lines of a paragraph to appear at the bottom and top of each page, adjusting the bottom margin, if necessary, to make sure that one line doesn't end up standing alone at the bottom or top of a page. Make sure, too, that words aren't divided across pages.

White space. When preparing each page of the business report, avoid leaving excessive space without type. This space distracts the reader and takes away from the appearance, organization, and format of the page. If white space is necessary before and after an illustration, artwork, or visual, leave not more than 2 inches.

Tables, figures, and illustrations. The placement of tables, figures, and illustrations in the body of the business report is very important and must be carefully done. Each visual (whether a table, figure, or other type of illustration) must have its own identification number (Table 1, Table 2, and so forth;

Population Under Investigation

    The population under investigation for this study is the
administration of the College, the Business and Economics
Division, the Secretarial Administration Department, the students
enrolled in the secretarial program, the surrounding business
community, and the certificated and classified staff of San
Bernardino Valley College.

Definition of Terms

    Mag Card II Typewriter. Paula Cecil states in her word
processing textbook:

> In April 1973 IBM introduced the use of "memory" in word
> processing typewriters with its new Mag Card II. Previously,
> recording of typing had been made directly onto the magnetic
> tape. But on the Mag Card II the recording is made "in
> memory" from which it can be played back. If the operator
> wants to store the recording on a card, a button is depressed
> which records all information that was typed into memory.[4]

> Memory Typewriter. In the same textbook Ms. Cecil describes
the Memory Typewriter:

> In March 1974, another member of the IBM family was
> introduced: the Memory Typewriter. This unit has all the
> features of the Mag Card II except the use of cards, thereby
> eliminating long storage and merging applications. The Memory
> Typewriter has a 50-page memory storage and a 4000-character-
> per-page capacity for revising, which means a total memory
> capacity of 200,000 characters. This unit is sold mainly to
> small offices for production of regular correspondence, some
> stored letters or paragraphs, and short-turnaround revisions.[5]

---

[4]Paula B. Cecil. *Word Processing in the Modern Office*
(Menlo Park, California: Cummings Publishing Co., 1976), pp.
85-86.

[5]*Ibid.*, p. 87.

Example Page from the Body of a Report

Figure 1, Figure 2, and so forth). Tables may present quantitative or qualitative
data, and the data should be arranged so that the significance of different items
is obvious at a glance. Allow ample spacing between rows and columns; white
space helps lend order to the data being displayed. Turning a report sideways
to read a table or study a figure is often an inconvenience to the reader. If
possible, reduce the visual enough so that it conforms to the margins but

retains its readability. Again, computer software may do much of the work for you.

Headings. The main heading is centered in uppercase letters at the beginning of the report. As a rule, no other heading should be typed in uppercase letters. If the report has a subheading (a secondary heading that explains or amplifies the main heading), separate it from the main heading with a double space, and then use a triple space between the subheading and the body of the report. The subheading should be centered, and the initial letter of the main word or words should be uppercase.

First-order subheadings are preceded by a triple space and followed by a double space. Side headings should be placed flush left, underlined with main words capitalized, and have no terminal period (or other terminal punctuation).

Second-order subheadings or paragraph headings are preceded by a double space. They are indented to the paragraph point (usually only the first word is capitalized), underlined, and followed by a period. Begin typing the paragraph on the same line as the heading.

Footnotes/Endnotes. Footnotes have a number of purposes: They may confirm or add meaning to the author's statements; they may refer to other parts of the report that have a bearing on the topic discussed; they may make acknowledgments; or they sometimes make additional explanations of the content or terms used.

Footnotes are marked in the text by figures called *superscripts*. The superscript is typed one-half space above the line of writing where it occurs and immediately follows the word or statement to which the footnote applies.

Most software packages have a footnote feature that makes the spacing and arrangement of footnotes fast and easy.

Footnotes may be numbered in one of two ways: consecutively throughout the article or chapter; or consecutively on each page, beginning with the number 1 for each new page. Be uniform in numbering the references. In rough-draft work and thesis work, numbering footnotes consecutively on each page simplifies the typing. Then, if there is an addition, deletion, or correction, subsequent footnotes need not be renumbered.

When using footnotes, put the reference figure in the text following the passage to which the footnote refers.

Most word processing software will automatically position the footnote on the page in the appropriate place with the superscript number. Single-space footnotes, using a slightly smaller typeface than the text size, if possible.

Double-space between two footnotes that appear on one page. If there are many footnote references throughout the report, consider having them appear as endnotes that go (no surprise) at the end of the document or at the end of a section. Endnotes can make the report more readable, although they force the reader to flip back and forth to use the references.

For a footnote that refers to published material, give the same information that is given in a bibliographical reference plus the page number of the cited material. The following two examples follow the *Chicago Manual of Style.*

```
      ──────────
      ³Rosemary T. Fruehling and Constance K. Weaver, Electronic
      Office Procedures (New York: McGraw-Hill Book Company, 1987),
      p. 29.
```

Example of a Footnote: Book with Two Authors

```
      ──────────
      ⁴Stephen McMillen, "Secretarial Development: The Other Side of
      the Coin," The Secretary (June/July, 1987), p. 26.
```

Example of a Footnote: Magazine Article

If two or more footnotes are identical, you do not need to retype the details. Use one of the following abbreviations for Latin phrases:

Ibid., meaning "in the same place." Use *Ibid.* when referring to the work cited in the immediately preceding footnote, without an intervening footnote. This abbreviation may be used several times in succession. Here is an example:

```
      ──────────
      ⁵Ibid. (Use when the reference is identical to the one in the
      preceding footnote. )

      ⁶Ibid., p. 35. (Use when the reference is identical to the one
      in the preceding footnote but on a different page.)
```

Example of an "Ibid." Footnote

Loc. cit., meaning "in the place cited." Use *loc. cit.* with nonconsecutive footnotes that refer to the same material, the same work, and the same page or pages. Repeat the author's name before *loc. cit.*

Op. cit., meaning "in the work cited." Use *op. cit.* with nonconsecutive footnotes that refer to the same work, but to different pages. Repeat the author's last name. Here is an example:

```
_____
⁸Walshe, loc. cit.

⁹Baker, op. cit., p. 77.
```

Example of an "Op. cit." Footnote

Sometimes, footnotes appear at the end of a report on a separate sheet titled "Works Cited."

Header/footer. Once again, computers make this element easier to execute. A *header* is a line or two at the top of each page in the report or at the top of the first page of the report that contains identifying information. Usually, the header contains the topic or subtopic in that particular section of the report. It may also identify a specific section of the report by number. Following is an example of a header:

```
                    TypeRight Software Version 4.0
                    Chapter 1.3: Compatibility

     The program design of major software is copyrighted.
  Moreover, some programs are compatible with major manufacturer's
  equipment. However, caution must be taken as to [...]
```

Example of a Header

A *footer,* located at the bottom of a page, also has identifying information. Generally, it contains the date of the report, page number, and other data. Following is an example of a footer:

```
     Recommendation:     Specifications must be drafted by the end of
                         the third quarter. The feasibilitiy study will
                         cost $30,000.

     September 1, 200_                              Confidential
```

Example of a Footer

Bibliography and Appendices

A *bibliography* includes the references used in the preparation of the report. Arrange it alphabetically by authors' last names. When listing books, copy the information from the title page, rather than from the outside cover. When listing references from periodicals, take the title from the article itself.

Depending on the content of some reports and the company's policy, items in the bibliography may be numbered in order of their appearance in the report. Sometimes, you may be asked to use abbreviated (shortened) forms of citations in your draft copy and complete forms in the final copy.

Each reference lists the surname of the author, followed by given name or initials, the title of the work, the publisher, the place of publication, and the date of publication. When using references from periodicals, you may include such identifying information as volume and page numbers. Observe these rules:

- Use italics for the titles of books and magazines.

- Enclose the titles of magazine articles in quotation marks.

- Type the author's initials after the surname. If some references use a full name and others only initials, be consistent, particularly when the references come close together. Usually, it is better to use the full name.

- If the author has written some books alone and collaborated with other authors on other projects, list first those books the author wrote alone.

- If the publication has more than three authors, list the publication under the name of the first mentioned author and then use the words "and others" or *et al.*

- If the publication is out of print, indicate this in parentheses following the reference.

- Volume numbers of periodicals are written with Arabic numerals.

- To make the author's name stand out, type the first line of the entry at the left margin and indent all other lines.

- If there are many sources of reference material, classify them according to books, periodicals, pamphlets, or other media.

- When two or more books by the same author are listed in succession, instead of retyping the author's name each time, simply use a solid line of five underscores followed by a comma. See the example on the opposite page.

References. Only citations used or referred to in the report are listed in the bibliography. Some reports provide a listing of suggested or recommended readings. These are separate from the bibliography and should be noted as

Popyk, Marilyn K., *Word Processing: Essential Concepts,* New York: McGraw-Hill Book Company, 1983.

———, *Word Processing and Information Systems: A Practical Approach to Concepts,* New York: McGraw-Hill Book Company, 1986.

Example of Two Sequential Books by the Same Author in a Bibliography

such. In other words, the suggested or recommended readings (books, magazines, films, and so on) are neither cited nor used in the preparation of the report; they are intended for further study or review only.

There are a number of style manuals that can be used in preparing a bibliography (or other parts of a report). Whatever manual you choose, use it properly: consistency, clarity, and common sense must prevail. See the example of one type of bibliography on the next page.

Appendix. Material supportive to the report should be placed in a supplementary section called an appendix. It should follow the bibliography. Examples of items placed in the appendix are copies of questionnaires, maps, lists, tables, sample forms and letters, and detailed summaries of data, notes, tables, a glossary of terms, and any other material that might be considered supplementary to the text itself.

The appendix may be preceded by an introductory page entitled APPENDIX, typed in all uppercase letters, and centered both horizontally and vertically. This page may also include a list of the items included in the appendix. If a list is included, both the title and the list are centered vertically, or the title may be placed two inches from the top of the paper with the listing beginning a triple space below the title. When more than one item is appended, each item should be numbered or lettered and placed under a separate heading, such as Appendix A, Appendix B, and so on. If you have more than 26 appendices, begin the 27th by doubling the letter as AA, BB, CC, and so forth.

If an appendix is rather lengthy and bulky, label it "Enclosure" and attach it after the last appendix. If there is only one appendix, no letter or number is necessary. The word "Appendix" is sufficient. Triple-space and begin the text of that single appendix.

In cases in which there are only one or two items to follow the end of a report, they may be labeled as "attachments." A sample questionnaire at the end of a survey is a good example of an item that could be called an attachment. Although there are no formal rules for naming attachments, the term may be considered appropriate for material supplementary to the text in a letter or report. It is not appropriate for anything more formal, such as a monograph or book.

B I B L I O G R A P H Y

<u>Books</u>

Fruehling, Rosemary T., and Weaver, Constance K. *Electronic Office Procedures*. New York: McGraw-Hill Book Co., 1987. 544 pp.

Keene, Michael L. *Effective Professional Writing*. Lexington, MA: D.C. Heath and Co., 1987. 450 pp.

Popyk, Marilyn K. *Word Processing and Information Systems: A Practical Approach to Concepts*. New York: McGraw-Hill Book Co., 1983. 336 pp.

<u>Journals</u>

Hart, M.B. "Status of OS in 29 Texas Companies (With Implications for OS Curricula)," *Office Systems Research Journal*. (1986).

McEntee, A. "Determining Core Competencies Necessary for Success in the Automated Office," *Journal of the Business Education Association of New York*. (1985).

Munter, M. "Using the Computer in Business Communication Courses," *The Journal of Business Communication*. (1986).

<u>Unpublished Work</u>

Xavier, Chris. "Office Needs" (Assessment Criteria, Star Associations, 1988), "Mimeographed."

Example of a Bibliography

Short Reports

Somewhere between the informality of a memo and the large-scale business or technical report described earlier lies a document commonly referred to as a *short report*. Very often an update between fewer people than might receive a full-blown business report, a short report has an objective to convey certain information less formally, and in fewer than four or five pages.

TECHNICAL REPORTS

Preparing reports for engineers, chemists, mathematicians, scientists, and other professionals often involves what used to be called "technical typing."

Today's word processing software has eased the burden of preparing such reports a bit, but the task still requires a mastery of such seldom-used skills as equation typing. And because the various disciplines demand an understanding of uncommon symbols and terminology, accuracy in report preparation becomes more important than speed.

Check the help manual for your word processing software. It will tell you what special typing rules you can set up to help you prepare technical documents. Even if you aren't a word processing whiz, here are a few guidelines that may help you make some headway:

- It is essential to double-space a technical report to accommodate the superscripts and subscripts required by many equations. Most word processing software can let even the casual keyboarder enter these symbols.

- Check your computer application's help menu to find out where to find mathematical symbols or Greek letters that are often necessary in a technical document.

- As a rule, leave a space before and after the arithmetical operational symbols: $=, +, -, \div, \times$. However, if the symbol is used adjectivally (-3, for example), there should be no space between the minus sign and the 3.

- Multiplication is expressed by using the "$\times$" or a centered period ($4 \cdot 6$), or by parentheses enclosing an expression to be multiplied. Often, the multiplication sign is omitted and the letters are typed together, as ab. Thus, in the equation $7ad(s - y) = mx$, there is no space between d and the opening parenthesis, but there is a space before and after the equal sign and the minus sign.

- Type fractions as follows: If the equation is short, the fraction may be part of the running text and is typed in the shilling style, which looks like this: 4/5. If you use mixed numbers, put a space between the whole number and the shilling fraction (for example, 43 5/6).

continues

TECHNICAL REPORTS *continued*

■ Equations are numbered consecutively throughout a report to make it easy to refer to any equation in the text. Each equation number is put in parentheses at the right margin. When making reference to these equation numbers, abbreviate equation to "Eq." Your reference will look like this: (Eq. 5).

Usually punctuation is not used with equations. If your author requests punctuation in equations, observe these rules:

■ Consider each equation as a clause of a complex sentence, and follow it with either a comma or semicolon.

■ If the equation concludes the sentence, a period follows it.

■ If you have a series of equations, introduce them by a colon in the line preceding the equations.

Sometimes, equations are too long for one line and must be placed on several lines. Break them before the equal sign when possible. Another good place to divide an equation is before any one of the operational signs ($+$, $-$, $\times$, $\div$). You may also divide it between fractions, or after brackets and parentheses. Do not put part of an equation on one page and the rest of it on the next page.

Some authors help their typists to read the symbols in an equation by writing all lowercase symbols and printing uppercase symbols. It may also be helpful to draft all the equations in the report before typing. Let the author check your arrangement of the equations. If the author has no objection, then you are ready to do the finished report and can proceed with confidence that the material is arranged in the very best form.

Very often, the structure of the short report is determined by the needs of the recipient. It might be delivered with some regularity (monthly, for example), and always follow a prescribed format.

In the content, there's less reliance on providing every detail and more action orientation. Some recipients prefer that the short reports they receive begin with the conclusion, and then paint the supporting background with broad strokes. Typically, the short or informal report answers the classic five Ws (who, what, when, where, why), and also tells how. If charts, figures, or other data are required, they are typically handled as attachments—referred to less formally in the body of the report.

VISUAL AIDS

Visual aids are any display materials in business reports, formal presentations, or other documents circulated to people both in and out of the company. They often present an easy way to communicate complicated sales data or growth numbers. Today's software programs make it much easier to not only create relevant and attractive graphs and charts, but to also share them between programs. It is easier to create a graph or chart in a spreadsheet program, include it in the written report, add captions and text, and then include the new graphic in the slide presentation that will accompany the report. With a little judicious use of color printing or copying—maybe a page or two—visuals can greatly increase the professional appearance of information. From photos scanned in and added to reports, to animated bullet points in a slide presentation, the office professional can help create effective visuals for reports or presentations.

One of the easiest ways to manipulate data or information is in spreadsheet or database programs, such as Microsoft Excel or Access. Using features like graphs, charts, and pivot tables gives you many ways to present the same data in different formats.

For example, let's say you have a spreadsheet in Microsoft Excel 97 with the following data in four different columns:

Customer	Product	Order Date	Amount of Order

From this data, you could reorganize information by using pivot tables to display a table organized by product, by ascending or descending dollar amounts, or by order dates. Simply go to the data menu and click on the pivot table feature.

Some guidelines for pivot table creation are as follows:

- Label the columns. Because pivot tables use column labels to cross-tabulate data, you can summarize data by customer, product, or amount of order.

- Use one worksheet row for each record. Pivot tables summarize data stored in rows.

- Use date format for any column with dates. See the format menu and date category to select the type of date display you want.

In addition, you can display the data graphically as either a bar chart, column, pie chart, or scatter diagram by clicking on the Excel Chart Wizard. Even stock charts are easy to create.

Other business-strength features worth exploring are sales forecasts created by predicting future sales based on the results of recent months, determining sales trends and predicting sales trends when you have a certain number of months of known years, and future assumptions you build into a formula. Again, you can chart a trend line by using the Excel Chart Wizard. One of the secrets of being a valued office professional is to get comfortable with the advanced features of the word processing and database programs in your office.

Tables and charts aren't static illustrations any more, either. If your team is giving a report in a formal presentation, you can take the same tables and charts used in the report, import them into the PowerPoint program, and create color slides with several clicks of the mouse or keyboard commands. Learning how to do this adds value to your skills in any professional setting. And it's fairly easy to accomplish: All it takes is time and effort. But the payoff is worth it.

In general, visuals are used to enhance the aesthetics of the page, clarify a key point in the text, add emphasis to the subject, arouse the reader's interest, simplify the explanation of technical or other complex subjects, and make the treatment of the subject stand out from similar materials. For example, if you are preparing a divisional report for a headquarters presentation with many other division heads, or if you are preparing a request for funds for a group of investors with other entrepreneurs, visual aids can add a lot to the absorption and interest level of the audience.

TYPES OF VISUALS

The type of visual to use depends on the intended purpose of the visual, the audience, the subject, the type of paper to be used, and the printing process to be used for reproduction.

Basically, there are two types of visuals: pictorial, and numerical or other data. Pictorials include photographs, figures, and illustrations. Numerical data include tables, charts, and graphs.

Choosing a Chart Style

Today's software programs do everything from basic pie charts to full-blown 3-D animated slide shows. We may not all be professional designers, but by following a few guidelines, we all can produce a professional-looking presentation.

As you look at a set of raw numbers and wonder whether they'd be best shown as a pie chart, line graph, or stacked bar chart, remember that choosing the appropriate style is probably the single hardest part of creating a chart.

The three basic styles for charts are Pie, Bar, and Line. More sophisticated styles—such as Histogram, Dual Y-Axis, or High/Low/Close—are just hybrids of the basics. When selecting a chart style, ask yourself what message you are trying to convey and to whom. Then, choose the simplest style that will most effectively communicate this message.

The good news is that most software programs allow you to change styles after you have created the chart without having to re-key the data. For example, the Chart Wizard feature of Microsoft Word allows you to create many different looks at the same data, as mentioned previously. In addition, you can reorganize the data in a spreadsheet by columns. Take advantage of this feature to "try on" different styles; just be sure to save the chart "as is" before moving to the next style. Most programs also allow you to save the chart and import it into another program such as a word processing program.

Pie Charts

Pie charts are the simplest of all. From fourth grade on, most of us can easily "read" a pie chart. Therefore, it's most effective when illustrating a simple concept.

Pie charts are used to compare parts to a whole or percentages of a whole. The pieces of pie, or wedges, are the parts; the entire pie is the whole. You can compare the pieces to each other, and to the sum of the pieces.

Use a pie chart when your data sets add up to a meaningful number or whole—to compare regional sales to each other and to the national total, for example.

When choosing pie charts, be sure that the color selection has enough contrast so that the different colored segments are readable. Also be careful about contrasting type to the colors selected if the type will appear beside the segments on anything other than white paper, or if the legends will appear on top of the colors in the segments themselves.

If the pie chart is in black and white, then check to make sure that the shading, textures, or crosshatching (or whatever you have available in your individual software bundle) are readable. The best way to check for readability is to print the chart because what you see on the screen is not necessarily the same thing you get on paper.

Bar Charts

Bar charts are the most popular chart style in business use, perhaps because the bar has a substantial feel, lending a sense of weight or importance to the presentation.

Single bar charts show single factors, such as sales or expenses, changing over equal time periods such as months, quarters, or years. As a variation, cluster bar charts can display multiple factors side by side, also over equal time periods.

Stacked bar charts, in which the multiple factors are placed on top of each other, are best used to show how parts of a whole change over equal time periods, such as quarterly sales broken out by region. Like the pie chart, use the stacked bar chart only when your parts add up to a meaningful whole.

Here's a little practical advice about bar charts: Stacked charts are a simple device for overlaying multiple factors in a single illustration, but they can be hard to read when using different colors. In black and white, the various shadings must be high-contrast to show up well. Also, if the differences in the factors are not significant they might be almost imperceptible to the reader and can minimize the impact of your information. Pie charts are often a better choice in this situation.

Line Charts

Line charts are useful to compare trends over time, particularly when dramatic changes have taken place. If your data turns out to be a boring flat line, adjust the scaling of the Y-axis by reducing the minimum or maximum value settings, or choose a completely different chart style.

You may choose a straight line to connect each data point (also known as a "zigzag" or "Alpine" line); a trend line, which is drawn straight through the average of data points; or a curved line, which draws a smooth curving line through the average of the data points.

THE FOUR Cs OF CHART DESIGN

Once you've chosen the style that best conveys your message, your next consideration is designing the chart itself. Keep the chart as simple as possible. If a design element, such as a grid or 3-D effect, does not enhance the message, get rid of it!

The following guidelines, which we call the "Four Cs of Chart Design," will help you make design decisions. You should be concise, conservative, consistent, and careful!

Be Concise

Keep your data and text simple and clear. Avoid using more than five sets of data in any chart. To reduce the number of data sets, look for ways to consolidate: Instead of 12 months, try four quarters; instead of 50 states, try four geographical regions.

In a text chart, pretend that each word costs $50 and edit accordingly. Eliminate articles and prepositions whenever possible.

Be Conservative

Use colors, fonts, and special effects sparingly. Just because you can use 12 different fonts in a single chart doesn't mean you should; you want to avoid the appearance of a "ransom note" or an explosion in a font factory.

When choosing colors and patterns, aim for strong contrast between colors and patterns so that viewers can readily distinguish one series from the next. Watch out for colors or patterns that conflict or create optical illusions.

Be Consistent

Use uniform patterns, colors, formats, and fonts throughout an entire presentation. You may even want to unify the look of all corporate presentations across departments.

In text charts, particularly in bulleted lists, check that grammar and phrasing are consistent. For example, don't put "Running," "Jumping," and "Swim" at the start of three bullets. The parallel structure of bulleted lists emphasizes any discrepancies in verb tense and voice or in noun pluralization.

A consistent format helps viewers to understand more quickly and easily; they don't have to waste time trying to figure out different chart formats.

If you are designing charts that will go into a slide or other presentation program, think about which colors will look best and be most readable and professional looking. Don't make the callouts yellow or pink.

Be Careful

Nothing is more embarrassing than to see a mistake magnified 100 times on the boardroom projection screen! Check your work carefully. Use your spell checker, then proofread a hard copy as well. Make sure that all data points are labeled correctly. Verify that percentage amounts add up to 100; sometimes, due to mathematical rounding, the percentages may be slightly off, adding up to 99 or 101. If this is the case, simply "nudge" your data a bit so that it adds up to 100—or use an asterisk to explain at the bottom.

PRESENTATIONS

Chances are that, as an office professional, you won't often have to get up in front of the board of executives and make a formal presentation. However, there are times when it might be necessary for you to address a group or other members of your team or office. Whatever the circumstances, whether explaining that your boss will be delayed and the agenda has been rearranged, or expressing your opinion in a staff meeting, it is always best to present yourself in the most organized and professional manner possible.

What are the secrets of speaking effectively before a group, whether delivering a formal speech or just standing up in a committee meeting "to say a few words"? Dale Carnegie, who founded an entire school of public speaking, thought the secrets involved making our listeners like us. He offered 12 specific points on ways to achieve this end.

- *If you're honored to speak before an audience, say so.* And say why. Even if a group is unimportant, the mere invitation to speak before it is a compliment. If the group is large or in some way important to you, the compliment and the honor are that much greater.

- *Compliment your listeners in turn.* Talk about the good works the group does or the fascinating reason that brings its members together. If you're new to the group and to the area, find out a few facts about both and work these into your speech. Personalizing your speech shows your listeners you know who they are—and you like them. They'll be ready to like you back.

- *Mention a few listeners by name.* This further personalization is a highly effective move, but to be successful it must be worked into your speech at logical and sincere moments. "When Mr. Jones first asked me to speak . . ."; "When Mrs. Rivera was showing me the grounds this morning. . . ." The technique also must be used sparingly because it would be awkward to try to mention every single member of the audience.

- *Be humble.* Your listeners already know your abilities—that's why they asked you to speak. If you downplay these abilities, your listeners will eagerly build you up in their own minds.

- *Say "we" instead of "you."* To get listeners on your side, it's better to join them rather than to preach or to be condescending. "If we could all pull together on this project" sounds more inviting than "If you could all pull together on this project."

- *Let both your face and your voice smile and be friendly.* Too harsh or scolding an expression—even if you have some bad news to impart during the speech—will turn listeners off. Keep your tone mild.

- *Appeal to your listeners' self-interests.* What are their problems? How can you help their work be easier, faster, or cheaper? How can you help them stop worrying or expand their business? What do they want to hear? If you have a set subject on which you're going to talk, meet a few group members ahead of time to see where their concerns are. With a little juggling, you can connect their interests to your own so that your topic will appeal to their self-interests.

- *Have a good time talking.* Be enthusiastic about your subject and you will sweep your listeners up into the emotion. When you enjoy yourself, they will enjoy themselves and will count your speech a great success.

- *Don't apologize.* Apologize for nothing except being late, which is common courtesy. If you're not ready for your speech, for example, apologizing will only antagonize your audience, making it seem as if you thought little enough of them not to prepare ahead of time. It's better to simply forge ahead. Even when apologies don't antagonize the listeners, they make you seem unsure of yourself. You may be, in truth, but why make it more noticeable by pointing it out?

- *Appeal to your listeners' better emotions.* Even supposedly cynical people respond to what's good in the world: it's what they want for themselves and their families. You needn't try to gush emotion at every turn of phrase. Just remember that what moves and inspires you will probably move and inspire your audience.

- *Welcome criticism.* If your message is controversial or apt to upset people, in your speech invite possible critics to later offer you suggestions. If you think you're ill-spoken, acknowledge it, then say, "But it's my message, not my style, that's important."

- *Speak with sincerity and honesty.* An eloquent speaking ability only impresses listeners in the very beginning. What they'll take home with them is your character, your integrity, and your own belief in the subject.

PRESENTATION AND GRAPHICS SOFTWARE

Chances are that if your boss or team has been preparing a lengthy report or document, someone is going to have to give a formal presentation. Given the data that needs to be explained, and given the fact that nothing is more boring than a person standing motionless at the podium while he or she reads, you will probably want to prepare visual aids.

Computers to the rescue again. Presentation software gives most computer-literate offices the capability to create at least passable charts and graphics. These can be output as paper documents, of course, but they also can be made into projectable slides or overheads, saved for display on other computer screens, or transmitted electronically to other sites.

Resist temptation. Relatively easy to master presentation desktopping skills, coupled with clip art packages loaded with tens of thousands of illustrations and a palette more colorful than any rainbow, provide a strong temptation to create presentation graphics that rival the ceiling of the Sistine Chapel. But even if you have the skill of Michelangelo, do not use it here.

Here are some rules of thumb:

- A good highway billboard has no more than six words. Present one idea on each visual and choose your words carefully. It's easier to read short bullet points than long lines of text.

- Keep the text of a slide or screen to a maximum of six lines of text, with no more than six words per line.

- Use graphics to support main ideas and crucial facts. Choose a graphic theme. Use it consistently. Try using charts for comparison information.

- Adjust your type. Choose one or two classic faces that are easy to read. All uppercase can be difficult to read; use uppercase and lowercase. Save the all uppercase to emphasize one word or concept.

■ Don't sweat the punctuation. You're grouping information visually, so let good design serve as punctuation. Bullet points can help.

WEB PAGES

Although you can learn more about the World Wide Web in Chapter 5, for the purposes of office documents, you should know that the Web is a computer network that allows you to view documents by using a browser such as Internet Explorer or Netscape Communicator. A Web page is simply a document that may contain text and graphics.

Nowadays, the Internet, and intranets or internal Web sites are fairly common. Although most companies today have at least a rudimentary site up and running, many companies have e-commerce or actual business transactions taking place on their sites. As we move into the next decade, more and more companies will disseminate more and more information—such as regular company updates, bulletins, and HR-type messages over their intranets. In some areas like sales, the regular output of the department will be put up on the company intranet for distribution to all departments. As the office professional, you may be the one preparing this information for the Web or even posting the document. Very active companies post Web pages daily (customer service, warehouse). Some departments may post weekly (human resources), monthly (sales), or quarterly (finance).

While building a simple Web page may seem like an intimidating task, it's incredibly simple to prepare a document to go on the Web—usually it's as simple as changing the way you save it. In Microsoft Word, for example, click the File menu and you'll see the command Save as HTML. (HTML is the language that browsers use to "read" the document on the Web.) In the Edit menu, you can place a portion of a document (or all of it) as a hyperlink in another document, so the reader can refer to it by simply clicking on the link retrieving the related text. This helps readers who may want more information about a particular term or concept they are reading about in a Web document. They simply click on the term or hyperlinked word, and jump to another hyperlinked document with more detailed information.

Many word processing programs, such as Microsoft Word, give users the option to save a document as a Web page. Most office packages now offer a Web page building program such as FrontPage or Publisher. Many companies that use the Web for internal documents might have an internal application for converting the file. The important thing is not to be mystified or afraid of using technology to save, convert, and work with documents. Take the time to learn a technique that works for you, the office pro, on your computer with the software at hand. If your company is just launching a Web site or a Web page, be sure to recommend that you and your department (the whole company, for that matter) get upgraded software to handle Web documents easily.

COMPANY NEWSLETTERS

Newsletters are an ideal way to establish your company as an expert in its field, remind clients of various products or services, and introduce the company to potential new clients. Newsletters are very useful within large companies to keep employees informed about what's going on inside the company, to improve morale, and to pass along things like motivational messages or recognition for a job well done.

Service businesses are a natural for newsletters, especially businesses that may be visited only once or twice a year. Lawyers and accountants can spotlight tax and legal issues that clients may not otherwise be aware of. Physicians can distribute a profile of a new medicine or describe an illness, such as the symptoms of a stroke. Dentists can report new advancements in "painless" or cosmetic dentistry.

No matter what the focus of your company—services or products—a newsletter should also contain personalized news about employees or community announcements that may affect workers. Maybe one of the company sales reps is involved in community service or has qualified for a national award, or the municipality may have instituted special emergency regulations to take effect in the event of a snowstorm. These are little extras that give the "house organ," as organizational newsletters are called, a unique look. It gives employees a reason to read the newsletters and increases the editor's visibility inside the company.

The editor of the newsletter will decide what the newsletter should cover, the frequency of publication, and the distribution list. However, the office professionals will most likely be in charge of producing it. As such, they have many duties and responsibilities. Here are some general tips and suggestions for handling newsletter production like a seasoned hand:

- Verify all grammar and spelling. Although this sounds simple, even the best spelling and grammar features of software programs won't cover such things as misuse of properly spelled words like "there" for "their," completely wrong words spelled right in the middle of a sentence, floating letters, and other chaff that just won't be picked up unless you proofread the material yourself.

- Don't use too many fancy fonts or clip art. If your business has a formal, all-business atmosphere, keep it professional, clean, and simple. Use a roman typeface for text and a sans-serif or display type for headings and callouts. If you work at a funky new age or neo-tech company, you can pull out all the stops and experiment. But this is generally better left to professional graphics people. Try getting friendly with them and you'll get some good advice based on experience. Resist the temptation to use more than a couple or three fonts per page or document.

- Use a standard paper size that can be folded into a business envelope. Legal-size paper may be an attractive size to use when you want the newsletter to stand out in a pile on someone's desk, but it requires a custom fold or a larger size envelope to stuff and mail.

- Provide room for an address label if you don't plan to mail the issues in an envelope. Check with the post office regarding requirements. By using heavier paper stock, such as 50-pound bright white, a simple fold in half once and then in half again, and the application of a stamp gets the newsletter in the mail as a self-mailer. This saves the company money in envelopes and insertion charges. And for small mailings you do yourself, it saves you time and labor.

- Keep a stack of current issues in your waiting room or reception lobby. It's a good public relations vehicle for new employees and applicants.

- Make sure that copies of back issues with articles by the boss or on topics relevant to the client are handed to the client or are on the reception area table.

- Find out who will receive the newsletter. Will it be employees only? Current and former clients and customers? Members of boards, committees, and organizations you and the boss attend? Referral sources? Suggest to the editor that topics of interest to the constituent readers be featured in future issues.

- Keep a file of sample publications from other companies. Identify what you like about them, and see if it's possible to incorporate some of their best features into your own newsletter.

You get what you pay for. Simply put, professionals get the most professional results. True, desktop publishing makes attractive documents possible, but it's no substitute for the polished skills of a graphic artist. You may find that an amateur design doesn't look as good or pack the wallop you expect or need.

Most of what's provided here is a quick and proven formula for producing a professional looking standard newsletter for the business. If you are trying to produce a one-of-a-kind look or using more than two colors it's a good idea to get some advice from a graphics professional. Do not be tempted to spend thousands of dollars on fancy hardware and software that you have no familiarity with unless you are the intrepid tinkerer who likes to go it alone and you have the time to do so.

FOR MORE INFORMATION

If you can't find what you need in this chapter, you may need to expand your search.

- For more information on preparing formal business reports, check your local library or bookstore in the reference section for resources.

- For more information on creating visuals using software applications, check your local library or bookstore in the computer book section. Books are available for any user level.

- For more information on style specifics, consult the Grammar and Punctuation Guide at the back of this book.

- For more information on formal presentations, check the library or bookstore in the business communications section.

3

OFFICE EQUIPMENT AND SUPPLIES

◆

Equipment and supplies encompass the wide variety of items needed in the day-to-day running of an office—items that the office professional is often responsible for choosing, buying, and keeping in stock. The umbrella term "equipment and supplies" includes everything: the pencils and scratch pads at everyone's desk, the business cards a salesperson hands out at a trade exhibit, and the phone system that links your company with customers halfway around the world.

The selection of equipment and supplies involves a great deal more than product demonstrations and price comparisons, especially at the high-tech, high-cost end of the spectrum. In a large organization, the office professional's involvement in assessing the organization's needs likely will include determining the type of work done, assessing the ease of use of equipment or software, listing any special features required, recording functions currently being used, and identifying desired functions. On the other hand, the office professional in a small company might participate directly in the processes of equipment selection, purchasing, and maintenance because he or she is probably the person most knowledgeable about what is needed.

EQUIPMENT SELECTION

Before selecting high-end office equipment (such as phone systems, computers, copiers, and so on), a careful analysis of the company's needs should be performed: What does the company want to do? Who will be doing it? How easy will it be to do? What technical and informational support will the user have? After this analysis is reviewed and a piece of equipment is selected, there's another question to address: Should the piece be leased or bought outright? This section discusses advantages and disadvantages of each option.

This overview concludes with a look at the equipment basics found in most offices and those pieces that are most likely to fall under the responsibility of the office professional when a new item must be selected.

NEEDS ANALYSIS

Before any piece of equipment is purchased, an analysis of the office or company needs should consider the expected applications of the new equipment, its users, and its ease of use. For the users' sake, a demonstration is crucial, as is an assurance of the level of documentation, instruction, and support services that come with the equipment. With today's constantly changing technology, it is also important to know whether a piece of equipment is versatile and whether it can be upgraded.

Using a high-end copier as an example, each of these elements will be considered in the following sections.

Applications

When considering the purchase, first address the equipment's applications. Put simply, what do you want the copier to do? Of course, you want it to make multiple-page copies for individual employee use, but what else? To make copies of a special fifty-page report for internal distribution? To provide an alternative to an outside printer for a small-run customer newsletter? Consider these special uses as well as the more frequent ones.

After determining the general applications, examine specific needs. What features are required? Just black-and-white copying? Photographic color copying? Two-sided enlarged or reduced copies? Simple collating? Folding, inserting into covers, and stapling? What level of monthly volume is the copier designed for? Can the machine be programmed to do lengthy jobs after-hours to prevent tie-ups during the day? Can it be linked to PCs for remote programming? Samples of actual or anticipated applications should be carefully analyzed to determine the features needed.

Still other considerations must be addressed. Does it make sense to have a multifunction machine that incorporates scanning, faxing, and so on besides its copying capability? If the copier has fax capability, does it have an anti-junk-mail filter for incoming faxes? Does it have storage memory? Can it physically manipulate the image?

Is security an issue? What about expensive unauthorized use? Can the copier be programmed to accept passwords? Can it diagnose its own problems? Can it be fixed from the manufacturer's remote location via modem?

Users

Think about who will use the equipment (in this case, the copier). How many individual users will share it? How many departments? Can it be shared by departments, or will each department require its own? Does one department have less need for a special features machine? Would that department be better served by buying a second small machine that handles only basic black-and-white copies?

Ease of Use

Many copiers use icons or pictures to represent the task to be performed. Users make choices by touching a control panel to change the number of copies, the size of the reproduced image, the darkness or lightness, and so on. Similarly, multifunction machines should quickly switch from one use to another, and each function's special features should be clearly labeled.

Loading paper trays and clearing jams also should be easily accomplished by all users, reducing the need to call on the office professional for help. Additional tasks that are usually performed by the office professional, such as changing toner cartridges, should be simply and neatly accomplished.

Demonstration

Although a vendor demonstration will highlight the good features of the piece of equipment being sold, there are a few points to remember. Because demonstrations are done by experienced personnel who know the product well, features that may be difficult to use sometimes only *look* as if they are very simple. Also, features that are important to you might not even be part of the demonstration. Make sure that the product demonstration is done with the application of the user in mind.

Again, let's use the example of the copier. Actual jobs should be performed—on both the copiers and the multifunction machines. Be sure to include the most complex combinations of functions. These functions should be tried by one or more people other than the office professionals who are familiar with the department or company's copying needs. Some vendors also might arrange for an in-house trial period of a piece of equipment—a "free trial" or a brief rental period. This tryout provides the best test because it happens under actual user conditions.

For both demonstrations and trial periods, the machine should be the exact make and model as the one being considered for purchase.

Documentation and Support

Documentation and support are primary areas of concern, especially for novice users and for users of more sophisticated pieces of equipment such as telephone systems, multifunction copiers, and computers. Equipment should come with detailed setup instructions, as in a tutorial disk. No matter which pieces are selected, the instruction manuals should be well organized and clearly written for beginners, not veteran users or technicians.

For computer users, templates that fit over the keyboard and list the functions performed by various keys or combinations can offer great help. An extensive selection of "how-to" books on PCs, operating systems, and software packages also can help simplify use.

For all kinds of equipment and software, ask if the company has a toll-free number to call with questions, at least for an initial period. In general, the level of support provided is greater with larger purchases; a desktop shredder, for example, comes with less support than an industrial-quality shredder. The level of support is also greater for a large company buying in quantity. Often a computer or office superstore also can provide more guidance than a mail-order house.

Vendors who provide training on the higher-end pieces generally train a certain number of employees to use the equipment. After the initial training, vendors usually charge a fee for each additional person trained. Some types of training—particularly for PCs on large systems—must be provided for newly hired, upgraded, and transferred personnel. Although an in-house training department might be appropriate for a large corporation, a smaller company might bring a trainer in-house. Individual users then might have to attend a seminar or course, or purchase an audiovisual training package.

Versatility and Upgradability

A major concern when purchasing equipment and software is the continual advances in technology. While purchases should include the needs of the foreseeable future, overbuying now can be much more expensive than upgrading later, especially as the cost of technology keeps dropping. Upgrades for computer hardware and software are familiar to everyone, but these are not the only products that can be upgraded. In analyzing the copier, for example, do you foresee the possibility that the company computers might become networked? In that case, can the copier be upgraded later to add network printing? Or can it be upgraded to scan to the network, individual PC, or e-mail? Ask about a machine's future capabilities as well as its current ones.

Other Considerations

Other important considerations exist for all types of equipment: guaranties, warranties, responsibility for repairs, extended warranties, and so on. In short, what happens when a problem occurs with the functioning of the equipment? What is covered under the original guaranty, by whom, and for how long a period? Is a maintenance contract available through the vendor? Is the repair provided by the vendor, or is it contracted to a third party? If the equipment is purchased from a computer store, does it have to be brought in for repair? Is on-site service available? Is a substitute available while the equipment is being repaired? All questions should be answered before any purchase takes place.

OFFICE EQUIPMENT LEASES

Years ago, most office equipment was bought as a matter of routine. Now, the office professional with purchasing duties faces an additional choice: to buy or lease? Basically, a lease is a rental agreement for a limited period of time. An estimated 80 percent of all companies now lease some, if not all, of their equipment because a lease offers the following distinct advantages:

- *A short-term lease is ideal for ever-changing technology.* This is perhaps the single most important reason for leasing pieces of equipment such as computers, which quickly become obsolete.

- *Repairs and servicing are usually covered by the agreement.* Except for routine wear and tear, major problems are not the company's responsibility. What constitutes wear and tear, however, should be spelled out.

- *Tax advantages make leasing very attractive.* Instead of averaging tax deductions for the cost of the item over what current tax law says is the life of the item, the company can deduct the lease payments in full as they are made.

On the other hand, leasing carries the following *disadvantages:*

■ *Poor terms.* The company could get locked into a lease with unfavorable terms, or one that is too long for what the company later discovers is its true needs.

■ *More costly than buying.* The lease could end up being as or more expensive than ownership over the full term of the lease. If the company decides to buy the item at the end of the term, the total of all lease payments plus the final purchase price almost always costs more than buying the piece in the beginning.

■ *No extras.* The lease may not include such expected items as maintenance, repairs, insurance, and so on.

■ *Too long.* If the lease extends beyond the life of the item, the company is forced to essentially pay rental money on outdated equipment. If the company breaks the lease to update its equipment, it may have to pay an early-termination penalty.

■ *Poor quality.* The rental equipment is not brand-new, as expected. Although these disadvantages do not apply to the best leases (which is why lease arrangements are so popular), the office professional should approach leasing with the idea that it has as many, if not more, risks as buying.

As with all purchasing deals, the office professional should specify to the vendors what the company wants: Be sure to establish the type and frequency of equipment servicing, get written bids from several vendors, make sure that contracts spell out details of maintenance and repair, try to ensure that equipment can be upgraded without breaking the old lease (upgrading won't be necessary for many items), and hand over the final negotiated contract for legal approval.

EQUIPMENT BASICS

Whether a company is a five-person ad agency, a factory employing hundreds of shift workers, or a national financial firm with thousands of stockbrokers, certain pieces of equipment are basic to every office.

TELEPHONES AND TELEPHONE SYSTEMS

Telephones have always been critical to a company's profitability because they are major sources of client contact. Now, those same lines are the heart of most of today's business communications systems because they send and receive voice, video, and data—both within a company's own boundaries and out to the world. The lone telecommuter working at midnight, the company's internal network, faxes to customers, and the company Web site handling hundreds of hits a day are all part of what was once the plain old telephone.

Features and Accessories

The telephone itself may have several features: speed dialing, last number recall, memory keys for frequently called numbers, caller ID, a built-in modem jack, a speakerphone, and an indicator light to show that a message is waiting. In a standard telephone, the message is transmitted through underground and above-ground phone wires.

Headsets. If the office professional or other employees spend long periods of time on the phone (especially while doing other tasks), a telephone headset is a smart investment. The newest models are very small and lightweight, help ease neck cramps, and leave hands free to use the keyboard, search files, and so on. Headsets must be compatible with the company's current phone system.

Cellular phones. Though once reserved for the salesperson on the road, cell phones are now in use everywhere and by everyone, from the busy manager who's in touch with the office while roaming the plant floor, to the technician who returns calls while on another job site.

When trying to decide on a cell phone, the confusing terminology may appear to be written by the same demons who write the tax laws. Part of the problem is common usage of the terms *cell phone* and *wireless phone* to refer to the same thing, as well as advancing and overlapping technology. Basically, cellular phones operate like a radio station, sending and receiving signals from a transmitter that covers a certain geographic location called a *cell*. The signal is transferred from cell to cell as the caller moves. Wireless phones operate like cellular phones, but instead of using radio signals and analog technology, they use high-frequency microwaves and digital technology. Although they can be cheaper to use, wireless phones are subject to interference from weather and terrain (in flat-lying regions, interference is not a problem). Some phones combine the two technologies and use both radio and microwaves.

Because the term *cell phone* has become almost generic, this book uses that term. The important thing in selecting a cell phone is to look for digital technology. The analog technology of most existing cell phones is subject to interference or "cross-talk" from radios and other phone users. Thus, an analog cell phone poses a security risk in two ways: The phone number and sometimes the PIN number can be scanned and cloned by phone thieves monitoring the air; and the conversation itself sometimes can be overheard, making cell phones a poor choice for discussing confidential business matters. Digital technology is much less subject to these security problems, plus it provides better sound and a stronger resistance to interference. Not all areas are equipped with digital technology yet, but the number of cities offering it is constantly increasing. In the meantime, if a caller is in such an area, the digital phones automatically switch to analog (they are subject to the same vulnerabilities as analog phones during that time).

Cell phones can be purchased with the monthly phone service, or sometimes are even given away. Rates are continually dropping, but other important considerations exist when pricing phones and service. Telecommunications providers offer a bewildering number of package deals, with so many free minutes, free weekends, peak hours, off hours, and so on. Be sure to compare a package deal against actual usage patterns and costs. In addition, check out the issue of roaming charges—fees for traveling outside the caller's local area. Cell phones using analog technology may impose roaming charges of as much as $1.50 per minute in addition to the cost of the call itself, as well as a daily fee just for roaming. Obviously, these telephone charges can mean enormous company expense for its employees on the road. Many digital phones have dropped roaming charges or include them in a cheaper flat rate within a package that includes a certain geographical area. Again, check actual usage against package costs.

Beepers and pagers. Before everyone had a phone in their pocket, beepers were the most common way to stay in touch while away from the office. Beepers are essentially tiny radio receivers that are always tuned to one station. When someone calls the beeper number, the call is picked up by the beeper service and transmitted to the beeper, the tiny machine chirps, and the individual knows it is time to phone in. Though just a multifunction version of the same thing, *pager* is now the preferred term—*beeper* is considered to be less upscale. A pager still beeps, but it may also silently vibrate. And instead of simply offering a way to say "Call in now," a pager can show the individual caller's number, his or her name, and printed text. Depending on the model, pagers can even supply a voice message.

Prices vary, depending on what features are wanted. Many paging companies offer the pager itself at low or no cost because the monthly service must be purchased at the same time. The price of this service depends on whether the individual wants to be paged within a local area only, within a wider geographical region, or nationwide. Currently, a pager is less expensive than a cell phone, but as pagers add features and raise their costs, and as telephone technology improves its quality and reduces cost, the cell phone eventually could win out entirely as the more useful of the two because of its immediacy.

Telephone Systems

The kind of phone system that the office professional recommends depends on the size of the company and the type of features wanted or needed. It's important to find the right balance between a system size that will accommodate growth (because phone systems are estimated to last seven to ten years) and one that is needlessly big (and usually needlessly expensive). A general rule of thumb is to purchase a capability of 50 percent more lines than currently used. For example, if a company now has 200 lines, its new system should rewire for 300 lines. Of course, if a company has a pattern of exceptionally rapid growth, that 50 percent figure should be adjusted upward accordingly.

The appropriateness of the following systems is based on the employee number, as well as the features desired. (*Employee number* refers to the number of employees who actually use the phones. The number of phone lines needed for a factory, for example, would not be based on the number of plant workers.)

Intercom. If a company has fewer than ten employees and most of them work in the same room, the company might want to use an intercom system. This is basically a single phone number, answered by a receptionist, with extension lines on each desk. The call comes into one of the available lines, and the receptionist announces the call over an overhead intercom: "Pat, call on Line 3." An intercom system involves buying only the receptionist's main phone and the intercom, and the individual phones with buttons to show which lines are open. The system uses the existing wiring and works through the usual service from the phone company, but it is very limited as far as expanding for employee growth or for adding features such as voice mail.

Centrex. Another option for small companies with twenty or fewer employees is a Centrex system. Basically, the local phone company acts as the business' phone system. Each employee has his or her own touch-tone phone and phone number. A company's existing phones can be used, and no rewiring is necessary. Unlike installing a larger system, Centrex involves no upfront capital costs, service contracts, or ongoing hassles with vendors. Features such as voice mail, call forwarding, three-way calling, and call transfer can be arranged for each number through the phone company.

Besides the simplicity of operation, another benefit of Centrex is that it makes small companies appear—by phone—to be much larger than they are. For example, with a single regular phone, the office professional of the one-room, start-up accounting firm might say, "She's not here," when a call comes in for the boss. The absence is obvious because the boss's empty desk is a cramped 6 inches away. With Centrex, the office professional can say, "She's in a meeting right now. May I connect you to her voice mail?" The caller is now imagining that the boss is down the hall in the conference room with all those junior partners.

Because each line is charged individually, Centrex price-per-minute charges on some features can mount up. Although this is the only major drawback of the system, it may be a sizable one for some smaller companies.

"Keyless" systems. Another system for small companies (with less than thirty employees) is called a "keyless" system, which also works on standard wiring. The company buys special phones that are plugged into current telephone jacks that provide up to three separate phone lines, with several more extensions for each line. That's all the equipment that must be purchased. Within the office, the phones can transfer calls, handle standard teleconferencing, and handle station-to-station intercom calls. Other features require a more sophisticated system, however.

"Key" systems. Larger companies (with up to 200 employees) or smaller companies with special needs (such as music-on-hold) must be connected to a "key" system, a central processing unit that organizes and routes calls automatically. Existing phones can be used, but the central processing unit must be purchased. Every company phone then must be wired to it. Although key systems used to be limited to basics such as voice mail and automated answering, they are now actually hybrids and are beginning to pick up many of the additional features of the PBX (discussed next).

PBX (Private Branch Exchange). A PBX system fills the needs of the largest companies (with up to thousands of employees) and those that want maximum phone features. Some smaller companies also might opt for a PBX if their phone demands are extensive because a PBX provides features less expensively than Centrex. PBX features include multiparty conferencing, automatic call distribution ("Please wait and the next available representative will answer your call"), voice mail, automated answering, and other standard features (call forwarding, call waiting, and so on). Special equipment and wiring are necessary; the company buys these and installs them on company property. Because of the complexity of the setup, however, the vendor or outside firm must supply ongoing maintenance. A market for used equipment does exist, so buying certain used components is a way to reduce costs; still, an expert's guidance is needed for the selection. By the same token, this serves as a way for unscrupulous vendors to raise profits by charging new-equipment prices, so be sure of the vendor's reputation for integrity.

T-1 lines. For even higher-volume (and better sounding) calling, companies may want to investigate T-1 lines, which are dedicated lines that use a high-speed digital circuit. Each line can carry twenty-four conversations at the same time—and for less money than twenty-four separate phone lines cost. The company enjoys a discount because the T-1 lines bypass the local phone company and tie in directly to the long-distance carrier. A T-1 line can be upgraded to double its capacity to forty-eight conversations per line. (A T-3 line has the capacity of twenty-eight T-1s.)

T-1s are used by companies with substantial long-distance calling costs. Because installing the T-1 wiring and equipment is expensive, a company's long-distance bills should be at least $3,000 to $5,000 per month per location before a T-1 is considered cost-effective. In some states, however (such as in those on the two seaboards), so much competition exists between phone companies that sometimes having a T-1 offers only minimal savings. Compare carefully. A T-1 line can be divided among customers (this is called a *fractional T-1*), but the same expensive equipment and wiring must be installed.

Cost is not the only reason to consider a T-1 line. One of its major advantages is its speed. Because its bandwidth is wider, a T-1 line can transmit much more information per second than traditional phone lines. This speed becomes increasingly important when a company is online. Modems over traditional analog phone lines transmit 56Kbps (kilobytes per second), which is adequate for many business needs, including e-mail, general Web searches, and maintenance of a Web site with limited daily hits. However, when a Web site has extensive graphics, includes a multimedia presentation, or attracts (or is trying to attract) hundreds of hits a day, a company should consider a faster line. You know from your own experience how many online sites you've abandoned without ever visiting because the site simply took too much time to load. If the site is commercial—an online shopping site, for example—slowness can spell disaster.

A step up from the traditional phone line is the wider bandwidth provided by ISDN (Integrated Services Digital Network). Using the existing copper phone lines available from local phone companies, ISDN offers a speed of 128Kbps, which, depending on the application, can be more than four times faster than traditional telephone service. ISDN provides better and faster connections to the Internet, as well as between two computers, two networks, and the telecommuter and the office. Telecommuters even can split the bandwidth and use 64Kbps for voice communication and 64Kbps for online use at the same time—and on a single line.

When an ISDN is too slow to hold the amount of data per second being transmitted, a T-1 line may be the answer because it can transmit 1.544Mbps. When Web page traffic approaches 500 hits a day, at least a half T-1 should be considered.

Voice-mail systems. In theory, voice mail is a way to expand and enhance the company's telephone capabilities. Voice mail can reduce or eliminate the need for a receptionist or operator, thus freeing up that person to handle other work as well. It enables personnel to work without interruptions, and to receive messages and make calls at their convenience. It even can work as a marketing tool, providing callers with new product information and describing existing services. In practice, however, voice mail can be a message-eating nightmare from which there's no escape.

Buying a voice mail system can be almost as complicated as buying the phone system itself. The simplest units are little more than answering machines for each line. As with phone systems, the more sophisticated systems require vendor installation and maintenance and enable users to do the following:

- Listen to, erase, store, or transfer messages

- Pre-record messages to send to other mailboxes at later scheduled times

- Record and choose from multiple greetings ("I'm either away from my desk right now or on the other line . . ."; "I'm out of the office until next Tuesday. For emergencies, please call . . ."; "I'm in, but I'm working on deadline . . ."; and so on)

- Route messages

- Give the same message to multiple people, as in fax polling

- Notify the individual's pager when there's voice mail

- Be linked to e-mail and faxes

Certain systems have "automated attendants" that answer the company's main phone and route the call, eliminating busy signals, the need to put callers on hold, and so on.

Although features such as these are always attractive, the office professional should ask the following important questions before choosing a voice-mail system:

- Will the proposed voice-mail system be compatible with the existing phone system?

- Must the voice-mail system come from the vendor who sold or is selling the company its phone system? (The answer should be no.)

- Can the voice-mail system store old messages until the recipient decides to erase them?

- Does each mailbox have its own security pass code?

- Can messages be retrieved while away from the office?

- Is the caller at each prompt able to repeat the menu by pushing a certain button?

- Is the caller at each prompt always able to reach a live voice, usually by dialing "0" to get the operator?

New voice-mail systems are as dreaded by employees as by customers, so make sure that the vendor includes full training in the package by the vendor.

What does an office professional do in the face of these bewildering choices? The best course may be to determine what features the company wants or needs in its phone system. Then, armed with the answers, the office professional can seek help from a competent vendor. Because the vendor not

TELEPHONES AND THE FUTURE

Telephone systems are on the brink of a revolution. Although existing systems will continue to be used for years, new technology involving PCs and the Internet are transforming the future. For example, PC PBXs and PC-based telephony make it easy and much less expensive for smaller companies to set up PBX systems and maintain these systems themselves without an outside vendor. Computer telephony integration links the individual's PC to the phone system. For example, caller ID will send the caller's name and number to the employee's PC; if the caller is a customer, his or her account will automatically appear on the employee's screen—and the phone may not even be answered yet. Internet telephony enables companies to route calls over existing phone lines, over a private network, or over the Internet. A main advantage of this is the reduction of long-distance call costs.

only bases its profits on the size and brand of the system purchased but also often works as the administrator of the system, choose carefully. When considering recommendations for vendors, the office professional should ask these questions:

- Does the particular system leave room for growth? How much?

- Can extra features be added onto a particular system later? If so, which ones?

- Can the company use its own telephones with the system? (Being limited to the vendor's phones may indicate a way the vendor is trying to boost cost.)

- If the company must buy vendor phones, do the phones use standard dial tones, ringing, busy signals, and out-of-order signals? (If not, this again could indicate a way to boost costs because unusual signals will not respond to standard signals, thus making it impossible to buy, say, voice mail from another vendor.)

- How experienced is the vendor?

- Is the vendor licensed by the state as a contractor to do the work?

- Is the vendor insured and bonded? Ask for proof.

- Does the vendor have 24-hour technical support for the new telephone system?

- How fast is the vendor's emergency response time?

- Is the vendor factory authorized and factory-certified for the brand desired by the company?

- Will the vendor supply recommendations from other customers?

- Will the vendor supply an itemized bid (not a package deal) for better comparison?

- How much time will it take to add new lines or services?

- Is leasing the telephone equipment an option with this particular vendor, and is leasing a good option for your company?

FAX MACHINES

Just as traditional postal delivery is often replaced by priority and overnight mail, overnight mail is often replaced by the fax. "Quickly" has come to mean "instantaneously."

Fax transmission is a flexible, inexpensive, and simple method of sending information instantly in the form of image replication (facsimile). A fax transmission can be generated in two ways: (1) from a fax machine, or (2) from a computer with faxing capability.

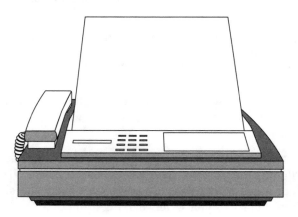

Although fax machines are standard in offices today, faxing from computers is less common. To fax directly from your computer, you need a system with a fax modem and a phone line. After installing the required fax software, you can send a fax as if you were printing a letter. When you go to output the document, the software dials the number and faxes the document.

Many people use the fax to instantly send a single letter to a single recipient. They dial the number into the telephone keypad and press the Start button. Fax machines have many other strengths that are often overlooked.

Suppose a business must notify all its customers immediately that an error was found, or must notify the entire sales force that an important deadline has been changed. The time involved in telephoning or mailing a letter to each recipient would be prohibitive. This is where fax transmissions come in. The fax has the capability of broadcasting—that is, automatically sending a list of fax numbers with the same transmission.

A WORD OF CAUTION ABOUT BROADCASTING

Although junk mail still clogs regular postal delivery, it is illegal to send electronic junk mail—unsolicited fax transmissions that advertise or sell services or products. Check in advance to see that all recipients on a broadcast list want to be included.

Not every machine has the same capabilities. The office professional should read the user's manual in detail or contact the dealer to become familiar with the full capabilities of the machine currently in use. Following are some of its possible features, or features to look for in a new machine (certain features require being linked to a computer):

- Message confirmation and/or error printouts
- Multiple-number speed dial
- Capability of storing pages as they arrive and printing when available, so as not to tie up the phone line while printing pages
- Memory for scanning documents and sending later, for delayed sending or so the sender doesn't have to wait for each page to transmit, or for sending when rates are lower
- Capability of sending the same document to multiple locations without having to rescan the document each time
- Capability of storing incoming messages in mailboxes so that the person with the proper access code can retrieve them
- Gray-scale controls that can adjust the resolution of the graphics
- Built-in surge protector
- Upgradable memory to store hundreds of pages
- Capability of creating logos, letterheads, forms, and protected signatures
- Prioritization of faxes so that urgent ones transmit first

- Data compression that substitutes symbols for words and phrases in a process that condenses information and enables faster transmissions (similar to disk compression)

- Capability of exporting transmission histories to spreadsheets, databases, and so on

With today's lower long-distance rates and higher postage charges, it is sometimes actually less expensive to send a fax than to send a letter. Unless urgency preempts all other reasons, the office professional should use the more cost-effective method. However, he or she also should be sensitive to the contents of the fax. Confidentiality has always been a significant risk with faxes: The machines are often located in open areas, so messages are usually seen by at least one other person before they reach the recipient. Newer machines store messages for individuals and require passwords before each mailbox can be opened, but not every recipient has this feature.

Another cost factor in fax usage is the full-size cover sheet. It is estimated that billions of dollars are spent each year on this single sheet, which is immediately discarded. A small sticky note attached at the top may suffice; letters that have an address and closing signature may not need a cover sheet at all.

COPIERS

The essential reason for buying a copier is, of course, to make copies, but the added features of the newest machines often can obscure that basic fact. Once-impressive features such as two-sided copying, color copying, and size reduction or enlargement are now taken for granted because copiers have become miniprinting systems. Depending on the model, they can print as many as two copies per second, can edit and store copy, and can be programmed to work off-hours. A copier's printing capability is joined by the capability to collate, sort, staple, and add a heavy-stock cover, if desired. Other models work as multifunction machines, giving the copier scanning capability. Add a phone line, and the copier is also a phone, answering machine, and fax (with anti-junk-fax function). In addition, some copiers can be linked to the office network to work as printers, with all the instructions—down to delayed printing—programmable from the user's desktop PC.

The new generation of copiers are digital machines. Although very expensive at the moment and therefore not yet widely used, these new machines can scan a document once and store it in memory to produce other originals, not copies. Image manipulation is also possible with digital machines, as are remote diagnosis and trouble-shooting.

Because all these features add considerably to the cost, the office professional should choose with care. Salespeople or in-house employees will persuasively explain how certain features are an absolute necessity. Vendors will try to sell package deals that *seem* to throw in the extra features at no cost. But absolute necessities are often just a wish list, and each feature has a cost even within a special package. Therefore, it is better to decide beforehand exactly what is needed by the company, and then to shop for only what is needed. The savings can be significant.

In contrast with employees generating an extravagant features wish list are those employees who will *not* use the special features at all. The individual may be afraid of doing something wrong and breaking the machine, or he or she may be too reluctant (or even too lazy) to learn a new procedure. A simple example is the employee who always uses two pieces of paper rather than making a double-sided copy (clearly a waste of money and resources) or the clerk who would rather spend hours stapling a cover to a collated report rather than programming the copier to do it. If certain complicated jobs must be done by using the special features, employees who resist learning will try to turn these copying projects over to the office professional. Training these people (and retraining them, if necessary) is essential if the company is to recoup its investment in terms of greater employee efficiency and time savings.

One of the most critical aspects of buying a copier is knowing its volume-per-month capability. Don't underestimate the company's usage. Although lower-volume machines are less expensive, underestimating usage makes lines at the copier longer and also can result in frequent problems and breakdowns. Keep careful watch of the present usage before selecting a model. Plan for growth. If usage is low but the number of employees per machine is about fifty or more, a second copier is often a good idea. If one machine has features, the second can be the most basic of models.

Copier Paper

The selection of the right copy paper is crucial to the machine's performance. To prevent jamming, choose the manufacturer's recommended paper weight. Also look for paper that is evenly trimmed, that can withstand copier heat, and that doesn't have a tendency to curl.

Copier paper is generally available from any office supply store, office superstore, or catalog company. Businesses with high paper consumption may want to consider buying paper directly from paper manufacturers. For information on how to buy from these major companies directly (or through their regional representatives), see the following Web sites:

Boise Cascade, at www.bcop.com

Georgia Pacific, at www.gp.com

Hammermill, at www.hammermill.com

The company's rate of usage will help determine whether paper can be bought in money-saving bulk. If paper is kept in a low-humidity, moderate-temperature environment, it may keep for extended periods as well. So even if a company does not use paper rapidly, it may still see some savings with bulk-buying if proper storage space is available. For a beginning rule of thumb, plan on reordering when the stock falls to 25 percent of the original quantity. This should accommodate even large rush jobs while the stock is being replenished. Adjust this 25 percent figure later, when you're familiar with the company's copying needs and patterns.

ELECTRONIC TYPEWRITERS

The birth of the electronic typewriter was sandwiched somewhere between the older electric typewriter and the word processor; as a piece of equipment, it is a hybrid of the two. Electronic typewriters do not have separate monitors or printers, but they do have small electronic display screens above the keyboard that show a partial page. These machines have become more sophisticated in recent years; many have built-in spell-checkers, text-editing capabilities, spreadsheet and mail-merge capabilities, limited font selections, timer alerts, formatting functions, upgradable memory, and security passwords. Some include a 100-key buffer zone so that even the fastest typist won't end up with snarled keys, as with an electric typewriter. Some electronic typewriters can be networked to computers and used as printers.

Although the market for electronic typewriters has plummeted, a viable niche still exists for them. They are durable and easy to use, and an electronic typewriter can handle some jobs faster and better than a computer. For example, electronic typewriters are more practical than computers for printing on checks or index cards, to generate printed paper forms that have not been computerized, to type on preprinted forms, and so on.

For example, to address a single envelope by computer, the office professional must boot up the computer, pull up the word processing program, click Envelopes, type in the return and main addresses, select the font style and size, remove the paper from the paper tray, adjust the tray to accommodate the wider-width envelope, insert an envelope, and then click Print. By contrast, he or she merely needs to turn on an electronic typewriter, insert an envelope, type, and it's done. Obviously, the electronic typewriter is not a replacement for the computer, but it can be a handy accessory.

RECORDING AND DICTATION EQUIPMENT

Suppose that your boss is eating a brown-bag lunch while stuck on the freeway. Sudden inspiration hits and he wants to change the opening of his motivational speech to the Lions Club next week. He takes out his pocket recorder and creates a new opening about how to succeed despite being stuck in life's traffic jams. That afternoon, he drops the disk on your desk and asks you to make the changes to his typed speech.

Although the old phrase "Take a letter" may not have been spoken in years, executives are still dictating letters, reports, random thoughts, and more—all into tiny recorders that go wherever they travel. Today, two types of portable models exist: much smaller versions of the old tape recorder and new digital machines that use disks.

Tape machines now come with special features such as the capability to screen out background noises (angry motorists in the next lane and the rustling of sandwiches being unwrapped, for example). They also can be switched on by voice activation, prevent accidental erasing of tapes, erase tapes rapidly, go at once to the end of the dictation, stamp the time and date, and so on. Digital machines can do the same and also insert urgent items at the front of the disk without erasing the rest, allow random access to any message on the disk, use electronic indexing, provide a bigger capacity, and use access codes for security. Some models can be linked to a PC. These can send contents automatically to a word processing program or e-mail, which eliminates the office assistant's need to transcribe.

Larger table-top recorders, sometimes called *conference recorders,* have sensitive recording capabilities that can follow all the proceedings of a meeting without having to be moved as the speakers change.

Many recorders, including the smaller ones, come with a foot-pedal attachment to control the playback speed as the material is played and keyboarded. Some larger transcription models only play back, although they have many of the recorder's features that are useful for transcription, such as electronic indexing, end of dictation codes, and so on.

VCRs AND PROJECTORS

Though the technology is relatively new, people have become spoiled very quickly: They now expect presentations to be in color and contain either live action or animation, even though a sophisticated presentation used to be a slide show. Today, *low-tech* is no longer a flip chart but a VCR, and *high-tech* means an LCD projector that produces computer graphics, millions of colors, and multimedia presentations.

VCRs

Basically, the same VCRs for use at home for recording favorite programs are used by businesses today for training and presentation purposes. The office professional should not forget that videotapes also can be made from special company occasions such as picnics, parties, charitable affairs, and more. In addition, press releases to cable and network news shows are bolstered when they are accompanied by footage of a person or event, as well as general scenes of the company itself.

When choosing a VCR, many of the features that are personally attractive also are important for business use: four heads rather than two for clearer images during pauses or searches, onscreen menus for easier programming, a digital tape counter that measures in real time rather than numbers, an automatic clock set to adjust for power outages and daylight saving time, automatic picture control to adjust for lower-grade or worn tapes, automatic tracking, electronic index searching to bookmark spots for easy reference, and an automatic head cleaner.

If the company plans to record its own videotapes, look for these extra features: jog/shuttle control, which enables the user to browse a tape either quickly or frame by frame for editing; an audio/video insert, which provides for both audio dubbing and inserting new video clips while maintaining a single soundtrack; and a flying erase head, which helps smooth scene transitions and recording starts and stops.

Projectors

Computers can produce amazing presentations with colors, graphics, sounds, and animation. But only a bare handful of people can view a monitor at the same time. To display a computer-generated program to a large audience, the LCD (liquid crystal display) projector was developed.

Now, armed with a laptop and a portable LCD projector, a salesperson can present a pitch to audiences of various sizes. In the past, if any information on a product or service changed while the salesperson was on the road, he or she had to wait until new charts or slides were made up and delivered by special courier. With LCD technology, he or she can easily connect back to the company's computer via modem and receive the updated program from the office professional.

LCD panels are positioned on top of the light of an overhead projector. LCD projectors come equipped with their own light source. The panel itself hooks up to the computer—often a laptop—and as the presentation data comes up on the computer monitor, the LCD panel projects the images onto a regular projection screen or, if necessary, onto a blank wall. Some models use just one panel or matrix that produces a single image on the screen; others use multiple panels and a series of lenses, producing multiple images that are then united on the screen. Multiple panels provide a brighter image, but they may face convergence problems if all the separate images are not exactly aligned. The future of projectors seems to lie with DLP (digital light processing) technology, although this is still in development. DLP projectors use many more panels than LCDs do, and each panel is covered by tiny mirrors that reflect light outward. The image is projected onto the screen one color at a time, but in such rapid succession that the brain fills in the gaps to create what appears to be a solid picture. The image is brighter than that from an LCD projector and presents a seamless surface, unlike the pixel-dotted surface of LCDs. But

DLPs are still being refined; at the moment, they are too large and expensive by comparison and can't yet compete with the performance of the best LCDs.

When choosing an LCD panel or projector, an office professional should come prepared with answers to the following questions, which determine the type of projector best suited to the company's needs:

- What is the typical size of the audience for whom presentations are given?
- What is the typical room size?
- What are the typical lighting conditions: complete darkness, some light, or fully lit rooms?
- How clear a picture resolution is desired?
- Will the presentation incorporate photos, video clips, or sound?
- How much travel is planned for a typical projector?
- How portable should the projector be?
- Will the company be projecting special images, such as high-resolution photography, CAD (computer-aided design) drawings, or maps?
- Are special features desired, such as a remote control, stereo Surround-sound, or simultaneous computer and video display?

When comparing projectors, check how much light reaches the screen (whether the actual screen or the room wall). This is reported in the product specifications in terms of ANSI lumens: The higher the number, the more light there is, and the better the image appears. Both LCD projectors and today's new overhead projectors use either a metal halide bulb or a halogen bulb. Although metal halide bulbs can cost ten times as much as halogen bulbs, the price usually evens out because halide bulbs last much longer. Halogen bulbs are best for projectors that see a lot of travel because the bulb is common and can be more easily replaced on the road if broken. The projector's lamp is wired for only one or the other; the choice must be made at the time of purchase because the bulbs are not interchangeable.

PURCHASING NOTE

The process of creating LCD panels is so complex that nearly every projector shows a few defective pixels—dots that are either permanently bright or permanently dark. The manufacturer tolerates a set number of these (find out specifically how many); only when this number is exceeded is the projector itself considered defective.

In general, look at the projector's focusing capability, the quality of its images, its fidelity to the original colors, and the uniformity of the brightness on the screen. Specifically, look for the type of image controls on the unit itself. What can be adjusted? In addition, some models come with a memory card if the user wants to run presentations without the laptop. Most projectors come with built-in stereo speakers; some also have a microphone jack so the presenter can speak over the same system.

SHREDDERS

Suppose that an executive has asked for a copy of a confidential report that has been sent to her before she forwards it to the next person on the routing list. You don't notice that the person ahead of you has adjusted the controls and you make a copy that, while readable, is too light. Tearing the paper into pieces is time-consuming and unreliable. That's one good reason why a small shredder should be next to every copier.

Paper shredders cannot make paper disappear, but they can make personal or confidential information disappear. Payroll lists, customer records, telephone logs, meeting minutes, personnel evaluations, pay scales, product specifications, market analyses, customer lists, design changes, and canceled checks are just a few types of sensitive materials that should remain confidential. Industrial espionage is a major concern today; many research companies not only shred top secret information but also keep the shreds. And with increasing lawsuits on all fronts, companies are less likely to put anything in the simple wastebasket.

The need for a shredder goes far beyond the business world. Law firms, medical offices, and pharmacists also regularly deal with confidential information that should be shredded. Schools should not put student and personnel files into the regular trash, even if they have expired. Anyone who has private information of any kind has a need for a shredder.

Shredders come in a wide range of styles, capabilities, prices, and shredding options. Flat paper can be shredded into long strips as wide as egg noodles or as fine as angel-hair pasta; for maximum security, it can even be cross-cut into confetti-like particles. The style selection ranges from desktop models to large free-standing units that can handle thick wads of paper and folders (including staples and paper clips)—as well as disks, cassettes, microfilm, and microfiche—and still run continuously without overheating. Popular features include an electronic eye that turns the shredder on and off, a function that stops the shredder when the waste bin beneath is full, and casters to move the shredder to the documents rather than add the extra security risk of transporting sensitive documents from their locked location.

When selecting a shredder, consider the level of security desired, the volume that the shredder must handle, and the kinds of material it is expected to shred (checks, letter-size paper, folders, computer printouts, and so on). Also consider the company's multiple shredding needs. You may want a desktop unit for you and the executive, another to put in the copy room, and a larger unit to be located in the central records department.

Shredding services are available from outside firms (look under Recycling in the Yellow Pages). However, many firms that are already concerned about privacy may be reluctant to place their confidential papers in the hands of an outside party, even for the time it takes to shred the papers. For companies with extensive files, owning one of the larger shredders may make sense.

Shredded material can be recycled or internally recycled by certain model shredding machines that turn old files and such into packing material.

No matter what the company or organization, buying a shredder is only the first step in its proper use. Employees must learn how to make the decision about what should be shredded and what should be kept. The office professional may want to draw up a memo detailing the types of documents that should be shredded, along with instructions about how it should be done—whether the material is to be left with you or brought to a central shredding location, or whether an appointment should be made for the portable shredder to be wheeled to a particular location.

EQUIPMENT MAINTENANCE AND ORDERING OFFICE SUPPLIES

Among the many duties of office professionals is the job of office management. This all-encompassing term can range from tracking lost change in the vending machine, to purchasing office supplies, to arranging maintenance and repairs of office equipment.

Although such petty duties as change-tracking might accompany the job, two office-management duties are critical to the efficient running of the department or the whole company. These responsibilities are maintaining the equipment and ordering office supplies.

EQUIPMENT MAINTENANCE

Basic equipment maintenance ranges from the scheduled visits of the copier repair team to the employees' basic understanding of how to put paper in the fax machine. When dealing with office equipment, employees must know enough about a machine's operation to understand whether it is broken when it stops working. Employees also must know that the office professional—or whoever else is maintaining the files of warranties, service contracts, and lists of repair people—should be notified immediately if there's a problem. So often a line of people will walk into the copy room, discover that the copier is out of paper, and then lazily decide that their copy was not important enough to warrant either filling the machine themselves or notifying you. Likewise, many people will attempt to use a machine, find out that it's malfunctioning, and then simply walk away from it rather than tell anyone.

When any new piece of equipment comes into the office—whether purchased by the office professional or not, whether to be used by the office professional or not—he or she should become familiar with the user's manual as soon as possible. Even if the equipment is not for the office professional's use, the actual user is likely to come to you to see how it works—and will definitely come to you when there is a problem.

For each piece of equipment, read the manual carefully. Note anything that might become difficult to operate under the company's specific conditions. Note any necessary accessories or attachments that require special ordering: cords, covers, uncommon battery sizes, and so on. Fill out the warranty card at once to register the equipment. Make two copies of the warranty card that shows the equipment's make, model, and serial number. Tape one copy of the card to a discreet location on the equipment itself (inside a hard cover, for example, or on the side of the machine). Do not give it to the user; employees come and go while equipment remains. File the other copy with the warranty itself, the service contract if any, and the manual (once the user is done with it). Following up on getting the manual will probably be necessary because in the beginning the user may not want to part with it.

Check for technical-support numbers, recommended service dealers, and so on, all of which might be listed in separate publications that come with the equipment. File these as well.

If the equipment is for general use (a copier or fax machine, for example), make a copy of the basic instructions and post it on the nearest wall. If there's no single list of instructions in the manual conveniently written up for this, condense one from your own understanding of the guide, type it up, and post it. File the copy as above with the warranty. This procedure helps prevent loss of important paperwork regarding the machines and accommodates faster servicing.

General Troubleshooting Instructions

The most important part of troubleshooting is the correct use and regular maintenance of equipment. This keeps problems to a minimum.

Scheduled maintenance. Just as a car needs regular oil changes and lube jobs even if it is running well, pieces of office equipment need regular maintenance to prevent cash- and time-consuming emergencies. In the user's manual for each piece of equipment, the manufacturer often includes a list of recommended maintenance practices. Some of these involve simple cleaning and can be performed in the office by the user. Others must be scheduled, whether through the manufacturer or through a service contract with an outside firm.

For each piece of equipment, use the same file folder that holds the warranty and user's manual. Write the basic warranty-registration information on

☎ **800 SERVICE AND SUPPORT NUMBERS FOR OFFICE EQUIPMENT MANUFACTURERS**

Brother International	800-276-7746
Canon	800-652-2666
Epson America	800-289-3776
Hewlett-Packard, Co.	800-752-0900
IBM	800-426-2968
Konica	800-256-6422
Kyocera Electronics, Inc.	800-232-6797
Lexmark International, Inc.	800-358-5835
Mita Copystar America	800-222-6482
Murata Business Systems	800-543-4636
NEC America	800-632-4636
Okidata	800-654-3282
Panasonic	800-742-8086
Ricoh	800-637-4264
Sharp Electronics	800-237-4277
Toshiba	800-334-3445
Xerox	800-862-6567

the inside cover of the folder, as well as the phone numbers of the manufacturer, the place of purchase, and the service company. Note the cost of the equipment as well. When the file becomes thick, having this information right on the inside cover will save much thumbing through of papers. It is handy to have all the information in one place when calling to schedule service or a repair because the make and model will be one of the first questions asked.

If the company has a service contract, be sure to note whether the technician comes automatically or whether the service call must be scheduled.

Each time a piece of equipment is serviced or repaired, note it in the file. Include the nature of the problem, the amount of time lost, and the cost involved. Tracking the actual maintenance will help determine the machine's overall efficiency over time and its actual price to run—both details necessary for making new purchasing decisions at a later time.

Enter all recommendations for regular maintenance on a yearly calendar. This enables timely scheduling of appointments and prepares users for periods of downtime.

Trouble-shooting. Besides instructions, most manuals have a list of troubleshooting directions: "If X goes wrong, try doing Y." These directions offer quick and simple solutions to the equipment's most common problems. Both the users and the office professional should confine their activities to those on the trouble-shooting list. If the trouble-shooting list recommends something that makes either person uncomfortable—going under the hood of the computer, for example—leave that for the repair person.

Certain troubleshooting recommendations will be basic to all equipment and are the common-sense directions often forgotten when something goes wrong: Check that the batteries have life, that the machine is switched on, that extension cords are plugged in firmly at both ends, that peripherals are firmly attached at both ends, that the paper or ink supply is filled, and so on. Do not overlook the obvious. Because machines work under only a specific set of conditions, make sure that all the conditions are fulfilled. The office professional might have to try to get the machine to operate after it has been reported as broken. Often, the user might skip a step in procedure, while the office professional will automatically perform it. It may be annoying to be called away from work to fix something that wasn't broken, but this can prevent a loss of downtime while an "Out of order" sign is taped up—and it also prevents calling a repair person for a needless (and pricey) appointment.

ORDERING OFFICE SUPPLIES

Ordering office supplies is another critical responsibility of office management. Sufficient supplies always should be on hand to finish the job and to prevent idle time caused by lack of supplies. On the other hand, the inventory should not be so bloated that supplies dry up, pass critical expiration dates, or otherwise become useless.

Catalogs and Superstores

In lieu of dealing with vendors and manufacturers, catalogs and superstores may offer great convenience and sometimes significant savings. But there also can be hidden costs. For example, superstores must factor in the cost of regional and national advertising, the cost of rental space for the retail operation in addition to warehouse space for the items, and the cost of retail staff salaries. Superstores often carry mostly name brands, while lower-priced, no-name clones could be of equal quality. In addition, the office professional must figure in the time spent traveling to and shopping in superstores.

Catalogs—without a showroom—solve many of these problems. But look for reputable companies that others can recommend. When dealing with a catalog company for the first time, order cautiously to test delivery speed and the

TIPS FOR PURCHASING SUPPLIES

Purchasing involves much more than just selecting a particular brand and model of office machine. The office professional also might be responsible for choosing the vendor, shopping by store or catalog, putting in verbal orders, changing the numbers of items ordered to take advantage of quantity discounts, negotiating prices and services, approving invoices, and more. Keep these hints in mind when purchasing supplies and equipment:

- Always take several bids on major purchases; take bids on reorders from time to time to keep prices competitive.

- Negotiate prices, but know which items are not worth negotiating.

- Consider the savings of close-out items, but weigh them carefully in terms of long-term use and maintenance if they are used for constantly updated items such as computers.

- Use more than one vendor so that a backup is always available.

- Get specific delivery dates, confirm them later in writing, and follow-up quickly when they pass; if timeliness is not important to you, it will not be important to the vendor.

- Remember that small companies often can give better attention to rush jobs than larger companies.

- Make sure that the specifications provided to vendors are exact, and are checked and rechecked.

quality of the items. Be certain of return policies and return shipping. Check that equipment is new and not someone else's reconditioned lemon.

Logging and Ordering

A simple notebook or computer file begins the process of establishing a regular and efficient ordering system. For each item, record the name of the item, its place of purchase, its stock number, when it was ordered, how long the actual delivery took, and how long the supply lasted. This process will help determine when it's time to reorder. For example, if an order takes a week to be delivered, order it a month in advance, which allows for three weeks leeway. Of course, if an item must be special-ordered, or if back orders often take longer than usual or promised, include extra time.

As a safety measure, put a note on the box or container of each item (on the side that faces outward when in the supply closet). The note should read,

☎	800 NUMBERS FOR OFFICE SUPPLY RESOURCES	
	Global Computer Supplies	800-845-6225
	Modern Service Office Supplies	800-672-6767
	Office Depot	800-685-8800
	Office Max	800-788-8080
	Penny Wise	800-942-3311
	Staples	800-333-3330
	Viking Office Products	800-421-1222

"Notify (office professional's name) when only (XX) are left." This note will help during times when an item is used up unusually quickly.

Because of the myriad supplies used in today's offices, an office professional might be placing an order each day if he or she ordered each item separately as needed. So try to look for ordering patterns, especially within the same place of purchase. For example, ten items regularly come from Catalog X. Four items are fairly slow-moving; the other six items are used up almost three times as quickly. Instead of ordering each of the ten items separately, order the six fast-moving items together; once every third time, add the four slow-moving items to the order. Or, if the company has the space, double up on the quantity for each of the six items and order only half as often. The slow-moving items might be added in every time or every other time, depending on whether their number also was doubled. Check for quantity discounts—they may make it worthwhile to find the space.

Depending on company policy, the office professional might be required to keep an individual log of personal use and a log of general use to help prevent waste and pilferage. At its strictest, this policy could involve keeping supply cabinets locked and not handing out a new item until the empty is handed in. Although the practice might garner complaints, follow it closely because maintaining and ordering supplies involves a tremendous responsibility.

What sort of products come under ordering and logging duties? The following list shows the wide variety possible in the area of consumables—items that are ordered, used up, and ordered again:

- *Paper and filing products.* Writing pads, legal pads, steno pads, memo pads, scratch pads, message pads, notebooks, index cards, business cards, sticky notes, labels, invoices, other forms, covers, portfolios, ring binders, dividers, name tags, letterhead and stationery, business envelopes, manila envelopes, shipping envelopes, printer paper, copier paper, fax machine paper, manila file folders, hanging folders, file pockets, file wallets, storage boxes.

- *Computer supplies.* Floppy disks, ZIP disks, backup tapes, printer toner cartridges, recordable CD-ROMs, compressed air spray.

- *Duplicating and dictating supplies.* Steno pads, tapes of all sizes, disks, batteries, fax machine toner cartridges, fax machine drum cartridges, fax cartridges, printer ribbons.

- *Desk supplies.* Pens, pencils, highlighters, markers, correction pens, ink refills, lead refills, erasers, gluesticks, staples, clear tape, packing tape, masking tape, mailing tape, mailing tubes, paper clips, binder clips, hole reinforcements, rubber bands, rubber stamps, ink, pushpins, calendars, planners.

- *Miscellaneous.* Light bulbs, clipboards, camera film, transparency film, videotapes, easel pads, coffee, tea, cleaning supplies, first-aid supplies, wastebasket liners, toilet paper, paper towels, tissues, lunchroom supplies, bottled water.

STORAGE

Because office supplies must be kept somewhere, storage is always a consideration when ordering. Unlike the local store that can run an inventory clearance sale when it wants to stock up on new items, the office professional works under the same strict limitations but without such a quick and easy way to make space. For every item that is brought into the company, these questions must be asked: Where will it go? If it is a replacement item, will the old item be stored, moved to another branch of the company, or thrown out? Can delivery of the new and moving of the old be timed so that two of the same aren't competing for the same space (even temporarily) or leaving users without any equipment at all?

Even ordinary items might have special storage needs. Printer cartridges, for example, come with expiration dates; if the package is opened, it should be used within a few months, regardless of expiration date. Cartridges and disks are sensitive to extreme temperatures and direct sunlight. Envelopes should be used within two years or the glue may no longer seal properly. Improperly stored paper picks up heat and humidity and begins to curl, causing jams. For every item, check with the manufacturer for the proper storage technique and shelf life.

COMMON OFFICE SUPPLIES CHECKLIST

Paper and Filing Products

- ☐ Typing paper
- ☐ Stationery (letterhead)
- ☐ Envelopes
- ☐ Correction fluid (with thinner; white and color as needed)
- ☐ Scratch pads and paper
- ☐ Manila or plastic file folders (color-coded as needed)
- ☐ Hanging file folders
- ☐ File folder tabs and labels
- ☐ Memo pads
- ☐ Dictation notebooks
- ☐ Alphabetized dividers
- ☐ Telephone message pads
- ☐ File baskets, trays, and stacks
- ☐ 3 × 5 cards

- ☐ 4 × 6 cards
- ☐ Transparent tape
- ☐ Bookmarks
- ☐ Card files
- ☐ Calendars
- ☐ Planning diaries
- ☐ Business envelopes
- ☐ Manila envelopes
- ☐ Padded envelopes
- ☐ Binders
- ☐ Loose-leaf covers and fillers
- ☐ Mailing tape
- ☐ Telex paper (in rolls)
- ☐ Address labels
- ☐ Paper for calculating machines
- ☐ Postage stamps

Computer Supplies

- ☐ Printer ribbons
- ☐ Printer cartridges

- ☐ Floppy disks
- ☐ Floppy disk trays

Duplicating and Dictating Supplies

- ☐ Cassette tapes
- ☐ Tape storage unit
- ☐ Tape demagnetizer
- ☐ Tape splicer

- ☐ Microfilm
- ☐ Microfiche film
- ☐ Microfiche index
- ☐ Copier toner

Desk Supplies

- ☐ Staplers
- ☐ Staples
- ☐ Staple removers
- ☐ Letter openers
- ☐ Pen and pencil holders
- ☐ Tape dispensers
- ☐ Rulers
- ☐ Fine-line, broad-nib, or felt-tip pens
- ☐ Paper clips
- ☐ Rubber bands

- ☐ Writing and marking pencils
- ☐ Magnifying glasses
- ☐ Erasers
- ☐ Scissors
- ☐ Rubber stamps, including date stamps
- ☐ Ink pads
- ☐ Push pins
- ☐ Book holders
- ☐ Bookends

Miscellaneous

- ☐ Postal scales
- ☐ Globe
- ☐ First-aid kit
- ☐ Maps
- ☐ Fire extinguisher

- ☐ Easels
- ☐ Keys
- ☐ Planning boards
- ☐ Batteries

Desk Reference Sources

- ☐ Desk dictionary
- ☐ International area code booklet
- ☐ Secretarial handbook
- ☐ Current office supply catalog
- ☐ Office address and/or telephone directory (booklet, sheet, or rotary file)

- ☐ Style manual
- ☐ Almanac
- ☐ Chart for current postal rates
- ☐ ZIP code directory
- ☐ Telephone directory
- ☐ Telex directory, if needed

REFERENCES AND PUBLICATIONS FOR OFFICES

A good reference library will save the office professional countless questions and searches. For correspondence needs, include a college dictionary, a thesaurus, and a grammar and usage guide. Combination books and dictionary or thesaurus programs in word processing will not provide the in-depth knowledge of separate volumes, although a good-quality dictionary on a CD-ROM may work as well. For most offices, an unabridged dictionary (which may run two or more volumes and carry a hefty price tag) provides too much information, while a pocket dictionary provides too little. A college dictionary—which will be identified as such in its title—will handle almost all your needs.

In addition to this absolute minimum, it is useful to have a desk reference—a single-volume encyclopedia on a subject (in this case, a business reference). *The New York Public Library Business Desk Reference* is one such title, as is the *Wall Street Journal Almanac*. A collection of ready-to-use business letters can be helpful, too, as can a handbook for technical writing and a book on business etiquette.

If the executive travels or clients are far-flung, include both a world atlas and a road atlas on the shelf, as well as a time-conversion table or universal clock, and an area-code/country-code chart for phone calls. If clients speak languages other than English, add foreign-language volumes, such as an English-to-Spanish/Spanish-to-English dictionary. Even if the office professional does not speak the language or is required to have client contact, these books can be invaluable because words may appear in files, letters, and so on.

If the office professional attends or chairs many meetings, a copy of the *New Roberts Rules of Order* describes ways to organize and run meetings in the parliamentary style. This resource also includes helpful hints for making meetings a success.

Phone books of major cities—at least the neighboring ones—have much valuable information.

Also look for a dictionary of business terms. If the company works in a specialized area or has frequent contact with one, specialty dictionaries are also available, such as a dictionary of legal or medical terms.

Finally, don't overlook sources of information already in your office. If the company deals in a specialized area such as technology, pharmaceuticals, or manufacturing, it's likely that it subscribes to numerous magazines, newspapers, and trade journals that relate specifically to that industry. These can be a tremendous reference, so file them after they've been routed and read. If publications are not routed but are left in a common area, allow them to remain a certain amount of time before filing (for example, two to three days for daily newspapers, two weeks for weeklies, one month for monthlies, and two months for quarterlies).

Each office has its own reference needs, and each office professional has his or her own reference preferences. The best way to decide on yours is to be familiar with what's available, with the needs of the company's employees, and with your own needs and habits of working.

LETTERHEAD AND BUSINESS CARDS

A company's letterhead stationery and business cards are more than simple paper on which to convey a message—they present a distinct image to employees, clients, and potential clients. The letterhead might be a person's first introduction to the company, and first impressions do count. Over time, the letterhead itself creates brand awareness and becomes in itself a type of publicity for the company—especially if it incorporates a logo.

When changing or choosing stationery or business cards, the office professional must be aware of three things: the quality of the paper, the type of printing, and the design of the image. The 20-pound stock paper that people are so accustomed to seeing in reports and photocopies is insufficient for stationery. A professional printer can display a variety of weights, colors, and textures.

Laid paper has a smooth surface, with very fine lines and crosslines. *Wove paper* has a thicker pattern, so that a mesh can be seen when the paper is held to the light. *Parchment* is an off-white paper treated to resemble actual parchment. A *linen finish* adds a noticeable texture to the paper's surface as if it were cloth. *Bond paper* has cotton fibers incorporated into it. In the right weight, any of these is suitable for business stationery, though some texture is preferred by many people for no other reason than that it feels substantial—and *substantial* is a word most companies like to have associated with them.

Whites, ivories, and light grays are standard colors; soft, muted pastels also can be used with care.

Different types of printing are also acceptable: Lithography provides a flat surface, and thermography has a raised surface. Stationery also can be engraved (in which the letters and design are cut into the paper) or embossed (in which the letters and design are pressed into the surface from the back, also creating a raised surface). Foil stamping involves a very thin sheet of metal pressed into the stationery as all or part of the design. Any of these is suitable for business stationery, although thermographic printing cannot tolerate the high heat of fax machines and the printing may melt inside the fax.

The design of the logo should be clear and clean. It does not matter whether the logo is a representation or an abstract image, as long as it is immediately recognizable. The letters should be large enough to be easily read without seeming egotistical or without overpowering the contents of the letter itself. As technology progresses, designers must keep in mind the extra lines of information that are needed—not only company name, address, and phone number (and perhaps an individual's name and title), but also a fax number and Web address. It's important that the design not look cluttered.

When ordering letterhead, office professionals also should order a supply of matching plain paper for those letters that are longer than one page.

Envelopes should match stationery in paper quality, color, type of printing, and font type. If a logo is used, it may be repeated in a smaller version on the envelope.

Many laser and ink jet printers now come with stationery programs to print letterhead, envelopes, and even business cards. At its best, with the purchase of quality paper, printers can simulate lithography. At its worst, the result looks like the company ran out of stationery and is copying its last blank sheet of letterhead, which creates a very poor impression. For that very reason, watch supplies carefully and reorder them with a safe margin of time.

Business cards use the same types of printing as letterhead and mimic its design and color on a heavy paper or light cardboard. Just as too-thin stationery gives a bad impression, so do lightweight business cards. Whenever possible, card stock rather than a heavy paper should be chosen. Preferably, an individual should use business cards imprinted with his or her own name and title, rather than just a company card with the name inked in. The latter makes the person seem insignificant and might prompt clients to search for someone more important. If the company does not provide the executive and/or the office professional with individual business cards, it is worth the small investment to have them made at a personal cost.

A variety of vendors will print stationery and business cards. Open the Yellow Pages under Printers, and you will see dozens of listings, from private commercial printers to nationally franchised instant printers. Weigh the company's needs of quality against price and speed when choosing. After you've decided upon a place (unless you have recommendations and have seen samples from people you know), make the initial order modest (even though it will cost more). If the first order is satisfactory, you can increase the size of later orders.

Other sources of letterheads and business cards can be found online. Note, however, that if you are using a search engine that rates its listings, this function rates the attractiveness, speed, informativeness, and usefulness only of the site itself—*not* the printer.

FOR MORE INFORMATION

If you can't find what you need from the phone numbers and Web sites listed in this chapter, you may need to expand your search.

- For more information on large office equipment such as copiers and fax machines, check in your phone directory under Office Equipment. Most stores will have sales people who will talk you through the basics.

- For more information on small office supplies and where to order, check in your phone directory under Office Supplies. Often, office "super-stores" will have catalogs and delivery services.

- For more information on telephones and office phone systems, check in your Yellow Pages under telecommunications and/or telephones. Many companies have sales reps who will help you assess your needs.

- For more information on obtaining or renting VCRs, projectors, video monitors and other equipment, check in your Yellow Pages under Audio/Visual. Many companies provide daily rental services and will pick up and deliver.

4

MAILING AND SHIPPING

◆

■ **The Office Mail**

 Incoming Mail

 Outgoing Mail

■ **Mailing and Shipping Services**

 Basic Shipping Services

 Mailing and Shipping on the Grand Scale

 Commercial Package-Delivery Services

 Air Freight

 Counter-to-Counter Shipping

 Couriers and Messengers

 Foreign Mail and Shipping

■ **Other Types of Office Communication**

 Telegram

 Cablegram

 Telex

 Fax

■ **U.S. Postal Service**

 Types and Classes of Mail

 Types of USPS Services

 International Mail

 Postage Meters

■ **For More Information**

Effective and efficient communication methods are essential for any business and its employees. These methods increasingly involve high-tech communication, such as e-mail and faxes. Nevertheless, some of the basic methods of communication—namely, mailing and shipping—will always remain necessary. They have also remained largely unchanged. Like most office technologies, though, mailing and shipping have become more complicated with time. In the past, office professionals only had to know how to seal a package and address a letter. Today, they must know everything from airline cargo schedules to overnight pickup times. They must have such varied skills as running postage meters for hundreds of letters and tracking packages on the Internet.

THE OFFICE MAIL

The processing and handling of the mail—U.S. Postal Service mail, express and courier deliveries, and faxes—constitutes one of the most important daily tasks in business. The office mail delivery may represent orders, contracts, inquiries, and many other transactions integral to business. And the office mail may come in several stages: overnight packages, U.S. mail, and nonpriority deliveries. The smooth operation of the office literally depends on the manner in which mail is handled before it leaves the office—or once it arrives.

INCOMING MAIL

The size of an organization has a great bearing on its system for handling mail. In a small office, one person might sort and open all mail except that marked "Personal" or "Confidential." In bigger offices, a designated person might sort the mail, placing mail in folders that are delivered to the recipients' offices, putting the folders in individual mail boxes, or giving them to a designated person. In some offices, faxes might also be delivered to the same boxes or perhaps placed in separate folders near the fax machine. Each office professional will need to work out a system that most efficiently sorts and distributes faxes.

A large organization usually has an entire department where both incoming and outgoing mail are handled according to a standardized system. Mail is sorted—but not opened—and then distributed to mail centers or boxes, or in some cases to individual employees. Either way, the key to effective mail handling is a routine that works for that office.

Courier and overnight express packages should be delivered to addressees as soon as they arrive. Packages that are shipped overnight or by courier are usually important and/or time sensitive.

No matter which system you use for handling mail, letters marked as "Personal" or "Confidential" or any mail that looks particularly personal should be delivered unopened to the addressee. Keep in mind that all mail should be treated as confidential within the office, and the office professional should take care not to repeat or share any information that he or she comes across while opening the company mail.

Picking Up the Mail

Mail will arrive at your office one of two ways: If you have a street address, it will be delivered; if you have a post office box, you will have to pick it up. Most offices have mail delivered. However, if you have a small office with few staff who are not always there, for example a small consulting office or a business that has no foot traffic, a post office box might be best for you.

If you do have a post office box, assign someone to check it every day. It's not a good idea to have someone check it at the end of the day and take the mail home with them; that could lead to problems. The best plan is to find out when the mail is usually sorted (sometimes midmorning, sometimes early afternoon, depending on your post office) and have someone check it then.

Of course, a large mail room or department will have a regular delivery of mail for the entire company from the post office. If you are an assistant for a manager, group, or executive that depends heavily on postal mail, make sure you know when the daily delivery is to the mail room and approximately how much time elapses between delivery to the mail room and delivery to your box or desk.

> **TIP:** If your company wants mail from a post office box delivered to the office, it can hire a service to pick up the mail every day. Such services will make daily deliveries for a fee.

Opening Mail

If you are employed in a small company, you might be responsible for opening and sorting the mail. In a larger company, if you are an assistant for a department or executive, you will be responsible for opening the mail delivered to you by the mail room. If you are responsible for opening the mail on a daily basis, take a minute to prepare before you begin. Use a clear space and keep items you might need close at hand. To efficiently process the mail, here are some items you will want to keep handy:

- Envelope opener
- Stapler
- Paper clips
- Date and time stamp
- Routing slips
- Transparent tape

- Pencils/pens (at least two different colors)

- Memo pad

- Mail register or log, if needed

- Staple remover

If electric equipment, such as a mail opener, stapler, or time stamp, is available, use it. It will save two-thirds of the time as compared with manual equipment, depending on the amount of mail you have to handle every day.

The mail should be opened as soon as it is delivered to your desk, and an orderly procedure should be followed to ensure that nothing is misplaced or lost. Time spent organizing your mail processing system is time saved in the long run. With a system in place, you can quickly and efficiently get important documents to the proper recipients.

Opening the envelopes. All envelopes should be opened before the contents are removed from any of them. To ensure that the contents will not be torn while the letter is being opened, tap the envelope firmly on the edge of the desk so that the contents will slip away from the top. Slit the top of the envelope with a letter opener. If the contents of a letter are cut by the opener, use transparent tape to join the parts together.

Checking the contents. After removing the contents of an envelope, check the letter for a return address. If there is none, staple or paper-clip the envelope containing the return address to the contents. The envelope should also be retained if the signature on the letter is not easily legible.

Check to determine that all enclosures stipulated in the letter are accounted for. If not, a notation should be made immediately on the face of the letter, indicating what is missing.

Even though annotating a letter is one of the procedures encouraged, some companies do not like correspondence marked up, especially legal or business firms that might have to submit a piece of correspondence as evidence in a court of law. Always follow company policy. Some companies prefer that you place a sticky note with the notation on the face of the letter. It serves the same purpose and doesn't alter the document itself.

Dating the mail. It is always wise to affix each day's date on incoming mail. The easiest procedure is to use a rubber stamp. Such a procedure is helpful if the letter has arrived too late to meet a requested deadline, has been in transit longer than it should have been, or is undated. In either of the last two cases, it is best to staple the envelope to the letter, in addition to dating the letter. This will give evidence of the date of mailing as well as the date of receipt.

Envelopes. In general you may destroy the envelope after you have ascertained that everything has been removed and that there are no problems concerning the names, addresses, or dates. However, in certain situations, especially legal matters, an envelope sometimes serves as evidence of date and time received (from the canceled postage stamp). In such situations, keep the envelope and clip or staple it to the back of the letter.

Preparing Mail

If you are an assistant for an executive or manager who receives large amounts of mail, he or she may want you to "prepare" the mail, which means that you read through it, make notes, and help prioritize. Some specifics include:

1. Read each letter or document, underlining important points that will aid you and your employer in answering the letter. Underline only those things that are of significance, such as publications, dates, and names of people.

2. Make annotations on documents, where appropriate, using removable notes. Do not write directly on any legal documents. Generally, annotations fall into four categories:

   a. Documents to be signed, such as contracts, agreements, employee documents, and expense reports. Make a separate folder for documents requiring a signature, and use multiple categories if your boss needs to prioritize the documents when there isn't time to sign them all at once.

   b. Action required by the letter—date, such as an appointment for the correspondent or reservations for a trip the employer may have to make as a result of the correspondence, and so on.

   c. Procedures to be followed. These may depend upon former correspondence with the same person or related correspondence, which will have to be sought in the files.

   d. The priority the letter should receive, symbolized by a code. In an agreement with the employer, a given place on each letter should be established for this code. For example, a red number may be written in the upper-left corner. Such codes might be:

      Code 1. Mail and reports having high priority and requiring a decision. These should be answered the same day they are received. (It is assumed that personal or confidential mail is delivered unopened to the addressee as soon as it arrives on the office professional's desk.)

      Code 2. Mail for which additional information must be procured and for which an answer may have to be deferred for a day or two while data are being collected. *All mail should be answered within 48 hours of receipt,* except under very unusual circumstances.

      Code 3. Routine mail that an office professional may be able to handle. Many employers want to see all mail; it is wise to determine an employer's preference in this regard. After the relationship is well established, many support personnel have their employers' permission to reply to routine letters. In such instances, it is usually good procedure to supply the employer with copies of the letters sent as well as the original letter.

Code 4. Letters that require notations but no reply.

This type of procedure makes it a simple matter to encode and sort the mail as you are preparing it for the employer. A fifth or even a sixth category may be added as needed. Important reports usually require a special category, while weekly, monthly, or semimonthly periodicals may require no encoding. Most employers prefer to examine the periodicals before they are made available to others in the office.

Preparing supplementary material. As the letters are being annotated, an efficient office professional will also make a list of files or pieces of correspondence and other information to be looked up before presenting the correspondence to the employer.

Some employers wish to see the mail as soon as it has been opened. In that case, bring the mail in as soon as you have annotated it. While the mail is being read, you can take the compiled list and seek the necessary files, reports, and other information for acting upon the urgent mail. To keep all papers pertaining to each piece of correspondence together, use file folders or small clips.

Arranging the mail. After the sorting process has been completed, arrange the mail either in one pile with the high-priority mail on top or in any other arrangement that has been agreed upon. Whenever the mail is placed on the desk of the employer, some provision should be made to prevent others from reading the top letter; for example, simply place the top letter face down.

Absence of the employer. When the employer is away from the office, letters requiring immediate replies may be handled in either of two ways. First, if a decision must be made immediately, give the mail to the person in charge during the employer's absence. Second, if the employer will be in the office within a day or two and the decision can wait, contact the sender immediately and explain when a reply may be expected and the reason for the delay.

The efficient assistant to whom the employer has entrusted routine correspondence will maintain a file of materials handled during the employer's absence. The folder should be readily at hand upon the employer's return.

OUTGOING MAIL

Even if your company is large enough to have a mailing and shipping department, chances are you will in some way be responsible for preparing outgoing mail. Time and expense can be saved by learning about the various postal and shipping services available and the general regulations and normal charges pertinent to these services. It is important to be alert to frequent changes. If your company is small, remember to talk with your post office representative

Preparing a Package for Shipping

If your company doesn't have a mail room, chances are high that you will prepare packages for shipping. Whether it's a box of magazines or a laptop computer, some basic rules apply for shipping items safely. The goal is to get a package from your office to its destination without the contents breaking or the package getting lost.

- Use a sturdy box. Avoid using boxes that have worn corners or torn tops or sides, even if they are reinforced with tape.

- Use packing material all around the item. If you are shipping something fragile, remember to use packing material underneath it and all around it.

- Stuff glass and fragile hollow items like glasses or vases with newspaper or packing material.

- Remove batteries from electronic equipment such as laptops and calculators. Wrap separately.

- Use tape that is designed for shipping, such as pressure-sensitive tape, nylon-reinforced paper tape, or glass-reinforced pressure-sensitive tape.

- Tape the bottom and sides of the package, especially if it is heavy.

- Don't use wrapping paper, string, masking tape, or cellophane tape.

- Type or print the label clearly; then place it in the center of the top of the box. Tape over the label with clear tape to keep it in place and to keep it from smearing. Make sure you put the delivery and return addresses on one side of the package only.

- Make sure you include a clear return address for the package.

- If shipping by UPS or other commercial shipper, make sure you affix all the proper stamps, weight notations, and tracking documents.

- If shipping internationally, make sure you have included all the appropriate customs documents.

before preparing a large mailing. There may be certain size and weight restrictions that you'll want to know about before you start a large project.

For preparing outgoing mail, keep a few supplies at your desk to save time. For overnight delivery, have some overnight folders or packages handy. Keep the name of the courier service (and the contact's name), along with the account information, in your card file or in another list of contacts. For regular mailings, keep these items handy:

- Number 10 and Number 6³⁄₄ envelopes
- Preprinted labels and/or return address stickers
- Water bottle for moistening envelopes

For larger mail rooms or mail spaces in offices, have on hand:

- Clear or reinforced packing tape
- Packing material (used computer print-out paper works well, or styrofoam "peanuts" available from any shipping store)
- Large labels for boxes
- Small postage scale for letters
- Large scale for packages (make sure it's calibrated)
- Postage meter for letters (larger meters will both seal and stamp envelopes)
- Assorted stamps
- Tracking book for overnight shipping

Getting Mail Out

With today's services, there are a multitude of ways to send packages and documents. In a large company, make sure you know where to drop off mail and packages for pickup—and when the last pickup of the day is. Also make sure you note the cutoff for overnight deliveries and shipping other packages. Each mail department will have a slightly different policy. For smaller offices, make sure someone is responsible every day for dropping the mail at the post office before the last pickup of the day. If packages need to be shipped or must go overnight, someone should be responsible for calling UPS, FedEx, or any other shipping or overnight delivery service for pickup. If your shipping person makes a daily stop at your office, make sure everyone is aware what time the cutoff is for having packages fully prepared. The pickup person is usually on a tight schedule, so don't keep him or her waiting while you add labels, re-tape, or otherwise prepare your package for shipping.

MINIMUM AND NONSTANDARD MAIL SIZES

Minimum Size Standards

Pieces ¼-inch thick or less are mailable if they are rectangular and:

- At least 3½ inches high
- At least 5 inches long (items sent to foreign countries must be at least 5½ inches long)
- At least .007 inch thick (about the thickness of a postcard)

Mail not meeting these standards is returned to sender.

Nonstandard Size Mail

Nonstandard size mail is more costly to handle because it usually cannot be mechanically processed. First-Class Mail, single-piece Standard Mail (A), and international letters are nonstandard if they weigh 1 ounce or less and if they exceed any of these size limits:

- Height exceeds 6⅛ inches
- Length exceeds 11½ inches
- Thickness exceeds ¼ inch
- Length divided by height is less than 1.3 or more than 2.5 inches

A surcharge, in addition to the applicable postage and fees, is applied to each piece of nonstandard size mail for two reasons: It compensates the U.S. Postal Service for the added cost of manually handling nonstandard mail, and it promotes the design and use of mail that can be processed mechanically.

TIP: Make sure everyone in the office knows the regular pickup schedule for packages and letters. If the mail room is closing early, send out an e-mail so employees can get any critical mail or overnight packages out.

MAILING AND SHIPPING SERVICES

Sometimes, for any of a variety of reasons, an office professional needs help with mailing and shipping. Whether it's the odd-shaped office chair that needs to be shipped to an employee who works from home, or 100,000 brochures that need to go to customers, the task can be daunting. Often, it is worth the money to have an outside, professional service tackle the job.

BASIC SHIPPING SERVICES

For the packages and large items that need to be shipped, commercial mail and parcel centers have sprung up as retail businesses. These centers can handle many of the office functions that you might have to tackle, for a fee, naturally. Typical services include making photocopies, wrapping and shipping packages, and providing private postal boxes.

If your business is willing to pay the premium for the convenience these services offer, this can be a time- and effort-saving way to go, especially for the small office or home office that doesn't warrant the investment in, say, higher-volume, higher-speed copiers. It can pay to shop for service, price, and convenience.

Some operations are linked as part of large franchises, some may operate as semiautonomous "departments" in office supply stores, and still others are independently owned and operated. Typically they're located for convenience in downtown centers or easy-to-reach malls. Look for them in the advertising pages of the phone book under "Mailing Services" or in the white pages under their franchise name.

> **TIP:** Retail shipping centers are great places to pack and ship odd-size packages safely, but you should keep close track of your expenses if you use them to send overnight mail or to rent a postal box. If you work at home in a small office, it is probably worth your while to get your own company account with a shipping company—and the company will usually come to your office for a pickup when you call.

MAILING AND SHIPPING ON THE GRAND SCALE

The large-scale direct mail campaign or shipping effort requires proportionately greater planning. There are, for example, significant postal economies to be gained by doing a number of things in a very deliberate and specific way. But managing the requisite elements is usually beyond the scope of the daily routine in most office settings.

Examples of such large-scale efforts include designing direct mail promotional pieces for your company that qualify for significant "bulk" postal discounts; placing logos and advertising copy; and ZIP-sequencing a significant quantity of letter-type mail, delivering it to the post office in order, and arranging for reply mail. The preceding are just a few elements of a very complicated and sophisticated business. If these tasks are not a big part of your company's primary business, you should probably not tackle a large-scale mailing or shipping effort alone.

In advertising agencies, commercial printing companies, and full-time mailing services, you'll find people who make it their business to execute direct marketing campaigns professionally. Get them to work for you when the mailing/shipping stakes are high.

COMMERCIAL PACKAGE-DELIVERY SERVICES

Beyond the U.S. Postal Service, there are any number of commercial package-delivery services. Currently they are used most often to ship larger packages than what the U.S. Postal Service (USPS) handles easily or conveniently, or when extra-speedy service is worth the extra cost that such shippers typically charge.

> **TIP:** Often, when working on big projects and tight schedules, a package or document will need to be shipped or scheduled for overnight delivery after the appointed pickup time. Keep a list available for everyone in the office giving the deadlines and drop-offs for other shipping services or stations. For example, in California, UPS makes office pickups for overnight shipping around 4:00 P.M.; even if you drive to the UPS office at the airport, the latest you can ship a package overnight might be 6:45 P.M. On the East Coast, packages can be shipped overnight often as late as 9:00 P.M. All of these times change often, so always check before sending someone out.

Several high-profile companies, such as United Parcel Service (UPS), FedEx, Airborne Express, and DHL are synonymous with "overnight" delivery.

There are, it should be noted, numerous alternatives to these high-profile shippers. To find shippers, check your telephone directory under "Delivery Services" or "Package Express Service."

Commercial package shippers typically offer overnight service with multiple levels: usually, early morning next day, midday or early afternoon, and next day delivery. Other services might include two- to three-day service for a discounted rate, package tracking, door-to-door pickup and delivery, etc. Some shipping companies also offer "ground" service as a regular package shipping option. Picking the best service for the package is key. If you are shipping important documents for an early morning meeting, then priority next day is what you'll need. If morning delivery isn't necessary, the less-expensive next day or two-day service will suffice. Ground or overland shipping is usually best for large packages that don't need to arrive right away.

The type of service, costs, and speed of delivery vary from service to service. Individual companies can provide comparative information on rates and limitations on items transported. Just remember, the needs of the business should drive the decision making process. Volume discounts can be negotiated. Electronic connection to the shipper might speed the process and cut your paperwork.

COMMERCIAL PACKAGE-DELIVERY SERVICES					
Company	*Same Day*	*Next Morning*	*Next Afternoon*	*2–3 Day*	*Door-to-Door Delivery*
Airborne Express		X	X	X	X
American Airlines	X	X	X	X	X[1]
Associated Global Systems	X	X	X	X	X
Burlington Air Express	X	X[1]	X	X	X
Continental Airlines	X	X	X	X	X[1]
Delta Airlines DASH	X[1]	X[1]	X[1]	X[1]	X[1]
DHL Worldwide	X	X			X
Emery Worldwide		X	X	X	X
FedEx		X	X	X	X
Roadway Express	X	X	X	X	X[1]
Roadway Package Service				X	X[1]
Sky Courier	X[1]	X[1]	X[1]		X[1]
Sonic Air	X	X	X	X	X
TNT Express Worldwide	X	X	X	X	X
TWA	X	X	X	X	X
United Airlines	X	X	X	X	X[1]
UPS		X[1]	X[1]	X[1]	X[1]
US Airways	X	X	X	X	X[1]
USPS Express Mail		X[1]	X	X	X

[1] Domestic shipments only.

TIP: Always record the tracking number! Most overnight shipping companies now offer Web sites that let you instantly find out where your package is, if it's been delivered, and who signed for it. Don't hesitate to track it down if it hasn't arrived on time. Often you can get credit back to your account if your package doesn't arrive on time.

Don't buy more service than you need. If the volume of any one kind of shipment does not warrant using a special shipper, then consolidating your mixed bag of shipping with a single service source may be the most sensible course, even though it may not be the most economical for all types of shipments.

AIR FREIGHT

Air freight, also known as air cargo shipping, is a service typically offered by airline companies for shipping packages on passenger airline flights. The cargo is loaded on the plane and rides in the cargo hold with passenger luggage. It can be used for any size package, as long as it doesn't exceed the airline size and weight requirements. The service is timely, but packages need to be delivered and picked up to and from the airport. However, air freight services will often deliver the cargo on the other end as part of the service. Such service is only a bit more costly and works best for large and awkward packages, but make sure you call ahead to package the cargo correctly. Often there is also a weight limit.

TIP: Air freight terminals are located at major airports, away from the main passenger terminal buildings. If you are picking up or dropping off a package for air freight, make sure you get directions to the building. Also make sure you get a price and find out the method of payment. It's frustrating to make a long trek to the freight terminal only to find out that the company check you brought is unacceptable and they take only credit cards.

COUNTER-TO-COUNTER SHIPPING

Counter-to-counter shipping is another type of shipping service offered by airline companies. It varies from air freight in several important ways. Packages shipped counter-to-counter travel in the cargo hold of an aircraft with passenger luggage, the same as air freight, but they are processsed in the main passenger terminal as if they were luggage—unlike air freight which goes to and

---

TIPS FOR RETAINING A COURIER SERVICE

- There are more than 10,000 courier services in the United States.
- Most are dedicated to servicing a particular region.
- Some operate 24 hours a day.
- Most require you to set up an account in advance.
- Ask for references in advance.
- Compare reliability and variety of services offered, as well as cost.
- Most offer regular and rush services.

---

from a separate airline freight terminal. When packages are shipped counter-to-counter, you drop them off in the baggage office at the airline terminal and they come off the conveyer belt in baggage claim with passenger baggage.

While air freight is good for large or awkward packages, counter-to-counter is better for small packages that must arrive faster than overnight in another city. Suppose you are supporting staff who are running an important conference in Washington, D.C., and you are in the home office in San Francisco; you can get those brochures to them that they need for an 8:00 A.M. meeting. Just call the airline and specify when you want the packages to arrive. They'll give you the flight info, and you drive the package to the airport just as if you were dropping off a passenger. Payment is made at the drop-off. It's a bit more expensive than standard air freight, but worth it when the situation is time critical. There are weight limits and time limits, so call ahead. And make sure you forward the flight arrival info to the recipients—someone will have to go to the airport to pick up the package.

COURIERS AND MESSENGERS

Here's a service that is, by and large, truly local. Need to get a packet of information across town in a hurry? Well, if you've ever been downtown in a large city and almost run over by a bicycle or, in a smaller city or town, seen delivery vehicles zipping between offices, you've seen the couriers and messengers that are largely relied upon in many cities for door-to-door communications.

If you will be using a service in the near future, call ahead to set up an account. If you wait to call until the first time you need them, it could take longer. Often, to set up an account, courier services will check credit worthiness. You should do a similar degree of reference checking, especially about punctuality of such services and the company's reputation for courteous and professional service.

Make sure you brief office staff on the delivery windows and costs. Usually courier services are set up so that anyone can schedule a pickup. Make sure anyone who schedules a pickup is aware that there is usually a significant cost difference between, say, one- to two-hour service and three- to four-hour service.

FOREIGN MAIL AND SHIPPING

Most of today's commercial shipping services can deliver packages internationally. Even though they may not guarantee overnight service to some areas, they are often the fastest way to ship overseas. Documents are usually required for packages that are shipped internationally, whether by airlines or by commercial shipping services like UPS. However, some shipping companies do not require documentation for letter-size envelopes. If you have a mail or shipping department, they will usually take care of this for you. If you prepare your own packages, however, call ahead to verify what will be required and to find out size, weight limits, documentation required, which items you can and cannot ship, etc.

OTHER TYPES OF OFFICE COMMUNICATION

Long before faxing was a common occurrence and e-mail deluged office and home computers everywhere, there were other "electronic" forms of communication. Cables and telegrams were the primary way urgent messages were communicated between businesses for much of this century. In the 1970s and 1980s, telex was popular, especially among international business, but as the facsimile machine came on the scene and more companies were able to communicate via computer networks and the Internet, many of these once popular forms of office communication fell by the wayside. Most are still available today, although it may take some research to find a service. Try the local phone directory or the Post Office.

Note that these services are still utilized in many foreign countries. Even though they are not frequently used in the United States, a good office professional should at least know what the service is and where to find it.

TELEGRAM

A telegram is still a valid method for sending messages anywhere in the continental United States. A *telegram* is a message transmitted through a company called Western Union, and the message typically is phoned to the recipient. If the sender wants a printed message delivered as well, that must be

WEB SITES FOR SHIPPING SERVICES

FedEx	http://www.fedex.com
Institute of Management and Administration's Mail Center Management Report Site	http://www.ioma.com/ioma/mcmr
Mail Boxes, Etc.	http://www.mbe.com
United Parcel Service	http://www.ups.com
United States Postal Service	http://www.usps.gov

indicated. Many offices require a typed copy for their files. The typed telegram is spaced to fit printed lines on a form. The cost of a telegram may be charged to the sender's phone number. The message is usually brief because the number of words determines the cost.

Telegrams are accepted for immediate transmission for delivery within two hours by telephone and five hours by messenger, subject to the open hours of the delivery office and special holiday concerns.

CABLEGRAM

A *cablegram* is essentially an international telegram that can be sent to almost every country in the world in the language of the recipient. A cablegram is also sent by Western Union and is usually delivered within 24 hours. It is most often printed out and hand delivered, but in some areas of the world it may be mailed or phoned to the recipient.

TELEX

Most telexes today are international and are used where e-mail or fax aren't available. *Telexes* are basically connected-by-phone typewriters that only handle numbers and letters, and cannot transmit graphic images. Some companies maintain their own networks. Others use Western Union's teletypewriter network. Either way, telexes offer the timeliness of a phone call and the convenience of a paper copy.

FAX

Once called by its full name "facsimile transmission" and requiring sizeable pieces of equipment that used chemically coated thermal paper, technological advances have made the *fax* another must-have piece of communications equipment for most modern offices. Today's machines send instantly and receive on regular copy paper.

Virtually any type of document—photographs, diagrams, statistical information, handwritten or typewritten messages—can be faxed within a matter of minutes. And the received document looks substantially like the original.

☎ 800 NUMBERS FOR COMMERCIAL PACKAGE-DELIVERY SERVICES

Airborne Express	800-247-2676
American Airlines	800-443-7300
Associated Global Systems	800-645-8300
Burlington Air Express	800-225-5229
Continental Airlines	800-421-2456
Delta Airlines DASH	800-638-7333
DHL Worldwide	800-272-7345
Emery Worldwide	800-443-6379
FedEx	800-238-5355
Roadway Express	800-257-2837
Roadway Package Service	800-762-3725
Sky Courier	800-336-3344
Sonic Air	800-782-7892
TNT Express Worldwide	800-368-3400
TWA	800-892-2746
United Airlines	800-825-3788
United Parcel Service	800-742-5877
US Airways	800-428-4322
U.S. Postal Service Express Mail	800-222-1811

U.S. POSTAL SERVICE

Despite the number of commercial package delivery services, the U.S. Postal Service still carries the bulk of all mail that is delivered in this country every day. If your company does a large amount of bulk or commercial mailing, chances are you already have talked to an agent at the post office who works with companies having bulk mail accounts. To get a bulk mail permit, you need an account with the post office. They will coordinate with you the postage amounts and payments to ensure that your business mail is delivered on time.

Sometimes the policies can be so confusing for different weights, sizes, ZIP codes, etc., that it's best to talk to the post office before you plan your marketing piece or brochure. That way you can design your piece around the most cost effective mode of delivery. It also saves surprises when you're all finished with your mailing and find out you have made it too large, too small, or too heavy to fit in a price range.

For updates and changes, check the USPS Web site for the latest pricing and addressing information. Electronic tools such as the Postal Explorer CD-ROM from USPS provide a minimally priced desktop toolbox of information. And finally, if your shipping and mailing volumes are sizeable, membership in organizations such as local Mail Councils may be useful, as well as training by, or subscriptions from, nonprofit or for-profit third parties. Check out the Web site.

There are several primary sources of authoritative information about services offered by the U.S. Postal Service. A comprehensive, yet understandable, overview source that is good for office reference is the *Quick Service Guide,* available from your local post office, from a Postal Business Center, or directly from the Postal Service, National Customer Support Center, 6060 Primacy Parkway, Memphis, TN 38188-0001; telephone: 800-238-3150. Or you can find it easily at the USPS Web site.

TYPES AND CLASSES OF MAIL

From personal letters to business correspondence and from advertisements to magazines and packages, the U.S. Postal Service (USPS) handles a huge volume of mail. It also offers a wide range of services, many of which are not provided by any other mail delivery entity. Although the USPS does offer overnight shipping, it really specializes in handling bulk and commercial mail at a reasonable rate—and in a timely manner. Before you choose a rate or service, make sure you call the Post Office for additional information on special mailing rates for books, catalogs, and international mailings.

First-Class Mail

Use *First-Class Mail* for sending letters, postcards, stamped cards, greeting cards, personal notes, checks, and money orders. If you have mail that weighs over 13 ounces, such as a package or large letter packet, you must send it Priority Mail. The post office can tell you how much the postage will be, or if you have a postage meter at the office, it will automatically calculate the rate.

All First-Class Mail receives prompt handling and transportation. If your First-Class Mail is not letter size, make sure to mark it "First Class." First-Class Mail moves fairly well, but expect delivery domestically to take three to seven days depending on the distance.

Express Mail

Express Mail is the USPS overnight delivery service. It is also offered internationally. Important letters, documents, and merchandise may be sent Express Mail. A full postage refund is made for all domestic shipments delivered later than the guaranteed commitment for that particular service.

To use Express Mail Next Day Service, take your shipment to a post office that offers the service, generally by 5:00 P.M.; deposit it in the Express Mail collection box or call for on-demand pickup or hand it to your letter carrier. Your local post office can give you specific Express Mail acceptance times for your area. Depending on the destination, your mailing will be delivered to the addressee either by noon or by 3:00 P.M. the next day. Express Mail Post Office to Post Office service can also be picked up at the destination post office by 10:00 A.M. the next day.

Priority Mail

Priority Mail offers expedited delivery, usually two to three days, but not overnight service. The rate is slightly higher than regular mail but significantly lower than overnight delivery. Priority Mail should be stickered and can be used for packages up to 70 pounds.

Periodicals

Only publishers and registered news agents approved for Periodicals mailing privileges may mail at the *Periodicals* rates. For magazines and newspapers mailed by the general public, other rates such as First-Class or Standard Mail (A) must be paid.

Standard Mail (A)

Standard Mail (A) is used primarily by retailers, catalogers, and other advertisers to promote their products and services. Churches and other eligible nonprofit organizations may apply to take advantage of nonprofit rates for their large mailings.

Currently, the minimum volume needed for using either the Standard Mail (A) rates or the Nonprofit Standard Mail rate is 200 pieces or 50 pounds per mailing. The pieces must each weigh less than 16 ounces and be prepared in a manner that allows for efficient handling. Standard Mail (A) also includes rates that anyone may use to send individual parcels weighing less than 1 pound.

Standard Mail (B)

Standard Mail (B) is a parcel rate for packages weighing more than 1 pound. (The rate varies if First-Class Mail is attached or enclosed.) Insurance is not included in this rate but is easily purchasable.

TYPES OF USPS SERVICES

There are several services offered by the United States Postal Service not offered by any other company or organization.

General Delivery

General delivery is used primarily at post offices without carrier delivery or those serving travelers and other customers who do not have a permanent mailing address. Mail endorsed "General Delivery" is placed in a general delivery case. The mail can be picked up by the addressee on request at a retail window. Proper identification is required.

Mail Forwarding

If your office is moving, your mail will follow you! By filling out the proper forms—Form 3575, *Change of Address Order*—your service will be uninterrupted. You must include the effective date of the change on all notification forms. Your complete new address should be included. All Express Mail, Priority Mail, and First-Class Mail such as cards and letters are forwarded for one year. There is no charge for this service.

Periodicals mail, including magazines and newspapers, is forwarded at no charge for 60 days from the effective date of your change of address order. Publishers are required to subscribe to the USPS address correction service. Normally, magazines will not need to be forwarded for longer than 60 days.

Certificate of Mailing

A *certificate of mailing* is a receipt showing evidence of mailing. It can be purchased only at the time of mailing. The certificate does not provide insurance coverage for loss or damage, nor does it provide proof of delivery. No record is kept at the mailing office, and a receipt is not obtained when mail is delivered to the addressee.

Certified Mail

Certified mail provides proof of mailing and delivery of mail. The sender receives a mailing receipt at the time of mailing, and a record of delivery is kept at the recipient's post office. A return receipt to provide the sender with proof of delivery can also be purchased for an additional fee. Certified mail service is available only for First-Class Mail or Priority Mail. Certified mail is not available for international mail, nor does it offer insurance protection.

Collect on Delivery

Collect on Delivery, COD, service is used when the mailer wants to collect payment for the merchandise and/or postage when the merchandise is delivered. COD service can be used for merchandise sent by First-Class Mail, registered mail, Express Mail, Priority Mail, or Standard Mail. The addressee has the choice of paying for the COD at the time of delivery, either by cash or by personal check, and the merchandise must have been ordered by the addressee.

Fees charged for this service include insurance protection against loss or damage.

Merchandise Return Service

Merchandise return service allows permit holders to pay the postage and fees for merchandise returned to them. The service enables the recipient to return a parcel and have the postage paid by the sender. Under this arrangement, the shipper provides a special label with instructions to attach it to the returning parcel. Apply this label to the parcel and deposit the parcel at a post office or, if it is under 16 ounces, place it in a mailbox.

POST OFFICE BOXES

Post office box service is available for businesses and individuals at most post offices for a small semiannual or annual fee. There are five post office box sizes from which to choose. The fee varies with the size of the box and the classification category of the post office. Post office box delivery is a secure and private means of getting your mail anytime the lobby of the post office is open. With post offices conveniently located near most businesses, you can get a jump on your day by receiving your mail at a post office box near where you work.

Registered Mail

Registered mail is the most secure service option offered by the Postal Service. It provides added protection for valuable and important mail. Registered articles are placed under tight security from the point of mailing to the point of delivery. First-Class Mail or Priority Mail postage is required on domestic registered mail. Return receipt and restricted delivery services are available for additional fees, and insurance up to $25,000 can be purchased on domestic registered mail at the mailer's option. Registered mail to Canada is subject to $1,000 indemnity limit. For all other countries the indemnity limit is currently $42.30.

Restricted Delivery

Restricted delivery means that the sender's mail is delivered only to a specific addressee or to someone authorized in writing to receive mail for the addressee. Restricted delivery mail addressed to officials of government agencies, members of the legislative and judicial branches of federal and state governments, members of the diplomatic corps, minors, and individuals under guardianship can be delivered to an agent without the addressee's written authorization. Restricted delivery is available only for registered mail, certified mail, COD mail, and mail insured for more than $50.

Return Receipt

A *return receipt* can be purchased for COD mail, Express Mail, mail insured for more than $50, and registered or certified mail. The return receipt shows who signed for the item and the date that it was delivered. Unless prohibited by law, the return receipt also provides the delivery address if the address on the mailpiece is no longer correct. Return receipt service can be purchased in conjunction with restricted delivery service. It can also be requested before or after mailing.

Return Receipt for Merchandise

This form of *return receipt* service provides a mailing receipt, return receipt, and record of delivery. It is available for merchandise sent at the First-Class Mail, Priority Mail, and Standard Mail postage rates.

Special Handling

Special handling service is required for parcels whose unusual contents require additional care in transit and handling.

Special handling is not required for those parcels sent by First-Class Mail, Express Mail, or Priority Mail. Examples of such contents include live poultry or bees. Special handling is available for Standard Mail only, including insured and COD mail. This service provides preferential handling to the extent practical in dispatch and transportation.

INTERNATIONAL MAIL

All mail originating in foreign countries and U.S. overseas territories, other than the Commonwealth of Puerto Rico, is subject to U.S. Customs Service examination upon entering the United States. Many imported goods are subject to the payment of U.S. Customs duty. When dutiable merchandise enters the United States by mail, the amount due is determined by the Customs Service but is collected by the Postal Service. When the duty is collected on behalf of the Customs Service, the Postal Service also collects a customs clearance and delivery fee on each dutiable item.

Types of International Mail

LC Mail—lettres et cartes—includes aerograms, letters, postcards, and postal cards. LC Mail is defined as "personal handwritten or typewritten communications having the character of current correspondence." The weight limit for LC Mail is 4 pounds. Type the word *letter* or *lettre* on the envelope. If the contents are not duty-free, you must attach *Customs Douane C-1* (Form 2976) or *Customs Declaration C-2* (Form 2976A) for packages valued above $400.

AO Mail—autre objets—includes printed matter, books, sheet music, small packets, periodicals, and audio and videotapes. The weight limit for AO Mail varies. Printed matter weighing between 11 and 66 pounds that is to go to a single address can be packaged in a *direct sack* or *M-bag*. Type the words "Printed Matter," or "Printed Matter—Periodicals," or "Printed Matter—Videotapes" on the package. If the contents are not duty-free, you must attach *Customs Douane C-1* (Form 2976) or *Customs Declaration C-2* (Form 2976A) for packages valued above $400.

Small Packet Mail covers gifts, merchandise, and commercial documents that don't fall under the definition of LC Mail can be shipped as AO Mail. Type the words "Small Packet" on the package. You must attach *Customs Douane C-1* (Form 2976) or *Customs Declaration C-2* (Form 2976A) for packages valued above $400. Cambodia, Cuba, and North Korea do not accept these Small Packets.

TIPS FOR OVERSEAS SHIPPING AND MAILING

Follow USPS address quality standards when addressing international packages. On the last line, include only the name of the destination country in capital letters. The same is true for the return address.

Include the destination country's postal codes if known. These should go on the second to last line after the city, state, or province name.

The U.S. Customs Service requires you to declare the content and value of mail shipped internationally.

*CP International Mail—colis postaux—*is very similar to USPS parcel post. It includes merchandise and nonletter mail. The weight limit for CP International Mail is 22 to 44 pounds. You must attach *Parcel Post Customs Declaration* (Form 2966-A) or *Parcel Post Customs Declaration and Dispatch Note* (Form 2966-B).

*EMS Mail—Express Mail International Service—*is very similar to USPS Express Mail; however, the service is not guaranteed. Packages can be insured. Corporate accounts can be established. Not all countries worldwide provide this service—check with the USPS. You must attach *Customs Douane C-1* (Form 2976) or *Parcel Post Customs Declaration* (Form 2966-A).

*IPA Mail—International Priority Airmail—*includes all LC and AP Mail. Volume and sorting requirements must be met. IPA Mail is designed to provide an international fast delivery alternative—check with the USPS for rates and requirements.

*ISAL Mail—International Surface Air Lift—*includes printed matter and is designed to provide faster service than surface mail at less cost than airmail. Drop-off sites are specified by the USPS—check with the USPS for rates and sites.

*WPL Mail—Worldpost Priority Letter—*is available in two flat-rate sizes: $9 \times 11\frac{1}{2}$ and 5×9. WPL Mail is delivered within four days on average.

All printed matter items, small packets, and parcel post packages may be sent either airmail or surface mail. Check with your local post office for specific information about the mail service in the country to which you are mailing.

Customs Forms

Customs forms are required when you send dutiable letter packages, small packets, printed matter, and parcels to international destinations. The specific customs form is governed by the type of mail, the weight of the item, and the regulations of the destination country.

Individual countries may restrict or prohibit certain articles, which makes them nonmailable. Articles that are restricted are subject to the import requirements of that country. The *International Mail Manual,* available at your local post office, gives specific information about restrictions and prohibitions for individual countries and about the forms required for mailing.

POSTAGE METERS

When a mailer uses a postage meter, the postage, place of mailing, and date are imprinted at the mailer's place of business. Many mailers, including those mailing a relatively small volume of mail, have found that this convenience more than offsets the costs of maintaining an account and leasing the machine.

POSTAGE METER VENDORS

Ascom Hasler Mailing Systems
19 Forest Parkway
Shelton, CT 06484-0903
203-926-1087

Friden Neopost
30955 Huntwood Avenue
Hayward, CA 94544-7085
800-624-7892

Pitney-Bowes, Inc.
Walter H. Wheeler Jr. Drive
Stamford, CT 06926-0001
203-356-5000

Postalia, Inc.
1980 University Lane
Lisle, IL 60532-2152
708-241-9090

Currently four companies are authorized by the USPS to manufacture and rent you postage meters. They are: Pitney-Bowes, Inc., Postalia, Friden Neopost, and Ascom Hasler Mailing Systems. Your phone book should reveal dealers in your area who will help you assess the costs and benefits, help complete the necessary paperwork, show you how to operate the equipment, and get you started with the USPS.

What do postage meters do? How do they work?

- Postage meters help monitor shipping costs.

- Metered mail is processed more quickly.

- Use fluorescent ink to ensure speedy processing.

- Postage meters can only be rented, not purchased.

- A license from the U.S. Postal Service is required.

- Postage meters must be reset every three months.

- Older model meters must be taken to a post office to be reset.

- Newer models can often be reset by calling the manufacturer, sometimes even via a modem.

- Most models can hold enough postage ($100 to $10,000) for the entire quarter.

- Payment for postage must be received by the U.S. Postal Service before a meter can be reset (except for Neopost machines).

FOR MORE INFORMATION

If you can't find what you need from the phone numbers and Web sites listed in this chapter, you may need to expand your search.

- For more information on mailing: Try the United States Postal Service Web Site (www.usps.gov). For more specific information, call your local post office.

- For more information on shipping: Check Web sites for individual shipping companies. Call airlines directly for all information on air cargo and air freight shipping. Most Web sites for individual shipping companies can now process tracking numbers for packages.

- For more information on other forms of office communication: Check your Yellow Pages for information on Telex, Telegram, and other services. Call Western Union directly if you have questions about types of service or costs.

5

COMPUTERS

◆

- **Personal Computers**
    - Parts of the PC
    - Peripherals
    - Types of PCs
- **Networks**
    - Two Kinds of Networks
    - Network and Internet Communications
- **Operating Systems**

- **Software Applications**
    - Word Processing Software
    - Spreadsheet Software
    - Database Management (DBM)
    - Presentation Software
    - Desktop Publishing
    - Communications Software
    - Other Applications
- **Basic Guidelines for Selecting Software**
    - Understanding Upgrades
    - Software Bundles
- **For More Information**

The impact of the computer on the office and personal environment grown exponentially since the first computer was introduced just after World War II. The first-generation machines were expensive, often room-sized mainframes capable of processing a few millions of instructions per minute. Next came smaller, general-purpose minicomputers tailored to meet the needs of small to medium-sized businesses. In the early 1980s, the smallest and fastest-growing category of computers evolved: personal computers (PCs). Originally known as microcomputers, these computers earned their names from the microprocessor chips that function as the brain.

Today's desktop computers, or PCs, are faster and more powerful than earlier mainframes and can process many millions of instructions per second. Chip-processing speed is measured in Hertz (Hz). One Hertz equals a million instructions per second. That means that a Pentium processor with a speed of 450 megahertz (MHz) is capable of processing 450 million instructions per second. PCs have grown in speed, memory, and capability; they are used in businesses, schools, and homes and now make up the largest and fastest-growing category of computers.

PERSONAL COMPUTERS

Most of the processing parts of the computer are invisible to the eye. As a user, you mainly are concerned with the applications of the PC and the most popular software packages to run those applications. Today's PCs most commonly are used for the following functions: word processing of letters and all forms of written communications (Word, WordPerfect); spreadsheets (Excel, Lotus); accounting and bookkeeping (Quicken, QuickBooks); presentation graphics (PowerPoint); database applications (Access, Approach, FileMaker, Oracle, Paradox); networking and e-mail (Outlook, Outlook Express, Lotus Notes, cc:Mail, Lotus Domino, HotMail, Juno); desktop publishing and multimedia graphics (Adobe Illustrator, AutoCAD, CorelDraw, Macromedia Director, Microsoft Publisher, Pagemaker, QuarkExpress); project management (Microsoft Project); and image creation and management (CorelDraw, Photoshop, Adobe PhotoMagic, Freehand). Many new office installations with late-model computers come with popular multiple software applications (word processing, spreadsheets, database, and so on) bundled into suites (Office, Works). These are the names of the applications you are likely to see when you boot up the computer and look at your desktop onscreen display.

PARTS OF THE PC

The basic desktop computer system consists of a monitor, a central processing unit (CPU), disk drives, a keyboard, a printer, and a mouse. This equipment is known as the *hardware;* the various programs are called the *software*.

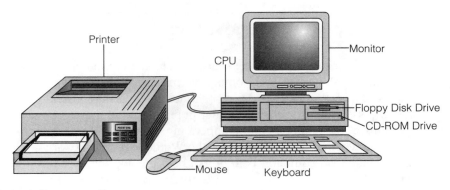

Typical Computer Setup

Monitors

The monitor is a television-like viewscreen, also called the screen or cathode ray tube (CRT). Many monitors have tilt-and-swivel bases so the user can position them for comfortable viewing. The sharpness of the image depends on the resolution, which is the number of pixels (dots) that make up the monitor's image. More pixels on the screen mean a higher resolution and, therefore, a sharper image. So, if resolution is expressed as 640 × 480 (which is standard VGA resolution), that means there are 640 pixels per line on the horizontal axis and 480 pixels per line on the vertical axis. This is okay for word processing applications but is not as good for multiple windows, graphics, or complex images. That's where SVGA comes in. Here the standard is 800 × 600, up to 1600 × 1280 pixels per line. Super VGA standards enable users to see additional rows of spreadsheets and to see as many as two full pages simultaneously.

The choice of a monitor depends on how the PC will be used. Is it for calculations and spreadsheets? Graphics? Desktop publishing? Multiple uses? Also consider interlaced versus non-interlaced display. (Interlaced versions display odd lines and then even lines, every other line first, and then fill in the gaps by generating a refreshed image at every other pass.) Users who sit in front of a monitor for several hours a day will prefer the non-interlaced monitors, which refresh every line on every pass—the result is less annoying flickering and jumping of horizontal lines. BuyersZone recommends a dot pitch of 0.28mm or better and a 72Hz vertical refresh rate in every resolution you expect to use. For larger 20- or 21-inch monitors, a dot pitch of 0.30 or 0.31 is acceptable.

If you don't know what kind of monitor you have or its age, check the model number and manufacturer's name (usually found on the back or bottom of the unit), call the manufacturer's help line, ask for customer service, and give the technical support staff the information. The staff should be able to help you determine the type of monitor and its age. To determine the size of the screen display, just measure diagonally across the screen with a ruler.

PC vs. Mac

The vast majority of the market share in personal computers that sit on desktops belongs to IBM-compatible machines running the Windows operating system. Apple or Macintosh users represent a smaller part of the installed computer population, but these are very loyal fans of the company and its operating system. A simple way to determine whether to go with either the Windows-based PC or an Apple/Macintosh computer is to think about the applications you plan for the equipment. In a standard office environment with professional services (accounting, legal, medical) and business services (landscaping, equipment repair, contracting), and one whose main functions and outputs include word processing, accounting, financial spreadsheets, and database management (with some creative or graphics communications applications thrown in), the Windows-compatible computer is the usual choice (although you could choose either one, depending upon price and your willingness to tinker with programs). PCs have the largest installed based in business and usually cost less than comparable Macintosh units.

If your desired applications include heavy graphics creation (such as brochures, display ads, newsletters, desktop publishing, and print production), the Apple computer still is considered by many professionals to be the best choice for businesses in advertising, graphic arts services, Web site development, and video game creation. However, most home-office workers, small-computer users, and entrepreneurs will use PCs.

Both Apple and Microsoft, the maker of the Windows operating system, constantly are creating new versions of their software to be more compatible. As to whether the current Apple users will have to change over to PCs due to the eventual disappearance of Mac machines, that's no longer an issue. For a variety of reasons, including competitive considerations, Apple's Mac machines are likely to be around for the foreseeable future.

Central Processing Unit (CPU)

The operation of the PC takes place in the central processing unit (CPU); it's the computer's brain. In PCs, the CPU is a single processing chip; in minicomputers, it can be contained in one or more printed circuit boards. In mainframes, the CPU is contained in several boards.

The CPU of the PC is housed in a rectangular case or box that sits on your desktop, which might be under or beside the monitor. Sometimes it sits under the desk in a tower arrangement that is a taller, narrower, and free-standing array for the CPU. The CPU houses the following: the motherboard, the processing chip, the processor memory (RAM), input/output devices that transfer data between the CPU and any peripheral devices, the hard drive or permanent storage memory device, a floppy disk drive, the CD-ROM drive, and any fixed disk drive (such as a ZIP, Syquest, or Inmation drive).

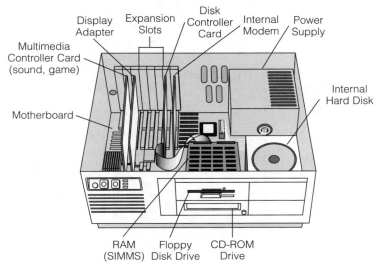

CPU Components

Memory

The computer has two kinds of memory: read-only memory (ROM) and random access memory (RAM).

ROM is the permanent memory that contains the information to make the computer run. Even when the computer is turned off, ROM is not affected. RAM is the memory discussed when buying a computer: It is a temporary workspace in which the computer runs and stores the information on which the user is working. RAM is wiped out as soon as the computer is turned off. RAM capacity is measured in kilobytes (K or KB, meaning thousands of bytes) and megabytes (M or MB, meaning millions of bytes). Early computers had RAM capacities of 64K, which expanded to 640K. Today, computers have RAM capacities of 256M, and RAM can be added to computers by placing an additional RAM chip on the motherboard. This is an effective way of increasing the working speed of the computer because it decreases the need for the processor to access data from the hard drive.

As with RAM, ROM also can be increased. One way is to have a technician install a new higher-capacity hard drive for you (hard drives are relatively inexpensive and the process is not difficult). But an integral part of the process involves transferring the data from your old drive to your new drive. Software programs can make this process easier if you prefer to do it yourself,

WEB SITES FOR COMPUTER
HARDWARE AND SOFTWARE SUPPORT

Acer	www.acer.com
AST	www.ast.com
Brother	www.brother.com
Canon	www.ccsi.canon.com
Casio	www.casio.com
Compaq	www.compaq.com
CTX	www.ctxintl.com
Dell	www.dell.com
Digital	www.digital.com
Epson	www.epson.com
Hewlett Packard	www.hp.com
IBM	www.ibm.com
Info Peripherals	www.infoconnection.com
Inteva	www.inteva.com
KLH	www.sierrainc.com
Logitech	www.logitech.com
Mustek	www.mustek.com
Packard Bell	www.packardbell.com
Panasonic	www.panasonic.com
PC Brand	www.sierrainc.com
Pionex	www.pionex.com
Positive	www.sierrainc.com
Premier	www.sierrainc.com
Sharp	www.sharp-usa.com
Toshiba	www.toshiba.com

but the technician can perform this task for you when installing the new drive. Also be sure to ask the technician to partition the drive that divides large drives into smaller segments. This makes file storage less cumbersome and enables you to store different programs on different parts of the drive. Another way of adding storage is to add a second hard drive. Newer computers have additional ports into which the new drive can plug, much like the auxiliary input/output ports on a stereo system.

Hard Disk Drives

The early PCs used floppy disks only, but as the amount of information and the size of programs grew, storage capacity needs increased. The hard disk drive then became available. This type of drive is built into the computer and stores data and programs. Information can be transferred to and from disks for portability. A hard disk can store much more information than a floppy disk, typically from 500M to more than 17 gigabytes (GB, meaning 1000M of data, or 1 billion bytes). Information retrieval also works much faster on hard disk drives.

Floppy Disks

Floppy disks are 3½-inch hard plastic disks, formerly called *diskettes*. The disks are inserted into slots called disk drives, which copy and record information. Floppies are portable and can be interchanged from one computer to another. Disk capacity equals sides plus density: The *density* of the disk refers to the spacing of the magnetic storage units used in recording data. Double-sided (DS) double-density disks can record information on the top and bottom. In general, a high-density drive can accommodate either a low-density or a high-density disk; a low-density drive can accommodate only a low-density disk. Today's computers come with only high-density drives.

Disks must be formatted before they can store information. When you buy a box of disks, you can buy them preformatted to run on most IBM computers, or you can format them yourself on your own machine.

> **TIP:** A floppy disk drive—usually the A drive—is subject to a lot of use and sometimes will fail to read a disk. Before calling in a computer repair service, try a disk drive cleaner system available from the local computer store. That and a shot of compressed air (available in spray cans) often will restore the drive to working order.
>
> Another obvious but sometimes overlooked reason that a computer fails to read the disk is that sometimes disks are damaged or faulty right out of the box. Be sure to try another disk in the drive to verify that a problem exists with the drive and not the disk. If time permits, and if you don't have a lot of extra disks on hand, you also might try reformatting the disk in an attempt to get rid of the error or fault that caused it to fail the first time.

CD-ROMs

A CD-ROM (compact disc, read-only memory) is a plastic permanent storage compact disc that is read by an optical laser. A CD-ROM is capable of storing more than 600M of data, up to 300,000 pages of text, tens of thousands of images, and stereo sound. A CD-ROM drive can be either internal or external, and it connects to the computer through a controller card. The transfer rate for data is 150K per second. Current speeds are measured in multiples of that rate ($32X = 32 \times 150K$).

CD-ROMs are helpful for holding vast amounts of data, such as encyclopedias, which would take up a lot of room on a hard drive. The computer CD-ROM also can play stereo music, but audio CD players cannot read computer CD-ROMs. Although originally a read-only drive, a recordable CD-ROM (CD-R) drive now permits you to record data that can be played on any CD-ROM player. Rewritable drives (CD-RW) accommodate updating and deleting of files, as needed. If your computer doesn't have a CD-ROM drive, you can purchase an external one to hook up to your machine.

Keyboard

The letters on the keyboard are laid out like a typewriter. In addition, the keyboard contains cursor control keys (arrows pointing up, down, left, and right) that are used to move the cursor around the screen, function keys (labeled F1 through F12) that act as shortcuts to performing certain operations, and a numeric keypad that looks like a calculator for computational input.

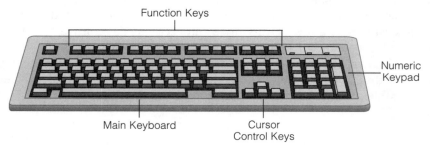

A Standard Keyboard

Redesign of keyboards is inviting a lot of attention as more people spend a large part of their time in front of the PC. Some of the more ergonomic designs include keyboards with built-in wrist pads and a more user-friendly design that optimizes the way the user positions the hands when typing to counteract repetitive stress syndrome (RSS) problems such as carpal tunnel syndrome. But here's an old-fashioned tip that, although not medically endorsed or guaranteed, can help save you needless pain: In the days before flat keyboards and even electric typewriters, carpal tunnel syndrome was almost unheard of because of the placement of the hands at the typewriter and the attitude of the typist. To get the old typewriter keys to strike the paper, it took some effort and strength—the hands had to be placed so that the user could strike the keys with some authority.

Quite simply, this involves keeping your wrists straight while typing and keeping your hands elevated above the keys. Take a look around the office today and you'll find many people with their hands flat on the keyboards and many wrists resting flat on the desk surface behind the keyboard, which is like heavy lifting without using your legs. Although recent developments in keyboards have tried to compensate for this tendency, try this simple old-fashioned approach and see whether it helps.

An Ergonomic Keyboard

Mouse

The mouse is a hand-held pointing device that takes the place of the cursor control keys and many function keys in performing routine computing tasks. When the cursor moves, a small arrow or bar-shaped pointer moves on the screen. The mouse can be used to select words, sentences, or paragraphs from the text that must be manipulated. Although some people find the mouse difficult to get used to at first, it is an indispensable tool for certain tasks and is easy to use once you become familiar with it.

Mouse users are also subject to wrist injury, but because of the way the mouse is used, the old-fashioned tip described previously is not likely to solve the problem. Here, a wrist support pad (available at your local computer supply store) comes in handy. Other innovative mouse designs incorporate wrist support, but these are available only from specialty suppliers.

COMPUTER BACKUPS

Backing up systems regularly helps businesses avoid the catastrophes that can happen at any time, such as fires, floods, or burglary. Many companies experience smaller losses, such as system crashes, accidental erasures, and computer viruses. It's rare for a company not to have experienced any of these problems, so a computer backup system and a regular policy of backing up valuable data makes for a good business practice.

Although different types exist, a backup generally involves the creation of a duplicate copy of certain files stored separately and used to restore data to the computer in the event of either a hard drive crash (a hard disk failure), corruption of files by viruses, or software failure. In a complete system backup, a copy is made of all installed software, as well as all files stored on the computer's hard drive. This backup usually requires a lot of floppy disks—and with today's memory-hungry programs, it is more likely to require a heavier-duty storage medium such as a ZIP, Syquest, or Inmation drive; a tape drive; or a separate tape storage device. In a data-only backup, copies are made of all files stored in the computer; if need be, the software is reloaded from the original CD-ROMs or disks.

After performing a complete system backup and complete file backup, subsequent backups might be incremental (in which case, the files that have been changed or added since the last backup are copied and all other files are left alone). This takes a lot less time than another complete backup.

Make sure that the data is stored in a safe and secure place, preferably at a completely different location than the primary site. In a small office, this process might mean having someone take home the disks on a regular basis. Why is this so important? Two reasons: Fires and floods can destroy not only the primary computer and storage medium, but also the entire site where backups are contained.

PERIPHERALS

Peripherals are the devices that hook up to a computer to help it—and you—do the job better. Peripherals include everything from additional drives to printers and speakers.

TIP: When you do backups and/or make copies of files, check the disk to make sure that the data you think you backed up or copied is actually there. Sometimes, backups are made and files copied on disks that, when needed for purposes of restoring data, are found to contain no data. To cover yourself when making a copy of a file on a disk, simply use the File Open command to determine whether the file does in fact exist on the disk.

Mei-Yun Lee, president of BuyersZone, adds the following special tips on data recovery or computer backup systems:

- Clean drives often. If you are using a tape drive to back up your data, remember that tape drives require frequent cleaning to remain in good working condition. Buy a tape head cleaner, and set a regular schedule for cleaning the drive to prolong its life.

- Frequently used tapes should be retired after one year of use.

- Store offsite. Businesses should keep one complete set of data offsite at all times. In small offices, one person can collect all copies of files and literally take them home each day. In larger offices, a backup to a network is a good approach. The network itself usually is backed up regularly with an offsite location. In highly sensitive environments, a multiple backup should be made with three copies of data. If a backup does not go as planned, two recent copies of the data are still available.

- A final word of advice: Even small businesses can afford the services of an outside vendor to perform needed backups of sensitive or valuable data and then store it offsite.

Modems

The modem (modulator-demodulator) is the device that enables a computer to connect to a telephone line or another computer network. The modem translates digital signals into analog signals so they can travel over a telephone line, and then translates them back into digital signals that can be read by the receiving computer. Modems communicate at various speeds; the more that computer communications grow, the more need for speed grows also. Current modems are rated at 56K, or 56,000 bits per second (bps), but most functional transmission speeds are limited to 33.6Kbps—especially over the Internet, where an Internet service provider (ISP) works as an intermediary.

You need a modem for a lot of reasons, such as to telecommute or work from home (and dial up the office or corporate computer network), to dial into your ISP, and to retrieve your e-mail.

Personal and small-business computer users can manage with the current crop of modems as long as they comply with the v90 Standards set by the International Telecommunications Union (ITU). However, the number of smaller businesses using the Internet is increasing enormously, with an estimated 41 percent currently. There will be an estimated 4.3 million businesses by 2001, according to a study by the International Data Group (IDG). This surge in growth will drive the industry to provide newer, higher-speed technology for accessing the Internet at more affordable prices. The following sections discuss current choices for businesses and entrepreneurs to consider.

Removable Cartridge Drives

Cartridge drives (such as ZIP, JAZ, and SyQuest) hold around 2GB of data—double the amount with compression—making them a good method for backing up individual computers. Data-access rates are fast, but the disks are expensive, so backing up many gigabytes of data is impractical. Networked computers usually are backed up to a remote site, either inside the office or an outside site via the network or the Internet.

Printers

Given the amount of documentation created in business, a printer is the most necessary piece of equipment needed next to the computer. The most common printers today are laser printers, inkjet printers, and dot-matrix printers. All three might be found in an office if connected output can be directed to any one of them for desired purpose.

Laser printers offer the fastest, most efficient way to produce text and images, offering high speeds and good resolution at relatively low cost. The laser printer uses a technology similar to a dry copy machine, electrostatically charging a photosensitive image drum. Toner particles are attracted to those areas of the drum that are charged; when paper passes over the drum, the particles are deposited onto the paper. Heat then fuses the toner particles to the paper.

TIP: In offices with PCs, look for printers that support PCL5 printer language—anything less will not support complex document printing. If the business outputs to service bureaus or has Macintosh computers in its network, it needs a printer that uses the Postscript language. This is universally accepted printer language that prints documents the same way, no matter what equipment exists on the other end. However, because Postscript printers are more expensive than PCL printers, PCL types might be just fine for a small office application. Although laser printers are most popular because they are quiet and fast, they have a few drawbacks: They cannot handle multiple forms, and they usually cannot accept anything larger than legal-size paper.

Inkjet printers use tiny jets to spray droplets of ink onto the page, and the refinement in the ink compound has made this technology attractive and highly affordable. To the untrained eye, little difference exists between the quality of an inkjet printer and a laser printer. Most offices can get by with 300dpi (dots per inch) printing, especially for text and black-and-white work. 600dpi is becoming the norm on many printers (it offers four times the clarity of 300dpi), but the naked eye can scarcely tell the difference, especially on text. A major advantage of the inkjet is its portability—it can be taken on the road and used with either a laptop or a portable computer.

Dot-matrix printers are impact printers that use a row of small pins, wires, and hammers that shoot up to make dots on the paper, creating text and graphics. Their most common use is for printing invoices, purchase orders, shipping forms, labels, and other multipart forms. Dot-matrix printers can print through multipart forms in a single pass, allowing them to produce more pages than even high-speed laser printers. Two types of printers exist: 9-pin and 24-pin. At one time, the trend was moving from 9- to 24-pin but recently has moved back to 9-pin. In the applications for dot-matrix printing, 9-pin is fine—in most cases, it is faster and less expensive. These printers can print in letter-quality mode for correspondence-quality output, or draft mode or near letter quality for forms applications.

The only other important consideration involves the number of parts you might have in a printing application for forms (invoices, purchase orders, and shipping labels). Dot-matrix printers use continuous-form paper, which runs through a tractor mechanism. The paper attaches to the tractor with holes that are part of a perforated strip that can be pulled away. Continuous-form envelopes, labels, and forms are also available. Although laser printers have become the office standard for letters and proposals, dot-matrix printers remain an important part of back-office operations in many firms.

Color printers are now within the reach of most users and have a lot to offer to low- to high-end users. Five types of color printers exist: inkjet, laser, solid ink, dry wax, and dye sublimation. The laser printers work ideally for high-end graphics and commercial presentations, for which precise imaging and reproduction are important. For home and small office use, the color inkjet printer will do the job adequately for a fraction of the cost of a color laser machine. Inkjet printers are more than sufficient when printing a color proof of a job to check the overall look before sending it to the printer. The drawback of an inkjet, however, is dealing with smudgy, wet-looking paper when heavily inked images are laid down.

Color printers also can function as black-and-white printers. In busy offices, however, most inkjets are too slow. If speed is important, a laser printer offers the best option. For advertising, marketing, and high-end graphics printing and presentation needs, one of the other top-of-the-line laser printers might serve as a better choice. A visit to online buying/advisory services such as BuyersZone (www.buyerszone.com) or the local professional vendor in your area can point you in the right direction.

CHOOSING A PRINTER

Printers are pretty much a commodity product, so pricing is very competitive among the major brands. You might ask your colleagues and friends what their experiences have been with various brands, and what potential problems exist in interactions with your software programs. For example, I once purchased a brand-new printer that wasn't listed on the setup menu in my computer, so I used a default setting. The printer gave me problems for more than two years, even after replacing the printer drivers and spending hours with tech support. I finally had to replace it.

Another item is cartridges: If you use the printer heavily, you might want to go for a laser printer because its cartridges can last for several thousand copies before being replaced. Inkjets that use separate ink cartridges for black ink and three different colors must be replaced much more often. Some low-end models have combined the various color inks into one cartridge, so you have to replace all colors whenever one of them runs out. If your main application involves printing word processing documents, you need not bother with the extra added expense of a color printer.

- *Printing speed.* This is the number of pages per minute that the printer can spit out. (In actual use, however, the speeds are slower.) Speed is determined by the processor in the printer; higher-speed printers cost more. Determine what your needs are and buy accordingly. Also ask whether the printing speed refers to regular letter-quality mode or draft mode (which can be almost twice as fast as letter quality, but is not suitable for either copying or printing).

- *Paper tray capacity.* This factor is important even for small offices. A capacity of up to 250 pages in one tray is adequate for some and not for others. Some printers offer more than one tray, which is a valuable feature if you switch from plain paper to letterhead and also handle envelopes and documents with the same printer. For heavy envelope work, consider a dedicated envelope printer.

- *Toner cartridges, drums, corona wires, and ozone filters.* It's a good idea to figure these costs into the buying process.

- *Black-and-white versus color.* Word processors and most communications-only functions in the firm, as well as accounting and finance users, don't need color printers. Graphic artists and people involved in marketing communications probably have a regular need for color printing. So, too, do the folks who produce your newsletters in-house. If the need is only occasional, it's a good idea to price having color jobs printed at the office supply superstore or copy places. If you work from home and share the printer with other family members—and, yes, that includes kids—a color printer is a no-brainer decision.

Plotter

A plotter is a type of printer used to print certain graphs and charts. Many types of plotters produce pages or transparencies and also draw curved lines, three-dimensional figures, bar charts, graphs, and so on with computer-based instruction. Some plotters even add text labels to the charts or transparencies. Engineering applications can include blueprints and schematics; business applications can include sales projections and presentation graphics. Few differences in quality exist between the low-end and high-end plotters—mainly, these involve ease of use, features, and budget.

Scanner

A scanner is a device that can "read" text and graphics. A copy of the scanned image is stored on magnetic media as it simultaneously reproduces on a monitor. Text, photographs, drawings, and charts can be scanned and used in desktop publishing or electronic filing. Accuracy depends on the quality of the document being scanned, so the smart user should review the scanned image for the occasional error resulting from the scanner misreading data. Most scanners come bundled with Optical Character Recognition (OCR) capability that can convert images into computer-editable format.

Scanners are available at affordable prices for every level of user. They range from hand-held portable models costing less than a couple hundred dollars, to moderately priced flatbed scanners, to sophisticated drum scanners costing much more. High-end multi-function devices also offer the capability of printing, copying, and collating right from your desk via the print and processing options menu. Many national office equipment dealers offer a huge variety of brand-name models. Office products superstores also can be a good place to shop locally. Online shoppers can consult a number of good Internet Office buying services, such as BuyersZone (www.buyers.zone.com).

Uninterruptible Power Supplies (UPS)

Although not technically a peripheral, the most useful additional item you can add to your computer is an uninterruptible power supply (UPS). Depending on the integrity of local electrical lines—how often you experience surges or spikes, such as when light bulbs flicker suddenly or how often your power goes off—you should consider a UPS. Even if your power goes off only once a year, a UPS can save you valuable time and work. This device contains a large battery and circuitry. When the circuitry detects a surge or spike, it switches the computer from AC to DC power. The battery in the UPS gives you enough time to stop working, save your work on a disk, and conduct an orderly shutdown of your system. Normally, you get about a 10-minute window to safely save and close down your system. If this is not enough time, some units can provide alternative power for a day or more, but these are expensive. Many manufacturers sell power-management systems that can be integrated with your computer equipment. These systems are outlet strips with surge protection; each outlet is designed for a specific piece of equipment or peripheral. For more information on other consumer electronics products and accessories, see the Consumer Electronics Manufacturers Association Web site (www.eia.org/cema).

The cost of UPSs vary from very inexpensive to expensive, depending on how much capacity you need—how many machines are hooked up—and how much time you need in reserve power to safely save open or working files and then shut down all systems. These devices are now available wherever computer and computer peripherals are sold.

Video Equipment

The growth of home-based businesses and entrepreneurs has pushed technology into accommodating independent business people to reach out and touch customers while running their businesses from home. Desktop videoconferencing systems typically include the following equipment you'll have to add to your computer: a video camera, a video capture card (installed internally), a modem (you may already have this, but check to see if the one with the video system is faster or is a later model with newer software), speakers (already standard equipment on most PCs), a microphone, and a software bundle. You can use videoconferencing to connect business owners, to customers, to remote employees, and to suppliers around the world without having to leave home.

The biggest barrier to quality so far is the use of old copper wire telephone cable to broadcast images. Television broadcasts 30 frames per second, whereas copper phone lines broadcast 3 to 13 frames per second. Two new standards developed by the International Telecommunications Union (ITU) have emerged, however: H.324, which improves video quality; and H.323, which improves communication in Internet, intranet, and local area network (LAN) environments. Digital Video Systems are available from 3Com Corp. (www.3com.com/bigpicture), Connectix Corp. (www.quickcam.com), Cubic VideoComm (www.cvideomail.com), and Intel Corp. (www.intel.com).

TYPES OF PCs

Offices today have many different types of PCs. You are likely to encounter familiar names such as IBM, as well as Compaq, NEC, Micron, Dell, Gateway, and many others—all are PCs or IBM-compatibles. With Macs, it's pretty much a Macintosh computer—although some clones were made for a few years, the clone population is small. Different types of PCs also exist in terms of function. Some high-end workstation computers serve a single user application, such as graphics or simulation, or a database application. These might have brand names such as Digital or Sun if they are running a UNIX operating system. They also might run Windows NT and look like any other PC or PC-compatible; or they might be a workstation or terminal connected to a network and referred to as a client (same as user), running routine applications such as word processing and spreadsheets.

Desktop Systems

Any computer that sits on a desktop is referred to as a desktop computer, whether it is a PC or a Mac. If it is networked to other computers, the computer is part of a desktop system. Desktop equipment also includes workstations or personal computer look-alikes in a graphics, computer-aided design (CAD), computer-aided manufacturing (CAM), or other high-end application. These might be made by Sun Microsystems, Hewlett Packard, Digital, Silicon Graphics, IBM, Dell, Gateway, or Compaq.

Laptop or Notebook Computers

Laptop, or *notebook,* refers to computers that can easily be carried around. These terms have given way to a newer term, *mobile computing,* which includes portables, laptops, palm computing devices, and personal digital assistants.

Laptops or notebook computers are highly functional for individuals on the go, such as executives or salespeople. They double as desktops because they have the capability of connecting to peripherals such as monitors, keyboards, CD-ROM drives, and printers. They also can connect to mainframes and other networked computers through communications ports, enabling telecommuters to keep in touch with the office and salespeople to demonstrate online services. Laptops or portables are typically more expensive than comparably equipped desktop PCs, but their advantages for the mobile professional or person who needs a virtual office usually make the extra cost worthwhile. Consider the following when buying a portable computer:

- *Size of the screen display.* Go for the largest available viewing area. Even an inch can make a big difference if you spend quite a bit of time at the machine or are doing demos for clients. After all, not every client's computer will be capable of running your applications on a PC. In fact, a recent survey shows that the largest installed operating system is still Windows 3.1. To sidestep problems with the client's equipment, bring your own.

■ *Battery life.* If you work frequently in places where electric power isn't available—such as on airplanes, buses, and trains—you'll appreciate batteries that have a life longer than that of a May fly. Batteries can last up to several hours, and many laptops have extra slots where you can add extra battery capacity. Some also have removable batteries that you can charge and bring along as extras.

■ *Storage capacity.* Hard drive sizes have increased to meet the needs of the new software applications. If you have the option of purchasing more hard drive capacity, it's a worthwhile option if you want to add after-market software or other applications that didn't come with the computer originally. The better purchase option is RAM because it increases your computer's capability of handling any industrial-strength graphics or presentation software you might add after the purchase.

■ *Navigation type.* Most portable keyboards incorporate a mouse-type device that enables you to navigate without tabbing and shifting. Often you can use attachable rollerballs (similar to a mouse) and pointers that are little nubs (not quite like a joystick) to move around on the screen.

■ *Docking station capability.* This worthwhile feature in a virtual office setup (that's an office where a desk might exist for any visiting employee who needs it at the time) enables you to hook up a laptop to a base station with a power supply, keyboard, and monitor. Multiple location setups have a network and network storage. When in the office, the user inserts the portable into the docking station, which functions with the ease of a desktop unit. When the user leaves, he or she simply takes the portables.

On a smaller scale, you can purchase a computer with a docking station configuration so that when you are at home base, you sit in front of a standard size monitor, with a regular power supply and other stationary peripherals such as a high-speed printer or scanner. When you leave the office, you simply pull the portable out of the docking station and your office, taking necessary files and portable computing power with you. This is an especially useful feature for people who travel regularly. If you have several associates in different locations, each can use a docking mechanism with a networked hard drive and then remove his or her laptop with any files needed for travel; use the home base for printing, e-mailing messages, faxing, and perhaps providing workgroup file access.

800 SERVICE AND SUPPORT NUMBERS FOR HARDWARE AND SOFTWARE MANUFACTURERS

Acer	800-445-6495
Adobe Systems	800-833-6687
Apple Computer, Inc.	800-538-9696
AST Computer, Inc.	800-758-0278
Brother International	800-276-7746
Canon	800-423-2366
Casio	800-634-1895
Citizen America	800-477-4683
Claris Corporation	800-325-2747
Compaq	800-652-6672
Consumer Technology Northwest	800-356-3983
CTX	
Desktops	800-367-0533
Monitors	800-888-2120
Notebooks	800-285-1889
Corel	800-772-6735
Dell Computer Corporation	800-247-9362
Digital	
Computers	800-354-9000
Printers	800-365-0696
Epson America	800-922-8911
Gateway 2000	800-846-2000
Hewlett-Packard, Co.	800-243-9816
IBM	800-772-2227
Info Peripherals	800-777-3280
Inteva	800-480-4519
Intuit	800-816-8025
Iomega	800-697-8833

continues

800 Service and Support Numbers for Hardware and Software Manufacturers *continued*

JASC	800-622-2793
KLH	800-347-1222
Konica	800-256-6422
Kyocera Electronics, Inc.	800-232-6797
Lanier Information Services	800-708-7088
Lexmark International, Inc.	800-891-0331
Logitech	800-231-7717
Microsoft	800-426-9400
NEC America	800-632-4636
Netscape	800-320-2099
Novell	800-451-5151
Okidata	800-654-3282
Packard Bell	800-244-0049
Panasonic	800-222-0584
PC Brand	800-255-5245
Peachtree Software	800-247-3224
Pionex	800-313-1995
Positive	800-452-6345
Premier	800-347-1222
Quark	800-788-7835
Sharp Electronics	800-237-4277
Sony	800-352-7669
Symantec	800-441-7234
Tektronix	800-835-6100
Texas Instruments	800-527-3500
Toshiba	800-334-3445
Visio Corporation	800-248-4746
Zenith Data Systems	800-533-0331

Personal Digital Assistants

Personal digital assistants (or PDAs) are computers that literally fit in the palm of your hand. Although limited in storage and applications capability, these machines are very convenient when traveling light and in situations when a simpler hand-held device is preferable. Some hand-held PCs run a scaled-down operating system called Window CE, which is a version of Windows 95 that includes many programs and applications. Other PDAs offer the capability of handwriting notes with a stylus right on the screen of the machine and later backing it up into a PC. With many hand-held computers, you can plug in desktop-size peripherals, such as keyboards or modems, and access the Internet, get your e-mail, or type long documents. Some enable you to download data, schedules, and documents directly from your desktop system using docking capabilities.

Some popular uses of PDAs include the following:

- Taking notes at an offsite meeting with a client when a laptop is unavailable or inconvenient to use.

- Jotting down memos and scheduling meetings or appointments on the spot with a device you can keep in your breast pocket. You can later update your scheduling on the PC or laptop.

- Replacing spiral notebooks and other memo pads. Instead of writing cramped handwritten notes that you have to type into the PC, you can jot down thoughts, digest a meeting on the spot, and then transfer the notes into a word processing document on your PC without rekeying by using a synchronizing device.

NETWORKS

Technology has brought the network up to the speed of light, at least figuratively. Formerly, networks of individuals, professionals, or companies used to communicate or get together via phone, association meetings, mail, and newsletters. In the office, documents used to be routed in hard copy. Now affinity groups, business partners, employees, stockholders, and even team members working on the same project can connect via computer. People in offices even at the most basic levels share applications, documents, and files.

TWO KINDS OF NETWORKS

Computer networks can be constructed in two basic ways: All the computers can be connected to a central host computer or server (a large computer containing data and shared programs); or all the computers can be hooked up to each other, enabling users to access certain files and data on other users' hard drives. In networking terminology, a user (called an "end user") works on a computer or workstation (also called a "client"). When the client works with the central host computer (the "server"), it creates a client-server relationship.

Networks communicate by using a network operating system (such as Novell NetWare, UNIX, Windows NT, or Apple Talk) and some form of communications medium. Each computer in the network is connected via a twisted cable—copper, fiber optic, or coaxial—and a network adapter card that is installed in each computer on the network. In a simple or local area network configuration (called a peer-to-peer network) in which all the computers exist in the same location, computers are linked directly via wires with no central server or host computer. Each computer has its own data, files, and storage. This creates a simple but effective—and relatively inexpensive—network on a small scale. In this configuration, each of the computers in the network can function as a server, and all members in the network can share or access their data files.

At the next level, all computers connect to a central server that manages the network. Each computer might or might not have hard disks with data files, but the network data is stored in a host computer. If the computer is just a workstation, it accesses its information, files, and data from a central computer and might have only floppy disk storage.

Either of these two types of networks, implemented in a single office or location, is called a local area network (LAN). Most LANs connect or share data using Ethernet, Token Ring, FDDI, or ATM technology.

Wide area networks (WANs) connect computers that might exist in a number of different locations, through a communications service provider such as a phone company, a satellite broadcaster, or a cable company. WANs can be used for hooking branch offices of a company together. Within each company office might be a LAN, and the LANs connect to the WAN to function as a single network. The Internet serves as a good example of a WAN in which a single or server computer connects via modem over the phone line to the Internet, which in turn connects to one of the networked computer databases anywhere in the world.

Advantages and Disadvantages of a LAN

Because a LAN is a multiuser computer system, administrators face pros and cons in deciding what kind of LAN is right for the office. Some LANs enable PCs to share software programs as well as hardware, such as printers and storage devices. What are the advantages and the disadvantages of these kinds of networks? What kind of questions do you need to ask before you decide which is right for you? Let's take a look at some of the advantages and disadvantages of both to help your organization make the right choice.

LAN Advantages

- *Shared software.* Some companies computerize their operations on a piecemeal basis, adding PCs and software as needed. Over time, this practice can lead to a lot of software proliferating in the organization, which might or might not be compatible with all users. From an internal viewpoint, this complicates technical support and also makes the installation process complicated for less-sophisticated users. The advantages of everyone using the same software are obvious, yet copying programs to share among separate users is illegal. A LAN solves that problem. The preferred or company-specified standard software for generalized applications (spreadsheets, word processing, presentations, and contact management) resides on the company server and easily can be downloaded for new or added users as needed. In workgroups where many people on different PCs must get into their copy of the same file to provide editing or other inputs, a LAN automatically keeps the file updated for all users.

- *Shared hardware.* One printer per PC might suit individuals but might not be cost-effective when printers sit idle for blocks of time. A LAN enables users to share printers and other peripherals.

- *Shared file storage.* By storing company files and workgroup documents on a communal server in a LAN setup, less need exists for upgrading the hard drives on each computer desktop. You can add large central storage devices for less cost per gigabyte of storage in a central server location than you can on each individual desktop.

- *Centralized backup.* If backing up on individual PCs occurs only occasionally, a LAN is ideal. Regularly accessed files are maintained on the network server and stored in a central location. If an individual PC goes down, the files still can be accessed by another computer; if your computer has a terminal crash and a new computer must be installed, the latest version of the files can be downloaded, along with the application software, right from the network server.

- *Support for flexible needs.* A LAN can be "hard-wired," with cables connecting each individual workstation to the central computer. Or, it can be wireless, with ranges of 5 miles and more possible. This provides excellent support for companies that have shifting staff need; that are changing to the fluidity of virtual offices; that use mobile sites; or that are subject to frequent flooding, hurricanes, and the like.

LAN Disadvantages

- *Cost.* The cost of installing a LAN can seem prohibitive and must be spread among the system's workstations. For maximum results, you must find the break-even point for your company: Determine how many workstations are needed before costs are lower than the combined costs of separate PCs. The number of printers on a LAN and how much they're shared is also a key to costs.

■ *Downtime.* Depending on your network configuration, PCs, or certain applications (such as e-mail or Internet access) can be unavailable when the LAN is down. Extra care in the selection of your network configuration and installation process can help reduce downtime. In any case, take certain precautions, such as duplicating certain emergency files as a matter of routine to a separate hard drive.

■ *Administration.* After you commit to a LAN, depending on the size, you might need a specific person to oversee the system. The duties of this administrator include providing new and ongoing training on LAN use,

---

CHOOSING A LAN SYSTEM

■ *Consider users first.* Talk to the people who will be on the network. What do they do on their current PCs? What would they like to do? What software do they use now? What specific applications are they running?

■ *Overestimate needs.* Most offices find that the actual use of their LAN is much greater than what they projected. If growth hasn't been built into the system, the LAN will quickly become obsolete. A professional guideline is to plan for 50 percent growth in LAN usage each year.

■ *Inventory hardware.* Take an inventory of all existing hardware to see how much of it can be incorporated into the new LAN.

■ *Piece it together.* Arranging the location of workstations and printers is like piecing together a jigsaw puzzle. Consider the personalities as you draw up floor plans and decide who will share equipment.

■ *Let vendors help.* LANs are more complex that PCs. Consequently, vendors offer more assistance in deciding whether a LAN makes sense and what equipment might be needed.

■ *Allow for training.* With any new technology-based system, you must build in time and cost for training key individuals. If no individual has been named as network administrator, you can look initially to the vendor for support and training. Although training is expensive in both time and money, you might see long-term returns.

adding and deleting users on the network, backing up data, maintaining security, and performing a host of computer housekeeping chores. With a small LAN of about twenty users, the duties likely will fall to a current employee who is computer-literate. If your company has some technical types on board, these people are perfect for the work. If not, the job could fall to you, which will even seem natural if you've been involved in selecting the system. A larger LAN needs a full-time employee to oversee its operations. Many companies make the mistake of buying the system without being willing to hire the needed administrator.

- *LAN security.* Security on a network starts at the very beginning. A well-designed system can without a doubt provide more security than that available from a PC. On the other hand, poorly designed security turns each separate workstation into a possible information leak.

NETWORK AND INTERNET COMMUNICATIONS

Computers on a network might be Macintosh, IBM PCs, or clones. To facilitate communication, computers need a common standard for communicating, as well as certain protocols or a universal set of rules about how to do certain things, from sending messages, to downloading files or programs. Computers on a LAN communicate with a protocol such as Ethernet. However, when computers from different networks work together to create or communicate on a WAN, they must communicate with a common protocol.

To connect to a WAN, computers usually communicate one-to-one over a phone line via a modem, which transfers digital information from the computer into analog information that can travel over the phone line. At the receiving end, the analog data is translated back into digital data that the receiving computer understands. Modems use communication software, containing additional rules such as file transfer protocols, which accommodate the transfer of files between two computers that are directly hooked together.

Internet Protocols

Computers connecting over the Internet use a universal protocol, called Transmission Control Protocol/Internet Protocol (TCP/IP). This is the standard for communication between computers and servers that was developed in the early days of the Internet. At that time, it was known as the ARPANET and fell under the control of the Department of Defense. TCP/IP enables computers and servers of all types (PCs or Macs) that use different forms of operating systems and hardware configurations to directly get in touch with one another. TCP, the transmission control protocol part of TCP/IP, enables computers to connect and exchange data, and ensures that the data is delivered in the order sent. The IP protocol contains the format of the data and the address or unique mailbox of the computer to which the data is to be sent.

TOPICS YOU CAN FIND ON THE INTERNET

You can find almost anything on the Internet, whether it be information on your favorite hobby or much-needed research for that business presentation. These are a few examples of what you can do on the Internet:

- *Hobbies and entertainment.* You can play online games, get movie reviews, be privy to hobbyist discussions, obtain travel information, and make travel arrangements.

- *Databases and research.* Virtually every important trade journal and reference publication is offered online. Access government, academic, and business information via online encyclopedias, magazines, textbooks, and newspapers.

- *News and finance.* Get up-to-the-minute news from the newswire services the newspapers use. Stay informed about local and international weather forecasts, stock quotations, brokerage services, company information, Dun & Bradstreet's profiles, Standard & Poor's profiles, and treasury fund rates.

After your computer connects to the Internet, it continues to communicate using TCP/IP. However, when it begins to load and run programs from certain parts of the Internet, such as the World Wide Web, it uses other computer and scripting languages to accomplish its goals.

The Internet is a large network in which your computer acts as a client. Through the Internet, you now can do just about everything, including watching the stock market ticker-tape, checking fast-breaking industry news, getting PC support services, conducting industrial research, making travel arrangements, getting detailed driving maps and directions, playing interactive games, finding medical advice, and much more.

To access information, your computer must use several client applications. Some applications, such as Telnet, Gopher, and FTP, help you transfer files and text data between other computers on the network. Two of the most well-known clients, Netscape Navigator and Internet Explorer, are browsers that give you access to the World Wide Web.

The Web is a graphical interface to the Internet. Using a markup language called HTML, anyone can post text, pictures, movies, or sound on the Web. To view these pages, you need the client, or browser.

One of several programming languages that have facilitated communications on the World Wide Web is Java, which is similar to the C++ language but easier to use. Java enables programmers to write applications that run on Web-capable browsers such as Netscape Navigator and Internet Explorer. The appeal of Java is that it is designed for writing programs that can safely be downloaded from the Internet and immediately run by the receiving computers without having to worry about the infection of a virus. Using a mini-Java application called an *applet,* programmers can create stand-alone applications such as spreadsheets, animation, or other functions that can be run on any computer.

Hypertext Markup Language (HTML) is the Web's programming language or source code used to create documents and forms on the Web. HTML displays information easily and has interactive forms capability. It explains to the browser how to display the various documents on the Web; documents created in HTML can support graphics, video, and audio. Javascript, the independent and open language developed by Netscape, interfaces well with HTML and enables Web authors to develop interactive sites rich with features.

Intranets

An intranet is a network based on Internet protocols (TCP/IP) that contains information internal to the organization. This information can be shared by members, employees, and others in such areas as operations, inventory, job postings, logistics, approved vendors, and more. Because this information is considered to be proprietary, access is restricted; the network is protected by a firewall or security screen to prevent unauthorized access. An intranet works like a company's own private Internet—it is a very inexpensive way for a company to connect its employees to needed information about the company. No customized software development is required, nor does a private network have to be developed. Intranets use the language of the Internet and can be read by anyone who has a browser and the proper authorization. The intranet uses the same programming languages and browsers that computers need to access the Internet.

Extranets

As with intranets, an extranet is a small, private Internet. This is a network that contains information about the organization that it then shares with certain people outside the company, such as vendors, customers, and other business partners. The extranet is a secure network that is protected by a firewall to prevent unauthorized access; registered users access it via a password. An extranet can have different levels of access built into it, and it often connects information contained on more than one intranet. For example, an extranet can permit vendors or suppliers to obtain inventory and shipping status (as FedEx and UPS have with their customer tracking systems), and it can enable investors and customers to access financial and corporate news information. Because extranets are relatively new, innovative uses for them are still developing. Extranets have great potential appeal to joint venture partners and project developers who can use extranets to hold virtual meetings.

Connecting to the Internet

Consumers and businesses have quickly taken to using the Internet. In fact, the popularity of the Internet is its own worst enemy in the short term because the network is nearly collapsing from its own weight. The main problem is traffic, or the number of people trying to access the Internet and the amount of information being requested or transferred at any given time at a single location.

SOME ONLINE SERVICE AND INTERNET SERVICE PROVIDERS

Online services: America Online, CompuServe, Dow Jones News/ Retrieval Service, and Genie

National ISPs: Microsoft News, MCI Worldcomm, AT&T Worldnet, NewsNet, Prodigy, Netcom, Spry, PSINET, IDT, and GTE Internet, to name a few

---

As a single user, you can connect to the Internet right from your own personal computer. (A good computer will have at least a Pentium processor, at least 32M of RAM and a run speed of more than 200MHz.) You need a browser (the piece of software that gets you to the online universe), a modem (what connects you over the phone line), a plain copper telephone line, and an Internet service provider (ISP), which provides your gateway to the Internet. Your modem should have a speed of at least 56Kbps, although many service providers still do not support that speed. If you are a business user who need to be online most of the time, you'll want a dedicated separate phone line to connect you to the Internet. With more than one employee, a single phone line can be a problem. If you are at a business site, you should consider how many people will seek access and how many times per day they will need to connect.

Connection Speed

With a standard connection to the Internet via a computer, modem, and phone line, your transmission speed is limited by the speed of your modem and the speed that your local or national service provider supports. In addition, you might be limited by the capacity of your particular phone line. Limitations such as old lines, faulty connections, and line leaks can seriously affect your connection speed. For example, I have a 56Kbps modem and a regular but dedicated copper phone line to connect to my national service provider. My download speeds, however, never exceed 33Kbps; most of the time, I connect at 26.4Kbps or 24Kbps. An optional connection line will get me in at 56Kbps, but this fee-based line costs around 10 cents per minute.

For a business, consider other options. One alternative is to connect several of your organization's computers to a network, and then connect the network to a faster T-1 line that gets you to the Internet at 1.5Mbps—or nearly 50 times faster than the 33Kbps mentioned previously. This is especially valuable if you download Web pages with graphics, which slow page-capture time considerably. Other alternatives range from cheap to expensive. A good ISP or local Net services firm can provide guidance in this area. Of course, if you plan to conduct commerce on the Net, you will need a computer and your own server online 24 hours a day. In that case, a high-speed connection to the Net is crucial for you and your customers. Here again, alternatives exist, such as leasing space on a server at your ISP or Web-hosting firm.

- *Integrated Services Digital Network (ISDN).* An ISDN line accommodates voice and data over a single line provided by local phone companies. It uses two bearer channels (B-channels) that enable data and voice to synchronously download and upload at rates up to 64Kbps, or a total data rate of 128Kbps—this is twice the speed of the fastest current v.90 standard modem. Connecting an ISDN line to a computer requires special equipment: an ISDN terminal adapter (sometimes called an ISDN modem) that plugs into the computer, and an NT-1 (or network terminator) that plugs into the ISDN line itself.

- *T-1.* T-1 is a direct cable connection from point to point over a copper wire line, with a total capability of 1.5Mbps (million bits per second). Ideal for entrepreneurs, Web sites, and companies with moderate-to-heavy Internet needs, the T-1 line offers the advantage of fast continual Internet access for a host of computers at an office. Each connection supports up to 24 channels of 64Kbps communication. Other advantages include supersonic file transfer (FTP) and downloads. Requirements include special hardware, setup costs, and monthly rates in the range of $1,000.

- *Digital subscriber line (DSL).* A cost-effective and speedy alternative to T-1, digital subscriber line technology is fairly new and somewhat unproved, but it is catching on rapidly because of its promise. The DSL provides ultrafast information pull from the Internet at 1.5Mbps and speedy 64Kbps transmission uploads to the Internet. This option is ideal for businesses in which the greatest need is to download or receive information instead of uploading or sending information over the Internet. Bell Atlantic recently launched a version of DSL called ASDL that works over copper lines and is considerably more affordable than T-1.

Connection Method

Depending on the size of your office, the number of employees, and how many e-mail accounts you'll need, your office will have a variety of options for Internet service. Although from home you can connect through an online service, for the office you should look at an Internet service provider. Some ISPs specialize in providing Internet services to businesses—your local phone company might be a good place to start. Ultimately, you'll want a cost-effective service provider to which your corporate LAN will connect directly. You'll probably want your own domain name for e-mail accounts, and maybe a Web site, too. Most full-service Internet access providers offer services that will get your domain, set up your individual e-mail accounts, and even design your Web page. Consider all these factors and more when you determine your company's Internet needs.

Online Services. Online services are commercial communications networks that grant subscribers access to their data. Online services include anything from Lexis-Nexis databases, to law libraries, to America Online— anything that charges you a fee to access just their data and network is an online service. To retrieve their information, you must access the provider, either through another Internet link or via a direct dial-up connection from your computer. Online services either charge flat monthly rates, charge by the hour, or charge by the document accessed.

ONLINE SERVICES

The following represent just a few of the online features that are available from the major ISPs. Make sure you check the availability of these features before you join.

- *Bulletin board systems (BBSs) (also called message boards).* With BBSs, you can retrieve messages and reply to other people's messages, get answers to technical questions, obtain driving and weather updates, get information on shareware (public-domain software), improve vendor responsiveness, and so on. BBSs also enable you to post a message and see a posted response from another user.

- *Chat rooms.* Chat rooms are real-time message boards. These are useful for online interviews and press conferences, as well as other collaborative events. They are also heavily featured for everything from fans gathering to discuss their favorite TV show to real-time news updates.

- *Instant messaging.* When you are online and want to know who else in your community of interest is online, you can sign on to the instant messaging board by using one of several versions of software that can be downloaded. You'll then be in real-time chat with them, no matter which ISP the other person uses.

- *Access to the other Internet services.* Getting to the Internet and to search engines or bulletin boards can be a snap because most online services provide basic Internet access.

CHOOSING AN ISP

This list of questions can help you decide on the right service provider:

- *Monthly charges.* Some ISPs provide unlimited service; others provide service for a flat fee for a certain number of hours, currently around 150 hours per month.

- *Local access numbers.* If you plan to spend a lot of time online, then you'll want a local access number to avoid long-distance charges.

- *Connection.* Find out if your service has a T-1 or a T-3 connection. Depending on how many customers they have, it could make a difference.

- *Backup connection.* Does the ISP provide an alternative connection through another carrier if its connection is down?

- *Number of subscribers per modem.* If too many users exist per modem connection, you will encounter a lot of busy signals during peak load time.

- *Web space.* Do you get free Web space of your own for setting up your own business or personal site?

- *Backups.* Does the provider back up the system regularly?

- *E-mail auto responders.* Does the ISP provide a way to automatically respond to inquirers?

- *Rating.* Regularly published reliability ratings exist; ask for this number.

- *High bandwidth connection options.* Can you connect directly to their network?

Internet service providers (ISPs). The Internet is simply a huge global network that connects millions of computers, most of which host a database of specific information. To get a connection to the Internet, you need an Internet service provider. Both local and national service providers exist. Although both provide comparable service, the local provider can be a good choice for a home office business or sole proprietor because it is usually available if you run into trouble. (On the other hand, most national service providers provide 24-hour technical support.) To find a good local provider, the best bet is to ask colleagues and area users for a reference. Among the national providers, the universe is expanding rapidly as the number of users expands. You might want to investigate an ISP that offers free server space for Web pages or an ISP connected with your long-distance service for combined billing. Most ISPs bill a flat monthly rate for unlimited usage.

OPERATING SYSTEMS

The operating system (OS) is the underlying program that runs the computer and all its applications. This is the first program that loads when the computer is turned on, and it tells the computer what to do in language and instructions that the machine understands. Operating systems have names that often depend on the type of computer or when the system was released. When you select an application to run on your computer (such as a word processing or spreadsheet program), you must make sure it runs on the operating system you have.

The original operating system for PCs was called DOS, which stands for disk operating system. DOS had limitations, however, because it accommodated only one program at a time and required a lot of commands to properly instruct the computer. DOS was followed by Microsoft's Windows program, which mimicked the Macintosh graphics-based operating system developed by Apple Computer. As a shell program with DOS running in the background, the first Windows program was not a true operating system; it was an improvement that allowed more than one program to run at a time. Windows 95 and Windows 98 are true operating systems that represent major improvements over each preceding system.

These newer OSs also require a lot more computer horsepower to run applications and multiple software programs. Each new Windows version comes closer to making computer instruction invisible to the user. All that's required is to click on a broad-based menu of icons to run software programs for the Windows platform. All programs run inside their own window on the computer. Microsoft worked with the developers of most programs for Windows, so they operate pretty much the same way. For example, instructions such as printing setups; printing, copying, and merging; filing; and saving are very similar and often use the same keystrokes.

As with DOS, Windows was meant for a single computer user. Other types of operating systems work better for some types of offices. Offices with many networked computers, workgroups, and other networked multiuser environments run Windows NT and UNIX. Other PC operating systems include OS/2, SCO, Xenix, and AIX. Macintosh computers from Apple run System 7 or 8 and A/UX (Apple's UNIX-based system). Digital's VAX computers (now part of Compaq Computer) use VMS and ULTRIX (UNIX). IBM mainframes use MVS VM and VSE.

Common Operating Systems

System	Description
DOS and Windows 3.*x*	The most popular operating systems in business today
Windows 95	Popular 16-bit operating system that succeeded Windows 3.*x*, adding a graphical user interface (GUI) like the Apple OSs
Windows 98	The current version and last 16-bit Windows OS from Microsoft
System 7	Apple's Macintosh operating system
Mac OS	System 8*x* for the Macintosh
AIX	IBM variant of UNIX for workstations
OS/2	IBM's multitasking operating systems with a GUI that runs DOS, OS/2, and Windows applications
Windows NT.*x*	A 32-bit system from Microsoft that runs DOS and Windows applications
BeOS	Multitasking operating system for the Power Mac
Solaris	Sunsoft variant of UNIX for PCs, the Power PC, and SPARC computers
VMS	Digital's multitasking, multiuser virtual memory operating system
Ultrix	Digital's variant of the UNIX OS for the VAX and PDP-11 series
Windows CE	A limited-application Windows operating system from Microsoft that runs hand-held PCs such as the Palm Pilot

SOFTWARE APPLICATIONS

Computer software falls into two major categories: system software and software applications. System software includes the control programs for the operating system, the communications system, and database management. Applications software packages process data in specific ways, such as word processing, spreadsheets, inventory, and packages available for business in several categories. The following table contains just a few relevant categories and subcategories (courtesy of Beyond.com, www.beyond.com, an Internet software superstore):

Common Types of Software

Category	*Application*
Business	Presentation graphics
	Legal
	Database/statistics
	Project/time management
	Finance
	General business
	Writing/spreadsheet tools
Communications	E-mail
	Communication
	Fax and document imaging
	Palm Pilot accessories
	Macintosh software
	Windows software—Palm Pilot/Win CE
Graphics	Clip art and fonts
	CAD
	Desktop publishing
	Graphics and presentations
	Multimedia
	Adobe typefaces
Utilities	Antivirus
	Backup and security
	File conversion and transfer
	Operating systems
Reference	Legal
	Encyclopedia
	Dictionary and thesaurus
	Atlas and mapping
	Directories
	Medical
	Career
	Foreign language

WORD PROCESSING SOFTWARE

In the early days of computers, a major distinction arose among people who were word processing experts, people who created graphics, and people who designed page layout. With the new software currently on the market, those lines are becoming blurred. Today, virtually anyone who can type, write clearly, and develop an eye for design can produce all kinds of documents. In the past, you had to use several pieces of software to design a document that would require a layout function: one for word processing and one for desktop publishing. Today, most word processing software applications offer more robust options for users who want to do a little more.

Most of the software packages on the market have the basic functions: text editing tools, cut and paste tools, print preview capability, search and replace tools, file management capability, a spell checker, a thesaurus, an electronic clipboard, font manipulation tools, and so on. The following are some of the special features that you should look for in word processing and/or desktop publishing (WP/DTP) software, if a combination is needed. Not all positions in offices require desktop publishing skills, so analyze the situation realistically. Desktop publishing software can be expensive and time-consuming to learn and use.

- *Styles.* Can the software apply multiple formats to words, phrases, headers, footers, paragraphs, and documents? For example, if you are preparing a newsletter and need assorted fonts, is there an option for creating a style sheet?

- *Columnization.* Does the software set up a page for multiple columns that can automatically wrap?

- *Importing graphics.* Can graphics be created in another source—chart, paint or draw program, clip art, or spreadsheet—and be imported? Once imported, is the image static, or can it be adjusted for size and shape?

- *Boxes and lines.* Can boxes and horizontal and vertical lines be created without using a line draw feature? Can the inside of a box be shaded to emphasize the text?

- *Leading and kerning. Leading* adjusts the spacing between lines and paragraphs; *kerning* adjusts the spacing between characters. Can leading and kerning be adjusted to make the page more readable?

- *Headers and footers.* A *header* is information repeated at the top of several or all pages; and a *footer* is information repeated at the bottom of several or all pages. Does the software handle headers and footers with the versatility of odd and even pages?

- *Large document handling.* Can the software separate files for sections of a large document, keep track of their order, and paginate for internal numbering (1-1, 1-2, 2-1, 2-2)?

- *Index and table of contents generation.* Can the software generate an index and/or table of contents electronically? Does it perform automatic updates when changes are made to the document?

- *WYSIWYG (what you see is what you get).* Does the software display on the screen what the printed page will look like?

Electronic Clip Art

Electronic clip art is a variety of ready-made graphics that can be used to improve the appearance of presentations, reports, newsletters, and so on. It can be electronically cut and pasted into documents, and it can be imported into most WP/DTP software. Electronic clip art is available for a wide variety of businesses and industries, educational institutions, and personal uses.

BASIC SOFTWARE NEEDS ASSESSMENT QUESTIONS

1. What are the required tasks?

2. What are the current software applications in use?

3. Do the current applications perform the required tasks adequately?

4. What software applications are needed to perform required tasks that are not currently being addressed?

5. How often will the software be used?

6. Who will be using the software?

7. What is the users' level of computer expertise?

8. What kind of training programs are currently in place?

9. What is the budget for new training programs?

10. What types of documents are currently produced?

11. What types of documents will a new software application produce?

12. Will these new documents require a change in printers?

13. What type of computer hardware is currently in use?

14. What is the budget if different hardware is needed?

15. What is the current operating system?

16. What is the budget if a different operating system is needed?

SPREADSHEET SOFTWARE

The development of the electronic spreadsheet was the fuel that sent PC sales skyrocketing in the early years. Spreadsheets are arranged in a grid, with columns (vertical) and rows (horizontal). The intersection of a column and a row is called a *cell*. Cells can be assigned a number or a formula, or can be identified in a special way. Text, mathematical formulas, and values are entered in the cells. The beauty of the spreadsheet is that if a value or formula is changed, everything affected by the change can be automatically recalculated. The format can be saved so that only new information need be entered. A year-to-date report, for example, requires simply calling up the last report and adding the current month's figures. The spreadsheet recalculates the year-to-date numbers automatically.

Add-on packages have been developed to give additional functions to spreadsheet information. For example, a word processing add-on that links a table to a spreadsheet updates the information in the document to reflect the changes made in the spreadsheet. Graphic add-ons enable the user to display the spreadsheet information by using a variety of graphs. The benefit is that the user does not have to exit the spreadsheet to utilize the add-on. The following is an example of an electronic spreadsheet:

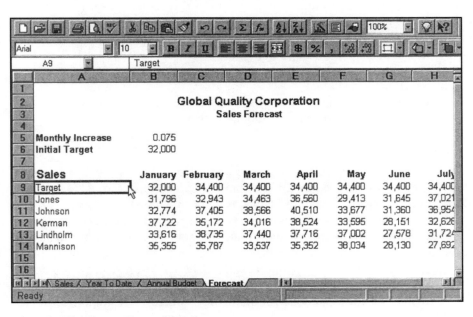

Sample Electronic Spreadsheet

DATABASE MANAGEMENT (DBM)

Database management software (DBMS) enters, organizes, stores, and retrieves data. These programs organize data in a manner similar to a filing cabinet. Data first is organized into files relating to a particular subject, such as customer lists, accounts receivable, employees, and inventory. Within the files are individual records, which can be compared to the folders in the file cabinet. Specific information in each record is broken down and contained in fields. For example, an employee record might have fields such as Last Name, First Name, Date of Birth, Address, Department, Date of Hire, and Position.

DBM software directs the computer to search the files and assemble specific information from the records into a report form that can be used to make informed decisions. Knowing what type of information will be needed aids the structure of the database so that retrieval is efficient.

Databases come in all shapes and sizes. For example, a database for contact names and addresses is a familiar one in offices. Customer names, addresses, phone numbers, and particles purchased, for example, all can be documented in a database. You can access that database to do a mailing, contact the customers, get a history of their purchases, or find out how many socks were sold on any given day. The most common example of a database is a spreadsheet application such as Microsoft Excel or Lotus 1-2-3. The database holds the data in a predefined format (dollar, general, or scientific), organized the way you defined it—by the rows (type of expense) and columns (date). The data can be stored either as inputted or as derived from a calculation. To access the information, start the application package (Excel) and open a spreadsheet (database).

A step up from a spreadsheet, you can create a database of items and information about items and then link them together.

Types of Databases

Two types of databases exist: flat file and relational. In a flat file database, each record is contained in a single table. You can page through each table to find data, but the individual tables have no relational capability with any other table. In a relational database, records are maintained in a collection of tables, each containing information about one subject. However, the tables are related so that you can use or collect information from more than one table at a time. Access is the most common example. In Microsoft Access, you define the items in which you are interested (Customer and Past Orders, for instance) and what you want to know about the items of interest (Customer: Customer Address, Customer Telephone; Past Orders: What was ordered, quality, when). Your access mechanism (MS Access) enables you to ask questions that would link the items of interest (which customers who live in New York City ordered more than one regular pizza in June).

Access and most other Windows-based databases are relational, but some offices still run other UNIX or DOS flat-file databases that are not relational.

Again, databases come in all different sizes. Many technologies exist today to assist you in obtaining answers to questions. One of the primary technology areas on everyone's mind is the Internet. Though extremely important, this offers a communication mechanism to information. The Internet provides access to more information for the corporation and provides a communication facility to reach a wider audience.

The key words in the above paragraph are *access* and *communication of information*. The Internet is *not* the information nor the data that provides information. It is *not* the storage of data. It is *not* the completeness or consistency of data. To be complete, consistent, and accessible in a timely manner, data must be kept in a well-designed database.

This is the purpose of a database: to store clear, concise, and consistent data in a format that is easily and quickly accessible. A database is the automated filing cabinet of all data. It comes or can be built in all shapes and sizes.

Today's businesses capture crucial information in databases, such as customer lists, product inventory, payroll schedules, employee history, sales by territory, and so forth. Many corporations separate operational data from informational data: Operational data is data gathered from business transaction-oriented information systems. Examples are order-entry type systems, online banking systems, or billing systems.

PRESENTATION SOFTWARE

Increasingly, sales, marketing, and communications employees (as well as company executives) are conducting their own presentations in a professional manner by using easy-to-learn, easy-to-use software. Although many presentation programs are available, you probably have the software bundled with the most popular office suite of software products out there: That's PowerPoint. With PowerPoint, you have the option of creating the following:

- A slide presentation for overheads

- An electronic presentation from your computer or laptop

- Audience handouts

- Speaker notes that the presenter can use at the lectern

PowerPoint is easy to use, and with a feature called the AutoContent Wizard, you can get step-by-step guidance in creating any number of reports or presentation formats, such as the following:

- Progress reports

- Financial overviews

- Strategy recommendations
- Business plans
- Marketing plans
- Status reports

The AutoContent Wizard has templates for the structure and organization of the material, as well as several different styles of presentation graphics. In short, even the most timid of new software users will want to try this easy-to use program.

For example, the Business Plan Wizard tiles the outline for the following slides or presentation windows:

- Mission Statement
- The Management Team
- Market Summary
- Opportunities
- Business Concept
- Competition
- Goals and Objectives
- Financial Plans
- Resource Requirements
- Risks & Rewards
- Key Issues

By following this template, all you need to do is state the information in the areas provided—and voila! You have a complete and professional looking business plan. This is just one of PowerPoint's more than 50 prebuilt content templates that give you a head start on creating top-notch presentations.

Corel Presentations 8, which is packaged with its WordPerfect suite, also comes with predesigned slide shows that you can customize, as well as tools to help you create and move through the presentation. These programs make it easier than ever for even the first-time user to develop quality presentations.

DESKTOP PUBLISHING

Desktop publishing (DTP) systems are becoming extremely popular as prices come down, and software programs come with an increasing number of user-friendly features. DTP eliminates many time-consuming steps in creating

TIPS FOR BUYING THE RIGHT SOFTWARE

- Start your search at least 90 days before you need the software.

- Conduct a needs assessment.

- Identify the tasks the software must perform.

- Make a list of the available software packages that meet your needs.

- Determine the features and benefits that differentiate one package from another.

- Create a grid to help compare the packages.

- Consult current users of the different packages for references.

- Determine how easy the packages' features will be to learn.

- Research the packages' general availability.

- Determine which packages will be compatible with hardware already in use.

- Determine which packages will be compatible with other software already in use.

- Determine the kind of training available.

- Verify that support is available after the sale.

- Make sure that support is provided by a reputable and well-established company.

- Make sure a toll-free number is available for technical support.

- Determine whether you can join a user group.

- Make sure you understand what kind of maintenance, if any, will be required.

- Determine whether the software package is easily upgradable.

- Determine whether the software company will provide upgrades for free or at a discount.

- Identify which add-on packages, if any, are available for the software.

- Request a demonstration or trial use.

camera-ready art. The layout occurs directly on the computer screen, with changes in type size and style made with a click of the mouse or a key. Headlines, graphics, and text can be moved easily. When you're finally satisfied with the result of your creative efforts, your computer printer produces camera-ready art for the printer. No more paste-ups—just neat, clean, simple, and fast. You also can save on typesetting and printing costs through desktop publishing.

You can learn to do many tasks in-house with a little DTP experience and the easy-to-learn software programs currently available:

- Newsletters
- Stationery
- Calendars
- Banners
- Awards
- Flyers
- Holiday greeting cards
- Awards
- Brochures
- Business cards
- Ads
- Marketing brochures
- Mailers
- Catalogs

Another convenient feature in DTP is the capability of creating a file on disk that is ready for the printer. This feature tells the printer what it needs to know to print without any further design specifications from you. With DTP becoming the next logical step up from word processing—and given the potentially significant savings to be realized from the output—the only remaining question becomes whether to do it. Here are some things to ponder before pushing forward:

- *Planning ahead.* How much time is there to devote to the effort? Getting the same kind of results as a professional printer and typesetter doesn't happen quickly (or maybe ever). If time is valuable and limited, desktop publishing might not be a bargain in the short term.

- *Equipment needs.* Although feature-rich programs make DTP appealing, they also require a lot of memory and fast processors to work well. This could mean upgrading to a faster processor and a more expensive laser printer to get the quality output desired. The laser also might not have a sufficient selection of typeface fonts to meet your needs.

- *Proficiency.* Even if you are a successful do-it-yourselfer, very few people can get professional results from DTP if it's a "sometime" thing. Professionals get the most professional results. Although acceptable and attractive documents can be obtained, don't expect to outproduce a graphic artist.

- *Learning curves.* DTP software can be very friendly, with all kinds of help screens and pull-down menus. However, there is no substitute for formal training. You almost certainly will invest a significant amount of money in new equipment. It's a good idea to back up that investment with the kind of basic training that will help get you up to speed in a hurry. Look for formalized classes in your area, particularly those given by national training centers and sometimes local colleges. This training certainly won't turn a novice into a DTP professional overnight, but at least it might keep you from the maddening tinkering that chews up hours of precious time. If you want to be able to keep working at the business full-time while learning, search for evening training classes.

> **TIP:** Don't take training classes before you have your own equipment to work with. DTP is a hands-on experience; if you take classes, you need to use the newfound skills you've gained as quickly as possible—or risk losing them.

COMMUNICATIONS SOFTWARE

Communications packages enable PCs to "talk" to each other. Such software requires a modem and a connection to telephone lines. The communications software handles logging on and off the communications network, dialing, saving messages, and sending or receiving information from a central computer.

E-mail

E-mail is becoming a necessity for many of today's businesses. Although the adoption rate has been slower in some professions than others, executives and office professionals alike are integrating e-mail into their work life. When you set up your system or log on in the morning to your network, you access your e-mail account, which probably has a password to safeguard your privacy.

After you log on to your e-mail application, you can compose, send, receive, and reply to messages. Depending on the application, you can file, archive, automatically reply to, and sort your messages. The application you use depends on your network because the same application will be deployed for every user.

Fax Software

You can take advantage of creating and sending a fax without leaving the desk if you have a fax program on your computer. Daily faxing in quantity costs a lot of money over the phone lines, especially at peak hourly rates (the phone companies have carefully calculated peak hours to take advantage of this business activity). With fax software comes store and forward options that enable you to send during off-peak hours—and save money, too.

If you do not have fax software, it's inexpensive and easy to install in Windows or Mac machines. You need a modem on your machine with fax capability, however. If you have no modem, the simple solution is to purchase one with fax and modem capability. The software will come bundled with the product. The third option is to use a fax-forwarding service that operates off your e-mail by way of your Internet service provider: You create a fax document in your e-mail program, add the appropriate names to the fax header, and then e-mail the whole thing to your ISP, where it is routed to all the appropriate addresses at Internet calling rates.

Electronic Data Interchange (EDI)

Electronic data exchange (EDI), which is a worldwide movement, is the computer-to-computer exchange of business information. EDI is rapidly changing the way companies do business because any company that sells goods and/or services can benefit from EDI. A company can send purchase orders, invoices, confirmations, shipping papers, inquiries, financial reports, and so on directly from its computer to the computer of the trading partner. The information is keyed in a standardized, structured format. The information must be keyed in only once and then can be processed for all related transactions. The following are just some of the industries using EDI: manufacturers, government offices, health care agencies, grocery retailers, transportation branches, publishing companies, and retail businesses.

The American National Standards Institute (ANSI) is the recognized coordinator for national and international standards information. For detailed information about EDI standards, contact the Publications Department, Data Interchange Standards Association, Inc., 1800 Diagonal Road, Suite 355, Alexandria, VA 22314-2852; 703-548-7005.

OTHER APPLICATIONS

Although the following list of applications barely begins to skim the surface, it will give you an idea of the variety of software that is on the market.

Project planning. Project planning is essential for the success of an office professional. Look for software that helps with scheduling calendars, planning projects, writing reports, and preparing Gantt and PERT charts.

Employee handbooks. If you must create an office or employee handbook, find a software application that can help. Such software includes information on how to find good employees, employment application forms, interview questions, a new employee orientation guide, performance evaluations, and so on.

Bookkeeping and accounting. Available programs range from entry-level bookkeeping to advanced accounting "what-if" scenarios, cash control, credit card tracking, job costing, a general ledger, accounts receivable and payable, payroll, inventory control, invoicing, income tax preparation, and much more. Packages are available for companies of all sizes, from those with one employee to those with hundreds.

Money management. Some programs help take control of finances. Use these programs to set budgets, write checks, track investments and expenses, collect financial data, set and modify financial goals, judge whether investments are performing as they should, learn how loans are front-loaded with interest, calculate interest rates, and much more.

Starting a business. For those entrepreneurs who want to start their own businesses, software can lead you to sources for business loans, grants, venture capital, and government contracts.

Maps. Get instant route planning and maps of major national and international cities.

BASIC GUIDELINES FOR SELECTING SOFTWARE

Buying computer software is like buying a plane ticket: Purchase on impulse or at the full retail rate, and you are wasting possibly hundreds of dollars per unit. On the other hand, if you're prepared to do some homework, planning, and comparison shopping, you can find real bargains. If you're buying for other employees besides yourself, the company savings can add up fast.

To begin saving money on software, you need to know your options in upgrades, software bundles, and integrated packages.

UNDERSTANDING UPGRADES

Software manufacturers realize that it's easier to sell their new products to a user already committed to its old products. Because of this, upgrades now account for an estimated one in every six software units sold. Upgrades offer registered computer users a great opportunity to save money.

Software vendors offer two kinds of upgrade pricing plans: a standard or traditional upgrade, and a competitive upgrade. In a standard upgrade purchase, you pay a reduced price for the latest edition of a software product because you already own an older version of the same product. Most software upgrades are mailed directly to registered users by the manufacturers (and it is a good reason for returning those registration cards to the manufacturers). When you receive vendor upgrade notifications, compare the upgrade price offered directly from the manufacturer to other special offers from software resellers. Sometimes, high-volume resellers can beat the vendor's price.

Competitive upgrades are designed to lure you away from one product to a similar product by a competing vendor. Competitive upgrade offers might arrive in the mail, and also can be found on specially marked software boxes on reseller shelves and in the pages of mail-order catalogs and PC magazines. To take advantage of a competitive upgrade, you usually must provide the original title page from the manual for the software you currently are using as proof of ownership.

Besides the new versions of software that are changing to incorporate more bells and whistles, existing software is subject to frequent minor revisions. Some of these changes come in response to consumer demand; others are a result of companies finding and fixing little bugs that the original developers didn't notice before the software was released. These are usually fixed with patches.

Next are device drivers, the program routines that enable the operating system to communicate with the device in question to get it to perform requested functions such as printing or displaying a graphic onscreen. Manufacturers release new drivers in response to complaints that the original drivers didn't work that well. Many troubles that users have with new software can be traced back to inadequate drivers. Although patches are nice-to-have fixes, they aren't necessary. Device drivers are often a necessity for users who want to use their hardware with the latest software, however.

Most popular software can be updated for new patches and device drivers via the World Wide Web, including the following:

- Windows 95 (www.microsoft.com/windows95/info/updates.htm)

- Windows 98 (www.microsoft.com/windows98/info/updates.htm)

- Microsoft Internet Explorer (www.microsoft.com/ie4)

- Netscape Navigator (www.netscape.com)

- Lotus (www.lotus.com)

- Corel (www.corel.com)

- Microsoft Office (www.microsoft.com/office)

- Quicken (www.intuit.com/support/updates)

If it sounds like a time-consuming hassle to update software, it certainly can be. A couple of software packages have taken the mystery out of updating your favorite programs by searching the Internet for the updates and automatically downloading them: Cybermedia's Oil Change and Symantec's Norton Live Update are two of these.

Watch for the availability of updates for your software because no matter how carefully designed the new software bundles are (and even if you are getting one of the newest releases out there at the time you read this book), responsible software companies fix user-discovered glitches as they are reported. You might even discover a fix for a problem you think you have discovered. For example, when Office 97 first shipped, the new versions of Word and Excel that were included could not read files saved in earlier versions. As soon as Microsoft discovered the problem, the company posted a downloadable patch or fix for the problem.

SOFTWARE BUNDLES

Software bundling is a marketing tactic: A manufacturer groups several of its own products into a unit or *bundle,* usually a group of popular software programs that perform functions necessary for most office and home users. The price on the bundles is reduced so that it is significantly less than if each product were purchased separately. Manufacturers' bundles are usually made up of high-end, expensive products that offer industrial-strength features. You'll also find bundles assembled by major resellers and mail-order outfits that combine products from assorted vendors. The resellers can purchase programs directly from the manufacturers at a discount because of their volume. These programs are packaged with rebates, coupons, or smaller inexpensive products to make an attractively priced group.

In choosing any bundle, evaluate each program individually. Make sure that you actually need each one of them. If not, add up the cost of the ones you really will use and compare this to the bundle price. Bundles are often a good deal for users or small businesses that are starting from scratch with new computers, or for anyone moving all at once to a new operating environment, such as from Windows 3.*x* to Windows 95 or 98. Less can be more if you don't

PURCHASING APPLICATIONS

Purchasing the right applications program can be easy if you follow a few simple steps:

- *Determine how involved your business needs are.* Will you be writing vanilla letters, interoffice memos, fax transmittals, and routine office correspondence; or creating reports, graphics, and slick presentations?

- *Decide what features you want to have.* Do you like to create from scratch, and are you very experienced at building fancy documents? Do you like applying factory features? Simple test: Are you a point-and-shoot photographer, or do you like to go to manual programming? If point-and-shoot is your response, one of the full-featured professional office suites will satisfy most of your needs.

- *Check PC magazines.* Publications such as *PC World* and *PC Magazine* print reviews of the latest and best-selling programs in the category you seek.

- *Look for references.* Ask fellow users or colleagues about their likes and dislikes about various programs.

The software recommendations in the table on pages 214-215 were compiled from a general listing of the best of the 1997 software. This list appeared in the January 1998 issue of *PC Magazine,* published by Ziff-Davis and is available online at www.zdnet.com/ pcmag/special/bestof97/software.htm.

really need an industrial-strength product. Often, a single, simpler product that combines several functions is a better solution.

Integrated packages, or suites, often combine several functions and have improved greatly (they frequently appear on the top-ten software sales lists). Generally, suites include a word processor, a spreadsheet, and a database application. Software developers trim some of the features of their flagship product for the "lite" version. For example, the word processor might not handle snake or newspaper-style columns, or the spreadsheet might contain 70 built-in mathematical functions instead of 750. Despite the reduction in features, the programs are streamlined to work well together. As a result, incorporating a chart into a document (for example, an Excel spreadsheet into a Word document) takes a couple of keystrokes instead of 20 and involves no translation at all. Look for bargains by comparison shopping at local computer supply stores, national chains, and mail-order catalogs. Also consider shopping direct from your office through companies such as Beyond.com.

No discussion of software bundles would be complete without mentioning Microsoft Office. This package has an installed base of more than 22 million licensed users and can be found at the sites of more than 90 percent of Fortune 500 companies. A new version (Microsoft Office 2000) currently is planned for 1999.

Office 2000 probably will come in more versions, but the flavors listed here show how Microsoft bundles different applications to target different segments of the market.

Office 97 comes in three versions:

- *Office 97 Regular Edition.* All Office bundles include Word 97, Excel 97, and Outlook 97. The standard edition of the bundle adds PowerPoint 97. This edition is perfectly adequate for most home users and small offices.

- *Office 97 Professional Edition.* In addition to the standard package, the professional edition adds Access 97 (a database program), PowerPoint presentation software, Binder 97 document-management software, and Bookshelf Basics (a reference program). This is a good package for most professional and larger offices.

- *Office 97 Small Business Edition.* This package has the standard three programs as well as Publisher 97, Financial Manager 97, and AutoMap Streets Plus. This o.ne is a good choice for business people on the go who typically work with laptops. If you purchase a PC today, it most likely comes with Microsoft's Office suite as well as its operating system. Your choice of versions depends upon your planned use. One universal feature of all Office bundles is that they are designed to create Web pages from Word and Excel documents. This is done by saving the document or worksheet in HTML format.

Although Office was designed to offer a broad package for a large constituency of users, at times you might want to choose a version without some features, and to get an industrial-strength, dedicated program that has options such as desktop publishing (such as Adobe PageMaker, if you are a professional publisher) or Web page design (such as Microsoft Front Page, if you plan to run a commercial business that generates a lot of activity or visits).

Software Recommendations

Category	Product	Comments
Application suite	Microsoft Office 97 Redmond, Washington Microsoft Corp. 800-426-9400 www.microsoft.com	Available in a standard edition including Word, Excel, and PowerPoint. A Professional Edition adds Access (a database program), Outlook (a new information manager and e-mail client), an animated Office Assistant, and new Internet tools.
Graphics: Professional Desktop Publishing	Adobe Pagemaker 6.5 Adobe Systems Inc. San Jose, California 800-843-7263 www.adobe.com	Offers nearly all the features that print designers require, combined with new, innovative Web-publishing tools.
Graphics: Personal Desktop Publishing	Microsoft Publisher 97	Fit for the novice desktop publisher, this program is capable of designing projects for both print and the Web.
Graphics: Professional Image Editing	Corel Photo-Pain 7 Plus Corel Corp. Ottowa, Ontario 800-772-6735 www.corel.com	A rival of Adobe Photoshop. Contains new editing tools: object-editing modes, transparency tools, and lens objects that allow preview of color and tonal adjustments without affecting the image. Can export client- or server-side maps.
Graphics: Personal Image Editing	Microsoft Picture It! 2.0	Powerful and easy-to-use image editor for the consumer market. Enables novices to work with images easily.

Category	Product	Comments
Graphics: Illustration	Macromedia FreeHand 7 Macromedia Inc. San Francisco, California 800-288-4797 www.macromedia.com	Illustration package for both artists and Webmasters. Has WYSIWYG features and Web format support.
Video Editing: Professional Video Editing	Adobe Premiere 4.2	The pioneer tool of choice for desktop video editing.
Video Editing: Personal Video Editing	MGI Video Wave. MGI Software Corp. Richmond Hill, Ontario 888-644-7638 www.mgisoft.com	Makes video editing understandable for beginners.
Business Diagramming	Visio Professional 5.0 Visio Corp. Seattle, Washington 800-246-4746 www.visio.com	Visio pioneered business graphics programs, enabling those who can't draw a straight line to create professional-looking charts.
Personal Finance	Quicken Deluxe 6.0 Intuit Inc. Mountain View, California 800-446-8848 www.quicken.com	A popular personal finance program with many new features.
Applications Development	Microsoft Visual Basic 5.0	The clear choice for powerful, yet easy-to-use programming development. Available in three versions: Professional, a high-end Enterprise, and a low-end Learners Edition.

FOR MORE INFORMATION

If you can't find what you need from the phone numbers and Web sites listed in this chapter, you may need to expand your search.

■ For more information and definitions of computer terminology, see *Webster's New World Dictionary of Computer Terms* from Que or check with your local bookstore in the computer or reference section.

■ For more information on the parts of computers and how they work, see *How Computers Work* by Ron White, published by Que. Its detailed full-color drawings explain the intricate details of computers and their peripherals allowing you to select what's best for you.

■ For more information on the Internet, intranets and how they work, see *How the Internet Works,* published by Que. It contains color illustrations showing how e-mail, the Web, and other aspects of the Internet work.

■ For more information on purchasing computer equipment, the Internet is the best place to start. See the Web sites in the chapter and ask lots of questions.

6

OFFICE ENVIRONMENTS AND WORKSTATIONS

◆

■ **Selecting and Optimizing Workspace**

Using a Floor Plan

Office Lighting

Office Furniture

Computers in the Office

■ **Workstations in the Office**

Components of Workstations

Workstation Adjustment Ergonomics

Organization of the Workstation

■ **Office Safety, Health, and Security**

Office Health and Safety

Disaster Planning

Security

Office Maintenance

Policies and Procedures Manuals

■ **Moving Without Headaches**

■ **For More Information**

Nothing affects an office as much as its environment. The image of the office, its productivity, and the contentment of its employees and clients are all directly affected by the design of the office. An office must be functional, aesthetic, and comfortable while still remaining efficient and cost-effective. This is a lot to juggle, but decisions made regarding the office environment have ramifications that will determine even the success or failure of the business. Therefore, it is imperative to ensure that any decision made regarding furniture, equipment, and standards is the right one.

SELECTING AND OPTIMIZING WORKSPACE

The optimal workspace varies from office to office. However, several factors remain constant when determining what is best suited for your business. The optimal workspace will be one that lends itself to the needs of your office, that contributes to efficiency, and that promotes employee contentment. The optimal workspace also will be determined by the constraints of the building and what is cost-effective. Pre-planning is essential to accomplishing these goals— the more time spent planning before implementing, the greater your chances of reducing the probability of error afterward.

USING A FLOOR PLAN

The most popular method by which to decide the layout of the office is certainly trial and error. This is unfortunate, however, because a significant amount of time and expense is dedicated to the error portion of the equation. With a small amount of effort and foresight, office workspace can be planned to be efficient and cost-effective.

A thoroughly developed floor plan represents the first, biggest, and most important step in workspace planning. To start, obtain documentation of the available space; the building manager generally can provide a copy of the design or architectural plans of the building. If this is not available, simply measure the space and transfer the measurements to grid paper. Each grid should represent a set distance, such as one box representing one foot. Include the measurements of any obstructions or permanent fixtures, such as columns or divider walls, and ensure that they are accurately represented on the page. In addition, include items such as doors, hallways, windows, and other structures that will affect the workflow. Finally, mark the position and location of all electrical outlets.

In addition to grid paper, office supply stores carry kits designed to aid in effective space planning. These kits usually contain generic cutouts of office furniture and equipment, as well as detailed instructions on their applications. When using these kits, ensure that the size and shape of all items directly reflect your own space and equipment. A recent innovation growing in popularity is the space planner software kit for the computer. These software kits enable users to try different arrangements and resize all items with the touch of a button.

After the floor plan has been laid out, it can be used to determine the size of furniture and equipment that will fit in the office. If furniture and equipment already have been purchased, measure these items, draw them to the scale established on the floor plan, and then cut out the representations. These cutouts can then be used to try out different arrangements on the floor plan so that you can avoid physically moving furniture and equipment around the office.

When designing the floor plan, consider the following issues:

- *Noise level.* Some employees need a more quiet workspace than others.

- *Privacy.* Besides quiet, some employees need a workspace where they can carry on confidential conversations.

- *Workflow.* Individuals who work together on the same kind of work should be placed together to facilitate the flow of assignments and communications.

- *Need for team discussion.* Set aside space for group discussions, with sufficient room at least for a round table and a few chairs for a team meeting.

- *Visitors.* Sometimes, a visitor will have to wait outside the workspace. Set up a quiet place, away from the flow of office traffic, where a visitor can sit until the person with whom he or she has an appointment is available.

- *Flow of traffic.* Consider the comings and goings not only of visitors but also of staff members, to minimize disruptions from co-workers as they go from one area of the office to another.

- *Key resources.* Consider where to place the network printer, office supply cabinets, and other resources used by all within the office so everything is accessible.

Many computer software programs offer planning tools to help create a floor plan. Visit your local software supplier to discuss the pros and cons of various offerings.

The final floor plan should be made up of large and small boxes—the larger boxes illustrate offices or cubicles, and the smaller boxes inside or outside these larger boxes illustrate desks and other office furniture.

OFFICE LIGHTING

Lighting is essential for productivity. Whenever possible, natural light should be used in the office because it provides a sense of openness and is the most familiar for human eyes. Artificial lighting will still be required, however, because natural lighting is not always possible and because detailed work such as graphic design requires stronger illumination than can be provided by natural light. Although specialized lighting exists for every function, three basic choices work for general purposes, as discussed in the following sections.

Incandescent Lighting

Incandescent lights are the standard light bulbs used in the home. Incandescent lighting is popular because of its availability, its capability to be easily directed, and the low cost of the bulbs. In addition, the illumination quality of an incandescent bulb is very warm. On the downside, however, incandescent bulbs require frequent replacement and burn substantially more electricity than other bulbs, thereby lowering their cost-effectiveness.

Fluorescent Lighting

Fluorescent lights are long tubes most often used in businesses and offices. Although the most expensive to purchase initially, fluorescent bulbs last significantly longer than incandescent bulbs and burn the least electricity, making them the most cost-effective and thereby contributing to their popularity. Fluorescent lighting is strongly artificial and not easily directed, however, so it works primarily for general-purpose overall lighting.

Halogen Lighting

On the rise in popularity, halogen lights come in a variety of shapes, produce a more natural and warm light than that of fluorescent bulbs, and can easily be directed. Halogen lights burn more electricity than fluorescents, but not as much as incandescents. Also, although they cost much more initially than fluorescents, you don't have to replace them as often, which makes them more cost-efficient in the long run.

The Best Light for the Workspace

Besides cost, consider the most appropriate lighting for your workspace. Halogen bulbs are used often in restaurants and other public places, but fluorescents don't create the tiring glare that halogens can.

The best-lit office is one that offers various degrees of lighting required for each area or task yet blends the different illumination levels harmoniously. To accomplish this, install general lighting, such as fluorescents, overhead so that all areas of the room are evenly lit. As much as possible, ensure that furniture, walls, and other obstructions don't create shadows. In addition, position overhead lights in relation to windows and computers to minimize glare. General lighting should mimic the illumination of natural light to avoid eye strain.

After establishing the overhead lighting levels and positions, determine which areas require more specific lighting. Desks, credenzas, and audiovisual rooms all require different types of lighting and should be addressed individually. Desk lamps, spotlights, and sconces provide varying degrees of illumination and can be placed to correspond to the varying light requirements. Don't limit the types and styles of lighting—mixing and matching can yield great results. An incandescent floor lamp can add a homey feel in a reception area, while halogen track lighting along hallways may add a sense of style. Above all, ensure that sufficient lighting exists. Although excessive lighting can always be reduced or dimmed, insufficient lighting may be difficult to address later, can lead to accidents, and can create eye strain and headaches.

Natural light or soft light generally works better than high-intensity lighting. But those who do close work, such as proofreading spreadsheets, manuscripts, or reports, need high-intensity lighting. If you get complaints about eye strain, headaches, fatigue—and, yes, mistakes—you probably have a lighting problem.

OFFICE FURNITURE

The selection of office furniture is a subjective decision based almost entirely on the taste of the individual. Rich woods, antiques, and leather-upholstered furniture once were the domain of executive offices, while computers and other technology were confined to minimalist styles composed of steel and plastic. Happily, furniture is being created today in all styles and price ranges that also accommodate technology and adhere to a predetermined sense of style. Therefore, selection of furniture can include functionality, size, and comfort.

Desks and Other Furnishings

In addition to simply providing a workspace, a desk can portray the success of the office, the level of the employee, and the style of both. Aesthetics, then, certainly are an important component of desk selection. The primary purpose of the desk is to be functional, however, so take care to ensure that the desk is comfortable and sufficiently meets the requirements of the job. A receptionist may need a counter, or a draftsperson may need a canted surface. Fortunately, no shortage of styles, colors, shapes, and models of desks exists—most can address even the most demanding needs.

Much of the new furniture today is modular, which means that it is capable of fitting together in various arrangements. As you develop the floor plans for individual workspaces, consider not only the size of desk needed, but also other furnishings that the employee will need—from file cabinets that can attach to the desk to overhead storage bins. Some individuals will want a

LEASING VS. BUYING FURNITURE AND EQUIPMENT

Carefully think through the decision to buy or lease office furniture and equipment by weighing all options and the circumstances of your business.

The most obvious benefit of leasing is the capability to fully furnish an office with the necessary furniture and equipment without tying up a significant amount of capital. Leasing generally doesn't require a down payment, and the monthly payments are almost always lower than finance payments for furniture or equipment that is purchased over time. This demands significant consideration for a start-up business or a business with little capital. In addition, because of the rapid pace of technological advances, leasing office equipment such as computers, printers, and copiers enables a company to return the equipment for more state-of-the-art models later. For companies that need the furniture or equipment for a limited time, leasing also makes a particularly viable option. However, monthly payments for leased equipment include charges to cover the leasing company's overhead and profit, which creates an unnecessary business expense that adds no value to your company.

Companies are better advised to purchase furniture and equipment whenever possible because buying creates an asset for the company. Furniture will be around for a long time and portray an image, so companies also should buy the best quality possible. This raises the cost, but remember that the best does not always mean the most expensive. When cost is an issue, this can be minimized by several methods, such as purchasing wholesale for larger offices or negotiating better deals from retailers. Purchasing used or slightly damaged furniture is also an option, as is buying equipment that is less than top-of-the-line, such as discontinued or demonstration models and floor models. The exception to this is computers, which never should be purchased damaged or after they are obsolete. Businesses also should check out overlooked retail channels such as auctions, estate sales, and business liquidation sales, as well as the classified section of the local newspaper.

counter on which they can store magazines or stacks of folders they are currently completing. Others prefer overhead cabinets, in which they can put these same materials. The more suitable the furnishings are to the employees' work styles or personal needs, the more productive those people will be. For instance, an employee may prefer a desk at standing height if he or she dislikes constantly sitting, whereas another might want a table rather than traditional desk, with side cabinets to store materials traditionally kept in a desk.

Ensure that your desk is the appropriate height. A height of 30 inches is recommended for most writing tasks; desks for typing and keyboard carrels should average about 26 inches from the floor. Desks also should be high enough to provide sufficient space for leg and knee comfort. Desks that are high enough might offer sufficient space for small file cabinets or other case goods to be placed under them, thereby preserving office space and providing a spot for files and paperwork that is used regularly.

In the past, desks were placed in the center of rooms, with a minimum of 4 feet of open space around the sides. Today's offices are considerably smaller than those of the past, given rental costs for office space. As a result, most desks are positioned against a wall, and other furnishings are placed on either side of the desk and/or opposite the desk.

If you will be interacting often with clients or other employees across your desk, you may want to consider a separate meeting table. Meeting tables are less formal and provide a more open feel, making others feel more comfortable and less confined.

Even if your desk is in a small cubicle, adding a chair next to it makes your workspace more inviting.

Computer Furniture

The proliferation of computers in the workplace has caused a similar proliferation of computer furniture. *Computer furniture* is a generic term that encompasses any furniture related to computers, from an adjustable stand for a monitor or printer, to an entire office system. As a general rule, referring to computer furniture also takes into account individual pieces. This type of furniture is the optimal choice for anyone who works with a computer because it is specifically designed to accommodate the needs raised by computers and their use. Due to its relatively recent invention, computer furniture also can encompass recent innovations and new discoveries in such areas as ergonomics, acoustics, and lighting. Although early offerings were over-engineered and often prohibitively expensive, most computer furniture today is relatively inexpensive and better designed. As a result, its popularity continues to increase. The National Products Association reports that one-fourth of all office furniture purchased today is computer-related.

File Storage

Today's paperless society is anything but paperless. Not only are offices generating increasing amounts of paper, but their storage space requirements also are growing in proportion. File cabinets can provide the necessary storage for this mass of paper generated by all offices. Fortunately, file cabinets are no longer solely utilitarian and are available in rich woods, jazzy plastics, and even padded fabric covers. This type of storage is not limited to file cabinets, however, so you should determine whether your needs might not be better met with rolling file racks, disposable cardboard file cabinets, or the services of a file archive firm.

Two basic types of file cabinets exist: vertical and lateral.

Vertical. When opened, vertical file cabinets position files to face the person. These cabinets are the most common, possibly because of their minimal space requirements. Most come with two drawers, which stand about 3 feet high; or four drawers, which stand about 5½ feet high. Because of its low height, the two-drawer style is particularly useful in offices with limited space because it can be placed under desks or tables. Always take care when opening the drawers; the stacking design and the unevenly distributed weight caused by open drawers can cause the unit to tip.

Lateral. Lateral file cabinets position files so that their side faces the person opening the drawer. These files are much more stable and therefore often are used as space dividers or credenzas. Lateral files come primarily with two drawers that stand about 3 feet high, four drawers that stand about 4 feet high, and five drawers that stand about 5½ feet high. Lateral file cabinets are particularly popular for legal files because the depth of these cabinets easily accommodates the additional length of these files. When both legal (8½ inches × 14 inches) and letter (8½ inches × 11 inches) files are used, lateral files are the best choice because most are built with moveable tracks to accommodate both sizes.

Storage needs should determine the kind of file cabinets selected. Some cabinets have two drawers; others have three; still others have five. The amount of materials with which you work and must maintain in your work area should determine the kinds of cabinets you choose.

COMPUTERS IN THE OFFICE

The computer revolution has arrived, changing the way we conduct business. Computers are now an integral part of the office (see chapter 5). Computers represent a large investment and come in a dizzying assortment of sizes, types, and capabilities.

There's more to purchasing computers than selecting a vendor and comparing prices. For instance, computers draw considerable power, so you must be sure that your facility is wired to accommodate the equipment you purchase. Review information on computers you are considering, and compare that information with the information contained in your lease or discuss this issue with potential vendors. Besides purchasing hardware within the limits set forth on your building blueprints, you should use power strips for each computer. A *power strip* is a heavy-duty extension cord with enough outlets to accommodate all the plugs in your system. The power strip has an on-off switch that enables you to control all the outlets at once; you can leave your computer, monitor, and printer permanently switched on and control them through the strip. More importantly, you can keep power surges or spikes from damaging your computers and other electronic equipment in use in your office.

A loss of power, on the other hand, can be prevented by a power-backup system, which provides emergency power for as little as ten minutes or up to an hour or more. Because even a brief power outage can wipe out considerable work, be sure to discuss a power-backup system with systems personnel. These systems cost considerably more than a power strip, so you may have to obtain written authorization from senior management.

WORKSTATIONS IN THE OFFICE

Workstations evolved from the open-office concept in Germany after World War II. Attempts to absorb excessive noise through the use of fabric-covered screens eventually developed into the construction of systems furniture that, in turn, evolved into today's workstations.

As you walk through an office of this type, you can see row after row of small cubicles in which employees work. In marketing firms, for instance, each cubicle might house telemarketers on the phone with potential customers. In open-landscaped offices, such as those found in insurance agencies or government offices, you can see desks lined up in rows, with filing cabinets on a side wall. These setups have become more popular because of their rental space savings.

As the workplace continues to evolve, workstations have secured a place for themselves through their adaptability to changing needs, space, and technology. It is this same adaptability that accounts for the millions of possible types of workstations through the use of interchangeable components and styles. It's virtually impossible not to find a workstation that addresses the specific needs of the individual as well as the dictates of the office: Determining *which* one to choose is the task.

COMPONENTS OF WORKSTATIONS

The use of computers has made the workstation a frequent site in offices. Depending on the work in the office, these workstations now are the standard for employees. Managers have a modified version, with space for a more traditional desk in the center of their offices and modularized furnishings for storage purposes. Workstations appear in insurance companies, telemarketing organizations, purchasing departments, and advertising agencies, to name a few organizations.

Most workstations are designed specifically for computers, as well as for peripherals such as printers, cables, and necessary electrical outlets. In addition to more effectively handling modern technology, many models are better designed ergonomically and look more aesthetically pleasing. Workstations can come predesigned or can be standardized for an entire corporation or building. The current trend, however, is to create a customized workstation from a variety of modularized components that is specific to the needs of the individual. Typically, these workstations include a minimum of desktop space, computer accommodations, file space, and bookshelves. However, they also can mix and match the following components:

- Desktops
- Meeting tables
- Printer stands
- Credenzas
- Shelves or bookcases
- Electrical strips or raceways
- Chairs
- Dividers or wall panels
- Keyboard carrels
- Filing cabinets

WORKSTATION ADJUSTMENT ERGONOMICS

Ergonomics is the study of the effects of physical design of equipment on the physical and emotional well-being of its users. In considering the ergonomics of a workstation, for instance, you would be concerned about how far the user must stretch to reach the phone on his or her desk, as well as how much the chair can adjust to minimize stress on the user's neck or back muscles. Ergonomics also deals with the size and shape of armrests on the chair, and whether the on/off switch is labeled so it can be read from a comfortable position.

Specifically, ergonomics is defined by *Webster's New World Dictionary* as "the science that seeks to adapt work or working conditions to suit the worker."

In practice, ergonomics is concerned with adapting the work environment to fit your body and to reduce and eliminate pain, discomfort, and strain. Ergonomics affects more than just your body, however, because physical discomfort contributes to mental fatigue, irritability, and an inability to concentrate. All this leads to reduced productivity. Almost half of all workers' compensation claims are based on repetitive stress injuries brought about by bad ergonomic design or adjustment. Employers are well advised, therefore, to provide ergonomically correct and adjustable furniture, while employees should ensure they are adjusted optimally.

Increasingly, as employees spend more time on their computers, the issue of ergonomics has become important. Often, employees will petition for ergonomically designed equipment when organizations undertake redesign. The issue can become a subject of employee-organized wellness programs and have prompted many organizations to invest in ergonomically designed equipment to increase employee satisfaction.

The Chair

Proper seating is the single most important aspect of any workstation because the average office worker spends 75 percent of his or her time seated. A good chair should adjust for height, back support, and tilt. In addition, the upholstery should absorb moisture and not permit sliding. The back of the chair should come up to the shoulder blades and support the lower spine. If necessary, a back support cushion can be added to provide additional support. The seat should tip slightly forward so as not to restrict blood flow to the legs. The height of the chair should place hands and wrists level with the keyboard, yet keep feet flat on the floor. If feet dangle, use a foot rest. Armrests, if provided, should not interfere with movement.

Most of this equipment can be purchased at office supply firms or orthopedic suppliers.

The Monitor

The computer monitor should be from one arm's length to 28 inches away. The top of the screen should be level with your forehead or slightly lower. The monitor should be placed directly in front of you or in the opposite direction of your predominant hand and tilted slightly upward. Use an anti-glare screen or computer filter to minimize eye fatigue caused by glare and reduce radiation emissions. Adjust the brightness and contrast controls until you find a display that is comfortable. If you use a copy stand, it should be at the same height and distance from you as the monitor. Take frequent breaks, and focus your eyes at distant objects often. Again, necessary items are available at office supply firms.

The Keyboard

Keyboard carrels or platforms should place your forearms parallel to the floor and place your hands comfortably in front of you. Mouse pads or trackballs should be immediately next to the keyboard and at the same height. When typing, use a light touch; use your entire arm when moving the mouse or trackball. A padded wrist rest should be placed in front of the keyboard to reduce the chances of developing carpal tunnel syndrome.

The latest keyboards come in a curved shape or in two parts. The keyboard has been redesigned so the arms and elbows are positioned ergonomically, to reduce stress on shoulders. These newer designs can be purchased in a computer equipment supplier or office supply firm, along with wrist pads or wrist/mouse pads.

Shelves and Bookcases

Shelves and bookcases should be designed and adjusted to be reached without having to get up from your chair. Therefore, shelves and bookcases that stand on the floor are the best, ergonomically speaking. Shelves and bookcases installed above you should be placed in the direction of your predominant hand. Never stuff or force anything into these shelves or bookcases because the items may fall out when the case is opened and cause injury.

Other Accessories

New computer accessories are being released almost every day, and each comes with an ergonomic promise. Whether you want the larger-sized mouse or the bigger trackball, visit a supply store before purchasing one of the new goodies on sale. Be sure that they do for you what the ads promise before buying them.

ORGANIZATION OF THE WORKSTATION

Workstations should be organized with several factors in mind: ergonomics, the frequency of use of the various pieces, and the design of the workstation itself. The most predominant feature of the workstation is likely to be the placement of the computer because this is almost certainly the equipment that will be used most during the workday. Most workstations are designed with this in mind, and holes and raceways for the necessary cords are positioned to correspond accordingly.

> **TIP:** The placement of electrical equipment should never necessitate the use of extension cords. If optimal positioning of these items is contradicted by the design of the workstation, consult an electrician about possible solutions, or consider replacing the workstation with a more appropriate design.

Especially with modular units, however, the decision of where to place other components is often left up to the individual. A good method to determine the correct placement of each item is to make a list of all items that are used throughout the workday, and then to divide this list into constantly used items, frequently used items, and seldom used items. Compare this list with a list of the components, and a trend will begin to appear. For example, if you frequently meet with clients or other employees, it might be a good idea to place a small meeting table at the end of the workstation close to the working area. If you seldom use certain files and records, place them in file cabinets in a different location. Files and records you constantly use should be placed in file cabinets under the desk.

In addition, it is a good idea to determine your position in the office and its consequences. If you are near a high-traffic area, for example, your workstation should be organized to minimize disruption and avoid injuries. As another example, being close to a window might dictate the placement of your monitor to reduce glare.

Workstation Accessories

Accessories such as Rolodexes, office supply caddies, and desk mats are the most individual and frequently used items in the workplace. The selection of these items should be left to the discretion of the individual employee, whenever possible, because he or she is best qualified to determine individual work habits and personal taste. A common method is to provide a catalog from which employees can choose individual items. Another method is to purchase items in several different styles, and allow the employee to take what he or she wants or needs from a centralized supply location. Some offices even enable employees to purchase items from any source, and then later reimburse them for the cost.

Many offices require a more uniform look, however. If this is the case, a clearly worded policy is essential for maintaining office standards. Employees also should be informed of the reasons for these decisions. Explaining to employees that standardization is required because of cost-effectiveness, safety factors, or the desire to portray a certain image for the office will make such measures more palatable and increase compliance.

In either case, the positioning of these items on the workstation always should be left to the employee, who should place these items in relation to what is most comfortable and effective for his or her work habits. This will increase productivity and reduce the likelihood of injury or discomfort.

Reducing Paper Waste and Recycling

Awareness of our responsibility to our planet continues to grow. Natural resources are being depleted at an alarming rate, and finding space for our increasing production of garbage is a monumental problem. In response, a variety of environmentally superior products are being produced and initiatives are being implemented to address this situation. Most buildings and offices, for example, are required to recycle and separate recyclable waste from other garbage. As an added bonus to the company, this policy also reduces costs, clutter, accidents, and the likelihood of fire.

Employees should be encouraged to participate in recycling initiatives; seek their input to find new ways to reduce the use of paper. Environmental groups, such as Earth Now and Greenpeace, are also excellent sources of information on how to promote recycling in the office and reduce the excessive use of paper. Before taking too much time and energy to set up a recycling program, however, check with the facilities or building management to determine the policy for recycling. Sometimes recycled trash is automatically removed with regular trash; you may, however, need to contract with an outside firm. Make

WORKSTATION EVALUATION CHECKLIST

Chairs

Yes No

☐ ☐   Is the chair comfortable?

☐ ☐   Can the chair be easily cleaned and maintained?

☐ ☐   Does the chair swivel?

☐ ☐   Can the seat height be adjusted to a height equal to the distance from the crease at the back of your knee to the floor?

☐ ☐   Can the seat height be adjusted so that your arms stay at the correct angle for keyboard use?

☐ ☐   Can height adjustments be made easily?

☐ ☐   If you are a short person, are footrests available?

☐ ☐   Does the lumbar support maintain the proper curvature of you back (as if you were standing)?

☐ ☐   Can the backrest recline and lock in at least two positions?

☐ ☐   Can you adjust the backrest to tilt forward for extended work periods in front of a computer monitor?

☐ ☐   Do the armrests interfere with movement?

☐ ☐   Do the armrests take enough pressure off your wrists when keyboarding?

☐ ☐   Do the armrests support leaning positions?

☐ ☐   Does the seat have a rounded front edge that maintains good circulation?

☐ ☐   Can the seat tilt and lock in a forward position for prolonged keyboarding?

☐ ☐   Does the chair have a five-leg base to prevent tipping?

☐ ☐   Are casters dual-wheeled to enable easy rolling?

Work Surfaces

Yes No

☐ ☐   Is the work surface at least 30 inches deep to accommodate all necessary equipment?

☐ ☐   Is the work surface between 26 and 29 inches high, or at least slightly above elbow height when seated?

☐ ☐   Can the workspace be adjusted to accommodate you if you are either right- or left-handed?

☐ ☐ Is all equipment within your arm's normal reach?

☐ ☐ Is adequate storage available for handbooks, documents, personal belongings, and other items?

☐ ☐ Are different work surface heights and angles necessary and available for different tasks?

☐ ☐ Does the area under the work surface provide adequate leg room, and is it free of obstacles?

Computers

Yes *No*

☐ ☐ Can you position the center line of the monitor screen slightly below eye level?

☐ ☐ Is the keyboard position adjustable to ensure that your lower arm and hand form a straight line parallel to the keycaps?

☐ ☐ Does your copy holder maintain the proper alignment with the monitor level?

☐ ☐ Can the mouse and its pad be positioned within your elbow's free movement range to avoid shoulder strain?

☐ ☐ Is your seating position a minimum of 30 inches (or arm's length) away from the monitor to minimize any electronic or radiation emissions?

Lighting

Yes *No*

☐ ☐ Can workstation overhead lighting be dimmed?

☐ ☐ Is task lighting available?

☐ ☐ Is the lighting level appropriate for hard-copy tasks?

☐ ☐ Is the lighting level appropriate for computer monitor use?

☐ ☐ Is the fluorescent lighting flicker-free?

☐ ☐ Is the workstation free from glare and reflection?

☐ ☐ Are workstations positioned in relation to windows to avoid glare and reflections?

☐ ☐ Do window treatments provide an adequate means of controlling incoming light?

☐ ☐ Are filters available to reduce reflections on monitor screens?

TIPS FOR RECYCLING AND REDUCING PAPER WASTE

- Review and change documents on the computer screen.
- Print only the number of copies you need.
- Use the print preview feature of your word processing program, if it has one.
- Use e-mail whenever appropriate.
- Archive e-mail messages on your computer instead of printing and filing hard copies.
- Reuse paper that has already been printed on one side for printing drafts.
- Make double-sided photocopies whenever feasible.
- Use bulletin boards (electronic or otherwise).
- Use white legal pads instead of colored ones; they are easier to recycle.
- Adopt a white-paper recycling program; many waste-management companies can help you set this up.
- Reuse shipping boxes and packing whenever possible.
- Use bad photocopies and obsolete stationery for drafts, internal memos, and notepads.
- Have clear plans about how recyclables will be delivered to recycling facilities.
- Coordinate with the building management's recycling plans to ensure their support.
- Post memos in a central location rather than providing individual copies.
- Consolidate files to one location.
- Edit documents onscreen rather than printing drafts.
- Provide separate wastebaskets for paper and other garbage.
- Limit the amount of file space in individual offices.
- Provide documents on disk rather than hard copy.
- Provide one copy and route it with a circulation list rather than a distributing multiple copies.

sure that processes are in place to get the recycled material to the recycling plant—instead of sorting paper to have it all go back in the building trash again.

OFFICE SAFETY, HEALTH, AND SECURITY

Organizations have a responsibility to their employees to ensure that facilities are safe and secure. It's to their advantage to create an environment in which employees are safe from accidents, illnesses, theft, or the violent acts of visitors or coworkers. Employees are more productive when they believe their companies are concerned for their well-being.

OFFICE HEALTH AND SAFETY

No one likes to think about the chances of injury or illness in the office. However, we probably spend more time in the office than anywhere else except our homes. It is in all of our best interests, therefore, to ensure that the conditions for injury or illness are minimized as much as possible, and that we are suitably prepared to deal with any situation before it arises. This responsibility is set forth in the Occupational Safety and Health Act.

The Occupational Safety and Health Administration

The Occupational Safety and Health Administration (OSHA) was created in 1970, when Congress passed the Occupational Safety and Health Act to establish minimum standards for worker health and safety, and to provide protection for employees from hazardous working conditions. OSHA regulations cover a variety of areas, including first aid, protective equipment, fire protection, workplace ventilation, and exposure to dangerous chemicals or conditions.

OSHA requires that companies with a minimum of eleven employees maintain documentation logs of job injuries that required medical attention, and make these logs available to all employees. These logs, which are known as 101 and 200 reports, are submitted to and reviewed by OSHA investigators, who may determine that an inspection of the work site is in order. Inspections also can be called in response to an accident or a complaint filed by an employee, can be regularly scheduled, or can occur unannounced at random.

Accidents take various forms. We all know it's bad luck to walk under ladders, but employees who are preoccupied with their work may still do so and be hit by some object that slips from the hands of the person on the ladder. If the top drawer in a file cabinet is filled first, the cabinet may topple on the worker who did not think to fill the cabinet from the bottom drawer. Employees might slip or trip, and break a leg or arm. More serious accidents could maim, even kill. If an accident occurs in the workplace, it must be investigated by the

BASIC OFFICE SAFETY

A few tips to avoid frequent problems follow:

- Keep floors clean and clear to avoid slips and falls.

- Spills and litter should be dealt with immediately, not left for the janitorial crew.

- Frayed carpets and loose tiles should be replaced or repaired immediately, and the area should be blocked off until action is taken.

- Desk and file drawers should be closed when not in use to prevent tripping.

- File cabinet tops should not be used for storage because items may fall off by the vibrations of opening and closing drawers.

- Avoid the use of extension cords whenever possible because they can cause tripping and are a fire hazard.

- Ensure that all areas of the office are adequately lit at all times.

- Employees should never run or engage in horseplay in the office.

person responsible for the facility's safety; this might be the safety director, a manager, or a floor monitor. OSHA demands a report on all accidents that occur—even those that seem to occur from personal clumsiness. Sometimes accidents credited to the accident-prone are due to individuals who may be overworked or tired from long shifts; such incidents must be investigated to identify and eliminate the cause.

If unsafe conditions or discrepancies are discovered during the inspection, the investigator will issue a citation that establishes a timeframe within which the condition must be rectified. A fine, penalty, or (in extreme situations) prison sentence also might be levied, depending on the circumstances or severity of the problem. Employers can challenge these citations and present the case to a judge in a court of law. It's a much better idea to avoid these situations by ensuring that the office complies with the standards set by OSHA. The free *OSHA Handbook for Small Business* can be obtained at the following address:

Occupational Safety and Health Administration
Department of Labor
200 Constitution Avenue NW
Room N3700
Washington, DC 20210
202-219-7266

SMOKING IN THE WORKPLACE

Smoking in the workplace is now rare in any form. Recent legislation has effectively banned smoking in public places, and Corporate America has eagerly followed suit with policies that further restrict smoking in the office. In spite of this trend and the general public's growing intolerance, odds are that at least a couple of employees in any company will be affirmed smokers. This doesn't usually lead to problems with the implementation of a clear and complete policy (for example, "Absolutely no smoking anywhere in the building") that all employees know is uniformly enforced.

If your office has several smokers, you may want to consider providing a smoking room. The time saved by employees not having to leave the building will increase productivity as well as increase smokers' morale. Smoking rooms should be as far away from the general areas of the building as possible and should have airtight doors. An independent ventilation system, or "smoke-eater," will keep the room bearable if there are many smokers and will help to keep the smell of smoke from traveling outside the room. It is also a good idea to check with your local fire department regarding pertinent regulations, as well as tips to avoid fire accidents.

Your best bet, however, is the arrangement of programs to help your smokers quit. Most smokers don't want to smoke, but they are unsure of how to go about giving up the addiction. The American Lung Association is a good source of programs and referrals to outside programs designed to help people kick the habit. Hypnotherapists, nicotine patches, and drug programs are effective and easily available, and new methods are being developed every day. Ensure that your smokers know these programs are available whenever they want them—and it's a good idea to offer them more than once. Research indicates that almost no one successfully quits on the first try, so it's important that office smokers know that they haven't failed if they don't quit on the first, second, or even third attempt. It's far more important that they continue to try.

Employees who are injured on the job or who suffer from illnesses related to their work are covered by workers' compensation. This compensation replaces their salary until they have recovered and can return to work. State statutes vary about workers' compensation: The trend is to reduce the time employees stay away from work by identifying alternative jobs that they can do while they recover.

REPETITIVE STRESS INJURIES

General Symptoms

Most repetitive stress injuries are localized in the areas of the fingers, hands, wrists, forearms, shoulders, and neck. The most common include these:

- Stiffness

- Inflammation

- Persistent tingling

- Persistent numbness

- Being awakened at night by this tingling and/or numbness

- Chronic change in hand temperature

- Generalized weakness

- Shooting pains

- Tendency to drop small, lightweight objects

Tips for Prevention

Here are several tips for preventing repetitive stress injuries:

- Exercise regularly outside of the office.

- Include aerobic exercise for better circulation.

- Include resistance training to build muscle mass.

- Practice yoga, tai chi, or other relaxation exercises.

- Use basic ergonomic principles when setting up (or changing) your workstation.

- Stretch at your desk frequently.

- Take frequent short breaks away from your desk at approximately half-hour intervals; use these breaks to move around and stretch your entire body.

- If keyboarding, keep wrists in a relaxed, comfortable position.

- At the first signs of an injury, use ice, braces, and anti-inflammatory medications, and consult your doctor.

Preventing Accidents and Work-Related Injuries

More than six million job-related accidents occur annually, costing companies fifty-seven million lost work days, $420 per worker, and more than $50 billion in workers' compensation programs. To prevent accidents, offices should implement a safety incentive program. This type of program should enlist the participation of all employees to pinpoint problems, determine solutions, and provide insight into the circumstances surrounding past accidents.

In addition to formalized safety incentive programs, however, employees should be reminded that they are responsible for their own safety and should be encouraged to bring to the attention of management anything they believe could threaten the safety of themselves or their co-workers. Employee-run wellness programs have developed from exactly this kind of initiative.

Employees are increasingly coming together to put on programs in which authorities on a variety of health-related issues address staff members. Relevant issues include health-related (as in weight control, diabetes, high blood pressure) or ergonomic ones, such as repetitive stress injuries from excessive typing or eyestrain from staring for long periods at the computer screen. Companies also sponsor memberships in health clubs or pay a portion of the costs. Organizations have found that healthy employees mean higher productivity. Furthermore, such initiatives demonstrate concern for the workers, which translates into motivated employees.

First Aid

Many injuries and illnesses can be addressed directly in the office with a minimum of care and fuss. A few preparations can help you effectively deal with them when they occur. First, ensure that your office has a first-aid kit. Determine the most probable incidents for your office, and consult appropriate salespersons or office supply distributors about which first-aid kit is most appropriate. As a minimum, however, the kid should contain bandages, hot and cold compresses, eyewashes, and minor pain relievers. In addition, place the phone numbers of the nearest hospital and emergency services in the kit for immediate access.

Keep on hand a list of anyone in the office who has any type of medical training: These include Emergency Medical Technicians (EMTs), nurses, and physicians. Don't hesitate to consult these individuals in any situation that requires medical attention. If no one in the office has any type of medical training, contact your local office of the American Red Cross. This organization runs first-aid training sessions on a regular basis, covering areas such as choking, CPR, and basic first aid for a variety of situations. A training session for the entire office can be arranged onsite, but as a minimum, several representatives of the office should be sent for training.

CHECKLIST FOR OFFICE FIRST-AID KIT

- ☐ 100 assorted adhesive bandages
- ☐ 1 roll 2-inch elastic-wrap bandage
- ☐ 1 roll 3-inch elastic-wrap bandage
- ☐ 2 rolls soft gauze bandages
- ☐ 3 gauze pads, 2×2, 3×3, 4×4
- ☐ 4 butterfly bandages
- ☐ 2 sterile eye pads
- ☐ 2 large triangular bandages, $40 \times 40 \times 55$
- ☐ 1 roll ½-inch hypoallergenic first-aid tape
- ☐ 10 cotton swabs
- ☐ 10 antiseptic wipes
- ☐ 1 container antiseptic soap
- ☐ 1 tube antimicrobial skin ointment (mycin family or triple antibiotic)
- ☐ 1 tube burn cream
- ☐ 1 bottle of aspirin or other analgesic pain reliever
- ☐ 1 container activated charcoal
- ☐ 3 cylinders of smelling salts
- ☐ 1 over-the-counter antihistamine
- ☐ 1 insect-sting kit
- ☐ 1 eyewash cup and solution
- ☐ 1 instant ice pack
- ☐ 1 pair blunt-nosed scissors
- ☐ 1 pair tweezers
- ☐ 1 thermometer
- ☐ 10 assorted safety pins
- ☐ 5 assorted splints
- ☐ 5 pair disposable rubber/latex gloves
- ☐ 1 sterile mouth protector for CPR
- ☐ 1 small flashlight
- ☐ 1 first-aid handbook

DISASTER PLANNING

Major disasters such as fire and flood in the office are rare. When they do occur, however, they are usually debilitating enough to completely suspend all work activity and, in many cases, cause the office to go out of business altogether. In spite of this, little thought is given to the office's response to a disaster even though the amount of preparation before a disaster is directly proportional to the office's capability to survive and recover in the event of an emergency. This poor planning is unfortunate; once established, disaster plans require little attention and yield positive results.

Most offices deal in the commodity of information. In addition, as most offices are computerized, it is relatively easy to minimize the disruption of work by ensuring that computerized information is available from another source. This can be done in several ways. Offices can secure the services of an outside disaster recovery firm that will download all computerized information on a regular basis, as well as provide office space in the event of a disaster. In addition, companies can connect their internal computer networks to a mainframe outside the office that is reserved specifically for this purpose. Companies also can download all information once a week to a tape, which is then stored off-premises. Files and information such as personnel files, client lists, and financial records that will be necessary to resume business also should be duplicated and stored offsite. Remember to update these files periodically.

Most organizations practice risk management to ensure that an accident or other disaster will not keep them from immediately resuming business. Insurance advisors can come into the facility and review operating procedures to minimize risks. These procedures might include ensuring that critical paper files are copied and stored elsewhere, reviewing hiring procedures to avoid negligent hiring or bringing individuals onboard with criminal records, or reviewing warehousing or manufacturing processes to avoid hazardous conditions.

To keep employees working, employers should consider providing temporary at-home computers for their employees, or purchasing software that will enable employees to connect their personal computers to the office network or mainframe. If the cost is prohibitive, a contract can be established to rent or lease computers for employees to use at home until the situation is resolved. When cost is an issue, companies can create innovative solutions. For example, consider a buddy system with another company, in which each company provides space and equipment for the other in the case of a disaster. These types of solutions require minimum expense and can be equally effective.

On an individual level, you can take actions to personally safeguard yourself and help your co-workers in a crisis such as a major fire.

Fire

The hazard of fire is a very real concern in the office. The biggest problem with fire safety is that it is rarely an issue until after the fact.

- Create a written plan for fire safety that specifies the actions to be taken by all employees to reduce the likelihood of a fire in the office. Also specify actions to be taken in the event of a fire. This plan should consider the office layout, available exits, and routes for evacuation. For instance, most organizational plans note that evacuation of the building should be by stairway, not elevators, unless instructed by a firefighter. Besides health reasons, smoking by employees should be discouraged because smoking is a major cause of fire in offices (second only to electrical fires). The plan should be shared with all employees, and fire drills should be held at least twice a year to ensure that new employees are familiar with the steps to take in the event of a fire. Your local fire department will be happy to work with you to devise and evaluate your plan. Experts want to come to your office *before* there is a need—they will review the procedures you have set, identify better actions if they exist, and answer employees' questions so they are clear not only about how to ensure their safety but also how to avoid endangering their co-workers.

- Establish a date once every six months to ensure that smoke detectors and fire extinguishers are in good working order. Use this same date, at a minimum, to conduct a fire drill. Predetermine a location outside the building where employees are to gather, and charge one employee with headcount responsibility. Remind all employees that elevators are not to be used in a fire.

- Ensure that office fire extinguishers have an ABC rating, which indicates that they can be used on all types of fires. Periodically demonstrate their proper use to all staff.

- The fire department provides free stickers that display an emergency fire telephone number—these should be attached to every office telephone. When possible, the company's alarm system should be linked directly to the local fire department.

- Electrical-code violations are the leading cause of fires in the office. Check the office for overloaded sockets; frayed electrical cords; light bulbs that exceed wattage recommendations; and wires under or near rugs, upholstery, or drapes. Rectify any violations immediately.

If you must evacuate a building because of a fire, walk calmly down the stairwell; don't push or shove. Follow instructions given by fire personnel, which often means that you should exit the building, although occasionally it may be sufficient to exit to a floor beneath the fire.

Most organizations have a fire monitor on each floor of their buildings. When you hear the fire alarm, don't worry about personal possessions. Go immediately to the area designated by your fire plan, which is usually near a fire exit.

TIP: Because some stairwells aren't well-lit, you may want to keep a flashlight in your workspace in case of a fire or other emergency that requires you to walk down the stairs.

SECURITY

Employees have a right to office security. Legislation constantly verifies that employees must be provided a work environment that is safe and that offers no threat to their well-being. As a result, offices are liable for almost any incident or situation that brings harm to an employee. Therefore, reasonable safety precautions should be taken to provide employee security and reduce incidents such as theft.

Beyond those concerning human life, establish security procedures to safeguard equipment or other items of worth within the organization, including proprietary information. Whatever your business—from software production, to publishing to manufacturing—you have records that should be protected by security systems and security personnel.

Access to the workplace should always be limited and, if possible, guarded. Receptionists and entrance guards can successfully limit access by unauthorized personnel. In larger offices, employees should be issued badges or other forms of identification for access whenever possible. In addition, internal phones or intercoms should be provided to identify visitors before they enter the premises.

In addition, doors and windows should automatically lock from the outside upon closing. Employees should be reminded never to prop open windows or doors because this could endanger their security. Delivery personnel and suppliers should have a centralized location to deposit their items, and the receiving employee should be contacted to retrieve the items from this location. Delivery personnel should never be allowed to freely roam through the workplace.

Finally, visitors and clients should be provided with a waiting area in the front of the office. Employees should meet them there and stay with them the entire time they are in the office. Employees should be reminded to question strangers who are unaccompanied in the workplace and never to provide access to the office to unknown people.

The treatment of visitors will vary with the size of the office. Most organizations have a waiting area—on every floor or on only one floor. In any case, ask visitors to come to the nearest visitors' area and identify themselves to the receptionist. Then you can go and get them.

Some organizations don't have receptionists. Instead, there is a phone for visitors to use to alert the party they have come to visit. Be sure that your visitor has your extension. Periodically check to see that the phone is indeed working. You also might want to list the names and extensions of all those on that floor.

Smaller organizations depend on the building's security system. At the very least, the system might include a sign-in system with careful control of the comings and goings of visitors and those with packages.

Within your organization, distribute rules about the treatment of visitors. For instance, they should not be allowed to wander around the office, no matter who they are. Furthermore, you should not allow strangers to follow you through office doors that lead to the work area. If you feel unsure about confronting them yourself, you should have the number of security or another person designated for security handy.

It is also unwise to stay in a building alone late into the night. Plan with co-workers to work together either in the evening or on a weekend.

Terrorism and Disgruntled Employees

Fortunately, the number of incidents of terrorism and sabotage from disgruntled employees and former employees is low. A situation is unlikely to occur in your own organization, but it is better to be prepared. The consequences and repercussions are severe enough to warrant attention and action.

The office is most susceptible to sabotage from current employees because they have access to the workplace. Obviously, no one wants to institute a police state within the office because this would only increase feelings of ill will and make for an uncomfortable work environment. However, if circumstances predict the possibility of sabotage, this can be minimized by limiting employee access to areas that directly pertain to their job, as well as requiring that employees leave at a certain time and not work unaccompanied after hours. A better method of addressing this danger, however, is by ensuring that the lines of communication in the office remain open and honest. Employees who feel empowered to express their concerns and feelings and who are given the truth regarding unpleasant situations are far less likely to react with violence, hostility, or sabotage. Not only will they feel safer, but they also will feel that their organization truly understands its responsibility for their well-being.

A bigger danger is the threat of attack by former disgruntled employees. Terminations and layoffs are always unpleasant situations and often are accompanied by enormous hostility and anger. Employees who are let go always should be accompanied while they clear their desk and should be escorted out of the building immediately. Ensure that all keys, passes, and office identification are collected at this time, and withhold final checks until these items are returned. Although re-entry is sometimes inevitable, former employees should have restricted access to the office as any stranger would, and they should be accompanied at all times while on the premises. In any situation in which the threat of violence is present, contact your local police station immediately.

OFFICE MAINTENANCE

A clean office is an effective office. Although your firm probably pays for janitorial services, you should work to keep your office neat. Cleanliness promotes productivity, increases employee morale, and projects a good image. Sadly, the issue of cleanliness in the office often is relegated solely to contracted cleaning staff and building maintenance. This is unfortunate because a cluttered and dirty office can be a safety hazard, contributing to illness and possible injury, as well as making the office an unpleasant place to work.

Janitorial Services

Most organizations contract for cleaning services, which include vacuuming, dusting, and emptying waste cans. Some services take on the responsibility for taking recycled paper to a recycling center, and some shred documents for firms whose tossed paperwork may contain proprietary information.

Some businesses contract for this service. Sometimes the landlord of a building leases the service for all corporate tenants. Janitorial services will clean kitchens or break areas but won't deal with personal items. They also won't deal with messy offices, cluttered workspaces, and other barriers to an office. Even though your office has janitorial service, there are a few basic ways to keep the office tidy and make it better for everyone.

- *Post signs.* This is the single best way to remind employees throughout the workday. Create signs for common areas such as kitchens, copier areas, and meeting rooms. Signs might read, "The refrigerator is cleaned Friday at 5 p.m. Take home any containers." Post whatever is appropriate for the work area.

- *Establish cleaning days.* As warranted by the condition of your office, periodically reserve workdays for the purpose of cleaning. Allow employees to dress casually and, if possible, provide things that will make the day enjoyable, such as a company-sponsored lunch, music, or contests for the cleanest office.

- *Develop a written policy.* Circulate a written policy with the office's expectations and standards for cleanliness. Remind employees to dispose of old files, keep food in the appropriate areas, and reduce clutter in common areas. Be careful not to lecture, however, because this may put off employees and create feelings of resentment.

- *Set an example for others.* If you want others to keep their work areas and common areas neat, you should do so yourself.

POLICIES AND PROCEDURES MANUALS

It is easier to run an office if employees have a clear sense of their responsibilities, how the company expects to achieve its mission, and the rules that the organization expects its employees to follow as they carry out their responsibilities and work toward accomplishing that mission.

That's where policies and procedures manuals come in handy. These are particularly valued by new and part-time workers because they can fill in the gaps left from orientation efforts or remind them about specific rules or activities. Policy manuals cover general guidelines governing how the company will operate. Procedures manuals—or employee manuals, as they are sometimes called—provide instructions for performing specific activities or tasks. A procedures manual might contain a variety of information: job descriptions of every employee, and advice on developing new ones or updating one's own; job aids to ensure that an employee does his or her work correctly; software and other operating tips to maximize productivity; instruction about such details as the preferred corporate format for memos, reports, and e-mail; and correct letterhead paper and style for correspondence. Alternatively, an organization might create separate manuals to cover each of these issues.

As companies install corporate intranets, materials that previously appeared in policies and procedures manuals are posted to the intranet. Many companies also maintain hard copies of these rules and instructions.

Usually, the manuals themselves come in the form of loose-leaf binders so that sheets can be added or updated as the need arises. The following section examines the kinds of content that should be covered in policy and procedures manuals. (In the case of procedures manuals, note that the text might refer to a single book or the beginnings of a manager's personal library.)

Office professionals sometimes might be called upon to help assemble or create a policy manual. Keep in mind a few simple ways to make it usable:

- Outline the contents if you are producing your first policies and procedures manual. Your outline should include the kinds of information you want to include in the manual, such as department job descriptions, phone etiquette, filing, business travel, memos and letters, supplies, procedures for handling complaints, and grievance procedures.

- Use a brightly colored binder, and give a title to the manual so that its purpose is obvious. A manager should provide a manual for each employee who reports to him or her, and should encourage each individual to place the manual in a prominent place on or near the desk, where it is easily accessible to those who may need it in the employee's absence.

■ Number all the pages. Because there may be changes to the contents, number each page by tab (if you separate multiple parts with tabbed pages) instead of numbering pages continuously throughout the manual Starting with page 1, number all pages consecutively for all material within that part.

■ Include a table of contents and an index so that someone new to the organization can easily find the information he or she needs.

■ Be complete but brief. The manual shouldn't go overboard in its explanations, but critical points should not be left out. For instance, if a computer problem occurs, the worker should know not only to call technical support, but he or she also should also know the name of the individual and any extension numbers.

What to Include

Policies manuals reflect the governance of the company, contain policy statements that reflect the basis of management decision making, and spell out the rules that everyone within the organization is expected to follow. Most policies manuals are divided into two categories: corporate information and general personnel policies.

Corporate information includes the organization's values or basic beliefs (including commitments to shareholders, customers, and employees), the corporate structure as a whole (for instance, subsidiaries or branch offices, and their locations and functions), and operations within each facility (with special attention to departments at headquarters and their responsibilities). If the organization takes a strong stand on a specific issue, such as diversity or the environment, this is also noted in this section of the manual.

The remainder of the manual is made up of general personnel policies: the organization's adherence to federal and state laws and regulations (such as Title VII); personnel issues such as recruiting, interviewing, hiring, termination, and the privacy guaranteed to employee personnel files; issues of attendance and punctuality; dress code; payroll provisions (including exempt and non-exempt qualifications); business travel; and grievance, safety, sexual harassment, and other corporate programs designed to ensure the rights of employees.

Policies should be organized by categories and should be cross-referenced when an issue pertains to more than a single policy. Policies increasingly are being placed on corporate intranets in addition to being stored in policies manuals. A numbering system should be used that includes both numbers and letters to permit the addition of new policies when the need arises. Pages can be printed on both sides or on one side only, but a manager should keep each policy separate to allow for changes. All policy statements should begin on a right-hand page (if you print on both sides of the page). As mentioned earlier, do not number policy manual pages consecutively. Instead, number the pages by policy (as in, page 1 of 3).

Job Descriptions

Job descriptions provide valuable information for managers so they can make the best hiring, placement, and promotion decisions. In today's workplace, as organizations realign and then realign once more, the information also can be useful for restructuring or eliminating jobs. Certainly, screening applicants for job openings is simpler if the interviewer has a clear idea of the tasks required and knows the specific educational and experiential requirements for job candidates.

POSITION DESCRIPTION

Position: Manager, Purchasing

Div/Department: Office of the President

Location: Corporate Headquarters

Grade: 19

Complement: Budget 79.53.100

Exempt: X   **Non-exempt:**

Purpose: To oversee corporate-wide purchasing program to ensure that quality products are purchased at the least cost to the organization. Responsible for the staff and staffing needs necessary to execute various purchasing programs in branch offices.

Essential Functions:

• Develop annual purchasing budget for office supplies, coordinating with branch office managers to maximize savings from corporatewide purchases.

• Inaugurate programs to control office supply inventory.

• Conduct annual audit of existing suppliers to determine if new suppliers should be sought, either to provide better quality or cost savings.

• Monitor operating budgets and initiate programs to address negative variances and communicate to appropriate staff positive variances.

Qualifications:

• Five to ten years as purchasing manager in company in similar field.

• Business degree.

• Knowledge of Excel and Lotus.

Measurements:

• Cost savings during the year.

• Variances from budget.

• Identification of better quality and less expensive sources for supplies.

Sample Job Description

VERBS FOR DESCRIBING THE JOB

These verbs can help an entrepreneur, a manager, or an office professional write a job description:

accelerate	deliver	identify	plan
achieve	design	implement	prepare
administer	develop	improve	prioritize
advise	devise	incorporate	process
analyze	direct	increase	produce
apply	draft	initiative	program
arrange	enhance	institute	promote
assess	establish	instruct	provide
author	evaluate	interface	recommend
automate	exceed	launch	reconcile
brief	excel	maintain	recruit
catalog	execute	manage	represent
collaborate	exhibit	maximize	research
communicate	expand	mentor	revise
compile	expedite	monitor	schedule
compose	facilitate	negotiate	streamline
computerize	fashion	operate	supervise
conceptualize	formulate	orchestrate	support
conduct	furnish	organize	train
coordinate	generate	originate	upgrade
create	handle	oversee	utilize
delegate	head	perform	

Procedures manuals can include a section that includes the job descriptions for all employees and managers, or a separate manual can be created solely for job descriptions. Most management experts recommend that job descriptions be updated annually to reflect the ongoing changes in a person's job. An up-to-date job description clarifies expectations between managers and their employees, and eliminates any problems at appraisal time. The best descriptions use active verbs to describe the work that is expected. When updated, the revisions usually are best handled by a manager and employee working together.

Each job description should list the job title, organizational department, classification (whether exempt from provisions of the Fair Labor Standards Act or non-exempt from those provisions), grade (which reflects the worth of the job and subsequent salary an occupant in the job will receive), work area location, budget from which money to pay the individual comes, and supervisor's title. If the organization is a startup and the owner needs to create job titles, he or she can contact the U.S. Department of Labor, Employment, and Training Administration (200 Constitution Avenue NW, Washington, DC 20001) for an up-to-date copy of *The Dictionary of Occupational Titles.* Trade associations also might have publications that include work characteristics, education, training requirements, and earnings and benefits within specific industries.

The first section of the job description should provide an overview of the job or a brief description. Below that usually comes a list of the duties that the job entails. Duties should be listed in order of priority. Write the primary or most frequently performed duty first, followed by the second most frequent duty, and then the third, and so on. Keep in mind that duties, rather than specific tasks, should be listed. For example, "conducts department planning sessions" is preferred over "develops agendas for department planning meetings."

In addition to the essential functions associated with the job, a manager or other person developing a job description should identify the level of supervision the position demands, as well as the job-holder's supervisory responsibilities, if any, and intercompany contacts. Finally, devote a section to the minimum qualifications for a candidate for the job and the general standards by which a holder of the job is measured.

Workstation Manual

Many organizations now place the following types of forms on their intranets: supply requisitions, customer invoices, travel information and expenses requests for petty-cash compensation, attendance, travel arrangements and expenditures, and so forth. Each form also should include samples either in the section of the procedures manual dedicated to workstation issues or in a separate binder for the workstation manual. Besides clean forms, the manual should contain a correctly filled-out copy of each form to help first-time users fill them out appropriately. The manual should include directions about accessing them on the intranet and to whom completed forms should be e-mailed.

If an organization still uses paper forms, information on who provides specific forms should be a part of the workstation manual.

Managers who operate in organizations with sophisticated intranets should include information on accessing and utilizing the intranet in their own workstation manuals, and in the manuals of those who report to them. An index of work activities that can be done on the intranet, such as requests for travel advances and hotel and plane reservations, also should be part of the workstation manual.

A directory of company personnel should be present at every workstation, with both telephone numbers and e-mail addresses. This information already might be part of a corporate intranet, but a manager might want to reproduce the directory and insert the information into a workstation manual after highlighting key contacts for the person at the workstation with a red or yellow magic marker. The names, addresses, telephone numbers, and e-mail addresses of outside contacts also should be kept up-to-date in the manual.

Be sure to include an up-to-date organization chart that includes accurate job titles and the names of the job holders (spelled correctly).

If the occupant of the workstation is involved in projects, the workstation manual should include a client list and projects done by the firm, with some file reference (either paper or computer) to enable the occupant to quickly access finished project reports.

Finally, a workstation manual should have an abbreviated version of user instructions for the software program(s) required in the workstation. Instructions for voice-mail systems also belong in the manual, including guidelines for updating messages when employees are away for extended periods from the workstation.

Job Instructions

Within the workstation manual or the larger and more encompassing procedures manual, a manager should include job instructions for performing specific tasks. The nature of the tasks determines the need for those instructions.

Some tasks must be done exactly as instructed; others can be revised based on ingenuity and creativity. For the former, a manager, entrepreneur, or office professional should detail in writing the steps to do the work. Also identify the work's purpose in terms of corporate and department objectives. This sometimes can clarify the reason behind some step that will ensure the likelihood it will be followed. Hard skills or infrequent tasks, such as processing an invoice or preparing a spreadsheet, more often need such job aids than do soft skills (such as putting together a team meeting or delegating a task).

Written job instructions, sometimes called *job aides,* begin with a description of the purpose of the task. In discussing office safety, for example, the introduction might explain what kinds of safety issues the office might encounter and then provide direction in adhering to local, state, and federal regulations on workplace safety. With project management, this could include a to-do list to ensure that the project leader has clearly identified the project's purpose, has adequate resources to accomplish the objective, and uses appropriate problem-solving and critical-thinking techniques.

When preparing the instructions for a task, a manager should visualize how the work is done and then write down each step. An entrepreneur should explain and train new office help to do this work; the job instructions serve as a reminder. Consequently, a manager wants to be sure that no aspect of a job is forgotten when recording the instructions.

The job aide should be typed as double-spaced or with large margins. During training, the manager should refer the employee to the job aide in the policies and procedures manual or workstation manual, and allow him or her to take notes in the margins.

A manager should devote a single page or group of pages to each procedure. This way, he or she won't have to redo the entire manual just to update a procedure. Just remove and replace the outdated pages.

Besides the "dos," a policies and procedures manual should include the "don'ts," such as policies limiting expenditures for meals while on business travel or the authority for signing off (approving) such expenditures (specifying those requests that demand a second signature).

Corporate Style

The policies and procedures manual might include a section devoted to preferred methods of correspondence, including the how and when of e-mail, and how to handle correspondence and printed internal memos and reports.

Increasingly, companies are looking for timesaving correspondence methods. A manager should consider how he or she wants to handle brief messages. For instance, is a letter preferable, or will a brief message on a standard-size postal card suffice? Should each piece of correspondence and each memo get a formal reply, or is it acceptable to respond by returning the original document with marginal notations after copying it? Brief notes at the bottom of a letter or report save time and cut costs, and they also reduce the number of file copies. Likewise, rather than instruct the recipient of a report or letter to respond with a written note, a manager might use a stamp that asks the recipient of the document to "Reply here to save time. Photocopy for your files."

These techniques may not be suitable for handling every report, memo, or piece of correspondence, and the policies and procedures manual or workstation manual should specify when such informality is acceptable.

Various letter styles also exist. The corporate style may be the simplified letter form (without a salutation, but containing a subject line in all capital letters); the block format (in which all elements are flush left and a salutation exists); a modified block format (with dateline, complimentary close, and signature block all aligned at the center, toward the right margin, or at the right margin); and the modified semi-block letter format (in which the dateline may appear either to the right of dead center or flush right, and the inside address and salutation are aligned flush left while the paragraphs are indented).

The preferred formats to follow in e-mail, status reports, meeting minutes, and memos should be covered in the policies and procedures manual, too. For instance, does the manager want the list of attendees at the top of meeting minutes, or does he or she prefer to focus on the substance of the minutes and put the names of attendees at the end of the minutes?

If the job holder must develop handouts as part of the job, the manual might indicate the specific color of paper stock for various handouts (for instance, yellow for computer procedures, pink for access codes, blue for client lists, and so on). Restrictions about the use of the corporate logo and changes (even small ones) that can be made to the logo also should be included in a policies and procedures manual.

Corporate style governs the letterhead and other stationery used. Department guidelines might govern the color for interoffice correspondence.

Different colors for each department will help recipients distinguish between memos and reports from accounting and those from marketing or another department more easily. Or, bright colors might be used to signify documents that need immediate attention. Corporate style, as described in the policies and procedures manual, should address these issues.

Chapter 2 contains further details as well as examples of these different types of correspondence.

Office Library

In many offices, reference materials are not kept in a central location. However, a better setup organizes these materials in one centralized place, where they are accessible to everyone in the office, from its managers to office professionals. You will want to have several reference books in your "library," but you also might want to store at least one copy of a complete procedural manual, with or without all job descriptions for the office; recent issues of management and trade magazines received by the office; and copies of each finished report, or reports on projects-in-progress, so everything is accessible to all in the workspace.

These reference books should be on hand in the department or corporate library:

- *Dictionaries.* Standard unabridged dictionaries (or even abridged dictionaries) are helpful for spelling, definitions, word divisions, and pronunciations. Some dictionaries also contain grammar rules, abbreviations, forms of address, directories of colleges and universities, signs and symbols, and common English names and their sources. Specialized dictionaries exist for such areas as law, medicine, electronics ("computerese"), and accounting.

- *Thesauruses.* A thesaurus can be helpful for editing documents because it provides alternatives for words that are used frequently. Ideally, within the same paragraph a word should not be repeated; a thesaurus can provide a synonym.

- *Directories.* Trade directories list the names, addresses, and special data about companies. Telephone companies have business-to-business directories, and a corporate library should include one for its area in addition to the more traditional Yellow and White Pages.

An office library also should have a book of business quotations, corporate manners, state and federal government agencies, and parliamentary procedure manuals. To facilitate editing and printing, include a style book such as *The Chicago Manual of Style.*

To ensure that books aren't borrowed and then never returned, managers should institute a policy that requires those who borrow a book from the reference library to sign out when they borrow the book and sign in when they return it.

MOVING WITHOUT HEADACHES

Offices move for a variety of reasons. They outgrow their space, lose their lease, downsize staff, consolidate, and so on. Moving to a new location can be a positive experience and can be done with minimal disruption if there is sufficient time and effective planning beforehand.

Moving plans depend on the size of the office and location to which it is moving. A move down the street takes considerably less work than a move out of state. Generally, offices begin to pack about a week before the actual move. The best way to pack is to number cartons so the material that needs to be unpacked first is placed in carton 1, the next-important office supplies and papers are placed in carton 2, and so on. Each employee should have his or her own set of numbered boxes that include the employee's name or location. Actual packing should be in reverse of the carton numbers, with the least important materials packaged first. This allows the office to continue to operate up until the last day or so of the move.

The move itself is likely to occur over a weekend. Individuals can tour the new facility prior to the move. Ideally, they have input into the arrangement of their furnishings in their new workspace. To speed unpacking, it is helpful to allow employees access to the new quarters once all the cartons have been moved to the new location.

If several floors of an organization are moving to a new location, identify one individual on each floor to act as the move monitor and see that the staff is kept informed of developments associated with the move. Many organizations find it helpful to set up a team made up of individuals from different parts of the organization to work together to plan the relocation.

Ideally, cartons are requisitioned and left on various floors for employees to begin packing. Prior to packing, a day may be set aside for housekeeping to ensure that materials that might rightfully be tossed aren't unnecessarily relocated. After unpacking the cartons, stack them at a single location in the new facility, where they can be picked up and either thrown out or sent for recycling each evening.

The move itself may take only a day or two, but don't underestimate the full time line, which can take from four weeks to two months in planning (or even longer if the office is moving into newly built facilities with brand-new furnishings).

To begin, take a full inventory of every item in the office, and encourage employees to do the same for their individual work areas. Depending on the size of the office, you may want to assign individuals responsibility for common areas. Determine which items should be discarded, and provide a clean-up day to accomplish this. Take measurements of all equipment and furniture that will be moving with you—you will need them for the new space. In addition, make notes on any items such as artwork, plants, and antiques that will require special handling. Take this list, the measurements, and your notes to the company contracted to perform the actual moving. With this information, you will be better equipped to intelligently discuss any concerns or questions you may have.

Obtain a floor plan of the new space you will be occupying. Post it or distribute copies to each employee with specifics about available space, restrooms, and assigned work areas. Include information about the new neighborhood and surrounding amenities such as restaurants and public transportation. This information is usually available from the building manager or the local chamber of commerce. When possible, set up a day before the move for employees to tour and become familiar with the new space. Keep a list of questions they may have and ensure that they receive thorough answers to minimize concerns about the new location.

If everyone numbered cartons not only in the order in which they should be emptied, but also by his or her name and/or new room number, employees should find their cartons at their specific workstation for unpacking.

Notify all clients and suppliers of your move. Your local post office will provide change-of-address kits free of charge. In addition, it's a good idea to create stickers to announce the move, complete with the effective date and the address and telephone number of the new location. Place these stickers on all correspondence that leaves the office. Draw up another list of everyone who should be notified to ensure that no one is accidentally overlooked. In addition to clients and suppliers, the list should include magazine subscriptions, independent contractors, and anything or anyone else associated with your office.

Systems personnel will handle moving the computers and printers. The duration in which computers are unavailable will depend on the size of the office and the changes that the new facility demands. In some instances, a company might decide to make systems changes at the same time it moves, such as updating its current network.

The switchboard will coordinate telephone systems. Ideally, employees should retain their old telephone numbers, assuming that the move is a short one. All extensions should provide a message to callers during the move to alert them that they will be unable to reach their party until the move is completed.

Although a move can be a major endeavor, there is a sense of accomplishment when it is completed.

FOR MORE INFORMATION

If you can't find what you need from the phone numbers and Web sites listed in this chapter, you may need to expand your search.

- For more information on workstations, workstation design, and office layout, check your local library or bookstore in the architecture sections. Also, look for books on occupational design.

- For more information on workstation furniture and help in planning a workable design or structure, check in the Yellow Pages under office furniture. Most large office furniture showrooms will have sales reps who can walk you through the basics of modular workspace.

- For more information on office lighting, look in the Yellow Pages under lighting or office furniture. Many office lighting products are modular and come as part of office workstations.

- For more information on first aid, check with your companies' health insurance provider. Also, check with your local hospital. First-aid classes may be available.

- For more information on federal and state government regulations and for occupational safety and health, check the government listings in your telephone directory.

- For more information on office fire safety, check with your local fire department. They may be available to help plan escape routes, evaluate office fire safety, or conduct a drill.

- For more information on office reference books, check your local bookstore or library in the reference section.

- For more information on moving, check the Yellow Pages under moving or relocation.

7

OFFICE OPERATIONS

◆

- **Forms Management**
    - Generic Forms
- **Filing Systems**
    - Traditional Filing Systems
    - Electronic Filing Systems
    - Physical Setup of Files
    - Preparation of Material for Filing
    - Finding and Using Files
    - Indexing and Alphabetizing
    - Long-Term File Maintenance
- **Managing Money**
    - Managing Cash Transactions
    - Handling the Bank Account
    - Handling Cash Payments
    - Bookkeeping
    - Payroll
- **For More Information**

Increasingly, office professionals are finding themselves involved in continuous improvement projects concerned with office operations. Because of their familiarity with the various aspects of office operations, they are valued additions to these planning teams. Not only are they familiar with the work done in general, but they can suggest ways to minimize the many steps in processing paper, whether the paper is a simple form, a letter, a complex report, or another document. A team's objective may be to computerize some forms currently on paper, or it may be to do away with any forms at all by eliminating unnecessary steps.

This involvement of office professionals in restructuring office operations has grown. In fact, some organizations have given support to project teams that are made up exclusively of office professionals who meet to recommend processes or other procedures to help run the office more efficiently. The savings have been substantial in both time and money.

How broad are these teams' charters? As broad as office operations themselves, which means that office professionals increasingly are having a voice in record maintenance, recordkeeping, and much more—including bookkeeping, the processing of payroll, handling of bank deposits, and maintenance of tax records. The extent of their involvement in the planning of office operations is a reflection of their job descriptions and the needs of the offices in which they work.

One of the first places in which office professionals, either individually or in continuous improvement teams, can have an impact is in forms management.

FORMS MANAGEMENT

Forms today are very different from the forms of the past. Many companies are now putting their forms—from personnel descriptions to travel expenditure forms and requisition forms—on company intranets. Departments that maintain their own intranet, and have forms specific to their function, may also have computerized their most frequently used forms. Certainly, most companies use spreadsheets for budgeting, and still others use variations of spreadsheets for project management. Forms have gone way beyond the simple, single-page format that could be filled out on an electric typewriter.

Many forms with which office professionals work are developed by others, but forms are also developed by the office professionals themselves to minimize repetition of a memo or letter. Rather than write a memo requesting supplies, for instance, it is much simpler to have a form to send to purchasing. If the professional also coordinates supply needs for the department, he or she might create a form that lists those office supplies most frequently requested. Each staff member has copies of the form and periodically gives a copy to the office professional, who collates all requests onto a single form that is submitted to purchasing.

The secret to creating a worthwhile form for yourself and others is to think ahead about the information it will contain. To make sure that your form deals with all the issues that might arise, put yourself in the shoes not only of those who will fill out the form, but also of those who will use it.

Think about the format of the form. A factor in choosing the format—paper or electronic—is the number of individuals who will be using the form. Some forms lend themselves to paper (for example, attendance sheets, which require managerial signoff); others, which might be needed by every member of the department or corporation, may be better installed on the department or corporate computer network (for example, meeting room allocations, including audiovisual needs).

Another factor that influences the format of a form is the technological level of its user. Although most organizations are moving quickly to computerized forms, there are still occasions when it is simpler to have a form that can be kept in a manila folder and handed out to staff members as needed, usually when the need is infrequent. A case in point would be a form used by staff members to order business cards. The form would contain all the pertinent information needed by the organization to produce the cards. This would include name and title of the staff member, company address and telephone number, fax number and e-mail address, and, if there is one, the corporate Web site address.

GENERIC FORMS

In the course of your job, you will undoubtedly work with many different forms used by your department or company. You probably will even be called upon to create or implement some. Although it can seem like a fairly simple task, there are a few factors to take into account. Consider whether the form should be created from scratch or whether a preprinted form already exists that will work, whether duplicate copies will be needed, whether the form has to be printed or can be copied, what information is required, and so on. Also, don't overlook forms that were already created by a predecessor; they may be just what you need.

Before simply reordering a form that you currently use, consider whether the form is still practical. It may be time to update the form to reflect changes in office processes.

If you decide to create a form or update an existing one, first determine the information that your finished form should contain. For instance, a request for office supplies will need a requisition or budget number, but should it also have the extension number of the person making the request? What about the date when the supplies are needed? How about the date when the form is submitted?

Besides the information itself, you next need to consider the order of the information that you are requesting on the form. Does it make sense? You wouldn't ask for someone's address before asking for that person's name, for instance. Neither would you ask a manager to sign off on a new software program before he or she had specified the program. Finally, you want to think about who, besides the person for whom the form is intended, will need a copy, or even who needs to sign off on the form to get it processed.

Now sit down and type your form. Once you have created your form or chosen an existing one, take a look. Is it:

- Properly spaced, with sufficient room to be filled out either by a typewriter or by hand?

- Logical and arranged in a sequential order, according to its intended use?

- Free from obscure jargon?

- Free from the clutter of unnecessary information?

Before committing yourself to numerous printed forms or copies, ask for suggestions from the people who actually use the form. Also, check filed copies of the current form to see whether people are routinely adding information not accounted for in the form itself. Make sure all the information needed is included.

Make sure that the form is convenient for the user. The purpose of any form is efficiency. Completing a form is supposed to be easier and faster than writing all the information from scratch on a blank sheet of paper. But proper design and regular periodic review are essential for maintaining this efficiency.

Experts suggest these additional tips:

- Look for opportunities to construct multipurpose forms.

- Test your new form before your final printing. This will help you work out any bugs that you may have missed. Make sure that you proofread and run a spell checker!

- Be sure to check spacing. Too much or too little makes the form inefficient.

- Note the forms from other businesses as they cross your desk. They may provide ideas for your revisions.

- Be aware that elements on certain technical forms are essential. Before revising, have the company's legal staff review them.

FILING SYSTEMS

An efficient filing system is one that reduces clutter, separates information into recognizable categories, and makes possible the rapid and accurate retrieval of documents. There are several standard methods, and each has its advantages and disadvantages. Nevertheless, it is not the system but the use of it that determines its effectiveness. Documents need to be filed so they can be found. This applies especially to information needed for making day-to-day management decisions. Given the system, the professional should be able to pull a document from a file within five minutes of a request. What if you had to wait for more than a few minutes for professionals in a doctor's office to retrieve your file? Or a financial advisor, an insurance agent, or your family lawyer? Each of these individuals has information that is critical to your situation, and you depend on them to keep good records about you.

A large organization may employ a number of office professionals who are responsible for maintaining all the company's records in a central area. In a small office, there may be only a few file cabinets, or assistants may each keep their own. In either case, you should be familiar with all the filing systems commonly used because every office depends on one or another of them.

Of course, in today's offices, chances are that the office professional will be dealing with both paper and electronic files and filing systems. Individual desktops may be tied into a central file server or other system. Even with this proliferation of technology, the "paperless office" is still not a reality. Office professionals today must be prepared to deal with both hard copy and electronic files, and be able to access both types of documents quickly and efficiently.

TRADITIONAL FILING SYSTEMS

The basic hard-copy filing systems in use in the modern office are alphabetic, combination subject, numeric, and phonetic. *Alphabetic filing* entails filing papers by name, subject, or geographic location in alphabetical order. *Combination subject* systems use both numbers and words, or numbers and letters arranged in alphabetical order. Such names as alphanumeric, subject-numeric, and duplex-numeric are used to describe systems in this category. *Numeric,* or *nonalphabetic, filing* exercises the use of numbers for filing purposes; and such names as numeric, decimal, terminal digit, triple digit, and middle digit are used to describe systems in this category. The *phonetic filing* system involves using letters and sounds in code number form.

Filing systems may be direct or indirect. In a *direct* method of filing, a person can locate a file immediately without first having to refer to a cross-index file to find out where to look. In an *indirect* filing system, a person cannot immediately locate the file but must refer to a cross-index file to determine where to locate it. For example, if the basic filing system is a subject system and the professional wishes to locate the file for a specific firm, he or she must either know the subject under which the firm is filed or refer to an alphabetical cross-index, looking up the firm name and finding out in which subject file the file is located.

Alphabetic Systems

Almost 90 percent of all filing that is done in the office is alphabetical. In an alphabetic system, office correspondence and other papers are filed alphabetically according to name, geographic location, or subject.

Name

In a *name file,* all papers are filed alphabetically according to the last name of the person or the name of a company. It is a direct method of filing and very simple to expand because any new name is filed alphabetically without disturbing the name before or after it.

Geographic Location

In the *geographic system,* the papers are filed alphabetically according to the name of the state; then alphabetically according to the town or city within that state; then alphabetically according to the name of the correspondent within the town or city. Mail-order houses, public-utility companies, publishing houses, and organizations that serve a geographic district or have branch offices in different areas use this system of filing.

The geographic system of filing is an indirect system. It is not possible to locate the file for a specific firm without first referring to a cross-index that lists the names of all the firms in alphabetical order and gives the location of each firm. In other words, if you do not know the location of the firm, you must refer to the cross-index under the firm name and determine under what geographic location to find the file.

Subject

When a company deals with products, supplies, materials, advertising, and so forth, the *subject system* is used. It is an indirect system because a cross-index file is used in order to save time in filing and finding material, and to locate correspondence by firm name when the subject is in doubt. The folders in the subject file are arranged alphabetically by the name of the product. The material within the folders is arranged by date, with the latest date in the front of the folder.

Often, a combination of subject filing and name filing is used. If there is not enough material to set up a separate subject file, the subject captions can be set up in a name file.

Combination Subject Systems

Some companies that use the subject filing system have found it necessary to use major subject titles, with separate subcategories relating to that major topic, to more quickly locate specific information. A major subject outline containing the most important titles is set up in alphabetical order. Next, subcategory subject titles within each area are placed beneath the major subject titles. Then, numbers are used in combination with the subjects in the outline to make up the *combination subject filing system.*

When a company uses the combination subject filing system, it is extremely important that an up-to-date list be kept of all subjects and their code letters and numbers. This list should be circulated to all persons and departments needing access to the files. Likewise, a *relative index* should be made, listing all possible subjects and the location of all pertinent information pertaining to each subject. This list, too, should be updated frequently and distributed to those using the files.

Subject-Numeric

The *subject-numeric system* uses the major subject title with numbers assigned to the subcategories underneath it. For example, the subject heading "Automobile Accessories" would be treated in this manner:

AUTOMOBILE ACCESSORIES

1 Automobile Accessories: Tires

1-1 Standard Black

1-2 Whitewall

Duplex-Numeric

The *duplex-numeric system* makes use of both numbers and letters of the alphabet. A digit is selected for the subject; this is followed by a dash and another digit for a division of the subject, plus a letter for further subdivision. For example, the subject heading "Automobile Accessories" might be given the number 13, the division "Automobile Accessories: Tires" would be numbered 13-1; a further subdivision, "Automobile Accessories: Tires, Standard Black," would be numbered 13-1a; "Automobile Accessories: Tires, Whitewall" would be numbered 13-1b. The outline would look like this:

13 AUTOMOBILE ACCESSORIES

13-1 Automobile Accessories: Tires

13-1a Standard Black

13-1b Whitewall

Alphanumeric

The *alphanumeric system* uses letters of the alphabet for the major subject titles, along with letters and numbers for subtopics:

A	ADMINISTRATION
A 1	Long-Range Planning
A 1 - 1	Guidelines and Schedules
A:	Competition
A2-1	Survey Reports
A3	Public Relations
G	GOVERNMENT RELATIONS
G1	Air Pollution Control
G1-1	Vehicle Emissions
G1-1-1	Health Hazards

Numeric Systems

Numeric filing systems are nonalphabetical. All records are filed solely by numbers. Numeric systems tend to be used in highly specialized businesses.

When the numeric system is used, an *accession register* must be kept so that a particular file can be retrieved quickly. The accession register is a book or card file that contains each file number, beginning with the first number, as well as the correspondent's name on that file. The correspondents' names should be alphabetized so that you can get the file quickly if a correspondent's file number has been forgotten.

Straight Numeric

In the *straight-numeric system,* records are filed according to strict numeric sequence. Folder number 1 is given to the first client or account, folder number 2 is given to the second, and so forth, in strict numeric order. Often, these file numbers correspond to order numbers or invoices. Consequently, you might find such a system in offices of manufacturers or wholesalers.

Terminal Digit

In the *terminal-digit system,* numbers on a file are read from right to left. Usually, the last (or terminal) two digits are the drawer number, the next two digits are the folder number, and any other numbers indicate the sequence within the folders. For example, an insurance policy numbered 567,123 would be stored in drawer 23, folder 71; and the 56 would refer to its sequence in the folder. This kind of system might be found in hospitals or insurance companies.

Triple Digit

The *triple-digit system* is similar to the terminal-digit system, except that the numbers are read in three-digit units instead of two. The terminal three digits of a number are called the *primary* numbers, and the remaining digits refer to the sequence of the papers in the folders bearing the primary numbers. For example, the insurance policy numbered 567,123 would be found in folder 123, and 567 would refer to its sequence in the folder.

Middle Digit

In the *middle-digit system,* the third and fourth digits from the right are separated from the last two digits on the right. For example, in the insurance policy number 567,123, the policy would be filed in folder 71, and 23 would refer to its sequence in the folder.

Decimal System

The *decimal system* is used only in highly specialized businesses. The system may be based on the Dewey decimal system, which is the system commonly used by public libraries, although many are switching to the Library of Congress Catalog cataloging system.

Phonetic Systems

The *phonetic filing system* is a filing method based on the use of letters and sounds. Organizations that file records by individuals' surnames encounter the problem of filing names that sound alike but are spelled differently, such as Smith and Smyth, or Schmidt and Schmitt. To eliminate this problem, the Remington Rand Office Systems Division of the Sperry Rand Corporation developed the Soundex Phonetic Filing System.

Soundex is a combination of spelling, or sounds and numbers. Basic sounds are represented by six fundamental letters: the consonants *B, C, D, L, M,* and *R,* which make up the entire Soundex alphabet. Each of these consonants is given a separate code number: *B* is 1, *C* is 2, *D* is 3, *L* is 4, *M* is 5, and *R* is 6. The remaining consonants in the alphabet have the same relative sounds as the six basic Soundex consonants and are grouped with the *basic* consonant. All vowels and the letters *W, H,* and *Y* have no number and are not coded. To use this system, look at the *first* letter of the *surname* and sort by *that letter* first. Then code the *remaining* letters in the surname by looking at the following chart.

The phonetic system is used in large hospitals, police departments, and the Social Security office. It is used where there are lots of records, where requests for information come over the phone, and where retrieval must be done quickly. You'll also find such systems in mail-order firms that take orders over the phone.

Code	Key Letters and Equivalents
1	BFPV
2	CGJKQSXZ
3	DT
4	L
5	MN
6	R

To file the surname "Snyder," the first letter, *S,* is recorded. The next letter to be coded is *N,* which is code 5. *Y* is disregarded, *D* is code 3, *E* is disregarded, and *R* is code 6. The surname "Snyder" is thus coded S536.

To file the surname "Day," code the letter *D* and three zeros to show that only vowels follow the first consonant, *D.* When no consonants or not enough consonants follow the first letter in the surname, use one, two, or three zeros to give the name a three-digit code. The code for "Day" is D000. The surname "Straw" is S360, "Levy" is L100, and "Kelly" is K400.

ELECTRONIC FILING SYSTEMS

As computers spread throughout businesses and offices, the problems of locating computer files spread as well. Often the "storage" of computer files is far from the control of any one individual. Central file servers, floppy disk storage, hard drives, networked computers, tape drives, cartridge drives, writeable CDs, and who-knows-what tomorrow, mean that a "file" can be virtually anywhere. So, for starters, an office or an enterprise must come to some consensus about who is responsible for what when it comes to recordkeeping and file maintenance.

The good news for the already-burdened office professional is that, as computer-related filing tasks grow, the information technology specialist assumes some of the burden for establishing company-wide standards for what would be the equivalent of filing electronic documents.

Assuming that your company lacks someone with that assignment in your company—and simply as a matter of personal convenience for you and those you influence—here are some broad guidelines for managing electronic files. They apply, no matter what commercial software you may be using or which internal systems have been established.

Be consistent. Use a file-naming methodology that makes it easy for you and others to identify the electronic files you may end up searching for.

Remember file extensions. Missing electronic documents may not be appearing on your search screen because the search is underway for a *.DOC* file that's been inadvertently tagged as *.TXT*.

Expand your horizons. Encourage computer file users to agree to major categories of items that will be retained in the system and to make their entries consistent. A filing system is no good if only one person can discern what's in a computer record by its name alone (even though some programs allow a preview of the document).

Watch your folders and subdirectories. Get agreement from all likely file users about how certain types of material will be grouped: for example, by territory, customer name, customer number, salesperson, product, project, order date—whatever.

Tag paper documents with electronic file names. Even the so-called paperless office generates a great deal of paper, especially hard copies because the file user is afraid something may happen to the electronic file. Simply recording the file name on the paper copies of the document can save much time hunting for a "lost" electronic file.

Divide and conquer. Saving multipage material as a single file may not be efficient. A year's worth of correspondence packed into a single file and added to week after week results in a long document that must be opened and scanned to find a particular bit of old info. Unique document files may be easier to handle.

Print appropriate directories. From time to time, make a hard copy record of what's on a disk or what's in a particular area of the network. Eyeballing the list may be a faster way to search for what you seek than chugging through the listing on the screen.

Back up files. Making backup files always was worthwhile. It still is. Lost files can be recovered from the backup only if the backup has been made.

Clean up files. What's valid for file cabinets is valid for computer records. On some periodic schedule, purge the system of stuff you no longer need. Dump it or store it to a medium such as disk or tape. Less clutter on a computer or in a system server leaves fewer places for "lost" files to hide and can speed the search process.

PHYSICAL SETUP OF FILES

Several kinds of file cabinets are standard in offices today. One is the *traditional vertical filing cabinet,* which has four drawers that hold file folders enclosing material on the regulation 8½-by-11-inch typing paper. A law office or a company with many legal papers will need a wider cabinet to accommodate the longer legal paper. The standard drawer will carry a load of from 60 to 70 pounds. For efficient filing, the file drawers should not be overcrowded.

Also standard in offices today is the *lateral or horizontal file cabinet.* These cabinets can hold either letter- or legal-size folders in much larger drawers. Lateral filing is particularly useful for active files in which papers are inserted and withdrawn constantly and which are not to be retained for a long period of time. Proponents of lateral filing claim much time is saved by having the files immediately at hand and in sight.

Another option is the *open-shelf method.* It is popular in medical offices, where files are color coded and need to be viewed. Lateral or open shelf filing can result in a savings of as much as 40 percent of office floor space. The aisles between the shelves can be considerably narrower than those needed between cabinets with drawers because the additional space for pulling out drawers is not needed. Also, files can be stacked higher than drawers—in many instances, stacked to the ceiling.

Arranging Files

Files should be arranged to minimize the amount of walking required to and from the files. The file drawers may be labeled in either vertical (top to bottom) or horizontal (left to right) order. Space may be saved if the file cabinets are backed up against a wall. If there are many cabinets, it may be more efficient to arrange them in a cluster in the center of a room. Floor space is expensive; therefore, some consideration should be given to arranging cabinets economically. Adequate aisle space between cabinets must be allowed. At least 28 inches must be allowed for a file drawer when it is opened into the aisle. Long rows of cabinets should have gaps between them to save time in getting from one row to another.

To make the most productive use of your time, you may want to keep your active project files in your desk until you have completed the work. Most desks, or tables in office cubicles, have at least two drawers that are deep enough to maintain files.

Setting Up the File Drawer

The basic file drawer is divided into alphabetic sections or numeric sections. The first division consists of metal or plastic dividers that you can purchase from an office supply catalog. These fit snugly into the drawer, hanging on the drawer framework. Guides are sold in sets, based on file size. The tabs may be on the left side or in the middle of the file drawer. Behind these dividers are hanging files that subdivide sections or that call attention to important names or numbers. Individual folders, arranged alphabetically, chronologically, or numerically, are placed directly within the hanging files. These folders are used for correspondents who communicate frequently with the firm.

When five to eight pieces of correspondence from the same source have accumulated, an individual folder is set up. The full name of the correspondent is on the tab. Tabs are usually alternated in position so that one does not come directly behind another. When material is arranged in an individual folder, the latest date is always in the front of the folder.

File drawers, incidentally, come in two sizes: letter size and legal size. If your filing cabinet doesn't have legal-sized drawers, you can still accommodate legal-sized documents by filing them sideways in the drawer.

When material is placed in a miscellaneous folder, it should be arranged alphabetically, with the latest date in front for each person or subject.

Miscellaneous folders follow the individual folders at the end of each major division. They are used for correspondence that does not warrant individual folders. The tab on the miscellaneous folder may be a different size or be marked with a distinctive color so that it can easily located.

When preparing index tabs and labels for guides and folders, type the letter of the alphabet or the name. Use the first typing space below the fold of the file drawer label, and start typing two spaces from the left of the label.

Use initial capitals, and indent the second line two spaces, so that the first word on the top line will stand out. Use abbreviations if the name or subject is long. Tabs are best created on a typewriter.

Sometimes, you will want to include more than a name or number on the folder. In that case, use a label for the cuts of file folders. Cuts come left, right, and center, and you can purchase boxes of either. Most boxes contain an assortment with tabs at the left, right, and center, allowing you to stagger the folders for maximum visibility. Labels for cuts can be typed or printed. If you print them, besides measuring carefully for fit, you will want to purchase the right kind of paper so your sheet doesn't get caught in your printer.

PREPARATION OF MATERIAL FOR FILING

So, you've decided which system you're going to use, how you will divide your files, and where they're going to go. Now you're ready to begin filing. Before you start, check all papers to see whether they are to be filed and have been released for filing. Sort the material into relevant groupings. For example, if you were filing correspondence, you might want to separate it into personal, business, or contracts, etc. Remove all staples, paper clips, or other paper holders.

As you file, it's helpful to highlight or underline the name in colored pencil to indicate where the letter is to be filed. If you are using a numerical system, indicate the guide number in the upper right corner. It's also helpful to use a highlighter or colored pencil to circle important words that will help you locate a particular paper when it is needed. Make any cross-reference sheets that are required.

> **TIP:** When a letter or a record may be filed in one of two places, make out a *cross-reference sheet.* File the letter or record under the more important name, and cross-refer the second name or subject. For example, suppose you are filing a letter using the alphabetic system based on an individual account. A letter is received from Sam Crawford at Jordan Marsh Company. It would be filed under Sam Crawford. The cross-reference would be under *J* for the Marsh Jordan Company.
>
> Crawford, Sam
>
> SEE
>
> Jordan Marsh Company

Based on whichever filing system you'll be using, the following is a simple step-by-step checklist to use when you are getting ready to file material:

1. *Inspection.* Read or scan the material. Put a check mark in the upper left corner to signal that this material should be filed.

2. *Indexing.* Determine which name or subject to use for filing the material. This is vital because poor indexing means "poor finding" and a loss of time.

3. *Coding.* Coding is the physical act of marking the name, subject, and so on under which the material is to be filed. Put the code in the upper right corner. Make cross-reference sheets at this point.

4. *Sorting.* Sort the material in a rough, superficial manner: all *As* together, all *Bs* together, and so on in alphabetical order. Put all *10s* together, all *20s* together, and so on for numeric filing. Then sort each stack according to "strict sorting," using the standard filing rules that your firm uses.

5. *Filing.* Place correspondence in the folders, placing the top to the left of the folder. Put material in the miscellaneous folder alphabetically, with the latest date on top. Place material in individual folders chronologically, with the latest date on top.

FINDING AND USING FILES

The reason office professionals spend so much time deciding on, organizing, and maintaining a record-filing system is so that the information is easy to find when needed. When it is necessary to remove material from a file for use, replace the record or correspondence with an "out" guide or card. Plastic placeholders can be purchased from an office supply firm, but you can also make them yourself by using old file folders or construction paper. If you make your own, attach an index card or sheet of paper. Alternatively, you can tape an envelope inside the file folder. In this envelope, you can keep not only notes about records that have been charged out, but also new documents. The "out" folder is a good place to store new documents until the charged-out file is returned.

On the "out" card or paper, you should record the date, the name of the record taken, who has it, and the date it is to be returned. The word *Out* should be printed on the folder or sheet, or the plastic placeholder. A different color should be used, so that the guide stands out.

Be sure to record the withdrawal of any material that goes out of the office for a period of time or any material that someone is going to use away from the office. Confidential records should be used in the office and returned to the files immediately.

Card File

A card file represents an excellent way to keep track of critical files. It can be used to keep a record of files that are charged out, or used as an index for faster retrieval of documents. The cards contain the location and status of all records. It's a particularly helpful addition to your major filing system if you have a large number of documents whose location in the filing system could be forgotten. A card file (usually with 3-by-5-inch cards) is normally arranged alphabetically by name of correspondent or subject matter.

Color Coding

Color coding can be a worthwhile expedient, permitting the easier location of specific files or file sections. Before making a decision about color coding, study the various methods available and determine which would be best for the particular type of material filed in the office for which the system is intended.

Simple color coding of files can involve file folders available in a wide variety of colors, or a color tab affixed to manila folders or hanging dividers. One of the common ways to use these files is to select a new color for each year within an alphabetical file.

Different offices use color codes for different purposes. Some use colors simply to differentiate file years. Others use colors to differentiate accounts (for example, consumer versus business-to-business); others, with multiple divisions, use different colors to differentiate the in-house relationships; still others use colors to separate some accounts, customers, or other correspondents from others. For instance, some charitable organizations might use different colors to signify the level of donation.

Color coding is usually employed to identify a filing series that has been categorized by the alphabetic system or any of the several numeric systems discussed earlier in this chapter. A specific color is assigned to each number or letter. One manufacturer of filing materials (Datafile) uses twelve colors twice—the second time with a white bar that sets it apart from the first. These twenty-four colors, with white for *Y* and gray for *Z*, serve for the twenty-six letters of the alphabet.

The pattern used depends on the complexity of the material to be filed. Datafile, using its twelve colors, also has folders with two color bands for identification of the first two letters of a word or name. By identifying two letters, the file is expanded from the twenty-six letters of the alphabet to about three or four hundred segments. The possible total is 26×26, or 676, but all combinations of letters do not occur at the beginning of words or names.

All of these variations—from bars to dots to labels—can be purchased from any office supply catalog.

> **TIP:** The key to successful use of color coding—for that matter, any filing system—is consistency. Failure just once to color code a new folder or place an "out" guide in the drawer with information on the material taken will defeat the entire purpose of having the system.

Another type of color coding, popular for use with open-shelf filing systems, involves a simpler color code. One company that keeps order files for exactly two years before discarding uses a color-coded dot on the folders holding the records for alternate years. Thus, the file at any particular time consists of folders marked in one color for one of the years represented, unmarked folders for another, and a second colored dot for the third. If, for example, the date is March 2005, the folders for April through December of 2003 (January through March having been discarded) have dots of one color, the folders for 2004 are plain, and the folders for January to date in 2005 have dots of a second color. Folders for 2006 will be plain, and then the system will repeat.

INDEXING AND ALPHABETIZING

The value of your filing system is based on your ability to quickly access files or documents within existing systems. If your system is alphabetic, it is important that you set specific rules and consistently follow them.

The following indexing rules are standard rules for filing. ARMA, the Association of Records Managers and Administrators, Inc., uses these guidelines with minor exceptions.

Individual names. Names of individuals are indexed by the last name (the surname) first, then the first name, and then the middle initial or middle name:

Name	Indexing Order
Alfred M. Amell	Amell, Alfred M.
Grace R. Gladd	Gladd, Grace R.
J. Thomas Williams	Williams, J. Thomas

Business names. The names of business establishments, institutions, and organizations are indexed as they are written, unless they embody the name of an individual. Exceptions to this rule are the names of schools. When the individual's name is part of a firm name, index by considering the last name (surname) first, and then the first name and the middle initial or middle name, if any.

Name	Indexing Order
Atlantic Service Station	Atlantic Service Station
Earl A. Stone Book Publishers	Stone, Earl A. Book Publishers
General Department Store	General Department Store
James A. Carson Company	Carson, James A. Company
J. M. Morgan Sign Company	Morgan, J. M. Sign Company
Nathan Hale Junior High School	Nathan Hale Junior High School
Rose and Peter Beauty Supplies	Rose and Peter Beauty Supplies
Rose Peter Beauty Shoppe	Peter, Rose Beauty Shoppe
Rose's Beauty Salon	Rose's Beauty Salon
Stone and Book Publishing Company	Stone and Book Publishing Company
Stone Book Publishers	Stone Book Publishers
Thomas Milford Stiles Florist Shop	Thomas Milford Stiles Florist Shop
Troy Sand and Gravel, Inc.	Troy Sand and Gravel, Inc.

Alphabetical order. Names are alphabetized by comparing each of their letters. If the first units are alike, compare the second units. If there is no second unit, the single name is filed first. The rule of "nothing before something" applies here. A surname followed by a first initial only goes before the same surname, followed by a complete first name beginning with the same letter as the initial. Again, "nothing before something."

Indexing Order

Name	Unit 1	Unit 2
Carson	Carson	
Carson Brothers	Carson	Brothers
J. Carson	Carson	J.
James Carson	Carson	James

Letters used as words. Consider any single letter as a word— not part of a cluster or part of an acronym.

Indexing Order

Name	Unit 1	Unit 2	Unit 3	Unit 4
NAPA Jobbers	N	A	P	A
NCR Accounting Company	N	C	R	Accounting
Pacific Car Company	Pacific	Car	Company	
R & B Auto Service	R	B	Auto	Service

Abbreviations. Abbreviations are indexed as if the words they represent are written out in full; hence, *Mme.* is indexed as *Madame*.

Indexing Order

Name	Unit 1	Unit 2	Unit 3
Mme. Sophie's Boutique	Madame	Sophie's	Boutique
Mr. Pete's Grocery	Mister	Pete's	Grocery
St. Alexis Hospital	Saint	Alexis	Hospital

Article *the*. When *the* is part of the name, it is disregarded in filing. If it is the initial word, it is placed at the end of the name in parentheses. If *the* occurs in the body of the name, it is placed in parentheses and disregarded.

Name	Indexing Order
The Cleveland Boat Company	Cleveland Boat Company (The)
Danny the Tailor	Danny (the) Tailor
Stanley of the Ritz	Stanley (of the) Ritz

Such words as *and, for, on, in, by,* and *of the* are disregarded in indexing and filing. However, they are placed in parentheses when writing names on folders and cards.

Hyphenated names. Hyphenated firm names are treated as separate names because they represent separate individuals. When listed among other proper names, the second name is regarded as a given name for alphabetizing purposes.

Name	Indexing Order
Branch-Merrill Company	Branch Merrill Company
Richard T. Branch	Branch, Richard T.

Winifred I. Wilson   Wilson, Winifred I.

Wilson-Wyman, Inc.   Wilson Wyman, Inc.

Hyphenated individual names are treated as one name because they represent one individual.

Name	Indexing Order
James A. Gladd-Monroe	GladdMonroe, James A.
Patricia Lloyd-Taylor	LloydTaylor, Patricia
Jane L. Marin-Jones	MarinJones, Jane L.

One- or two-word names. Names that may be spelled as one word or two words are usually considered to be one word.

Indexing Order

Name	Unit 1	Unit 2	Unit 3
Raybrook Cleaners	Raybrook	Cleaners	
Ray Brook Paint Company	RayBrook	Paint	Company
South East Electric Shop	SouthEast	Electric	Shop
Southeast Supply Company	Southeast	Supply	Company
Good Will Cleaners	GoodWill	Cleaners	
Goodwill Industries	Goodwill	Industries	

Individual surnames with prefixes. Prefixes such as *D', d', De, de, Del, Des, Di, Du, Fitz, l', La, Le, M', Mac, Mc, O', Van, Von,* and so on, are indexed as written and treated as one word.

Indexing Order

Name	Unit 1	Unit 2	Unit 3
D'Aoust, James	D'Aoust	James	
Darling, John E.	Darling	John	E.
De Lancett, Morris	De Lancett	Morris	
DeLancey, Lincoln	DeLancey	Lincoln	
MacDonald, George H.	MacDonald	George	H.
McCasland, Raymond A.	McCasland	Raymond	A.
Van Cour, Elsie A.	Van Cour	Elsie	A.
Von Ottenfeld, Oscar M.	Von Ottenfeld	Oscar	M.

Words ending in S. When a name ends in *s'* or *'s*, the *s* is considered part of the name.

Indexing Order

Name	*Unit 1*	*Unit 2*	*Unit 3*
Bob's Sport Shop	Bob's	Sport	Shop
Boy Scout Camp	Boy	Scout	Camp
Boys' Clothing Store	Boys'	Clothing	Store
Williams' Dry Cleaning	Williams'	Dry	Cleaning
William's Service Station	William's	Service	Station

Titles. A personal or professional title or degree is usually not considered in indexing and filing. When the name is written, the title is placed in parentheses at the end of the name.

Name	**Indexed as**
Dr. Richard P. Bellaire	Bellaire, Richard P. (Dr.)
Ms. Helen Hayles	Hayles, Helen (Ms.)
Grace M. Janson, D. D.	Janson, Grace M. (D. D.)

A religious or foreign title is considered as the first indexing unit when it is followed by a given name only.

Indexed and filed as

Brother Francis

Madame Eugenie

Prince Charles

Princess Anne

Sister Mary Megan

Married women's names. The name of a married woman is indexed according to the name by which she prefers to be known. Some women retain their maiden names after marriage, and this preference should be respected. A married name could be a woman's given first name, her maiden surname, and her husband's surname, or it could be her given first and middle names (or initial for the middle name) and her husband's surname. The title *Mrs.* is disregarded in filing, but it is placed in parentheses after the name. If signatures on correspondence from a married woman indicate that she prefers *Ms.,* then that is the title placed in parentheses after her name. The name of the husband may be given in parentheses below the woman's legal name.

Name	Indexing Order
Mrs. John F. Matson (Mary Nelson)	Matson, Mary Nelson (Mrs.) (Mrs. John F. Matson)
Mrs. Lucien (Louise S.) Platt	Platt, Louise S. (Mrs.) (Mrs. Lucien Platt)
Mrs. Robert (Mary Lee) Young	Young, Mary Lee (Mrs.) (Mrs. Robert Young)

Names with numbers. When a name contains a number, it is considered as if the number were written as a single unit and is spelled as it is pronounced.

Indexing Order

Name	Unit 1	Unit 2	Unit 3
A 1 Garage	A	One	Garage
The 400 Club	Fourhundred	Club (The)	
7th Ave. Building	Seventh	Avenue	Building

Geographic names. An easy rule to follow in arranging geographic names is to treat them as they are written. Each element in a compound name of a geographic location is indexed as a separate unit.

Indexing Order

Name	Unit 1	Unit 2	Unit 3	Unit 4
Mount Holly, New Jersey	Mount	Holly	New	Jersey
New Bedford, Massachusetts	New	Bedford	Massachusetts	
Newburgh, New York	Newburgh	New	York	

When the first element of a geographic name is not of English origin, that element is considered part of the first unit.

Indexing Order

Name	Unit 1	Unit 2
Des Moines, Iowa	DesMoines	Iowa
Las Vegas Hotel	LasVegas	Hotel
Los Angeles, California	LosAngeles	California
San Francisco, California	SanFrancisco	California

THE ASSOCIATION OF RECORDS MANAGERS AND ADMINISTRATORS INDEXING AND FILING RULES

ARMA, the Association of Records Managers and Administrators, Inc., in its book of indexing rules, *Rules for Alphabetical Filing*, has established three classifications for indexing: individual names, business establishment names, and government/political designations. ARMA recommends separating index units with the diagonal (/). ARMA rules are essentially the same as the ones listed previously, with the following differences:

1. The hyphenated company name is treated as one unit.

   Brown-Jacobs/Company/

2. Compound geographical names are treated as separate units.

   Las/Vegas/Construction/Company

   Del/Rio/Music/Store/

3. Company names that have compass points as part of the name are indexed as separate units.

Name	Indexing Order
North East Alignment	North/East/Alignment/
Southeastern Transfer	South/eastern/Transfer/

4. The *'s* is included as part of the indexing unit; that is, the apostrophe is disregarded.

Name	Indexing Order
Leon's Barbecue	Leon's/Barbecue/
Leons' Music Store	Leons'/Music/Store/

5. Company names that are numbers and written in figure form, such as 500 Club, are arranged in strict numeric sequence and are not spelled out. They are filed at the front of the entire alphabetic file.

Name	Indexing Order
1 Hour Cleaners	1/Hour/Cleaners/
7th Street Auto Shop	7(th)/Street/Shop/
8 Ball Eatery	8/Ball/Eatery/
400 Executive Clothiers	400/Executive/Clothiers/
500 Club	500/Club/

Government offices and departments. The name of a federal government office is indexed as follows:

1. *United States Government* (whether or not it is written as part of the name)

2. Principal word or words in the name of the department

3. Principal word or words in the name of the bureau

4. Principal word or words in the name of the division

Department of, Bureau of, and *Division of* are disregarded, but they are usually placed in parentheses.

Name	Indexing Order

Bureau of the Census
   U.S. Department of Commerce
	United States Government
	   Commerce (Department of)
	   Census (Bureau of the)

Office of Indian Affairs
   U.S. Department of the Interior
	United States Government
	   Interior (Department of)
	   Indian Affairs (Office of)

U.S. Postal Service
   Bureau of Accounts
   Division of Cost Ascertainment
	United States Government
	   Postal Service
	   Accounts (Bureau of)
	   Cost Ascertainment
	   (Division of)

Foreign government names. Names pertaining to foreign governments are indexed under names of countries and subdivided by title of the department; and then by bureau, division, commission, or board.

Name	Indexing Order

Republic of India
   Department of Energy
	India (Republic of)
	   Energy Department

Other political divisions. Names pertaining to other political divisions are indexed under the name of the political division and followed by its classification (such as state, county, or city); and then subdivided by the title of the department, bureau, division, commission, or board.

Name	Indexing Order

Bureau of Statistics
   State of Maine
	Maine, State (of)
	   Statistics (Bureau of)

Harris County
   Bureau of Personnel
	Harris, County (of)
	   Personnel (Bureau of)

Department of Safety
   City of Anaheim
	Anaheim, City (of)
	   Safety (Department of)

Banks. Banks are indexed under the names of the communities in which they are located, and then by bank name. The state is the last indexing unit.

Name	Indexing Order
First National Bank Cleveland, Ohio	Cleveland: First National Bank Ohio
Bank of New Jersey Newark	Newark: Bank of New Jersey New Jersey
Wells Savings Bank Wells, Maine	Wells Savings Bank Maine

If the name of the community is a part of the name of the bank, the name of the community is not repeated, but it is considered the first unit as it occurs.

Churches, schools, and other organizations. The names of churches, schools, and other organizations are indexed as follows. Cross-references may be used, when necessary, to file or find these names more efficiently.

Name	Indexing Order
American Legion	American Legion
University of California	California, University (of)
Lakewood Kiwanis Club	Kiwanis Club, Lakewood
First Lutheran Church	Lutheran Church, First
Martin Luther King High School	Martin Luther King High School
The Salvation Army	Salvation Army, The

Addresses. If two or more persons or firms have the same name but different addresses, alphabetize them according to city or town. If the persons or firms also have the same city or town name, then alphabetize according to the state name. If the persons or firms having the same name are in the same community but have different addresses, alphabetize these names according to the name of the street. If the same name has more than one address on the same street of that city or town, then index from the lowest to highest street number. 125 Main Street goes before 126 Main Street.

LONG-TERM FILE MAINTENANCE

When records become inactive in the office file, they should be transferred to storage files. Thus, the expensive filing equipment is used only for active material. The material that is removed from the active files and placed in the *inactive,* or *transfer,* files should be well arranged, so that no time is wasted in locating this material if it is needed. Many firms transfer the material in the files annually—the entire file drawer is transferred to the inactive file. The professional needs to make new guides and prepare new folders for the new files.

Records Management

Records management is the term for the systematic control of the maintenance, retention, protection, and preservation of records. Many business papers— from correspondence to reports and records—may not be needed in the future and can be destroyed to conserve file space. But other documents must be retained, sometimes indefinitely. Which documents to retain is determined by legal counsel or senior management. Duration may be a matter of federal or state statute, or it may be a management issue. For instance, a company will have to retain records of its incorporation indefinitely. Financial records must be retained not only for administrative purposes but also for government tax reports. Corporate historical documents are also frequently preserved by management, in case they want to catalog the growth of their organization. Historical records that identify the bases on which past decisions were made can also help with future decisions. Your responsibility is to know not only the length of time each document should be kept, but also the storage location of records that have been removed from file cabinets and relocated to a warehouse or other storage facility.

A time frame is usually set for purging file drawers or transferring files to a storage facility. You will also have a *retention schedule,* on which is listed instructions for how long each type of record should be kept. There will probably be instructions on the way specific documents should be treated—for instance, whether they should be transferred to an inactive file, destroyed, microfilmed, or scanned and put on CD for storage. The retention schedule is prepared by management in consultation with legal counsel. Although computer advancement enables the inexpensive storage of inactive files, government statutes still require original documents in many instances. The retention list will indicate those files that must be kept as hard copy.

If the guides and folders are going to be kept in the office, the transferred material should be labeled with the same captions as those in the active-file drawer.

If files are going to storage, they should be packed into file boxes and labeled to indicate their contents, dates, and so forth, so that they can easily be located when needed. It's also helpful to label boxes with a discard date.

Micrographics

Micrographics is the term used to designate reproduced information in miniature form on film. Storing information on microfilm has saved firms great amounts of money, space, and retrieval time. Records are photographed onto film in a microfilmer so that many small images in color or black and white

RECORDS RETENTION SCHEDULE

Here is an example of a retention schedule for various types of documents.

Classification	Document Type	Retention Time
Legal	Annual reports	Permanently
	Affadavits	10 years
	Contracts	5 years
	Copyrights	Permanently
	Correspondence	10 years
	Deeds, titles	Permanently
	Expired insurance policy	10 years
	Leases	6 years
	Licenses, federal, state, local	Permanently
	Maintenance and repair to facilities	10 years
	Mortgages	5 years
	Patents and trademarks	Permanently
	Research reports	20 years
	Speeches, publications	10 years
Personnel	Accident reports	8 years
	Attendance records	3 years
	Claims, workers' compensation	10 years
	Daily time reports	3 years
	Employee file (after separation)	5 years
	Medical folders	25 years
	Pension plan	Permanently
	Time cards	3 years
Manufacturing	Bills of materials	20 years
	Blueprints	30 years
	Correspondence	6 years
	Customer specifications	20 years
	Drafting records	8 years
	Inspection records	10 years

	Operating reports	10 years
	Production reports	5 years
	Quality control reports	5 years
	Test data	20 years
	Work orders	2 years
Accounting	Accounts payable ledger	6 years
	Accounts receivable ledger	25 years
	Bank reconciliation	2 years
	Bonds	Permanently
	Budget worksheets	6 years
	Capital stock records	Permanently
	Cash disbursement ledgers	6 years
	Cash receipt registers	15 years
	Check register	6 years
	Checks, cancelled	6 years
	Contracts	Permanently
	Correspondence	6 years
	Cost accounting records	6 years
	Dividend register	Permanently
	Donations	10 years
	Expense reports	6 years
	External audit reports	Permanently
	Financial statements	Permanently
	General journal	10 years
	Internal audit reports	10 years
	Inventory records	Permanently
	Invoices	6 years
	Payroll register, year end	Permanently
	Payroll register, weekly/monthly	15 years
	Profit and loss statement	Permanently
	Stock certificates, cancelled	15 years
	Stock ledger, reports and records	Permanently
	Trial balance sheets	Permanently

will appear on a reel of 16-millimeter or 35-millimeter film. Records can be viewed in enlarged form on a reader.

Storage on film is less expensive than on microfiche, but film is not as easy to handle. Microfiche is easier to use and makes retrieval of documents simpler, and consequently is better to use when the information is frequently referred to. Increasingly, however, companies are storing files on computer disks. Data stored on CDs can be sorted and then resorted alphabetically, numerically, or in many other ways. They can be easily retrieved, and cost is decreasing, which makes CD storage a convenient alternative to microfilming.

MANAGING MONEY

An office professional may be required to handle financial transactions during the work day. The mail may contain checks that need to be forwarded to the appropriate department. There may be payroll records or other financial records that must be processed and kept up to date. In some offices, an office professional may be responsible for petty cash, or handing out cash for travel and other business expenses. Whatever the transactions, they will need to be recorded. Such information may be used in preparing income tax returns and/or determining the profitability of the firm's operations.

Depending on your responsibilities, you need either to develop your own system or to follow your organization's established system to ensure that you keep track of these transactions. There will probably be different processes for different situations. For instance, you may need to keep only an informal record of incoming checks before putting them into interdepartmental mail, whereas you may have to keep a more formal record of cash given out for travel and other business expenses.

MANAGING CASH TRANSACTIONS

In today's parlance, cash transactions refer to cash and checks, but for the office professional they also include credit cards. Cash will come into the company from various sources, including fees collected for services, and payment of bills or accounts. For the executive assistant, there will also be personal funds of the employer such as salaries, interests, dividends, rents, and so on. An office professional who opens the mail on a regular basis will become used to seeing payments and should know how to route checks and credit card numbers in a secure manner.

It is important that all received monies be processed and deposited into the appropriate bank account on the day they are received. This procedure is the best insurance against thefts, robberies, and fraud. Examine checks to determine whether they are properly made out. Pay attention to the date; postdated checks cannot be deposited or cashed before the date written on the check. Set aside checks that are made out incorrectly and discuss them with your employer. If your company accepts credit cards and you receive credit card payments, they need to be processed through the credit card company and need an authorization number before they can be submitted.

The person who processes payments should also be responsible for the record keeping (entries should be made in the proper records). Arrangements for night deposits should be made if funds cannot be deposited before the bank closes.

HANDLING THE BANK ACCOUNT

Banks offer different services to client firms. The office professional needs to be familiar with the inner workings of the bank that the company uses. Such knowledge will be helpful when handling any problems that arise, and will help optimize opportunities for the company.

Making Bank Deposits

When cash is to be deposited in a bank, make out a deposit slip, detailing the specific checks and amounts. The company bank-deposit slips are usually imprinted with the company name and the bank account number. If these are not available, then fill out this information on a blank slip. The account number is important because it is the number, rather than the name, that the bank uses for its records.

Count the currency, and enter the total on the slip. If there are large quantities of coins, roll them in wrappers provided by the bank. List separately each check included in the deposit. Occasionally, traveler's checks or money orders may be a part of the deposit. Enter these in the same manner as ordinary checks. After all checks have been listed, add the amounts of all items on the slip and enter the total in the space provided. Deposit slips can be handwritten as long as writing and numbers are neatly written. If handwriting is illegible or the form is incorrectly filled out, the bank can reject it.

The bank will give you a receipt for the deposit. Retain the receipt until the bank statement is received, and then use it to check the statement to ensure that all deposits have been properly recorded.

Endorsing Checks

Technically, checks are written orders by which the depositor, known as the *drawer,* directs the bank, referred to as the *drawee,* to pay money to the *payee* or to a third party designated by the payee. Checks are sometimes made payable to *bearer,* a practice generally frowned upon because they are negotiated by simple delivery and can be cashed by persons who wrongfully receive them. Checks need not be made payable to real persons. Business checks are

BASIC BOOKKEEPING TERMS

Accrual method—An accounting system in which the right to receive payments and the establishment of obligations are recorded as transactions take place, rather than when cash is received or paid. Because both receivables and payables are matters of value, this system gives management a truer picture of the net worth than the cash method does.

Assets—Anything owned that has cash or exchange value. Collectively, the assets of a person or business are the means that may be used to offset liabilities. In accounting, the assets are all of the entries on a balance sheet, showing the entire resources of a person or business, which, when compared with liabilities, become a disclosure of net worth.

Balance sheet—A financial statement itemizing the assets, liabilities, and capital accounts of a business; and giving its net worth on a given date, such as the end of a fiscal year. A balance sheet is so called because it shows that the sum of the assets equals the total of the liabilities plus the net worth.

Bookkeeping—The work of keeping a systematic record of business transactions.

Capital—In accounting, the excess of assets over liabilities; the net worth of a business.

Cash method—An accounting system in which the receipts and payments of a business are recorded when made rather than when the transactions take place.

Current asset—Any of the liquid assets of a business, including cash, securities, goods, and materials that are expected to be sold or consumed within the fiscal year, and accounts receivable.

Current liability—Any of the liabilities of a business that are payable and that must be satisfied within the fiscal year.

Double-entry bookkeeping—A bookkeeping system in which a transaction is recorded as both a credit and a debit, in conformity with the accounting principle that assets equal liabilities plus net worth.

Expense—A cost met in doing business.

General ledger—The principal book of accounts for a business, in which all money transactions are recorded, including subsidiary accounts that may be summarized.

> **Income statement**—A statement that summarizes the various transactions of a business during a specified period, showing the net profit or loss.
>
> **Journal**—In accounting, the book in which the first entry of a transaction is recorded: Journal entries are chronological and are later posted to a ledger, in which they are classified by account.
>
> **Ledger**—In accounting, the book of final entry, in which debits, credits, and all money transactions are recorded.
>
> **Liability**—In accounting, any of the debts of a business, such as accounts and notes payable, obligations incurred but not paid, and long-term debentures.
>
> **Revenue**—The aggregate of income to a business, individual, or government.
>
> **Single-entry bookkeeping**—A bookkeeping system, used principally in small businesses, in which a transaction is entered only once.

frequently made out to "Petty Cash" or to "Payroll." A check is made payable to Payroll, for example, when money is needed to make up pay envelopes.

If a check is made out to a definite payee, such as the company or a specific person, there must be a matching signature on the back of the check. This signature is known as an *endorsement*. Endorsements are placed on the back of the check on the left-hand side. The endorser should sign the name exactly as it is written on the face of the check. If the name is misspelled or differs in any manner from the way it appears on the bank records, the payee should sign twice, first as it is written on the face of the check and then correctly. Many companies use stamps, which qualify as endorsements. You can also include the account number. It is also recommended that you note "For Deposit Only" to prevent checks from being cashed illegally.

Forms of Endorsement

There are three principal forms of endorsement: blank, in full, and restrictive.

Blank endorsement. In a blank endorsement, the endorser's signature is simply written across the back of the check. The effect of a blank endorsement is to make the check payable to the bearer. If it is lost or stolen, it can be cashed by the holder without further endorsement. Although commonly used, blank endorsements are not recommended. They should be made only at the time a check is being cashed or deposited at the bank.

Blank Endorsement: Payable to Bearer Without Further Endorsement

Blank Endorsement: for Misspelled Name

Endorsement in full. In an endorsement in full, the endorser transfers the check to a designated party by writing the words "Pay to the order of," followed by the name of the person to whom payment is to be made, and then signs the check. A check so endorsed can be cashed or negotiated only after the person named in the endorsement has signed it. It is not negotiable by another person.

Endorsement in Full: Payable as James Cavanaugh Directs

Restrictive endorsement. In a restrictive endorsement, the endorser limits further negotiation of the check by writing definite instructions, above his or her signature, about what may be done with the check. Thus, a check might be made payable to one person only or it might be endorsed "For deposit only." Except when checks are being deposited in the bank, restrictive endorsements are almost never used. Business checks are usually endorsed for deposit with a rubber stamp; no written signature is needed.

FOR DEPOSIT ONLY IN
MECHANICS NATIONAL BANK
TO THE CREDIT OF
Grace Nelson

Restrictive Endorsement: Further Negotiation Prohibited

Dishonored Checks

A bank accepts checks for deposit subject to its final payment. If the drawer has directed the bank to refuse payment or if there are insufficient funds on deposit, the bank will return the check and charge it to the drawer's account. Such a check is known as a *dishonored check,* or an "NSF (nonsufficient funds) check." Informal arrangements for payment or redeposit of a dishonored check are usually made with the drawer. However, if the drawer is a stranger, it would be advisable for the holder of a dishonored check to take legal steps and file a formal notice of protest. In this way, the holder is assured of protecting full rights against the drawer. A fee is often also charged to the account holder for a refused check. This fee is usually charged back to the drawer in addition to the regular payment.

Dishonored checks that have been returned by the bank should be deducted from the bank balance on the depositor's cash records, and then be redeposited or filed for safekeeping until the drawer has made settlement. Any fees that may have been paid for the protest or collection can rightfully be collected from the drawer.

Bank Statements

At regular intervals (usually monthly, or sometimes upon request of the depositor), the bank renders a bank statement, showing what has taken place in the account since the last statement was prepared. It also shows the present balance, according to the bank's records. The statement shows the balance carried forward from the previous statement, all deposits and all charges made to the account during the period, and the balance on the date the statement was rendered. Sometimes sent along with the statements are canceled checks, credit memos, and debit memos. Otherwise, the bank keeps these documents on file for reference, for a period of time—usually five years.

Today, many financial institutions provide checkbooks that make self-carbon copies of checks written. These copies remain in the check register and are used to balance the account at the end of the statement period, just like the traditional canceled and returned checks.

Canceled checks are the depositor's checks that have been returned to the bank, charged against the account, and stamped "PAID." *Credit memos* are notices of amounts added to the account for such sums as interest allowed by the bank or proceeds of items left with the bank for collection—notes and bond coupons, for example. *Debit memos* are notices of deductions made from the account for service charges, interest on bank loans, and the like.

Bank Reconciliation

Seldom will the balance showing in the checkbook agree with the balance reported on the bank statement, even though no errors have been made in either place. Disagreement results from the following causes:

- Deposits that were made near or after the date of the statement have not yet been posted on the bank records. They do, however, appear in the checkbook.

- Credits that have been made to the account by the bank, as indicated on the credit memos, have not yet been entered in the checkbook.

- Checks issued by the depositor and deducted in the checkbook are still outstanding; that is, they have not yet been presented to the bank for payment and therefore do not appear on the bank statement.

- Charges that have been made against the account by the bank, as indicated on the debit memos, have not yet been entered in the checkbook.

- Errors have been made in the checkbook, in the bank's records, or in both places.

As soon as possible after receiving a statement, the depositor should locate the reasons for differences between the bank statement and the checkbook, and find the correct balance in the account. This is done on a bank reconciliation statement, prepared by following these steps:

1. Compare deposits entered in the checkbook with those recorded on the bank statement. Check discrepancies against deposit slips to determine which record is correct. Make a note of deposits that do not appear on the bank statement and credits made by the bank that have not been added in the checkbook.

2. Take checks returned by the bank or self-carbon copies in the checkbook and arrange them in numerical order. Compare them with their stubs or other notations in the checkbook, taking careful notice to see whether the amounts agree. Make a note of differences. Place a check mark or other symbol on stubs of the checks that have been returned. Prepare a list of the outstanding checks, noting the check numbers, the dates, and the names of the payees. Do not include certified checks on this list because they have already been charged against the account. Make a note of any bank charges that have not been entered in the checkbook.

3. Arrange the information that has been assembled on a bank reconciliation statement. The form and the preparation of this statement are explained and illustrated in the following material.

If the checkbook and bank statement are both correct, the balances can be brought into agreement and the reconciliation is complete. If the accounts cannot be reconciled after adjustments have been made for omissions. there is probably an error in addition or subtraction in the checkbook. Check the check stubs, paying particular attention to the balances carried forward from one stub to another.

Bank Reconciliation Statements

Bank reconciliation statements are prepared in three ways:

1. Adjustments are made to the balance reported by the bank to bring it into agreement with the checkbook balance.

2. Adjustments are made in the checkbook balance to bring it into agreement with the balance shown in the bank statement.

3. Adjustments are made to both balances to get the correct balance.

Because neither of the first two methods provides the correct balance, the third method is the preferred procedure and is the one explained here. The sources of the data are the bank statement and the checkbook or a cash ledger account, if one was prepared.

Comparison of the deposits that were made during the month with those recorded on the bank statement reveals that the bank has not entered a deposit of $1,000 made on July 31; this amount is added to the balance reported by the bank. Comparison of the canceled checks returned by the bank with the checks drawn during the period shows that the following checks are still outstanding:

Check No.	Date	Payee	Amount
633	7/22	Bean & Co.	$2,180
634	7/28	Blue Cross	$50
			$2,230

The total of the outstanding checks is deducted from the balance reported on the bank statement. Adding the unrecorded deposits and deducting the outstanding checks takes care of all omissions on the bank statement. The correct bank balance is determined to be $6,098.

The bank statement shows a service charge of $2 that has not been entered in the cash records; this amount is deducted from the checkbook balance. Now, the corrected checkbook balance is also $6,098, and it has been proved that no errors have been made.

After the reconciliation has been completed, errors should be corrected and entries should be made in the depositor's cash records and checkbook for any omissions (such as the service charge discussed previously), so that the records will reflect the correct balance. Adjustments in the checkbook can be made on the stub for the last check drawn. It is not necessary to correct all preceding balances. Any bank errors uncovered in the reconciliation should be reported to the bank immediately.

The bank reconciliation statement should be filed for future reference. It will prove useful when the next reconciliation is made. The canceled checks are receipts for payments that have been made. They should be kept on file as long as proof of payment might be necessary.

Reconciliation Statement (July 31)

Balance on bank statement	$7,328
Deposits made after date of statement	1,000
Add	$8,328

Checks Outstanding

Check No.	Date	Payee	Amount
633	7/22	Bean & Co.	$2,180
634	7/28	Blue Cross	50
			$2,230

Deduct checks outstanding	2,230
Corrected bank balance	6,098
Balance according to checkbook	6,100
Service charge not recorded	2
Corrected checkbook balance	$6,098

Reconciliation Statement

Investigating Outstanding Checks

Ordinarily, checks should clear through the bank and be returned to the depositor within a few weeks after issue (this is not the case with self-carbon checks). Checks that have been outstanding for unreasonably long periods of time should be investigated. Outstanding checks not only are annoying when bank accounts are being reconciled, but also pose a question as to what may have happened to them. Perhaps the checks have been lost or mislaid by the payee. Communication with the payee is in order.

If the payee claims not to have received a check, a new one will have to be issued in its place. This should be done, however, only after a stop-payment notice has been filed on the old check. How to stop payment on a check is described later in this chapter.

HANDLING CASH PAYMENTS

Large organizations issue credit cards to their managers to use for business expenses. In smaller firms, a manager may use a personal card to handle some of his or her operating expenses. Just as the office professional checks outstanding bills for accuracy, the professional needs to review credit card bills and compare them to credit card receipts, to ensure the accuracy of the bills before preparing a check.

Compare the charges listed on the statement with the sales slips that are attached or other supporting evidence, and make sure that proper credits have been allowed for returns and payments that have been made on the account. The mathematical accuracy of all calculations on the statement should be verified.

Prompt payment of all bills is desirable; on some bills, payment on or before a given date is essential. Pay particular attention to insurance premiums because policies lapse if premiums are not paid before a certain date. Also pay attention to those bills that are subject to some form of additional charge if payment is not made within a stated period. Bills that allow for a cash discount if paid within a certain time should be earmarked for timely payment. For example, the expression "2/10: n/30" stands for a 2 percent discount if paid within ten days; if not taken, the total is due within thirty days. In terms of annual notes, this is the equivalent of almost a 35 percent interest charge if the discount is not taken. One method of ensuring payment at the right time is the use of a tickler file, in which bills are filed by the dates on which they should be paid.

Occasionally, payments must be made in a foreign currency. The easiest means of making remittances to foreign countries is a draft, payable in the funds of the country to which payment is to be sent. Drafts can be purchased at any bank. Personal checks can be used in some instances; however, this poses the problem of exchange rates and presents the possibility of over- or underpayment. The exchange rates fluctuate.

Writing Checks

Exercise care in writing checks. It is a good policy to fill in the check stub first; this prevents you from possibly drawing a check without recording it. On the stub, list the date, the check number, the name of the payee, and the reason for the payment. The reason for payment should contain enough information to permit later entry in the cash records. Fill in the check with the number (if not preprinted), the date, the name of payee, the amount in both figures and words, and the signature. Make sure the check is written legibly, and don't leave any blank spaces that might be used to alter the check. The amount in figures is placed close to the dollar sign, and the amount in words is started close to the left side. The amount in words should agree with the amount in figures. In case of disagreement, the bank may refuse to honor the check. If the check is

Example of a Filled-Out Check

honored, the amount written in words governs. If the amount of the check is less than one dollar, it is customary to cross out the word "Dollars" and write "Only . . . cents."

Information about the payee and amount of the check can be typed or handwritten, depending on managerial preference. Many organizations prefer typed checks, simply because some individuals' handwriting is indecipherable.

Titles such as "Dr." or "Rev." are not used; it is "Ben Kildare," not "Dr. Ben Kildare." "Mrs." is used only in connection with the husband's name; it is either "Mrs. Roy Roe" or "Ruth Roe." Checks issued to organizations should be made payable to the organization, not to some individual in the organization. Likewise, checks should be made payable to companies rather than to their agents. Checks for insurance premiums, for example, should be drawn in favor of the insurance company rather than the agent who handles the account.

It is not wise to sign blank checks. If this is necessary when the employer will be absent from the office, keep the checkbook in a place where it will be safe from theft. Checks, like money, are a medium of exchange and should be guarded as carefully as money.

Erasures and alterations should never be made on checks. Banks are reluctant to accept a check if there is any suspicion that it has been tampered with. If you make a mistake in preparing a check, write the word "VOID" across the face of the check and on its stub. If the checks are prenumbered, don't discard the spoiled check; keep it with the canceled checks so that there can be no question concerning the whereabouts of a missing check.

Certified Checks

Often, checks for large amounts drawn by a person whose financial status is unknown to the payee must be certified by the bank before they are issued. To secure certification, the depositor takes a completed check to the bank. After the cashier has ascertained that the account has sufficient funds to cover it, the cashier stamps the check "CERTIFIED" and signs it. Immediately upon certification, the amount of the check is charged against the depositor's account.

There can be no question concerning whether funds are available for payment when the check is presented. As far as the bank is concerned, it has already been paid. Thus, in a bank reconciliation, a certified check is never outstanding because it has been charged in advance.

Certified checks should never be destroyed. In the event that they are not sent to the payee, they should be redeposited in the bank.

Stopping Payment on a Check

The drawer of a check has the power to stop payment on it at any time prior to its presentation to the bank for payment. This is accomplished by filing a stop-payment notice at the bank on a form that the bank will provide. Oral notice is insufficient. So that the bank can identify the check when it is presented, it will ask for information such as the number of the check, its date, the name of the payee, and the amount. If a check is lost, file a stop-payment notice immediately.

As soon as the stop-payment notice is filed with the bank, mark the check stub "Payment stopped." The amount of the check should then be added to the current balance. This can be done on the check stub open at the time; it is not necessary to go back and correct all preceding balances.

Petty Cash Fund

It is good policy to make all payments by check because a check provides a written record of the transaction and serves as a receipt. But it is impractical to write checks for small amounts to cover items such as collect telegrams, postage due, carfare, supper money, and incidental purchases of office supplies. In some instances, too, cash is needed immediately. To meet these needs, it is customary to set up what is generally called a "petty cash fund." Operation of the petty cash fund is described in the following paragraphs.

Establishing the petty cash fund. First, decide how much cash should be placed in the fund. This is determined by the expenditures that are anticipated. The amount should not be too high, yet it should not be so low that too-frequent reimbursements are required. When the amount has been set, draw up a check, payable to Petty Cash. Cash the check and place the funds in a locked cash box or drawer, generally referred to as the petty cash drawer. One person should be responsible for the fund, and this person alone should have access to it.

Payments from the petty cash fund. All payments from the petty cash fund should be supported by documentary evidence in the form of a petty cash voucher, showing the date of payment, the name of the payee, the reason for payment, and the amount paid out. The petty cash voucher is initialed by the person making payment and signed by the person who has received the cash. Printed forms for this purpose can be purchased at any stationery store.

```
AMOUNT. $  3.75                      NO. 124

RECEIVED OF PETTY CASH
                    Jan.   9,      19

FOR      Almanac

CHARGE TO  Sales Dept.


APPROVED BY              RECEIVED BY

                         Leslie Adams
```

Petty Cash Voucher

Paid vouchers are placed in the petty cash drawer or in a special envelope kept for this purpose. In addition, some firms maintain a petty cash record. This is simply a form on which paid vouchers can be summarized. Columns are provided for the voucher number, date, name of payee, explanation of payment, and a summary of the expenditures made. Seldom is there a real need for such a record; the petty cash vouchers themselves usually provide an adequate record. However, in a company with a system of bookkeeping that accounts for every expenditure, regardless of how small, the inclusion of petty cash payments in the accounting books as part of the daily record may be the best procedure.

Replenishing the petty cash fund. Whenever the cash in the petty cash fund gets low, the fund is replenished. A check is written payable to Petty Cash for the amount that has been spent from the fund. The check is cashed, and the proceeds are placed in the petty cash drawer. After replenishment, the cash in the fund should amount to the fund originally established. If replenishment of the fund is taking place too often, consideration should be given to increasing the size of the fund.

BOOKKEEPING

There are two reasons for properly recording the income and expense transactions of any business operation. The first reason is to determine the profitability of the business. When a company is able to calculate the profit or loss of the operation, and then analyze in detail the individual items of income and expense, the company is in a position to make decisions with greater knowledge. The second reason is to gather the necessary information required by governmental tax agencies such as the Internal Revenue Service. These tax reports not only require a calculation of net income (income less total expense), but also require detailed substantiation of individual amounts.

The preparation of these financial statements is usually the responsibility of the accountant. Much of the initial work, however, may be done by the bookkeeper, and a professional may be called upon to handle these bookkeeping duties. The next section briefly describes these duties. It should be understood that some of these tasks can be handled with little or no experience, while others require complete training as an accountant.

Business Records

Careful records of all payments, expenses, and other transactions must be kept to determine the profits (or losses) of a business. Some of the tasks involved in keeping complete business records are:

- Recording business transactions originally in journals. Most companies use what is referred to as a *double-entry* system that has a debit and credit entry for each item.

- Posting the journal to the ledger. There will be a general ledger, and there may be subsidiary ledgers for specific accounts, such as accounts receivable and accounts payable.

- Calculating a trial balance of all accounts in the ledger to determine whether the accounts are in balance in terms of debits and credits.

- Adjusting journal entries to bring all accounts up-to-date. For example, any bills owed at the end of the year are recorded, even though they will not be paid until the next year.

- Preparing the financial statements, primarily the Balance Sheet and the Income Statement. This usually involves the use of a worksheet.

The first two items, and possibly the third, are considered to be work normally done by the bookkeeper. The last two items are more often the job of the accountant. How a professional fits into this process will depend upon the practice of the individual company.

Tax Records

Aside from the bookkeeping described previously, there is a need to keep adequate tax records. Every business must pay a tax on its profits. A corporation pays its own income tax; income from a partnership or an individually owned business is added to the personal tax return of the individual owner. In each case, there must be proof of the amounts recorded in the tax returns for income and expense. Save all receipts.

A sales invoice, a bill, a receipt for cash payment—all of these can be useful in providing the necessary documentation. A filing system that allows the accountant to find the necessary papers easily should be maintained.

A filing system can be set up on the basis of (1) date, with bills and invoices filed according to month; (2) type of expense—for example, office supplies or utilities; or (3) type of document—for example, invoice, cash receipt, or bill. Combinations of these systems are often used. The main point is that the system should be based on a common-sense approach that other people can follow. The professional is in a central position to see to it that the filing is correctly handled.

Travel and Entertainment Expenses

There are specific expense items for which the IRS requires a detailed record. An example of this type of expense and the additional recordkeeping involved is the travel and entertainment deduction (T & E). Adequate records include the following:

■ The amount of the expenditure

■ The dates of departure and return for each trip, and the number of days spent on business

■ The business purpose of the expenditure

■ The place of travel or entertainment

■ The nature of the business relationship of the person(s) being entertained to the taxpayer

Documentary evidence in the form of credit card stubs and receipts of paid bills is required for all expenditures for lodging while traveling away from

Expense Report

home and for any expenditure over the amount specified by the Internal Revenue Service. It is good practice to record all expenditures in an account book or diary, and to attach receipts, paid bills, and other substantiating documents to the back of the page on which the expenditure is recorded. Employers will expect professionals to handle this type of detailed recordkeeping. Usually the employer will turn over the raw information to the professional and expect the professional to put it together in a formal record.

Automobile Expense Record

The taxpayer who uses a personal automobile in connection with business or employment is entitled to deduct automobile expenses (in total if the auto is used exclusively for business, or in part if it is used for both business and pleasure) on the income tax return. Expenses include not only all the operating costs, but also a reasonable allowance for depreciation. To ensure receiving full benefit from allowable deductions, the taxpayer should keep careful account of expenses and mileage on an automobile-expense record. An assistant can keep the record by using information supplied by the employer or, better yet, by making entries from bills that are routinely filed. The calculation for depreciation can best be made by the accountant responsible for preparing the tax return.

If records are not kept on automobile expenses, an optional tax-deduction method is allowed by the IRS. A standard mileage rate for business use each year, instead of a record of the actual operating and fixed expenses and a separate deduction for depreciation, may be used by an individual. Interest payments on loans, and state and local taxes (other than the gasoline tax) attributable to the business use of the car are deductible in addition to the standard mileage rate.

Always check current IRS booklets for detailed information and for rules on necessary record keeping.

RECORD OF AUTOMOBILE UPKEEP FOR THE   Month of *January*   1994

DATE	MILEAGE	GASOLINE		OIL AND GREASE	STORAGE and PARKING	AUTO REPAIRS	CLEANING AND WASHING	ACCESS-ORIES	MISCEL-LANEOUS
		No. Gals.	Amount						
1									
2	22,346	10	11 40						
3					2 00				
4							3 75		
5					2 75				
6				16 00		18 00			54 30
7		14	15 96						
28									
29					3 15				
30		12	13 72						
31	24,180								
TOTAL	1,834				16 00	10 70	18 00	7 50	54 30

Automobile Expense Form

Employer's Personal Tax Records

A number of different nonbusiness expenses are deductible on the individual's personal income tax return. As with business expenses, it is important that there exist adequate evidence of the payment of these expenses.

The office professional may be called upon by the employer to keep an additional set of records for these personal expenses. The expense deductions include: contributions to charities, colleges, and so on; medical and dental expenses; interest on mortgages, loans, and so on; and taxes. The most important proof is the canceled check indicating payment. Although this is usually sufficient, more evidence is occasionally required. Thus, a file of the bills would be helpful in substantiating a tax deduction. The employer should turn over personal bank statements with the canceled checks, or at least the ones to be recorded, along with the bills received. The degree that the employer wants the professional involved in personal financial matters will obviously affect the amount of record keeping that will be necessary.

PAYROLL

The bookkeeper may be called in to handle the payroll of the company. This will involve calculating the net amount to be paid out, and keeping payroll records required for computing the various kinds of payroll taxes and for the government reports. The following section describes these procedures in some detail.

The federal government requires that the employer withhold from each employee's salary a sufficient amount that will add up to the amount of income tax due at year's end. The employee, when first hired, must fill out a form indicating the number of exemptions claimed. The number of exemptions is then used to calculate how much tax should be withheld for each salary level, according to IRS guidelines.

There also may be state and city income taxes that will require additional withholdings from the employee's payroll check. Although the general procedures are basically the same, it is important that the professional follow the specific requirements of each governmental agency.

Besides the various income taxes, the Federal Insurance Contributions Act (FICA) requires employees to pay a percentage of their salary as their contribution to the Social Security program. (There is a matching contribution that is paid by the employer.) The rate is fixed at a certain percentage of the annual salary, up to a given amount. After this figure is reached, no more FICA tax has to be paid. Each year FICA tables are prepared for the various salary levels.

The following example uses the figure 7.65% FICA tax to be withheld from the annual salary:

Employee A, married with two children, may claim four exemptions. If A's weekly salary is $300, the payroll check is calculated as follows:

Gross Pay	$300.00
Less: Federal Income Tax Withheld	33.30
FICA Tax Withheld (7.65% × $300)	22.95
Total Withheld	– 56.25
Net Pay—Amount of Check	$243. 75

The illustration would have been more complex if state and city income taxes had been included. Besides the taxes that are withheld, the company sometimes withholds medical insurance, union dues, contributions to charity or retirement programs, and other agreed-upon items.

The monies withheld from the employee's paycheck have to be remitted periodically to the respective agencies. Thus, for example, the federal income tax withheld, plus the FICA tax withheld, and the employer's matching FICA tax contribution must be sent to the Internal Revenue Service (or a bank authorized to act as the depositor). How often this is to be done depends upon the dollar amount:

Dollar Amount	**Periodic Due Date**
Less than $500 a month	Every three months
More than $500, but less than $3,000 a month	Every month
More than $3,000 a month	Every two weeks

At the end of each three-month period, the IRS requires that a payroll tax return form be filed. Although this requirement normally is not the responsibility of the professional, keeping the detailed payroll records may be one of the duties. This will require a record of each pay period that shows the dates, hours, and earnings of each employee. Also required is a record of each employee's earnings that shows date of employment and discharge, Social Security number, rate or method of pay, and summary of wages and all deductions by quarter and calendar year.

There are additional reports required at the end of each year. These include the *Employer's Annual Federal Tax Return* (Form 940) and a *Wage and Tax Statement* (Form W-2) for each employee. On the state and local government level, quarterly and annual income and unemployment tax returns may be required, depending on state and local regulations.

TIP: It is essential that any information you know about salaries be kept confidential. At many organizations, disclosure of this information to others can be grounds for dismissal. If office professionals deal with salary and tax records, they must be just that—professionals.

It is important to point out that the ability to manage all of these tax and payroll reports is normally *not* the responsibility of the professional. Usually, the company has an accountant who handles these items. However, the accountant may delegate much of the work to the bookkeeper or the professional, and act only as a supervisor. Therefore, it is helpful to be familiar with payroll procedures and tax reports, in case these areas become your responsibility.

When individuals think about office operations, they usually immediately think of record keeping. But record management isn't the only responsibility in office operations. As the role of office professionals grows, they

NECESSARY PAYROLL TAX FORMS

OOAN-7003   Employee Change of Name Form.

SS-4   For employers without an employer identification number.

SS-5   For employees without a Social Security number.

W-2   Employee's Wage and Tax Statements. The employer must provide these to the employee on or before January 31. Employers also send copies to the Social Security Administration and to state, city, and local tax agencies.

W-3   Transmittal of Income and Tax Statements. The employer sends this, along with every employee's W-2 forms, to the Social Security Administration. These statements are due on the last day of February. Because the W-3 form is scanned, entries must be typed in and no dollar signs may be used.

W-4   Employee's Withholding Allowance Certificate. Used to calculate federal and state income tax deductions. Employees are responsible for requesting any changes.

8109   Federal Tax Deposit Form. Employers must submit this form every time they deposit income tax and FICA deductions and contributions. The form must include the amount of tax deposited, the type of tax, and the tax period.

940   Employer's Annual Federal Unemployment Tax Return. The employer reports the amount already deposited during the year. This form is due on January 31 of the following year.

941   Employer's Quarterly Federal Tax Return. Employers report the amount of income taxes and FICA taxes deducted or contributed every three months. This form is due one month after the quarter ends.

will increasingly be involved in financial transactions, both incoming and outgoing. It's a very big responsibility. Aside from the monetary value, in this role you represent your company, and manage customers and vendors. It's imperative that you understand your responsibilities fully.

FOR MORE INFORMATION

If you can't find what you need from the phone numbers and Web sites listed in this chapter, you may need to expand your search.

- For more information on formal letters and their formats, consult "1001 Essential Letters," on the CD-ROM that accompanies this book. It has letter templates ready to load on your computer and use.

- For more information, check your local library or bookstore for the following books:

  - Association of Records Managers and Administrators. *Rules for Alphabetical Filing as Standardized by ARMA.*

  - Clements, Jonathan. *25 Myths You've Got to Avoid If You Want to Manage Your Money Right: The New Rules for Financial Success.* New York: Simon & Schuster.

  - Gallapher, Stephanie. *Money Secrets the Pros Don't Want You to Know: 365 Ways to Outsmart Your Banker, Broker, Insurance Agent, Car Dealer, Realtor, Travel Agent, Lawyer, Credit Agent.* New York: AMACOM.

  - General Services Administration. *A Guide to Record Retention Requirements.* Washington, DC: Government Printing Office.

  - Pool, John Charles, et al. *The ABCs of Personal Finance: An Essential Money Management Guide.* Shenandoah University Durell.

8

ORGANIZING PEOPLE AND TIME

◆

■ **Organizing Meetings and Conferences**

Planning

Facilities

Supplies

Keeping a Budget

Notification

Teleconference and Video Conferences

Minutes

■ **Time Management**

Basic Timesaving Strategies

Manage the Executive Efficiently

■ **For More Information**

A large part of the office professional's time and energy each day is taken up with managing multiple tasks effectively. This might range from structuring his or her own day and time to planning and managing others.

ORGANIZING MEETINGS AND CONFERENCES

Whenever people gather for a specific purpose—whether for weekly meetings or annual sales conferences—the event organizers must spend time and effort before, during, and after the activity to oversee both the event and its results. Even if the office professional does not attend the function as an active participant, he or she plays a crucial role behind the scenes. Even after the initial planning—and even when the office professional does not have to be onsite for the day or days of the meeting—he or she still must perform endless follow-up tasks. All arrangements should be checked and verified, if not by the office professional directly, then through someone else—and then the office professional should check with *that* person. Nothing can be left to chance. Nothing can be assumed to be okay.

In short, it takes enormous organizational skill to arrange a large-scale meeting or conference. Only those who have done it fully know the innumerable details involved. In fact, the task is so important and so time-consuming that many companies employ full-time meeting planners.

Because meeting planning accounts for only one part of an office professional's job, the skill may not always be fully acknowledged, even when the event is a success. But this is no place to cut corners and hope it won't be noticed. The meeting that ends in disaster makes both the organizer and his or her boss look bad and speaks poorly of the company.

PLANNING

In planning any meeting or conference, the most basic elements are the most important: Why is the event being called? Who are the people attending? How many people will be there? Where will they come from? How long will the meeting last? Obviously, a department-wide presentation of a new benefits package differs from a new-product presentation to overseas clients. A meeting to award salespeople differs from a meeting of the board of directors. Each event will have its own budget, atmosphere, setting, and so on—and each will treat the same element with a different procedure. For example, booking a professional speaker for a national conference is not the same as arranging for one of the company's retired sales stars to come back and give a motivational speech at an awards dinner. Similarly, the invitations sent to executives for an

COUNTDOWN FOR PLANNING MEETINGS AND CONFERENCES

This three-month countdown serves as a guideline for a mid-sized event. Because of their size, some functions might require a year or more of planning. Professional speakers also tend to book their engagements a year or two in advance. Adjust the early part of this schedule as needed.

Three Months Out

☐ Reserve the meeting location.

☐ Contact and draw up contracts with the conference center/hotel coordinator, the audiovisual coordinator, caterers, and others.

☐ Notify participants of dates and location.

☐ Make travel arrangements for participants.

☐ Contact the chamber of commerce, and select local events and entertainment venues for after-meeting sessions.

☐ Plan a program of structured group entertainment activities.

☐ Provide information on individual free-time entertainment possibilities.

☐ Plan agenda topics and book speakers.

☐ Send invitations to VIPs.

One Month Out

☐ Confirm menus, caterers, room arrangements, and business services and supplies with the conference center/hotel coordinator in writing.

☐ Confirm speakers and group entertainment events.

☐ Mail final agenda and information packets.

☐ Reconfirm RSVPs of participants.

One Week Out

☐ Ship materials to the conference center/hotel.

☐ Send a small backup supply of general office supplies, such as tape, shipping labels, paper clips, pens, pencils, note pads, badges, scissors, masking tape, magic markers, and so on.

continues

☐ Make arrangements with the conference center/hotel to collect, pack, and ship any unused materials back to your office.

48 Hours Prior to Departure

☐ Confirm arrival of conference materials.

☐ Reconfirm menus or catering arrangements.

Upon Departure

☐ Bring a master set of conference materials with you, just in case.

Upon Arrival

☐ Meet with the conference center/hotel coordinator and confirm all details.

☐ Meet with the audiovisual coordinator and confirm that required equipment is functional and in place.

☐ Walk through the meeting site.

☐ Introduce yourself to the bell captain and the maitre d' of the hotel(s).

☐ Confirm participants' room assignments with hotel registration.

☐ Confirm any special services to be rendered to participants, such as bed-time chocolates or complimentary breakfast.

☐ Confirm that the location of the meeting room(s) is clearly posted in the conference center/hotel lobby.

☐ Confirm that the speaker(s) have arrived, and introduce yourself.

☐ Review with the speaker(s) any audiovisual operating procedures that they might need to know.

Day(s) of the Meeting

☐ Do a final walkthrough of the meeting room(s) at least one hour prior to the beginning of the meeting each day.

☐ Confirm that all audiovisual equipment is functional and in place.

☐   Set up a command center so that you are instantly available during the meeting(s).

☐   Provide methods of contacting you in case of an emergency.

After the Meeting(s)

☐   Meet with the conference center/hotel coordinator to review billing.

☐   Confirm arrangements for the return of unused materials.

☐   Pay appropriate gratuities.

Back at the Office

☐   Distribute copies of the minutes to the appropriate individuals.

☐   Distribute, store, or destroy any unused materials, as appropriate.

☐   Review charges and receipts when they arrive.

☐   Write thank-you notes to speakers, VIPs, and conference center/hotel staff.

---

in-house meeting will not be the printer-produced announcements and invitations sent about a meeting that attracts those from outside the organization.

Regardless of the size of the meeting, its purpose, or its location, the heart of its success always lies in the details.

The Offsite Large Meeting or Conference

The larger the meeting or conference, the more important it is to begin planning the physical setup first. For functions held in hotels or other outside facilities, preparations should begin at least a year ahead of time—longer, if possible. For the moment, agendas, invitations, and other details can wait. With the budget in mind, look for facilities that best match both the tone set by the participants and the space, location, and equipment needs of the meeting. Understand the terms used by hotels to describe set packages: What's the difference between a Full American, European, and Bermuda Plan? What about between a rack, flat, and run-of-the-house rate?

Take bids from several appropriate facilities. Each facility will want to know the date(s) of the meeting, the flexibility of the dates, the number of expected attendees, the type of meeting space desired, the need for overnight accommodations and for how many, and the number and type of meals prepared by the facility.

Although taking bids was once a time-consuming process consisting of multiple letters, faxes, and phone calls, online "request for proposals" systems now help search out those hotels worldwide that meet your criteria. After you select the venues you want to consider, the system sends a request for a bid. Make sure that submitted bids are completely itemized to ensure that all your points have been covered and to better compare results. Also make sure that each bid includes the facility's policy on gratuities and taxes (and the specific percentage for each), deposits, cancellations, no-shows, and other relevant points.

The In-house Meeting or Conference

Far fewer details require planning in this case, but reserving space still rates as one of the first things to do in planning an in-house meeting. Check with office management to see whether the desired room is available and to reserve both the space and any company audiovisual equipment required. If outside partici-

---

BOOKING SPEAKERS

No matter where the meeting is held, another element that requires advance planning is the booking of a speaker. For instance, your conference might include an industry professional who will present an informational program to all attendees at a general session or a motivational speaker who will address the closing banquet. Better-known or celebrity speakers book their schedules one and two years in advance. They sometimes work through a manager or agent, and charge a substantial fee. Don't plan on having a specific person attend (or mention it in early agendas) until you have a written contract. Until then, also investigate alternates because speakers' schedules—and your budget for them—can be subject to change.

When you confirm any speakers, make sure to finalize every term with them or their agents, including fees (if applicable), who will cover travel and hotel expenses, and any other special details, such as literature they might want to distribute or books to be sold.

Even non-professional speakers require advance notice. For example, if you work for an association or society, its annual conference might include a keynote speaker and several guest speakers—one or more of whom might be well-known. But the rest of the conference might consist of workshops given by the society's own members. These presentations will be generated by a call for papers about the conference theme, which is sent to the society's members six or nine months before the meeting date. The extra months are needed to gather and approve responses, and then to advertise the workshop topics when the conference notice is sent to the membership at large.

pants will be attending—whether from other divisions or other companies—see whether these people require hotel accommodations.

If the in-house meeting is large or lengthy enough, you also should make arrangements for meals and refreshments. These refreshments could be provided by the company's cafeteria (which is often serviced by an outside firm), by a caterer, or even by the hotel where guests are staying. If dealing with the hotel, find out whether delivery is included or if you must pick up the food. Because of the setup and clean-up involved, be sure to reserve a separate room for conference meals.

FACILITIES

Although meetings must be held *someplace,* they need not be limited to an official meeting room. Besides traditional places such as a company conference room, a hotel, or a meeting center, don't overlook an airport's business suite, the private dining room of a restaurant, or even a college auditorium or lecture hall during semester or summer break. The smaller the meeting, the more alternatives will be available. Just be sure that the venue can accommodate any special needs (such as audiovisual equipment or meals), that the place is easy to find, and that it's near sources of major transportation if out-of-towners are attending.

The Offsite Large Meeting or Conference

When your request for a bid has narrowed your search to a few choices, it's time to begin asking specific questions.

- How old is the facility? When was the last time substantial renovations were done?

- Where is the place located in terms of the airport or train station?

- What's the size of the available meeting room(s)?

- What are its furnishings?

- What audiovisual equipment is available? Is it available on your specific date?

- What are the overnight accommodations?

- What hotel amenities will be available to your group (restaurant, pool, steam room, golf course)? Are extra charges involved?

- What entertainment or extracurricular activities are available for attendees of multiday conferences? What can the facility arrange?

- What other conferences or events are being scheduled at the same or overlapping times as yours? Check not only those being held at the facility itself, but also those in the same town or city.

The best way to make a final decision on a facility is to personally inspect the site, preferably as a surprise visit so that you see the facility as the average guest would. Check the general layout of the facility: its security measures and its loading docks and freight elevators (if equipment or elaborate exhibits will be shipped there). Go to its meeting rooms and check their acoustics, sound systems, temperature and lighting controls, ventilation, and other relevant features. Eat in the restaurant to check its quality and service.

Although this in-person inspection offers a good opportunity to see what details might be negotiable (cost or service breaks, for example), prices written in ink aren't written in stone until the contract is signed. So gather up your advantages and see what better deal the hotel or conference center can offer. You eventually will want to meet the conference coordinator because this person will be handling the actual planning and setup. But now you want someone who has the authority to negotiate and to provide you with extras: That's the sales manager—or, even better, the director of sales.

Why would a hotel or conference center be willing to negotiate the price it just stated? Here are some reasons:

- Your company will be renting a proportionately large amount of its space.

- You're holding a multiday conference.

- Many overnight accommodations are needed.

- The hotel or center is providing meals.

- It's the hotel's off-season.

- You know from prior company events at this hotel or center that the just-quoted price is high.

- This is a first-time visit to the site with a chance of repeat businessl.

- Your company has used this same site every year.

- Your company's repeated use proves a history of very few no-shows, or heavy food and beverage consumption.

All these things provide you with negotiating leverage. Obviously, the hotel won't cut its rate in half—nor should you expect it to, in all fairness—but it might make concessions. For example, if a large number of guests are staying for one or more nights, the hotel might include the daytime meeting rooms at no charge. Or it may include one free room for every X number reserved. Or it may give you the room reserved for the hospitality suite at no charge, provided that you use the hotel's food and liquor. If the hotel has its own audiovisual equipment, it might let you use the equipment at no charge. If VIPs are expected, the hotel might include pickup from and return to the airport, free newspapers, and/or complimentary fruit and cheese baskets. Depending on what else is scheduled at the time, the hotel might even include a complimentary suite—the perfect place for the company CEO if attending.

TIP: Don't be intimidated by the word *negotiation*. It doesn't mean playing hardball or being nasty. In fact, you want to avoid pressure and bad feelings because you'll be working with these same people on an almost daily basis for a very long time—you want the relationship to remain cordial. If the sales manager doesn't automatically bring up the topic of "Here's what I can do for you," say something like, "Last year's site provided complimentary airport limousine service for our chairman. Is anything like that possible?"

Not every hotel will give you everything, and what one can or will give won't be the same as another. For example, a non-union hotel might include meeting room setup at no charge, which often means the conference coordinator personally sets up the room. In a union hotel, everything from unloading meeting equipment off the truck to plugging in a projector must be done by union personnel and thus comes at a price tag with little or no margin for negotiation. Substantial breaks on meals and liquor generally are not offered because they represent a high percentage of the hotel's profit. One exception for food could be if another large group will be attending at the same time as yours and already has planned its menu: If your group accepts the same menu, you might be able to get a break because the kitchen has to prepare only one type of meal rather than two. However, equipment, rooms, and services provided by staff are more likely to be negotiated because the hotel has them on hand anyway.

Whatever is negotiated as extra should be put into writing in the contract with the regular charges so that no misunderstandings occur later. This also protects you if there's a change of personnel before your event and you end up working with new people.

The In-house Meeting or Conference

The needs of both the large meeting or conference and the in-house meeting converge at the point of the actual room used for the presentation. Here are some questions to ask about the room.

- How large a group must it hold?

- What is the best seating arrangement: classroom style with all attendees at tables facing a podium, horseshoe style to encourage whole-group interaction, or roundtable style for small-group discussion?

WHO NEEDS A/V EQUIPMENT? WHO SUPPLIES IT?

For a room of even moderate size, a microphone is required for all speakers. Some speakers have distinct preferences: a cordless hand mike or a lapel mike. If the speaker has any sort of experience, he or she also will want other audiovisual equipment as a way to vary the presentation and engage the audience. Although this equipment might be as simple as a flip chart and markers, the question remains: Who provides it?

At least a month ahead of time, find out the speaker's needs and whether he or she will be bringing equipment. Does the speaker's LCD presentation require an LCD panel, projector, and screen; a projector and screen; or just a screen?

Then ask whether the hotel has this available or can arrange for it on that day. Many hotels and conference centers do not own their A/V equipment; they use an outside leasing firm, passing the cost along to you. Some have their own equipment and a staff trained to set it up.

Be specific in asking the speaker his or her needs, and be specific when conveying them to the hotel. The hotel can comply with your request only with a reasonable lead time.

- What are the speakers' audiovisual requirements? Their needs could run from a flip chart and magic markers all the way to LCD or CRT projectors that show computerized graphics.

- Is the existing sound system adequate? Will the speaker prefer a wireless lapel microphone to one attached to a stand? If the meeting is important, you might want to consider renting a sound system for the occasion.

- How is the lighting and visibility? Will charts or slide screens be clearly seen? Do supporting columns block anyone's line of sight? For an in-house meeting, check the room ahead of time. That flickering fluorescent tube—annoying in itself—could be out by next week, and maintenance might not be able to respond as quickly as you need.

When you've finally decided upon a facility for the larger meeting or conference, get the name of the individual who will be directly planning your event. Titles may vary: convention service planner, conference manager, or conference coordinator. Try to meet in person and establish rapport as soon as possible. This is the individual you'll be calling more frequently as the months and weeks go by.

SUPPLIES

What sort of supplies or giveaways will attendees receive at the meeting? These will be determined not only by the size and importance of the event, but also by your budget.

On the one end, you might provide attendees only with a duplicate copy of the agenda at an in-house meeting; in this case, pads and pens are their own responsibility. At the other end, you might want to arrange for color-and-design coordinated materials at an outside conference that include agendas, maps, reports, name tags, handouts, certificates of attendance, certificates of achievement, pads, imprinted items such as pens or keychains, and imprinted folders or plastic bags to hold all the materials. Leave adequate time for getting bids and ordering these materials. New-product launches might be even more lavish, especially to get salespeople and buyers excited. For example, a bound first chapter of a book, sample sizes of consumables, or demo video game disks can be given away.

TIP: Don't forget your own emergency supply kit. Include all those little extras found to be useful over the years, such as extension cords, an assortment of batteries, and all-purpose duct tape. Among a dozen other uses, duct tape can fasten wires to the rug and quickly mend torn rugs—both reduce risks of tripping.

Beverages and light refreshments can prove to be an ongoing distraction if set up in the back of the meeting room; it's better to set them up in another room or the hallway outside and to make sure that lengthy presentations allow for a brief break.

Supplies for the speaker should include at the minimum a carafe of water and a glass. Tissues and hard candies for a dry throat also are helpful. Ask each speaker if there's anything else in particular he or she would appreciate having at the podium.

Shipping

Getting everything you need to the site—from printed agendas, supplies, and giveaways, to audiovisual equipment coming from your company—is another key last-minute detail, but don't wait until the last minute to plan it. The best method of transportation is one that gets the materials there quickly and safely—and that can be tracked at every point.

Even if you use overnight delivery, mail the supplies two or three days ahead of time. Delays can happen, and the hotel needs a day to sort through its daily mail and packages. Have each package clearly addressed to you if you're going to be onsite, or address it to the appropriate person from your company

PLANNING FOR GIVEAWAYS

Having even simple giveaway supplies such as pens or pads imprinted can take several weeks. The more elaborate the meeting giveaway, the more lead time is needed. Add in even more time if this is the first time you're using a particular item or particular company. Samples such as those mentioned previously won't be under your direct responsibility the way imprinted folders will because they are likely to come from other departments. You'll need extra time to coordinate efforts.

Also leave enough time to check the finished item personally before sending it to the conference. Even if you're running late and you've seen proofs or mocked-up items, don't have the finished batch sent directly to the meeting location. Proofs are not an infallible indicator of the finished product. If you worked for FAST—Frank's American Steak Temptations—you wouldn't want to find out the morning of the conference that you have 200 canvas bags imprinted FATS.

who is coordinating the event at that end. After this name, put the word "guest" to make it absolutely clear to the hotel: "To Jackie Sinisi, Guest/Hotel Hanover."

If you must use overnight shipping the day before the event, try air freight or counter-to-counter service. Find out which service or airline is being used; get phone numbers, tracking numbers, and delivery locations; and then get all this information to the person on the other end.

No matter what type of service you use or what lead time you have, ask the conference coordinator to notify you when the shipment has arrived.

KEEPING A BUDGET

Except for the in-house event, which typically involves very few expenses, few steps in meeting planning can be taken without having a budget. In the early stages of planning, this may be as exact as a precise dollar limit or as open as a comment from the boss such as, "Everyone complained about the food last year. Let's see about upgrading all the menus." Without at least a rough budget, the office professional doesn't know whether to take bids from economy sites or luxury sites, whether attendees or the company will be responsible for meals and/or lodgings, whether refreshments will be catered, or whether the office professional will be making a fast trip to the local bakery that morning.

First-time planners should look up files of past events. These will provide a general idea of what events cost, as well as provide a breakdown of dozens of easily overlooked items that must be included and itemized. Draw up some rough figures based on estimates: These can be adjusted later as you get actual costs and head counts.

Budget for 4-Day Annual National Sales Convention

Airfare	Est $ pp × Est #	Estimated Cost	Actual Cost
Coach	$500pp × 139	$69,500	$74,128
First class	$1,200pp × 8	$9,600	$9,003
Total	$79,100	$83,131	

Hotel Rooms	Est $ pp × Est # × 3 Nights	Estimated Cost	Actual Cost
Block	$150 × 160 × 3	$72,000	$69,723
Suite	$425 × 2 × 3	$2,550	0
Meeting	$375 × 4 × 3	4,500	$4,230
Hospitality	$525 × 1 × 3	$1,575	0
Total		$80,625	$73,953

Other expenses to be itemized include:

Food and beverages: Total number of breakfasts, coffee breaks, lunches, and dinners over the four days and three nights—multiplied by the number of people

Audiovisual expenses: Production of presentations, professional graphics designer (if desired), and equipment rental (if needed)

Promotional materials: Design, printing, and mailing of invitations and replies; imprinted pens, pads, and cups; and folders, bags, and name tags

And so on. Although airfare, space rental, and food and beverages constitute the greater share of almost every budget, these other items add up and can completely throw off a budget if forgotten or underestimated.

NOTIFICATION

During this preparation phase, when should the office professional notify the meeting's attendees? The larger the function, the more notice is preferred—as much as several months—because the event might involve considerable travel and a stay of one or more nights. This requires arrangements and schedule-shuffling on the part of each attendee. Smaller, in-house meetings need less advance notice, of course, but take into consideration the staff, directors, and other persons who do not reside close to the branch site where the meeting will be held.

For the simple in-house meeting, a phone call or brief memo serves as the usual form of notification. A conference is better announced through a written invitation, which also can give further particulars about the meeting location, hotel accommodations, and so on. A single list of those to be notified makes it handy to track when notification is actually sent and what the response is. Prepare your final list of attendees from this list.

Unless the list of invitees is too long (for example, an association membership generated from computer files), make sure that every name is spelled correctly and that the person's business title is up-to-date.

For all large meetings and for smaller in-house meetings where attendance is optional, request a reply. The written invitation should include a reply card and self-addressed envelope. All notifications should include the name of a contact person and a phone number and/or e-mail address.

Press Releases

For conferences and meetings that cover significant items, you might want to seek press coverage for the event. In calculating when to send press releases, allow for individual deadlines: Monthly trade magazines may require as much as three months' lead time, while daily newspapers and local news shows can provide overnight coverage if the topic is deemed important enough.

The Agenda

At some point after notification and before the meeting date, all attendees should receive a copy of the agenda, even though they also might receive a duplicate at the door at larger meetings. A meeting without an agenda is a meeting without a purpose. Even though at its simplest an agenda is just a list of topics to be covered, it helps prepare the participants to focus on key issues. It also alerts them to the time limits: Conclusions should be reached before a certain hour to allow for the next item. More detailed agendas might include copies of supporting documentation if attendees are expected to make decisions on the issues at the meeting.

TIP: A helpful tip for preparing agendas—particularly more detailed ones—is to look at previous copies, which will help you decide on the appropriate style and format. The descriptions of the separate items and the supplementary documentation often originate in separate departments and require some coordination in pulling together the information. Estimate the time you'll need for preparation so that the agenda can be printed and distributed before the meeting. As you plan more meetings, keep detailed files so that you have documentation to which you can return. Templates also can be helpful for frequently held meetings.

Here are two examples of a simple agenda.

Agenda for Monthly Staff Meeting
January 15, 200_

SCHEDULE	EVENT	PLACE
9:30 a.m.	Call to Order	Suite 1215
	Old Business	
	Read Minutes of Last Meeting	
	Committee Reports	
10:00 a.m.	New Business	Suite 1221

	1. Peter Spinella—
	   Demonstration of New Computer
	   System for Accounting	

	2. Ravi Dalal— Overlooked Markets	
Noon	President's Report	Suite 1221
1:00-2:00 p.m.	Lunch	Suite 1232

Daily Agenda for a Conference
Monday, February 15, 200_

SCHEDULE	EVENT	PLACE
9:00 a.m.-Noon	Letitia Johnson, Philip Boyle	Harrison Rm
	Our New Line of Software	
Noon-1:00 p.m.	Informal Discussion	Harrison Rm
1:00-2:30 p.m.	Lunch Dorotea Chavez Dealing with Executive Stress: New Techniques	Sky Terrace

Tuesday, February 16, 200_

SCHEDULE	EVENT	PLACE
9:00-11:00 a.m.	Ben Isaacs, Ginny Williams	Columbia Rm
	Hardware: Old and New	
11:35-1:00 p.m	Plenary	Wintergreen Rm
	George Takahashi and Martin Snow Management Systems for Small Companies	
1:15-2:30 p.m.	Lunch	Sky Rm
	Karen Trainer Businesses Run by Women	

Typical Simple Agendas

TELECONFERENCE AND VIDEO CONFERENCES

With today's leaner budgets and widespread staff and customers, companies often choose teleconferences or videoconferences as alternates to face-to-face meetings. A teleconference is simply a multiway phone meeting. Local phone companies or voiceconferencing services can provide teleconferencing within minutes by patching a third party into a conversation. Private branch exchange

TIPS FOR MAKING THE MOST OF A MEETING

- Remember, the purpose of any meeting is to communicate.

- Determine whether a formal or an informal format would facilitate communication—a formal format ensures greater organization and closer attention, and an informal format ensures more opportunity for brainstorming and creativity.

- Include only those people who are directly affected by the information you have to communicate.

- Try to keep the number of people in attendance to fewer than ten whenever possible.

- Hold meetings that include everyone and that cover a large range of topics quarterly or on an as-needed basis.

- Discuss three topics at the most in a single meeting, if possible.

- Hold more shorter meetings that cover fewer topics.

- Prepare an agenda—even if the meeting is an informal one.

- Designate a chairperson to keep things on track—even if the meeting is an informal one. The person calling the meeting is usually regarded as the *de facto* chairperson.

- Open the meeting in a friendly, congenial manner.

- Make eye contact with the participants, especially if you're speaking.

- Pay attention to your body language.

- Maintain a professional tone of voice.

- Clearly state the topic or problem.

- Make any presentations succinctly and get directly to the point.

- Guest speakers should speak for a maximum of 20 minutes, unless the meeting is a seminar.

- Listen to all viewpoints carefully.

- Utilize a white board or flip chart to track the discussion visually.

- Ensure that all views are expressed.

- Utilize techniques of constructive criticism.

- Accept comments and criticism in a professional manner.

- Keep disagreements on a professional instead of personal level.

- Maintain control of your emotions.

- Be sure to clear up any misunderstandings as they occur. Remember, a meeting's true purpose is to communicate.

- Set a time limit for the meeting and stick to it.

- Select a time for a follow-up meeting or second session, if necessary, before dismissing everyone.

(PBX) systems also can merge several lines. Although some teleconferencing calls must be operator-assisted, technology provides for complete automation in many cases, with callers using a special toll-free number and a password. Meetings can be set up so that either all callers participate, or only a few do while many more listen in. Teleconferences also can be easily recorded for transcription for those unable to attend.

Teleconferencing is popular for many reasons beyond the obvious cost savings over travel. Telephones are easy and not intimidating to use, and conferences can be set up within minutes. On the other hand, if the equipment is older or if standard speakerphones are used, voices can echo or create feedback; it's also necessary that only one person speak at a time or the other conversation will be clipped. In addition, participants must deal with the artificiality of group conversations aimed at a single point, confusion about who is talking unless speakers identify themselves, and the lack of visual cues and body language. Frequent teleconferences and familiarity with the other parties help avoid some of this limitations, as does advanced teleconferencing technology, which accommodates a more normal back-and-forth flow of conversation, including overlapping voices. Headsets and handsets provide the participants with their own microphones so that a crowd need not cluster around one point. Customized conferencing phones with special microphones and speakers also are available.

Videoconferences combine the audio benefits of teleconferences with images of the participants, either in full motion or in freeze-frame. This currently involves special technology because of the need to match up the hardware and software compatibility of each participant. Rather than purchase the expensive and always-changing equipment, many companies rent time by the hour in videoconference centers. However, the technology already exists to change any PC equipped with a video camera into a videoconferencing unit, which allows for spontaneous meetings. One exciting possibility is the creation of virtual meetings, in which participants actually will perceive the other attendees as being in the same room as themselves.

Despite the advantages of being able to see the speaker, many people are camera-shy and are reluctant to have themselves filmed. As with teleconferencing, the method sometimes can feel forced, particularly if participants have never met. Watching a single talking head on a screen can be as removed and boring as watching a dull newscast.

Methods to increase the effectiveness of both teleconferences and videoconferences are similar to producing more effective face-to-face meetings. Having the participants meet beforehand at some point is very helpful. Handouts, slides, and other graphics for all ends increases involvement, as does carefully planned use of questions to participants, small group discussions, group problem solving, and other regular meeting strategies.

MINUTES

The request "Take the minutes" can cause even experienced office professionals to hesitate. In the old days, *minutes* meant shorthand and a word-for-word account of the entire meeting. Because shorthand is required less frequently today, office professionals wonder how they'll ever keep up when asked to take the minutes now. In addition, the formality of minutes with their suggestion of legal overtones still seems to demand absolute word-for-word accuracy.

Although meetings of any significance require minutes, all this really entails is a point-by-point record of what happened during the meeting. Accuracy and completeness are necessary because the minutes might later be used as evidence to settle legal or tax disputes, but these qualities are trademarks of top office professionals anyway.

The first step in taking the minutes is to look at those for previous meetings; the hard copies are usually kept loose in a ring binder to be bound into volumes later. Each book contains a copy of the corporation's charter and bylaws at the beginning, followed by the minutes. Study these minutes for tone and style, the type of matters that come up during meetings, and the format used by your company.

Follow the format for capitalization, indentation, use of captions, and line spacing. Generally, an inch-and-a-half margin on all sides of every page is used, with double-spaced text and triple-spacing between separate points. Materials that are read into the minutes, such as letters or documents, are single-spaced; resolutions are single-spaced and indented. Numbers, including sums of money, are written in words first, with the numbers following in parentheses.

Although the format itself is strict, there's nothing inherently legal in minutes, so formats do vary slightly from company to company. It's possible to suggest reducing double- and triple-spacing to single- and double-spacing to save paper, or to suggest other changes that seem economical and reasonable.

The contents of most minutes begin with the meeting's time and place, a statement that the meeting was properly called with advance notice given (get a copy of the notice given), and the names of the chairperson and secretary (as well as the attendees). Key people who did not attend—in a directors' meeting, for example—are noted; stockholders should be noted, whether present in person or by proxy. If attendees come late or leave early, mention the names and the point at which they came or left because their absences during certain discussions or votes might later become important. State whether the minutes of the last meeting were read and approved or corrected, or whether the reading was waived. For these initial points, the language from previous minutes usually can be copied with only the pertinent changes made.

After this standard opening, note each item on the agenda as it is addressed in the meeting, plus items not on the agenda that spontaneously come up. For the most part, this is not a word-for-word transcription of the meeting; it is a summary of the points made and by whom, as well as a neutral interpretation of the feelings expressed. So, although an attendee might bang a desk and yell, "You're crazy. This idea will never work," the minutes might read, "Committee head Robert Green strongly disagreed with the proposal." Decisions are set down as resolutions; resolutions and motions must be recorded word for word. If you don't hear something clearly, it's acceptable and even desirable for you to interrupt the proceedings and ask to have a statement repeated.

Even so, meetings in general often can have vague conclusions. If you're not quite sure what happened or what was decided upon after the meeting, talk to the chairperson to make sure that your record is accurate. In any case, try to type up the minutes as soon as possible, while your memory is freshest. Occasionally, minutes must be corrected when they're read at a subsequent meeting. This is not necessarily a reflection on your accuracy—people might remember events differently. Put a single red line through the incorrect statement so that it still can be read, and insert the new one between the lines (a reason for double-spacing if minutes tend to be frequently corrected). If a substantial part of the minutes must be corrected, cross out the original in red, keep the original page, and then include a separate new page with the corrected version.

After a meeting or conference, you might have to distribute copies of the minutes to the attendees on paper or via e-mail, depending on the company's practice.

TIME MANAGEMENT

When surveyed about workplace concerns, office professionals list the following: handling stress, reducing paperwork, keeping up with ever-changing software, improving human relations, reading faster, and comprehending better. However, almost without exception, the single topic that appears most often on their lists is *time management*.

Some office professionals can deal with a tremendous workload within the normal working day without appearing frazzled. They rarely need to stay late to catch up on correspondence, get out a critical mailing, meet a deadline, or develop a training plan. As the popular saying goes, it's not that they work harder—they work smarter.

The key to working smarter is time management. This is both a skill and a discipline, but it can be mastered and can yield many benefits. Effective control and use of time can restore confidence and job satisfaction—and ultimately even help the office professional advance his or her career.

Effective time management begins with a few basic strategies regarding habits and overall working patterns. Concrete tools, such as planners and calendars, also can help organize the day more efficiently.

BASIC TIMESAVING STRATEGIES

No one best way exists to save time. What's best is what actually works for you, your work habits, and your job. The following strategies, however, do seem to be successful with many different types of people and activities. See which of these you can adapt to your own situation.

Analyze the Way You Use Time Now

Before you can draw up meaningful rules for streamlining your performance and managing your time, you must diagnose the specific problems that plague you. In short, try to determine how your time is now being spent, and then decide whether it is being used to the best advantage in each instance. After this analysis, you'll be able to plan how to make better use of your time in the future.

Just as a research-oriented employer might bring in a time-study expert to watch employees in action, you must watch *yourself* in action. Keep a log of your daily expenditure of time. To do this, jot down your activities every half-hour for a period of two weeks. Then study the log and focus on recurring items that cause you to use time inefficiently. Are they repeated interruptions by staff members that you're training? Frequent visits from co-workers who want to socialize? Numerous periods of waiting for the busy executive to return to the office to answer your questions?

With the patterns apparent, you will find it easier to change habits, draw up a more effective schedule, and eliminate wasted time.

Ask: "Is This the Best Use of My Time *Right Now?*"

Besides writing down activities as they are performed, ask yourself at several points during each day, "Is this the best use of my time *right now?*" If you have to arrange a meeting, but you're politely smiling through a coworker's third folder of vacation photos, the question can bring you back into focus. Get into the habit of asking it of yourself frequently and then—if the answer is *no*—do what *is* the most profitable use of your time at the moment.

This same question can be applied to groups of activities when you're trying to prioritize: "*Which* is the best use of my time?" Another way to phrase it is: "If I had time to do only *one* of these things, which should it be?" Together, these questions repeatedly should lead you to the most important, most profitable activity.

Sometimes, however, when you ask yourself this question, you might be in the middle of a routine duty (such as filing or delivering mail). Although these tasks might not be the most profitable use of your time, you really cannot choose between writing up a procedures manual and filing: Both must be done. Accomplishing both in the most effective manner is another element of time management.

Learn How to Delegate

Few situations are more frustrating than an executive who refuses to delegate responsibility to an office professional who is eager, qualified, and competent. When this executive at last enrolls in a time-saving seminar, learning how to delegate is one of the first lessons he or she will learn.

Are you guilty of the same behavior, clinging to every chore as if each one were of equal importance? Is it really necessary for you to photocopy agendas, staple newsletters, or run envelopes through a postage meter? Are clerical assistants available for such tasks? Assuming that help is available, executive office professionals should learn how to delegate. Properly trained, most assistants will be able to take over routine duties, freeing you for those tasks that you and only you were hired to do. This also frees you to take on even greater responsibilities, which, hopefully, the executive will in turn have delegated to you.

> **TIP:** When delegating to assistants, do not give them only the worst and most boring of your tasks; assign jobs that make delegation worthwhile to *them*. After all, you hope for the same consideration from the executive.

Live with a Schedule

Another useful step in time-saving organization is a daily schedule.

Of course, individual assignments will make it necessary to vary routines, but a general schedule for each day can be helpful. Here's a sample schedule.

Within that schedule, variations always will come up. Vendors might not come every day, and meetings don't always end when lunchtime is supposed to begin. You'll face coffee breaks, emergencies, and days you're working through a cold. Nevertheless, those office professionals who are guided in general by a flexible schedule often find they have extra minutes each day to accomplish the tasks they need to complete.

```
 9:00-9:30 a.m.      —Play back telephone messages; sort and deliver
                       mail; file
 9:30-10:00 a.m.     —Transcribe executive's taped notes
10:00-10:30 a.m.     —Executive's correspondence
10:30-11:00 a.m.     —Personal correspondence, follow-up memos
11:00-12:00 p.m.     —Take meeting minutes; transcribe them
12:00-12:45 p.m.     —Lunch
12:45-1:30 p.m.      —Meet with vendors; review written bids
 1:30-2:30 p.m.      —Make business calls; set up appointments;
                       respond to inquiries and complaints
 2:30-3:30 p.m.      —Staff training
 3:30-4:30 p.m.      —Make conference arrangements
 4:30-5:00 p.m.      —Meet with executive to discuss tomorrow's work
                       and changes to schedule
```

Sample Schedule

Know the Times You Work Your Best

A schedule enables the office professional to take advantage of his or her natural rhythms and to find the time of day for his or her own peak performance. Work is done faster when done at peak performance. In the previous example, the office professional is obviously not a morning person. As much quiet work as possible has been scheduled for the morning, while people contact has been scheduled for the afternoon.

Work with a "To Do" List

Going hand-in-hand with a daily schedule is the "to do" list, a compilation of outstanding matters that require the office professional's attention. A typical "to do" list might include the following:

- Write to the new sales rep.

- Call the service company about the copy machine.

- Order office supplies.

- Write and place a help-wanted ad for a clerk-typist.

- Call DHL for pickup of the letter to the Bangkok office.

- Confirm Ms. Behrman's night flight to Atlanta with Delta Airlines.

- Research dining etiquette for Ms. Behrman's Thailand trip next month.

- Order business cards for Ms. Behrman and self.

- Follow up on memo to marketing.

- Draw up the guest list for the retirement party.

The "to do" list should be drawn up at the start of the week, should be reviewed daily, and should be updated as progress is made.

Some tasks on the list, such as a phone call, will take five minutes; some will be multistep challenges, such as reviewing the minutes of all unit meetings for the previous year and preparing an executive summary. In addition, some tasks require immediate attention; others are long-range in nature.

After drawing up the "to do" list, group the routine tasks that can be promptly accomplished in one column; group the more complex and time-consuming tasks in another column. The tasks in each column can be prioritized so that the more important ones and/or the ones to which the executive gives greater weight appear at the top. Also divide the larger tasks into smaller parts, and do one part at a time.

Don't put every single activity of the day onto your list, just for the sake of crossing them off. Include only the important items that *must* be done and the items you're likely to forget if they're not in writing. Some people advocate limiting such a list to no more than the three most important jobs of each day so that the list doesn't seem overwhelming. Do what works for you.

Learn to Say "No"

The office professional naturally wants to cooperate not only with the executive but also with coworkers. This cooperation sometimes can lead to problems if the office professional takes on others' responsibilities and becomes so overburdened that his or her own work suffers.

For example, suppose your coworker Jack surfs the Web all day. As a result, he doesn't have enough time to complete an important assignment, so he asks for your help. This is not the first time this has happened. Although fellow employees should pitch in and help each other, this has become a case of your good nature and willingness to work being taken advantage of. You might say (in your sincerest voice), "Jack, I'm sorry, but I'm too busy with my own assignments to help you out again. Should I talk to Ms. Behrman about how over-scheduled you are?" This tactfully lets you say no without lecturing Jack about his misuse of the Internet, thus keeping relations between you cordial. It also should prevent Jack from asking you again because he will not want you to go to bat for him to Ms. Behrman, who will probably then want to know why he can't get his work done on his own.

As another example, suppose Ms. Behrman asks you to shop for her daughter's birthday present, return a purchase for a credit, pick up theater tickets, and so on. She tells you to take a two-hour lunch, to leave the office an hour early, or to punch in an hour late tomorrow as compensation. If this will make you late on projects, you might say, "Ms. Behrman, I'm always happy to help you out. My one question is that you also wanted the sales figures from the fourth quarter by nine o'clock tomorrow. Should I postpone the figures until a later time?" Now the executive will either see where the better use of your time lies or extend your deadline.

Handle Paper Only Once

One of the most frustrating—and time-consuming—elements of paperwork is the number of times each piece of paper is picked up. You read a memo and don't quite know what to do with it, so you set it down to make a decision later. When later comes, you have to re-read the memo to refresh your memory. And this is just a simple example. Some documents are handled four, five, or six times before they leave your desk.

The best way to handle paper is to deal with it quickly and to deal with it only once. You have nothing to gain from reading every word of every document, or from reading mail or a memo and then putting off action until a later time only to have to re-read it to refresh your memory. Just determine the importance of the paper the first time you handle it, and then immediately do one of four things: Take action, pass it on, file it, or throw it out. Don't keep it on your desk, where it's subject to multiple handling.

Avoid Interruptions

Often, a steady swirl of people winds around the office professional's desk, which naturally leads to both needless questions and socializing. The placement of your office furniture can help reduce both. A person who can be seen from the hallway is often the one who is interrupted. Consider moving your desk, if your situation permits it, to prevent direct eye contact with passersby.

Another source of interruptions is people who repeatedly ask the same questions. It may be well worth the time to write up a simple set of directions for these people and have them photocopy it for their own reference.

Of course, for some people, it's their job to be interrupted—the receptionist, for example. In all fairness, these necessary interruptions should be taken into account when other duties are assigned. However, if no receptionist is present, the first person encountered on entering the office—no matter what his or her title is—will end up filling that role and will be forced to deal with visitors, salespeople, deliveries, and so on. This situation must be addressed. The "front desk" could be made a rotating position, an official receptionist could be hired, or the front door could be locked and visitors buzzed in only when they have an appointment and have been identified by an intercom.

Don't forget the times when you interrupt yourself by making or taking personal phone calls. Try to limit these to lunchtime. Besides being time-eaters, personal calls are much more obvious to others than the caller assumes and can be detrimental to career growth.

Keep Your Desk Neat and Clean

An office professional should have a clean and orderly desk for many reasons: It makes a good impression on visitors and staff. It reflects well on the executive. It also is much easier and less distracting to work on the task at hand than if a dozen other assignments are sitting on the desk at the same time.

Another important reason for neatness is the countless time spent each week looking for something that's lost on a cluttered desk. This lost time spent searching for misplaced notes, files, or messages can never be retrieved. Use temporary file folders for the materials you're currently working on until they are ready to be filed in the central system.

MANAGE THE EXECUTIVE EFFICIENTLY

Though it's not often thought of in these terms, the time-savvy office professional also must learn how to manage the executive. Too much time is lost when the executive and the office professional are not working in synchronization. You waste time pulling multiple files for a meeting that the executive rescheduled, you make multiple phone calls only to discover that the executive already has called personally, and so on.

First thing every morning (or last thing every night), sit down with the executive to discuss what needs to be done next, which changes have been made in appointments and schedules, and what your own priorities and deadlines for the upcoming day are. Your strategies for managing time and the executive's strategies for managing time must be a team effort for either of you to be successful.

Tools for Time Management

Many products on the market today can help office professionals and executives manage their time more effectively. Some of these products are varieties of calendars, and some are types of worksheets for individual projects. Together with multicolored pens and markers, these tools can be very useful for gaining better control of time. They gather key information—from frequently called phone numbers, to a list of who's doing what on a project—into one place that can be grasped with just a single glance. Planners also can be used to track the amount of time spent on each project, which is invaluable for pricing what a project really costs and deciding whether it's worth doing again in the same way.

Software finally has helped resolve the issue of keeping two separate calendars (one for the office professional and one for the executive), with each inevitably having different appointments and tasks. Networked scheduling systems enable both the office professional and the executive to work from the same calendar so that each can see what the other has added or changed.

Wall and Day Planners

Day planners are the basic calendar tool: You write assignments inside a portable daily calendar. These planners might have a page for each day or, if not many notes are needed, a week to each double-page spread. Most people often write down only the due date of an upcoming job. But this is a bad way to jog

CALENDAR TIME

The early Roman calendar was based on the lunar month of 29½ days, and it had 354 days. But the solar year (the time it takes the Earth to circle the sun) is about 365½ days. The Romans added an extra month from time to time to bring the calendar into agreement with the seasons.

A more consistent calendar was instituted by Julius Caesar in 46 B.C. Its year had 365 days, with an extra day added in February every fourth year (leap year). The Julian calendar set the length of a month at 30 or 31 days, except for February.

By 1582, the calendar again was out of sync with the seasons. In October of that year, Pope Gregory XIII dropped ten days from the calendar to correct the error that had accumulated. To keep the error from recurring, the Gregorian calendar includes a leap year every fourth year, except in those centesimal years that can be divided by 400. Many countries adopted the new calendar at once, but Great Britain and its American colonies waited until 1752. Sometimes, two dates are specified for an early event: "Old Style" means the Julian calendar and "New Style" means the Gregorian calendar.

A year is divided into 12 months, 52 weeks, or 365 days (except in a leap year, which has 366 days):

Months with 31 Days		*Months with 30 Days (or Less!)*	
January	31 days	February	28 days
March	31 days	April	30 days
May	31 days	June	30 days
July	31 days	September	30 days
August	31 days	November	30 days
October	31 days		
December	31 days		

one's memory: When the day is actually here, it's too late to be reminded that the work is due. A more effective use of day planners is to break large jobs into smaller parts, to give yourself due dates for each, and to write them down. Write reminders of the coming due dates several days ahead of time so you'll know how you're progressing. And don't forget a starting date: Make an appointment for when you actually will begin a specific task.

If you're not quite sure how a job will be broken down, first brainstorm on a piece of scratch paper, and then copy the results to the planner. This minimizes cross-outs and squeezed-in notes. Even so, on a project you might want to use a pencil because Step A and Step B invariably become Step A1, Step A2, Step A3, and then finally Step B.

Also use planners to schedule an appointment with yourself. These extra hours of free time sprinkled throughout the week provide opportunities to catch up on unfinished business, do specific jobs, or just catch your breath. Don't simply promise yourself you will leave Friday morning from ten to eleven free; write down the appointment, or the time will disappear.

Just as you might add birthdays and anniversaries to a personal calendar, add to your planner any significant recurring business events. You might have never missed handing in the updated quarterly budget report—yet. It takes just minutes to add this routine to the calendar, and it can save you work and embarrassment later.

Keep your "to do" list in the day planner as well. At the end of each day, look at the planner, note the tasks you finished, and mark them off. Seeing each crossed-off item gives you concrete proof of how much you actually achieved that day. Then plan for the next day, making whatever notes and changes are needed. A simple way to prioritize the next day's list is to ask, "What would happen if I don't do *this*?" Prioritize according to consequences.

Use the executive's day planner to track travel and entertainment expenses; some planners come with handy pockets to hold the receipts. The executive need only turn the whole thing over to you at the end of a trip.

Because of its portability, a day planner is an excellent place for you to write down personal goals. The act of writing something down automatically gives the thing more importance in the mind; no longer just a wish, it has its own life and constitutes its own reality. Write down goals frequently until you achieve them.

Wall planners are ideal for larger projects that have interim deadlines (whether assigned or imposed by you) or that are multifaceted in other ways. Wall planners are also useful when whole jobs or pieces of jobs have been delegated to different individuals. Each person's separate progress can be noted on the planner; use a different color pen for each person for easy tracking.

Appointment Calendars

Perhaps the most important thing for the office professional to keep in mind regarding appointment calendars is that your calendar and the executive's always should agree. Changes in the one must be marked on the other as soon as possible. Not having identical appointment calendars is a frequent complaint of office professionals, one that must be addressed to the executive in straightforward terms. Because it is almost always the executive who has gone ahead and made changes without saying anything, it's usually the office professional's time that is lost. This can become a serious problem—one that not only wastes time unnecessarily, but also that can threaten the sense of teamwork that the executive and office professional need.

As mentioned before, software calendars that can be accessed by both the office professional and the executive can offer a solution to this problem.

Project Planners and Flowcharts

Rather than being keyed into the yearly calendar, project planners focus on a specific piece of work. They track a project from the initial planning stages until its very end, breaking down the elements as work progresses. Use color coding for each person involved in a project; you also might find it useful to break down the type of work by color as well.

Flowcharts can be an enormous timesaver, even though they function differently from calendar-type tools. A flowchart is a schematic tracking of a process. The simplest example is a family tree, which is a schematic tracking of a family name over time. A flowchart tracks a particular job or project. Where does the task originate? Where does it end? What are the many steps along the way? Each time a job changes hands, it should be noted on the flowchart.

The timesaving benefit of making a flow chart is that when you see how a piece of work is actually routed, patterns become more obvious. It's easier to see which steps take the longest or create a bottleneck, which steps duplicate each other, or which steps can be eliminated. A flowchart also presents a broad picture of how the separate elements of a group relate to each other.

Software programs are available for ready-to-use flow charts or to help in designing your own.

FOR MORE INFORMATION

If you can't find what you need from the phone numbers and Web sites listed in this chapter, you may need to expand your search.

- For more information on meeting planning, check your local library or bookstore for books. Meeting planning titles will most likely be found in the business/management section. Or search www.amazon.com with the keywords "meeting planning."

- For more information on time management, check your local library or bookstore in the self-help section.

- For more information on conference supplies and corporate give away items, check the Yellow Pages under "promotions". Marketing or promotional companies will be able to help you get these.

- For more information on shipping materials, see chapter 4.

9

HUMAN RESOURCES

◆

■ **Organizational Structures and Charts**

■ **Hiring a New Employee**

Deciding on the New Job

Handling Resumes and References

Finding Job Candidates

Interviewing

Advertising the Position

Preparing for a New Employee

■ **Training and Supervising Employees**

Performance Reviews

Firing

Discipline

Severance

Scheduling

Unemployment

■ **Employee Rights and Responsibilities**

Sexual Harassment

The Americans with Disabilities Act

Workplace Violence

The Family and Medical Leave Act

Diversity

■ **Benefits**

Health Benefits

Pay for Time Not Worked

Insurance

Employee Services

Retirement Plans

■ **Etiquette**

Dealing with Office Politics

Gift Giving

Dress

Dating

Invitations

Congratulations and Condolences

Parties and Social Functions

■ **For More Information**

Effective *human resources,* also known as personnel management, is the basis for a happy office and successful employees. Without employees, companies simply don't exist. Although the current strides in technology have greatly changed the way we do business and have reduced the time required for many tasks, no amount of technology will ever replace the presence and abilities of people in the office. Even as technology makes our workday easier, however, it also presents new challenges and increases expectations in areas such as productivity, personal service, and quality. Coupled with more time constraints, the challenge to ensure that staff is qualified, content, and well-cared for has never been greater. To address this, the science of human resources is evolving to meet the changes in the American workplace. Innovations, tips, and standards for creating a productive workplace continue to be created and revised, and many of these are discussed in detail here.

ORGANIZATIONAL STRUCTURES AND CHARTS

You can get a better perspective of your own company's human resources if you look at its organizational chart. Within companies, organizational charts serve as an invaluable tool to help understand reporting relationships, manage workflow effectively, and maintain good communications. During reorganizations, they enable the planners to better understand the way the organization currently operates and the impact that changes may have on current communications or workflow. Companies are structured to maximize productivity and performance, and organizational charts, correctly done, can provide both new employees and existing ones with clear direction about whom to consult on a specific matter and how to get information or assistance with a problem or project.

Office professionals may not plan the original organizational charts, but they often are asked to update them and/or oversee review and approval of the final charts prior to their distribution—which is also a charge they frequently are given.

If you are asked to do one of these tasks, know that you can get help from one of a number of software programs. The most popular is actually PowerPoint, which contains standard templates you can use. To do the work, you need to know the following:

■ The source of information. Whether it is a new chart or revisions to an old one, you need to have one resource to whom you can go, should questions arise about the accuracy of the chart. This person should also review the final draft prior to its distribution to the remainder of the organization.

- The number of levels within your organization that will be depicted on the chart. Some charts include all job titles and levels; others go only to the first supervisory level.

- Whether the chart will reflect both formal and informal (dotted line) relationships.

> **TIP:** When putting on paper the organization of your company, it's important to realize that the chart depicts the formal structure of your company, not necessarily the interactions that occur daily in your organization as work is accomplished.

HIRING A NEW EMPLOYEE

One human resources responsibility is hiring new employees. Most people think of hiring only as the interview, but there is more to it than that. Rather, recruitment begins when you determine the need for someone—whether a replacement upon loss of a staff member or addition of a new position. The process doesn't end until someone has been chosen to fill the position. Some human resource authorities would say that recruitment isn't completed until a new hire has been oriented to the employer.

As you can see, hiring isn't a single step but rather a process, and office professionals will often be involved in it. They will be the individuals who process much of the paperwork associated with recruitment. As their responsibilities grow, they increasingly are also finding themselves developing the paperwork, conducting the interviews, and making the final selection of a candidate.

DECIDING ON THE NEW JOB

When you begin the hiring process, it's unwise to work with past documentation without giving careful consideration to your current needs. The earlier description may no longer reflect the work as done by the former job holder, or it may be time to rethink how the work should be done and the qualifications of the person you need to do the tasks.

Staff Requirements

Are staff positions required to effectively and efficiently handle the workload? Would alternatives such as overtime, temporary staff, or outsourcing be a more cost-effective solution? Often, when workloads increase, the situation can be addressed with more temporary solutions or a redistribution of duties among existing employees.

Job Descriptions

Job descriptions should include specific functions, required duties, and the tools needed to fulfill the expectations of the position. The job description should also include a measurable method of evaluating the success of the employee. The job description should clearly define what each job contributes to the organization as a whole and should be reevaluated and updated, with the employee's input, at least once a year.

Look at the past job description. If one does not exist, sit down and develop one, identifying not only the responsibilities the job will entail but also the qualifications for the position and the measures by which the job holder will be evaluated.

Consider the reporting structure. How does the position relate and contribute to other jobs within the firm? What level of supervision will the position require? It is important to take into account the workload requirements of each position before assigning direct reports, because time spent on the functions of the position may preclude an employee from being able to effectively manage other employees.

FINDING JOB CANDIDATES

Finding and hiring new employees tops the list of unpleasant, difficult, and time-consuming tasks for most offices. The time and effort involved in screening and interviewing candidates can be disruptive in the office, and, if you're having trouble finding the right person, it can be just plain frustrating. The more critical it is to find and hire someone, the more pressure is felt—particularly if, in this interim period, the existing staff has to assume the work in addition to their regular tasks. The time involved and amount of personal interaction is distasteful for both the potential employer and the employee. It's no wonder, then, that services such as personnel or recruiting firms (headhunters) and temporary services continue to grow at bounding rates. Rather than conduct your own screening, you may want to hire an outside firm to do your initial screening. Until you find someone, you may want to bring on board a temporary worker contracted from a temporary agency.

An interviewer may have to go through hundreds of resumes—in print and online—to identify ten to fifteen likely prospects for a job. Phone calls have to be made to interesting candidates to set up interviews; the telephone tag that often ensues can make even this phase time-consuming. Some interesting candidates may turn out to want higher salaries than you are able to pay or may lack critical qualifications and thus have to be eliminated. Good interviews take an hour or more for each candidate, and they are often conducted at lunch or after work to accommodate candidates who can come for an interview only

AGENCIES CAN LEND ASSISTANCE

Sometimes you will be working solely with your own human resources department to find a person to fill a vacancy; other times, you and your company will also have the aid of a recruitment agency. It will undertake the initial screening process, including advertising for the position for you. For a fee upon your selection of several possible candidates from those the agency has found, the agency will identify one or two candidates for you to meet. Thus, you save the time you might have had to spend in reviewing resumes or interviewing lots of candidates to identify the one or two likely ones.

Depending on the nature of the position you are trying to fill, you may want to give an agency exclusivity in finding someone for the position. If you have had good experiences with an agency, you may want to allow it exclusivity for two weeks or so. If it's not successful, then you may want to alert other agencies to help you in your search. That firm that identifies the candidate you hire gets its fee. Often the fee is calculated on the basis of the annual salary of the position to be filled.

Besides recruitment or placement agencies, there are also temporary agencies that will identify for you individuals for short-term assignments. This is a good option when your company has a short-term assignment, lasting a few days or a few months, but for economic or organizational reasons doesn't want to commit to a full-time staff member. The temporary agency should provide you with someone who meets your job needs in the same way that a placement firm would identify candidates for a full-time position. Some temporary agencies are willing to contract to provide temporary help that can become full-time if circumstances change or if you are extremely impressed with the individual's abilities and want to hire that person.

at these times because they already have a job. One of the most depressing aspects of interviewing is that you may finally identify a wonderful candidate and call to tell the person the good news, only to learn that the individual has taken a job elsewhere.

ADVERTISING THE POSITION

Because of their ability to reach a large number of potential applicants at a relatively low cost, newspaper ads remain one of the most common methods of external recruiting. Newspaper ads are also very versatile and can be used to recruit for all types of positions from unskilled to top managerial. Running your ad in the Sunday edition will generate the greatest response; avoid holiday weekends, however, since many people leave town and may miss your ad.

If cost is an issue, consider running the ad on a weekday and running a smaller, more concise ad. While a larger ad may seem to be more effective because it catches the applicant's eye, people do not respond on the basis of an ad's size. Also consider placing your ad in a trade journal to reach a more specific group of applicants. Be aware, however, that longer lead times are usually required and the ad can become dated.

The placement of the ad will be influenced by the nature of the position you are attempting to fill. If it's a technical position and there is a technical organization with a "positions available" column in its membership newsletter or journal, you may want to advertise there even if it will lengthen the time needed to fill the position. As you move up to senior management positions, you may want to supplement the ad in the employment section of your newspaper with an ad in the business section of the same newspaper. For some critical positions, if you are willing to pay relocation fees, you may want to advertise outside your geographical area. The more difficult the position you have to fill, the wider your search should be and the more money you may have to spend in advertising for suitable candidates.

> **TIP:** If you are located in a suburban locale, you may want to advertise not only in your own local newspaper but in newspapers from nearby metropolitan areas. You may find someone who is more willing to commute for your job.

You can choose from two types of ads:

- *Open ads.* In an open ad, the company name and address are included, as well as a contact person and a telephone or fax number, so that a direct response may be made. This type of ad will generate the greatest response and is particularly useful if your company has a recognizable name and a good reputation. You should, however, be prepared for a significant number of responses from unqualified applicants as well.

- *Blind ads.* In a blind ad, the company name is not listed, and responses to the ad are directed to a post office box or a box provided by the newspaper. This type of ad makes the responses much more manageable; however, it also decreases the number of responses. In addition, some qualified candidates may not respond to an unknown company.

JOBS ON THE INTERNET

Increasingly, companies are using the Internet to advertise job openings. Many ads provide an e-mail address for replies. Usually these are blind ads; the firms create a special e-mail address just for responses rather than give their identity. They may also set up a separate phone line or voice mail box to receive responses without identifying themselves. They may also take advantage of the many, many job boards that are growing on the web. For certain positions—like computer-related jobs—these postings make much more sense than an advertisement in a newspaper.

How Much Does It Cost?

Advertising in a newspaper isn't cheap. Rates are based on publication circulation; the larger a newspaper is, the higher the price you will have to pay. Of course, too, the wider the newspaper's distribution, the more likely it is that you will get many individuals from which to make your final selection. Most newspapers charge by the space—whether classified or display ads—rather than by the word. If you choose to identify your firm, you will have to provide your firm's logo. For a simple classified ad, you need only provide the copy for the ad. If you choose to pay the much higher price of a display ad in the business section of a newspaper, and you have a certain graphical idea in mind, you may want to provide artwork.

Whatever the medium or type of ad, use care when deciding what information you will include. At the minimum, the ad should state the type of position, required qualifications, method of response (phone, fax, P.O. box), and any information that should be forwarded, such as resume, salary history, and references. In addition, you may want to consider including in the ad a salary range, job location, identifying codes (if advertising for more than one position), and any other information you believe relevant to the position.

HANDLING RESUMES AND REFERENCES

Because the writer of a resume wants to gain your attention, he or she may exaggerate, omit negative information, and sometimes lie about his or her credentials. References are infrequently sent, but if you do receive any, you can expect that they will give a glowing report of the candidate's personality, work ethic, and qualifications. However, you shouldn't assume that the references are necessarily untrue. Just as you would investigate the facts in a resume during an interview with its writer, you will want to verify the facts in a reference.

This kind of investigation is unnecessary with every candidate, only those final candidates from whom you are making your final choice. Then it is imperative that you check resumes and references with an eye for implied and less-obvious indicators of the applicant's past.

During your search, you will receive resumes for several days, even weeks, after placing an advertisement. Give respondents about a week; then read those you have received and select five to ten candidates to screen either in person or via phone. Often a phone call will be sufficient to determine whether you want to see the candidate. If you have a human resources department, this initial screening can be handled by it.

You may want to label the resumes "A" (really interesting, most likely), "B" (maybe but some concerns), "C" (intriguing for some reason but unlikely to be worthy of consideration). Begin with the "As," then "Bs." If you find yourself at the "Cs," you may want to look at those resumes that have trickled in since you last screened the original stack, or you may want to extend your search, maybe even consider placing another advertisement. While reviewing resumes or references, you should pay particular attention to some of the following details:

- *Extended time between jobs.* This in itself is not necessarily indicative of a problem; however, it is important for an applicant to explain the gap, and you should, if possible, check the truthfulness of the explanation. Difficulty in finding a new position, being laid off, and taking time to return to school or care for a family member with an extended illness are all plausible explanations and should not deter an employer from considering a candidate for a position.

- *Glowing or excessively qualified reports.* It could be that you have uncovered the world's only perfect employee. However, if the employee's past history is excessively positive or fits the job qualifications perfectly, it's more likely that the candidate is selectively presenting one-sided information. When speaking about references, ask them for other contacts who may be able to provide further information.

- *Frequent job changes.* This may indicate a problem with the employee's work habits or ability to adjust within the work environment. It is important to request employer contacts and compare their stories with each other as well as with the applicant's version of why he or she left each position.

- *Vague, missing, or incorrect information.* It is not uncommon for applicants to be unable to provide some information; companies do close, people change jobs, and time may change some specifics without the applicant being aware. Some information, however, such as length of employment, salary, positions, and duties should be relatively stable. Depending on the disparity of the discrepancy, you may want to allow the applicant the option of providing corrected information before discounting him or her as a candidate. If further information is provided, it should always be checked.

INTERVIEWING

The process of interviewing has two sides. Even as the prospective employer should obtain as much information as possible regarding the applicant's ability to do the job and fit into the workplace, so too should the prospective employee use this opportunity to determine particulars of the job, such as the work level, hours, company personality, and his or her appropriateness for the position. There will be other issues, too, that prospective candidates

---

REFERENCES TODAY

Because of today's litigious environment, many firms discourage managers from giving references when they are asked for feedback on a former employee. The managers are told to refer the inquirer to human resources, where he or she may get only confirmation that the person did, indeed, work for the firm as indicated and may be told the circumstances under which the person left.

If you do get the chance to talk to a former supervisor, have a list of prepared questions that call for more than "yes" or "no" answers. For instance, you can ask the manager to describe the climate or culture of the company and ask how it was evident that the candidate fit within that climate. Then compare the climate described by the former supervisor to your current climate. If the job you have to fill demands someone who can juggle multiple assignments and work in a pressure-cooker environment, ask for examples of how the employee worked under pressure. Don't ask, "Can he work under pressure?" or, "Did she ever have any problems doing more than one task at one time?"

If a manager or another person has provided a written reference, you may want to call and ask for specifics about the glowing assessment. A personal reference is very different from a professional one, and is irrelevant unless it addresses some aspect of the job you are attempting to fill and there is no professional reference. If you can't check with a former employer, then you may want to talk to someone's professor or minister or rabbi about the candidate's trustworthiness and honesty if the person will be handling money or making decisions that could be self-serving.

BASIC INTERVIEW QUESTIONS

As the job of office professionals changes, they find themselves responsible for interviewing and making decisions about prospective hires. Here are some questions to consider:

Why do you wish to leave your current position?

What do you like most/least about your current position?

Which accomplishments are your greatest source of pride?

What is your educational/professional background?

Why does this position appeal to you?

Why are you the best candidate for this position?

What are your professional strengths/weaknesses?

What are your career goals?

What questions do you have for me?

---

may be looking at—some that we tend to ignore once we have worked at an organization over time, but that can influence a candidate's decision about working for you.

First impressions count. And not just from your perspective. Job candidates will be looking at your work space to decide if they want to work in your company. Ask yourself if you would work at your firm if you knew nothing about it except what you see; then look around you. Would a visitor to your office be turned off because it looked messy? You expect your candidates to come dressed professionally. What impression would you give, in turn, if you showed up in jeans, even if it was a dress-down day? What if you wanted a candidate to meet with others in your organization, but you asked the person to hang around for 15 minutes to a half hour to see someone because you hadn't prepared for this situation? It's these little details that can influence a prospective candidate's impression.

Other factors can help candidates have a successful interview experience with your company. If they are expected to meet with several people, help set up a schedule for them. Determine who will be responsible for getting them from appointment to appointment and try not to leave them alone for too long. The office professional can provide a very pivital role in the interview process, whether sending a quick e-mail to remind everyone that a candidate will be in or screening initial interviews for an executive.

Think of the candidates you will be interviewing as visitors, and prepare for their visit. This includes deciding in advance how you will conduct the

QUESTIONS TO AVOID

Usually, when a candidate arrives in the office for an interview, they will need to fill out a standard employment form. Make sure your form clearly states that questions or discussion on the following topics are strictly prohibited by antidiscrimination laws.

- Age
- Race
- Sex
- National origin
- Religion
- Credit record
- Marital status
- Parental status
- Sexual orientation
- Disabilities

interview. The three most common types of interviews are unstructured, structured, and panel.

Unstructured. In an unstructured interview, the interviewer has only a general idea of which topics to cover. Unstructured interviews enable both parties to focus on the areas that are specific to the individual being interviewed as well as allow them to interact on a more personal level. This type of interview is most appropriate when the personality of the interviewee is of paramount importance. For example, employees, such as receptionists, who will need to deal with the public on a constant basis, fall into this category. This type of interview, however, also provides the greatest opportunity to be swayed by the presentation of information, personal tastes and prejudices, and the interviewing skill of both parties.

For the most part, you will want to avoid unstructured interviews. Although they can give you insights into the character and personality of the candidate, they often give little information about previous job history or qualifications for the position you are attempting to fill.

Keep in mind that unless you are constantly alert in an unstructured interview, an articulate candidate can move the interview in directions that will show them only in a good light.

Structured. A structured interview resembles an oral questionnaire as the interviewer has a prepared list of questions he or she asks each interviewee.

This interview type, by its prepared nature, ensures consistency and minimizes personal interjection. Validation studies have shown that the patterned interview consistently predicts job success and is applicable for almost any position. You need to be a little flexible if you use this style, however. You should be willing to allow a candidate to lead the discussion for brief periods, and you should be willing to return to a comment by the candidate to get more insights.

Panel. Panel interviews require the participation of several individuals to interview the candidate at the same time. The panel members then discuss their impressions and reach a consensus regarding each interviewee. Panel interviews harvest the greatest amount of information on each candidate and allow for the least amount of personal influence. Panel interviews are, however, costly and time-consuming, and can make interviewees highly uncomfortable.

Note that as organizations move toward self-directed teams with responsibility for hiring new members, team-conducted interviews are occurring.

A version of a panel interview is one in which a candidate is interviewed separately by several members of the organization, rather than just the individual to whom the candidate would be reporting. Such an interview allows the company to get more than one person's perspective of the candidate. Usually the other individuals who participate would be peers of the new employee. Sometimes the person to whom the individual would report may ask his or her superior to meet with the final candidates in order to get a second view of them.

Which type of interview is preferable? There are benefits to be had in all three. You may want to choose the best from each. You might want to have a prepared list of questions that are critical to making a good hiring decision. On the other hand, you want to be flexible. If the candidate says something that interests you, you may want to pursue the issue unless you feel that the person is trying to distract you from another issue that would put him or her in a poor light. If so, after you have pursued the candidate's track, return to the original question that prompted the side trip.

If you aren't sure which of two candidates to choose or if you still have some doubts about an applicant, you may want to get a second opinion, either from a colleague or your own manager. Ask the candidate(s) back for a second interview with this other person.

In some cases, you will want others in your company to give their view of a candidate. If you want to conduct a panel interview, you may want to e-mail all likely participants to set up a schedule for a joint interview or a series of single interviews with your final applicant(s). The most important thing is to be sure that those with whom you want the applicant(s) to meet have sufficient advance notice.

PROS AND CONS OF TEMPORARY SERVICES

There are many benefits of temporary workers. Companies don't have to deal with the time, energy, and expense of hiring new employees, and some hard-to-find skills are more readily accessible through temporary agencies. Organizations often need extra help only for a limited time. Finally, in many instances, the hourly rate paid to temporary workers is less than what a full-time employee would have to be paid. For these reasons, over 3,000 agencies currently provide temporary employment for over 2.5 million people, representing a $3 billion industry. And that figure is growing.

Before hiring temps, however, your company should consider the dangers and drawbacks. Because they are placed and screened by their agencies, little, if any, information is provided regarding their skills and employment history. Often the temp who is sent may simply be the most available, not the most qualified. And because temps are employees of their respective agencies, a significant amount of control over their work habits is lost. Finally, as the name implies, temps have little or no reason to remain at an assignment when faced with a better employment prospect, and a significant amount of turnover is to be expected.

Here are a few considerations to keep in mind both when you call the agency and when the temp has arrived at your office:

- Tell the agency how long the position is needed. Do you need a data entry person for a week or an executive assistant for six months?

- Tell the agency whether it is a temp-to-perm situation. Some temp agencies get a commission if the person is hired and thus will send you a person looking for a permanent job. Other temps don't want permanent positions. Giving the agency this information in advance will prevent you from getting a person who doesn't want to stay.

- Make sure you gauge the amount of in-house training that the temp will need to the job length and the difficulty level. For example, you don't want to spend a lot of time training a temp if the job lasts only a week, or if the agency sends a different person every week. Let the agency know there is training involved.

- Make sure you monitor the performance of a temp. Remember, if the person isn't working out, you can call the agency and request another person. Of course, it's a two-way street and if the temp isn't happy, he or she can request reassignment also.

PREPARING FOR A NEW EMPLOYEE

Introducing a new employee immediately is imperative to making him or her feel comfortable and welcome in strange new surroundings. While generally it is the responsibility of the new employee's boss to make the introductions, when this is not possible, someone else, especially a co-worker, should take the responsibility. On the new employee's first day, wait until he or she is situated at his or her desk or office, then introduce yourself with a handshake, a smile, and a sincere "Welcome." It is also a good idea to tell the new employee where you sit and what your function is. Offer to take the employee around the office with a simple comment such as "Come on, I'll show you around."

Combine your introductions with a tour of the areas of the office with which the employee will come in frequent contact during the workday, including the kitchen area, restrooms, mailroom, and other facilities. Introduce the employee to his or her co-workers first, support staff second, and, if possible, executives last. When introducing the employee, include the function of both parties. For example, "John, I'd like for you to meet Bob Smith, our new director of marketing. Bob, this is John Anderson, our public relations manager." Avoid mentioning the person whom the new employee is replacing, since this can lead to embarrassment on the part of the new employee, as well as hostility or sadness from co-workers, depending on the circumstances surrounding the replacement.

After the tour, take the employee back to his or her work area. Take your leave with an offer of future assistance. For example, "I'm right over here. If you need anything, please don't hesitate to let me know." Remember that he or she will probably not be able to remember everyone's name or location at the office, so checking back periodically is a good idea. Above all, ensure that the employee feels comfortable and welcome.

You should prepare for the new employee before he or she arrives. Take a look at his or her workstation. Does the individual have all the supplies he or she will need the first week on the job? Has systems been notified that the person should be on the network? Has the switchboard been informed so that calls can be forwarded? Even more basic, if the job is new, does the desk have a phone and a computer and all other equipment the individual will need to get to work?

This kind of thinking is as applicable to the arrival of a temp as it is to a new hire. Most importantly, you want to set aside time in the morning to spend with the individual to review the job description and tasks and give him or her the first assignment. And you should be available for a few minutes at the end of the day to see how the individual has done.

If there are individuals you wish the new employee to know, you should schedule meetings prior to his or her arrival. Taking your new hire to lunch is another way to say, "Welcome aboard."

TRAINING AND SUPERVISING EMPLOYEES

Increasingly office professionals have to train coworkers as well as temps and interns. They may also have their own employees, such as assistants and temps, to supervise. These responsibilities are relatively new to many office professionals but are becoming more common, and all office professionals should be prepared to take them on.

It is the supervisor's responsibility to ensure that the employee grows professionally. Training and supervision are tools that can aid in this effort. The employee's supervisor should assign the training and determine the appropriate level of supervision.

The functions of training and supervision are both critical to the well-being of employees and employers. Unfortunately, these duties are too often pushed aside in the attempt to keep up with increasing workloads and a diminishing workforce. The ramifications of poorly trained and supervised employees are severe enough to endanger the future of the organization. It is imperative, therefore, to ensure that sufficient time, expertise, and importance be devoted to these areas.

PERFORMANCE REVIEWS

As you assume supervisory duties, one such duty will be providing feedback to those who report to you—even conducting performance reviews.

Performance reviews are an essential tool in determining how well an employee is doing his or her job. They provide the employee with valuable feedback about the areas in which he or she is excelling and also the areas that may need improvement. For the supervisor, this same information can be used to determine in which areas, if any, further training or closer supervision may be required. Performance reviews may also provide information on which an employer can determine promotions, raises, or bonuses as well as required corrective action and terminations.

For many office professionals, this responsibility represents a new and uncomfortable role—making judgments about others' work. Thus, it is important to keep in mind the positive goal of this task: providing feedback that the individual can use to perform his or her job better.

There are several different types of performance reviews; however, most require an accurate reflection of the job components and the criteria used for appraisal. The two most common are the subjective and the objective review.

- *Subjective reviews.* Subjective reviews evaluate the employee on personal attributes such as leadership, ability to work with others, and flexibility. These personal attributes are also referred to as *performance factors.* Subjective reviews are popular because their general nature allows companies to use the same form across all areas. They require little training to be effectively completed and give a clear picture of the employee's work habits. By their subjective nature, however, it is difficult to uniformly apply the same criteria to each employee, and personal feelings may distort the evaluation.

■ *Objective reviews.* Objective reviews evaluate specifically defined behaviors and quantifiable outcomes such as level of output, measurable tasks, and attendance. These reviews are often composed from employee feedback, and include objectives culled from the employee's job description. These reviews are popular because of their effectiveness in evaluating actual job performance. However, the time and the effort involved in creating and applying them are substantial, and as a result, they are often incorrectly applied, or avoided altogether.

DISCIPLINE

Disciplining employees is never a pleasant task. Through effective supervision and open communication, most problems can be resolved before they ever reach the stage of punitive action. Situations do arise, however, that require direct address, even in the best-run organizations. This process is known as the *corrective action process* and involves four steps.

1. Oral warning

2. First written warning

3. Final written warning

4. Termination

When addressing these situations, it is important to remember several things:

■ Always explain the disciplinary action in private so that you do not embarrass the employee.

■ Focus on the problem or behavior rather than the employee or the employee's personality.

■ Keep an open mind and listen carefully to the employee's comments and explanations.

■ Sincerely offer your support and help to rectify the problem.

If you are relatively new at applying discipline, it is best to go by corporate rules. Talk to your own supervisor to ensure that you are clear about corporate policy in issuing discipline; then follow that policy closely. Here are some general guidelines.

When administering an oral warning, explain the situation and its ramifications as they affect the company's well-being. Ask for the employee's input, and attempt to discover any underlying problems or situations you may not be aware of that may be contributing to the situation. Ensure that the employee is clear on all points, and seek his or her commitment to correct the problem.

If, after a reasonable amount of time, no improvement is visible, the first written warning is in order. The first written warning is the first official documentation of a problem, and can be used by both parties in later disputes or legal action. Take care, therefore, to fully document all aspects of the problem and the ramifications. Also document the fact that an oral warning has already been provided. Detail the expected improvement of the situation, the benchmarks that will determine the improvement, and the time frame in which this improvement is expected. Provide a space for the employee to sign acknowledging receipt of the warning as well as a space for his or her comments or rebuttal. Provide a copy for the employee and one for his or her personnel file.

If the problem persists, the final written warning is in order. The final written warning should contain the same information as the first written warning, but with the additional information that the employee has received a first written warning and that failure to rectify the situation will result in termination.

SCHEDULING

While most scheduling is a direct result of the requirements of the office, some flexibility in scheduling should exist. Creative and alternative scheduling can be implemented to accommodate the special needs of employees. By doing this, an employer can reduce lateness and absenteeism as well as boost the morale of employees. Three of the most popular approaches to alternative scheduling—flextime, the compressed workweek, and time-sharing—are discussed next.

Flextime

Of the three types of alternative scheduling, flextime is the most common approach. An employee works a required number of hours during an established time period and then has the flexibility to make up the remaining hours at his or her discretion. For example, the employee must be at the office between the hours of 11:00 A.M. and 3:00 P.M.; however, the balance of the eight-hour workday can be covered either before 11:00 A.M. or after 3:00 P.M.

Compressed Workweek

The compressed workweek is gaining in popularity and involves determining the required number of hours that must be worked per week and then compressing these hours into a set number of days (usually four). For example, a forty-hour workweek compressed into four days would require the employee to work ten hours per day for four days, rather than the standard eight-hour day over a five-day period. Other variations involve a two-week cycle of nine-hour days followed by a three-day weekend.

Time-sharing

Some office professionals share either their jobs or their offices, or both, with a second person. Individuals may come to the same workstation on alternate days, working at home in between. Neither one has to work in the office every day, and each can work at home effectively given new office technology.

FIRING

One of the most distasteful jobs you may have to perform is to fire someone. In cases involving ongoing problems, termination is unfortunately the only option available after disciplinary and other supervisory options have been exhausted.

Employees can be fired for any number of reasons. As a general rule, however, most terminations can be grouped into one of two categories:

1. Ongoing problems that have been brought to the employee's attention a number of times without satisfactory improvement or change. Terminating an employee in this case is the final step in what is known as the *corrective action process.*

2. Immediate termination for gross misconduct. Actions that would prompt this type of firing include being physical violent; being under the influence of, or buying or selling, drugs or alcohol while at work; falsifying credentials or company documents; and stealing company property. This process is known as *termination for cause.*

For legal recourse, any employee who is fired should receive an official letter on company letterhead that specifies the reasons for termination, the effective date, and any prior corrective action.

As a supervisor, you may find yourself having to make a termination decision about an employee after counseling shows no improvement. If you work for a manager who has terminated a staff member, you may find yourself typing the termination documents or otherwise having access to the records. From a professional standpoint, these documents are confidential. Their contents should be kept secret; you should not talk to anyone about them.

SEVERANCE

Depending on the circumstances of the termination, an employer may decide to offer the terminated employee *severance pay.* Severance pay is a voluntary allowance based on a preset formula, generally the length of time an individual has been employed. Recent trends have broadened to include other severance benefits such as use of company equipment (fax, computers, etc.) to assist in looking for another job, the right to apply for other jobs within the company, and the continuation of such benefits as health insurance. The benefits are referred to as a *severance package*.

When companies downsize or reorganize and have to let staff go, they frequently provide severance packages to those terminated. Some companies that are downsizing will offer generous packages to those who volunteer to be let go or who choose to take early retirement.

UNEMPLOYMENT

Employees who are terminated are generally eligible for *unemployment compensation benefits*. The purpose of unemployment compensation benefits is to provide income to a person seeking a job. Unemployment benefits are administered jointly by federal and state agencies, so eligibility requirements, compensation levels, and length of coverage vary. Terminated employees file a claim at the state unemployment office. The unemployment office mails the terminating company a questionnaire requesting such information as salary, length of employment, and details regarding the termination. This information, together with the employee's input, is used to determine the employee's eligibility for benefits.

Benefits are paid by the *Unemployment Compensation Fund*. This fund is supported solely through mandatory employer contributions, except in Alabama, Alaska, and New Jersey where employees also contribute. Employer contributions are determined by the number of unemployed people receiving benefits, so it is in an employer's best interest to keep firings to a minimum.

EMPLOYEE RIGHTS AND RESPONSIBILITIES

A variety of legal issues affect the office professional these days. Both state and federal government continue to pass and reform legislation. At the same time, rulings in the court system have a direct effect on policy and enforcement. While the aim of this increasing legislation is generally to protect and aid both employers and employees, compliance has become a nightmare. A variety of information regarding legal issues in the workplace is available directly from the government and, where appropriate, contact information has been provided in the following sections. This information is presented for informative purposes only; for any situation with legal or potentially legal ramifications, consult an attorney directly.

SEXUAL HARASSMENT

Sexual harassment is *"uninvited and unwelcome verbal or physical contact directed at an employee because of his or her sex."* Because sexual harassment is so subjective, however, it is often difficult to define which behaviors are unwanted. Overt action, such as groping, is clear and unambiguous, but more subtle actions such as sexually explicit jokes, gestures, or even pet names could be considered unwanted by someone—even if the same behavior would be acceptable to someone else.

Employees of either sex can be harassed by members of either sex. A principle of sexual harassment is that the person being harassed will be vulnerable if he or she objects to the harasser's behavior. While it's currently correct that sexual harassment doesn't legally go up the corporate ladder, the way the courts are handling the hostile workplace issue, the definition may soon change to find sexual harassment going up and down the corporate ladder. As sexual harassment is still largely determined by the relationship of the people involved, the first and most important step to stopping offensive behavior is to tell the person to stop.

It is the responsibility of employers to educate employees about their firm's policy. This issue should be treated with a high degree of seriousness, with a very carefully worded policy that tells employees these things are not permitted in the workplace. The policy should be disseminated, communicated, and accessible. In addition, it is important that the policy be enforced and be nonthreatening so that employees don't fear repercussions if they speak up. One bit of advice, if you think yourself a victim of harassment, immediately bring the matter to the attention of two parties, one male and one female.

WORKPLACE VIOLENCE

Physical violence or the threat of physical violence is not acceptable in any form in the workplace. Physical violence or the threat of physical violence from an employee is grounds for immediate termination or *termination for cause*. This area is not confined to employees, however; previous cases have included clients, suppliers, delivery personnel, and others with whom an employee comes in contact within a normal workday.

Courts have ruled that employers have a responsibility to provide a safe workplace for their employees and have ruled against employers in situations where an employee has suffered injury, been attacked, or been threatened while at work. In any situation where an employee is harmed or threatened, he or she should immediately inform management and, if the situation warrants, the appropriate legal authorities.

So far we have been talking about physical violence, but there is also emotional trauma, which can stem from verbal abuse. Sometimes the abuser is a colleague, sometimes a supervisor, a client, or a vendor or one of his or her representatives. While such abuse doesn't leave physical scars, it does impact self-esteem and performance. If you feel that you are being verbally abused— harangued or taunted by another—report such conduct to human resources or to your manager if he or she isn't the abuser. If your own supervisor is guilty of this, then go over his or her head. Often the intervention of a third party will put an end to such behavior.

Unfortunately, the Occupational Safety and Health Act does not cover verbal abuse, although it does cover situations that could lead to physical violence. When the problem lies with your manager and it continues, sometimes your only solution is to seek a transfer to another part of the company.

DIVERSITY

Workforce diversity is a growing reality. In 1987, 48 percent of the population entering the American workforce consisted of American-born white males; in the year 2000, this figure is projected to be a mere 15 percent. People of various ages, races, genders, physical abilities, sexual orientations, religions, socioeconomic classes, education, and national origins will continue to enter the American workforce in growing numbers. Even as this diversity creates challenges, it also provides for substantial benefits and opportunities. While misunderstandings in the office are bound to arise as a result of differences in behaviors, beliefs, and communication styles, the key to understanding people is learning to respect their differences. Hatred, prejudice, racism, sexism, ageism, and homophobia cannot be tolerated in the workplace in any form. The disruptive nature of such attitudes only hinders employees from achieving their full potential.

Even as more legislation is enacted, and courts rule to protect employees, it is heartening to observe the astonishing number of companies that have embraced diversity with such steps as broader recruitment, diversity training, and the establishment of inclusive policies and procedures. These steps pay off as study after study proves that companies who value a diverse workforce have saved million of dollars, lowered employee turnover, and improved their methods and products. There is a wealth of resources available, including training programs, videos, books, and consulting firms to address any aspect of diversity. Diversity in the workplace will continue to grow, directly mirroring the increasing diversity in the world in which we live.

THE AMERICANS WITH DISABILITIES ACT

Over 40 million Americans are disabled in some capacity. Recent studies have shown that over two-thirds of these people are unemployed, and over 80 percent of those unemployed would like to be employed. In response, the

Americans with Disabilities Act (ADA) was passed in 1990 to provide any disabled person with, among other things, equal access to employment.

ADA covers anyone who has a physical or mental impairment that limits one or more major life activity. Examples include blindness, deafness, or mental retardation; incapacitation in such areas as standing, walking, or speaking; and life-threatening illnesses such as cancer, epilepsy, or AIDS. Individuals who have a record of being substantially limited in any of these areas are also covered. For example, an individual who had cancer but has since recovered may qualify even though no visible impairment may remain. Finally, the act also applies to anyone who is regarded as being substantially limited. "Regarded," however, is subjective, and new interpretations are constantly being raised through ongoing discrimination lawsuits, further adding to the confusion.

The ADA is a complicated act divided into titles dealing with areas as broad as access to public transportation and services. Title I, *Fair Employment for People with Disabilities,* is specifically directed to employment issues. It prohibits discrimination in such areas as hiring, benefits, and medical examinations by any business that has fifteen or more employees. Title III, *Reasonable Accommodation,* requires employers to address qualified employees' physical and mental limitations. Accommodations include wheelchair ramps, Braille signage, or modified work schedules. Accommodations that would place an undue hardship on a business financially or logistically, or would otherwise have a negative impact on other employees, are exempt. Be aware, however, that this is extremely subjective and defined on a case-by-case basis. For specifics, clarification, or questions, contact the Office of the ADA or the Equal Employment Commission.

> Office of the ADA
> U.S. Department of Justice
> P.O. Box 66738
> Washington, DC 20035
> 800-669-4000
>
> U.S. Equal Employment Opportunity Commission
> 1801 L Street NW
> Washington, DC 20507
> 800-663-4900

THE FAMILY AND MEDICAL LEAVE ACT

To allow family members the opportunity to help each other without jeopardizing their work situation, as well as allow employees to take leaves of absence for personal illness without loss of employment, Congress passed the Family and Medical Leave Act (FMLA) in 1993.

The FMLA applies to any employee who must care for a child recently born, adopted, or placed in the employee's care through a foster agency, or who must care for a child, spouse, or parent with a serious health condition or illness requiring continuing treatment. Employees with a health condition that directly affects their own professional performance are also eligible. Employees must have worked for the company at least twelve months and worked at least 1,250 hours during that time. Employers with fewer than fifty employees and any branch office with fewer than fifty employees within a 75-mile radius are exempt. Employers may also exempt the 10 percent highest-paid employees if their absence would cause "substantial and grievous injury" to the company.

The Act grants eligible employees twelve weeks of leave per year to address these issues, with the guarantee that, on return, the worker will be returned to his or her formal position or its equivalent in pay benefits and working conditions. Payment during this leave is at the discretion of the employer, and employees are not eligible for unemployment benefits. Employees may also be required to exhaust their accumulated vacation, personal, and sick time first. Leave may be taken intermittently or all at once, again at the discretion of the employer. Employers must continue to pay any health-insurance premiums; however, if the employee paid any part of the premium, he or she is still responsible for it during the leave. The Act is enforced by the U.S. Labor Department, which can be contacted for further information at:

The U.S. Department of Labor
200 Constitution Avenue NW
Washington, DC 20210
800-366-0547

BENEFITS

Benefits, also known as *indirect compensation,* fall into three major categories: protection programs, pay for time not worked, and employee services. *Protection programs* ensure that employees and their dependents are cared for in the event the employee is incapacitated. These programs include pension, unemployment, disability, and medical benefits. *Pay for time not worked* covers vacation, personal days, and holidays as well as time during the day such as rest periods or lunch breaks. *Employee services* consist of "perks," which vary enormously, and may include such standard benefits as employee counseling, assistance programs, scholarship or tuition assistance, day care for children, food services, use of company vehicles, and expense accounts.

Benefits also fall into one of two different types. *Mandated benefits* are required by law, and their guidelines are determined by legislation and government entities. Examples of mandated benefits include Social Security, workers' compensation, and unemployment insurance. *Voluntary benefits* are not required by law, and the decision to provide them, as well as their terms and conditions, is largely left to the employer. Examples of voluntary benefits include medical and dental plans; life, health, and disability insurance; and savings, stock, or retirement programs.

Through indirect compensation, employers hope to attract and retain employees, increase morale and job satisfaction, and enhance their own image. Accomplishing all this while remaining cost-effective is, however, tricky because benefits packages usually average around a third of payroll costs. Several of the more standard benefits are discussed next.

HEALTH BENEFITS

Health benefits are an excellent form of protection for employees and their families. They can include health and dental plans and insurance, vision care, and even discount memberships to gyms and health clubs. Coverage may be *basic,* covering only one aspect of an employee's health needs, or *comprehensive,* covering several or all medical requirements. Employees may be responsible for a percentage of the cost of these benefits, the percentage being determined by the employer.

An employee can get coverage for his or her own medical expenses and those of dependents, such as children or a spouse, and, in some organizations, for a "domestic partner."

The three most common types of coverage are health maintenance organizations, known as HMOs; indemnity and reimbursement plans; and preferred provider organizations, known as PPOs. Each is discussed next.

Health Maintenance Organizations (HMOs)

In *health maintenance organizations,* or HMOs, a predetermined network of hospitals and doctors provides medical services to employees and their dependents for a monthly fee. HMOs have become increasingly popular through their attention to preventive care and their ability to offer one-stop shopping for most or all health care needs. Patients are assigned a primary care physician, usually a general practitioner or internist, who refers patients to specialists within the network, as needed. Patients who receive medical care outside of the network are not covered and are responsible for all charges incurred. HMO patients usually pay a small fee, called a *copayment,* each time they see their medical practitioner. The copayment is for services rendered within the network and for medication.

Indemnity and Reimbursement Plans

Indemnity and reimbursement plans are also referred to as traditional health insurance. Patients are free to select health care from any physician or hospital and are responsible for a percentage of the cost up to a predetermined limit. In an indemnity plan, physicians and hospitals bill the insurance provider directly for services rendered, with the patient paying the balance at the time of service. In a reimbursement plan, as the name implies, the patient is responsible for all charges incurred at the time of service and later files a claim with the insurance provider for reimbursement.

Preferred Provider Organizations (PPOs)

Preferred provider organizations, or PPOs, are a fusion of HMOs and traditional indemnity and reimbursement plans. PPOs are similar to HMOs in that a predetermined network of hospitals and doctors agrees to provide medical services to employees and their dependents for a set fee. PPOs allow patients to see physicians outside of the network, however, and still cover a percentage of the costs. This coverage is referred to as *point of service* (POS). Copayments for services within the network are substantially lower than those outside of the network in order to encourage patients to seek care within the network.

INSURANCE

A variety of insurance is almost always available to employees, particularly since it is one of the least expensive benefits an employer can provide. Insurance is popular with employees, as well, and the cost to employees for premiums is usually nominal. The importance of insurance should not be underestimated. Disability insurance, for example, provides income for employees or their dependents in the event that the employee is incapacitated. Other types of insurance provide income for retirement or payment in case of accidental loss of life or the loss of a sense or limb. Several popular forms of insurance are discussed next.

Life Insurance

There are various types of life insurance, including *whole life,* in which a policy, once fully paid, pays survivors whenever the employee dies; and *group term,* in which an employee must die during the policy term in order for payment to occur. Employers are free to decide which types, if any, they will offer. Most employers will pay the premiums for a set amount of coverage and allow their employees to purchase additional coverage as needed. Premiums are tax-deductible for both employer and employees, further enhancing life insurance's accessibility and popularity. Life insurance for employees with families is of major importance to ensure that survivors of the deceased have the necessary funds for burial costs and also as a means of replacing, at least partially, the income of the deceased.

Accidental Death and Dismemberment Insurance (AD&D)

Similar to life insurance, *AD&D insurance* provides a lump sum payment to the survivors of a deceased employee. As the name implies, however, the condition of death must generally be accidental and unforeseen as opposed to extended illness, for example. AD&D will also provide payment to the employee in the event of the loss of a sense or limb. These payments are generally less, although specifics vary from provider to plan.

Disability Insurance

Disability insurance provides income to an employee who suffers a debilitating injury or illness. There are two types of disability insurance: *short-term* and *long-term;* and both are designed to supplement state and federal disability programs. Corporate programs vary, but most employers pay the entire premium for short-term disability insurance since the premiums are small and tax-deductible; some companies self-insure their employees directly. Long-term disability insurance is usually part of a group policy in which the premium payments are split between the employee and employer. Because of these costs, short-term disability insurance is more common, being offered by 80 percent of employers as opposed to 70 percent for long-term.

RETIREMENT PLANS

Retirement plans have evolved to reflect the changes in the American workforce and to reflect recent legislation such as the Employee Retirement Income Security Act (ERISA). About 85 percent of all office workers are covered by their employer's pension programs, as opposed to 50-percent coverage in the general population. A recent trend is to offer retirement to younger employees. This enables employers to promote new employees more quickly, lower costs, and provide for better morale within the workforce. Retirement plans, once offered, must be available uniformly to all employees at least 21 years of age who have worked 1,000 hours or more within the past twelve months. Retirement plans fall into two categories: defined benefit and defined contribution.

Defined Benefit

Defined benefit plans are rapidly disappearing, reflecting the changes in the American workforce. Under a *defined benefit plan,* employers invest enough to pay a guaranteed, predetermined amount, usually a percentage of the employee's salary, upon the employee's retirement. This type of plan requires no contribution from the employee, involves enormous financial commitment from the company, and requires adherence to heavy administration and government regulations. Originally designed to encourage employees to stay with a company for life, defined benefit plans remain the domain of large corporations because of their expense. As the American workforce continues to move toward self-employment, contractual employment, and small business, defined benefit plans will continue to diminish.

Defined Contribution

Defined contribution plans continue to proliferate, replacing defined benefit plans. Employees in *defined contribution plans* have the opportunity to invest in their retirement themselves, up to a given percentage of their annual income. This money, along with a set portion from their employer, goes into a savings and investment program.

The most popular defined contribution plan today is the *401(k) plan* in which employees invest regularly on a pretax basis. Most employers make matching contributions, which are vested to the employee after a set amount of time. While still regulated by the government, 401(k) contributions and investment earnings are tax-free, allowing accelerated growth of employees' retirement accounts and further adding to the popularity of the 401(k) plan. Heavy tax penalties exist to discourage early withdrawal, although many plans do make provisions for employees to borrow from their accounts.

Investors suggest that you should be investing as much as 10 percent of your pretax income, or $3,000 per year if you are earning $30,000 annually, in a 401(k) to ensure sufficient retirement funds.

PAY FOR TIME NOT WORKED

Paid time off, such as holidays and sick days, is so commonplace in the office environment that employees are often under the impression that it is a mandated right. Make no mistake, offering pay for time not worked under any condition is completely determined by employers. It is also one of the most expensive benefits offered, accounting for about 10 percent of the average company's payroll costs. Still, paid time off continues to grow. For example, the average number of paid holidays per year in 1955 was six compared to today's twelve. Employers have long since recognized the effect of these benefits on employee morale and the need for time-off benefits as employees juggle the demands of their personal and professional life. Payment for time not worked falls into two categories: on the job and off the job.

On the Job

In the past, office workers were officially given a 15-minute coffee break about midmorning and a second formal coffee break between noon and the end of the day. During these time periods, everyone took time off. At the end of that time, everyone was expected to get back to work. Lunch, too, was structured, with 30 minutes being the norm rather than the 60- and 90-minute lunch times common today.

Generally, today's offices aren't so regimented. Most managers understand that their employees need some time to rest and socialize, and will say little about breaks or lunch times. On the other hand, abuse of the privilege can incur criticism from a supervisor. Excessive abuse by the staff as a whole can generate a very restrictive approach, with managers prowling the workplace to see if some worker has a newspaper out or is staring into space.

If you need a break, it is better to take a walk outside the building. Since confusion about a lunch break can arise if you eat at your desk, you may want to take your lunch breaks in the office cafeteria or nearby coffee shop.

Off the Job

Paid time off when you are off the job includes paid vacation, personal and sick days, and holidays. It can also include less orthodox time off, such as floating holidays, bereavement days, and accommodations for jury duty. These benefits may be offered on an accumulated basis, may have eligibility requirements, or may be carried over from year to year. Since these benefits are strictly voluntary, conditions and specifics are as different as the employers who offer them. Most employers apply their policies uniformly, however, and have written policies available for new employees or employees who request them.

EMPLOYEE SERVICES

Employee services have changed considerably as companies have discovered the positive impact such services can have on productivity. Given the time constraints that we live under, these services can be of real value. For example, some companies contract to provide their employees with concierge services that range from picking up cleaning to picking up tickets for a children's outing.

During summer months, many companies offer a number of half days on Fridays. During the winters, in the two-week period between Christmas and New Year's, some offices close; others implement dress-down days. Many companies in summer allow dress-down everyday; the rest of the year, they allow dress-down every Friday. Some firms have a tradition of summer picnics or other social events for the company as a whole.

Other special benefits for employees can include company-paid snacks or dinners for those who work late in the evening, even limousine service home; child care; tuition reimbursement; and, increasingly, health club memberships or, at least, a portion of the membership fee. Employees at a certain level within their organization may get special perks, from extra vacation time to a company car.

For employees with personal problems, companies offer employee assistance programs (EAPs) that provide personal counseling and help with everything from drug or alcohol addiction to delinquency in a child to eldercare.

ETIQUETTE

The daily news is full of reports about huge, faceless entities that are merging with other companies, implementing new technology, or addressing stock fluctuations. When business is conducted on such a mega scale, we can easily forget that it is people who conduct business, not faceless entities. It is important, therefore, that we learn to treat each other with respect and consideration in the workplace. Office etiquette provides common-sense guidelines on how to do this in the easiest manner. Office etiquette increases the quality of life in the workplace, contributes to employee morale, and embellishes the company image—all with a minimum of effort. Having a knowledge of office etiquette is a quality that can separate an assistant from an office professional and can draw attention to his or her promotability.

General guidelines on some of the most common office situations follow. Two excellent and comprehensive sources of more detailed information are *Amy Vanderbilt's Complete Book of Etiquette* and *Letitia Baldrige's Complete Guide to Executive Manners.*

- When greeting a visitor to the office in your supervisor's absence, introduce yourself by name, then title, and ask, "May I help you?"

- When you answer the phone, don't just identify your company; identify yourself, as well. Say, "This is (your name)."

- Always introduce a younger person or junior person to an older or more senior person. An exception is that staff people should be introduced to clients or customers.

- Exchange business cards at the start of a meeting. Offer your card by saying, "May I give you my card?" if the other person doesn't offer his or hers. If you are given a card by another, offer yours in turn. Take the card and keep it before you if seated. Treat the card with the same respect as you do the person who is there with you. You can put the card in your Rolodex after the individual has left.

- If you are attending a large group meeting, the chair will likely ask each member to introduce himself or herself, going around the room. When you introduce yourself, give both your name and job title. If you don't know many people, take the opportunity before the meeting to introduce yourself to as many people as you can.

- Greet visitors and offer to take their coats. If they must wait for your manager, lead them to a chair and tell them you will return for them shortly. If the wait is longer than you thought, revisit to assure them that you haven't forgotten them.

- If you have been asked to help with a visitor—for instance, to take him or her on a tour of the office—introduce yourself to the visitor. If you must absent yourself from the visitor for a period of time, be sure to leave him or her in a colleague's care. Introduce the visitor to your colleague and tell the visitor when you will be back. When the visit is over, escort the guest to the office door and thank him or her for coming.

DEALING WITH OFFICE POLITICS

When people interact with each other on a daily basis, politics are bound to arise. It is important to keep office politics to a minimum by treating everyone fairly and refraining from participation in politics; this includes gossiping with or about co-workers. When conversation becomes uncomfortable, try to direct the conversation to a more neutral topic, or simply excuse yourself and leave. Gossip will almost always make its way back to the original person and lead to hostility, discomfort, and an unhappy work environment.

Avoiding gossip in today's offices is hard. But, if you want to be seen as a professional, it's imperative that you neither repeat gossip nor begin it yourself. If a co-worker wants to share some gossip with you, and you don't want to offend the person, you can use the excuse that you are too busy to hear.

THE ASSISTANT/BOSS PARTNERSHIP

In today's organizations, you and your boss are a team. Thus, it's imperative that you help your teammate look good. This means that you have to make that little extra effort to see that your boss is on time for meetings and that his or her letters do not have typographical errors. You also should ensure that your boss completes work on schedule by alerting him or her to due dates and assisting whenever you can. Never put your boss in a position to be surprised by a mistake. Let him or her know if there is a problem so that, together, you can resolve the problem.

The more you can make your boss look good, the better you will look. Many office professionals have built reputations based on their support of their boss. The demonstration of their professionalism ultimately resulted in obtaining their own managerial position. Being a partner with your boss may be the best career move you can make.

DRESS

Even though many offices have relaxed their dress standards, allowing employees to dress casually, it is critical that your clothing and grooming still portray a professional image. The most important aspect of dressing well for the office is appropriateness. What is acceptable in one office may not be appropriate in another. Banking and law, for example, still command a much more formal appearance than more creative industries such as journalism. Your position within the office should also be reflected in the way you dress. CEOs, for example, are expected to dress formally at all times, regardless of the policy for the office at large. Finally, employees who have direct contact with clients or others outside of the company should adopt a more conservative dress to portray a favorable and professional image.

If you are unsure whether your clothing is appropriate, a good model to follow is the dress of co-workers you respect. Other sources of information include consultants and salespeople in clothing stores, fashion magazines, books and other media, and friends or family with a good sense of style. When determining what is appropriate, consider your coloring and body type. Avoid trendy fashions and fads because they quickly go out of style. Invest in the best fabric and workmanship you can afford. It pays off in the long run because good-quality clothing wears better, never goes out of style, and looks better on you.

For men, a well-fitting suit is almost always appropriate dress in an office environment, and men should invest in a minimum of three good-quality suits. Styles and types vary and project different images, and should be carefully chosen to reflect the image of the individual and the profession. A double-breasted suit, for example, is considered more formal than a three-button suit, which is currently considered very stylish. A navy blue blazer should also be a staple in an office professional's closet. This garment is incredibly versatile and can be worn in place of a suit in the office as well as worn in more casual environments. Long-sleeved shirts project a better image than short-sleeved and are more appropriate for the office. If a man does wear a short-sleeved shirt, however, he should remember not to remove his jacket while in view of the public. Ties should subtly complement the colors, textures, and patterns of both the suit and the shirt, and should never be loud or distracting. Lace-up, dress shoes are most appropriate for the office, although tasseled loafers are also considered acceptable. Shoes should be clean, well-polished, and in good condition.

Women have much more versatility in what is acceptable dress in the office. With that versatility, however, comes more decisions. A professional woman's closet should contain a minimum of three business suits. Business pants suits are completely appropriate; however, a skirt suit is still considered more formal and professional. Daytime dresses are also a staple of office wear and should be chosen with care to project a good image. Women should also invest in good-quality blazers that can be coupled with skirts or pants. Blouses are the easiest garment to replace as fashion changes, so they can be stylish and project a more personal image. Blouses for the office should, however, remain somewhat conservative and subtle. Women should always wear stockings in the office. Hose with patterns, pictures, or runs is not appropriate and should be replaced. Shoes should be flat or medium-heeled, cleaned daily, and in good condition.

Always in Style by Doris Pooser is an excellent resource to help create your own personal style.

INVITATIONS

Invitations to office parties and socials should directly reflect the formality of the function. If the office is gathering after work to celebrate a co-worker's birthday, for example, it is fine to invite people verbally. A formal dinner or holiday party, however, requires a printed invitation that contains the time, date, location, dress, and type of function. In either case, it is a good idea to have a prepared list of invitees to ensure that no one is accidentally overlooked and omitted. For formal functions, the list also serves as a check-off of who has responded to an RSVP. On printed invitations, hand-write on the envelope the name of the recipient and also the address if the invitation will be mailed. Distribute printed invitations at least four weeks in advance; for verbal invitations or informal get-togethers, a week or two is sufficient.

Your responsibilities to your manager may include screening invitations to events and responding for him or her. You may want to discuss this issue with your boss to be sure that a key business opportunity isn't inadvertently declined. Until you are certain, it is better to take the information if the invitation is via phone. If he or she receives a printed invitation, make sure that your boss knows about it and has told you whether to accept. If your boss chooses to accept, note it on his or her calendar and also on yours when you make the acceptance..

If your boss decides not to attend, you still need to call. That's what *RSVP* means—*Respondez s'il vous plait* (Reply, if you please—in French). If your boss wants to take a guest, ask about this when you call. If there is a question of dress, you can use this occasion to ask about that, too.

If your boss will need the invitation to enter the gathering, you may want to keep it in your own work files and give him or her the invitation on the day of the event.

PARTIES AND SOCIAL FUNCTIONS

Office parties and social functions boost morale, encourage people to celebrate, and promote interaction on a personal level. They also vary greatly, depending on the event, the size of the company, and available resources.

When planning a party, take into consideration the size, cost, objective, theme, and image you wish to project. Preparing for a large function can quickly become overwhelming; the menu, guest list, location, decorations, and entertainment must all be decided on. In these situations, hotel and restaurant facility managers, caterers, and professional party consultants are an excellent source of information and ideas.

When attending an office party, use the opportunity to mingle and meet and talk with co-workers you don't know well or with whom you have little contact at the office. Keep conversation light and avoid office politics as a topic. Above all, maintain a professional image. While the purpose of the party is for employees to enjoy themselves, remember that anything said or done will be remembered the next day at the office. When alcohol is served, drinking in moderation is of paramount importance.

Here are some questions to ask yourself as you plan the party:

- Given the purpose of the occasion, where is the best location for it?

- Is this party solely for staff members, or should clients or customers be invited?

- Will guests bring family members—not just a spouse but children? If so, how should I adapt the menu?

- Should there be background music? If so, live or recorded?

- Should I arrange for transportation home if the event lasts late into the night?

GIFT GIVING

Corporate gift giving in the United States is a $2 billion industry. This is not surprising; giving gifts has long been an ingrained part of American culture. Gifts to clients and employees promote goodwill and loyalty, and let people know they are appreciated. Whenever possible, it is important to carefully select gifts that are individualized and will be personally appreciated rather than mass distributing identical items. In larger companies, budget guidelines can be set for representatives of individual departments, and gift purchasing can be on a smaller and more personal level. Even gifts to thousands of employees or clients can be creatively done so as to impress the recipient with your thoughtfulness. Tickets to sporting or cultural events; parties or receptions for employees, clients, and their guests; and gift certificates for products or services are good examples of gifts designed to make the individual feel singled out and appreciated.

In addition to a company's budgetary constraints, there are other reasons to keep the cost of corporate gifts in perspective. While there is no limit on what can be spent, excessively expensive gifts may make the recipient feel uncomfortable, may be construed as bribery, or may violate gift recipient rules of other companies. In addition, the IRS limits the tax-deductible amount for business gifts to $25. Twelve of the most popular gift items, which are not excessively expensive, are:

- Gift subscriptions
- Pen and pencil sets
- Clocks
- Coffee mugs
- Hats
- Food baskets

- Desk folios and folders
- Calendars
- Calculators
- Golf items
- Liquor
- Desk sets

Most of these gifts can also be imprinted with your company's logo. However, to avoid having your gift construed as cheap or an attempt at free advertising, you may want to consider imprinting the logo in an inconspicuous place or perhaps printing it only on the wrapping paper—or leaving it off altogether. Finally, a handwritten note or card should accompany every gift.

Personal gifts

A gift marks a special relationship with a person and should never be given by rote or obligation. Employees who give their coworkers gifts are under no obligation to give something to everyone; however, it is best to be as inconspicuous as possible to avoid hurt feelings. It is generally accepted that gift giving goes down the corporate ladder, so consideration should be given to staff and employees to show appreciation for their support. Employees are free to give their bosses a small token of their esteem, but the expense should be kept to a minimum and excessively personal gifts, which could be misconstrued, should be avoided.

DATING

In a perfect world, interoffice romance would not occur at all. The opportunity for hazardous situations is just too great. The reality, however, is that we spend most of our waking hours in the office, and attraction doesn't always conform to what is in our best interests. Because romance on the job will affect how an employee is perceived by his or her coworkers, care should be taken to keep the repercussions to a minimum. A few tips follow.

1. Be wary of a romance with someone from the same department. Even in the best of circumstances, you will both be under intense scrutiny, and your romance is going to be a topic of conversation in the office. In the event that the romance does not work out, you will be left in the

uncomfortable situation of having to face and work with the other person on a daily basis.

2. Under no circumstances engage in a romance with your boss or an employee who reports to you. The possible repercussions are severe enough to endanger your job. Should you find yourself involved in a mutual attraction, seriously consider transferring to a different department or finding a new job.

3. Keep your personal life private. Even though gossip and rumors may eventually circulate through the office regarding your romance, avoid providing verbal and behavioral confirmation as well as making references to your personal life.

4. In every area of the company, refrain from public displays of affection, pet names, arguments or disagreements, and plans for personal time. This includes cafeterias, break areas, and parking lots. Also avoid being together alone in isolated areas or behind closed doors.

5. Show no favoritism, and set priorities as always.

CONGRATULATIONS AND CONDOLENCES

Letters and cards of congratulations and condolences are in excellent taste. It is always appropriate and uplifting to let someone know how highly he or she is regarded both in celebration and in times of mourning. Such a gesture also demonstrates your thoughtfulness. Even though the two circumstances are opposites, several rules apply to both situations.

Don't let the opportunity pass you by. Write your note as soon as you hear the news. Delays imply that the news isn't as important to you as to the recipient. If you have learned of the event after the fact, address the situation with a simple phrase such as "I've only just recently returned from vacation and heard the great/terrible news." Available time should not constrain your response. If your time is limited, a two- or three-sentence note or a signed card is all that is required.

The same advice applies to your boss's response. Often, your boss will get so involved in office details that he or she will forget to ask you to send his or her requests/congratulations. Knowing your boss, you need to judge whether you should purchase a card for his or her signature and brief message.

Address the situation directly, and keep your response sincere and concise. Use a straightforward phrase such as "I was very happy to learn of your recent promotion" or "I was saddened to learn of the death of your mother." While writing congratulations, avoid gushing or using insincere flattery. When writing condolences, be as concise as possible to avoid making the recipient feel worse in an already difficult time.

Don't refer to other business or news or ask for favors. This is not an opportunity to "sneak one in." There will be time later to address circumstances that may arise due to the situation. Congratulations should never refer to how you can benefit from the situation. When writing condolences, it is appropriate, however, to let the recipient know you are available for anything he or she may need with a simple phrase such as "Please don't hesitate to let me know if there is anything I can do to help."

FOR MORE INFORMATION

If you can't find what you need from the phone numbers and Web sites listed in this chapter, you may need to expand your search.

- For more information on placing an ad for a job, call your local newspaper. Their classified advertising department will be able to assist you.

- For more information on temporary employment agencies, look in your Yellow Pages under "employment agencies."

- For more information on human resources, organizational management or employee management, check the business section of your local library or bookstore.

- For more information on your state's labor laws, including compliance requirements for ADA and other legislation, check your government listings for Labor Relations.

- For more information on your company's exposure to lawsuits regarding sexual harassment and other workplace issues, check with you attorney or local labor relations board. Seminars and on-site training courses are often available.

- For more information on business etiquette, check your local bookstore for the business category and business life subcategory.

10

TRAVEL PLANNING

◆

- **Business Travel Today**

- **The Itinerary**

    Compiling the Details
    Making Reservations
    Internet Travel Services

- **International Travel**

    International Airline Travel
    Passport, Visa, Immunizations, and Customs
    Getting Extra Business Help While Away
    Money: Yours and Theirs
    Legal Help Abroad
    Medical Help Abroad
    Renting and Driving Cars in Other Countries
    Business Etiquette Abroad
    Post-Travel Tasks

- **For More Information**

As advanced communications turn the world into a global village, businesses increasingly consider the entire country their market—and are rapidly expanding their interests into international areas as well. That means travel is the norm these days, no longer the exception. Sales people roam further and further to meet new clients, executives scour new locations for sources of cheaper manufacturing, and technical staffs shuttle between remote offices. Even the office professional, who years ago rarely left the office, now might accompany the boss to give a sales presentation, go on-site to arrange a conference, or fly cross-country to staff a trade show. All employees, including office professionals, are more likely today to go anywhere to make and maintain contacts, attend meetings and conventions, present lectures, and just relax.

Making travel arrangements for the entire staff often is a key part of the office professional's job. To ensure a smooth, enjoyable, and profitable trip, the office professional must be familiar with everything from the best means of transportation to the culture and politics of the intended location. And that's in addition to overseeing the innumerable details of collecting all the supplies and documents needed to make the trip a success.

BUSINESS TRAVEL TODAY

Once considered a perk, business travel is now more often seen as a chore, a disadvantage that sometimes prompts people to change or refuse jobs. After all, travel is time-consuming to prepare for and to do, employees often lose productive work time enroute, and travel isolates employees not only from their families, but from the critical events of everyday company life.

Good office professionals can do a lot to solve these problems. They track the traveler's mileage to upgrade flights for more comfort. They make seamless arrangements that don't force the traveler into either sprinting to connections or killing hours during changeovers. They route travel on airlines with up-to-date business lounges. They discover—and avoid—the worst travel times at individual airports. They facilitate communications between the traveler and the office, both en route to and at his or her destination. They make sure that the traveler has the necessary files and documents for business purposes. And, depending on their work, office professionals may be handling these same details for half a dozen different people traveling to half a dozen different destinations.

Large organizations sometimes have in-house travel services that handle all the pertinent arrangements. If the company has such a department, the office professional submits the details (such as arrival and departure dates, hotel requirements, and so on), and then helps coordinate the information with the traveler. The in-house travel service works out the itinerary with the traveler's approval, makes reservations for transportation and accommodations,

FINDING A GOOD TRAVEL AGENCY

The choice of a travel agency is crucial, not only to the success of any specific trip but also to the company's overall success as well. If the executive is late for a meeting because he or she missed a connecting flight that was too closely timed, if the hotel that was a "good deal" is actually so shabby that it gives a poor impression, or if the executive ends up overseas three days too early in one place and two days too late in another because of jumbled last-minute changes to the itinerary—these problems can result in a loss of clients and a drastic drop in profits.

Although many large companies put out bids or surveys before choosing an agency (and repeat this process at intervals), most companies want an agency they can use all the time. Today's business demands instant responses. If the company's manufacturing plant in Thailand is facing a crisis, the office assistant can't spend two weeks polling agencies about their practices. A reliable agency delivers every time, taking care of the major details of travel and transportation and also providing extra services for its clients. Therefore, the office professional will want to choose an agency that will do the following:

- Prepare a tentative itinerary, which the executive can approve or change.

- Handle all the arrangements for travel and transportation, for hotel reservations, and perhaps for sightseeing and other extracurricular activities.

- Arrange to have a rental car waiting for the executive at the destination point, if desired; explain relevant driving concerns; and arrange for necessary documents in a foreign country.

- Handle both personal and baggage insurance, if desired.

- Provide information about exactly which documents will be needed for foreign travel (such as passports, visas, and health and police certificates) and how to obtain them.

- Obtain as many of these documents as possible (certain documents must be obtained by the traveler personally).

- List the vaccinations required by each country to be visited.

continues

- Supply the name of a desirable hotel in the country of destination, and provide a letter of introduction to the hotel manager if the executive's accommodations are not finalized ahead of time.

- Inform the traveler of the country's culture, politics, and customs that might affect his or her business dealings.

- Alert the traveler to state department travel advisories regarding the political climate in areas to be visited.

Because an agency's true capability to handle these items will not be discovered until its services actually have been engaged, what should the office professional look for in selecting a travel agency?

Begin with recommendations from other departments and divisions, from fellow office professionals, and from the company's clients and vendors. Whether you have recommendations or must make cold calls from the telephone book, ask each agency the following questions:

- *What is the agency's professional affiliation?* Membership in professional travel societies usually indicates at least a minimum level of competence because certain qualifications must be met before the agency is awarded membership. The most important of these is the American Society of Travel Agents (ASTA). Other key organizations are Airline Reporting Corporation (ARC), International Air Transport Association (IATA), Meeting Planners International (PI), and Cruise Line Industry Association (CLIA).

- *Are one or more of its agents certified?* To become a certified travel counselor or certified travel consultant (CTC), an agent must log hours of study of a set curriculum. Certification is a good indication of the personnel's professionalism.

- *Can the agency write its own tickets?* Although many agencies today write e-tickets, written tickets are still very common. (An e-ticket is an electronic version of your ticket filed with the airline. To travel on an e-ticket, the traveler only needs a confirmation number and identification.) Having the capability to issue an airline ticket on the spot shows that the agency has experience and financial strength.

- *Does the agency specialize in corporate travel?* Package tours require very different planning from the more difficult individualized itineraries of business executives. Look for an agency that is familiar with the needs of business travelers.

- *Is its technology up-to-date?* A fully computerized office can find you the best travel schedules and rates instantly and can make adjustments for changes on either end.

- *Does it have a 24-hour toll-free phone number?* It's important that the agency can be reached after hours and on weekends through a toll-free phone number. This helps the traveler whose flight arrangements have been fouled up or whose sudden change in plans require new departure times.

- *Is the agency multilingual?* An agent's capability to communicate in the language of the destination country can help prevent problems.

- *Does it supply recordkeeping?* If the agency can supply a fully itemized bill matched to the itinerary afterward, a large part of the recordkeeping duties are done. This itemization can satisfy requirements for both company reimbursements and tax purposes.

- *Will the agency provide recommendations from other business travelers?* The agency's willingness to do so often says as much as any customer's individual comments about it.

If this search does not yield a satisfactory agency, contact the American Society of Travel Agents (www.astanet.com/) for members closest to you. This organization can be reached at 1101 King Street, Alexandria, VA 22314; 703-739-2782.

When it comes to the particulars of the executive's trip, the agency relies largely on the information that comes from the office assistant. He or she should provide the agency with the executive's name, business and home telephone numbers, credit card number (if necessary), detailed information on dates and times of desired arrival and departure for each city to be visited, and the type of transportation preferred. Although the agent will report periodically on the progress made, it is the office professional's responsibility to keep in touch with the agent to see that tickets and reservations arrive at the office in plenty of time to check the dates, times, destinations, and so forth before they are turned over to the traveler.

If the office professional makes the arrangements without the use of an agency, he or she must see to all the details personally. All these details will be brought together in the itinerary.

and obtains confirmations. The details then are sent to the executive's office well before the departure date.

If a company does not have its own in-house travel department, it is often wise to use an outside agency. The services generally are free (except for rail travel), are backed by more specific experience and contacts than office professionals have in this area, can usually obtain better and faster service than an individual, and can save untold hours of time and effort.

However, even if help is available through an in-house agency or an outside firm, the office professional still plays a major role in travel planning. Not only does the office professional have the responsibility of providing the agencies with all the information regarding destinations, arrivals, departures, and accommodations, but he or she is also responsible for following up. If the department or agency makes the wrong arrangements or overlooks a detail, it's up to the office professional to catch the mistake and correct it.

The office professional also might be responsible for making sure that details of travel plans comply with the company's travel policies. This goes far beyond obtaining the proper signatures to authorize a trip beforehand, and collecting and filing receipts afterward. It involves planning both travel and accommodations within a limited budget—and sometimes within strict procedures. For example, some companies designate a travel level for each employee, which could mean that only CEOs fly first-class and only top executives fly business class. Middle managers, sales people, and other staff might be limited to coach, even if they've accumulated enough frequent-flyer miles to upgrade their own ticket. Accommodations are similarly graded. Policies might also require the filing of a travel profile, a document on file with the travel planner including preferred seating, meals, cars, and so on. Travel policies also might include handling appropriate accommodations, filing travel profiles, tracking personal days, or submitting an executive's frequent-flyer miles to an airline.

THE ITINERARY

For the most part, business travel has come to mean air travel. This means that the office assistant's travel-planning duties will largely involve booking flights and perhaps arranging for a rental car at each destination. But what sounds simple in theory becomes complicated in practice.

For example, let's say that an executive must fly from San Francisco to Washington, DC, and asks the office professional to book a nonstop flight from California's Oakland Airport to Washington's Ronald Reagan Airport. A simple request, right? Then the assistant discovers (or already knows from experience) that neither Oakland nor Ronald Reagan handles nonstop, coast-to-coast flights. Before coming up with alternatives, the assistant needs to know which is most important to the executive: leaving from Oakland, taking a nonstop flight, or arriving directly at Ronald Reagan. Knowing the traveler's priority determines whether the alternative is a flight from Oakland to Chicago with a brief layover, and then a flight from Chicago into DC; or whether it's a nonstop flight from San Francisco into Washington Dulles Airport with a limo, bus, or rental car ride into DC.

This is just the smallest example of the kind of creative thinking that an assistant must use when making travel plans. And given how ordinary business travel has become for just about every industry, the assistant must be ready to come up with creative solutions on any given day.

COMPILING THE DETAILS

An itinerary is a travel schedule, a chronological listing of each place to be visited, the separate appointments at each location, and the method of transportation between each point. To begin compiling an itinerary, ask the traveler his or her destination, the dates of the trip, the preferred time and method of travel, hotel accommodations, the daily appointments (if known), the preferred airports, and whether any options are possible. Write these facts up as a tentative itinerary, or enter them in a file.

Keep in mind the company's travel policy when drawing up even the initial itinerary, and include flights that fit the fare requirements. Some companies require only that flights be booked the standard 14 or 21 days in advance. Others require that the cheapest flight must be booked, no matter what. In addition, some policies might not allow the traveler to choose the method of transportation.

OBTAINING REFUNDS FOR UNUSED TICKETS

With today's hectic schedules that are always subject to change, travelers might need to change travel plans en route. In such a case, the traveler is entitled to a refund on the unused portion of the ticket. The airline should be informed immediately when the need for cancellation becomes apparent.

If the ticket was handwritten and not an e-ticket, the ticket must be physically returned to the travel agency or airline before the traveler can be issued a refund or credit, depending on the company's policy. If the unused ticket is mailed, include a cover letter mentioning the date of the flight, departure city, destination, ticket number, flight number, credit card number, and cost. Keep the letter in a follow-up folder to make sure that the company credit card is actually credited with the refund or to track credits to be applied to the next trip.

Charles Murray

Itinerary February 19, 200_

Tuesday, February 19 (New York to Raleigh)

10:00 a.m.	Leave West Side Airline Terminal, New York, by limousine or van for Newark airport.
11:10 a.m.	Leave Newark airport on Eastern Airlines Flight #275 (lunch). (Ticket attached)
1:19 p.m.	Arrive Raleigh. Van to Hotel Hilton. (Reservation attached)
2:00 p.m.	Yvonne Lee, Office Manager at Raleigh branch, will pick you up at the Hilton. Conference scheduled at branch office. (File #1 in briefcase)

Wednesday, February 20 (Raleigh)

9:00 a.m.	Yvonne Lee will pick you up at the hotel for inspection of Raleigh plant. (File #2 in briefcase contains facts and statistics on plant operation)
1:00 p.m.	Lunch with Yvonne Lee and Neil Jordan, Raleigh Plant Manager.
3:00 p.m.	Conference with plant shift managers.
8:00 p.m.	Company dinner at Hotel Hilton. (Speech in File #3 in briefcase)

Thursday, February 21 (Raleigh to Winston-Sale, via Greensboro)

9:30 a.m.	Yvonne Lee will pick you up at the hotel and drive you to the airport.
9:56 a.m.	Leave Raleigh on Delta Airlines Flight #101. (Ticket attached)
10:18 a.m.	Arrive Greensboro airport. Limousine or van to Winston-Salem Hotel in Winston-Salem. (Reservation attached) Lunch at hotel.
3:00 p.m.	Appointment with John Spaaks, Office Manager at Winston-Salem branch, and Teresa Kopecky, Sales Director. Hotel Winston-Salem, Green Room. (File #4 in briefcase)
7:00 p.m.	Dinner at Bill Lawson's home. (Telephone 722-1234)

Sample Itinerary (page 1 of 2)

If no limitations exist concerning the travel method, obtain complete information on all airlines and railroads serving the city of destination, including arrival and departure times and the costs of each. Also include information about car rental agencies at the various destinations. List all the choices available, and let the executive decide which to use.

As further pieces of information about the trip are gathered, the assistant can fill in the details of the itinerary. These details might include departure

Friday, February 22 (Winston-Salem)

9:00 a.m.   Golf with Bill Lawson.

1:00 p.m.   Conference with staff at Winston-Salem offices.
               (File #5 in briefcase)

8:00 p.m.   Company dinner at Winston-Salem Hotel. (Speech in
               File #6 in briefcase)

**Saturday, February 23 (Winston-Salem to Greenville via
             Asheville)**

9:02 a.m.   Leave Winston-Salem on Southern Airlines Flight
               #501. (Ticket attached)

10:10 a.m.   Arrive Asheville. Limousine or van to Greenville
               Hotel in Greenville. (Reservation attached) Lunch
               at hotel.

2:00 p.m.   Conference with Greenville branch office manager
               Nasim Borzorg at Greenville Hotel, Mezzanine
               Lounge. (File #7 in briefcase)

7:00 p.m.   Company dinner at hotel. (Speech in File #8 in
               briefcase)

Sunday, February 24 (Greenville to Columbia)

3:00 p.m.   Leave Greenville/Spartanburg airport on Southern
               Airlines commuter flight #38. (Ticket attached)

4:00 p.m.   Arrive Columbia. George Lewis, Office Manager, will
               meet you at the airport. Magnolia Hotel.
               (Reservation attached)

Monday, February 25 (Columbia)

9:00 a.m.   Conference at Columbia offices. George Lewis will
               pick you up at the hotel. (File #9 in briefcase
               contains statistics and progress reports from this
               branch)

7:00 p.m.   Dinner meeting of Columbia staff at Magnolia Hotel.
               (Speech in File #10 in briefcase)

Tuesday, February 26 (Columbia to New York)

10:00 a.m.   George Lewis will pick you up to take you to the
               airport.

11:07 a.m.   Leave Columbia on Eastern Airlines Flight #666
               (lunch). (Ticket attached)

2:33 p.m.   Arrive Newark airport. Limousine to New York
               offices.

Sample Itinerary (page 2 of 2)

times, optional flight times, layovers, connections, arrival times, ground transportation, times and locations of appointments, people attending appointments, reference material needed for each, special meals, scheduled events, and so on.

In planning an itinerary, bear in mind that while en route to each destination, the traveler must have the time and a place to eat regularly, to rest, to travel from a terminal to the place of an appointment, and so forth. Therefore, the following information should be included in the schedule:

- Eating locations (plane, train, hotel, restaurant).

- Sufficient time to travel from the place of arrival to the appointment.

- Event times, listed in both the time zone of the destination and the time zone of the home office.

- Two copies of the final itinerary, meeting files, confirmation documents, and any other relevant travel information—one for the traveler and one for the office professional. Keep yours handy, in case the traveler calls while on the road with a problem. Additional copies of the schedule alone may be given to supervisors, family members, and others in the organization who might need to contact the traveler.

MAKING RESERVATIONS

For both domestic and international travel, the phone proves handy for finding information and making reservations quickly. The major airlines all have toll-free numbers listed in the Yellow Pages of the phone book (see the following section for numbers and Web site addresses). Most major hotel chains and car-rental agencies also maintain international branches, so arrangements for both can be made easily from the office. The Yellow Pages have toll-free numbers for these, too.

To make a plane reservation, call the reservation desk of the airline and give your boss's name, the name and address of the firm, the credit card number, the desired flight number, the city of departure and city of destination, and the time the flight is scheduled to leave. If the flight is already filled, or if a considerable change in departure time has occurred, ask for alternatives. If none of the suggestions is acceptable, ask to be put on standby, and then try to make reservations on another airline. As soon as a reservation is available and confirmed, immediately cancel the other arrangements, including the standby reservation.

When a reservation has been confirmed, ask for the confirmation in writing, and get the confirmation number over the phone. All future conversations and transactions will refer to that number—keep it safe and make sure that the traveler has a copy. Reservations for hotel rooms and rental cars also will give you a confirmation number.

When renting a car, be persistent in asking for the lowest rate possible. Check for promotional offers that may be lower than the corporate rate. Also know the travel itinerary before making the reservation; a difference in a few dozen driving miles per day can result in a lower-priced category. Before the reservation is finalized, check such details as late charges, city and state sales taxes, fuel charges, drop-off charges, insurance extras, backup cars in case of breakdown, emergency services, and so on.

If the executive travels frequently, the office professional may want to add the following resources to the office reference library:

TRAIN TRAVEL

Trains are of decreasing importance as a travel method in the United States: Disappearing railroad connections to desired cities reflect this. A rail trip takes longer than air travel and can be more expensive. However, some executives may not be able to fly (for health reasons, for example). For specific details about available rail destinations, call Amtrak at 800-872-7245.

Once overseas, however, trains still provide a viable form of transportation. Your travel agent will be able to supply you with information about the condition of the railroads in any particular country.

- *The Official Airlines Guide.* This guide provides information on airlines that service each city in the United States, its possessions, and Canada. It also includes information on car rental and taxi service in each city. The book is available by writing to *The Official Airlines Guide,* 2000 Clearwater Drive, Oak Brook, IL 60521; or by calling 800-323-3537.

- *Hotel and Motel Red Book.* This guide lists hotels and motels by city and state; indicates the number of rooms, rates, and plans (e.g., American, with meals; European, without meals); lists recreational facilities; gives toll-free telephone numbers for each; and indicates whether the hotel or motel is part of a chain. A special section lists the number and types of meeting rooms of various seating capacities, along with their audiovisual capabilities. Published annually, the *Hotel and Motel Red Book* is available from the American Hotel and Motel Association Directory Corporation, 1201 New York Avenue NW, Washington, DC 20036.

- *AAA Tour Books.* These guidebooks from the American Automobile Association describe one or more states per volume and list motels, hotels, inns, restaurants, and recreational spots for automobile travelers. Books for every state are available from local AAA offices and are free to members.

INTERNET TRAVEL SERVICES

More travel information is now available on the Web, and with encryption techniques improving, more actual transactions are being conducted. Travel is no exception to this; it's an industry that has embraced the Web enthusiastically from the beginning. Not only is it possible to research, book, and pay for an entire trip online, but Web sites also enable you to indicate seating preferences and meal selection, discover the length of travel time, find out about fare restrictions, hunt for fare discounts, and more.

An especially valuable feature of online travel services is the capability to compare up-to-the-minute flight prices and times. A few of these services are PC Travel (located at pctravel.net), easySabre (at easysabre.com) and the Official Airline Guide Electronic Travel Services (go to the home page at www.oag.com).

For comprehensive services that provide one-stop shopping for air travel, hotel reservations, and car rental, check expedia.com, previewtravel.com, travel.com, and airtravel.net.

Sites that specialize in booking air travel and providing discounted tickets are airline-fares.com, 4airlines.com, air-fare.com, and bestfares.com. For hotel and motel information and reservations, check travelWeb.com and hotelamerica.com.

Airlines, hotels, or car rental agencies also can be reached at their individual home sites. Here are several, with their Web addresses and toll-free numbers.

Travel Services: Web Sites and 800 Numbers

Company	Web Address	800 Number
Airlines		
Airline Aer Lingus	aerlingus.ie	800-474-7424
AeroMexico	aeromexico.com	800-237-6639
Air Canada	aircanada.com	800-776-3000
American Airlines	aa.com	800-433-7300
British Airways	britishairways.com	800-247-9297
China Air	china-air.com	800-227-5118
Continental	flycontinental.com	800-523-3273
Delta	delta-air.com	800-221-1212 (Dom) 800-241-4141 (Int'l)
El Al	elal.com	800-223-6700
Finnair	finnair.com	800-950-5000
Iberia	iberia.com	800-772-4642
Japan Airlines	japanair.com	800-525-3663
Korean Air	koreanair.com	800-438-5000
Lan-Chile Airlines	lanchile.com	800-488-0070
Lufthansa	lufthansa.com	800-645-3880
Northwest Airlines	nwa.com	800-225-2525 (Dom) 800-447-4747 (Int'l)
Qantas	qantas.com	800-227-4500

Swissair	swissair.com	800-221-4750
TWA	twa.com	800-221-2000
United Airlines	ual.com	800-241-6522
US Airways	usair.com	800-428-4322

Hotels and Motels

Best Western	bestwestern.com	800-780-7234
Embassy Suites	embassysuites.com	800-362-2779
Hilton	hilton.com	800-445-8667
Holiday Inn	holidayinn.com	800-465-4329
Howard Johnson	hojo.com	800-446-4656
Hyatt	hyatt.com	800-233-1234
Marriott	marriott.com	800-228-9290
Radisson	radisson.com	800-333-3333
Sheraton	sheraton.com	800-325-3535

Car-Rental Agencies

Alamo	goalamo.com	800-327-9633
Avis	avis.com	800-831-2847
Budget	budgetrentacar.com	800-527-0700
Enterprise	enterprise.com	800-327-8007
Hertz	hertz.com	800-654-3131
National	national.com	800-227-7368
Thrifty	thrifty.com	800-367-2277

INTERNATIONAL TRAVEL

The world is now a global village, meaning that today's traveler is as likely to be flying to Riyadh as to Richmond. But although the frequency of flying overseas has increased to the point of everyday business, international travel still requires extra preparations to smooth the trip and extra care to smooth the face-to-face encounter.

To begin planning, you'll need a bit more basic information. In addition to the list of countries to be visited and the trip dates, you'll need to find out the following:

- *Any requirements that the United States has for travelers.* Most of these requirements include customs for travelers re-entering the country and limits and/or fees based on the nature and amount of items being brought back. Business samples could be exempt from these limits or fees;

however, the business traveler must fill out specific exemption forms. Likewise, no more than $10,000 may be brought into or taken out of the country without filing a report.

■ *Any requirements that the destination country has for travelers.* These requirements vary from place to place and can include a visa for entry, a return ticket, sufficient funds for the stay, vaccinations, health insurance, and, in some cases, a test for Human Immunodeficiency Virus (HIV/AIDS). Some countries also limit the amount of currency that can be brought into or taken out of its borders.

■ *Any conditions imposed on business travelers that are not imposed on tourists.* For example, business travelers cannot use a tourist visa; they must obtain a business visa. Next, assemble a list of the names, nationalities, and citizenship of all employees who will be traveling; the countries to which they will travel; and the length of the trips. You'll need this basic information as you determine who needs visas, entry permits, and other official documents.

> **TIP:** Once again, assembling a detailed travel folder for each traveler is important. For foreign travel, it is useful to provide each traveler with a small ticket case (easily obtainable from travel agencies or office supply stores) for all transport tickets, official travel documents, and a passport. Travelers should be advised to keep this ticket case with them at all times.

In making foreign transportation arrangements, the agency or in-house travel service should be competent and experienced not only in international travel, but in corporate travel as well. Arranging a package tour to Italy, where a group of tourists could then be handed off to a sightseeing bus, differs significantly from arranging the detailed itinerary of a jewelry executive who will meet with a dozen new and prospective sources of Italian silver chains. If the agency is not fully experienced, make sure that you find a service that specializes or has some skill in international corporate travel. It's also invaluable that the agency have a toll-free number to call anytime for problems. This number can be helpful for the traveler on the road who might have lost a ticket, missed a connection, or changed his or her schedule.

> **TIP:** Although travel agencies often provide basic information about foreign countries, it's helpful for the visitor who is new to a particular place to have a guidebook, which the office assistant can pick up at most bookstores. A good guidebook can brief travelers on the country's customs and local sites and provide information on hotels and restaurants as well.

Travel is sometimes a bit different in foreign countries. In Europe, for example, it's common (and not that expensive) to hire a car and driver for the few days an executive might be in town. It's also more common to take the bus. Taxis are ubiquitous, but as in the United States, check first to make sure that they'll be available on both ends before committing your traveler to taxis between meetings. Train travel is much more common; between London and Paris it now replaces a short shuttle flight or a bumpy channel ferry. See what works best for your travelers and their schedules. In some foreign countries, guides are required (or at least recommended). Often, foreign business contacts can help arrange local transportation, a translator, or a guide, if necessary.

TIP: When scheduling a trip, bear in mind that many countries celebrate holidays and holy days that differ from those in the United States. Make sure that you check a calendar for the country of travel. This will prevent the executive from scheduling a business lunch in Saudi Arabia during Ramadan, when business clients are likely to be fasting till sundown; or from counting on bank services in Sri Lanka on May 22, National Heroes Day, which is also a bank holiday.

Make sure that you keep track of time differences as well. Make a note on the itinerary so that travelers know when they can call the office—and so the office knows when to call them. Nothing is as annoying for travelers as spending a late night out at a long business dinner, only to be rung up by the office shortly after going to bed.

INTERNATIONAL AIRLINE TRAVEL

For domestic flights, travelers have the option of first-class, business class, or economy (coach). The main differences arise in the size and comfort of the seats, the types of meals, and the amount of leg space. First-class travelers enjoy wider seats and more leg room. They are served restaurant-like meals and complimentary alcoholic beverages. Business-class passengers sit in slightly smaller seats, have no middle seats in the rows, and eat meals similar to those in first-class. The coach section of the plane accommodates many more passengers; thus, there's decreased leg room and the seats are set much more closely together. Meals are less elaborate, and alcoholic beverages are purchased separately.

On international flights, travel classes offer a much larger range of service. First-class often offers seats that recline for sleeping, elaborate multicourse meals, and fine wines and liquors. International business class is similar to domestic first class and is quite comfortable for business travelers. International coach or economy service is similar to coach service in the United States. Keep in mind that services will also vary depending on the airline, the region, and the length of the flight. Short flights won't provide the services that long flights do.

If you are booking travelers on international first- or business class, make sure you clarify with the ticket agent the services actually being offered, and weigh these against the traveler's needs. For example, in most cases the executive can fly business class (instead of first-class) and arrive just as comfortably for considerably less cost. On the other hand, if no business class is provided and the executive is expected to arrive in Europe rested for a morning meeting, it may be worth the additional cost to fly first-class. Always confirm your company's travel policy before upgrading.

Business- and first-class passengers are usually granted use of special terminal lounges. In larger international airports such as Tokyo, London, or Paris, these lounges include such services as meals, showers, and valet service.

PASSPORT, VISA, IMMUNIZATIONS, AND CUSTOMS

Every country has some requirements for visitors, although these vary widely from place to place. For a country-by-country listing, visit the State Department's Web site at http://travel.state.gov. Although the list is updated once a year, political events can rapidly change both the climate of a country and its travel status. For up-to-date changes, check the same Web site for the State Department's list of travel warnings and consular information sheets. The consular information sheets list the location of the U.S. embassy or consulate, health conditions, minor political disturbances, facts about currency, and entry penalties for each country.

Passport

All U.S. citizens traveling abroad should carry a passport at all times. This is strongly recommended, even in countries such as Mexico and Canada, where one is not required. These countries require proof of U.S. citizenship anyway, which the passport proves. In all cases, emergency itinerary changes, accidents, and sudden medical or legal problems may be handled more smoothly if a passport can be shown.

Before departure, two photocopies of the passport's identification page should be made to help facilitate replacement if the passport is lost or stolen. One copy should be kept with the traveler, and one should be kept at the office.

Anyone requiring a passport can apply for one at a passport agent's office; through a clerk of a Federal court, state court, or court of record; through a judge or clerk of a probate court; or through a designated postal clerk. Passport agencies are located in Boston, Chicago, Honolulu, Houston, Los Angeles, Miami, New Orleans, New York, Philadelphia, Portsmouth (New Hampshire), San Francisco, Seattle, Stanford (Connecticut), and Washington, DC. For passport information, contact Passport Services, Bureau of Consular Affairs,

1425 K Street NW, Washington, DC 20524; or call 202-647-0518. Forms are available from your local post office. Downloadable, printable passport applications are also available from the following Web site: www.travel.state. gov/passport_services.html.

The traveler should allow several weeks for a passport because processing normally takes 25 days. An expedited passport can be arranged in about three working days, but this requires an additional fee, as well as proof (such as plane tickets) that the applicant is leaving the country in less than two weeks (or in less than three weeks if a visa is also required). Expedited passports can be applied for in person at one of the passport agencies, but note that lines tend to be longest during the first half of the year, from January to July. These passports also may be applied for by mail, but payment for overnight return delivery must be included.

For all passports, the applicant is required to show proof of citizenship (birth certificate with embossed seal, certificate of naturalization, baptismal certificate, or voter registration certificate). Two full-face, front-view passport photos also must be presented. Many photo shops offer this service and develop the picture while the traveler waits. After a passport is issued, it is valid for 10 years.

A passport may be renewed by mail by submitting the previous passport if it has been less than 12 years since originally issued. In addition, the traveler's name on the original passport must be the same. If the name has been changed by marriage or a court order, the passport still can be renewed by mail if proper documentation of the name change is provided.

Visas

In addition to a passport, some countries require visitors to obtain permission to enter that country through a document called an entry permit or a visa. Call the consulates or embassies of the countries to be visited for their current requirements. (A travel agent or library should be able to provide the address and telephone number.) Also check the visa requirements posted on the State Department's Web site (http://travel.state.gov). If a visa or entry permit is necessary, the traveler must present a passport at the consulate and fill out a form. Some countries do not charge for their visas; others base the fee on the length of the visit. Be sure that you know the dates involved when applying. Because the length of time necessary to process a visa varies by country, this must be done well in advance of the set departure date.

Immunizations

The country's consulate determines which immunizations are needed, if any. A Certificate of Vaccination, as well as the shots themselves, can be obtained at a local board of health. The traveler also should be sure that personal immunizations are up-to-date, including those for measles, mumps, rubella, polio, diphtheria, tetanus, and pertussis. An increasing number of countries now require foreigners to be tested for Human Immunodeficiency Virus (HIV) prior to entry, especially for long-term visits.

Customs

To help the traveler avoid difficulties when entering the country of destination and returning to this country, the office professional should obtain information about customs regulations. The details can be found in pamphlets issued by the U.S. Treasury Department, located at the Bureau of Commerce in Washington, D.C. Further information can be obtained from the travel agent arranging the trip, from the individual consulates, and from the Department of Customs Web site at www.customs.ustreas.gov/.

Customs requirements vary depending on the individual country. Mexico, for example, limits the value of goods brought into the country to $300; Israel requires that all equipment (including laptops, cameras, and video cameras) be registered.

GETTING EXTRA BUSINESS HELP WHILE AWAY

Often travelers will find that they need office or secretarial services to help them conduct their business while away. It's very common, especially in Europe, for the hotel itself to have an extensive business center. This will accommodate business people in the hotel for just a day or two, as well as business people there for longer stays. Services can include faxing to and from the travelers' office at odd times; printing, copying or typing files; and arranging for private conference rooms or for a temporary assistant or secretary. If the company has several people in the hotel at once who need space for meetings or formal entertaining, it might be worthwhile to book a suite. Private rooms that accommodate several people often can be added on to the suite. Dining rooms or common rooms can be used for small meetings, lunches, dinners, or receptions.

If the hotel does not offer these services, or if the executive expects frequent or long-term office requirements, it is possible to rent furnished offices and office services in almost any country on a daily, weekly, monthly, or annual basis. The hotel concierge can be a great help in referring foreign business travelers to the appropriate place. The in-house hotel business center also can make recommendations if their own facilities do not suffice.

Services to expect from such companies include the following:

- Private office space/conference rooms/showrooms
- Business mailing address
- Mail-collecting and forwarding service
- 24-hour telephone answering service

- Multilingual office-assistant services

- Communication services, including photocopying, dictation, fax, telex, modem

- Internet, teleconferencing, videoconferencing

- Document safekeeping

In addition, these companies might provide assistance in making business contacts in the country in which the executive rents space or services, or in obtaining legal and financial advice. Costs, of course, vary depending on the space or services required.

MONEY: YOURS AND THEIRS

Don't wait too long before purchasing funds for the traveler's trip. Between the time a trip is first booked and the actual departure, the exchange rate can vary widely. Follow the rate in the financial pages of the newspaper, and buy when the dollar is strong. Because the rate changes daily, do not buy funds with a check or a credit card. By the time the check is actually cashed or the credit-card order actually processed, the rate can be much lower. Electronic transfer is best.

Traveler's checks are probably the safest and most convenient form in which to carry money while traveling abroad. They can be cashed easily in most cities, and in case of loss or theft, they can be replaced when a report is filed with the bank or agency from which they were purchased. For this purpose, the traveler should keep a copy of the checks' serial numbers in a place other than a wallet; a copy of the serial numbers also should be kept at the home office. Travelers' checks are usually available in the currency of the country to be visited and can be bought in the United States when the exchange rate is optimal. Also keep in mind that the exchange rate, as well as the service charge, can vary from bank to bank.

The office professional should obtain for the traveler a small amount of cash in the local currency to pay for taxis and porters on arrival. Banks may be closed at the destination, or the tired traveler simply might wish to leave the airport quickly without battling the crowds to cash a check. U.S. banks with an international department or currency exchange branches usually can provide a limited amount of funds in the desired currencies. Currency dealers, hotels, and most international airports are other sources, but a bank offers the best rate of exchange. Although the exchange rate on the "black market" may be tempting, it's inadvisable, foolish, and possibly even dangerous to use it.

When large amounts of cash will be needed in a foreign country, it is best to arrange for a line of credit with a U.S. bank before leaving. This line of credit then can be used to obtain funds from associated banks en route.

Some countries have currency restrictions that limit the amount of local currency that may be brought into or taken out of its borders. Check with the appropriate consulate or embassy for the latest information.

LEGAL HELP ABROAD

Legal difficulties abroad can be as complicated as legal difficulties at home, particularly in suits involving drug trafficking, personal injury, divorce, child custody, nationality, paternity, wills and estates, immigration violations, customs violations, drunk driving, and so on. Because of the complicated and varied legal systems in many other parts of the world, it is advisable to consult a law firm with experience in these matters. One such firm is the International Legal Defense Counsel, which is staffed by experienced American attorneys and has been providing this type of assistance for many years. The address is 111 South 15th Street, 24th Floor, Philadelphia, PA 19102; 215-977-9982.

The U.S. citizen must remember that he or she is subject to the laws and regulations of the country being visited. These laws sometimes differ significantly from those in the United States and might not provide the civil liberties taken for granted in this country. Laws also differ significantly from country to country and sometimes involve unexpected criminal penalties. For example, a traffic accident in Japan automatically becomes a criminal offense if an injury is involved. In case of arrest, the traveler should immediately contact the U.S. consul, whose range of services includes providing a list of local attorneys, providing information about the country's legal procedures, relaying information and requests to family and friends, and more. However, the services themselves are limited to the country's laws: A consul cannot get the traveler released on the simple basis of being an American citizen.

MEDICAL HELP ABROAD

A few simple first-aid items carried in a personal emergency kit can help cure uncomplicated illnesses and make life much more comfortable. Such items include aspirin (or an aspirin substitute), bandages, an antiseptic cream, a thermometer, sunscreen, antihistamines, nasal decongestants, antidiarrheal medication, and sunglasses. An extra pair of prescription glasses—or at least a written copy of the prescription (available from the traveler's optometrist)—should be included in case glasses are broken or contact lenses are lost.

If the traveler takes medication, it should be carried in its original container with the prescription attached; this will lessen problems with customs or during security checks in the foreign country. The name of the medication, along with the doctor's name and telephone number, should be carried separately in case the medication is lost. A letter from the doctor is also useful. Even with the written prescription and letter, however, certain medications that are legal in the United States might be considered illegal narcotics in the country to be visited. For example, Japan prohibits inhalers and allergy and sinus medication. Check the particular country's consul beforehand. If the medication is necessary, it may be possible for the consul to recommend a native doctor who can prescribe a similar (though not illegal) drug as a replacement for the duration of the trip.

Before traveling overseas, it is advisable to contact a travelers' clinic in the major city nearest the company. These clinics offer counseling on travel health, especially in countries in which water or disease problems exist. The clinics receive continual updates from the Centers for Disease Control in Atlanta and the World Health Organization to provide this information to their clients. One such clinic is the International Travel Clinic, 601 North Caroline Street, Baltimore, MD 21287; (410) 955-8931. As an alternative, the traveler can consult his or her private physician.

Another suggestion is to join the International Association for Medical Assistance to Travelers (IAMAT), a nonprofit, donation-supported foundation. Its home page is www.sentex.net/~iamat/; the address is 417 Center Street, Lewiston, NY 14092; 716-754-4883. No membership fee is required, although donations are accepted. Upon joining, the member will be sent a directory of doctors serving in 125 countries and territories worldwide. The physicians have been educated in international medical practices, with skills meeting Western standards. All speak English and are available to members 24 hours a day. A fixed fee is charged for office visits and house or hotel calls, as well as for holiday and Sunday visits. The traveler also will receive a Travelers Clinical Record (to be completed by a family doctor and carried with the traveler) in addition to world immunization and malaria risk charts.

Another organization that provides personal and medical service for international travelers is International SOS Assistance, Inc., 8 Neshaminy Interplex, Suite 207, Trevose, PA 19053; 215-244-1500. If the local medical center is inadequate, International SOS Assistance arranges for the patient to be evacuated to the nearest medical facility for treatment of the illness or injury. After stabilization, the patient is returned to facilities near home. More details are available by contacting the organization directly.

Most major hotels around the world also have a doctor on call and can make arrangements with the nearest clinic or hospital to treat guests who become ill.

In case of serious illness, the U.S. consul can help in finding appropriate medical services and medical evacuation.

Medical Insurance

Before departure, the traveler should determine what, if anything, his or her existing health insurance covers. Some policies provide coverage outside the United States, while others do not. Very few pay for medical evacuation back to this country, which may cost as much as $10,000. Check with either the

Compiling a Travel File

Each copy of the complete file (the traveler's and the office professional's) should contain the following, whether as documents or spreadsheets, copies of e-mail, or scanned-in forms:

- An appointment calendar listing the days, dates, and times of each meeting
- The name and address of each company to be visited
- A list of the individuals to see and their positions in the company
- A list of the officers and executives of the organization
- A list of the individuals with whom the executive has had contact in the past (other than those with whom appointments are scheduled), and the circumstances of these contacts
- Telephone numbers of the company and individuals to be seen
- Past correspondence with the firm or individual
- Letters or memos concerning the problem to be discussed
- All confirmations for hotel accommodations
- All confirmations for transportation, airline tickets, and other relevant materials
- Directions from hotels to meetings
- Miscellaneous items, such as notes for speeches and descriptions of customs for foreign countries

Except for necessary hard-copy documents (such as hotel confirmations, contracts, and so on), much of the previous information might be stored on disk for the traveler's laptop. Be sure that the battery is fully charged before the executive leaves—security checkpoints will ask that the laptop be taken out of its case and turned on. Also check to see what electrical adapters, if any, are needed for power sources in the places to be visited.

An excellent way to arrange all this travel material is with an accordion folder with section dividers. Mark the tabs with headings such as "Flights," "Hotel," "Car rental," "Jackson meeting," "Lundquist contract," and so on. In each section, put all the information pertinent to that subject; for example, a Meeting section would contain copies of correspondence about the meeting's subject, relevant files and documents, directions to the meeting location, method of transportation, names and phone numbers of people to be seen, and so on. Keeping all the information at an executive's fingertips simplifies the many problems of traveling. Then when the executive first arrives and the hotel says, "We have no record of your reservation," he or she can immediately turn to the Hotel section and pull out a copy of the confirmation letter without having to rummage.

employer or the insurance agent to get all the details of coverage, including exceptions, deductibles, maximum limits, and procedures to follow in case of need.

If the traveler is not covered by an existing policy, contact International Health Service, Georgetown University Medical Center, 3800 Reservoir Road, NW, Washington, DC 20007; 202-687-1872 for information.

RENTING AND DRIVING CARS IN OTHER COUNTRIES

If a traveler intends to drive overseas, the office professional should check with the embassy or consulate of each country for its requirements for a driver's license, road permits, and automobile insurance. If possible, also obtain road maps of the countries.

Although many countries do not recognize a U.S. driver's license, most will accept an international driving permit, which the traveler should obtain before departure. The State Department has authorized only two organizations to issue international driver permits: the American Automobile Association (AAA) and the American Automobile Touring Alliance. To obtain an international driving permit, the traveler must be at least 18 years of age and must present two passport-size photos and a valid U.S. driver's license.

Even with the international permit, however, it is wise to check with the consulate for requirements for drivers. Each country has its own age requirement for licenses, which may supersede the requirements for the international permit. In addition, many countries require a road permit, which is used in place of tolls on highways. The traveler could be fined if found driving without one. The consulate also can advise the traveler on road and parking signs, speed limits, insurance requirements, and other key information. Great Britain, for example, is not the only country whose drivers drive on the left side of the road.

Much of the procedure of renting a car overseas is similar to renting one at home. The traveler should read the rental agreement carefully to note significant differences, as well as to check for such details as late charges, city and state sales taxes, fuel charges, drop-off charges, back-up cars in case of breakdown, emergency service, and so on. Car-rental agencies usually provide automobile insurance, but it is often minimal. The traveler should purchase the equivalent of what he or she uses at home.

The traveler should be especially aware of the country's borders when driving a rental car. Cars rented in certain countries are not allowed in others. For example, a rental car from Austria is not allowed into Greece, luxury rentals are not allowed into Italy, and rental cars in Morocco must stay completely within its borders. Again, the office professional should check with the individual embassy beforehand.

BUSINESS ETIQUETTE ABROAD

Although people are more alike than different, they can easily take offense when their differences are ignored or unintentionally insulted. To be effective, the international business executive must make an effort to have a passing knowledge of the cultures and customs of the countries to be visited—especially their etiquette rules.

The following practices may vary greatly from culture to culture: religious customs, dietary laws, table manners, humor, style of dress, gift-giving practices, privacy issues, degrees of formality in person and in writing, tipping, local superstitions, and more. International etiquette involves many elements, each of which differ among countries. The next sections describe just a few that affect business travelers.

Timeliness

Although punctuality is a valued courtesy for Americans, it is a critical element of etiquette for the Germans, Romanians, and Japanese. On the other hand, clients in the Middle East, the Caribbean, and many Latin countries have a much more relaxed notion of time. Because being a half-hour late for an appointment is not necessarily an offense, the traveler should not necessarily read a hidden meaning into it if he or she is made to wait in these countries.

Gifts

At some point during the trip, the traveler is likely to be a dinner guest either at a restaurant or in the home of a business client. Although it is almost universally accepted for a guest to bring a gift (except in China, where gift-giving is discouraged), what makes it suitable varies from place to place. For example, the common gift of wine in the United States would offend a client in an Islamic country. Candy, pastries, or fruit make a safe choice for most countries, and small age-appropriate gifts for the host's children are encouraged. Souvenirs from the United States, such as landmark-site gift-shop items or foods such as maple syrup or macadamia nuts, are both intriguing and inoffensive.

Flowers are usually welcome, but be careful not to offend within that broad category. In some countries (Belgium, Italy, Luxembourg, and Spain), chrysanthemums suggest funerals; in Japan, chrysanthemums are acceptable as long as they are not the ones reserved for the imperial family. Roses suggest a lover's intimacy in Germany, Switzerland, and Poland and therefore are unsuitable for a business contact. The number and color of flowers in the arrangement is also important and varies from country to country.

Imprinted Items

No matter how expensive the gift and how subtle the imprint, items with the traveler's company logo should not be considered when the traveler is a guest. Some countries such as Japan consider imprinted items to be in poor taste in all situations.

Gift-wrapping

In Germany and Japan, the wrapping is as important as the gift inside. In Japan, several hundred ways to wrap gifts exist, each one having a different meaning. No matter which country, what looks like bright paper and festive ribbons may seem gauche to the recipient. Consult a local gift shop for help.

Body Language

A quick and firm handshake appropriate in the United States becomes much softer in France, is repeatedly frequently throughout a conversation in Latin and Middle-Eastern countries, and is seldom used at all in the East. Eye contact in France is maintained much longer than is the custom in the United States. Hispanic, southern European, and Middle-Eastern people also maintain a long and steady eye contact, while people in Asian countries are more likely to avoid direct eye contact altogether.

Common gestures in the United States may have unsuspected meanings in other countries, so the traveler should be conscious of hand and foot movements. Pointing with one's finger is rude in Asian countries, for example, as is crossing the legs. Middle-Eastern countries also dislike crossing the legs. Shorthand expressions also carry a risk of offending one's contacts: In many areas of the world, the "V-for-Victory" sign of two extended fingers is a vulgarity.

Formality

The American business traveler who is accustomed to using first names and knowing a great deal of personal information about clients should be prepared for a higher degree of formality in other countries. The safest course is to address all people by their surnames (Mr. Dudley, Señora Ramirez, Monsieur Guignard), unless specifically invited to do otherwise. Information about the other person's family could be sparse, and relationships may take longer to develop.

HANDLING BUSINESS WHILE THE BOSS IS AWAY

One of the ways the office professional is most useful to the traveling executive is by handling matters smoothly and capably while he or she is away. Following are a few basic steps:

- *Set a chain of authority.* Prior to departure, the office professional should work out with the executive which matters should be forwarded at once to his or her attention, which should be forwarded to other executives, and which should be handled personally. If some of these matters fall beyond the office professional's usual area of responsibilities, the executive should send a memo to everyone involved, granting the assistant authority to act in his or her absence.

- *Adjust the calendar.* While the executive is still in the office, cancel or reschedule appointments that fall during the business trip. Also make sure that the executive signs any documents or forms that will be needed in the office during this period.

- *Know how to make contact.* Even if the executive does not wish material to be forwarded, the office professional might need to contact the traveler about an urgent item. The executive's itinerary should be handy and up-to-date with any changes, and the assistant should know at all times how and when (depending on the time change) to make contact—whether through e-mail, fax, phone, telegram, or cablegram. If the traveler is calling in on a regular basis, keep a list of issues that need to be resolved, and address them all at once.

- *Know what to tell callers.* The executive may not wish people outside the company to know that he or she is away from the office, where he or she is, or for how long the trip will last. Before departure, establish what should be said and if there are any exceptions.

- *Keep a record.* The office professional should keep a log of each day's events, which can be used to provide a brief recap when the executive returns. Some travelers might even want the log forwarded to them regularly through fax or e-mail, especially if the trip is lengthy.

- *Divide incoming work.* Though the traveler is away, his or her work continues to pile up. So that the executive is not overwhelmed upon return, it is helpful for the office professional to prioritize the material. This can be done simply though the use of separate manila folders. Urgent items that must be handled at once by the executive can be placed in one folder, copies of work forwarded to other executives can go into another folder, and copies of what the assistant handled personally can go into still another folder. Additional folders can be made for less-critical items such as magazines and newsletters, advertising, and so on.

- *Provide a transition period.* When the traveler returns, he or she might need a period of adjustment to cope with jet lag, the sometimes considerable difference in climate and environment, and the piles of materials labeled Urgent. The office professional should try to keep visitors, appointments, and phone calls to a minimum for a day or two to allow for a smoother transition.

The style of correspondence used in these countries reflects this formality. The flowery introductions and closings now considered to be old-fashioned in the United States are considered a point of etiquette elsewhere. The traveler should take his or her cue from the host. The office professional also should take cues from correspondence arriving from abroad and should imitate its style when preparing responses.

In addition, formal customs might mark business occasions, such as ordering champagne in Germany to signify the closing of a deal. It would be rude to refuse, so the traveler should at all times be prepared to follow the lead of his or her host.

This brief overview indicates how varied and complicated international business etiquette can be. The office professional can be of enormous help here by compiling pertinent information for the traveler about the country to be visited. Just one of the sources that can be tapped is *Letitia Baldridge's New Complete Guide to Executive Manners,* published by Macmillan, which is available from both amazon.com and barnesandnoble.com. In addition, information is available from the Industry and Trade Division of the Department of Commerce in Washington, D.C. The State Department also publishes *Background Notes,* pamphlets on 170 countries that provide brief factual information on culture, history, geography, economy, government, and current political situation. To purchase copies, contact the Superintendent of Documents, U.S. Government Printing Office, Washington, DC 20402; 202-512-1800. Select issues are also available on the State Department's home page at www.state.gov or by fax-on-demand by calling 202-736-7720. The country's own consulate is an ideal source of information, as is the travel agency handling the executive's trip.

POST-TRAVEL TASKS

Upon the traveler's return, the office professional might have to deal with urgent items: contracts, rush orders, special requests by clients, and so on. When the immediate tasks have been handled, the assistant should sort through the materials brought back by the executive and either file them or pass them on for the appropriate action. Thank-you notes to clients for their hospitality should be written for his or her signature. These notes should always be handwritten by the executive personally, but often the assistant can provide a few helpful phrases to get the process started.

Unused currency and traveler's checks in the foreign denomination may be kept if the country is a frequent destination. They can be converted to dollars if trips are infrequent or if the exchange rate is favorable.

The travel agency should already have been notified that all bills not already charged to a credit card must be sent to the attention of either the executive or the assistant. As bills and credit-card statements come in, the office professional should check them carefully before forwarding them to the accounting department or preparing an expense report. This includes canceled checks and credit-card statements, which should be kept for proof of expenses paid.

Expense Reports

Many of the expenses incurred by the traveler abroad are reimbursable. They also might be tax-deductible (either personally or by the company), which requires detailed and accurate recordkeeping. The office professional often coordinates and maintains these records. But can encourage the executive to keep good recordkeeping habits, which will simplify these task reporting tasks.

Some travelers compile their own expense reports. Not only do they total up how much is owed them in each category (or by day), but they also usually attach receipts for documentation of all expenses. When the traveler prepares his or her own expense report, the office professional should look it over to make sure that it conforms to protocol before passing it along for signature. Other travelers—usually executives with their own assistants—will turn expense reports over to their assistants. The assistant then compiles the report, based on the form provided, and assembles the appropriate receipts. Daily records should be annotated as fully as possible: A credit-card slip for a restaurant meal should note who was present and what business was discussed.

Records and receipts should be turned over to the office professional as soon after the trip as possible so that questions can be addressed while the trip is still fresh in mind. If the executive travels frequently, a routine biweekly or monthly timetable might be more convenient for handling records.

If the executive has combined business and pleasure on a trip (for example, has brought his or her family along or extended the length of stay for sightseeing), make sure that the records clearly show which expenses are purely personal.

In case records are lost or stolen, check the company policy for how to handle reimbursements and tax deductions.

Travel-planning duties are an increasingly important part of any office assistant's job, but, fortunately, resources for travel planning are also increasing. For further information on international travel, check the library, bookstores, Web sites, travel agencies, government agencies, and foreign consulates.

FOR MORE INFORMATION

If you can't find what you need from the phone numbers and Web sites listed in this chapter, you may need to expand your search.

- For more information on locating travel agencies, try your local Yellow Pages under travel.

- For more information on travel agency associations and obtaining ratings for agencies, try a Web search for the organization you want, or call information for 800 numbers.

- For more information on e-tickets and if they are the right solution for your travel needs, call any airline directly or check on the Web site.

- For more information on State Department travel advisories, immunization advisories or other international travel requirements, check the State Department Web site (http://travel.state.gov) or call your nearest U.S. consulate.

- For more information on obtaining a passport including requirements and time limits, call the passport agency in your city or your local post office.

- For more information on business customs, holidays, and etiquette for foreign travel, check your local bookstore or library in the business section. You can also check the travel section for any guidebooks or phrase books you might need.

GRAMMAR AND PUNCTUATION GUIDE

◆

- **Introduction**

- **Grammar**

- **Punctuation**

- **Capitalization**

- **Numbers**

- **Compound Words**

- **Usage**

- **Abbreviations**

- **Forms of Address**

INTRODUCTION

This reference contains a complete and concise review of English grammar as well as the basic rules of punctuation and capitalization. It also contains guidelines for the proper treatment of compound words including many commonly used business and technical terms. The section on numbers outlines the proper way to include numbers in both formal and informal writing. The usage section clarifies the appropriate use of words and expressions that are often confused or misused. The rules and guidelines in all sections are clearly illustrated with hundreds of examples. Also included are handy alphabetical lists of standard abbreviations, abbreviations of units of measure, and Latin abbreviations with definitions for each entry. Finally, for letter writing, useful tables indicate the correct forms of address for government and religious officials. With this reference in hand, you will never again be puzzled by such questions as the following:

- Does *XYZ Corporation* need a singular or plural verb?

- Is it *differ from* or *differ with* in this sentence?

- Does this sentence need a comma or a semicolon?

- Should the word *English* in English literature be capitalized?

- Should *1984* be spelled out at the beginning of a sentence?

- Which compound words need a hyphen and which do not?

- What is the difference between *abbreviate* and *abridge*? *allege* and *claim*? *farther* and *further*?

- Are abbreviations acceptable in a letter or report?

- How do you address a letter to a member of Congress?

GRAMMAR

This section provides a brief review of English grammar, concentrating on common errors.

PARTS OF SPEECH

Noun

A noun is a word used to name a person, place, idea, thing, or quality.

Shakespeare, Paris, desk, truth

Pronoun

A pronoun is a word used in place of a noun.

I, we, who, these, each, himself

Verb

A verb is a word or group of words that denotes action, occurrence, or state of being. The verb, together with any words that complete or modify its meaning, forms the predicate of the sentence.

am, has washed, ran, will be seen

Adjective

An adjective is a word that describes or limits (modifies) the meaning of a noun or pronoun.

higher morale, *net* income, *rolling* stone

Adverb

An adverb is a word that modifies a verb, an adjective, or another adverb. It answers the questions where, how or how much, or when.

write *legibly,* long *enough, very* high production, do it *soon,* go *there*

Preposition

A preposition is a word used to relate a noun or pronoun to some other word in the sentence.

at, in, by, from, toward

Conjunction

A conjunction is a word used to join words, phrases, or clauses.

and, but, nor, since, although, when

Interjection

An interjection is an exclamation that expresses strong feeling.

Ah! Nonsense! Shh! Bravo!

Note that the part of speech (grammatical function) represented by a given word is determined by its use in a sentence. For instance, *but* may be an adverb, a preposition, or a conjunction, depending on how it is used.

PHRASES AND CLAUSES

Phrases and clauses are groups of grammatically related words that function as a single part of speech (*noun, adjective,* or *adverb*) or as a sentence.

Phrase

A phrase is a group of grammatically related words *without a subject, a predicate, or both.* A phrase is used as a *noun, adjective,* or *adverb.* Phrases are classified as:

Prepositional:	Put the finished letter *in the mail.* (also adverbial phrase)
	The man *in the red swimsuit* is looking for attention. (also adjective phrase)
Participial:	The woman *giving the talk* speaks with conviction. (also adjective phrase)
Gerund:	*Skiing deep powder* is both exciting and challenging. (also noun phrase)
Infinitive:	Our purpose is *to eat as inexpensively as we can.* (also noun phrase)
	The teacher assigned work *to be done quickly.* (also adjective phrase)
	She ran *to catch the horse.* (also adverbial phrase)

Clause

A clause is a group of grammatically related words containing both a subject and a predicate.

Independent (or main) clauses make a complete statement and are not introduced by any subordinating word. When it stands alone, it is a simple sentence.

We will return the favor.

Dependent (or subordinate) clauses cannot stand alone as simple sentences, usually because they are introduced by a subordinating word. Dependent clauses are classified as:

Adjective:	This is the man *who wrote to us for information.*
	I have the video *he is looking for.* ("that" understood)
Adverb:	*As soon as you have finished icing the cake,* bring it to the table.

Noun: *Whoever conducts the meeting* will be able to answer your questions.

Can you tell me *what my charges will total?*

TYPES OF SENTENCES

Simple Sentence

A simple sentence contains only one independent clause. This does not mean, however, that it must be short. It may include many phrases, a compound subject or predicate, and/or a number of modifiers.

The prisoner escaped.

You should run to the store next door and buy as many tortillas as you can.

Compound Sentence

A compound sentence contains two or more independent clauses, each of which could be written as a simple sentence.

You may want to vacation in the Bahamas, or you may prefer Acapulco instead.

Complex Sentence

A complex sentence contains one independent clause and one or more dependent clauses.

Since the freeway was jammed, we looked for an alternate route.

Compound-Complex Sentence

A compound-complex sentence contains two or more independent clauses and one or more dependent clauses.

Since they moved to town, the river flooded three times, and the stores all shut down.

PARTS OF A SENTENCE

The basic parts of a sentence are the *subject, verb,* and *complement. Modifiers* and *connectives* support this basic sentence structure—modifiers by making the meaning more exact and connectives by showing the relationship between parts.

Subject

The subject of a sentence is the word or group of words that names the thing, person, place, or idea about which a sentence makes a statement. These words or groups of words can include *nouns; pronouns; gerunds; infinitives; demonstrative, interrogative,* and *indefinite pronouns; phrases;* and *clauses.*

Nouns and **pronouns** are the single words most often used as subjects.

> The *director* called the meeting for 3 o'clock. (noun)

> *He* wants everybody to attend. (personal pronoun)

Gerunds and, less often, **infinitives,** are two verbals that may also be the subject of a sentence.

> *Walking* is good exercise. (gerund)

> *To run* is more tiring than to walk. (infinitive)

Demonstrative, interrogative, and **indefinite pronouns** are among the other parts of speech used as subjects.

> *That* is going to be a difficult task. (demonstrative)

> *What* are your plans for doing it? (interrogative)

> *Everyone* is eager to have you succeed. (indefinite)

Phrases serving as a noun may be the subject of a sentence.

> *Adopting that kitten* was the smartest thing he did.

> *To learn as many languages as possible* is his objective.

Clauses in their entirety may be used as the subject.

> *Whoever answers the telephone* will get a chance to win the prize.

> *Whether the wild burro has been released or not* will determine our action.

Verb

The verb tells what the subject itself does, what something else does to the subject, or what the subject is. Verbals, although they come from verbs, cannot serve as verbs in the predicate of a sentence. (For more on verbs and verbals, see the comprehensive section that follows.)

There are three types of verbs: *transitive verbs; intransitive verbs;* and *copulative* or *linking verbs.*

Transitive verbs take a direct object.

> He *hit* the ball.

Intransitive verbs take no direct object.

> She *fell* down.

Copulative or **linking verbs** take a predicate noun or predicate adjective.

> Jim *is* captain.

> Jim *seems* strong.

The properties of a verb are *number, person, tense, mood,* and *voice.* To indicate these properties we either change the form of the verb itself or add other verb forms called *auxiliary verbs—be, have, can, may, might, shall, will, should, would, could, must, do.*

Number tells whether the verb is singular or plural.

Person tells whether the first person (*I*), second person (*you*), or third person (*he, it, she*) is performing the action. A verb and its subject must agree in number and person. (This problem of agreement—so essential to the writing of clear sentences—is discussed in the section on Agreement and Reference.)

Tense is the means by which we show the time of an action—whether it happened in the past, is happening in the present, or will happen in the future.

Mood (indicative, imperative, subjunctive) indicates the manner of assertion—statement, command, wish, or condition.

Voice is the property of a verb that indicates whether the subject is performing or receiving the action of the verb. A verb in the *active voice* tells what the subject is doing; a verb in the *passive voice* tells what is being done to the subject.

> The *athlete completed* his training on time. (The verb *completed,* in the active voice, tells what the subject, *athlete,* did.)

> The *cereal was dropped* on the floor. (The verb *was dropped,* in the passive voice, tells what was done to the subject, *cereal.*)

Complement

The complement is the word or group of words that follows the verb and completes its meaning. A complement may be a *direct object,* an *indirect object,* a *predicate nominative,* or a *predicate adjective.*

Direct objects are nouns or other parts of speech functioning as nouns that receive the action of the verb.

He gave the *map* to the tourist. (*Map* is the direct object of the verb.)

We are trying *to launch a probe to Jupiter.* (The infinitive phrase is the direct object of the verb.)

Give me *whatever information you have.* (The noun clause is the direct object of the verb.)

Indirect objects are nouns or other parts of speech functioning as nouns that indicate to whom (what) or for whom (what) the action of the verb is done.

He gave [to] *her* the tickets. (*Her* is the indirect object of the verb; *tickets* is the direct object.)

Give [to] *whoever answers the door* the bouquet of flowers. (The noun clause is the indirect object of the verb.)

David did [for] *Jerry* a big favor. (*Jerry* is the indirect object; *favor* is the direct object.)

Predicate nominatives are also called predicate nouns, predicate complements, or subjective complements. The predicate nominative follows copulative, or linking, verbs and renames the subject. It can be a noun, a pronoun, a verbal, a phrase, or a clause.

Noun:	He is *chairman* of the committee.
Pronoun:	They thought the author was *she.*
Gerund:	My favorite exercise is *swimming.*
Infinitive phrase:	The purpose of this experiment is *to test the new engine.*
Noun clause:	The next president should be *whoever is best qualified.*

Predicate adjectives are adjectives (or adjective phrases) appearing in the predicate that modify the subject. A predicate adjective occurs only after copulative, or linking, verbs.

The flower smells *sweet.*

The meeting we are planning for Tuesday will be *on that subject.*

This material is *over my head.*

He appears *enthusiastic* about learning to dance.

Modifiers

Modifiers are single words, phrases, or clauses used to limit, describe, or define some element of the sentence. These are classed as either *adjectives* or *adverbs*. A modifier is said to "dangle" when it cannot attach both logically and grammatically to a specific element in the sentence. (For more on modifiers and modification, see the comprehensive section that follows.)

Adjectives describe or limit the meaning of nouns or pronouns.

> The *wily* raccoon was caught in the *baited* trap and transported to an *animal* shelter for *medical* tests.

> The statistics *on juvenile crime* are alarming. (prepositional phrase used as an adjective)

> The report *submitted by the audit committee* is being studied. (participial phrase used as an adjective)

Adverbs modify verbs, verbals, adjectives, or other adverbs. They answer the questions where, how or how much, when, and why?

> We will hold the meeting *here.* (Where?)

> The car accelerated *rapidly.* (How?)

> Spending *excessively,* he ran out of funds. (How much?)

> Let's eat the lasagna *as soon as it is finished cooking.* (When?)

> Pete went downtown *to buy a tie.* (Why?)

Connectives

Connectives join one part of a sentence with another and show the relationship between the parts they connect. Connectives joining elements of equal rank include: *coordinate conjunctions, correlative conjunctions,* and *conjunctive adverbs.* Connectives joining elements of unequal rank include: *subordinate conjunctions, relative pronouns,* and *relative adverbs. Prepositions* are also some of the most important connectives. (For more on the usage of these and other connectives, see the Connectives section.)

Coordinate conjunctions are perhaps the most frequently used connectives. They join sentence elements of equal grammatical importance—words with words, phrases with phrases, independent clauses with independent clauses. The commonly used coordinate conjunctions are:

> *and, but, or, nor, for, yet*

Correlative conjunctions work in pairs to connect sentence elements of equal rank. Each member of a pair of correlative conjunctions must be followed by the same part of speech. Examples of these conjunctions are:

> *either . . . or, neither . . . nor, not only . . . but also, both . . . and*

Conjunctive adverbs connect independent clauses and show a relation of equal rank between them. Although the clause introduced by the conjunctive adverb is *grammatically* independent, it is *logically* dependent upon the preceding clause for its complete meaning. These are some conjunctive adverbs:

> *therefore, however, consequently, accordingly, furthermore, moreover, nevertheless*

Subordinate conjunctions introduce dependent adverb clauses and join them to independent clauses. Some of these conjunctions are:

> *before, since, after, as, because, if, unless, until, although*

NOTE: The subordinate conjunction *that* introduces a noun clause:

When he calls, tell him that *I had to leave for a meeting.*

Relative pronouns not only introduce noun and adjective clauses but also act as pronouns within their own clauses. These pronouns include:

> *that, which, who, whom, whatever, whichever, whoever*

> The salesperson *who called for an appointment* has just arrived. (adjective clause)

> Tell me the news *that you just heard.* (noun clause)

Relative adverbs introduce subordinate clauses. The most common of these connectives are:

> *how, where, when, while*

Prepositions show the relationship between a word that follows them, called the object, and a word before them to which they relate. Some prepositions are:

> *to, of, by, from, between, in, over, under, for*

Verbals

Verbals are nonfinite verbs used as a noun, an adjective, or an adverb. A nonfinite verb can never stand as the only verb in a sentence. There are three verbal forms: *infinitives, participles, gerunds.* (For more on verbs and verbals, see the Verbs and Verbals section that follows.)

Infinitives (to go, to run, to see, etc.) may act as a noun *or* an adjective *or* an adverb.

I like *to swim.* (noun)

A book *to read* is what she wants. (adjective)

He went *to play* golf. (adverb)

Participles may be either a present participle (going, seeing, feeling, etc.) or a past participle (having gone, having seen, having felt, etc.). A participle acts *only* as an adjective.

Going to the store, Jamal slipped. (adjective)

Having seen the entire movie, Judy left the theater. (adjective)

Gerunds (knowing, running, hearing, etc.) act *only* as nouns.

Charlie enjoys *running.* (noun)

Dancing is a good way to enjoy music. (noun)

NOUNS AND PRONOUNS

A noun names a person, thing, idea, place, or quality. There are five classes of nouns: *proper, common, collective, concrete,* and *abstract.*

Pronouns stand in place of nouns. The six classes of pronouns are: *personal, relative, interrogative, indefinite, demonstrative,* and *reflexive.*

Proper Nouns

A proper noun names a particular place, person, or thing. The writer's chief problem with proper nouns is recognizing them in order to capitalize them.

Atlanta, Mr. Jones, the Commissioner of Education, Form 1040

Common Nouns

A common noun names a member of a class or group of persons, places, or things.

hope, banana, education, form

Collective Nouns

A collective noun, singular in form, names a group or collection of individuals. The chief problem with collective nouns is determining the form of the verb to use with the collective noun. For this reason, it is discussed at length in the section on agreement and reference.

> committee, jury, council, task force

Concrete Nouns

A concrete noun names a particular or specific member of a class or group.

> apple, *not* fruit; chair, *not* furniture

Abstract Nouns

An abstract noun names a quality, state, or idea.

> beauty, truth, objectivity

> Notice that common nouns can be concrete or abstract.

Personal Pronouns

The personal pronoun shows which person (first, second, or third) is the subject. Personal pronouns are troublesome because of their many forms; they change form to indicate number, person, and case.

The personal pronouns are:

> I, my, mine, me, you, your, yours, he, his, him, she, her, hers, it, and its, *and their plurals*—we, you, they, it, our, ours, your, yours, their, theirs, us, and them

Relative Pronouns

The relative pronoun serves two purposes: (1) it takes the place of a noun in the clause it introduces, and (2) like a conjunction, it connects its clause with the rest of the sentence.

The relative pronouns are:

> who, whom, which, that, what, whoever, whomever, whichever, whatever

> The relative pronoun has the same number, person, and case as its antecedent.

Interrogative Pronouns

The interrogative pronoun is the same in form as the relative pronoun, but different in function. The interrogative pronoun asks a question.

who ——————————→ refer to persons

whom ——

what   refers to things

which   refers to person or things

As an adjective, *which* and *what* may be used.

. . . which book? . . . what time?

Indefinite Pronouns

The indefinite pronouns listed here are singular, as are most indefinites:

another, anyone, each, either, everyone, no one, nothing . . .

Demonstrative Pronouns

The demonstrative pronouns (*this, that, these, those*) point out or refer to a substantive (usually a noun) which has been clearly expressed or just as clearly implied. They may be used as pronouns

These are the letters he wants.

or as adjectives

Bring me *those* letters.

Reflexive Pronouns

The reflexive pronouns are compound personal pronouns:

myself, yourself, yourselves, himself, themselves, ourselves, herself, itself

A reflexive pronoun emphasizes or intensifies a meaning. It is not set off by commas.

I *myself* will see that it is done.

The director *himself* gave the order.

You will take it to her *yourself.*

A reflexive pronoun often appears as the direct object of a verb; its antecedent, as the subject of the verb.

I taught *myself* how to type.

He hurt *himself* when he fell.

It can, however, be the object of a preposition,

He finished the job by *himself.*

He was beside *himself* with joy.

the indirect object of a verb,

I bought *myself* a new suit yesterday.

They gave *themselves* a pat on the back.

or a predicate nominative.

I am just not *myself* today.

They just were not *themselves* at the party.

In formal usage, the reflexive pronoun is not used where the shorter personal pronoun can be substituted for it with no change in meaning.

Not: Both the director and *myself* endorse the policy.

But: Both the director and *I* endorse the policy.

Avoid the following pronoun errors:

The use of *hisself* for *himself.*

The use of *theirselves* for *themselves.*

The use of *myself* or *yourself* instead of the personal pronoun *me, I,* or *you* in such constructions as "The secretary and *myself* opened the mail. It's ideal for a professional person such as *yourself*."

CASE

Case is the property of a noun or pronoun which shows, either by inflection (change in form) or by position, the relation of the word to other parts of the sentence.

English has three cases: *nominative, objective,* and *possessive.*

All nouns and a few pronouns keep the same form in the nominative and in the objective cases. Consequently, we must depend on the position of these words in the sentence to indicate their function. Since nouns don't change form to indicate nominative and objective case, our only real difficulty with them comes in the formation and use of the possessive case.

On the other hand, some pronouns are inflected (change form) in the nominative and objective cases, as well as in the possessive. Because of this, the case of pronouns causes us more trouble than does the case of nouns.

Nominative Case

The nominative (or subjective) case is used primarily to name the subject of a verb or the predicate complement after a copulative, or linking, verb (such as *seem, appear,* or any form of *be*).

> Not: Either *she* or *me* will be responsible.

> But: Either *she* or *I* will be responsible. (Either *she* will be . . . or *I* will be . . .)

NOTE: An appositive, which is a word or group of words standing next to another word and denoting the same person or thing, is always in the same case as its antecedent (the word to which it stands in apposition). Therefore, if the antecedent is in the nominative case, the appositive must also be in the nominative case. If the antecedent is in the objective case, the appositive is also in the objective case.

> Not: The representatives, *John and me,* are to meet on Friday.

> But: The representatives, *John and I,* are to meet on Friday. (*John and I* are to meet. . . .)

Subject of a Verb in a Main Clause

A noun or pronoun serving as the subject of a verb (except the subject of an infinitive) is in the nominative case.

> *I* was late for work this morning.

> *He* is planning to finish his pancakes this morning.

> Neither *she nor I* had heard of this before.

> The culprits, *she and I,* were reprimanded.

Subject of a Relative Clause

A relative pronoun (*who, whoever, which, whichever*) used as the subject of a clause is in the nominative case.

Give the letter to *whoever* answers the door.

You'll want to decide *whichever* is best.

The clause itself may be a subject or an object; however, the case of the relative pronoun depends upon its use *within the clause.*

Whoever is selected must board the plane immediately.

The pronoun *who* used as the subject of a verb is not affected by a parenthetical expression such as *I think, he believes, they say* intervening between the subject and the verb.

She is the person *who* I think is best qualified. (*Who* is the subject of the clause.)

We asked Susan, *who* we knew *had always been* a climber of mountains. (*Who* is the subject of the clause.)

Ms. Mann is the attorney *who* we suppose *will prepare* the brief. (*Who* is the subject of the clause.)

Subject of a Clause Introduced by *than* or *as*

If the word following *than* or *as* introduces a clause, even if part of the clause is understood, that word must be in the nominative case. But if the word following *than* or *as* does not introduce a clause, it must be in the objective case. To test whether the word should be in the nominative or objective case, complete the clause.

He has been here longer than *she.* (than *she has*)

Mary is a better mathematician than *I.* (than *I am*)

They were as late as *we* in filing our tax returns. (as *we were*)

We were seated as promptly as *they.* (as *they were*)

In the following examples, the word following *than* or *as* may be in either the nominative or the objective case, depending on the intended meaning. If there is any chance your meaning might be misunderstood, complete the clause.

She likes this work better than *I.* (than *I like it*)

She likes this work better than *me.* (than *she likes me*)

I have known John as long as *she.* (as *she has*)

I have known John as long as *her.* (as *I have known her*)

Words Following Forms of *be* (Predicate Nominative)

A noun or pronoun following a form of the verb *be* (except for the infinitive if it has its own subject) must be in the nominative case. (This word is called the *predicate nominative*—or, if a noun, the *predicate noun.*) The general rule applying to this construction is that the word following the verb *be* must be in the same case as the word before the verb. Imagine that the verb *be* has the same meaning as the equals sign (=) in mathematics.

Not: They thought I was *him.*

But: They thought I was *he.* (*I* = *he*)

A noun or pronoun following the infinitive *to be* is in the nominative case if the infinitive has no subject.

He was thought to be *I.*

My brother was taken to be *I.*

> **NOTE:** You may have trouble when one or both of the members of the compound subject or predicate nominative are pronouns. Try this simple test: Decide which case would be appropriate if *one* pronoun were the simple subject or predicate nominative, and then use the same case for both.
>
> Example: The new chairmen are *he* and *I.*
>
> Reverse positions: *He* and *I* are the new chairmen.
>
> Example: If any one of the free agents is chosen, *it* should be *he.*
>
> Reverse positions: If any one of the free agents is chosen, *he* should be *it.*
>
> Example: The *author* was thought to be *I.*
>
> Reverse positions: *I* was thought to be the *author.*
>
> These examples show the proper forms for formal use. In informal English, the objective case forms are often encountered.

Direct Address

Direct address is a construction used parenthetically to direct spoken language to some particular person. Nouns or pronouns in direct address are in the nominative case and are set off by commas. This construction will cause little trouble, since proper names, which are the main examples of direct address, do not change form to indicate case.

Jim, come here for a minute.

It is true, *sir,* that I made that remark.

Tell me, *doctor,* is he showing much improvement?

Objective Case

The objective (or accusative) case is used chiefly to name the receiver or object of the action of a verb, or to name the object of a preposition.

When one part of a compound expression (joined by a coordinate conjunction) is in the objective case, all other parts of the same expression must also be in the objective case.

When you reach the station call either *him* or *me.*

The work was given to *you* and *me.*

When the antecedent of an appositive is in the objective case because it is serving a function that requires that case, the appositive must also be in the objective case.

The teacher has appointed *us, you and me,* to the group.

He gave *us passengers* a copy of the schedule.

The principle is basic to *us Americans.*

Direct Object of a Verb or Verbal

A noun or pronoun serving as the direct object of a verb or verbal is in the objective case.

The driver returned *him* to his home.

My father called *him* and *me* to come back inside.

They will invite *us fans* to the football game.

Whomever you called on Monday night is certainly upset.

BUT

Call *whoever* is responsible before the alarm sounds.

I enjoyed meeting *him.*

I didn't intend to ask *them* again.

Having called *him* and told *him* of our plan, we left for the evening.

We have a letter from her cousin thanking *us* for our courtesy.

Indirect Object of a Verb or Verbal

A word used as the indirect object of a verb or verbal is in the objective case.

The ballplayer gave *me* his autograph.

The supervisor assigned *him* and *me* the task of cleaning up the boardroom.

The inspector showed *us employees* the operation of the meat grinder.

A letter giving *him* authority to represent his mother is being prepared.

Object of a Preposition

A noun or pronoun serving as the object of a preposition is in the objective case.

From *whom* did you receive the letter? (*Whom* is the object of the preposition *from.*)

NOTE: *But* is a preposition when *except* may be substituted for it with no change in meaning.

Everyone is going but *me.*

A special troublemaker is the compound object *you and me* after the preposition *between.* Do not say *between you and I;* say *between you and me.*

Subject of an Infinitive

A noun or pronoun used as the subject of an infinitive is in the objective case.

I want *him* to have this car.

We expect *him* to finish that job.

They invited *her and me* to attend the reception.

Whom will he cast to play the lead character?

Words Following Infinitive *to be*

The verb *to be* takes the same case after it as before it. Since the subject of an infinitive is in the objective case, a word following the infinitive is also in the objective case.

They thought him to be *me.* (Reverse, to test choice of case: They thought *me* to be *him.*)

We assumed the author of the letter to be *him.* (Reverse: We assumed *him* to be the *author . . . .*)

They did not expect the representatives to be *him and me.* (Reverse: They did not expect *him and me* to be the *representatives.*)

Subject of a Participle and of a Gerund

The subject of a participle is in the objective case. The problem comes in determining whether a verbal is a participle or a gerund. Both may have the same form (the *-ing* form of the verb), but only the subject of the *participle* is in the objective case. The subject of the *gerund* is in the possessive case.

Imagine *him flying* an airplane. (The verbal *flying* is a participle modifying *him,* and the pronoun *him* is in the objective case.)

Imagine *his flying* to Paris. (The verbal *flying* is a gerund, and the pronoun *his* is in the possessive case.)

His rushing to catch the plane was in vain. (*Rushing* is a gerund, and its subject must be in the possessive case.)

We watched *him rushing* to catch the plane. (The verbal, *rushing,* is a participle modifying *him;* therefore, the subject, *him,* is in the objective case.)

NOTE: In the gerund expression *its being,* the subject that follows must be in the objective case.

In our search for the thief, we never thought of its being *him* (not *he*).

Possessive Case (and Its Proper Punctuation)

The possessive (or genitive) case is used to indicate possession.

Possessive of Singular Words

To form the possessive of singular words not ending in *s* (including the indefinite pronouns), add the apostrophe and *s.*

the *student's* report; the *neighbor's* car; the *widow's* cat; *anyone's* guess; *somebody's* coat

> **NOTE:** When *else* is used with an indefinite pronoun, form the possessive by adding the apostrophe and *s* to *else,* rather than to the indefinite pronoun.
>
> *somebody's* coat   But: *somebody else's* coat
>
> *anyone's* idea   But: *anyone else's* idea

To form the possessive of singular words ending in *s,* add the apostrophe and *s* or simply the apostrophe alone.

Singular form	Possessive form
boss	boss's or boss'
hostess	hostess's or hostess'

> **NOTE:** The possessive of some proper names ending in *s,* however, is traditionally formed by adding only the apostrophe:
>
> Jesus' disciples   Moses' staff
>
> Some names of more than one syllable ending in *s,* as well as some ancient Greek names, also form the possessive in this way:
>
> John Quincy Adams' presidency
>
> Epimenides' paradox

The apostrophe is omitted in some organizational or geographical names that contain a possessive thought. Follow the form used by the organization itself.

Harpers Ferry   Pikes Peak

Governors Island   Citizens National Bank

Do not use the apostrophe in forming the possessive of the personal and relative pronouns. The possessive forms of these pronouns are:

Relative: whose

Personal: her, hers (*not* her's) his, their, theirs, our, ours, my, mine, your, yours, its

NOTE: *Its* is the possessive form of the personal pronoun *it*; *it's* is a contraction of *it is*. Similarly, *whose* is the possessive form of the relative pronoun *who*, and *who's* is a contraction of *who is* or *who has*. The examples below illustrate the correct use of these words.

Its operation is simple.
It's (*it is*) simple to operate.

Don't drive that car; *its* tires need changing.
Don't drive that car; *it's* in need of new tires.

Whose mailbox is that?
Who's (*who is*) going with me?

Theirs is in the closet.
There's very little time left.

Possessive of Plural Words
To form the possessive of a plural word not ending in *s,* add the apostrophe and *s.*

men's, children's, women's, people's

To form the possessive of a plural word ending in *s,* add the apostrophe only.

All of the *mechanics'* tools were lost.

NOTE: Avoid placing the apostrophe before the final *s* of a word if the *s* is actually a part of the singular or plural form. To test, first form the plural; then add the correct possessive sign.

Not: ladie's

But: ladies'

(*Ladies* is the plural form; since the word ends in *s,* add the apostrophe alone to form the possessive, *ladies'.*)

Use of the *of* Phrase to Form Possessive

Use the *of* phrase in forming the possessive to avoid the "piling up" of possessives.

Not: The *taxpayer's wife's income* must be reported.

But: The *income of the taxpayer's wife* must be reported.

Not: Her *brother's friend's bicycle* was red.

But: The *bicycle of her brother's friend* was red.

In order to avoid an awkward construction, use the *of* phrase to form the possessive of names consisting of several words.

Not: The local chapter of the National Association of Radio and Television Broadcasters' first meeting was held Thursday.

But: The first meeting of the local chapter of the National Association of Radio and Television Broadcasters was held Thursday.

Not: The Director of the Alcohol and Tobacco Tax Division's report . . .

But: The report of the Director of the Alcohol and Tobacco Tax Division . . .

Use the *of* phrase to avoid adding a possessive to a pronoun that is already possessive.

Not: We are going to a *friend of mine's* house.

But: We are going to the *house of a friend of mine*.

Possessive of Compound Words

Form the possessive on the last word of a compound word, whether or not the compound is hyphenated. A point to remember is that even though the plural of a compound word is formed by adding *s* to the principal noun in the compound, the possessive is always formed by adding the sign of the possessive to the last word in the compound.

Singular	**Singular Possessive**
notary public	notary public's
comptroller general	comptroller general's
supervisor in charge	supervisor in charge's
Plural	**Plural Possessive**
notaries public	notaries public's
comptrollers general	comptrollers general's
supervisors in charge	supervisors in charge's

If a possessive is followed by an appositive or an explanatory phrase, form the possessive on the explanatory word.

That was *Mr. Smith the auditor's* idea.

I was acting on my *friend John's* advice.

Have you read the *senator from Arizona's* speech?

If the appositive or explanatory words are set off by commas, the possessive may be found on both the main word and the explanatory word.

Either: This is *Mary, my assistant's,* day off.

Or: This is *Mary's, my assistant's,* day off.

Either: I sent it to *Mr. Smith, the collector's,* office.

Or: I sent it to *Mr. Smith's, the collector's,* office.

NOTE: The methods just illustrated are grammatically correct ways to show possession; they do, however, sound awkward. To be more effective (and just as correct), try using an *of* phrase to form the possessive of compound words.

Not: This is the supervisor in charge's office.

But: This is the office of the supervisor in charge.

Not: I was acting on my friend John's advice.

But: I was acting on the advice of my friend, John.

Not: I sent it to Mr. Smith's, the collector's, office.

But: I sent it to the office of Mr. Smith, the collector.

Joint, Separate, and Alternative Possession

When two or more people possess the same thing jointly, form the possessive on the last word only.

She is *Mr. Smith and Ms. Henry's* cousin. (She is cousin to both people.)

These pictures are from *John and Mary's* vacation trip.

I bought my coat at *Woodward and Lothrop's.* (*store* understood)

> **NOTE:** When one of the words involved in the joint possession is a pronoun, each word must be in the possessive.
>
> This is *John's, Bob's,* and *my* neighborhood.
>
> Have you seen *Mary's* and *his* new home?

When it is intended that each of the words in a series possess something individually, form the possessive on each word.

Barbara's and *Mary's* singing are certainly different.

The *drivers'* and the *owners'* associations are meeting here this week.

When alternative possession is intended, each word must be in the possessive.

I wouldn't want either *John's* or *Harry's* job.

Is that the *author's* or the *editor's* opinion?

Possessive of Abbreviations
Possessives of abbreviations are formed in the same way as are other possessives. Ordinarily the possessive sign is placed after the final period of the abbreviation where one is present.

Singular Possessive	Plural	Plural Possessive
MD's	MDs	MDs'
Dr.'s	Drs.	Drs.'

John Blank, *Jr.'s* account has been closed. (Note that there is no comma after *Jr.* when the possessive is used.)

Parallel Possessives
Be sure that a word standing parallel with a possessive is itself possessive in form.

Not: *His* work, like an *accountant,* is exacting.

But: *His* work, like an *accountant's,* is exacting.

Not: The *agent's* job differs from the *auditor.*

But: The *agent's* job differs from the *auditor's.*

Not: *His* task is no more difficult than his *neighbor.*

But: *His* task is no more difficult than his *neighbor's.*

Possessive with a Gerund

A noun or pronoun immediately preceding a gerund is in the possessive case. A gerund is a verbal noun naming an action. A participle, which may have the same form as a gerund, functions as an adjective; its subject is in the objective case.

> *Our* being late delayed the meeting.

> *Mr. Jones's* being late delayed the meeting.

> You can always depend on *his* being a good friend.

> *Jim's* singing the anthem made all the difference.

> *Washington's* being the capital makes it different from other cities.

NOTE: There are two exceptions to this general rule:

Do not use the possessive case for the subject of a gerund unless the subject immediately precedes the gerund. If the subject and gerund are separated by other words, the subject must be in the objective case.

Not: I can see no reason for a *man's* with his background *failing* to pass the test.

But: I can see no reason for a *man* with his background *failing* to pass the test. (Without intervening words: I can see no reason for a *man failing* to pass the test.)

There are no possessive forms for the demonstrative pronouns *that, this, these,* and *those.* Therefore, when these words are used as subjects of a gerund they do not change form.

Not: We cannot be sure of *that's* being true.

But: We cannot be sure of *that* being true.

Not: What are the chances of *this'* being sold?

But: What are the chances of *this* being sold?

He/She

Traditionally, the personal pronoun *he* has been used in English when the gender of its antecedent is unknown.

> Each child (boy or girl) develops at *his* own pace.

This usage is still widely accepted, but it is changing. If you prefer a more neutral form (he/she, for example), or if you think your reader may be offended, use instead a form of *he or she.*

Each child develops at *his or her* own pace.

Since the *he or she* form is somewhat clumsy, a frequent repetition of it may make your writing awkward. Avoid the problem by rewording.

All children develop at *their* own pace.

Take care to make pronouns and antecedents consistent within a passage.

AGREEMENT AND REFERENCE

Many grammatical errors result from failing to make different parts of a sentence agree in number, person, or gender.

The verb must agree with the subject in number and in person. If the subject is singular, the verb form must also be singular; if the subject is in the third person—*she, it, he*—the verb must be in the third person. The chief problem is identifying the true subject of the sentence and determining whether it is singular or plural.

The pronoun must agree with its antecedent (the word to which it refers—sometimes called its *referent*) in number, in person, and in gender. Of the three, gender causes the writer the least difficulty. The chief problem is identifying the antecedent and determining its number, person, and gender.

Often the subject of the verb is also the antecedent of the pronoun. You might think that this would greatly simplify things, and to some extent it does, for once you have determined that the subject-antecedent is singular, you know where you stand—both verb and pronoun must likewise be singular. A word of caution: be consistent. Don't shift from a singular verb (which properly agrees with its singular subject) to a plural pronoun later in the sentence.

Subject Problems

The first step in making the parts of a sentence agree is to identify the subject. In this section, therefore, we will discuss only those subjects that may present special problems.

Collective Words

A collective is a single word that names a group of people or things. Although usually singular in form, a collective is treated as either singular or plural according to the sense of the sentence.

A collective is treated as singular when members of the group act, or are considered, as a *unit*.

The survey committee *is visiting* the district this week.

The national office evaluation team *has* five trips scheduled for this quarter.

A collective is treated as plural when the members act, or are considered, *individually.*

The jury *are* unable to agree on a verdict.

The national office evaluation team *pool* the data *they* gather and *prepare their* report.

Common collectives include:

assembly, association, audience, board, cabinet, class, commission, company, corporation, council, counsel, couple, crowd, department, family, firm, group, jury, majority, minority, number, pair, press, public, staff, United States

Company names also qualify as collectives and may be either singular or plural. Usually those ending with a plural signifier such as *s* are plural.

Flowers, Inc., *mails its* advertisements in envelopes with floral decorations.

Jones Brothers *have sent their* representative to the conference.

Short collectives include the following short words. Though seldom listed as collectives, these words are governed by the rule for collectives. They are singular or plural according to the intended meaning of the sentence.

all, any, more, most, none, some, who, which

When a prepositional phrase follows the short collective, the number of the noun in the phrase controls the number of the verb. When no such phrase follows, the writer signals the intended meaning by the choice of the singular or the plural verb.

Some of the *work has been done.*
Some of the *returns have been filed.*

Most of the *correspondence is* routine.
Most of the *letters are* acceptable.

Is there *any* left? (any portion—any money, any ink)
Are there *any* left? (any individual items—any forms, any copies)

Which is to be posted? (which one?)
Which are to be posted? (which ones?)

Either: None of the items *is* deductible.
Or: None of the items *are* deductible.

NOTE: Many writers treat *none* as singular in every instance, since it is a compound of *no one.* This usage is correct. It is equally correct, however, to treat *none* as plural (meaning *not any*) when it is followed by a prepositional phrase that has a plural object. Those who want to emphasize the singular meaning often substitute *not one* for *none*:

Not one of the birds *is* building a nest.

Special collectives include certain words called *abstract collectives* by some grammarians. These words are also treated as collectives, even though they do not name a group of persons or things. Their singular form is used when they refer to qualities, emotions, or feelings common to a group of persons or things; or to actions common to such a group. Their plural form is used when this common or general idea is not present.

Use the singular under such circumstances as these:

attention	We called their *attention* to the plan's advantages. (not *attentions*)
consent	Several gave their *consent* to the guru.
failure	The dogs' *failure* to heed commands delayed their finding new homes.
interest	Their *interest* was in winning at all costs.
sense	Our interpretation is based on the *sense* of the amendment.
work	Rain will not interfere with their *work.*

Use either the singular or the plural with:

opinion	The students and their teacher expressed their *opinion* (or *opinions*) on the matter.
time	The only *time* these restrictions are in order is when the airlines . . . *OR* The only *times* these restrictions are in order are when the airlines . . .
use	What *use* (or *uses*) can be made of the timber?

Units of Measure

When a number is used with a plural noun to indicate a unit of measurement (money, time, fractions, portions, distance, weight, quantity, etc.), a singular verb is used. When the term is thought of as individual parts, a plural verb is used.

> *Ten years seems* like a long time.
>
> *Ten years have gone* by since I last saw him.
>
> *Twenty-one pages is* our homework for each day.
>
> *Twenty-one pages are* needed to finish the job.

When fractions and expressions such as *the rest of, the remainder of, a part of, percent of,* etc., are followed by a prepositional phrase, the noun or pronoun in that phrase governs the number of the verb.

> *Four-fifths* of the job *was* finished on time.
>
> *Four-fifths* of the students *were* finished on time.
>
> The *rest* (or *remainder*) of the work *is* due Friday.
>
> The *rest* (or *remainder*) of the cards *were* mailed today.
>
> What *percentage* of the information *is* available?
>
> What *percentage* of the items *were* lost?

Confusing Singular and Plural Forms

It is sometimes hard to tell by its form whether a word is singular or plural. Some words that end in *-s* may be singular, and some seemingly singular words may be plural.

These words are singular, though they may seem plural in form:

> apparatus, news, summons, whereabouts
>
> The *news* is disturbing.

These words are plural, though they are singular (or collective) in meaning:

> assets, earnings, means (*income*), odds, premises, proceeds, quarters, savings, wages, winnings
>
> His *assets are* listed on the attached statement.
>
> *Earnings are* up this quarter.
>
> The *odds are* against our getting home on time.
>
> The *proceeds are* earmarked for the most needy.

These words may be either singular or plural, depending on their meaning, even though they may seem plural in form:

ethics, goods, gross, headquarters, mechanics, politics, series, species, statistics, tactics

Ethics is a subject on which he is well qualified to speak.

His business *ethics are* above question.

Statistics is the only course I failed in school.

The *statistics prove* that I am right.

A *gross* of pencils *is* not enough.

A *gross* of pencils *are* being sent.

These nouns are plural, though they may appear to be singular because they have foreign or unusual plural forms.

The *analyses* have been completed. (*Analyses* is the plural of *analysis.*)

What *are* your *bases* for these conclusions? (*Bases* is the plural of *basis.*)

Some interesting *phenomena are* disclosed in this report. (*Phenomena* is the plural of *phenomenon.*)

His conclusion seems sound, but his *criteria are* not valid. (*Criteria* is the plural of *criterion.*)

Hyphenated compound nouns usually take their pluralization on the important part.

editors-in-chief, daughters-in-law

Solid compound nouns always take their pluralization at the end of the word.

stepdaughters, spoonfuls, bookshelves

Indefinite Pronouns

These indefinite pronouns are singular. When they are used as subjects, they require singular verbs; when used as antecedents, they require singular pronouns.

anybody, anyone, any one (any one of a group), anything, each, either, every, everybody, everyone, every one (every one of a group), everything, neither, nobody, no one, nothing, one, somebody, someone, some one (some one of a group), something

Anyone is welcome, as long as *he or she* (not *they*) behaves appropriately.

Any one of the men *is* capable of doing it. (written as two words when followed by a phrase)

Each of us *is* obliged to sign *his or her* own name.

Either of the alternatives *is* suitable.

Everyone must buy *his or her* book for the course.

Every one of the relatives *wishes* to sign the card. (written as two words when followed by a phrase)

Everything seems to be going smoothly now.

Neither of the plans *is* workable.

No one believes that our plan will work.

Someone has to finish this dessert.

Even when two indefinite pronouns are joined by *and,* they remain singular in meaning.

Anyone and everyone is invited.

Nothing and *no one escapes* her attention.

When *each* or *every* is used to modify a compound subject (subjects joined by *and*), the subject is considered singular.

Every ticket holder and *fan has sent* in a request.

When *each* is inserted (as a parenthetic or explanatory element) between a plural or a compound subject and its plural verb, neither the plural form of the verb nor the plural form of the pronoun is affected.

Region A, region B, and region C *each expect* to increase *their* investments.

They *each want* the same thing.

The customers *each have requested* permission to change *their* method of payment.

Many a (unlike *many*) is singular in meaning and takes a singular verb and pronoun.

Many a new leaf falls prey to insects during its first few weeks.

But: *Many new leaves* fall prey to insects during *their* first few weeks.

More than one, though its meaning is plural, is used in the singular.

More than one vacation plan *was* changed last night.

More than one detail *is* often overlooked.

These words are plural:

both, few, many, several, others

Both of us *have received* new assignments.

Few will be able to finish *their* work on time.

Many plan to leave in the morning.

Several writers *have submitted their* stories.

Others have not yet *finished theirs.*

Relative Pronouns

The verb in a relative clause must agree in number and in person with the relative pronoun (*who, which, that, what*) serving as the subject of the clause. The relative pronoun, in turn, must agree with its antecedent. Therefore, before we can make the verb agree with the relative pronoun, we must find the antecedent and determine its person and number.

Have you talked with the man *who was* waiting to see you? (*Man* is the antecedent of the relative pronoun *who,* and the verb *was* must agree with this antecedent in person and number.)

Where are the books *that were* left on the table? (The verb in the relative clause—*were*—must agree with the relative pronoun—*that*—which must agree with its antecedent—*books.*)

We *who have* met him do not doubt his ability. (The relative pronoun is *who;* the verb in the relative clause is *have;* the antecedent of the relative pronoun is *we.*)

In sentences that contain the phrases *one of the* or *one of those,* the antecedent of the relative pronoun is not *one,* but the plural words that follow.

One of the tools *that were* on my table has disappeared.

Here is one of the men *who are* moving the piano.

One of the women *who are* attending the conference is wanted on the telephone.

Who, that, or *which* may be used to refer to a collective noun. When the members of the group act, or are considered, as a unit, either *that* or *which* should be used—*that* is usually preferred if the group comprises persons rather than things. *Who* is used when the persons comprising a group act, or are considered, individually.

> The editorial suggests that there *is* a *group* of citizens *that* is unhappy with progress.

> We have heard from an *association* of homeowners *who feel* strongly opposed to cutting down trees.

Subjects Joined by *and*

When two or more subjects are joined by *and,* whether the subjects are singular or plural, they form a compound subject, which is considered plural.

> The *date and the time* of the party *have* not been decided.

> The *host and his guests are* giving their toasts.

> The *coins, pencils, and other papers are* on the table where you left *them.*

> *He and I* will deliver *our* newspapers in the morning.

Phrases or clauses serving as subjects follow the same rule. When two or more phrases or clauses serving as the subject of a sentence are joined by *and,* the resulting compound subject is considered plural.

> *Rising early in the morning and taking a walk before breakfast make* a person feel invigorated all day.

> *That your work is usually done properly* and *that you are usually prompt are* the factors I considered.

Exception: When the subjects joined by *and* refer to the same person or object or represent a single idea, the whole subject is considered singular.

> *Ham and eggs is* a traditional American breakfast.

> The *growth and development* of our country *is* described in this book.

The article or personal pronoun used before each member of the compound subject indicates whether we see the subject as a single idea or as different ideas.

> *My teacher and friend helps* me with my problems. (one person)

> *My teacher* and *my friend help* me with my problems. (two people)

> *The lead actress and star* of the film *has* arrived.

> *The lead actress* and *the star* of the film *have* arrived.

Subjects Joined by *or* or *nor*

When singular subjects are joined by *or* or *nor,* the subject is considered singular.

> Neither the *cat nor* the *mouse knows* that *he* is being watched.
>
> *One or* the *other* of us *has* to go.
>
> Neither *love nor money is* sufficient in such situations.
>
> Neither *heat nor cold nor sun nor wind affects* this material.

When one singular and one plural subject are joined by *or* or *nor,* the subject closer to the verb determines the number of the verb.

> I believe that *she or* her *sisters have* the keys to the car.
>
> I believe that her *sisters* or *she has* the keys to the car.

When one antecedent is singular and the other antecedent is plural, the pronoun agrees with the closer antecedent.

> Is it the general or the rebels who *merit* praise?
>
> Is it the rebels or the general who *merits* praise?

> **NOTE:** Because your reader may be distracted by your use of a singular verb with a subject containing a plural element, place the plural element nearer the verb whenever possible.
>
> *Ask* him whether the *card or* the *letters have* been signed.
>
> Neither the *equipment nor* the *drivers are* capable of maintaining that pace.
>
> When the subjects joined by *or* or *nor* are of different persons, the subject nearer the verb determines its person.
>
> I was told that *she or you were* to be responsible.
>
> I was told that *you or she was* to be responsible.

Shifts in Number or Person

Once you establish a word as either singular or plural, keep it the same throughout the sentence. Be sure that all verbs and all pronouns referring to that word agree with it in number.

Not: Because this *country* bases *its* economy on voluntary compliance with *its* tax laws, we must all pay our share if *they are* to carry out the necessary functions of government.

But: Because this *country* bases *its* economy on voluntary compliance with *its* tax laws, we must all pay our share if *it is* to carry out the necessary function of government.

Not: A *person needs* someone to turn to when *they are* in trouble.

But: A *person needs* someone to turn to when *he or she* is in trouble.

Not: When *one* has had a difficult day, it is important that *they* be able to relax in the evening.

But: When *one* has had a difficult day, it is important that *one* (or *he or she*) be able to relax in the evening.

Be consistent. If you decide that a collective is singular, keep it singular throughout the sentence—use a singular verb to agree with it and a singular pronoun to refer to it. If you establish the collective as plural, see that both the verb and the pronoun are plural.

The committee *has* announced *its* decision.

The committee *have* adjourned and gone to *their* homes.

Our staff *is* always glad to offer *its* advice and assistance.

Most indefinite pronouns are singular and require singular verbs and pronouns.

Not: *Has anyone* turned in *their* report?

But: *Has anyone* turned in *his or her* report?

(The indefinite pronoun *anyone* takes both a singular verb and a singular pronoun.)

Do not apply a verb form from one part of the sentence to another (elliptically) unless the same form is grammatically correct in both parts.

Not: The *numbers were* checked and the total verified.

But: The *numbers were* checked and the *total was* verified.

Avoid shifting the person of pronouns referring to the same antecedent.

Not: When *one* is happy, it often seems as if everyone around *you* is happy, too.

But: When *one* is happy, it often seems as if everyone around *one* (or *him or her*) is happy, too.

Not: *As the ship* entered *her* berth, *its* huge gray shadow seemed to swallow us.

But: As the *ship* entered *its* berth, *its* huge gray shadow seemed to swallow us.

or: As the *ship* entered *her* berth, *her* huge gray shadow seemed to swallow us.

Structure Problems

Usually it is easy for us to identify the subject or antecedent and determine its number and person. But occasionally a puzzling sentence comes along. The subject is there, as clear as can be, but something in the structure of the sentence tries to make us believe that another word is the subject.

Verb Precedes Subject

When the verb precedes the subject in the sentence (either in a question or in a declarative sentence), locate the true subject and make the verb agree with it.

Are the *lamp* and the *bookcase* in this room?

Walking down the hall *are* the *men* we were waiting for.

Clearly visible in the sky *were* the *kites* he had previously admired.

From these books *come some* of our best *ideas.*

To us *falls* the *task* of repairing the environment.

Among those attending *were* two former *teachers.*

Where, here, and *there* do not influence the number or person of the verb when introducing a sentence. In such sentences, find the real subject and make the verb agree with it.

Where *are* the individual *sessions* to be held?

Where *is* the *case* filed?

Here *are* the *songs* for which we were waiting.

Here *is* the *song* for which we were waiting.

There *are* two *books* on the table.

There *is* a *book* on the table.

What, who, which, the interrogative pronouns, do not affect the number of the verb. Again, find the subject of the sentence and make the verb agree with it.

What *is* the *point* of your argument?

What *are* your *recommendations* on this problem?

Who *is* going to accompany you to the dentist?

Who, in this group, *are* members of your family?

Which *is* the *light* that he means?

Which *are* the *standards* that we are to apply?

The expletives *it* or *there* may introduce the verb and stand for the subject, which comes later in the clause. *It* requires a singular verb, even when the real subject is plural. Following *there,* the verb is singular or plural according to the subject which follows it.

It *is* solutions we are looking for, not problems.

It *is* doubtful that he will start today.

There *are* enclosed five copies of the pamphlet you requested.

There *is* attached a letter from your mom.

NOTE: Avoid confusing your reader by using the expletive *it* and the personal pronoun *it* in the same sentence.

Not: I haven't read the book yet; *it* has been hard for me to find time for *it.*

But: I haven't read the *book* yet; I haven't been able to find time for *it.*

Words Intervening Between Subject and Verb

The presence of explanatory or parenthetical phrases, or other modifiers, between the subject and verb does not change the number or person of the subject. Locate the real subject of the sentence and make the verb agree with it.

His sworn *statement,* together with statements from other witnesses, *was* heard in court.

The *amount* shown, plus interest, *is* due within 30 days.

The *letter* with its several attachments *was* received this morning.

Our *manners,* like our speech, *are* indicators of character.

The *policeman,* instead of the agents who had been assigned the case, *is* scheduled to visit our neighbor.

His *appraisal,* including extensive notes on the furnishings of the office, *was* well received.

That *fact,* in addition to our already large file on the case, *means* our assumptions were correct.

No one but those present *knows* of this bargain.

Subject and Predicate Differ in Number

After forms of the verb *to be* we often find a construction (called the *predicate nominative*) which means the same thing as the subject. When the predicate nominative differs in number from the subject, the verb must agree with the element that precedes it (the subject).

Our main *problem is* writing complete stories and keeping them short enough for fast reading.

Writing complete stories and keeping them short enough for fast reading are our main problem.

As always, the *question was* sufficient funds.

As always, *sufficient funds were* the question.

The electrician said that a dangerous *problem is* the old lines.

The electrician said that the *old lines are* a dangerous problem.

Construction Shift and Parallelism

Use the same grammatical construction for each of the words or ideas in a sentence if these words or ideas require balance, according to the meaning that the sentence is conveying.

Not: *Singing* and *to dance* are not permitted here.

But: *Singing* and *dancing* (or *To sing* and *to dance*) are not permitted here.

Not: The children are learning the value of *courtesy* and *being kind.*

But: The children are learning the value of *courtesy* and *kindness.*

Special Problems of Pronoun Reference

Pronouns should follow as closely and as logically as possible the antecedent (subject) to which they refer.

Ambiguous Antecedents

Do not use forms of the same pronoun to refer to different antecedents.

Not: The letter is on the conference table *that* we received yesterday.

But: The *letter that* we received yesterday is on the conference table.

Indefinite Antecedents

Be sure that the reference to an antecedent is quite specific.

Not: The copies of these letters were not initialed by the writers, so we are sending *them* back. (What are we sending back? The copies, the letters, or the writers?)

But: We are sending back the copies of the letters because *they* were not initialed by the writers.

Not: When you have finished the book and written your summary, please return *it* to the library. (What is going to be returned, the book or the summary?)

But: When you have finished the book and written your summary, please return the book to the library.

Implied Antecedents

As a general rule, the antecedent of a pronoun must appear in the sentence—not merely be implied. And the antecedent should be a specific word, not an idea expressed in a phrase or clause. *It, which, this,* and *that* are the pronouns that most often lead meaning astray. Any of these pronouns may refer to an idea expressed in a preceding passage if the idea and the reference are *unmistakably* clear. But too often the idea that is unmistakably clear to the speaker or writer is nowhere to be found when the listener or reader looks for it.

Not: Although the doctor operated at once, *it* was not a success and the patient died.

But: Although the doctor performed the *operation* at once, *it* was not a success and the patient died.

or: Although the doctor operated at once, the *operation* was not a success and the patient died.

Vague Reference

The usage illustrated below—the impersonal use of *it, they,* and *you*—is correct, but may produce vague, wordy sentences.

Not: In the instructions *it* says to make three copies.

But: The instructions say to make three copies.

Not: In the letter *it* says he will be here on Thursday.

But: The letter says he will be here on Thursday.

or: He says, in his letter, that he will be here on Thursday.

Not: *They* say in the almanac that we are in for a cold, wet winter.

But: The almanac predicts a cold, wet winter.

Not: From this report *you* can easily recognize the cause of the accident.

But: From this report *one* can easily recognize the cause of the accident. (The first example is correct if the writer is addressing his remarks to a specific person.)

or: The cause of the accident can be easily recognized from this report.

VERBS AND VERBALS

We know that, as their main function, verbs describe an action or a state of being on the part of the subject. But verbs also tell *when* the action took place or *when* the state existed. This property of verbs is called **tense.**

Tense

English has six tenses: three simple tenses (**present, past,** and **future**) in which an action may be considered as simply occurring; and three compound—called **perfect**—tenses in which an action may be considered as completed. (To be *perfected* means to be *completed.*)

Present Tense:	I walk, he walks
Present Perfect Tense:	I have walked, he has walked
Past Tense:	I walked, he walked
Past Perfect Tense:	I had walked, he had walked
Future Tense:	I shall walk, he will walk
Future Perfect Tense:	I shall have walked, he will have walked

Each of the six tenses has a companion form—the **progressive** form. As its name indicates, the progressive says that the action named by the verb is a continued or progressive action. The progressive consists of the present participle (the *-ing* form of the verb—that is, *walking*) plus the proper form of the verb *to be*. The progressive forms of the verb *to walk* are:

Present Tense:	I am walking, he is walking
Present Perfect Tense:	I have been walking, he has been walking
Past Tense:	I was walking, he was walking
Past Perfect Tense:	I had been walking, he had been walking
Future Tense:	I shall be walking, he will be walking
Future Perfect Tense:	I shall have been walking, he will have been walking

The present tense and the past tense also have an **emphatic** form, which uses *do, does, did* as auxiliaries:

Present Tense:	I do understand, she does understand
Past Tense:	You did understand, they did understand

We indicate tense by changing the verb itself or by combining certain forms of the verb with auxiliary verbs. The verb tenses from which we derive every form of a verb are called **principal parts.** The principal parts of a verb are:

The Present Tense:	talk, write
The Past Tense:	talked, wrote
The Present Perfect:	have talked, has written

Verbs are classified as **regular** (or *weak*) and **irregular** (or *strong*), according to the way in which their principal parts are formed. Regular verbs form their past tense and present perfect tense by the addition of *-ed* to the infinitive:

Present Tense	Past Tense	Present Perfect Tense
talk	talked	has (have) talked
help	helped	has (have) helped
walk	walked	has (have) walked

The principal parts of irregular verbs are formed by changes in the verb itself:

Present Tense	Past Tense	Present Perfect Tense
see	saw	has (have) seen
say	said	has (have) said
go	went	has (have) gone

Principal Parts of Troublesome Verbs

Some irregular verbs are particularly troublesome. The following list shows
how the principal parts of these irregular verbs change to reflect the tense.

Present Tense	Past Tense	Present Perfect Tense
abide	abode, abided	has abode
arise	arose	has arisen
bear (carry)	bore	has borne
bear (bring forth)	bore	has borne
bid	bade, bid	has bid, bidden
bide	bode, bided	has bode, bided
bleed	bled	has bled
broadcast	broadcast, broadcasted	has broadcast(ed)
burst	burst	has burst
chide	chid, chidded	has chid, chidded, chidden
choose	chose	has chosen
cleave (adhere)	cleaved	has cleaved
cleave (split)	cleft, cleaved	has cleft, cleaved, cloven
cling	clung	has clung
drink	drank	has drunk
drown	drowned	has drowned
flee	fled	has fled
fling	flung	has flung
flow	flowed	has flowed
fly	flew or flied	has flown
forsake	forsook	has forsaken
freeze	froze	has frozen
grind	ground	has ground
hang (a picture)	hung	has hung
hang (a person)	hanged	has hanged
lay (place)	laid	has laid
lead	led	has led
lend	lent	has lent
lie (rest)	lay	has lain
light	lit, lighted	has lit, lighted
raise	raised	has raised

continues

PRINCIPAL PARTS OF TROUBLESOME VERBS *continued*

Present Tense	Past Tense	Present Perfect Tense
rid	rid, ridded	has rid, ridded
ring	rang	has rung
set	set	has set
sew	sewed	has sewed, sewn
shrink	shrank, shrunk	has shrunk, shrunken
sink	sank, sunk	has sunk
sit	sat	has sat
ski	skied (rhymes with *seed*)	has skied
slay	slew, slayed	has slain
slide	slid	has slid, slidden
sling	slung	has slung
slink	slunk	has slunk
smite	smote	has smitten
spring	sprang, sprung	has sprung
steal	stole	has stolen
sting	stung	has stung
stink	stank, stunk	has stunk
stride	strode	has stridden
strive	strove, strived	has striven
swim	swam	has swum
swing	swung	has swung
thrust	thrust	has thrust
weave	wove, weaved	has woven
wring	wrung	has wrung

NOTE: When two forms are given, one or the other may be restricted to a particular sense of the verb. Consult a dictionary to establish if this is so.

He wove fine cloth.

She weaved in and out of traffic.

Past Tense vs. Past Perfect Tense

The past perfect indicates that the action or condition described was completed (perfected) earlier than some other action that also occurred in the past. Distinguish carefully between this tense and the simple past tense.

> When I *came* back from lunch, she *finished* the letter. (Both verbs are in the past tense; therefore, both actions happened at approximately the same time in the past.)

> When I *came* back from lunch, she *had finished* the letter. (Again, both actions occurred in the past, but the use of the past perfect *had finished* tells us that this action was completed before the other action.)

> We *discovered* that a detective *was following* us. (Both actions happened at the same time in the past.)

> We *discovered* that a detective *had been following* us. (He had been following us some time before we discovered it.)

Mood

The mood of a verb tells what kind of utterance is being made. An English verb may be **indicative, imperative,** or **subjunctive** in mood.

Indicative Mood

The indicative mood—used to make a statement or ask a question—is used in almost all our writing and speaking.

> The planting *was scheduled* for May 15.

> What *is* the correct form to be used?

> It *seems* likely to rain.

Imperative Mood

The imperative mood expresses a command, a request, or a suggestion. The subject of an imperative sentence is ordinarily the pronoun *you* (not expressed, simply understood.)

> *Lock* the safe before you leave the office.

> *Let* me give you directions to the interstate.

> Please *sign* the receipt before returning it to us. (Note that the word *please* may be inserted with no effect on the use of the imperative, but often with a desirable effect on the listener or reader.)

Probably the greatest mistake we make in using the imperative mood is in *not using it enough.* An order or a request stated in the imperative is usually not only more emphatic but much more quickly and easily understood.

Indicative: It would be appreciated if you would open the envelope promptly.

Imperative: Please open them envelope promptly.

Subjunctive Mood

The subjunctive expresses a hypothetical or conditional situation, or an indirect command. It is going out of use in English, but the subjunctive can still be seen in the following forms:

The third person singular present (which in the indicative has an *-s* and in the subjunctive has none):

Indicative: The plane usually *arrives* on schedule.

Subjunctive: Should the plane *arrive* on schedule, we will be able to make our connection.

Indicative: The detective *prepares* his reports as soon as he completes a case.

Subjunctive: We suggested that the detective *prepare* his reports immediately.

The forms of the verb *be:*

He requested that we *be* there.

If I *were* rich, I would buy a house.

Present: If he *were* able to do it, I am sure he would.

Past: If he *had been* able to do it, I am sure he would have.

Uses of the subjunctive include the following:

1. To express a wish not likely to be fulfilled or impossible to be realized:

    I wish it *were* possible for us to approve the loan. (It is *not* possible.)

    I wish she *were* here to hear your praise of her work. (She is *not* here.)

    Would that I *were* able to take this trip in your place. (I am *not* able to go.)

    I wish I *were* able to help you.

2. To express a parliamentary motion:

    I move that the meeting *be* adjourned.

    Resolved, that a committee *be* appointed to study this matter.

3. In a subordinate clause after a verb that expresses a command, a request, or a suggestion:

He asked *that* the flowers *be* watered in his absence.

It is recommended *that* this office *be* responsible for preparing the statements.

We suggest *that* he *be* aware of the situation.

We ask *that* he *consider* the possibility of a reversal.

It is highly desirable *that* they *be* given the keys to the apartment.

4. To express a condition known or supposed to be contrary to fact:

If this *were* up to me, we wouldn't be going.

If I *were* you, I wouldn't wait in the car.

5. After *as if* or *as though*. In formal writing and speech, *as if* and *as though* are followed by the subjunctive, since they introduce as supposition something not factual. In informal writing and speaking, the indicative is sometimes used:

He talked *as if* he *were* an expert on karate. (He's not.)

This drawing looks *as though* it *were* the work of a master.

Shifts in Mood

Be consistent in your point of view. Once you have decided on the mood that properly expresses your message, use that mood throughout the sentence or the paragraph. A shift in mood is confusing to the listener or reader; it indicates that the speaker or writer himself has changed his way of looking at the conditions.

Not: The hospital suggests that newborns *be* fed by their mothers and *should be* changed by their fathers. (*Be* is subjunctive; *should be*, indicative.)

But: The hospital suggests that newborns *be* fed by their mothers and *be* changed by their fathers.

Voice

Voice indicates whether the subject of the verb is performing or receiving the action described by the verb. There are two voices: **active** and **passive.**

If the subject is performing the action, the verb is in the active voice.

The *mechanic fixed* our car.

The *article summarizes* the problem.

The *hostess asked* that everyone be seated.

If the subject is being acted upon, the verb is in the passive voice. (The passive form always consists of some form of *be* plus the past participle.)

Our *car was fixed* by the mechanic.

The *problem is summarized* in this article.

Everyone was asked by the hostess to be seated.

Active and Passive Voice

In general, the active voice is preferable to the passive: it is simpler and more direct. If, however, you wish to emphasize the action itself or the object of the action and not the agent, use the passive.

Smoking is prohibited. (emphasizing the object, smoking)

Lori is employed by the college. (emphasizing Lori)

Shifts in Voice

Shifts in voice—often accompanied by shifts in subject—usually occur in compound or complex sentences. Although it is not essential that all clauses in a sentence be the same in structure, any unnecessary shifts may result in a disorganized sentence. Therefore, unless you have a good reason for changing, use the same subject and voice in the second clause that you used in the first.

Not: As *I searched* through my dresser drawers, the missing sock *was found.* (The first subject is *I*—its verb is active; the second subject is *sock*—its verb is passive.)

But: As *I searched* through my dresser drawers, *I found* the missing sock. (Subject is *I* in both clauses; both verbs are active.)

MODIFIERS

Modifiers are words or groups of words that describe, qualify, or limit another word or group of words.

Classification of Modifiers

Modifiers fall generally into two categories: **adjectives** (and phrases or clauses used as adjectives) and **adverbs** (and phrases or clauses used as adverbs). Sometimes the form of the modifier clearly shows whether it is an adjective or an adverb; sometimes the form is the same for both.

Adjectives describe, limit, or make more exact the meaning of a noun or pronoun (any substantive).

> He liked the *red* car.

> The dresser *that is made of oak* is my favorite.

Adverbs describe, limit, or make more exact the meaning of a verb, an adjective, or another adverb.

> He liked the *enchantingly* beautiful actress.

> Run around the track *as quickly as you can.*

Articles

Articles are a type of adjective. The indefinite articles are *a* and *an,* and the definite article is *the.* Use *a* before words beginning with a consonant sound, *an* before those beginning with a vowel sound.

> *a* desk, *a* book

> *an* agent, *an* error, *an* unusual occurrence, *an* honor (the *h* is not pronounced)

The article used before each of two connected nouns or adjectives signals that the words refer to different people or things.

> We elected *a* secretary and *a* treasurer. (two persons)

> He uses *a* tan and green typewriter. (one machine, two colors)

Do not use *a* or *an* after *sort of, kind of, manner of, style of,* or *type of.*

> Not: What *kind of a* book do you want?

> But: What *kind of* book do you want?

Do not use *the* before *both.*

> Not: We'll buy *the both* of them.

> But: We'll buy *both* of them.

The following words may be either adjectives or adverbs depending on their use:

above, bad, better, cheap, close, deep, early, fast, first, hard, late, long, much, only, quick, slow, very, well

Adverbs with Two Forms

Some adverbs have two forms—one ending in *-ly,* the other not. The longer form is nearly always correct and is preferable in formal writing. The short form is properly used in brief, forceful sentences (in commands, such as the road sign "Drive Slow") and may be used informally. The *-ly* form should, however, always be used to modify an adjective.

Following are examples of adverbs having two forms:

cheap, cheaply	direct, directly	sharp, sharply
clear, clearly	loud, loudly	slow, slowly
deep, deeply	quick, quickly	soft, softly

Sometimes the meaning desired will determine which form should be used. Notice that either *direct* or *directly* may be used when the meaning is "in a straight line," but *directly* is the only choice when *soon* is meant.

NOTE: In informal speech, we sometimes drop the *-ly* ending from some often-used adverbs. This practice is not appropriate in formal writing.

Correct usage:

I am *really* glad you could come. (Not *real* glad)

Adjectives and Adverbs (Degrees of Comparison)

Adjectives and adverbs change form to show a greater or lesser degree of the characteristic named by the simple word. There are three degrees of comparison.

Positive Degree

The positive degree names the *quality* expressed by the adjective or adverb. It does not imply a comparison with, or a relation to, a similar quality in any other thing.

high morale, a *dependable* worker, work *fast,* prepared *carefully*

Comparative Degree

The comparative degree indicates that the quality described by the modifier exists to a greater or lesser degree in one thing than in another. It is formed by adding *-er* to the positive degree or by inserting *more* or *less* before the positive form.

> Our club has *higher* morale now than ever before.

> Jan is a *more dependable* worker than Tim.

> She can work *faster* than I.

> This meal was prepared *more carefully* than the one we had last night.

Superlative Degree

The superlative degree denotes the greatest or least amount of the quality named. It is formed by adding *-est* to the positive degree of the adjective or adverb or by inserting *most* or *least* before the positive form.

> That club has the *highest* morale of any club.

> Jan is the *most dependable* worker in the office.

> This is the *most carefully* prepared meal I have ever eaten.

The comparative degree is used to refer to only two things, the superlative to more than two.

> This boat is the *longer* of the two.

> This boat is the *longest* of the three.

Using *-er* and *-est* vs. *more* and *most*

There is no difference in meaning between *-er* and *more* or between *-est* and *most.* Either method may be used with some modifiers. However, most adjectives of three syllables or more and almost all adverbs are compared by the use of *more* and *most* (or *less* and *least*) rather than by the endings *-er* and *-est*. In choosing which method should be used with the modifiers that may take either method, you may base your choice on emphasis. By adding *-er* and *-est* to the root word you emphasize the *quality,* while by using *more* or *most* you stress the *degree* of comparison.

> Should I have been *kinder* or *harsher* in handling that call?

> That boat is the *longest* of the three.

> Should I have been *more firm* or *less firm* in handling that caller?

> Of all the forms, this one is the *most simple* and that one is the *least simple* to fill out.

Irregular Comparisons

Some modifiers are compared by changes in the words themselves. A few of these irregular comparisons are given below; consult your dictionary whenever you are in doubt about the comparison of any adjective or adverb.

Positive	Comparative	Superlative
good	better	best
well	better	best
bad (evil, ill)	worse	worst
badly (ill)	worse	worst
far	farther,	farthest, further, furthest
late	later, latter	latest, last
little	less, lesser	least
many, much	more	most

Problems with Comparison (Adjectives and Adverbs)

Some adjectives and adverbs express qualities that do not admit freely of comparison. They represent the highest degree of a quality and, as a result, cannot be improved. Some of these words are listed below.

complete	infinitely	square
correct	perfect	squarely
dead	perfectly	supreme
deadly	perpendicularly	totally
exact	preferable	unique
horizontally	round	uniquely
immortally	secondly	universally

However, there may be times when the comparison of these words is justified. If we use these modifiers in a relative or approximate sense, they may be compared. But proceed with care. It is usually better, for example, to say *more nearly round* or *more nearly perfect* than *rounder* or *more perfect*.

Comparison with *other* and *else*

When we use the comparative in such an expression as *this thing is better than any other,* we imply that *this thing* is separate from the group or class to which it is being compared. In these expressions we must use a word such as *other* or *else* to separate the thing being compared from the rest of the group of which it is a part.

Not: Our house is cooler than any house on the block. (The mistake here is not separating the item being compared—*house*—from the group to which it is being compared.)

But: Our house is cooler than any *other* house on the block. (Our house is one of the houses on the block.)

Not: He has a better record than any coach in our conference.

But: He has a better record than any *other* coach in our conference. (He himself is one of the coaches in the conference.)

Incomplete Comparison—Improper Ellipsis

When you make a comparison between two items, be sure that both terms of the comparison are named. Violation of this rule places the burden on the listener or reader, who may or may not clearly understand which of two items you are comparing. Be sure the listener or reader knows exactly what you mean when you say:

There have been more successful ad campaigns in our district this year. (Do you mean *more than in any other district?* or *more than in any previous year?*)

Whenever a comparison is not completed, the meaning of the sentence is obscured.

Incomplete comparison with possessive:

Obscure: Joe's letter states the problem better than John. (We cannot tell whether it is *John* or *John's letter* that is stating the problem.)

Improved: Joe's letter states the problem better than *John's*.

Ambiguous: John's proposed form is less complicated than management.

Improved: John's proposed form is less complicated than *management's*. (Or: than the one proposed by management.)

Incomplete comparison with conjunction:

Obscure: This text is as good, if not better than that one. (Because of the omission of the second *as* after *good*, this sentence reads " . . . as good *than*.")

Improved: This text is as good *as*, if not better than, that one.

or: This text is as good as that one, if not better.

Obscure: This book is shorter, but just as comprehensive as that one.

Improved:	This book is shorter *than,* but just as comprehensive as, that one.
or:	This book is shorter than that one, but just as comprehensive.

Incomplete comparison with verb:

Ambiguous:	I enjoy this kind of work more than John. (This could be interpreted as: I enjoy this kind of work more than I enjoy *John.*)
Improved:	I enjoy this kind of work more than John *does.*
Obscure:	I have known him longer than John.
Could mean:	I have known him longer than John *has.*
or:	I have known him longer than *I have known* John.

Split Infinitives

Inserting an adverb between *to* and the rest of an infinitive creates a split infinitive. In the past, writers have been told unequivocally to avoid this construction and to reposition the adverb or recast the entire sentence. Today, however, this rule has been relaxed to a great extent, even by careful writers. Still, avoiding the split infinitive can result in clearer, more graceful writing.

Not:	He wished to *completely* forget the matter.
But:	He wished to forget the matter *completely.*

Verbals and Verbal Phrases as Modifiers

Verbals are sometimes used as modifiers, either singly or in phrases.

To get the most out of the course, you must study regularly. (infinitive phrase modifying *you*)

Rising, the lion roared. (present participle modifying *lion*)

The card, *signed by all of us,* was mailed today. (past participles modifying *card*)

The letter, *having been corrected,* was dropped in the mailbox. (perfect participle modifying *letter*)

Dangling Verbal Phrases

A dangling phrase is one that cannot logically modify the noun or pronoun to which it refers. Corrective action may be taken in either of two ways: (1) by changing the subject of the main clause to one that the phrase can refer to, or (2) by changing the phrase itself into a dependent clause, so that it has a subject of its own.

Dangling: *To get the most out of this course,* careful *study* is necessary. (The phrase cannot logically modify *study;* it dangles.)

Corrected: *To get the most out of this course, you* must study it carefully.

or: If you are to get the most out of this course, you must study it carefully.

Dangling: *To apply for this job,* an *application* must be completed. (Dangles; an *application* can't apply.)

Corrected: *To apply for this job,* the *applicant* must complete an applicaton.

or: When the applicant applies for the job, an application must be completed.

Dangling: *By summarizing the information,* a clear *picture* of the situation was presented. (Dangles; a *picture* cannot perform the act of summarizing information.)

Corrected: *By summarizing the information, we* were able to present a clear picture of the situation.

or: After we had summarized the information, a clear picture of the situation was presented.

An infinitive or a participial phrase that modifies the whole sentence—designating general action rather than action by a specific agent—may be correctly used without relation to the subject of the main clause.

Generally speaking, these plants grow better in sunlight.

To summarize, Albuquerque has many spectacular sunsets.

Prepositional Phrases as Modifiers

The prepositional phrase can serve as an adjective or adverb.

The letter was addressed to the office *of the registrar.* (adjective modifying *office*)

They have gone *to the rally.* (adverb modifying *have gone*)

A prepositional phrase *dangles* when it does not, both logically and grammatically, refer to the subject of the main clause.

Dangling: *With much effort,* the *assignment* was completed on time.

Corrected: *With much effort, we* completed the assignment on time.

Dependent Clauses as Modifiers

Dependent clauses can serve as adjectives or adverbs. Parts of a dependent clause are sometimes omitted because the missing elements can be easily supplied. These incomplete clauses are known as **elliptical clauses.** An elliptical clause must be able to modify, both logically and grammatically, the subject of the main clause. If it does not, it dangles.

Dangling: *Unless compiled by early June,* we cannot include the figures in this year's crop report.

Corrected: *Unless compiled by early June,* the figures cannot be included in this year's crop report.

or: Unless *the figures are* compiled by early June, we cannot include them in this year's crop report.

Dangling: *While making his periodic tour of the state,* a few changes in the planned itinerary were necessary.

Corrected: *While making his periodic tour of the state,* he made a few changes in the planned itinerary.

or: While *he was* making his periodic tour of the state, a few changes in planned itinerary were made.

Relative Pronouns Introducing Clauses

Be careful to select the correct relative pronoun to introduce the adjective clause. *Who* refers to persons; *what, that,* and *which* refer to things; *that* usually refers to things, but is sometimes used to refer to persons.

The trainer *who tamed this lion* has had extensive experience.

The homework assignment, *which is due tomorrow,* will contain that information.

The time card *that you have been submitting weekly* will be required once a month from now on.

Placement of Modifiers

Modifiers should be placed as close as possible to the words they modify. This is true whether the modifier is a single word, a phrase, or a clause. In English, sometimes the only way the reader can tell which word is being modified is by the location of the modifier. It's often simply a matter of proximity.

Many ambiguous (and unintentionally humorous) sentences result from the misplacement of modifiers.

Modifier Between Subject and Verb

Wherever possible, avoid placing the modifier between subject and verb and between verb and object.

Not: The driver, *to save money on fuel,* switched to a smaller car.

But: *To save money on fuel,* the driver switched to a smaller car.

Single Adverbs

Some adverbs—*only, almost, nearly, also, quite, merely, actually*—are frequent troublemakers. Be sure they are placed as close as possible to the words they modify.

Example: The problem can *only* be defined by this committee.

Could mean: *Only* this committee can define the problem.

or: This committee can *only define* the problem, not solve it.

Do not use *hardly, only, scarcely, barely*—so-called subtractive adverbs—together with a negative construction. If you do, you will have a double negative.

Not: They *haven't only* a single blanket.

But: They *have only* a single blanket.

Not: He *hasn't scarcely* done anything worthwhile.

But: He *has scarcely* done anything worthwhile.

Phrases and Clauses

Phrases and clauses, like single-word modifiers, should be placed as close as possible to the words they modify; this way there will be no danger of their attaching themselves to the wrong sentence element.

Not: We need someone to design buildings *with architectural experience.*

But: We need someone *with architectural experience* to design buildings.

Not: Mr. Dough has resigned from Congress after having served four years *to the regret of all the members.*

But: *To the regret of all the members,* Mr. Dough has resigned from Congress after having served four years.

Relative Clauses

Relative clauses should also be placed immediately after the word they modify, since they attach themselves to the sentence element nearest them.

Not: The man has an appointment *who is waiting in my office.*

But: The man *who is waiting in my office* has an appointment.

Not: She mentioned the number of cases closed by agents in her group *which are over a year old.*

But: She mentioned the number of cases *over a year old* which have been closed by agents in her group.

Squinting Constructions

Avoid **squinting** constructions—that is, modifiers that are so placed that one cannot tell whether they are modifying the words immediately preceding them or those immediately following them.

Obscure: The city agreed *after the papers were signed* to allow the march.

Could mean: The city agreed to allow the march *after the papers were signed.*

or: *After the papers were signed,* the city agreed to allow the march.

Obscure: He agreed *that morning* to marry her.

Could mean: He agreed to marry her *that morning.*

or: *That morning,* he agreed to marry her.

CONNECTIVES

Four kinds of words can serve as connectives: **prepositions, conjunctions, relative pronouns,** and **relative adverbs.** Each not only connects two sentence elements but also shows the relationship between them.

Prepositions

A preposition *connects* the word, phrase, or clause that follows it (its object) with some other element in the sentence *and shows the relationship* between them. A preposition can be a single word (*to, with*) or a phrase (*according to, as well as, because of, contrary to*).

Prepositional Idioms

The use of many prepositions in English is purely idiomatic: there is no logical reason that one preposition is wrong and another correct in a given expression. There are no rules for choosing the correct preposition; the idioms must simply be memorized. Study the following list of some of the more common prepositional idioms.

accede **to**	We cannot *accede to* the request.
accessory **of**	He was an *accessory of* the criminal.
accessory **to**	He was an *accessory to* the act.
accommodate **to**	He finds it hard to *accommodate* himself *to* new situations. (changed conditions)
accommodate **with**	We *accommodated* her *with* a loan of five dollars.
accompany **by**	Sheba was *accompanied by* a friend. (a person)
accompany **with**	The flowers were *accompanied with* a note. (a thing)
accountable **for**	I am *accountable for* my actions.
accountable **to**	I am *accountable to* my parents.
accused **by**	He was *accused by* the customer of giving poor service.
accused **of**	Edwin was *accused of* eating the last cookie.
acquiesce **in**	The commissioner *acquiesced in* the decision.
acquit **of**	The group was *acquitted of* the crime.
acquit **with**	She *acquitted* herself *with* honor.
adapt **for**	The stairway was *adapted for* our use.
adapt **from**	The movie was *adapted from* the book.
adapt **to**	Evelyn finds it difficult to *adapt to* new procedures.
adequate **for**	His golf game was not *adequate for* the course.
adequate **to**	Her ability was *adequate to* the job.
averse **to**	Fernandez was not *averse to* hard work.

advise **of**	The skaters were *advised of* the new regulations.
affix **to**	A stamp was *affixed to* the container.
agree **on**	They cannot *agree on* the best course of action.
agree **to**	They state that they *agree to* the compromise.
agree **with**	The boys and their fathers *agree with* us.
amenable **to**	Francis was *amenable to* our suggestion.
analogous **to**	This situation is *analogous to* the one we faced last year.
annoy **by**	The librarian was *annoyed by* the frequent interruptions.
annoy **with**	I was *annoyed with* many of the suggestions.
apparent **in**	Marv's attitude is *apparent in* his actions.
apparent **to**	The trouble is *apparent to* everyone.
append **to**	A rider was *appended to* the bill.
appreciation **for**	The student had a deep *appreciation for* the arts.
appreciation **of**	He expressed *appreciation of* their hard work.
appreciative **of**	They are *appreciative of* Jim's efforts.
authority **in**	Dr. Rollin is an *authority in* the field of radiology.
authority **on**	Professor Haslem is an *authority on* Renaissance literature.
basis **for**	They had a sound *basis for* agreement.
basis **in**	Janet's argument has no *basis in* fact.
cater **to**	This magazine *caters to* coin collectors.
commensurate **with**	His salary was *commensurate with* his abilities.
comply **with**	We must *comply with* the request.
concur **in**	We *concur in* the decision of the survey committee.
concur **with**	One member did not *concur with* the others.
conform **to**	All campers must *conform to* the regulations.
consist **in**	Her chief value *consists in* her ability to work with others.
consist **of**	The handbook *consists of* mathematical formulas.

consistent **in**	Parents should be *consistent in* rearing their children.
correspond **to**	His description of the planet *corresponds to* the known facts.
correspond **with**	Lakeisha has been *corresponding with* her boyfriend.
demand **from**	What did Oscar *demand from* them in payment?
demand **of**	They had *demanded* an accounting *of* the company funds.
differ **from**	Trent's estimate of the amount due *differs from* Jarlyn's.
differ **in**	We *differ in* our political opinions.
differ **on**	They *differ on* the amount to be assessed.
differ **with**	I *differ with* him about the evaluation method to be used.
discrepancy **between**	There is a *discrepancy between* the two totals.
discrepancy **in**	There is a *discrepancy in* Felix's account.
displeased **at**	Jeff was *displeased at* the way the employee wasted time.
displeased **with**	Rolando was *displeased with* Michael's comments.
eligible **for**	He is *eligible for* the job.
equivalent **in**	His shirt and mine are *equivalent in* size.
equivalent **of**	This is the *equivalent of* a full payment.
equivalent **to**	Each payment is *equivalent to* a week's salary.
excepted **from**	He was *excepted from* further responsibility.
excluded **from**	This item may be *excluded from* the questionnaire.
exempt **from**	This type of income is *exempt from* tax.
expect **from**	What favor do you *expect from* your friend?
expect **of**	What does Bacon *expect of* his assistant?
familiar **to**	The name is *familiar to* me.
familiar **with**	I am quite *familiar with* motorcycles.
find **for**	The jury *found for* the defendant.

furnish **to**	Adequate supplies were *furnished to* them.
furnish **with**	Please *furnish* us *with* background information on this matter.
habit **of**	Carlos made a *habit of* checking his facts.
identical **with**	That case is *identical with* the one I am working on.
identify **by**	The girl was *identified by* the tattoo on her arm.
identify **with**	He was *identified with* the opposing members.
ignorant **of**	He was *ignorant of* his rights.
improvement **in**	The *improvement in* his singing was soon noted.
improvement **on**	His second pasta dish was an *improvement on* the first.
inconsistent **with**	Cruelty is *inconsistent with* civilized behavior.
infer **from**	We *infer from* Karen's statement that she plans to visit Paul.
influence **by**	The actors were all *influenced by* the director's exhortations.
influence **on (upon)**	The moon at perigee has a dramatic *influence on* (*upon*) the tides.
influence **over**	The minister had a strong *influence over* his congregation.
influence **with**	Mark referred frequently to his *influence with* those in authority.
inform **of**	Patients should keep their doctors *informed of* any changes in their health.
inherent **in**	A capacity for growth is *inherent in* all people.
insert **in**	This pin should be *inserted in* the slot.
intercede **for**	My best friend *interceded for* me.
intercede **with**	Doug *interceded with* the board in my behalf.
invest **in**	The police said he had *invested* the money *in* stocks.
invest **with**	She was *invested with* full power to act.
irrelevant **to**	This statement is *irrelevant to* the matter under discussion.

irrespective **of**	They decided to appoint him *irrespective of* the criticism that might result.
liable **for**	Trudi is *liable for* damages.
liable **to**	The employee is *liable to* his employer.
liberal **in**	He was very *liberal in* his views.
liberal **with**	My boss was *liberal with* her praise.
necessity **for**	There is no *necessity for* our launching the boat.
necessity **of**	We are faced with the *necessity of* reducing travel expenses.
oblivious **of (to)**	He was *oblivious of* (*to*) the effect that his remarks had on his friends.
precedent **for**	Is there a *precedent for* this action?
precedent **in**	His decision established a *precedent in* law.
recompense **for**	Miguel was fully *recompensed for* the time he spent on the job.
reconcile **to**	We have become *reconciled to* our fate.
reconcile **with**	Our views cannot be *reconciled with* his.
similarity **in**	I agree that there is much *similarity in* their appearance.
similarity **of**	The *similarity of* these odd vegetables caused a great deal of confusion.
similarity **to**	This camera shows a *similarity to* one I have.
talk **of**	The traveler *talked* long *of* his experiences.
talk **to**	The teacher *talked to* his class.
talk **with**	The lawyer *talked with* her client.
transfer **from**	He has been *transferred from* his former position.
transfer **to**	They *transferred* him *to* another department.
unequal **in**	The contestants were *unequal in* strength.
unequal **to**	She was *unequal to* the demands placed on her.
use **for**	He had no *use for* the extra table.
use **of**	She made good *use of* her opportunity.
wait **for**	Marci seemed to be *waiting for* someone.

Placement of Prepositions

It is now considered acceptable to end a sentence with a preposition.

> What did you do that *for?*

> We had too many ideas to talk *about.*

Superfluous Prepositions

In formal writing, avoid superfluous prepositions.

> Not: He is standing near *to* the ledge.

> But: He is standing near the ledge.

> Not: When are you going to start *in* to write that letter?

> But: When are you going to start to write that letter?

Faulty Omission of Prepositions

The preference in more formal writing is to repeat the preposition before the second of two connected elements.

> He seemed interested *in* us and our problems.

> He seemed interested *in* us and *in* our problems.

> He was able to complete the renovation *by* planning carefully and working diligently.

> He was able to complete the renovation *by* planning carefully and *by* working diligently.

In the so-called *split* (or *suspended*) construction, in which two words are completed by different prepositions, be especially careful to use both prepositions.

> Not: He has an interest and an aptitude *for* his work.

> But: He has an interest *in* and an aptitude *for* his work. (Commas may be used in this construction: He has an interest in, and an aptitude for, his work.)

> Not: They were puzzled and concerned *about* her erratic behavior.

> But: They were puzzled *by* and concerned *about* her erratic behavior.

Conjunctions and Parallelism

Sentence elements are said to be *coordinate* (or *parallel*) when they are of equal rank (of equal importance) both grammatically and logically.

Determining equal grammatical importance is relatively simple: words = words; phrases = phrases; subordinate clauses = subordinate clauses; principal clauses = principal clauses.

Elements not grammatically equal (not parallel) are shown in this example:

> His main virtues are *that he is sincere* and *his generosity.* (a clause linked to a word)

Improved:

> His main virtues are *that he is sincere* and *that he is generous.* (two noun clauses, now parallel; noun clause = noun clause)

> His main virtues are his *sincerity* and his *generosity.* (two words)

Coordinate Conjunctions Showing

The coordinate conjunctions, including *and, but, or, nor, for, yet, moreover,* are the connectives most frequently used to show that two ideas are equal (are parallel). Notice in the following illustrations that the two ideas connected are parallel.

> The *director and* the *assistant director* will attend the meeting. (connecting a word with a word)

> He is a man *of great capability but of little experience.* (connecting a phrase with a phrase)

> He said *that he had filed a claim for a refund but that he had not heard anything further from this store.* (connecting a subordinate clause with a subordinate clause)

> *I was eager to attend the seminar; moreover, I knew that the exchange of ideas would be helpful.* (connecting an independent clause with an independent clause)

Correlative Conjunctions Showing Coordination (Parallelism)

The correlative conjunctions—*either . . . or, neither . . . nor, not only . . . but also, both . . . and, if . . . then, since . . . therefore*—work in pairs to show that words and ideas are parallel (equal in importance).

> *Either* the *doctor or* the *lawyer* must attend. (connecting a word with a word)

> The report is designed *not only to present a list of the problems facing us but also to recommend possible solutions to these problems.* (connecting a phrase with a phrase)

The significant point in the use of pairs of correlatives is that each member of the pair must be followed by the same part of speech (same grammatical construction). That is, if *not only* is followed by a verb, then *but also* must be followed by a verb; if *either* is followed by a phrase, *or* must likewise be followed by a phrase.

Not: *Either* fish of this type are much fewer in number *or* are not easily caught. (*Either* is followed by a noun, *fish;* or is followed by a verb phrase.)

But: Fish of this type *either* are much fewer in number *or* are not easily caught.

Not: His reply *not only* was prompt *but also* complete.

But: His reply was *not only* prompt *but also* complete.

When this plan is not followed, the result is "faulty parallelism." To turn faulty parallelism into effective parallelism, sometimes we need add only a word or two.

Not: The picnic was a disappointment *not only* to me *but also* my boyfriend. (*Not only* is followed by the prepositional phrase *to me; but also* is followed by a noun.)

But: The picnic was a disappointment *not only* to me *but also* to my boyfriend. (Note that each of the correlative conjunctions is followed by a prepositional phrase.)

Not: His assignment was *both* to conduct the course *and* the evaluation of it.

But: His assignment was *both* to conduct the course *and* to evaluate it.

NOTE: The correlative *as . . . as* is used both affirmatively and negatively; the correlative *so . . . as* is used only negatively.

This melon is *as* sweet *as* that one.

This melon is not *as* sweet *as* that one

This melon is not *so* sweet *as* that one.

Troublesome Conjunctions

and vs. *also*

Also, a weak connective, should not be used in place of *and* in sentences such as:

He writes poems, stories, *and* (not *also*) art reviews.

and etc.

The abbreviation *etc.* stands for the Latin *et cetera,* meaning *and so forth.* Obviously, then, an additional *and* is not only unnecessary but incorrect.

> Not: He used all our paper, pencils, pens, *and etc.*

> But: He used all our paper, pencils, pens, *etc.*

and which, and who, but which

Avoid using *and which, and who, but which, but that,* etc., when there is no preceding *who, which,* or *that* in the sentence to complete the parallel construction.

> Not: We are looking for a car more economical to operate *and which* will be easy to maintain.

> But: We are looking for a car *which* will be more economical to operate *and which* will be easy to maintain.

too many *and's*

Avoid stringing together a group of sentence elements connected by *and's.*

> Not: The evaluation of the training program was planned *and* conducted *and* reported to the appropriate officials.

> But: The evaluation of the training program was planned and conducted; then it was reported to the appropriate officials.

and vs. *but*

Use *and* to show addition; use *but* to show contrast.

> Not: The boy and his mother have been called to a short meeting, *and* the principal will be out of the office all afternoon.

> But: The boy and his mother have been called to a short meeting, *but* the principal will be out of the office all afternoon.

and or *but* to begin a sentence

We may begin a sentence—or even a paragraph—with *and, but,* or any other coordinating conjunction. A coordinate conjunction or a conjunctive adverb at the beginning of a sentence is often a handy signpost for the reader, pointing out the direction this new sentence will carry him.

as, since, because

These conjunctions can be used interchangeably to introduce clauses of cause or reason.

> *Because* the book was due at the library, I returned it.

> *Since* the book was due at the library, I returned it.

> *As* the book was due at the library, I returned it.

However, *since* and *as* have another function: *since* introduces clauses of sequence of time, and *as* introduces clauses of duration of time. Because of the double function of these two words, we must be careful to use them only in sentences in which they cannot be misunderstood.

> Not: *Since* this study was conducted to analyze the effects of . . .
> (Could mean: *Since the time that* the study was conducted . . .)

> But: *Because* this study was conducted to analyze the effects of . . .

> Not: *As* I was writing the lab report, he gave the correct answers to Beth. (Could mean: *During the time that* I was writing the lab report . . .)

> But: *Because* I was writing the lab report . . .

NOTE: When an *as* or *since* clause comes last in the sentence, the meaning of the conjunction can be made clear by the punctuation of the clause. If *as* or *since* is used as a time indicator, the clause it introduces is not set off from the sentence. But if the conjunction introduces a clause of cause or reason, the clause is set off.

There have been several changes in policy *since* the committee released its findings. (No punctuation; *since* means *since the time that*.)

There have been several changes in policy, *since* the committee released its findings. (. . . *because* the committee released its findings)

---

as vs. *that* or *whether*

Avoid using *as* in place of *that* or *whether* to introduce clauses following such verbs as *say, think, know*.

> Not: I don't know *as* I believe you.

> But: I don't know *that* I believe you.

> or: I don't know *whether* I believe you.

if vs. *whether*

If is used to introduce clauses of condition or supposition.

> We will stay *if* the fish are biting.

> *If* you cannot answer the phone immediately, please ask Erin to do it.

Whether introduces clauses indicating an alternative. The alternative may be expressed in the sentence or understood.

It will not make any difference *whether* John agrees or disagrees with the outcome of the polling.

Please let me know *whether* you received the check.

Today, many grammarians endorse the use of either *if* or *whether* in such constructions as:

Please let me know *if* (or *whether*) you received the check.

I wonder *if* (or *whether*) he is qualified for that position.

If there is any danger that the reader may fail to understand the meaning, use the preferred *whether*.

whether vs. *whether or not*
It is not essential that *or not* be used with *whether* to complete the alternative choice. These words may be added if they are needed for emphasis.

Either: Please let me know *whether or not* you received our letter.

Or: Please let me know *whether* you received our letter.

that introducing parallel clauses
When either *that* or *which* introduces one of a series of parallel clauses, the same conjunction must introduce the other clauses in the series. Do not shift conjunctions or omit the conjunction in later clauses.

Not: He said *that* he would call me before noon and his brother would meet me. (conjunction omitted)

But: He said *that* he would call me before noon and *that* his brother would meet me. (conjunction supplied)

Shift in conjunction:

Not: We painted the boat *that* we liked so much and *which* we bought.

But: We painted the boat *that* we liked so much and *that* we bought.

proper omission of *that*
That may be omitted in noun clauses (especially those following such verbs as *say, think, feel, believe, hope*) and in adjective clauses, if the meaning of the sentence is clear.
Noun clauses:

He said (*that*) he would call me before noon.

I hope (*that*) we can finish this painting today.

Adjective clauses:

The book (*that*) I asked for is out on loan.

The instructions (*that*) she gave were perfectly clear.

faulty repetition of *that*

Do not use *that* twice to introduce the same noun clause. This error most often occurs in a long sentence in which a long interrupting expression occurs between *that* and the rest of its clause.

Not: I am sure you can appreciate *that,* in order to serve as many guests as possible, *that* we must open the veranda.

But: I am sure you can appreciate *that,* in order to serve as many guests as possible, we must open the veranda.

when

Avoid using *when* to introduce a definition unless the definition pertains to time.

Not: Their first important step in the improvement of the conditions was *when* they thoroughly surveyed the situation. (The step was not "when.")

But: Their first important step in the improvement of the conditions was *the thorough survey* of the situation.

Correct usage: Three o'clock is *when* the meeting will be held.

where

Avoid using *where* to introduce a definition unless the definition pertains to place or location.

Not: A sentence is *where* you have a subject and a verb. (A sentence is not "where.")

But: A sentence is a group of words containing a subject and a verb.

Correct usage: The large conference room is *where* the meeting is being held.

Avoid substituting *where* for *that.*

Not: I saw in the bulletin *where* the new law has been put into effect.

But: I saw in the bulletin *that* the new law has been put into effect.

while* vs. *when

While indicates duration of time; *when* indicates a fixed or stated period of time.

> *When* I return to work, I will take you out to lunch. (at that fixed time)

> *While* I am shopping, I will look for that skirt. (During the time I am shopping . . .)

while* vs. *though, although, and, but

While pertains to time and should not be substituted loosely for *though, although, whereas, and,* or *but.*

> Not: *While* I did not remember the woman's name, I thought I could recognize her face.

> But: *Although* I did not remember the woman's name, I thought I could recognize her face.

> Not: I assembled the material for the manual *while* he wrote the outline. (Could mean: *during the time that he* . . .)

> But: I assembled the material for the manual, *but* he wrote the outline.

PUNCTUATION

The purpose of punctuation is to clarify the meaning of written language. In general, punctuation marks should prevent misreading by bringing out clearly the author's intended meaning.

APOSTROPHE

Do not space to set off an apostrophe.

1. In a contraction, insert an apostrophe in place of the omitted letter or letters.

> have + not = haven't

> we + are = we're

> let + us = let's

> class of 2001 = class of '01

2. When indicating possession, the apostrophe means *belonging to every- thing to the left of the apostrophe.*

> lady's = belonging to the lady
>
> ladies' = belonging to the ladies
>
> children's = belonging to the children

Observe the following forms:

> man's, men's
>
> hostess's, hostesses'
>
> prince's, princes'

In set phrases, nouns ending in *-s* or *-ce* and followed by a word begin- ning with an *s* may form the possessive by adding an apostrophe only, with no following *s*.

> for goodness' sake
>
> for old times' sake

In compound nouns, the *'s* is added to the element nearest the object possessed.

> comptroller general's office
>
> John White, Jr.'s account
>
> attorney at law's fee

Joint possession is indicated by placing an apostrophe on the last element of a series; individual or alternative possession requires the use of an apostrophe on each element in the series.

> soldiers and sailors' home
>
> Brown & Nelson's store
>
> men's, women's, or children's clothing
>
> editor's or proofreader's opinion

Possessive pronouns do not take an apostrophe.

> its (belongs to it)
>
> theirs

Do not confuse *its* with the contraction *it's* (it is).

3. Use an apostrophe to form the plural of numbers and letters, and words referred to as words.

49'ers	a's, 7's, ¶'s
YMCA's	three R's
2's, 3's,	*but* twos and threes

Observe the following forms:

ands, ifs, and buts

do's and don'ts

ins and outs

Years may be typed as follows:

1990's or 1990s, the '90s, *not* the '90's

BRACKETS

Do not space to set off brackets from the material they enclose.

1. Brackets are used to enclose interpolations that are not specifically a part of transcribed or quoted material. An interpolation in brackets is often a correction, an explanation, or a warning that the material quoted is in error.

"The bill had *not* been paid." [Emphasis added.]

"July 3 [sic] is a national holiday."

2. Brackets are used to enclose parenthetical material within a parenthesis.

(The result [see fig. 2] is most surprising.)

COLON

Check carefully the spacing for colons. See each example below.

1. Use a colon after the salutation in a business letter.

Dear Board Member:

2. Use a colon (or a slash) to separate the initials of the dictator from the initials of the typist. Do not space after the colon.

RLT:pop

3. Use a colon to separate hours from minutes. Do not space after the colon.

   The eclipse occurred at 10:36 A.M.

4. A colon may (but need not always) be used to introduce a list, a long quotation, and a question.

   My question is this: Are you willing to punch a time clock?

5. Use a colon before a final clause that extends or explains what is said in the preceding matter.

   Railroading is not a variety of outdoor sport: it is a service.

6. Use a colon to indicate proportion and a double colon to indicate ratio. Space before and after the colon.

   concrete mixed 5 : 3 : 1

   1 : 2 :: 4 : 12

COMMA

Leave one space after the comma.

1. The salutation of a personal letter is followed by a comma.

   Dear Mary,

2. The complimentary close of a letter is ordinarily followed by a comma, though this use is optional.

   Cordially yours,

3. An appositive must be set off by commas.

   Jim Rodgers, my next-door neighbor, is an excellent baby-sitter.

4. A noun of address is set apart by commas.

   When you finish your homework, Jeff, please take out the garbage.

5. Use commas to set off parenthetical words.

   I think, however, that move might not be wise at this time.

6. When two or more adjectives (called coordinate adjectives) all modify a noun equally, all but the last must be followed by commas. Test: if you can add the word *and* between the adjectives without changing the sense of the sentence, then use commas.

   The jolly, fat man stood at the top of the stairs.

7. An introductory phrase or clause of five or more words is usually followed by a comma.

   Because the prisoner had a history of attempted jailbreaks, he was put under heavy guard.

8. After a short introductory phrase, the comma is optional. The comma should be used where needed for clarity.

   As a child she was a tomboy. (comma unnecessary)

   To Dan, Phil was friend as well as brother. (comma clarifies)

   In 1978, 300 people lost their lives in one air disaster. (comma clarifies)

9. A comma is not generally used before a subordinate clause that ends a sentence, though in long, unwieldy sentences, use of such a comma is optional.

10. A comma precedes the coordinating conjunction unless the two clauses are very short.

    The boy wanted to borrow a book from the library, but the librarian would not allow him to take it until he had paid his fines.

    Roy washed the dishes and Helen dried them.

11. Words, phrases, or clauses in a series are separated by commas. The use of a comma before *and* is optional. If the series ends in *etc.,* use a comma before *etc.* Do not use a comma after *etc.* in a series, even if the sentence continues.

    Coats, umbrellas, and boots should be placed in the closet at the end of the hall.

    Pencils, scissors, paper clips, etc. belong in your top desk drawer.

12. A comma separates a short direct quotation from the speaker.

    She said, "I must leave work on time today."

    "Tomorrow I begin my new job," he told us.

13. Use a comma to indicate that you have omitted a word or words, such as *of* or *of the.*

    President, XYZ Corporation

14. Use a comma to separate a name from a title or personal-name suffix.

    Linda Feiner, Chairman

    Carl Andrew Pforzheimer, Jr.

15. Use a comma when first and last names are reversed.

    Bernbach, Melissa

16. Use a comma to separate parts of addresses.

> Please come to a party at "The Old Mill" on Drake Road, Cheswold, Delaware.

The use of a comma between the name of a city and a two-letter postal abbreviation of a state is optional. Do not use a comma between the postal abbreviation of a state and the ZIP code.

> Cleveland OH 44114

> Scarsdale, NY 10583

17. A comma may or may not be used to separate parts of a date. But note that in European and military style dates the comma is never used.

> We will be leaving for Paris on October 6, 1999.

> I think she will arrive on April 14 1998.

> He joined the navy 31 October 1956.

18. A comma ordinarily separates thousands, millions, billions, and trillions. There is no space before or after the comma.

> 75,281,646

19. A nonrestrictive adjective phrase or clause must be set off by commas. A nonrestrictive phrase or clause is one that can be omitted without changing the meaning of the sentence.

> Our new sailboat, which has bright orange sails, is very seaworthy.

A restrictive phrase or clause is vital to the meaning of a sentence and cannot be omitted. Do not set it off with commas.

> A sailboat without sails is useless.

20. A comma must be used if the sentence might be subject to different interpretation without it.

> He saw the woman who had rejected him, and blushed.

21. If a pause would make the sentence clearer and easier to read, insert a comma.

> Inside the people were dancing. (confusing)

> Inside, the people were dancing. (clearer)

> After all crime must be punished. (confusing)

> After all, crime must be punished. (clearer)

The pause rule is not infallible, but it is an acceptable resort when all other comma rules fail to suit the situation.

DASH

Leave no space on either side of a dash.

1. You may use a dash—or parentheses—for emphasis or to set off an explanatory group of words.

   The tools of his trade—probe, mirror, cotton swabs—were neatly arranged on the dentist's tray.

2. Dashes must be used in pairs unless the set-off expression ends a sentence or marks a sudden break in thought or speech that leaves a sentence unfinished.

   The elections will take place in November—if we remain at peace.

   "No! Don't open that—"

ELLIPSIS

An ellipsis is three spaced periods. If the material deleted includes a final period, type four spaced periods.

1. An ellipsis indicates that something has been left out of a quoted text.

   "The country is excited from one end to the other by a great question of principle. On that question the Government has taken one side."

becomes

   "The country is excited . . . by a great question . . . . On that question the Government has taken one side."

2. Four spaced periods may be used to indicate that a sentence or more has been omitted. To indicate the omission of an entire paragraph or more, terminate the preceding paragraph with a period and ellipsis (four dots) and initiate the next paragraph with an ellipsis (three dots).

EXCLAMATION MARK

Leave two spaces after the exclamation mark.

1. An exclamation mark indicates strong feeling or emotion.

   Congratulations! You broke the record.

   Rush! Perishable contents.

   Don't touch that dial!

HYPHEN

There is no space on either side of a hyphen unless it is used at the end of the line.

1. Use a hyphen to divide a word at the end of a line.

2. Use a hyphen to connect the elements of some compounds. (See the section on Compound Words.)

3. Use a hyphen to separate the letters of a spelled word.

> In front of the children she asked me if I had brought the c-a-n-d-y.

PARENTHESES

Do not space to set off parentheses from the material they enclose.

1. Use parentheses to set off matter that is not intended to be part of the main statement or that is not a grammatical element of the sentence, yet important enough to be included.

> This case (124 US 329) is not relevant.
>
> The result (see fig. 2) is most surprising.
>
> The Galesburg (IL) Chamber of Commerce

A reference in parentheses at the end of a sentence is placed before the period, unless it is a complete sentence in itself.

> The specimens show great variation. (See pl. 6.)
>
> The specimens show great variation (pl. 6).

2. Use parentheses to enclose a figure following a spelled-out number in a legal document.

> The tenant shall vacate within thirty (30) days.

3. Use parentheses to enclose numbers or letters designating items in a series.

> The order of delivery will be (a) food, (b) medicines, and (c) clothing.

PERIOD

Leave two spaces after the period at the end of a sentence.

1. Use a period at the end of a sentence that makes a statement, gives a command, or makes a polite request in the form of a question that does not require an answer.

    I am brushing up on my archery skills.

    Give generously of yourself.

    Please read that menu to me.

2. Use a period after some abbreviations, including the initials of a personal name. (See the comprehensive section in this volume on abbreviations.)

    Gen. Robert E. Lee led the Confederate forces.

3. Use a period as a decimal point in numbers. Do not leave a space before or after the period.

    A sales tax of 5.5 percent amounts to $7.47 on a $135.80 purchase.

QUESTION MARK

Leave two spaces after the question mark.

1. Use a question mark at the end of a direct and genuine question.

    Why do you wish to return to Peru?

2. Do not use a question mark after an indirect question; use a period.

    He asked if they wanted to accompany him.

    I wonder where the fire is.

3. A direct question must end with a question mark even if the question does not encompass the entire sentence.

    "Daddy, are we there yet?" the child asked.

    The man cried "Who would do such a thing?" when he saw his vandalized car.

4. Use a question mark (within parentheses) to indicate uncertainty as to the correctness of a fact.

    John Carver, first governor of Plymouth colony, was born in 1575 (?) and died in 1621.

QUOTATION MARKS

Do not space to set off quotation marks from the material they enclose.

1. All directly quoted material must be enclosed by quotation marks. Words not quoted must remain outside the quotation marks.

   "If it is hot on Sunday," she said, "we will go to the beach."

2. An indirect quote must not be enclosed by quotation marks.

   She said that we might go to the beach on Sunday.

3. When a multiple-paragraph passage is quoted, each paragraph of the quotation must begin with quotation marks, but ending quotation marks are used only at the end of the last quoted paragraph.

4. A period always goes inside the quotation marks, whether the quotation marks are used to denote quoted material, to set off titles—such as chapters in a book or titles of short stories—or to isolate words used in a special sense.

   Jane explained, "The house is just around the corner."

   The first chapter of *The Andromeda Strain* is entitled "The Country of Lost Borders."

   Pornography is sold under the euphemism "adult books."

5. A comma always goes inside the quotation marks.

   "I really must go home," said the dinner guest.

   If your skills have become "rusty," you must study before you apply for the job.

   Three stories in Kurt Vonnegut's *Welcome to the Monkey House* are "Harrison Bergeron," "Next Door," and "Epicae."

6. A question mark goes inside the quotation marks if it is part of the quotation. If the whole sentence containing the quotation is a question, the question mark goes outside the quotation marks.

   He asked, "Was the airplane on time?"

   What did you really mean when you said, "I do"?

7. An exclamation mark goes inside the quotation marks if the quoted words are an exclamation, outside if the entire sentence including the quotation is an exclamation.

   The sentry shouted, "Drop your gun!"

   Save us from our "friends"!

8. A colon and a semicolon always go outside the quotation marks.

   He said, "War is destructive"; she added, "peace is constructive."

9. Words used in an unusual way may be placed inside quotation marks.

   A surfer who "hangs ten" is performing a tricky maneuver on a surfboard.

10. A quotation within a quotation may be set apart by single quotes (apostrophes).

    George said, "The philosophy 'I think, therefore I am' may be attributed to Descartes."

SEMICOLON

Always single-space after a semicolon.

1. A semicolon may be used to join two short, related independent clauses.

   Anne is working at the front desk on Monday; Pedro will take over on Tuesday.

   Two independent clauses must be joined by a conjunction (and comma) or by a semicolon (or colon) or must be written as two sentences. A semicolon never precedes a coordinating conjunction. The same two clauses may be written:

   Autumn had come to our mountain home, and the trees were almost bare. (Use a comma when conjoining longer independent clauses.)

   Autumn had come to our mountain home; the trees were almost bare. (Use a semicolon when conjoining two independent clauses.)

   Autumn had come to our mountain home. The trees were almost bare.

2. A semicolon may be used to join two independent clauses which are connected by an adverb such as *however, therefore, otherwise,* or *nevertheless.* The adverb must be followed by a comma.

   We went to the track; however, the race was rained out.

   You may use a semicolon to join one clause with the next; however, you will not be incorrect if you choose to write two separate sentences.

   We went to the track. However, the race was rained out.

   If you are uncertain how to use the semicolon to connect independent clauses, write two sentences instead.

3. A semicolon should be used to separate a series of phrases or clauses, especially when those phrases and clauses contain commas.

The old gentleman's heirs were Margaret Whitlock, his half-sister; James Bagley, the butler; William Frame, companion to his late cousin, Robert Bone; and his favorite charity, the Salvation Army.

CAPITALIZATION

1. Capitalize the first word of a complete sentence.

Your favorite television program is on now.

2. Capitalize the first word of a quoted sentence.

The bookkeeper said, "Please identify your personal long-distance phone calls."

Do *not* capitalize the first word within quotation marks if it does not begin a complete sentence.

"I tore my stocking," she told us, "because the drawer was left open."

3. Capitalize the letter *I* when it stands alone.

4. Capitalize the first letter of the first, last, and each important word in the title of a book, play, article, etc.

"The Mystery of the Green Ghost"

A Night at the Opera

5. Capitalize a title when it is used with the name of a person, group, or document.

Senator Jane Doe is a leading figure in the Republican Party.

Do *not* capitalize the same type of title when it does not make a specific reference.

The congressman is a liberal; his opponent is a conservative.

It would be useful for our club to write a constitution.

6. Capitalize days of the week, months of the year, and holidays, but do *not* capitalize the seasons.

Labor Day, the last holiday of the summer, falls on the first Monday in September.

7. Capitalize the points of the compass only when referring to a specific place or region.

   Many retired persons spend the winter in the South.

   Do not capitalize the points of the compass when they refer to a direction.

   The birds were flying south.

8. The only school subjects that are regularly capitalized are languages and specific place names used as modifiers.

   Next year we will offer French, English literature, biology, mathematics, European history, and ancient philosophy.

9. A noun not regularly capitalized should be capitalized when it is used as part of a proper name.

   Yesterday I visited Uncle Fester, my favorite uncle.

10. In a letter, capitalize all titles in the address and closing.

    Mr. John Jones, President

    Mary Smith, Chairman of the Board

    Capitalize the first and last words, titles, and proper names in the salutation.

    Dear Dr. Williams,

    My dear Sir:

    Capitalize only the first word in a complimentary closing.

    Very truly yours,

11. Capitalize all proper names—including, but not limited to, the names of people (*John F. Smith*); buildings (*World Trade Center*); events (*Veterans Day*); places (*Panama*) and words formed using those places (*Panamanian*); organizations (*The United Fund*); and words referring to a sole God (*Allah*).

    Some words derived from proper names have lost their proper-name meaning and have acquired an independent meaning in a different context. Many of these words are no longer capitalized. Below is a list of some lowercased derivatives of proper names. Consult a dictionary if in doubt.

angstrom unit	artesian well	bourbon whisky
apache (Paris)	astrakhan fabric	bowie knife
argyle wool	bologna sausage	britannia metal

burley tobacco	herculean task	neon light
cashmere shawl	holland cloth	newton
chesterfield coat	italic type	oriental rug
china clay	japan varnish	osnaburg cloth
chinook salmon	jersey fabric	oxford cloth
coulumb	joule	parkerhouse roll
curie	klieg light	pasteurized milk
degaussing apparatus	knickerbocker	petri dish
delftware	kraft paper	philistinism
diesel engine	lambert	pitman arm
dotted swiss	lynch law	pitot-static tube
fedora hat	lyonnaise potatoes	portland cement
frankfurter	macadamized road	quisling
frankfurt sausage	madras cloth	quixotic idea
fuller's earth	maraschino cherry	roentgen
gargantuan	maxwell	surah silk
gauss	mercerized fabric	timothy grass
georgette crepe	merino sheep	utopianism
gilbert	morocco leather	venturi tube
graham bread	navy blue	zeppelin

NUMBERS

SPELLED OUT

1. Two general rules apply to expressing numbers. One or the other should be followed consistently within a piece of writing.

   a. Spell out numbers through nine; use figures from 10 on.

   > two people
   >
   > three times as large
   >
   > 14 recommendations

b. Spell out numbers through ninety-nine; use figures from 100 on.

    eighty-six apples

    forty people

    163 pages

2. Any number that begins a sentence:

    Nineteen eighty-three was the company's best year.

    Two hundred forty workers were hired.

3. Centuries, round numbers, and indefinite expressions:

    hundreds of men

    the early seventies, *but* the 1890s, mid-1964

    the nineteenth century

4. Large numbers in very formal writing such as legal work. Use the following forms as models:

    sixteen hundred and twenty

    exactly four thousand

    fifty-two thousand one hundred and ninety-five

    nineteen hundred and eighty-four

5. Fractions standing alone or followed by *of a* or *of an:*

    one-half inch

    three-fourths of a pie

    one-third of an acre

6. Ordinal numbers less than one hundred:

    twentieth century

    eighty-second congress

    Fifth Fleet

    Twelfth Avenue

EXPRESSED IN FIGURES

1. Numbers over one hundred within ordinary text:

    Enrollment reached 16,847.

    952 ballots

    101 districts

2. All numbers in tabular material.

3. Measurements of physical properties in scientific or technical writing, and any number used with a symbol or abbreviated unit of measurement:

20/20 vision	43 mm
6 pounds	13 lb. 2 oz.
32° F	1 yd.
17½"	8:30 A.M.

4. Serial numbers, including numbers designating the pages and other parts of a book:

    Bulletin 756

    pages 322–345

    diagram 4

5. Years:

53 B.C.	in A.D. 7
1925	1255 B.C.E.

6. Fractions that would be awkward if spelled out:

    8½-by-11-inch bond

7. Decimal fractions and percentages:

    10.5 percent return

    $83.95

    a grade point average of 3.42

8. All numbers referring to the same category in a single passage if the largest is over one hundred:

    Of the 137 delegates at the twelve o'clock meeting, only 9 opposed the plan.

LARGE NUMBERS

Large numbers are usually expressed in figures; however, numbers from a million up which end in four or more zeros may be expressed in text by combining figures and words. In the examples that follow, preference is based on the ease with which the number can be grasped in reading.

Figures:	299,789,655
Preferred:	299,789,655
Figures:	$12,000,000
Preferred:	$12 million
Acceptable:	12 million dollars
Figures:	3,250,000
Preferred:	3.25 million
Acceptable:	3¼ million
or:	three and one-fourth million
or:	three and one-quarter million
Figures:	9,000,000 to 1,000,000,000
Preferred:	9 million to 1 billion
Acceptable:	nine million to one billion

ROMAN NUMERALS

It is generally preferable to use Arabic numbers, as they are more easily understood than Roman numerals.

A repeated letter repeats its value; a letter placed after one of greater value adds to it; a letter placed before one of greater value subtracts from it; a dashline over a letter denotes multiplied by 1,000.

I	1	X	10	XL	40
II	2	XV	15	XLV	45
III	3	XIX	19	XLIX	49
IV	4	XX	20	L	50
V	5	XXV	25	LV	55
VI	6	XXIX	29	LIX	59
VII	7	XXX	30	LX	60
VIII	8	XXXV	35	LXV	65
IX	9	XXXIX	39	LXIX	69

LXX	70	C	100	CM	900
LXXV	75	CL	150	M	1,000
LXXIX	79	CC	200	MD	1,500
LXXX	80	CCC	300	MM	2,000
LXXXV	85	CD	400	MMM	3,000
LXXXIX	89	D	500	MMMM or MV	4,000
XC	90	DC	600		
XCV	95	DCC	700	V	5,000
XCIX	99	DCCC	800	M	1,000,000

Dates

MDC	1600	MCMLXX	1970
MDCC	1700	MCMLXXX	1980
MDCCC	1800	MCMXC	1990
MCM or MDCCCC	1900	MM	2000
MCMX	1910	MMX	2010
MCMXX	1920	MMXX	2020
MCMXXX	1930	MMXXX	2030
MCMXL	1940	MMXL	2040
MCML	1950	MML	2050
MCMLX	1960	MMLX	2060

COMPOUND WORDS

A compound is a union of two or more words; it conveys a unit idea that is not as clearly or quickly conveyed by the component words in unconnected succession. Compounds may be spelled open (with a space), solid (with no space), or with a hyphen.

Since ours is a fluid, changing language, the rules that follow can only provide guidelines to common practice. Word forms constantly undergo modification. Two-word forms often acquire the hyphen first and are later printed solid. Sometimes the transition is from open to solid, bypassing the hyphenated form. The trend recently has been toward solid spellings; for instance, the once-common spellings *life style* and *life-style* have now generally given way to *lifestyle*. Check a current, reliable dictionary for guidance.

GENERAL RULES

1. In general, omit the hyphen when words appear in regular order and the omission causes no ambiguity in sense or sound.

banking hours	fellow citizen	real estate
blood pressure	living costs	rock candy
book value	palm oil	training ship
census taker	patent right	violin teacher

2. Words are usually combined to express a literal or nonliteral (figurative) unit idea that would not be as clearly expressed in unconnected succession.

afterglow	eye-opener	newsprint
bookkeeping	forget-me-not	right-handed
cupboard	gentleman	whitewash

3. Unless otherwise indicated, a derivative of a compound, that is, a compound which is derived from another compound, retains the solid or hyphenated form of the original compound.

coldbloodedness	outlawry	X-rayer
footnoting	praiseworthiness	Y-shaped
ill-advisable	railroader	

4. Except after the short prefixes *co, de, pre, pro,* and *re,* which are generally typed solid, a hyphen is used to avoid doubling the same vowel or tripling the same consonant.

Solid	**Hypenated**
antiaircraft	semi-independent
cooperation	thimble-eye
preexisting	ultra-atomic
semiannual	shell-like

SOLID COMPOUNDS

1. Consider solid (as one word) two nouns that form a third when the compound has only one primary accent, especially when the prefixed noun consists of only one syllable or when one of the elements loses its original accent.

airship	cupboard	footnote
bathroom	dressmaker	locksmith
bookseller	fishmonger	workman

2. Consider solid a noun consisting of a short verb and a terminal adverb, except when the use of the solid form would interfere with comprehension.

blowout	pickup	*BUT* cut-in
flareback	runoff	run-in
giveaway	setup	tie-in
hangover	throwaway	
makeready		

3. Compounds beginning with the following nouns are usually considered solid.

book(end)	mill(work)	snow(fall)
eye	play	way
horse	school	wood
house	shop	work

4. Compounds ending in the following are usually considered solid, especially when the prefixed word consists of one syllable.

(blue)berry	(devil)fish	(lime)light
blossom	flower	like
boat	grower	wise
book	hearted	woman
borne	holder	maker
bound	house	making
brained	keeper	man
bush	keeping	master

mate	stone	woman
mill	store	wood
mistress	tail	work
monger	tight	worker
owner	time (*not* clock)	working
piece	ward	worm
power	way	wort
proof	weed	writer
room	wide	writing
shop	wise	yard
smith		

5. Consider solid *any, every, no,* and *some* when combined with *body, thing,* and *where.* When *one* is the second element, print as two words if meaning a single or particular person or thing. To avoid mispronunciation, print *no one* as two words at all times.

anybody	everywhere	somebody
anything	everyone	something
anywhere	nobody	somewhere
anyone	nothing	someone
everybody	nowhere	
everything	no one	

BUT Any one of us may stay.

Every one of the pilots is responsible.

6. Consider solid compound personal pronouns.

herself	oneself	thyself
himself	ourselves	yourself
itself	themselves	yourselves
myself		

7. Consider solid compass directions consisting of two points, but use a hyphen after the first point when three points are combined.

northeast	north-northwest
southwest	south-southeast

UNIT MODIFIERS

1. Except as indicated in the other rules in this chapter, type a hyphen between words, or abbreviations and words, combined to form a unit modifier immediately preceding the word modified. This applies particularly to combinations in which the second element is a present or past participle.

Baltimore-Washington road	long-term loan
collective-bargaining talks	long-term-payment loan
contested-election case	lump-sum payment
contract-bar rule	most-favored-nation clause
drought-stricken area	multiple-purpose uses
English-speaking nation	no-par-value stock
fire-tested material	part-time personnel
Federal-State-local cooperation	rust-resistant covering
German-English descent	service-connected disability
guided-missile program	tool-and-die maker
hard-of-hearing class	two-inch-diameter pipe
high-speed line	ten-word telegram
large-scale project	a 4-percent increase,
law-abiding citizen	the 10-percent rise
	U.S.-owned property

2. Where meaning is clear and readability is not aided, it is not necessary to use a hyphen to form a temporary (or made) compound. Restraint should be exercised in forming unnecessary combinations of words used in normal sequence.

atomic energy power	high school student; elementary school grade
bituminous coal industry	
child welfare plan	income tax form
civil rights case	land bank loan
civil service examination	land use program
durable goods industry	life insurance company
flood control study	mutual security funds
free enterprise system	national defense appropriation

natural gas company

parcel post delivery

per capita expenditure

portland cement plant

production credit loan

public utility plant

real estate tax

small businessman

Social Security pension

soil conservation measures

special delivery mail

speech correction class

BUT no-growth policy (readability aided); *NOT* no growth policy

3. When the second element is a present or past participle and the unit modifier does not immediately precede the thing modified, omit the hyphen.

The effects were far reaching.

The shale was oil bearing.

The area is drought stricken.

The reporters are best informed.

These cars are higher priced.

4. Use without a hyphen a two-word modifier when the first element is a comparative or superlative.

better drained soil

best liked books

higher level decision

highest priced apartment

larger sized dress

better paying job

lower income group

BUT lowercase, uppercase type (printing)

upperclassman

bestseller (noun)

lighter-than-air craft

higher-than-market price

5. Do not use a hyphen in a two-word unit modifier when the first element is an adverb ending in -ly. Do not use hyphens in a three-word unit modifier the first two elements of which are adverbs.

eagerly awaited moment

wholly owned subsidiary

unusually well preserved specimen

very well defined usage

longer than usual lunch period

very well worth reading

not too distant future

often heard phrase

BUT still-new car, because still is an adverb and new is an adjective

ever-rising flood

still-lingering doubt

well-known lawyer

well-kept farm

6. Proper nouns used as unit modifiers—either in their basic or derived form—retain their original form, but the hyphen is used after combining forms of proper nouns.

Latin American countries	*BUT* Winston-Salem festival
North Carolina roads	Washington–Wilkes-Barre route
a Mexican American	African-American program
South American trade	Anglo-Saxon period

7. Do not confuse a modifier with the word it modifies.

American flagship	light blue hat
American-flag ship	old-clothes man
average taxpayer	prudent stockholder
canning factory	service men and women
competent shoemaker	stockownership
elderly clothesman	tomato-canning factory
elementary school teacher	well-trained schoolteacher
gallant serviceman	wooden-shoe maker
income-tax payer	

8. Where two or more hyphenated compounds have a common basic element and this element is omitted in all but the last term, the hyphens are retained.

two- to three-ton trucks

8-, 10-, and 16-foot boards

moss- and ivy-covered walls, *NOT* moss and ivy-covered walls

long- and short-term money rates, *NOT* long and short-term money rates

BUT twofold or threefold, *NOT* two or threefold

goat, sheep, and calf skins, *NOT* goat, sheep, and calfskins

American owned and managed companies

preoperative and postoperative examination

9. Omit the hyphen in a unit modifier containing a letter or numeral as its second element.

abstract B pages	grade A milk
article 3 provisions	class II railroad

PREFIXES, SUFFIXES, AND COMBINING FORMS

1. Compounds formed with prefixes and suffixes are typed solid, except as indicated elsewhere.

*after*birth	*in*bound	oper*ate*
*Anglo*mania	*infra*red	*out*back
*ante*date	inner*most*	out*let*
*anti*slavery	*inter*view	*over*act
*bi*weekly	*intra*specific	*pan*cosmic
*by*law	*intro*vert	*para*centric
*circum*navigation	*iso*metric	partner*ship*
*cis*alpine	kilo*gram*	*peri*patetic
clock*wise*	lone*some*	*plano*graphy
*co*operate	man*hood*	plebis*cite*
*contra*position	*macro*biotics	*poly*morph
*counter*charge	meat*less*	port*able*
cover*age*	*meso*thorax	*post*script
*de*cry	*meta*genesis	*pre*exist
*demi*tasse	*micro*phone	*pro*consul
*ex*communicate	*mis*state	procure*ment*
*extra*curricular	*mono*gram	*pseudo*science
*fore*tell	*multi*color	pump*kin*
geo*graphy*	*neo*phyte	*re*enact
home*stead*	*non*neutral	*retro*spect
*hyper*sensitive	north*ward*	self*ish*
*hypo*center	*off*set	*semi*official

spoon*ful*	*thermo*couple	twenty*fold*
*step*father	*trans*onic	*ultra*violet
*sub*group	*trans*ship	*under*coat
*super*market	*tri*color	*un*necessary

2. Consider solid words ending in *like*, but use a hyphen to avoid tripling a consonant or when the first element is a proper name.

lifelike	*BUT* bell-like
lilylike	Florida-like
girllike	Truman-like

3. Use a hyphen or hyphens to prevent mispronunciation, to insure a definite accent on each element of the compound, or to avoid ambiguity.

anti-hog-cholera	re-cover (cover serum again)
co-op	re-sort (sort again)
mid-ice	re-treat (treat again)
non-civil-service	un-ionized position
non-tumor-bearing tissue	

4. Use with a hyphen the prefixes *ex, self,* and *quasi.*

ex-governor	quasi-academic	self-control
ex-serviceman	quasi-argument	self-educated
ex-trader	quasi-corporate	*BUT* selfhood
ex-vice-president	quasi-young	selfsame

5. Unless usage demands otherwise, use a hyphen to join a prefix or combining form to a capitalized word. (The hyphen is retained in words of this class set in caps.)

anti-Arab	post–World War II	*BUT* nongovernmental
un-American	post–Second World War	overanglicize
non-Government	pro-British	*OR* transatlantic

6. The adjectives *elect* and *designate,* as the last element of a title, require a hyphen.

president-elect	ambassador-designate
mayor-elect	minister-designate

NUMERICAL, SCIENTIFIC, AND TECHNICAL COMPOUNDS

1. Do not type a hyphen in scientific terms (names of chemicals, diseases, animals, insects, plants) used as unit modifiers if no hyphen appears in their original form.

   carbon monoxide poisoning   *BUT* screw-worm raising

   guinea pig raising   Russian-olive plantings

   methyl bromide solution   white-pine weevil

2. Chemical elements used in combination with figures use a hyphen, except with superior figures.

   polonium-210

   uranium-235; *BUT* U^{225}; Sr^{90}; 92^{U234}

   Freon-12

3. Use a hyphen between the elements of technical compound units of measurement.

   candle-hour   light-year

   horsepower-hour   passenger-mile

   kilowatt-hour

IMPROVISED COMPOUNDS

1. Use with a hyphen the elements of an improvised compound.

   blue-pencil (v.)   one-man-one-vote principle

   18-year-old (n.)   stick-in-the-mud (n.)

   first-come-first-served basis let-George-do-it attitude

   know-it-all (n.)   how-to-be-beautiful course

   know-how (n.)   hard-and-fast rule

   make-believe (n.)   penny-wise and pound-foolish policy

   BUT a basis of first come, first served; easy come, easy go

2. Use a hyphen to join a single capital letter to a noun or participle.

H-bomb	X-raying
I-beam	T-shaped
V-necked	U-boat

USAGE

This section is a guide to the correct use of words and phrases that are frequently misused.

abbreviate—means *to shorten by omitting.*
abridge—means *to shorten by condensing.*
　　New York is *abbreviated* to NY, Tennessee to TN.
　　In order to save time in the reading, the report was *abridged.*

ability—means a *developed, actual* power.
capacity—means an *undeveloped, potential* power.
　　He now has fair writing *ability,* but additional courses in college will
　　　develop his *capacity* beyond the average level.

above—Avoid *above* except in business forms where it may be used in refer-
　　ence to a preceding part of the text.
　　In normal writing use *foregoing* or *preceding,* instead of *above.*
　　Unacceptable: The *above* books are available in the library.
　　Acceptable: The *above* prices are subject to change without notice.

accede—means *to agree with.*
concede—means *to yield,* but not necessarily in agreement.
exceed—means *to be more than.*
　　We *accede* to your request for more evidence.
　　The candidate *conceded* the victory to his opponent.
　　My expenses often *exceed* my income.

accept—means *to take when offered.*
except—means *excluding.* (preposition)
except—means *to leave out.* (verb)
　　I *accept* the proposition that all men are created equal.
　　All eighteen-year-olds *except* seniors will be called.
　　The final report will *except* all data that doesn't conform to standards.

access—means *availability.*
excess—means *too much.*
> The lawyer was given *access* to the grand jury records.
> Their expenditures this month are far in *excess* of their income.

in accord with—means in agreement with *a person.*
> I am *in accord with* you about this.

in accordance with—means in agreement with a *thing.*
> The police officer acted *in accordance with* the law.

acoustics—when used as a singular noun means the *science* of sound.
> *Acoustics* is a subdivision of physics.

acoustics—when used as a plural noun denotes the *qualities* of sound.
> The *acoustics* of Carnegie Hall are incomparable.

acquiesce in—means *to accept,* with or without objection.
> Although there is some doubt about your plan, I *acquiesce in* its adoption.

ad—is a colloquial, clipped form for *advertisement;* it is not to be used in formal writing. Other colloquial words of this type are *exam* (*examination*), *auto* (*automobile*), *lab* (*laboratory*), *demo* (*demonstration*), and *dorm* (*dormitory*).

adapt—means *to adjust* or *change.*
adopt—means to *take as one's own.*
adept—means *skillful.*
> Children can *adapt* to changing conditions very easily.
> The war orphan was *adopted* by the general and his wife.
> Proper instruction makes children *adept* in various games.

addicted to—means *accustomed to by strong habit.*
subject to—means *exposed to* or *liable to.*
> People *addicted to* drugs or alcohol need constant medical care.
> The coast of Wales is *subject to* extremely heavy fogs.

addition—means *the act or process of adding.*
edition—means *a printing of a publication.*
> In *addition* to a dictionary, she always used a thesaurus.
> The first *edition* of Shakespeare's plays appeared in 1623.

advantage—means *a superior position.*
benefit—means *a favor conferred or earned* (as a profit).
> He had an *advantage* in experience over his opponent.
> The rules were changed for her *benefit.*
> NOTE: To *take* advantage *of,* to *have* an advantage *over.*

adverse—means *unfavorable.*
averse—means *disliking* or *reluctant.*
   He took the *adverse* decision in poor spirit.
   Many students are *averse* to criticism by their classmates.

affect—means *to influence* or *to pretend.* (a verb)
effect—means *an influence* or *result.* (a noun)
effect—means *to bring about.* (a verb)
   Your education must *affect* your future.
   He *affected* a great love for opera, though in fact it bored him.
   The *effect* of the last war is still being felt.
   A diploma *effected* a tremendous change in his attitude.

affection—means *feeling.*
affectation—means *pose* or *artificial behavior.*
   Alumni often develop a strong *affection* for their former schools.
   The *affectation* of a Harvard accent is no guarantee of success.

affinity—means an *attraction to a person or thing.*
infinity—means an *unlimited time, space, or quantity.*
   She has an *affinity* for men with beards.
   It is impossible to visualize an *infinity* of anything.

after—is unnecessary with the past participle.
   Not: *After having checked* the timetable, she left.
   But: *Having checked* the timetable, she left.

aggravate—means *to make worse.*
exasperate—means *to irritate* or *annoy.*
   Her cold was *aggravated* by faulty medication.
   His inability to make a quick recovery *exasperated* him exceedingly.

ain't—is an unacceptable contraction for *am not, are not,* or *is not.*

aisle—is *a passageway* between seats.
isle—is *a small island.*

alibi—is an explanation on *the basis of being in another place.*
excuse—is an explanation on *any basis.*
   The *alibi* offered at the trial was that he was twenty miles away from the
      scene of the crime.
   His *excuse* for failing on the test was that he was sick.

alimentary—refers to *the process of nutrition.*
elementary—means *primary.*
The *alimentary* canal includes the stomach and the intestines.
Elementary education is the foundation of all human development.

all ready—means *everybody or everything ready.*
already—means *previously.*
They were *all ready* to write when the teacher arrived.
They had *already* begun writing when the teacher arrived.

all-round—means *versatile* or *general.*
all around—means *all over a given area.*
Rafer Johnson, decathlon champion, is an *all-round* athlete.
The police were scouring for evidence for miles *all around.*

all together—means *everybody or everything together.*
altogether—means *completely.*
The boys and girls sang *all together.*
This was *altogether* strange for a person of her age.

all ways—means *in every possible way.*
always—means *at all times.*
She was in *all ways* acceptable to the voters.
Their reputation had *always* been spotless.

allow—means *to give permission.*
Acceptable: The teacher *allows* adequate time for study in class.
Unacceptable: I *allow* I haven't ever seen anything like this.

allude—means *to make an indirect reference to.*
elude—means *to escape from.*
Only incidentally does Coleridge *allude* to Shakespeare's puns.
It is almost impossible for one to *elude* tax collectors.

allusion—means *an indirect reference.*
illusion—means *a deception of the eye or mind.*
The student made *allusions* to his teacher's habits.
Illusions of the mind, unlike those of the eye, cannot be corrected with
   glasses.

alongside of—means *side by side with.*
alongside—means *parallel to the side.*
Bill stood *alongside of* Henry.
Park the car *alongside* the curb.

allot—means *apportion.*

alot—is an unacceptable spelling for *a lot. A lot,* meaning *very much,* should be avoided in formal writing.

They *allotted* the prize money equally among the winners.

Not: We like the proposal *a lot.*

But: We like the proposal *very much.*

alumnus—means *a male graduate.*

alumna—means *a female graduate.*

With the granting of the diploma, he became an *alumnus* of the school.

She is an *alumna* of Hunter College.

NOTE: The masculine plural form of *alumnus* is *alumni* (*-ni* rhymes with *hi*). The feminine plural form is *alumnae* (*-ae* rhymes with *key*). Use *alumni* when referring to both men and women.

amend—means *to correct.*

emend—means *to correct a literary work; to edit.*

Our Constitution, as *amended* by the Bill of Rights, was finally ratified.

Before publication, several chapters of the book had to be *emended.*

among—is used with *more than two persons or things.*

NOTE: *Amongst* should be avoided.

between—is used with *two persons or things.*

The inheritance was equally divided *among* the four children.

The business, however, was divided *between* the oldest and the youngest one.

amount—applies to quantities *that cannot be counted one by one.*

number—applies to quantities *that can be counted one by one.*

A large *amount* of grain was delivered to the store.

A large *number* of bags were delivered.

and etc.—is unacceptable for *etc.,* a Latin abbreviation meaning *and other things.* It is best to use *etc.* only when you are sure your reader will understand what other items or kinds of items you are referring to—for instance, when referring to a list of things already mentioned in full. Beware of *etc.* as a cover for vague or sloppy thinking.

annual—means *yearly.*

biannual and **semiannual**—mean *twice a year.*

biennial—means *once in two years, every two years.*

The Saint Patrick's Day parade is an *annual* event in New York City.

Some schools have *biannual* promotion, in January and June.

The *biennial* election of congressmen is held in the even numbered years.

another such—is *acceptable.*
such another—is *unacceptable.*
> *Another such* error may lead to legal prosecution.
> After his illness, he seemed *quite another* (**not** *such another*) person from what he had been.

ante—is a prefix meaning *before.*
anti—is a prefix meaning *against.*
> The *ante*chamber is the room just before the main room.
> An *anti*fascist is one who is opposed to fascists.

anxious—means *worried.*
eager—means *keenly desirous.*
> We were *anxious* about our first airplane flight.
> We are *eager* to fly again.

Any other—indicates a comparison. Do not use *any* by itself for a comparison.
> He likes France better than *any other* country.

anywheres—is *unacceptable.*
anywhere—is *acceptable.*
> We can't find it *anywhere.*
> Similarly, use *nowhere* (**not** *nowheres*) and *somewhere* (**not** *somewheres*).

appraise—means *to set a value.*
apprise—means *to inform.*
> The jeweler *appraised* the diamond at a very high value.
> We were *apprised* of their arrival by the honking of the car horn.

apprehend—means to *catch the meaning of something.*
comprehend—means *to understand a thing completely.*
> At first I didn't *apprehend* his true intent.
> It is often difficult to *comprehend* the Euclidean postulates.
> NOTE: Apprehend may also mean to take into custody.
> The sheriff succeeded in *apprehending* the rustler.

apt—suggests *habitual behavior.*
likely—suggests *probable behavior.*
liable—suggests an *exposure to something harmful.*
> Children are *apt* to be rather lazy in the morning.
> A cat, if annoyed, is *likely* to scratch.
> Cheating on a test may make one *liable* to expulsion from school.

argue—means *to prove something by logical methods.*
quarrel—means *to dispute without reason or logic.*
   The opposing lawyers *argued* before the judge.
   The lawyers became emotional and *quarreled.*

artisan—means *mechanic* or *craftsman.*
artist—means *one who practices the fine arts.*
   Many *artisans* participated in the building of the Sistine Chapel.
   The basic design, however, was prepared by the *artist* Michelangelo.

as—(used as a conjunction) is followed by a verb.
like—(used as a preposition) is not followed by a verb.
   Do *as* I do, not *as* I say.
   Try not to behave *like* a child.
   Unacceptable: He acts *like* I do.

as good as—should be used *for comparisons only.*
   This motel is *as good as* the next one.
   Do not use *as good as* to mean *practically.*
   Unacceptable: They *as good as* promised us a place in the hall.
   Acceptable: They *practically* promised us a place in the hall.

as if—is correctly used in the expression, "He talked *as if* his jaw hurt him."
   Unacceptable: "He talked *like* his jaw hurt him."

as per—is poor usage for *according to* or *in accordance with.*
   He assembled the bicycle *in accordance with* (**not** *as per*) the directions.

as to whether—is *unacceptable. Whether* includes the unnecessary words *as to.*
   I don't know *whether* it is going to rain.

ascent—is *the act of rising.*
assent—means *approval.*
   The *ascent* to the top of the mountain was perilous.
   Congress gave its *assent* to the President's emergency directive.

assay—means *to try* or *experiment.*
essay—means *to make an intellectual effort.*
   We shall *assay* the ascent of the mountain tomorrow.
   Why not *essay* a description of the mountain in composition?

astonish—means *to strike with sudden wonder.*
surprise—means *to catch unaware.*
  The extreme violence of the hurricane *astonished* everybody.
  A heat wave in January would *surprise* us.

at—should be avoided where it does not contribute to the meaning.
  Acceptable: Where shall I meet you?
  Unacceptable: Where shall we meet *at*?
at about—should not be used for *about.*
  The group will arrive *about* noon.

attend to—means *to take care of.*
tend to—means *to be inclined to.*
  One of the clerks will *attend to* my mail in my absence.
  Lazy people *tend to* lack ambition.

audience—means *a group of listeners.*
spectators—refers to *a group of watchers.*
  Leonard Bernstein conducted a concert for the school *audience.*
  The slow baseball game bored the *spectators.*
  NOTE: A group that both watches and listens is called an *audience.*

average—means *conforming to norms or standards.*
ordinary—means *usual, customary,* or *without distinction.*
  A book of about 300 pages is of *average* length.
  The contents of the book were rather *ordinary.*

back—should **not** be used with such words as *refer* and *return* since the prefix *re-* means *back.*
  Refer to the text if you have difficulty recalling the facts.

balance—meaning *remainder,* is *acceptable* only in commercial usage. Use *remainder* or *rest* otherwise.
  Even after the withdrawal, his bank *balance* was considerable.
  Three of the students voted for John; the *rest* voted for Jim.

bazaar—is a *marketplace* or a *fair.*
bizarre—means *odd* or *strange.*
  We are going to the *bazaar* to buy things.
  He dresses in a *bizarre* manner.

being that—is *unacceptable* for *since* or *because.*
  Acceptable: Since you have come a long way, why not remain here for the night.

berth—is a *resting place.*
birth—means *the beginning of life.*
>The new liner was given a wide *berth* in the harbor.
>She was a fortunate woman from *birth.*

beside—means *close to.*
besides—means *in addition.*
>He lived *beside* the stream.
>He found wildflowers and weeds *besides.*

better—means *recovering.*
well—means *completely recovered.*
>Ivan is *better* now than he was a week ago.
>In a few more weeks, he will be *well.*

both—means *two considered together.*
each—means *one of two or more.*
>*Both* of the applicants qualified for the position.
>*Each* applicant was given a generous reference.

bouillon—is a *soup.*
bullion—means *gold* or *silver* in the form of bars.
>This restaurant serves tasty *bouillon.*
>A mint makes coins out of *bullion.*

breath—means an *intake of air.*
breathe—means *to draw air in and give it out.*
breadth—means *width.*
>Before you dive in, take a very deep *breath.*
>It is impossible *to breathe* under water.
>In a square, the *breadth* is equal to the length.

bridal—means *of a wedding.*
bridle—means to *hold back.*
>The *bridal* party was late to the church.
>You must learn to *bridle* your temper.

bring—means *to carry toward the person who is speaking.*
take—means *to carry away from the speaker.*
>*Bring* the books here.
>*Take* your raincoat with you when you go out.

broach—means *to mention for the first time.*
brooch—means an *ornament* for clothing.
> At the meeting, one of the speakers *broached* the question of salary increases.
> The model was wearing an expensive *brooch.*

bunch—refers to *things.*
group—refers to *persons* or *things.*
> This looks like a delicious *bunch* of bananas.
> What a well-behaved *group* of children!
> NOTE: The colloquial use of *bunch* applied to *persons* should be avoided.

burst—is acceptable for broke.
bust—is unacceptable for broke (or broken).
> *Acceptable:* The balloon burst.
> *Unacceptable:* My pen is busted.

business—is sometimes incorrectly used for *work.*
> *Unacceptable:* I went to *business* very late today.
> *Acceptable:* He owns a thriving *business.*

but—should **not** be used after the expression *cannot help.*
> *Acceptable:* One cannot help noticing the errors.
> *Unacceptable:* One cannot help but notice . . .

byword—is *a pet expression.*
password—is *a secret word uttered to gain passage.*
> In ancient Greece, truth and beauty were *bywords.*
> The sentry asked the scout for the *password.*

calculate—means *to determine mathematically.* It does **not** mean *to think.*
> Some students still know how to *calculate* on an abacus.
> *Unacceptable:* I *calculate* it's going to rain.

calendar—is *a system of time.*
calender—is *a smoothing and glazing machine.*
colander—is *a kind of sieve.*
> In this part of the world, most people prefer the twelve-month *calendar.*
> In ceramic work, the potting wheel and the *calender* are indispensable.
> Vegetables should be washed in a *colander* before cooking.

Calvary—is *the name of the place of the Crucifixion.*
cavalry—is *a military unit on horseback.*
> *Calvary* and Gethsemane are place-names in the Bible.
> Most of our modern *cavalry* is now motorized.

can—means *physically able.*
may—implies *permission.*
   I *can* lift this chair over my head.
   You *may* leave after you finish your work.

cannon—is a *gun* for heavy firing.
canon—is a *rule* or *law,* usually of a church.
   Don't remain near the *cannon* when it is being fired.
   Churchgoers are expected to observe the *canons.*

cannot help—must be followed by an *-ing* form.
   We cannot help *feeling* (**not** *feel*) distressed about this.
   NOTE: *cannot help but* is unacceptable.

can't hardly—is a double negative. It is *unacceptable.*
   The child *can hardly* walk in those shoes.

capital—is *the city* or *money.*
capitol—is *the building.*
   Paris is the *capital* of France.
   The *Capitol* in Washington is occupied by the Congress. (The Washington
      Capitol is capitalized.)
   NOTE: *capital* also means wealth.

catalog—is a *systematic list.* (also **catalogue**)
category—is a *class* of things.
   The item is precisely described in the sales *catalog.*
   A trowel is included in the *category* of farm tools.

cease—means *to end.*
seize—means *to take hold of.*
   Will you please *cease* making those sounds?
   Seize the cat as it rounds the corner.

censer—is *a container which holds burning incense.*
censor—means *to examine for the purpose of judging moral aspects.*
censure—means *to find fault with.*
   One often finds a *censer* in church.
   The government *censors* films in some countries.
   She *censured* her husband for coming home late.

center around—is *unacceptable.* Use *center in* or *center on.*
   The maximum power was *centered in* the nuclear reactor.
   All attention was *centered on* the launching pad.

certainly—is an *adverb*.
sure—is an *adjective*.
>He was *certainly* learning fast.
>*Colloquial:* He *sure* was learning fast.

cession—means *a yielding*.
session—means *a meeting*.
>The *cession* of a piece of territory could have avoided the war.
>The legislative *session* lasted three months.

childish—means *silly, immature*.
childlike—means *innocent, unspoiled*.
>Pouting appears *childish* in an adult.
>His *childlike* appreciation of art gave him great pleasure.

choice—means *a selection*.
choose—means *to select*.
chose—means *selected*.
>My *choice* for a career is teaching.
>We may *choose* our own leader.
>I finally *chose* teaching for a career.

cite—means *to quote*.
sight—means *seeing*.
site—means *a place for a building*.
>He was fond of *citing* from the Scriptures.
>The *sight* of the wreck was appalling.
>The Board of Education is seeking a *site* for the new school.

climate—is the average weather *over a period of many years*.
weather—is the *hour by hour* or *day by day* condition of the atmosphere.
>He likes the *climate* of California better than that of New York.
>The *weather* is sometimes hard to predict.

coarse—means *vulgar* or *harsh*.
course—means a *path* or a *subject of study*.
>He was shunned because of his *coarse* behavior.
>The ship took its usual *course*.
>Which *course* in English are you taking?

comic—means *intentionally funny*.
comical—means *unintentionally funny*.
>A clown is a *comic* figure.
>The peculiar hat she wore gave her a *comical* appearance.

comma—is *a mark of punctuation.*
coma—(rhymes with *aroma*) means *a period of prolonged unconsciousness.*
   A *comma* should never separate two complete sentences.
   The accident put him into a *coma* lasting three days.

common—means *shared equally* by two or more.
mutual—means *interchanged.*
   The town hall is the *common* pride of every citizen.
   We can do business to our *mutual* profit and satisfaction.

compare to—means to liken to something *which has a different form.*
compare with—means to compare persons or things with each other *when they are of the same kind.*
contrast with—means to show the *difference between two things.*
   A minister is sometimes *compared to* a shepherd.
   Shakespeare's plays are often *compared with* those of Marlowe.
   The writer *contrasted* the sensitivity of the dancer *with* the grossness of the pugilist.

complement—means *a completing part.*
compliment—is *an expression of admiration.*
   His wit was a *complement* to her beauty.
   He received many *compliments* on his valedictory speech.

comprehensible—means *understandable.*
comprehensive—means *including a great deal.*
   Under the circumstances, your doubts were *comprehensible.*
   Toynbee's *comprehensive* study of history covers many centuries.

comprise—means *to include.*
compose—means *to form the substance of.*
   Toynbee's study of history *comprises* seven volumes.
   Some modern novels are *composed* of as little as three chapters.

concur in—must be followed by *an action.*
concur with—must be followed by *a person.*
   I shall *concur in* the decision reached by the majority.
   I cannot *concur with* the chairman, however much I respect his opinion.

conducive to—means *leading to.*
conducive for—is *unacceptable.*
   Your proposals for compromise are *conducive to* a settlement of our disagreement.

conform to—means *to adapt oneself to.*
conform with—means *to be in harmony with.*
> Youngsters are inclined to *conform to* a group pattern.
> They feel it is dangerous not to *conform with* the rules of the group.

conscience—means *sense of right.*
conscientious—means *faithful.*
conscious—means *aware.*
> Man's *conscience* prevents him from becoming completely selfish.
> We value her because she is *conscientious.*
> The injured man was completely *conscious.*

considerable—is properly used *only as an adjective,* **not** as a noun.
> *Acceptable:* The fraternal organization invested a *considerable* amount in government bonds.
> *Unacceptable:* He lost *considerable* in the stock market.

consistently—means *in harmony.*
constantly—means *regularly, steadily.*
> If you choose to give advice, act *consistently* with that advice.
> Doctors *constantly* warn against overexertion.

consul—means *a government representative.*
council—means *an assembly which meets for deliberation.*
counsel—means *advice.*
> Americans abroad should keep in touch with their *consuls.*
> The City *Council* enacts local laws and regulations.
> The defendant heeded the *counsel* of his friends.

contemptible—means *worthy of contempt.*
contemptuous—means *feeling contempt.*
> His spying activities were *contemptible.*
> It was plain to all that he was *contemptuous* of his co-workers.

continual—means happening *again and again at short intervals.*
continuous—means *without interruption.*
> The teacher gave the class *continual* warnings.
> Noah experienced *continuous* rain for forty days.

convenient to—should be followed by a *person.*
convenient for—should be followed by a *purpose.*
> Will these plans be *convenient to* you?
> You must agree that they are *convenient for* the occasion.

copy—is *an imitation of an original work.* (not necessarily an exact imitation)
facsimile—is *an exact imitation of an original work.*
> The counterfeiters made a crude *copy* of the hundred-dollar bill.
> The official government engraver, however, prepared a *facsimile* of the bill.

core—means the *heart of something.*
corps—(pronounced like *core*) means *an organized military body.*
corpse—means *a dead body.*
> The *core* of the apple was rotten.
> The *corps* consisted of three full-sized armies.
> The *corpse* was quietly slipped overboard after a brief service.

corespondent—is *a joint defendant in a divorce case.*
correspondent—is *one who communicates.*
> The *corespondent* declared that he loved the other man's wife.
> Max Frankel is a special *correspondent* for the *New York Times.*

corporeal—means *bodily as opposed to spiritual.*
corporal—means *bodily as it pertains to a person.*
> Many believe that our *corporeal* existence changes to a spiritual one after death.
> *Corporal* punishment is not recommended in modern schools.

could of—is unacceptable for *could have.* Similarly, avoid *should of, must of,* and *would of.*
> Not: I *could of* won.
> But: I *could have* won.

credible—means *believable.*
creditable—means *worthy of receiving praise.*
credulous—means *believing too easily.*
> The pupil gave a *credible* explanation for his lateness.
> Considering all the handicaps, he gave a *creditable* performance.
> Politicians might prefer to address *credulous* people.

decease—means *death.*
disease—means *illness.*
> His friend is *deceased.*
> Leukemia is a deadly *disease.*

decent—means *suitable*.
descent—means *going down*.
dissent—means *disagreement*.
> The *decent* thing to do is to admit your fault.
> The *descent* into the cave was treacherous.
> Two of the nine justices filed a *dissenting* opinion.

deduction—means *reasoning from the general* (laws or principles) *to the particular* (facts).
induction—means *reasoning from the particular* (facts) *to the general* (laws or principles).
> All men are mortal. Since John is a man, he is mortal. (*deduction*)
> There are 1,000 oranges in this truckload. I have examined 100 from various parts of the load and find them all of the same quality. I therefore conclude that the 1,000 oranges are of this quality. (*induction*)

deference—means *respect*.
difference—means *unlikeness*.
> In *deference* to his memory, we did not play yesterday.
> The *difference* between the two boys is unmistakable.

definite—means *clear, with set limits*.
definitive—means *final, decisive*.
> We would prefer a *definite* answer to our *definite* question.
> The dictionary is the *definitive* authority for word meanings.

deprecate—means *to disapprove*.
depreciate—means *to lower the value*.
> His classmates *deprecated* his discourtesy.
> The service station *depreciated* the value of our house.

desirable—means *that which is desired*.
desirous—means *desiring* or *wanting*.
> It was a most *desirable* position.
> She was *desirous* of obtaining it.

despise—means *to look down upon*.
detest—means *to hate*.
> Some wealthy persons *despise* the poor.
> I *detest* cold weather.

desert—(pronounced DEZ-ert) means *an arid area.*

desert—(pronounced di-ZERT) means *to abandon;* it is also *a reward or punishment.*

dessert—(pronounced di-ZERT) means *the final course of a meal.*
> The Sahara is the world's most famous *desert.*
> A husband must not *desert* his wife.
> Execution was a just *desert* for his crime.
> We had plum pudding for *dessert.*

device—means *a way to do something.* (a noun)

devise—means *to find the way.* (a verb)
> A hook is a good fishing *device.*
> Some fishermen prefer to *devise* other ways for catching fish.

differ from—is used when there is a difference *between things.*

differ with—is used when there is a difference *in opinion.*
> A coat *differs from* a cape.
> You have the right to *differ with* me on public affairs.

different from—is *acceptable.*

different than—is *unacceptable.*
> Acceptable: Jack is different from his brother.
> *Unacceptable:* Florida's climate is *different than* New York's climate.

discover—means *to find something already in existence.*

invent—means *to create something that never existed before.*
> Pasteur *discovered* germs.
> Whitney *invented* the cotton gin.

discreet—means *cautious.*

discrete—means *separate.*
> The employee was *discreet* in her comments about her employer.
> Since these two questions are *discrete,* you must provide two separate answers.

disinterested—means *impartial.*

uninterested—means *not interested.*
> The judge must always be a *disinterested* party in a trial.
> As an *uninterested* observer, he was inclined to yawn at times.

divers—(pronounced DI-vurz) means *several.*

diverse—(pronounced di-VERS) means *different.*
> The store had *divers* foodstuffs for sale.
> Many of the items were completely *diverse* from staple foods.

doubt that—is *acceptable*.
doubt whether—is *unacceptable*.
    Acceptable: I *doubt that* you will pass this term.
    Unacceptable: I *doubt whether* you will succeed.

doubtless—is *acceptable*.
doubtlessly—is *unacceptable*.
    Acceptable: You *doubtless* know your work; why, then, don't you pass?
    Unacceptable: He *doubtlessly* thinks that you can do the job well.

dual—means *relating to two*.
duel—means *a contest between two persons*.
    Dr. Jekyl had a *dual* personality.
    Alexander Hamilton was fatally injured in a *duel* with Aaron Burr.

each other—refers to *two persons*.
one another—may also refer to *more than two persons*.
    The two girls have known *each other* for many years.
    Several of the girls have known *one another* for many years.

economic—refers to the *subject of economics*.
economical—means *thrifty*.
    An *economic* discussion was held at the United Nations.
    A smart shopper is usually *economical*.

either . . . or—is used when referring to choices.
neither . . . nor—is the *negative* form.
    Either you *or* I will win the election.
    Neither Bill *nor* Ellen is expected to have a chance.

elegy—is a *mournful or melancholy poem*.
eulogy—is a *speech in praise of a deceased person*.
    Gray's "*Elegy* Written in a Country Churchyard" is a melancholy poem.
    The minister delivered the *eulogy*.

eligible—means *fit to be chosen*.
illegible—means *impossible to read* or *hard to read*.
    Not all persons are *eligible* to be president.
    His childish handwriting was *illegible*.

eliminate—means *to get rid of*.
illuminate—means *to supply with light*.
    Let us try to *eliminate* the unnecessary steps.
    Several lamps were needed to *illuminate* the corridor.

else—is superfluous in such expressions as the following:
Unacceptable: We want *no one else* but you.
Acceptable: We want *no one* but you.

emigrate—means *to leave one's country for another.*
immigrate—means *to enter another country.*
The Norwegians *emigrated* to America in mid-1860.
Many of the Norwegian *immigrants* settled in the Midwest.

enclosed herewith—is *redundant.*
enclosed—is *acceptable.*
You will find *enclosed* one copy of our brochure.

endorse—means to write on the back of.
Acceptable: He endorsed the check.
Unacceptable: He endorsed the check on the back.

enormity—means *viciousness or great wickedness.*
enormousness—means *vastness.*
The *enormity* of his crime was appalling.
The *enormousness* of the Sahara exceeds that of any other desert.

enthused—should be avoided.
enthusiastic—is preferred.
Acceptable: We were *enthusiastic* over the performance.
Unacceptable: I am truly *enthused* about coming.

equally as good—is *unacceptable.*
just as good—is *acceptable.*
Acceptable: This book is *just as good* as that.
Unacceptable: Your marks are *equally as good* as mine.

everyone—is written as one word when it is a *pronoun.*
every one—(two words) is used when *each individual* is stressed.
Everyone present voted for the proposal.
Every one of the voters accepted the proposal.
NOTE: *Everybody* is written as one word.

every bit—is used colloquially for *just as.*
Acceptable: You are *just as* clever as she is.
Colloquial: He is *every bit* as lazy as his father.

everywheres—is *unacceptable.*
everywhere—is *acceptable.*
We searched *everywhere* for the missing book.

every which way—meaning *in all directions* is colloquial.
every way—is *acceptable.*
   He tried to solve the problem *every way* he could.

exceed—means *going beyond the limit.*
excel—refers to *superior quality.*
   You have *exceeded* the time allotted to you.
   All-round athletes are expected to *excel* in many sports.

except—is *acceptable.*
excepting—is *unacceptable.*
   Acceptable: All *except* Joe are going.
   Unacceptable: All cities, *excepting* Washington, are in a state.
   NOTE: Don't use *except* for *unless.*
   He won't consent *unless* you give him the money.

exceptional—means *extraordinary.*
exceptionable—means *objectionable.*
   Exceptional children learn to read before the age of five.
   The behavior of exceptional children is sometimes *exceptionable.*

excessively—means *beyond acceptable limits.*
exceedingly—means *to a very great degree.*
   In view of our recent feud, he was *excessively* friendly.
   The weather in July was *exceedingly* hot.

expand—means *to spread out.*
expend—means *to use up.*
   As the staff increases, we shall have to *expand* our office space.
   Don't *expend* all your energy on one project.

factitious—means *unnatural* or *artificial.*
fictitious—means *imaginary.*
   His *factitious* enthusiasm did not deceive us.
   Jim Hawkins is a *fictitious* character.

faint—means *to lose consciousness.*
feint—means *to make a pretended attack.*
   The lack of fresh air caused her to *faint.*
   First he *feinted* to the left; then he lobbed the ball over the net.

farther—is used to describe *concrete distance.*
further—is used to describe *an extension of time or degree.*
   Chicago is *farther* from New York than is Cincinnati.
   I'll explain *further* my point of view.

feel bad—means to feel ill or sorry.
feel badly—is *unacceptable*.
>   *Acceptable:* I *feel bad* about the accident I saw.
>   *Unacceptable:* I *felt badly* when I saw her fall.

fever—refers to an *undue rise of temperature*.
temperature—refers to the *degree of heat* which may be normal.
>   We had better call the doctor—he has a *fever*.
>   The *temperature* is 80 degrees.

fewer—refers to *persons or things that can be counted*.
less—refers to *something considered as a mass*.
>   We have *fewer* customers this week than last week.
>   I have *less* money in my pocket than you have.
>   *But idiom:* One *less* thing to worry about.

financial—refers to money matters in a *general sense*.
fiscal—refers to the *public treasury*.
>   Scholars are usually not *financial* successes.
>   The government's *fiscal year* begins July 1 and ends June 30.

flout—means *to show contempt for*.
flaunt—means *to make a display of*.
>   He *flouted* the authority of the principal.
>   She *flaunted* her wealth.

flowed—is the past participle of *flow*.
flown—is the past participle of *fly*.
>   The flood waters had *flowed* over the levee before nightfall.
>   He had *flown* for 500 hours before he crashed.

forbear—means *to refrain from doing something*.
forebear—means *ancestor*.
>   *Forbear* seeking vengeance.
>   Most of the family's *forebears* came from Ghana.

formally—means *in a formal way*.
formerly—means *at an earlier time*.
>   The letter of reference was *formally* written.
>   He was *formerly* a delegate to the convention.

former—means *the first of two*.
latter—means *the second of two*.
>   The *former* half of the book was prose.
>   The *latter* half of the book was poetry.

fort—means *a fortified place.*
forte—means *a strong point.*
>A small garrison was able to hold the *fort.*
>Conducting Wagner's music was Toscanini's *forte.*

forth—means *forward.*
fourth—*comes after third.*
>They went *forth* like warriors of old.
>The *Fourth* of July is our Independence Day.

freeze—means *to turn to ice.*
frieze—is *a decorated band in or on a building.*
>As the temperature dropped, the water began to *freeze.*
>The *friezes* on the Parthenon are wonders of art.

funny—means *humorous* or *laughable.*
>That clown is truly *funny.*
>*Funny* meaning *odd* or *strange* is a colloquial use.

genial—means *cheerful.*
congenial—means *agreeing in spirit.*
>*Genial* landlords are rare today.
>A successful party depends on *congenial* guests.

genius—means *extraordinary natural ability, or one so gifted.*
genus—means *class* or *kind.*
>Mozart showed his *genius* for music at a very early age.
>That flower probably does not belong to the *genus* of roses.

gibe / jibe—(pronounced alike)—both mean *to scoff.*
>We are inclined to *gibe* at awkward speakers.
jibe also means *to agree.*
>The two stories are now beginning to *jibe.*

got—means *obtained.* Colloquially, *got* conveys a sense of *obligation* or *possession.*
>He *got* the tickets yesterday.
>Not: We *have got* no sympathy for them.
>But: We *have* no sympathy for them.
>Colloquial: You've *got* to do it.
>I've *got* two cats.

gourmand—is *one who eats large quantities of food.*
gourmet—(rhymes with poor-MAY) is *one who eats fastidiously; a connoisseur.*
His uncontrollable appetite soon turned him into a *gourmand.*
The *gourmet* chooses the right wine for each course.

graduated—is followed by *from.*
He *graduated* (or *was graduated) from* high school in 1997.
Unacceptable: He *graduated* college.
NOTE: A *graduated* test tube is one that has markings on it to indicate volume or capacity.

guess—is *colloquial* for *think* or *suppose.* I *think* I'll go downtown.

habit—means an *individual* tendency to repeat a thing.
custom—means *group habit.*
He had a *habit* of breaking his glasses before each ball game.
The *custom* of the country was to eat fish raw.

had ought—is *unacceptable.*
You *ought* not to eat fish if you are allergic to it.

hanged—is used in reference to a *person.*
hung—is used in reference to a *thing.*
The prisoner was *hanged* at dawn.
The picture was *hung* above the fireplace.

healthy—means *having health.*
healthful—means *giving health.*
The man is *healthy.*
Fruit is *healthful.*

heap—means a *pile.*
heaps—is *slang* in the sense of *very much.*
Slang: Thanks *heaps* for the gift.
Lots is also *slang* for very much.

holy—means *sacred.*
holey—means *with holes.*
wholly—means *completely* or *altogether.*
Easter Week is a *holy* time in many lands.
Old socks tend to become *holey* after a while.
We are *wholly* in agreement with your decision.

hypercritical—refers to a person *who finds fault easily.*
hypocritical—refers to a person *who pretends.*
   Don't be *hypercritical* about meals at low prices.
   It is better to be sincere than to be *hypocritical.*

idle—means *unemployed or unoccupied.*
idol—means *image* or *object of worship.*
   Idle men, like *idle* machines, are inclined to lose their sharpness.
   Some dictators prefer to be looked upon as *idols* by the masses.

immunity—implies *resistance to a disease.*
impunity—means *freedom from punishment.*
   The Salk vaccine helps develop an *immunity* to poliomyelitis.
   Because he was an only child, he frequently misbehaved with *impunity.*

imply—means *to suggest* or *hint at.* (The speaker *implies.*)
infer—means *to deduce* or *conclude.* (The listener *infers.*)
   Are you *implying* that I have disobeyed orders?
   From your carefree attitude, what else are we to *infer?*

inclement—(pronounced in-CLEM-ent) refers to *severe weather,* such as a
   heavy rainfall or storm. It does **not** mean threatening.
   Because of the *inclement* weather, we were soaked to the skin.

indict—(pronounced in-DITE) means *to charge with a crime.*
indite—means *to write.*
   The Grand Jury *indicted* him for embezzlement.
   Modern authors prefer the expression *to write,* rather than *indite;* the latter
      is now a stuffy sort of expression.

ingenious—means *skillful, imaginative.*
ingenuous—means *naive, frank,* or *candid.*
   The *ingenious* boy created his own rocket.
   One must be *ingenuous* to accept the Communist definition of freedom.

inside / inside of—When referring to time, use *within.*
   She is arriving *within* two hours.

irregardless—is *unacceptable.*
regardless—is *acceptable.*
   Not: *Irregardless* of the weather, I am going to the game.
   But: *Regardless* of his ability, he is not likely to win.

irresponsible—means *having no sense of responsibility.*
not responsible for—means *not accountable for something.*
   Irresponsible people are frequently late for appointments.
   Since you came late, we are *not responsible for* your having missed the
     first act.

its—means *belonging to it.*
it's—means *it is.*
   The house lost *its* roof.
   It's an exposed house, now.

join together—means to *unite* or *connect.* Omit the redundant *together.*
   Acceptable: I want to *join* these pieces of wood.
   Unacceptable: All of us should *join together* to fight intolerance.

judicial—means *pertaining to courts or to the law.*
judicious—means *wise.*
   The problem required the *judicial* consideration of an expert.
   We were certainly in no position to make a *judicious* decision.

kind of / sort of—are *colloquial* for *rather.*
   What *kind of* car do you prefer?
   We are *rather* disappointed in you.

last—refers to *the final member in a series.*
latest—refers to *the most recent in time.*
latter—refers to *the second of two.*
   This is the *last* bulletin. (There won't be any other bulletins.)
   This is the *latest* bulletin. (There will be other bulletins.)
   Of the two most recent bulletins, the *latter* is more encouraging.

later on—is *unacceptable* for *later.*
   Later, we shall give your request fuller attention.

least—means *the smallest.*
less—means *the smaller of two.*
   This was the *least* desirable of all the locations we have seen.
   We may finally have to accept the *less* desirable of the two locations we
     last saw.

leave—means *to go away from.*
let—means *to permit.*
   Leave this house at once.
   Let me remain in peace in my own house.

legible—means *able to be read.*
readable—means *able to be read with pleasure.*
   Your reports have become increasingly *legible.*
   In fact, I now find most of them extremely *readable.*

lengthened—means *made longer.*
lengthy—means *annoyingly long.*
   The essay, now *lengthened,* is more readable.
   However, try to avoid writing *lengthy* explanations of obvious facts.

levy—means *to impose a tax.*
levee—means *an embankment.*
   It is the duty of Congress to *levy* taxes.
   The Mississippi River is contained by massive *levees.*

libel—is *a written and published statement injurious to a person's character.*
slander—is *a spoken statement of the same sort.*
   The unfavorable references to me in your book are *libel.*
   When you say these vicious things about me, you are committing *slander.*

lightening—is the present participle of *to lighten.*
lightning—means *the flashes of light accompanied by thunder.*
   Lightening the pack made it easier to carry.
   Summer thunderstorms produce startling *lightning* bolts.

line—meaning *occupation* is *unacceptable.*
   Acceptable: He is in the engineering *profession.*
   Unacceptable: What *line* are you in?

lineament—means *outline* or *contour.*
liniment—is *a medicated liquid.*
   His face had the *lineaments* of a Greek Adonis.
   After the football games, we all applied *liniment* to our legs.

loan—is a *noun.*
lend—is a *verb.*
   The bank was willing to grant him a *loan* of $500.
   The bank was willing to *lend* him $500.

lonely—means *longing for companionship.*
solitary—means *isolated.*
   Some people are forced to live *lonely* lives.
   Sometimes *solitary* surroundings are conducive to deep thought.

luxuriant—means *abundant growth*.
luxurious—implies *wealth*.
>One expects to see *luxuriant* plants in the tropics.
>The *luxurious* surroundings indicated both wealth and good taste.

majority—means *more than half of the total number.*
plurality—means *an excess of votes received by the leading candidate over those received by the next candidate.*
>*Example:*   A received 251 votes.
>   B received 127 votes.
>   C received 123 votes.
>A received a *majority,* or one vote more than half of the total.
>A received a *plurality* of 124 votes over B.

many—refers to *a number*.
much—refers to *a quantity in bulk*.
>How *many* inches of rain fell last night?
>I don't know, but I would say *much* rain fell last night.

material—means *of or pertaining to matter.*
materiel—(accent the last syllable) is French, and means *material equipment,* the opposite of *personnel* (*manpower*).
>His *material* assets included an automobile and two suits of clothing.
>The small army was rich in *materiel,* poor in personnel.

may—is used in the *present tense*.
might—is used in the *past tense*.
>We are hoping that he *may* come today.
>He *might* have done it if you had encouraged him.

it's I—is always *acceptable*.
it's me—is *acceptable* in informal speech or writing.

It's he / This is she / It was they—are always *acceptable*.
It's him / This is her / It was them—are informal.

measles—is plural in form, singular in meaning.
>*Measles* is now a minor childhood disease.
>NOTE: *Mumps* and *shingles* are also singular in meaning.

medieval—means of or pertaining to *the Middle Ages*.
middle-aged—refers to persons *in the middle period of life*.
>Serfs and feudal baronies were part of *medieval* times.
>According to the Bible, the *middle-aged* man has thirty-five more years of life to look forward to.

Messrs.—(rhymes with *guessers*) is the plural of *Mr.*
Misters is *unacceptable.*
The meeting was attended by *Messrs.* Smith, Jones, Brown, and Swift.

metal—is a type of *substance.*
mettle—means *spirit.*
Lead is one of the more familiar *metals.*
One had to admire his *mettle* in the face of a crisis.

minutiae—(pronounced min-EW-she-ee) is the plural of *minutia,* and means *minor details.*
A meticulous person spends much time on *minutiae.*

Mmes.—(pronounced me-DAM) is the abbreviation for *Mesdames,* the plural of *Madam.* It introduces a series of names of married women.
The party was attended by the *Mmes.* Jones, Smith, and Wilson.
The plural of *Miss* is *Misses.*

moneys—is *the plural of money.* (also monies)
We shall vote on the disposition of the various *moneys* in the treasury.

moral—means *good or ethical;* also, an *ethical lesson to be drawn.*
morale—(pronounced more-AL) means *spirit.*
The *moral* of the story is that it pays to be honest.
The *morale* of the troops rose after the general's inspiring speech.

most—is an adverb in the *superlative degree.*
almost—is an adverb meaning *nearly.*
He is the *most* courteous boy in the class.
It's *almost* time to go to school.

nauseous—means *causing sickness.*
nauseated—means *being sick.*
The odor is *nauseous.*
I feel *nauseated.*

naval—refers to *ships.*
nautical—refers to *navigation and seamen.*
John Paul Jones was a famous *naval* commander.
A *nautical* mile is a little longer than a land mile.

neither—means *not either of two,* and should **not** be used for *none* or *not one.*
Neither of his two books was very popular.
Of the many plays he has written, *not one* (or *none*) was good.

noplace—is *unacceptable* for *no place* or *nowhere*.
You now have *nowhere* to go.

nohow—is *unacceptable for regardless.*
Unacceptable: I can't do this nohow.

notable—means *remarkable*.
notorious—means *of bad reputation*.
December 7, 1941, was a *notable* day.
At that time, the *notorious* Tojo commanded the Japanese forces.

nothing more or less—is *unacceptable* for *nothing more nor less*.
Using correct English is *nothing more nor less* than a matter of careful practice.

nowhere near—is *unacceptable* for *not nearly*.
The work was *not nearly* finished by nightfall.

nowheres—is *unacceptable*.
nowhere—is *acceptable*.
The child was *nowhere* to be found.

number—is singular *when the total is intended*.
number—is plural when the individual units are referred to.
The *number* of pages in the book is 500.
A *number* of pages were printed in italic type.

obligate—implies a *moral or legal responsibility*.
oblige—means *to do as a favor* or *to accommodate*.
The principal felt *obligated* to disqualify himself in the dispute between the pupils.
Please *oblige* me by refraining from discussing this matter with anyone else.

observance—means the *act of complying*.
observation—means the *act of noting*.
In *observance* of the new regulation, we shall omit further tests.
His scientific *observations* became the basis for a new rocket theory.

occupancy—refers to *the mere act of occupying*, usually legally.
occupation—means *the forceful act of occupying*.
According to the lease, the tenant still had *occupancy* of the apartment for another month.
The *occupation* of the town by troops worried the townspeople.

oculist or ophthalmologist—is an MD who *treats diseases of the eye.*
optometrist—is a person who *measures the eye* to prescribe glasses.
optician—is a person who *makes the glasses.*
> An *oculist* is also called an *ophthalmologist.*
> An *optometrist* may also be an *optician.*

of any—(and *of anyone*) is *unacceptable* for *of all.*
> His was the highest mark *of all.*

off of—is *unacceptable.* Omit *of.*
> He took the book *off* the table.

OK—(or *okay*) is used for *acceptable* or *approved* in informal business and informal social usage. Avoid the use of OK in formal situations.

on account of—is *unacceptable* for *because.*
> We could not meet you *because* we did not receive your message in time.

oral—means *spoken.*
verbal—means *expressed in words,* either spoken or written.
> In international intrigue, *oral* messages are less risky than written ones.
> Shorthand must usually be transcribed into *verbal* form.

ordinance—means *regulation.*
ordnance—refers to *guns, cannon, and the like.*
> The local *ordinance* restricted driving speeds to 35 miles an hour.
> Some rockets and guided missiles are now included in military *ordnance.*

ostensible—means *shown* (usually for the purpose of deceiving others).
ostentatious—means *showy.*
> Although he was known to be ambitious, his *ostensible* motive was civic pride.
> His *ostentatious* efforts in behalf of civic improvement impressed no one.

other . . . than—is acceptable.
other . . . but—is unacceptable.
other . . . except—is unacceptable.
> Acceptable: We have no *other* motive *than* friendship.

other—is an adjective and means *different.*
otherwise—is an adverb and means *in a different way.*
> What you did was *other* than what you had promised.
> I cannot look *otherwise* than with delight at the improvement in your work.

out loud—is *colloquial* for *aloud.*
He read *aloud* to his family every evening.

outdoor—is an adjective.
outdoors—is an adverb.
We spent most of the summer at an *outdoor* music camp.
Most of the time we played string quartets *outdoors.*
Out-of-doors is *acceptable* in either case.

part from—*a person.*
part with—*a thing.*
It was difficult for her to *part from* her classmates.
It will be difficult for him to *part with* his car.

party—refers to a *group,* **not** an *individual.*
person—refers to an *individual.*
A *party* of men went on a scouting mission.
Who is the *person* you came with?
NOTE: *Party* may be used for the word *person* in a legal document.

pedal—means *a lever operated by foot.* (avoid foot pedal)
peddle—means *to sell from door to door.*
It is impossible to ride a bicycle without moving the *pedals.*
The traveling salesman *peddling* brushes is a thing of the past.

percent—(also **per cent**) expresses *rate of interest.*
percentage—means *a part or proportion of the whole.*
The interest rate of some banks is 4 *percent.*
The census showed the *percentage* of unmarried people to have increased.

persecute—means *to make life miserable for someone.*
prosecute—means *to conduct a criminal investigation.*
Some racial groups insist upon *persecuting* other groups.
The District Attorney is *prosecuting* the racketeers.

personal—refers to *a person.*
personnel—means *an organized body of individuals.*
The general took a *personal* interest in every one of his men.
He believed that this was necessary in order to maintain the morale of the
personnel in his division.

physic—means *a drug.*
physics—is *a branch of science.*
physique—means *body structure.*
A doctor should determine the safe dose of a *physic.*
Nuclear *physics* is one of the most challenging of the sciences.
Athletes must take care of their *physiques.*

plenty—is a noun; it means *abundance.*
America is a land of *plenty.*
There is *plenty of* (**not** *plenty*) room in the compact car for me.
Plenty as an adverb is *colloquial.*
The compact car is *quite* large enough for me.

pole—means a long stick.
poll—means *vote.*
We bought a new *pole* for the flag.
The seniors took a *poll* to determine the graduate most likely to succeed.

poorly—meaning *in poor health* is *unacceptable in formal usage.*
Grandfather was feeling *in poor health* all last winter.

pour—is *to send flowing with direction and control.*
spill—is *to send flowing accidentally.*
Please *pour* some cream into my cup of coffee.
Careless people *spill* things.

practicable—means *usable* or *workable* and is applied only to objects.
practical—means *realistic, having to do with action.* It applies to persons and
things.
There is as yet no *practicable* method for resisting atomic bomb attacks.
Practical technicians, nevertheless, are attempting to translate the theories
of the atomic scientists into some form of defense.

precede—means *to come before.*
proceed—means *to go ahead.* (*procedure* is the noun)
supersede—means *to replace.*
What are the circumstances that *preceded* the attack?
We can then *proceed* with our plan for resisting a second attack.
It is then possible that Plan B will *supersede* Plan A.

prescribe—means *to lay down a course of action.*
proscribe—means *to outlaw* or *forbid.*
The doctor *prescribed* plenty of rest and good food for the man.
Some towns may *proscribe* various forms of expression.

principal—means *chief* or *main* (as an adjective); *a leader* (as a noun).
principle—means *a fundamental truth* or *belief.*
  His *principal* supporters came from among the peasants.
  The *principal* of the school asked for cooperation from the staff.
  Humility was the guiding *principle* of Buddha's life.
  NOTE: *principal* may also mean a sum placed at interest.
  Part of his monthly payment was applied as interest on the *principal.*

prodigy—means a *person endowed with extraordinary gifts or powers.*
protégé—means *someone under the protection of another.*
  Mozart was a musical *prodigy* at the age of three.
  For a time, Schumann was the *protégé* of Johannes Brahms.

prophecy—(rhymes with *sea*) is the noun meaning *prediction.*
prophesy—(rhymes with *sigh*) is a verb meaning *to predict.*
  The *prophecy* of the three witches eventually misled Macbeth.
  The witches had *prophesied* that Macbeth would become king.

put in—meaning *to spend, make,* or *devote* is *colloquial.*
  Every good student should *spend* (or *put in*) at least four hours a day
    studying.
  Be sure to *make* (or *put in*) an appearance at the council meeting.

rain—means *water from the clouds.*
reign—means *rule.*
rein—means *a strap for guiding a horse.*
  The *rain* in Spain falls mainly on the plain.
  A queen now *reigns* over England.
  When the *reins* were pulled too tightly, the horse reared.

real—meaning *very* or *extremely* is *colloquial.*
  He is a *very* handsome young man.
  He is *really* handsome.

reason is because—is *unacceptable* for *reason is that.*
  The *reason* young people do not read Trollope today *is that* his sentences
    are too involved.
  Avoid *due to* after *reason is.*
  The *reason* he refused *was that* he was proud (**not** *due to* his pride).

rebellion—means *open, armed, or organized resistance to authority.*
revolt—means *similar resistance on a smaller scale.*
revolution—means *the overthrowing of one government and the setting up of another.*
> Bootlegging has sometimes been referred to as a *rebellion* against high whiskey taxes.
> An increase in the grain tax caused a peasants' *revolt* against the land-owners.
> Unpopular regimes are often overthrown in violent *revolutions.*

reckon—meaning *suppose* or *think* is *unacceptable.*
> I *think* it may rain this afternoon.

recollect—means *to bring back to memory.*
remember—means *to keep in memory.*
> Now I can *recollect* your returning the money to me.
> I *remember* the occasion well.

reconcile to—means *resign to* or *adjust to.*
reconcile with—means *to become friendly again with someone;* also, *to bring one set of facts into harmony with another one.*
> I am now *reconciled to* this chronic ache in my back.
> George was *reconciled with* his parents after many years.
> How does one *reconcile* the politician's shabby accomplishments *with* the same politician's noble promises?

regular—meaning *real* or *true* is *colloquial.*
> *Colloquial:* He was a *regular* tyrant.
> *Preferred:* He was a *true* tyrant.

respectably—means *in a manner deserving respect.*
respectfully—means *with respect and decency.*
respectively—means *as relating to each, in the order given.*
> Young people should conduct themselves *respectably* in school as well as in church.
> The students listened *respectfully* to the principal.
> John and Bill are the sons *respectively* of Mr. Smith and Mr. Brown.

reverend—means *worthy of reverence or respect.*
reverent—means *feeling or showing respect.*
> Shakespeare, the *reverend* master of the drama, still inspires most readers.
> Sometimes a too *reverent* attitude toward Shakespeare causes the reader to miss much of the fun in his plays.

rob—One *robs a person or institution.*
steal—One *steals* a *thing.*
   They *robbed* the man of his money.
   He *stole* my wallet.

rout—(rhymes with *stout*) means *a defeat.*
route—(rhymes with either *boot* or *stout*) means *a way of travel.*
   The *rout* of the army was near.
   The salesman has a steady *route.*

same as—is *colloquial* for *in the same way as* and *just as.*
   The owner's son was treated *in the same way as* any other worker.
   Avoid *same* as a pronoun, except in *legal* usage.
   If the books are available, please send *them* (**not** *same*) by parcel post.

self-confessed—is *redundant* for *confessed.* Omit *self.*
   He was a *confessed* lover of chocolate.

sensible of—means *aware of.*
sensitive to—means *affected by.*
   I am very *sensible of* my shortcomings.
   He is *sensitive to* criticism.

shape—meaning *condition* is *colloquial.*
   The refugees were in a serious *condition* (or *shape*) when they arrived here.

show up—meaning *to expose* is *unacceptable.*
   It is my firm intention to *expose* (**not** *show up*) your hypocrisy.

simple reason—is *unacceptable* for *reason.* Omit the word *simple* in similar
   expressions: *simple truth, simple purpose,* etc.
   Unacceptable: I refuse to do it for the *simple reason* that I don't like your
      attitude.
   Acceptable: The *truth* is that I feel tired.

simply—meaning *absolutely* or *extremely* is often redundant.
   Not: The performance was *simply* thrilling.
   But: The performance was thrilling.

size up—meaning *to estimate* is *colloquial.*
   The detectives were able *to estimate* (or *size up*) the fugitive's remaining
      ammunition supply.

sociable—means *friendly.*
social—means *relating to people in general.*
   Sociable individuals prefer to have plenty of people around them.
   The President's *social* program was just another waste.

sole—means *all alone.*
soul—means *human spirit.*
   He was the *sole* owner of the business.
   Man's *soul* is unconquerable.

some time—means *a portion of time.*
sometime—means *at an indefinite time in the future.*
sometimes—means *occasionally.*
   I'll need *some time* to make a decision.
   Let us meet *sometime* after noon.
   Sometimes it is better to hesitate before signing a contract.

somewheres—is *unacceptable.*
somewhere—is *acceptable.*

specie—means *money as coins.* (*Specie* is singular only.)
species—means *a member of a group of related things.* (*Species* is singular
   and plural.)
   He preferred to be paid in *specie,* rather than in bank notes.
   The human *species* is relatively young. (singular)
   Many animal *species* existed before man. (plural)

stand—meaning *to tolerate* is *colloquial.*
   I refuse *to tolerate* (or *to stand for*) crime.

state—means *to declare formally.*
say—means *to speak.*
   Our ambassador *stated* the terms for a ceasefire.
   We *said* that we would not attend the meeting.

stationary—means *standing still.*
stationery—means *writing materials.*
   In ancient times people thought the earth was *stationary.*
   We bought writing paper at the *stationery* store.

statue—means *a piece of sculpture.*
statute—is *a law.*
   The *Statue* of Liberty stands in New York Harbor.
   Compulsory education was established by *statute.*

summons—is singular; *summonses* is the plural.
> We received a *summons* to appear in court.
> This was the first of three *summonses* we were to receive that week.

surround—means *to enclose on all sides*. Do **not** add *on all sides* to it.
> The camp was *surrounded* by heavy woods.

take in—is *colloquial* in the sense of *deceive* or *attend*.
> We were *deceived* (or *taken in*) by her charming manner.
> We should like to *attend* (or *take in*) a few plays during our vacation.

tasteful—means *having good taste.*
tasty—means *pleasing to the taste.*
> The home of our host was decorated in a *tasteful* manner.
> Our host also served us very *tasty* meals.

tenants—are *occupants.*
tenets—are *principles.*
> Several *tenants* occupied that apartment during the first month.
> His religious *tenets* led him to perform many good deeds.

tender—means *to offer officially or formally.*
give—means *to donate* or *surrender something willingly.*
> The discredited official decided to *tender* his resignation.
> He *gave* testimony readily before the grand jury.

testimony—means *information given orally only.*
evidence—means *information given orally or in writing.*
> He gave *testimony* to the grand jury.
> The defendant presented written *evidence* to prove he was not at the scene of the crime.

that there / this here—are *unacceptable*. Omit *there, here.*
> *That* person is taller than *this* one.

their—means *belonging to them.*
there—means *in that place.*
they're—means *they are.*
> We took *their* books home with us.
> You will find your books over *there* on the desk.
> *They're* not as young as we expected them to be.

theirselves—is *unacceptable* for *themselves.*
> Most children of school age are able to care for *themselves* in many ways.

therefor—means *for that.*
therefore—means *because of that.*
> One day's detention is the punishment *therefor.*
> You will, *therefore,* have to remain in school after dismissal time.

these kind—is *unacceptable.*
this kind—is *acceptable.*
> I am fond of *this kind* of apples.
> (*These kinds* would also be *acceptable.*)

tortuous—means *twisting.*
torturing—means *causing pain.*
> The wagon train followed a *tortuous* trail through the mountains.
> The *torturing* memory of his defeat kept him awake all night.

track—means *a path* or *road.*
tract—means *a brief but serious piece of writing* or *a piece of land.*
> The horses raced around the *track.*
> John Locke wrote a famous *tract* on education.
> The heavily wooded *tract* was sold to a lumber company.

ulterior—means *lying beyond or hidden underneath.*
underlying—means *fundamental.*
> His noble words were contradicted by his *ulterior* motives.
> Shakespeare's *underlying* motive in *Hamlet* was to criticize the moral climate of his own times.

unique—means *the only one of its kind,* and therefore does not take *very, most,* or *extremely* before it.
> The First Folio edition of Shakespeare's works is *unique* (**not** *very unique*).
> NOTE: The same rule applies to *perfect.*

upwards of—is *colloquial* for *more than.*
> There are *more than* (or *upwards of*) one million people living in Idaho today.

valuable—means *of great worth.*
valued—means *held in high regard.*
invaluable—means *priceless.*
> This is a *valuable* manuscript.
> The expert gave him highly *valued* advice.
> A good name is an *invaluable* possession.

venal—means *corrupted.*
> The *venal* councilwoman accepted the bribe.

veracity—means *truthfulness.*
truth—is *a true statement, a fact.*
> Because he had a reputation for *veracity,* we could not doubt his story.
> We would have questioned the *truth* of his story otherwise.

via—means *by way of* and should be used in connection with travel or motion only.
> We shipped the merchandise *via* motor express.
> I received the information *through* (**not** *via*) his letter.

virtue—means *goodness.*
virtuosity—means *technical skill.*
> We should expect a considerable degree of *virtue* in our public officials.
> The young pianist played with amazing *virtuosity* at his debut.

virtually—means *in effect.*
actually—means *in fact.*
> A tie in the final game was *virtually* a defeat for us.
> We had *actually* won more games than they.

waive—means *to give up.*
wave—means *a swell* or *roll of water.*
> As a citizen, I refuse to *waive* my right of free speech.
> The *waves* reached the top deck of the ship.

whereabouts—is *colloquial* for *where* but only as a noun meaning *location.*
> Not: *Whereabouts* do you live?
> But: Do you know his *whereabouts?*

whose—means *of whom.*
who's—means *who is.*
> *Whose* is this notebook?
> *Who's* in the next office?

would have—is *unacceptable* for *had.*
> I wish you *had* (**not** *would have*) called earlier.

ABBREVIATIONS

Established abbreviations are acceptable in all but the most formal writing. For reading ease, use only well-known abbreviations. If it is desirable to use an abbreviation that may not be familiar to the reader, spell out the word or phrase in parentheses after the abbreviation the first time you use it. After this first definition, the abbreviation may be used without further explanation. Abbreviations should be consistent throughout a text.

PUNCTUATION

1. In general, an abbreviation follows the capitalization and hyphenation of the original word or phrase. Each element may or may not be followed by a period. The current trend is to omit the periods where they used to be required. Note, however, that abbreviations of courtesy titles, initials, addresses, business names, calendar dates, and Latin terms generally retain their periods.

AFL-CIO	NATO	SW (in an address following a street name)
KGB	NT (New Testament)	USMC

2. Periods are omitted from abbreviations of units of measure in scientific or technical writing:

cm^3	FM	g
dB	ft-lb	km

   In non-technical writing, abbreviated units of English measure may be typed with or without periods. Use a period if leaving it out would create confusion.

3. Abbreviations with periods should be typed without spaces, except for initials in personal names:

A.D.	R. S. Baker, MD
etc.	T. S. Eliot

   The initials of American presidents, however, are typed without spaces or periods:

JFK	RMN	WJC

GEOGRAPHIC TERMS

1. You may abbreviate *United States* when preceding *Government* or the name of a Government organization, except in formal writing. Spell out *United States* when it is used as a noun or when it is used as an adjective in association with names of other countries.

   US Government

   US Congress

US Department of Agriculture

US monitor *Nantucket*

USS *Brooklyn* (note abbreviation for ship)

BUT The position taken by the United States, British, and French governments.

2. With the exceptions just noted, the abbreviation US is used in the adjective position, but is spelled out when used as a noun.

US foreign policy	*BUT* foreign policy of the United States
US economy	the economy of the United States
US attorney	United States Code (official title)
US troops	United States Steel Corp. (legal title)

3. Words in an address are usually spelled out. Where brevity is required, the following abbreviations may be used. Note that compass directions do not use periods.

Ave.—Avenue	Pl.—Place	NE—Northeast
Bldg.—Building	Sq.—Square	NW—Northwest
Blvd.—Boulevard	St.—Street	SE—Southeast
Ct.—Court	Terr.—Terrace	SW—Southwest
Dr.—Drive		

4. Spell out the names of the US states and territories when they are used alone or follow another name (such as that of a city) in ordinary text. If space is limited, as in tabular work, use the abbreviations given on the left. Use the official two-letter postal abbreviations with ZIP code for anything being mailed. The names of countries are usually not abbreviated.

Ala.	AL	Fla.	FL
Alaska	AK	Ga.	GA
Ariz.	AZ	Guam	GU
Ark.	AR	Hawaii	HI
Calif.	CA	Idaho	ID
Colo.	CO	Ill.	IL
Conn.	CT	Ind.	IN
Del.	DE	Iowa	IA
DC	DC	Kans.	KS

Ky.	KY	Okla.	OK
La.	LA	Ore.	OR
Maine	ME	Pa.	PA
Md.	MD	PR	PR (Puerto Rico)
Mass.	MA	RI	RI
Mich.	MI	Amer. Samoa	AS
Minn.	MN	SC	SC
Miss.	MS	S. Dak.	SD
Mo.	MO	Tenn.	TN
Mont.	MT	Tex.	TX
Nebr.	NE	Utah	UT
Nev.	NV	Vt.	VT
NH	NH	Va.	VA
NJ	NJ	VI	VI (Virgin Islands)
N. Mex.	NM	Wash.	WA
NY	NY	W. Va.	WV
NC	NC	Wis.	WI (or Wisc.)
N. Dak.	ND	Wyo.	WY
Ohio	OH		

NAMES AND TITLES

1. Use abbreviations in company names as they are shown on the company's letterhead.

   J. Dillard & Sons, Inc.

2. Where brevity in company names is required, the following abbreviations may be used:

Bros.—Brothers		Inc.—Incorporated	
Co.—Company		Ltd.—Limited	
Corp.—Corporation		&—and	

Do not abbreviate *Company* and *Corporation* in names of Federal Government units.

> Metals Reserve Company

> Commodity Credit Corporation

3. In other than formal usage, you may abbreviate a civil or a military title preceding a name if followed by the person's given name or initial as well as the surname.

Adj.—Adjutant	LTJG—Lieutenant, junior grade)
Adm. (or ADM)—Admiral	
Asst. Surg.—Assistant Surgeon	Maj.—Major
	Maj. Gen.—Major General
Brig. Gen.—Brigadier General	M. Sgt.—Master Sergeant
	Pfc. (or PFC)—Private, first class
Capt.—Captain	PO—Petty Officer
Col.—Colonel	Prof.—Professor
Comdr.—Commander	Pvt.—Private
Cpl.—Corporal	Rear Adm.—Rear Admiral
CWO—Chief Warrant Officer	2d Lt.—Second Lieutenant
1st Lt.—First Lieutenant	Sfc.—Sergeant, first class
1st Sgt.—First Sergeant	Sgt.—Sergeant
Gen.—General	SGM (or Sgt. Maj)—Sergeant Major
Gov.—Governor	
Lt. (or Lieut.)—Lieutenant	S. Sgt.—Staff Sergeant
Lt. Comdr.—Lieutenant Commander	Supt.—Superintendent
	Surg.—Surgeon
LTC (or Lt. Col.)—Lieutenant Colonel	TSgt.—Technical Sergeant
LTG (or Lt. Gen.)—Lieutenant General	Vice Adm.—Vice Admiral
	WO—Warrant Officer

4. Use the following abbreviations after a name:

> Jr., Sr.

> 2d, 3d, II, III (not preceded by a comma)

5. Fellowships, orders, etc.:

   BPOE (Benevolent and Protective Order of Elks),

   KCB (Knight Commander of the Order of Bath)

6. *Sr.* and *Jr.* should be used with the full given name and initials, and in combination with any title.

   Anthony Baxter Jones, Jr.; *or* A. B. Jones, Sr.

7. Do not use titles such as *Mr., Mrs., Ms., Dr.,* or *Esq.* in combination with another title or with abbreviations indicating academic degrees.

   John Jones, MA, PhD; *not* Mr. John Jones, MA, PhD

   David Roe, MD; *not* Dr. David Roe, MD, *nor* Mr. David Roe, MD

   Gerald West, Esq. *not* Mr. Gerald West, Esq., *nor* Gerald West, Esq., PhD

8. Although academic degrees are abbreviations of Latin terms, the punctuation and, in some cases, the spacing are often omitted.

   MA, PhD, LLD

9. When a name is followed by abbreviations designating religious and fraternal orders and academic and honorary degrees, arrange the abbreviations in this sequence: Orders, religious first; theological degrees; academic degrees earned in course; and honorary degrees in order of bestowal.

   John J. Jones, DD, MA, DLit

   Richard R. Row, CSC, PhD, LLD

PARTS OF PUBLICATIONS

Abbreviations may be used to designate parts of publications mentioned in parentheses, brackets, footnotes, lists of references, and tables, and followed by figures, letters, or Roman numerals. Note that these abbreviations retain their periods.

App., apps.,—appendix, appendixes

art., arts.—article, articles

bull., bulls.—bulletin, bulletins

cl., cls.—clause, clauses

chap., chaps.—chapter, chapters

col., cols.—column, columns

fig., figs.—figure, figures

no., nos.—number, numbers

p., pp.—page, pages

par., pars.—paragraph, paragraphs

pl., pls.—plate, plates

pt., pts.—part, parts

sec., secs.—section, sections

subchap., subchaps.—subchapter, subchapters

subpar., subpars.—subparagraph, sub-paragraphs

subsec., subsecs.—subsection, subsections

supp., supps.—supplement, supplements

vol., vols.—volume, volumes

CALENDAR DIVISIONS

When brevity is required, you may abbreviate the names of months—except May, June, and July—when used with day, or year, or both.

Jan. Feb. Mar. Apr. Aug. Sept. (or Sep.) Oct. Nov. Dec.

Similarly the names of days of the week may be abbreviated.

Sun. Mon. Tues. Wed. Thurs. Fri. Sat.

STANDARD WORD ABBREVIATIONS

AA or **A.A.,** Alcoholics Annonymous, antiaircraft, Associate in Arts, Administration on Aging

AAA, American Automobile Association, antiaircraft artillery

AB or **A.B.** or **BA** or **B.A.,** bachelor of arts

abbr. or **abbrev.,** abbreviated or abbreviation

ABC, American Bowling Congress; American Broadcasting Company; atomic, biological, and chemical

abs., absolute, abstract

AC or **A.C.,** alternating current, Athletic Club

A/C, air conditioning

acct., account, accountant
ACDA, Arms Control and Disarmament Agency
ACTH, adrenocorticotropic hormone
ACTION, not an acronym, but an independent Federal agency
AD or **A.D.,** active duty; Anno Domini, in the year of our Lord
ADP, automatic data processing
AEC, Atomic Energy Commission
AEF, American Expeditionary Force (or Forces)
AFB, Air Force Base
AFL-CIO, American Federation of Labor and Congress of Industrial Organizations
AID, Agency for International Development
aka, also known as
ALR, American Law Reports
AM or **A.M.,** *ante meridiem,* before noon; master of arts (see also **MA** or **M.A.**)
AMC, American Maritime Cases
Am Dec, American Decisions
AMG, Allied Military Government
Am Repts, American Reports
AMVETS, American Veterans of World War II, Amvet(s) (individual)
antilog, antilogarithm
API, American Petroleum Institute
APO, Army and Air Force Post Office (overseas)
App DC, District of Columbia Appeal Cases
App Div, Appellate Division
APPR, Army Package Power Reactor
approx., approximate, approximately
ARC, American Red Cross, AIDS-related complex
ARPA, Advanced Research Projects Agency
ARS, Agricultural Research Service
ASCS, Agricultural Stabilization and Conservation Service
ASME, American Society of Mechanical Engineers
ASN, Army Service Number
Asst. Surg., assistant surgeon
AST, Atlantic Standard Time
ASTM, American Society for Testing and Materials
AT, Atlantic Time
Atl, Atlantic; Atlantic Reporter; **A.(2d),** Atlantic Reporter, second series
AUS, Austria, Army of the United States
AWL, Absent With Leave
AWOL, Absent Without Official Leave
BAE, Bureau of Agricultural Economics
BCG, (bacillus Calmette-Guerin), anti-tuberculosis vaccine
BDSA, Business and Defense Services Administration

Bé, Baumé
BEC, Bureau of Employees' Compensation
bf, boldface
BIA, Bureau of Indian Affairs
BIS, Bank for International Settlements
Blatch Pr Cas, Blatchford's Prize Cases
bldg., building
BLit(t) or **B.Lit(t)** or **Lit(t)B** or **Lit(t).B.,** Bachelor of Letters (or Literature)
BLM, Bureau of Land Management
BLS, Bachelor of Library Science, Bureau of Labor Statistics
BNDD, Bureau of Narcotics and Dangerous Drugs
bo, back order, bad order, buyer's option
BS or **B.S.,** Bachelor of Science
CAB, Civil Aeronautics Board
CACM, Central American Common Market
c. and sc., caps and small caps
CAP, Civil Air Patrol
CARE, Cooperative for American Relief Everywhere, Inc.
cbd, cash before delivery
CCA, Circuit Court of Appeals
CCC, Civilian Conservation Corps, Commodity Credit Corporation
CCls, Court of Claims
CClsR, Court of Claims Reports
CCPA, Court of Customs and Patent Appeals
CCR, Commission on Civil Rights
CE, Christian (or Common) Era
CEA, Council of Economic Advisers, Commodity Exchange Authority
CEC, Commodity Exchange Commission
Cento., Central Treaty Organization
CFR, Code of Federal Regulations
CFR Suppl., Code of Federal Regulations Supplement
CIA, Central Intelligence Agency
CIC, Counterintelligence Corps
CJ, *corpus juris,* body of law; Chief Justice
CMS, Consumer Marketing Service
CO, Commanding Officer
COD or **cod,** cash (or collect) on delivery
col., collateral, collected, collector, college, colony, color, column
COL, cost of living
Comp. Dec., Comptroller's Decisions (Treasury)
Comp. Gen. Dec., Comptroller General Decisions
con., consolidated, consul, continued
CONELRAD, control of electromagnetic radiation (civil defense)
cos, cash on shipment, companies, cosine, counties
cosh, hyperbolic cosine

cot, cotangent
coth, hyperbolic cotangent
cp, candlepower, chemically pure, compare
CPA, Certified Public Accountant
CPI, Consumer Price Index
CPR, cardiopulmonary resuscitation
cr, credit, creditor
CRP, C-reactive protein
CSC, Civil Service Commission
csc, cosecant
csch, hyperbolic cosecant
CSS, Commodity Stabilization Service
CST, Central Standard Time
ct or **ct.,** cent, county, court
CT, Central Time
CWO, cash with order (cwo), Chief Warrant Officer
Dall, Dallas (U.S. Supreme Court Reports)
DAR, Daughters of the American Revolution
DATA, Defense Air Transportation Administration
dba, doing business as
dbh, diameter at breast height
DC, direct current, District of Columbia
DD or **D.D.,** Doctor of Divinity
DDS or **D.D.S.,** Doctor of Dental Surgery
DDT, dichlorodiphenyltrichloroethane
DEW, distant early warning (DEW line)
Dist. Ct., District Court
DLF, Development Loan Fund
Dlit(t) or **D.Lit(t)** or **Lit(t)D** or **Lit(t).D.,** Doctor of Literature
DMB, Defense Mobilization Board
DOD, Department of Defense
DOT, Department of Transportation
DP, dew point, displaced person, double play
DPH, Doctor of Public Health
DPHy, Doctor of Public Hygiene
dr, debit, debtor, drachma, dram
DSA, Defense Supply Agency
DV, distinguished visitor (Air Force) (see also **VIP**)
DVM, Doctor of Veterinary Medicine
Ecosoc, Economic and Social Council
EDT, Eastern Daylight Time
EEC, European Economic Community
EEE, Eastern Equine Encephalitis
EFTA, European Free Trade Association
EHS, Environmental Health Services

8°, octavo
emcee, master of ceremony
eom, end of month
EOP, Executive Office of the President
EPA, Environmental Protection Agency
ERP, European Recovery Program
ESSA, Environmental Science Services Administration
EST, Eastern Standard Time
ET, Eastern Time
Euratom, European Atomic Energy Community
Euromarket, European Common Market (European Economic Community)
Euromart, see Euromarket
Ex. Doc., executive document
FAA, Federal Aviation Administration
FAO, Food and Agriculture Organization
fas, free alongside ship
FAS, Foreign Agricultural Service
FBI, Federal Bureau of Investigation
FCA, Farm Credit Administration
FCC, Federal Communications Commission
FCIC, Federal Crop Insurance Corporation
FCSC, Foreign Claims Settlement Commission
FDA, Food and Drug Administration
FDIC, Federal Deposit Insurance Corporation
FDL, fast deployment logistic (ship)
Fed, Federal, Federation
FHA, Federal Housing Administration, Farmers Home Administration
FHLBB, Federal Home Loan Bank Board
FICA, Federal Insurance Contributions Act
FLSA, Fair Labor Standards Act
FM, frequency modulation
FMC, Federal Maritime Commission
FMCS, Federal Mediation and Conciliation Service
FNMA, Federal National Mortgage Association (Fannie May)
FNS, Food and Nutrition Service
FOB or **fob,** free on board
FPC, Federal Power Commission
FPIS, forward propagation ionospheric scatter
FPO, Fleet Post Office
FPV, free piston vessel
FR, Federal Register (publication)
FRS, Fellow of the Royal Society, Federal Reserve System
FS, Forest Service
FSA, Federal Security Agency
FSS, Federal Supply Service

Fsuppl., Federal Supplement
FTC, Federal Trade Commission
FWS, Fish and Wildlife Service
GAO, General Accounting Office
GAR, Grand Army of the Republic
GARIOA, Government and Relief in Occupied Areas
GATT, General Agreement on Tariffs and Trade
GAW, guaranteed annual wage
GCA, ground-control approach
GCD or **gcd,** greatest common divisor
GCI, ground control intercept
GCT, Greenwich Civil Time
GI, gastrointestinal, general issue, Government issue
GMAT, Greenwich Mean Astronomical Time
GM & S, general, medical, and surgical
GMT, Greenwich Mean Time
GNMA, Government National Mortgage Association (Ginnie Mae)
GNP, gross national product
GPO, Government Printing Office
gr. Wt., gross weight
GS, Geological Survey
GSA, General Services Administration
GTS, gas turbine ship
HC, House of Commons
hcf, highest common factor
H Con. Res. (with number), House concurrent resolution
H Doc. (with number), House document
HE, high explosive
HHFA, Housing and Home Finance Agency
HHS, or **DHHS,** Department of Health and Human Services
HJ Res (with number), House joint resolution
HL, House of Lords
Hosp. Steward, hospital steward
How., Howard (U.S. Supreme Court Reports)
HR or **H.R.** (with numbers), House bill
H Rept. (with number), House report
H Res. (with number), House resolution
HUD, Department of Housing and Urban Development
IADB, Inter-American Defense Board
IAEA, International Atomic Energy Agency
ICBM, intercontinental ballistic missile
ICC, Interstate Commerce Commission, Indian Claims Commission
id, inside diameter
IDA, International Development Association
IF, infield, intermediate frequency

IFC, International Finance Corporation
IFF, Identification, Friend or Foe
ILO, International Labor Organization
IMCO, Intergovernmental Maritime Consultative Organization
IMF, International Monetary Fund
INS, Immigration and Naturalization Service
Insp. Gen., Inspector General
Interpol, International Criminal Police Organization
IOU, I owe you
IQ, intelligence quotient
IRAC, Interdepartment Radio Advisory Committee
IRBM, intermediate range ballistic missile
IRE, Institute of Radio Engineers
IRO, International Refugee Organization
IRS, International Revenue Service
ITO, International Trade Organization
ITU, International Telecommunication Union, International Typographical Union
JAG, Judge Advocate General
jato or **JATO,** jet-assisted takeoff
JD., *jurum doctor,* doctor of laws
JOBS, Job Opportunities in the Business Sector
Judge Adv. Gen., Judge Advocate General
KCB, Knight Commander of the Bath
LAFTA, Latin American Free Trade Association
lat. or **lat,** latitude
LC, Library of Congress
lc, lowercase
lcl, less-than-carload lot
lcm, least common multiple
L Ed., Lawyer's edition (U.S. Supreme Court Reports)
LitD or **Lit.D,** Doctor of Literature
LLB or **LL.B.,** Bachelor of Laws
LLD or **LL.D.,** Doctor of Laws
log, logarithm
long or **long.,** longitude
loran, long-range navigation
lox or **LOX,** liquid oxygen
LPG, liquefied petroleum gas
LST, Local Standard Time
LT, Local Time
LTL, less than truckload
lwl, load waterline
lwm, low watermark

MA or **M.A.,** Master of Arts, Maritime Administration, Manpower Administration

MAC, Military Airlift Command (formerly MATS)

maf, moisture and ash free (coal)

MAG, Military Advisory Group

MB, Manitoba, megabyte

MC or **M.C.,** Member of Congress, emcee (master of ceremonies)

MCA, Model Cities Administration

MD or **M.D.,** Doctor of Medicine, Medical Department

MDAP, Mutual Defense Assistance Program

mf, machine finish, medium frequency

Misc. Doc. (with number), miscellaneous document

mmf, magnetomotive force

mol wt, molecular weight

MOS, military occupational specialty

MP or **M.P.,** Member of Parliament, Military Police, Mounted Police

mp, melting point

MS, or **M.S.,** or **MSc,** or **M.Sc.,** Master of Science

MSC, Military Sealift Command

msl, mean sea level

MST, Mountain Standard Time

MT, Mountain Time

N, normal

NA, not available

NAC, national agency check

NAS, National Academy of Science

NASA, National Aeronautics and Space Administration

NATO, North Atlantic Treaty Organization

NB, New Brunswick

NBS, National Bureau of Standards

NCUA, National Credit Union Administration

nec, not elsewhere classified

nes, not elsewhere specified

net wt., net weight

NF, Newfoundland, National Formulary

NFAH, National Foundation on the Arts and the Humanities

n-fe, nitrogen-free extract

NFSN, French-Speaking Nations of NATO

NIH, National Institutes of Health

nl, natural log or logarithm

NLRB, National Labor Relations Board

NOAA, National Oceanic and Atmospheric Administration

noibn, not otherwise indexed by name

nop, not otherwise provided (for)

nos, not otherwise specified

NOS, National Ocean Survey (formerly Coast and Geodetic Survey)
NOVS, National Office of Vital Statistic
NPS, National Park Service
NS, naval station, new series, New Style, Nova Scotia, nuclear ship
NSA, National Shipping Authority
NSC, National Security Council
NSF, National Science Foundation
nsk, not specified by kind
nspf, not specifically provided for
NT or **N.T.,** New Testament, Northern Territory, Northwest Territories
OASDHI, Old-Age, Survivors, Disability, and Health Insurance Program
OASI, Old-Age and Survivors Insurance
OCD, Office of Civil Defense
OD or **O.D.,** Doctor Optometry, Officer of the Day
od, olive drab, outside diameter
OE, Office of Education
OEO, Office of Economic Opportunity
OEP, Office of Emergency Preparedness, Office of Emergency Planning
OIT, Office of International Trade
OK, OK'd, OK'ing, OK's
OMB, Office of Management and Budget (formerly **BOB,** Bureau of the Budget)
ON, Old Norse, Ontario
OSD, Office of the Secretary of Defense
OTC, Organization for Trade Cooperation
PA, physician assistant, Post Adjutant, power of attorney, public-address system
Passed Asst. Surg., Passed Assistant Surgeon
PBS, Public Broadcasting Service
PE, physical education, Prince Edward Island
Pet, Peters (US Supreme Court Reports)
Ph, phenyl
ph, phase
PHA, Public Housing Administration
Phar D, Doctor of Pharmacy
PhB or **BPh,** Bachelor of Philosophy
PhD or **Ph.D.,** Doctor of Philosophy
PhG, Graduate in Pharmacy
PHS, Public Health Service
pl or **pl.,** plate, plural
PO Box (with number), *but* post office box (in general sense)
pod, pay on delivery
por, pay on return
POW, prisoner of war
PP, parcel post, postpaid, prepaid

PPI, plan position indicator
ppi, policy proof of interest
pq, previous question
PQ, Province of Quebec
Private Res. (with number), private resolution
PST, Pacific Standard Time
PT, Pacific Time
PTA, Parent-Teacher Association
pto, please turn over
Public Res. (with number), public resolution
PX, Post Exchange
QT, on the quiet
racon, radar beacon
radar, radio detection and ranging
R & D, research and development
rato, rocket-assisted takeoff
RB, Renegotiation Board
RDB, Research and Development Board
REA, Rural Electrification Administration
Rev., Revelation, Reverend
Rev. Stat., Revised Statutes
rf, radio frequency
RFD or **R.F.D.,** Rural Free Delivery
Rh, Rhesus (blood factor)
RN or **R.N.,** Registered Nurse, Royal Navy
ROP, run of paper
ROTC, Reserve Officer's Training Corps
RR or **R.R.,** railroad, Right Reverend, Rural Route
RRB, Railroad Retirement Board
Rwy or **Rwy.,** Railway
SAC, Strategic Air Command
SACEUR, Supreme Allied Commander Europe
SAE, Society of Automotive Engineers
SAGE, semiautomatic ground environment
s and sc, sized and supercalendered
SAR, Sons of the American Revolution
SBA, Small Business Administration
SCAP, Supreme Commander of the Allied Powers (Japan)
S Con. Res. (with number), Senate Concurrent Resolution
S Doc. (with number), Senate document
SEATO, Southeast Asia Treaty Organization
SEC, Securities and Exchange Commission
sec or **sec.,** secant, seconds, secondary, secretary, section
sech, hyperbolic secant
2d, **3d,** second, third

ser., series, sermon
Sf, Svedberg floatation
SHAPE, Supreme Headquarters Allied Powers (Europe)
SHF, superhigh frequency
shoran, short range (radio)
SI, Systeme International d' Unites
sin, sine
sinh, hyperbolic sine
SJ Res (with number), Senate Joint Resolution
SK, Saskatchewan
so, seller's option
sofar, sound fixing and ranging
sonar, sound, navigation, and ranging
SOP or **S.O.P.,** standard operating procedure
SOS, wireless distress signal
SP, Shore Patrol, Submarine Patrol
SPAR, Coast Guard Women's Reserve (*Semper Paratus—Always Ready*)
sp gr or **sp. gr.,** specific gravity
S Rept. (with number), Senate Report
S Res. (with number), Senate Resolution
SRS, Social and Rehabilitation Service
SS or **S.S.,** Social Security, steamship
SSA, Social Security Administration
SSS, Selective Service System
St., Saint, Strait, Street
Ste., SS., Sainte, Saints
Stat., Statutes at Large
STP, standard temperature and pressure
SUNFED, Special United Nations Fund for Economic Development
Sup. Ct., Supreme Court Reporter
Supp. Rev. Stat., Supplement to the Revised Statutes
Surg. Gen., Surgeon General
tan, tangent
tanh, hyperbolic tangent
TB, tuberculosis
TD, touchdown, Treasury Department, Treasury Decisions
TDN, total digestible nutrients
ter., terrace, territory
tlo, total loss only
tm, true mean
TNT, trinitrotoluene
TOFC, trailer-on-flatcar
Tp., township
TV, television
TVA, Tennessee Valley Authority

2,4-D, insecticide
uc., uppercase
UHF or **uhf,** ultrahigh frequency
UMTS, Universal Military Training Service (or System)
UN, United Nations
UNESCO, United Nations Educational, Scientific, and Cultural Organization
UNICEF, United Nations Children's Fund
URA, Urban Renewal Administration
USA or **U.S.A.,** United States of America, US Army
USAF, US Air Force
USAREUR, US Army, Europe
USC, United States Code
USCA, United States Code Annotated
USC Suppl, United States Code Supplement
USCG, US Coast Guard
USDA, United States Department of Agriculture
USES, US Employment Service
USIA, US Information Agency
USMC, US Marine Corps
USN, US Navy
USNR, US Naval Reserve
USP or **U.S.P.,** United States Pharmacopoeia
USS, US Senate, US ship
USSR or **U.S.S.R.,** Union of Soviet Socialist Republics
ut, universal time
VA, Veterans' Administration
VAR, visual-aural range
VCR, video cassette recorder
VHF, very high frequency
VIP, very important person (see also **DV**)
VLF or **vlf,** very low frequency
WAC, Women's Army Corps
wae, when actually employed
WAF, Women in the Air Force
Wall, Wallace (US Supreme Court Reports)
WAVES, Women Accepted for Volunteer Emergency Service
wf, wrong font
Wheat., Wheaton (US Supreme Court Reports)
WHO, World Health Organization
wi, when issued
WMAL, WRC, etc., radio stations
woc, without compensation
YT, Yukon Territory
ZIP Code, zone improvement plan code (Postal Service)

METRIC ABBREVIATIONS

Metric abbreviations are typed in lowercase, the same form being used for both singular and plural. The preferred abbreviation for *cubic centimeter* is cm^3, rather than *cc*.

Prefixes for Multiples and Submultiples			
T	tera (10^{12})	c	centi (10^{-2})
G	giga (10^9)	m	milli (10^{-3})
M	mega (10^6)	μ	micro (10^{-6})
k	kilo (10^3)	n	nano (10^{-9})
h	hecto (10^2)	p	pico (10^{-12})
da	deka (10)	f	femto (10^{-15})
d	deci (10^{-1})	a	atto (10^{-18})

Length		Area	
m	meter	m^2	square meter
mym	myriameter	mya	myriare
km	kilometer	km^2	square kilometer
hm	hectometer	hm^2	square hectometer
dam	dekameter	dam^2	square dekameter
dm	decimeter	dm^2	square decimeter
cm	centimeter	cm^2	square centimeter
mm	millimeter	mm^2	square millimeter

Volume		Weight	
m^3	cubic meter	g	gram
km^3	cubic kilometer	myg	myriagram
hm^3	cubic hectometer	kg	kilogram
dam^3	cubic dekameter	hg	hectogram
dm^3	cubic decimeter	dag	dekagram
cm^3	cubic centimeter	dg	decigram
mm^3	cubic millimeter	cg	centigram
		mg	milligram
		μg	microgram

Land Area		Capacity of Containers	
a	are	l	liter
ha	hectare	myl	myrialiter
ca	centiare	kl	kiloliter
		hl	hectoliter
		dal	dekaliter
		dl	deciliter
		cl	centiliter
		ml	milliliter

A similar plan of abbreviation applies to any unit based on the metric system:

Units Based on the Metric System			
A	ampere	V	volt
Å	angstrom	W	Watt
c	cycle (radio)	kc	kilocycle
dyn	dyne	kV	kilovolt
erg	erg	kVA	kilovolt-ampere
F	farad	kW	kilowatt
H	henry	mF	millifarad
J	joule	mH	millihenry
mho	(not abbreviated)	mF	microfarad (one millionth of a farad)
ohm	(not abbreviated)		

STANDARD ABBREVIATIONS FOR OTHER UNITS OF MEASURE

a, are (unit of area), atto (prefix, one-quintillionth)
aA, attoampere
abs, absolute (temperature and gravity)
AF or **af,** audio-frequency
AM, amplitude modulation
asb, apostilb
at, atmosphere, technical
atm, atmosphere (infrequently, A_s)
at wt, atomic weight
avdp., avoirdupois

b, barn, bit
B, bel
bbl, barrel
bbl/d, barrel per day
Bd, baud
bd ft, board foot
Bhn, Brinell hardness number
bhp, brake horsepower
bm, board measure
bp, boiling point
Btu's or **BTU'S,** British thermal units
bu, bushel
C, coulomb, Celsius (preferred), also Centigrade
C or **C.** or **c** or **¢** or **ct,** cent
°C, degree Celsius
cal, calorie
cal., caliber
cd, candela
cd-ft, cord-foot
cd/in^2, candela per square inch
cd/m^2, candela per square meter
cfm, cubic feet per minute
cfs, cubic feet per second
c-h, candle-hour
Ci, curie
cp, candle power
cP, centipoise
cSt, centistokes
cu ft (obsolete), see **ft^3**
cu in (obsolete), see **in^3**
cu yd (obsolete), see **yd^3**
cwt, hundredweight
D, darcy
d, day, degree, diameter, penny, pence, deci (prefix, one-tenth)
db or **dB,** decibel
dbu, decibel unit
dol, dollar
doz or **doz.,** dozen(s)
dr, dram
dwt, deadweight tons
EHF or **ehf,** extremely high frequency
EMF or **emf,** electromotive force
esu, electrostatic unit
°F, degree Fahrenheit
F, Fahrenheit; femi

fbm, feet board measure
fc, foot-candle
fL, footlambert
FM, frequency modulation
ft or **ft.,** foot, feet
ft^2, square foot
ft^3, cubic foot
ftH$_2$0, conventional foot of water
ft-lb, foot-pound
ft-lbf, foot pound-force
ft/min, foot per minute
ft^2/min, square foot per minute
ft^3/min, cubic foot per minute
ft-pdl, foot poundal
ft/s, foot per second
ft^2/s, square foot per second
ft^3/s, cubic foot per second
ft/s^2, foot per second squared
ft/s^3, foot per second cubed
G, gauss, giga (prefix, 1 billion), gravity
Gal, gal (acceleration)
gal or **gal.,** gallon
gal/min, gallons per minute
gal/s, gallons per second
Gb, gilbert
g/cm^3, gram per cubic centimeter
GeV, giga-electron-volt
GHz, gigahertz, gigacycle per second
gr, grain, gram, gross
h, hour, hecto (prefix, 100)
ha, hectare
hf, half, high frequency
HP or **hp,** horsepower
hph, horsepowerhour
Hz, hertz (cycles per second)
ihp, indicated horsepower
in, inch
in^2, square inch
in^3, cubic inch
in/h, inch per hour
inH$_2$O, conventional inch of water
inHg, conventional inch of mercury
in-lb, inch-pound
in/s, inch per second
K, karat, kayser, kilobyte, Kelvin (no degree symbol °)

k, karat, kilo (prefix, 1,000)
kHz or **khz,** kilohertz (kilocycles per second)
klbf, kilopound-force
kt, karat, kiloton, knot
L, lambert
lb or **lb.,** pound(s)
lb ap, apothecary, pound
lb, **avdp,** avoirdupois, pound
lbf, pound-force
lbf/ft, pound-force foot
lbf/ft^2, pound-force per square foot
lfg/ft^3, pound-force per cubic foot
lbf/in^2, pound-force per square inch
lb/ft, pound per foot
lb/ft^2, pound per square foot
lb/ft^3, pound per cubic foot
lb/in^{2}a, pounds per square inch absolute
lb/in^{2}g, pounds per square inch gage
lct, long calcined ton
ldt, long dry ton
LF or **lf,** low frequency
lin ft, linear foot
l/m, lines per minute
lm, lumen
lm/ft^2, lumen per square foot
lm/m^2, lumen per square meter
lm-s, lumen second
lm/W, lumen per watt
l/s, lines per second
l/s, liter per second
lx, lux
M, Roman numeral for 1,000
M#bm, thousand (feet) board measure
mD, millidarcy
meq, milliequivalent
M#ft^3, thousand cubic feet
Mgal/d, million gallons per day
MHz or **Mhz,** megahertz
mHz, millihertz
mi or **mi.,** mile
mi^2, square mile
mi/h, mile per hour
min., minute (time)
mol, mole (unit of substance)
ms, millisecond

MT, megaton
Mx, maxwell
N, newton
N•m, newton meter
N/m^2, newton per square meter
nmi, nautical mile
Np, neper
ns, nanosecond
N•s/m^2, newton second per square meter
nt, nit
Oe, oersted (use of **A/m,** amperes permeter, preferred)
oz or **oz.,** ounce(s)
P, poise
Pa, pascal
pct, percent
pdl, poundal
pF, water-holding energy
pH, hydrogen-ion concentration
ph, phot
pk, peck
p/m, parts per million
ps, picosecond
pt or **pt.,** pint(s)
pwt, pennyweight
ql, quintal
qt or **qt.,** quart(s)
R, rankine; roentgen
°R, degree rankine; degree reaumur
rad, radian
rd, rad
rem, rem
rms, root mean square
rpm, revolutions per minute
rps, revolutions per second
s or **s.,** second(s) (time)
S, siemens
sb, stilb
scp, spherical candlepower
s-ft, second-foot
shp, shaft horsepower
slug, slug
sr, steradian
sSf, standard saybolt fural
sSu, standard saybolt universal
stdft^3, standard cubic foot (feet)

Sus, saybolt universal second
t or **t.,** ton
tbs or **tbs.** or **tbsp** or **tbsp.,** tablespoon
thm, therm
Twad, twaddell
u (unified), atomic mass unit
var, var
VHF or **vhf,** very high frequency
Wb, weber
W/sr, watt per steradian
W/(sr•m^2), watt per steradian square meter
yd or **yd.,** yard(s)
yd^2, square yard
yd^3, cubic yard
yr or **yr.,** year(s)

LATIN ABBREVIATIONS

a., *annus,* year; *ante,* before
A.A.C., *anno ante Christum,* in the year before Christ
A.A.S., *Academiae Americanae Socius,* Fellow of the American Academy [Academy of Arts and Sciences]
AB or **A.B.,** *artium baccalaureus,* bachelor of arts
ab init., *ab initio,* from the beginning
abs. re., *absente reo,* the defendant being absent
AC or **A.C.,** *ante Christum,* before Christ
AD or **A.D.,** *anno Domini,* in the year of our Lord
a.d., *ante diem,* before the day
ad fin., *ad finem,* at the end, to one end
ad h.l., *ad hunc locum,* to this place, on this passage
ad inf., *ad infinitum,* to infinity
ad init., *ad initium,* at the beginning
ad int., *ad interim,* in the meantime
ad lib., *ad libitum,* at pleasure
ad loc., *ad locum,* at the place
ad val., *ad valorem,* according to value
A.I., *anno inventionis,* in the year of the discovery
al., *alia, alii,* other things, other persons
AM or **A.M.,** *anno mundi,* in the year of the world; *Annus mirabilis,* the wonderful year [1666]; a.m., *ante meridiem,* before noon
an., *anno,* in the year; *ante,* before
ann., *annales,* annals; *anni,* years
A.R.S.S., *Antiquariorum Regiae Societatis Socius,* Fellow of the Royal Society of Antiquaries

A.U.C., *anno urbis conditae, ab urbe condita,* in [the year from] the building of the City [Rome], 753 B.C.

BA or **B.A.,** *baccalaureus artium,* bachelor of arts

BS or **B. Sc.,** *baccalaureus scientiae,* bachelor of science

C., *centum,* a hundred; *condemno,* I condemn, find guilty

c., *circa,* about

cent., *centum,* a hundred

cf., *confer,* compare

CM or **C.M.,** *chirurgiae magister,* master of surgery

coch., *cochlear,* a spoon, spoonful

coch. amp., *cochlear amplum,* a tablespoonful

coch. mag., *cochlear magnum,* a large spoonful

coch. med., *cochlear medium,* a dessert spoonful

coch. parv., *cochlear parvum,* a teaspoonful

con., *contra,* against; *conjunx,* wife

C.P.S., *custos privati sigilli,* keeper of the privy seal

C.S., *custos sigilli,* keeper of the seal

D., *Deus,* God; *Dominus,* Lord; **d.,** *decretum,* a decree; *denarius,* a penny; *da,* give

DD or **D.D.,** *divinitatis doctor,* doctor of divinity

D.G., *Dei gratia,* by the grace of God; *Deo gratias,* thanks to God

D.N., *Dominus noster,* our Lord

DSc or **D.Sc.,** *doctor scientiae,* doctor of science

d.s.p., *decessit sine prole,* died without issue

D.V., *Deo volente,* God willing

e.g., *exempli gratia,* for example

et al., *et alibi,* and elsewhere; *et alii,* or *aliae,* and others

etc., *et cetera,* and others, and so forth

et seq., *et sequentes,* and those that follow

et ux., *et uxor,* and wife

F., *filius,* son

f., *fiat,* let it be made; *forte,* strong

fac., *factum similis,* facsimile, an exact copy

fasc., *fasciculus,* a bundle

fl., *flores,* flowers; *floruit,* flourished; *fluidus,* fluid

f.r., *folio recto,* right-hand page

F.R.S., *Franternitatis Regiae Socius,* Fellow of the Royal Society

f.v., *folio verso,* on the back of the leaf

guttat., *guttatim,* by drops

H., *hora,* hour

h.a., *hoc anno,* in this year; *hujus anni,* this year's

hab. corp., *habeas corpus,* have the body—a writ

h.e., *hic est,* this is; *hoc est,* that is

h.m., *hoc mense,* in the month; *huius mensis,* this month's

h.q., *hoc quaere,* look for this

H.R.I.P., *hic requiescat in pace,* here rests in peace
H.S., *hic sepultus,* here is buried; *hic situs,* here lies; h.s., *hoc sensu,* in this sense
H.S.S., *Historiae Societatis Socius,* Fellow of the Historical Society
h.t., *hoc tempore,* at this time; *hoc titulo,* in or under this title
I., *Idus,* the Ides; i., *id,* that; *immortalis,* immortal
ib. or **ibid.,** *ibidem,* in the same place
id., *idem,* the same
i.e., *id est,* that is
imp., *imprimatur, sanction,* let it be printed
I.N.D., *in nomine Dei,* in the name of God
in f., *in fine,* at the end
inf., *infra,* below
init., *initio,* in the beginning
in lim., *in limine,* on the threshold, at the outset
in loc., *in loco,* in its place
in loc. cit., *in loco citato,* in the place cited
in pr., *in principio,* in the beginning
in trans., *in transitu,* on the way
i.q., *idem quod,* the same as
i.q.e.d., *id quod erat demonstrandum,* what was to be proved
J., *judex,* judge
JCD or **J.C.D.,** *juris civilis doctor,* doctor of civil law
JD or **J.D.,** *jurum doctor,* doctor of laws
JUD or **J.U.D.,** *juris utriusque doctor,* doctor of both civil and canon law
L., *liber,* a book; *locus,* a place
L, *libra,* pound; placed before figures, thus L10; if l., to be placed after, as 40l.
LAM or **L.A.M.,** *liberalium artium magister,* master of the liberal arts
LB or **L.B.,** *baccalaureus literarum,* bachelor of letters
lb., *libra,* pound (singular and plural)
LHD or **L.H.D.,** *literarum humaniorum doctor,* doctor of the more humane letters
LittD or **Litt. D.** or **Dlit(t),** *literarum doctor,* doctor of letters
LLB or **LL.B.,** *legum baccalaureus,* bachelor of laws
LLD or **LL.D.,** *legum doctor,* doctor of laws
LLM or **LL.M.,** *legum magister,* master of laws
loc. cit., *loco citato,* in the place cited
loq., *loquitur,* he, or she, speaks
L.S., *locus sigilli,* the place of the seal
l.s.c., *loco supra citato,* in the place above cited
L s.d., *librae, solidi, denarii,* pounds, shillings, pence
M., *magister,* master; *manipulus,* handful; *medicinae,* of medicine
m., *meridies,* noon
MA or **M.A.,** *magister artium,* master of arts

MB or **M.B.**, *medicinae baccalaureus*, bachelor of medicine

MCh or **M.Ch.**, *magister chirurgiae*, master of surgery

MD or **M.D.**, *medicinae doctor*, doctor of medicine

m.m., *mutatis mutandis*, with the necessary changes

m.n., *mutato nomine*, the name being changed

MS., *manuscriptum*, manuscript; **MSS.**, *manuscripta*, manuscripts

MusB or **Mus. B.**, *musicae baccalaureus*, bachelor of music

MusD or **Mus. D.**, *musicae doctor*, doctor of music

MusM or **Mus. M.**, *musicae magister*, master of music

N., *Nepos*, grandson; *nomen*, name; *nomina*, names; *noster*, our; n., *natus*, born; *nocte*, at night

N.B., *nota bene*, mark well

ni. pri., *nisi prius*, unless before

nob., *nobis*, for (or on) our part

nol. pros., *nolle prosequi*, will not prosecute

non cul., *non culpabilis*, not guilty

n.l., *non licet*, it is not permitted; *non liquet*, it is not clear; *non longe*, not far

non obs., *non obstante*, notwithstanding

non pros., *non prosequitur*, he does not prosecute

non seq., *non sequitur*, it does not follow logically

O., *octarius*, a pint

ob., *obiit*, he, or she, died; *obiter*, incidentally

ob. s.p., *obiit sine prole*, died without issue

o.c., *opere citato*, in the work cited

op., *opus*, work; *opera*, works

op. cit., *opere citato*, in the work cited

P., *papa*, pope; *pater*, father; *pontifex*, bishop; *populus*, people; p., *partim*, in part; *per*, by, for; *pius*, holy; *pondere*, by weight; *post*, after; *primus*, first; *pro*, for

p.a. or **per ann.**, *per annum*, yearly; *pro anno*, for the year

p. ae., *partes aequales*, equal parts

pass., *passim*, everywhere

percent., *per centum*, by the hundred

pil., *pilula*, pill

PhB or **Ph.B.**, *philosophiae baccalaureus*, bachelor of philosophy

pm or **p.m.**, *post mortem*, after death

PM or **P.M.**, *post meridem*, afternoon

pro tem., *pro tempore*, for the time being

prox., *proximo*, in or of the next [month]

P.S., *postscriptum*, postscript; **P.SS.**, *post scripta*, postscripts

q.d., *quasi dicat*, as if one should say; *quais dictum*, as if said; *quasi dixisset*, as if he had said

q.e., *quod est*, which is

Q.E.D., *quod erat demonstrandum*, which was to be demonstrated

Q.E.F., *quod erat faciendum,* which was to be done

Q.E.I., *quod erat inveniendum,* which was to be found out

q.l., *quantum libet,* as much as you please

q. pl., *quantum placet,* as much as seems good

q.s., *quantum sufficit,* sufficient quantity

q.v., *quantum vis,* as much as you will; *quem, quam, quod vide,* which see; qq. v., *quos, quas,* or *quae vide,* which see (plural)

R., *regina,* queen; *recto,* right-hand page; *respublica,* commonwealth

R, *recipe,* take

R.I.P., *requiescat,* or *requiescant,* in pace, may he, she, or they, rest in peace

R.P.D., *rerum politicarum doctor,* doctor of political science

t. or **temp.,** *tempore,* in the time of

tal. qual., *talis qualis,* just as they come, average quality

R.S.S., *Ragiae Societatis Sodalis,* Fellow of the Royal Society

S., *sepultus,* buried; *situs,* lies; *societas,* society; *socius* or *sodalis,* fellow; s., *semi,* half; *solidus,* shilling

s.a., *sine anno,* without date; *secundum artem,* according to art

S.A.S., *Societatis Antiquariorum Socius,* Fellow of the Society of Antiquaries

sc., *scilicet,* namely; *sculpsit,* he, or she, carved or engraved it

ScB or **Sc.B.,** *scientiae baccalaureus,* bachelor of science

ScD or **Sc.D.,** *scientiae doctor,* doctor of science

S.D., *salutem dicit,* sends greetings

s.d., *sine die,* indefinitely

sec., *secundum,* according to

sec. leg., *secundum legem,* according to law

sec. nat., *secundum naturam,* according to nature, or naturally

sec. reg., *secundum regulam,* according to rule

seq., *sequens, sequentes, sequentia,* the following

S.H.S., *Societatis Historiae Socius,* Fellow of the Historical Society

s.h.v., *sub hac voce* or *sub hoc verbo,* under this word

s.l.a.n., *sine loco, anno, vel nomine,* without place, date or name

s.l.p., *sine legitima prole,* without lawful issue

s.m.p., *sine mascula prole,* without male issue

s.n., *sine nomine,* without name

s.p., *sine prole,* without issue

S.P.A.S., *Societatis Philosophiae Americanae Socius,* Fellow of the American Philosophical Society

s.p.s., *sine prole superstite,* without surviving issue

S.R.S., *Societatis Regiae Socius or Sodalis,* Fellow of the Royal Society

ss., *scilicet,* namely (in law)

S.S.C., *Societas Sanctae Crucis,* Society of the Holy Cross

stat., *statim,* immediately

STB or **S.T.B.,** *sacrae theologiae baccalaureus,* bachelor of sacred theology

STD or **S.T.D.,** *sacrae theologiae doctor,* doctor of sacred theology

STP or **S.T.P.,** *sacrae theologiae professor,* professor of sacred theology
sub., *subaudi,* understand, supply
sup., *supra,* above
ult., *ultimo,* last month (may be abbreviated in writing but should be spelled
   out in printing)
ung., *unguentum,* ointment
u.s., *ubi supra,* in the place above mentioned
ut dict., *ut dictum,* as directed
ut sup., *ut supra,* as above
ux., *uxor,* wife
v. or **vs.,** *versus,* against; *vide,* see; *voce,* voice, word
v.—a., *vixit—annos,* lived [so many] years
verb. sap., *verbum [satis] sapienti,* a word to the wise suffices
v.g., *verbi gratia,* for example
viz., *videlicet,* namely
v.s., *vide supra,* see above

FORMS OF ADDRESS

The following are conventional forms of address in general use. They may be
varied where appropriate. Use them as guides for other addresses.

All presidential and federal and state elective officials are addressed as
Honorable. A person once entitled to *Governor, Judge, General, Honorable,*
or a similar distinctive title may retain the title for his or her lifetime.

When a woman occupies the position, substitute *Ms.* for *Mr.* However,
before such formal titles as *President, Vice President, Chairman, Secretary,
Ambassador,* or *Minister,* use *Madam* or *Mme.* If in doubt err on the side of formality and use *Mme.* Use the title *Senator* for a female member of the Senate
and *Ms.* for a female member of the House of Representatives, Senator-elect,
or Representative-elect.

In most States, the lower branch of the legislature is the House of
Representatives. In some States, such as California, New York, New Jersey,
Nevada, and Wisconsin, the lower house is known as the Assembly. In others,
such as Maryland, Virginia, and West Virginia, it is known as the House of
Delegates. Nebraska has a one-house legislature. Its members are classed as
Senators.

Academic or professional titles replace *Mr.* or *Ms.* Don't use two titles
with the same meaning with one name: write *Dr. Paula White* or *Paula White,
MD,* not *Dr. Paula White, MD* or *Ms. Paula White, MD.* Spell out all titles in
an address except *Dr., Mr., Mrs.,* and *Ms.* Use *Ms.* for women generally, unless
the woman addressed has expressed a preference for *Miss* or *Mrs.*

The term *pastor* applies to a minister who leads a congregation. It is
appropriately used in conversation or direct address, but not in formal, written
address.

Forms of Address

Addressee	Address on Letter and Envelope	Salutation	Complimentary Close
The President	The President The White House Washington, DC 20500	Dear Mr./Mme. President:	Respectfully,
Spouse of the President	Mr./Mrs. [full name] The White House Washington, DC 20500	Dear Mr./Mrs. [surname]:	Sincerely,
Assistant to the President	Honorable [full name] Assistant to the President The White House Washington, DC 20500	Dear Mr./Ms. [surname]:	Sincerely,
The Vice-President	The Vice-President United States Senate Washington, DC 20510	Dear Mr./Mme. Vice-President	Sincerely,
The Chief Justice	The Chief Justice of the United States The Supreme Court of the United States Washington, DC 20543	Dear Mr./Mme. Chief Justice: *or* Dear Chief Justice [surname]:	Sincerely,
Associate Justice	Mr./Mme. Justice [surname] The Supreme Court of the United States Washington, DC 20543	Dear Mr./Mme. Justice *or* Dear Justice [surname]:	Sincerely,

Addressee	Address on Letter and Envelope	Salutation	Complimentary Close
United States Senator	Honorable *[full name]* United States Senate Washington, DC 20510 *or* Honorable *[full name]* United States Senator *[local address]* *[City], [State] [ZIP]*	Dear Senator *[surname]*:	Sincerely,
United States Representative	Honorable *[full name]* House of Representatives Washington, DC 20515 *or* Honorable *[full name]* Member, United States House of Representatives *[local address]* *[City], [State] [ZIP]*	Dear Mr./Ms. *[surname]*:	Sincerely,
Committee Chairman	Honorable *[full name]* Chairman, Committee on *[name]* United States Senate Washington, DC 20510 *or* Honorable *[full name]* Chairman, Committee on *[name]* House of Representatives Washington, DC 20515	Dear Mr./Mme. Chairman:	Sincerely,

continues

Forms of Address *(Continued)*

Addressee	Address on Letter and Envelope	Salutation	Complimentary Close
Subcommittee Chairman	Honorable *[full name]* Chairman, Subcommittee on *[name]* *[name of parent Committee]* United States Senate Washington, DC 20510 *or* Honorable *[full name]* Chairman, Subcommittee on *[name]* House of Representatives Washington, DC 20515	Dear Senator *[surname]*: Dear Mr./Mme. *[surname]*:	Sincerely, Sincerely,
Speaker of the House of Representatives	Honorable *[full name]* Speaker of the House of Representatives Washington, DC 20515	Dear Mr./Ms. Speaker:	Sincerely,
Cabinet Members	Honorable *[full name]* Secretary of *[name of Department]* Washington, DC *[ZIP]* *or* Honorable *[full name]* Postmaster General Washington, DC 20260 *or* Honorable *[full name]* Attorney General Washington, DC 20530	Dear Mr./Mme. Secretary: Dear Mr./Ms. Postmaster General: Dear Mr./Ms. Attorney General:	Sincerely, Sincerely, Sincerely,

Addressee	Address on Letter and Envelope	Salutation	Complimentary Close
Deputy Secretaries, Assistants, or Under Secretaries	Honorable *[full name]* Deputy Secretary of *[name of Department]* Washington, DC *[ZIP]* *or* Honorable *[full name]* Assistant Secretary of *[name of Department]* Washington, DC *[ZIP]* *or* Honorable *[full name]* Under Secretary of *[name of Department]* Washington, DC *[ZIP]*	Dear Mr./Mme. *[surname]*:	Sincerely,
Head of Independent Offices and Agencies	Honorable *[full name]* Comptroller General of the United States General Accounting Office Washington, DC 20548 *or* Honorable *[full name]* Chairman, *[name of Commission]* Washington, DC *[ZIP]* *or* Honorable *[full name]* Director, Bureau of the Budget Washington, DC 20503	Dear Mr./Ms. *[surname]*: Dear Mr./Mme. Chairman: Dear Mr./Ms. *[surname]*:	Sincerely, Sincerely, Sincerely,

continues

Forms of Address *(Continued)*

Addressee	Address on Letter and Envelope	Salutation	Complimentary Close
Librarian of Congress	Honorable *[full name]* Librarian of Congress Library of Congress Washington, DC 20540	Dear Mr./Ms. *[surname]*:	Sincerely,
Public Printer	Honorable *[full name]* Public Printer US Government Printing Office Washington, DC 20401	Dear Mr./Ms. *[surname]*:	Sincerely,
American Ambassador	Honorable *[full name]* American Ambassador *[City]*, *[Country]*	Sir/Madam: (formal) Dear Mr./Mme. Ambassador: (informal)	Very truly yours, (formal) Sincerely, (informal)
American Consul General	*[full name]* or American Consul General (or American Consul) *[City]*, *[Country]*	Dear Mr./Ms. American Consul *[surname]*:	Sincerely,
Foreign Ambassador in the United States	His Excellency *[full name]* Ambassador of *[Country]* *[local address]* *[City]*, *[State]* *[ZIP]*	Excellency (formal) Dear Mr./Mme. Ambassador: (informal)	Very truly yours, (formal) Sincerely, (informal)

Addressee	Address on Letter and Envelope	Salutation	Complimentary Close
United States Representative to the United Nations or Organization of American States	Honorable *[full name]* United States Representative to the United Nations (or Organization of American States) Ambassador: *[local address]* *[City], [State] [ZIP]*	Sir/Madame: (formal) Dear Mr./Mme. (informal)	Very truly yours, (formal) Sincerely, (informal)
Governor of State	Honorable *[full name]* Governor of *[name of State]* *[City], [State] [ZIP]*	Dear Governor *[surname]*:	Sincerely,
Lieutenant Governor	Honorable *[full name]* Lieutenant Governor of *[name of State]* *[City], [State] [ZIP]*	Dear Mr./Ms. *[surname]*:	Sincerely,
State Senator	Honorable *[full name]* *[name of State]* Senate *[City], [State] [ZIP]*	Dear Mr./Ms. *[surname]*:	Sincerely,
State Representative, Assemblyman, or Delegate	Honorable *[full name]* *[name of State]* House of Representatives (or Assembly or House of Delegates) *[City], [State] [ZIP]*	Dear Mr./Ms. *[surname]*:	Sincerely,

continues

Forms of Address *(Continued)*

Addressee	Address on Letter and Envelope	Salutation	Complimentary Close
Mayor	Honorable *[full name]* Mayor of *[name of City]* *[City], [State] [ZIP]*	Dear Mayor *[surname]*:	Sincerely,
President of a Board of Commissioners	Honorable *[full name]* President, Board of Commissioners of *[name of City]* *[City], [State] [ZIP]*	Dear Mr./Ms. *[surname]*:	Sincerely,
Protestant Clergy			
—Episcopalian	The Most Reverend Archbishop of (Canterbury or York) *[local address]* *[City], [State] [ZIP]*	Most Reverend Sir *[full name]*: (formal) Dear Archbishop *[surname]*: (informal)	Sincerely, (formal) Sincerely, (informal)
	The Right Reverend Bishop of *[name of church]* *[local address]* *[City], [State] [ZIP]*	Right Reverend Sir: *[full name]* (formal) Dear Bishop *[surname]*: (informal)	Sincerely, (formal) Sincerely, (informal)
—Lutheran	The Reverend *[full name]* Bishop of *[name]* *[local address]* *[City], [State] [ZIP]*	Dear Bishop *[surname]*: (informal)	Sincerely, (informal)

Addressee	Address on Letter and Envelope	Salutation	Complimentary Close
—Methodist	The Reverend *[full name]* Bishop of *[name]* *[local address]* *[City]*, *[State]* *[ZIP]*	Reverend Sir/Madam: (formal)	Sincerely, (formal)
—Baptist —Christian (church) —Episcopalian —Lutheran —Methodist —Presbyterian —Quaker	The Reverend *[full name]* *[Title]*, *[name of church]* *[local address]* *[City]*, *[State]* *[ZIP]*	Dear Mr./Ms. *[surname]*:	Sincerely,
Catholic Clergy			
—Roman	His Holiness The Pope Apostolic Palace 00210 Vatican City	Your Holiness:	Your obedient servant,
	His Eminence *[given name]* Cardinal *[surname]* Archbishop of *[Diocese]* *[local address]* *[City]*, *[State]* *[ZIP]*	Your Eminence: (formal) Dear Cardinal *[surname]*: (informal)	Yours faithfully, (formal) Yours faithfully, (informal)

continues

Forms of Address (Continued)

Addressee	Address on Letter and Envelope	Salutation	Complimentary Close
	The Most Reverend [full name] Archbishop of [Diocese] [local address] [City], [State] [ZIP]	Your Excellency: (formal) Dear Archbishop [surname]: (informal)	Yours faithfully, (formal) Yours faithfully, (informal)
	The Most Reverend [full name] Bishop of [City] [local address] [City], [State] [ZIP]	Your Excellency: (formal) Dear Bishop [surname]: (informal)	Yours faithfully, (formal) Yours faithfully, (informal)
	The Reverend [full name] [Title], [name of church] [local address] [City], [State] [ZIP]	Dear Monsignor/Father [surname]:	Yours sincerely,
—Orthodox	His Holiness The Patriarch [local address] [City], [State] [ZIP]	Your Holiness:	Your obedient servant,
	The Most Reverend [full name] Metropolitan or Archbishop of [Diocese] [local address] [City], [State] [ZIP]	Your Grace or Eminence: (formal) Dear Metropolitan or [surname]: Archbishop (informal)	Your obedient servant, (formal) Your obedient servant, (informal)
	The Right Reverend Bishop [full name] [local address] [City], [State] [ZIP]	Right Reverend Bishop: (formal) Dear Bishop [surname]: (informal)	Yours faithfully, (formal) Yours faithfully, (informal)

Addressee	Address on Letter and Envelope	Salutation	Complimentary Close
—Roman and Orthodox	The Reverend *[full name]* *[Title]*, *[name of church]* *[local address]* 00000	Dear Monsignor/Father *[surname]*:	Yours sincerely,
Jewish Clergy	Rabbi *[full name]* *[Name of Congregation]* *[local address]* 00000	Dear Rabbi *[surname]*:	Sincerely,
Islamic Clergy			
—Sunni	His Eminence *[full name]* The Grand Mufti of *[area]* *[local address]* 00000	Your Eminence:	Sincerely,
—Shiite	His Eminence *[full name]* The Ayatollah of *[area]* *[local address]* 00000	Your Eminence:	Sincerely,
—Sunni and Shiite	Imam *[full name]* *[name of mosque]* *[local address]* 00000	Imam *[surname]*:	Sincerely,

Index

G

M

S

U

WEBSTER'S NEW WORLD™ 1001 ESSENTIAL LETTERS

When you don't have time to start from scratch, Webster's New World 1001 Essential Letters helps you get a head start on writing the perfect letter. From this extensive library of letters to fit every purpose, you can conduct a key-word search to find the right one. The CD's easy-to-use interface lets you customize letters in a flash.

System Requirements

- Windows® 3.1, 3.11 or Windows 95 or 98 operating system
- 486 SX 33 Mhz or faster processor
- 8 MB Minimum System Memory (RAM)
- 2 MB Hard Disk Space
- CD-ROM drive
- Compatible with Microsoft Word, WordPerfect, and MS Write word processing software.

Installation Instructions

Windows 95 and 98:

1. Insert Webster's New World™ 1001 Essential Letters disc into your CD-ROM drive.

2. From the Start Menu, select Run.

3. Type "d:\setup" (where "d" is the letter of your CD-ROM drive) and press Enter.

4. Follow the instructions that appear on the screen to complete the installation.

5. To start the program, click on the Start menu, roll your mouse over the 1001 Essential Letters Group, and choose the 1001 Essential Letters icon. You may also choose the Release Notes icon to learn more.

Windows 3.1 and 3.11:

1. Put the Webster's New World™ 1001 Essential Letters disc into your CD-ROM drive.

2. From the Program Manager, open the File Menu and then choose Run.

3. Type "d:\setup" (where "d" is the letter of your CD-ROM drive) and press Enter.

4. Follow the instructions that appear on your screen to complete the installation.

5. To start the program, double-click on the Program Group labeled 1001 Essential Letters from your Program Manager. Double-click on the 1001 Essential Letters icon to run the program, or choose the Release Notes to learn more.